AMERICAN
DECADES
2000 - 2009

AMERICAN
DECADES
2 0 0 0 - 2 0 0 9

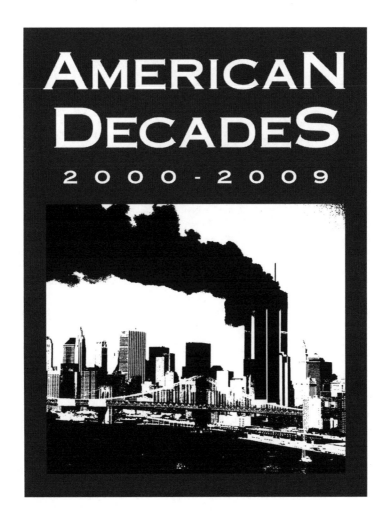

EDITED BY
ERIC BARGERON
WITH
JAMES F. TIDD JR.

A MANLY, INC. BOOK

GALE
CENGAGE Learning

Detroit • New York • San Francisco • New Haven, Conn • Waterville, Maine • London

American Decades: 2000–2009
A Manly, Inc. book

Edited by Eric Bargeron
with James F. Tidd Jr.

Editorial Director: Richard Layman
Production Manager: Janet E. Hill

For product information and technology assistance, contact us at
Gale Customer Support, 1-800-877-4253.

For permission to use material from this text or product,
submit all requests online at **www.cengage.com/permissions**
Further permissions questions can be e-mailed to
permissionrequest@cengage.com

Library of Congress Control Number: 2011930906

Gale
27500 Drake Rd.
Farmington Hills, MI 48331-3535

ISBN-13: 978-1-4144-3606-7   ISBN-10: 1-4144-3606-8

This title is also available at as e-book.
ISBN-13: 978-1-4144-3709-5   ISBN-10: 1-4144-3709-9
Contact your Gale, a part of Cengage Learning, sales representative for ordering information.

Printed in Mexico
1 2 3 4 5 6 7 14 13 12 11

CONTENTS

INTRODUCTION

A New Century. At the close of the 1990s, America stood alone as the world's superpower. For better or for worse, Henry Luce's 1941 call to make the twentieth century "the first great American Century" had been borne out. The United States' entry into World War II was decisive in the victory over fascism. America prevailed over the Soviet Union after decades of cold war. As the 1990s came to an end, the military, economic, and cultural power of the United States reached the farthest corners of the globe. A late-century technological boom lit a fire under the U.S. economy. Americans had invented the Internet and laid claim to being the most technologically advanced nation on the planet, an imposing advantage when it was clear that, whatever else might happen, the twenty-first century would be driven by technology. Still, as Americans planned their celebrations marking the dawn of a new century, they were also preparing for the worst. For months news outlets had warned of the doomsday scenario created by the so-called Y2K bug, a programming glitch that could cause computer systems across the country to crash. It was a simple problem: for decades programmers had shortsightedly neglected to allot an extra two digits denoting the century and millenium when coding their timekeeping software. If the software was not retrofitted in time, many feared the Cinderella story of American technological prowess might just come to an end. Computers, blindly setting their dates to 1 January 1900, could lose the ability to keep accurate time, setting off a series of internal failures that threatened to erase much of the progress of the American century.

"Decade from Hell." The world's computer systems did not melt down in the first seconds of 2000, but by the end of the year, the "dot-com" economic boom begun in the 1990s had collapsed. The NASDAQ index hit its record level of 5,049 in March. By October it had fallen to 1,114, losing 78 percent of its value. Investors had been too exuberant in the belief of the limitless expansion of the Internet age, and the United States entered a painful recession. The dot-com crash was prelude to a decade's worth of difficulties. The 2000 presidential election ended in a stalemate that had to be decided by the Supreme Court in a controversial and divisive 5-4 ruling. The new president, George W. Bush, had won the electoral-college vote by the slimmest of margins and had lost the popular vote outright.

Economic woes in the early Bush presidency dimmed in comparison with the horrific tragedy of the terrorist attacks of 11 September 2001, in which international terrorists associated with al Qaeda hijacked planes and turned them into weapons. The terrorists destroyed New York's World Trade Center by crashing a plane into each of its twin towers. Another jet slammed into the Pentagon; still another crashed near Shanksville, Pennsylvania, after the heroic efforts of passengers to stop the hijackers' plans. 9/11 brought about a major shift in the way Americans viewed themselves and their place in the world. It remade the Bush administration as well; President Bush had campaigned in part on limiting U.S. involvement overseas, but his prosecution of a worldwide war on terror included two major wars in Iraq and Afghanistan. There were other disasters as well. In 2005 Hurricane Katrina struck the Gulf Coast, causing widespread damage and leading to flooding that left much of the city of New Orleans under water. As the decade wore on, optimism about quick U.S. victories in Afghanistan and Iraq faded; both wars dragged on as American soldiers transitioned to the fight against insurgency. The stock market crashed again in 2008 as a result of overconfidence in the housing boom and Wall Street investors gone wild in an era of deregulation, but the fallout was widespread as banks had overleveraged themselves in pursuit of record profits. Major Wall Street financial institutions went bankrupt. Credit, which had been so freely available, suddenly dried up, and the U.S. economic outlook was as bleak as it had been since the stock market crash of 1929, which marked the beginning of the Great Depression. The headline of *Time* magazine's review of the decade summed up the American mood: "The '00s: Goodbye (at Last) to the Decade from Hell."

Terrorism. The biggest nightmare in a hellish decade was the threat of terrorism. In the aftermath of 9/11, the Bush administration quickly adopted an aggressive domestic and international strategy to combat terrorism. It oversaw the creation of the first new Cabinet-level department in decades, the Department of Homeland Security, charged with protecting the nation from terrorist attack. In the early days it was not altogether clear to most Americans what they should do to take part in the effort. President Bush enjoined Americans to go about their lives as usual:

"do your business around the country. Fly and enjoy America's great destination spots." But it soon became clear that life was not returning to normal anytime soon. The Department of Homeland Security created an advisory system with a color-coded guide to terror threat levels, but in the course of the decade it never fell below the midpoint, which represented "Elevated: Significant Risk of Terrorist Attacks." For most of the decade, American opinion was split over the proper boundary between the protection of civil liberties and protection against terrorist attacks. The Patriot Act expanded the power of law-enforcement agencies to obtain and share information about American citizens. Passed with overwhelming support after the attacks, it quickly became a sore point for civil libertarians and other critics of the Bush administration's policies in the war on terror. Revelations of a warrantless wiretapping program, authorized in secret and conducted by the National Security Administration, further unsettled Bush critics. Two overseas wars also proved divisive. That the United States would go to war against Afghanistan in late 2001 was almost a foregone conclusion. The central Asian nation was ruled by a fundamentalist regime called the Taliban that had provided a haven for al Qaeda, the group headed by Osama bin Laden that was responsible for the 9/11 attacks. But two years later, many greeted the Bush administration's call for a war against Iraq with skepticism. That nation had a long and troubled history with the United States, but the case for any connection between ruler Saddam Hussein's Baathist regime and al Qaeda seemed tenuous at best. By and large, however, Americans took the administration's claims of an Iraqi threat to democracy seriously, and early support for an invasion ran high after spurious claims by the Bush administration that the nation was on the verge of developing nuclear weapons. The overwhelming power of the U.S. military made it easy to topple the governments of Afghanistan and Iraq. What proved elusive was the settlement of a stable peace in either country, as the American presence became a source of agitation throughout the Middle East and sparked widening insurgencies. The wars in Iraq and Afghanistan were central issues in the deeply partisan presidential elections of 2004 and 2008. By the end of the decade, Americans were still fighting in both countries with little hope for long-term success.

Distraction. In a decade of grim news, it was little wonder that many sought distraction from the headlines. Americans tuned in by the millions to the spectacular diversions of reality television. The shows took many forms, with some offering cash prizes to everyday people for completing gruelling challenges, and others promising fame and fortune to talented amateur musical performers. The format proved a hit with audiences and a cash cow for flagging networks, since reality shows were much cheaper to produce than traditional drama. Game shows got bigger as well: the long-running quiz show *Jeopardy* doubled its prize money; *Who Wants to Be a Millionaire* offered the promise of a $1 million grand prize to contestants who could correctly answer fifteen multiple-choice questions. Viewership levels for sports generally increased with the proliferation of cable channels devoted to coverage. Football, long America's most watched sport, continued to grow in popularity, while NASCAR racing had the largest increase.

Breakthroughs. The 2000s was a decade of breakthroughs for minorities. In 2001 Colin Powell became the first African American secretary of state; in 2005 Condoleezza Rice became the first African American woman in that position. Alberto Gonzales became the first Hispanic to serve as attorney general in 2005 and in 2009 Eric Holder became the first African American to hold the post. In 2007 Nancy Pelosi became the first female Speaker of the House. After winning a legendary primary battle with Hillary Clinton for the Democratic nomination in 2008, Barack Obama defeated John McCain to become the first African American president of the United States. Gains for minorities were not limited to the world of politics. In sports, the African American sisters Venus and Serena Williams were a dominant force in women's tennis. Tiger Woods towered over the golfing world. Danica Patrick became the first woman to win an Indy Car race. Though the issue of gay rights remained contentious, gay Americans experienced growing levels of acceptance in general over the course of the decade. Outdated sodomy laws were finally overturned by the Supreme Court, and several states legalized gay marriage or domestic partnership. In 2004 the first gay marriage license in America was issued in San Francisco.

Technology. Despite the bursting of the dot-com bubble, digital technology proved an enduring bright spot for American capitalism. Cell phones overtook landlines in popularity, and pay phones all but disappeared from the landscape. Computers got smaller and faster. The iconic consumer item of the decade was the smartphone, a tiny handheld device that was a telephone, computer, digital music player, and more. In 1999 computers with a five hundred megahertz Pentium III microchip weighed over twenty-five pounds and took up most of a desktop. In 2009 Apple's popular iPhone 3GS offered a processor speed of six hundred megahertz in a lightweight device that was slightly larger than a deck of playing cards at less than half the cost. Americans lined up to purchase flat-screen, high-definition televisions (HDTVs) that took up far less space than traditional sets and offered eye-popping clarity of picture. Luxury items in 2000, HDTVs could be purchased at Wal-Mart by the end of the decade. The growth in broadband service meant that music and video could be instantly accessed and enjoyed via the Internet, a development that fueled the popularity of the iPod and other digital media players. Tablet devices and ereaders promised to remake the publishing industry as improved screen technology made the convenience of digital books into a palatable reading experience.

Environment. Concerns over global climate change loomed large in the decade. Al Gore's 2006 documentary

An Inconvenient Truth sparked a national debate over the role of humans in changing the natural environment. While most scientists agreed that human activity, especially the burning of fossil fuels, had a detrimental effect on the earth's ecology, Americans remained divided on the topic. The issue of global warming became fodder for political argument, with many decrying the Bush administration's failure to join the international Kyoto protocol for limiting greenhouse gas emissions and its stance on domestic oil exploration. Critics of climate-change claims charged that science offered no definitive proof of human environmental impact, and that in a weakening economy the cost of implementing scientists' recommendations would be felt in terms of lost jobs and diminished growth. While political action remained elusive, many Americans took it upon themselves to limit their "carbon footprint," their personal contribution to carbon emissions. Green living took many shapes: recycling, car pooling or taking advantage of public transportation, planting gardens or buying local foods, and making homes more energy efficient. The market also responded to consumer desire for green products. The Toyota Prius hybrid automobile became a hot seller and a totem of environmental consciousness. Energy-saving fluorescent light bulbs became widely available along with a host of more-efficient appliances. Major food retailers took steps to increase the amount of locally grown food on offer, while many restaurants made prominent mention of their commitment to sustainable food.

Change. Taking the pulse of the nation in the run-up to the 2008 presidential election, Barack Obama and his advisers settled on the theme of "change" for the campaign. They chose well. Americans of all political stripes were weary, if not of Bush administration policies, then of the decade as a whole, with all its setbacks and disappointments. Obama's victory in the 2008 election, forty years after the assassination of Martin Luther King Jr. and almost a century and a half after the end of slavery, was greeted as a milestone of American progress. It was also seen as a much-needed opportunity to restore the battered image of the United States in the rest of the world. Like his predecessor, Obama was greeted in office by massive problems. It soon became clear that the recession begun in 2007 was a much deeper, more long-term crisis than the nation had faced in generations. Backed by Democratic majorities in both houses of Congress, the incoming president had planned a broad overhaul of foreign and domestic policy. Instead, dealing with the economic crisis consumed much of Obama's first term in office, and some of the president's erstwhile allies saw more continuity than change in his approach to the war on terror. Still, despite the nation's myriad problems, the default national mood remained as it had been, one of optimism tempered with a faith in hard work. In his inaugural address, Obama channeled that spirit in a challenge to Americans as they closed one decade and opened another. "Starting today," he said, "we must pick ourselves up, dust ourselves off, and begin again the work of remaking America."

—*Eric Bargeron,*
University of South Carolina

ACKNOWLEDGMENTS

This book was produced by Manly, Inc. George Parker Anderson and Philip B. Dematteis were the in-house editors.

Production manager is Janet E. Hill.

Senior editor is Philip B. Dematteis.

Editorial assistant is Katherine E. Macedon.

Copyediting supervisor is Phyllis A. Avant. The copyediting staff includes Eileen R. Newman. Freelance copyeditors are Brenda L. Cabra, Jennifer Cooper, David C. King, Katherine E. Macedon, Rebecca Mayo, and Nancy E. Smith.

Digital photographic copy work and photo editing was performed by photo/permissions editor Dickson Monk.

The typesetting and graphics department includes Kathleen M. Flanagan and Patricia M. Flanagan.

Systems manager is James Sellers.

Office manager is Kathy Lawler Merlette.

Accountant is Ann-Marie Holland.

AMERICAN DECADES
2000 - 2009

WORLD EVENTS: SELECTED OCCURRENCES OUTSIDE THE UNITED STATES

2000

- The world population is 6.08 billion people.
- Andrew Lloyd Webber's musical *Cats* ends its nineteen-year run in London and also closes on Broadway.
- J. K. Rowling publishes *Harry Potter and the Goblet of Fire.*
- Outbreaks of Bovine Spongiform Encephalopathy, popularly known as mad cow disease, occur in Europe.
- Chinese author Gao Xingjian wins the Nobel Prize in Literature.
- Scottish film director Guy Ritchie marries singer Madonna.
- Chinese film *Crouching Tiger, Hidden Dragon* debuts.
- Sony introduces the PlayStation 2 video-game console.

Jan.	Pressure mounts from around the world to return Elian Gonzalez to his father in Cuba; the six-year-old boy had survived an escape attempt from the island to Florida that had claimed the lives of his mother and stepfather.
1 Jan.	Predictions of widespread worldwide computer shutdowns due to the Y2K bug prove false as the new millennium begins.
2 Jan.	Muslims and Coptic Christians clash in southern Egypt.
3 Jan.	Israeli prime minister Ehud Barak and Syrian foreign minister Farouk al-Shara meet in Shepherdstown, New York, to discuss security and economic issues.
3 Jan.	The deposed president of Ivory Coast, Konan Bedie, arrives in France. His successor, military ruler Robert Guéï, will suspend payments on the foreign debt within the week.
4 Jan.	Israel agrees to begin giving land in the West Bank to the Palestinian Authority.
4 Jan.	Italy opens diplomatic relations with North Korea.
5 Jan.	A suicide bomber from the Liberation Tigers of Tamil Eelam strikes in Colombo, Sri Lanka, part of an ongoing struggle to gain a homeland for Tamils. In June of this year another attack will kill a government minister.
5 Jan.	The Dalai Lama welcomes the seventeenth lama of the Karmapa Buddhist order, Ogyen Trinley Dorje, to Dharmsala, India, after he leaves Tibet in opposition to Chinese oppression of the country.
9 Jan.	Chechen rebels attack Grozny, Russia.

10 Jan.	The UN Security Council convenes to discuss the spread of AIDS, especially in Africa.
10 Jan.	Truck drivers in France block highways in protest against higher gas prices and fewer work hours.
10 Jan.	Islam Karimov wins a second term as president of Uzbekistan.
12 Jan.	Great Britain ends its ban on homosexuals in the military.
15 Jan.	Serbian paramilitary leader and accused war criminal Zĕljko Ražnatović is assassinated in Belgrade.
30 Jan.	A Kenyan airliner crashes into the Atlantic Ocean near Ivory Coast.
7 Mar.	Bangladesh ratifies the Comprehensive Nuclear Test Ban Treaty (CNTBT).
11 Mar.	Socialist Ricardo Froilán Lagos Escobar becomes president of Chile, the country's first leftist leader since the death of Salvador Allende in 1973.
17 Mar.	More than seven hundred members of a religious cult called the Movement for the Restoration of the Ten Commandments of God in Uganda commit mass suicide.
26 Mar.	Vladimir Putin is elected president of Russia. One of his first official acts is to visit the troubled Republic of Chechnya.
17 Apr.	Morocco ratifies the CNTBT.
24 May	Israeli troops withdraw from all of southern Lebanon except the Shebaa Farms area.
28 May	Putin signs a Nuclear Test Ban law, opening the way for Russia to approve the CNTBT.
13 June	South Korean president Kim Dae Jung visits North Korea, a first for a South Korean leader.
26 June	The CNTBT is signed by representatives of Iceland and Portugal. Four days later Russia signs the treaty.
28 June	Elian Gonzalez is returned to Cuba to live with his father.
July	Colombian president Andrés Pastrana initiates "Plan Colombia" to curtail drug trafficking; the United States will contribute $1.3 billion for helicopters and training.
2 July	Mexicans elect Vincente Fox president of their country over the Partido Revolucionario Institucional (PRI), which has ruled for more than seven decades.
10 July	More than 250 Nigerians die in a pipeline explosion.
25 July	Air France's supersonic plane *Concorde* crashes while taking off from Paris, killing 114 people (four on the ground). Most of the passengers are German tourists.
30 July	Hugo Chávez is reelected as president of Venezuela.
12 Aug.	The Russian nuclear submarine *Kursk* sinks in the Barents Sea. Allegations are made that some of the 118 sailors killed could have been saved with faster action by the navy and the acceptance of international aid, which was refused.
Sept.	Belarus and the United Arab Emirates (UAE) ratify the CNTBT.
11 Sept.	The World Economic Forum meets in Melbourne, Australia.
15 Sept.–1 Oct.	The twenty-seventh Olympics are hosted by Sydney, Australia.

26 Sept.	International Monetary Fund and World Bank meetings in Prague are hampered by massive antiglobalization protests.
26 Sept.	The Greek ferry *Express Samina* sinks off the island of Páros, with the loss of 82 passengers and crew; more than 450 are saved.
28 Sept.	Rock throwing erupts as Israeli politician Ariel Sharon visits the Temple Mount in Jerusalem, igniting several days of clashes between Palestinians and Israelis. Termed the Second Intifada, actions by youthful protesters against Israeli rule are gradually taken over by militant groups.
28 Sept.	Former Canadian prime minister Pierre Trudeau dies.
5 Oct.	Serbian president Slobodan Milŏsević is forced to step down as the leader of Yugoslavia.
12 Oct.	Seventeen U.S. sailors perish in an al Qaeda suicide attack against the destroyer USS *Cole* in Aden, Yemen.
26 Oct.	Laurent Gbagbo becomes president of Ivory Coast, replacing Robert Guéï.
2 Nov.	Two Russian cosmonauts and an American astronaut become the first crew to man the International Space Station in orbit.
11 Nov.	An Alpine cable-car fire in a tunnel in Kaprun, Austria, kills more than one hundred people.
13 Nov.	Philippine president Joseph Estrada is impeached.
16 Nov.	U.S. president Bill Clinton visits Vietnam.
17 Nov.	Peruvian president Alberto Fujimoro is removed from office on corruption charges. He will later be convicted for misuse of power and human-rights violations.
24 Nov.	A meeting is held in Zagreb, Croatia, between representatives of the European Union (E.U.) and former parts of Yugoslavia (Croatia, Bosnia and Herzegovina, Macedonia, and Albania) concerning regional stability and entry into the E.U.
10 Dec.	Former prime minister of Pakistan, Nawaz Sharif, who was overthrown by Pervez Musharraf, enters exile in Saudi Arabia.
30 Dec.	A string of bombs explode in Manila, killing more than twenty people.
31 Dec.	Massive riots erupt in Algeria.

2001

- Wikipedia goes online.
- *Nature* magazine publishes the first map of the human genome.
- A self-contained artificial heart is invented.
- Canadian author Yann Martel publishes *Life of Pi*.
- Trinidadian novelist V. S. Naipaul wins the Nobel Prize in Literature.
- The movies *Harry Potter and the Sorcerer's Stone* and *The Fellowship of the Ring* debut.
- The Nintendo GameCube gaming system is introduced.

Jan.	Amr Moussa replaces Egyptian Ismat Abdel Meguid as secretary general of the Arab League.
9 Jan.	China launches an unmanned space vehicle.

13 Jan.	A strong earthquake hits El Salvador, taking nearly nine hundred lives.
16 Jan.	President Laurent-Désiré Kabila of the Democratic Republic of Congo is assassinated.
20 Jan.	Joseph Estrada is replaced as the president of the Philippines by Gloria Macapagal-Arroyo.
23 Jan.	Revolutionary Armed Forces of Colombia (FARC) rebels kidnap two American journalists.
26 Jan.	Gujarat, India, is destroyed by an earthquake that kills more than twenty thousand people.
29 Jan.	Corruption charges against the president of Indonesia inspire thousands of students to storm the parliament building.
6 Feb.	Ariel Sharon is elected prime minister of Israel.
7 Feb.	Jean-Bertrand Aristide begins his third term as president of Haiti.
9 Feb.	A Japanese trawler is sunk off Hawaii after it is struck accidentally by an American submarine.
12 Feb.	A spacecraft (Near Earth Asteroid Rendezvous *Shoemaker*) lands for the first time on an asteroid.
26 Feb.	Two huge Buddhist statues carved into the side of a mountain near Bamian are destroyed by the ruling Taliban in Afghanistan. The act is widely condemned.
Mar.	Ethnic Albanians in Macedonia seek autonomy.
4 Mar.	A bomb, attributed to the Irish Republican Army, explodes in front of the BBC building in London.
23 Mar.	The Russian *Mir* space station falls back to Earth and is incinerated during atmospheric descent.
Apr.	Berbers protest in Kabylia, Algeria.
1 Apr.	Netherlands legalizes same-sex marriages.
2 Apr.	A U.S. spy plane and crew are forced down in China after a midair collision. The crew is released on 11 April.
6 May	Pope John Paul II visits a mosque in Syria.
1 June	Nepalese crown prince Dipendra shoots and kills his parents and other members of the royal family before attempting to commit suicide; he dies three days later and the former king's brother Gyanendra becomes king.
7 June	The Labour Party in Britain handily wins in the national elections. Tony Blair retains the post of prime minister.
14 June	The Shanghai Cooperation Organization is formed (China, Kazakhstan, Kyrgyzstan, Russia, Tajikistan, and Uzbekistan).
20 June	Musharraf assumes the presidency of Pakistan.
23 June	Pope John Paul II visits Ukraine.
July	In Sudan, the antigovernment Darfur Liberation Front is formed.
16 July	Russia and China sign a treaty of cooperation and friendly relations.
20 July	The members of the Group of Eight (G8) meet in Genoa, Italy, amid protests that cost at least one life.
6 Aug.	Brazilian author Jorge Amado de Faria dies.

10 Aug.	Coalition jets strike Iraqi air-defense sites.
21 Aug.	NATO plans to send peacekeepers to Macedonia.
2 Sept.	South African surgeon Christiaan Barnard, who performed the first human heart transplant, dies.
9 Sept.	Taliban suicide bombers posing as journalists kill Afghanistan Northern Alliance leader Ahmad Shah Massoud.
11 Sept.	Al Qaeda hijackers from Saudi Arabia, United Arab Emirates, Egypt, and Lebanon crash commercial airplanes into the World Trade Center towers in New York and the Pentagon in Washington, D.C. Nations around the globe quickly condemn the terrorist attacks.
18 Sept.	Iranian leader Ayatollah Ali Khamenei denounces the World Trade Center's attack.
22 Sept.	Ukrainian-born violinist Isaac Stern dies.
24 Sept.	Taliban leaders respond defiantly to U.S. demands that Afghanistan turn over Osama bin Laden.
25 Sept.	Saudi Arabia, a major contributor to humanitarian and radical activities in Afghanistan, breaks ties with the Taliban.
7 Oct.	American and British planes bomb Taliban targets in Afghanistan. Protests against the attacks erupt in several Muslim countries, including Pakistan. Special forces are secretly inserted into the country, largely to link up with anti-Taliban factions in the Northern Alliance.
19 Oct.	An Indonesian ship sinks en route to Easter Island; more than 350 passengers perish.
23 Oct.	The Provisional Irish Republican Army begins disarmament.
14 Nov.	Kabul is captured by forces from the Northern Alliance.
29 Nov.	Musician and former Beatles member George Harrison dies.
11–17 Dec.	Taliban forces withdraw from Qandahar. Many Taliban and al Qaeda fighters are trapped in the Tora Bora region and are routed by coalition troops. Reports surface that bin Laden has been wounded, but he escapes into the Pashtun-controlled region of Pakistan.
13 Dec.	Terrorists attack the Indian parliament.
19–20 Dec.	Riots caused by economic measures to shore up the banking system in Argentina force President Fernando de la Rua from office.
22 Dec.	Hamid Karzai is made interim president of Afghanistan.
22 Dec.	An al Qaeda sympathizer, Richard Reid, using a bomb hidden in his shoe, attempts to blow up an American Airways jet over the Atlantic Ocean as it travels from Britain to the United States.
29 Dec.	Nearly three hundred people die in a shopping-complex fire in Lima, Peru.

2002

- The euro (currency of the European Union) begins circulation in coin and paper.
- Hungarian writer Imre Kertész wins the Nobel Prize in Literature.

	• French archaeologists unearth the seven-million-year-old skull of a human ancestor in Chad.
16 Jan.	All assets of bin Laden, al Qaeda, and the Taliban are frozen by order of the UN Security Council.
17 Jan.	Spanish writer and Nobel Prize laureate Camilo José Cela dies.
20 Jan.	The FARC agrees to establish peace talks with the Colombia government.
23 Jan.	*Wall Street Journal* reporter Daniel Pearl is kidnapped and later brutally murdered in Pakistan.
8–24 Feb.	The Winter Olympics are held in Salt Lake City, Utah.
9 Feb.	Great Britain's Princess Margaret dies.
10 Feb.	Antar Zuabri, leader of the Islamic Army Group (blamed for killing thousands of civilians), is killed by Algerian antiterrorist forces.
12 Feb.	Former Serbian leader Milŏsević goes on trial before a UN war-crimes tribunal at The Hague.
22 Feb.	Rebel leader Jonas Savimbi is killed in Angola.
27 Feb.	More than fifty Hindus are burned to death in a Muslim attack on a trainload of pilgrims in Godhra, India. Hindu mobs strike back killing around sixty Muslims in Ahmadabad the following day.
1 Mar.	U.S. troops invade eastern Afghanistan. Operation Anaconda will eliminate approximately five hundred Taliban during two and a half weeks of battle.
27 Mar.	A Hamas suicide bomber attacks a Passover dinner in Netanya, Israel, killing twenty-eight attendees.
30 Mar.	Great Britain's Queen Mother, Elizabeth Bowes-Lyon, dies.
2 Apr.	Israel initiates Operation Defensive Shield in the West Bank.
11 Apr.	Twenty-one tourists are killed in a suicide attack at the Ghriba Synagogue on the island of Jerba, Tunisia.
12 Apr.	A coup in Venezuela temporarily deposes President Chávez; he regains the leadership of the country two days later.
5 May	Jacques Chirac is elected president of France.
12 May	Cuban president Fidel Castro welcomes former U.S. president Jimmy Carter.
20 May	East Timor becomes an independent country; it was formerly part of Indonesia.
23 May	Iceland becomes the fifty-fifth country to ratify the Kyoto Accords, the UN convention on climate control.
25 May	Nearly two hundred people die in a train crash in Mozambique.
	A Chinese airliner crashes into the Taiwan Strait, leaving 225 passengers dead.
22 June	Western Iran is struck by a strong earthquake; more than 250 people perish.
29 June	Naval forces from North and South Korea exchange fire.
30 June	Brazil defeats Germany in the World Cup, hosted by Japan and South Korea, earning its fifth crown.
1 July	The UN International Criminal Court (established to prosecute individuals charged with war crimes and genocide) is formally established.

2 July	The first nonstop balloon circumnavigation of the earth is completed by American Steve Fossett when he lands his vessel, *Spirit of Freedom,* in Australia.
9 July	The African Union is formed.
14 July	An assassination attempt is made on French president Jacques Chirac.
22 July	Hamas military leader Salah Shahade is assassinated by Israeli forces.
27 July	An accident at an air show held in L'viv, Ukraine, kills more than eighty spectators.
7 Aug.	Alvaro Uribe Velez assumes office as president of Colombia. His Patriot Plan steps up action against both leftist rebels and narcotics traffickers. FARC rebels mortar the inauguration.
16 Aug.	Palestinian terrorist Abu Nidal is assassinated in Iraq.
20 Aug.	The Iraqi embassy in Berlin is overrun by expatriate Iraqi dissidents.
5 Sept.	An assassination attempt is made against Afghan president Karzai; he survives, but around thirty others are killed.
10 Sept.	Switzerland joins the United Nations.
12 Sept.	Before the UN Security Council, U.S. president George Bush claims Iraq has been sheltering terrorists and harboring weapons of mass destruction (WMD).
19 Sept.	A military rebellion in Ivory Coast results in half the country being controlled by rebel forces. French troops are requested to help the government and block rebel advances.
26 Sept.	More than one thousand passengers die when a ferry sinks off the coast of Gambia.
27 Sept.	East Timor joins the United Nations.
12 Oct.	Terrorists explode bombs at popular nightclubs in Bali, killing more than two hundred people, many of them Australian tourists.
23 Oct.	Fifty Chechen rebels take hostage more than seven hundred theatergoers in Moscow. Russian forces storm the building three days later, killing most of the rebels; more than a hundred hostages die.
8 Nov.	UN Resolution 1441 urges Iraq to disarm or face military consequences.
21 Nov.	Bulgaria, Estonia, Latvia, Lithuania, Romania, Slovakia, and Slovenia are invited to join NATO.
22–27 Nov.	Muslim rioting in Nigeria leads to more than one hundred deaths and forces the Miss World pageant to relocate to England.
28 Nov.	Fifteen tourists and workers are killed in a terrorist attack against Israeli visitors at a hotel in Kenya.
7 Dec.	Iraq provides documentation to the United Nations supporting its claim that it does not have WMD.
27 Dec.	A government building in Chechnya is bombed, killing more than seventy people.

2003

- Many countries struggle with outbreaks of Severe Acute Respiratory Syndrome (SARS) during the year, although the first incidents occurred as early as November 2002.

- Volkswagen ceases production of the traditional "beetle" design.

- J. K. Rowling publishes *Harry Potter and the Order of the Phoenix.*

- Afghan author Khaled Hosseini publishes *The Kite Runner.*

- Iranian human-rights activist Shirin Ebadi wins the Nobel Peace Prize; South Africa writer J. M. Coetzee wins the Nobel Prize in Literature.

- A planet thought to be more than twelve billion years old is discovered by the Hubble telescope.

31 Jan.   A train derails in New South Wales, Australia, killing seven people.

1 Feb.   The space shuttle *Columbia* disintegrates upon reentry on its return trip to Earth; the first Israeli astronaut and an Indian American perish alongside five fellow crew members.

5 Feb.   U.S. Secretary of State Colin Powell addresses the UN Security Council; he claims that the United States has "undeniable" evidence that Iraq has WMD. In the following weeks, millions of people throughout the world protest against possible war in Iraq.

18 Feb.   A subway fire in South Korea kills nearly two hundred people.

1 Mar.   British prime minister Tony Blair backs the U.S. claims against Iraq, and calls for military action if Saddam Hussein does not comply with UN dictates.

5 Mar.   Seventeen civilians are killed when a bomb destroys a bus in Haifa, Israel.

12 Mar.   Serbian prime minister Zoran Djindjic is assassinated.

15 Mar.   Hu Jintao becomes president of the People's Republic of China.

19 Mar.   The war against Iraq begins. British and American troops invade.

23 Mar.   A U.S. Army maintenance unit blunders into an ambush in An Nasiriyah. Lori Piestewa becomes the first Native American woman to die in battle while serving in the U.S. Army. Of seven soldiers captured by the Iraqis, Jessica Lynch becomes best known. Ten days later American commandos rescue the POWs.

24 Mar.   The Arab League calls for the removal of foreign troops from Iraq.

7 Apr.   Baghdad falls to U.S. forces.

14 Apr.   Palestinian terrorist Muhammed "Abu Abbas" Zaidan, mastermind of the *Achille Lauro* hijacking, is captured in Baghdad.

25 Apr.   Soldiers of the Sudan Liberation Movement and Sudanese Liberation Army (SLM/SLA), which is formed out of the Darfur Liberation Front, attack Sudanese government garrisons.

1 May   U.S. president Bush announces "mission accomplished" in Iraq in a ceremony aboard the USS *Abraham Lincoln* aircraft carrier.

12 May   A powerful bomb explodes in a compound for foreign workers in Riyadh, Saudi Arabia, killing more than thirty people; al Qaeda claims responsibility.

14 May   A suicide-bombing attempt is made against Chechen administrator Akhmad Kadyrov.

16 May   Thirty-three people are killed and more than a hundred wounded in terrorist attacks in Casablanca, Morocco.

21 May   More than two thousand die in an earthquake in Algeria.

25 May   Néstor Kirchner becomes president of Argentina.

28 May   Israel accepts the U.S.-backed peace plan known as the "road map to peace."

28 May	Peter Hollingworth resigns as governor-general of Australia.
1 June	Popular Myanmar (Burma) leader Aung San Suu Kyi is arrested by the ruling military.
2 June	The European Space Agency launches a Mars probe from Kazakhstan.
3 June	Zimbabwean opposition leader Morgan Tsvangirai (Movement for Democratic Change) is arrested. Strikes break out against President Robert Mugabe. Hundreds are arrested by the military.
5 June	Sixteen soldiers and civilians on a bus in Chechnya are killed in a suicide attack.
18 June	The International Atomic Energy Agency (IAEA) claims that Iran is actively hiding its nuclear program.
1 July	Nearly half a million protesters in Hong Kong peacefully march against restrictive security measures.
8 July	An airplane crash in Sudan takes the lives of 116, with only one survivor.
22 July	Saddam Hussein's sons, Uday and Qusay, are killed in a firefight with U.S. troops.
Aug.	A heat wave in France leads to nearly 15,000 deaths, mostly in the first half of the month.
1 Aug.	A Russian military hospital in Chechnya is attacked; more than fifty perish.
5 Aug.	A car-bomb attack on a Marriott hotel in Jakarta, Indonesia, results in twelve deaths and hundreds of injuries.
11 Aug.	NATO takes over International Security Assistance Force (ISAF) operations in Afghanistan.
13 Aug.	Thai police and the C.I.A. arrest Jemaah Islamiyah leader Hambali (Riduan Isamuddin), believed to be a top al Qaeda member.
19 Aug.	A massive bomb destroys the UN headquarters in Baghdad; among the dead is human-rights commissioner Sérgio Vieira de Mello of Brazil. More than twenty other employees also perish.
26 Aug.	Islamic militants set off two car bombs in Mumbai, India, killing more than fifty people.
28 Aug.	London is hit with a widespread electrical blackout.
29 Aug.	Shia leader Sayed Mohammed Baqir al-Hakim is assassinated in a bombing that also kills almost one hundred worshipers at a mosque in An Najaf, Iraq.
10 Sept.	Swedish foreign minister Anna Lindh is attacked by a mentally ill Swedish citizen originally from Yugoslavia. Lindh dies the following day.
12 Sept.	The United Nations lifts its sanctions against Libya; the restrictions had been placed in response to the 1988 Pan Am bombing.
20 Sept.	Rioting erupts in Male, Maldives, after a prisoner dies in custody.
2 Oct.	North Korea announces successful plutonium extraction.
2 Oct.	Pakistan strikes al Qaeda militants within its borders, killing at least a dozen suspected terrorists.
4 Oct.	A suicide bomber attacks a restaurant in Haifa, Israel, killing twenty-one people.
15 Oct.	Yang Liwei pilots China's first manned space flight.
17 Oct.	Taipei finishes construction on Taipei 101, claimed to be the highest building in the world.

18 Oct.   Bolivian president Gonzalo Sánchez de Lozada resigns in the face of widespread protests by impoverished indigenous citizens.

31 Oct.   Malaysian prime minister Mahathir bin Mohamad resigns, ending more than two decades in office; he is replaced by Abdullah Ahmad Badawi.

12 Nov.   Italian troops are killed in a suicide bombing in An Nasiriyah, Iraq.

15 and 20 Nov.   Terrorists carry out bombings in Istanbul, Turkey.

23 Nov.   Georgian president Eduard Shevardnadze resigns.

9 Dec.   A suicide bomber attacks the National Hotel in Moscow; five people die.

13 Dec.   Saddam Hussein is captured by American forces near Tikrit, Iraq.

14 and 25 Dec.   Pakistan president Musharraf survives two assassination attempts.

17 Dec.   The privately financed rocket plane *SpaceShipOne* makes its first supersonic flight; on 21 June 2004 it makes its first trip into space.

23 Dec.   More than 230 people die in a natural-gas field explosion in Chongqing, China.

26 Dec.   Thousands die in an earthquake centered around Bam, Iran.

2004

- Google introduces its Gmail electronic mail service.

- Kenyan environmental and political activist Wangari Maathai wins the Nobel Peace Prize; Austrian writer Elfriede Jelinek wins the Nobel Prize in Literature.

1 Jan.   President Musharraf wins a vote of confidence in Pakistan.

3 Jan.   An Egyptian airliner crashes into the Red Sea, killing all aboard.

4 Jan.   A NASA rover *(Spirit)* lands on Mars and, along with a companion vehicle *(Opportunity)* at another location, will far exceed expectations, supplying pictures and scientific data. Despite several small glitches, the rover will continue to operate into 2009.

12 Jan.   The RMS *Queen Mary 2,* the largest ocean liner in the world, begins her maiden voyage. On 16 April she will begin her first cross-Atlantic voyage.

14 Jan.   Libya ratifies the CNTBT.

26 Jan.   Afghanistan establishes a new constitution.

1 Feb.   Hundreds are trampled at Mecca, Saudi Arabia, during the annual Hajj.

1 Feb.   Some 124 members of Iran's parliament resign in protest of the refusal of the government to allow reformists to run for offices throughout the country.

2 Feb.   Israel plans to remove settlements from Gaza.

2 Feb.   Abdul Qadeer Kahn, a respected Pakistani nuclear scientist, admits to helping Iran, North Korea, and Libya develop nuclear technology.

5 Feb.   Members of the Revolutionary Artibonite Resistance Front initiate a rebellion in Haiti.

14 Feb.   The collapse of a roof covering a water park in Moscow kills more than two dozen attendees.

18 Feb.	A train crash and explosion in Neyshābūr, Iran, causes the death of nearly three hundred passengers and rescue personnel.
26 Feb.	Macedonian president Boris Trajkovski is killed in a plane crash.
27 Feb.	More than one hundred passengers are killed when the Philippine Islamic terrorist organization Abu Sayyaf bombs a ferry.
28 Feb.	President Aristide is deposed and forced to leave Haiti in a rightist coup.
2 Mar.	Nearly two hundred die, and five hundred are wounded in Karbala, Iraq, after terrorist bombings during celebrations of Ashura. Other attacks occur in Baghdad, mostly against Shia worshipers.
11 Mar.	Nearly two hundred commuters are killed, and around seventeen hundred are wounded in coordinated terrorist bombings against commuter trains in Madrid, Spain.
12 Mar.	South Korean president Roh Moo Hyun is impeached, but the impeachment will later be overturned by the Supreme Court.
17 Mar.	José Luis Rodriguez Zapatero becomes Spanish prime minister, partly on his promise to remove soldiers from the Iraq conflict.
19 Mar.	Taiwanese president Chen Shui-bian survives an assassination attempt.
22 Mar.	An Israeli rocket attack kills Hamas cofounder Ahmed Yassin and his bodyguards in Gaza.
29 Mar.	Bulgaria, Estonia, Latvia, Lithuania, Romania, Slovakia, and Slovenia join NATO.
29 Mar.	Smoking is banned in public places in Ireland, the first such nationwide ban to be instituted.
31 Mar.	Four Blackwater contractors are murdered and publicly displayed in Al Fallujah, Iraq. U.S. forces will assault the city on 5 April.
6 Apr.	Lithuanian president Rolandas Paksas is impeached and removed from office.
8 Apr.	A cease-fire is called in the troubled region of Darfur.
22 Apr.	Hundreds are killed as a result of two trains colliding in Ryongchon, North Korea.
24 Apr.	South Waziristan leader Nek Mohammed agrees to stop fighting against the Pakistani army.
30 Apr.	The release of photographs revealing rampant abuse and humiliation of Iraqi prisoners in Abu Ghraib prison by American guards shocks the allies and sparks protests in the Islamic world.
1 May	Cyprus, the Czech Republic, Estonia, Hungary, Latvia, Lithuania, Malta, Poland, Slovakia, and Slovenia join the European Union.
2 May	A Christian mob in Yelwa, Nigeria, massacres more than six hundred Muslims. Muslims will retaliate by killing Christians and burning churches.
9 May	Russian-backed Chechen president Akhmad Kadyrov is assassinated in Grozny.
29 May	Islamic militants seize and kill more than twenty in an attack on a residential compound for foreigners in Al Khobar, Saudi Arabia.
1 June	An interim government headed by Iyad Allawi is established in Iraq. The UN Security Council eventually recognizes the new government.
18 June	Nek Mohammed is killed by a U.S. missile strike after reneging on his commitment to the Pakistani army.

14 July   The Butler Review, which is critical of British intelligence gathering leading up to the war in Iraq, is released.

1 Aug.   Nearly four hundred people die in a supermarket fire in Asunción, Paraguay.

12–29 Aug.   The Olympic Games are held in Athens, Greece.

14 Aug.   Polish author and Nobel Prize laureate Czesław Miłosz dies.

22 Aug.   Edvard Munch's paintings *The Scream* and *Madonna* are stolen from a museum in Oslo, Norway.

24 Aug.   Chechen suicide bombers bring down two commercial airplanes near Moscow, killing eighty-nine people.

31 Aug.   Hamas suicide bombers attack in Beersheba, Israel; sixteen people are killed, and more than sixty are wounded.

31 Aug.   A female Chechen suicide bomber strikes the subway in Moscow, taking ten lives.

2 Sept.   The UN Security Council calls for Syrian troops to withdraw from Lebanon.

3 Sept.   Nearly 350 people, mostly children, die in a shoot-out with Russian forces after a two-day hostage incident orchestrated by Chechen rebels in Beslan, North Ossetia.

7 Sept.   Hurricane Ivan kills nearly forty people when it strikes Grenada.

9 Sept.   Australia's embassy in Jakarta, Indonesia, is attacked. Eleven die, and more than one hundred are wounded.

10–13 Sept.   Hurricane Ivan strikes Cuba, causing massive destruction but few deaths.

15 Sept.   UN secretary-general Kofi Annan criticizes the Iraq War.

17 Sept.   Representatives from Japan and Mexico sign a free-trade agreement.

23 Sept.   Floods caused by Hurricane Jeanne ravage Haiti, leaving at least one thousand dead.

8 Oct.   Algerian-French philosopher Jacques Derrida dies.

23 Oct.   Brazil launches a rocket into space from Alcântara Launch Center in Maranhão.

23 Oct.   Northern Japan is struck by a strong earthquake; thirty-five are killed, and thousands are left homeless.

2 Nov.   Filmmaker Theo van Gogh is assassinated in Amsterdam by a Muslim extremist upset about van Gogh's August release of a movie that depicted the mistreatment of women in Islam.

8 Nov.   American troops encircle and assault the insurgent stronghold of Al Fallujah, Iraq. An estimated fifteen hundred to sixteen hundred militants will be killed during the month-long battle.

11 Nov.   Palestinian leader and Nobel Peace Prize–winner Yasser Arafat dies of a blood disease. He is succeeded by Mahmoud Abbas.

14 Nov.   Burmese troops attack Karen villages.

18 Nov.   Russia ratifies the Kyoto Accords.

21 Nov.   Viktor Yanukovych wins the presidency of Ukraine. Opponents claim fraud, and in late December the Supreme Court annuls the election and orders a new one. The political unrest leads to the Orange Revolution.

21 Nov.	A strong earthquake strikes the northern half of the Caribbean island nation of Dominica.
13 Dec.	Former Chilean president Augusto Pinochet is placed under house arrest.
26 Dec.	Tsunamis triggered by a massive earthquake destroy coastal towns in Thailand and Indonesia, and cause death and damage as far away as Myanmar, Bangladesh, India, the Maldives, and the east African coast. More than two hundred thousand perish.

2005

- The video-sharing and -viewing Internet site called YouTube is launched.

- Boeing announces it will produce a stretched version of its popular 747 airliner.

- French doctors perform the first partial human-face transplant.

- J. K. Rowling publishes *Harry Potter and the Half-Blood Prince.*

- Swedish author Stieg Larsson's *Män som hatar kvinnor (The Girl with the Dragon Tattoo),* is posthumously published.

- Egyptian IAEA director Mohamed ElBaradei is awarded the Nobel Peace Prize; British writer Harold Pinter wins the Nobel Prize in Literature.

9 Jan.	Rawhi Fattouh is elected to head the Palestine Liberation Organization (PLO).
13 Jan.	Militants from Gaza enter Israel and kill six people. Palestinian leader Mahmoud Abbas promises to control such attacks.
17 Jan.	The former premier of the People's Republic of China, Zhao Ziyang, dies.
21 Jan.	Antitax protesters riot in Belize.
25 Jan.	More than two hundred die in a stampede at the Mandher Devi temple in India.
29 Jan.	China resumes commercial air traffic with Taiwan.
30 Jan.	Iraqis vote for representatives to a national assembly.
2 Feb.	German heavyweight-boxing champion Max Schmeling dies.
10 Feb.	Municipal elections are held in Saudi Arabia for the first time. Only men are allowed to vote.
14 Feb.	Former Lebanese prime minister Rafik Hariri is assassinated, allegedly by pro-Syrian elements within the country.
14 Feb.	Three cities in the Philippines are bombed by al Qaeda–linked terrorists; at least eleven people are killed and 150 wounded.
16 Feb.	The Kyoto Protocol is now in force.
23 Feb.	U.S. president Bush and Russian president Putin visit Slovakia to attend a summit.
25 Feb.	Islamic Jihad stages attacks in Tel Aviv, Israel, killing five and wounding more than fifty.
25 Feb.	The founder of Amnesty International, Peter Benenson, dies.
28 Feb.	Lebanese prime minister Omar Karami resigns from office in response to anti-Syrian demonstrations.
4 Mar.	Italian journalist Giuliana Sgrena is accidentally wounded by American gunfire at a roadblock.
7 Mar.	Women in Kuwait march for equal voting rights.

14 Mar.	A train derailment in Vietnam takes the lives of eleven passengers and injures hundreds of others.
24 Mar.	President Askar Alayev is overthrown in Kyrgyzstan in what becomes known as the Tulip Revolution.
2 Apr.	Pope John Paul II dies.
6 Apr.	Jalal Talabani, a Kurd, becomes the president of Iraq.
9 Apr.	Charles, Prince of Wales, marries Camilla Parker Bowles.
19 Apr.	The College of Cardinals in Rome elects German-born Joseph Ratzinger as pope; he begins his papacy as Benedict XVI on the twenty-fourth.
26 Apr.	The last Syrian troops withdraw from Lebanon.
4 May	More than sixty people are killed in a suicide-bombing attack against a police recruiting center in Arbil, Kurdish northern Iraq.
10 May	An assassination attempt is made on President Bush during a state visit to Tbilisi, Georgia.
25 May	Egyptian thugs in Cairo molest and beat women participating in protests against undemocratic elections. The actions by police who allowed the outrage lead to a movement to reform the political process in Egypt.
14 June	Jamaican sprinter Asafa Powell sets the men's one-hundred-meter world record at 9.77 seconds.
24 June	Mahmoud Ahmadinejad wins the presidency of Iran.
30 June	Spain allows same-sex marriages.
6 July	French writer and Nobel Prize laureate Claude Simon dies.
7 July	Suicide bombers, Muslim radicals with British backgrounds, attack the London subway and a bus; almost forty people are killed. Another coordinated bombing attempt against the transportation system fails two weeks later.
10 July	Kurmanbek Bakiyev wins the presidency of Kyrgyzstan.
12 July	Ethiopian raiders stage an attack across the Kenyan border, killing more than one hundred villagers.
28 July	The Provisional Irish Republican Army ceases armed conflict with the British.
3 Aug.	Mauritanian president Maaouya Ould Sid'Ahmed Taya's rule is overthrown while he is on a state visit to Saudi Arabia.
15–23 Aug.	Israel removes more than eight thousand settlers from Gaza and the West Bank.
7 Sept.	Hosni Mubarak is elected president of Egypt.
19 Sept.	North Korea asks for aid in return for stopping their nuclear program.
25 Sept.	News reporter May Chidiac is seriously wounded in a car bombing attributed to pro-Syrian elements in Lebanon.
30 Sept.	The Danish newspaper *Jyllands-Posten* publishes a cartoon with a physical depiction of the prophet Muhammad that sparks protests and threats of violence in the Islamic world.
1 Oct.	A bomb kills twenty-six people in Bali.
2 Oct.	The Arizona Cardinals and San Francisco 49ers of the National Football League play a regular season game for the first time outside the United States, in Mexico City.

8 Oct.	A massive earthquake in Kashmir, Pakistan leads to the deaths of more than eighty thousand people.
19 Oct.	Saddam Hussein goes on trial.
26 Oct.	Iranian president Ahmadinejad calls for the elimination of Israel.
27 Oct.	Weeks of rioting by young immigrant men from Africa and the Middle East begin in the underprivileged outskirts of Paris.
Nov.	Ellen Johnson-Sirleaf is elected president of Liberia. She is sworn in on 16 January 2006 as the first democratically elected female leader in Africa.
9 Nov.	More than sixty people are killed as three hotels in Amman, Jordan, are bombed by followers of Abu Musab al-Zarqawi.
21 Nov.	Ariel Sharon steps down as leader of the Likud Party in Israel.
22 Nov.	Germany elects its first female chancellor, Angela Merkel of the conservative Christian Democratic Union.
28 Nov.	The Canadian parliament is dissolved after a vote of no confidence.
15 Dec.	Iraqis elect their first parliament since Hussein's overthrow with more than 70 percent turnout.
18 Dec.	War breaks out between Chad and Sudan.

2006

- The Internet social network Twitter is launched.
- The Svalbard Global Seed Vault, a project to preserve biodiversity, is established in Spitsbergen, Norway.
- Bangladeshi economist and banker Muhammad Yunus, who promotes the idea of microloans to entrepreneurs in developing countries, is awarded the Nobel Peace Prize; Turkish novelist Orhan Pamuk wins the Nobel Prize in Literature.
- The Nintendo Wii gaming system is introduced (the concept was revealed in 2005); Sony answers with the PlayStation 3.

5 Jan.	Ehud Olmert replaces Sharon as Israel's prime minister.
12 Jan.	More than 350 people are killed in a stampede at the Hajj in Mina, Saudi Arabia.
15 Jan.	Kuwaiti emir Jaber Al-Ahmad Al-Jaber Al-Sabah dies.
22 Jan.	Juan Evo Morales Ayma, a member of the Aymara nation, becomes Bolivia's first indigenous president.
Feb.	Muslims worldwide protest the depiction of Muhammad in cartoons originally published in a Danish newspaper in September 2005.
4 Feb.	A stampede in Manila kills more than seventy people.
16 Feb.	René Préval is elected president of Haiti; he is inaugurated 14 March.
17 Feb.	More than one thousand people are killed in a mudslide in Leyte, Philippines.
22 Feb.	In Samarra, Iraq, the famous Shia al-Askari mosque's dome is destroyed in sectarian violence.
22 Feb.	With a haul larger than $90 million, robbers in Great Britain pull off one of the largest bank heists in history in Tonbridge, Kent.
24 Feb.	The Philippines goes under martial law to counter a possible coup attempt.

11 Mar.	Socialist Michelle Bachelet Jeria becomes president of Chile.
11 Mar.	Slobodan Milŏsević is found dead at the UN Detention Center at The Hague.
20 Mar.	Rebels slaughter more than 150 Chadian soldiers.
21 Mar.	Immigrant workers riot in Dubai, causing millions of dollars of damage.
28 Mar.	Workers in France riot over new employment laws.
30 Mar.	Brazilian astronaut Marcos Pontes becomes the first from his country to travel in space.
11 Apr.	Iran announces it has produced a small amount of enriched uranium.
22 Apr.	Prodemocracy protestors in Nepal clash with police. Two days later King Gyanendra restores the parliament. Within a month the country will have a secular government that will diminish the power of the king.
1 May	Bolivia nationalizes its oil industry.
12–15 May	Prison riots and street attacks on police—believed to be coordinated by the criminal organization the First Command of the Capital (PCC)—erupt in the state of São Paulo in Brazil. More than eighty people die in widespread weekend violence.
27 May	Nearly six thousand people are killed in an earthquake in central Java.
28 May	Uribe is reelected president of Colombia after restrictions against second presidential terms are overthrown.
3 June	Montenegro becomes an independent state and on 28 June joins the United Nations. Serbia declares its independence on 5 June.
25 June	A Palestinian raid—in which two Israeli soldiers are killed and one, Gilad Shalit, is taken hostage—prompts an Israeli incursion into Gaza.
4–5 July	North Korea tests several long-range missiles, sparking UN meetings on the potential threat.
9 July	Italy defeats France in the World Cup, which is hosted by Germany.
9 July	124 of 203 people aboard a Russian airliner perish after a runway accident in Siberia.
11 July	Terrorist bombings in Mumbai kill more than two hundred people.
12 July	Israel bombs Hezbollah targets in Lebanon. Hezbollah tries to bargain captured Israeli soldiers for the release of Israeli-held prisoners. On 13 July, Haifa is struck by rockets, and the next day Israel responds by destroying sites in Beirut, Lebanon.
24 July	Nearly two hundred passengers and crew die, and more than eight hundred are wounded, in the bombing of a commuter train in Mumbai, India, allegedly by an extremist Islamic group.
31 July	Raúl Castro is given presidential powers in Cuba by his brother, Fidel.
3 Aug.	German/Austrian/English opera star Elisabeth Schwarzkopf dies.
14 Aug.	The United Nations helps broker a truce between Israel and Hezbollah forces and establishes a peacekeeping presence along the southern border of Lebanon.
22 Aug.	All 169 people aboard a Russian airliner die in a crash in the Ukraine. President Vladimir Putin orders an investigation into possible violation of air-safety rules.
30 Aug.	Egyptian author and Nobel Prize laureate Naguib Mahfouz dies.
31 Aug.	Munch's *The Scream* and *Madonna* are recovered.

4 Sept.	Australian naturalist Steve Irwin, who hosts the popular television show *The Crocodile Hunter,* is killed by a stingray-barb strike to his heart.
10 Sept.	Tongan king Taufa'ahau Tupou IV dies and is succeeded by his son, Tupou V.
19 Sept.	Martial law is declared in Bangkok as a military coup overthrows the government.
7 Oct.	Russian journalist Anna Politkovskaya is murdered in Moscow, the thirteenth such killing of critics of Putin.
9 Oct.	North Korea tests a nuclear device.
5 Nov.	Saddam Hussein is convicted by an Iraqi court and later sentenced to death.
12 Nov.	Israel warns that it may be forced to strike Iran's nuclear facilities.
15 Nov.	Joseph Kabila is elected president of the Democratic Republic of Congo.
21 Nov.	Lebanese minister Pierre Amine Gemayel is assassinated.
10 Dec.	Former Chilean president Augusto Pinochet dies; he had been indicted at home and in Europe on human-rights violations that occurred during his dictatorial rule (1973–1990) and was under house arrest.
28 Dec.	Ethiopian troops drive Muslim soldiers from Mogadishu, Somalia. Fighting will continue into January 2007, as rebels are pushed into Kenya.
30 Dec.	Saddam Hussein is executed by hanging.

2007

•	Apple introduces the iPhone, a heavily-hyped, full-featured cell phone and media player.
•	The tomb of the first-century B.C. Jewish king Herod is discovered by archaeologists.
•	The last surviving clipper ship, the *Cutty Sark,* burns at its dock in London.
•	J. K. Rowling's *Harry Potter and the Deathly Hallows,* the final volume in the Harry Potter series, is published.
•	Khaled Hosseini publishes *A Thousand Splendid Suns.*
•	The double-decked, wide-bodied European airliner, the *Airbus A380,* enters passenger service.
•	British author Doris Lessing wins the Nobel Prize in Literature.

1 Jan.	Bulgaria and Romania join the European Union.
	More than one hundred people die in an Indonesian airliner crash.
10 Jan.	Venezuelan president Hugo Chávez begins his third term as president.
10 Jan.	Former Sandinista leader Daniel Ortega is inaugurated president of Nicaragua.
15 Jan.	Saddam Hussein's half brother Barzan Ibrahim al-Tikriti and former Iraqi chief judge Awad Hamad al-Bandar are executed in Iraq.
16 Jan.	Rafael Correa becomes president of Ecuador.
18 Jan.	Strong storms assault Europe, with damage and deaths ranging from the coast of England to Germany.
19 Jan.	Journalist Hrant Dink is killed in Turkey by teenagers who allege he had insulted Islam.

3 Feb.	A bomb explosion in a Baghdad market kills more than 135 people.
10–12 Feb.	Antigovernment protestors riot in Guinea.
15 Feb.	More than seventy members of the Muslim Brotherhood are arrested in Egypt.
1 Mar.	Riots break out in Copenhagen, Denmark, after a popular building, the Ung-domshuset, is cleared for demolition.
11 Mar.	Opposition leader Morgan Tsvangirai and fellow protestors are arrested and beaten by police in Harare, Zimbabwe. They are released by 13 March.
22 Mar.	Violence wracks the Democratic Republic of Congo as rebels led by Jean-Pierre Bemba protest their defeat in presidential elections. Bemba will seek sanctuary in the South African embassy, and his soldiers lay down their arms on 28 March.
23 Mar.	Fifteen British sailors are detained by Iran for straying into Iranian waters; they will be released on 4 April.
2 Apr.	Sunni and Shia factions battle in Parachinar, Pakistan; more than forty people die.
11 Apr.	More than thirty people are killed in bombings in Algiers, Algeria.
15 Apr.	Thousands of Pakistanis march against extremist violence in their country.
18 Apr.	Three employees of a Christian publishing house are killed in Turkey.
27 Apr.	Abdullah Gul is elected president of Turkey, but without secular support. His election will be annulled on 1 May.
11 May	Samoan ruler Malietoa Tanumafili II dies.
28 May	U.S. and Iranian officials meet in Baghdad to discuss the need for stability in Iraq.
10–17 June	Fighting erupts between Fatah and Hamas factions in Gaza.
14 June	Austrian politician and former head of the United Nations Kurt Waldheim dies.
17 June	Author Salman Rushdie is knighted by Queen Elizabeth II, sparking demonstrations in Muslim countries.
27 June	Brazilian military police battle with drug dealers in the slums *(favelas)* of Rio de Janeiro; approximately twenty people are killed.
28 June	Egypt outlaws the practice of female circumcision.
July	Price controls are established in Zimbabwe to control high inflation. By October citizens are still finding it hard to buy necessities, such as bread.
1 July	England bans smoking in public areas.
16 July	A strong earthquake rattles Niigata, Japan.
17 July	Nearly two hundred people die in an airliner crash in São Paulo, Brazil.
25 July	President Pratibha Patil is sworn in; she is the first woman to hold the position in India.
6 Aug.	Israeli prime minister Ehud Olmert meets with Palestinian president Mahmoud Abbas in Jericho in the West Bank.
14 Aug.	More than four hundred (some reports claim seven hundred) people perish in multiple suicide bombings in the Kurdish region of northern Iraq.
15 Aug.	A strong earthquake in Peru kills more than five hundred people and injures more than one thousand.
6 Sept.	Famous Italian tenor Luciano Pavarotti dies.

10 Sept.	Nawaz Sharif returns to Pakistan.
18 Sept.	Prodemocracy protesters in Myanmar are joined by Buddhist monks.
2 Oct.	South Korean president Moo Hyun holds a summit with North Korean leader Kim Jong Il.
7 Oct.	Musharraf is reelected president of Pakistan.
10 Oct.	Malaysia's first astronaut, Sheikh Muszaphar Shukor, travels to the International Space Station aboard a Russian rocket.
17 Oct.	Togo holds democratic elections.
18 Oct.	Former prime minister Benazir Bhutto returns to Pakistan. Terrorist bombers attack crowds of well-wishers.
21 Oct.	Growing anti-immigrant sentiment in Switzerland is expressed in increased representation by members of the Swiss People's Party in the National Council.
28 Oct.	Cristina Fernández de Kirchner is elected president of Argentina.
3 Nov.	Musharraf declares a state of emergency in Pakistan. Pakistani troops begin operations in the northeast, capturing and killing pro-Taliban forces—by early December nearly three hundred have been killed.
5 Nov.	China positions its first lunar satellite.
7 Nov.	Nine people are killed in a school shooting in Tuusula, Finland.
13 Nov.	A congressman and three others are killed in a bombing of the House of Representatives in Quezon City, Philippines.
15 Nov.	Approximately five thousand people die in a cyclone that strikes Bangladesh.
20 Nov.	Former Rhodesian prime minister Ian Smith dies.
29 Nov.	A mutiny in Manila is quickly defeated by Philippine forces.
3 Dec.	Australia signs the Kyoto Protocol.
11 Dec.	Algiers is again rocked by car bombs; more than forty people die.
12 Dec.	A UN agency is attacked in Algiers, with the death toll more than thirty.
17 Dec.	Saudi king Abdullah pardons a gang-rape victim who had been given a six-month jail sentence and two hundred lashes for being alone with a man with whom she was neither related nor married.
20 Dec.	Paintings by Pablo Picasso and Candido Portinari are stolen from the São Paulo Museum of Art.
27 Dec.	Former Pakistani prime minister and candidate Benazir Bhutto is assassinated, allegedly by supporters of Baitullah Mehsud of South Waziristan.

2008

- Former Finnish president Martti Ahtisaari wins the Nobel Peace Prize; the Nobel Prize in Literature is awarded to French author J. M. G. Le Clézio.

- The European Organization for Nuclear Research (CERN) smashes two accelerated particle beams at the Large Hadron Collider (LHC) on the Swiss-French border.

Jan.	Kenya is wracked by serious rioting over contested presidential elections; more than eight hundred people will die.
6 Jan.	Georgian president Mikheil Saakashvili is reelected.

7 Jan.	Riots break out in Kenya.
11 Jan.	New Zealand mountain climber and philanthropist Sir Edmund Hillary, the first person to summit Everest (1953), dies.
15 Jan.	Uzbekistan president Islam Karimov starts his third term.
21 Jan.	Stock markets worldwide experience major losses.
27 Jan.	Former Indonesian dictator Suharto dies.
4 Feb.	Serbian president Boris Tadic wins reelection.
5 Feb.	Indian guru and founder of transcendental meditation, Maharishi Mahesh Yogi, dies.
12 Feb.	Senior Hezbollah official Imad Fayez Mugniyah is assassinated.
17 Feb.	Kosovo declares its independence from Serbia.
19 Feb.	Fidel Castro permanently gives up power in Cuba.
2 Mar.	Dmitry Medvedev is elected president of Russia.
14 Mar.	Tibetan rioting against Chinese rule commences.
24 Mar.	Bhutan holds its first general elections.
Apr.	Rising worldwide prices on food—caused in part by rising oil prices—spur rioting in many countries.
11 Apr.	Nepalese voters choose a new parliament to write a constitution.
22 Apr.	Two female journalists are assassinated in Oaxaca Province, Mexico.
22 Apr.	Fernando Lugo wins the presidency of Paraguay.
2 May	More than twenty thousand people die as Myanmar is hit by a cyclone.
12 May	Central China is struck by a massive earthquake. More than eighty-five thousand are killed.
25 May	A U.S. spacecraft lands on Mars.
25 May	Michel Suleiman is elected president of Lebanon.
28 May	The Nepalese monarchy is abolished.
30 May	Mexico initiates measures to counter the effects of rising food prices on the poor.
2 July	Colombian soldiers free politician Ingrid Betancourt, who has been a hostage of leftist FARC rebels since 2002.
14 July	The International Criminal Court charges Sudanese president Omar Hassan al-Bashir with acts of genocide.
21 July	War criminal Radovan Karadžić is arrested in Serbia.
6 Aug.	Mohamed Ould Abdel Aziz overthrows President Sidi Ould Cheikh Abdallahi in Mauritania.
7–11 Aug.	Troops from Georgia and Russia fight in South Ossetia.
20 Sept.	A car bomb outside the Marriott Hotel in Islamabad, Pakistan, kills more than fifty people.
21 Sept.	South African president Thabo Mbeki resigns (effective four days later).
21 Sept.	Israeli prime minister Olmert resigns his office.
1 Oct.	The Iraqi government begins taking control of its own military forces.

10 Nov.	South African singer and activist Miriam Makeba dies.
26 Nov.	A terrorist group based out of Pakistan attacks sites in Mumbai. More than 150 people are killed in the assault.
14 Dec.	An Iraqi reporter makes international headlines for throwing a shoe in protest at President Bush while he is making a speech in Baghdad.
15 Dec.	Abhisit Vejjajiva becomes the prime minister of Thailand.
22 Dec.	Guinean president Lansana Conté dies. Two days later a military coup places Moussa Camara in power.

2009

- German author Herta Müller wins the Nobel Prize in Literature.
- A vaccine against the AIDS virus shows some promise.
- The H1N1 (swine flu) virus cause international concerns.

1 Jan.	Slovakia begins using the euro.
1 Jan.	A nightclub fire in Bangkok, Thailand, takes the lives of more than sixty people.
3 Jan.	Israel invades Gaza.
1 Feb.	Iceland elects Jóhanna Sigurðardóttir, who becomes the first openly gay prime minister.
7 Feb.	Wildfires in Australia kill more than 170 people.
25–26 Feb.	Around seventy Bangladesh Rifles officers and family members are massacred by mutinous border guards possibly loyal to a militant Islamic group.
3 Mar.	A six-story historical archive building in Cologne, Germany, collapses, possibly due to nearby construction. Two other buildings collapse as well, with the loss of two lives. Many medieval records are destroyed.
3 Mar.	Pakistani gunmen attack a bus carrying cricket players from Sri Lanka; six policemen and the driver are killed.
4 Mar.	Sudanese president Omar Hassan al-Bashir is indicted by the International Criminal Court for war crimes committed in Darfur.
1 Apr.	Albania and Croatia join NATO.
6 Apr.	L'Aquila, Italy, is struck by an earthquake that kills more than 250 people.
7 Apr.	Former Peruvian president Alberto Fujimori is sentenced to twenty-five years in prison.
11 Apr.	Previously unknown Scottish singer Susan Boyle becomes a worldwide sensation following a broadcast of the television show *Britain's Got Talent.*
12 Apr.	U.S. naval forces free the captain of the *Maersk Alabama* from Somali pirates, who had taken him aboard a life vessel after the ship's crew initially thwarted the attack; three pirates are killed by sniper fire.
28 Apr.	Russian ballerina Ekaterina Maximova dies.
1 May	Sweden allows same-sex marriages.
10 May	Iranian American journalist Roxana Saberi is released from custody by Iran after being detained for months.
18–19 May	The Sri Lankan civil war, which had lasted for twenty-seven years, comes to an end.

1 June	A French airliner crashes into the Atlantic Ocean off Brazil with the loss of all aboard.
13 June	Ahmadinejad retains the presidency of Iran, despite strong opposition by Mir Hossein Mousavi. Allegations of voter fraud are widespread, and protests continue for weeks before being quieted by government crackdown.
20 June	An Iranian woman, Neda Agha-Soltan, is shot and killed during street demonstrations over Iran's disputed election results. Images of her death are posted worldwide and spark sympathy for the protesters.
30 June	One passenger survives the crash of a Yemeni airliner off the coast of Comoros.
17 July	The Marriott and Ritz-Carlton Hotels in Jakarta, Indonesia, are bombed by terrorists; nine people are killed.
31 July	Three American hikers are arrested along the Iran-Iraq border and are imprisoned. Some accounts claim Iranian forces crossed the border to apprehend the Americans.
18 Aug.	Former South Korean president and winner of the Nobel Peace Prize, Kim Dae Jung, dies.
26–30 Sept.	Typhoon Ketsana sweeps through the Philippines, China, Vietnam, Cambodia, Laos, and Thailand; more than seven hundred people are killed.
29 Sept.	The Samoan Islands are struck by a strong earthquake.
2 Oct.	Rio de Janeiro is announced as the winner to host the 2016 Olympics.
10 Oct.	The border between Armenia and Turkey is officially opened.
20 Oct.	Pope Benedict approves rules that make it easier for Episcopalians, many angry at their church's acceptance of women and homosexual priests, to join the Roman Catholic Church.
23 Nov.	Supporters of the Ampatuan clan in Maguindanao, Philippines, attack and kill nearly sixty political activists and media members.
25 Nov.	Floods ravage Jedda, Saudi Arabia, killing more than 150 people.

CHAPTER TWO

THE ARTS

by GEORGE PARKER ANDERSON, PHILIP B. DEMATTEIS, HEATHER PENFIELD

CONTENTS

Sidebars and tables are listed in italics.

2000

Movies

All the Pretty Horses, directed by Billy Bob Thornton and starring Penélope Cruz, Matt Damon, and Henry Thomas; *Almost Famous,* directed by Cameron Crowe and starring Billy Crudup, Kate Hudson, and Frances McDormand; *American Psycho,* directed by Mary Harron and starring Christian Bale, Josh Lucas, and Justin Theroux; *Bring It On,* directed by Peyton Reed and starring Jesse Bradford, Kirsten Dunst, and Eliza Dushku; *Cast Away,* directed by Robert Zemeckis and starring Tom Hanks, Helen Hunt, and Paul Sanchez; *The Cell,* directed by Tarsem Singh and starring Vincent D'Onofrio, Jennifer Lopez, and Vince Vaughn; *Dinosaur,* animated feature, directed by Eric Leighton and Ralph Zondag; *Dude, Where's My Car?,* directed by Danny Leiner and starring Jennifer Garner, Ashton Kutcher, and Seann William Scott; *The Emperor's New Groove,* animated feature, directed by Mark Dindal; *Erin Brockovich,* directed by Steven Soderbergh and starring Albert Finney and Julia Roberts; *Gladiator,* directed by Ridley Scott and starring Russell Crowe, Connie Nielsen, and Joaquin Phoenix; *High Fidelity,* directed by Stephen Frears and starring John Cusack, Iben Hjejle, and Todd Louiso; *How the Grinch Stole Christmas,* directed by Ron Howard and starring Jim Carrey; *Me, Myself & Irene,* directed by Bobby Farrelly and Peter Farrelly and starring Jim Carrey and Renée Zellweger; *Meet the Parents,* directed by Jay Roach and starring Robert De Niro and Ben Stiller; *Memento,* directed by Christopher Nolan and starring Carrie-Anne Moss, Guy Pearce, and Joe Pantoliano; *Mission: Impossible II,* directed by John Woo and starring Tom Cruise, Thandie Newton, and Dougray Scott; *Mission to Mars,* directed by Brian De Palma and starring Don Cheadle, Tim Robbins, and Gary Sinise; *Oh Brother, Where Art Thou?,* directed by Joel Coen and starring George Clooney, Tim Blake Nelson, and John Turturro; *The Patriot,* directed by Roland Emmerich and starring Mel Gibson, Heath Ledger, and Joely Richardson; *Pay It Forward,* directed by Mimi Leder and starring Helen Hunt, Haley Joel Osment, and Kevin Spacey; *The Perfect Storm,* directed by Wolfgang Petersen and starring George Clooney, Diane Lane, and Mark Wahlberg; *Pollock,* directed by Ed Harris and starring Harris and Marcia Gay Harden; *Remember the Titans,* directed by Boaz Yakin and starring Wood Harris, Will Patton, and Denzel Washington; *Requiem for a Dream,* directed by Darren Aronofsky and starring Ellen Burstyn, Jared Leto, and Jennifer Connelly; *Scream 3,* directed by Wes Craven and starring David Arquette, Neve Campbell, and Courteney Cox; *Sexy Beast,* directed by Jonathan Glazer and starring Ben Kingsley, Ian McShane, and Ray Winstone; *Snatch,* directed by Guy Ritchie and starring Benicio Del Toro, Brad Pitt, and Jason Statham; *Traffic,* directed by Steven Soderbergh and starring Benicio Del Toro, Michael Douglas, and Catherine Zeta-Jones; *Unbreakable,* directed by M. Night Shyamalan and starring Samuel L. Jackson, Bruce Willis, and Robin Wright; *Wonder Boys,* directed by Curtis Hanson and starring Michael Douglas, Tobey Maguire, and Frances McDormand; *X-Men,* directed by Bryan Singer and starring Hugh Jackman, Ian McKellen, and Patrick Stewart.

Novels

Charles Baxter, *Feast of Love;* Michael Chabon, *The Amazing Adventures of Kavalier and Clay;* Tom Clancy, *The Bear and the Dragon;* Mary Higgins Clark, *Before I Say Goodbye;* Patricia Cornwell, *The Last Precinct;* Mark Z. Danielewski, *House of Leaves;* Tony Earley, *Jim the Boy;* Dave Eggers, *A Heartbreaking Work of Staggering Genius;* Janet Evanovich, *Hot Six;* Maureen Gibbon, *Swimming Sweet Arrow;* Myla Goldberg, *Bee Season;* John Grisham, *The Brethren;* Stephen Harrigan, *The Gates of the Alamo;* Joseph Heller, *Portrait of an Artist, as an Old Man;* Denis Johnson, *The Name of the World;* Robert Jordan, *Winter's Heart;* Heidi Julavits, *The Mineral Palace;* Dean Koontz, *From the Corner of His Eye;* Tim LaHaye and Jerry B. Jenkins, *The Indwelling: The Beast Takes Possession* and *The Mark: The Beast Rules the World;* Jhumpa Lahiri, *Interpreter of Maladies;* Jeffrey Lent, *In the Fall;* Joyce Carol Oates, *Blonde;* Rosamunde Pilcher, *Winter Solstice;* Tim Powers, *Declare;* Francine Prose, *Blue Angel;* Philip Roth, *The Human Stain;* John Sandford, *Easy Prey;* Christina Schwarz, *Drowning Ruth;* Nicholas Sparks, *The Rescue;* Danielle Steel, *The House on Hope Street* and *The Wedding;* Darin Strauss, *Chang and Eng;* James Welch, *The Heartsong of Charging Elk.*

Popular Songs   Aaliyah, "Try Again"; Christina Aguilera, "What a Girl Wants"; Toni Braxton, "He Wasn't Man Enough"; Creed, "Higher"; Destiny's Child, "Jumpin', Jumpin'" and "Say My Name"; Faith Hill, "Breathe"; Janet Jackson, "Doesn't Really Matter"; Joe, "I Wanna Know"; Lonestar, "Amazed"; Madonna, "Music"; Matchbox Twenty, "Bent"; Pink, "There You Go"; Santana, featuring The Product G&B, "Maria Maria"; Santana, featuring Rob Thomas, "Smooth"; Savage Garden, "I Knew I Loved You"; Sisqo, "Thong Song"; 3 Doors Down, "Kryptonite"; Vertical Horizon, "Everything You Want."

14 Mar.   Stephen King publishes his ghost story *Riding the Bullet* exclusively in electronic form.

20 Apr.   The heirs of a U.S. Army lieutenant who stole artwork while stationed in Germany during World War I agree to pay fines for nonpayment of taxes after owning and selling some of the works. Criminal charges for trafficking in stolen art were dismissed earlier.

May   The popular band Smashing Pumpkins announces they will disband.

26 Oct.   The Broadway musical *The Full Monty* (based on a British movie) opens on Broadway.

17 Nov.   The musical *Mamma Mia!* debuts in San Francisco and has a three-month run; it is produced in Los Angeles and Chicago before opening on 18 October 2001 on Broadway, where it becomes a major, long-running hit.

18 Nov.   Actors Michael Douglas and Catherine Zeta-Jones marry in New York City.

2001

Movies   *A.I.: Artificial Intelligence,* directed by Steven Spielberg and starring Jude Law, Frances O'Connor, and Haley Joel Osment; *Ali,* directed by Michael Mann and starring Jamie Foxx, Will Smith, and Jon Voight; *A Beautiful Mind,* directed by Ron Howard and starring Jennifer Connelly, Russell Crowe, and Ed Harris; *Black Hawk Down,* directed by Ridley Scott and starring Josh Hartnett, Ewan McGregor, and Tom Sizemore; *Blow,* directed by Ted Demme and starring Penélope Cruz and Johnny Depp; *Bridget Jones's Diary,* directed by Sharon Maguire and starring Colin Firth, Hugh Grant, and Renée Zellweger; *Donnie Darko,* directed by Richard Kelly and starring Jake Gyllenhaal, Jena Malone, and Mary McDonnell; *Enemy at the Gates,* directed by Jean-Jacques Annaud and starring Joseph Fiennes, Ed Harris, and Jude Law; *The Fast and the Furious,* directed by Rob Cohen and starring Vin Diesel, Michelle Rodriguez, and Paul Walker; *Hannibal,* directed by Ridley Scott and starring Anthony Hopkins, Julianne Moore, and Gary Oldman; *Harry Potter and the Sorcerer's Stone,* directed by Chris Columbus and starring Rupert Grint, Richard Harris, and Daniel Radcliffe; *I Am Sam,* directed by Jessie Nelson and starring Dakota Fanning, Sean Penn, and Michelle Pfeiffer; *The Lord of the Rings: Fellowship of the Ring,* directed by Peter Jackson and starring Orlando Bloom, Ian McKellen, and Elijah Wood; *Monster's Ball,* directed by Marc Forster and starring Halle Berry, Taylor Simpson, and Billy Bob Thornton; *Monsters, Inc.,* animated feature, directed by Pete Docter and David Silverman; *Moulin Rouge!,* directed by Baz Luhrmann and starring Nicole Kidman, John Leguizamo, and Ewan McGregor; *Mulholland Dr.,* directed by David Lynch and starring Laura Harring, Justin Theroux, and Naomi Watts; *Ocean's Eleven,* directed by Steven Soderbergh and starring George Clooney, Brad Pitt, and Julia Roberts; *The Others,* directed by Alejandro

Amenábar and starring Christopher Eccleston, Fionnula Flanagan, and Nicole Kidman; *The Royal Tenenbaums,* directed by Wes Anderson and starring Gene Hackman, Anjelica Huston, and Gwyneth Paltrow; *Shrek,* animated feature, directed by Andrew Adamson and Vicky Jenson; *Spy Game,* directed by Tony Scott and starring Brad Pitt and Robert Redford; *Swordfish,* directed by Dominic Sena and starring Halle Berry, Hugh Jackman, and John Travolta; *Training Day,* directed by Antoine Fuqua and starring Scott Glenn, Ethan Hawke, and Denzel Washington; *Vanilla Sky,* directed by Cameron Crowe and starring Tom Cruise, Penélope Cruz, and Cameron Diaz; *Zoolander,* directed by Ben Stiller and starring Stiller, Christine Taylor, and Owen Wilson.

Novels

Elizabeth Benedict, *Almost;* Mary Higgins Clark, *On the Street Where You Live;* Michael Connelly, *A Darkness More than Night;* Clive Cussler, *Valhalla Rising;* Jennifer Egan, *Look at Me;* Louise Erdrich, *The Last Report on the Miracles at Little No Horse;* Janet Evanovich, *Seven Up;* Jonathan Franzen, *The Corrections;* Sue Grafton, *"P" Is for Peril;* John Grisham, *A Painted House* and *Skipping Christmas;* Charlaine Harris, *Dead Until Dark;* John Irving, *The Fourth Hand;* Jan Karon, *A Common Life;* Stephen King, *Dreamcatcher;* King and Peter Straub, *Black House;* Dean Koontz, *One Door Away from Heaven;* Tim LaHaye and Jerry B. Jenkins, *Desecration;* Dennis Lehane, *Mystic River;* Heather McGowan, *Schooling;* Terry McMillan, *Day Late and a Dollar Short;* Alice Munro, *A Quiet Genius;* Ann Patchett, *Bel Canto;* James Patterson, *1st to Die* and *Suzanne's Diary for Nicholas;* Dawn Powell, *The Country and the City;* Nora Roberts, *Midnight Bayou;* Mary Robison, *Why Did I Ever;* Brian Ascalon Roley, *American Son;* Richard Russo, *Empire Falls;* John Sandford, *Chosen Prey;* W. G. Sebald, *Austerlitz;* Danielle Steel, *The Kiss* and *Leap of Faith;* Mattie J. T. Stepanek, *Journey Through Heartsongs;* Anne Tyler, *Ordinary People;* Brady Udall, *The Miracle Life of Edgar Mint;* Colson Whitehead, *John Henry Days.*

Popular Songs

Aerosmith, "Jaded"; Christina Aguilera, Lil' Kim, Mýa, and Pink, "Lady Marmalade"; Mary J. Blige, "Family Affair"; Blu Cantrell, "Hit 'Em Up Style (Oops!)"; Crazy Town, "Butterfly"; Destiny's Child, "Survivor"; Dido, "Thank You"; Dream, "He Loves U Not"; Enrique Iglesias, "Hero"; Janet Jackson, "All for You"; Alicia Keys, "Fallin'"; Lifehouse, "Hanging By a Moment"; Jennifer Lopez, "I'm Real" and "Love Don't Cost a Thing"; Madonna, "Don't Tell Me"; *NSYNC, "Gone"; Shaggy, featuring Rayvon, "Angel"; Shaggy, featuring Ricardo "Rikrok" Ducent, "It Wasn't Me"; Train, "Drops of Jupiter"; Usher, "U Remind Me."

Apr.

Responding to complaints by construction workers and the Catholic League for Religious and Civil Rights, Deborah Masters paints a loincloth on a 12-inch image of a naked Christ, part of her three-hundred-foot-long mural of New York street life at Kennedy International Airport.

12 Apr.

Actor Steve Buscemi suffers stab wounds to his head and upper body outside a bar in Wilmington, North Carolina.

19 Apr.

The Broadway hit musical *The Producers,* starring Matthew Broderick and Nathan Lane, opens.

3 July

The Screen Actors Guild and American Federation of Television and Radio Artists reach an agreement with studios that forestalls an actors' strike.

25 Aug.

Popular singer and emerging actor Aaliyah and eight others die in the crash of an overloaded plane after takeoff from the Bahamas.

11 Sept.

In addition to the thousands of lives lost in the terrorist attack on the World Trade Center, artwork valued in the tens of millions was destroyed, including a large tapestry by Joan Miró, sculptures by Auguste Rodin and Alexander Calder, and paintings by Pablo Picasso, Roy Lichtenstein, and David Hockney. Broadway shows are cancelled and many concerts are postponed.

Nov.	The animated movie *Monster's, Inc.*, by Pixar, dominates the box office, earning approximately $63 million in its first weekend.
16 Nov.	*Harry Potter and the Sorcerer's Stone* opens to large crowds in theaters across the United States.
20 Nov.	The Andrew Mellon Foundation announces it will provide $50 million to assist New York City cultural and performing arts organizations affected by 9/11.
29 Nov.	British superstar George Harrison, formerly lead guitarist for The Beatles, dies in Los Angeles.
19 Dec.	Tony Kushner's play *Homebody/Kabul* opens at The New York Theatre workshop.
20 Dec.	Michael Hammond is confirmed as Chairman of the National Endowment for the Arts. He dies one week after taking office.

2002

Movies

About Schmidt, directed by Alexander Payne and starring Hope Davis, Dermot Mulroney, and Jack Nicholson; *Adaptation*, directed by Spike Jonze and starring Nicolas Cage, Chris Cooper, and Meryl Streep; *The Bourne Identity*, directed by Doug Liman and starring Chris Cooper, Matt Damon and Franka Potente; *Catch Me If You Can*, directed by Steven Spielberg and starring Leonardo DiCaprio, Tom Hanks, and Christopher Walken; *Chicago*, directed by Rob Marshall and starring Richard Gere, Renée Zellweger, and Catherine Zeta-Jones; *Collateral Damage*, directed by Andrew Davis and starring John Leguizamo and Arnold Schwarzenegger; *Confessions of a Dangerous Mind*, directed by George Clooney and starring Drew Barrymore, Clooney, and Sam Rockwell; *Die Another Day*, directed by Lee Tamahori and starring Halle Berry, Pierce Brosnan, and Rosamund Pike; *8 Mile*, directed by Curtis Hanson and starring Kim Basinger, Eminem, and Brittany Murphy; *Equilibrium*, directed by Kurt Wimmer and starring Christian Bale, Sean Bean, and Emily Watson; *Gangs of New York*, directed by Martin Scorsese and starring Daniel Day-Lewis, Leonardo DiCaprio, and Cameron Diaz; *Harry Potter and the Chamber of Secrets*, directed by Chris Columbus and starring Rupert Grint, Daniel Radcliffe, and Emma Watson; *The Hours*, directed by Stephen Daldry and starring Nicole Kidman, Julianne Moore, and Meryl Streep; *Ice Age*, animated feature, directed by Carlos Saldanha and Chris Wedge; *Insomnia*, directed by Christopher Nolan and starring Al Pacino, Hilary Swank, and Robin Williams; *John Q*, directed by Nick Cassavetes and starring Robert Duvall and Denzel Washington; *The Lord of the Rings: The Two Towers*, directed by Peter Jackson and starring Ian McKellen, Viggo Mortensen, and Elijah Wood; *Minority Report*, directed by Steven Spielberg and starring Tom Cruise, Colin Farrell, and Samantha Morton; *My Big Fat Greek Wedding*, directed by Joel Zwick and starring Michael Constantine, John Corbett, and Nia Vardalos; *The Pianist*, directed by Roman Polanski and starring Adrien Brody, Frank Finlay, and Thomas Kretschmann; *Red Dragon*, directed by Brett Ratner and starring Ralph Fiennes, Anthony Hopkins, and Edward Norton; *The Ring*, directed by Gore Verbinski and starring Brian Cox, Martin Henderson, and Naomi Watts; *Road to Perdition*, directed by Sam Mendes and starring Tom Hanks, Jude Law, and Paul Newman; *Signs*, directed by M. Night Shyamalan and starring Rory Culkin, Mel Gibson, and Joaquin Phoenix; *Spider-Man*, directed by Sam Raimi and starring Willem Dafoe, Kirsten Dunst, and Tobey Maguire; *Star Trek: Nemesis*, directed by Stuart Baird and starring Jonathan Frakes, Brent Spiner, and Patrick Stewart; *Star Wars: Episode II—Attack of the Clones*, directed by George Lucas and starring Hayden Christensen, Ewan McGregor, and Natalie Portman; *The Transporter*, directed by Louis Leterrier and Corey Yuen and starring Matt Schulze, Jason Statham, and Qi Shu; *Tuck Everlasting*, directed by Jay Russell and starring Alexis Bledel,

Jonathan Jackson, and Sissy Spacek; *A Walk to Remember*, directed by Adam Shankman and starring Peter Coyote, Mandy Moore, and Shane West; *We Were Soldiers*, directed by Randall Wallace and starring Mel Gibson, Greg Kinnear, and Madeleine Stowe; *Wind Talkers*, directed by John Woo and starring Adam Beach, Nicolas Cage, and Peter Stormare.

Novels   Jean M. Auel, *The Shelters of Stone;* James Lee Burke, *Jolie Blon's Bounce;* Tom Clancy, *Red Rabbit;* Mary Higgins Clark, *Daddy's Little Girl;* Michael Connelly, *City of Bones;* Michael Crichton, *Prey;* Jeffrey Eugenides, *Middlesex;* Janet Evanovich, *Hard Eight;* Michel Faber, *The Crimson Petal and the White;* Jonathan Safran Foer, *Everything Is Illuminated;* Alan Furst, *Blood of Victory;* Sue Grafton, *"Q" Is for Quarry;* John Grisham, *The Summons;* Jan Karon, *In This Mountain;* Stephen King, *Everything's Eventual* and *From a Buick 8;* Tim LaHaye and Jerry B. Jenkins, *The Remnant;* Robert Littell, *The Company: A Novel of the CIA;* Alice McDermott, *Child of My Heart;* Emma McLaughlin and Nicola Kraus, *The Nanny Diaries;* China Miéville, *Perdido Street Station;* Walter Mosley, *Bad Boy Brawley Brown;* James Patterson, *Four Blind Mice;* Patterson and Andrew Gross, *2nd Chance;* Patterson and Peter de Jonge, *The Beach House;* Nora Roberts, *Chesapeake Blue* and *Three Fates;* Alice Sebold, *The Lovely Bones;* Nicholas Sparks, *Nights in Rodanthe;* Danielle Steel, *Answered Prayers;* Donna Tratt, *The Little Friend;* William Trevor, *The Story of Lucy Gault.*

**Popular
Songs**   Michelle Branch, "All You Wanted"; The Calling, "Wherever You Will Go"; Vanessa Carlton, "A Thousand Miles"; Creed, "My Sacrifice"; Eminem, "Lose Yourself"; Jimmy Eat World, "The Middle"; Avril Lavigne, "Complicated"; Linkin Park, "In the End"; Jennifer Lopez, "Ain't It Funny"; Kylie Minogue, "Can't Get You out of My Head"; *NSYNC, "Girlfriend"; Nelly, "Hot in Here"; Nelly, featuring Kelly Rowland, "Dilemma"; No Doubt, "Hey Baby"; Pink, "Don't Let Me Get Me" and "Get the Party Started"; Santana, featuring Michelle Branch, "The Game of Love"; Justin Timberlake, "Like I Love You"; Usher, "U Don't Have to Call" and "U Got It Bad."

Apr.   A 1714 Stradivarius "Le Maurien" violin, worth more than $1.5 million, is stolen from Christophe Landon's rare violin workshop and instrument store on Broadway near Lincoln Center, New York.

3 May   The movie *Spider-Man* is released and by August grosses more than $400 million.

15 Aug.   With Harvey Fierstein starring, the hit musical *Hairspray* debuts on Broadway.

2003   **Movies**   *The Cat in the Hat*, directed by Bo Welch and starring Mike Myers; *Cheaper By the Dozen*, directed by Shawn Levy and starring Hilary Duff, Bonnie Hunt, and Steve Martin; *Cold Mountain*, directed by Anthony Minghella and starring Nicole Kidman, Jude Law, and Renée Zellweger; *Finding Nemo*, animated feature, directed by Andrew Stanton and Lee Unkrich; *Holes*, directed by Andrew Davis and starring Shia LaBeouf, Jon Voight, and Sigourney Weaver; *Hulk*, directed by Ang Lee and starring Eric Bana, Jennifer Connelly, and Sam Elliott; *Identity*, directed by James Mangold and starring John Cusack and Ray Liotta; *The Italian Job*, directed by F. Gary Gray and starring Edward Norton, Donald Sutherland, and Mark Wahlberg; *Kill Bill: Vol. 1*, directed by Quentin Tarantino and starring David Carradine, Daryl Hannah, and Uma Thurman; *The Last Samurai*, directed by Edward Zwick and starring Billy Connolly, Tom Cruise, and Ken Watanabe; *The Lord of the Rings: The Return of the King*, directed by Peter Jackson and starring Ian McKellen, Viggo Mortensen, and Elijah Wood; *Lost in Translation*, directed by Sofia Coppola and starring Scarlett Johansson, Bill Murray, and Giovanni Ribisi; *Love Actually*, directed by Richard Curtis and starring Hugh Grant, Martine McCutcheon, and Liam Neeson; *Master and*

Commander: The Far Side of the World, directed by Peter Weir and starring Russell Crowe; *The Matrix Reloaded* and *The Matrix Revolutions,* directed by Andy Wachowski and Lana Wachowski and starring Laurence Fishburne, Carrie-Anne Moss, and Keanu Reeves; *Mystic River,* directed by Clint Eastwood and starring Kevin Bacon, Sean Penn, and Tim Robbins; *Pirates of the Caribbean: The Curse of the Black Pearl,* directed by Gore Verbinski and starring Orlando Bloom, Johnny Depp, and Geoffrey Rush; *Seabiscuit,* directed by Gary Ross and starring Elizabeth Banks, Jeff Bridges, and Tobey Maguire; *Shanghai Knights,* directed by David Dobkin and starring Jackie Chan and Owen Wilson; *Something's Gotta Give,* directed by Nancy Meyers and starring Diane Keaton, Jack Nicholson, and Keanu Reeves; *Terminator 3: Rise of the Machines,* directed by Jonathan Mostow and starring Arnold Schwarzenegger; *The Texas Chainsaw Massacre,* directed by Marcus Nispel and starring Jessica Biel, Andrew Bryniarski, and Jonathan Tucker; *Underworld,* directed by Len Wiseman and starring Kate Beckinsale, Shane Brolly, and Scott Speedman; *X2,* directed by Bryan Singer and starring Halle Berry, Hugh Jackman, and Patrick Stewart.

Novels

Mitch Albom, *The Five People You Meet In Heaven;* Jane Alison, *The Marriage of the Sea;* Paul Auster, *Oracle Night;* Nicholson Baker, *A Box of Matches;* Thomas Berger, *Best Friends;* T. C. Boyle, *Drop City;* Anita Brookner, *Making Things Better;* Dan Brown, *The Da Vinci Code;* John Burdett, *Bangkok 8;* Frederick Busch, *A Memory of War;* Jay Cantor, *Great Neck;* Tom Carson, *Gilligan's Wake;* Susan Choi, *American Woman;* Tom Clancy, *The Teeth of the Tiger;* Michael Connelly, *Lost Light;* Patricia Cornwell, *Blow Fly;* Meghan Daum, *The Quality of Life Report;* Don DeLillo, *Cosmopolis;* Pete Dexter, *Train;* Louise Erdrich, *The Master Butcher's Singing Club;* Janet Evanovich, *To the Nines;* Kinky Friedman, *Kill Two Birds and Get Stones;* Cristina García, *Monkey Hunting;* William Gibson, *Pattern of Recognition;* Neil Gordon, *The Company You Keep;* Katherine Govier, *Creation;* John Grisham, *Bleachers* and *The King of Torts;* David Guterson, *Our Lady of the Forest;* Khaled Hosseini, *The Kite Runner;* Michael Ignatieff, *Charlie Johnson in the Flames;* Pico Iyer, *Abandon;* Diane Johnson, *L'Affaire;* Edward P. Jones, *The Known World;* Robert Jordan, *Crossroads of Twilight;* Ken Kalfus, *The Commissariat of Enlightenment;* Garrison Keillor, *Love Me;* Thomas Keneally, *Office of Innocence;* Tim LaHaye and Jerry B. Jenkins, *Armageddon;* Jhumpa Lahiri, *The Namesake;* Chang-rae Lee, *Aloft;* Jonathan Lethem, *The Fortress of Solitude;* Jim Lewis, *The King Is Dead;* David Liss, *The Coffee Trader;* Simon Mawer, *The Fall;* Donald Miller, *Blue Like Jazz;* Thomas Moran, *Anja the Liar;* Toni Morrison, *Love;* Walter Mosley, *Six Easy Pieces: Easy Rawlins Stories;* Ruth Ozeki, *All Over Creation;* Carolyn Parkhurst, *The Dogs of Babel;* Suzan-Lori Parks, *Getting Mother's Body;* James Patterson, *The Lake House;* Patterson and Andrew Gross, *The Jester;* George P. Pelecanos, *Soul Circus;* Richard Powers, *The Time of Our Singing;* Richard Price, *Samaritan;* Sara Pritchard, *Crackpots;* Annie Proulx, *That Old Ace in the Hole;* Nora Roberts, *Birthright;* Norman Rush, *Mortals;* John Sandford, *Naked Prey;* Jane Smiley, *Good Faith;* Danielle Steel, *Johnny Angel;* Robert Stone, *Bay of Souls;* Ellen Ullman, *The Bug;* Vendela Vida, *And Now You Can Go;* Marianne Wiggins, *Evidence of Things Unseen;* Tobias Wolff, *Old School.*

Popular Songs

Christina Aguilera, "Beautiful"; Aguilera, featuring Lil' Kim, "Can't Hold Us Down"; Black Eyed Peas, featuring Justin Timberlake, "Where Is the Love?"; Kelly Clarkson, "Miss Independent"; Evanescence, "Bring Me to Life"; 50 Cent, "In da Club"; Kid Rock and Sheryl Crow, "Picture"; Beyoncé, featuring Jay-Z, "Crazy in Love"; Beyoncé, featuring Sean Paul, "Baby Boy"; Avril Lavigne, "I'm With You"; Jennifer Lopez, featuring LL Cool J, "All I Have"; Maroon 5, "Harder to Breathe"; Matchbox Twenty, "Unwell"; Nelly, P. Diddy, and Murphy Lee, "Shake Ya Tailfeather"; Outkast, "Hey Ya!"; Santana, featuring Alex Band, "Why Don't You and I"; 3 Doors Down, "Here without You" and "When I'm Gone"; Justin Timberlake, "Cry Me a River" and "Rock Your Body."

22 Jan.–
30 Mar.   The Metropolitan Museum of Art in New York hosts a major exhibit of drawings by Leonardo da Vinci.

9 Sept.   Twelve-year-old Brianna LaHara is among 261 people sued by the Recording Industry of America for illegally downloading music. LaHara's family paid a fee to belong to a music-swapping service, and the honor student did not realize she was doing anything wrong.

24 Sept.   Facing budget deficits, the musicians of the Pittsburgh Symphony Orchestra ratify a three-year contract in which they accept a 7.8 percent pay cut in the first two years before a major raise in the 2005–2006 season.

30 Oct.   The musical *Wicked*, starring Kristin Chenoweth and Idina Menzel, opens on Broadway.

17 Dec.   *The Lord of the Rings: The Return of the King* is released and by next year earns more than $1 billion worldwide.

2004

Movies   *Anchorman: The Legend of Ron Burgundy*, directed by Adam McKay and starring Christina Applegate, Steve Carell, and Will Ferrell; *The Aviator*, directed by Martin Scorsese and starring Kate Beckinsale, Cate Blanchett, and Leonardo DiCaprio; *The Bourne Supremacy*, directed by Paul Greengrass and starring Joan Allen, Matt Damon, and Franka Potente; *Collateral*, directed by Michael Mann and starring Tom Cruise, Jamie Foxx, and Jada Pinkett Smith; *Crash*, directed by Paul Haggis and starring Sandra Bullock, Don Cheadle, and Thandie Newton; *Dawn of the Dead*, directed by Zack Snyder and starring Mekhi Phifer, Sarah Polley, and Ving Rhames; *Dodgeball: A True Underdog Story*, directed by Rawson Marshall Thurber and starring Ben Stiller, Christine Taylor, and Vince Vaughn; *Eternal Sunshine of the Spotless Mind*, directed by Michel Gondry and starring Jim Carrey and Kate Winslet; *Friday Night Lights*, directed by Peter Berg and starring Derek Luke, Jay Hernandez, and Billy Bob Thornton; *Harry Potter and the Prisoner of Azkaban*, directed by Alfonso Cuarón and starring Rupert Grint, Daniel Radcliffe, and Emma Watson; *Hellboy*, directed by Guillermo del Toro and starring Selma Blair, Doug Jones, and Ron Perlman; *Hotel Rwanda*, directed by Terry George and starring Don Cheadle and Joaquin Phoenix;*The Incredibles*, animated feature, directed by Brad Bird; *Kill Bill: Vol. 2*, directed by Quentin Tarantino and starring David Carradine, Michael Madsen, and Uma Thurman; *Ladder 49*, directed by Jay Russell and starring Joaquin Phoenix and John Travolta; *Lemony Snicket's A Series of Unfortunate Events*, directed by Brad Silberling and starring Jim Carrey, Jude Law, and Meryl Streep; *Man on Fire*, directed by Tony Scott and starring Dakota Fanning, Christopher Walken, and Denzel Washington; *Mean Girls*, directed by Mark Waters and starring Jonathan Bennett, Lindsay Lohan, and Rachel McAdams; *Million Dollar Baby*, directed by Clint Eastwood and starring Eastwood, Morgan Freeman, and Hilary Swank; *The Notebook*, directed by Nick Cassavetes and starring James Garner, Rachel McAdams, and Gena Rowlands; *Ray*, directed by Taylor Hackford and starring Jamie Foxx, Regina King, and Kerry Washington; *Shark Tale*, animated feature, directed by Bibo Bergeron and Vicky Jenson; *Shrek 2*, animated feature, directed by Andrew Adamson and Kelly Asbury; *Sideways*, directed by Alexander Payne and starring Thomas Haden Church, Paul Giamatti, and Virginia Madsen; *Spider-Man 2*, directed by Sam Raimi and starring Kirsten Dunst, Tobey Maguire, and Alfred Molina; *The Stepford Wives*, directed by Frank Oz and starring Matthew Broderick, Nicole Kidman, and Bette Midler; *The Terminal*, directed by Steven Spielberg and starring Tom Hanks and Catherine Zeta-Jones; *Troy*, directed by Wolfgang Petersen and starring Eric Bana, Orlando Bloom, and Brad Pitt; *The Village,* directed by M. Night Shyamalan and starring William Hurt, Joaquin Phoenix, and Sigourney Weaver.

Novels

Jonathan Ames, *Wake Up, Sir!;* Kate Atkinson, *Case Histories;* David Baldacci, *Hour Game;* Russell Banks, *The Darling;* T. C. Boyle, *The Inner Circle;* Michael Connelly, *The Narrows;* Patricia Cornwell, *Trace;* Nelson DeMille, *Night Fall;* Janet Evanovich, *Metro Girl* and *Ten Big Ones;* Sue Grafton, *"R" Is For Ricochet;* John Grisham, *The Last Juror;* Thomas Keneally, *The Tyrant's Novel;* Stephen King, *The Dark Tower* and *Song of Susannah;* Tim LaHaye and Jerry B. Jenkins, *Glorious Appearing;* Walter Mosley, *Little Scarlet;* Joyce Carol Oates, *The Falls;* James Patterson, *London Bridges* and *Sam's Letters to Jennifer;* Patterson and Andrew Gross, *3rd Degree;* Tom Perrotta, *Little Children;* Nancy Reisman, *The First Desire;* Nora Roberts, *Northern Lights;* Marilynne Robinson, *Gilead;* Philip Roth, *The Plot Against America;* John Updike, *Villages;* Kate Walbert, *Our Kind;* Tom Wolfe, *I Am Charlotte Simmons.*

Popular Songs

Black Eyed Peas, "Hey Mama"; Kelly Clarkson, "Breakaway"; Evanescence, "My Immortal"; Hoobastank, "The Reason"; JoJo, "Leave (Get Out)"; Alicia Keys, "If I Ain't Got You"; Avril Lavigne, "My Happy Ending"; Maroon 5, "She Will Be Loved" and "This Love"; Christina Milian, "Dip It Low"; Nelly, featuring Tim McGraw, "Over and Over"; OutKast, "The Way You Move"; Ashlee Simpson, "Pieces of Me"; Jessica Simpson, "With You"; Britney Spears, "Toxic"; Switchfoot, "Dare You to Move" and "Meant to Live"; Usher, "Burn"; Usher, featuring Ludacris and Lil' Jon, "Yeah!"; Usher and Alicia Keys, "My Boo."

Feb.

Mel Gibson's movie *The Passion of the Christ,* a violent depiction of the death of Jesus Christ, is criticized as anti-Semitic but does well at the box office.

Mar.

The New Museum of Contemporary Art in New York, Museum of Contemporary Art in Chicago, and U.C.L.A. Hammer Museum in Los Angeles combine resources to purchase works by emerging artists.

2005

Movies

Batman Begins, directed by Christopher Nolan and starring Christian Bale, Michael Caine, and Ken Watanabe; *Brokeback Mountain,* directed by Ang Lee and starring Jake Gyllenhaal and Heath Ledger; *Capote,* directed by Bennett Miller and starring Philip Seymour Hoffman; *Charlie and the Chocolate Factory,* directed by Tim Burton and starring Johnny Depp; *The Chronicles of Narnia: The Lion, the Witch and the Wardrobe,* directed by Andrew Adamson and starring Georgie Henley, William Moseley, and Tilda Swinton; *Cinderella Man,* directed by Ron Howard and starring Russell Crowe and Renée Zellweger; *Coach Carter,* directed by Thomas Carter and starring Rick Gonzalez, Samuel L. Jackson, and Robert Ri'chard; *Fantastic Four,* directed by Tim Story and starring Jessica Alba, Michael Chiklis, and Chris Evans; *The 40 Year Old Virgin,* directed by Judd Apatow and starring Steve Carell, Catherine Keener, and Paul Rudd; *Four Brothers,* directed by John Singleton and starring Tyrese Gibson, Garrett Hedlund, and Mark Wahlberg; *Good Night, and Good Luck,* directed by George Clooney and starring Patricia Clarkson, Clooney, and David Strathairn; *Harry Potter and the Goblet of Fire,* directed by Mike Newell and starring Rupert Grint, Daniel Radcliffe, and Emma Watson; *The Interpreter,* directed by Sydney Pollack and starring Catherine Keener, Nicole Kidman, and Sean Penn; *Jarhead,* directed by Sam Mendes and starring Lucas Black, Jamie Foxx, and Jake Gyllenhaal; *Kingdom of Heaven,* directed by Ridley Scott and starring Orlando Bloom, Eva Green, and Liam Neeson; *Madagascar,* animated feature, directed by Eric Darnell and Tom McGrath; *Memoirs of a Geisha,* directed by Rob Marshall and starring Ken Watanabe, Michelle Yeoh, and Ziyi Zhang; *Mr. & Mrs. Smith,* directed by Doug Liman and starring Angelina Jolie, Brad Pitt, and Vince

Vaughn; *Munich,* directed by Steven Spielberg and starring Eric Bana, Daniel Craig, and Marie-Josée Croze; *Rent,* directed by Chris Columbus and starring Rosario Dawson, Taye Diggs, and Wilson Jermaine Heredia; *The Ring Two,* directed by Hideo Nakata and starring David Dorfman, Sissy Spacek, and Naomi Watts; *Serenity,* directed by Joss Whedon and starring Chiwetel Ejiofor, Nathan Fillion, and Gina Torres; *Sin City,* directed by Frank Miller and Robert Rodriguez and starring Mickey Rourke, Clive Owen, and Bruce Willis; *Star Wars: Episode III–Revenge of the Sith,* directed by George Lucas and starring Hayden Christensen, Natalie Portman, and Ewan McGregor; *Syriana,* directed by Stephen Gaghan and starring George Clooney, Matt Damon, and Amanda Peet; *Walk the Line,* directed by James Mangold and starring Joaquin Phoenix and Reese Witherspoon; *War of the Worlds,* directed by Steven Spielberg and starring Tom Cruise, Dakota Fanning, and Tim Robbins; *Wedding Crashers,* directed by David Dobkin and starring Rachel McAdams, Vince Vaughn, and Owen Wilson; *White Noise,* directed by Geoffrey Sax and starring Michael Keaton.

Novels Sandra Brown, *Chill Factor;* Mary Higgins Clark, *No Place Like Home;* Michael Connelly, *The Closers* and *The Lincoln Lawyer;* Patricia Cornwell, *Predator;* Catherine Coulter, *Point Blank;* Clive Cussler with Paul Kemprecos, *Polar Shift;* E. L. Doctorow, *The March;* Bret Easton Ellis, *Lunar Park;* Louise Erdrich, *The Painted Drum;* Janet Evanovich, *Eleven on Top;* Diana Gabaldon, *A Breath of Snow and Ashes;* Sue Grafton, *"S" Is For Silence;* W. E. B. Griffin, *The Hostage;* John Grisham, *The Broker;* Kathryn Harrison, *Envy;* Robert Jordan, *Knife of Dreams;* Thomas Kelly, *Empire Rising;* Sue Monk Kidd, *The Mermaid Chair;* Elizabeth Kostova, *The Historian;* Tim LaHaye and Jerry B. Jenkins, *The Rising;* Elmore Leonard, *The Hot Kid;* Sam Lipsyte, *Home Land;* George R. R. Martin, *A Feast for Crows;* Cormac McCarthy, *No Country for Old Men;* Walter Mosley, *Cinnamon Kiss;* James Patterson, *Mary, Mary;* Patterson and Andrew Gross, *The Lifeguard;* Patterson and Maxine Paetro, *4th of July;* Patterson and Howard Roughan, *Honeymoon;* Francine Prose, *A Changed Man;* Nicholas Sparks, *At First Sight* and *True Believer;* William T. Vollman, *Europe Central.*

Popular Songs Black Eyed Peas, "Don't Phunk with My Heart"; Chris Brown, "Run It"; Mariah Carey, "Don't Forget about Us"; "Shake It Off"; and "We Belong Together"; Ciara featuring Missy Elliott, "One, Two Step"; Kelly Clarkson, "Because of You," "Behind These Hazel Eyes," and "Since U Been Gone"; Green Day, "Boulevard of Broken Dreams"; Alicia Keys, "Karma"; Lifehouse, "You and Me"; Mario, "Let Me Love You"; Nickelback, "Photograph"; Pussycat Dolls, featuring Busta Rhymes, "Don't Cha"; Rihanna, "Pon de Replay"; Gwen Stefani, "Hollaback Girl"; Usher, "Caught Up"; Weezer, "Beverly Hills"; Kanye West, featuring Jaime Foxx, "Gold Digger."

Feb. Conceptual artists Christo and Jeanne-Claude debut the two-week display called "The Gates," more than seven thousand individual saffron nylon sheets suspended from steel posts in Central Park in New York City.

17 Mar. The musical *Spamalot,* inspired by the zany antics of the comedy troupe Monty Python, debuts on Broadway. Two other blockbuster musicals debut during the year, *Jersey Boys* and *The Color Purple.*

14 June Singer Michael Jackson is acquitted of felony charges of child molestation, conspiracy, and alcohol charges by a California jury.

18 Nov. An oil painting by Jackson Pollock (valued at $11.6 million) and a silkscreen by Andy Warhol are stolen from the Everhart Museum in Scranton, Pennsylvania.

2006

Movies

Apocalypto, directed by Mel Gibson and starring Dalia Hernández, Gerardo Taracena, and Raoul Trujillo; *Babel,* directed by Alejandro González Iñárritu and starring Gael García Bernal, Cate Blanchett, and Brad Pitt; *Barnyard,* animated feature, directed by Steve Oedekerk; *Blood Diamond,* directed by Edward Zwick and starring Jennifer Connelly, Leonardo DiCaprio, and Djimon Hounsou; *Borat,* directed by Larry Charles and starring Sacha Baron Cohen; *Cars,* animated feature, directed by John Lasseter and Joe Ranft; *Casino Royale,* directed by Martin Campbell and starring Judi Dench, Daniel Craig, and Eva Green; *Charlotte's Web,* animated feature, directed by Gary Winick; *Children of Men,* directed by Alfonso Cuarón and starring Chiwetel Ejiofor, Julianne Moore, and Clive Owen; *The Da Vinci Code,* directed by Ron Howard and starring Tom Hanks, Jean Reno, and Audrey Tautou; *Déjà vu,* directed by Tony Scott and starring James Caviezel, Paula Patton, and Denzel Washington; *The Departed,* directed by Martin Scorsese and starring Matt Damon, Leonardo DiCaprio, and Jack Nicholson; *The Devil Wears Prada,* directed by David Frankel and starring Adrian Grenier, Anne Hathaway, and Meryl Streep; *Dreamgirls,* directed by Bill Condon and starring Jamie Foxx, Beyoncé Knowles, and Eddie Murphy; *Eragon,* directed by Stefen Fangmeier and starring Sienna Guillory, Jeremy Irons, and Ed Speleers; *Flags of Our Fathers,* directed by Clint Eastwood and starring Joseph Cross, Barry Pepper, and Ryan Phillippe; *Ice Age: The Meltdown,* animated feature, directed by Carlos Saldanha; *Inside Man,* directed by Spike Lee and starring Jodie Foster, Clive Owen, and Denzel Washington; *Little Miss Sunshine,* directed by Jonathan Dayton and Valerie Faris and starring Steve Carell, Toni Collette, and Greg Kinnear; *Mission: Impossible III,* directed by J. J. Abrams and starring Tom Cruise, Michelle Monaghan, and Ving Rhames; *Pirates of the Caribbean: Dead Man's Chest,* directed by Gore Verbinski and starring Orlando Bloom, Johnny Depp, and Keira Knightley; *The Prestige,* directed by Christopher Nolan and starring Christian Bale, Hugh Jackman, and Scarlett Johansson; *The Pursuit of Happyness,* directed by Gabriele Muccino and starring Thandie Newton, Jaden Smith, and Will Smith; *The Queen,* directed by Stephen Frears and starring James Cromwell, Helen Mirren, and Michael Sheen; *Superman Returns,* directed by Bryan Singer and starring Kate Bosworth, Brandon Routh, and Kevin Spacey; *Talladega Nights: The Ballad of Ricky Bobby,* directed by Adam McKay and starring Sacha Baron Cohen, Will Ferrell, and John C. Reilly; *300,* directed by Zack Snyder and starring Gerard Butler, Lena Headley, and David Wenham; *V for Vendetta,* directed by James McTeigue and starring Rupert Graves, Natalie Portman, and Hugo Weaving; *World Trade Center,* directed by Oliver Stone and starring Maria Bello, Nicolas Cage, and Michael Peña; *X-Men: The Last Stand,* directed by Brett Ratner and starring Halle Berry, Hugh Jackman, and Patrick Stewart.

Novels

Mitch Albom, *For One More Day;* Monica Ali, *Alentejo Blue;* Howard Bahr, *The Judas Field;* Julian Barnes, *Arthur and George;* Mary Higgins Clark, *Two Little Girls in Blue;* Michael Connelly, *Echo Park;* Patricia Cornwell, *At Risk;* Ivan Doig, *The Whistling Season;* Jennifer Egan, *The Keep;* Janet Evanovich, *Twelve Sharp;* Richard Ford, *The Lay of the Land;* Nell Freudenberger, *The Dissident;* Terry Goodkind, *Phantom;* Allegra Goodman, *Intuition;* Ward Just, *Forgetfulness;* Ken Kalfus, *A Disorder Peculiar to the Country;* Jonathan Kellerman, *Gone;* Stephen King, *The Cell* and *Lisey's Story;* Dean Koontz, *The Husband;* David Long, *The Inhabited World;* Cormac McCarthy, *The Road;* Alice McDermott, *After This;* Brad Melzer, *The Book of Fate;* Claire Messud, *The Emperor's Children;* Stephenie Meyer, *New Moon;* David Mitchell, *Black Swan Green;* James Patterson, *Cross;* Patterson and Andrew Gross, *Judge & Jury;* Patterson and Peter de Jonge, *Beach Road;* Patterson and Maxine Paetro, *The 5th Horseman;* Marisha Pessl, *Special Topics in Calamity Physics;* Richard Powers, *The Echo Maker;* Thomas Pynchon, *Against the Day;* Anna Quindlen, *Rise and Shine;* Nora Roberts, *Angels Fall;* Philip Roth, *Everyman;* Diane Setterfield, *The Thirteenth Tale;* Gary Shetyngart, *Absurdistan;* Scott Smith, *The Ruins;* Nicholas Sparks, *Dear John;* Danielle Steel,

The House; Anne Tyler, *Digging to America;* John Updike, *Terrorist;* Colson Whitehead, *Apex Hides the Hurt;* Daniel Woodrell, *Winter's Bone.*

Popular Songs

Gnarls Barkley, "Crazy"; Natasha Bedingfield, "Unwritten"; Beyoncé, featuring Slim Thug, "Check on It"; Mary J. Blige, "Be Without You"; James Blunt, "You're Beautiful"; Chris Brown, "Run It"; Cassie, "Me & U"; Chamillionaire, featuring Krayzie Bone, "Ridin'"; The Fray, "Over My Head (Cable Car)"; Nelly, featuring Paul Wall, Ali & Gipp, "Grillz"; Nelly Furtado, featuring Timbaland, "Promiscuous"; Ne-Yo, "So Sick"; Panic! At The Disco, "I Write Sins Not Tragedies"; Sean Paul, "Temperature"; Daniel Powter, "Bad Day"; Pussycat Dolls, featuring Snoop Dogg, "Buttons"; Rihanna, "SOS"; Shakira, featuring Wyclef Jean, "Hips Don't Lie"; Justin Timberlake, "Sexy Back"; Yung Joc, "It's Goin' Down."

7 July

Pirates of the Caribbean: Dead Man's Chest is released; the film earns more than $1 billion worldwide.

**19 Sept.–
10 Dec.**

Art photographs by Robert Polidori of the damage left by Hurricane Katrina in New Orleans are displayed at the Metropolitan Museum of Art.

Nov.

David Geffen sells Jackson Pollock's painting *Number 5, 1948* (1948) for $140 million and Willem de Kooning's *Woman III* (1952–1953) for $137.5 million.

8 Nov.

Francisco Goya's painting "Children With a Cart" is stolen in Pennsylvania during transport to a museum exhibition in Toledo, Ohio; the painting is recovered later in the month.

2007

Movies

American Gangster, directed by Ridley Scott and starring Russell Crowe, Chiwetel Ejiofor, and Denzel Washington; *Beowulf,* directed by Robert Zemeckis and starring Crispin Glover, Angelina Jolie, and Ray Winstoner; *The Bourne Ultimatum,* directed by Paul Greengrass and starring Joan Allen, Matt Damon, and Édgar Ramírez; *Charlie Wilson's War,* directed by Mike Nichols and starring Tom Hanks, Philip Seymour Hoffman, and Julia Roberts; *Enchanted,* directed by Kevin Lima and starring Amy Adams, James Marsden, and Susan Sarandon; *The Game Plan,* directed by Andy Fickman and starring Dwayne Johnson, Madison Pettis, and Kyra Sedgwick; *Ghost Rider,* directed by Mark Steven Johnson and starring Nicolas Cage, Sam Elliott, and Eva Mendes; *The Golden Compass,* directed by Chris Weitz and starring Daniel Craig, Nicole Kidman, and Dakota Blue Richards; *Hairspray,* directed by Adam Shankman and starring Nikki Blonsky, Queen Latifah, and John Travolta; *Halloween,* directed by Rob Zombie and starring Tyler Mane, Malcolm McDowell, and Scout Taylor-Compton; *Harry Potter and the Order of the Phoenix,* directed by David Yates and starring Rupert Grint, Daniel Radcliffe, and Emma Watson; *I Am Legend,* directed by Francis Lawrence and starring Alice Braga, Will Smith, and Charlie Tahan; *Into the Wild,* directed by Sean Penn and starring Emile Hirsch, Catherine Keener, and Vince Vaughn; *Juno,* directed by Jason Reitman and starring Michael Cera, Jennifer Garner, and Ellen Page; *Knocked Up,* directed by Judd Apatow and starring Katherine Heigl, Seth Rogen, and Paul Rudd; *Live Free or Die Hard,* directed by Len Wiseman and starring Justin Long, Timothy Olyphant, and Bruce Willis; *Meet the Robinsons,* animated feature, directed by Stephen J. Anderson; *Michael Clayton,* directed by Tony Gilroy and starring George Clooney, Tilda Swinton, and Tom Wilkinson; *No Country for Old Men,* directed by Ethan Coen and Joel Coen and starring Javier Bardem, Josh Brolin, and Tommy Lee Jones; *Pirates of the Caribbean: At World's End,* directed by Gore Verbinski and starring Orlando Bloom, Johnny Depp, and Keira Knightley; *Ratatouille,* animated feature, directed by Brad Bird and Jan Pinkava; *Shrek the*

Third, animated feature, directed by Raman Hui and Chris Miller; *The Simpsons Movie*, animated feature, directed by David Silverman; *Spider-Man 3*, directed by Sam Raimi and starring Kirsten Dunst, Topher Grace, and Tobey Maguire; *There Will Be Blood*, directed by Paul Thomas Anderson and starring Paul Dano, Daniel Day-Lewis, and Ciarán Hinds; *Transformers*, directed by Michael Bay and starring Josh Duhamel, Megan Fox, and Shia LaBeouf.

Novels   Sherman Alexie, *The Absolutely True Diary of a Part-Time Indian;* Martin Amis, *House of Meetings;* David Baldacci, *Simple Genius* and *Stone Cold;* Michael Chabon, *The Yiddish Policeman's Union;* Mary Higgins Clark, *I Heard That Song Before;* Leah Hager Cohen, *House Lights;* Patricia Cornwell, *Book of the Dead;* Don DeLillio, *Falling Man;* Junot Diaz, *The Brief Wondrous Life of Oscar Wao;* Janet Evanovich, *Lean Mean Thirteen* and *Plum Lovin';* Joshua Ferris, *Then We Came to the End;* Vince Flynn, *Protect and Defend;* Ken Follett, *World without End;* Sue Grafton, *"T" Is for Trespass;* John Grisham, *Playing for Pizza;* Steven Hall, *The Raw Shark Texts;* Khaled Hosseini, *A Thousand Splendid Suns;* Denis Johnson, *Tree of Smoke;* Sophie Kinsella, *Shopaholic & Baby;* Thomas Mallon, *Fellow Travelers;* Stephenie Meyer, *Eclipse;* Walter Mosley, *Blonde Faith;* Alice Munro, *The View from Castle Rock;* James Patterson, *Double Cross;* Patterson and Michael Ledwidge, *Step on a Crack* and *The Quickie;* Patterson and Maxine Paetro, *The 6th Target;* Patterson and Howard Roughan, *You've Been Warned;* Tom Perrotta, *The Abstinence Teacher;* Jodi Picoult, *Nineteen Minutes;* J. D. Robb, *Innocent in Death;* Philip Roth, *Exit Ghost;* Richard Russo, *Bridge of Sighs;* William Trevor, *Cheating at Canasta*.

Popular Songs   Akon, "Don't Matter"; Akon, featuring Eminem, "Smack That"; Akon, featuring Snoop Dogg, "I Wanna Love You"; Beyoncé, "Irreplaceable"; Daughtry, "It's Not Over"; Fergie, "Big Girls Don't Cry" and "Fergalicious"; Fergie, featuring Ludacris, "Glamorous"; Nelly Furtado, "Say It Right"; Avril Lavigne, "Girlfriend"; Maroon 5, "Makes Me Wonder"; Mims, "This Is Why I'm Hot"; Plain White T's, "Hey There Delilah"; Rihanna, featuring Jay-Z, "Umbrella"; Shop Boyz, "Party Like a Rock Star"; Soulja Boy, "Crank That"; Gwen Stefani, featuring Akon, "The Sweet Escape"; T-Pain, featuring Yung Joc, "Buy U a Drank (Shawty Snappin')"; Timbaland, featuring Keri Hilson, "The Way I Are"; Carrie Underwood, "Before He Cheats."

17 Jan.   On a Friday morning during the rush hour, Joshua Bell performs incognito as a street musician in the L'Enfant Plaza Metro Station in Washington, D.C.

**18 Sept.–
6 Jan. 2008**   The Metropolitan Museum of Art mounts a major exhibit of more than two hundred Dutch masterpieces from its collection, including works by Aelbert Cuyp, Rembrandt, and Johannes Vermeer.

2008

Movies   *Appaloosa*, directed by Ed Harris and starring Harris, Viggo Mortensen, and Renée Zellweger; *Bolt*, animated feature, directed by Byron Howard and Chris Williams; *The Chronicles of Narnia: Prince Caspian*, directed by Andrew Adamson and starring Ben Barnes, Georgie Henley, and Skandar Keynes; *The Dark Knight*, directed by Christopher Nolan and starring Christian Bale, Aaron Eckhart, and Heath Ledger; *Eagle Eye*, directed by D. J. Caruso and starring Rosario Dawson, Shia LaBeouf, and Michelle Monaghan; *Gran Torino*, directed by Clint Eastwood and starring Christopher Carley, Eastwood, and Bee Vang; *Horton Hears a Who!*, animated feature, directed by Jimmy Hayward and Steve Martino; *The Hurt Locker*, directed by Kathryn Bigelow and starring Brian Geraghty, Anthony Mackie, and Jeremy Renner; *The Incredible Hulk*, directed by Louis Leterrier and starring Edward Norton, Tim Roth, and Liv Tyler; *Indiana Jones* *and the Kingdom of the Crystal Skull,* directed by Steven Spielberg and starring Cate Blanchett, Harrison Ford, and Shia LaBeouf; *Iron Man,* directed by Jon Favreau and starring Robert Downey Jr., Terrence Howard, and Gwyneth Paltrow; *Mamma Mia!,* directed by Phyllida Lloyd and starring Pierce Brosnan, Amanda Seyfried, and Meryl Streep; *Milk,* directed by Gus Van Sant and starring Josh Brolin, Emile Hirsch, and Sean Penn; *Pineapple Express,* directed by David Gordon Green and starring Gary Cole, James Franco, and Seth Rogen; *Quantum of Solace,* directed by Marc Forster and starring Mathieu Amalric, Daniel Craig, and Olga Kurylenko; *Sex and the City,* directed by Michael Patrick King and starring Kim Cattrall, Cynthia Nixon, and Sarah Jessica Parker; *Slumdog Millionaire,* directed by Danny Boyle and Loveleen Tandan and starring Dev Patel, Freida Pinto, and Saurabh Shukla; *The Spiderwick Chronicles,* directed by Mark Waters and starring Sarah Bolger, Freddie Highmore, and David Strathairn; *Taken,* directed by Pierre Morel and starring Maggie Grace, Famke Janssen, and Liam Neeson; *10,000 BC,* directed by Roland Emmerich and starring Camilla Belle, Marco Khan, and Steven Strait; *Tropic Thunder,* directed by Ben Stiller and starring Jack Black, Robert Downey Jr., and Stiller; *21,* directed by Robert Luketic and starring Kate Bosworth, Kevin Spacey, and Jim Sturgess; *Twilight,* directed by Catherine Hardwicke and starring Billy Burke, Robert Pattinson, and Kristen Stewart; *Valkyrie,* directed by Bryan Singer and starring Tom Cruise, Bill Nighy, and Carice Van Houten; *Vantage Point,* directed by Pete Travis and starring Matthew Fox, Dennis Quaid, and Forest Whitaker; *WALL-E,* animated feature, directed by Andrew Stanton; *The Wrestler,* directed by Darren Aronofsky and starring Mickey Rourke, Marisa Tomei, and Evan Rachel Wood.

Novels

Kate Atkinson, *When Will There Be Good News?;* David Baldacci, *Divine Justice* and *The Whole Truth;* Charles Bock, *Beautiful Children;* Sandra Brown, *Smoke Screen;* Shannon Burke, *Black Flies;* Lee Child, *Nothing to Lose;* Mary Higgins Clark, *Where Are You Now?;* Harlan Coben, *Hold Tight;* James Collins, *Beginner's Greek;* Michael Connelly, *The Brass Verdict;* Helene Cooper, *The House at Sugar Beach;* Patricia Cornwell, *Scarpetta;* Nelson DeMille, *The Gate House;* Tony Earley, *The Blue Star;* Janet Evanovich, *Fearless Fourteen* and *Plum Lucky;* Christine Feehan, *Dark Curse;* Vince Flynn, *Extreme Measures;* W. E. B. Griffin, *Black Ops;* John Grisham, *The Appeal;* Lauren Groff, *The Monsters of Templeton;* Laurell K. Hamilton, *Blood Noir;* Jonathan Kellerman, *Compulsion;* Sherrilyn Kenyon, *Acheron;* Stephen King, *Duma Key;* Chuck Klosterman, *Downtown Owl;* Dean Koontz, *Odd Hours;* Jhumpa Lahiri, *Unaccustomed Earth;* Dennis Lehane, *The Given Day;* Stephenie Meyer, *The Host;* Sue Miller, *The Senator's Wife;* James Patterson, *Cross Country;* Patterson and Gabrielle Charbonnet, *Sundays at Tiffany's;* Patterson and Howard Roughan, *Sail;* Jodi Picoult, *Change of Heart;* Richard Price, *Lush Life;* Kathy Reichs, *Devil Bones;* Nora Roberts, *Tribute;* Marilynne Robinson, *Home;* Philip Roth, *Indignation;* Daniel Silva, *Moscow Rules;* Curtis Sittenfeld, *American Wife;* Nicholas Sparks, *The Lucky One;* Neal Stephenson, *Anathem;* Brad Thor, *The Last Patriot;* John Updike, *The Widows of Eastwick;* Sean Williams, *The Force Unleashed;* Tobias Wolff, *Our Story Begins;* David Wroblewski, *The Story of Edgar Sawtelle.*

Popular Songs

Sara Bareilles, "Love Song"; Natasha Bedingfield, "Pocketful of Sunshine"; Chris Brown, "Forever" and "With You"; Chris Brown, featuring T-Pain, "Kiss Kiss"; Coldplay, "Viva la Vida"; Flo Rida, featuring T-Pain, "Low"; Alicia Keys, "No One"; Leona Lewis, "Bleeding Love"; Ne-Yo, "Closer"; Katy Perry, "I Kissed a Girl"; Ray J and Yung Berg, "Sexy Can I"; Rihanna, "Disturbia," "Don't Stop the Music," and "Take a Bow"; Jordin Sparks duet with Chris Brown, "No Air"; T.I, "Whatever You Like"; Timbaland, featuring One Republic, "Apologize"; Usher, featuring Young Jeezy, "Love in This Club"; Lil Wayne, featuring Static Major, "Lollipop."

7 Sept.	Jonathan Larson's *Rent* ends its twelve-year run on Broadway.
16 Oct.	The revival of Arthur Miller's *All My Sons*—starring John Lithgow, Dianne Wiest, Patrick Wilson, and Katie Holmes—opens on Broadway to brisk business.
8 Nov.	The Taubman Museum of Art (formerly the Art Museum of Western Virginia), located in a modern building designed by Frank Gehry protégé architect Randall Stout, opens in Roanoke.
13 Nov.	The musical *Billy Elliot*, about a young boy more interested in ballet than sports and based on a hit British film of the same name, debuts on Broadway.

2009

Movies   *Angels & Demons*, directed by Ron Howard and starring Tom Hanks, Ewan McGregor, and Ayelet Zurer; *Avatar*, directed by James Cameron and starring Zoe Saldana, Sigourney Weaver, and Sam Worthington; *The Blind Side*, directed by John Lee Hancock and starring Quinton Aaron, Sandra Bullock, and Tim McGraw; *A Christmas Carol*, animated feature, directed by Robert Zemeckis; *Coraline*, animated feature, directed by Henry Selick; *The Hangover*, directed by Todd Phillips and starring Justin Bartha, Bradley Cooper, and Zach Galifianakis; *Harry Potter and the Half-Blood Prince*, directed by David Yates and starring Rupert Grint, Daniel Radcliffe, and Emma Watson; *Ice Age: Dawn of the Dinosaurs*, animated feature, directed by Carlos Saldanha and Mike Thurmeier; *Inglourious Basterds*, directed by Quentin Tarantino and starring Diane Kruger, Brad Pitt, and Eli Roth; *Invictus*, directed by Clint Eastwood and starring Matt Damon and Morgan Freeman; *It's Complicated*, directed by Nancy Meyers and starring Alec Baldwin, Steve Martin, and Meryl Streep; *Julie & Julia*, directed by Nora Ephron and starring Amy Adams, Chris Messina, and Meryl Streep; *Knowing*, directed by Alex Proyas and starring Rose Byrne, Nicolas Cage, and Chandler Canterbury; *Law Abiding Citizen*, directed by F. Gary Gray and starring Gerard Butler and Jamie Foxx; *Night at the Museum: Battle of the Smithsonian*, directed by Shawn Levy and starring Amy Adams, Ben Stiller, and Owen Wilson; *Precious*, directed by Lee Daniels and starring Mo'Nique, Paula Patton, and Gabourey Sidibe; *The Princess and the Frog*, animated feature, directed by Ron Clements and John Musker; *The Proposal*, directed by Anne Fletcher and starring Sandra Bullock, Ryan Reynolds, and Mary Steenburgen; *Public Enemies*, directed by Michael Mann and starring Christian Bale, Johnny Depp, and James Russo; *Sherlock Holmes*, directed by Guy Ritchie and starring Robert Downey Jr., Jude Law, and Rachel McAdams; *The Soloist*, directed by Joe Wright and starring Robert Downey Jr., Jamie Foxx, and Catherine Keener; *Star Trek*, directed by J. J. Abrams and starring Simon Pegg, Chris Pine, and Zachary Quinto; *Surrogates*, directed by Jonathan Mostow and starring Radha Mitchell, Ving Rhames, and Bruce Willis; *The Taking of Pelham 1 2 3*, directed by Tony Scott and starring Luis Guzmán, John Travolta, and Denzel Washington; *Up*, animated feature, directed by Pete Docter and Bob Peterson; *Up in the Air*, directed by Jason Reitman and starring George Clooney and Vera Farmiga; *Watchmen*, animated feature, directed by Zack Snyder; *Where the Wild Things Are*, directed by Spike Jonze and starring Catherine O'Hara, Max Records, and Forest Whitaker; *X-Men Origins: Wolverine*, directed by Gavin Hood and starring Hugh Jackman, Ryan Reynolds, and Liev Schreiber; *Zombieland*, directed by Ruben Fleischer and starring Jesse Eisenberg, Woody Harrelson, and Emma Stone.

Novels   Paul Auster, *Invisible;* Nicholson Baker, *The Anthologist;* David Baldacci, *First Family;* Dan Brown, *The Lost Symbol;* Jim Butcher, *Turn Coat;* Lee Child, *Gone Tomorrow;* Mary Higgins Clark, *Just Take My Heart;* Chris Cleave, *Little Bee;*

Harlan Coben, *Long Lost;* Michael Connelly, *Nine Dragons* and *The Scarecrow;* Pat Conroy, *South of Broad;* Catherine Coulter, *Knockout;* Guillermo Del Toro and Chuck Hogan, *The Strain;* Janet Evanovich, *Finger Lickin' Fifteen* and *Plum Spooky;* Christine Feehan, *Dark Slayer;* Sue Grafton, *"U" Is for Undertow;* John Grisham, *The Associate;* Laurell K. Hamilton, *Skin Trade;* Charlaine Harris, *Dead and Gone;* Robert Jordan and Brandon Sanderson, *The Gathering Storm;* Jonathan Kellerman, *True Detectives;* Sherrilyn Kenyon, *Bad Moon Rising;* Stephen King, *Under the Dome;* Barbara Kingsolver, *The Lacuna;* Dean Koontz, *Relentless;* Brad Leithauser, *The Art Student's War;* Jonathan Lethem, *Chronic City;* Penelope Lively, *Family Album;* Valerie Martin, *The Confessions of Edward Day;* Colum McCann, *Let the Great World Spin;* Maile Meloy, *Both Ways Is the Only Way I Want It;* Philipp Meyer, *American Rust;* Lonnie Moore, *A Gate at the Stars;* Alice Munro, *Too Much Happiness;* Audrey Niffenegger, *Her Fearful Symmetry;* James Patterson, *I, Alex Cross;* Patterson and Richard DiLallo, *Alex Cross's Trial;* Patterson and Maxine Paetro, *The 8th Confession* and *Swimsuit;* Jayne Anne Phillips, *Lark and Termite;* Jodi Picoult, *Handle with Care;* J. D. Robb, *Promises in Death;* Nora Roberts, *Black Hills;* John Sandford, *Wicked Prey;* Joanna Scott, *Follow Me;* Daniel Silva, *The Defector;* Nicholas Sparks, *The Last Song;* Kathryn Stockett, *The Help;* Colm Toibin, *Brooklyn;* Abraham Verghese, *Cutting for Stone;* Jennifer Weiner, *Best Friends Forever;* Colson Whitehead, *Sag Harbor.*

Popular Songs

The All-American Rejects, "Gives You Hell"; Beyoncé, "Single Ladies (Put a Ring on It)"; The Black Eyed Peas, "Boom Boom Pow" and "I Gotta Feeling"; Flo Rida, "Right Round"; Jamie Foxx, featuring T-Pain, "Blame It"; The Fray, "You Found Me"; Keri Hilson, featuring Kanye West and Ne-Yo, "Knock You Down"; Kings of Leon, "Use Somebody"; Lady Gaga, "Poker Face"; Lady Gaga, featuring Colby O'Donis, "Just Dance"; Jason Mraz, "I'm Yours"; Pitbull, "I Know You Want Me (Calle Ocho)"; Jay Sean, featuring Lil Wayne, "Down"; Soulja Boy Tell 'Em, featuring Sammie, "Kiss Me thru the Phone"; Taylor Swift, "Love Story" and "You Belong with Me"; T.I., featuring Rihanna, "Live Your Life"; T.I., featuring Justin Timberlake, "Dead and Gone"; Kanye West, "Heartless."

10 Apr.   The Hearst Castle in California returns two sixteenth-century Venetian oil paintings to the heirs of a Jewish couple who had the pieces confiscated from them in Nazi Germany in 1935.

June   Geoffrey Naylor's fountain sculpture on the campus of the University of Florida, installed in 1975, is removed and scheduled for scrapping because of years of vandalism and rising costs for restoration.

7 July   Using funds provided by the American Economic Recovery and Reinvestment Act, the National Endowment for the Arts announces direct grants worth $29,775,000 to more than six hundred arts groups.

7 Aug.   Rocco Landesman is confirmed by the Senate as chairman of the National Endowment for the Arts.

10 Sept.– 29 Nov.   The Metropolitan Museum of Art displays Vermeer's masterpiece *The Milkmaid,* the first time it has been shown in the United States since the 1939 World's Fair.

15 Oct.   The Margot and Bill Winspear Opera House, supporting the Dallas Opera, opens in Texas.

11 Nov.   Andy Warhol's "200 One Dollar Bills" is sold for $43.7 million at Sotheby's; later in the month newspapers report that in a private sale completed the previous year Warhol's "Eight Elvises" sold for $100 million.

18 Dec.   *Avatar* is released and by next year becomes the highest grossing movie ever, earning worldwide box office receipts of more than $2 billion by the end of January.

OVERVIEW

Art after 9/11. The experience of 9/11 and the subsequent war on terror set the tone for art in the decade. Filmmakers at first avoided touching on the tragedy. Martin Scorsese's movie *Gangs of New York*, which took place in lower Manhattan and featured a closing shot of the twin towers of the World Trade center, was initially scheduled to debut in December 2001. Though the film's release was eventually moved back a year, the filmmaker and producers continued to agonize over the propriety of such imagery in the wake of the tragedy. Trailers for the film *Spider Man* were edited to remove images of the towers, and many other films released in late 2001 or early 2002 were digitally altered to remove the World Trade Center from the city's skyline. As the decade progressed, artists found their voices. In literature, Jonathan Safran Foer became the first important American novelist to grapple with 9/11; later in the decade experienced writers John Updike and Don DeLillo weighed in with their own novels touching on the subject of terrorism. Musicians were less reticent in dealing with the subject. Singers from Bruce Springsteen to Alan Jackson channeled the sense of national unity after the attacks, as they and others penned successful tribute songs. Rowdy country- music star Toby Keith produced the theme song of American post-9/11 defiance, the jingoistic anthem "Courtesy of the Red White and Blue" (2002), which warned potential enemies, "we'll put a boot up your ass, it's the American way."

Technology. No innovation in publishing received greater fanfare in the decade than the proliferation of the ebook. Electronic tablet devices allowed readers to simply download digital versions of published works, storing hundreds or thousands of titles in a single, slim case. Though critics were skeptical of the kind of reading experience one could expect from such devices, booming sales quickly caught the attention of the industry, and major booksellers Barnes & Noble and Amazon.com as well as computer giant Apple all produced devices. Among the benefits of digital readership was the ability to quickly highlight words to search for definitions or search within the text for a specific phrase. Additionally, thousands of works in the public domain could be downloaded free of charge. Though traditional book sales remained strong through much of the 2000s, ebooks sat poised to overtake printed works at

decade's close. Technology loomed large in other areas as well. The use of computer-generated imagery (CGI) in movies allowed filmmakers created fantastic digital worlds for their characters to inhabit, and the Pixar and DreamWorks studios dominated the genre of animated feature films with their CGI offerings. Smaller filmmakers also benefited from the changes. With the advent of digital video, the cost of creating high-quality film footage dropped significantly. Armed with handheld high-definition digital cameras, as well as editing software that could run on a home computer, independent filmmakers created films that looked and sounded nearly as good as the productions of major studios. The proliferation of the iPod and other handheld digital music devices not only allowed users to carry thousands of songs with them at all times but also changed the way music was sold. Sales of CD albums continued to wane while MP3 downloads skyrocketed. Some feared the death of the album, as customers of online stores such as Apple's iTunes could listen to samples of songs before deciding which individual tracks they wanted to purchase. Musical artists sought new ways to promote their work in the digital age. Late-decade pop sensation Justin Bieber was discovered after a talent manager saw videos of him on the video-sharing site YouTube.

Return to Reading. In an era when many bemoaned a supposed national decline in readership, two cultural phenomena stood out as bright spots for the future of the book. Television host Oprah Winfrey's book club, begun in 1996 to showcase contemporary novels, developed a large following. Her selections, announced on air, flew off bookstore shelves as devoted fans rushed to purchase the latest Oprah pick. Across the country, people met to discuss characters, plots, and themes as they progressed through the novels. Publishers understood Oprah's power in the marketplace: the selections were quickly reprinted to prominently showcase her seal of approval. After she claimed to have difficulty choosing contemporary novels she found compelling, Winfrey began to revise her selection schedule to include established works of authors such as William Faulkner and John Steinbeck. If Oprah was responsible for getting middle-aged Americans reading and talking about books again, British author J. K. Rowling did the same for young readers. Her *Harry Potter* series became a national sensation, and the release of each new installment in the series became occasion for celebrations in bookstores across the country, with fans—many of them in costume as characters—forming huge lines for the chance to buy the book at the stroke of midnight. Other young-adult series flourished as well, including Stephenie Meyers's wildly popular *Twilight* novels.

Trends in Music. Hip-hop, which emerged in the 1980s and moved into the mainstream in the 1990s, established itself as a dominant force in popular music in the 2000s. On *Billboard*'s list of the top ten artists of the decade, four were hip-hop artists. Rapper Eminem had five consecutive number-one albums and became the top-selling artist of the decade. By 2009 hip-hop's influence could be felt in nearly every genre, including country music; stars such as Toby Keith and Tim McGraw collaborated with hip-hop artists and even tried their hand at rapping. As a genre, country music moved in several directions. Country musicians such as *American Idol* winner Carrie Underwood adopted a more mainstream pop sound, earning crossover hits on the country and pop charts. Meanwhile a nationwide fascination with American roots music, owing in part to the popularity of the soundtrack to the 2001 film *O Brother, Where Art Thou?*, helped to reinvigorate the bluegrass scene. While the British band Radiohead loomed large in rock music, American rock was reinvigorated by the brash, raw creativity of bands such as The White Stripes and Wilco that emerged from the indie music scene to experience mainstream success. Young pop stars Britney Spears, Christina Aguilera, and Justin Timberlake dominated the charts and were among the most talked-about artists of the decade.

Film. There were several notable breakthroughs in Hollywood's representation of minorities. Halle Berry became the first African American woman to receive the Oscar for Best Actress for her role in *Monster's Ball* (2001). Previously taboo subjects of gender and sexuality were addressed by Hillary Swank's performance as a transgender man in *Boys Don't Cry* (1999), an effort that won her the Oscar for Best Actress in 2000. as well as by Felicity Huffman's role as a transgender woman in *Transamerica* (2005). Ang Lee's *Brokeback Mountain* (2005) told the story of a long affair between two closeted gay men, and featured a homosexual love scene between stars Heath Ledger and Jake Gyllenhaal. While some movies broke new ground, filmmakers found box-office success in more-traditional fare. The fantasy genre was bolstered by Peter Jackson's hit adaptation of J. R. R. Tolkien's *Lord of the Rings* trilogy, as well as the *Harry Potter* series of films based on J. K. Rowling's popular youth novels. The last two installments in the *Star Wars* prequel trilogy, *Attack of the Clones* (2002) and *Revenge of the Sith* (2005), were panned by critics but drew massive audiences. Films featuring established superheroes from comic books proliferated, with movies such as *X-Men* (2000) and *Spider-Man* (2002) sparking multiple sequels.

Song and Dance. Broadway productions remained the most important source for musical theater in the 2000s. The movies proved fertile ground for subject matter, as *The Producers* (2005), *The Lion King* (1994), and *Monty Python and the Holy Grail* (1975) were all successfully adapted to the Broadway stage. More-serious fare was popular as well. The 2006 musical *Spring Awakening* explored sexual repression in nineteenth-century Germany; the Tony Award–winning *In the Heights* (2007) became one of the first Broadway musicals to include hip-hop-inspired beats. In popular culture, the growth of reality-television programming during the decade fostered a resurgence of interest in song and dance. The smash hit *American Idol*, which pitted amateur singers against one another in a competition to earn a record contract, helped to launch the careers of several new pop stars. The series *Dancing with the Stars* fueled a revival in ballroom dance.

Tween Market. The interests of preteen or "tween" audiences drove sales as scores of young adults became popular trendsetters in literature, movies, television, and music during the decade. Romantic stories featuring wizards and vampires filled bookshelves and theaters. The *Harry Potter* series (books and movies) dominated sales in the United States and worldwide. The final installment, *Harry Potter and the Deathly Hollows* (2007), became the fastest-selling book in history with more than 15 million sold worldwide on the first day of release. Once the appetite for fantasy literature was established, new series such as *Twilight* by Stephenie Meyer and *The Hunger Games* by Suzanne Collins became popular with girls, while the *Percy Jackson* series, based on Greek mythology, garnered male readers. Tweens flocked to the cinemas in support of movies based on these books. Tween television stars (from series such as *Lizzie McGuire*, *High School Musical*, and *That's So Raven*) often combined their popularity on the small screen with musical careers, creating a crossover category that included such entertainers as Hannah Montana/Miley Cyrus, the Jonas Brothers, Hilary Duff, Vanessa Hudgens, and Zac Efron. Tween voting also heavily influenced the winners of television-reality shows such as *American Idol*, and youngsters catapulted the careers of such young rappers as Soulja Boy, Lil' Romeo, and Bow Wow.

TOPICS IN THE NEWS

ART

NEA Funding. Government support for the National Endowment for the Arts (NEA) slightly increased over the course of the first decade of the twenty-first century, though inflation reduced the purchasing power of the dollars that art organizations received. In a 2003 appearance before Congress, NEA chairman Dana Gioia (2002–2009) broke down the allocation of federal arts funding, noting that about 40 percent went to state arts agencies and regional arts groups on a matching basis. A large portion of the budget of approximately $115 million went to more than a thousand projects across the country to "support performances of opera, chamber music, symphony, theatre, dance, jazz, and folk arts" as well as for "exhibitions in museums and community centers, large and small." Federal money also went to the Challenge America program—designed to bring the arts to underserved communities—and to promote arts programs that serve as models for adoption by local groups for schools. Gioia emphasized the importance of the arts in education: "Without instruction and experience in the arts, no child's education is com-

Glass artist Dale Chihuly with his piece *The Sun* during a 2006 exhibition of his work at the Fairchild Tropical Botanic Gardens in Coral Gables, Florida (AP Photo/Mitchell Zachs)

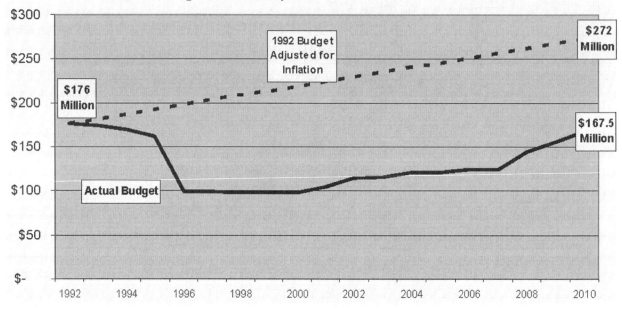

NEA Funding Fails to Keep Pace with Inflation: 1992 to 2010

$300

$250

$200

$150

$100

$50

$-

1992 1994 1996 1998 2000 2002 2004 2006 2008 2010

$176 Million

1992 Budget Adjusted for Inflation

$272 Million

$167.5 Million

Actual Budget

Graph showing the real drop in funding for the National Endowment for the Arts since 1992 (National Endowment for the Arts, U.S. Office of Management and Budget, 2010. Analysis by Americans for the Arts)

plete." While the increasing funding for the NEA during the decade in some measure recouped the cuts made to the agency as a result of political battles in the latter 1990s, government support for the arts continued to lag far behind that provided by other nations. In 2003 a cross-country analysis by the Canada Council for the Arts ranked the United States last among countries providing government support for the arts. The per-capita arts funding through the NEA that year was approximately 51¢, while the per-capita funding through the Arts Council in England, for example, was nearly $25.

Modern Expansions. Although plans for an innovative $950 million Guggenheim Museum designed by Frank Gehry for Lower Manhattan fell through in 2002, the first decade was notable for major expansions of important museums showcasing modern art. On 20 November 2004, its seventy-fifth anniversary, the Museum of Modern Art (MoMA) reopened in New York after an $858 million renovation that lasted more than two years. With the demolition of the Hotel Dorset on West 54th Street, architect Yoshio Taniguchi was able to expand the museum to practically double the square footage. As critic Arthur Lubow noted, the MoMA, the first museum in the world to be dedicated to modern art, has long been regarded as "the arbiter and guardian of progressive art," and the new space allowed the story of modern art to be told more flexibly: "No longer does one room lead inescapably into the next. Some of the new painting and sculpture galleries will have four doorways, allowing the curators to express their understanding that history can move sideways as well as forward." In 2006, with the opening of the Lewis B. and

Dorothy Cullman Education and Research Building adding classrooms, performance space, and exhibit space, the final stage of the reinvigoration of the MoMA was completed. In May 2009 the Art Institute of Chicago opened its Modern Wing, designed by Renzo Piano, adding 264,000 square feet of interior space and making the museum the second largest in the nation after the Metropolitan Museum of Art. Critic Roberta Smith calls the addition "a rarity: a work of genuinely good architecture that is also kind to art."

Street Art. One of the important art trends in the early years of the century was the continued development of "street art," which captured the notice of art lovers and critics alike. A form of graffiti art, street art makes use of materials and methods such as stencils, posters, and stickers that are easier to remove or efface than is the paint of traditional graffiti artists. In his study of the street art subculture in Los Angeles, Damien Droney found that the major street artists—including Buff Monster, Obey (Shepard Fairey), Branded, 20 mg, Tiki Jay One, Zoso, Kof, and Vader One—were generally white, middle-class males, 18–35; sometimes former graffiti artists; and often current or former art students. These artists place their iconic images and objects all over the city—"wheatpasting" posters, spray painting stencils on sidewalks, and plastering stickers to the backs of street signs and any other available surface. Kof of Project Rabbit offers a rationale for his art that several other street artists share:

> You can't turn on the television or go on the internet without having some sort of ad pop up right in your face and tell you to buy something or subliminally tell you how to

be. And a lot of people walk around and they've got their little lives and they've got their jewelry and their little gear that they wear and that's them and that's who they are. And that's who they feel they have to be in order to get by. And I feel if they can look at something and be distracted from that crazed mentality for a second they're being set free in a way. They're kind of having a break from knowing exactly what it is that they're being told by every message. And I really don't feel that my street art has a message at all. I mean, I put up rabbit posters.

The line between art and marketing, however, is sometimes blurred in the world of these street artists, as some street artists have made their art into valuable commodities. Vader One, for example, considers Shepard Fairey, the most commercially successful street artist, a sellout: "He makes guitars for Guitar Center, he makes skateboards, he makes clothes. What the hell is that? I can respect him for a street artist, I can respect him as marketing genius, but keep them separate."

Sources:
Roger Armbrust, "Equity Pushes NEA Funding," *Back Stage*, 44 (18 July 2003): 3–4;

Sarah Birke, "Painting the Town," *New Statesman*, 9 April 2007, pp. 15–16;

Holland Cotter, "Depending on the Culture of Strangers," *New York Times*, 3 January 2010;

Damien Droney, "The Business of 'Getting Up': Street Art and Marketing in Los Angeles," *Visual Anthropology*, 23, no. 2 (2010): 98–114;

David W. Dunlap, "Guggenheim Drops Plans for Elaborate New Museum on East River," *New York Times*, 31 December 2002;

James Gardner, "The High Church of Modern Art," *New York Sun*, 28 November 2006;

Natalia Grincheva, "U.S. Arts and Cultural Diplomacy: Post-Cold War Decline and the Twenty-First Century Debate," *Journal of Arts Management, Law, and Society*, 40 (2010): 169–183;

Arthur Lubow, "Re-Moderning," *New York Times Magazine*, 3 October 2004;

Jeff McMahon, "Follow the Money?: Location, Community, and Artist Funding," *TDR: Drama Review*, 50 (Summer 2006): 5–11;

Roberta Smith, "A Grand and Intimate Modern Art Trove," *New York Times*, 13 May 2009.

DANCE

Ballet. The ballet repertory in the United States in the 2000–2009 decade did not change much from that of the 1990s. The major choreographers were Jorma Elo, Trey McIntyre, Peter Martins, Mark Morris, Yuri Possokhov, Alexei Ratmansky, Twyla Tharp, and Christopher Wheeldon. Notable dancers included Ashley Bouder and Joaquin De Luz of the New York City Ballet; Gennadi Nedvigin, Davit Karapetyan, Taras Domitro, and Sara Van Patten of the San Francisco Ballet; and Desmond Richardson of the Complexions Contemporary Ballet in New York City. American ballet technique still harked back to the Russian-born choreographer George Balanchine, who had come to the United States from London in 1933, cofounded the School of American Ballet in 1934 and the New York City Ballet in 1948. Balanchine trained several generations of dancers, and the major companies in the 2000–2009 decade were still headed by dancers who had worked with

him. Between 1920 and his death in 1983 Balanchine created 425 dances. Between 12 and 24 September 2000 the John F. Kennedy Center for the Performing Arts in Washington, D.C., presented fourteen of his works by companies that included the Miami City Ballet, the San Francisco Ballet, the Pennsylvania Ballet, and the Kennedy Center's resident troupe, the Suzanne Farrell Ballet, established by Balanchine's final muse. In the aftermath of the terrorist attacks of 11 September 2001, the New York City Ballet opened its 2001–2002 season on 20 November with a benefit performance, "Tribute to the Spirit of New York," featuring works by Balanchine. The audience had to negotiate car barriers set up on the Lincoln Center Plaza, and their bags were examined at the entrance to the theater. The 1934 "Serenade" was included because it was the first ballet created by Balanchine in the United States and because of its final image of loss and solace. Jazz great Wynton Marsalis appeared as a surprise guest to play "America the Beautiful" on the trumpet, and the evening ended with "The Star-Spangled Banner" sung by the dancers with the audience standing in the house and the orchestra on their feet in the pit. The centennial of Balanchine's birth was 22 January 2004, and a gala in New York attended by such luminaries as Mayor Michael Bloomberg, author Salman Rushdie, designer Donna Karan, actress Isabella Rossellini, and model Iman Bowie kicked off a yearlong celebration of the choreographer. In May 2006 the U.S. Congress recognized New York's American Ballet Theatre as America's National Ballet Company.

Dancing with the Stars. When *Dancing with the Stars* (based on a British program, *Strictly Come Dancing*) pre-

SPOLETO FESTIVAL USA

Founded by Giancarlo Menotti in 1977 as an American counterpart to the Festival of Two Worlds in Spoleto, Italy, the Spoleto Festival USA quickly became an essential venue for new works of opera, dance, theater, jazz, and classical music. By the 2000s, Spoleto was widely recognized as one of the premier festivals of the fine arts in the world. Hosted every summer in Charleston, South Carolina, the festival has helped launch high-profile careers, including those of choreographers Paul Taylor and Twyla Tharp, as well as singer Shirley Verrett. Ties between Spoleto USA and the Festival of Two Worlds were strained in 1993 when their mutual founder Menotti left the Charleston organization over a financial dispute. The two festivals reaffirmed their partnership and mutual interest in 2008, working together to honor Menotti after his 2007 death. In his welcome speech at the opening of the 2008 festival, Charleston Mayor Joe Riley announced, "our family is back together."

Source: "Festival Joins With Italy Again," *Los Angeles Times*, 24 May 2008; *spoletousa.org.*

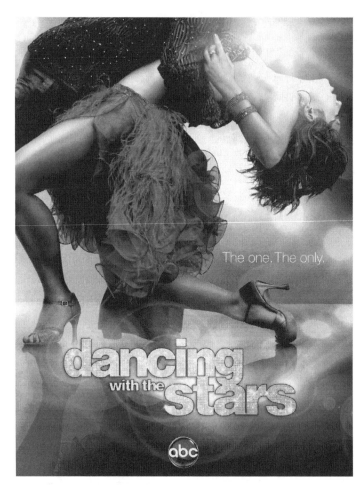

The one. The only.

An advertisement for the popular reality-television dance show (<www.impawards.com>)

miered on the ABC television network on 1 June 2005, thirteen million viewers tuned in—the most for any reality show that started in the summer. Six couples, each consisting of a celebrity amateur dancer and a professional dancer, competed in a ballroom-dancing contest; the show had grown to sixteen couples by the time the ninth season began in the fall of 2009, and the viewership had increased to more than twenty million. The professional dancers and the "stars"—minor or past-their-prime celebrities from television, movies, music, sports, or other fields (including an astronaut)—performed choreographed routines of about ninety seconds in duration and then faced a panel of three judges who critiqued their performances and awarded points for them; the television audience could also vote via a toll-free phone number or online. The couple with the lowest combined score was eliminated; the process continued each week until only one couple was left. Although a few celebrity dancers faced real physical obstacles, such as animal-welfare activist Heather Mills's prosthetic leg or actor Marlee Matlin's deafness, most of the drama resulted from the contestants' emotions during clips from rehearsals as the likes of Jerry Springer and Marie Osmond attempted to learn the finer points of the foxtrot; during the judging; and when the results were announced. Many male viewers

were also attracted by the scanty costumes worn by the female dancers. Since the professionals, however, were bigger stars in their field than the celebrities in theirs, viewers could also see the posture, grace, and naturalness of movement exhibited by real dancers. Those intrigued by the dancing, which took up less than ten minutes on the television show, could attend a three-hour performance of *Dancing with the Stars: The Tour*. The 2008–2009 tour, for example, visited thirty-eight cities from California to Connecticut and featured the celebrities Matlin, singer Lance Bass, Olympic gold-medal-winning sprinter Maurice Greene, and R&B star and Broadway actress Toni Braxton and ten professional dancers, including Mark Ballas, Cheryl Burke, Derek Hough, and Edyta Sliwinska. Ballroom-dance schools experienced an explosion of interest after the show premiered.

Sources:

Joan Acocella, "Mambo! 'Dancing with the Stars,'" *New Yorker* (14 April 2008);

Acocella, "Pacific Heights," *New Yorker* (3 November 2008);

Cathy Lynn Grossman, "Dance World Honors Ballet of 'Mr. B.': Kennedy Center Presents 14 Works from Balanchine," *USA Today*, 12 September 2000, p. 4D;

Peter Hartlaub, "'Dancing with the Stars' Tour Leaves the Humiliation at Home," *San Francisco Chronicle*, 22 December 2008, p. E1;

Mark Kappel, "Ballet Stars of the 21st Century," *Dancers Magazine* (2007): 37–39;

Anna Kisselgoff, "Ballet as Balm in a Tribute to a City on the Mend," *nytimes.com* (22 November 2001);

Lewis Segal, "Dance: The 21st Century Awaits Its Next Cue," *Los Angeles Times*, 20 December 2009.

LITERATURE

Literary Stars. Among the multitude of authors who published important work in the 2000s, a few stand out for their notable contributions. Nobel Prize–winning author Toni Morrison wrote of the effect of one man on the lives of the women he knew in *Love* (2003) and the roots of slavery in *A Mercy* (2008). One of the great chroniclers of contemporary American life, Philip Roth, who published his first book, *Goodbye Columbus and Five Other Stories* in 1959, continued his prolific career with several books in the decade, including *The Human Stain* (2000), the much-praised conclusion of his trilogy of novels, preceded by *American Pastoral* (1997) and *I Married a Communist* (1998), in which Roth's alter ego Nathan Zuckerman narrates the fall of classics professor Coleman Silk, an ironic victim of political correctness. Cormac McCarthy added to his growing reputation with two more eloquent, violent novels, the modern Western *No Country for Old Men* (2005) and the apocalyptic fable *The Road* (2006), which won a Pulitzer Prize. Don DeLillo, best known for his dark comedy *White Noise* (1985), continued to explore the essence and variety of the American character in such works as *The Body Artist* (2001) and *Cosmopolis* (2003). Thomas Pynchon, who made his reputation with the massive novel *Gravity's Rainbow* (1973), published his longest novel yet in *Against the Day* (2006), which treats hundreds of characters and is set in the period between the Chicago World's Fair of 1893 and the aftermath of World War I. Marilynne Robinson, a writer, like Pynchon, given to long silences, won her second Pulitzer Prize for her second novel, *Gilead* (2004), published twenty-three years after her debut novel *Housekeeping* (1980). Some of the most distinguished work of the decade was published by a younger generation of authors, born in the late 1950s and thereafter. Jonathan Franzen's third novel, *The Corrections* (2001), which examines the disintegration of a Midwestern family, established him as a major literary artist. Other acclaimed literary authors and novels included Michael Chabon's *The Amazing Adventures of Kavalier & Clay* (2000) and *The Yiddish Policemen's Union* (2007), Ann Patchett's *Bel Canto* (2001), Glen David Gold's *Carter Beats the Devil* (2001), Jeffrey Eugenides's *Middlesex* (2002), Jonathan Lethem's *Fortress of Solitude* (2003) and *Chronic City* (2009), and Junot Díaz's *Brief Wondrous Life of Oscar Wao* (2007). The decade was also outstanding for the continued excellence of genre artists, among them Tom Clancy, Michael Connelly, Walter Mosley, Sara Paretsky, and John Sandford. John Grisham added to his extensive list

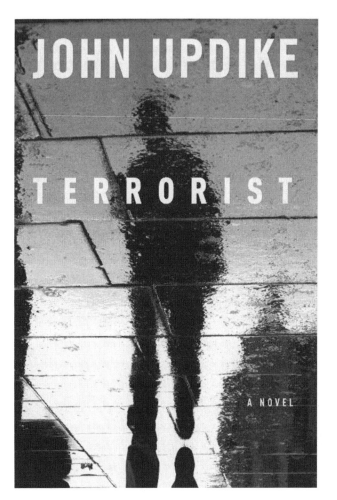

Dust jacket for Updike's 2006 novel
(Richland County Public Library)

of publications with twelve full-length books. Grisham typically wrote legal thrillers, and though he strayed from his proven formula in his 2001 book *Skipping Christmas* and his 2006 nonfiction book *The Innocent Man: Murder and Injustice in a Small Town,* he retained a wide readership.

9/11 Novels. During the first part of the decade dozens of novelists incorporated the terrorist attacks of 11 September 2001 into their works, though no single book emerged as a consensus choice among critics as *the* 9/11 novel. Perhaps a certain cultural distance from the events was an asset as two of the most-praised novels that examined the consequences of the tragedy came from abroad—English author Ian McEwan's *Saturday* (2005) and Irish writer Joseph O'Neill's *Netherland* (2008). One of the earliest American 9/11 novels to attract attention was *Extremely Loud and Incredibly Close* (2005), the second novel by the young author Jonathan Safran Foer, whose first novel was the well-received *Everything Is Illuminated* (2002). Foer's main character is the precocious and extraordinarily knowledgeable nine-year-old boy Oskar Schell, whose father died in the attacks on the Twin Towers. The narrative follows

Among the many thousands of poets across the nation, known and unknown, who responded in their work to the tragedy of September 11 was Billy Collins, the U.S. poet laureate. During a special joint session of Congress held in New York City on 6 September 2002, he read his poem "The Names" to commemorate the first anniversary of the attacks. In his poem, which was entered into the *Congressional Record,* Collins recalls how he began to remember the victims:

> Yesterday, I lay awake in the palm of the night.
> A soft rain stole in, unhelped by any breeze,
> And when I saw the silver glaze on the windows,
> I started with A, with Ackerman, as it happened,
> Then Baxter and Calabro,
> Davis and Eberling, names falling into place
> As droplets fell through the dark.

After "the final jolt of Z," the poem ends:

> Names of citizens, workers, mothers and fathers,
> The bright-eyed daughter, the quick son.
> Alphabet of names in a green field.
> Names in the small tracks of birds.
> Names lifted from a hat
> Or balanced on the tip of the tongue.
> Names wheeled into the dim warehouse of memory.
> So many names, there is barely room on the walls of the heart.

Source: *Congressional Record,* 108th Congress, 2nd session, 2004, 150, pt. 13: 17839.

---

describes the novel as "a stinging portrait of life among Manhattan's junior glitterati." Also inspired by 9/11 were two of America's most celebrated novelists, John Updike and DeLillo. In *Terrorist* (2006), a chilling and illuminating work, Updike goes inside the mind of eighteen-year-old Ahmad Mulloy, the son of a long-absent Egyptian father and an Irish American mother. The novelist tries to show how this intelligent boy growing up in New Jersey is led through his disdain for the excesses of American culture and by his Islamist faith to contemplate a suicide bombing of the Lincoln Tunnel. In *Falling Man* (2007), his last novel of the decade, DeLillo raises questions about how the artist can deal with such a tragedy as the terrorist attacks through the image of the falling man—in his story a performance artist reenacts the fatal leaps of those who escaped the burning towers at the cost of their lives. The novel focuses on Keith Neudecker, a survivor of the World Trade Center attacks who returns to his estranged wife and son and attempts to rebuild his life in a world wholly loosened from its moorings.

Google Books. In October 2004 at the Frankfurt Book Fair, Google formally announced a monumental

Cover for DeLillo's 2007 novel (Richland County Public Library)

Oskar as he searches for the owner of a key, labeled "Black," that he found among his father's things. Yet, this book is much more a psychological journey of a family's struggle with the aftermath of tragedy. In tandem with Oskar's quest, his paternal grandparents struggle with the loss of their son and memories of surviving the Dresden firebombing of 1945. While Foer treats the attacks as the driving force behind his characters' motivations, other novelists portray the effects of the disaster less directly. Jay McInerney begins *The Good Life* (2006), which Louis Menand in *The New Yorker* calls "an intelligent venture in a tricky genre," on the tenth of September with his two protagonists, Luke and Corrine, strangers who are both dissatisfied and restless in their current lives. The novel skips to the morning of 12 September, when Luke and Corrine meet and develop a relationship. In Claire Messud's *The Emperor's Children* (2006), the fall of the towers provides the background for her piercing examination of three Brown University friends, whose lives a few years out of college have failed to meet their grand expectations. A *Kirkus Reviews* critic project that had been in development for several years: the intention to digitize and index all published books and make them fully searchable online for free. The project, which at first was called Google Print and later was renamed Google Book Search, was supported from the first by several publishers who submitted books to be scanned. In December 2004 Google announced the Library Project, which began with five major institutions— the New York Public Library and university libraries at Harvard, Michigan, Oxford, and Stanford—participating in the digitazation of texts. As the project progressed and more libraries became involved, one of the problems that had to be overcome arose from font variations—especially in older texts—as scanners were not always able to correctly recognize text and provide accurate digitization. Technical issues, however, were more easily dealt with than were cultural and legal objections. While material in the public domain—texts that were no longer legally owned—could be searched or presented online in full, the digitization of copyrighted material was controversial, particularly as Google's practice was often to scan such material without seeking permission. Groups such as the Authors Guild and the Association of American University Presses (AAUP) brought lawsuits, contending that Google was violating copyright law and abusing the doctrine of fair use. Google contended that copyright was being respected as users were allowed to see only small portions of protected texts as a result of searches. Another concern raised was that, once scanned, the original texts would no longer be properly preserved or appreciated. Despite the controversies that were not fully settled by the end of the decade, Google Book Search established itself as a useful and widely accessed resource on the World Wide Web. While users sacrifice the physical experience of browsing the shelves of bookstores and libraries and turning the pages of books, twenty-first-century readers seem to have embraced the idea of digitized texts, made more attractive by Google Book Search. While most readers continued to prefer the actual printed page, more and more people embraced the digital era, with the ultimate consequences for the traditional publishing industry still unclear at the end of the decade.

Surprise Best Seller. Once it became a huge success in Europe, the so-called Millenium trilogy written by former Swedish journalist Stieg Larsson was acquired by Knopf and published in the United States. After the release in Sweden of the first volume in 2005—a year after Larsson suffered a fatal heart attack—the trilogy gained popularity with the annual release of each subsequent book. By 2007, when the final novel was published, sales in Europe rivaled those of the *Harry Potter* series, with more than 2.7 million copies sold in Sweden, more than a million in France, and more than 400,000 in Germany. The first book in the series, *Men Who Hate Women*, was released by American publisher Knopf in 2008 under a new title—*The Girl with the Dragon Tattoo*. The reasoning behind the change in title is not entirely clear; an article in the Newsletters section of Knopf publishers' website claims the title was changed to connect all three works of the trilogy through the central figure of Lisbeth Salander, the "girl" of the title. Other sources claim the original title was a potential deterrent for readers and was thus changed for marketability. *The Girl with the Dragon Tattoo* follows the lives of investigative journalist Mikael Blomkvist and the brilliant, tattooed hacker Lisbeth Salander as they attempt to solve the cold-case murder of Harriet Vanger, a favorite great-niece of the wealthy Swedish businessman, Henrik Vanger. Salander and Blomkvist return in the second novel of the series, *The Girl Who Played with Fire*, which Knopf released in 2009 under its original title. The final book, *The Girl Who Kicked the Hornet's Nest* (originally *The Air Castle that Blew Up*), was to be published in 2010. While some American critics praised the fast-paced plot and intriguing story, others found fault with stereotypical or superficial characterizations and the graphic undertones of the contemporary horror and suspense film genres. Despite the mixed critical reception, U.S. sales figures for Larsson's trilogy have been particularly impressive for a translated novel. The film version of *The Girl with the Dragon Tattoo*, produced in Denmark in 2009, garnered enough popularity that an English remake is scheduled for release in 2011 by MGM. *The New York Times* estimates that the trilogy has sold more than 27 million copies in forty countries.

Oprah's Book Club. Begun in September 1996, Oprah Winfrey's television book club maintained its popularity and influence as it evolved through the first decade of the century. From 1996 to 2002, Winfrey picked contemporary authors whom she interviewed on her show. Her selection of a novel could typically boost its sales from twenty thousand copies—a figure considered a success for a literary novel—to more than a million copies. Even when author Jonathan Franzen's disparagement of her book club so irritated Winfrey that she rescinded her invitation for him to appear on her show, his novel *The Corrections* (2001) increased its sales dramatically, benefiting immensely from the attention and controversy. In April 2002 Winfrey announced that she was ending her book club, saying that she struggled to find compelling novels—a decision that deeply disappointed the publishing industry. Several other television programs then started their own book clubs; and while none was as successful as Winfrey's club, some—including the reading clubs begun on *Today* and *Good Morning America*—continued to operate even after Winfrey's book club was reinstated in summer 2003. In restarting her book club after a fourteen-month hiatus, Winfrey decided to focus on classic literature, choosing books such as *East of Eden* (1952) by John Steinbeck, *Anna Karenina* (1873–1877) by Leo Tolstoy, and three novels by William Faulkner. Although her influence was not as strong for classic novels as when she endorsed contemporary works, it was still powerful. Random House executive Sonny Mehta remarked that the television host was deserving of a Cabinet post for having "had 300,000 people reading William Faulkner over the summer." In September 2005 Winfrey decided to reintroduce contemporary authors to her book club. Her first choice was *A Million Little Pieces* (2003), a memoir about drug and alcohol addiction by James Frey, which sold two million copies the last three months of 2005, placing it only behind J. K. Rowling's *Harry Potter and the Half-Blood Prince* (2005). When it was revealed in January 2006 that Frey had misrepresented himself and fabricated portions of his supposedly nonfiction work, Winfrey initially defended the author and was widely criticized. In her 26 January 2006 show, however, she reversed her position by confronting Frey and denouncing his work. After the Frey controversy, Winfrey's next book choice was *Night* (1960), a memoir of his experience of the Holocaust by Elie Wiesel, an author who, in contrast to Frey, did not need to exaggerate to make his story compelling. To close out the decade, Winfrey primarily continued to choose contemporary works, boosting sales with each new selection.

Scholastic and Harry Potter. British author J. K. Rowling's series of novels featuring the boy wizard Harry Potter, which set worldwide publication records, was paced by sales in the United States. Nearly nine years after Scholastic put the first Harry Potter book, *Harry Potter and the Sorcerer's Stone*, on America's bookshelves in September 1998, the series came to an end in July 2007 with the publication of *Harry Potter and the Deathly Hallows*, the seventh and final installment in the fantasy epic that captivated readers of all ages. When the fifth book, *Harry Potter and the Order of the Phoenix*, was released in 2003 by Scholastic, publication-industry records in the United States were shattered with 5 million copies sold in the first twenty-four hours and sales reaching 11 million within twelve weeks. Two years later, *Harry Potter and the Half-Blood Prince* sold 6.9 million copies in the first twenty-four hours and reached the 11 million sales mark in only nine weeks. Scholastic's release of the final Harry Potter novel in 2007 again toppled the publication record, selling 8.3 million copies in the first twenty-four hours and surpassing 11.5 million sales in just ten days. Scholastic, however, was not the only company reaping the benefits of "Pottermania"; other publishers profited as fantasy books such as C. S. Lewis's *The Chronicles of Narnia* (1949–1954) series, Brian Jacques's *Redwall* series (1986), J. R. R. Tolkien's *The Hobbit* (1937), and Madeleine L'Engle's *A Wrinkle in Time* (1962) experienced increased sales during the decade, as devotion to the Harry Potter series evidently whetted readers' appetites for similar fare. While many publishers reaped profits thanks to "the boy who lived," it seems that the entertainment industry will not be able to ride Harry's coattails forever; in the fiscal years following the release of *The Deathly Hallows*, Scholastic's revenue dropped $309.8 million, highlighting not only the impact of Potter sales but also the precarious and trend-dependent nature of the children's book industry.

The *Twilight* Saga. A Mormon and an Arizona mother of three young boys, Stephenie Meyer brought

---

INTERVIEW WITH STEPHENIE MEYER

Stephenie Meyer: I'm not really an expert on the subject of vampires. I haven't read many vampire novels—maybe one, but I don't remember its title, and I don't think I have ever seen a vampire movie. I have been asked in interviews, one for Amazon.com, for example, to name my favorite vampire book and favorite vampire movie, and I can't. Some people would like me to be more of a vampire-ophile than I really am for some reason; in fact, one interviewer wrote up the story of my visit saying that I was wearing all black, and nothing could have been farther from the truth (I had on burgundy and white). The Goth thing is really not me.

Actually, the *Twilight* premise came to me in a dream. In my dream, the basics of which would become the meadow scene in chapter 13, I can see a young woman in the embrace of a very handsome young man, in a beautiful meadow surrounded by forest, and somehow I know that he is a vampire. In the dream there is a powerful attraction between the two. When I started to write this, I had no idea where it was going; I had no idea at all in the beginning that I was writing a book, I started writing out the scene from my dream, and when I got done I was so interested in the characters that I wanted to see what would happen to them next. And so, I just wrote and let whatever happened happen.

I wrote from chapter 13 to the end, and then I went back and wrote the beginning, now having a better idea of where I was going because I knew I had to match up the beginning and the ending. I didn't really know that I was writing a book until I was almost finished. I just started writing the story for fun, and so I was never intimidated by the immensity of writing a novel; I never felt like I had to get this done or had to get that done. I didn't even think I would let anyone else read it, let alone was I thinking that I would try to get it published—it was just for me, for fun, and I never felt any self-imposed pressure.

Source: "Interview with Stephenie Meyer" *Journal of Adolescent & Adult Literacy*, 49 (April 2006): 630–631, reprinted by permission of the publisher.

THE END OF EASY RAWLINS?

At the conclusion of his tenth Easy Rawlins mystery, Walter Mosley apparently kills off his popular African American detective. Readers of the series—among them former president Bill Clinton—followed Easy as he made his way through a tumultuous period in America's racial history, from his return to Los Angeles as a World War II veteran in *Devil in a Blue Dress* (1990) into the aftermath of the Watts riots in *Blonde Faith* (2007). At the beginning of *Blonde Faith*, Easy finds a runaway sixteen-year-old, Chevette Johnson, and at its end he is enjoying a momentary "state of grace" on the Pacific Coast Highway, his car heading north into the early morning darkness, all his windows down, smoking cigarettes, taking hits from a pint of cognac placed between his legs, and thinking of the "dead men and women" he had "known and lost over the decades."

A big sixteen-wheeler was having trouble with the rise. I moved out a little to make sure there was no one coming and then hit the gas. I had just about cleared the cab when I saw the headlights of an oncoming car.

That was no problem. There was a shoulder to the left. I widened the arc of my turn and tapped the brake to slow down. I had no idea that the shoulder would thin out and then fade away. I jammed down on the brakes, but by that time the wheels were no longer on solid ground. The engine stalled out, and the wind through the windows was a woman howling for help that would never come.

"No," I said, remembering all the times I had almost died at the hands of others: German soldiers, American soldiers, drunkards, crooks, and women who wanted me in the grave.

The back of my car hit something hard, a boulder, no doubt. Something clenched down on my left foot, and pain lanced up my leg. I ignored this, though, realizing that in a few seconds I'd be dead.

Quickly I tried to come up with the image I needed to see before I died. My mind reached toward the top of the cliff. I was grasping for Bonnie, Faith, and my mother. But none of them was around for my last seconds.

The front of the car hit something, making a loud bang and a wrenching metal sound. Chevette Johnson rushed into my mind then. She was sleeping on my new couch, safe from an evil world.

I think I smiled, and then the world went black.

"There are no more Easy Rawlins books in my head," Mosley told *All Things Considered* host Robert Siegel. "But I guess it's always possible that I could write another one, but I'm not thinking about writing another one, and this feels like a nice ending to me."

Sources: Walter Mosley, *Blonde Faith* (New York, Boston London: Little, Brown, 2007);

Robert Siegel, "Easy Rawlins and the Unbearable Sadness of Being," *All Things Considered*, NPR (10 October 2007).

vampires to the young-adult literary world in the second half of the first decade with her *Twilight* series. Although Meyer's series did not rival Rowling's Harry Potter series in terms of sales, her books, like Rowling's, began as a surprise publishing hit and grew a passionate following, becoming best sellers. According to Meyer, the key scene that inspired her romantic saga came to her in a dream in June 2003. She started to write and published her first book, *Twilight* (2005), with a seemingly unprecedented ease. After the quick acceptance of *Twilight*, Meyer went on to complete the series with *New Moon* (2006), *Eclipse* (2007), and *Breaking Dawn* (2008). The novels involve a love triangle between Bella Swan, a teenage girl caught between her admirer Jacob Black, a werewolf, and Edward Cullen, the vampire with whom Bella falls in love. Although some literary critics have faulted the *Twilight* books as predictable and lacking the sophistication and finesse of literature, proponents have touted the story as a compelling young adult drama that captures the social frustrations and sexual complexities of teenage life.

Sources:
Stephen Barbara, "How Stephenie Meyer Cramps My Style," *Publishers Weekly* (7 December 2009): 54;

James Blasingame, "Interview with Stephenie Meyer," *Journal of Adolescent & Adult Literacy*, 49 (April 2006): 630–632;

Ed Caesar, "Don DeLillo: A Writer Like No Other," *Sunday Times*, 21 February 2010;

Doreen Carvajal, "Booksellers Grab a Young Wizard's Cloaktails," *New York Times*, 28 February 2000, p. A16;

Rachel Deahl, "The Tattooed Girl: Knopf Touting Swedish Hit," *Publishers Weekly* (19 May 2008): 6;

Anne Galligan, "Truth is Stranger than Magic: The Marketing of Harry Potter," *Australian Screen Education*, 35 (Summer 2004): 36–41;

Bill Goldstein, "Technology & Media; TV Book Clubs Try to Fill Oprah's Shoes," *New York Times*, 16 December 2002;

June Harris, "John Grisham," *Critical Survey of Long Fiction*, fourth edition, January 2010, pp. 1–4;

"Harry Potter Decade: Scholastic Media Room," *scholastic.com*;

Tom Holman, "Google Brings Books to Net," *Bookseller*, 5149 (2004): 6;

Caryn James, "CRITIC'S NOTEBOOK; Online Book Clubs as Lit 101 Fun," *New York Times*, 12 March 2004, pp. E27, E36;

Malcolm Jones, "Up from the Ashes," *Newsweek*, 149 (14 May 2007): 72–74;

David D. Kirkpatrick, "Oprah Will Curtail 'Book Club' Picks, And Authors Weep," *New York Times*, 6 April 2002, p. C3;

Robert J. Lackie, "From *Google Print* to *Google Book Search*: The Controversial Initiative and Its Impact on Other Remarkable Digitization Projects," *Reference Librarian*, 49, no. 1 (2008): 35–53;

Shawn Martin, "To Google or Not to Google, That Is the Question: Supplementing Google Book Search to Make It More Useful for Scholarship," *Journal of Library Administration*, 47 no. 1–2 (2008): 141–150;

Charles McGrath, "A Cautious Novelist, a Dangerous Subject; John Updike's Latest, a 'Loving Portrait of a Terrorist'," *New York Times*, 31 May 2006, pp. E1, E7;

Louis Menand, "The Earthquake," *New Yorker*, Books Section (6 February 2006);

Alex Mindlin, "Harry Potter and the Gyrating Book Sales," *nytimes.com*, (2 July 2007);

oprah.com;

Laurie Penny, "Girls, tattoos and men who hate women," *New Statesman* (6 September 2010): 12;

Review of *The Emperor's Children, Kirkus Reviews,* 74 (15 June 2006): 596;

Motoko Rich, "Record First-Day Sales for Last 'Harry Potter' Book," *nytimes.com* (22 July 2007);

Peggy Samedi, "The Jacket Journey of Stieg Larsson's The Girl With the Dragon Tattoo," *knopfdoubleday.com*;

Liesl Schillinger, "Children's Books/Young Adult: Book Review for *Eclipse* by Stephenie Meyer," *nytimes.com* (12 August 2007);

Robert Stone, "Updike's Other America," *nytimes.com* (18 June 2006);

Sien Uytterschout and Kristiaan Versluys, "Melancholy and Mourning in Jonathan Safran Foer's *Extremely Loud and Incredibly Close*," *Orbis Litterarum*, 63, no. 3 (2008): 216–236;

Edward Wyatt, "Author Is Kicked out of Oprah Winfrey's Book Club," *New York Times*, 27 January 2006, p. A1;

Wyatt, "Oprah's Book Club to Add Contemporary Writers," *nytimes.com* (23 September 2005).

MOVIES

The Coen Brothers. The filmmaking team of brothers Joel and Ethan Coen established a reputation in the 1990s for quirky, offbeat, and often dark comedies, reveling in the level of stress they could induce in the lives of their characters as their audiences squirmed in their seats. They revealed a deft hand at creating strange and unforgettable characters, and proved talented at casting the right actors for the roles, utilizing a stable of great character actors including Steve Buscemi, John Turturro, and John Goodman. With such films as *Barton Fink* (1991), *The Hudsucker Proxy* (1994), and *The Big Lebowski* (1998), the brothers exploited this loose formula to critical acclaim and box-office success. Their 1996 film *Fargo,* starring Frances McDormand and Steve Buscemi, won the Oscar for Best Picture. Despite their varied subject matter, Coen brothers' films were instantly recognizable for their deadpan humor, their imaginative cinematography, and their consistent ability to shock, often through the twists and turns of their intricate plots. The Coens put the audience on notice, critic David Denby wrote, that they "were going to pull any rug it might be standing on." Their 2000 film *O Brother, Where Art Thou?,* which they claimed was a loose adaptation of Homer's *Odyssey,* followed a trio of chain-gang fugitives through the Depression-era South. The film's soundtrack, produced by T-Bone Burnett, and featuring bluegrass and folk music, was awarded the Grammy for best soundtrack in 2001 and helped fuel a nationwide fascination with so-called roots music. *O Brother, Where Art Thou?* was followed by the light comedies *Intolerable Cruelty* (2003) and *The Ladykillers* (2004), neither of which was very well regarded by critics or audiences. In 2007 the Coens reclaimed their reputation as leading filmmakers, shifting from dark comedy with the penetrating dramatic thriller *No Country for Old Men* (2007), adapted from Cormac McCarthy's 2005 novel of the same name. The film was nominated for eight Academy Awards and won four, including Best Picture.

Wes Anderson. Few directors in the decade were more successful at creating a distinctive and recognizable aesthetic than hipster auteur Wes Anderson. His first film *Bottle Rocket* (1996) was coauthored with college roommate Owen Wilson, whose starring role launched his own acting career. Produced on a small budget, the rollicking comedy garnered enough attention and acclaim that Anderson was able to procure greater funding for his second film. *Rushmore* (1998), which was also co-authored with Wilson, set the tone for what became known as the Anderson template: intricate set and costume design, both pleasantly retro and thoroughly modern, finely tuned soundtracks featuring back-catalog pop gems of the 1960s and 1970s, and ensemble casts. Veteran comedic actor Bill Murray found a late-career resurgence after his role as Herman Blume in *Rushmore*; Anderson cast him for a supporting role in *The Royal Tenenbaums* (2001) and as the lead in his 2004 film *The Life Aquatic with Steve Zissou*. Set design and location were critical elements of Anderson's films. For *The Royal Tenenbaums,* which centered on a dysfunctional family of child geniuses now long past their prime, he renovated a huge Manhattan mansion, filling it with the artifacts of youth—childhood paintings, portable record players, encyclopedia sets, a hallway closet stacked from floor to ceiling with brightly colored board games. In *The Life Aquatic,* too, Anderson located his comic-Ahab story of oceanographer and documentarian Steve Zissou on a refitted World War II–era naval minesweeper ship, and much of the film was shot on the ocean. Despite his waning fortunes, the film's title character is driven out to sea to seek revenge on a shark that killed his longtime partner. When asked at a meeting before the mission for the "scientific purpose" of such an undertaking, Zissou, played brilliantly by Bill Murray, replied simply, "revenge." Anderson's next film, *The Darjeeling Limited* (2007), found a setting in another pleasantly nostalgic mode of transportation, as its main characters—three brothers on a vaguely spiritual voyage of discovery after the death of their father—make their way across India on a crowded passenger train. His 2009 film *The Fantastic Mr. Fox* represented in many ways a departure, as the film—adapted from the Roald Dahl children's classic—was made through stop-motion animation. Yet, in other ways the film's reliance on an older, analog form of animation in a world of computer-generated graphics matched well with Anderson's sensibilities.

Paul Thomas Anderson. After a positive reception of his first film *Hard Eight* at the 1996 Cannes Film Festival, director Paul Thomas Anderson established a reputation as a critics' darling nearly overnight with his second and third films *Boogie Nights* (1997) and *Magnolia* (1999). His 2002 film *Punch Drunk Love* featured the unlikely casting choice of Adam Sandler in the lead role of the socially awkward and anchorless small-business man Barry Egan. The film itself was hard to classify: funny, but rife with escalating tension; part crime thriller, part romantic comedy. Despite

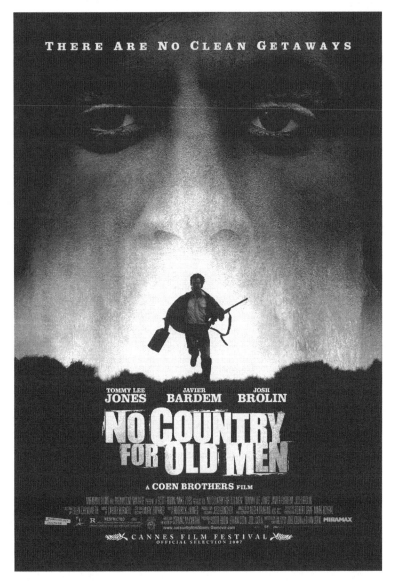

THERE ARE NO CLEAN GETAWAYS

TOMMY LEE JONES   JAVIER BARDEM   JOSH BROLIN

NO COUNTRY
FOR OLD MEN

A COEN BROTHERS FILM

CANNES FILM FESTIVAL
OFFICIAL SELECTION 2007

Poster for Joel Coen and Ethan Coen's 2007 film adaptation of Cormac McCarthy's 2005 novel (<www.impawards.com>)

limited box-office success, it earned Anderson best director honors at the 2002 Cannes Film Festival. *There Will Be Blood* (2007), adapted from an Upton Sinclair novella, told the early-twentieth-century story of Daniel Plainview, a driving and ruthless oilman brought to life by the performance of actor Daniel Day-Lewis. The movie earned eight Oscar nominations and won two, with Day-Lewis taking home Best Actor honors and Robert Elswit winning for his cinematography work. Roger Ebert wrote of *There Will Be Blood,* "watching the movie is like viewing a natural disaster that you cannot turn away from. By that I do not mean that the movie is bad, any more than it is good. It is a force beyond category."

Sofia Coppola. Daughter of filmmaker Francis Ford Coppola, Sofia Coppola made her film debut early in life, playing the uncredited role of infant Michael Francis Rizzi in the famous baptism scene of *The Godfather* (1972). She made a name for herself as a talented young director with her film *The Virgin Suicides* (1999), based on a novel by Jeffrey Eugenides. Her film *Lost in Translation* (2003), starring Bill Murray and Scarlett Johansson, was a relative box-office success and earned Coppola the Oscar for Best Original Screenplay. After these relatively small-scale character studies, Coppola switched gears for *Marie Antoinette* (2006), a chic and updated biopic of the famous French queen. Coppola was granted unprecedented access to the palace of Versailles, lavish costume design, and substantial budget. Still, she offered viewers a more intimate and sympathetic view of Marie Antoinette than had been seen on film before, investigating the difficulties of being a young queen, the problems of her marriage to Louis XVI, and above all her youthfulness, wit, and vitality. *Marie Antoinette* was a box-office hit and received praise from critics, winning the Academy Award for Costume Design.

Poster for Wes Anderson's 2001 comedy (<www.impawards.com>)

Books into Movies. As usual, many of the biggest Hollywood successes of the past decade found their way from the pages of novels to the big screen. Although film adaptations often strayed from the book in many details, a fact perennially annoying to devotees of the page, filmmakers and novelists continued to find symbiosis with one another, mining the pages of best sellers for great stories and experiencing boosts in book sales concurrent with film releases. The first decade of the twenty-first century saw a variety of books transformed into films, from children's literature, pop fiction, action and thriller, and more. The fantasy genre got a boost when Tolkien's *Lord of the Rings* series hit the cinemas to great popular fanfare. The epic trilogy, which included *The Fellowship of the Ring* (2001), *The Two Towers* (2002), and *The Return of the King* (2003), earned nearly $3 billion combined at the box office

worldwide. Maurice Sendak's children's book *Where the Wild Things Are* also was adapted for the screen by director Spike Jonze and writer Dave Eggers. Many books experienced an increase in popularity following the subsequent film adaptation, including *Julie & Julia* (2009) based on Nora Ephron's 2006 novel, and *Precious* (2009), adapted from author Sapphire's *Push* (1996). Action-packed thrillers also saw success in the translation to film. Robert Ludlum's series of Bourne novels, *The Bourne Identity* (1980), *The Bourne Supremacy* (1986), and *The Bourne Ultimatum* (1990), became a successful franchise starring Matt Damon with releases in 2002, 2004, and 2007, respectively. In 2006 Dan Brown's best-selling *The Da Vinci Code* (2003), was brought to the screen in a film directed by Ron Howard and starring Tom Hanks; the two teamed up again in 2009 for the movie version of Brown's earlier novel *Angels and*

The mystery-thriller *The Da Vinci Code*, released in 2003, sold over eighty million copies worldwide and spent more than two years on *The New York Times* best-seller list, with fifty-one weeks in first place. In an era of waning book sales, Dan Brown's book invigorated the market, helping to raise Barnes and Noble and Amazon stock prices. The astronomical success of *The Da Vinci Code* also boosted the sales of Brown's earlier book, *Angels and Demons* (2000). In September 2009, *The Lost Symbol*, sequel to *The Da Vinci Code*, broke one-day sales records, selling over one million copies in a day.

A worldwide controversy was spurred by *The Da Vinci Code*, as critics accused the book of depicting the Catholic Church as a villainous, secretive, and misogynistic organization. Many saw the book as encouraging beliefs inconsistent with the foundations of Christianity, such as the existence of a sexual relationship between Jesus and Mary Magdalene and the Holy Grail as a reference to the bloodline created by their union—secrets so powerful that for centuries the Church had been willing to kill to preserve them. The Vatican finally denounced the book two years after its publication, but by then it had already sold twenty-five million copies and had been translated into forty-four languages. The book was banned in some countries and put on "trial" to separate religious fact from fiction in others; it spawned documentaries, copycat books, public discussions, rebuttals, and encouraged a surge of tourism to the historical locations highlighted in its pages. Spin-off products were as varied as cookbooks, video games, diet books, paint-by-numbers kits, and

pornography. It was no surprise that the movies based on the books were also successful: U.S. ticket sales were $217 million for *The Da Vinci Code* (2006) and $133 million for *Angels and Demons* (2009).

In 2006, British authors Michael Baigent and Richard Leigh brought suit against Random House, U.K., accusing Brown of stealing "the whole architecture" of *The Da Vinci Code* from their book, released in the United States as *Holy Blood, Holy Grail*, which asserted as historical fact some of the ideas in Brown's fictional work. The judge ruled that, although Brown had borrowed ideas from it, the earlier book did not "have a central theme as contended by the claimants: it was an artificial creation for the purposes of the litigation working back from 'The Da Vinci Code.'"

Speaking at the height of the craze, Brown said, "In some ways, my life has changed dramatically." He explained how he had been at an airport when he suddenly realized that he had forgotten his picture ID. "Fortunately, the guy behind me in line had a copy of 'Da Vinci Code,'" he said. "I borrowed it, showed security the author photo and made my flight."

Sources: Julie Bosman, "'Da Vinci' as a Brand: From Soup to Nuts," *New York Times*, 20 May 2006;

"Dan Brown Novel Breaks One-Day Sales Records," Reuters, 16 September 2009;

Maureen Dowd, "The Vatican Code," *New York Times*, 27 March 2005;

Sarah Lyall, "Idea for 'Da Vinci Code' Was Not Stolen, Judge Says," *New York Times*, 8 April 2006;

Edward Wyatt, "For 'Code' Author, 24 Months in a Circus," *New York Times*, 21 March 2005.

Demons (2000). Thomas Harris's unforgettable serial killer Hannibal Lecter returned to the screen with Ridley Scott's 2001 film adaptation of *Hannibal* (1999); a version of Brown's earlier work *Red Dragon* (1981) hit theaters in 2002. Mark Wahlberg and Rachel Weisz starred in the 2009 film based on Alice Sebold's *The Lovely Bones* (2002). Young-adult novels in the *Harry Potter* and *Twilight* series loomed large during the decade, with the release of each new installment a cause for celebration among fans. Six Harry Potter films were released in quick succession during the decade, drawing legions of devoted fans. Other popular titles made into movies included Cormac McCarthy's *The Road* (2006), Jodi Picoult's *My Sister's Keeper* (2004), and Janet Fitch's *White Oleander* (2009).

Return of the Superhero. Comic-book heroes made an impressive comeback during the first decade of the twenty-first century. At the turn of the century, Marvel Comics was in dire financial straits; however, when the superheroes of Marvel Comics began appearing on the

big screens, the company was soon posting profits and the superhero resurgence began. The industry shot forward with films such as *Spider-Man* (2002), *The Hulk* (2003), *Batman Begins* (2005), and *Superman Returns* (2006). The *X-Men* series debuted in 2000, followed by sequels *X2* (2003) and *X-Men: The Last Stand* (2006). Batman's Hollywood story line was rebooted with *The Dark Knight* in 2008, featuring a standout performance by actor Heath Ledger as the Joker. *The Fantastic Four* (2005), *Catwoman* (2004), and *Iron Man* (2008) were also revived. The superhero became a staple of summer blockbuster fare, featuring massive budgets and showcasing the latest in computer-generated graphic imagery. These comic-book translations were more than simple popcorn fare, however. Well-regarded directors such as Ang Lee *(Hulk)* and Christopher Nolan (*The Dark Knight*) helped lend credibility to the genre.

Tribeca Film Festival. The Sundance Film Festival, held annually in Park City, Utah, was the anchor of the independent film industry since its inception in 1978. Despite a proliferation of smaller film festivals around the country, Sundance remained the largest and most important venue in the United States to promote an independent film. In 2001 prominent New Yorkers, including actor Robert DeNiro, conceived of a festival that could not only rival Sundance but also help restore the vitality of Manhattan's downtown Tribeca neighborhood, once a creative hub of the city, that suffered after the September 11 attacks. The Tribeca Film Festival was founded in 2002 and quickly rose to become one of the most important showcases of independent movies in the country. As a tribute to the philosophy behind its inception, the Tribeca Film Festival retained a separate category for New York films. The festival, DeNiro said, was "the next logical step in the evolution of New York as the independent film capital of the world. Our commitment to New York and the downtown area has never been stronger."

Sources:

John Anderson, "Tribeca Film Festival Turns 10," *newsday.com* (19 April 2011);

Mike Atkinson, "That's Entertainment," *Sight & Sound*, 17 (April 2007): 18–22;

Peter Bart, "Superheroes Get Super Makeovers," *Variety* (20 June–13 July 2008): 3, 57;

Richard Brody, "Wild, Wild West" *New Yorker* (2 November 2009);

Pam Cook, "Portrait of a Lady Sofia Coppola," *Sight & Sound*, 16 (November 2006): 36–40;

David Denby, "Killing Joke," *New Yorker* (25 February 2008);

Arnaud Desplechin, "Wes Anderson," *Brant Publications*, (July 2009): 210–211, 238;

Mary Ann Gwinn, "When Books Get a Second Wind," *seattletimes.com* (24 August 2009);

imdb.com;

Matthew P. McAllister, Ian Gordon, and Mark Jancovich, "Blockbuster Meets Supero Comic, or Art House Meets Graphic Novel?: The Contradictory Relationship between Film and Comic Art," *JPF&T* (2007): 108–114;

Cade Metz, "Making an Indie Film," *PC Magazine* (23 May 2006): 76–82;

"Read The Book or See the Movie?," *People*, 66 (16 October 2006): 55;

John H. Richardson, "The Secret History of Paul Thomas Anderson," *Esquire*, 150 (October 2008): 239–312;

Scott Simon, "Analysis: Comic Book Stories Made Into Movies," *npr.org* (11 May 2002);

Sharon Swart, "Have Films, Will Travel: Fests Test Self-Distribution," *Variety* (25–31 January 2010): 1, 29.

MUSIC

Hip-Hop. Over the course of the first decade of the twenty-first century the hip-hop or rap genre, which had originated in the United States during the 1970s, achieved solid footing in the global music industry. Hip-hop was second only to rock in U.S. record sales from 1999 to 2008; by 2009 half of the top ten songs globally were hip-hop. Dr. Dre, Eminem, Ice Cube, Jay-Z, LL Cool J, Usher, Ludacris, Nas, Nelly, Snoop Dogg, Kanye West, Wu-Tang Clan, and 50 Cent were some of the top rap artists of the 2000s. The decade also brought a rise in the number of books about hip-hop, indicating an increase in credibility for the genre. In February 2006 the Smithsonian Institu-

Cover for Justin Timberlake's last solo album of the decade, released in 2006 (Jive Records)

tion's National Museum of American History announced that it would start collecting such items as vinyl records, turntables, and boom boxes for an exhibit titled "Hip-Hop Won't Stop: The Beat, the Rhymes, the Life" that was expected to cost up to $2 million and take as long as five years to complete; a museum spokeswoman said that hip-hop was "here to stay" and was as much a part of American music history as jazz. On 4 January 2006 Queen Latifah became the first hip-hop artist to be given a star on the Hollywood Walk of Fame.

Country Music. Major country-music stars during the first decade of the twenty-first century included George Strait, Alan Jackson, Toby Keith, Kenny Chesney, Rascal Flatts, Faith Hill, Tim McGraw, Keith Urban, Brad Paisley, Brooks & Dunn, Taylor Swift, Carrie Underwood, and LeAnn Womack. According to the Nielsen SoundScan rating service, the top ten best-selling recording artists in all genres for the years 2000 to 2009 included McGraw in third place, Keith in fourth, and Chesney in sixth. The Dixie Chicks trio was highly popular at the beginning of the period; the music video of their song "Goodbye, Earl," about two women who kill the abusive husband of one of them by poisoning his black-eyed peas, won the Country Music Association (CMA) and Academy of Country Music (ACM) Video of the Year Awards in 2000. But their career was damaged by comments made by their lead singer, Natalie Maines. In August 2002 Maines initiated a feud with Keith by criticizing his chart-topping patriotic single, "Courtesy of the Red, White and Blue (The Angry American)," written in response to the 11 September 2001 terrorist attacks, as jingoistic and "ignorant." Then, on 10 March 2003, she protested the impending U.S. invasion of Iraq by telling the audience at a concert in London that the

Chicks were "ashamed" that President George W. Bush was from their home state of Texas. Their single "Travelin' Soldier," which had been number one in sales, disappeared from the charts within two weeks; fans boycotted their concerts; their CDs were publicly crushed and thrown into dumpsters; and many country-music radio stations refused to play their songs. The second half of the decade was largely dominated by Underwood and Swift. Underwood achieved fame when she won the fourth season of *American Idol* in 2005. Her debut album, *Some Hearts*, was released that year and ultimately sold more than seven million copies; it was ranked by Billboard.com as the number one country album of the decade. Between 2006 and 2009 she won two Grammy Awards, five ACM Awards, five CMA Awards, and five Country Music Television (CMT) Music Awards. In 2006 the fifteen-year-old Swift became a country-music star with her self-titled first album; her fourth album, *Fearless*, was the highest-grossing album of 2008 in any musical genre. In 2009 *Fearless* won multiple awards, including an MTV Video Music Award; a scandal erupted when rapper Kanye West jumped on the stage during Swift's acceptance speech during the MTV show to assert that the award should have gone to Beyoncé.

Jazz at Lincoln Center. In November 2004 New York City welcomed an expansive new venue dedicated to jazz. Jazz at Lincoln Center (JLC) was the first significant permanent home for an American musical tradition whose origins traced back to the southern United States and the merging of African rhythms and European instrumentation in the nineteenth and early twentieth centuries. The JLC was not located in the Lincoln Center for the Performing Arts itself, at 70 North Broadway; instead, its various components—Rose Hall, the Allen Room, Dizzy's Club Coca-Cola, and the Jazz Hall of Fame—were ensconced several blocks to the south in a retail mall in the Time Warner Center at 80 Columbus Circle, with neighbors such as a Whole Foods Market and the flagship Williams-Sonoma kitchenware store. Regardless of the location, the facilities were designed and built with the utmost attention to acoustic detail under the supervision of American jazz great Wynton Marsalis. Marsalis hoped that the new, permanent performance space would help the American public to begin to realize the importance of jazz to the country's cultural heritage. In the years before the JLC opened, record labels such as Columbia, Atlantic, and Verve had reduced the size of their jazz collections, and New York's Carnegie Hall had discontinued its jazz orchestra in 2002. The grand opening of the JLC seemed to promise a revival, or at least the continuation, of the art form. The inaugural production at the JLC, *Jazz in Motion* on 3–5 November 2004, combined jazz with dance to provide a feast for both the eye and the ear.

Death of Michael Jackson. Celebrated singer Michael Jackson died on 25 June 2009, at age fifty, as he was in the midst of preparing for a series of concerts in London that would have been his major performances since 2002. Jackson's personal physician, Dr. Conrad Murray, had adminis-

Wynton Marsalis performing at the Oskar Schindler Performing Arts Center Jazz Festival in 2009 (photograph by Eric Delmar)

tered a high dose of propofol, a potent anesthetic used during surgery, just prior to Jackson's death; he had been doing so nightly for the previous six weeks to treat Jackson's insomnia. Murray was accused of manslaughter after an autopsy found that the cause of Jackson's death was a heart attack induced by a mixture of propofol and lorazepam, an antianxiety drug that Murray had also been administering to help the singer sleep. The circumstances of Jackson's death not only brought to light the singer's narcotics dependency but also brought forth a public outpouring of grief. Twitter and other Internet sites experienced unusually heavy volume, and television news programs devoted their leading segments to the death of the King of Pop. Jackson's celebrity status in the years preceding his death had been rife with controversy, including accusations of child molestation (he had settled a lawsuit on the charge for about $20 million in 1991 and had been acquitted in a criminal case in June 2005 after a four-month trial); video footage of Jackson holding his son Prince Michael II in one arm and dangling him over a balcony railing with a towel draped over the baby's head; and the altering of his appearance through repeated plastic surgeries. Jackson's many oddities were for the most part set aside while the United

States and the rest of the world mourned the loss of one of music's greatest legends. A public memorial service was held on 7 July at the Staples Center in Los Angeles with 17,500 people in attendance and millions of others watching on television. Tickets for the service had been distributed by a lottery system after more than 1.6 million applications were submitted. On 3 September Jackson was laid to rest at Forest Lawn Memorial Park; around two hundred mourners were present for the funeral, including his former wife, Lisa Marie Presley; his longtime friend Elizabeth Taylor; his children, Prince Michael, Paris, and Prince Michael II; and his parents and siblings.

Pop Stars. Three cast members of the 1993–1994 season of the Disney Channel's *The All New Mickey Mouse Club*—Justin Timberlake, Britney Spears, and Christina Aguilera—went on to rise to the top of the American popular-music industry in the twenty-first century. In 1996 Timberlake and fellow former Mouseketeer J. C. Chasez formed the boy band *NSYNC with Lance Bass, Joey Fatone, and Chris Kirkpatrick. The group had top-selling albums and hit songs in 2000, 2001, and 2002. In 2002, after *NSYNC went on a hiatus that was supposed to be temporary but turned out to be permanent, Timberlake pursued a solo singing career. In February 2004 he and Janet Jackson were involved in the notorious "wardrobe malfunction" incident during the Super Bowl XXXVIII halftime show during which Jackson's breast was exposed briefly. After *FutureSex/LoveSounds* in 2006, he did not release any new solo albums but collaborated with other artists, such as The Black Eyed Peas and Snoop Dogg. He also acted in several films. Spears transformed her image from innocent teen to controversial sex symbol and became one of the highest-selling recording artists of the decade. Her 1999 debut album, . . . *Baby One More Time,* sold 22 million copies. It was followed in 2000 by *Oops! I Did It Again,* which sold 1.3 million copies in the week of its release—the most successful debut week for a solo artist in American history. With *Britney* (2002) she became the first female artist to have three albums debut at number one, and *Forbes* magazine named her the most powerful celebrity in the world. Around that time her four-year relationship with Timberlake came to an end; the following year she revealed that she had lost her celebrated virginity to him. She won her first Grammy for her fourth album, *In the Zone* (2003). Her personal life became fodder for the tabloids, with a fifty-five-hour marriage to a childhood friend followed nine months later by one to backup dancer Kevin Federline that produced two children and ended in divorce in less than two years; drug rehabilitation; a child-custody battle with Federline; and hospitalizations for psychiatric observation. After a disastrous attempted comeback at the 2007 MTV Video Music Awards, she made a triumphant return on the 2008 show and remained a dominant figure in the music industry. Aguilera began the decade by beating out Spears for the Best New Artist Grammy. Later in 2000 she released the Spanish-language album *Mi Reflejo,* for which she had to learn the lyrics phonetically; the following year she was named the world's best-selling Latin female artist at the World Music Awards. She adopted a sexy, provocative image for her 2001 U.S. tour and her multiplatinum 2002 album *Stripped,* posed nude on the cover of *Rolling Stone* and topless on the cover of the men's magazine *Maxim,* and joined Spears in exchanging passionate kisses with fellow pop star Madonna at the 2003 MTV Video Music Awards. Aguilera produced top-selling albums every year of the decade except for 2005 and 2008.

Downloaded Music. In 1999 Northeastern University freshman Shawn Fanning wrote a computer program to find and index music files in the compact MP3 format on the Internet. He thereby launched a peer-to-peer (P2P) music file-sharing network that allowed users to upload their music collections to the World Wide Web and download those of other users free of charge. With the assistance of his uncle, John Fanning, Shawn Fanning joined with his friend Sean Parker and computer programmer Jordan Ritter to incorporate the idea; they named the company Napster, after Shawn Fanning's high-school nickname (which was derived from his nappy hairstyle), and moved its headquarters from Boston to the San Francisco Bay area. Napster was the first of what became a torrent of online sites devoted to sharing music; others included Gnutella, Kazaa, Morpheus, BearShare, LimeWire, AudioGalaxy, Freenet, and Grokster. Within months of its incorporation, Napster was hit with copyright-infringement lawsuits by the rock band Metallica and the rapper Dr. Dre. The suit that ultimately brought Napster down, however, had already been filed in federal court in December 1999 by the Recording Industry Association of America (RIAA). Record companies blamed file sharing for the decline in sales of albums on compact discs; surveys, however, indicated that music fans objected to being forced to pay the high prices for entire albums when they might only be interested in one or two of the songs on them. Calling Napster a "monster," Ninth Circuit U.S. district judge Marilyn Hall Patel issued two injunctions against the service. After attempting, in partnership with the German publishing conglomerate Bertelsmann, which owned the BMG record label, to become a legitimate music-purchasing service, Napster shut down its website in July 2001. In November 2002 software maker Roxio Inc. bought Napster in bankruptcy court and relaunched it as a fee-based music-subscription service that paid royalties to record companies and artists. By then, however, the dominant Internet music service was Apple Inc.'s iTunes, which had been launched in January 2001 and was given a major boost by the introduction in October 2001 of Apple's portable iPod MP3 player. In April 2003 Apple introduced the iTunes Music Store, a website from which customers could legally purchase and download albums and individual songs—the latter for less than a dollar each. Nevertheless, illegal file sharing continued, and the music industry turned its attention to tracking down and suing individual downloaders.

Concert Ticket Prices. While the recording industry faced declining CD sales at the beginning of the twenty-

In an experiment arranged by *The Washington Post*, the celebrated violinist Joshua Bell performed as a street musician in the nation's capital at the L'Enfant Plaza Metro Station. Wearing a Washington Nationals baseball cap and dressed in jeans and a long-sleeved T-shirt, Bell played six classical pieces for forty-three minutes on 12 January 2007, during the Friday morning rush hour. He used his favorite violin, handcrafted in 1713 by Antonio Stradivari.

The *Post* writer first asks his reader, "So, what do you think happened?" and then seeks the opinion of an expert.

Leonard Slatkin, music director of the National Symphony Orchestra, was asked the same question. What did he think would occur, hypothetically, if one of the world's great violinists had performed incognito before a traveling rush-hour audience of 1,000-odd people?

"Let's assume," Slatkin said, "that he is not recognized and just taken for granted as a street musician . . . Still, I don't think that if he's really good, he's going to go unnoticed. He'd get a larger audience in Europe . . . but, okay, out of 1,000 people, my guess is there might be 35 or 40 who will recognize the quality for what it is. Maybe 75 to 100 will stop and spend some time listening."

So, a crowd would gather?

"Oh, yes."

And how much will he make?

"About $150."

Thanks, Maestro. As it happens, this is not hypothetical. It really happened.

"How'd I do?"

We'll tell you in a minute.

"Well, who was the musician?"

Joshua Bell.

"NO!!!"

The *Post* writer later gives the accounting: "In the three-quarters of an hour that Joshua Bell played, seven people stopped what they were doing to hang around and take in the performance, at least for a minute. Twenty-seven gave money, most of them on the run—for a total of $32 and change. That leaves the 1,070 people who hurried by, oblivious, many only three feet away, few even turning to look. No, Mr. Slatkin, there was never a crowd, not even for a second."

One of the few who did pay attention was John Picarello, a U.S. Postal Service supervisor, who listened for nine minutes before dropping $5 into the open violin case. "It was a treat," he said, "just a brilliant, incredible way to start the day."

Source: Gene Weingarten, "Pearls Before Breakfast," *washingtonpost.com* (8 April 2007).

first century, the live-music industry also struggled: during the first half of the 2000s attendance at concerts decreased by more than 6 percent. In apparent violation of the law of supply and demand, ticket prices rose by just over 20 percent in the same period. Part of the explanation was with fewer people buying tickets, concert promoters had to raise the price to cover the minimum payments guaranteed to performing artists. Prices were also driven up by scalpers who purchased large blocks of tickets and resold for a profit. Luckily for those who enjoyed concerts, performers began to react to the drop in attendance by agreeing to lower guarantees, which allowed ticket sellers to lower their prices. Some performers also offered special concerts with inexpensive tickets. Many in the industry hoped that, with the cooperation of artists and stabilization in the economy, live concerts would continue to be an option for music fans.

Live Simulcasts. Another solution to the high price of tickets came from advances in the technologies of high-definition digital sound and video recording, transmission, and projection, which allowed the entertainment industry to develop a new concept: simultaneous broadcasts, or "simulcasts." Simulcasts enabled audiences to experience rock concerts and operas "live" in their local movie theaters. The Denver-based company Big Screen Concerts, which was owned jointly by the AMC, Cinemark, and Regal theater chains, broadcast twenty-one rock concerts in 2004, including performances by Phish, Jimmy Buffett, and Prince. On 9 May 2006 a Widespread Panic show at the Fox Theater in Atlanta was sent live to 114 theaters, from California to Florida. New York's Metropolitan Opera, which had broadcast its Saturday matinee performances on the radio since the 1930s, entered into simulcasting with the 30 December 2006 production of Mozart's *The Magic Flute;* it was viewed by about 21,000 people in 98 theaters across the United States and Canada and in a few other countries. The Met beamed six operas live to movie theaters that season; the final one, Puccini's *Il Trittico* on 28 April 2007, reached an audience of 48,000 on 248 screens. Advantages of simulcasting for audiences included cheaper tickets (as low as $7.00), reduced travel time to the venue, free and convenient parking, and close-up and unobstructed views from all seats in the house; as one fan said about viewing the Widespread Panic concert on a theater screen, "You can see a lot better and you can hear the music and there's no smoke." Performers and promoters benefited from increased revenue and the ability to reach out to fans without undergoing the rigors of touring, and theater owners had a way to attract customers on days and at times when movie attendance was generally low. Furthermore, some local opera companies used the Met simulcasts to create interest in their own performances. Yet, as with all new ideas, there were also some concerns. Opera singers, for example, are trained to project their voices throughout the house without electronic enhancement; if an opera is being simulcast, however, the performers must wear microphones. One fear was that if simulcasting became widespread, the ability to project would eventually be lost. Another concern was that the use of close-ups in simulcasts would lead to an emphasis on the physical appearance of the performers at the expense of their vocal talents. Such effects had not appeared during the brief history of simulcasting in the first decade of the twenty-first century, and some insiders considered the fears overblown; the general director of the Seattle Opera, for instance, said, "I do not now cast for the movies, nor do I ever intend to." While there was general agreement that the in-person experience was still the best one, simulcasts made "live" performances accessible to many who would not otherwise be able to experience them at all.

Satellite Radio. Another option for music fans that arose during the decade was satellite digital radio, which offered hundreds of CD-quality channels, many of them free of commercials, for a monthly subscription fee. The world's first such service, Washington, D.C.–based XM Satellite Radio, was scheduled to begin operation on a trial basis in San Diego and Dallas on 11 September 2001, but the terrorist attacks on that day delayed the launch until 26 September. Full nationwide service began in November 2001. The first satellite radios cost around $300, and the monthly fee was $9.95 a month. A competitor, New York–based Sirius, began broadcasting in February 2002. XM broadcast its programs through two geostationary satellites positioned above the United States, while Sirius used three nongeostationary satellites in high elliptical orbits that ensured that one satellite was always above the United States. Both services also used ground-based repeater stations for areas where the satellite signal was obscured by buildings or terrain. In addition to the specialized, crystal-clear music channels, the satellite services also offered channels devoted to sports, news, talk, comedy, old-time radio, traffic reports for major cities, and much more. The radio displays provided information about the program to which the listener was tuned. The radios could be mounted in boom boxes for home use or in automobiles with special kits; manufacturers began installing them permanently in automobiles. Since they were not subject to Federal Communications Commission (FCC) content regulation, the

services could present uncensored lyrics and stand-up comedy acts; and "shock jocks" such as Opie and Anthony and Howard Stern could cast off the restraints imposed on them by terrestrial radio. Nevertheless, the market would not support two satellite-radio providers, and both companies lost money. In July 2008, after a sixteen-month battle with U.S. Department of Justice and Federal Communications Commission regulators who were concerned about a possible monopoly, Sirius and XM completed an all-stock merger valued at $13 billion to form Sirius XM Radio Inc. The merged company had more than 18.5 million subscribers.

Sources:

Bryan Alexander, "Jackson's Funeral: Family and Friends Say Goodbye," *time.com* (4 September 2009);

Spencer Ante, "Shawn Fanning's Struggle," *Business Week*, no. 3679 (1 May 2000): 197–198;

Randal C. Archibald, "Doctor Is Charged in Death of Jackson," *New York Times*, 9 February 2010, p. A12;

M. K. Asante Jr., *It's Bigger Than Hip Hop: The Rise of the Post-Hip Hop Generation* (New York: St. Martin's Press, 2008);

Associated Press, "Over 1.6M Apply for Jackson Memorial Tickets: LAPD Braces for Huge Crowds but Only 17,500 Fans Will Gain Entry to Events," *today.msnbc.com* (4 July 2009);

Associated Press, "Rock Concerts Moving to Big Screens: Rolling Stones, Green Day among Bands Simulcasting Shows," *today.msnbc.com* (7 June 2006);

"Best of the 2000s: Artists of the Decade," "Christina Aguilera," "Britney Spears," "Justin Timberlake," "*NSYNC," *billboard.com*;

Sudip Bhattacharjee, Ram D. Gopal, Kaveepan Lertwachara, and James R. Marsden, "Consumer Search and Retailer Strategies in the Presence of Online Music Sharing," *Journal of Management Information Systems*, 23 (Summer 2006): 129–159;

Lee B. Brown, "Jazz: America's Classical Music?" *Philosophy and Literature*, 26 (April 2002): 157–172;

Jon Caramanica, "Country's New Face: It's Young and Blond," *nytimes.com* (31 July 2009);

Caramanica, "My Music, MySpace, My Life," *nytimes.com* (7 November 2008);

Adam Cohen and Jennifer L. Schenker, "In Search of Napster II," *time.com* (26 February 2001);

Rachel Deahl, "Hip-Hop Loses Bad Rap with Publishers," *Publishers Weekly*, 252 (19 December 2005): 10–11;

"Ex-Mouseketeers: Where Are They Now?" *abcnews.com* (18 January 2008);

Ram D. Gopal, Sudip Bhattacharjee, and G. Lawrence Sanders, "Do Artists Benefit from Online Music Sharing?" *Journal of Business*, 79 (May 2006): 1503–1533;

David Hajdu, "Wynton's Blues," *Atlantic Monthly*, 291 (March 2003): 43–58;

Mike Hale, "The Swift-West Spectacle, Stoked on Screen," *nytimes.com* (15 September 2009);

Mickey Hess, ed., *Icons of Hip-Hop: An Encyclopedia of the Movement, Music, and Culture*, 2 volumes (Westport, Conn.: Greenwood Press, 2007);

Paul Hollander, "Michael Jackson, the Celebrity Cult, and Popular Culture," *Society*, 47 (2010): 147–152;

Malcolm Jones, "Wynton Marsalis and the Temple of Jazz," *Newsweek*, 144 (18 October 2004): 62–64;

Brad King, "The Day the Napster Died," *wired.com* (15 May 2002);

Steve Knopper, "The Cheap Seats," *Rolling Stone*, no. 926 (10 July 2003): 17;

Knopper, "In Tough Times, Promoters Slash Prices on Top Tours," *Rolling Stone*, no. 1091 (12 November 2009): 15–16;

Knopper, "Why Tickets Cost So Much," *Rolling Stone*, no. 1016–1017 (28 December 2006): 20;

Amy Kover, "It's Back, But Can the New Napster Survive?" *New York Times*, 17 August 2003, p. C4;

Kover, "Napster: The Hot Idea of the Year," *Fortune*, 142 (26 July 2000): 128;

Kover, "Who's Afraid of This Kid?" *Fortune*, 141 (20 March 2000): 129;

Steven Levy, "The Man Can't Stop Our Music," *Newsweek*, 135 (27 March 2000): 68;

George Loomis, "Opera's Unlikely Embrace of the Telecast," *nytimes.com* (12 January 2010);

Bob Mehr, "Justin Timberlake: Highlights from his Career in Music," *gomemphis.com* (30 January 2011);

Joseph Menn, *All the Rave: The Rise and Fall of Shawn Fanning's Napster* (New York: Crown Business, 2003);

Marcyliena Morgan and Dionne Bennett, "Hip-Hop and the Global Imprint of a Black Cultural Forum," *Daedalus*, 140 (Spring 2011): 176–196;

Edward Ortiz, "More Operas, More Theaters for the Met's HD Simulcasts," *Sacramento Bee*, 5 September 2010, p. 12;

Joseph Palenchar, "Execs: Digital Music Future Still Unclear (at the sixth annual Digital Music Forum)," *Twice* (13 March 2006): 6, 40;

Laura Robinson and David Halle, "Digitization, the Internet, and the Arts: eBay, Napster, SAG, and e-Books," *Qualitative Sociology*, 25 (Fall 2002): 359–383;

Susanna Sleat, "Jazz in Motion at Jazz at Lincoln Center," *Attitude: The Dancers' Magazine*, 18 (Winter 2005): 46–49;

Ryan E. Smith, "More Than Movies: Local Cinema Simulcasts Live Operas and Concerts," *Toledo Blade*, 14 December 2007;

Warren St. John, "The Backlash Grows against Celebrity Activists," *nytimes.com* (23 March 2003);

Neil Strauss, "The Pop Life: The Sound of Silence?" *nytimes.com* (20 March 2003);

Daniel Wakin, "Met Opera to Expand Simulcasts in Theaters," *nytimes.com* (17 May 2007);

S. Craig Watkins, *Hip-Hop Matters: Politics, Pop Culture, and the Struggle for the Soul of a Movement* (Boston: Beacon Press, 2006).

Playbill cover for the 2003 Broadway production
(<www.playbill.com>)

THEATER

Theater Subscriptions. While commercial theaters such as those on Broadway sell tickets to individual shows, non-profit local and regional theater companies gain a substantial portion of their revenue from the sale of season tickets—also known as subscriptions. Symphonies and museums had long sold memberships to their elite patrons, but the idea of selling subscriptions to middle-class theatergoers received its major impetus from public-relations expert Danny Newman's 1977 book *Subscribe Now!* Newman advised non-profits to cultivate the "saintly season subscriber" who "commits himself in advance" instead of relying on the "slothful, fickle single-ticket buyer" who "stays home if it snows, if there's ice on the roads, sleet in the air, or if any of those unfavorable weather conditions so much as threatens." By the beginning of the twenty-first century, however, fewer people were willing to commit themselves to preset packages and preferred to pick and choose the productions they saw. Part of the reason was the proliferation of entertainment options, including national tours of big Broadway shows. In response, some theaters began using email and the Internet to market single tickets; the Mark Taper Forum in Los Angeles increased its sale of single tickets from 2 percent in 1998 to 20 percent in 2001. Losing the

subscription base and marketing individual shows, however, meant that there was no safety net for presenting riskier plays; thus, theaters could have been forced to stick to more-conservative works. As a result, some theaters went in the opposite direction and developed more-flexible subscription plans. For example, PCPA Theaterfest in Santa Maria, California, offered the "Passport": six tickets that could be used in any combination for any of the nine plays in the company's season. The Actors Theatre of Louisville devised several season-ticket packages: the Brown-Forman Series, which granted admission to all seven Mainstage productions and guaranteed seats for $121; Choose Your Plays, which allowed the ticket holder to pick any three plays from the Brown-Forman series, Humana Festival, or holiday shows and receive the best seats available at the time of purchase starting at $120; Build It Up, which permitted the purchaser to add additional productions to the Choose Your Plays package for $35 for weekday or matinee packages and $40 for weekends; and the Flex Pass, consisting of eight vouchers to use any way the holder chose (eight tickets to one play, one ticket each to eight different plays, or any other combination) for $360. Seattle's A Contemporary Theatre continued to offer traditional guaranteed-seat subscriptions at $300 a year but also created the ACTPass, which worked like a gym membership or the Netflix video service: for $25 a month, theatergoers received a small plastic card that admitted them to any show for which seats were available; they could attend as often as they liked and could even see the same show more than once; they received discounts on concessions and free ticket exchanges; and friends who attended with them could receive up to 50 percent off the price of their own tickets. The cost of the ACTPass, of course, was the same as a year's subscription, but patrons did not have to plan their theatergoing in advance; in addition, by merely flashing their pass for admission, they almost felt that they were getting in for free and were more willing to take a chance on productions they might not otherwise have attended. Also, while the traditional subscription provided a lump sum that had to last through the year, the ACTPass provided the theater with a monthly income. Unlike a traditional subscription that could be renewed or cancelled annually, the ACTPass continued indefinitely with an automatic credit-card charge. The ACTPass had a high retention rate; few holders of the card deactivated their accounts after the three-month minimum membership period. On the other hand, Salt Lake City's Pioneer Theatre Company instituted a season pass that had only a 25 percent renewal rate. Their customers told them, "It doesn't fit our needs because we don't know until the last minute whether we're going or not, and you can't guarantee seats." Also, lacking specific performance dates, they forgot about it and never used the passes. Overall, according to *Theatre Facts,* the Theatre Communications Group's annual in-depth report on the nonprofit theater industry, between 2001 and 2009, subscription renewals averaged 70 percent to 76 percent annually, ending at 73 percent in 2009, while total subscription packages sold and total subscriber attendance, both of which were at ten-year highs in 2001, were at their lowest in 2009, declining by 26 percent and 16 percent, respectively, over the period. Average single-ticket income exceeded average subscription income every year except 2001 and 2005.

Broadway Musicals. Classic Broadway tunes could still be heard in the first decade of the twenty-first century with revivals of shows such as Richard Rodgers and Oscar Hammerstein's *South Pacific* (1949) in 2008 and *Guys and Dolls* (1950) in 2009; but rock 'n' roll, political satire, and social commentary were more prominent in Broadway musicals of the period. Most of the hits climbed up through local theater and Off Broadway before opening on Great White Way; several were based on movies. *Rent,* about a group of impoverished young artists and musicians, moved Giacomo Puccini's 1896 opera *La Bohème* from Paris's Latin Quarter in the nineteenth century to New York's East Village in the twentieth century and introduced the specter of HIV/AIDS; the play opened in 1996 and did not close until 2008. *Urinetown* (2001–2004) told the story of the Urine Good Company, a pay-toilet monopoly that thrives after the government outlaws toilets in homes. *Avenue Q* (2003–2009) had human performers interacting with giant *Sesame Street*–style puppets. *Wicked* (2003–   ), based on Gregory Maguire's 1995 novel *Wicked: The Life and Times of the Wicked Witch of the West,* traced the origins of the witches from L. Frank Baum's novel *The Wonderful Wizard of Oz* (1900) and the 1939 movie version of Baum's work. Mel Brooks's *The Producers* (2001–2007) was based on his 1968 mostly nonmusical movie about two unscrupulous impresarios who try to come up with a play so atrocious that it will be sure to close on opening night, allowing them to keep their backers' money; to their chagrin, *Springtime for Hitler* turns out to be a hit. *The Producers* was, in turn, made into a film in 2005 with most of the Broadway cast reappearing in the movie. The Arthurian farce *Monty Python's Spamalot* (2005–2009) derived from the British comedy troupe's 1975 movie *Monty Python and the Holy Grail.* The "jukebox musical" *Mamma Mia!* (2001–   ) used a story about a wedding on a Greek island, at which the bride's mother confronts the three men who might be her daughter's father, to showcase the songs of the 1970s Swedish pop quartet ABBA; it was adapted as a movie starring Meryl Streep and Pierce Brosnan in 2008. *Hairspray* (2002–2009), about an overweight teenager who auditions for a 1960s television dance program, was based on the 1988 John Waters movie and, like *The Producers,* was itself filmed in 2007 (with John Travolta in drag replacing Harvey Fierstein as the heroine's mother). *Jersey Boys* (2005–   ) was a jukebox musical that dramatized the lives of the members of the 1960s–1970s rock band Frankie Valli and the Four Seasons and included many of their hit songs. *Spring Awakening* (2006–2009) was a rock musical adapted from the German dramatist Frank Wedekind's 1891 play *Frühlings Erwachen,* about teenagers discovering sex; it retained the time period and locale of the original work. While none of the hit musicals was likely to become a timeless classic that would be revived over and over for many years like those of the 1940s and 1950s by Rodgers and Hammerstein or Alan Jay Lerner and Frederick Loewe, they brought in a great deal of revenue from tourists (with tickets for *The Producers* priced as high as $485) and refuted the often-repeated fear that the Broadway musical was "dead."

Sources:

Anne Beggs, "'For Urinetown is your town . . .': The Fringes of Broadway," *Theatre Journal,* 62 (March 2010): 41–56;

Eliza Bent, "Paper or Plastic?" *American Theatre* (April 2011): 56–57;

Robert Edwin, "What's Going on on Broadway?" *Journal of Singing,* 66 (September–October 2009): 71–73;

Jeffrey Eric Jenkins, "Through a Glass, Nostalgically: The Death and Life of Broadway," *American Literary History,* 19 (Spring 2007): 190–210;

Stephen Nunns, "Shifting Currents: TCG's *Theatre Facts 2001* Tracks the Field's Course through Troubled Waters," *American Theatre* (September 2002): 52–54.

HEADLINE MAKERS

SHEPARD FAIREY

1970–

STREET ARTIST, GRAPHIC DESIGNER

OBEY. Born in Charleston, South Carolina, on 15 February 1970, Frank Shepard Fairey as a youth was part of a skateboarding and punk-rock subculture. Among his influences were the Sex Pistols, the British graffiti artist Banksy, and the guerilla poster artist Robbie Conal. While still a student at the Rhode Island School of Design, he attracted attention with his black-and-white stickers featuring the image of the wrestler and actor Andre Roussimoff and the words "ANDRE THE GIANT HAS A POSSE/ 7'4in, 520lb," which he plastered in unusual places all around Providence. When a legal objection was raised to his use of the trademarked phrase "Andre the Giant," he substituted the word "Obey"—which he subsequently used by itself and in other work and then chose as the name of his first company. In a 1990 manifesto on his Obeygiant website, Fairey explained the rationale for his OBEY campaign and much of his art:

> The OBEY sticker attempts to stimulate curiosity and bring people to question both the sticker and their relationship with their surroundings. Because people are not used to seeing advertisements or propaganda for which the product or motive is not obvious, frequent and novel encounters with the sticker provoke thought and possible frustration, nevertheless revitalizing the viewer's perception and attention to detail. The sticker has no meaning but exists only to cause people to react, to contemplate and search for meaning in the sticker. Because OBEY has no actual meaning, the various reactions and interpretations of those who view it reflect their personality and the nature of their sensibilities.

Building on the prominence gained from his street art, Fairey developed a successful design and marketing career. His clients included corporations such as Pepsi, Nike, and Hasbro. His designs appeared as album art and film posters and on skateboards and clothing. Yet, he also remained an unrepentant street artist, being arrested more than a dozen times during the course of his career for vandalism.

Obama Poster. Shepard Fairey became a widely known artist in 2008 through the popularity of a "grass roots" poster he created in support of presidential candidate Barack Obama. Without being officially connected to the campaign, Fairey chose an Associated Press (AP) photograph of Obama as the basis of his design. He described the image as Obama "gazing off into the future, saying, 'I can guide you.'" Making a stylized stencil portrait of the candidate, Fairey used a patriotic palette of red, beige, and two shades of blue, printing the word "progress" underneath. The poster was used locally in Los Angeles prior to a rally and the portrait was also posted on the Internet, where it went viral and became the iconic image associated with the campaign. Fairey later designed posters at the request of the Obama campaign, using the words "Hope" and "Change" and "Vote." An estimated 300,000 posters as well as some 500,000 stickers and badges were eventually produced. As payment, Fairey received a thank-you note from the future president: "Your images have a profound effect on people, whether seen in a gallery or on a stop sign. I'm privileged to be part of your art work and proud to have your support."

Controversy. Following the explosion in popularity of his Obama art, Fairey was sued by the AP for copyright infringement—a legal case not wholly settled by the end of the decade. With his commercial success, Fairey was also attacked as a sellout by other artists. His noncommercial efforts, too, were sometimes harshly criticized. In his *New York Times* review of Fairey's 2007 "E Pluribus Venom" show at the Jonathan LeVine Gallery, Benjamin Genocchio called his art "generic": "It's Norman Rockwell crossed with the Dead Kennedys crossed with Communist-era propaganda." Undaunted at the close of the decade, Fairey continued his career on the street as well as in the gallery.

Sources:

William Booth, "Obama's On-the-Wall Endorsement," *Washington Post*, 18 May 2008;

Alex Cohen, "What's with That Obama Poster?" *Day to Day*, NPR, 7 April 2008;

Benjamin Genocchio, "'E Pluribus Venom," *New York Times*, 29 June 2007;

obeygiant.com;

Melena Ryzik, "Closer to Mainstream, Still a Bit Rebellious," *New York Times*, 1 October 2008.

JONATHAN FRANZEN

1959–

NOVELIST

Achievement and Disillusionment. Franzen was born on 17 August 1959 in Western Springs, Illinois, and grew up in Webster Groves, Missouri, a suburb of St. Louis. He graduated from Swarthmore College with a B.A. in German, and was awarded a Fulbright Fellowship to study abroad for a year at the Freie Universität in Berlin. He married another aspiring writer and began to work seriously on his first novel while employed at a seismology lab at Harvard University on weekends. "I began my first novel as a twenty-two-year-old dreaming of changing the world," Franzen wrote in 1996. His first two novels, *The Twenty-Seventh City* (1988) and *Strong Motion* (1992)—elaborately plotted works set in cities Franzen knew well, St. Louis and Boston, respectively—were praised by critics, but neither amounted to the success their author envisioned. Franzen's doubts about his profession as a novelist were compounded by personal troubles, as in the 1990s he suffered the deaths of his parents and the disintegration of his marriage. For a time he turned from writing novels to investigative journalism for *The New Yorker:* "I began doing regular work for them, partly because I needed to keep paying the bills, but also because that which I was not getting from novel writing—especially after the disappointment of the second book—I was finding doing *The New Yorker* pieces: a sense of engagement with public life." Franzen was encouraged to return to the novel in part through his relationships with such writers as Don DeLillo, Donald Antrim, and David Foster Wallace.

Career Maker. Franzen's *The Corrections* (2001), a National Book Award Winner, was one of the most discussed literary works of the decade. In structuring the book as five interrelated novellas, "each compelling on its own," Franzen intended to "get rid of the big plot" and "make a long book work without that sense of big machinery, gears turning, *issues, issues.*" Critics praised Franzen's satirical treatment of American society and his compelling focus on the lives of Alfred and Enid Lambert. "Despite a complex and involved plot," observed Stewart O'Nan of *The Atlantic Monthly,* "the driving force of the book is that simplest, most intricate of engines, the unhappy family."

The Oprah Affair. A solitary creature of routine, Franzen wrote his third novel in the isolation of an office on the fourth floor of an old Manhattan bank building that he commuted to five days a week. With the publication of *The Corrections,* he suddenly reemerged as a public figure, apparently unprepared for the degree of engagement with the culture that he and his book achieved. After Oprah Winfrey selected *The Corrections* for her book club—an honor that typically assured a work of being a best seller—Franzen expressed ambivalence about his association with the television celebrity and his reluctance to have the Winfrey stamp of selection on the book's jacket. His public comments so offended Winfrey that she rescinded her invitation for Franzen to appear on her show. He was subsequently attacked for ingratitude and arrogance, while the public spat reignited the old debate over the popular versus the "literary" novel. The controversy no doubt attracted even more readers to Franzen's work.

After *The Corrections.* Later in the decade Franzen wrote *How to Be Alone: Essays* (2002), a collection that included a discussion of his father's death from Alzheimer's, and also a memoir titled *The Discomfort Zone: A Personal History* (2006). In 2007 he published *Spring Awakening,* a translation of Frank Wedekind's 1891 German play. In the last years of the decade, Franzen was again sequestered in his writing routine at work on another long novel.

Sources:

Thomas R. Edwards, "Oprah's Choice," *Raritan,* 21 (Spring 2002): 75–86;

Jonathan Franzen, "Perchance to Dream: In an Age of Images, a Reason to Write Novels," *Harper's,* 292 (April 1996): 35–55;

Philip Hensher, "Writing beyond His Means," *Spectator,* 287 (24 November 2001): 44–45;

Stewart O'Nan, Review of *The Corrections, Atlantic Monthly,* 288 (September 2001): 136;

Joanna Smith Rakoff, "Making *The Corrections:* An Interview with Jonathan Franzen," *Poets & Writers,* 29 (September/October 2001): 27–33.

MEL GIBSON

1956–

ACTOR, DIRECTOR

Golden Boy. Mel Gibson was born in Peekskill, New York, on 3 January 1956, moving with his family to his grandmother's native Australia in 1968. He achieved international fame in the title role of the low-budget film *Mad Max* (1979), set in a dystopian future Australia. He made two sequels, *Mad Max 2: The Road Warrior* (1981) and *Mad Max beyond Thunderdome* (1985). His American film debut was as Fletcher Christian in *The Bounty* (1984). In 1987 he played the violent, alcoholic, near-suicidal Los Angeles police detective Martin Riggs in the first of four *Lethal Weapon* movies. He departed from the action roles for which he had become known in 1990 to star in director Franco Zeffirelli's *Hamlet*. Gibson won an Academy Award for directing *Braveheart* (1995), in which he starred as the thirteenth-century Scottish rebel William Wallace; the film received the Best Picture Oscar. He was selected *People* magazine's "Sexiest Man Alive" in 1985 and one of its "50 Most Beautiful People" in the world in 1990, 1991, and 1996; *Empire* magazine ranked him thirty-seventh among its "100 Sexiest Stars" in movie history in 1995. In 2000 Gibson played a reluctant fighter in the American Revolution in *The Patriot* and a man who suddenly finds himself with the power to overhear women's thoughts in the romantic comedy *What Women Want*. Two years later, he starred as a colonel in the Vietnam War film *We Were Soldiers*.

Controversy over *The Passion of the Christ*. In 2004 Gibson confronted a storm of criticism when he co-authored the screenplay for and directed *The Passion of the Christ*, about the final hours in the life of Jesus. The film's dialogue was entirely in Aramaic, Latin, and Hebrew; Gibson originally intended not to include subtitles but ultimately did so. Despite its popularity with many Christian groups, the estimated $30 million film, which became the highest-grossing R-rated movie in U.S. box-office history at $370 million (plus $241 million overseas), was attacked for its extremely brutal and bloody depiction of Jesus' scourging and Crucifixion. More serious were charges that the movie promoted anti-Semitism by exonerating the Romans and blaming the Jews for Christ's death. Gibson claimed that he was merely being faithful to the Gospel accounts. He did remove from the subtitles the translation of the verse in Matthew 27:25 in which the Jewish mob cries, "His blood be on our heads and on the heads of our children!" The line, spoken in Aramaic, remained on the soundtrack. Many speculated that Gibson's conservative religious beliefs were motivation for the film's controversial account of the passion. His father, Hutton, was an outspoken ultraconservative Catholic who opposed the modernizing of the church, believing, for example, that John XXIII (1958-1963) was the last legitimate Pope.

The Rant Heard round the World. The anti-Semitism charges were revived when Gibson was arrested by a Los Angeles County deputy sheriff for drunk driving on the Pacific Coast Highway in Malibu at 2:30 A.M. on 28 July 2006. The arrest report was "sanitized" for public release, but the original version was obtained by the celebrity-gossip website *TMZ*. It stated that "Gib-

son blurted out a barrage of anti-Semitic remarks about 'f—king Jews.' Gibson called out, 'The Jews are responsible for all the wars in the world.' Gibson then asked, 'Are you a Jew?'" At the police station he reportedly said to a female deputy, "What are you looking at, sugartits?" (On 22 February 2009 Gibson said on the ABC *Jimmy Kimmel Live Post-Oscar Special* that it was the arresting officer, not he, who used the term "sugartits," which Kimmel called "the greatest new word of the decade.") Five days after his arrest, Gibson released a statement that began: "There is no excuse, nor should there be any tolerance, for anyone who thinks or expresses any kind of anti-Semitic remark. I want to apologize specifically to everyone in the Jewish community for the vitriolic and harmful words that I said to a law enforcement officer the night I was arrested on a DUI charge." He pleaded no contest to a misdemeanor DUI charge, paid a fine, was placed on three years' probation, and entered an outpatient alcohol-rehabilitation program. There was speculation that the incident might have destroyed his career.

"Mad Mel"? Concern over Gibson's fascination with violence grew when *Apocalypto* was released in December 2006; he produced and directed the film and co-authored the screenplay but did not appear in it. The film, set amidst the 16th-century disintegration of Mayan civilization, featured graphic depictions of human sacrifice. Describing the brutality of this and other Gibson films, critic Richard Schickel noted that the director "loves to get people painfully restrained and then do really bad things to them," as in "the drawing-and-quartering scene in 'Braveheart' and the ghastly flogging of Jesus in 'The Passion.'" We are not, in these instances, dealing with mere 'violence.' We are dealing with ritualized sadomasochism—an open manifestation of one of those dark fantasies that those in thrall to them must endlessly repeat and that have, of course, some sort of psychosexual component." Similarly, Mick LaSalle wrote in the *San Francisco Chronicle* that while "it would be inappropriate and probably inaccurate for any critic to pronounce on the mental health of a filmmaker based on his movie, *Apocalypto* seems like something made by a crazy person."

Sources:

Peter Carrick, *Mel Gibson* (London: Robert Hale, 1998);

Zev Garber, *Mel Gibson's Passion: The Film, the Controversy, and Its Implications* (West Lafayette, Ind.: Purdue University Press, 2006);

J. Hoberman, "Mel Gibson Is Responsible for All the Wars in the World: OK, Slight Exaggeration, but He's at Least to Blame for This One He Made Up," *Village Voice,* 28 November 2006;

Mick LaSalle, "Rape, Murder, Mayhem—There Goes the Civilization," *San Francisco Chronicle,* 8 December 2006, p. E1;

Richard Schickel, "What's with Mel's Bloody Porn? Gory Scenes of Torture in 'The Passion of the Christ' and 'Apocalypto' Tell Us Much about Gibson's Sensibilities," *Los Angeles Times,* 13 December 2006.

JAY-Z

1969–

RAP ARTIST, HIP-HOP MOGUL

Out of Brooklyn. Shawn Corey Carter was born on 4 December 1969 in the Bedford Stuyvesant section of Brooklyn, New York. He grew up in the Marcy Houses, a public housing project, and attended several high schools but never graduated. Carter's early life was plagued by difficulty; his father left the family when he was only eleven years old, and the Marcy Houses was notorious for gun violence and drug trade. Fascinated with the burgeoning rap scene in New York, he began writing lyrics and rapping with friends, freestyling and honing his craft.

Jay-Z. In 1989 he collaborated with an older rapper called Jaz-O on a song titled "The Originators," an effort that earned him a spot on the seminal rap television program "Yo! MTV Raps." He began calling himself "Jay-Z" as an homage to the mentorship of Jaz-O and in reference to his childhood nickname, "Jazzy." Unable to sign with a major record label, Jay-Z and friends Damon Dash and Kareem Burke created their own in 1996, naming it Roc-A-Fella Records. His debut album, *Reasonable Doubt*, released in June 1996, benefited from the notable appearance of established rapper Notorious B.I.G. and reached number twenty-three on the Billboard charts. In 1997 Jay-Z followed up with *In My Lifetime . . . vol. 1*, which peaked at number three on the Billboard album charts. In 1998 he released *Volume 2 . . . Hard Knock Life* and scored a major hit with the album's title track "Hard Knock Life (Ghetto Anthem)," which sampled a song from the Broadway musical *Annie*. The single went gold and was nominated for a Grammy in 1999. His next album, *Vol. 3 . . . Life and Times of S. Carter*, featured the hit single "Big Pimpin'." At the close of the 1990s, Jay-Z was quickly becoming one of the most recognizable and successful young hip-hop artists in America.

Controversy. In 2001 a growing rivalry between Jay-Z and rapper Nas for the unofficial title of best New York rapper became an outright feud when Jay-Z recited a verse of the track "Takeover" from his upcoming *Blueprint* album at a music festival. The song was written as a direct slight or "diss" of Nas and his collaborators. In response, Nas performed a freestyle attack on Jay-Z and other acts associated with Roc-A-Fella records. A four-year battle ensued in which the two hip-hop giants traded lyrical blows, and which many feared might spill over into violence, especially after the tragic deaths of rappers Tupac Shakur and Biggie Smalls (Notorious B.I.G.) in the East Coast-West Coast battles of the 1990s. The feud ended when Jay-Z invited Nas onstage during an October 2005 concert. "All that beef sh-- is done, we had our fun," he said, "let's get this money."

Black Album and "Retirement." In 2003 Jay-Z released *The Black Album*, which debuted at number one on the Billboard chart. With hit singles such as "Dirt Off Your Shoulder" and "Change Clothes," the album was a commercial and critical success, nominated for the album of the year Grammy and ranked number seven on *Slant* magazine's list of the top albums of the 2000s. Before *The Black Album*'s release, he announced that it would be his last studio album. Jay-Z's retirement from rapping was part of a shift in the focus of his career, as he became increasingly involved with record production and developing new talent at Roc-A-Fella records of which he took sole control in 2004. Also in 2004 Jay-Z was named the president of Def-Jam Records, and during his tenure there he signed such artists as Rihanna and Young Jeezy before departing in 2007.

Business Mogul. In addition to his success in the music industry, the Jay-Z brand proved bankable in other areas. His clothing line "RocaWear," founded in 1999 with Damon Dash, was purchased by Iconix Brand Group in 2007 for more than $200 million. He opened several nightclubs across the country and became part owner of the New Jersey Nets basketball franchise. His net worth at the end of the decade was estimated at more than $300 million. Despite his well-publicized retirement, Jay-Z found it difficult to stay out of the studio for long, releasing *Kingdom Come*, his ninth album, in 2006, followed by *American Gangster* (2007) and *The Blueprint 3* (2009). As an artist, producer, businessman, and mentor to up-and-coming rappers, Jay-Z was an influential presence in the hip-hop world in the 2000s.

Sources:
Jeff Leeds, "Jay-Z to Quit His Day Job as President of Def Jam," *New York Times*, 25 December 2007;

Kelefa Sanneh, "Gettin' Paid," *New Yorker* (20 August 2001);

Josh Tyrangiel, "Jay-Z: Music's $150 Million Man," *Time*, 3 April 2008;

Malcolm Venable, "Jay-Z and Nas' Feud of Words," *Entertainment Weekly*, 11 January 2002.

ANGELA LANSBURY

1925–

ACTOR

A Life of Acting. Born in London on 16 October 1925, Angela Lansbury moved to the United States in her teens at the outbreak of World War II. She received an Oscar nomination for her film debut in *Gaslight* (1944) and another, shortly thereafter, for *The Picture of Dorian Gray* (1945). As her film career progressed she played more-mature female characters, though she was often only a few years older than her onscreen sons or daughters. In *The Manchurian Candidate* (1962), which many critics considered her finest film role, Lansbury convincingly played the mother of an actor two years her junior, creating one of the screen's most unforgettable villains. For her work on the stage she won her first Best Actress Tony in 1966 for *Mame;* she later won Best Actress in a Musical for her roles in *Dear World* (1969), *Gypsy* (1975), and *Sweeney Todd* (1979). Her portrayal of mystery writer-turned-sleuth Jessica Fletcher in the television series *Murder, She Wrote* (1984–1996) earned her four Golden Globe Awards. Lansbury also lent her voice to the animated films *The Last Unicorn* (1982) and *Anastasia* (1997), and perhaps most memorably to *Beauty and the Beast* (1991) as Mrs. Potts, the singing teapot, a role she reprised in *Beauty and the Beast: The Enchanted Christmas* (1997).

Blithe Spirit. A beloved and accomplished performer whose varied career began in the 1940s, Lansbury returned to the stage in 2007 at age eighty-one to play a retired tennis champion in *Deuce,* receiving a Tony nomination. At a 2008 benefit, "The Ladies Who Sing Sondheim," she brought down the house with her performance of "The Worst Pies in London" from *Sweeney Todd,* in the role of Nellie Lovett which she originated on Broadway in 1979. In 2009 she tied with Julie Harris's record number of Tony Awards with her fifth Tony for her role in Noel Coward's play *Blithe Spirit,* in which she played an eccentric spirit medium. *New York Times* reviewer Ben Brantley singled out Lansbury's performance: "If 'Blithe Spirit' itself misses comic greatness, Coward did create a genuinely great comic character in Madame Arcati, and Ms. Lansbury gleefully makes it her own."

"Back Where I Belong." The eighty-three-year-old Lansbury left no doubt about her plans to continue acting when she told producers at the 2009 Drama Awards League luncheon, "Give me another job in the next five years," and then, amidst cheers from the crowd, continued, "I'll see you all on Broadway." Apparently the producers could not wait that long, as that fall she was cast as another madame, Madame Armfeldt, in Stephen Sondheim's *A Little Night Music,* and nominated for yet another Tony. The stage, she said, is "the place I am most comfortable as an actress. It's like Dolly: 'I'm back where I belong' when I'm in the theater."

Sources:

Ben Bradley, "The Medium as the Messenger," *New York Times,* 16 March 2009;

Kathy Henderson, "This is Your (Broadway) Life, Angela Lansbury!" *www.broadway.com* (26 May 2009);

Michael Portantiere, "Together Again: Lansbury and Sondheim Offer Rare Champagne and a Sumptuous Feast," *Sondheim Review,* 16 (Spring 2010).

PEOPLE IN THE NEWS

Artist **Robert Anderson** was selected to paint President George W. Bush's official portrait, to be hung at the National Portrait Gallery in Washington D.C. Russian-born **Aleksander Titovets** of El Paso, Texas, painted First Lady Laura Bush's portrait.

Nicholson Baker published three novels during the decade: *A Box of Matches* (2003), *Checkpoint* (2004), and *The Anthologist* (2009). A vocal critic of overreliance on archival digitization, he also wrote *Double Fold: Libraries and the Assault on Paper* (2001), a book critical of the destruction of paper-based materials by many libraries. He was inspired to write *Human Smoke: The Beginnings of World War II, the End of Civilization* (2008) after reading daily accounts of the outbreak of World War II from his personal collection of rescued historical newspapers; the book, a pacifist history of the war's beginning, was composed entirely of newspaper articles, journal entries, letters, and other materials, which Baker edited and arranged to form a narrative.

In 2001 **Halle Berry** became the first African American woman to receive the Academy Award for Best Actress for her role in *Monster's Ball,* directed by **Marc Foster.** Her portrayal also garnered a Screen Actors Guild Award and a Golden Globe nomination.

Hip-hop artists **Big Boi** and **André 3000** of rap group **OutKast** released their landmark double-album *Speakerboxxx/The Love Below* in September 2003. Two singles from the album, "Hey Ya," and "The Way You Move," reached number one on the billboard charts, and it won a Grammy Award for album of the year.

In February 2005 *The Gates,* a work of public art by Bulgarian-born artist **Christo** and his wife and collaborator **Jeanne-Claude,** was displayed in Central Park in New York City. The controversial installation featured over seven thousand vinyl gates hung with flowing saffron fabric throughout the park.

Actor **Robert Downey Jr.** was repeatedly arrested for drug-related charges, spending time in prison and also rehabilitation clinics. Despite his personal challenges, he achieved award-winning performances on television and screen, in such hits as *Iron Man* (2008), *Tropic Thunder* (2008), and *Sherlock Holmes* (2009).

In September 2006 the work of German-born modernist sculptor **Ruth Duckworth,** who escaped Nazi Germany in 1936 and was trained in Britain, and later taught at the University of Chicago, was exhibited as part of a retrospective at the Smithsonian American Art Museum.

Dave Eggers, author of the critically acclaimed memoir *A Heartbreaking Work of Staggering Genius* (2000), and founder of independent publishing house McSweeney's, published two novels: *You Shall Know Our Velocity* (2002) and *What Is the What: The Autobiography of Valentino Achak Deng* (2006). He co-wrote the screenplay with Spike Jonze for the 2009 film *Where the Wild Things Are.*

James Frey sparked controversy in January 2006 when it was alleged that his memoir, *A Million Little Pieces* (2003), contained fabrications and exaggerations of his criminal past. Television host **Oprah Winfrey,** who had selected the work for her book club, took Frey to task on her show, where he admitted that much of his account was fictional.

Director **Ron Howard** received the Academy Award for Best Director for his film *A Beautiful Mind* in 2001. He was also nominated for his direction of *Frost/Nixon* (2008), and in 2003 he was awarded the National Medal of Arts.

A twenty-five-foot-tall statue by **J. Seward Johnson** titled *Unconditional Surrender* was unveiled in New York in 2005. The sculpture re-created the iconic World War II photograph by **Alfred Eisenstaedt** of a sailor and nurse kissing in Times Square after news of Japan's surrender was announced in August 1945.

Actor **Nathan Lane** received his second Tony Award for Best Actor in a musical in 2001 for his portrayal of Max Bialystock in *The Producers.* One of Broadway's most recognizable stars, Lane also starred in a successful revival of *The Odd Couple* in 2006 and was inducted into the American Theatre Hall of Fame in 2008.

Rapper **Lil' Kim** was found guilty of lying to a federal grand jury on 17 March 2005, after it was proven that, contrary to her testimony, she had been present on the scene of a 2001 shooting that involved her manager and her bodyguard. Kim was sentenced to one year and one day in federal prison and was released in July 2006.

In March 2003 singer **Natalie Maines** of the country-music group the **Dixie Chicks** sparked controversy when, during a London concert, she criticized President **George W. Bush** and U.S. policy toward Iraq. Many country-music radio stations removed the band's songs from airplay in response, and sales of the band's music plummeted.

In 2006 the Museum of Modern Art in New York City featured a retrospective of the artist **Brice Marden.** The exhibition, which showcased his evolution as an artist, contained over fifty paintings, including two new works.

On 8 October 2003 **Idina Menzel** played the lead role of Elphaba in the Broadway debut of **Stephen Schwartz**'s musical *Wicked.* In 2004 she received the Tony Award for Best Actress in a musical for her performance.

The documentary *The Cats of Mirikitani* debuted at the Tribeca Film Festival in 2006, featuring the life and art of Japanese American painter **Jimmy Mirikitani,** who survived internment during World War II and was found homeless on the streets of New York City, creating his distinctive portraits of cats and other subjects.

Director **Michael Moore**'s documentary *Fahrenheit 9/11,* which criticized the Bush administration's handling of the war on terror, won the top prize at the Cannes International Film Festival and went on to gross over $200 million worldwide. Two other Moore documentaries, *Bowling for Columbine* (2002) and *Sicko* (2007), also garnered critical acclaim and drew large audiences.

Nathan Sawaya's exhibit "The Art of the Brick" toured the country during the decade, starting in 2007, and featured sculptures created with Lego building blocks.

Veteran director **Martin Scorsese** received his first Academy Award for Best Director in 2007 for *The Departed.* Other major films directed by Scorsese in the decade included *Gangs of New York* (2002), *The Aviator* (2004), and documentaries *The Blues* (2003) and *No Direction Home* (2005), about the life of Bob Dylan.

William Starrett's ballet *Off the Wall and onto the Stage,* based on the paintings of Gullah artist **Jonathan Green,** debuted in Columbia, South Carolina, in February 2005.

In December 2007 four songs featuring vocal hooks provided by rapper **T-Pain** reached the top ten of the Billboard Hot 100 song list. His contributions utilized auto-tune technology, which digitally altered his voice to achieve a unique sound. The success sparked an auto-tune craze in the industry, with rappers **Snoop Dogg** and **Lil Wayne,** among others, quickly releasing their own tracks featuring auto tune.

Brian K. Vaughan's graphic novel *Pride of Baghdad* (2006), illustrated by Niko Henrichon, won the IGN (Imagine Games Network) Award for best graphic novel in 2006. The work was a fictionalized retelling of the true story of four lions who escaped from the Baghdad zoo shortly after the U.S. bombing in 2003.

In August 2004 **Jack Valenti** retired as president of the Motion Picture Association of America (MPAA). In his 38-year tenure as head of the organization, Valenti oversaw the creation of the MPAA ratings system and lobbied successfully for the Digital Millenium Copyright Act (1998), which strengthened U.S. copyright law against digital piracy.

David Foster Wallace, author of the influential novel *Infinite Jest* (1996), released his third collection of short stories, *Oblivion: Stories,* in 2004. *Consider the Lobster: And Other Essays,* a volume of his most celebrated work as an essayist, was published in 2005.

AWARDS

PULITZER PRIZES

2000

Fiction: *Interpreter of Maladies*, by Jhumpa Lahiri

Drama: *Dinner with Friends*, by Donald Margulies

Poetry: *Repair*, by C. K. Williams

Music: *Life Is a Dream, Opera in Three Acts: Act II, Concert Version*, by Lewis Spratian

2001

Fiction: *The Amazing Adventures of Kavalier & Clay*, by Michael Chabon

Drama: *Proof*, by David Auburn

Poetry: *Different Hours*, by Stephen Dunn

Music: *Symphony No. 2 for String Orchestra*, by John Corigliano

2002

Fiction: *Empire Falls*, by Richard Russo

Drama: *Topdog/Underdog*, by Suzan-Lori Parks

Poetry: *Practical Gods*, by Carl Dennis

Music: *Ice Field*, by Henry Brant

2003

Fiction: *Middlesex*, by Jeffrey Eugenides

Drama: *Anna in the Tropics*, by Nilo Cruz

Poetry: *Moy Sand and Gravel*, by Paul Muldoon

Music: *On the Transmigration of Souls*, by John Adams

2004

Fiction: *The Known World*, by Edward P. Jones

Drama: *I Am My Own Wife*, by Doug Wright

Poetry: *Walking to Martha's Vineyard*, by Franz Wright

Music: *Tempest Fantasy*, by Paul Moravec

2005

Fiction: *Gilead*, by Marilynne Robinson

Drama: *Doubt: A Parable*, by John Patrick Shanley

Poetry: *Delights & Shadows*, by Ted Kooser

Music: *Second Concerto for Orchestra*, by Steven Stucky

2006

Fiction: *March*, by Geraldine Brooks

Drama: No Winner

Poetry: *Late Wife*, by Claudia Emerson

Music: *Piano Concerto: Chiavi in Mano*, by Yehudi Wyner

2007

Fiction: *The Road*, by Cormac McCarthy

Drama: *Rabbit Hole*, by David Lindsay-Abaire

Poetry: *Native Guard*, by Natasha Trethewey

Music: *Sound Grammar*, by Ornette Coleman

2008

Fiction: *The Brief Wondrous Life of Oscar Wao*, by Junot Díaz

Drama: *August: Osage County*, by Tracy Letts

Poetry: *Time and Materials*, by Robert Hass

Music: *The Little Match Girl Passion*, by David Lang

2009

Fiction: *Olive Kitteridge*, by Elizabeth Strout

Drama: *Ruined*, by Lynn Nottage

Poetry: *The Shadow of Sirius*, by W. S. Merwin

Music: *Double Sextet*, by Steve Reich

ANTOINETTE PERRY AWARDS (TONYS)

2000

Play: *Copenhagen,* by Michael Frayn

Actor, Dramatic Star: Stephen Dillane, *The Real Thing*

Actress, Dramatic Star: Jennifer Ehle, *The Real Thing*

Musical: *Contact,* produced by Lincoln Center Theater, André Bishop, and Bernard Gersten

Actor, Musical Star: Brian Stokes Mitchell, *Kiss Me Kate*

Actress, Musical Star: Heather Headley, *Aida*

2001

Play: *Proof,* by David Auburn

Actor, Dramatic Star: Richard Easton, *The Invention of Love*

Actress, Dramatic Star: Mary-Louise Parker, *Proof*

Musical: *The Producers,* produced by Rocco Landesman, SFX Theatrical Group, The Frankel-Baruch-Viertel-Routh Group, Bob Weinstein and Harvey Weinstein, Rick Steiner, Robert F. X. Sillerman, Mel Brooks, and James D. Stern/Douglas L. Meyer

Actress, Musical Star: Christine Ebersole, *42nd Street*

2002

Play: *The Goat or Who Is Sylvia?* by Edward Albee

Actor, Dramatic Star: Alan Bates, *Fortune's Fool*

Actress, Dramatic Star: Lindsay Duncan, *Private Lives*

Musical: *Thoroughly Modern Millie,* produced by Michael Leavitt, Fox Theatricals, Hal Luftig, Stewart F. Lane, James L. Nederlander, Independent Presenters Network, L. Mages/M. Glick, Berinstein/Manocherian/Dramatic Forces, John York Noble, and Whoopi Goldberg

Actor, Musical Star: John Lithgow, *Sweet Smell of Success*

Actress, Musical Star: Sutton Foster, *Thoroughly Modern Millie*

2003

Play: *Take Me Out,* by Richard Greenberg

Actor, Dramatic Star: Brian Dennehy, *Long Day's Journey into Night*

Actress, Dramatic Star: Vanessa Redgrave, *Long Day's Journey into Night*

Musical: *Hairspray,* produced by Margo Lion, Adam Epstein, The Frankel-Baruch-Viertel-Routh Group, James D. Stern/Douglas L. Meyer, Rick Steiner/Frederic H. Mayerson, SEL & GFO, New Line Cinema, Clear Channel Entertainment, A. Gordon/E. McAllister, D. Harris/M. Swinsky, and J. & B. Osher

Actor, Musical Star: Harvey Fierstein, *Hairspray*

Actress, Musical Star: Marissa Jaret Winokur, *Hairspray*

2004

Play: *I Am My Own Wife,* by Doug Wright

Actor, Dramatic Star: Jefferson Mays, *I Am My Own Wife*

Actress, Dramatic Star: Phylicia Rashad, *A Raisin in the Sun*

Musical: *Avenue Q,* produced by Kevin McCollum, Robyn Goodman, Jeffrey Seller, Vineyard Theatre, and The New Group

Actor, Musical Star: Hugh Jackman, *The Boy from Oz*

Actress, Musical Star: Idina Menzel, *Wicked*

2005

Play: *Doubt,* by John Patrick Shanley

Actor, Dramatic Star: Bill Irwin, *Who's Afraid of Virginia Woolf?*

Actress, Dramatic Star: Cherry Jones, *Doubt*

Musical: *Monty Python's Spamalot,* produced by Boyett Ostar Productions, the Shubert Organization, Arielle Tepper, Stephanie McClelland/Lawrence Horowitz, Ean V. McAllister/Allan S. Gordon, Independent Presenters Network, Roy Furman, GRS Associates, Jam Theatricals, TGA Entertainment, and Clear Channel Entertainment

Actor, Musical Star: Norbert Leo Butz, *Dirty Rotten Scoundrels*

Actress, Musical Star: Victoria Clark, *The Light in the Piazza*

2006

Play: *The History Boys,* by Alan Bennett

Actor, Dramatic Star: Richard Griffiths, *The History Boys*

Actress, Dramatic Star: Cynthia Nixon, *The Rabbit Hole*

Musical: *Jersey Boys,* produced by Dodger Theatricals, Joseph J. Grano, Pelican Group, Tamara Kinsella and Kevin Kinsella, Latitude Link, and Rick Steiner/Osher/Staton/Bell/Mayerson Group

Actor, Musical Star: John Lloyd Young, *Jersey Boys*

Actress, Musical Star: LaChanze, *The Color Purple*

2007

Play: *The Coast of Utopia,* by Tom Stoppard

Actor, Dramatic Star: Frank Langella, *Frost/Nixon*

Actress, Dramatic Star: Julie White, *The Little Dog Laughed*

Musical: *Spring Awakening,* produced by Ira Pittelman, Tom Hulce, Jeffrey Richards, Jerry Frankel, Atlantic Theater Company, Jeffrey Sine, Freddy DeMann, Max Cooper, Mort Swinsky/Cindy Gutterman and Jay Gutterman/Joe McGinnis/Judith Ann Abrams, ZenDog Productions/CarJac Productions, Aron Bergson Productions/Jennifer Manocherian/Ted Snowdon, Harold Thau/Terry Schnuck/Cold Spring Productions, Amanda DuBois/Elizabeth Eynon Wetherell, and Jennifer Maloney/Tamara Tunie/Joe Cilibrasi/StyleFour Productions

Actor, Musical Star: David Hyde Pierce, *Curtains*

Actress, Musical Star: Christine Ebersole, *Grey Gardens*

2008

Play: *August: Osage County,* by Tracy Letts

Actor, Dramatic Star: Mark Rylance, *Boeing–Boeing*

Actress, Dramatic Star: Deanna Dunagan, *August: Osage County*

Musical: *In the Heights,* produced by Kevin McCollum, Jeffrey Seller, Jill Furman, Sander Jacobs, Goodman/Grossman, Peter Fine, and Everett/Skipper

Actor, Musical Star: Paulo Szot, *South Pacific*

Actress, Musical Star: Patti LuPone, *Gypsy*

2009

Play: *God of Carnage,* by Yasmina Reza

Actor, Dramatic Star: Geoffrey Rush, *Exit the King*

Actress, Dramatic Star: Marcia Gay Harden, *God of Carnage*

Musical: *Billy Elliott, the Musical,* produced by Universal Pictures Stage Productions, Working Title Films, Old Vic Productions, and Weinstein Live Entertainment

Actor, Musical Star: David Alvarez, Trent Kowalike, and Kiril Kulish, *Billy Elliott, the Musical*

Actress, Musical Star: Alice Ripley, *Next to Normal*

ACADEMY OF MOTION PICTURE ARTS AND SCIENCES AWARDS (OSCARS)
2000

Actor: Russell Crowe, *Gladiator*

Actress: Julia Roberts, *Erin Brockovich*

Director: Steven Soderbergh, *Traffic*

Picture: *Gladiator*

2001

Actor: Denzel Washington, *Training Day*

Actress: Halle Berry, *Monster's Ball*

Director: Ron Howard, *A Beautiful Mind*

Picture: *A Beautiful Mind*

2002

Actor: Adrien Brody, *The Pianist*

Actress: Nicole Kidman, *The Hours*

Director: Roman Polanski, *The Pianist*

Picture: *Chicago*

2003

Actor: Sean Penn, *Mystic River*

Actress: Charlize Theron, *Monster*

Director: Peter Jackson, *The Lord of the Rings: The Return of the King*

Picture: *The Lord of the Rings: The Return of the King*

2004

Actor: Jamie Foxx, *Ray*

Actress: Hilary Swank, *Million Dollar Baby*

Director: Clint Eastwood, *Million Dollar Baby*

Picture: *Million Dollar Baby*

2005

Actor: Philip Seymour Hoffman, *Capote*

Actress: Reese Witherspoon, *Walk the Line*

Director: Ang Lee, *Brokeback Mountain*

Picture: *Crash*

2006

Actor: Forest Whitaker, *The Last King of Scotland*

Actress: Helen Mirren, *The Queen*

Director: Martin Scorsese, *The Departed*

Picture: *The Departed*

2007

Actor: Daniel Day-Lewis, *There Will Be Blood*

Actress: Marion Cotillard, *La Vie En Rose*

Director: Joel Coen and Ethan Coen, *No Country for Old Men*

Picture: *No Country for Old Men*

2008

Actor: Sean Penn, *Milk*

Actress: Kate Winslet, *The Reader*

Director: Danny Boyle, *Slumdog Millionaire*

Picture: *Slumdog Millionaire*

2009

Actor: Jeff Bridges, *Crazy Heart*

Actress: Sandra Bullock, *The Blind Side*

Director: Kathryn Bigelow, *The Hurt Locker*

Picture: *The Hurt Locker*

THE NATIONAL ACADEMY OF RECORDING ARTS AND SCIENCES AWARDS (GRAMMYS)

2000

Record: **U2,** "Beautiful Day"

Album: Steely Dan, *Two against Nature*

2001

Record: **U2,** "Walk On"

Album: Alison Krauss and the Union Station, *O Brother Where Art Thou?*

2002

Record: Norah Jones, "Don't Know Why"

Album: Norah Jones, *Come Away with Me*

2003

Record: Coldplay, "Clocks"

Album: OutKast, *Speakerboxxx/The Love Below*

2004

Record: Norah Jones and Ray Charles, "Here We Go Again"

Album: Ray Charles, *Genius Loves Company*

2005

Record: Green Day, "Boulevard of Broken Dreams"

Album: U2, *How to Dismantle an Atomic Bomb*

2006

Record: Dixie Chicks, "Not Ready to Make Nice"

Album: Dixie Chicks, *Taking the Long Way*

2007

Record: Amy Winehouse, "Rehab"

Album: Herbie Hancock, *River: The Joni Letters*

2008

Record: Alison Krauss and Robert Plant, "Please Read the Letter"

Album: Alison Krauss and Robert Plant, *Raising Sand*

2009

Record: Kings of Leon, "Use Somebody"

Album: Taylor Swift, *Fearless*

NOBEL PRIZE IN LITERATURE

2000: Gao Xingjian

2001: V. S. Naipaul

2002: Imre Kertész

2003: John M. Coetzee

2004: Elfriede Jelinek

2005: Harold Pinter

2006: Orhan Pamuk

2007: Doris Lessing

2008: Jean-Marie Gustave Le Clézio

2009: Herta Müller

DEATHS

Aaliyah (Aaliyah Dana Haughton), 22, singer and actor, appeared in *Romeo Must Die* (2000) and *Queen of the Damned* (2002), 25 August 2001.

Darrell "Dimebag" Abbott, 38, guitarist with heavy-metal band Pantera, mortally wounded by gunman at concert, 8 December 2004.

Burna Acquanetta, 83, actor, born in Wyoming; often typecast by Hollywood studios as a "native woman," appeared in eleven movies, including *Tarzan and the Leopard Woman* (1946), 16 August 2004.

Virginia Adair, 91, poet, published *Ants on the Melon* (1996), *Beliefs and Blasphemies* (1998), and *Living on Fire* (2000), 16 September 2004.

Eddie Albert, 99, actor, starred in television show *Green Acres* (1965–1971), performed in movies *Roman Holiday* (1953) and *The Heartbreak Kid* (1972), 26 May 2005.

Chris Alcaide, 80, character actor, appeared in more than one hundred films and television programs, mostly Westerns, 30 June 2004.

Dayton Allen, 85, comedian, voice of Deputy Dawg, Phineas T. Bluster on *The Howdy Doody Show,* and other cartoon characters, 11 November 2004.

Donald M. Allen, 92, scholar, edited poetry of Jack Kerouac, 29 August 2004.

Tina Allen, 58, sculptor, known for her bronze statues of African American activists, 9 September 2008.

Vernon Alley, 89, jazz bassist, played with Lionel Hampton and Count Basie, 3 October 2004.

Robert Altman, 81, director, best known for *MASH* (1970), *Nashville* (1975), and *Gosford Park* (2001), 20 November 2006.

Joe Ames, 86, baritone, sang with the Ames Brothers (1950s and 1960s), 22 December 2007.

Muriel Angelus (Findlay), 95, British-born singer and actor, appeared on Broadway (*The Boys from Syracuse,* 1938) and in sixteen movies, 22 August 2004.

Izora Rhodes Armstead, 62, singer, founding member of The Weather Girls, best known for disco hit "It's Raining Men" (1982), 16 September 2004.

Eddy Arnold, 89, country/pop singer, sang "Make the World Go Away," 8 May 2008.

Gerald Arpino, 85, dancer and choreographer, cofounder of the Joffrey Ballet, 29 October 2008.

Mark Arvin, 40, ballet and modern dancer, performed in Broadway shows (*Fosse, Chicago*), 5 December 2004.

Edward Avedisian, 71, painter, abstract style, 17 August 2007.

Richard Avedon, 81, photographer, specialized in portraiture, fashion, and advertising; defined the look of Calvin Klein, Versace, and Revlon, 1 October 2004.

Rose Bampton, 99, mezzo-soprano and soprano, sang at the Metropolitan Opera (1932–1950), 21 August 2007.

Anne Bancroft, 73, actor, portrayed Annie Sullivan in *The Miracle Worker* (1962), Mrs. Robinson in *The Graduate* (1967), and Mother Miriam Ruth in *Agnes of God* (1985), 6 June 2005.

Joseph Barbera, 95, animator, cocreator of cartoons "Tom and Jerry," "Yogi Bear," "The Jetsons," "Scooby Doo," and "The Flintstones" with Bill Hanna, 18 December 2006.

Saul Bellow, 89, novelist, won Nobel Prize in Literature (1976), best-known novel was *The Adventures of Augie March* (1953), 5 April 2005.

Peter Benchley, 65, author, best known for novel *Jaws* (1974), 11 February 2006.

Ara Berberian, 74, bass opera singer, performed with New York City Metropolitan Opera, San Francisco Opera, and Michigan Opera Theatre, 21 February 2005.

Stan Berenstain, 82, author, created with his wife Jan the children's book characters the Berenstain Bears, 26 November 2005.

Charles Biederman, 98, modernist painter and sculptor, known for geometric paintings and reliefs based on nature, 26 December 2004.

Joey Bishop, 89, comedian, actor, talk-show host; best known as member of the Rat Pack (1960s), 17 October 2007.

Hyman Bloom, 96, painter, abstract expressionist, 26 August 2009.

Natalie Bodanya, 98, soprano, performed with the Metropolitan Opera (1930s and 1940s), 4 March 2007.

Todd Bolender, 92, dancer and choreographer, studied under George Balanchine, danced from 1936 to 1972, 12 October 2006.

Mike Botts, 61, drummer for the band Bread (1970s), 9 December 2005.

William Boyett, 77, character actor, best known for Sgt. "Mac" MacDonald on *Adam-12* (1968–75), as well as roles on *Perry Mason, Sea Hunt, Family Affair, My Three Sons,* and *Knots Landing,* 29 December 2004.

Peter Boyle, 71, actor, best known for roles in *Joe* (1970), *The Candidate* (1972), *Young Frankenstein* (1974), and television series *Everybody Loves Raymond* (1996–2005), Emmy winner, 12 December 2006.

Jocelyn Brando, 86, character actor, sister of Marlon Brando, 27 November 2005.

Marlon Brando, 80, actor, won an Oscar for *The Godfather* (1972); best known for roles in *A Streetcar Named Desire* (1951), *On the Waterfront* (1954), *Mutiny on the Bounty* (1962), and *Apocalypse Now* (1979), 1 July 2004.

Henry Brant, 94, composer, won Pulitzer Prize for "Ice Field," 26 April 2008.

Michael Brecker, 57, saxophonist, won eleven Grammy Awards, recorded jazz and pop, 13 January 2007.

Charles Bronson, 81, actor, best known for roles in the *Death Wish* series, *The Magnificent Seven* (1960), *Once Upon a Time in the West* (1968), 30 August 2003.

Danny Joe Brown, 53, lead singer of rock band Molly Hatchet, 10 March 2005.

James Brown, 73, singer, seminal rhythm and blues artist, pioneered funk, known as the "Godfather of Soul," 25 December 2006.

Lawrence Lloyd Brown Sr., 63, tenor with Harold Melvin & the Blue Notes, 6 April 2008.

Fernando Bujones, 50, dancer, first American male to win gold medal at the International Ballet Competition; danced with American Ballet Theatre and other companies, 10 November 2005.

Hiram Bullock, 52, guitarist, played with such stars as Billy Joel, Sting, and Barbra Streisand, 25 July 2008.

Ralph Burgard, 81, first director of the Arts Councils of America (1965–1970), 3 July 2008.

Octavia Butler, 58, novelist, wrote *Kindred* (1979); won Hugo and Nebula Awards, first science-fiction writer to win a MacArthur Foundation Genius Grant, 24 February 2006.

Red Buttons, 87, comedian and actor, won an Oscar as supporting actor in *Sayonara* (1957), also known for roles in *The Longest Day* (1962) and *The Poseidon Adventure* (1972), 13 July 2006.

Randy Cain, 63, singer, member of The Delfonics, 9 April 2009.

George Carlin, 71, comedian, actor, and author, famous for "Seven Words You Can Never Say on Television" routine; won Grammy Award and Mark Twain Prize for American Humor, 22 June 2008.

Kitty Carlisle (Hart), 96, actor, appeared in *A Night at the Opera* (1935); known as panelist on television game show *To Tell the Truth* (1956–1967), 17 April 2007.

David Carradine, 72, actor, played in *Kill Bill* movies (2003–2004), best known as star of television show *Kung Fu* (1972–1975), 3 June 2009.

Jim Carroll, 60, poet and author, wrote *The Basketball Diaries* (1978), 11 September 2009.

Hayden Carruth, 87, poet, won National Book Award for *Scrambled Eggs & Whiskey* (1996), 29 September 2008.

Jean Carson, 82, actor, appeared in television, movies and on Broadway, best known as character Daphne on *The Andy Griffith Show,* 2 November 2005.

Johnny Carson, 79, comedian, legendary host of NBC's *The Tonight Show* (1962–1992), won Presidential Medal of Freedom (1992), 23 January 2005.

Johnny Cash, 71, musician, best known for "I Walk the Line," and "Ring of Fire"; inducted into Country Music and Rock and Roll Halls of Fame, enjoyed late-career resurgence after partnering with producer Rick Rubin, 12 September 2003.

June Carter Cash, 73, musician, member of the Carter Family, wife of Johnny Cash, 15 May 2003.

Victor Castelli, 52, dancer with New York City Ballet, performed in George Balanchine's "Mozartiana" (1981), 8 February 2005.

Jack L. Chalker, 60, author, wrote *Midnight at the Well of Souls* (1977), founded the Baltimore Science Fiction Society, 11 February 2005.

Cyd Charisse, 86, dancer, appeared in musicals with Fred Astaire and Gene Kelly, best known for role in *Singin' in the Rain* (1952), 17 June 2008.

Ray Charles, 73, singer and composer, pioneer of rhythm and blues, earned many hits, including "Georgia on My Mind" (1960), 10 June 2004.

Cy Coleman, 75, jazz pianist and composer, wrote "Big Spender" and "If My Friends Could See Me Now" for Broadway, 18 November 2004.

Perry Como, 88, singer, starred on *The Perry Como Show* (1948–1963), 12 May 2001.

Alistair Cooke, 95, author and broadcaster, best known for his *Letters from America* documentary series and as host of PBS *Masterpiece Theater,* 30 March 2004.

Leroy Cooper, 80, saxophonist, played with Ray Charles, 15 January 2009.

Patrick Crankshaw, 86, character actor, played in movies and television, appeared in *Bonnie and Clyde* (1967) and *The Hudsucker Proxy* (1994), appeared on television shows such as *Alice* and *The Dukes of Hazzard,* 28 December 2005.

Ernest Crichlow, 91, artist, worked during the Harlem Renaissance, 10 November 2005.

Michael Crichton, 66, author, best known for *The Andromeda Strain* (1969), *Jurassic Park* (1990), and as creator of TV series *ER* (1994–2009), 4 November 2008.

Hume Cronyn, 91, actor, starred on stage and screen, won Tony Award for Lifetime Achievement (1994), 15 June 2003.

Celia Cruz, 77, singer, known as the Queen of Salsa, 16 July 2003.

Emilio Antonio Cruz Jr., 66, New York poet, painter, playwright, and professor of art, 10 December 2004.

Merce Cunningham, 90, choreographer and dancer, pioneered modern dance, 26 July 2009.

Art Davis, 73, bassist, played with John Coltrane and New York Philharmonic, 29 July 2007.

Ossie Davis, 87, actor and director, longtime civil-rights activist, delivered eulogy for Malcolm X; appeared in *Do the Right Thing* (1989) and *Jungle Fever* (1991), as well as on many television shows, 4 February 2005.

Talmadge Davis, 43, Cherokee artist, won Cherokee Medal of Honor (2004), 3 November 2005.

Tyrone Davis, 66, rhythm-and-blues singer, best known for "Can I Change My Mind" and "Turn Back the Hands of Time", 9 February 2005.

Mary Day, 96, dancer, cofounded the Washington School of Ballet and The Washington Ballet, 11 July 2006.

Bill DeArango, 85, jazz guitarist, played with Sarah Vaughan and Dizzy Gillespie, 26 December 2005.

Sandra Dee, 62, actor, teen idol in 1950s and 1960s, best known for roles in *The Reluctant Debutante* (1958), *Gidget* (1959), and *A Summer Place* (1959), 20 February 2005.

Nicole DeHuff, 31, actor, appeared in *Meet the Parents* (2000), 16 February 2005.

Dom DeLuise, 75, comedic actor, appeared in movies, cartoons, and television shows, 4 May 2009.

Bo Diddley, 79, guitarist and singer, innovator of the blues, rock-and-roll pioneer, 2 June 2008.

William Diehl, 81, author of *Sharky's Machine* (1978) and *Primal Fear* (1993), 24 November 2006.

Spencer Dryden, 66, drummer for Jefferson Airplane, played at Woodstock Festival, 11 January 2005.

Kevin DuBrow, 52, singer, fronted heavy-metal band Quiet Riot, 25 November 2007.

Will Eisner, 87, comic-book artist, popularized the graphic novel, created "The Spirit," 3 January 2005.

Dale Evans, 88, actor and songwriter, starred in Westerns alongside husband Roy Rogers, wrote "Happy Trails," 7 February 2001.

Ray Evans, 92, lyricist, helped write "Mona Lisa," "Buttons and Bows," and "Que Sera, Sera (Whatever Will Be, Will Be), 15 February 2007.

Douglas Fairbanks Jr., 90, actor, best known for swashbuckling roles, including roles in *The Prisoner of Zenda* (1937) and *Gunga Din* (1939), 7 May 2000.

Eileen Farrell, 82, soprano, operatic star, 23 March 2002.

Danny Federici, 58, keyboard player for Bruce Springsteen and the E Street Band, 17 April 2008.

Maynard Ferguson, 78, jazz trumpeter, best known for "Gonna Fly Now," the main theme from the movie *Rocky* (1976), 23 August 2006.

Mel Ferrer, 90, actor, starred in *War and Peace* (1956) and *The Sun Also Rises* (1957), was married to Audrey Hepburn (1954–1968), 2 June 2008.

Joseph E. Fields, 53, pianist and composer, worked with Dance Theater of Harlem, 4 July 2008.

John Flynn, 75, movie director, directed *Rolling Thunder* (1977), 4 April 2007.

Dan Fogelberg, 56, singer and songwriter, 16 December 2007.

Horton Foote, 92, playwright, adapted Harper Lee's *To Kill a Mockingbird* (1962) for the screen, wrote *Tender Mercies* (1983) and *The Trip to Bountiful* (1985), 4 March 2009.

Shelby Foote, 88, author, wrote novels *Love in a Dry Season* (1951) and *Shiloh* (1952), best known for three-volume narrative history of the Civil War, 27 June 2005.

Glenn Ford, 90, actor, best known for roles in *The Big Heat* (1953) and *The Blackboard Jungle* (1955), 30 August 2006.

Anthony "Tony" Franciosa, 77, actor, star during 1950s and 1960s, 19 January 2006.

Reginald Gammon, 84, painter, founding member of Spiral Group (black artists who sought to aid the civil-rights movement), 4 November 2005.

Hank Garland, 74, guitarist, performed with Elvis Presley, Roy Orbison, and Patsy Cline, 27 December 2004.

George Garrett, 78, writer and poet, author of novel *Death of the Fox* (1971), 25 May 2008.

Paul Gleason, 67, actor, best known for roles in *The Breakfast Club* (1985) and *Die Hard* (1988), 27 May 2006.

Michael Goldberg, 83, painter, member of abstract expressionist movement (New York School), 30 December 2007.

Leon Golub, 82, award-winning painter, 8 August 2004.

Bernard Gordon, 88, screenwriter, blacklisted during the 1950s, wrote *Day of the Triffids* (1962), 11 May 2007.

R. C. Gorman, 74, Navajo artist, who lived and worked in the Taos Valley in New Mexico, 3 November 2005.

Frank Gorshin, 72, impressionist and actor, played The Riddler on television series *Batman* (1966–1967), 17 May 2005.

Robert Goulet, 73, singer and actor, best known for song "If Ever I Would Leave You" from *Camelot* (1960), won Emmy, Tony, and Grammy Awards, 30 October 2007.

Cleve Gray, 86, painter, known for colorful large compositions, 8 December 2004.

Gene Greif, 50, graphic artist, designed album covers and worked for *Rolling Stone*, 20 November 2004.

Jimmy Griffin, 61, singer, helped found pop group Bread, cowrote Oscar-winning "For All We Know" for movie *Lovers and Other Strangers* (1970), 11 January 2005.

Buddy Hackett, 78, comedian and actor, appeared in many movies and television shows, 30 June 2003.

Frederick Hammersley, 90, painter, known for abstract paintings, 31 May 2009.

Joseph Hansen, 81, novelist and poet, best known for creating the gay detective: the Dave Brandstetter series, 24 November 2004.

Mark Harris, 84, author, best known for *Bang the Drum Slowly* (1956), 30 May 2007.

Johnny Hart, 76, cartoonist, created the "B.C." comic strip (1958), 7 April 2007.

Melissa Hayden, 83, ballerina, performed with the New York City Ballet, 9 August 2006.

Isaac Hayes, 65, singer, songwriter, best known for "Theme from *Shaft*," 10 August 2008.

Al Held, 76, painter, abstract expressionist, 27 July 2005.

Billy Henderson, 67, singer, member of The Spinners, 2 February 2007.

Skitch Henderson, 87, conductor, founded the New York Pops, bandleader for original *Tonight Show*, 1 November 2005.

Richard "Big Boy" Henry, 83, blues singer, one of few remaining practitioners of Piedmont Blues style, 9 December 2004.

Katharine Hepburn, 96, actor, four-time Oscar winner, starred in *The Philadelphia Story* (1940), *The African Queen* (1951), and *On Golden Pond* (1981), 29 June 2003.

Charlton Heston, 84, actor, best known for playing Moses in *The Ten Commandments* (1956) and the lead in *Ben-Hur* (1959), 5 April 2008.

Rosella Hightower, 88, Native American ballet dancer, 3 November 2008.

Debra Hill, 54, screenwriter, coauthor of movie *Halloween* (1979), 7 March 2005.

Tony Hillerman, 83, author, best known for a series of detective novels set on a Navajo reservation, 26 October 2008.

Gregory Hines, 57, dancer and actor, appeared in the musical *Jelly's Last Jam* and movies *The Cotton Club* (1984) and *White Nights* (1985), 9 August 2003.

Al Hirschfeld, 99, caricaturist, known for legendary sketches of theater and film stars, 20 January 2003.

Don Ho, 76, Hawaiian singer, best known for "Tiny Bubbles" (1966), 14 April 2007.

John Lee Hooker, 83, blues guitarist, influenced rock-and-roll bands, inducted into the Rock and Roll Hall of Fame (1991), 21 June 2001.

Bob Hope, 100, comedian and actor, starred in many comedic movies, perhaps best known for his service entertaining American troops and for his television specials, 27 July 2003.

Wilson Hurley, 84, landscape painter, 29 August 2008.

Makoto "Mako" Iwamatsu, 72, actor, Japanese-born, best known for role in *The Sand Pebbles* (1966), 21 July 2006.

Michael Jackson, 50, singer, known as the "King of Pop," had eight platinum or multiplatinum albums, with hits such as "I'll Be There," "Bad," "Beat It," "Billie Jean," "Black or White," "Man in the Mirror," and "Thriller," 25 June 2009.

Jam Master Jay, 37, rap artist, born Jason William Mizell, founding member of pioneering rap group Run-DMC, 30 October 2002.

Rick James, 56, guitarist, pioneered funk, best known for his hit "Super Freak," 6 August 2004.

Elizabeth Janeway, 91, feminist critic and novelist, 15 January 2005.

Waylon Jennings, 64, singer, pioneer of outlaw country-music sound, 13 February 2002.

Luis Jimenez, 65, Mexican American sculptor, known for colorful fiberglass sculptures often depicting Western themes, 13 June 2006.

Pauline Kael, 82, movie critic, known for her influential reviews in *The New Yorker*, 3 September 2001.

Howard Kanovitz, 79, painter, leader in photo-realism style, 2 February 2009.

Millard Kaufman, 92, screenwriter, wrote *Bad Day at Black Rock* (1955), cocreated cartoon character Mr. Magoo, 14 March 2009.

Elia Kazan, 94, director, won Oscars for *Gentleman's Agreement* (1947) and *On the Waterfront* (1954), directed such classics as *A Streetcar Named Desire* (1951), *East of Eden* (1955), and *Splendor in the Grass* (1961); cooperated with the House Un-American Activities Committee, cofounded The Actors Studio, 28 September 2003.

Alton Kelley, 67, 1960s and 1970s graphic artist, known for psychedelic art, 1 June 2008.

Ken Kesey, 66, author, best known for *One Flew over the Cuckoo's Nest* (1962), 10 November 2001.

Evelyn Keyes, 91, actor, appeared in *Gone with the Wind* (1939) and *The Jolson Story* (1946), 4 July 2008.

Keith Knudsen, 56, drummer with the Doobie Brothers (1974–1982), formed group Southern Pacific, 8 February 2005.

Harvey Korman, 81, comic actor, best known for role in movie *Blazing Saddles* (1974) and as cast member on *The Carol Burnett Show* (1967–1977), 29 May 2008.

Stanley Kramer, 87, director, best known for movies including *The Defiant Ones* (1958), *It's a Mad, Mad, Mad, Mad World* (1963), and *Guess Who's Coming to Dinner* (1967), 19 February 2001.

Stanley Kunitz, 100, poet laureate, Pulitzer Prize winner, 14 May 2006.

Erich Kunzel, 74, conductor, led the Cincinnati Pops Orchestra, 1 September 2009.

Frankie Laine, 93, singer, popular during the 1950s, 6 February 2007.

Philip Lamantia, 77, surrealist poet, member of the Beat generation, 7 March 2005.

Francess Lantz, 52, author, created *Luna Bay* series, 22 November 2004.

Jacob Lawrence, 82, painter, depicted the African American experience, married to fellow artist Gwendolyn Knight, 9 June 2000.

Jack Lemmon, 76, actor, best known for comedic roles in *Mister Roberts* (1955), *Some Like It Hot* (1959), and *The Odd Couple* (1968), 27 June 2001.

Madeleine L'Engle, 88, author, wrote *A Wrinkle in Time* (1962), 6 September 2007.

Ira Levin, 78, author, wrote *Rosemary's Baby* (1967), *The Stepford Wives* (1972), and *The Boys from Brazil* (1976), 12 November 2007.

Lisa Lopes, 30, singer, member of pop group TLC, known by nickname "Left Eye," 25 April 2002.

Jimmy Lovelace, 64, jazz drummer who performed with Wes Montgomery and George Benson, 29 October 2004.

Charlotte MacLeod, 82, Canadian-born mystery writer, 14 January 2005.

Jackson Mac Low, 82, poet and composer, 8 December 2004.

Mae Madison, 90, Hungarian-born actor, played in Warner Bros. movies, worked with John Wayne and Busby Berkeley, 1 November 2004.

Norman Mailer, 84, author, wrote *The Naked and the Dead* (1948), won Pulitzer Prizes for *Armies of the Night* (1968) and *The Executioner's Song* (1979), 10 November 2007.

Bob Maize, 59, jazz bassist who worked with Billy Eckstine, Sarah Vaughan, and Mel Tormé, 20 November 2004.

Karl Malden, 97, actor, won an Oscar for role in *A Streetcar Named Desire* (1951), also known for role in television show *The Streets of San Francisco* (1972–1977), 1 July 2009.

Ruth Manning, 84, character actor on stage and film, appeared in *All in the Family* and *Three's Company*, 19 November 2004.

Agnes Martin, 92, abstract painter, won National Medal of Art from the National Endowment for the Arts (1998), 16 December 2004.

Dewey Martin, 68, drummer, played with Buffalo Springfield, 1 February 2009.

Donald Martino, 74, composer and teacher, wrote "Notturno" (1974) and "Fantasies and Impromptus" (1981), 8 December 2005.

Walter Matthau, 79, actor, best known for his comedic role on Broadway in *The Odd Couple* (1965), and later in the movie (1968), won an Oscar for *The Fortune Cookie* (1966), 1 July 2000.

Virginia Mayo, 84, actor, had roles in *The Best Years of Our Lives* (1946) and *White Heat* (1949), 17 January 2005.

Frank McCourt, 78, author, best known for his Pulitzer Prize-winning memoir, *Angela's Ashes*, 19 July 2009.

Ann Wyeth McCoy, 90, painter and composer, daughter of N. C. Wyeth and sister of Andrew Wyeth, 10 November 2005.

Gene McFadden, 57, singer, known for McFadden and Whitehead's disco hit "Ain't No Stoppin' Us Now" (1979), 27 January 2006.

Patrick McGoohan, 80, actor, best known as creator and star of cult television show *The Prisoner* (1967–1968), also starred in the series *Secret Agent* (1964–1967) and appeared in the movies *Silver Streak* (1976) and *Braveheart* (1995), 13 January 2009.

Anne Meacham, 80, actor, worked on Broadway and in television soap operas (*Another World)*, won two Obie Awards, 12 January 2006.

Giancarlo Menotti, 95, Italian American composer and librettist, founded Spoleto Arts Festivals in Italy and the United States, 1 February 2007.

Arthur Miller, 89, playwright, among his award-winning plays were *Death of a Salesman* (1949) and *The Crucible* (1953), married to Marilyn Monroe, 10 February 2005.

Richard McDermott Miller, 82, sculptor, best known for lifelike nudes, 25 December 2004.

John Parr Miller, 91, animator and illustrator, worked for Disney Studios, provided art for many Little Golden books, 29 October 2004.

John Monks Jr., 94, playwright and screenwriter, cowrote *Brother Rat* (1938), *Strike Up the Band* (1940), *The West Point Story* (1950), as well as episodes of television shows, 10 December 2004.

LeRoi Moore, 46, saxophonist with the Dave Matthews Band, 19 August 2008.

Robin Moore, 82, writer, best known for *The French Connection* (1969) and *The Green Berets* (1965), 21 February 2008.

Pat Morita, 73, actor, best known as character Mr. Miyagi in *The Karate Kid* series, also played on television show *Happy Days*, 24 November 2005.

Howard Morris, 85, comedian and actor, costarred on *Your Show of Shows* (1950–1954), best known for portrayal of Ernest T. Bass on *The Andy Griffith Show* (1963–1965), 21 May 2005.

Sal Mosca, 80, jazz pianist, played with Miles Davis and Sarah Vaughan, 28 July 2007.

Roy Newell, 92, painter, abstract expressionist, 22 November 2006.

Paul Newman, 83, actor and philanthropist, won an Oscar for *The Color of Money* (1986), also starred in *Cat on a Hot Tin Roof* (1958), *Hud* (1963), *Cool Hand Luke* (1967), *Butch Cassidy and the Sundance Kid* (1969), *The Sting* (1973), and *Road to Perdition* (2002), 26 September 2008.

Fayard Nicholas, 91, tap dancer, starred with brother Harold, danced in many movies in the 1930s and 1940s, famous for acrobatic dancing, appeared in *Stormy Weather* (1943); won Tony Award for choreo-

graphy of Broadway revue *Black and Blue* (1989), 24 January 2006.

Sheree North, 72, actor, appeared in *How to Be Very, Very Popular* (1955) and many television shows, 4 November 2005.

Ol' Dirty Bastard, 35, rap artist, born Russell Tyrone Jones, founding member of rap group Wu-Tang Clan, 13 November 2004.

Jules Olitski, 84, painter, part of 1960s color field movement, 4 February 2007.

Jerry Orbach, 69, actor, appeared in many movies and television shows, but best known for role in *Dirty Dancing* (1987) and recurring role from 1991 to 2004 on *Law & Order,* 28 December 2004.

Buck Owens, 76, country singer, pioneer of the "Bakersfield sound," cohost of long-running television show *Hee Haw,* elected to Country Music Hall of Fame (1996), 25 March 2006.

Jack Palance, 87, actor, starred in *Shane* (1953), won an Emmy for *Requiem for a Heavyweight* (1956), won an Oscar for comic role in *City Slickers* (1991), 10 November 2006.

Gordon Parks, 93, photographer and filmmaker, chronicled the African American experience, directed *Shaft* (1971), 7 March 2006.

Ed Paschke, 65, painter, known for neon-colored, acid-toned, urban Pop Art, 25 November 2004.

Les Paul, 94, guitarist, developed the solid-body electric guitar, 13 August 2009.

Johnny Paycheck (Donald Lytle), 64, country singer, best known for hit "Take This Job and Shove It," 19 February 2003.

Gregory Peck, 87, actor, major film star of the mid twentieth century, nominated for five Academy Awards, won an Oscar for the role of Atticus Finch in *To Kill a Mockingbird* (1962), 12 June 2003.

Irving Petite, 84, author, wrote *Mister B.* (1963), *The Elderberry Tree* (1964), and *Life on Tiger Mountain* (1968), 27 November 2004.

Wilson Pickett, 64, soul singer, famous for "In the Midnight Hour" (1965) and "Mustang Sally" (1966), inducted into the Rock and Roll Hall of Fame (2005), 19 January 2006.

Joe Pinckney, 75, painter, famous for depictions of Gullah (descendants of African slaves in the South Carolina and Georgia lowcountry) culture, 22 November 2005.

Bill Pinkney, 81, singer, member of The Drifters, 4 July 2007.

George Plimpton, 76, writer, cofounder of *The Paris Review* literary magazine, championed "participatory journalism," 25 September 2003.

June Pointer, 52, singer, member of The Pointer Sisters during the 1970s and 1980s, 11 April 2006.

Sydney Pollack, 73, director and actor, directed and appeared in *Tootsie* (1982), won an Oscar for *Out of Africa* (1985), 26 May 2008.

Billy Powell, 56, keyboardist with Lynyrd Skynyrd, 28 January 2009.

Billy Preston, 59, singer-songwriter, known for hit song "Nothing from Nothing," wrote "You Are So Beautiful," performed with The Beatles and Rolling Stones, nicknamed "the fifth Beatle," 6 June 2006.

Richard Pryor, 65, comedian and actor, starred in *Uptown Saturday Night* (1974), *Silver Streak* (1976), and *Stir Crazy* (1980); won many awards, including the Kennedy Center Mark Twain Prize for American Humor, 10 December 2005.

Anthony Quinn, 86, actor, first Mexican American to win an Oscar, won Oscars for *Viva Zapata!* (1952), and *Lust for Life* (1956), best known for lead role in *Zorba the Greek* (1964), 3 June 2001.

John Raitt, 88, actor, played on Broadway in *Carousel* (1947), in movie *Pajama Game* (1957), father of singer Bonnie Raitt, 20 February 2005.

Dee Dee Ramone, 50, musician, bassist for punk-rock group The Ramones, 5 June 2002.

Johnny Ramone, 55, guitarist, cofounded the Ramones, 15 September 2004.

Nell Rankin, 81, mezzo-soprano, starred with the Metropolitan Opera, 13 January 2005.

Lou Rawls, 72, singer, best-known for "You'll Never Find (Another Love Like Mine)" (1976) and "Lady Love" (1978), supported United Negro College Fund, 6 January 2006.

Jerry Reed, 71, country musician and actor, known for finger-picking guitar style, played in *Smokey and the Bandit* (1977); hits included "When You're Hot, You're Hot" and "East Bound and Down," 1 September 2008;

Christopher Reeve, 52, actor, starred in *Superman* (1978), paralyzed following fall from horse in 1995, advocate for stem-cell research, 10 October 2004.

Nick Reynolds, 75, member of The Kingston Trio, 1 October 2008.

Jason Rhoades, 41, sculptor and performance artist, 1 August 2006.

Lloyd Richards, 87, theater director, staged *A Raisin in the Sun* (1959), 29 June 2006.

Robert Richenburg, 89, abstract expressionist painter, 10 October 2006.

Leonard Rosenman, 83, provided scores for *East of Eden* (1955); *Rebel without a Cause* (1955), *Barry Lyndon* (1975), and *Bound for Glory* (1976), won Oscars for latter two, 4 March 2008.

Max Roach, 83, jazz percussionist and composer, innovator of bebop style, vocal supporter of civil-rights movement, 1988 recipient of MacArthur Foundation "genius" grant, 16 August 2007.

Bobby Rosengarden, 82, jazz drummer, worked with Jimi Hendrix, part of house band on *The Dick Cavett Show*, 27 February 2007.

Roy Scheider, 75, actor, best known for performances in *The French Connection* (1971), *Jaws* (1975), and *All That Jazz* (1979), 10 February 2008.

Budd Schulberg, 95, author and screenwriter, wrote the novel *What Makes Sammy Run?* (1941), won Oscar for *On the Waterfront* (1954), 5 August 2009.

Charles Schulz, 77, cartoonist, created *Peanuts* comic strip, 12 February 2000.

Barbara Schwartz, 58, abstract painter and teacher, associated with Pattern and Decoration movement, 8 May 2006.

Jerry Scoggins, 93, singer, performed with the Cass County Boys, songs often used in Gene Autry movies; best known for "The Ballad of Jed Clampett" from *The Beverly Hillbillies* television series (1962–1971), 7 December 2004.

Frank "Son" Seals, 62, blues guitarist, helped establish Alligator Records, 20 December 2004.

Hubert Selby, 75, novelist, best known for *Last Exit to Brooklyn* (1964), 26 April 2004.

Artie Shaw, 94, jazz clarinetist and big-band leader, rivaled Benny Goodman as the "King of Swing" with his breakthrough hit "Begin the Beguine" (1938), 30 December 2004.

Sidney Sheldon, 89, writer, wrote popular novels often made into television miniseries; 30 January 2007.

Marion Shilling, 93, actor, appeared in *Shadow of the Law* (1930) and more than forty films (mostly Westerns), 6 November 2004.

Beverly Sills, 78, soprano, later ran the Metropolitan Opera and New York City Opera, 2 July 2007.

Hal Sitowitz, 71, screenwriter for such television series as *Gunsmoke, Streets of San Francisco,* and *Cannon,* 31 October 2004.

Robert Slutzky, 75, painter, professor of art and architecture at the Cooper Union for the Advancement of Science and Art in New York, 3 May 2005.

Charles Smith, 57, guitarist for group Kool & the Gang, 20 June 2006.

Sammi Smith, 61, singer, best known for "Help Me Make It through the Night" (written by Kris Kristofferson, 1970), 12 February 2005.

Lowell Smith, 56, dancer, principal with Dance Theater of Harlem, 22 October 2007.

W. D. Snodgrass, 83, poet, won 1960 Pulitzer Prize for *Heart's Needle* (1959), 13 January 2009.

Dash Snow, 27, artist, worked in collage and photography, 13 July 2009.

V. Douglas Snow, 82, painter, known for impressionist murals, 20 October 2009.

Joseph Solman, 99, modernist painter, 16 April 2008.

Susan Sontag, 71, author, activist, and critic, wrote *In America* (2000), 28 December 2004.

Warren Spears, 50, dancer and choreographer, performed with Alvin Ailey American Dance Theater (1974–1977), 8 January 2005.

Mickey Spillane, 88, writer, created character detective Mike Hammer, 17 July 2006.

Maureen Stapleton, 80, character actor, won Oscar for *Reds* (1981), 13 March 2006.

William Steig, 95, cartoonist and author, cartoons appeared in *The New Yorker*, wrote *Shrek!* (1993), 3 October 2003.

Rod Steiger, 77, actor, starred in *On the Waterfront* (1954) and *The Pawnbroker* (1964), won 1968 Oscar for *In the Heat of the Night* (1967); 9 July 2002.

Isaac Stern, 81, violinist, considered one of the greatest musicians of all time, helped save Carnegie Hall from demolition, 22 September 2001.

Levi Stubbs, 72, singer, member of The Four Tops, 17 October 2008.

William Styron, 81, author, wrote *Lie Down in Darkness* (1951), *The Confessions of Nat Turner* (1967), and *Sophie's Choice* (1979), 1 November 2006.

Patrick Swayze, 57, dancer and movie actor, best known for roles in *Dirty Dancing* (1987) and *Ghost* (1990), 14 September 2009.

Louis "Studs" Terkel, 96, author and radio broadcast personality, best known for oral histories such as *Hard Times* (1970), 31 October 2008.

Hunter S. Thompson, 67, journalist and author, wrote *Fear and Loathing in Las Vegas* (1972), pioneered gonzo journalism, writer for *Rolling Stone*, 20 February 2005.

Mary Travers, 72, singer, member of folk group Peter, Paul and Mary, 16 September 2009.

Anne Truitt, 83, sculptor and author, known for minimalist three-dimensional sculptures, 23 December 2004.

Tasha Tudor, 92, illustrator and author of children's books, 18 June 2008.

Walter Turnbull, 62, founder of the Boys Choir of Harlem, 23 March 2007.

Ike Turner, 76, singer, performed with wife Tina Turner, 12 December 2007.

John Updike, 76, novelist, won Pulitzer Prizes for *Rabbit Is Rich* (1961) and *Rabbit at Rest* (1990), 27 January 2009.

Leon Uris, 78, novelist, wrote *Exodus* (1958), 21 June 2003.

Luther Vandross, 54, eight-time Grammy Award–winning singer/songwriter, 1 July 2005.

Mona Van Duyn, 83, poet laureate, won 1991 Pulitzer Prize for *Near Changes* (1990) and 1971 National Book Award for *To See, To Take* (1970), 2 December 2004.

Peter Viertel, 86, screenwriter and author, wrote *White Hunter, Black Heart* (1953), 4 November 2007.

Kurt Vonnegut, 84, author, wrote fourteen novels, including *Cat's Cradle* (1963), *Slaughterhouse-Five* (1969), and *Breakfast of Champions* (1973), 11 April 2007.

Porter Wagoner, 80, country singer, member of the Country Music Hall of Fame, star of *The Porter Wagoner Show* (1960–1981), discovered Dolly Parton, 28 October 2007.

Malvin Wald, 90, screenwriter, wrote screenplay for *The Naked City* (1948); member of Hollywood 10, who refused to testify before the House Un-American Activities Committee, 6 March 2008.

David Foster Wallace, 46, author, essayist, best known for novel *Infinite Jest* (1996), 12 September 2008.

Ruth Warrick, 88, actor, played in *Citizen Kane* (1941), best known as Phoebe Tyler Wallingford on television soap opera *All My Children*, 15 January 2005.

Wendy Wasserstein, 55, playwright, wrote play *The Heidi Chronicles* (1989) and screenplay for *The Object of My Affection* (1998), 30 January 2006.

Edward S. Waters, 74, screenwriter on television series such as *Kung Fu, Police Story, Mannix, Baretta, T. J. Hooker,* and *Jake and the Fatman*, 9 November 2004.

Vince Welnick, 55, keyboardist, played with the Grateful Dead (1990–1995), 2 June 2006.

Barry White, 58, singer and composer, founded the Love Unlimited Orchestra, hits included "Can't Get Enough of Your Love, Babe" and "You're the First, the Last, My Everything," 4 July 2003.

Onna White, 83, dancer and choreographer, won special honorary Oscar for *Oliver!* (1968), 8 April 2005.

Thelma White, 94, actor, played in cult-classic movie *Reefer Madness* (1936), 11 January 2005.

Vantile Whitfield, 74, playwright, cofounded D.C. Black Repertory Company, 9 January 2005.

James Whitmore, 87, character actor, appeared in movies *Battleground* (1949), *The Asphalt Jungle* (1950),

Planet of the Apes (1968), and *The Shawshank Redemption* (1994), 6 February 2009.

John Wilde, 86, surrealist painter associated with the Magic Realist school, 9 March 2006.

Billy (Samuel) Wilder, 95, director, six-time Academy Award winner, 27 March 2002.

Johnnie Wilder Jr., 56, singer, headed 1970s funk/disco band Heatwave, 13 May 2006.

Al Wilson, 68, singer, top hit was "Show and Tell" (1973), 21 April 2008.

August Wilson, 60, Pulitzer Prize–winning playwright, best known for his ten-play Pittsburgh Cycle, 2 October 2005.

Shelley Winters, 85, actor, won Oscars as supporting actor in the movies *The Diary of Anne Frank* (1959) and *A Patch of Blue* (1965), 14 January 2006.

Jade Snow Wong, 84, Chinese American author, wrote *Fifth Chinese Daughter* (1950), 16 March 2006.

Fay Wray, 96, actor, best known for her role as the damsel in distress in *King Kong* (1933), 8 August 2004.

Teresa Wright, 86, actor, won an Oscar (1942); starred in *The Little Foxes* (1941), *The Pride of the Yankees* (1942), *Mrs. Miniver* (1942), *Shadow of a Doubt* (1943), *The Best Years of Our Lives* (1946), 6 March 2005.

Andrew Wyeth, 91, painter, most famous work was *Christina's World* (1948); son of N. C. Wyeth, 16 January 2009.

Jane Wyman, 90, actor, appeared in *The Yearling* (1946) and won Oscar for role in *Johnny Belinda* (1948); married to Ronald Reagan (1940–1948), 10 September 2007.

Hy Zaret, 99, lyricist, wrote "Unchained Melody" (1955), 2 July 2007.

Warren Zevon, 56, musician, wrote and sang "Werewolves of London" (1978), 7 September 2003.

PUBLICATIONS

Bruce Altshuler, ed., *Collecting the New: Museums and Contemporary Art* (Princeton: Princeton University Press, 2005);

Saul Austerlitz, *Another Fine Mess: A History of American Film Comedy* (Chicago: Chicago Review Press, 2010);

Julius Bailey, ed., *Jay-Z: Essays on Hip Hop's Philosopher King* (Jefferson, N.C.: McFarland, 2011);

Matthew Biberman and Julia Reinhard Lupton, eds., *Shakespeare after 9/11: How a Social Trauma Reshapes Interpretation* (Lewiston, N.Y.: Edwin Mellen Press, 2010);

Casey Nelson Blake, ed., *The Arts of Democracy: Art, Public Culture, and the State* (Washington, D.C.: Woodrow Wilson Center Press; Philadelphia: University of Pennsylvania Press, 2007);

M. Keith Booker, *Disney, Pixar, and the Hidden Messages of Children's Films* (Santa Barbara, Cal.: Praeger, 2010);

Gerald Bordman and Richard Norton, *American Musical Theatre: A Chronicle*, fourth edition (Oxford & New York: Oxford University Press, 2011);

Oscar G. Brockett and Robert J. Ball, *The Essential Theatre*, ninth edition (Boston: Wadsworth, 2008);

Paul R. Cappucci, *William Carlos Williams, Frank O'Hara, and the New York Art Scene* (Madison, N.J.: Fairleigh Dickinson University Press, 2010);

Joni Maya Cherbo, Ruth Ann Stewart, and Margaret Jane Wyszomirski, eds., *Understanding the Arts and Creative Sector in the United States* (New Brunswick, N.J.: Rutgers University Press, 2008);

Tyler Cowen, *Good & Plenty: The Creative Successes of American Arts Funding* (Princeton, N.J.: Princeton University Press, 2006);

Jessica Hoffmann Davis, *Why Our Schools Need the Arts* (New York: Teachers College Press, 2008);

Nancy Day, *Censorship, or Freedom of Expression?* (Minneapolis: Lerner Publications, 2001);

Jill Dolan, *Theatre & Sexuality* (New York: Palgrave Macmillan, 2010);

Denis Donoghue, *Speaking of Beauty* (New Haven: Yale University Press, 2003);

Charles Dorn and Penelope Orr, *Art Education in a Climate of Reform: The Need for Measurable Goals in Art Instruction* (Lanham, Md.: Rowman & Littlefield Education, 2008);

Astrid Franke, *Pursue the Illusion: Problems of Public Poetry in America* (Heidelberg: Winter, 2010);

Krin Gabbard, *Hotter than That: The Trumpet, Jazz, and American Culture* (New York: Faber & Faber, 2008);

Stanley Green, *Broadway Musicals, Show by Show*, sixth edition, revised by Kay Green (New York: Applause Theatre and Cinema Books, 2008);

Adam Gussow, *Journeyman's Road: Modern Blues Lives from Faulkner's Mississippi to Post-9/11 New York* (Knoxville: University of Tennessee Press, 2007);

Bill Ivey, *Arts, Inc.: How Greed and Neglect Have Destroyed Our Cultural Rights* (Berkeley: University of California Press, 2008);

Patricia Johnston, ed., *Seeing High & Low: Representing Social Conflict in American Visual Culture* (Berkeley: University of California Press, 2006);

Gayle Kassing, *History of Dance: An Interactive Arts Approach* (Champaign, Ill.: Human Kinetics, 2007);

Herbert H. Keyser, *Geniuses of the American Musical Theatre: The Composers and Lyricists* (New York: Applause Theatre and Cinema Books, 2009);

Dustin Kidd, *Legislating Creativity: The Intersections of Art and Politics* (New York: Routledge, 2010);

Raymond Knapp, *The American Musical and the Performance of Personal Identity* (Princeton: Princeton University Press, 2006);

Pam Korza, Barbara Schaffer Bacon, and Andrea Assaf, *Civic Dialogue, Arts & Culture: Findings from Animating Democracy* (Washington, D.C.: Americans for the Arts, 2005);

Cameron Lazerine and Devin Lazerine, *Rap-up: The Ultimate Guide to Hip-Hop and R&B* (New York: Grand Central, 2008);

Ellen Levy, *Criminal Ingenuity: Moore, Cornell, Ashbery, and the Struggle between the Arts* (Oxford & New York: Oxford University Press, 2011);

Jeffrey D. Mason, *Stone Tower: The Political Theater of Arthur Miller* (Ann Arbor: University of Michigan Press, 2008);

Kevin F. McCarthy and others, *A Portrait of the Visual Arts: Meeting the Challenges of a New Era* (Santa Monica, Cal.: RAND, 2005);

Angela L. Miller and others, *American Encounters: Art, History, and Cultural Identity* (Upper Saddle River, N.J.: Pearson/Prentice Hall, 2008);

William Murray, *Fortissimo: Backstage at the Opera with Sacred Monsters and Young Singers* (New York: Crown, 2005);

Philip Nel, *The Avant-Garde and American Postmodernity: Small Incisive Shocks* (Jackson: University Press of Mississippi, 2002);

Karen Paik, *To Infinity and Beyond!: The Story of Pixar Animation Studios* (San Francisco: Chronicle Books, 2007);

David B. Pruett, *MuzikMafia: From the Local Nashville Scene to the National Mainstream* (Jackson: University Press of Mississippi, 2010);

Annette J. Saddik, *Contemporary American Drama* (Edinburgh: Edinburgh University Press, 2007);

Anthony Shay, *Dancing across Borders: The American Fascination with Exotic Dance Forms* (Jefferson, N.C.: McFarland, 2008);

Barry Singer, *Ever After: The Last Years of Musical Theater and Beyond* (New York: Applause Theatre and Cinema Books, 2004);

Thomas M. Smith, *Raising the Barre: The Geographic, Financial, and Economic Trends of Nonprofit Dance Companies: A Study*, edited by Bonnie Nichols (Washington, D.C.: National Endowment for the Arts, 2003);

Willard Spiegelman, *How Poets See the World: The Art of Description in Contemporary Poetry* (New York: Oxford University Press, 2005);

Janis P. Stout, *Picturing a Different West: Vision, Illustration, and the Tradition of Austin and Cather* (Lubbock: Texas Tech University Press, 2007);

Steven J. Tepper and Bill Ivey, eds., *Engaging Art: The Next Great Transformation of America's Cultural Life* (New York: Routledge, 2008);

U.S. Congress, House Committee on Education and Labor, *The Economic and Employment Impact of the Arts and Music Industry: Hearing before the Committee on Education and Labor, U.S. House of Representatives, One Hundred Eleventh Congress, First Session, Hearing Held in Washington, D.C., March 26, 2009* (Washington, D.C.: Government Printing Office, 2009);

Art in America, periodical;

Art News, periodical;

Billboard, periodical;

Dance, periodical;

Entertainment Weekly, periodical;

Harper's, periodical;

Januarymagazine.com;

Jazz Review, periodical;

New Yorker, periodical;

Paris Review, periodical;

Poetry, periodical;

Rolling Stone, periodical;

Salon.com;

Spin, periodical;

Variety, periodical;

XXL, periodical.

CHAPTER THREE

BUSINESS AND THE ECONOMY

by JOE MORRIS

CONTENTS

Sidebars and tables are listed in italics.

2000

1 Jan. Computer clocks turn over with only minor glitches, following $8.8 billion in government spending and $100 billion by private businesses to prepare for the "Y2K bug."

4 Jan. Alan Greenspan is nominated for fourth term as chairman of the Federal Reserve Board.

10 Jan. America Online Inc. announces deal to buy Time Warner Inc. for over $160 billion in stock and debt.

13 Jan. Bill Gates announces that he will step down as CEO of Microsoft Corp.

7 Feb. Pfizer Inc. announces deal to buy Warner-Lambert Co. for $90 billion in stock, forming the world's second-largest drug company.

13 Mar. *Chicago Tribune* publisher Tribune Co. announces an $8 billion deal to buy Times Mirror Co., publisher of the *Los Angeles Times, Baltimore Sun,* and *Newsday.*

9 Aug. Bridgestone-Firestone Inc. announces it is recalling 6.5 million tires following reports of blowouts and peeling treads on sport-utility vehicles and light trucks.

13 Sept. Chase Manhattan Corp. announces a $34.3 billion deal to buy J.P. Morgan & Co., uniting the third- and fifth-largest U.S. banks.

16 Oct. Chevron Corp. announces plan to buy Texaco Inc. for $36 billion, creating the world's fourth-largest oil company.

25 Oct. AT&T Corp. announces its split into four companies providing long-distance, wireless, cable television, and Internet services.

16 Nov. Coca-Cola Co. settles a racial-discrimination class-action suit for $192.5 million with about 2,000 current and former black employees.

2001

17 Jan. California utility Pacific Gas & Electric, squeezed by rising power prices and laws barring rate hikes, orders rolling blackouts cutting off two million electricity customers in Northern California. Governor Gray Davis declares state of emergency and orders the state Department of Water Resources to buy power for ratepayers.

20 Jan. President Bill Clinton pardons commodities trader Marc Rich, who had fled the United States in 1983 to avoid prosecution on conspiracy, tax evasion, racketeering, and illegal trading with Iran.

26 May Congress approves $1.35 trillion tax cut spread over ten years. President George W. Bush signs the legislation on 7 June.

28 June A U.S. appeals court overturns a ruling ordering that Microsoft Corp. be broken up. The Justice Department abandoned its case, demanding the dissolution on 6 September.

11 Sept. Federal Aviation Administration grounds all commercial flights following the disasters in New York, Washington, D.C., and Pennsylvania caused by planes hijacked by terrorists; international flights are diverted to Canada or sent back to their originating airports. The New York Stock Exchange (NYSE), the American Stock Exchange (ASE), and the National Association of Securities Dealers Automated Quotations (NASDAQ) do not open, remaining closed until 17 September, when the Dow Jones Industrial Average falls 684 points, or 7.1 percent, the index's biggest one-day drop up to that time.

21 Sept.	Congress approves a $15 billion bailout package for airlines, ailing from 9/11-related losses.
12 Oct.	Camera and film manufacturer Polaroid files for Chapter 11 bankruptcy protection.
26 Oct.	The Pentagon chooses Lockheed Martin Corp. for a $200 billion contract to build more than 3,000 supersonic jet fighters.
2 Dec.	Enron Corp. files for bankruptcy, its stock practically worthless following Dynegy's decision to back out of its planned acquisition.
28 Dec.	President Bush formally grants permanent normal-trade status to China, effective 1 January 2002.

2002

11 Jan.	Ford Motor Co. announces plans to lay off 35,000 workers, close four plants, and drop four models.
22 Jan.	Kmart Corp. files for Chapter 11 protection from creditors in the nation's biggest retail bankruptcy, listing $16.29 billion in assets and $10.35 billion in debt.
5 Mar.	President Bush imposes tariffs of up to 30 percent on steel imported from Europe, Asia, and South America.
14 Mar.	The Justice Department indicts Enron accounting firm Arthur Andersen LLP, alleging it destroyed documents related to a fraud probe. The firm was convicted on 15 June, but the Supreme Court overturned the conviction in 2005.
25 June	WorldCom Inc. announces it overstated cash flow by $3.8 billion over the past fifteen months and will lay off 17,000 of its 85,000 employees. The Securities and Exchange Commission (SEC) files fraud charges on 26 June, and the company declares bankruptcy on 21 July.
15 July	The euro trades ahead of the dollar for the first time.
24 July	Adelphia Communications Corp. founder John Rigas is arrested on fraud charges following the company's bankruptcy filing.
30 July	President Bush signs into law the Sarbanes-Oxley Act, a package of corporate governance and accounting reforms.
7 Aug.	Federal authorities indict Samuel Waksal, founder and former chief of pharmaceutical company ImClone LLC, on charges of obstruction of justice and bank fraud.
5 Nov.	SEC chairman Harvey Pitt resigns amid criticism over mounting accounting scandals.
6 Dec.	Treasury secretary Paul O'Neill and National Economic Council chairman Lawrence Lindsey resign. CSX Corp. chief John Snow is nominated to succeed O'Neill and former Goldman Sachs Group Inc. chairman Stephen Friedman to succeed Lindsey.

2003

12 Jan.	AOL-Time Warner Inc. chairman Steve M. Case announces his resignation, ahead of the decision to write down the value of his company's AOL division by $35 billion and its cable division by $10 billion.

28 Apr. Ten of the nation's biggest investment banks reach a settlement with the SEC, National Association of Securities Dealers, and the NYSE to avoid prosecution over tainted research reports.

23 May Congress approves the Jobs and Growth Tax Relief Reconciliation Act of 2003, providing $318 billion in tax cuts over eight years; President Bush signs the legislation a week later.

2 June The Federal Communications Commission votes 3-2 to rescind a ruling barring any one media company from owning both a television station and a newspaper in the same market.

4 June Martha Stewart is indicted in federal court on conspiracy, obstruction of justice, and securities fraud charges related to trades of ImClone stock. She pleads not guilty and steps down as chairwoman and chief of Martha Stewart Living Omnimedia Inc.

14 Aug. A blackout eventually blamed on Ohio utility FirstEnergy Corp. leaves 50 million people in the Northeast and Midwest without power, some for as long as two days.

3 Sept. New York attorney general Eliot Spitzer announces fraud charges against hedge fund Canary Capital Partners LLC, alleging improper trading of mutual-fund shares. The case initiates a wave of charges by Spitzer's office and the Securities and Exchange Commission against mutual-fund companies.

17 Sept. NYSE chairman and chief Richard Grasso resigns amid criticism of his compensation by SEC and several large pension funds.

4 Nov. HealthSouth CEO Richard Scrushy becomes the first executive indicted under the Sarbanes-Oxley Act.

18 Dec. California governor Arnold Schwarzenegger declares a fiscal crisis following downgrades of the state's bond ratings, allowing him to reduce government spending by $150 million without legislative approval.

2004

2 Mar. Former WorldCom Inc. chief Bernard Ebbers is charged with securities fraud, conspiracy, and false regulatory filings; he pleads not guilty. The company's former chief financial officer, Scott Sullivan, pleads guilty on the same day to securities fraud and agrees to cooperate with prosecutors. Ebbers is convicted on 15 March 2005.

5 Mar. Martha Stewart is convicted on charges of conspiracy and obstruction. She will be sentenced to five months in prison, five months' house arrest, and nineteen months of probation and be ordered to pay a $30,000 fine, plus court fees.

2 Apr. The fraud trial of former Tyco International Ltd. executives ends in a mistrial. The executives are found guilty of conspiracy, grand larceny, securities fraud, and falsifying business records in a 17 June 2005 decision.

17 May Oil prices reach a twenty-one-year high of $41.85 per barrel of light sweet crude, reflecting Middle East tensions and surging demand from China.

18 May President Bush nominates Alan Greenspan to an unprecedented fifth term as Federal Reserve chairman.

30 June The Federal Reserve Board raises the benchmark interchange rate from 1 percent to 1.25 percent, the first hike in four years for the overnight-loans rate.

7 July   Federal prosecutors indict former Enron chief Kenneth Lay on charges including conspiracy and bank, securities, and wire fraud. He is convicted on 15 May 2006.

8 July   Adelphia Communications Corp. founder John Rigas is convicted of conspiracy, bank fraud, and securities fraud.

2005

2 Feb.   President Bush calls for a partial privatization of the Social Security program in his State of the Union Address.

1 June   William Donaldson announces his resignation as SEC chairman. He is succeeded by California congressman Christopher Cox.

7 June   General Motors Corp. announces it will cut 25,000 jobs by 2008.

23 June   The Supreme Court rules in *Kelo* v. *City of New London* that the city could invoke eminent domain to take private property in order for private developers to build office space and a hotel, expanding the justification of eminent domain beyond public works or transportation projects.

27 June   The Supreme Court rules in *MGM Studios* v. *Grokster Ltd.* that software companies producing Internet file-sharing software are liable to suits when they intend for customers to use the software in violation of copyright laws.

25 July   The Teamsters and Service Employees International Union announce their secession from the American Federation of Labor and Congress of Industrial Organizations (AFL-CIO) at the labor coalition's national convention.

28 July   Congress passes the Central American Free Trade Agreement. President Bush signs it into law on 5 August.

29 July   Congress passes energy legislation authorizing $12.3 billion in incentives for new technology, alternative fuels, and nuclear power. President Bush signs it into law on 8 August.

29 Aug.   Hurricane Katrina strikes the Gulf Coast, leaving 80 percent of New Orleans underwater and causing extensive damage in Gulfport and Biloxi, Mississippi, and Mobile, Alabama, while hobbling the Gulf's petrochemical, maritime cargo, fishing, sugarcane, rice, cotton, and tourism industries. Light sweet crude oil hits $71 per barrel on 30 August owing to Gulf shortages. Congress approves $62 billion in emergency spending for hurricane relief on 8 September. The cost to private insurers tops $40 billion.

14 Sept.   Delta Air Lines Inc. and Northwest Airlines Inc. file for bankruptcy protection, blaming high fuel costs.

20 Dec.   New York City transit workers begin a three-day strike, halting bus and subway service.

2006

2 Jan.   Twelve miners die in a methane gas explosion at International Coal Group Inc.'s Sago Mine in Tallmansville, West Virginia.

24 Jan.   Ford Motor Co. announces plans to cut up to 30,000 jobs over six years and close as many as fourteen factories.

1 Feb.   Ben Bernanke is sworn in as chairman of the Federal Reserve Board.

1 May   Amid national debate on legislation to curb illegal immigration, more than one million people take part in "Day Without Immigrants" demonstrations around the country to highlight the role of immigrant workers in the economy.

30 May   Treasury secretary John Snow announces his resignation; Goldman Sachs chief Henry Paulson is named as his successor.

6 July   Florida's Supreme Court rejects a $145 billion judgment in a class action against five tobacco companies, calling the award excessive.

2007

14 May   DaimlerChrysler AG announces it will sell 80.1 percent of its Chrysler division to private equity firm Cerberus Capital Management LP for $7.4 billion.

24 Sept.   Seventy-three thousand United Auto Workers union members take part in a strike of General Motors plants; a deal between labor and management ends the walkout on 26 September.

9 Oct.   The Dow Jones Industrial Average closes above 14,000 for the first time, hitting 14,164.53.

30 Oct.   Merrill Lynch & Co. chief E. Stanley O'Neal announces his resignation less than a week after the company's disclosure of an $8.4 billion write-down on bad subprime mortgage investments. He is succeeded on 14 November by NYSE chief John A. Thain.

4 Nov.   Citigroup Inc. reveals it is writing down $8 to $11 billion in assets owing to bad subprime mortgage investments, following a $5.9 billion write-down the previous month. Chairman and chief Charles O. Prince III also announces his resignation.

5 Nov.   The Writers Guild of America's East and West unions strike as contract negotiations with the Alliance of Motion Picture and Television Producers break down. The walkout ceases production for all scripted television programming and lasts until 12 February 2008.

6 Dec.   President Bush announces an agreement among major mortgage lenders to help cash-strapped homeowners with adjustable-rate subprime mortgages by placing temporary freezes on rate hikes and refinancing through the Federal Housing Administration.

18 Dec.   Congress passes legislation requiring increases in automobile fuel economy standards to 35 miles per gallon by 2020. President Bush signs the bill into law the following day.

19 Dec.   Morgan Stanley & Co. discloses a $9.4 billion write-down of subprime mortgage assets.

2008

12 Feb.   General Motors Corp. announces losing $722 million in the fourth quarter and $38.7 billion for all of 2007.

16 Mar.   The Federal Reserve approves the sale of Bear Stearns, which had been crippled by subprime-related losses, to J.P. Morgan Chase & Co. at $2 per share following a 47 percent plunge in the stock, to $30 per share.

16 Mar.   The Federal Reserve begins letting securities dealers borrow from it on the same terms as banks.

12 May   Immigration agents raid the Agriprocessors Inc. meatpacking plant in Postville, Iowa, arresting 389 in what the government describes as the biggest immigration enforcement action at a single U.S. workplace.

11 July	The Federal Deposit Insurance Corp. (FDIC) places IndyMac Bank in conservatorship following a run on assets triggered by losses on defaulted mortgages. Parent IndyMac Bancorp files for bankruptcy protection on 31 July.
13 July	The Federal Reserve Board and the Treasury Department announce that they will request temporary authority from Congress to buy equity in the Federal National Mortgage Association (FNMA) and in the Federal Home Loan Mortgage Corporation (FHLMC), popularly known as Fannie Mae and Freddie Mac. They assume control of the quasi-public lending enterprises on 7 September.
14 Sept.	Bank of America Corp. reaches an agreement to buy Merrill Lynch & Co. for $50 billion.
15 Sept.	Lehman Brothers Holdings Inc. declares bankruptcy.
16 Sept.	The Federal Reserve takes a 79.9 percent equity stake in American International Group Inc. (AIG), also ailing from mortgage losses, and creates an $85 billion credit facility, subsequently expanding the line of credit to $144 billion by 31 October.
20 Sept.	The Treasury Department publicly proposes a $700 billion bailout plan to buy bad mortgage-backed securities. Companion legislation fails initially in the House of Representatives on 29 September, but a revised version passes both chambers on 3 October and is signed by President Bush the same day.
21 Sept.	The Federal Reserve announces that Goldman Sachs Group Inc. and Morgan Stanley & Co. will restructure as bank holding companies and submit to more government oversight.
25 Sept.	Federal regulators place Washington Mutual Bank, straining under subprime mortgage losses, into receivership following a ten-day run on the bank that drains $16.4 billion in deposits. The FDIC sells the banking subsidiaries to J.P. Morgan Chase & Co. for $1.9 billion.
29 Sept.	The Dow Jones Industrial Average drops a record 777 points in one day of trading.
3 Oct.	Wachovia Corp., under pressure from federal regulators to sell following a one-day $5 billion run on deposits, reaches a deal to be acquired by Wells Fargo & Co. for $15.4 billion.
10 Nov.	Electronics retailer Circuit City files for bankruptcy protection.
	The White House announces it will increase the AIG bailout from $123 billion to $150 billion. AIG discloses losses of $24.5 billion from July to September 2008.
12 Nov.	Treasury secretary Henry Paulson announces that Troubled Asset Relief Program (TARP) funds will be spent on stabilizing and stimulating credit markets in part by buying shares in banks.
18–19 Nov.	The chief executives of General Motors (GM), Chrysler, and Ford request a taxpayer-financed rescue in congressional hearings.
23 Nov.	Citigroup finalizes its rescue plan with the Treasury Department, Federal Reserve, and FDIC providing for the government to invest $20 billion in the bank and to partially guarantee more than $300 billion in assets.
25 Nov.	The Federal Reserve and the Treasury Department announce an $800 billion program to thaw frozen credit markets—$600 billion allocated to buying debt from Fannie Mae, Freddie Mac, and other mortgage financiers and $200 million to encourage investors to buy securities tied to car and student loans and other forms of consumer credit.

8 Dec.	Tribune Co. files for bankruptcy protection.
11 Dec.	Federal agents arrest investment adviser Bernard Madoff in New York, charging him with operating a $50 million Ponzi scheme. The size of the fraud is subsequently estimated at $65 billion.

2009

17 Feb.	President Barack Obama signs a $787 billion stimulus package, providing $212 billion in tax cuts and $575 billion in new federal spending.
18 Feb.	President Obama orders that $275 billion be allocated to help homeowners avoid foreclosure.
25 Feb.	Bank "stress tests" mandated by the stimulus legislation begin. Ten banks are ordered in May to raise a combined $74.6 billion in new capital.
2 Mar.	AIG posts a $61.7 billion loss for 2008's fourth quarter. The Treasury Department agrees to provide $30 billion more in financing.
12 Mar.	Madoff pleads guilty to eleven counts of fraud, money laundering, perjury, and theft. On 29 June he is sentenced to 150 years in prison.
23 Mar.	The Treasury Department announces the Public-Private Investment Program, in which the government will provide subsidies and other incentives to encourage private investors to buy up to $1 trillion in toxic loans and assets.
29 Mar.	A White House task force studying aid for struggling automakers forces the resignation of GM chief Rick Wagoner.
30 Mar.	President Obama, threatening to withdraw U.S. support to Chrysler and GM, issues a thirty-day deadline for Chrysler to merge with Fiat or find another suitable merger partner and a sixty-day deadline for GM to rework its business plan.
15 Apr.	"Tea Party" demonstrations across the country protest the Obama administration's stimulus programs.
30 Apr.	Chrysler files for bankruptcy protection after creditors reject a White House–brokered restructuring plan.
18 May	The Supreme Court agrees to hear a case challenging the 2002 Sarbanes-Oxley Act.
1 June	GM files for bankruptcy protection with $172.81 billion in debt and $82.29 billion in assets.
18 June	Federal authorities arrest Texas banker R. Allen Stanford, founder of the Stanford Group Co., after a federal grand jury indicts him on charges of fraud involving the misallocation of certificate-of-deposit assets into private-equity investments.
10 July	GM emerges from bankruptcy.
24 July	The federal government begins offering refund vouchers of up to $4,500 on trade-ins of older, low-fuel-efficiency automobiles. The initial $1 billion funding of the so-called Cash for Clunkers program runs out quickly, prompting Congress to pass a $2 billion extension.
16 Sept.	Richard Trumka is elected president of the AFL-CIO, succeeding the retiring John Sweeney.
22 Oct.	Christina Romer, head of the White House Council of Economic Advisers, predicts in congressional testimony that the unemployment rate will remain at or above 10 percent into 2010.

3 Nov. Warren Buffett's Berkshire Hathaway buys Burlington Northern Sante Fe railroad for $34 billion.

1 Dec. GM fires chief Fritz Henderson and names chairman Edward Whitacre as interim chief.

3 Dec. General Electric (GE) sells NBC Universal to Comcast in deal valued at $30 billion.

Robin Radaetz holds a sign in front of the Lehman Brothers headquarters in New York on 15 September 2008, the day the 158-year-old investment bank filed for Chapter 11 protection in the biggest bankruptcy filing ever (AP Photo/Mary Altaffer, file).

OVERVIEW

Introduction. The U.S. economy grew by more than 20 percent from 2000 through 2009, compared with annual growth rates around 3 percent in the three previous decades. What appeared simultaneously as a minor statistical decrease in production masked huge economic shifts that reverberated throughout the decade. Foreign competition increasingly displaced U.S. manufacturing, a trend that loomed especially large in the steel, electronics, and automotive sectors. Surging foreign demand for fuel, steel, and other raw materials constrained U.S. supply. The growth of computer networking technology, meanwhile, hastened shifts in the retail, media, communications, and financial industries. In this atmosphere of change, corporate fraud was rampant.

Global Pressures. General Motors began the decade as the nation's largest company but ten years later found itself just emerging from bankruptcy. Like competitors Ford and Chrysler, it was the victim of rising competition from foreign manufacturers, especially Japanese automakers. The U.S. trade deficit ballooned by 150 percent from 2000 to 2008, rising to $816.2 billion before falling with the onset of the late-decade recession. The same trend felled Bethlehem Steel, another iconic U.S. manufacturer, whose steel girds the Hoover Dam, Chrysler Building, and George Washington Bridge. It declared bankruptcy in 2001 and was followed by National Steel, Weirton Steel, and Georgetown Steel. Foreign manufacturers simultaneously muscled into the world's commodity markets, creating a buzz-saw effect that drove up the price for crucial raw materials, none more so than oil. Inflation-adjusted domestic crude oil prices shot up 150 percent over the course of the decade, a trend that forced nearly all the major U.S. airlines into bankruptcy.

Technology's Impact. Technology became the engine for growth in the United States. Of the decade's ten fastest-growing industries, seven were grounded in Internet technology, including the top four: providers of Internet-based phone service, search engines, electronic-commerce services, and online dating services. Among the slowest growers were banks, whose revenues fell 73 percent, and manufacturers of recordable media, down 64 percent. Newspapers, broadcast networks, and publishers also lost ground in their hesitancy to embrace digital technology. *Chicago Tribune* and *Los Angeles Times* publisher Tribune Co. descended into bankruptcy in 2008. *The New York Times* came close to bankruptcy in 2009 before Mexican billionaire Carlos Slim Helú saved it with a $250 million investment. In 2002, AOL-Time Warner recorded the country's biggest annual loss in corporate history, $99 billion, as it struggled in vain to adapt its "old-media" content warehouse to Internet use. No company benefited from the upheaval more than Google, which became a $200 billion media conglomerate during the decade.

Legacy of Scandal. American workers and consumers suffered greatly in the changing economy, often due to reckless and fraudulent corporate practices. The dot-com bubble's overnight fortunes had stoked reckless investment throughout the decade as venture capitalists sought out the next big stock boom. The nation witnessed corporate fraud on an equally grotesque scale. The Enron accounting abuses alone are estimated to have wiped out $74 billion belonging to investors, many of them Enron employees enrolled in the company's retirement plan, who lost their jobs as well. The Wall Street speculation, however, proved the costlier vice. It took increasingly arcane forms, devolving from bets on nascent technology to bets on bets on nascent technology, or on future commodity prices or, most devastatingly, on homeowners' creditworthiness. By one estimate, the wave of mortgage defaults that swept the world's financial markets starting in 2007—and that was ultimately shouldered by taxpayers and bondholders—erased more than $7.7 trillion in wealth.

TOPICS IN THE NEWS

'90S BOOM ENDS AND 9/11

Dot-Com Crash. The "dot-com bubble," an astounding surge in stock valuations powered by Internet-related public offerings, came to a crashing halt in March 2000. The rally's start is widely traced to the frenzied trading-floor reaction to Netscape Communication's initial stock offering in August 1995, signaling ripe demand for companies positioned for a boom in electronic commerce. The NASDAQ Composite Index, home to most technology companies' stocks, more than quadrupled from then to its 10 March 2000 peak. As the turn of the millennium neared, doubts about Internet ventures' multiplying valuations began to snowball, gaining momentum with a June 2000 federal court ruling that Microsoft Corp., the world's dominant software manufacturer, be broken up. From March to October 2000, the NASDAQ plunged 78 percent, eroding $5 trillion in market value. Shares of dot-com bellwether Yahoo!, having topped $100 in March 2000, fell below $6 the following March. A string of bankruptcies by web-focused companies ensued: NorthPoint Communications and Covad Communications in 2001; the following year, Global Crossing, XO Communications, and, in what was then the biggest filing in history, WorldCom. The most emblematic failure of the era was that of Pets.com, an online pet supplies company that made its name with a memorably quirky commercial during the 2000 Super Bowl broadcast starring a sock puppet; by November it was liquidated.

Microsoft Antitrust Case. The problems forecasted in the Microsoft verdict, however, never materialized. The Justice Department had accused the company in 1998 of exercising monopoly powers over the market for Internet browsers by bundling its Explorer product with its ubiquitous Windows operating systems. Federal judge Thomas Penfield Jackson sided with the government, mandating that Microsoft be divided into two companies—one producing the operating system and another focused on other software products. A year later, a federal appeals court overturned Jackson's ruling, finding that Microsoft had violated portions of the Sherman Antitrust Act but had not sought to monopolize the market. The decision also rebuked Jackson, accusing him of violating the judicial code of conduct by granting interviews with

reporters. The new ruling shunted the case to a different trial judge for rehearing. The Justice Department, whose leadership had since changed with the inauguration of President Bush, announced in September 2001 that it would not seek Microsoft's breakup. The two sides soon reached a settlement agreement resolving the suit; Microsoft was not to prevent computer makers from installing non-Microsoft software and had to share technical information with rivals that sought to design products relying on Windows. In 2003 Microsoft reached a related settlement with AOL-Time Warner, agreeing to pay $750 million to end a private antitrust suit brought by Netscape (which AOL bought in 2002).

9/11. Recessionary conditions had been in effect six months when the 11 September attacks occurred. The attacks did not merely cool the economy further, but froze whole sectors. Less than an hour after the first plane struck,

Microsoft chairman Bill Gates speaks to business and government leaders at the Microsoft Government Leaders' Conference in Seattle, 4 April 2000 (AP Photo/Stevan Morgian).

the Federal Aviation Administration suspended all civilian flights—the nation's first unplanned halt in air travel. The skies remained restricted for three days. The New York Stock Exchange and NASDAQ markets, so close in proximity to Ground Zero, as the World Trade Center (WTC) disaster site came to be known, remained closed for four trading days, the longest Wall Street shutdown since the Great Depression. When equities trading resumed on 17 September, the Dow Jones Industrial Average ended down more than 7 percent. The sheer cost of cleaning up, rebuilding, and financing new security infrastructures after 9/11 mounted rapidly. The WTC damage was estimated as high as $4.5 billion; the loss of air traffic revenue, $10 billion; the insurance industry tab, $40 billion; immediate federal emergency funds, another $40 billion. The spending, ironically, provided crucial stimulus, as did a sizable interest-rate cut, reducing the federal-funds rate by October 2001 to its lowest level since 1962. By November, before the Ground Zero fires had stopped burning, the economic recession that began in March 2001 officially lifted. Six months after 9/11, the Dow had climbed nearly 10.5 percent.

Global Settlement. Two years into the decade, the dot-com crash continued to reverberate, more so in the courtroom than on the trading floor. New York attorney general Eliot Spitzer and the Securities and Exchange Commission (SEC) leveled charges in 2002 against Wall Street's biggest investment banks, accusing them of stoking the stock-buying fury by pressuring their analysts to recommend stocks merely in order to help win investment-banking business. Ten banks—including Goldman Sachs, J.P. Morgan Chase, Merrill Lynch, and Morgan Stanley—settled the allegations in 2003 in a $1.4 billion "Global Settlement" requiring that they set up dividing walls between their research and investment-banking operations. Two of the best-known analysts were also fined and banned from the securities industry: Henry Blodget of Merrill Lynch and Jack Grubman of Salomon Smith Barney. The settlement sidetracked the trend among big banks of creating "financial supermarkets" through mergers. Embodied by Citigroup, the model entailed building up sundry financial business lines—banking, brokerage, insurance, investment products—for the sake of reaping economies of scale, consolidations that were made possible by the Gramm-Leach-Bliley Act of 1999. The threat of prosecution stemming from conflicts emerged as a fatal flaw, prompting Citigroup and other banking giants to shed ancillary units over the course of the decade.

Sources:

John Cassidy, *dot.com: How America Lost Its Mind and Money in the Internet Era* (New York: Harper, 2003);

Jamie Doward, "Ashes to ashes, boom to bust," *Observer* (U.K.), 8 September 2002;

Adam Lashinsky, "Remembering Netscape: The Birth of the Web," *Fortune* (25 July 2005);

"SEC, NY Attorney General, NASD, NASAA, NYSE and State Regulators Announce Historic Agreement to Reform Investment Practices," Office of the New York Attorney General, *ag.ny.gov* (20 December 2002);

Richard W. Stevenson and Leslie Kaufman, "Amid Anxiety, Markets Edge Back Toward Routines," *New York Times,* 14 September 2001.

AUTOMOBILE INDUSTRY

GM Goes Bankrupt. The Big Three automakers were all running on empty when the 2007 economic downturn hit, but General Motors faced the most difficult situation. It was quickly losing market share to foreign manufacturers, burdened by a gas-guzzling inventory and, most draining of all, struggling to meet massive worker-benefits obligations dating back to the 1950s. By 2005, when it posted a loss of $10.6 billion, GM was paying out $7.6 billion annually in benefits. After losing $2 billion in 2006, it hemorrhaged another $38.7 billion in 2007. In November 2008, amid contracting credit markets, the company disclosed it would run out of cash by mid 2009. Along with the heads of Ford and Chrysler, GM chief Rick Wagoner testified in Congress later that month, requesting federal aid to stay afloat. The outgoing Bush White House complied in December with a $13.4 billion bridge loan from the Troubled Asset Relief Program (TARP). But by February 2009, buried under 2008's $30.9 billion loss, GM was asking for more. President Obama convened the Auto Industry Financing and Restructuring Board and demanded

"THE GUY AT A SOUP KITCHEN IN HIGH HAT AND TUXEDO"

The CEOs of cash-strapped American automakers General Motors, Chrysler, and Ford committed a major public-relations error when they each flew in separate private luxury jets to Washington, D.C., in order to testify before Congress on 18 November 2008 on the need for a public bailout of the industry. Representative Gary Ackerman (D-N.Y.) submitted the chiefs to a public scolding:

"There's a delicious irony in seeing private luxury jets flying in to Washington, D.C., and people coming off of them with tin cups in their hand, saying that they're going to be trimming down and streamlining their businesses. It's almost like seeing a guy show up at a soup kitchen in high hat and tuxedo. Kind of makes you a little bit suspicious as to whether or not, as Mr. Mulally said, we've seen the future. And it causes at least some of us to think, 'have we seen the future?' I mean, there's a message there. Couldn't you all have downgraded to first class, or jet-pooled or something to get here?"

Sources: "Automotive Industry Assistance, Auto Executives," *C-spanvideo.org;*

Bill Vlasic and David Herszenhorn, "Auto Chiefs Fail to Get Bailout Aid," *New York Times,* 19 November 2008.

Auto executives, from left, General Motors chief executive officer Richard Wagoner, United Auto Workers president Ron Gettelfinger, Ford chief executive officer Alan Mulally, and Chrysler chief executive officer Robert Nardelli, testify on Capitol Hill in Washington on 4 December 2008, before a Senate Banking Committee hearing on the auto industry bailout (AP Photo/Gerald Herbert, File).

more thorough restructuring, forcing Wagoner out as chief. Another $6 billion in Treasury loans plus a $3.2 billion loan from Canada would be granted before GM proposed cuts including closing plants, phasing out the Pontiac and Saturn lines, and nearly halving its 6,000-member dealership network, over the complaints of dealers and some members of Congress. The administration agreed to inject $30 billion more, to be converted to a majority equity stake, with bondholders and the United Auto Workers also major shareholders. The agreements set the stage for a 1 June 2009 Chapter 11 filing. GM would be split into a new and old GM, with the "old" to be renamed Motors Liquidation and left with most of the bankruptcy liabilities. The new GM emerged from bankruptcy in July, retaining the Chevrolet, GMC, Buick, and Cadillac vehicle lines, and with the federal government owning 61 percent of the company. Before year's end, GM's board ousted Wagoner's successor, Fritz Henderson, contending the company was not changing fast enough.

Fiat Rescues Chrysler. Like GM, Chrysler was already flagging when the economic downturn hit in 2007. It too was losing market share to foreign manufacturers, falling behind Toyota in 2006 in the rankings for U.S. sales, and relying heavily on truck and SUV sales, which began to drop amid higher fuel prices. Germany's Daimler, which bought Chrysler in 1998, sold it to private equity firm

Cerberus Capital Management in 2007 for $7.4 billion. Daimler actually ended up paying for the sale under terms requiring it to invest $6 billion in Chrysler operations and another $1.6 billion to cover Chrysler's 2007 losses. Without Daimler's backing, Chrysler lost easy access to debt markets just as the nation's credit markets began seizing up, and by the fall of 2008 it was seeking a federal bailout to avert bankruptcy. The government responded in early 2009 with a $4 billion emergency loan and extended $11.5 billion more in aid through May. The newly installed Obama administration, meanwhile, brokered April negotiations with Chrysler's creditors, asking that they sign on to a restructuring in which Italy's Fiat assumed a 35 percent stake in exchange for access to Chrysler technology and overseas markets; the creditors were asked to forgive billions in debt. They said no, prompting a 30 April Chapter 11 filing designed to position Chrysler for a fuller partnership with Fiat. In bankruptcy, Chrysler was split into "new" and "old" versions—the new company, Chrysler Group, to be 20 percent owned by Fiat, 9.85 percent by the United States, 2.46 percent by Canada, and 67.69 percent by a United Auto Workers union retiree health-care trust fund. Fiat chief Sergio Marchionne was installed as Chrysler chief, and Fiat would have the option to boost its stake to 51 percent eventually. The old Chrysler, named Old Carco, would retain eight manufacturing sites, a real-estate portfolio, equipment leases, and contracts with 789 U.S. auto dealerships—all to be sold off under court supervision, with proceeds paid to creditors.

Ford Survives on Its Own. Ford had to contend with the same roiled auto market as its two big domestic competitors but managed to avoid bankruptcy or even a government bailout. Its salvation was a prophetic decision in November 2006 by newly installed chief executive Alan Mulally to take out $23.6 billion in loans. The funds, which Mulally sought in order to finance an overhaul of the company and as a cushion for any tough times, would have been impossible to secure in a year's time, after the credit market's collapse. Ford, it turned out, did need the cushion after a $6 billion loss in 2006, another $3.5 billion loss in 2007, and $14.6 billion in 2008. At the November Capitol Hill hearing with the Big Three automakers, Mulally testified in support of a bailout for his competitors, reasoning that their failure could jeopardize Ford by disrupting its parts-supply chain. Ford itself did not need government aid at the moment though it might in the future, Mulally said. Meanwhile, Mulally had proceeded with the restructuring he promised creditors in 2006—shifting Ford's fleet to smaller, more-fuel-efficient models; selling the company's ownership stakes in Jaguar, Land Rover, and Aston Martin while committing to sell its Volvo division; cutting factory capacity to reflect demand; culling more than one hundred dealerships; and announcing plans to close fourteen manufacturing plants in North America and eliminate between 25,000 to 30,000 jobs by 2012. By spurning bailouts and avoiding bankruptcy, Ford won favor with consumers. Sales fell in 2009 across the industry nearly 40 percent, but the decline was far smaller at Ford, just 15.6 percent. The cuts, meanwhile, helped Ford post net income in 2009 of $2.7 billion, its first full-year profit since 2005, and executives said they expected to remain profitable before taxes in 2010 and 2011.

Sources:

Andrew Clark, "Chrysler declares itself bankrupt," *Guardian,* 30 April 2009;

Jack Healy, "Back on Hill, Automakers Defend Dealer Closings," *New York Times,* 12 June 2009;

Chris Isidore, "Daimler Pays to Dump Chrysler," *cnnmoney.com* (14 May 2007);

Isidore, "Ford to Cut Up to 30,000 Jobs," *cnnmoney.com* (23 January 2006);

Michelle Krebs, "Ford Earns $2.7 Billion Profit in Tumultuous 2009," *autoobserver.com* (28 January 2010);

Roger Lowenstein, *While America Aged* (New York: Penguin, 2008);

Mike Ramsey and Lizzie O'Leary, "Fiat Said to Buy Chrysler Assets Today to Form New Automaker," *Bloomberg News,* 10 June 2009;

David E. Sanger, Jeff Zeleny, and Bill Vlasic, "G.M. to Seek Bankruptcy and a New Start," *New York Times,* 31 May 2009;

Vlasic, "How Ford Avoided the Meltdown that Hit GM, Chrysler," *New York Times,* 9 April 2009.

DISARRAY FOR THE AIRLINE INDUSTRY

9/11 Bailout. Of the seven major U.S. air carriers, all but Southwest and Continental went bankrupt and operated with fewer passengers and lower revenue over the course of the decade, and all but Southwest coped with lower wages, fewer employees, and smaller fleets. The September 11 terrorist attacks devastated the industry, though only initially. Forebodings of a lingering chill over airline flight caused by the fear of additional attacks were never borne out. Rather, more deeply seated economic forces gripped the industry, forcing older carriers to deal with lower-cost competitors such as Southwest and rising fuel costs. The 9/11 attacks represented the first crisis for the airline industry in a tumultuous decade. Less than an hour after the first plane struck, the Federal Aviation Administration suspended all civilian flights, and the skies remained restricted for three days. Carriers surrendered an estimated $10 billion in air-traffic revenue during the flight ban, and they faced still steeper expenses in complying with a new regime of plane and airport security. The strain proved too much, especially for airlines that were already reckoning with overcapacity. The same day that flights resumed, Continental announced it would cut 12,000 jobs. The other major carriers eventually made similar announcements: United and American would lay off 20,000 apiece, Northwest 10,000, and US Airways 11,000; Delta said it expected to cut 13,000 jobs. Industry lobbyists converged on Washington to press for federal support. Congress did come to the airlines' rescue, passing on 21 September a $15 billion bailout package designed to lessen the blow of the ban as well as losses likely to be incurred through the rest of the year owing to the attacks. A third of the bailout was to be paid in cash reimbursements and the rest pledged toward loan guarantees. United claimed the biggest grant, $774.2 million, while American garnered $694 million and Delta $635.7 million. Provisions in the bailout legislation requiring the government be granted equity in the airlines in exchange for the support generated well over $100 million in returns for the Treasury.

The Low-Fare Rivals. Along with rising fuel prices, the other enormous pressure on the big air carriers was the surging popularity of low-cost carriers such as Southwest and JetBlue. Southwest posted profits throughout the decade, while JetBlue suffered losses only in 2005, 2006, and 2008. Southwest's operating revenue climbed more than 83 percent in the decade, and passenger totals were up 35.5 percent, while the other major carriers lost ground, with the exception of Continental, where increases were marginal. Customers flocked to the low-fare model, prompting Delta and United to experiment with copycat low-fare brands—Delta's Song and United's Ted—as well as motivating the regional Atlantic Coast Airlines to revamp itself into a national low-fare carrier, Independence Airlines. Delta and United ultimately abandoned their ventures, and Independence was forced to liquidate in 2006, deeply indebted by soaring fuel costs. Southwest succeeded in large part because of its fuel price hedging, which insulated it from mid-decade fuel-cost spikes by locking in purchases at lower rates.

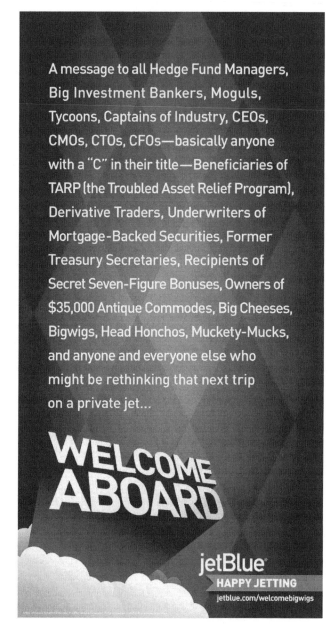

A February 2009 JetBlue airline advertisement capitalizes on popular dissatisfaction with Wall Street to promote its low-fare services (from <http://whengrowthstalls.com>).

Bankruptcies and Consolidation. The aid was insufficient for US Airways and United, both of which filed for bankruptcy protection in 2002. US Airways had been struggling even before the 9/11 attacks, and investors pressured it in 2000 to seek out a merger with United, though the talks collapsed in mid 2001. It managed to exit bankruptcy in 2003 with the assistance of a $900 million federally guaranteed loan, but a year later it filed again, wracked by rising fuel costs and stalled labor negotiations with pilots. While in bankruptcy, US Airways began merger talks with America West, which agreed in May 2005 to buy US Airways and take its name, a deal that broadened US Airways' market beyond that of the highly competitive Northeast and

ushered it out of bankruptcy four months later. United was still struggling with 9/11 losses, higher fuel costs, and cost overruns from its successful late-1990s period when it was forced to file for bankruptcy protection in December 2002. The airline was losing an estimated $22 million a day, and had bled $4 billion in the two prior years. The last straw was the federal government's refusal to grant a $1.8 billion loan guarantee on grounds that United had not prepared a sound business plan. In bankruptcy, United cut costs extensively, canceling routes, renegotiating employee contracts, and furloughing tens of thousands of workers while relinquishing its pension plan to federal control. But ever-rising fuel prices deepened the losses, and the original plan for exiting Chapter 11 in two and a half years had to be extended. United finally emerged from bankruptcy in February 2006, having secured a $3 billion loan from J.P. Morgan Chase and Citigroup. Northwest and Delta filed for bankruptcy protection within minutes of each other on 14 September 2005, both burdened by skyrocketing fuel prices and withering under competition from low-cost carriers. Both companies also emerged nearly simultaneously, having cut a combined 9,000 jobs and reaping additional savings through pay cuts and reduced capacity. Within a year, in April 2008, the two airlines announced a deal for Delta to acquire Northwest, creating the world's biggest airline. The deal closed in October, though Northwest continued to operate under the Northwest brand until year-end 2009. The combination accelerated consolidation negotiations among the major carriers, though no major deals were to follow. United held on-again-off-again merger talks with Continental and US Airways that ultimately proved unfruitful.

Sources:

"Airline Data and Analysis," *airlinefinancials.com* (2 July 2010);

Jeff Bailey, "Southwest Airlines Gains Advantage by Hedging on Long-Term Oil Contracts," *New York Times,* 28 November 2007;

Susan Carey, "United, Continental Had Exploratory Talks in 2006," *Wall Street Journal,* 25 June 2010;

"Independence Air to End Flights Thursday," *Bloomberg News,* 3 January 2006;

Chris Isidore, "Delta Air Lines Files for Bankruptcy," *cnnmoney.com* (15 September 2005);

Isidore, "Northwest Files for Bankruptcy," *cnnmoney.com* (14 September 2005);

"JetBlue Data and Analysis," *airlinefinancials.com* (2 July 2010);

Dan Reed, "United Files for Bankruptcy," *USA Today,* 9 December 2002;

"Southwest Data and Analysis," *airlinefinancials.com* (2 July 2010);

"US Air Files for Bankruptcy," *cnnmoney.com* (12 August 2002).

FRAUD IN THE CORPORATE WORLD

Financial Scandals. A small wave of financial restatements and accounting anomalies reported in late 2001 and 2002 gave way to a surge of unprecedented financial scandals ending in corporate bankruptcies and liquidations, prison sentences for corporate executives, and the loss of retirement savings by their employees. Separately, prosecu-

Martha Stewart, with U.S. Marshals, leaves the Manhattan federal court on 16 July 2004, after her sentencing (AP Photo/Bebeto Matthews).

ruptcy protection on 2 December, laying off 21,000 employees the next day. In congressional hearings in January and February 2002, Enron principals including Skilling, former chief financial officer Andrew Fastow (who resigned in October), and founder and chief Kenneth Lay were called to testify. Fastow and Lay refused to testify by citing their Fifth Amendment rights against self-incrimination, as did Enron's chief outside accountant, Arthur Andersen partner David Duncan. Skilling did testify, denying knowledge of any fraud. Other Enron employees maintained that the company was shredding incriminating documents, and in June Arthur Andersen was convicted of obstruction of justice by a federal jury for destroying thousands of records. The firm agreed to cease auditing public companies in the United States, effectively going out of business. Three years later, the Supreme Court overturned the Andersen conviction on the grounds that the jury was given incomplete instructions. Fastow, Skilling, and Lay also faced fraud and related charges. Fastow pleaded guilty in January 2004 and was sentenced to ten years in prison. Skilling and Lay were found guilty in May 2006.

tions of illegal trading by mutual funds and the singular case of insider trading involving television host and magazine publisher Martha Stewart helped to publicize the pattern of influential traders manipulating the stock markets at the expense of mainstream investors.

Enron. Nowhere was the accounting fraud more devastating than at Houston-based energy conglomerate Enron, where the spate of scandals began. By 2001, Enron had grown from a gas pipeline controller formed in the mid 1980s to an owner of transmission networks, generation facilities, and a vast energy trading business, valued at more than $60 billion. The secret to its towering growth, however, lay in fraudulent accounting designed to exceed Wall Street earnings expectations, thus fueling ever more investment in its stock. Most notorious was Enron's creation of "special purpose entities," or shell companies, in which it dumped mounting debt in order to keep the Enron balance sheet pristine. Enron's astounding rise began to look suspicious after a *Fortune* magazine article, published 5 March 2001, questioned the company's steep stock price and the minimal documentation it was providing to explain earnings. Analysts chimed in with doubts, sending the stock lower through the summer and prompting many executives to sell huge blocks of company shares. Chief executive Jeffrey Skilling resigned in August, and two months later Enron reported an unexpected quarterly loss of $618 million, triggering an SEC investigation and credit rating agencies' downgrades of its credit. In November, the company disclosed it overstated profits by $586 million over five years. Its stock price plunging, Enron quickly negotiated its sale to rival energy marketing company Dynegy, but Dynegy's offer was retracted less than three weeks later. With debt payments due and unable to tap the credit markets, Enron filed for bank-

MARTHA STEWART IMPRISONED

The wave of financial fraud sweeping the decade cast many an obscure executive into the ranks of household names. But one required no introduction. Martha Stewart, the popularizer of domestic crafts and simplified gourmet cooking, was charged in 2003 with insider trading and lying to prosecutors. Securities regulators alleged that Samuel Waksal, the founder of pharmaceutical company ImClone, had learned that federal regulators were about to block approval of a promising new ImClone drug. He urged family members and friends, including Stewart, to sell company shares ahead of the ruling, and Stewart took his advice, avoiding more than $45,000 in losses when the stock fell the next day. After a five-week jury trial, Stewart was found guilty in March 2004 of conspiracy, obstruction of justice, obstruction of an agency proceeding, and making false statements to federal investigators. The sentence was five months in a West Virginia federal prison. Stewart served out the term without appealing and quickly got back to business, writing a 750-page book, launching a twenty-four-hour radio channel, hosting a daily television show, and signing new merchandising deals. The terms of her sentence, however, prevented Stewart from resuming duties as chairwoman and chief executive of the company she formed, Martha Stewart Omnimedia.

Sources: Lloyd Allen, *Being Martha: The Inside Story of Martha Stewart and Her Amazing Life* (Hoboken, N.J.: Wiley, 2006);

Diane Brady, "The Reinvention Of Martha Stewart," *BusinessWeek* (6 November 2006).

Workers remove an Enron logo from the Houston Astros ballpark on 28 February 2002. The ballpark, named for Enron, briefly became Astros Field until Minute Maid bought the naming rights (AP Photo/Pat Sullivan).

Skilling's sentence was twenty-four years; Lay died of a heart attack in July 2006 before his sentence was handed down. Enron investors lost an estimated $74 billion in the four years leading up to the company's collapse. As the scandal unfolded, loyal employees who held stock in the company that they had received as matching funds to their 401(k) retirement accounts, provided a sympathetic human face to the downfall of Enron. Many had maintained their holdings of Enron shares because of reassurances from company executives who knew that the company was on its way to bankruptcy. A class action filed against Andersen and investment banks implicated in the fraud, including J.P. Morgan Chase, Citigroup, and the Canadian Imperial Bank of Commerce, netted $7.2 billion, $688 million of which was paid to the plaintiffs' law firm.

WorldCom. The telecommunications company WorldCom grew on a trajectory as steep as Enron's, and collapsed in a similar manner, even sharing the same outside accountant, Arthur Andersen. Formed in the early 1980s as a long-distance phone service provider, its market capitalization ballooned to $160 billion over the next twenty years owing to a series of late-1990s acquisitions, including CompuServe, MFS Communications, and MCI Communications, a $40 billion deal that at the time ranked as the biggest merger in history. Business slowed down dramatically starting in 2000, as

investment in the telecom industry ebbed and a bitter price war among long-distance carriers began eating into profit. WorldCom lined up another merger in 2000 with Sprint, but regulators in the United States and Europe blocked it later that year, further depressing WorldCom's stock. To prop up WorldCom's financial results, company executives led by chief executive Bernard Ebbers and chief financial officer Scott Sullivan began manipulating accounting practices to hide losses. Three internal auditors, their suspicions piqued by accounting irregularities, began in spring 2002 to scrutinize the company books without informing their superiors. Not long thereafter, SEC regulators, also curious how WorldCom was escaping the losses plaguing its rivals, requested information from the company on its accounting practices. In June, the WorldCom internal auditors uncovered at least $2 billion in suspicious accounting entries that company executives could not explain. The findings were presented to WorldCom's board of directors, who then scoured the books and went public on 24 June, announcing WorldCom had lost $3.8 billion over the previous fifteen months. The estimate of the losses subsequently grew to $11 billion. Sullivan was promptly fired, as were 17,000 of the company's employees, about 20 percent of the workforce. The next month, WorldCom filed for bankruptcy protection, listing $107 billion in assets and $41 billion in debt. It was at the time the largest Chapter 11 filing in history. In 2005 Sullivan was sentenced to five years in prison on fraud and related charges, while Ebbers was sentenced to twenty-five years on nine counts of conspiracy, securities fraud, and filing false reports with regulators. WorldCom exited bankruptcy in 2004, renamed MCI, and the next year reached terms to be sold to Verizon Communications for $8.44 billion.

Adelphia. The rapid demise of Adelphia Communications, a cable television company founded by Pennsylvania businessman John Rigas in 1952, began with a March 2002 securities filing footnote disclosing the company had fronted the Rigas family $2.3 billion in guaranteed loans used on largely personal expenses. Amid the backdrop of the then-unfolding Enron scandal, the revelations sent Adelphia's shares plunging. Rigas and his two sons Timothy and Michael, who worked as Adelphia executives, were forced to resign. In June, the company filed for bankruptcy protection, and in July the Rigases were arrested and charged with fraud. In their 2004 trial Adelphia executives testified that they regularly fabricated accounting documents for investors and lenders. The Rigases were found to have spent company funds on perks ranging from a private jet to a golf course, and were even said to have spent $6,000 in company funds to fly a Christmas tree to a family member. John Rigas and Timothy Rigas were convicted of conspiracy, bank fraud, and securities fraud and sentenced to fifteen years and twenty years respectively. Michael was acquitted, though later he did plead guilty to making a false entry in a financial record and was sentenced to terms of home confinement and probation. Adelphia's cable television assets were sold in bankruptcy in 2006 to Time Warner and Comcast, while Pioneer Telephone bought its telephone business in 2005.

Tyco. Almost simultaneously, a similar scandal played out at the manufacturing conglomerate Tyco International involving company officials' misappropriation of corporate funds. Tyco had grown during the 1990s at a rapid clip through acquisitions of companies making products ranging from medical devices to industrial piping and fire suppression materials. It raised suspicions with a January 2002 disclosure revealing that a Tyco director, Frank Walsh, received a $10 million fee for helping arrange a merger with lending company CIT Group, while another $10 million in Tyco money had been directed to a charity for which he was also a director. Six months later, chief Dennis Kozlowski resigned unexpectedly, shortly before the Manhattan district attorney was to indict him for conspiring to evade more than $1 million in state and city sales taxes on art purchases. Prosecutors soon broadened their charges against Kozlowski and former Tyco financial chief Mark Swartz, alleging they had defrauded the company through hidden loans and outright theft. Before their trial, Walsh pleaded guilty to scheming to hide his CIT

deal fee. At the 2003 trial, Kozlowski and Swartz stood accused of awarding themselves bonuses totaling more than $150 million that they concealed from company directors and of hiding loans they took out from Tyco and then had forgiven—Kozlowski for $25 million and Swartz for $12.5 million. Inflaming public sentiment against Kozlowski, prosecutors aired video footage of a Roman-themed birthday party he threw for his wife in Sardinia, featuring toga-clad entertainers and a performance by Jimmy Buffett—and costing $2 million, roughly half of which was paid for with Tyco funds. Another video showed a $6,000 shower curtain and other lavish furnishings at Kozlowski's Tyco-owned apartment in Manhattan. The trial ended in a mistrial after a juror claimed she had been urged in a letter to convict. A new trial began in January 2005, ending with convictions for both men on charges of conspiracy, grand larceny, securities fraud, and falsifying business records. They were sentenced to prison terms of at least eight years and four months.

Mutual Funds. The farthest-reaching of the corporate scandals, which eventually victimized millions of investors, involved fraudulent trading in mutual funds. Tipped off by a whistle-blower in the summer of 2003, New York attorney general Eliot Spitzer's office launched a probe of the hedge-fund manager Canary Capital Partners and its trading business with four mutual-fund firms: Janus Capital Management, Strong Funds, and the fund units of Bank of America and Bank One. Spitzer's investigators discovered and revealed in September that the mutual-fund firms were letting Canary execute trades in their funds after stock trading had closed for the day, while recording the trades as if they had been conducted prior to the day's close. Canary was also allowed to trade in and out of the funds rapidly, in an effort to time market changes. Mainstream investors in the mutual funds were forbidden from such trading, since it drives up fund costs by accumulating trading fees. In exchange for these privileges, Canary agreed to leave large sums of money in the mutual funds over a long period of time, racking up management fees for the mutual-fund firms. Spitzer's office negotiated a $40 million settlement with Canary and settlements worth $675 million with Bank of America, $226 million with Janus, $115 million with Strong, and $90 million with Bank One. For the next two and a half years, Spitzer and other state and federal regulators hammered out settlements with more than a dozen fund firms, including industry powerhouses Franklin Templeton, Putnam, and Federated Investors. A smaller group of brokerage firms, trade processors, and hedge funds implicated in such trades, including Bear Stearns and Prudential Financial, also consented to settlements. Shareholder lawsuits eventually took six years to reach settlements garnering more than $275 million for investors. More than $3 billion from state and federal settlements was earmarked to be returned to investors under the Sarbanes-Oxley Law's "Fair Fund" provision, which allows the agency to return funds gained in prosecuting fraud to be distributed to the investors harmed, rather than deposited into the treasury.

The SOX Solution. Congress's response to the widening gyre of corporate fraud was 2002's Sarbanes-Oxley Act, known informally as SOX. Crafted by Senator Paul Sarbanes (D-Md.) and Representative Michael Oxley (R-Ohio), it targeted fraud through new legal responsibilities for boards, auditors, and executives. For instance, the newly formed Public Company Accounting Oversight Board, housed within the Securities and Exchange Commission, had responsibility for regulating accountants in their capacity as auditors of public companies. Public companies were required to disclose more information with regulators, such as off-balance-sheet transactions, and issue annual reports assessing their "internal controls," or policies and procedures for guarding against accounting abuses. Another requirement: senior company executives were made person-

ally responsible for certifying the accuracy and completeness of their corporate financial reports, nullifying the defenses mustered by executives such as Enron's Jeffrey Skilling and WorldCom's Bernard Ebbers that they had no knowledge of the fraud enveloping their companies. Sarbanes-Oxley won widespread support in Congress, passing 423-3 in the House of Representatives and 99-0 in the Senate. But it engendered bitter criticism from business, most of it directed at the internal-controls regulations, which opponents including the U.S. Chamber of Commerce and American Bankers Association contended were too costly to carry out. They also pointed to research showing a drastic reduction in the number of U.S. companies registering with public stock exchanges soon after the law's enactment, presumably to escape its requirements. Many more companies also voluntarily restated their financial results in the first years of the law's taking effect, signaling sharper attention to accuracy. SOX was central to the airing of one major fraud case in 2008, when an official at the mutual-fund company Value Line balked at signing

CELEBRITY FORECLOSURES

In the widening economic crisis of 2008–2009, a downturn in real-estate values combined with the credit crunch to create financial woes for homeowners, many of whom found themselves unable to meet their payments on outsized mortgages. The rich were not immune to this, and many well-known celebrities faced foreclosure on their extravagant homes.

Nicolas Cage: Film star Nicolas Cage lost two homes in New Orleans's French Quarter district to a foreclosure auction in November 2009. Cage's financial troubles included being $5.5 million behind in mortgage payments on multiple properties and owing over $6 million in back taxes, a situation he blamed on the malfeasance of his business manager, Samuel J. Levin.

Jose Canseco: Retired Oakland Athletics baseball star Jose Canseco made headlines in 2005 with his confessional exposé of steroid use in Major League Baseball, *Juiced: Wild Times, Rampant 'Roids, Smash Hits, and How Baseball Got Big*. In 2008 he was in the news again, after losing his $2.5 million home to foreclosure. Despite claiming to earn up to $6 million per year, Canseco cited two costly divorces for his inability to make payments. Eventually, he stopped making them: "It didn't make financial sense for me to keep paying a mortgage on a home that was basically owned by someone else."

Lenny Dykstra: Former Major League Baseball player Lenny Dykstra purchased a lavish six-bedroom Thousand Oaks, California, estate from hockey great

Wayne Gretzky for $18.5 million in 2007. By 2009, after a series of financial setbacks, including the failure of a sports-magazine venture, Dykstra had his personal Gulfstream II jet repossessed and was $900,000 behind on his loan payments. Unable to find a buyer at the asking price of $25 million, Dykstra was forced to place the property up for auction in June 2009.

Victoria Gotti: The daughter of New York crime boss John Gotti and star of the reality-television series *Growing Up Gotti*, Victoria Gotti owned a six-bedroom, $4 million mansion in Long Island, New York. After struggling to pay off debts incurred by her ex-husband, however, the Mafia princess found herself $650,000 behind on her mortgage payments and facing foreclosure in May of 2009. She was able to save her home after convincing an appeals court that her ex-husband had unlawfully used her name to take out loans against the property.

Evander Holyfield: In June 2009 former heavyweight boxing champion Evander Holyfield's $10 million Atlanta, Georgia, estate fell into foreclosure. For the second time, Holyfield had trouble keeping up payments on the 109-room, 54,000-square-foot home; he was forced to strike a deal with creditors in June 2008 to remain in the property. The retired boxer's financial woes also included being sued over nonpayment of child support for one of his eleven children, and defaulting on a $550,000 loan to landscape his property.

Source: *forbes.com*

an internal code of ethics required by the law and affirming that he was not aware of any misconduct at the company. Pressured to sign, the official instead went to securities regulators, prompting an investigation finding the firm had collected more than $24 million in improper brokerage commissions on fund trades.

Sources:

Kris Axtman, "How Enron Awards Do, or Don't, Trickle Down," *Christian Science Monitor* (20 June 2005);

Jonathan D. Glater, "The S.E.C. Is Investigating Fee Practices at Value Line," *New York Times*, 2 August 2008;

Peter Grant and Christine Nuzum, "Adelphia Founder and One Son Are Found Guilty," *Wall Street Journal*, 9 July 2004;

Kristen Hays, "Enron payout plan approved," *Houston Chronicle*, 9 September 2008;

Mark Maremont, "Kozlowski, Swartz Are Found Guilty in Tyco Fraud Retrial," *Wall Street Journal*, 17 June 2005;

Brooke A. Masters, *Spoiling for a Fight: The Rise of Eliot Spitzer* (New York: Times Books, 2007);

Masters, "Tipster Set Fund Scandal Snowballing," *Washington Post*, 23 July 2006;

Bethany McLean and Peter Elkind, *The Smartest Guys in the Room: The Amazing Rise and Scandalous Fall of Enron* (London: Portfolio, 2006);

Susan Pulliam and Deborah Solomon, "Corporate Regulation Must Be Working—There's a Backlash," *Wall Street Journal*, 16 June 2004;

Pulliam and Solomon, "How Three Unlikely Sleuths Exposed Fraud at WorldCom," *Wall Street Journal*, 30 October 2002;

Jenny Strasburg, "Corporate backlash over Sarbanes-Oxley," *San Francisco Chronicle*, 23 March 2005.

NEW BUSINESS MODELS IN A DIGITAL WORLD

The Digital Revolution. The transformative promise of electronic commerce appeared wildly exaggerated in late 2000, as Internet-related stocks suffered stunning declines. The decade's subsequent years, however, vindicated the dot-com boom as merely premature. The crash's survivors, most notably Google, were building digital empires that would challenge dominant companies in industries ranging from retail and publishing to music production, newspapers, and software design.

Google. Just two years old in 2000 and shielded then from the market downturn by virtue of its private ownership, the Internet search company Google seized on the dot-com crash by hiring tech industry talent that was suddenly crowding the job market. It finished 2000 still shy of its first profit, but had by then indexed 1 billion web pages, creating the web's largest index, and signed on to become Yahoo!'s official search engine. The astounding ascent that Google was now beginning as a company coincided with and, in many accounts, accelerated the decline of businesses soon to be known collectively as "Old Media"—newspapers and magazines, music producers, motion pictures, the broadcast and cable television networks, and book publishing. The tipping point for Google came in February 2002, when it revamped its keyword-based AdWords advertising platform to charge by clicks rather than views, with the ads being stacked in an order determined by an adver-

tiser auction. Revenue more than quadrupled to $439 million, while profit surged fourteenfold, rising to $100 million. Prior to the AdWords makeover, Google executives were still struggling for a business model to capitalize on its search engine's massive reach; afterward, advertising comprised upward of 97 percent of revenue. A major ad and search syndication deal with AOL-Time Warner's portal followed, as did an ambitious stream of product rollouts—Google News, Books, Maps, Voice—staking Google's claim to one Old Media fortress after another. Google's initial stock offering in 2004 generated billions for further expansion. Floated with a floor price of $85 per share, the stock shot to $100 immediately, topping $200 in early 2005 on its way to a high of $747 in 2007. The public offering's proceeds funded two blockbuster acquisitions: $1.65 billion for the online video-sharing service YouTube in 2006 and, the following year, $3.1 billion for the Internet-ad servicing firm DoubleClick. The deal for DoubleClick, the dominant player in Internet advertising, gave Google 40 percent of money spent on online advertising. YouTube, reinforced with Google's backing, emerged as a formidable provider of video programming. DoubleClick's expertise in display advertising, adding the visual component that Google's textual advertising lacked, underscored the competitive threat to other media outlets. The broadcast and cable networks took notice, first with licensing negotiations that ultimately broke down, then with challenges of YouTube's airing of broadcast programming under copyright law. A suit filed in 2007 by Viacom—the owner of Paramount Pictures, DreamWorks, and cable channels including MTV and Comedy Central—charged Google with "massive intentional copyright infringement" and demanded $1 billion in damages. (The suit was decided in Google's favor in 2010.) Fox network parent News Corp. and NBC Universal chose instead to join forces in creating Hulu, a rival Internet video platform to air their programming. ABC parent Disney eventually joined Hulu as an equity partner, while CBS struck advertising ventures with YouTube in addition to devising its own Internet platform, TV.com. Google was able to strike a more conciliatory tone with the newspaper and publishing industries. It reached an accord in 2004 with the Associated Press and other wire services preventing lawsuits over Google News's content links. Four years later, it struck a similar settlement with book publishers, ending a copyright suit prompted by Google Books's digitization of public and university libraries' volumes. The agreements did little, however, to stem Google's amazing growth. By the end of 2008, the number of viewers watching prime-time network television shows had fallen nearly 10 percent, broadcast network advertising by 3.5 percent, book sales 2.8 percent, and daily newspaper ad revenue 17.7 percent. Google's ad revenues matched the combined ad revenues of the five broadcast networks (CBS, NBC, ABC, Fox, and the CW).

Google cofounders Larry Page, left, and Sergey Brin at their company's headquarters on 15 January 2004 in Mountain View, California (AP Photo/Ben Margot)

AOL-Time Warner. Old Media stalwart Time Warner sought a stake in the New Media's potential through its January 2000 deal to merge with Internet service provider America Online Inc. (AOL). The timing of the record $350 billion tie-up, however, proved disastrous, coming just two months before the dot-com bull market topped out. AOL's value and profitability sank

America Online's chairman and chief executive, Stephen Case, left, and Time Warner's chairman and chief executive, Gerald Levin, shake hands over the merger at a news conference on 10 January 2000, in New York (AP Photo/Kathy Willens).

with the broader e-commerce sector. Even more damaging was the slow unraveling of the deal's underlying logic: that combining a storehouse of entertainment content with a leading Internet distribution platform would command online attention. It turned out that the Internet dynamic instead favored platforms such as Google's, geared toward evolving, open-ended applications, over AOL-Time Warner's one-stop shop. By 2002 the combined company had posted a $99 billion loss, its worst annual loss in corporate history, and by 2003 the deal's key brokers, chief executive Gerald Levin and chairman Stephen Case, had been forced to step down, and the company opted to drop the initials "AOL" from its name. Time Warner went on to post profitable years—marred as they were by two settlements with regulators for $510 million resolving allegations of AOL accounting improprieties—until 2008, when it reverted to losses of more than $14 billion, owing again to AOL write-downs. The next year, it resolved to split its content businesses from its distribution businesses and proceeded to spin off first its cable television business and then AOL. At the end of 2009, the combined value of AOL and Time Warner was less than $40 billion.

Polaroid. Another company poorly positioned for the digital revolution was Polaroid, maker of the iconic One-Step instant camera. Besieged by the advance of digital camera technology, it had been losing money for

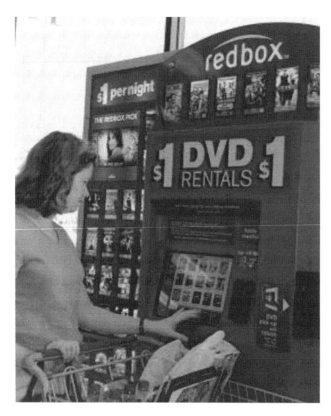

A grocery shopper uses an in-store automated Redbox kiosk to rent a DVD (<http://news.cnet.com>).

in 1999, Netflix built a subscriber base of 10 million over the next ten years and by 2007 had made its billionth DVD delivery. Customers did not have to contend with late fees, and for a monthly charge could rent an unlimited number of movies from home by using postage-paid envelopes to return and receive DVDs. Netflix's success spawned copycat ventures by Wal-Mart in 2002 and by in-store rental leader Blockbuster in 2004. Blockbuster's entry sparked a price war with Netflix that weakened both competitors, as well as a patent suit resolved by Blockbuster's payment of $4.1 million to Netflix in 2007. But the market continued to shift in Netflix's favor. In the last three years of the decade, Blockbuster suffered losses totaling more than $1 billion, and in 2009 it was forced to close 572 of its U.S. stores. In early 2010, a company official acknowledged that Blockbuster was near bankruptcy. Meanwhile, a new competitive challenge was creeping up on both: the kiosk rental company Redbox, which dispensed videos for $1 per day. The company was formed in 2003 by the investment arm of the restaurant chain McDonald's and launched business the next year with just twelve kiosks. Over the next five years, it added 22,000 kiosks across the country and at the decade's end claimed, along with other kiosk vendors, 19 percent of the rental market, compared with 36 percent for rent-by-mail companies and 45 percent for in-store providers. Industry market researchers NPD Group projected that the kiosk vend-

more than a decade when forced into bankruptcy in October 2001. In the late 1980s, company executives began digging their hole by issuing debt to fund stock repurchases and other expenditures aimed at fending off a hostile takeover attempt. Through the 1990s the company failed to invest in digital technologies that gradually began to overwhelm photographic film sales, and its camera sales-and-distribution agreements disappeared. Bank One's private equity unit bought up Polaroid's assets in 2002 for $265 million, and new management pursued a strategy of licensing the Polaroid brand for use on products including digital cameras, televisions, and digital video disc players. In 2005 the company was sold again to Petters Group Worldwide, a turnaround specialist, for $426 million. A year later it halted production of instant cameras, then announced its intention to exit the film business and close plants in the United States, Mexico, and the Netherlands, focusing instead on digital photography and flat-panel televisions. But Polaroid was forced to file bankruptcy again in 2008, amid fraud charges leveled against Petters. A joint venture of private-equity firms Hilco Consumer Capital and Gordon Brothers Group bought Polaroid in April 2009 for $88 million, stating its intention to pursue global licensing deals using the Polaroid brand.

Video Rentals. The innovation of Netflix's DVD subscription service and, later, of the video kiosk business chipped away at the conventional in-store video rental business model over the course of the decade. Launched

University of Chicago economics professor Steven Levitt poses with his book, coauthored with Stephen Dubner, *Freakonomics: A Rogue Economist Explores the Hidden Side of Everything*, in Chicago, 2005 (AP Photo/Charles Rex Arbogast).

Known as the dismal science, economics took on an uncharacteristically playful tone with the publication of *Freakonomics: A Rogue Economist Explores the Hidden Side of Everything* in 2005. The book, by economist Steven Levitt and journalist Stephen Dubner, explored the laws of supply and demand through counterintuitive case studies involving cheating sumo wrestlers, penny-pinching drug dealers, and trends in children's names. It was a sensation, selling more than 4 million copies over five years, and carving out a mass audience for topics typically reserved for graduate seminars.

One chapter probed the ways economic incentives can go horribly awry. Parsing the statistics of sumo-wrestling tournaments, Levitt and Dubner showed the lure of reaching the elite sumo divisions—which involves a vast increase in income—led to cheating rather than intensifying competition. Wrestlers facing elimination from the upper echelon were winning at inexplicably high rates when facing opponents whose elite status was safely assured, while the near-elimination wrestlers almost always lost the subsequent match with the same opponent. The clear implication to Levitt and Dubner was that the wrestlers had fixed the matches, each agreeing to lay down once in order to win easily in the match that was more important to him. Indeed, *Freakonomics* noted, the suspicions were confirmed by two former wrestlers who came forward with allegations of match-rigging, only to die under suspicious circumstances soon after.

The authors were in hot demand as speakers and writers; they signed on to appear regularly on ABC news programming, hosted a *New York Times* blog, and collaborated on a sequel, *SuperFreakonomics*, published in 2009. Copycat books followed in their wake—*The Undercover Economist, Discover Your Inner Economist*, and *Naked Economics*. "People are pitching everything from 'The Medical Freakonomics' to 'The Freakonomics of Parenting,'" said Suzanne Gluck, the authors' agent, in a *Fast Company* interview. "They're using freakonomics as a code word for unconventional wisdom."

Sources: Lucas Conley, "Year of the Economist," *Fast Company* (1 November 2005);

Noam Scheiber, "Superfreaky," *New Republic* (18 April 2007).

ing's market share would surge to 30 percent by the end of 2010. Again playing catch-up, Blockbuster began in 2009 rolling out more than five hundred of its own kiosks, dubbed Blockbuster Express. Redbox emerged not only as a threat to other video rental companies but also to Hollywood studios, which feared that its growth would undermine their DVD sales. Warner Bros., Universal, and 20th Century-Fox declared in 2009 that they would sell no DVDs to Redbox until at least twenty-eight days after their arrival in stores, prompting Redbox to file suit claiming antitrust violations.

Sources:
Matt Andrejczak and Steve Gelsi, "Blockbuster says it may file for bankruptcy; shares plunge," *MarketWatch*, 17 March 2010;

Tim Arango, "How the AOL-Time Warner Merger Went So Wrong," *New York Times*, 10 January 2010;

Ken Auletta, *Googled: The End of the World As We Know It* (New York: Penguin, 2009);

Brooks Barnes, "Movie Studios See a Threat in Growth of Redbox," *New York Times*, 6 September 2009;

Claudia Deutsch, "Deep in Debt Since 1988, Polaroid Files for Bankruptcy," *New York Times*, 13 October 2001;

Jonathan D. Glater, "The S.E.C. Is Investigating Fee Practices at Value Line," *New York Times*, 2 August 2008;

Erik Larson and Michael Bathon, "Polaroid in Bankruptcy Again, Cites Petters Charges," *Bloomberg News*, 19 December 2009;

"Why AOL Time Warner failed to change the world," *BBC* (9 December 2009).

RECKONINGS FOR RETAIL GIANTS

Wal-Mart. Wal-Mart emerged as the dominant force in retailing early in the decade. It proceeded to tighten its grip, despite challenges from organized labor and stiff competition from retail rivals, by replicating the proven formula of leveraging its unparalleled shelf space to drive supplier prices ever lower. In 2001 Wal-Mart's grocery sales hit $56 billion, making it the nation's biggest food retailer. The next year, its $219 billion in revenue elevated it to the position of America's largest company, as measured by *Fortune* magazine's Fortune 500 list, making it the first service company to top the list. Profit and revenue rose for the rest of the decade, and Wal-Mart maintained the number one spot every remaining year except 2006 and 2009, when Exxon Mobil overtook it.

Labor Woes. With such rapid growth came mounting opposition. Wal-Mart's chief antagonist throughout the decade was organized labor, whose attempts to organize Wal-Mart workers had been stymied time and time again. Labor resorted to lobbying efforts and public-relations campaigns, alleging Wal-Mart lowballed on wages and benefits, discriminated against women, and ran roughshod over small businesses and the environment. The critics scored a major victory in 2006, with passage in Maryland of legislation requiring Wal-Mart to spend more on employee health care, prompting the introduction of similar legislation in nearly two dozen states. Wal-Mart's relentless store expansions also suffered setbacks, as civic organizations, small businesses, and Wal-Mart's own corporate rivals mustered opposition campaigns warning that it would depress wages, bankrupt small businesses, and wreak havoc on traffic systems. Wal-Mart's biggest defeat came in 2004, when it proposed to build a Supercenter in Inglewood, California, outside Los Angeles. After the L.A. City Coun-

An Amish man unhooks his horse from a special buggy-only parking area outside the newly opened Wal-Mart store in Middlefield, Ohio, on 3 June 2005 (AP Photo/Amy Sancetta).

cil passed an ordinance blocking the development, Wal-Mart succeeded in having a referendum held on the plans, which it lost—garnering just 40 percent of the vote despite spending nearly $1 million in election advertising. Sullying the Wal-Mart image further, a 2004 federal court ruling certified a class action on behalf of 1.6 million current and former Wal-Mart employees alleging that female workers had been discriminated against through lower wages and fewer promotions than men. The ruling was upheld on appeal in 2007, but in 2009 Wal-Mart prevailed on a federal appeals court to rehear the case. By then, however, the size of the would-be class had swollen to 2 million. In 2008, meanwhile, Wal-Mart agreed to pay up to $640 million to settle sixty-three federal and state class actions claiming it had shortchanged hourly workers and forced them to work through breaks.

Slowdown and Recovery. Wal-Mart's growth appeared to be plateauing in 2006, as profit dipped to under 1 percent following a 13.4 percent jump in 2005. A 2007 *Wall Street Journal* article titled "Wal-Mart Era Wanes Amid Big Shifts in Retail" cited evidence that Wal-Mart's down-market appeal was withering in the face of rivals' emphasis on quality, service, and corporate responsibility as well as a burgeoning online marketplace. The slowdown instigated radical responses from Wal-Mart in 2006, including the discounting of all generic drugs to $4 per prescription, plans to remodel nearly half of its stores, creation of more-fashionable clothing lines, investments in its organic food line sufficient to make Wal-Mart the country's biggest seller of organic milk, and vast increase in its marketing bud-

get—funding among other things the hiring of civil-rights advocate and former United Nations ambassador Andrew Young to promote Wal-Mart's good deeds. Just as it seemed Wal-Mart's low-cost doctrine might have grown outdated, however, the recession hit. Suddenly more cost-conscious shoppers flocked back to Wal-Mart, reversing its decline in market share and restoring annual profit to double digits.

Sources:

Michale Barbaro, "Wal-Mart Tries to Find Its Customer," *New York Times,* 22 February 2006;

Larry Copeland, "Wal-Mart's Hired Advocate Takes Flak," *USA Today,* 15 March 2006;

Gary McWilliams, "Wal-Mart Era Wanes Amid Big Shifts in Retail," *Wall Street Journal,* 3 October 2007;

Stephanie Rosenbloom, "Wal-Mart Outpaces a Weak Economy," *New York Times,* 18 February 2009;

Ann Zimmerman, "Rival Chains Secretly Fund Opposition to Wal-Mart," *Wall Street Journal,* 7 June 2010.

SCARE OVER CHINESE EXPORTS

Tainted Pet Food. A string of product recalls from Chinese manufacturers pulled millions of toys, toothpaste tubes, and vast quantities of pet food and seafood from U.S. shelves in 2007, putting U.S. regulators on high alert and Chinese authorities on the defensive. Canada's Menu Foods Inc., a supplier to name-brand dog- and cat-food makers including Iams and Eukanuba, initiated the pet-food recalls in March, informing the U.S. Food and Drug Administration (FDA) that it was recalling food made with wheat gluten found to be tainted by the industrial chemical melamine. Chemical company officials in China told *The New York Times* that makers of animal feed had added

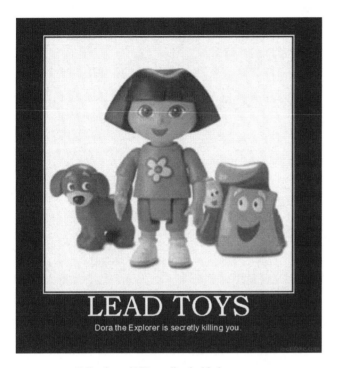

Following a 2007 recall a darkly humorous "de-motivational" Internet poster highlights the hidden dangers of lead-based paint used in toys produced in China (<www.motifake.com>).

melamine to their products for years in order to give the appearance of higher protein content. Within two weeks of the recall, the Veterinary Information Network reported that more than one hundred pets had died from kidney failure believed to have been caused by melamine ingestion. The recall then widened to include 5,300 pet-food products, packaged into tens of millions of containers of wet dog and cat food. The FDA also issued an import alert authorizing border inspections of Chinese products ranging from noodles to breakfast bars. By July, Chinese officials had outlawed melamine in animal feed and closed the two manufacturers found to have adulterated the wheat gluten. In 2008 Menu Foods and other manufacturers and suppliers agreed to a $24 million settlement resolving claims by pet owners.

FDA Response. On edge from the pet-food scare, the FDA responded in May to growing reports of tainted Chinese-made toothpaste in Central America by issuing a ban on Chinese toothpaste imports until they could be tested. Soon thereafter, Colgate-Palmolive announced it had found contaminated toothpaste falsely sold under its name in discount stores in New York, New Jersey, Pennsylvania, and Maryland. The toothpaste, labeled as having been made in South Africa, contained the poisonous solvent diethylene glycol (DEG), the same chemical contaminating the Chinese-made toothpaste in Central America. The FDA quickly issued recalls of more than two dozen off-brand Chinese-made toothpaste products found also to contain DEG. Approximately 900,000 tubes had been distributed to mental hospitals and hospitals for the general population, prisons, and juvenile detention centers in

Georgia, Florida, and the Carolinas. Chinese regulators contended that DEG in small amounts was safe in toothpaste because it was meant to be spat out, but in July the Chinese government bowed to international criticism, banning the ingredient in toothpaste.

Toys. The heightened scrutiny of Chinese products and components next began turning up toxic ingredients in toys. Illinois toymaker RC2 in April detected lead paint on the Thomas & Friends wooden train sets supplied from China, prompting a recall of 1.5 million toys in June. Leading toy manufacturer Mattel boasted in a July *New York Times* article that "we're doing more than anyone else" to monitor the Chinese supply chain, but it too was forced the next month to issue a recall of nearly 1 million of its own toys that were feared to contain hazardous levels of lead paint, including products featuring popular characters Elmo and Dora the Explorer. Less than two weeks later, Mattel began expanding the recalls, eventually reaching 21 million products thought to be coated with lead paint or to contain magnets presenting a swallowing hazard. The owner of the Chinese plant blamed for the Mattel lead paint applications committed suicide on 14 August, and a month later U.S. and Chinese regulators pledged to reform exporting procedures to protect against more lead paint hazards. Next, in a stunning admission, Mattel formally apologized to Chinese regulators, acknowledging that most of the health threats—in particular, ones involving potentially dangerous magnets—resulted from Mattel's own design flaws and that some of its recalls were not justified. But the wave of recalls from other quarters continued. One of the larger recalls involved Aqua Dots, or bead toys made in China and distributed by Canada-based Spin Master; the toys were found to contain the so-called date-rape drug, gamma-hydroxybutyrate. Some children swallowing the dots vomited or became comatose temporarily. About 4.2 million of the toys were recalled. Chinese officials suspended the license of the factory responsible and solicited U.S. help in methods for detecting the presence of the ingredient in other products.

Sources:
David Barboza and Alexei Barrionuevo, "Filler in animal feed is open secret in China," *New York Times*, 29 April 2007;

Walt Bogdanich, "China Prohibits Poisonous Industrial Solvent in Toothpaste," *New York Times*, 12 July 2007;

Bogdanich, "Wider Sale Is Seen for Toothpaste Tainted in China," *New York Times*, 28 June 2007;

Keith Bradsher, "China Confirms Poison Was on Toy Beads," *New York Times*, 11 November 2007;

Nicholas Casey, "Mattel Issues Third Major Recall," *Wall Street Journal*, 5 September 2007;

Casey, "Mattel Toys to Be Pulled Amid Lead Fears," *Wall Street Journal*, 2 August 2007;

"Menu Foods Announces $24 Mln Settlement Fund," *Reuters* (30 May 2008);

"104 Deaths Reported in Pet Food Recall," *Associated Press* (28 March 2007);

Louise Story and Barboza, "Toymaking in China, Mattel's Way," *New York Times*, 26 July 2007;

Story, "Toy-Train Maker Discusses Lead Paint Problem," *New York Times*, 26 July 2007;

Elizabeth Weise and Julie Schmit, "FDA Limits Chinese Food Additive Imports," *USA Today*, 1 May 2007;

Nicholas Zamiska and Casey, "Mattel Does Damage Control after New Recall," *Wall Street Journal*, 15 August 2007;

Zamiska and Casey, "Owner of Chinese Toy Factory Kills Himself," *Wall Street Journal*, 14 August 2007.

TOO BIG TO FAIL

The Banking Sector. Low interest rates designed to stimulate the economy in 2001 and vast inflows of foreign investment intensified competition for consumer-loan business, quickly fueling astronomical and ultimately unsustainable U.S. debt levels. Mass defaults on "subprime" loans, or those extended to borrowers with poor credit, began occurring in early 2007, radiating rapidly along with failures in other lending sectors. Exposure to the bad loans gradually deepened on Wall Street, whose biggest banks throughout the credit boom had marketed as well as invested themselves in complex loan portfolios. Starting in the fall of 2007, massive write-downs linked to subprime losses from the likes of Citigroup, Merrill Lynch, and Morgan Stanley cast a pall over credit markets, and lending began to contract. By March 2008, Bear Stearns faced bankruptcy, with payments on its mounting debt coming due and no one willing to lend to it. One after another, the big banks reached similar crisis points, their sobering disclosures of financial distress sowing panic and threatening the entire financial system with a domino-like collapse. Following the catastrophic bankruptcy of Lehman in mid September 2008, the nation's biggest filing ever, the Bush White House intervened in unprecedented bailouts and nationalizations. The rescues culminated, but by no means ended, with Congress's passage in October of legislation allocating $700 billion to the bailouts.

Bear Stearns. The first clouds on the horizon appeared in the second half of 2007, as big banks went public with punishing subprime-related losses—Bear Stearns's amounting to $3.2 billion, Merrill Lynch's $8.4 billion, Morgan Stanley's $9.4 billion, and Citigroup's estimated at $8 billion to $11 billion. The chief executives of both Merrill Lynch and Citigroup subsequently stepped down. Mounting losses at Bear Stearns led it to the government's doorstep, seeking the life-sustaining credit that no other banks would extend. The Federal Reserve agreed to make a $25

INVESTMENT BANK CLOSURES

The nation's five stand-alone investment banks, in spite of the buttoned-down image they long cultivated, were among the most reckless investors in high-risk subprime mortgages. In the aftermath of the economic downturn, the Wall Street neighborhood emerged with fewer marquee names, and, technically speaking, no more investment banks.

Bear Stearns: Facing bankruptcy, Bear Stearns was bought by J.P. Morgan Chase on 18 March 2008 for $2 per share, less than one-tenth Bear Stearnes's market price on the prior trading day, in a deal orchestrated and financed by the Federal Reserve. A week later the price was increased to $10, and the deal closed that month.

Lehman Brothers: Lehman filed for Chapter 11 bankruptcy protection on 15 September 2008, when it became clear that neither fellow banks nor the federal government would come to its rescue. The filing declared bank debt of $613 billion, bond debt of $155 billion, and assets worth $639 billion. Britain's Barclays Bank secured court approval the next day to buy Lehman's stronger assets for $1.75 billion. Japan's Nomura Holdings bought Lehman's Asia division and portions of its European operations. One of the strongest Lehman units, its Neuberger Berman asset management subsidiary, was sold to firm management.

Merrill Lynch: Bank of America reached terms to buy Merrill Lynch on 14 September 2008, rescuing it from certain bankruptcy. The price, roughly $50 billion, represented a 70 percent premium over Merrill's most recent trading price, despite its troubled balance sheet. The deal closed on 1 January 2009, and subsequent revelations of Merrill's problematic finances prompted the Treasury and Federal Reserve to pledge a $20 billion investment shielding Bank of America from Merrill's toxic assets.

Goldman Sachs: Goldman Sachs remained profitable during the subprime crisis, thanks to astute short-selling of the mortgage securities by its structured products group. Yet, it did need to take write-downs of just under $5 billion for ill-timed investments elsewhere, and revenue from investment banking slowed. On 22 September 2008, it agreed to surrender its investment bank designation to become instead a commercial bank, submitting to tighter regulation while gaining access to emergency Federal Reserve funds.

Morgan Stanley: Morgan Stanley also remained profitable, but for reasons remaining unclear, its stock price sank 44 percent during September 2008, raising the prospect of another government-financed sale. It reversed the plunge, however, by converting to a commercial bank with Goldman Sachs on 22 September and then striking a deal on 29 September to sell a 21 percent stake to Japan's Mitsubishi UFJ Financial Group. The following year, it bought the Smith Barney brokerage firm from Citigroup.

Sources: Steven M. Davidoff, "There Will Be Blood," *New York Times*, 15 September 2008;

John Dunbar and David Donald, "The Roots of the Financial Crisis: Who is to Blame?" *publicintegrity.org;*

"Shattering Glass-Steagall," *Newsweek* (15 September 2008).

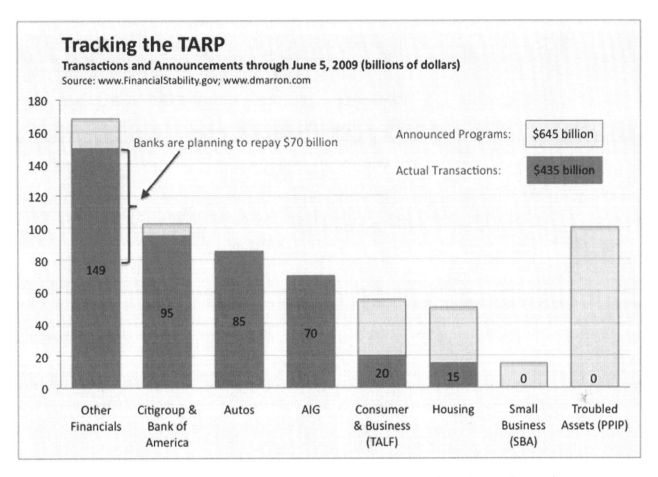

Tracking the TARP
Transactions and Announcements through June 5, 2009 (billions of dollars)
Source: www.FinancialStability.gov; www.dmarron.com

Banks are planning to repay $70 billion

Announced Programs: **$645 billion**

Actual Transactions: **$435 billion**

Other Financials	149
Citigroup & Bank of America	95
Autos	85
AIG	70
Consumer & Business (TALF)	20
Housing	15
Small Business (SBA)	0
Troubled Assets (PPIP)	0

Chart detailing federal payouts through the Troubled Asset Relief Program (<www.istockanalyst.com>)

billion loan in March but then quickly retracted the offer and instead brokered a deal with J.P. Morgan Chase involving the Fed's lending $30 billion to the company, which would then buy Bear Stearns at $2 per share, or about 7 percent less than its most recent trading price. At the same time the Federal Reserve took the unprecedented step of changing policy to allow securities dealers to borrow from it on the same terms as banks.

Two Weeks in September. Mounting subprime losses at the government-sponsored lending companies Fannie Mae and Freddie Mac similarly prompted the Fed and the Treasury to request congressional approval in July to take equity stakes aimed at buoying the companies. Less than two months later on 7 September, as their losses multiplied, the Treasury and the Fed assumed control, buying $1.4 trillion in mortgage-backed securities from them. As the Fannie/Freddie takeover was being hashed out, the Treasury and the Fed were simultaneously attempting to broker a takeover of Lehman Brothers, which teetered on the brink of bankruptcy after a year of disclosing subprime-related losses and an accompanying plunge in its stock value. At a 12 September meeting with Wall Street's biggest banks, Treasury secretary Henry Paulson and New York Federal Reserve Bank chief Timothy Geithner urged the banks to muster a

Lehman takeover or risk the consequences of its bankruptcy. Bank of America and Barclays were the most interested, but both refused unless the federal government agreed to sweeten the deal, as it had in the Bear Stearns's takeover. Paulson and Geithner would not budge, citing their fear of setting the expectation of unlimited bailouts, and Lehman was left with no recourse but to file for Chapter 11 protection, declaring bank debt of $613 billion, bond debt of $155 billion, and assets worth $639 billion. The next day, Barclays won court approval to buy Lehman's stronger assets for $1.75 billion.

Continued Fallout. The first victim of the market anxiety sowed by Lehman's failure was Merrill Lynch. Burdened by its subprime losses, it had lost more than $19 billion in the fiscal year ending July 2008. The once-unthinkable prospect of bankruptcy was suddenly very real, and lenders turned their backs. Simultaneous to the Lehman negotiations, Bank of America had begun confidential negotiations to buy the troubled firm, and on 14 September the two came to terms: Bank of America paid about $50 billion, a 70 percent premium over Merrill's most recent trading price. Subsequent revelations of Merrill's deteriorated finances prompted the Treasury and the Fed to pledge a $20 bil-

Jamie Dimon, chairman and chief executive officer of J.P. Morgan Chase, left, and Alan Schwartz, Bear Stearns president and chief executive officer, testify on Capitol Hill in Washington, D.C. on 3 April 2008, before the Senate Banking Committee hearing on the federal bailout of Bear Stearns (AP Photo/Lawrence Jackson).

lion investment in Bank of America to shield it from Merrill's toxic assets. Creditors were no more interested in lending to insurance giant American International Group (AIG), whose mortgage investments had contributed to more than $13 billion in losses through the first six months of the year and threatened far greater losses ahead. On 16 September, credit downgrades left it in near collapse, since they allowed counterparties to withdraw capital from their AIG contracts. The counterparties did indeed demand more than $10 billion in collateral be returned, leaving AIG effectively broke. Fed-convened talks with J.P. Morgan Chase, Goldman Sachs, and Morgan Stanley failed to produce a rescue, prompting the Fed to create an $85 billion lending facility in exchange for an 80 percent ownership stake. By the end of October, the facility would be enlarged to $144 billion as AIG losses mounted. The ever-widening bailouts convinced Fed chairman Ben Bernanke and Treasury secretary Paulson of the need to involve Congress, and on 17 September they formally requested lawmakers enact bailout legislation. A bill modeled on the Treasury's proposal, the Emergency Economic Stabilization Act, was approved by both chambers and signed by President Bush by 3 October. Its centerpiece was the Troubled Asset Relief Program, commonly

called TARP, authorizing the Treasury to spend up to $700 billion to buy troubled assets from financial companies, which would then issue equity stakes in return, with the overall aim of bolstering the financial system. Paulson subsequently interpreted the legislation as allowing Treasury to buy shares in the biggest banks instead of buying toxic assets, effectively nationalizing the banks. President Bush then authorized use of the funds for bailouts for struggling auto companies. When the Obama administration took over in January 2009, new Treasury secretary Timothy Geithner initiated a program to allocate $500 billion in TARP funds toward subsidies encouraging private banks to buy the toxic assets.

Washington Mutual and Wachovia. Despite the pledges of government support, depositors and investors in two other subprime-burdened depository banks, Washington Mutual (WaMu) and Wachovia, ran for cover. In mid September 2008, months of layoffs and write-downs at WaMu had whittled its share price down more than 90 percent over twelve months. A run on the bank began 15 September, the day of Lehman's bankruptcy filing, with customers yanking $16.7 billion in deposits, about 9 percent of overall deposits, over the next ten days. The Fed and the Treasury again tried, unsuccessfully, to orchestrate a third-party takeover. Regulators then seized the thrift, placing it into receivership, and the Federal Deposit Insurance Corp. proceeded to hold a secret auction. J.P. Morgan Chase emerged the winning bidder, agreeing to pay $1.9 billion and absorb $31 billion in bad loans (which the FDIC would otherwise have been responsible for) in exchange for WaMu's loan portfolio and banking operations. The government's WaMu takeover unwittingly touched off a panic at Wachovia the same day, as investors bid its share price down 27 percent and larger depositors pulled $5 billion in deposits. Federal regulators began pressuring bank officials to seek out buyers. After FDIC-brokered sale talks came up empty, the FDIC resolved to auction off Wachovia's assets before the bank had time to collapse, reaching a $2.16 billion deal on 29 September with Citigroup. Wachovia offi-cials, however, entered into talks with Wells Fargo and on 3 October announced a $15.4 billion deal. Within a week Citigroup had backed down.

Sources:
John Brinsley and Robert Schmidt, "Paulson Shifts Focus of Rescue to Consumer Lending," *Bloomberg News* (12 November 2008);

Eric Dash, "U.S. Gives Banks Urgent Warning to Solve Crisis," *New York Times*, 12 September 2008;

Matthew Karnitsching, Carrick Mollenkamp, and Dan Fitzpatrick, "Bank of America to Buy Merrill," *Wall Street Journal*, 15 September 2008;

Robin Sidel, David Enrich, and Dan Fitzpatrick, "WaMu Is Seized, Sold Off to J.P. Morgan, in Largest Failure in U.S. Banking History," *Wall Street Journal*, 26 September 2008;

Andrew Ross Sorkin, *Too Big to Fail: The Inside Story of How Wall Street and Washington Fought to Save the Financial System from Crisis—and Themselves* (New York: Penguin, 2009);

Louise Story and Jo Becker, "Bank Chief Tells of U.S. Pressure to Buy Merrill Lynch," *New York Times*, 11 June 2009;

Lorraine Woellert and John Gittelsohn, "Fannie-Freddie Fix at $160 Billion with $1 Trillion Worst Case," *Bloomberg News* (14 June 2010).

HEADLINE MAKERS

BEN BERNANKE

1953–

FEDERAL RESERVE CHAIRMAN

Background. Ben Bernanke was born in Augusta, Georgia, on 13 December 1953 and grew up in Dillon, South Carolina. He studied economics at Harvard University, earned his doctorate at Massachusetts Institute of Technology, and taught at the Stanford Graduate School of Business before joining the economics department at Princeton University. A 1999 paper he gave for the Federal Reserve Bank of Kansas City advocating a hands-off Fed in the mold of chairman Alan Greenspan drew not only harsh condemnation from liberal economists but also the endorsement of Greenspan himself. Three years later, Bernanke was chosen to become a Federal Reserve governor and, three years after that, he was tapped as President Bush's top economic adviser. Eight months later, in December 2005, Bush nominated Bernanke to succeed Greenspan as Fed chairman.

Filling Greenspan's Shoes. As a Fed governor and White House adviser, he remained the staunchest of Greenspan's allies, fully endorsing the central bank's program of cheap money and minimal financial regulation. There would be no change under a Bernanke-led Fed, he told his Senate confirmation panel. In fact, Bernanke presided over the most radical interventions in the central bank's seventy-year history. The Fed policies he inherited and promised to uphold—chief among them the easy availability of credit and light financial regulation—had fueled a staggering accumulation of consumer and commercial debt. A wave of mortgage defaults was poised to break in the summer of 2007, causing credit markets to seize up and unleashing a series of catastrophic financial failures. Yet, Bernanke never sensed the gathering storm, telling Congress in February that "we don't see it [the housing downturn] as being a broad financial concern or a major factor in assessing the course of the economy." By August, with contrary evidence mounting, Bernanke's Fed moved to stimulate lending by lowering the discount rate half a point, to 5.75 percent. Then he and Fed colleagues formulated a longer-term strategy if credit markets remained clogged, starting with rate cuts and ending with the Fed's commitment to become lender of last resort in the absence of private-market lending. That was the role Bernanke and the Fed assumed in short order.

Lessons of the Depression. In fashioning his response to the evolving crisis, Bernanke drew on his academic past—but not the studies that won Greenspan's approval—espousing a passive central bank deferring to the market's wisdom. Bernanke was also a student of the Great Depression. During his doctoral studies at MIT, his research articulated the impact of a "financial accelerator" effect, or the tendency during downturns like the Depression for the slowdown to poison consumer perceptions, which in turn worsen actual economic conditions. In 2007 Bernanke discerned close parallels to the Depression's financial accelerator. The primary lesson of the Depression, in his reading, was to avoid government inaction; the government needed instead to respond with overwhelming stimulus to forestall a deepening crisis of confidence. "People saw the Depression as a necessary thing, a chance to squeeze out the excesses, get back to Puritan morality," he said. "That just made things worse."

Crisis Measures. The first test of Bernanke's approach came in March 2008, when he authorized the Fed to finance a private takeover of a near-bankrupt Bear Stearns. Having lowered interest rates as much as possible, to no noticeable effect, Bernanke brazenly opened the Fed's bank-lending window to securities dealers. Next, he acceded to a series of unprecedented bailouts, taking over government-sponsored lending companies Fannie Mae and Freddie Mac, extending $20 billion in federal support for Bank of America's takeover of Merrill Lynch and blessing an $85 billion credit facility for American International Group that would balloon past $140 billion. The Fed ultimately handed out more than $1.6 trillion in loans and committed to buying more than $1.7 trillion of troubled assets.

Contentious in Congress. In breaking new ground, however, Bernanke also encountered new critics—from the Left and the Right, attacking Bernanke's interventions as both excessive and insufficient. "When I picked up my newspaper yesterday, I thought I woke up in France," Senator Jim Bunning (R-Ky.) lectured Bernanke in congressional testimony. "But no," he continued, "it turned out it was socialism here in the United States of America." Christine Lagarde, the French finance minister, meanwhile censured Bernanke for failing to come to the rescue of Lehman Brothers, calling its bankruptcy a "horrendous" error imperiling the global financial system. When renominated by President Barack Obama to his second Fed term, Bernanke won reconfirmation by the narrowest margin for any Fed chairman nominee. "Considerable economic devastation occurred as a result of Chairman Bernanke's loose monetary policy and weak regulatory oversight," said Senator Richard Shelby (R-Ala.) in urging that Bernanke's renomination be denied. Supporters, like Senator Judd Gregg (R-N.H.), cited the difficult choices that may have averted an even deeper crisis. "He basically allowed the Fed to become the lender of the nation," Gregg said. "The way he did it was extraordinary in its creativity, and the results were that the country's financial system did not collapse."

Sources:
John Cassidy, "Anatomy of a Meltdown: Ben Bernanke and the Financial Crisis," *New Yorker* (1 December 2008);

Sewell Chan, "Fed Chief Wins A Second Term Despite Critics," *New York Times*, 29 January 2010;

Michael Grunwald, "Person of the Year 2009," *Time* (16 December 2009).

STEVE JOBS

1955–

TECHNOLOGY TRAILBLAZER

Early Success. Steve Jobs was born on 24 February 1955 to University of Wisconsin graduate students who gave him up for adoption. He grew up in Mountain View, California. His adoptive father was a machinist for Spectra-Physics, a laser manufacturer, and his mother was an accountant. While still in high school, Jobs began attending lectures at the nearby Hewlett-Packard (HP) headquarters in Palo Alto, California, and was hired at the company as a summer intern. There, he met Stephen Wozniak, a recent university dropout and engineering whiz who also worked for HP. After Jobs himself dropped out of college in 1973 and took a job with videogame maker Atari, he made contact again with Wozniak, and the two began collaborating on Atari games before deciding to work together on designing a computer. They raised $1,300 between them, Jobs by selling his Volkswagen microbus and Wozniak by pawning his HP scientific calculator. Their design for the prototype, honed by Jobs's penchant for simplifying technology, resurrected Xerox's graphical user interface innovation, which allowed users to enter commands through visual prompts (aided by external input devices such as mouses) rather than solely by typing code. The two, together with financial backer A. C. "Mike" Markkula, formed Apple Corp. in 1977 upon filling their first big sale, fifty computers for $500 apiece, to a Mountain View computer store.

Apple's Rise and Fall. Apple next introduced the Apple II model in 1977 for the nascent personal-computer market. Industry leader IBM had spurned the niche, but Apple II sales exploded, and by 1981 Apple had become a $300 million corporation, ranking as the fastest-growing company in U.S. history. The Macintosh, introduced in January 1984, sold 72,000 units in one hundred days. Sales soon stumbled, however, amid an industrywide slowdown. Jobs had persuaded PepsiCo president John Sculley to join Apple as chief executive in 1983, but the relationship between the two became strained as Apple's growth began to slow. Employees across the company, meanwhile, increasingly complained about Jobs's propensity for angry outbursts. In May 1985, with Jobs and Sculley each lobbying for the other's removal, Apple's board sided with Sculley, and Jobs was fired. He formed NeXT Computer, a maker of high-end personal computers, but sales sputtered because of the models' steep cost and eventually the company slimmed down to focus on operating systems. In 1986 Jobs bought a foundering computer graphics maker, Graphics Group, later renamed Pixar, for $10 million. Pixar switched gears, partnering with Disney to make computer-animated feature films that rank among the studio's biggest box-office hits, including *Finding Nemo*, *The Incredibles*, and *Toy Story*. Meanwhile, Apple had never recovered, and in 1996 it bought Jobs's NeXT, with Jobs as an adviser. The next year, the board ousted Apple's chief and selected Jobs to head the company.

The iPod and iPhone. Jobs set about revamping Apple's product line, reorienting the company with his design aesthetics and acute sense of customer expectations, and soon the momentum had returned. The iMac, released in 1998, sold nearly 800,000 units in its first five months. Simultaneously Apple acquisitions added a suite of digital production software for future rollouts. Dust from the dot-com stock crash was still settling as Apple engineers began work on the iPod mobile digital audio player. Introduced in 2001, it sold more than 220 million units over the next eight years. The launch in 2003 of Apple's iTunes Store made singles available for iPod download at a cost of 99 cents, tapping into music sales at the expense of established distributors like Sony. From 2003 sales of digital music soared from less than 1 percent of all music sales to 15 percent in 2007; album sales fell 38 percent in the same time frame. Shortly after the iPod's release, Jobs turned his attention to developing a similarly novel mobile phone that could combine the functions of phones, handhelds, and music players. After a dead-end partnership with phone maker Motorola Inc., Apple designed a model itself, the iPhone, which it released in 2007. The user-friendly design proved spectacularly popular, and by the end of the decade more than 17 million had been sold. That response altered the dynamic in phone design, propelling the development of web-based applications. At the end of the decade, Apple derived twice as much revenue from handheld devices and music as it did from computer sales. It was also poised to overtake Microsoft Corp. as the biggest technology company as measured by market capitalization.

Health Scare. As Jobs revived Apple, his own health was deteriorating. In August 2004, he disclosed that he had recently been treated for a rare form of pancreatic cancer called islet-cell neuroendocrine tumor. Though Jobs maintained he was cancer-free, two years later he had become noticeably thin, sowing suspicions he had suffered a relapse. Apple's share price zigzagged as speculation about its rainmaker's health intensified. A few weeks into 2009, Jobs announced he suffered from a hormone imbalance that was "relatively simple and straightforward" to treat, but soon thereafter he revealed the ailment was more serious than first thought and that he would take a leave from the company. In fact, Jobs was stricken with end-stage liver disease and had placed himself on a transplant waiting list. He received a transplant in April, and in June was back at work on a half-week schedule.

Sources:

Ken Auletta, *Googled: The End of the World as We Know It* (New York: Penguin, 2009);

Miguel Helft and Ashlee Vance, "Apple Passes Microsoft as No. 1 in Tech," *New York Times*, 26 May 2010;

Andy Hertzfeld, "The Original Macintosh," *folklore.org* (8 July 2010);

Yukari Iwatani Kane and Joann S. Lublin, "Jobs Had Liver Transplant," *Wall Street Journal*, 20 June 2009;

Erica Ogg, "Apple's Steve Jobs back at work," *cnet.com* (8 July 2010);

Fred Vogelstein, "The Untold Story: How the iPhone Blew Up the Wireless Industry," *Wired* (9 January 2008).

BERNARD MADOFF

1938–

PONZI SCHEMER

Meteoric Rise. Bernard Madoff was born on 29 April 1938 in Queens, New York, the son of a plumber who became a stockbroker. He graduated from Hofstra College in 1960 and briefly attended Brooklyn Law School before founding Bernard L. Madoff Investment Securities LLC in New York, a penny-stock trading firm, which he capitalized with $5,000 of his own savings. The firm began attracting clients through referrals from Madoff's father-in-law, then took off in the 1970s, after regulatory changes allowed smaller-market makers like Madoff's to trade more expensive stocks. Madoff lured away orders from the New York Stock Exchange by paying clients a few pennies for every share they agreed to trade through him. This strategy, though legal and common among penny-stock traders, was frowned upon at the larger exchanges for its resemblance to a kickback. Madoff's firm claimed still more trading market share in the 1980s and 1990s by pioneering electronic trading systems that became precursors to the NASDAQ electronic market. Simultaneously, Madoff Securities discreetly operated as an investment adviser, accepting client assets on an invitation-only basis. It delivered steady investment returns in all markets, typically about 10 percent annually, a success Madoff attributed to his skill in trading futures and options to even out any losses on stock investments. Madoff recruited many of his clients among the affluent circles of Long Island and Palm Beach, Florida, where he had homes. His reputation as a powerful trader, for unsurpassed investment gains, and the air of exclusivity helped rake in billions in assets from hedge funds, endowments, and well-heeled individuals.

Suspicions Grow. The returns stupefied Madoff's competitors. One, Boston's Rampart Investment Management Co., tasked its derivatives expert, Harry Markopoulos, with cracking Madoff's code, but Markopoulos found it impossible. He met with the Securities and Exchange Commission (SEC) in 2001 to air suspicions about Madoff's investments, following up with a twenty-one-page analysis asserting, "Madoff Securities is the world's largest Ponzi scheme." The same month of Markopoulos's SEC meeting, two trade publications published articles suggesting Madoff could achieve his returns only by "front-running," or fraudulently trading ahead of the orders that his market-making business processed. The allegations were difficult to prove because Madoff ran his investments with minimal oversight. He did not have to register with the SEC for regular inspections. Similar investment houses typically contracted with outside broker-dealers to process their trades, exposing their holdings to new sets of eyes, but Madoff's processing arm handled his investment trades. Madoff even routinely denied his own investors access to his investment records. Far from seeming suspicious to the SEC, Madoff in fact was held in high esteem. For decades he had cultivated close ties with regulators and had served for years in a regulatory role as chairman of the board of directors of the National Association of Securities Dealers, a self-regulatory industry organization. Arthur Levitt, the SEC chairman from 1993 to early 2001, acknowledged in a *New York Times* interview that even he occasionally consulted Madoff for advice about how the market worked. Finally, in 2004, the SEC did launch an investigation of the accusations; it found no evidence of fraud. Another probe the next year concluded that Madoff had violated SEC rules requiring investment advisers with more than fourteen clients to register with the commission. But the investigators again turned up no evidence of fraud, and Madoff agreed to register with the SEC. Two years later, another SEC probe centered on allegations of a Madoff Ponzi scheme; it too came up empty.

Exposed. In truth, Madoff had been fabricating trades and concealing investment losses since the 1970s. His enigmatic investment process consisted simply of paying out returns to one investor from the principal of another. Investment assets were wired to Madoff's trading operation in London, ostensibly to process investments in Europe, but the money was instead channeled back to Madoff's New York trading business. Steady streams of new investment money fueled the scheme for decades, but the flows effectively stopped in 2008, amid a stock-market plunge and unprecedented credit shortage. Madoff clients were increasingly asking to cash out. In late November, Madoff frantically sought to raise money to stave off collapse, telling potential investors he was putting together a $1 billion investment fund. One of his oldest friends and earliest investors, Carl Shapiro, a ninety-five-year-old clothing entrepreneur and philanthropist, forwarded $250 million on 1 December. The first week of December, Madoff told one of his sons who worked with him that clients had demanded about $7 billion in redemptions. On 9 December, a noticeably distraught Madoff informed another firm employee that he wanted to distribute annual bonuses early; later that day he confessed to senior employees that he was "finished," describing the firm as "all just one big lie." The business had been insolvent for years and now faced losses of about $50 billion, he said. He intended to pass out $200 million remaining on hand to employees before surrendering. The employees then informed securities authorities, who dispatched FBI agent Theodore Cacioppi to Madoff's penthouse apartment. "We are here to find out if there is an innocent explanation," Cacioppi said to Madoff, who replied: "There is no innocent explanation."

Life in Prison. In custody, Madoff told prosecutors that he alone was responsible for the fraud. He had not invested any of his clients' assets in more than a decade, he said, and he always meant to end the scheme but over time it became impossible. Victims ranged from European hedge funds and South American banks to Jewish charities and medical research foundations. He pleaded guilty in March to eleven criminal charges, including securities fraud, wire fraud, mail fraud, and money laundering. At the June sentencing, Madoff issued a somber apology, "I have left a legacy of shame, as some of my victims have pointed out, to my family and my grandchildren. This is something I will live in for the rest of my life. I'm sorry." Judge Denny Chin noted that no letters attesting to Madoff's good deeds had been submitted to the court. "The absence of such support is telling," he said. Chin also noted Madoff's unwillingness to cooperate with investigators: "I have a sense Mr. Madoff has not done all that he could do or told all that he knows." He then sentenced Madoff to a prison term of 150 years and assigned a fine of $170 billion. No other Madoff employees were charged, though federal authorities continued investigations into 2010.

Sources:

Julie Creswell and Thomas Landon Jr., "The Talented Mr. Madoff," *New York Times,* 24 January 2009;

Michael De la Merced, "Effort Under Way to Sell Madoff Unit," *New York Times,* 24 December 2008;

Stephen Foley, "The Madoff Files: Bernie's Billions," *Independent* (29 January 2009);

Carlyn Kolker, Tiffany Kary, and Saijel Kishan, "Madoff Victims May Have to Return Profits, Principal," *Bloomberg News* (23 December 2008);

Thomas Zambito, Jose Martinez, and Corky Siemaszko, "Bye, Bye Bernie: Ponzi King Madoff Sentenced to 150 years," *New York Daily News,* 29 June 2009.

NOURIEL ROUBINI

1959–

CRISIS CASSANDRA

Student of Crisis. Nouriel Roubini was born in Istanbul in 1959, the son of an importer-exporter of carpets, and moved with his family in early childhood to Iran, then to Israel, and finally to Italy. While growing up in Milan, he first became interested in economics. "Economics had the tools to understand the world," he recalled realizing, "and not just understand it but also change it for the better." After graduating from Italy's Bocconi University, he earned a Ph.D. in economics from Harvard University in 1988 and began teaching at Yale and New York Universities. Ten years later, he joined the Clinton White House as senior economist in the Council of Economic Advisers, later becoming senior adviser to Treasury undersecretary Timothy Geithner, the future Treasury secretary. While still an academic, throughout the 1990s, Roubini became transfixed by a series of financial crises sweeping emerging markets—first in Mexico, then across Asia, Brazil, and Russia. He returned to the subject after leaving government to become a visiting scholar at the International Monetary Fund (IMF) in 2001, just in time to work on the IMF's response to an economic crisis unfolding in Argentina. His research eventually turned up a distinct pattern in the failures: leading up to the precipice, each economy had built up massive current-account deficits, which they usually financed at tremendous risk by borrowing from foreign lenders. Another common trait was insufficient banking regulation, which fostered excessive lending, and weak corporate governance. Having distilled these symptoms into the 2004 book *Bailouts or Bail-Ins? Responding to Financial Crises in Emerging Markets,* Roubini proceeded to scan the world's economies to discover the next crisis before it happened. The numbers all pointed to the United States.

Sounding the Alarm. The most worrisome sign was the U.S. current-account deficit, which in 2004 stood at $600 billion. Roubini began writing widely on the dangers that the deficit posed. "The rapid deterioration of U.S. net external debt position implied by large trade and current account deficits cannot continue indefinitely," he wrote in a 2004 paper. "The U.S. is on an unsustainable and dangerous path." Further analysis led him to one especially troubling omen: the U.S. housing bubble. He became convinced that more than any other credit market, housing was poised to collapse. "Since 1997, real home prices have increased by about 90 percent; there is no economic fundamental . . . that can explain this," he said in a 2006 interview. "It means there was a speculative bubble, and now that bubble is bursting." The predictions grew sharper. At a September 2006 presentation at the IMF, Roubini estimated trillions of dollars in mortgage-backed securities would blow up, imperiling hedge funds, investment banks, and other financial giants, including the government-sponsored mortgage companies Fannie Mae and Freddie Mac. A year later, at the World Economic Forum in Davos, Switzerland, he said record corporate profits and bonuses were disguising a "nightmare hard landing scenario" set to erupt within months.

Vindication. Few were convinced. Unemployment and inflation remained low, and though the housing market was beginning to soften, the economy continued to grow. Roubini was becoming known as a pessimist by nature. "He sounded like a madman in 2006," said IMF economist Prakash Loungani, who had invited Roubini to the 2006 conference. "He was a prophet when he returned in 2007." Indeed, the collapse in March 2007 of two Bear Stearns hedge funds laden with mortgage debt set the crisis on its path, much as Roubini had warned, with unsustainable housing debt dragging down hedge funds, investment banks, mortgage corporations Fannie Mae and Freddie

Mac, and finally national banks. "I was intellectually vindicated," Roubini told an interviewer. "But I was vindicated by having an economic disaster which has political and social consequences." His prescience transformed Roubini into a central figure in economic policy circles, drawing invitations to address central banks and finance ministers across the globe, testify before Congress, and write for general-circulation newspapers and magazines.

Call to Nationalize. Roubini endorsed the massive government bailouts following in the wake of the crisis, but he continued to argue the storm was far from over, that other forms of debt constituted bubbles, and that consequently an even more aggressive government response was warranted. "Reckless people have deluded themselves that this was a subprime crisis, but we have problems with credit-card debt, student-loan debt, auto loans, commercial real-estate loans, home-equity loans, corporate debt and loans that financed leveraged buyouts," he said. "We have a subprime financial system, not a subprime mortgage market." Instead of investing billions in federal money in banks and hoping that would stimulate new lending, regulators would be wiser to nationalize banks outright and dispatch the toxic assets themselves. "Nationalization is the only option that would permit us to solve the problem of toxic assets in an orderly fashion and finally allow lending to resume," he wrote in early 2009. "Of course, the economy would still stink, but the death spiral we are in would end."

Sources:
Simon Kennedy, "Roubini Sees Global Gloom after Davos Vindication," *Bloomberg News* (30 January 2009);

Stephen Mihm, "Dr. Doom," *New York Times,* 15 August 2008;

Matthew Richardson and Nouriel Roubini, "Nationalize the Banks! We're All Swedes Now," *Washington Post,* 15 February 2009;

Jhoanna S. Robledo, "The Descent: One extreme view of how long this market will last," *New Yorker* (24 September 2006).

ELIOT SPITZER

1959–

WALL STREET CRIME FIGHTER

District Attorney. Eliot Spitzer was born in the Bronx, New York, on 10 June 1959, the son of a real estate investor. He graduated from Princeton University and Harvard Law School, then went to work at the Manhattan district attorney's office. There he helped break the Gambino crime family's control over the trucking and garment businesses by setting up a decoy sweatshop allowing undercover agents to penetrate the crime syndicate. Spitzer next worked as a corporate lawyer at New York firms, then in 1994, at age thirty-five, he launched a long-shot campaign to be elected state attorney general, finishing last in a field of four for the Democratic nomination. Four years later, Spitzer ran again and won, owing in large part to campaign contributions by his father.

The Martin Act Resurrected. Soon after taking office, Spitzer transformed the attorney general's office into an aggressive prosecutor of corporate fraud. Exhibiting the same zeal and audacious creativity he drew upon to nab the Gambinos, Spitzer prosecuted Midwestern power plants for polluting New York air, citing an obscure provision within the federal Clean Air Act. He filed suit against gun manufacturers under public nuisance law, and compelled General Electric to clean up Hudson River pollution by charging it with disrupting river traffic. When the stock-market bubble burst in 2001, Spitzer turned his sights to Wall Street. In a now-characteristic move, he chose as his ammunition an obscure state law, the Martin Act. Enacted in 1921, the law arms New York's attorney general with far-reaching powers to prosecute financial fraud. Under it, civil or criminal charges can be filed; any document can be subpoenaed from anyone doing business in the state; witnesses brought in for questioning can be denied access to counsel or the right against self-incrimination; and fraud violations can hold even without proof that defendants intended to defraud or that anyone was in fact defrauded. "It's the legal equivalent of a weapon of mass destruction," said one New York lawyer representing defendants in Martin Act cases. "The damage that can be done under the statute is unlimited." For decades, attorneys general had limited Martin Act prosecutions to small-time fraud, and in the early 1990s state budget cuts had reduced the staff of lawyers specializing in prosecuting Martin Act cases.

War on Wall Street. The first opportunity to dust off the Martin Act came in early 2001, when Spitzer's office began receiving complaints about Merrill Lynch analysts' promotion of Internet stocks before their plunge in value. The law gained Spitzer's team access to thirty boxes of Merrill emails, a sample of which showed the analysts had recommended stocks to investors only because the company in question had promised banking business to Merrill. When settlement negotiations with Merrill broke down, Spitzer went public with his charges, sending Merrill's own shares into free fall. The bank had no choice but to settle on Spitzer's terms. Spitzer employed the same merciless combination—the Martin Act for filing charges, the news media for compelling settlements—in bringing Wall Street's biggest firms to their knees. Following the Merrill settlement, he hammered out settlements totaling $1.4 billion with New York's ten biggest investment banks on similar charges of tainted research. A tip in 2003 led to a string of prosecutions of mutual-fund firms unfolding over the course of two and a half years. The firms had been allowing their most affluent investors to execute fund trades after the market had closed for the day and to circumvent fund rules barring rapid in-and-out trading—at the expense of other fund investors. In the biggest of the settlements, Bank of America agreed to pay $675 million and Alliance Capital $600 million. Spitzer also picked fights with New York Stock Exchange chief Richard Grasso, suing to recover most of $140 million Grasso earned in deferred compensation because he had allegedly failed to inform the board about the size of the package. The fund scandal was still playing out when Spitzer announced he was charging insurance brokers with bid rigging, a case ending with an $850 million settlement with Marsh & McLennan.

Resignation in Disgrace. The prosecutions gained Spitzer a reputation as the antidote to the seeming epidemic of corporate fraud. Headline writers dubbed him the corporate world's Eliot Ness or "the Sheriff of Wall Street." In 2005 the Associated Press mentioned him as a potential candidate for president, and *The Nation* magazine endorsed him as an ideal Democratic vice-presidential nominee. With his second term as attorney general expiring, Spitzer chose to run for New York governor, an office he won in 2006 with 69 percent of the vote. One year and two months after taking office, Spitzer resigned in disgrace amid the stunning revelation that he had been patronizing prostitutes. Federal authorities were prompted to investigate after Spitzer's bank reported suspicious money transfers, and a federal wiretap then brought the prostitution to light. "The remorse I feel will always be with me," Spitzer said in his resignation speech on 13 March 2008. "I look at my time as governor with a sense of what might have been." Traders at the NYSE watching the television broadcast of the speech broke out in cheers and applause when he said he would step down. No charges were ever filed against Spitzer, who ended up working in his father's real estate firm.

Sources:

Chris Dolmetsch, "Cheers on NYSE Floor, Shock in Albany: Spitzer's Fall," *Bloomberg News* (13 March 2008);

Danny Hakim, "Gilded Path to Political Stardom, with Detours," *New York Times,* 12 October 2006;

Adi Ignatius, "Eliot Spitzer: Wall Street's Top Cop," *Time* (30 December 2002);

Nicholas Thompson, "The Sword of Spitzer," *Legal Affairs* (May/June 2004).

SHERRON WATKINS

1959–

ENRON'S FRAUD DETECTOR

"Buzzsaw." Sherron Watkins was born on 28 August 1959 in Tomball, Texas. She studied accounting at the University of Texas at Austin and, after graduating, worked as a commodities portfolio manager and in the auditing group of Arthur Andersen. In 1993 she joined the energy trading and generation company Enron in Houston, helping manage its portfolio of energy-related investments. There she became known as a quick study and blunt speaker, acquiring the nickname "Buzzsaw." By 2001 she had risen through the ranks to become vice president and was assigned to work with chief financial officer Andrew Fastow in managing Enron's mergers and acquisitions group. In that capacity, she soon uncovered the fraudulent accounting that Enron executives were employing to hide hundreds of millions in losses. Some of the losses were buried in "special purpose entities" (SPEs), or shell companies, with fanciful names like Project Condor and Project Raptor and created to keep debt off Enron's balance sheets; other debts were meant to be covered by Enron's once-soaring stock, which was falling rapidly. Watkins resolved to find another job but take her findings to Enron's brass before leaving.

Growing Concern. She typed up an anonymous letter to Enron chief executive Kenneth Lay in August. "I am incredibly nervous that we will implode in a wave of accounting scandals," she wrote. Too impatient to wait for a response from Lay, Watkins sought a face-to-face meeting. She came prepared with a much-expanded warning, including new details and her recommendation for Lay to clean up the mess. At the meeting, Lay reacted with surprise, though he had in fact signed off on the fraudulent accounting. "You haven't gone outside the company with this, have you?," Lay asked. Watkins had not, reasoning that Enron's only chance to save itself was to come clean. Lay assured Watkins that Enron's accountants had scrutinized the SPEs but that he would look into her allegations. Lay tasked Enron's lawyers with investigating Watkins's claims, but they refused to involve outside accountants or to question accounting work already performed on the SPEs by Andersen, Enron's primary outside accounting firm. Not surprisingly, the investigation concluded that Watkins's accusations were unwarranted. The letter was presented to Enron's board with the disclaimer that an independent investigation had found its charges baseless. Lay had also sent a memo to Enron lawyers asking if he had legal grounds to fire Watkins; they informed him that Texas did not have whistle-blower protections on its books but firing her was ill-advised because it could prompt a lawsuit and draw regulators' scrutiny.

Almost a Whistle-Blower. As news of Watkins's letter spread through the company, the office atmosphere became increasingly tense, Watkins later said. At one point she began fearing for her and her family's safety. Meanwhile, Enron's finances were deteriorating rapidly. In October, the company was forced to restate assets and disclose a quarterly loss of $618 million, triggering an investigation by the Securities and Exchange Commission. Watkins then met again with Lay to offer advice on how to handle the crisis: Lay was to blame his subordinates, explaining that Fastow and others had designed the scheme in secret. Lay, however, sought out his political connections for help, but none came to his rescue. The next month Enron admitted overstating profits by $586 million over five years. In December it filed for bankruptcy protection. Watkins's letter did not become public until January 2002, when Enron was in free fall. She testified in Congress on Enron's collapse in February, asserting that she believed Lay was largely oblivious to the fraud, whose true masterminds were Fastow and Jeffrey Skilling, Lay's predecessor as chief. Initially Watkins was celebrated as a courageous whistle-blower; *Time* named her one of its three 2002 People of the Year, along with whistle-blowers from WorldCom and the Federal Bureau of Investigation. But opinions cooled as the depths of the Enron fraud came to light, prompting the question of why, instead of counseling Lay in damage control, Watkins had not alerted regulators, the media, or Enron's board. Her oft-stated reply was that she feared she would hasten the company's collapse. "In truth," a *New York Times* editorial argued, "Enron's only hope for survival was for someone like Ms. Watkins . . . to go public with their concerns as early as possible. That would have given this sordid tale a true whistle-blower."

Sources:

Bethany McLean and Peter Elkind, *The Smartest Guys in the Room: The Amazing Rise and Scandalous Fall of Enron* (New York: Penguin, 2003);

"Not Quite a Whistle-Blower," *New York Times*, 15 February 2002;

Shaheen Pash, "Enron's whistle blower details sinking ship," *cnnmoney.com* (16 March 2002).

PEOPLE IN THE NEWS

Rap recording artist **Shawn Corey Carter,** better known as **Jay-Z,** reached terms to sell his Rocawear clothing line to Iconix Brand Group for $204 million on 6 March 2007, with Carter staying on as chief creative officer.

The board of computer maker Hewlett-Packard ousted chief executive **Carly Fiorina** on 9 February 2005, after five and a half years at the helm. Fiorina had pushed for HP's 2002 acquisition of Compaq Computer, despite strong opposition within the company, and was saddled with blame for the company's weak financial results following the deal.

New York Stock Exchange chairman **Richard Grasso** was forced out of his position on 17 September 2003, a month after the disclosure of his $140 million deferred-compensation package. The following year a New York court ruling ordered him to repay much of the compensation, but the order was overturned in 2008. Grasso was succeeded at the NYSE by Goldman Sachs president **John Thain,** who was credited with modernizing the exchange's technology and expanding its reach abroad through a merger with the pan-European Euronext exchange.

In a congressional hearing examining the financial crisis's causes on 23 October 2008, former Federal Reserve chairman **Alan Greenspan** testified that his policies at the Fed had contributed to the housing bubble. "I have found a flaw," he said. "I have been very distressed by that fact."

Noreen Harrington, a longtime Wall Street trader, called New York attorney general **Eliot Spitzer**'s office in June 2003 with a tip about illegal trading activities by her former employer, the hedge fund Canary Capital Partners. The tip touched off an investigation that uncovered rampant fraud in the mutual-fund industry.

Viacom agreed on 3 November 2000 to pay $3 billion for Black Entertainment Television, the network founded by **Robert Johnson,** who owned two-thirds of the company at the time.

News Corp., the company controlled by newspaper magnate **Rupert Murdoch,** reached terms to buy the *Wall Street Journal*'s parent company Dow Jones on 1 August 2007 for $5 billion.

Indra Nooyi was named chief executive officer of PepsiCo, Inc. on 1 October 2006, becoming the company's first female leader. Nooyi had been president and chief financial officer since 2001 and was credited with reshaping Pepsi's global strategy through the spin-off of its bottling operations and mergers with Tropicana and Quaker Oats.

Bush administration Treasury secretary **Paul O'Neill** announced on 6 December 2002 that he was resigning. O'Neill said later he was effectively fired for his frequent disagreements with the president, principally O'Neill's opposition to a series of tax cuts.

Fossil-fuel prospector and hedge-fund manager **T. Boone Pickens** committed in 2007 to building the world's biggest wind-power project, a 4,000-megawatt complex in west Texas. On 15 May 2008, he announced having ordered 667 turbines for a price of $2 billion. Two years later, Pickens abandoned the project and scrambled to assign the turbines to smaller wind projects elsewhere. He blamed the credit crunch and depressed natural gas prices, which had lowered demand for wind energy.

Professional baseball player **Alex Rodriguez** signed a ten-year contract for $275 million to play with the New York Yankees on 13 December 2007, the most lucrative contract in sports history.

Starbucks founder **Howard Schultz** unseated company chief executive officer **Jim Donald** and assumed the role himself on 7 January 2008, after leaving the position eight years prior. The move, Schultz said, was designed to revive the company following a 50 percent drop in Starbucks stock in 2007.

Richard Scrushy, founder of the Alabama-based rehab-hospital chain HealthSouth, was charged with a $2.7 billion accounting fraud on 19 March 2003. A Birmingham, Alabama, jury acquitted him of the charges in 2005, but he and a former Alabama governor, **Don Siegelman,** were indicted again four months later on charges including money laundering, extortion, obstruction of justice, racketeering, and bribery. Both were convicted on 29 June 2006.

Texas financier **R. Allen Stanford** was arrested on 18 June 2009 at his sister's house in Stafford, Virginia, after a federal grand jury indicted him on charges of running a $7 billion Ponzi scheme through his Stanford Group Co., involving the misallocation of certificate-of-deposits assets into private equity investments.

Meg Whitman stepped down as chief executive officer at eBay Inc. on 31 March 2008, ending a decade at the helm in which the company's annual revenues multiplied by 2000 times, to $8 billion. She became national cochair of Senator **John McCain**'s presidential campaign in 2008, and the following year she announced plans to run for governor of California.

Oprah Winfrey published the first edition of *O: The Oprah Magazine* on 19 April 2000. Two years later, *Fortune* magazine declared it "the most successful startup ever in the industry," having accumulated more than $140 million in revenue in 2001.

Harvard University student **Mark Zuckerberg** launched the social-media website Facebook from his dorm room on 4 February 2004. Three and a half years later, Microsoft announced it had bought a 1.6 percent stake in Facebook for $240 million.

AWARDS

THE SVERIGES RIKSBANK PRIZE IN ECONOMIC SCIENCES IN MEMORY OF ALFRED NOBEL

2000

James J. Heckman and Daniel L. McFadden, for contributions to microeconometrics, the statistical analysis of individual and household behavior.

2001

George A. Akerlof, A. Michael Spence, and Joseph E. Stiglitz, for analysis of markets with asymmetric information.

2002

Vernon L. Smith and Daniel Kahneman, for applying tools of laboratory experimentation and psychological research to economic decision making.

2003

Robert Engle and Clive Granger, for statistical work in measuring investment risks.

2004

Finn E. Kydland and Edward C. Prescott, for contributions to dynamic macroeconomics, the time consistency of economic policy, and the driving forces behind business cycles.

2005

Robert J. Aumann and Thomas C. Schelling, for using game-theory analysis to enhance understanding of conflict and cooperation.

2006

Edmund S. Phelps, for analysis of intertemporal trade-offs in macroeconomic policy.

2007

Leonid Hurwicz, Eric S. Maskin, and Roger B. Myerson, for formulating a mathematical framework for analyzing institutions that implement collective decision making.

2008

Paul Krugman, for analysis of trade patterns and location of economic activity.

2009

Elinor Ostrom and Oliver E. Williamson, for analysis of economic governance, especially the commons.

JOHN BATES CLARK MEDAL

Awarded by the American Economic Association to "that American economist under the age of 40 who is adjudged to have made a significant contribution to economic thought and knowledge."

2001: Matthew Rabin

2003: Steven Levitt

2005: Daron Acemoglu

2007: Susan C. Athey

2009: Emmanuel Saez

DEATHS

James Van Andel, 80, cofounder of Amway Corporation, 7 December 2004.

Walter Annenberg, 96, publishing magnate with holdings including *TV Guide* and *The Philadelphia Inquirer*, 1 October 2002.

Roone Arledge, 71, ABC television executive, creator of *The Wide World of Sports, World News Tonight*, and *20/20*, 5 December 2002.

Mary Kay Ash, 83, creator of Mary Kay Cosmetics, 22 November 2001.

Warren Avis, 92, founder of Avis rental car company, 24 April 2007.

Lloyd Bentsen, 85, former Secretary of the Treasury (1993–1994), 23 May 2006.

Richard A. Bloch, 78, cofounder with brother Henry of tax preparation firm H&R Block, 21 July 2004.

Daniel Carasso, 103, Dannon yogurt creator, 17 May 2009.

Ronald R. Carey, 72, president of the International Brotherhood of Teamsters, 11 December 2008.

Otis Chandler, 78, *Los Angeles Times* publisher (1960–1980), 27 February 2006.

Joseph Coors Sr., 85, beer magnate, 15 March 2003.

John DeLorean, 80, automobile executive, developed Pontiac GTO and Firebird, founded DeLorean Motor Co., 19 March 2005.

William T. Dillard, 87, Dillard's retail chain founder, 8 February 2002.

C. Dillon Douglas, 93, former Secretary of the Treasury (1961–1965), 10 January 2003.

Peter F. Drucker, 95, management theorist, author of *The Future of Industrial Man* (1942) and *Practice of Management* (1954), 11 November 2005.

Jack Eckerd, 91, founder of Eckerd drugstore chain, 19 May 2004.

Bob Evans, 89, founder of restaurant chain, 21 June 2007.

Bill R. France, 74, NASCAR entrepreneur, 4 June 2007.

Milton Friedman, 94, Nobel laureate economist, author of *Capitalism and Freedom* (1962), 16 November 2006.

John Kenneth Galbraith, 97, economist, presidential adviser, ambassador to India (1961–1963), 29 April 2006.

Ernest Gallo, 97, cofounder of E&J Gallo winery, 6 March 2007.

J. Paul Getty Jr., 70, philanthropist and heir to oil fortune, 17 April 2003.

Katharine Graham, 84, longtime *Washington Post* publisher, 17 July 2001.

Gary Gygax, 69, cocreator of the role-playing game Dungeons & Dragons, 4 March 2008.

Ruth Handler, 85, Mattel cofounder, Barbie-doll creator, 27 April 2002.

Robert Heilbroner, 85, economic historian, author of *The Worldly Philosophers: The Lives, Times & Ideas of the Great Economic Thinkers* (1953), 4 January 2005.

Leona Helmsley, 87, real-estate magnate, hotel owner, 20 August 2007.

William R. Hewlett, 87, cofounder of Hewlett-Packard computer company, 12 January 2001.

John Johnson, 87, founder of *Ebony* and *Jet* magazines, 8 August 2005.

Samuel Curtis Johnson, 76, longtime head of household-cleaning-product manufacturer SC Johnson & Son, 22 May 2004.

Reginald Jones, 86, chairman and CEO of General Electric (1972–1981), adviser to four presidents, 30 December 2003.

William A. Jovanovich, 81, Harcourt Brace Jovanovich publisher, 4 December 2001.

Clark Kerr, 92, economist, labor mediator and president of the University of California System, 1 December 2003.

Victor Kiam, 74, Remington Products chief executive, 27 May 2001.

Richard Knerr, 82, cofounder of toymaker Wham-O, 14 January 2008.

Estée Lauder, 97, founder of cosmetics company bearing her name, 24 April 2004.

Kenneth L. Lay, 64, chief executive of Enron, 5 July 2006.

Stanley Marcus, 96, oversaw creation of Neiman-Marcus chain, 22 January 2002.

Robert Mondavi, 94, Robert Mondavi Winery founder, 16 May 2008.

Victor Posner, 83, finance pioneer, oversaw earliest hostile takeovers, 11 February 2002.

Donald Regan, 84, Secretary of the Treasury under Ronald Reagan (1981–1985), 10 June 2003.

Victor Reuther, 92, leader of United Auto Workers' education department, survived 1949 assassination attempt, 3 June 2004.

Laurance Rockefeller, 94, venture capitalist and grandson of John D. Rockefeller, 11 July 2004.

William Rosenberg, 86, Dunkin' Donuts chain cofounder, 20 September 2002.

William V. Roth Jr., 82, Delaware senator, chief sponsor of law creating the Roth Individual Retirement Account, 13 December 2003.

Louis Rukeyser, 73, financial commentator, thirty-two-year host of *Wall Street Week* (1970–2002), 2 May 2006.

Roger Straus, 87, longtime publishing chief at Farrar, Straus & Co., 25 May 2004.

John Templeton, 95, founder of Templeton investment firm, 8 July 2008.

PUBLICATIONS

Chris Anderson, *The Long Tail: Why the Future of Business Is Selling Less of More* (New York: Hyperion, 2006);

Ken Auletta, *World War 3.0: Microsoft and Its Enemies* (New York: Random House, 2001);

John Battelle, *The Search: How Google and Its Rivals Rewrote the Rules of Business* (New York: Portfolio, 2005);

William D. Cohan, *The Last Tycoons: The Secret History of Lazard Frères & Co.* (New York: Doubleday, 2008);

Stephen Dubner and Steven D. Levitt, *Freakonomics: A Rogue Economist Explores the Hidden Side of Everything* (New York: Morrow, 2006);

Barbara Ehrenreich, *Nickel and Dimed: On (Not) Getting By in America* (New York: Metropolitan, 2001);

Mohamed El-Erian, *When Markets Collide: Investment Strategies for the Age of Global Economic Change* (New York: McGraw-Hill, 2008);

Charles Fishman, *The Wal-Mart Effect: How the World's Most Powerful Company Really Works, and How It's Transforming the American Economy* (New York: Penguin, 2006);

Malcolm Gladwell, *The Tipping Point: How Little Things Can Make a Big Difference* (Boston: Little, Brown, 2000);

Alan Greenspan, *The Age of Turbulence: Adventures in a New World* (New York: Penguin, 2007);

Michael Lewis, *Moneyball: The Art of Winning an Unfair Game* (New York: Norton, 2003);

Bethany McLean and Peter Elkind, *The Smartest Guys in the Room: The Amazing Rise and Scandalous Fall of Enron* (New York: Portfolio, 2003);

Ben Mezrich, *The Accidental Billionaires: The Founding of Facebook: A Tale of Sex, Money, Genius, and Betrayal* (New York: Doubleday, 2009);

Carmen Reinhart and Kenneth Rogoff, *This Time Is Different: Eight Centuries of Financial Folly* (Princeton, N.J.: Princeton University Press, 2009);

Pietra Rivoli, *The Travels of a T-Shirt in the Global Economy: An Economist Examines the Markets, Power, and Politics of World Trade* (New York: Wiley, 2005);

Alice Schroeder, *The Snowball: Warren Buffett and the Business of Life* (New York: Bantam, 2008);

Andrew Ross Sorkin, *Too Big to Fail: The Inside Story of How Wall Street and Washington Fought to Save the Financial System from Crisis—and Themselves* (New York: Viking, 2009);

James Stewart, *Disney War* (New York: Simon & Schuster, 2005);

James Surowiecki, *The Wisdom of Crowds: Why the Many are Smarter than the Few and How Collective Wisdom Shapes Business* (New York: Doubleday, 2004);

Nassim Nicholas Taleb, *The Black Swan: The Impact of the Highly Improbable* (New York: Random House, 2007);

Don Tapscott and Anthony D. Williams, *Wikinomics: How Mass Collaboration Changes Everything* (New York: Portfolio, 2006);

David Wessel, *In Fed We Trust: Ben Bernanke's War on the Great Panic* (New York: Random House, 2009).

Armed security guards outside the New York Stock Exchange building on Wall Street on 23 April 2004.
After 11 September 2001, the building was closed to the public and guarded against terrorist threats
(photograph by Eugene Zelenko).

EDUCATION

by ASHLEY COOK AND PAUL COOK

CONTENTS

Sidebars and tables are listed in italics.

2000

Feb.	Florida's legislature approves Governor Jeb Bush's "One Florida" initiative that bans colleges and universities from considering race as a factor in admission.
29 Feb.	A six-year-old boy in Mount Morris Township, Michigan, shoots and kills his classmate at their elementary school.
3 Mar.	Bob Jones University, a fundamentalist Christian institution in Greenville, South Carolina, lifts its long-standing ban on interracial dating.
14 Mar.	A Florida judge rules against vouchers, finding that the state constitution prohibits the use of public funds to send students to private schools, invalidating a school-voucher program begun eight months earlier.
8 May	The Philadelphia school board adopts a policy that requires all public-school students to wear a uniform to class, becoming the first major city to pass such a law.
19 June	In *Santa Fe Independent School District* v. *Doe,* the Supreme Court rules that the district should not be allowing student-led prayer prior to football games as it violates the establishment clause of the First Amendment. Prayers at any school-sponsored extracurricular activity are deemed unconstitutional.
28 June	The Supreme Court, by a six-to-three vote, rules in *Mitchell* v. *Helms* that a federal program (the Education Consolidation and Improvement Act of 1981) that provides computers and other equipment to private schools is constitutional.
1 Aug.	Kansas voters oust two conservative members of the state school board who had voted to remove any mention of evolution from the state curriculum.
11 Sept.	California enacts a plan to help needy students attend college: high-school students with good grades and financial need receive free tuition at public institutions or $10,000 a year toward tuition at a private school.
9 Nov.	Ruth J. Simmons, president of Smith College, is chosen to lead Brown University, becoming the first African American to head an Ivy League institution. She is sworn in on 3 July 2001.

2001

2 Feb.	William Michael Stankewicz attacks students and faculty with a machete at North Hopewell-Winterstown Elementary School in the Red Lion School District of York County, Pennsylvania. He is later convicted and sentenced to serve between 132 and 264 years in prison.
14 Feb.	The Kansas State Board of Education reverses its 1999 decision to remove the theory of evolution from the state's science curriculum.
5 Mar.	A freshman at Santana High School in Santee, California, opens fire with a handgun at school, killing two students and injuring thirteen others.
May	The William and Flora Hewlett Foundation pledges $400 million to Stanford University in the largest gift ever given to an institution of higher learning in the United States.
16 May	Fourteen-year-old Nathaniel Brazill is convicted of second-degree murder and is later sentenced to twenty-eight years in prison for shooting a teacher at Lake Worth Middle School in Florida.
26 June	The Bush administration nominates Gerald A. Reynolds, a lawyer and affirmative-action opponent, to head the Education Department's Office of Civil Rights.

25 Nov.   Police foil a Columbine-style murder plot at a New Bedford, Massachusetts, high school after one of three students involved in the plan comes forward. The leader of the group is eventually sentenced to three years of probation.

Dec.   After their original exams are quarantined in an anthrax scare, 7,500 students nationwide retake their Scholastic Aptitude Tests (SATs). The original tests never reached the scoring center.

2002

8 Jan.   The No Child Left Behind (NCLB) Act, which mandates that schools have to perform to new federal standards or face a range of penalties, is signed into law by President George W. Bush.

19 Feb.   The Supreme Court votes unanimously that the practice of allowing students to grade fellow students' classroom assignments does not violate privacy laws.

11 Apr.   The Walton Family Charitable Support Foundation, created by the family of Wal-Mart founder Sam Walton, donates $300 million to the University of Arkansas. It is the largest donation ever made to an American public university.

12 Apr.   After publicly feuding with Harvard president Lawrence Summers, prominent African American professor Cornel West announces that he has accepted a job at Princeton University.

7 May   University of Wisconsin-Stout student Lucas John Helder admits that he planted eighteen pipe bombs in mailboxes across five states, earning the nickname "The Midwest Pipe Bomber."

12 June   The Accreditation Council for Graduate Medical Education approves new regulations in which a medical resident's hours are not to exceed eighty hours a week, and single shifts can be no longer than twenty-four hours.

20 June   In a seven-to-two vote, the Supreme Court rules that an individual student cannot sue a school under the Family Educational Rights and Privacy Act for releasing personal information, a federal law that protects student privacy.

26 June   A Federal Appeals Court in San Francisco rules that requiring students to recite the Pledge of Allegiance is unconstitutional because of the phrase "under God."

27 June   The Supreme Court, in a five-to-four ruling, approves drug testing as a possible requisite for participation in interscholastic, extracurricular competition.

18 Oct.   Poet Quincy Troupe resigns after only four months as California's first poet laureate, after admitting that he falsified his resume, which stated that he had graduated from a college that he had only attended. He later resigns from his teaching position at the University of California at San Diego.

2003

15 Jan.   In a televised address, President Bush weighs in on the University of Michigan admissions controversy; he denounces the use of race in university admissions and plans to file a brief with the Supreme Court asking that they find the policy unconstitutional.

20 Feb.   Sami Al-Arian, a suspended University of South Florida computer engineering professor, is charged with funding and advising a Palestinian terrorist organization. He is fired on 26 February.

28 Feb.   The Ninth Circuit Court of Appeals refuses a request from the federal government to reconsider its ruling that making children recite the Pledge of Allegiance is unconstitutional.

24 Apr.   Two years after a machete attack that injures fourteen people at a Red Lion School District elementary school in Pennsylvania, eighth-grader James Sheets brings multiple weapons into Red Lion Area Junior High School. After fatally shooting the principal, Sheets turns the gun on himself.

21 May   An explosion inside the Sterling Law School at Yale University damages two rooms. No injuries are reported, and investigators believe the explosion was caused by a pipe bomb.

23 June   The Supreme Court rules that University of Michigan's law school admissions policy, which considers race as a factor, is constitutional while its similar undergraduate system is not, in *Grutter* v. *Bollinger* and *Gratz* v. *Bollinger* respectively.

July   New York City officials announce plans for Harvey Milk High School, the first public school aimed at protecting gay students from discrimination.

July   Evangelist Pat Robertson announces his massive prayer offensive called "Operation Supreme Court Freedom." Robertson asks his followers to pray that at least three Supreme Court justices retire so that conservative justices may take over and overturn rulings on school prayer.

23 Aug.   In Naples, Florida, Ave Maria University opens. Founded by Domino's Pizza owner Thomas S. Monaghan, it is the first Roman Catholic institution of higher learning established in the United States in forty years.

14 Oct.   The Supreme Court agrees to hear *Elk Grove Unified School District* v. *Newdow*, which will consider the constitutionality of school Pledge of Allegiance recitations.

2004

23 Feb.   Secretary of Education Rod Paige calls the National Education Association (NEA), the nation's largest teachers' union, a terrorist organization in reference to the group's persistent lobbying against No Child Left Behind reforms. Paige later apologizes.

25 Feb.   In a seven-to-two vote, the Supreme Court rules that states are not violating the First Amendment if they choose not to subsidize, with taxpayer-funded scholarships, students studying for the ministry.

17 May   President Bush and his presidential election opponent, Democratic senator John Kerry of Massachusetts, attend ceremonies in Topeka, Kansas, honoring the fiftieth anniversary of *Brown* v. *Board of Education* school desegregation.

14 June   In *Elk Grove Unified School District* v. *Newdow*, the Supreme Court rules unanimously that the words "under God" in the Pledge of Allegiance do not violate the establishment clause.

4 Aug.   Mary Kay Letourneau is released from prison after serving a seven-year sentence for having sex with her thirteen-year-old student while she was a teacher in Des Moines, Washington. Letourneau bore two children by the student and upon her release reunites with him. The two are married months later.

17 Aug.   A survey conducted by the National Assessment of Educational Progress finds that the test scores of charter-school students are considerably lower than those of students in public schools.

10 Nov.   The Association of International Educators reports that the number of foreign students enrolled in American graduate programs has declined.

15 Nov.   Secretary of Education Paige resigns.

17 Nov.   President Bush nominates White House special aide on domestic issues Margaret Spellings, one of the authors of No Child Left Behind, to become secretary of education. She assumes office 20 January 2005.

2005

7 Jan.   Conservative radio host Armstrong Williams admits that he accepted payments from the Department of Education to say favorable things about the Bush administration's education reform. Williams also admits an open-door policy with members of the administration, allowing them to come on his program whenever they chose.

Feb.   A bipartisan task force of legislators argues that No Child Left Behind is unconstitutional and sets schools up for failure.

16 Mar.   *The New England Journal of Medicine* predicts that if the childhood obesity epidemic continues, the current generation of children may have a life expectancy of two to five years shorter than adults today.

21 Mar.   Sixteen-year-old Jeff Weise shoots five fellow students (as well as a teacher and a security guard) at Red Lake High School in Minnesota before turning the gun on himself.

7 Apr.   Secretary of Education Spellings announces revisions to No Child Left Behind and promises increased flexibility to states that are attempting to comply.

20 Apr.   The NEA and school districts in Michigan, Texas, and Vermont file suit against the federal government for violation of No Child Left Behind; the plaintiffs argue that the government has not provided the proper funding for the mandates.

May   The documentary movie *Corridor of Shame: The Neglect of South Carolina's Rural Schools* debuts.

21 May   A third of the faculty of Calvin College protest President Bush's commencement speech. Their petition reads, "We believe your administration has launched an unjust and unjustified war in Iraq."

1 Aug.   In response to a question on the teaching of so-called intelligent-design theories, which argue for the presence of a divine creator of the natural world, Bush says, "I think that part of education is to expose people to different schools of thought. You're asking me whether or not people ought to be exposed to different ideas, the answer is yes."

26 Aug.   A federal bankruptcy judge rules that churches and schools of the Roman Catholic diocese of Spokane, Washington, can be liquidated to pay the claims of victims of sexual abuse at the hands of priests.

29 Aug.   Hurricane Katrina makes landfall in southeast Louisiana; many schools are closed for weeks or longer.

26 Sept.   A federal court hears opening arguments of *Kitzmiller* v. *Dover Area School District,* which challenges the teaching of intelligent design in a public-school curriculum.

30 Sept.   The Government Accountability Office rules that the Bush administration engaged in the illegal dissemination of propaganda when it paid for favorable coverage of its education reform.

1 Oct.   A bomb explodes outside the University of Oklahoma's memorial stadium during a football game. Bomber Joel Henry Hinrichs III is killed.

3 Oct.   The Open Content Alliance announces their plan to digitize thousands of books and scholarly papers, making them available on the Internet.

15 Nov.   Students at the University of Tennessee interrupt a keynote speech given by Dick Cheney, heckling the vice president and calling for an end of the war in Iraq.

7 Dec.   The Supreme Court rules that the government may hold a person's Social Security benefits in order to collect unpaid student loans.

20 Dec.   Judge John E. Jones III rules in *Kitzmiller* v. *Dover Area School District* that it is unconstitutional to teach intelligent design as an alternative to the theory of evolution in a public school.

2006

31 Jan.   President Bush calls for an increase in spending for science education in his State of the Union address.

21 Feb.   Controversial Harvard president Lawrence Summers resigns.

6 Mar.   The Supreme Court votes unanimously in *Rumsfeld* v. *Forum for Academic and Institutional Rights* to uphold a federal law that says colleges and universities must allow military recruiters the same access to students as they do other potential employers or else lose federal funds. A group of law schools had challenged the law, arguing that it violated their First-Amendment right to free speech and association. The schools objected to the military's exclusion of openly gay men and women.

3 May   The three largest soft-drink companies in the United States announce that they will remove sugary drinks such as soda and iced tea from cafeterias and vending machines in schools, replacing soft drinks with water, milk, and fruit juice.

Aug.   The National Center for Education Statistics releases a report that finds charter-school students score considerably lower in math compared to students in public schools.

21 Aug.   The Virginia Tech campus is closed and classes are canceled as police search for William C. Morva, suspected in the murder of a security guard and a police officer. Officials arrest and charge Morva a day and a half later. He is sentenced to receive the death penalty.

17 Sept. Five Duquesne University basketball players are shot on campus after trying to calm a disturbed man at the student union. Three of the student athletes are hospitalized.

27 Sept. During a hostage situation at Platte Canyon High School in Colorado, the gunman sexually assaults several female students and mortally wounds another before shooting himself.

29 Sept. Eric Hainstock, a fifteen-year-old high-school student, fatally shoots his principal, John Klang, at Weston High School in Cazenovia, Wisconsin. He is given a life sentence in prison, with the possibility of parole in thirty years.

2 Oct.   Charles Carl Roberts IV invades an Amish schoolhouse in Nickel Mines, Pennsylvania, with guns and restraints. After sending out all the boys and adults, he shoots the girls, killing five and wounding five. He then kills himself.

128

2 Oct.   Two schools in Las Vegas, Nevada, are locked down after a student brings an AK-47 assault rifle and other automatic weapons to school.

12 Oct.   Work begins on demolishing the one-room schoolhouse in Nickel Mines.

29 Oct.   The board of trustees at the world's premier school for the deaf, Gallaudet University in Washington, D.C., terminates the contract of incoming president Jane K. Fernandes after weeks of protests by students.

20 Nov.   A school bus careens from an Interstate 565 overpass in Huntsville, Alabama, killing four high-school girls.

5 Dec.   The U.S. Court of Appeals for the Ninth Circuit rules that Kamehameha, a preparatory school in Hawaii, can favor native Hawaiians in its admissions policy.

22 Dec.   Rape charges are dropped against three Duke University lacrosse players accused of assaulting a stripper at an off-campus party.

2007

11 Feb.   Harvard University announces that historian Drew Gilpin Faust will become the first female president in the school's 371-year history.

19 Mar.   The Supreme Court hears arguments in *Morse* v. *Frederick*, the case of an Alaskan student who was suspended for displaying a banner reading "Bong Hits 4 Jesus" in front of his high school.

11 Apr.   North Carolina attorney general Roy Cooper says the Duke University lacrosse players had been falsely accused and criticizes prosecutor Mike Nifong for his handling of the case, calling him a "rogue prosecutor."

11 Apr.   Don Imus's popular radio show and television simulcasts are canceled after public outrage over racist comments Imus made about the Rutgers University women's basketball team. Imus later issues an apology: "I want to take a moment to apologize for an insensitive and ill-conceived remark we made the other morning regarding the Rutgers women's basketball team[…] It was completely inappropriate and we can understand why people were offended. Our characterization was thoughtless and stupid, and we are sorry."

16 Apr.   Virginia Tech student Seung-Hui Cho kills thirty-two people and wounds fifteen more on campus in Blacksburg. Cho, a senior, also kills himself following the most deadly shooting rampage on American soil.

19 Apr.   University officials at Virginia Tech announce that students killed in the massacre will be posthumously awarded their degrees during the spring commencement ceremony.

15 June   Facing disbarment, Nifong resigns his position as district attorney for Durham County, North Carolina.

25 June   The Supreme Court rules in *Morse* v. *Frederick* that school administrators can prohibit students from displaying pro-drug-use messages.

28 June   The Supreme Court rules five to four that programs in Seattle, Washington, and Louisville, Kentucky, which maintain racial integration by considering race when assigning students to schools, are unconstitutional.

11 July   The House of Representatives votes to cut $19 billion in federal subsidies to student lenders. The law also increases Pell Grants by $500 over five years and creates loan-forgiveness programs for public servants.

24 July   The University of Colorado dismisses controversial professor Ward Churchill for academic misconduct. Churchill insists that he is being fired because of his political outspokenness.

8 Aug.	Barbara R. Morgan, a former teacher from Idaho, is aboard the space shuttle *Endeavour* as it lifts off. Morgan was the backup to Christa McAuliffe, the teacher who died in the 1986 *Challenger* explosion.
31 Aug.	Nifong is found in contempt of court for lying to a judge in the Duke University lacrosse case and is sentenced to one day in jail.
20 Sept.	More than 10,000 people march in Jena, Louisiana, to protest harsh measures taken against six black students for assaulting a white student. On hand are civil-rights activists Jesse Jackson, Al Sharpton, and Martin Luther King III.
21 Sept.	Freshman Loyer D. Braden shoots two female students (one fatally) on the Delaware State University campus.
10 Oct.	A fourteen-year-old high-school student opens fire at his school in Cleveland, Ohio, injuring two students and two teachers before killing himself.
28 Nov.	Officials at Arlington High School in LaGrange, New York, announce that the state police have thwarted a Columbine-style attack on the school.
Dec.	The Bush administration's abstinence-only sex education program's effectiveness is questioned when the birth rate for teens ages fifteen to nineteen rises 3 percent in 2006. It is the first time this statistic had risen since 1991.

2008

28 Jan.	During his last State of the Union address, President Bush urges Congress to reauthorize No Child Left Behind.
8 Feb.	A student shoots and kills two students and then kills herself at Louisiana Technical College in Baton Rouge, Louisiana.
14 Feb.	Alumnus Stephen P. Kazmierczak opens fire in a classroom at Northern Illinois University. He kills five students and wounds fifteen more before killing himself.
5 Apr.	A bus transporting a high-school band overturns on Interstate 94, northwest of Minneapolis, Minnesota. One person is killed, and three more are critically injured.
25 Apr.	Students across the country participate in the thirteenth annual Day of Silence, which protests the silencing of homosexual students by harassment, bullying, and intimidation.
21 Aug.	Fifteen-year-old Jamar B. Siler shoots and kills a classmate in the cafeteria of his Knoxville, Tennessee, high school.
23 Sept.	An effigy of presidential nominee Barack Obama is found hanging from a tree on the campus of George Fox University in Newberg, Oregon.
26 Oct.	Two students are killed on the campus of the University of Central Arkansas in Conway when a shooter opens fire from a passing car.
16 Dec.	Obama nominates Chicago school superintendent Arne Duncan as secretary of education.

2009

Apr.	The federal government declares the swine-flu outbreak a public-health emergency after confirming twenty cases in the United States. Schools across the country close in an attempt to isolate those who have been infected.

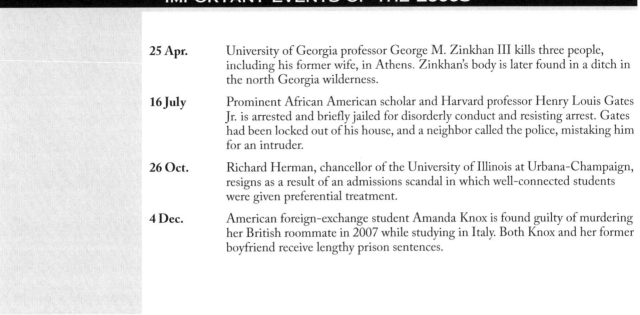

| 25 Apr. | University of Georgia professor George M. Zinkhan III kills three people, including his former wife, in Athens. Zinkhan's body is later found in a ditch in the north Georgia wilderness. |

25 Apr. University of Georgia professor George M. Zinkhan III kills three people, including his former wife, in Athens. Zinkhan's body is later found in a ditch in the north Georgia wilderness.

16 July Prominent African American scholar and Harvard professor Henry Louis Gates Jr. is arrested and briefly jailed for disorderly conduct and resisting arrest. Gates had been locked out of his house, and a neighbor called the police, mistaking him for an intruder.

26 Oct. Richard Herman, chancellor of the University of Illinois at Urbana-Champaign, resigns as a result of an admissions scandal in which well-connected students were given preferential treatment.

4 Dec. American foreign-exchange student Amanda Knox is found guilty of murdering her British roommate in 2007 while studying in Italy. Both Knox and her former boyfriend receive lengthy prison sentences.

First Lady Michelle Obama visits the Prager Child Development Center at Fort Bragg, North Carolina, for a reading of Dr. Seuss's *The Cat in the Hat*, 12 March 2009 (photograph by Joyce N. Boghosian).

OVERVIEW

Federal Reform Shapes the Decade. Many of the changes and trends in American primary education during the decade came as a result of the No Child Left Behind legislation, enacted early in 2002. The new law held schools to a new level of accountability and imposed serious penalties for those that did not perform. The law also brought standardized testing and assessment back into the spotlight, as many worried that children taught to do well on a defined set of questions missed out on a well-rounded education that promoted critical thinking. While states and schools struggled to conform to the regulations, many administrators, teachers, and parents began speaking out in opposition to No Child Left Behind. They claimed that while the government mandated sweeping changes, it was not providing funding for implementation. By the decade's end, newly elected president Barack Obama promised more money for reform, as well as easing punitive measures of the act.

Race Still an Issue. Public-school reform ignited debates about the so-called education gap between white and minority students. Many of the schools that could not meet the new standards were populated with inner-city children from underprivileged families. Some felt these schools needed help, not strict punitive measures. The battle over affirmative action continued, culminating in President George W. Bush's request that the Supreme Court strike down college-admission policies that consider race as a factor. The *Bollinger* cases in Michigan set a new precedent against affirmative action as schools began working around such bans, initiating economic versions in an attempt to keep minority enrollment on the rise. Career colleges enjoyed a successful decade of recruiting minorities, but were criticized by some for being predatory and unconcerned with the financial well-being of their students. Race remained a hot topic, from the civil-rights march in Jena, Louisiana, to the front-door arrest of Harvard professor Henry Louis Gates Jr.

Violence. Painful memories of the 1999 massacre at Columbine High School in Colorado remained fresh as schools sought to prevent violence by hiring security guards and installing metal detectors. Still, violence found its way inside schools, even in once unthinkable places. In Nickel Mines, Pennsylvania, a gunman killed five girls and wounded five more in a one-room Amish schoolhouse. The news reverberated across the country, making parents wonder if there was any safe place to send their children. Shootings plagued institutions of higher learning throughout the decade, culminating in one of the worst mass killings in U.S. history on the Virginia Tech campus in Blacksburg, Virginia. Senior Seung-Hui Cho killed thirty-two people in two separate attacks before turning the gun on himself. In the aftermath of the shooting, debates emerged over the release of student mental-health records and on-campus firearms possession.

Recession. In late 2008 the economy fell into one of the deepest recessions in history. States and school districts were hit hard as budgets dwindled and resources became scarce. The requirements of No Child Left Behind became almost unobtainable as money for new teachers, tests, and textbooks fell away. Another education casualty of the recession was electives such as arts education and foreign languages. There were mass teacher layoffs around the country. Both Bush and Obama passed stimulus packages that provided aid to struggling schools. More than $100 billion went to help schools update crumbling infrastructure and outdated technology. The Education Department initiated the Race to the Top grant program in which states could earn money for education by proving that they met No Child Left Behind standards.

Curriculum Debates Heat Up. While most public discussion was over how to improve education, just *what* to teach was often still in question. Trials in Kansas and Pennsylvania tested the constitutionality of teaching intelligent design, a theory devised by proponents of creationism, which argued that natural history was set in motion by a creator god. Mainstream scientists and many parents felt that religious undertones of the theory's "intelligent agent" violated the separation of church and state. The Supreme Court agreed. In an another arena, the conservative state school board in Texas created a controversy by downplaying global warming and leaving doubtful language about natural selection in its science textbooks. Bush, who spoke out in support of intelligent design, also favored and implemented abstinence-only education programs. Critics who supported comprehensive sex education raged against what they saw as the unrealistic expectation that teens would wait for marriage to have sex. Statistics published in the latter part of the decade seemed to support opponents of abstinence-only education, as the teen birth rate increased for the first time since the early 1990s. Obama promised to end Bush's policies and allocate more funding for comprehensive sex education.

Changes in Higher Education. By 2008 more than one-fifth of college students had taken a course online, and millions of Americans were pursuing a degree via the Internet. For-profit online schools such as Phoenix and Strayer

Universities soared in popularity for their convenience and affordability. Meanwhile, tuition at brick-and-mortar institutions continued to rise. As a result, Congress set new regulations for universities as well as student-loan companies, which had been enjoying historic profits. Student lenders struggled to adapt to the standards of transparency. Inside the academy, many graduating with humanities Ph.D.'s struggled to find jobs as tenured lines closed and many schools stopped hiring altogether. Many universities faced huge budget cuts as state legislatures slashed funding for higher education.

TOPICS IN THE NEWS

AFFIRMATIVE ACTION

Backlash. In the first decade of the 2000s universities struggled in the courts over the viability of affirmative-action policies. Many of these arguments hinged upon whether these policies had outlived their value. Backlash against affirmative action began in the late 1990s with a series of court decisions that banned universities and colleges from considering race in admissions standards, which had a profound effect on minority enrollment. When Texas ruled against affirmative-action policies, African American enrollment at the University of Texas Law School dropped from thirty-eight to four students. Likewise, minority enrollment fell from 25 to 11 percent after a similar ban was put in place at the University of California, Berkeley.

Bollinger Cases. *Gratz* v. *Bollinger* and *Grutter* v. *Bollinger* were a pair of cases that addressed the issue of affirmative action at the University of Michigan. Jennifer Gratz and Barbara Grutter were rejected from the undergraduate program and law school, respectively, in the late 1990s. Both brought suits against the school, claiming that race played a role in their rejection and that the admissions policy, which awarded automatic points to minorities, was unconstitutional. Lee Bollinger, then president of the university, served as defendant and stood by the school's policies and efforts to create a diverse student body. In *Gratz* v. *Bollinger*, the undergraduate case, the court ruled six to three that the admissions policy was unconstitutional because it was not "narrowly tailored" and seemed to support a quota system that had been struck down by the Supreme Court in the *Bakke* case (1978). In *Grutter* v. *Bollinger*, the law-school case, the court ruled five to four that

the admission policy was constitutional because it was "narrowly tailored," and used race as one part of a holistic approach that involved personal interviews. Race was merely a "plus" for the applicant. Justice Sandra Day O'Connor wrote for the majority that the state has a "compelling interest" in diversity because the "effective participation by members of all racial and ethnic groups in the civic life of our nation is essential if the dream of one nation, indivisible, is to be realized." The dual decision was celebrated by both opponents and proponents of affirmative action but left the door open for more lawsuits. Justice Antonin Scalia commented that "today's *Grutter-Gratz* [decision] seems perversely designed to prolong the controversy and the litigation."

New Methods. The courts and voters alike displayed growing disapproval for affirmative action. Legislators and administrators tried to maintain diversity in schools without traditional tools. Several states adopted programs designed to get around the rulings against affirmative action. In Texas, where affirmative action was banned, officials found creative ways to ensure minorities enrolled. The University of Texas asked high-profile African American alumni to write to minority students to encourage them to apply. Administrators encouraged alumni groups to create race-based scholarships. State officials enacted the "top 10%" law that guaranteed a place at a state school for any high-school student who graduated in the top 10 percent of her or his class. Because schools in Texas were so poorly integrated, this plan was expected to increase minority enrollment. Following its own legal setbacks, California began looking for ways to fight the decline of minority students in the absence of affirmative action. After considering

In 2006 the small town of Jena, Louisiana, some two hundred miles north of New Orleans, garnered national attention when six African American students, who became known as the Jena Six, were accused and tried for assaulting a white student. The conflict began when black students, during their lunch period, attempted to sit under a tree that had long been a place where white students gathered. The next day two nooses were hanging from the tree. Three white students claimed it was a practical joke and were given in-school suspensions. Racial tensions mounted for the next few months: someone tried to burn down Jena High School, and racially motivated fights broke out in the town. In December six black students attacked and injured a white student, who spent a few hours in the emergency room before attending a school event later that night. Instead of the expected charges of assault and battery, the six were charged with attempted second-degree murder, which carried a sentence of life in prison. Five of the six were to be tried as adults. The National Association for the Advancement of Colored People (NAACP) and American Civil Liberties Union (ACLU) publicized the case and soon reporters from major networks and newspapers filled the town. Singer John Mellencamp wrote a song about the incident and filmed a video in support of the six young men. During the trial, civil-rights leaders organized a rally on 20 September 2007 in which more than 10,000 people (including activists Jesse Jackson, Al Sharpton, and Martin Luther King III) marched on Jena to protest the charges. Eventually, the charges were reduced. Mychal Bell was convicted of second-degree battery, but the conviction was later thrown out by an appeals court ruling that Bell should not have been tried as an adult. (He spent ten months in jail.) The remaining five pleaded no contest and agreed to plea bargains with the punishment of a $500 fine and seven days of probation.

Source: Tom Mangold, "Racism Goes on Trial Again in America's Deep South," *Observer,* 20 May 2007.

Demonstration in Jena, Louisiana, 20 September 2007, in support of six black teenagers initially charged with attempted murder in the beating of Justin Barker, a white classmate (AP Photo/*The Chronicle,* Sharon Steinmann)

Governor Jeb Bush, left, in Tallahassee, Florida, during a meeting with representatives from women's organizations and black lawmakers about affirmative action and Bush's "One Florida" plan, 13 March 2000 (AP Photo/Mark Foley)

dropping Scholastic Aptitude Test (SAT) requirements from admission standards, lawmakers passed the 4 percent plan, akin to the Texas program. Florida governor Jeb Bush did away with affirmative action as a part of his "One Florida" plan. Harshly criticized by minority leaders, One Florida was approved by the legislature in early 2000. Like Texas and California, Florida guaranteed a spot in a public university to the top 20 percent of each high school's graduating class. Toward the end of the decade support for a new, economic version of affirmative action was growing. In the 2008 presidential debates, Democratic nominee Barack Obama expressed that his privileged daughters would not deserve affirmative-action aid but that a working-class white student might.

Sources:
Adam Cohen, "Coloring the Campus," *Time* (9 September 2001);

"Florida Ends Use of Race in College Admissions," *New York Times*, 23 February 2000;

Walter Nowinski, "Suit Against U. Michigan Admissions Policy Settled After 10 Years," *Michigan Daily*, 1 February 2007;

Timothy Starks, "Supreme Court Declares Diversity is Compelling," *New York Sun*, 24 June 2003.

CHARTER SCHOOLS

Choices. Charter schools were primary-education institutions that received public funding but operated under a contract (or charter) that promised a higher level of student achievement than traditional public schools. This arrangement was intended to allow administrators and teachers the freedom to be creative in encouraging student performance. While these schools adhered to certain guidelines—such as those set by No Child Left Behind—they were also under the guidance of their authorizing bodies, which could be for-profit entities, universities, and local school districts. If the charter was not met, the school faced closure by its authorizing body. The charter-school movement began in the 1990s and remained strong in the new millennium. By 2002–2003 more than 2,700 charter schools were operating in thirty-nine states and Washington, D.C. However, the effectiveness of these new schools was largely unknown. In 2004 the U.S. Department of Education published results of a three-year, intensive study of charter schools.

Kindergarten teacher Caroline Derr walks students to the playground at the World Of Wonder School, a charter school in
Dayton, Ohio, 16 May 2001 (AP Photo/David Kohl).

Money. The federal Public Charter Schools Grant Program awards money to states with charter-school legislation. States then allocate money to schools and school-planning groups. In 2001 the average charter school received $4.5 million in federal grant money. This funding was the most common type of start-up money used, with more than two-thirds of charters using public funds to get off the ground. Dissemination subgrants were also awarded to charter schools at the discretion of individual states. These funds were commonly used for technological and curricular instruments as well as professional development opportunities.

Students. In 2001 the average charter school served 190 students, considerably fewer than a traditional public school. The Department of Education survey found that charter schools served fewer white students and more minority students than traditional public schools. They were also more likely to serve children from low-income families but less likely to enroll special-education students. Charter schools were more likely to consolidate grade levels. For instance, K-8 and K-12 are common arrangements to prevent difficult transitions from elementary to middle to high school.

Authorizing Bodies and Penalization. The Department of Education report found that 45 percent of authorizing

bodies were local school districts and 41 percent were state departments of education. Institutions of higher education made up 12 percent of authorizing bodies, while the final 2 percent was composed of independent charter boards. Though smallest in number, the latter group included the most controversial authorizing bodies: education-management organizations. These for-profit entities faced criticism for their high administrative costs, low teacher salaries, and lack of services (such as counseling and special-education materials). In some cases, parents complained of a greater focus on advertising than education. Despite the emphasis on oversight, the report on charter schools noted that these authorizing bodies did not play a daily role in running the school and that only 36 percent had an office or staff dedicated to overseeing the school. The report added that even when the contract was not met, authorizing bodies had a difficult time shutting down the school.

Performance. Case studies showed that more than half of charter schools met state performance standards. Charter schools affiliated with local school districts were most likely to be on par with traditional public schools. However, the report also found that fourth-graders in traditional public schools scored considerably better than charter-school students in both reading and math. Proponents of charter schools criticized the report, claiming that it did not take into account the various backgrounds of students. Charter-school performance, supporters argued, was linked to the prior achievement of students, and these alternative schools serve high proportions of educationally disadvantaged students. Criticism of charter schools did not deter their proponents. George W. Bush pledged millions to open charter schools and the Obama administration declared its support of charters soon after taking power. By decade's end the Department of Education had awarded millions in federal funds to states with charter-school programs.

Sources:
Elissa Gootman, "Public vs. Charter Schools: A New Debate," *New York Times*, 5 April 2006;

Jodie Morse, "Do Charter Schools Pass the Test?" *Time* (4 June 2001);

Diana Jean Schemo, "Study of Test Scores Finds Charter Schools Lagging," *New York Times*, 23 August 2006;

U.S. Department of Education, Office of the Under Secretary, *www2.ed.gov/rschstat/eval/choice/pcsp* (Washington, D.C.: 2004).

DECLINE IN ARTS AND HUMANITIES

Effect of No Child Left Behind. One criticism of No Child Left Behind (NCLB) was the time and funding the program took away from electives such as art and music in favor of "testable" subjects like math and science. At the end of the decade the National Arts Education Foundation released a comprehensive survey on the effects of NCLB on arts education. The study, conducted by Purdue University, surveyed 3,000 arts educators in fifty states. Teachers said that NCLB had a moderately negative effect on staffing, teaching load, and enrollment, but that there had been numerous negative consequences in scheduling, workload, and funding. For instance, 14 percent of those surveyed had students pulled out of class for issues related to testing. Fifty-eight percent of teachers reported a heavier workload because they were asked to teach other "testable" subjects in addition to their regular schedule. And 43 percent reported budget cuts in their arts program. In general, arts educators had a negative opinion of NCLB and 89 percent said that the law had a detrimental impact on faculty morale.

Recession. If NCLB was detrimental to arts education, the 2008 recession was catastrophic. As school districts struggled to balance shrinking budgets, music and art were usually first on the chopping block. In a 2009 survey conducted by the Department of Education, only 16 percent of eighth-graders reported going on an arts-related field trip, down from 22 percent in 1997. Less than 60 percent attended schools that offered music class three times a week. As class time in the arts declined, so did test scores in those areas. In 2009 Secretary of Education Arne Duncan addressed concerns that art education was slipping. "Particularly in times when budgets are tough, we worry about the arts," Duncan said, "It's a real worry, that students aren't hav-

Los Angeles Unified School District teachers and others protest state and local cuts to school funding (AP Photo/Reed Saxon).

ing that chance to have that well-rounded education." Duncan urged administrators to take advantage of federal grants and funds provided by the Federal Stimulus Act of 2009.

Higher Education. The recession had a similar effect on liberal arts in higher education. The humanities experienced a period of sharp decline in the 1980s and 1990s, when market forces shifted favor toward "practical" degrees such as business and science. Managers, administrators, and taxpayers wanted programs that produced measurable results, often difficult in subjective disciplines. Furthermore, many argued, the humanities did not prepare students for a particular vocation. Richard M. Freeland, Massachusetts commissioner of higher education, explained that the humanities tend "to focus almost entirely on personal intellectual development. What we haven't paid a lot of attention to is how students can put those abilities effectively to use in the world. We've created a disjunc-

tion between the liberal arts and sciences and our role as citizens and professionals." This disjunction led to "a crisis of confidence" for professors in the liberal arts, producing two schools of thought: that the humanities had an intrinsic value that could not be monetized or that, in order to survive, humanities scholars would have to show what a degree in English (or visual arts, or Spanish) could do in the marketplace. The crisis of confidence worsened in 2008. When the recession began, the already dwindling funding for the humanities was in danger. Ph.D. candidates in the humanities faced a dismal job market. According to a 2008 survey conducted by the *Chronicle of Higher Education,* of 200 institutions, 5 percent were on a total hiring freeze while 43 percent were on a partial freeze. The Modern English Association's job listings in English, literature, and foreign languages dropped 21 percent in 2008–2009.

THE INFLUENCE OF TEXAS

Because Texas accounted for nearly 10 percent of the national textbook market, publishers often wrote their textbooks with the Lone Star State in mind. "The bottom line is that Texas and California are the biggest buyers of textbooks in the country, and what we adopt in Texas is what the rest of the country gets," said Carol Jones, field director of the Texas chapter of Citizens for a Sound Economy, an organization that monitored textbooks for political bias. Texas had long been a battleground for textbook wars, and the 2000s were no exception. The Texas Education Code explicitly stated that textbooks should promote democracy, patriotism, and the free-enterprise system. Conservatives worked hard to keep what they saw as a "liberal bias" out of textbooks, while liberals fought back against what they perceived as censorship. In 2001 conservative members of the Texas board scored a victory by voting to reject texts that they found "anti-Christian" and "anti-American"; they also voted to reject texts that concluded as scientific fact that the earth temperature was rising due to global warming. Of two books approved, one was funded in large part by mining and oil companies while the other was subjected to major changes. The publisher of *Environmental Science: How the World Works and Your Place in It* agreed to alter some passages about climate change. For instance, the sentence "Destruction of the tropical rain forest could affect weather over the entire planet" was changed to "Tropical rain forest ecosystems impact weather over the entire planet." Also added was: "In the past, the earth has been much warmer than it is now, and fossils of sea creatures show us that the sea level was much higher than it is today. So does it really matter if the world gets warmer?" One year after the

environmental studies battle, the board clashed over *Out of Many,* a history textbook for high-school students. Conservative members objected to passages that detailed rampant prostitution in the nineteenth-century West. "It makes it sound that every woman west of the Mississippi was a prostitute," said Grace Shore, Republican chairwoman. "The book says that there were 50,000 prostitutes west of the Mississippi. I doubt it, but even if there were, is that something that should be emphasized? Is that an important historical fact?" Pearson-Prentice Hall, the publisher, immediately removed the book from consideration. In 2009 the state's influence over textbooks made headlines again, when the board voted to uphold the teaching of evolution as mainstream science, removing the "strengths and weaknesses" language that teachers had been required to use when teaching the theory. Conservative members found other victories, however, in language they attached to the curriculum. For example, biology teachers were required to "analyze and evaluate the sufficiency or insufficiency of natural selection" to explain the complexity of the cell. Earth science teachers had to consider "current theories of the evolution of the universe including the estimates for the age of the universe." Critics of the board's conservative agenda were disappointed. "The State Board of Education pretty much slammed the door on 'strengths and weaknesses,'" said Dan Quinn of the Texas Freedom Network, an organization that promotes the teaching of evolution, "but went around and opened all the windows in the house."

Sources: Michael Brick, "Defeat and Some Success for Texas Evolution Foes," *New York Times,* 26 March 2009;

Alexander Stille, "Textbook Publishers Learn: Avoid Messing With Texas," *New York Times,* 29 June 2002.

Sources:

Patricia Cohen, "In Tough Times, Humanities Must Justify Their Worth," *New York Times,* 24 February 2009;

Francis Conroy, "In a Technocratic Age, Study of the Liberal Arts is Even More Important," *Christian Science Monitor* (17 July 2001);

Sam Dillon, "Study Finds Instruction in Art Lags in 8th Grade," *New York Times,* 15 June 2009;

Andrew Kahn and Aalok Mehta, "Obama Education Secretary Affirms Arts as 'Core Academic Subject,'" *Dana.org* (19 August 2009);

F. Robert Sabol, "NCLB: A Study of Its Impact on Art Education Programs," *arteducators.org* (3 February 2010).

EVOLUTION VS INTELLIGENT DESIGN

Controversy. In 1999 the Kansas State Board of Education made headlines when they ignored the opinions of an expert panel and removed any mention of the theory of evolution from the science curriculum. A year later voters ousted those who supported the change. Over the next few years, opponents of the teaching of evolution regained seats on the board and in 2005 they challenged the current curriculum standards. Specifically, the board discussed teaching that there was controversy over Charles Darwin's theory of evolution and that it was in fact, only theory. Many teachers and research scientists protested, arguing that there is no reasonable scientific argument against teaching evolution. In the end, the board ruled to adopt new standards that included not only teaching the controversy around evolution, but presenting intelligent design as an alternate theory.

Intelligent Design. "Teaching the controversy" was a slogan for the intelligent-design movement. Proponents claimed that there were holes in Darwin's theory, specifically the inability to explain fully the complexity of living beings and natural life. Intelligent design proposed that life could not be a coincidence or result of random mutations and was best explained by the influence of an outside agent of some sort. Though the word "God" was studiously avoided, many considered intelligent design simply a subtler form of creationism. The organization most associated with advocacy for intelligent design was the Discovery Institute of Seattle, Washington. In the 2000s the Institute focused on promoting the election of intelligent-design proponents on state school boards and then challenging curriculum standards. The plan was to draw attention to the controversy over evolution, raise public doubts about Darwin's theories, then gradually develop textbooks and teaching materials that explained the concept of intelligent design. Although few scientists considered intelligent design a viable theory, a survey of adults in 2005 found that 55 percent thought children should be taught creationism or intelligent design as an alternative to evolution. More than twenty states considered laws that would challenge the teaching of evolution.

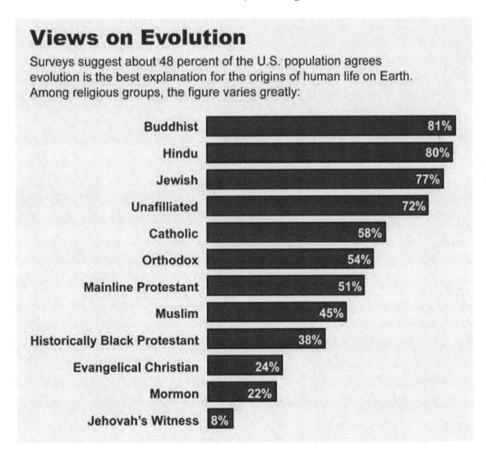

Chart detailing belief in the theory of evolution among various U.S. religious groups (from Pew Forum U.S. Religious Landscape Survey, conducted in 2007, released 2008)

Scientists React. Many scientists were reluctant to be a part of the intelligent-design debate for fear of legitimizing what they saw as a meaningless claim. "I'm concerned about implying that there is some sort of scientific argument going on," noted scholar Richard Dawkins; "there's not." Most argued that intelligent-design proponents played by a different set of rules. They did not, for example, publish their arguments in peer-reviewed journals or conduct experiments to test their theories. Scientists also argued that the theory of evolution in fact offered an answer to the problem of complexity because it described slow, gradual change over millions of years. *Kitzmiller* v. *Dover Area School District* was the first case heard by a federal court about the constitutionality of teaching intelligent design in schools. The suit was brought by parents of students in a district near York, Pennsylvania, after they learned that, before reading about the theory of evolution, ninth-grade students would hear the following statement, read by school administrators:

Because Darwin's Theory is just a theory, it is still being tested as new evidence is discovered. The Theory is not a fact. Gaps in the Theory exist for which there is no evidence. . . . Intelligent Design is an explanation of the origin of life that differs from Darwin's view. The reference book *Of Pandas and People* is available for students to see if they would like to explore this view . . . . As is true with any theory, students are encouraged to keep an open mind.

During the trial, President George W. Bush weighed in on the debate, stirring up more political controversy. "I felt like both sides ought to be properly taught," the president said, "so people can understand what the debate is about. I think that part of education is to expose people to different schools of thought." Scien-

tists and advocates of the separation of church and state were infuriated while social conservatives rallied around the president's comments. Regardless of Bush's support, a judge found that teaching intelligent design in schools was unconstitutional and promoted a "particular view of Christianity." He argued that intelligent design could not be considered science because it involved supernatural causation, made assertions that could not be tested, and caused students to doubt evolution without giving them any scientific reason to do so.

Sources:
Elisabeth Bumiller, "Bush Remarks Roil Debate on Teaching of Evolution," *New York Times*, 3 August 2005;

"Intelligent Design Derailed," *New York Times*, 22 December 2005;

Claudia Wallis, "The Evolution Wars," *Time* (7 August 2005);

Jodi Wilgoren, "In Kansas, Darwinism Goes on Trial Once More," *New York Times*, 6 May 2005.

HIGHER EDUCATION

Rise of For-Profit Universities. In the 2000s for-profit institutions such as the University of Phoenix, sometimes referred to as career colleges, saw a dramatic increase in their enrollments, particularly among minority students. These colleges came under criticism, accused of aggressively recruiting low-income students without regard to whether the student would benefit from the degree or be able to pay back the large sums of money borrowed in order to pay tuition. Students could also be trapped; many credits that students earned would not transfer to a traditional college due to differences in accreditation. According to the college board, students who pursued an associate degree at a for-profit college incurred 2.5 times more debt than those who attended a community college. Students who pursued a bachelor's degree at a for-profit school took on 58 percent more debt than those who attended a public four-

SCHOOL LUNCH REFORM

"School lunches are based on an outdated idea—that hungry kids only need calories," said Margo G. Wootan, director of nutrition policy at the Center for Science in the Public Interest, a health-advocacy group. "What hungry kids need is healthy food." During the decade the push for healthy food in schools reached the tipping point. Childhood obesity statistics soared, as did obesity-related diseases. Experts in the medical community warned that eating habits children learned in school—as well as their ailments—would stick with them for life. Public-health officials began vigorously advocating for more regulation and federal funding for school lunches. In 2004 many states passed laws regarding what could be sold in school vending machines. Schools in Washington, D.C.,

for example would not sell food or drink with more than seven fat grams and fifteen sugar grams. Beverage sizes could no longer exceed sixteen ounces, and fruit drinks were required to contain at least 20 percent juice. When Michelle Obama became first lady in 2009, she made childhood nutrition one of her top priorities, working to amend the Childhood Nutrition Act (1966) by increasing funding to schools. By the end of the decade, many schools sought to lead the way by improving their meals to offer whole grains and lean meats. Some schools even started providing children with locally grown produce.

Sources: Lesley Alderman, "Putting Nutrition at the Head of the School Lunch Line," *New York Times*, 5 November 2010;

Arlo Wagner, "School Vending Machines Shed Colas, Candy Bars," *Washington Times*, 30 September 2004.

year institution. In 2008 Congress passed the Higher Education Opportunity Act, a reauthorization of the Higher Education Act (1965). The new law required all colleges to be more transparent about the actual cost of attending and to provide real-cost calculators to potential students.

Federal Reform. In the middle of the decade, Congress passed several measures to ensure that lower-income families could afford higher education, despite soaring tuition costs. Under new regulations passed in 2007, the Department of Education began releasing a user-friendly list of the cost of colleges and universities. Any institution that significantly raised tuition would have to report why the price hike was needed and what it would do to keep costs down in the future. The reforms also required institutions of higher learning to report any relationship they had with student lenders, banning gift giving or profit sharing between lenders and educational institutions. George Miller (D-Cal.), chairman of the House Education Committee, said that the new law would "create a higher-education system that is more consumer-friendly, fairer and easier to navigate." To make the process easier for families seeking financial aid, the legislation called for a new two-page EZ FAFSA form. "Though it was only a seven-page form, you had to hire a financial services outfit to do it," Senator Barbara Mikulski (D-Md.) said. Though the new regulations were intended to lower costs and increase transparency for college students, many of the measures were negated by state education budget cuts.

Sources:
David Hawkins, "Who are For-Profit Colleges Serving, and at What Cost?" *Diverse Issues in Higher Education,* 24 (27 December 2007);

Vince Lechuga, *Minority Students Increasingly Choose For-Profit Schools,* interview by Tony Cox, *Npr.org* (13 March 2007);

Tamar Lewin, "House Acts to Overhaul College Loan Regulations," *New York Times,* 1 August 2008.

NO CHILD LEFT BEHIND

Rocky Start. On 11 September 2001, as the first plane crashed into the World Trade Center, President George W. Bush was reading to a group of schoolchildren in Sarasota, Florida. Education reform, a centerpiece of his 2000 bid for the presidency, was faltering in Congress and the administration sought to refocus public attention on the campaign for passage of No Child Left Behind (NCLB). Six months and one war later, Bush's goal became reality. On 8 January 2002 he signed NCLB. The bill, pushed through the House and Senate by a bipartisan group that included Edward Kennedy (D-Mass.) and John Boehner (R-Ohio), incorporated buzz-

A student buys snacks from one of the vending machines at Lane Tech High School in Chicago, 15 December 2005 (AP Photo/M. Spencer Green).

In 2003, spurred by increasing diagnoses of autism among American children, federal officials made their first move to produce a long-term plan to address the illness. A brain disorder that affects a person's ability to interact with the external world, autism can be mild or extreme, making it difficult for education policy makers to deal with it in any overarching way. The plan set forth by the government coordinated efforts from scientists, clinicians, policy makers, and educators. "The idea is to be challenging everyone in the field to be reaching for the best we can possibly do," said Dr. Steve Foote of the National Institute of Mental Health. By 2005 reported cases of autism had tripled, and education for those afflicted became a hot topic. Educators experimented with different methods; many began to favor early, intensive, one-on-one instruction. Unfortunately, that option was also prohibitively expensive. Some of the best programs cost up to $100,000, and the waiting list to participate was long. According to the federal Individuals with Disabilities Education Act (IDEA), public schools had to identify children with special needs and provide them with free and appropriate education, even if that meant reimbursing parents for private-school tuition. Many school districts were simply unable to pay for such care. Throughout the decade, parents of autistic children spoke out publicly to raise awareness of their struggle for support—both financially and educationally—and demanded more be done.

Sources: Faiza Akhtar, "For Autism Programs, Revolving Issues," *New York Times*, 12 March 2006;

Jane Gross, "Government Mapping Out A Strategy to Fight Autism," *New York Times*, 19 November 2003;

Polly Morrice, "Few Options for Treating Autism," *New York Times*, 12 November 2002.

words such as "measurable goals," "increased accountability," and "higher standards." As a bipartisan piece of legislation, NCLB mixed Democratic goals such as higher funding for public education with Republican concerns that states retain power to shape standards.

Specifics. Under NCLB, every state was required to develop and implement strict academic standards in reading and math. These standards had to cover every student—regardless of ethnicity, social class, or mental ability—to ensure that in twelve years, 100 percent of students could demonstrate satisfactory skills. The law also required states to create their own tests and assessments, to be administered to students in third through eighth grade annually. The results were published in annual "report cards" that detailed the progression toward student proficiency and also determined how much funding each district would receive from the federal government. Students had to show Adequate Yearly Progress (AYP). Underperforming schools were subject to punitive measures and corrective action, including government takeover or even shuttering. Children in a school that underperformed two years in a row would be allowed to transfer to a better district or attend free after-school programs and other supplementary sessions. The law required the federal government to provide funding for the requirements to be implemented. Language in the legislation excused states from NCLB requirements if the federal funding was not adequate.

Criticism. Opposition to NCLB was sharp and immediate. State officials felt the law asked too much while offering little financial support. In order to enact these changes, officials argued that schools would need to recruit highly trained teachers. New tests and assessments would also cost money and time and require new staff. Some officials felt that NCLB promoted increased government involvement. Education experts said guidelines were too narrow and warned that instructors would teach "to the test"—wherein students are taught only what was expected to appear on the test—threatening broad and well-rounded education. Critical thinking, opponents said, had no place under the new law. Standardized tests as a mode of assessment also encouraged what opponents called "gaming the system," by selectively testing or even tampering with results. Others questioned the standards, arguing that there was little oversight of the process for creating assessment tests. Opposition also came from arts educators, who argued that with so much attention and funding given to math and reading, classes that fell outside of these "testable" subjects would be replaced or diminished due to a lack of financial support.

Impossible Standards? While many educators and officials felt that public school reform was needed, they argued that 100 percent proficiency was an unattainable goal, no matter how dedicated the teachers and students. Also, they pointed out, total proficiency included children who were learning English as a second language as well as children with cognitive disabilities. NCLB ignored cultural backgrounds, social and economic stratification, and varying needs. The guidelines forced a "one size fits all" answer to a complex set of problems. Because funding was awarded based on school improvement, opponents of NCLB argued that it would create a vicious cycle for underprivileged and underperforming schools and students.

Protests. In 2005 several groups led by the National Education Association (NEA) initiated a legal challenge asserting that the federal government had yet to appropriate aid to states for test creation, administration, and assessment. Michigan, Texas, and Vermont joined the NEA and American Association of School Administrators in filing suit. After ten months of deliberation, the U.S. Court of Appeals for the Sixth Circuit declared itself unable to decide whether NCLB represented an unfunded mandate. Other states, Utah, for example, passed legislation allowing educators to focus on the accountability sys-

President George W. Bush with Carolyn Bailey and her daughter, Isabelle, at the signing of the Individuals with Disabilities Education Improvement Act of 2004 (AP Photo/Lawrence Jackson)

tem and not the federal government's standards in the case of a conflict. In the absence of judicial or legislative relief, Education Secretary Margaret Spellings quietly made more lax certain points of the law, increasing, for example, the number of children that could be excused from the test due to extreme mental disabilities, in order to appease teachers and state lawmakers.

Results. By decade's end the debate over NCLB still raged and the outcome seemed mixed at best. Despite a spike in test scores in 2007, results remained stagnant. Overall, students improved modestly since states began enforcing the requirements. The "achievement gap" (proficiency differences between white and minority students) had yet to close. In high schools, test scores of white students remained higher than those of African American students. In 2009 the Obama administration initiated talks in Congress about the best way to reform NCLB, while leaving intact most of its basic tenets. A new push to prepare children for college and a competitive global economy became the administration's focus.

Sources:
Nick Anderson and Bill Turque, "Reading Scores Stall Under 'No Child' Law, Report Finds D.C. Fourth-Graders a Bright Spot in Disappointing 2009 Data," *Washington Post,* 25 March 2010;

David S. Broder, "Long Road to Reform," *Washington Post,* 17 December 2001;

Sam Dillon, 'No Child' Law Is not Closing a Racial Gap," *New York Times,* 28 April 2009;

Michael Dobbs, "NEA, States Challenge 'No Child' Program," *Washington Post,* 21 April 2005;

"Even Top Schools Can Fall Short Under 'No Child Left Behind,'" *Washington Post,* 14 April 2005;

"The New Rules," *Frontline: Testing Our Schools: No Child Left Behind, pbs.org* (1 September 2010);

Dean Schabner, "Teachers Challenge No Child Left Behind," *ABCNews.com* (9 September 2004).

SEX EDUCATION

Abstinence Only. There were two major approaches to sex education in American schools in the 2000s, and they were punctuated by an ideological divide between social conservatives and liberals. Comprehensive sex education affirmed that sex after puberty was normal, even inevitable, and focused on sexual-health awareness, pregnancy prevention, and the use of contraceptives. Abstinence-only education promoted waiting until marriage for sexual intercourse. Many of these programs emphasized morality and the dangers of sexu-

More states decline abstinence funds

Currently, only 28 states participate in the federal abstinence education program that continues to shrink.

Federal dollars for abstinence education, FY 2008

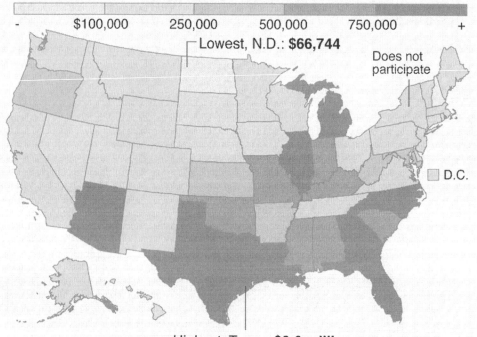

$100,000   250,000   500,000   750,000   +

Lowest, N.D.: **$66,744**

Does not participate

D.C.

Highest, Texas: **$3.6 million**

NOTE: Iowa and Arizona announced their intention to forgo their share of the federal grant at the start of the fiscal year that begins Oct. 1.

SOURCE: Administration for Children and Families, Department of Health and Human Services   AP

Map showing state participation in federal abstinence education program
(AP Photo/Damiko Morris)

ally transmitted diseases (STDs), fearing that the comprehensive approach represented a government endorsement of premarital sex. The federal government awarded more than $1 billion in funding to abstinence-only programs, which were initially created by Title V, an attachment to welfare reform in 1996. The Bush administration fought hard for these programs and made them a centerpiece of its policy. The stated goal was to promote the social, psychological, and health gains of abstaining until marriage. President George W. Bush also sought to export abstinence-only education worldwide to fight the AIDS epidemic. In 2002, more than one-third of high schools had incorporated abstinence-only education into their curriculums. In that same year, the Centers for Disease Control and Prevention reported that 60 percent of twelfth-graders admitted to being sexually active.

Opposition. Opponents criticized these programs for not discussing contraception and for misrepresenting statistics on contraceptive failure. James Wagoner, president of Advocates for Youth, complained of a "total disconnect between the [Bush] administration's spin and health policy research." Others charged that abstinence-only programs ignored teenagers' burgeoning sexuality and did not give them the tools or knowledge to deal with these changes. Groups that publicly denounced abstinence-only education in favor of a comprehensive program included the American Medical Association (AMA), American Public Health Association, and American Association of Pediatricians. There was also concern about the level of federal control over the abstinence-only programs. If states accepted funding, teachers were required to instruct that sex before marriage was "likely to have harmful psychological and physical effects," and that abstinence was the "only certain way" to

PREGNANCY PACT?

In May 2008 the principal of Gloucester High School in Massachusetts told reporters that a record number of pregnancies among her students that spring were due to a pact made by a group of girls who planned to have babies and raise them together. Though the school superintendent and mayor of the seaside town north of Boston quickly denied the story, it soon made national headlines. Superintendent Christopher Farmer argued that while some of the girls "expressed pleasure at being pregnant, that does not mean they made a pact." Staff at the high school's health clinic had been embroiled in a debate about offering contraceptives. Two of the three doctors resigned when it became clear that the hospital administering the clinic was opposed to offering students condoms and oral contraceptives. After the scandal broke, a committee formed to determine a way to lower the number of teen pregnancies. The committee eventually voted to allow contraceptives to be distributed with parental consent. Though it was never confirmed that the girls entered into a pact, the controversy reignited the debate over sex education and offering contraceptives in school. The controversy found its way into popular primetime shows such as *Dateline;* a Lifetime network dramatization, *Pregnancy Pact;* and a 2009 documentary, *The Gloucester 18.*

Sources: Kathy McCabe, "17 Gloucester High Students are Said to be Pregnant," *Boston Globe,* 29 May 2008;

Katie Zezima, "Officials Reject Report of Pregnancy Pact," *New York Times,* 24 June 2008.

prevent pregnancy and STDs. In order to receive federal funding, private health groups had to agree to follow eight strict criteria, including teaching that "a mutually faithful monogamous relationship in the context of marriage is the expected standard of human sexual activity," and that "sexual contact outside the context of marriage is likely to have harmful psychological and physical effects." Many opponents of abstinence-only felt that teaching children to wait until marriage was alienating and confusing for sexually abused children, homosexual children, and those with single parents.

Lackluster Results. Many abstinence-only proponents claimed that the programs were too recent to get an accurate reading of their effectiveness. A landmark eight-year nonpartisan federal research study showed in 2007 that an abstinence-only curriculum did not reduce the rate of teenage sexual activity. The General Accounting Office found similar results, in addition to finding that most programs were not scientifically reviewed and may have been promulgating inaccurate information. Polls found that parents were largely in favor of comprehensive sex education, or at least a compromise approach. While parents did not want

their teenagers having sex, they did want them to have the knowledge about how to stay safe. In 2009 President Barack Obama's proposed budget eliminated almost all funding for abstinence-only programs and instead directed money to teen-pregnancy prevention, but advocacy for abstinence-only education remained strong among religious groups and social conservatives.

Sources:
"Abstinence-Only Fails to Stop Early Pregnancies, Diseases," *USA Today,* 30 June 2007;

Sharon Jayson, "Obama Budget Cuts Funds for Abstinence-Only Sex Education," *USA Today,* 11 May 2009;

Debra Rosenburg, "The Battle Over Abstinence," *Newsweek* (9 December 2002);

Steve Sternberg, "Sex Education Stirs Controversy," *USA Today,* 10 July 2002.

VIOLENCE

Debates about the Causes. Memories of the 1999 Columbine school massacre were still fresh at the beginning of the decade, and the question of why students engaged in acts of spectacular violence was the subject of intense public debate. After Columbine, the federal government commissioned a study of thirty-seven school shootings from 1974 to 2000 to profile the shooters and gain insight into the causes of such tragedies. The study found that oft-cited causes such as the glorification of violence in the entertainment gaming industries were in fact negligible. In most cases, school shooters shared certain personality traits and psychological disorders. Narcissism, debilitating low self-esteem, depression, childhood trauma, and substance-abuse problems were common characteristics. The study also revealed that many of the shooters felt severely marginalized and powerless, but almost always confided in at least one person about their plans. While these findings provided insight, they did little to alleviate the pressure and fears parents and teachers felt.

Media Saturation and Zero Tolerance. Daytime talk shows and evening news programs were saturated with stories of school violence, although the incidence rate for these attacks had actually not changed in many decades. One study of California local news found that while 70 percent of reporting on violent crime featured young people, only 14 percent of violent crimes were committed by young people. Though many complained that the media exaggerated and sensationalized the problem, fear and worry were rampant among parents and students. To prevent further violence, many school districts and administrators began enforcing zero-tolerance policies. Under these guidelines, there was little individual consideration for rule breakers. In some cases, the possession of nail clippers could be punished as harshly as possession of a knife: both infractions triggering immediate suspension. Dozens of stories emerged of generally well-behaved children being suspended or sent to alternative schools for carrying aspirin in their book bag, spitting, or being late to class. The rate of expulsion doubled when these policies took effect.

Further Violence. On 2 October 2006 an attack at an Amish school in rural Nickel Mines, Pennsylvania, shocked the nation. Charles C. Roberts, a non-Amish man, entered West Nickel Mines Amish School with an assortment of weapons and restraints. He sent male students and some visiting adults out of the school, tied up the ten remaining female students, and shot at them while they faced the blackboard. Five girls were killed, five others injured, and Roberts was dead from a self-inflicted gunshot wound. Though Roberts was an adult from the community, the shootings reignited the national conversation about how to keep students safe. Less than a year later, the largest school massacre in American history took place on the campus of Virginia Tech University in Blacksburg. On 16 April 2007 senior Seung-Hui Cho killed thirty-two people before turning the gun on himself.

Outrage and Reform. The Virginia Tech massacre sparked unprecedented media attention and public outrage and concern. Cho, who had been diagnosed with an anxiety disorder and received special education during his youth, had alarmed administrators before the shooting. He had been accused of stalking two girls; an English professor had asked that Cho be counseled after he turned in disturbing assignments. Because of federal privacy laws, many administrators were not informed of Cho's illnesses. Those who sensed something was wrong thought it would be in violation of privacy rights to call his parents or a doctor. In response to the incident the Department of Education proposed regulations to make clearer when university officials could release student information and to reassure them that they would not be penalized. These regulations were the first updates on privacy laws since the Family Educational Rights and Privacy Act (1974). There was further concern over how a mentally disabled person could buy two handguns though federal law forbade anyone who had undergone involuntary psychiatric care from doing so. Virginia had not been sending those records to the National Instant Criminal Background Check System. In 2007 Virginia governor Tim Kaine signed an executive order to start submitting the records immediately.

Sources:
Jonathan Alter, "Between the Lines Online: Back-to-School Jitters," *Newsweek* (20 August 2001);

Kris Axtman, "Why Tolerance Is Fading for Zero Tolerance in Schools," *Christian Science Monitor* (31 March 2005);

John Cloud and others, "The Legacy of Columbine," *Time* (19 March 2001);

Jeffrey Kluger, "Inside a Mass Murderer's Mind," *Time* (19 April 2007);

David Kocieniewski and Shaila Dewan, "Elaborate Plan Seen by Police in School Seige," *New York Times*, 4 October 2006;

Tamar Lewin, "After Campus Shootings, U.S. to Ease Privacy Rules," *New York Times*, 25 March 2008.

VOUCHERS

School Choice. Voucher programs were part of the school-choice movement allowing public-school students to attend private schools using government funds. Some vouchers were awarded by lottery, while others were assigned to children in low-performing schools or low-income families. Like charter schools, voucher programs were controversial. Opponents argued that not only were vouchers unconstitutional because they violated the separation between church and state, they also were ineffective and ultimately created greater inequality. Proponents felt that school choice inspired competition for students and funding, and thus improved failing schools. Though vouchers had been discussed since the Reagan administration, the long-term results of such a program were largely unknown. In the 2000s Americans finally learned what effect voucher programs had on various school districts.

Florida. In 2003 the Manhattan Institute for Policy Research published a report on Florida's A+ voucher program, considered one of the most aggressive of its kind, which allowed students in chronically failing schools to use government vouchers to attend private schools. A chronically failing school was one that received an "F" rating for two years in a row on the Florida Comprehensive Assessment Test (FCAT). The study found that the threat of losing students and funding to private schools had an effect on how public schools performed. For instance, schools facing competition, particularly

HOMESCHOOLING

Homeschooling grew in popularity throughout the decade, while state governments struggled to develop an acceptable policy for regulating those parents who chose this alternative form of education. In February 2008, Judge H. Walter Croskey of the Second District Court of Appeals in Los Angeles ruled that in order to homeschool their children, parents needed to have a credentialed teaching degree or else their children would be considered truants. Parents of 200,000 homeschooled children in California rallied against the decision, as did Governor Arnold Schwarzenegger. In August, Croskey overturned his decision, saying that if parents filed the necessary paperwork to declare their home a private school then they would be free to continue homeschooling, even without the teaching degree. "This is a victory for California's students, parents, and education community," said Schwarzenegger, "I hope the ruling settles this matter for parents and homeschooled children once and for all in California, and assures them that we, as elected officials, will continue to defend parents' rights." Homeschooling parents also lobbied for their children's participation in public-school extracurricular activities. They were taxpayers, too, they reasoned. In 2005, fourteen state legislatures passed bills that required school districts to open their athletic programs, clubs, and even AP classes to home-schooled children.

Sources: James Dao, "Taught at Home, but Seeking to Join Activities at Public Schools," *New York Times*, 22 June 2005;

Kristin Kloberdanz, "A Homeschooling Win in California," *Time* (13 August 2003).

those that had poor ratings, showed the greatest improvement. Nevertheless, the Florida Supreme Court declared the program unconstitutional in 2006. After the ruling, students in chronically failing schools had the option to transfer to another public school but could not opt to attend private school with state funding.

Milwaukee. Since 1990, when the Milwaukee voucher program was initiated, public schools in the city lost a quarter of its students. In 2000 more than 8,000 students were using vouchers. By 2007 that number had nearly doubled. The Milwaukee system was troubled by criticism and scandal. Many residents resented that their property taxes were going to private schools at the expense of public institutions. Others criticized the lack of regulation of voucher-participating schools, while some were found to be lacking any accreditation and standardized testing to measure achievement. Despite the criticism, Milwaukee experienced some positive results. Compared to public schools, in which fewer than half of ninth-graders graduated from high school, voucher-accepting private schools sent 85 percent of their students to college.

Cleveland. Ohio initiated a voucher program modeled after Milwaukee in an attempt to improve the City of Cleveland School District. The Pilot Project Scholarship, a lottery-style voucher program, awarded funds to low-income students in failing public schools. By 2002, 96 percent of students using vouchers were attending religiously affiliated schools. Angry taxpayers felt the program violated the establishment clause, which prohibits Congress from promoting any one religion over another. In a five to four decision in *Zelman* v. *Simmons-Harris* (2002) the Supreme Court ruled the program constitutional. Writing for the majority, William Rehnquist stated that "the Ohio program is entirely neutral with respect to religion. It provides benefits directly to a wide spectrum of individuals, defined only by financial need and residence in a particular school district. It permits such individuals to exercise genuine choice among options public and private, secular and religious. The program is therefore a program of true private choice." The court developed a five-part test to determine whether a voucher program was constitutional. The Private Choice test dictates that the program must have a valid secular purpose; aid must go to parents and not the schools; a broad class of beneficiaries must be covered; the program must be neutral with respect to religion; and there must be adequate nonreligious options.

More Challenges. Throughout the decade, polling showed that the public generally did not support voucher programs, preferring instead that existing public schools be reformed. While alternative-school choices became more mainstream, teachers' unions and average Americans still generally opposed the movement. The challenges faced by voucher programs were similar to those of charter schools. Opponents criticized the lack of government oversight on private schools that received funding. These schools had a great deal of autonomy in hiring and curricular decisions. In one sensational case of

END OF SUMMER VACATION?

"**I** know longer school days and school years are not wildly popular ideas . . . but the challenges of a new century demand more time in the classroom."—President Barack Obama

As American test scores continued to pale in comparison to their global counterparts, experts and politicians began looking for solutions to keep students competitive. One of the most talked-about proposals was to shorten summer breaks. "Our school calendar is based upon an agrarian economy and not too many of our kids are working in the fields today," pointed out Secretary of Education Arne Duncan in 2009. Experts argued that a three-month gap in instruction could stunt intellectual growth. Some teachers called it "the summer slide," as students often forgot much of what they had learned in the previous year. Research showed that for lower-income, less-privileged students who were already prone to trouble in school, the "slide" was more pervasive; affluent students tended to have their education supplemented throughout the summer by trips to museums, vacations, or camps. In addition to longer school years, education advocates pushed for longer school days. Many charter schools enforced such hours and more public schools began offering optional afternoon instruction.

Sources: "Obama Proposes Longer School Day, Shorter Summer Vacation," *foxnews.com* (27 September 2009);

David Von Drehle, "The Case Against Summer Vacation," *Time* (22 July 2010).

inadequate oversight, a Cleveland school hired a convicted killer. Another controversy surrounding vouchers was over who should get the funds. Though typically vouchers were offered to low-income families, this was not always the case. Some programs were designed for special-education students or students in underperforming schools. In 2007 the Utah state legislature passed a universal voucher program, meaning *any* student could attend a private school, with voucher values depending on family income. Voters repealed the act in a statewide referendum, however, before the law was enacted. While alternative programs gained strength and popularity, questions about their efficacy and justice remained.

Sources:
Lynette Clemetson, "A Ticket to Private School," *Newsweek* (27 March 2000);

"Education Vouchers: Free to Choose, and Learn," *Economist* (3 May 2007);

Jay P. Greene and Marcus A. Winters, "When Schools Compete: The Effects of Vouchers on Florida Public School Achievement," *Education Working Paper*, Manhattan Institute for Policy Research (August 2003).

HEADLINE MAKERS

LAURA WELCH BUSH

1946–

FIRST LADY

Early Life. Laura Welch was born on 4 November 1946 in Midland, Texas. The only daughter of a home builder and a bookkeeper, Bush knew early on that her parents, though not college graduates themselves, had high educational hopes and expectations for her. Bush attended Southern Methodist University in Dallas and earned a bachelor's degree in education in 1968. She earned a master's in library science from the University of Texas in 1973. After college, Bush was a teacher and school librarian in Houston and Austin. In 1977 she met George W. Bush and three months later, they were married. She is the mother of twin daughters.

Fighting for Education. During the 1990s, George Bush served two terms as Texas governor, and his wife, once reserved and quiet, became an outspoken champion of education. As first lady, Bush established the Texas State Festival, which raised more than $1 million for state libraries. Literacy became one of her top priorities, and she helped write legislation to create reading-readiness programs for preschoolers. In 2001, Bush became the first lady of the United States. Her first initiative was to recruit retired military personnel as teachers because of their knowledge of math and science. She hosted the first National Book Festival, which featured well-known authors signing books and giving readings. She founded the Laura Bush Foundation, to provide school libraries with funds to buy up-to-date books, often overlooked in the budget battles in favor of technologies. Bush also spoke out for greater voting rights for women in the Middle East, established a teacher-training program in Afghanistan, as well as education campaigns against breast cancer and heart disease. In May 2006 she announced a $500,000 grant for school libraries that had been devastated by Hurricane Katrina. She is the

UNESCO Honorary Ambassador for the Decade of Literacy for the UN Literacy Decade (2003–2012).

Sources:
"First Lady Biography: Laura Bush," National First Ladies' Library, *firstladies.com;*
"Laura Welch Bush," *whitehouse.gov;*
"Laura Welch Bush as an Education Advocate," *UNESCO.org.*

DREW GILPIN FAUST

1947–

HISTORIAN AND HARVARD PRESIDENT

Early Life. Drew Gilpin Faust was born on 18 September 1947 in New York City. She grew up in Virginia and at a young age noticed segregation and inequality, even though her own circumstances were comfortable. In fifth grade, Faust wrote to then-president Dwight D. Eisenhower, expressing her support for integration. "Please Mr. Eisenhower please try and have schools and other things accept colored people," she wrote. Faust studied at the prestigious women's college Bryn Mawr and took part in civil-rights marches and Vietnam War protests. After graduating, Faust attended the University of Pennsylvania, earning her master's and Ph.D. in American civilization in 1975. She stayed at Penn and later became department chair. Her scholarship flourished and she wrote many groundbreaking books about the pre–Civil War South, including the award-winning *Mothers of Invention: Women of the Slaveholding South in the American Civil War* (1996).

Leading Harvard. Faust joined the faculty at Harvard in 2001. She became the founding dean for the Radcliffe Institute for Advanced Study, which she turned into a well-known center for gender studies. In 2005 Harvard president Lawrence Summers made infamous comments about the lack of women in the sciences. In response to the controversy, Faust was named to head a task force designed to hire and promote women in the sciences at Harvard. When Summers stepped down in 2006, the Harvard Corporation choose Faust from a long list of distinguished candidates to become the first female to lead the oldest university in the country.

Sources:

"Drew Gilpin Faust to Become Harvard University's President," *American Historical Association* (March 2007), *historians.org*;

"Up Front: Drew Gilpin Faust," *New York Times,* 3 September 2009.

HENRY LOUIS GATES JR.

1950–

EDUCATOR

Early Life. Henry Louis Gates Jr. was born on 16 September 1950 in Keyser, West Virginia. After graduating from Yale, Gates won a fellowship to study at Cambridge University in England. There, he met his mentor, Nigerian playwright Wole Soyinka, who convinced Gates to study African American literature. After earning his Ph.D., Gates was awarded a $150,000 grant from the MacArthur Foundation for his rediscovery and republication of the first novel, Harriet E. Wilson's *Our Nig; or, Sketches from the Life of a Free Black,* published by an African American in the United States (it had long been forgotten and attributed to a white writer). Throughout his early career, Gates worked to get more African American works included in the literary canon. He also advocated for the establishment of a body of African American literary criticism. In 1991 Gates became chair of the Afro-American studies department at Harvard University. At the time, there was only one other professor in the department. Gates transformed the department by recruiting top black intellectuals such as Cornel West, Evelyn Brooks Higginbotham, and William Julius Wilson.

Educating the Public. Gates's mission to educate the public about African American history and culture continued throughout the 2000s, both inside and outside classroom walls. Gates and his colleagues completed *Africana: The Encyclopedia of the African and African American Experience* (1999). When in 2000 the McDonald's Corporation devoted a year to celebrating African American heritage, Gates wrote a two-volume set called *Little Known Black History Facts,* which was sold at the restaurants. In 2006 Gates launched the PBS television program *African American Lives* (based in part on a 2004 publication coedited by Higginbotham), which examines the roots and ancestry of prominent African Americans, such as Oprah Winfrey, Whoopi Goldberg, and Quincy Jones.

A New Conversation. On 16 July 2009 Gates returned to his home in Cambridge, Massachusetts, following a trip to China. Upon finding that his front door was jammed, Gates enlisted the help of his driver to jar it open. Meanwhile, a neighbor dialed the police, thinking a break-in was in progress. When responding officer Sergeant James Crowley arrived, Gates said he provided the proper identification. But according to Crowley, Gates was antagonistic and uncooperative. Crowley arrested Gates for disorderly conduct. While the charges were eventually dropped, the matter became front-page news. Would Gates have been detained if he was white? Was it necessary to handcuff Gates, who walks with a cane? Soon, President Barack Obama weighed in on the matter, saying Cambridge police acted "stupidly." The president later admitted he should have chosen his words more carefully and apologized to Crowley by phone. Weeks later, the three men, along with the vice president, shared beers in the rose garden at the White House and had a conversation about race in America.

Sources:

Richard Thompson Ford, "The Depressing Cycle of Racial Accusation," *Slate* (23 July 2009), *slate.com*;

"Henry Louis Gates, Jr.," Program in the History of American Civilization, Harvard University, *fas.harvard.edu*;

"Henry Louis 'Skip' Gates, Jr.," *African American Lives,* 2, *pbs.org*.

ROD PAIGE

1933–

EDUCATION SECRETARY

Early Life. Roderick Raynor "Rod" Paige was born in Monticello, Mississippi, on 17 June 1933 and grew up in the segregated South. His father, a school principal, and mother, a librarian, taught their children the value of education, saying it was the answer to the world's problems. Paige took his parents encouragement to heart and graduated from Jackson State University with honors. After college, Paige took a football-coaching position at Utica Junior College and then with his alma mater. His career led him back to academia when he moved north to coach for the University of Cincinnati; while there he pursued a Ph.D. in physical education at Indiana University. In 1971 Paige was offered the job of head football coach at Texas Southern University in Houston. He accepted only after the university agreed to give him a faculty position as well; after four years, he was named dean of the School of Education. Paige was elected to Houston Independent School District in 1989, and in 1994 was appointed superintendent. Paige was extremely successful—during his tenure the number of students who passed the state achievement test increased by 36 percent, and school violence fell by 20 percent.

Secretary of Education. During his time in Houston, Paige worked closely with then-governor George W. Bush. During the 2000 presidential campaign, Paige expressed support for Bush's stance on school choice and voucher programs. Bush nominated Paige to be the first African American to serve as secretary of education, and he won bipartisan support. Paige promoted voucher programs and addressed the growing trend of school violence in America. His tenure was not without controversy. The centerpiece of the Bush administration's education reform, No Child Left Behind (NCLB), was often criticized by educators and administrators. Paige was on the front line of implementation, and after experiencing resistance from the National Education Association, the largest teachers union, he referred to the group as a "terrorist organization," in a private White House meeting. Allegations also surfaced that his success in Houston had been overblown and that dropout rates were seriously underreported. He resigned in 2004. Paige's tenure as secretary was later stained by revelations that his department had paid radio personality Armstrong Williams to make positive statements about NCLB.

Sources:
"Rod Paige: Former United States Secretary of Education (2001–2005)," *rodpaige.com*;

"Rod Paige, U.S. Secretary of Education—Biography," U.S. Department of Education, *ED.gov*.

LAWRENCE SUMMERS

1954–

SOCIAL SCIENTIST, HARVARD PRESIDENT

Early Life. Lawrence Summers was born on 30 November 1954 in New Haven, Connecticut, to a family of economists and educators. After graduating early from high school, Summers attended the Massachusetts Institute of Technology (MIT). By the time he earned his Ph.D. from Harvard in 1982, he was already an associate professor at MIT. Summers later became one of Harvard's youngest tenured professors at the age of twenty-eight.

Summers was the first social scientist to be awarded the National Science Foundation's Alan T. Waterman Award in 1987. In 1999 Summers was tapped for the position of secretary of the treasury by President Bill Clinton.

Harvard Presidency. Summers became the twenty-seventh president of Harvard University on 1 July 2001 and almost immediately alienated some faculty members with his brash manner and campaign for reform. The most famous of these conflicts was with distinguished African American studies professor, Cornel West, who claimed Summers had admonished him for recording a spoken-word compact disc and for missing too many classes due to extracurricular commitments. The rift caused West to leave Harvard for Princeton. Faculty and administrator resignations were common throughout Summers's tenure as president, though students continued to support him.

Resignation and Post-Harvard Career. In 2005 Summers claimed that "intrinsic aptitude" was to blame for the lack of women in math and science. Soon thereafter the faculty of the Department of Arts and Sciences issued a "no-confidence" vote, publicly criticizing Summers and making it clear his authority among staff had been compromised. The governing body, the Harvard Corporation, backed Summers, allowing him to retain his position. But the final straw came with the resignation of two high-ranking administrators whom many felt were pushed out by Summers. A second "no-confidence" vote was organized but Summers announced his resignation before it took place, making him one of the shortest-serving presidents in Harvard history. "Believing deeply that complacency is among the greatest risks facing Harvard, I have sought for the last five years to prod and challenge the University to reach for the most ambitious goals in creative ways. There surely have been times when I could have done this in wiser or more respectful ways," Summers wrote. After a sabbatical, Summers returned to Harvard as an endowed professor from 2007 to 2009, when president-elect Barack Obama appointed him director of the National Economic Council and assistant to the president for economic policy.

Sources:
"History: Larry H. Summers," Office of the President, Harvard University, *president.harvard.edu*;

David Pluviose, "Rifts Between Harvard President and Faculty Lead to Resignation,"*Diverse Issues in Higher Education* (9 March 2006);

Lawrence H. Summers, "Letter to the Harvard Community," Office of the President, Harvard University, *president.harvard.edu* (21 February 2006).

PEOPLE IN THE NEWS

Sami Al-Arian, a professor of computer science at the University of South Florida, was arrested and charged with conspiring to provide money and advice to the terrorist organization Palestinian Islamic Jihad. Al-Arian was found not guilty on eight of seventeen conspiracy charges, and a jury deadlocked on the others, though in 2006 he pleaded guilty to helping the organization.

Governor **Jeb Bush** defended his One Florida Initiative (2000), which banned race and gender preferences in university admissions, by saying it would "unite us, not divide us." Many Democrats and African American leaders denounced the plan, saying it would shut minorities out of higher education in Florida. Five years later, Bush did not regret his decision, saying, "we don't have one low criteria for one race at the expense of another. That, I think, is the morally right position."

Ethnic studies professor **Ward Churchill** stirred up controversy with "On the Justice of Roosting Chickens," an essay that claimed the attacks on 11 September 2001 were a result of U.S. foreign policy. When the University of Colorado at Boulder dismissed him in July 2007 for research misconduct, Churchill sued for wrongful termination, alleging that his unpopular politics were the real reason behind his firing. A court eventually determined that Churchill was wrongly terminated but awarded only one dollar in damages.

Former chief of Chicago public schools **Arne Duncan** was appointed U.S. secretary of education by President Barack Obama in 2009. In one of his first initiatives, Duncan asked states to compete for federal funds in the Race to the Top program.

Eighteen-year-old **Joseph Frederick** was suspended from school after hanging a banner that read "Bong Hits 4 Jesus" across from his school during the 2002 Olympic torch parade. Frederick sued the school district, and the case was eventually heard by the Supreme Court, which ruled that his First Amendment rights had not been violated because schools had a right to suppress speech that advocated drug use. Frederick eventually received $45,000 from the school district.

Richard Herman resigned as chancellor of the University of Illinois in 2009 after it was made public that he was a part of an admissions scandal in which high-ranking officials gave preference to lesser-qualified children of wealthy and well-connected individuals.

Tammy Kitzmiller, lead plaintiff in *Kitzmiller v. Dover Area School District* (2005), directly challenged the teaching of intelligent design. Kitzmiller's daughter was ridiculed by fellow students after expressing interest in evolution and was called "monkey girl." The court found that teaching intelligent design was unconstitutional based on earlier rulings that banned creationism from the curriculum.

Amanda Knox, a foreign-exchange student studying in Italy, was arrested and charged with murdering her British roommate. In 2009, after a long and controversial trial, Knox was found guilty and sentenced to twenty-six years in prison. Her parents and defense team argued that Knox, as an American, never got a fair trial.

Author and educator **Alfie Kohn,** a prominent figure in progressive-education theory and an outspoken opponent of George W. Bush's No Child Left Behind, claimed the act stole time from the teaching of critical thinking in favor of preparation for testing.

Former schoolteacher **Mary Kay Letourneau** was released from prison in 2004 after serving a seven-year sentence for having sex with a thirteen-year-old student; she reunited with the young man, with whom she has two children, and the couple married in 2005.

"My No. 1 priority now is to help as many people get to heaven as possible," said **Thomas Monaghan,** founder of Domino's Pizza. "I believe the best way to do that is education." In 2003 Monaghan founded the first Catholic university to open in a generation, the Ave Maria University in Florida. The school put faith at the center of its curriculum and students followed a strict behavioral and dress code.

In 2000 lawyer and atheist **Michael Newdow** sued on behalf of his daughter, charging that since the Pledge of Allegiance contains the words "under God" it should not be recited in schools because it violates the establishment clause of the First Amendment. The Supreme Court ruled that since Newdow did not have custody of his daughter, he could not file a suit on her behalf.

Michael Nifong, prosecutor in the Duke University lacrosse scandal in which three student athletes were charged with raping a stripper, dropped charges. After much criticism that he exaggerated the charges, interfered with the police investigation, and consistently referred to the defendants as "a bunch of hooligans" whose "daddies could buy them expensive lawyers," Nifong was disbarred in North Carolina for pushing ahead for his own political gain with an extremely weak case.

Televangelist **Pat Robertson** launched a twenty-one-day prayer offensive in 2003, asking followers to pray for the retirement of three liberal Supreme Court justices who had ruled to ban mandatory prayer in school.

Margaret Spellings, secretary of education under George W. Bush and a chief supporter of No Child Left Behind, in 2005 wrote a letter to Public Broadcasting Service (PBS) condemning a cartoon that featured a lesbian couple and their children. "Congress' and the Department's purpose in funding this programming certainly was not to introduce this kind of subject matter to children," she said. Her letter drew sharp criticism from Representative **Barney Frank,** who wrote in response: "I'm sorry that young people all over this country who happen to be gay or lesbian have now learned that the person who has been picked by the president of the United States to help with their education has such a fundamentally negative view of their very existence."

In 2002 **Quincy Troupe** served as California's poet laureate for less than a month before stepping down when it was discovered he had falsified his resume to reflect that he had graduated from Grambling State University in Louisiana. Troupe also resigned his professorship from the University of California, San Diego.

Cornel West resigned his prestigious professorship at Harvard in 2002 after he claimed he was treated poorly by university president Lawrence Summers. A longtime political activist and prominent African American studies and religion scholar, West had taken time off from teaching to record a rap album. Summers allegedly asked the professor to be more serious about his scholarship and teaching. West took a position at Princeton University.

It was revealed in 2005 that **Armstrong Williams** was paid $240,000 by the Department of Education to promote No Child Left Behind (NCLB) on his radio show. The agreement between Williams and the Bush administration required the conservative commentator to regularly mention NCLB and allow Education Secretary Rod Paige to be a guest on the show.

University of Georgia marketing professor **George M. Zinkhan III**'s body was found on 9 May 2009; he was the prime suspect in a triple homicide in which his estranged wife and two other men, one a Clemson University economist, were shot outside a theater in Athens.

DEATHS

Mortimer J. Adler, 98, prolific philosopher and educator who helped establish Great Books Foundation to introduce people to classic texts, director of the Institute for Philosophical Research in San Francisco, maintained long affiliation with *Encyclopædia Britannica,* 28 June 2001.

Stephen Ambrose, 66, history professor and writer who faced claims of plagiarism late in his career, 13 October 2002.

Daniel J. Boorstin, 89, Pulitzer Prize–winning historian and twelfth Librarian of Congress, 28 February 2004.

Matthew J. Bruccoli, 76, eminent F. Scott Fitzgerald scholar, Emily Brown Jeffries Distinguished Professor Emeritus of English at the University of South Carolina, co-founder of Bruccoli Clark Layman, 4 June 2008.

J. Robert Cade, 80, University of Florida professor and research scientist who developed Gatorade, 27 November 2007.

Kenneth B. Clark, 90, psychologist, whose research on effects of segregation on black children helped win *Brown* v. *Board of Education* (1954), 1 May 2005.

Gerald R. Ford Jr., 93, thirty-eighth president of the United States (1974–1977), signed the Education for All Handicapped Children Act (1975) establishing special-education programs, 26 December 2006.

Betty Friedan, 85, activist, author, wrote *The Feminine Mystique* (1963), encouraged women to pursue an education and professional success, 4 February 2006.

Milton Friedman, 94, Nobel Prize–winning economist who argued for educational voucher programs because they would promote competition and improve public schools, established Foundation for Educational Choice with his wife, Rose, 16 November 2006.

Clifford Geertz, 80, professor and cultural anthropologist whose contributions to the fields of anthropology, sociology, and cultural studies made him one of the most influential scholars of the twentieth century, 30 October 2006.

Stephen Jay Gould, 60, Harvard paleontologist and biologist whose research and publications contributed to the theory of evolution, 20 May 2002.

Joanne Grant, 74, journalist, documented civil-rights efforts in Black Protest (1968), 8 January 2005.

Jesse Helms, 86, senator (R) from North Carolina, introduced legislation to allow prayer in school and to ban sex education without parental consent, 4 July 2008.

William Redington Hewlett, 87, electrical engineer and cofounder of software giant Hewlett-Packard, founder of William and Flora Hewlett Foundation (which supports public schools and community colleges working toward a comprehensive and free online database of academic materials), 12 January 2001.

Lady Bird Johnson, 94, first lady of the United States (1963–1969), strong advocate for Head Start program that prepared underprivileged children for the classroom, 11 July 2007.

Edward M. Kennedy, 77, senator (D) from Massachusetts (1962–2009), longtime public-education advocate who defied his party and worked with George W. Bush to pass No Child Left Behind, 25 August 2009.

Nancy Larrick, 93, educator, advocated for diversity and complexity in children's literature, founder of International Reading Association, wrote *A Parent's Guide to Children's Reading* (1958), 14 November 2004.

Patricia A. Locke, 73, advocate for Native Americans, fought to preserve native languages and for greater control by Native American parents over education of their children, 20 October 2001.

Lester Maddox, 87, governor (D) of Georgia (1967–1971), outspoken opponent of school integration, 25 June 2003.

Burke Marshall, 80, law professor and head of the Justice Department's civil-rights division under President John F. Kennedy, instrumental in the desegregation of many southern schools, 2 June 2003.

Will Maslow, 99, lawyer for American Jewish Congress who fought against discrimination in education against Jews and African Americans, filed brief in support of *Brown* v. *Board of Education* (1954), 23 February 2007.

Vashti McCollum, 93, Illinois mother and atheist who brought successful lawsuit to Supreme Court challenging religious education in public schools, 20 August 2006.

Frank A. McCourt, 78, Irish American teacher, author, and Pulitzer Prize winner, who was honored by the New York City Department of Education with the Frank A. McCourt High School of Writing, 19 July 2009.

Lloyd Meeds, 77, representative (D) from Washington (1965–1979), fought for Head Start and Title IX of the Education Act, 17 August 2005.

Richard E. Neustadt, 84, presidential adviser and Harvard professor, known for research on the institution of the presidency, 31 October 2003.

Paul Newman, 83, actor, celebrity, and philanthropist who donated $10 million to his alma mater Kenyon College, cosponsored PEN/Newman's Own First Amendment Award (recognizes those who protect the amendment in written form), 26 September 2008.

Robert Nozick, 63, philosopher, distinguished Harvard professor, wrote *Anarchy, State, and Utopia* (1974), brought libertarianism into the mainstream academic conversation, 23 January 2002.

Frank L. O'Bannon, 73, governor (D) of Indiana (1997–2003), developed community-college system as well as alternative high schools and charter schools, 13 September 2003.

Rosa Parks, 92, civil-rights activist, founded scholarship foundation and civil-rights educational program, died 24 October 2005.

Claiborne Pell, 90, senator (D) from Rhode Island (1961–1997), sponsored federal funding for financially needy college students in the Basic Educational Opportunity Grants (Pell Grants), 1 January 2009.

Neil Postman, 72, New York University professor and social critic who warned that the entertainment industry was ruining the moral and intellectual education of children, 5 October 2003.

John Rawls, 82, Harvard professor widely regarded as one of the most significant scholars in modern political philosophy, 24 November 2002.

Ronald Reagan, 93, fortieth president (R) of the United States (1981–1989), sought to dismantle the Department of Education and give state and local governments greater authority over education, 5 June 2004.

Julius Benjamin Richmond, 91, medical doctor, first director of Project Head Start in the Johnson administration, 27 July 2008.

Michael Rossman, 68, helped organize the Free Speech Movement on the campus of University of California, Berkeley, 12 May 2008.

Claude Elwood Shannon, 84, mathematician, professor emeritus at Massachusetts Institute of Technology, considered "Father of Information Theory," 24 February 2001.

Herbert A. Simon, 84, economist, held endowed chair at Carnegie Mellon University, credited with many ideas behind modern curricula for master's of business administration, 9 February 2001.

Robert T. Stafford, 93, Vermont governor and senator (R), whose work on higher education led to the Federal Guaranteed Student Loan Program being renamed the Robert T. Stafford Student Loan Program, 23 December 2006.

Byron Raymond "Whizzer" White, 84, Supreme Court justice appointed by President John F. Kennedy who advocated affirmative action to cure educational segregation, 15 April 2002.

PUBLICATIONS

Karin Chenoweth, *It's Being Done: Academic Success in Unexpected Schools* (Cambridge, Mass.: Harvard Education Press, 2007);

Clayton M. Christensen, Michael B. Horn, and Curtis W. Johnson, *Disrupting Class: How Disruptive Innovation Will Change the Way the World Learns* (New York: McGraw-Hill, 2008);

David K. Cohen and Susan L. Moffitt, *The Ordeal of Equality: Did Federal Regulation Fix the Schools?* (Cambridge, Mass.: Harvard University Press, 2009);

Dave Cullen, *Columbine* (New York: Twelve, 2009);

Gareth Davies, *See Government Grow: Education Politics from Johnson to Reagan* (Lawrence: University Press of Kansas, 2007);

Richard F. Elmore, *School Reform from the Inside Out* (Cambridge, Mass.: Harvard Education Press, 2004);

Claudia D. Goldin and Lawrence F. Katz, *The Race between Education and Technology* (Cambridge, Mass.: Belknap Press of Harvard University Press, 2008);

Gerald Grant, *Hope and Despair in the American City: Why There Are No Bad Schools in Raleigh* (Cambridge, Mass.: Harvard University Press, 2009);

Jay P. Green, Greg Forster, and Marcus A. Winters, *Education Myths: What Special Interest Groups Want You to Believe about Our Schools—and Why It Isn't So* (Lanham, Md.: Rowman & Littlefield, 2005);

Eric A. Hanushek and Alfred A. Lindseth, *Schoolhouses, Courthouses, and Statehouses: Solving the Funding-Achievement Puzzle in America's Public Schools* (Princeton, N.J.: Princeton University Press, 2009);

Jeffrey R. Henig, *Spin Cycle: How Research Is Used in Policy Debates: The Case of Charter Schools* (New York: Russell Sage Foundation, 2008);

Frederick M. Hess, *Common Sense School Reform* (New York: Palgrave Macmillan, 2004);

E. D. Hirsch Jr., *The Knowledge Deficit: Closing the Shocking Education Gap for American Children* (Boston: Houghton Mifflin, 2006);

William G. Howell and Paul E. Peterson, *The Education Gap: Vouchers and Urban Schools* (Washington, D.C.: Brookings Institution Press, 2002);

Joanne Jacobs, *Our School: The Inspiring Idea of Two Teachers, One Big Idea, and the School that Beat the Odds* (New York: Palgrave Macmillan, 2005);

Richard D. Kahlenburg, *All Together Now: Creating Middle-Class Schools through Public School Choice* (Washington, D.C.: Brookings Institution Press, 2001);

Alfie Kohn, *The Homework Myth: Why Our Kids Get Too Much of a Bad Thing* (Cambridge, Mass.: Da Capo, 2006);

Daniel M. Koretz, *Measuring Up: What Educational Testing Really Tells Us* (Cambridge, Mass.: Harvard University Press, 2008);

Jay Matthews, *Work Hard. Be Nice: How Two Inspired Teachers Created the Most Promising Schools in America* (Chapel Hill, N.C.: Algonquin Books of Chapel Hill, 2009);

Deborah Meier, *In Schools We Trust: Creating Communities of Learning in an Era of Testing and Standardization* (Boston: Beacon, 2002);

Terry M. Moe, *Schools, Vouchers, and the American Public* (Washington, D.C.: Brookings Institution Press, 2001);

Moe and John E. Chubb, *Liberating Learning: Technology, Politics, and the Future of American Education* (San Francisco: Jossey-Bass, 2009);

Charles Murray, *Real Education: Four Simple Truths for Bringing America's Schools Back to Reality* (New York: Crown Forum, 2008);

William G. Ouchi and Lydia G. Segal, *Making Schools Work: A Revolutionary Plan to Get Your Children the Education They Need* (New York: Simon & Schuster, 2003);

Charles M. Payne, *So Much Reform, So Little Change: The Persistence of Failure in Urban Schools* (Cambridge, Mass.: Harvard Education Press, 2008);

Linda Perlstein, *Tested: One American School Struggles to Make the Grade* (New York: Holt, 2007);

Diane Ravitch, *Left Back: A Century of Failed School Reforms* (New York: Simon & Schuster, 2000);

Richard Rothstein, Rebecca Jacobsen, and Tamara Wilder, *Grading Education, Getting Accountability Right* (Washington, D.C.: Economic Policy Institute; New York: Teachers College Press, 2008);

Abigail Thernstrom and Stephan Thernstrom, *No Excuses: Closing the Racial Gap in Learning* (New York: Simon & Schuster, 2003);

Paul Tough, *Whatever It Takes: Geoffrey Canada's Quest to Change Harlem and America* (Boston: Houghton Mifflin, 2008);

Joe Williams, *Cheating Our Kids: How Politics and Greed Ruin Education* (New York: Palgrave Macmillan, 2005);

Daniel T. Willingham, *Why Don't Students Like School?: A Cognitive Scientist Answers Questions About How the Mind Works and What It Means for the Classroom* (San Francisco: Jossey-Bass, 2009);

Yong Zhao, *Catching Up or Leading the Way: American Education in the Age of Globalization* (Alexandria, Va.: Association for Supervision and Curriculum Development, 2009).

Teachers capitalized on students' interest in J. K. Rowling's *Harry Potter* and Stephenie Meyer's *Twilight* series to promote good reading habits, incorporating these popular novels into the curriculum. Dust jackets above are from the last two *Harry Potter* novels (2005, 2007, respectively), and the first two *Twilight* novels (2005, 2006, respectively).

FASHION

by EMILY MURRAY

CONTENTS

Sidebars and tables are listed in italics.

2000

Jan. The "green" Adam Joseph Lewis Center for Environmental Studies on the Oberlin College campus in Ohio includes a greenhouse wastewater-purification system.

23 Feb. Singer Jennifer Lopez makes a memorably revealing appearance at the Grammy Awards in a plunging sheer green Versace dress.

18 May The *Victoria's Secret Fashion Show* is webcast from Cannes, France, to American viewers, marking the first time the event takes place outside of the United States. Organizers raise $3.5 million for AIDS research.

Aug. Fashion notables Calvin Klein, Ralph Lauren, and Norman Norell are among the first inductees on the "Fashion Walk of Fame," on Seventh Avenue in New York City's garment district.

Oct. American fashion designer Tom Ford takes over as creative director of the French fashion house Yves Saint Laurent.

13 Oct. *Trading Spaces,* a television show that pitted two teams in redecorating a room in their rival's home, debuts on TLC.

2001

25 Mar. Icelandic pop star Björk turns heads in Los Angeles when she wears an unconventional swan-shaped dress on the red carpet at the seventy-third Academy Awards. Actress Julia Roberts wears a vintage Valentino black with white trim dress, considered by many to be the most beautiful on the red carpet for the decade.

22 June Clothing retailer Gap announces a 7 percent cut in its workforce.

28 Sept. Directed by and starring Ben Stiller, the movie *Zoolander* premieres, spoofing the shallowness of the fashion industry.

Nov. The last issue of the women's magazine *Mademoiselle* is published.

15 Nov. The *Victoria's Secret Fashion Show* airs on television (ABC) for the first time.

Dec. Sportswear designer Michael Kors launches his "leg shine" body-highlighting product.

2002

- Ford introduces a retro-style Thunderbird, which helps inspire a return to traditional car designs during the decade. Also introduced this year is the Hummer H2, a huge, boxy SUV, based on the military version; it is widely criticized as being energy inefficient and having high gas mileage.

Aug. The Levi Strauss company, which makes denim jeans and pants, announces it will close six of its U.S. factories and lay off more than 3,000 workers.

2003

- Jennifer Lopez introduces a new line of women's clothing, called Sweetface.

Feb. The first issue of *Teen Vogue,* a fashion magazine for young women, is published with singer Gwen Stefani featured on the cover.

May Cleveland, Ohio, opens its first annual fashion week. The event will grow to be the third largest in the country by the end of the decade.

20 May *America's Next Top Model*, a reality-television show, premieres on UPN. Created and hosted by supermodel Tyra Banks, the program features young models who compete for a break in the modeling industry.

17 July Architect David Childs is chosen to design the Freedom Tower, which will rise on the site of the destroyed World Trade Center in New York City.

2004

• New York socialite and model Nicky Hilton launches her clothing line, Chick.

23 May The Seattle Central Library building opens; a modernistic glass-covered set of geometric forms designed by architects Rem Koolhaas and Joshua Prince-Ramus of the radical Dutch architectural firm OMA, it is regarded as one of the most striking new structures in the United States.

26 May The Louisiana State legislature rejects a proposed bill that would have outlawed low-riding pants.

4 July The first stone of the Freedom Tower is laid at the former World Trade Center site.

28 Sept. Designer Geoffrey Beene dies in New York City; famous for his minimalist designs and the popular men's fragrance, Grey Flannel.

1 Dec. The Bravo Network's fashion-based reality-television show *Project Runway* premieres. Hosted by German American supermodel Heidi Klum, the program pits aspiring fashion designers in a competition to win a $100,000 prize and an editorial feature in *Elle* magazine.

2005

• Ford introduces the retro-style Mustang S197, a sleek update of its classic "muscle" car.

Summer The Boho Gypsy skirt sweeps the nation as a popular fashion statement.

6 Sept. The premier fall issue of *Men's Vogue* is released, with actor George Clooney featured on the cover.

2006

Feb. Renée Strauss (designer) and Martin Katz (jeweler) design a wedding dress featuring 150 carats of diamonds that is worth approximately $12 million.

• TOMS Shoes is founded by Blake Mycoskie. For every pair of shoes sold, the company donates a pair to a child in need.

30 June *The Devil Wears Prada*, starring Meryl Streep and Anne Hathaway, premieres. In the film, Streep portrays a thinly veiled fictional version of *Vogue* editor Anna Wintour.

27 June Revisions to the design of the Freedom Tower are made in response to criticisms that some aspects of the proposed structure are not aesthetically pleasing.

28 Sept. The television sitcom *Ugly Betty*, starring America Ferrara and Vanessa Williams, debuts on ABC. The series revolves around the experiences of a frumpy secretary at a fashion magazine.

2007

- Ray-Ban reintroduces its classic sunglasses design, the Wayfarer.

11 June The town of Delcambre, Louisiana, bans the wearing of saggy pants that expose men's underwear. Other towns in Louisiana will follow suit and ban the display of undergarments.

26 June Iconic Belgian American fashion designer Liz Claiborne dies in New York City.

19 July Period drama *Mad Men* premieres on AMC. Set in the early 1960s, the show features period-correct set and costume design and helps to launch a national retro fascination with the clean, modern look of the 1960s.

3 Aug. American clothing retailer Aéropostale opens its first store in Canada, as it begins to expand into international markets.

19 Aug. Style icons Mary-Kate and Ashley Olsen launch The Row, a high-end couture brand.

Sept. Protesters from People for the Ethical Treatment of Animals (PETA), dressed in sexy outfits, hand out citations to people wearing fur who are attending New York Fashion Week events.

Oct. The first annual Portland, Oregon, fashion week showcases ecofriendly designs and products.

Nov. The Los Angeles–based clothing company American Apparel sparks controversy by running a billboard in Manhattan depicting a topless model bent against a wall, which critics and feminists claim is pornographic and incites violence against women.

Dec. Public schools in Atlanta ban the wearing of "baggy oversize clothing."

2008

Apr. The cover of *Vogue*'s "Shape" issue, featuring basketball star LeBron James and Brazilian fashion model Gisele Bündchen, is criticized for allegedly playing on racial stereotypes.

13 May U.S. District Judge Richard Smoak rules that a junior at Ponce De Leon High School in Florida was denied her First Amendment rights when she was prohibited from wearing gay-pride clothing.

7 Aug. Antifur ads, sponsored by PETA, featuring Olympic swimmer Amanda Beard posing nude debut.

Oct. Reports reveal that the Republican National Committee spent more than $150,000 on clothes for vice-presidential candidate Sarah Palin, including items purchased at Saks Fifth Avenue and Neiman Marcus.

30 Oct. Condé Nast publications announces it will cease publication of *Men's Vogue*.

22 Dec. Donna Karan announces that her fall 2009 clothing lines will not include fur, after protests from the organization PETA.

2009

- Chris Yura, a former model and football player, founds SustainU, a clothing line that uses only recycled materials and domestic labor to produce its products.

Jan. Former competitive skater and fashion designer Vera Wang is inducted into the U.S. Figure Skating Hall of Fame for her costume designs.

Jan.	First Lady Michelle Obama selects twenty-six-year-old Taiwanese American designer Jason Wu to make her gown for the presidential inaugural ball.
14 Jan.	The foundation of the Freedom Tower, now known as the One World Trade Center, is completed.
11 Mar.	During a possible high-speed automobile race on the streets of Newport Beach, California, TapouT brand cofounder Charles "Mask" Lewis dies in a crash. Along with partner Dan "Punkass" Caldwell, Lewis had built the company from a start-up in 1997 to yearly sales of more than $200 million.
June	Jennifer Lopez closes the Sweetface brand.
June	The new modernistic, "green" Cooper Union academic building, designed by Thom Mayne, opens in New York City.
17 June	Clothing retailer Eddie Bauer files for Chapter 11 bankruptcy protection.
20 Aug.	*Project Runway* moves from Bravo to the Lifetime Network.
Nov.	*Glamour* magazine hosts a photo-shoot article on plus-size models. Several high-end fashion lines have begun to produce fashion for larger women.

Models backstage during the Time Warner *In Style* magazine fashion show in New York City, 7 September 2005 (AP Photo/Jennifer Graylock)

OVERVIEW

Mainstreaming Couture. Though known for its exclusivity in the past, the world of high fashion increasingly became the subject of popular discussion in the decade. Television programs such as Bravo's *Project Runway* introduced Americans not only to the ins and outs of creating fashionable clothing but also to many fashion-world stars through hosts Michael Kors (a noted fashion designer) and Nina Garcia (fashion director of *Elle* and *Marie Claire* magazines), as well as guest judges such as Betsey Johnson and Rachel Roy. Movies such as *The Devil Wears Prada* (2006) further popularized the high-fashion world. The publishing, television, and film phenomenon of *Sex and the City* (television, 1998–2004; movies, 2008, 2010) presented viewers with a parade of glamorous brands worn by empowered, successful women, and helped make shoe designer Manolo Blahnik a household name. With the proliferation of cable-television networks, a host of reality programs offered instruction for everyday viewers on the finer details of dressing well. As consumers developed a taste for top names in the fashion industry, even wholesale retailers (Target, Kmart) sought out partnerships with well-known designers such as Isaac Mizrahi, providing high concepts for low budgets.

Celebrity Fashion Lines. It often seemed as if one of the true badges of celebrity in the 2000s was to release a fashion line. Movie and television stars such as Jennifer Lopez, Jessica Simpson, Mary-Kate and Ashley Olsen, Reba McEntire, and Elizabeth Hurley all produced their own labels, to varied success. Sarah Jessica Parker's line, Bitten, was released to great fanfare as a high-fashion choice for consumers on a budget, though it met with only limited success. Hip-hop stars, in particular, entered the world of fashion with a vengeance. Following on the successes of rap mogul Russell Simmons and his popular Phat Farm brand, Jay-Z (Shawn Corey Carter) and Sean "Diddy" Combs released their own clothing lines. Jay-Z's Rocawear brand was an astounding success in the urban-wear department, selling for $206 million to Iconix group in 2006.

Nostalgia. As they faced a new century, Americans increasingly looked backward to earlier trends for fashion and style inspiration. Fashion offered a pastiche of styles that harked back many decades. Young hipsters embraced the tights and skinny jeans of the 1980s, even as couturiers found inspiration in the elegance of mid-twentieth-century formal wear. Vintage looks on the runway matched consumers' desire to find secondhand treasures, whether in the consignment shops or on resale websites such as eBay or Etsy. Automobile designs, too, reflected the backward gaze. Ford's redesigned Mustang evoked the muscle cars of the 1960s; indeed, the automaker released a special edition of its sports car called the Bullitt, after one driven by Steve McQueen in the 1968 movie of the same name.

Metrosexual. Masculine fashion experienced a dramatic overhaul, as young professional men began to embrace grooming and fashion habits previously thought to be outside the realm of acceptable male tastes. The term was a combination of metropolitan and heterosexual, and often described a straight man who did not fear being branded as too feminine for caring about his appearance. The modern metrosexual male was not shy about wearing fashionable clothes or visiting the spa. Television series such as *Queer Eye for the Straight Guy* (2003–2007) brought the metrosexual impulse into the mainstream, while salons offered services exclusively for men.

Patriotism. Following the terrorist attacks of 11 September 2001, there was an upsurge in patriotic feeling. Accordingly, displays of the flag and national colors became more ubiquitous, as America waged an international war against terrorism, as well as two ground wars in Afghanistan and Iraq. Sales of clothing featuring the American flag, from T-shirts to sports coats, skyrocketed in the months after 9/11. For politicians, wearing a flag lapel pin became standard procedure, so much so that when presidential candidate Barack Obama was seen without one on the campaign trail he was heavily criticized. In architectural design the nation's attention turned to replacing the destroyed World Trade Center towers with a new structure. Daniel Libeskind's initial design was meant to evoke the Statue of Liberty, and to reference the year of American independence by reaching 1,776 feet into the New York City skyline.

Green Design. The increasing concern shared by many Americans over human impact on the natural environment pervaded the design world. Designers began introducing clothing lines made only from organically grown natural fibers. The vintage craze touched on the desire by many to recycle and reuse items rather than waste resources by creating new clothing. Architects worked increasingly to make their designs more energy efficient and in harmony with the environment. The green-building movement sought to create a minimal impact through the use of innovative systems such as rainwater filtration, solar heating, and wastewater recycling. Renewable and recycled building materials were used to cut down on the carbon footprint created by building projects. Interior designers mixed old and new, finding vintage treasures in antique shops and secondhand stores, while incorporating elements made from recycled or renewable materials. Bamboo, an abundant, fast-growing grass, became a favorite for its multiple uses, from pillow stuffing to flooring. Automobiles reflected the change as well, as designers worked to create sleeker, more aerodynamic body styles to increase fuel efficiency. The easily recognizable look of hybrid or electric cars became a fashion statement in itself, as the ultimate symbol of the conscientious green consumer.

TOPICS IN THE NEWS

ARCHITECTURAL DESIGN

One World Trade Center. The destruction of the World Trade Center on 11 September 2001 left a scar on the American psyche as well as on the landscape of lower Manhattan. In the months and years following the attack, New York state and city officials formed the Lower Manhattan Development Corporation (LMDC), which began making plans to rebuild the complex. The architectural design of the project was approached with care, as it needed not only to satisfy the commercial demands of its owners and the city but also to aid in the national healing process after the devastating terrorist attacks, providing an affirmation of continued American strength. In 2002 the LMDC launched a competition to determine the design of the project, which became known first as "Freedom Tower." The winner was Daniel Libeskind, who had previously designed the Jewish Museum Berlin. His design, which included a spiraling, gracefully arching 1,776-foot tower, was eventually reworked after conflict with the World Trade Center lessee, real-estate developer Larry Silverstein, who chose his own architect, David Childs, changing the design to include a more traditional, symmetrical tower. The tower, which became known as "One World Trade Center," was still slated to reach 1,776 feet, making it the tallest building in the United States (as well as referencing the year of American independence), but Libeskind's design was largely written out. On 4 July 2004 New York governor George Pataki laid a ceremonial cornerstone for the rebuilding project, though various delays meant that construction did not begin in earnest until 2006. By the end of 2009, the first floor above ground level was just beginning to rise. With an estimated cost of $3.1 billion, the construction of One World Trade Center is projected for completion in 2013.

Sustainable Design. In the environmentally conscious 2000s, one area of largest growth in architecture was in the realm of sustainable design, which sought to incorporate into buildings elements that would reduce waste, make minimal impact on the natural environment, and, whenever possible, be highly efficient or even self-sustaining in regard to energy consumption. Taking inspiration from the natural world, sustainable design sought to eliminate waste, searching for renewable and recyclable elements. This model, known as "biomimicry," set as its goal the constant reuse of materials in closed cycles. Sustainable buildings used, wherever possible, renewable or low-impact resources in construction, replacing hardwood flooring with fast-growing and abundant bamboo, or recycled linoleum. A pioneer in the field was architect William McDonough, who won the contract to rebuild Ford Motor Company's River Rouge complex in Dearborn, Michigan. After his renovations, the site featured a cutting-edge green "living roof," which was covered with sedum, a plant that not only aided in the roof's built-in rainwater-treatment processes but also helped to cool the building and save on energy costs. Ford's ecoconsciousness was rewarded with millions of dollars in yearly savings on water expenditures alone. For his contributions to sustainable design, McDonough received a Smithsonian Institution National Design Award in 2004. In 2000 the U.S. Green Building Council, a nonprofit trade organization, set forth a certification system for buildings known as Leadership in Energy and Environmental Design (LEED). Earning this certification quickly became the most widely recognized international standard for green design, with many states and municipalities offer-

The Walt Disney Concert Hall (2003) in Los Angeles, designed by Frank Gehry (photograph by Arturo Ramos)

ing incentives to builders who adhered to LEED standards. In addition, many architectural schools began offering concentrations in the field, and in 2009 the American Institute of Architects began requiring its members to enroll in classes in sustainable design.

Disney Hall. Perhaps the most notable achievement in American architecture in the decade was Frank Gehry's Walt Disney Concert Hall in Los Angeles, completed in 2003. Begun after an initial gift of $50 million from Lillian Disney, widow of Walt Disney, to the city of Los Angeles, the construction project lasted more than a decade and ran to $274 million, including $110 million for an underground parking garage. Gehry's design utilized large, undulating arcs of stainless steel to create a free-flowing deconstructivist masterpiece similar in form to his earlier work for the Guggenheim Museum in Bilbao, Spain. Reviews of the building were overwhelmingly positive: Marcus Binney of the *Times* (London) called it a "silver galleon with full sails billowing in the wind": Cathleen McGuigan of *Newsweek* swooned, "its roller-coaster swoops and gleaming curves seem to mirror [Gehry's] formidable energies and ambitions"; and Paul Goldberger of

The New Yorker noted that "the outside of Disney Hall lifts the spirits of those who see it from the sidewalk or, this being Los Angeles, from the windows of their cars." With a 2,265-seat capacity, the auditorium serves as home to the Los Angeles Philharmonic, and the building includes a fine-dining restaurant, Patina. The hall's interior was praised for its excellent acoustics, with walls and ceiling of Douglas fir and oak flooring. Despite the positive reception by the design and music community for the hall, its neighbors proved to be tougher critics. The lustrous curves of the hall's exterior presented an unexpected problem, as they served to concentrate and reflect the ample southern California sunshine, creating spots on the sidewalk that exceeded 130 degrees Fahrenheit and a glare that made life miserable for nearby condominium owners. As a result, in 2005, workers began buffing the stainless-steel panels of the building's exterior in order to create a less-reflective matte finish.

Open-Air Malls. As the trend toward local, in-town shopping meant a downturn for many large shopping malls, a design focus changed to reflect consumers' desire to do their shopping in a more traditional environment

Leadership in Energy and Environmental Design (LEED)

Bank of America Tower, New York City

Opened for business in 2009, the fifty-five-floor, concrete, glass, and steel skyscraper featured a double-walled insulated facade, rainwater collection, filtered air ventilation, and self-sufficient energy production from a wind turbine. Built largely of recycled materials, it also utilizes new technologies for lighting and energy savings.

Boulder Community Hospital, Foothills Campus, Boulder, Colorado

First hospital to achieve Silver LEED rating by designing a sustainable, healthy environment that also featured "cost-saving motion-activated lights, an energy-saving central utility plan, recycling rooms, extensive Xeriscape techniques and waterless urinals."

Brooklyn Children's Museum, New York City

Opened in 2008, the museum used renewable and recycled materials in its construction, and features geothermal environmental control and multiple energy-saving sensors.

William J. Clinton Presidential Library, Little Rock, Arkansas

The only federally managed facility with a Platinum LEED certification (earned in 2007, after having received a Silver designation upon completion in 2004), the library features a green roof, a high level of recycling, and solar-power electricity production.

Hearst Tower, New York City

A forty-six-story steel-and-glass office building ("a faceted jewel") that features multiple-diamond shapes uses between 80 and 90 percent recycled steel, features rainwater collection, and has a reduced carbon footprint. The building reduced by one-third typical energy usage and features a three-story waterfall in the atrium.

Keystone Community Church, Ada, Michigan

Opened in 2004, the first LEED certified church can accommodate five hundred worshipers in the structure, which features radiant perimeter heat and precast flooring, expandable auditorium panels, low toxic paints and materials, and water-free urinals.

Nationals Park, Washington, D.C.

Home to the Major League Baseball Washington Nationals, this Silver LEED stadium used recycled materials and features newly designed ecofriendly irrigation systems, water-conserving plumbing, energy-saving light fixtures, drought-resistant landscaping, and reflective roofing materials.

Northland Pines High School, Eagle River, Wisconsin

Opened in 2006, the school is made from recycled material and features natural light.

Pasadena EcoHouse, Pasadena, California

Looking like a giant, white bird on the edge of a cliff, the ecofriendly concrete home features modern material and techniques that involved recycled materials, sound dampening, and energy efficiency.

Three PNC Plaza, Pittsburgh, Pennsylvania

The twenty-three-story steel and glass mixed-use skyscraper (offices, condos, apartments, stores, hotel, parking) utilizes "high-performance glazing, energy-efficient HVAC systems and low-emission materials to create an environmentally friendly interior."

Sources: Mahesh Basantani, "Three PNC Plaza: Pittsburgh's Shining Green Skyscraper," *inhabitat.com* (21 August 2008);

Jed Boal, "New 'Green' Skyscraper Sets Higher Standard for Healthy Workplace," *ksl.com* (7 October 2009);

"Clinton Presidential Library Receives Highest Green Building Rating," *clintonlibrary.gov;*

"First LEED Certified Hospital Built," *Interior Design* (29 January 2004);

"Green Ballpark," *washington.nationals.mlb.com;*

"The Green Museum," Brooklyn Children's Museum, *brooklynkids.com;*

Hearst Corporation, *hearst.com;*

Evelyn Lee, "Pasadena EcoHouse: First LEED Certified Concrete Home," *inhabitat.com* (7 March 2008);

New York City Architecture, *nyc-architecture.com;*

Julianne Winkler Smith, "Taking an Innovative Stand on Stewardship," *Worship Facilities* (March/April 2007);

"Uber-Eco Towers: The Top Ten Green Skyscrapers," *ecogeek.com* (June 2006).

while still taking advantage of the convenience of high-density retail space. So-called lifestyle centers began to replace the large, multistory enclosed mall environment with open-air shops, pedestrian-friendly sidewalks and promenades, as well as mixed commercial and residential development. The result was a mall that looked and felt in many ways like a stylized downtown area. Though composed of multiple freestanding stores, the lifestyle center usually incorporated a common design element with inviting landscape details, fountains, streetlamps, and even piped-in music. Suburban shoppers could enjoy the charm and nostalgia of Main Street without actually having to travel downtown or worry about finding a parking space. In-town developers sought to capitalize on the trend as well. The Hollywood and Highland center opened in November 2001 as part of a plan to revitalize the commercial center of the Hollywood district of Los Angeles, California. Anchored by the Kodak Theater, home to the annual Academy Awards ceremony, the center boasted dozens of shops, including such mall staples as American Eagle, Express, and Gap.

Sources:
"About the Building," *wtc.com;*

David W. Dunlap and Edward Wyatt, "Leaseholder Sees Limited Role for Libeskind at World Trade Center," *New York Times,* 30 May 2003;

"Enjoying the View from Out of Town," *Los Angeles Times,* 25 October 2003;

Paul Goldberger, "Urban Warriors," *New Yorker* (15 September 2003): 72–81;

Linda Hales, "At Design Awards, the Extraordinary that Touches the Everyday," *Washington Post,* 21 October 2004;

"The Inauguration of Walt Disney Hall," *npr.org* (23 October 2003);

Robin Pogrebin, "Architects Return to Class as Green Design Advances," *New York Times,* 19 August 2009;

Eric Roston, "New War on Waste," *Time* (26 August 2002);

Anna Sowa, "Trend Turns Bend Malls Inside Out," *The* (Bend) *Bulletin,* 8 May 2006;

Barbara Whitaker, "Hollywood's Newest Star is a Mall, and More," *New York Times,* 10 November 2001.

CLOTHING TRENDS

Green Fashion. A growing concern over materials used in the production of clothing led to a green movement in the fashion industry. Although no clear standard emerged, green fashion (or ecofashion) was concerned with using natural or recycled materials, being conscious of animal welfare, and using organically grown materials such as

Advertisement for fashion retailer H&M promoting its environmentally friendly Garden Collection
(from <www.pourfemme.it>)

CROWNING THE INAUGURAL

One of the most memorable fashion highlights of the 20 January 2009 inauguration of President Barack Obama was the hat sported by singer Aretha Franklin as she sang the national anthem. The grey felt hat featured a large bow on the front with crystal accents, and was created by Detroit designer Luke Song. "Three words describe how I felt," Song said, "Thrilled. Honored. And then just plain scared. I knew the hat would be seen by a billion people, and it had to be perfect." Song's millinery had been in operation for more than twenty-six years, but after garnering the national stage, business grew five-fold. More than five thousand copies of the hat were shipped in the months following the inauguration. Retailing for $180, and known simply as "The Aretha," the hat even got its own Facebook page with more than 96,000 fans.

Sources: Mr. Song Millinery, *mrsongmillinery.com*;

"Smithsonian Wants Aretha Franklin's Hat," *msnbc.com* (2 February 2009).

bamboo or cotton that left a minimal impact on the environment. In 2007 organic-fabric manufacturer Loomstate partnered with the high-end retail chain Barney's to create Loomstate for Barney's Green, the store's first ecofriendly label. On the more affordable end of the spectrum, Loomstate also teamed up with discount retailer Target to create Loomstate for Target, making ecofriendly fashion choices available to a wider consumer audience. From high-fashion designers such as Stella McCartney to discount department stores such as Target and Wal-Mart, a trend toward sustainability reached consumers on all levels. By the decade's end many recognizable clothing retailers were offering environmentally friendly fashion choices, including Banana Republic, Guess, and H&M.

Fresh Faces in Couture. Narciso Rodriguez was most famous in the 2000s for designing the stunning yet controversial black-and-red dress that Michelle Obama wore on election night in 2008. Though the first lady's fashion choice propelled him into mainstream awareness, the New Jersey–born designer was not unknown in the industry. He worked under accomplished designers such as Donna Karan and Calvin Klein and was the only American to win two Council of Fashion Designers of America (CFDA) Awards. When employed by Cerruti, he created Caroyln Bessette's wedding dress for her marriage to John Kennedy Jr. Another favorite of Obama was Chinese American designer Jason Wu, who was once an apprentice to Rodriguez. Previously working as creative director for Integrity Toys, he began releasing his own collections in 2006. Wu became a household name partly because of the ivory gown he designed for Obama to wear for the inaugural ball. Describing his inspiration, he said "I wanted it to look like

a sign of hope." Another fresh face on the fashion scene was Zac Posen, a rising New York designer. His first brush with fame came after he designed a dress for supermodel Naomi Campbell. He presented his first runway show in 2002. He was known for dressing stars such as Natalie Portman, Cameron Diaz, Gwyneth Paltrow, and Kate Winslet. He earned a CFDA award for Womenswear in 2004. His early style combined classic glamour with sharp edges and angular shapes. Later in the decade he became known for softer, more feminine pieces.

Celebrity Fashion. The decade produced many memorable celebrity fashion moments. At the 2000 Grammy Awards, actress and singer Jennifer Lopez wore a low-cut Versace dress that turned heads, as its dramatic V neck fell below her navel. Actress and musician Björk appeared at the 2001 Academy Awards wearing a dress that looked like a swan, complete with its neck wrapped around her neck for complete coverage. The feathery fashion statement, panned by most critics, was designed by Macedonian British designer Marjan Pejoski. Another fashion misstep occurred at the 2001 American Music Awards, as pop singers Justin Timberlake and Britney Spears arrived together in matching denim "formal wear." At the Golden Globe Awards in 2003, actress Lara Flynn Boyle appeared in a

Aretha Franklin sports a gray felt hat designed by Luke Song for her performance at the inauguration of President Barack Obama in 2009 (AP Photo/Ron Edmonds).

pink ballerina costume. High-waisted jeans made a brief comeback late in the decade, although not always with flattering results. In January 2009, actress Jessica Simpson was subjected to ridicule when a pair of the 1970s throwbacks was deemed to emphasize the fullness of her figure.

Vintage. The influence of vintage clothing expanded during the 2000s, with certain styles transcending any one particular moment in fashion. Vintage wear, in particular, increased in popularity, spurred perhaps by nostalgia, and changed the realm of shopping at secondhand clothing stores such as the Salvation Army or Goodwill into a boutique business all of its own. Designers presented vintage-inspired collections, along with a showcase of vintage pieces, in their shops. Another approach that gained popularity was using parts of vintage clothing and reworking old fabrics to create appealing products, allowing designers to reach a more current audience while recycling and reinventing. Sara George, owner of secondhand store Miami Twice, advised that "if you want to predict what's ahead, your best bet may be to look back." Chain resale stores such as Plato's Closet focused on a younger audience, offering used clothing but only accepting popular labels from Abercrombie and Fitch or Gap, giving shoppers a more economical option for keeping up with current trends. Shoppers could bring in clothes that were up to a year old and gain cash or store credit to buy used, but current, name-brand clothes for a discount.

Sources:

"All About Jason Wu," *wmagazine.com* (21 January 2009);

"High Fashion or Just Plain Weird?" *life.com* (9 July 2010);

Janet Ozzard, "Zac Posen," *style.com* (19 September 2002);

Marie-Joelle Parent, "She's Bringing the '60s Back," *Toronto Sun,* 29 March 2011;

Rachael Strugatz, "Narciso Rodriguez: Designer of Michelle Obama's Election Night Dress Looks Back," *huffingtonpost.com* (4 November 2009);

Feifei Sun and Claire Suddath, "The 25 Best and Worst Oscar Gowns of All Time," *Time* (22 February 2011);

Rajini Vaidyanathan, "Six Ways Alexander McQueen Changed Fashion," *bbc.com* (12 February 2010).

CLOTHING TRENDS FOR WOMEN

From the Past. In many ways the 2000s decade did not begin with a bold innovative style but took its direction from previous decades. The "grunge" era inspired by the Seattle music scene lingered with flannel shirts, distressed jeans, and work boots. Women wore minimalist styles with muted colors and simple lines most evident in designers such as Calvin Klein. The focus of the 1990s fashion trend was comfort and individual expression. Earlier decades, however, shaped new fashion as well. Marc Jacobs's 2003 runway collection was reminiscent of 1950s style. His attention to the past invited other designers to follow his lead, as retro chic consumed the middle part of the decade. Other trends fed into the retro craze as well. The desire for vintage clothing only grew with the advent of the television series *Mad Men* (2007–), which presented the clean mod-

MR. BLACKWELL'S LIST

Richard Sylvan Selzer, more commonly known as Mr. Blackwell, was an American fashion designer and critic famous for his annual Ten Worst Dressed Women list. He began the list in 1960 and published it on the second Tuesday of January every year. He was known for concise but devastating critiques, calling actress Sharon Stone "an over-the-hill Cruella DeVille," accusing Meryl Streep of looking like "a gypsy abandoned by a caravan," and calling Madonna "the bare-bottomed bore of Babylon." In addition to criticizing celebrity fashion choices, he also designed for clients such as Nancy Reagan, and worked as an actor, radio personality, and author. His final list was issued in January 2007; he died in Los Angeles on 19 October 2008.

Blackwell's Worst Dressed of the 2000s

2000:	Britney Spears
2001:	Anne Robinson
2002:	Anna Nicole Smith
2003:	Paris Hilton
2004:	Nicollette Sheridan
2005:	Britney Spears
2006:	Paris Hilton, Britney Spears (tie)
2007:	Victoria Beckham

Sources: Chris Ayers, "Fashion Critic Richard Blackwell Dies in Los Angeles," *Times* (London), 21 October 2008;

Kate Betts, "Mr. Blackwell," *Time* (23 October 2008);

Richard Lawson, "Mr. Blackwell's Worst Dressed List: The Past 20 Years," *gawker.com* (20 October 2008).

ern elegance of early 1960s women's fashion in a beautiful, stylized light.

Boho. By 2004 actress Sienna Miller, along with model Kate Moss and child stars turned business moguls Mary-Kate and Ashley Olsen, popularized the look known as "boho chic." Short for bohemian, boho style was characterized by oversized sunglasses, large hats, loose-fitting sweaters, and flowing skirts. Women wore peasant-style tops and donned cowboy boots with skirts and dresses. Hobo bags—large catch-all purses—were popular. The trend was rooted in the hippie style of the late 1960s with a revised, more elegant appeal. Boho's eclectic impulse invited women to mix and match patterns and styles, creating a look whose casual appearance was meant to seem effortlessly cool, despite the hard work that often went into the ensembles. The softness of the boho look was in many ways a reaction to the harder, metallic tones of high fashion in the previous decade. Although runway looks trended away

Leggings

Advertisement for clothing retailer American Apparel demonstrating the popularization of 1980s style elements (from <www.americanapparel.com>)

from the earthy style, boho remained an influential force in popular fashion, both among celebrities and at retail outlets.

Looks from the 1980s. Another popular style trend was the move away from an emphasis on uncomplicated comfort and toward a more glamorous aesthetic. Late in the decade, many highlights of fashion in the 1980s appeared, such as the return of hoop earrings and bright color combinations. Accessories of the 1980s resurfaced as well, with young women donning headbands and leggings. Retailers such as American Apparel helped to popularize this look

for a new generation. Leggings worn inside tall boots and ankle boots became prominent along with "skinny jeans" or tight-fitting, tapered-leg denims. The desire for ever-skinnier leg wear eventually led to the advent of "jegging," a combination of leggings and jeans meant to be worn as pants.

Casual Footwear. In the early 2000s Pamela Anderson popularized the UGG, a clunky, wool-lined sheepskin boot. The footwear soon became de riguer for young women, who wore them with jeans or even skirts. Anderson reversed course in 2007 and spoke against the company after "discovering" the boots were made of sheepskin. A

An unseen but ubiquitous fashion feature of the decade was the wildly popular women's undergarment known as "Spanx." The body-shaping "power panties" helped to create the appearance of slimmer waistlines for those who wore them. Launched in 2000 by entrepreneur Sara Blakely, Spanx experienced a meteoric rise after being featured on the *Oprah Winfrey Show* in November of that year, as a part of her annual "favorite things" episode in which she touted outstanding products. By the end of the decade the company had sold more than five million pairs. *InStyle* magazine named the formfitting hosiery the best body-shaping invention of the decade, and celebrities from Tyra Banks to Katy Perry admitted openly to using them. For men hoping to cut a more svelte silhouette, in 2008 the company began offering undershirts that promised to firm the chest and "eliminate bulk under clothes."

Sources: *oprah.com;*

Spanx.com;

Ellen Tien, "Dealing with Control Issues," *New York Times*, 4 February 2001.

vocal member of People for the Ethical Treatment of Animals (PETA), Anderson encouraged shoppers to buy brands that only used fake fur and leather. Another clunky but popular footwear choice that rose and fell in popularity were Crocs—the undeniably comfortable, however unattractive, lightweight clog with prominent vent holes that began as a boat shoe because of its breathability and quick drying. The item first experienced a wider popularity as an orthopedic shoe when it gained a seal of acceptance from the American Podiatric Medical Association. Popular with men and women, celebrity chef Mario Batali was seldom seen on his Food Network show without the brightly colored clogs. In a decade of casual footwear choices, the flip-flop was king. Once thought of primarily as a cheap, practical beach shoe, the flip-flop became everyday street wear and could even be seen at weddings and in the workplace. Designers dressed up the lowly slip-ons to match consumer demand. In 2009 Peche Platinum offered a pair for $400 with a strap made from crocodile skin; the ecoconscious could rest assured that 5 percent of profits on the product were destined for groups that worked against primate extinction.

High on Heels. High-heeled shoes experienced a renaissance in the decade. The fastest rise from obscure, high-end boutique item to household name belonged to Spanish shoemaker Manolo Blahnik. Popularized by *Sex and the City* (television, 1998–2004; movies, 2008, 2010), "Manolos" became the must-have shoe for those lucky *fashionistas* who could afford them. While they became a well-known product thanks to pop-culture publicity, they remained outrageously expensive. The handmade heels

could cost up to $14,000 a pair. French shoe designer Christian Louboutin introduced his signature red-sole shoes in the 1990s, but they gained popularity in the 2000s with the increased popularity of stilettos. The shoes eventually surpassed Manolos in sales and popularity. Other popular names in high-end high heels included Salvatore Ferragamo, Jimmy Choo, and Prada.

Sources:

Liz Appling, "Bringing Back the '80s," The Lariat Online, *baylor.edu* (8 October 2010);

Kate Betts, "Fashion: The School of Cool," *Time* (23 February 2004);

Suzanne S. Brown, "Mr. Blackwell's Dresses Impress at CSU Exhibit," *Denver Post*, 21 October 2010;

Gemma Champ, "Fashion: The Decade in Retrospect," *The National*, 27 December 2009;

Jo Craven, "Manolo Blahnik," *vogue.com* (20 April 2008);

Anita Hamilton, "The New Trend of Used Clothes," *Time* (31 May 2007);

Kate Novack, "Something Old, Something New," *Time* (1 March 2004);

Ray A. Smith, "Shades of Green: Decoding Eco Fashion's Claims," *Wall Street Journal*, 24 May 2008.

CLOTHING TRENDS FOR MEN

Suits. A return to color and retro tailoring occurred in men's formal wear in the 2000s. Celebrities such as singer/actor Justin Timberlake and television host Ryan Seacrest popularized three-piece suits. Near the end of the decade the double-breasted suit returned, most notably in fashion designer Valentino's 2007 runway show.

An American Movie Classics channel (AMC) period drama about an advertising agency on Madison Avenue, *Mad Men* made an immediate impact on the fashion world. Set in the early 1960s, the series reflected the stylized, modern fashion and culture of that decade. Many Americans were transfixed by the show's dapper advertising agents in tailored suits and thin ties, secretaries in pencil skirts, and housewives in elegant dresses. Costume designer Janie Bryant used fashion to delineate the changing roles for women in the 1960s: "Secretaries, they're working girls. I wanted to keep [their look] more about pleated skirts and pencil skirts and not have them wear trims and bows and lace kind of things to have that separation of lifestyle between the housewives and what's going on in the office." The show debuted in July 2007 and quickly influenced fashion designs on the runway. Designer Betsey Johnson, for instance, created dresses with a fitted waistline that reflected the period.

Sources: Robin Givhan, "A Rough Reality beneath a Slick Surface," *Washington Post*, 27 July 2008;

Clifford Pugh, "The 60's Revisited: TV's *Mad Men* Makes a Stylized Era Brand New," *Houston Chronicle*, 24 July 2008.

Promotional poster for the AMC series *Mad Men*. The series sparked a revival of early 1960s looks (<www.sundancechannel.com>).

Inspired by European fashion trends, as well as the early 1960s look popularized in the television series *Mad Men,* tailoring styles included tapering at the waist and narrower pants. Although skinny ties returned, the popularity of suits without ties grew even more. Fashion designer Thom Browne was a leading force in the popularity of slim-fitting suits. He saw the suit as a bold statement against an overly casual culture. Jeans and T-shirts had become standard attire he noted: "Everyone's dressed down. So actually putting on a jacket is the anti-establishment stance."

Metrosexual. Although the notion of a "metrosexual" was introduced in the 1990s, its popularity grew in the 2000s, especially in the wake of the Bravo television network's reality program *Queer Eye for the Straight Guy* (2003–2007), which dispatched a team of gay men to make over straight men who were mired in hopelessly conventional personal styles. A portmanteau of metropolitan and heterosexual, the metrosexual man was comfortable enough in his masculinity to pay attention to fashion trends, dote on personal grooming, work on his crêpe suzette technique in the kitchen, and have his closet well organized. In short, the metrosexual was a straight man who did not fear those stereotypes typically associated with femininity or homosexuality.

Casual. Brightly colored polo shirts returned to popularity as a casual staple for men, as the grungy-earth tones of the 1990s gave way to a more "preppy" aesthetic. The bohemian trend prevalent in women's fashion also inspired men's looks. Fashion-conscious men could be seen with mixed patterns and a combination of classic and new. The slimmer silhouette was not only restricted to formal attire but was also seen in sweaters and jeans. V-neck merino wool sweaters, worn over oxford shirts or by themselves, became a fashion staple. A shift toward more-casual attire also occurred in the workplace. Ties were no longer a staple of business attire. Many high-tech industries discouraged the wearing of ties as a way of promoting a youthful, creative company image.

Sources:
Cathy Horyn, "Review/Fashion; In Paris, Breathing New Life Into Men's Suits," *New York Times*, 2 July 2002;

LaMont Jones, "The Tie No Longer Binds Men's Fashion," *Pittsburgh Post-Gazette*, 29 March 2011;

Mark Simpson, "Here Come the Mirror Men," *Independent* (15 November 1994), reprinted in *marksimpson.com* (2006).

CLOTHING TRENDS FOR YOUTH

Showing Skin. The decade opened with pop icons such as singers Britney Spears and Christina Aguilera paving the way for youthful sexuality in mainstream fashion. Once popular on Disney's show *The All New Mickey Mouse Club* (1989–1994), these teen idols graduated to pop stardom bringing with them a generation of fans emulating the lat-

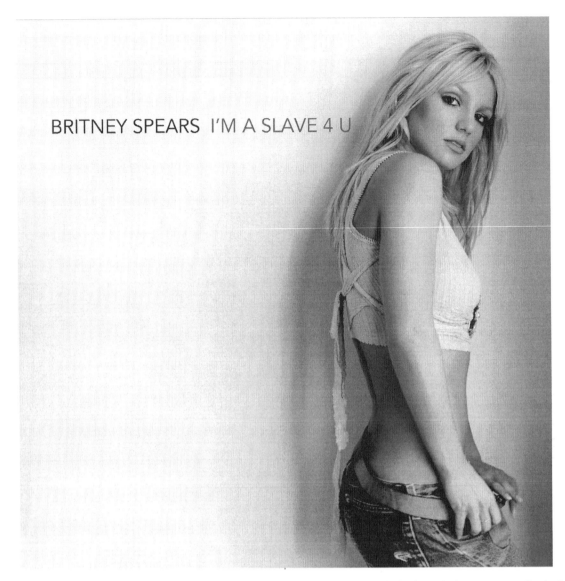

BRITNEY SPEARS I'M A SLAVE 4 U

Cover for Britney Spears's 2001 single "I Am a Slave 4 U." Spears and other pop stars helped popularize a more revealing look for teenagers that featured low waistbands and exposed midriffs (<www.chartstats.com>).

est styles. Tiny tops, exposed navels, and short shorts—however unsettling for many observers—dominated the media from awards ceremonies to music videos, such as Aguilera's "Genie in a Bottle" (1999) or Spears's "I'm a Slave 4 U" (2001). High-school and middle-grade students were not exempt from the growing fad. Tween boutique owner Jennifer Bruder explained how girls were testing the limits of school dress codes on how low waistbands could be: "[they] often roll them down twice." R&B singer Sisqó released the "Thong Song (Uncensored)" (2000) from his *Unleash the Dragon* album launching the "whale tail" trend, so named for describing the shape of woman's thong underwear showing above their pants as looking like a whale's tail flutes. As the decade drew to a close, American youth embraced a more mature style inspired from the past. Hemlines became lower, while texture, color, and detail in clothing gained ground. Designer David Wolfe explained, "This 'youth gone wild' theme in fashion is starting to fade away."

From Emo to Hipster. Emo or "emotive" music was a style that originated in the 1990s but moved to the mainstream by the early 2000s. Emo expressed sadness and teen isolation, and was represented by bands such as Jimmy Eat World. A closely associated distinct style emerged consisting of skinny jeans, band T-shirts, black-rimmed glasses, and Converse shoes. The style shifted during the decade from a more-tailored look to an intense appeal with darker clothes and dyed black hair. The term "hipster" came into popular use but was notoriously difficult to define. Like emo kids, hipsters were often seen in skinny jeans, oversized glasses, and thrift-store apparel. The sixteenth-century notion of *sprezzatura* (seeming effortlessly nonchalant while actually working quite hard) best described the hipster trend. In fact, the term carried a negative connotation, especially among middle-class youth. In the 1940s "hipster" was used to describe white youth who eschewed mainstream culture. By the 2000s, however, the term was appropriated and eventually usurped by mainstream culture. Trendy clothing stores such as Urban Outfitters and American Apparel mass produced a "hipster chic" for popular consumption.

Hip Hop. Hoodies and tracksuits, inspired by popular artists such as rapper Eminem, dominated hip-hop style, and in 2003 he introduced his own casual fashion line, Shady Ltd. Rap moguls Jay-Z and Sean Combs worked as hard at producing fashion trends through their respective labels as they did at releasing records. The overall look was one of muted colors and comfortable, loose-fitting clothing. Not all hip-hop fashion fit this mold, however. Rapper Kanye West introduced a "preppy" hip-hop look to match his debut album the *College Dropout* (2004). André 3000 of Atlanta rap group Outkast changed the image of hip-hop clothing with more tailored look, bold colors, and retro appearance. Baggy pants were replaced with a slimmer silhouette. He told *Esquire* magazine, "To me, that's real style, anything that feels comfortable and expresses your personality and makes you stand a little taller."

Sources:

"André 3000 Dubbed World's Best-Dressed Man," *msnbc.com* (11 August 2004);

Dan Fletcher, "Hipsters," *Time* (29 July 2009);

Isabel C. González, "Lessons in Style," *Time* (8 September 2003);

Mark Greif, "The Hipster in the Mirror," *New York Times,* 12 November 2010;

"The Origins of Emo," *worldofsubculture.com* (15 February 2010);

Helen A. S. Popkin, "What Exactly is 'Emo'," Anyway?" *msnbc.com* (26 March 2006);

Hitha Prabhakar, "10 Fashion Trends You Can't Ignore," *forbes.com* (28 August 2007).

FASHION INDUSTRY

Tom Ford and Gucci. When he was named creative director in 1994, Tom Ford brought a fresh approach that transformed the Gucci label. By 2000 he was a dominant force in the fashion industry as well as a popular celebrity. Ford sharpened Gucci's image to give the venerable fashion house an edge, a glamorous urban appeal that was instantly recognizable. Harold Koda, curator of the Costume Institute at the New York Metropolitan Museum, declared that Ford "had the pulse on the generation that everyone is trying to court . . . it's very much about nightlife: girls who are incredibly well maintained but look dirty. People on the prowl. And very sexy shoes." In 2004, however, because of irreconcilable differences between Ford and business partner Domenico De Sole, he left to pursue other options.

Celebrity Fashion Lines. After her success on the Home Box Office (HBO) series *Sex and the City,* Sarah Jessica Parker rocketed to fashion-icon status. In 2007 she announced her clothing line, Bitten, offering affordable fashion designs for women, available through discount-clothing retailer Steve and Barry's. "Women," she said "should be able to wear great clothes and not lie in bed at night feeling guilty about how much money they've spent." Despite much fanfare, the label never took hold, and shortly after, Steve and Barry's suffered financial problems, finally folding in 2008. Actress and singer Jennifer Lopez

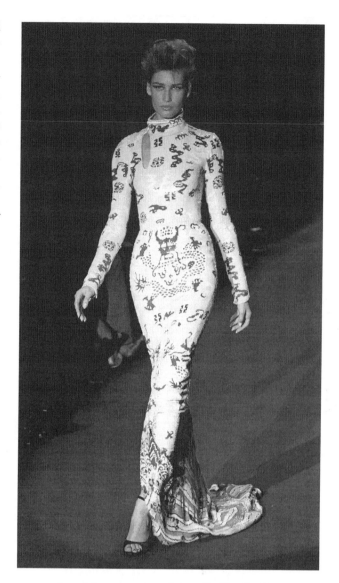

A model wearing a dress designed by Tom Ford for Yves Saint Laurent Rive Gauche's fall-winter 2004–2005 collection (AP Photo/Michel Euler)

moved from singer and actress to fashion designer. Her first line JLO had a young, sexy urban appeal while her later Sweetface presented a more mature look. More successful celebrity fashion offerings included singer and actress Jessica Simpson's self-titled line. She focused on handbags and shoes, but later expanded to include dresses, and in 2009 launched Intimates. Another pop star with fashion sense was Sean Combs. With the debut of Sean John in 1998, his style gained international attention and popularity as well as respect within the fashion industry. In addition to acclaim for his music career, in 2004 he was awarded the Council of Fashion Designers of America (CFDA) Men's Designer of the Year Award. American rapper Jay-Z created a clothing line in 1999 featuring men's sportswear, which gained popularity in both the domestic and international market. The brand, Rocawear, eventually expanded to include children's and junior's clothing as well as accessories. The label boasted a youthful street style that was fresh

In response to criticism of ultrathin models who risked health and life to achieve the tiniest possible runway figures, which resulted in several deaths and campaigns against the tragic effects of anorexia, the Council of Fashion Designers of America (CFDA) formed a committee in 2007 to develop these guidelines to maintain healthy lifestyles for models and reduce the incidence of eating disorders.

RECOMMENDATIONS

Educate the industry to identify the early warning signs in an individual at risk of developing an eating disorder.

Models who are identified as having an eating disorder should be required to seek professional help, and models who are receiving professional help for an eating disorder should not continue modeling without that professional's approval.

Develop workshops for the industry (including designers, agents, editors, and models and their families) on the nature of eating disorders, how they arise, how we identify and treat them, and complications that may arise if left untreated.

Support the well-being of younger individuals by not hiring models under the age of sixteen for runway shows; not allowing models under the age of eighteen to work past midnight at fittings or shoots; and providing regular breaks and rest. (Consult the applicable labor laws found at *www.labor.state.ny.us* when working with models under sixteen.)

Supply healthy meals, snacks, and water backstage and at shoots and provide nutrition and fitness education.

The **CFDA Health Initiative** is about awareness and education, not policing. Therefore, the committee does not recommend that models get a doctor's physical examination to assess their health or body-mass index to be permitted to work. Eating disorders are emotional disorders that have psychological, behavioral, social, and physical manifestations, of which body weight is only one.

The **CFDA Health Initiative** is committed to the notion of a healthy mind in a healthy body, and there cannot be one without the other. The industry is determined to foster a balanced approach to nutrition, recreation, exercise, work, and relationships.

Eating Disorders: Warning Signs

Members of the fashion industry—modeling agents, designers, magazine editors, stylists, and models themselves—are on the front line with regard to early recognition of eating disorders in our community. Identifying and treating eating disorders early can lead to improved outcomes. Yet early detection of eating disorders can be challenged by the fact that eating disorder symptoms often involve private behaviors or secret thoughts and beliefs that are not apparent from the outside. Below, we list a number of the more common warning signs. While alone, none of the warning signs listed below indicates a definite eating disorder, each of these behaviors and attitudes, particularly in combination, may warrant clinical attention.

- Drastic change in eating or exercise patterns
- Skipping meals; eating very little; denying hunger
- Avoiding situations that involve food or eating
- Unusual food rituals or behaviors (cutting food into little pieces, pushing food around on plate without eating it, hiding food in napkin)
- Adherence to a very strict diet or rules about food/eating
- Obsessive counting of calories, carbohydrates, or fat grams
- Regularly eating large amounts of food without weight gain
- Tendency to go to the bathroom after eating
- Hiding food; eating in secret
- Extreme fears of gaining weight
- Severe dissatisfaction with body weight, shape or appearance
- Rapid weight loss
- Using extreme measures to lose weight (e.g., laxatives, diet pills, diuretics)
- Compulsive or driven exercise; inflexible exercise routine
- Talking about weight, shape, and/or food all the time
- Irritability, moodiness, depression
- Withdrawing from friends and/or activities
- Cuts and calluses on the back of the hands
- Dental enamel problems
- Wearing loose-fitting clothing to conceal weight loss
- Irregular or absent menstrual cycles
- Sensitivity to the cold

Source: "Health Initiative," Council of Fashion Designers of America, cfda.com.

Actress and singer Jennifer Lopez at the Grammy
Awards in 2000 wearing a low-cut, sheer green dress
designed by Versace (AP Photo/Reed Saxon)

and modern, and that benefited from Jay-Z's name recognition and reputation. In 2007 Iconix Brand Group bought Rocawear for $204 million, with Jay-Z retaining his role as chief creative officer.

Modeling. Brazilian supermodel Gisele Bündchen solidified her modeling career during the 2000s as she was named the "Most Beautiful Woman in the World" by *Rolling Stone* magazine and became the prominent face of Victoria's Secret. In 2002 she was labeled "Fur Scum" by the animal activist group PETA during a Victoria's Secret runway taping (that featured only faux fur); she was also ranked number one on the *Forbes* list of "World's Sexiest Supermodels." In 2005 her modeling career expanded as she appeared in several commercials and movies, including an appearance in *The Devil Wears Prada* (2006). Other shows that featured models who used their career fame to launch their projects included Tyra Banks's television series, *America's Next Top Model* (2003–), and Heidi Klum's *Project Runway* (2004–). The modeling world, however, experienced criticism for promoting dangerous standards of beauty. Guy Trebay of *The New York Times*

pointed out that the industry continually reproduced a standard of beauty that was extremely thin and increasingly white. While "Irina Kulikova, a feline 17-year-old Russian, appeared on no fewer than 24 runways in New York last month, a success she went on to repeat in Milan with 14 shows, and in Paris with 24 more," he wrote, "Honorine Uwera, a young Canadian of Rwandan heritage, was hired during the New York season for just five runway shows."

Affordable Options. The decade began and ended with economic downturns, and many style-conscious Americans looked for high-end fashion at bargain prices. Brooklyn-born designer Isaac Mizrahi attended Parsons School of Design and established an early reputation in the fashion industry, winning four CFDA awards. In 2003 he partnered with Target to make his innovative style available to the mainstream consumer, jump-starting a trend that continued throughout the decade and redefining the relationship between consumer and designer. Vera Wang's name was synonymous with the modern wedding dress, designing for celebrities such as Kate Hudson and Anne Hathaway. She launched a ready-to-wear collection in 2000, and in 2005 she was named CFDA Womenswear Designer of the Year. In 2007 she created an affordable line called Simply Vera, available for the price-conscious shopper at the department store Kohl's. In 2006 Wal-Mart was featured in *Vogue* magazine, emphasizing affordable fashion. Spokeswoman Linda Blakely noted, "We're about attainable looks. We wanted to show everyday people could come out of Wal-Mart with smashing clothes."

Sources:

Allison Adato, "Frida Gets Gucchi," *People* (5 December 2005);

"Bitten Revealed!" *dailyfrontrow.com* (13 March 2007);

"Fur Protesters Disrupt Victoria's Secret Show," *cnn.com* (15 November 2002);

"Gisele Bündchen," *New York Magazine* (n.d,);

"Iconix to Buy Rocawear, Jay-Z's Clothing Brand," *New York Times*, 7 March 2007;

Isaacmizrahiny.com;

"Jennifer Lopez Closes Down Her Sweetface Clothing Line," *People* (24 June 2009);

Julee Kaplan, "Jessica Simpson Signs Deal for Dresses," *wwdmarkets.com* (23 July 2008);

Suzy Menkes, "Tom Ford: Is It Au Revoir Superstar?" *New York Times*, 24 February 2004;

SeanJohn.com;

Stephen M. Silverman, "Jennifer Lopez Unveils Her Fashion Line," *People* (14 February 2005);

Guy Trebay, "Ignoring Diversity, Runways Fade to White," *New York Times*, 14 October 2007;

Verawang.com;

"Wal-Mart Goes High Fashion in May *Vogue*," *Pittsburgh Tribune*, 5 May 2006.

FASHION AND REALITY TV

High Fashion. In 2003 producer and host Tyra Banks premiered her reality series *America's Next Top Model*. Over the course of the season prospective models learned about the modeling industry and practiced working in all aspects of the job, posing with photographers and going through

Tim Gunn, a former faculty member at the Parsons School of Design and on-air mentor for the fashion-design reality program
Project Runway, interviewed during New York fashion week 2009 (The Heart Truth)

fittings with designers. The contestants were given weekly goals to achieve and competed against one another. One contestant was eliminated at the end of each show. The winner was awarded a modeling contract, as well as a platform from which to launch a modeling career. In December 2004 *Project Runway* premiered, focusing on the design aspects of the fashion industry, with model Heidi Klum as host. The show featured hopeful contestants competing in fashion design and execution. Each week contestants engaged in different challenges and then presented their work. Tim Gunn of the Parsons School of Design acted as mentor and guide, and quickly became a household name and fan favorite for his friendly and compassionate demeanor, as well as his sound advice. Four judges—Klum, fashion designer Michael Kors, journalist Nina Garcia, and a special guest—weighed in on each offering. The finalists presented their collections during New York Fashion Week, and the winner was featured in a top fashion magazine. In 2008 TVLand aired a twist to the reality fashion

experience, presenting a modeling competition for women over the age of thirty-five. Hosted by model Kim Alexis, *She's Got the Look* introduced competitors to the modeling and fashion industry, and the winner earned a modeling contract with an internationally recognized agency.

Street Fashion. *What Not To Wear* premiered in January 2003 with hosts Stacy London and Clinton Kelly, who were on a mission to bring style to the masses. Unsuspecting makeover targets were nominated by friends and family before being selected for the program. After the surprise arrival of the hosts, the hosts critiqued the participant's daily wardrobe and eliminated undesirable clothing in his or her closet. Armed with fashion advice, the contestant was sent on a shopping spree and got a full makeover. A similar series offering fashion advice was *Queer Eye for the Straight Guy,* which premiered July 2003. The show had five hosts—known as the "Fab Five": Ted Allen, Kyan Douglas, Thom Filicia, Carson Kressley, and Jai Rodriguez. Each host had specific expertise in different areas of

Poster for the 2001 film *Zoolander,* directed by and starring Ben Stiller, which lampooned the fashion industry (from <www.impawards.com>)

style and fashion. Though some critics panned the show for perpetuating the common cultural stereotype that gay men had better fashion sense, others argued that its popularity brought greater social awareness and acceptance of gay people to television and American culture.

Fashion in the Movies. *Sex and the City: The Movie* (2008) was based on and inspired by the HBO series *Sex and the City,* centering on the lives and friendships of four successful and empowered women—Carrie, Miranda, Samantha, and Charlotte—in New York City. In May 2008 the movie premiered. Girls and women of all ages dressed up in their trendiest clothes to go to the movie, which featured a cavalcade of fashion, including shoes by Dior, Jimmy Choo, Gucci, and Manolo Blahnik as well as handbags by Louis Vuitton and Timmy Woods. The characters wore jewelry by Tiffany and dresses by Oscar de la Renta, Maggy London, and Versace. Another fashion-focused movie of the decade, *The Devil Wears Prada,* opened in 2006. Based on the book by Lauren Weisberger, the movie followed young college graduate Andy Sachs (Anne Hathaway) during her experience as an assistant with a famous fashion magazine and her interactions with the insufferable editor Miranda Priestly (Meryl Streep), a thinly veiled version of famed *Vogue* editor Anna Wintour. A more comedic take on the industry was offered in *Zoolander* (2001), which featured Ben Stiller as male model Derek Zoolander and Will Ferrell as Mugatu, a distinctly evil fashion mogul whose onscreen homeless-inspired fashion line *derelicte* was seen by many as a reference to real life Christian Dior designer John Galliano, who once introduced a line inspired by the homeless of Paris.

Sources:

Meghan A. Burke, "Insurance Plan for the Gay Man: Who Benefits from Media Stereotypes?" National Sexuality Resource Center, *nsrc.com* (28 July 2005);

Imdb.com;

"Sex and the City: The Movie," *instyle.com* (n.d.).

INTERIOR DESIGN

Bohemian Style. Interior design during the decade was shaped by many of the stylistic themes that dominated fashion design. Consumers retained a desire for comfort and familiarity, but moved toward more-decorative patterns and colorful designs. Boho- or bohemian-inspired style crossed over to the home-fashion world. A shift toward recycling and reusing pieces gained popularity in the growing impulse toward sustainability. Trendy designers incorporated vintage pieces and repurposed furniture and accessories to develop an eclectic and individual feel to a room. Boho chic combined flea-market finds with rich color palettes and incorporated natural elements such as flowers and branches to add asymmetrical dimensions to a space. Boho had a lived-in effect with an effortless appeal. The trend fit nicely with growing concern over the negative environmental impact of mass-produced furnishings.

Regreening. Consumer awareness of "going green" influenced how people decorated, including repurposing materials and employing products that were safe for the environment. The American Society of Interior Designers published "Regreen: The Nation's First Green Residential Remodeling Guidelines," which provided home decorators with resources on how best to make their remodeling projects environmentally friendly or low-impact. Green consumers sought out housewares manufactured from sustainable resources, energy-efficient appliances, flooring and paneling from renewable woods or alternative materials, and lower-energy lighting provided by fluorescent bulbs.

CRAFTING

Etsy, a website for buying and selling homemade goods, was launched in 2005 and by the decade's end counted more than 200,000 sellers. Bolstered by the growth of the green consumer movement and the frugality brought about by economic downturn, Etsy featured products that were sold between individuals, typically handcrafted, often made from recycled or natural products. The website provided a forum for selling many items, from jewelry and purses to pottery and housewares. While focused primarily on handmade crafts, the site also allowed members to offer vintage items, as long they were at least twenty years old. As the popularity of the site grew, it became an online gathering spot for the crafting movement. Etsy described its mission as "enabl[ing] people to make a living making things, and to reconnect makers with buyers. Our vision is to build a new economy and present a better choice: Buy, Sell, and Live Handmade."

Sources: *etsy.com;*

Thom Patterson, "Make Magic, Save Cash This Gift-Giving Season," *cnn.com* (19 November 2008).

Poster for the popular interior design television show, which aired from 2000 to 2008 (<www.impawards.com>)

Interior-Design TV. One measure of the popularity of interior design was the explosion in television programs devoted to the topic. *Trading Spaces* aired on The Learning Channel and ran from 2000 to 2008. The series, hosted by Paige Davis, featured two families in charge of redecorating a specific room in each others' homes. The families were given a small budget and with the help of a designer, they rebuilt, painted, and redecorated to create a new space in the home. The fact that the owners were not always pleased with the results only added to the fun and drama. Another design series that aired on Home and Garden Television (HGTV) in 2003, *Design on a Dime*, brought in talented designers to rework a specific room on a limited budget. Hosts Brice Cooper, Kristan Cunningham, Frank Fontana, Kahi Lee, and Lee Snijders led viewers through the interior transformations. The appeal of reality television infiltrated the design world as well with the premiere of *Design Star* on HGTV in 2006. Twelve contestants competed in different challenges to avoid elimination and to win their own design series. ABC's *Extreme Makeover: Home Edition*, hosted by Ty Pennington, premiered in 2003 and featured the story of a struggling family in need of a new house on each episode. The family was sent on a weeklong vacation while their original house was destroyed. Meanwhile, the design team, along with a host of volunteers, rebuilt a cleaner, greener, bigger, dream home. Interior designers made a special effort to learn about family members' personal interests, creating individualized rooms to reflect their tastes.

Global Influence. The meshing of many cultural influences in interior design increased throughout the decade. "You can see the impact at the local store, for example, with these little Japanese water fountains," designer George Gehringer explained. "Designers pick up on this international influence and then it becomes mass culture. The interior designer starts to see these trends reflected in other contexts and begins to incorporate them in his design work." Chain stores such as Cost Plus, World Market, and Pier One offered products from around the globe, capitalizing on this growing trend.

Sources:

"Design Star," *hgtv.com*;

"'Global' Fusion Seen Impacting Design Trends," *Kitchen and Bath Design News* (June 2002);

Emily Henderson, "17 Stylish Boho-Chic Designs," *hgtv.com* (n.d);

IMDb.com;

"The Nation's First Green Residential Remodeling Guidelines to be Unveiled at INTERIORS 08," American Society of Interior Designers, *asid.org* (30 January 2008);

"Sustainable Design FAQ," American Society of Interior Designers, *asid.org* (2011).

MOTORCAR DESIGN

Environmentally Friendly Design. The growing awareness of environmental issues was reflected in automotive design as many consumers began demanding more fuel-efficient, less-polluting options on the car lot. One of the earliest of the new pack of environmentally friendly cars was the result of collaboration between Mercedes Benz and watchmaker Swatch. The Smart car, a small, fuel-efficient vehicle, was also primarily made of recyclable materials, but only became available in the United States in 2008 with limited success. No vehicle symbolized the trend of ecoconsciousness more than the Toyota Prius, which began selling in the United States in 2001. The Prius was a hybrid gas-electric vehicle that could achieve more than forty miles per gallon fuel efficiency. Its 2004 redesign, which made it a larger hatchback, coincided with a rise in gasoline prices that propelled the vehicle to popularity. Its distinctive, aerodynamic egg-shaped design made the Prius easy to spot on the road, and ownership became a badge of honor for green consumers. The hybrid sold for around $20,000 in its first year, and *Automotive Engineering International Magazine* called it the "Best Engineered Car of 2001." American automakers quickly followed suit. In 2004 Ford introduced the first hybrid Sports Utility Vehicle (SUV) and in 2009 introduced hybrid versions of the Ford Fusion and Mercury Milan models.

Electric Cars. The electric car was not new to the United States, having debuted in 1891. By 1900 almost one-third of the cars in New York City were electric powered, but by 1908 with the invention of the Model T by Henry Ford, the gas-powered car redefined transportation. Electric cars made a brief comeback in the early 2000s with cars such as G.M.'s EV1 or Chevy's S-10 EV, but these were discontinued by 2004. In 2009 Nissan unveiled its new electric car, called the LEAF ("Leading, Environmentally Friendly, Affordable, Family Car"). Fighting off the reputation that electric vehicles were sluggish on the road, the LEAF topped out at 90 mph. It could travel 100 miles on its battery, which could be recharged to 80 percent capacity in only thirty minutes. Though electric cars still sought a wide market at the end of the decade, growing consumer demand, coupled with government incentives, promised continued movement toward ecofriendly automobile design.

An advertisement for the 2008 Dodge Challenger (from <spiritualoasis.org>)

Retro Returns. Despite the trend toward fuel efficiency and environmentally friendly vehicles, the automotive industry found success in reviving body styles more consistent with gas-guzzling muscle cars of the past. In 2002 Ford introduced the redesigned Thunderbird with nostalgic appeal. Inspired by the 1955 model, the new Thunderbird was praised as a luxury vehicle as well as a performance car. The Thunderbird was offered as a convertible or with a hardtop that featured a distinctive, retro round backseat window. Continuing the trend in 2005, Ford redesigned the Mustang, harking back to the larger-bodied models of the late 1960s and early 1970s. The large headlights and chrome nodded to the past, but it had newly redesigned features as well as a more efficient engine. In 2008 the Dodge Challenger returned, closely resembling its older counterpart. *Motortrend* noted that the first impression of getting into the new Challenger was "Wow. This is a big car." These cars focused on power, speed, and nostalgic style and were less concerned with environmental impact.

Road Hogs. The Hummer first gained popularity among Americans primarily because of media exposure of the Humvee during the Gulf War in the early 1990s. The vehicle was redesigned for mass appeal and marketed as an on-and-off road vehicle. By 2002 the second generation, H2, was revealed at the Los Angeles Auto Show. It was a smaller vehicle but retained an off-road capability and look with large wheels and boxy body shape. There were mixed emotions even early on. Although some criticized the Hummer for its inefficiency and enormous size, others were drawn to its power and the prestige it represented on the road, and for some consumers, the flashy appeal was hard to resist. Such eye-popping size, however, was sometimes a liability: according to an ISO Quality Planning study, the Hummer was the car most likely to be ticketed in 2009. Radical environmental groups often targeted Hummers, damaging or destroying them in protest. Increasing gas prices, an economic downturn, and an environmentally disastrous image ultimately doomed the Hummer, and the line was discontinued in 2008.

Sources:

Michael Frank, "2002 Ford Thunderbird," *forbes.com* (n.d.);

"Hummer H2 to Debut at 2002 Los Angeles Auto Show," *cardesignnews.com* (20 December 2001);

Andrew Kaufman, "The Life and Death of the Hummer," *carsdirect.com* (n.d.);

Adam Kress, "Aftermarket Parts Supplier Follows Hummer's Popularity," *Phoenix Business Journal* (8 June 2003);

Aaron Robinson, "2005 Ford Mustang—First Drive Review," *Car and Driver* (February 2004);

"Smart Vehicles Go USA—United Auto Group Selected as Future Exclusive Distributor," *daimlerchrysler.com* (28 June 2006);

SmartUSA.com;

Arthur St. Antoine, "First Test: 2008 Dodge ChallengerSRT8," *Motor Trend* (April 2008);

Matt Stone, "World Debut: 2005 Ford Mustang," *Motor Trend* (February 2004);

"Timeline: History of the Electric Car," *pbs.org* (30 October 2009);

"Toyota Prius Chronological History," *toyoland.com* (n.d.);

Brian Vance, "One Year Test Verdict: 2002 Ford Thunderbird," *Motor Trend* (January 2004);

Calvin Woodward, "Hummer Shocks and Awes the Open Road," *Lakeland Ledger*, 7 August 2003.

HUMMER MENTALITY

In this opinion piece from *Wired* magazine, Keith Barry commented on the love of men for the popular Hummer and their response to criticism of their choice of vehicle:

Researchers also interviewed Hummer haters. While the folks armed with digital cameras and middle fingers at *FUH2.com* may be more concerned about the environment than the Second Amendment, their criticism of the Hummer is similarly steeped in their own personal beliefs. Unfortunately for the Hummer haters, the moral indignation they bring to the debate may actually be driving up Hummer sales. "Our analysis of the underlying American identity discourses revealed that being under siege by (moral) critics is an historically established feature of being an American," the authors wrote. "The moralistic critique of their consumption choices readily inspired Hummer owners to adopt the role of the moral protagonist who defends American national ideals." Emboldened by the cavalcade of hate unleashed upon them by East Coast elites who've never even made their own gun racks, Hummer owners may be embracing the very stereotypes their vehicles confer on them in order to prove their full-blooded American-ness. Similarly, like-minded individuals may seek out Hummer ownership to prove and show off their beliefs. We wonder if they'll feel the same way when those H2s are built by a company called Sichuan Tengzhong Heavy Industrial Machinery. While we're not sure of the statistical merit of such a small study, it's at least a convenient explanation of why more than one dealer has tied in firearms ownership with the total Hummer experience.

Source: Keith Barry, "Conservative Ideals Drive Hummer Ownership," *wired.com* (24 September 2009).

HEADLINE MAKERS

TYRA BANKS

1973–

MODEL, TELEVISION HOST

Early Years. Tyra Banks shaped the modeling industry as well as influenced the shift in cultural ideas of beauty away from the narrowly defined thin blonde supermodel. Banks grew up in Inglewood, California, and attended Immaculate Heart High School. She began her modeling career in the eleventh grade with the support of her mother, Carolyn London-Johnson. Instead of attending college, she went to Paris and shifted from catalogue modeling to the high-fashion runway. She appeared in twenty-five shows her first season (1991). Four years later, Banks began modeling for the lingerie and clothing company, Victoria's Secret. She won the prestigious Michael Award for Supermodel of the Year in 1997. Banks paved the way for other minority models, appearing as the first African American on the cover of *Sports Illustrated* as well as *GQ*. She ended her runway career with a Victoria's Secret show in 2005. As her modeling career came to an end, Banks looked to other opportunities. "My mom always told me," she said, "'Plan for the end at the beginning. You're gonna have to retire really early like an athlete, and then what are you gonna do after?'"

America's Next Top Model. With the reality-television craze in full swing, in 2003 Banks launched *America's Next Top Model*, a series in which women learn about the modeling industry, complete challenges, and compete for a one-year modeling contract as well as an appearance in a notable fashion magazine. Banks used the show as a platform to highlight different types of beauty and act as a role model for young women. A common emphasis on the show is that modeling is not only about looking pretty but also about hard work and vision. In 2006 the program moved from United Paramount Network (UPN) to the CW Television Network and enjoyed rising success. The show was criticized for producing no supermodels thus far, as well as for sending mixed messages to viewers. Women are to be "empowered" and fit a normative idea of beauty at the same time.

The Tyra Banks Show. Banks's talk show premiered in 2005 and covered various topics from fashion to politics. Modeled on the format of the *Oprah Winfrey Show*, the emphasis was often on issues of self-esteem and body image. She promoted diversity in beauty and encouraged young women to accept so-called physical flaws. As the program rose in popularity, Banks was successful in garnering high-profile guests. She interviewed Barack Obama, Hillary Clinton, and others. In June 2008 the show won a Daytime Emmy Award for Outstanding Talk Show. In 1999 Banks founded TZONE, a camp that supports young girls, focusing on self-esteem and motivation. In 2005 TZONE moved away from the camp format and became a notable charity. In addition, Banks sponsors a scholarship at her former high school, Immaculate Heart.

Sources:

Lynn Hirschberg, "Banksable," *New York Times*, 1 June 2008;

Tim Stack, "Tyra Banks: America's Next Top Mogul," *Entertainment Weekly* (19 February 2008);

"Tyra Banks," *tyrashow.warnerbros.com*;

Naomi Wolf, "The Time 100," *Time* (3 May 2007).

MARC JACOBS

1963–

FASHION DESIGNER

Guru of Grunge. Marc Jacobs was born in New York City and grew up in Teaneck, New Jersey. He worked as a sales attendant for the Upper West Side boutique Charivari while attending Parsons School of Design in New York. He began the first Marc Jacobs label in 1986 with the support of

Canadian manufacturer Jack Atkins. He was the youngest designer ever to receive the Council of Fashion Designers of America Perry Ellis Award for New Fashion Talent (1987). In 1989 Jacobs joined Perry Ellis as vice president. In 1992 Jacobs won the Women's Designer of the Year Award for his Grunge Collection, influenced by grunge rock including bands such as Nirvana and Pearl Jam. *New York Times* reporter Rick Marin wrote, "When Marc Jacobs sent out a parade of the world's most beautiful women wearing wool ski caps, unlaced combat boots, clashing prints and dirty-looking hair (styled by Oribe) for his spring Perry Ellis collection, *Women's Wear Daily* dubbed him "the guru of grunge."

Continued Success. Marc Jacobs International was launched in fall 1993, and by 1997 Jacobs also worked as creative director for Louis Vuitton, revitalizing the classic name. He presented the venerable design house's first ready-to-wear collection. In 2001 he launched Marc by Marc Jacobs, which designed women's handbags and accessories. He has won seven Council of Fashion Designers of America Awards. In May 2005 he opened three stores in Los Angeles, and in January of 2006 he opened the first freestanding European store in Paris. A documentary highlighting his relationship with Vuitton—*Marc Jacobs & Louis Vuitton*—premiered in America in 2008, giving a behind-the-scenes look at the life and influence of Jacobs. In 2007 he launched a children's-wear line: Little Marc Jacobs.

On the Runway. Jacobs meshed high-fashion creativity without losing touch with youthful, popular culture. He was also a master storyteller. *New York Times* fashion critic Cathy Horyn praised his February 2007 show for giving "clothes the emotional charge of a film or painting." For his New York Fashion Week show in 2008, which spotlighted a fall collection of pleated pants and jersey dresses, the band Sonic Youth provided accompaniment. His runway shows were not without controversy, however; some criticized his use of his boyfriend as a prominent model. He was also charged with descending into narcissism after losing a great deal of weight and showing off his body in risque magazine photos. Despite the criticism, in 2008 Jacobs was named one of *Out* magazine's fifty most-powerful gay men and women in America.

Sources:

Jo Craven, "Mark Jacobs," *Vogue.com* (20 April 2008);

Michael Gross, "For Two Young Designers, A Change of Direction," *New York Times*, 4 January 1986;

Marcjacobs.com;

Rick Marin, "Grunge: A Success Story," *New York Times*, 15 November 1992;

David Ninh and Jason Sheeler, "Strong Finish for Fashion Week," *Dallas* (Texas) *Morning News*, 9 February 2008;

Eric Wilson, "Loving and Hating Marc Jacobs," *New York Times*, 15 November 2007.

TOM FORD

1961–

FASHION DESIGNER

Background. Tom Ford grew up in Austin, Texas, and moved to Sante Fe, New Mexico, at the age of thirteen. He later moved to New York to pursue a degree in art history. He attended Parsons School of Design, graduating with a focus in architecture. As a young designer, he garnered early accolades, including four Council of Fashion Designers of America Awards. Ford became the womenswear designer for Gucci in 1990 and by 1994 was the creative director. His glamorous sensibility challenged the "grunge" wave of the early 1990s. His velvet low-rise pants soared in popularity after hitting the runway in 1994.

Gucci. After Gucci Group procured Yves Saint Laurent in 2000, Ford became creative director of both. His suggestive advertising gained much attention and criticism. His controversial YSL advertisement for Opium perfume featured model Sophie Dahl naked, and the ad was banned by the Advertising Standards Authority in Great Britain. In response to another provocative ad featuring a woman with her pubic hair shaved in the shape of a "G," Ford responded "at that moment in time, that was meant as a bit of a tongue-in-cheek take on where we were with branding in our culture. And, of course, you know, I was at Gucci and branding everything, everything had a G on it." In 2001 Ford won the CFDA Womenswear Designer of the Year Award. In 2002 he became vice chairman of the management board of the Gucci Group. His influence revitalized the company, increasing sales from $230 million to over $4 billion during his ten-year tenure. Ford resigned in 2004 and created the Tom Ford Brand in 2005. He created partnerships with Marcolin Group, designing frames and sunglasses. He worked with Estée Lauder to create Tom Ford Beauty. In April 2007 he opened his first store on Madison Avenue in New York. He sought to move fashion toward "real luxury" and away from the mass-produced luxury that Gucci represented.

From Fashion to Film. In 2005 Ford created his own movie company, Fade to Black. He directed, produced, and coauthored *A Single Man* (2009). The movie was based on a novel by Christopher Isherwood and opened with a depressed man whose partner has just died in a car accident. His transition to filmmaking was met with mixed reviews. Stephanie Zacharek, writing for *Salon*, called the movie, "smug and arty," with an "aggressive artificiality." Despite criticism in some quarters, *A Single Man* was nominated for an Academy Award. Openly gay, Ford has been with his long-term partner Richard Buckley since 1986.

Sources:

David Ansen, "'A Single Man': Gucci-Goo," *Newsweek* (25 November 2009);

Laura M. Holson, "Tom Ford: Design Director," *New York Times*, 2 December 2009;

"Naked Sophie Dahl Ad Banned," *bbcnews* (18 December 2000);

"Tom Ford: The Man Behind the Brand," *cnn.com* (27 July 2007);

Tomford.com;

Stephanie Zacharek, "A Single Man": Tom Ford's Shallow but Compelling Debut," *salon.com* (9 December 2009).

DANIEL LIBESKIND

1946–

ARCHITECT

Early Life. Libeskind was born in Łódź, Poland, to Holocaust survivors who immigrated to the United States in 1959. An early talent on the accordion and other instruments, he began a career in music, but changed after earning a degree in architecture in 1970 from Cooper Union for the Advancement of Science and Art. He pursued graduate education at Essex University, England, in history and architectural theory. After working as a professor for many years, at the age of fifty-two Libeskind designed his first building, the Felix Nussbaum Haus in Osnabrück, Germany. The design was touted by *Time* magazine as one of the best designs of 1998. His Jewish Museum Berlin (1999) was a widely praised success and garnered him international attention.

Ground Zero. After the attacks of 11 September 2001 destroyed the World Trade Center, the Lower Manhattan Development Corporation solicited designers to produce plans for its rebuilding. Libeskind's design, a symbolic tower called Memory Foundations (for the sixteen-acre space), won the competition in February 2003. Robin Finn of *The New York Times* called it "a model of the Statue of Liberty, whose torch-bearing arm was an inspiration for the Freedom Tower's shape and height." The plans called for the structure to soar to 1,776 feet, a reference to the year of America's independence.

Other Work. Libeskind designed the Frederic C. Hamilton building, an extension to the Denver Art Museum (2006), and created the glass courtyard addition to the Jewish Museum Berlin (2007). In addition to many ongoing works through his international architectural design firm, Studio Daniel Libeskind, he has worked at times as a set designer for opera productions of the Norwegian National Theatre and German Berlin Orchestra. Libeskind has garnered many honors, winning three Royal Institute of British Architects Awards, the American Institute of Architects medal, and the Leo Baeck Medal for his humanitarian work.

Sources:

"Daniel Libeskind," *daniel-libeskind.com*;

Robin Finn, "Public Lives; Big Enough to be the Brainy Half," *New York Times*, 30 July 2004.

MICHELLE OBAMA

1964–

FIRST LADY OF THE UNITED STATES

Early Years. Michelle LaVaughn Robinson grew up on the south side of Chicago where her father worked for the city while her mother was a secretary. She attended public schools and earned her degree in sociology from Princeton University in 1985. She completed her law degree from Harvard in 1988 and took a position with Sidley Austin. She married Barack Obama in 1992. Her children Malia and Sasha were born in 1998 and 2001 respectively.

To the White House. Campaigning alongside her husband during his 2008 run for the White House, Obama was often praised for her chic, approachable fashion look. After her husband was inaugurated in January 2009, Michelle Obama's style came to the forefront in her role as first lady. Her classic feminine appeal reminded critics of Jacqueline Kennedy. She has a particular talent for combining designer clothing with off-the-rack options. In October 2008 she appeared on *The Tonight Show* with Jay Leno wearing a J. Crew outfit. She also appeared on *The View* wearing the affordable White House Black Market dress. Her department-store fashion sense appealed to the public, making her seem accessible and easy to identify with.

New Designers. Obama brought new, creative designers to the forefront. Thakoon Panichgul, Narciso Rodriguez, and Jason Wu were all young designers whose work was popularized by the first lady. In March 2009 she appeared on the cover of *Vogue* magazine, only the second first lady ever to do so. As a trendsetter, Obama was credited with promoting the revival of sleeveless dresses. Her promotion of frugal chic also included the use of several vintage gowns.

Sources:

Stephanie Clifford, "J. Crew Benefits As Mrs. Obama Wears the Brand," *New York Times*, 17 November 2008;

Cathy Horyn, "The First Lady Tells a Story with Fashion," *New York Times*, 20 January 2009;

Guy Trebay, "U.S. Fashion's One-Woman Bailout?" *New York Times*, 7 January 2009.

PEOPLE IN THE NEWS

Model and actress **Pamela Anderson** helped popularize UGG boots, before realizing they were made of sheepskin; a strong supporter of animal rights, Anderson later encouraged the public to wear synthetic versions of the boots.

Costume designer **Colleen Atwood** won the Academy Award for Best Costume Design for *Chicago* in 2003 and *Memoirs of a Geisha* in 2006. She was nominated in the category three other times during the decade.

Adrianne Curry won the first competition on *America's Next Top Model* (2003), hosted by **Tyra Banks.**

Katherine von Drachenberg emerged as a star from the television show *Miami Ink* (2005–2007) and later starred in her own show *L.A. Ink* (2007–), as women and men increasingly turn to tattooing and piercings as part of their personal fashion statements.

Pop star **Janet Jackson,** intending to reveal only a lace undergarment, instead exposed her breast in a "wardrobe malfunction" at the 1 February 2004 Super Bowl during the halftime performance with **Justin Timberlake.**

Landscape architects **James Corner Field Operations** in conjunction with **Diller Scofidio + Renfro** designed the High Line, a refurbished freight rail originally built in the 1930s that ran above the streets of New York City. Although the 1.5-mile stretch faced demolition in the 1990s, the idea to transform the space into a park gained support in 2002. Construction began in 2006, and the first section of the park opened in June 2009.

Motorcycle designer **Jesse James** starred in the hit television series *Monster Garage* (2002–2006) and married actress **Sandra Bullock** in 2005.

In May 2003 basketball star **LeBron James** signed a seven-year, $90 million contract with Nike to endorse a new line of shoes.

In March 2007 rapper **Jay-Z** sold his clothing company Rocawear (an urban-inspired clothing line that had expanded to include children's and juniors' clothing,

handbags, belts, and outerwear) to Iconix Brand Group for $204 million dollars.

In 2004 mother of pop star **Beyoncé Knowles, Tina Knowles,** who designed for musical group Destiny's Child, and Beyoncé started their own clothing line for young girls and women with their House of Deréon brand. The name and styles was inspired by Beyoncé's grandmother Agnéz Deréon, a skilled seamstress from Louisiana.

Actress and singer **Jennifer Lopez** received overwhelming media attention when she wore a low-cut, sheer green dress designed by Versace to the Grammy Awards in 2000.

Fashion designer **Lana Marks** designed a $250,000 Cleopatra clutch for British actress **Helen Mirren** at the 2007 Academy Awards.

Actresses **Mary-Kate** and **Ashley Olsen** produced the trendy and affordable line Elizabeth and James, as well as the high-end The Row, that debuted spring 2007.

After much controversy, construction began for the new Yankee Stadium in 2006. Architecture firm **Populous** headed the project, and the stadium in the Bronx opened in April of 2009. The stadium retains many design features of the original facility constructed in 1923.

Model, actress, and entrepreneur **Kimora Lee Simmons,** as creative director, expanded the Baby Phat line from T-shirts to popular urban wear for women; in 2004 she sold the apparel side of the company, but continued to develop jewelry, fragrances, cosmetics, and shoes under the label.

Created by **Gela Nash-Taylor** and **Pamela Skaist-Levy,** Juicy Couture—a casual, trendy label targeting teenagers and young women—in 2001 introduced the velour tracksuit that was popularized by singer Madonna.

In 2006 supermodel **Christy Turlington Burns** returned to work for Maybelline Cosmetics, the company that helped make her famous in the 1990s.

Anna Wintour, editor of the fashion magazine *Vogue,* supported new designers and introduced *Teen Vogue, Vogue Living,* and *Men's Vogue.* She provided inspiration for the novel *The Devil Wears Prada* (2003) by **Lauren Weisberger,** a former assistant to Wintour; the film adaptation (2006) starred Meryl Streep and Anne Hathaway.

In March 2009 **Catherine Zuber,** winner of the Merritt Award for Excellence in Design and Collaboration in 2007 and five-time Tony Award winner for costuming for Broadway, designed the costumes for the 125th Anniversary Gala of the Metropolitan Opera in New York City.

AWARDS

COUNCIL OF FASHION DESIGNERS OF AMERICA

2000

Womenswear Designer of the Year: Oscar de la Renta

Menswear Designer of the Year: Helmut Lang

Accessory Designer of the Year: Richard Lambertson and John Truex for Lambertson Truex

Perry Ellis Award for Womenswear: Miguel Adrover

Perry Ellis Award for Menswear: John Varvatos

Perry Ellis Award for Accessory Design: Dean Harris

International Award: Jean-Paul Gaultier

Lifetime Achievement Award: Valentino

Humanitarian Award: Liz Claiborne

Most Stylish Dot.com Award: PleatsPlease.com

Special Award: The Dean of American Fashion Bill Blass

Special Award: The American Regional Press Janet McCue

Special Award: The Academy of Motion Picture Arts and Sciences

2001

Womenswear Designer of the Year: Tom Ford

Menswear Designer of the Year: John Varvatos

Accessory Designer of the Year: Reed Krakoff for Coach

Swarovski's Perry Ellis Award for Womenswear: Daphne Gutierrez and Nicole Noselli for Bruce

Swarovski's Perry Ellis Award for Menswear: William Reid

Swarovski's Perry Ellis Award for Accessory Design: Edmundo Castillo

International Award: Nicolas Ghesquière for Balenciaga

Lifetime Achievement Award: Calvin Klein

Eugenia Sheppard Award: Bridget Foley

Humanitarian Award: Evelyn Lauder

Eleanor Lambert Award: Dawn Mello

Special Award: Bernard Arnault

Special Award: Bob Mackie

Special Award: Saks Fifth Avenue

2002

Womenswear Designer of the Year: Narciso Rodriguez

Menswear Designer of the Year: Marc Jacobs

Accessory Designer of the Year: Tom Ford for Yves Saint Laurent

Swarovski's Perry Ellis Award for Womenswear: Rick Owens

Eugenia Sheppard Award: Cathy Horyn

International Award: Hedi Slimane for Dior Homme

Lifetime Achievement Award: Grace Coddington and Karl Lagerfeld

Fashion Icon Award: C. Z. Guest

Creative Visionary Award: Stephen Gan

Eleanor Lambert Award: Kal Ruttenstein

2003

Womenswear Designer of the Year: Narciso Rodriguez

Menswear Designer of the Year: Michael Kors

Accessory Designer of the Year: Marc Jacobs

Swarovski's Perry Ellis Award for Ready-to-Wear: Lazaro Hernandez and Jack McCollough for Proenza Schouler

Swarovski's Perry Ellis Award for Accessory Design: Brian Atwood

Eugenia Sheppard Award: André Leon Talley

International Award: Alexander McQueen

Lifetime Achievement Award: Anna Wintour

Fashion Icon Award: Nicole Kidman

Eleanor Lambert Award: Rose Marie Bravo

Board of Directors' Special Tribute: Oleg Cassini

2004

Womenswear Designer of the Year: Carolina Herrera

Menswear Designer of the Year: Sean Combs for Sean John

Accessory Designer of the Year: Reed Krakoff for Coach

Swarovski's Perry Ellis Award for Womenswear: Zac Posen

Swarovski's Perry Ellis Award for Accessory Design: Eugenia Kim

Eugenia Sheppard Award: Teri Agins

International Award: Miuccia Prada

Lifetime Achievement Award: Donna Karan

Fashion Icon Award: Sarah Jessica Parker

Eleanor Lambert Award: Irving Penn

Board of Directors' Special Tribute: Tom Ford

2005

Womenswear Designer of the Year: Vera Wang

Menswear Designer of the Year: John Varvatos

Accessory Designer of the Year: Marc Jacobs for Marc Jacobs

Swarovski's Perry Ellis Award for Womenswear: Derek Lam

Swarovski's Perry Ellis Award for Menswear: Alexandre Plokhov for Cloak

Swarovski's Perry Ellis Award for Accessory Design: Nak Armstrong and Anthony Camargo for Anthony Nak

Eugenia Sheppard Award: Gilles Bensimon

International Award: Alber Elbaz for Lanvin

Lifetime Achievement Award: Diane von Furstenberg

Fashion Icon Award: Kate Moss

Board of Directors' Special Tribute: Norma Kamali

2006

Womenswear Designer of the Year: Francisco Costa for Calvin Klein

Menswear Designer of the Year: Thom Browne

Accessory Designer of the Year: Tom Binns

Swarovski's Perry Ellis Award for Womenswear: Doo-Ri Chung

Swarovski's Perry Ellis Award for Menswear: Jeff Halmos, Josia Lamberto-Egan, Sam Shipley, and John Whitledge for Trovata

Swarovski's Perry Ellis Award for Accessory Design: Devi Kroell

Eugenia Sheppard Award: Bruce Weber

International Award: Olivier Theyskens for Rochas

Lifetime Achievement Award: Stan Herman

Eleanor Lambert Award: Joan Kaner

Board of Directors' Special Tribute: Stephen Burrows

2007

Womenswear Designer of the Year: Oscar de la Renta; Lazaro Hernandez and Jack McCollough for Proenza Schouler

Menswear Designer of the Year: Ralph Lauren

Accessory Designer of the Year: Derek Lam

Swarovski Award for Womenswear: Phillip Lim

Swarovski Award for Menswear: David Neville and Marcus Wainwright for Rag & Bone

Swarovski Award for Accessory Design: Jessie Randall for Loeffler Randall

Eugenia Sheppard Award: Robin Givhan

International Award: Pierre Cardin

Geoffrey Beene Lifetime Achievement Award: Robert Lee Morris

American Fashion Legend Award: Ralph Lauren

Eleanor Lambert Award: Patrick Demarchelier

Board of Directors' Special Tribute: Bono and Ali Hewson

2008

Womenswear Designer of the Year: Francisco Costa for Calvin Klein

Menswear Designer of the Year: Tom Ford

Accessory Designer of the Year: Tory Burch

Swarovski Award for Womenswear: Kate and Laura Mulleavy for Rodarte

Swarovski Award for Menswear: Scott Sternberg for Band of Outsiders

Swarovski Award for Accessory Design: Philip Crangi

Eugenia Sheppard Award: Candy Pratts Price

International Award: Dries Van Noten

Geoffrey Beene Lifetime Achievement Award: Carolina Herrera

Board of Directors' Special Tribute: Mayor Michael R. Bloomberg

2009

Womenswear Designer of the Year: Kate and Laura Mulleavy for Rodarte

Menswear Designer of the Year: Scott Sternberg for Band of Outsiders and Italo Zucchelli for Calvin Klein

Accessory Designer of the Year: Jack McCollough and Lazaro Hernandez for Proenza Schouler

Swarovski Award for Womenswear: Alexander Wang

Swarovski Award for Menswear: Tim Hamilton

Swarovski Award for Accessory Design: Justin Giunta for Subversive Jewelry

Eugenia Sheppard Award: Edward Nardoza

International Award: Marc Jacobs for Louis Vuitton

Geoffrey Beene Lifetime Achievement Award: Anna Sui

Eleanor Lambert Award: Jim Moore

Board of Directors' Special Tribute: First Lady Michelle Obama

NATIONAL DESIGN AWARDS

Lifetime Achievement

2000: Frank Gehry

2001: Robert Wilson

2002: Dan Kiley

2003: Lella and Massimo Vignells and I. M. Pei

2004: Milton Glaser

2005: Eva Zeisel

2006: Paolo Soleri

2007: Antoine Predock

2008: Charles Harrison

2009: Bill Moggridge

Fashion

2003: Tom Ford

2004: Yeohlee Teng

2005: Toledo Studio

2006: Maria Cornejo

2007: Rick Owens

2008: Ralph Rucci

2009: Francisco Costa

Architecture

2001: Peter Eisenman

2002: Steven Holl

2003: Billie Tsien and Tod Williams

2004: Rick Joy and Polshek Partnership

2005: Diller Scofidio + Renfro

2006: Thom Mayne

2007: Office dA

2008: Tom Kundig

2009: SHoP Architects

Interior

2005: Richard Gluckman

2006: Michael Gabellini

2007: Lewis.Tsurumaki.Lewis

2008: Rockwell Group

2009: TsAO & McKOWN Architects

AMERICAN INSTITUTE OF ARCHITECTS

AIA Gold Medal (recognizes distinguished service to the architectural profession)

2000: Ricardo Legorreta

2001: Michael Graves

2002: Tadao Ando

2003: No Winner

2004*: Samuel "Sambo" Mockbee

2005: Santiago Calatrava

2006: Antoine Predock

2007*: Edward Larrabee Barnes

2008: Renzo Piano

2009: Glenn Marcus Murcutt

* Honored Posthumously

AMERICAN SOCIETY OF INTERIOR DESIGNERS

ASID Designer of Distinction Award (recognizes an ASID interior designer who has made outstanding contributions toward achieving the organization's goal of design excellence)

2000: Paul Vincent Wiseman

2001: William Hodgins

2002: Hugh Latta and Margaret McCurry

2003: Eleanor Brydone

2004: Deborah Lloyd Forrest

2005: Barbara Barry

2006: Penny Bonda

2007: Nila Leiserowitz

2008: No Winner

2009: Darrell Schmitt

ASID Design for Humanity Award (bestowed upon an individual or institution that has made a significant contribution toward improving the quality of the human environment through design-related activities)

2000: Victoria Schomer

2001: Tennessee Chapter—Chattanooga Association

2002: Cynthia Leibrock

2003: Habitat for Humanity International

2004: Cameron Sinclair, Architecture for Humanity

2005: Patricia Moore, Ph.D.

2006: Robin Hood Foundation

2007: Marianne Cusato, Katrina Cottages

2008: No Winner

2009: HOK Community Service Project

The Pritzker Architecture Prize (the profession's highest honor; international award established by the Pritzker family of Chicago)

2000: Rem Koolhaas

2001: Jacques Herzog and Pierre de Meuron

2002: Glenn Marcus Murcutt

2003: Jørn Utzon

2004: Zaha Hadid

2005: Thom Mayne

2006: Paulo Mendes da Rocha

2007: Richard Rogers

2008: Jean Nouvel

2009: Peter Zumthor

Motor Trend Car of the Year

2000: Lincoln LS

2001: Chrysler PT Cruiser

2002: Ford Thunderbird

2003: Infiniti G35

2004: Toyota Prius

2005: Chrysler 300C

2006: Honda Civic

2007: Toyota Camry

2008: Cadillac CTS

2009: Nissan GT-R

Motor Trend Truck of the Year

2000: Toyota Tundra

2001: Chevrolet Silverado Heavy Duty

2002: Chevrolet Avalanche

2003: Dodge Ram Heavy Duty

2004: Ford F-150

2005: Toyota Tacoma

2006: Honda Ridgeline

2007: Chevrolet Silverado

2008: Toyota Tundra

2009: Ford F-150

Motor Trend Sport/Utility of the Year

2000: Nissan Xterra

2001: Acura MDX

2002: GMC Envoy

2003: Volvo XC90

2004: Volkswagen Touareg

2005: Land Rover LR3

2006: Nissan Xterra

2007: Mercedes-Benz GL 450

2008: Mazda CX-9

2009: Subaru Forester

DEATHS

Max Abramovitz, 96, architect, designed Avery Fisher Hall at Lincoln Center, 12 September 2004.

Richard Avedon, 81, fashion and portrait photographer, featured frequently in *Vogue* and *Harper's Bazaar*, 1 October 2004.

Geoffrey Beene, 77, fashion designer, left medical school to study fashion in New York at the Traphagen School of Fashion (1947), created Geoffrey Beene, Inc. (1963), designed clothes for Nancy Reagan and Faye Dunaway, mentored young designers, 28 September 2004.

Lenore Benson, 80, executive director of Fashion Group International, promoted the advancement of women in the fashion industry, 1 September 2004.

Peter Blake, 86, architect, editor of Architectural Forum (1950–1972), 5 December 2006.

Bill Blass, 79, fashion designer, created wearable clothes rather than artistic fashion, designed for Ford Motor Company's Continental Mark automobiles, 12 June 2002.

Kenneth Paul Block, 84, fashion illustrator, sketch artist for McCall's Patterns early in his career, illustrator for *Women's Wear Daily* and *W*, sketched designs for the famous, including the Duchess of Windsor, Gloria Vanderbilt, Lauren Bacall, Barbra Streisand, and Sophia Loren, as well as for designers such as Beene, Blass, and Perry Ellis, 23 April 2009.

Donald Brooks, 77, fashion designer, created more than 3,500 costumes for the stage and film, Emmy Award winner, 1 August 2005.

Lily Carlson, 85, fashion model, early employee of Ford Modeling Agency, 14 December 2000.

Bonnie Cashin, 84, creator of sportswear, designer for Coach Leatherwear (1960s), inducted into Coty American Fashion Critics' Hall of Fame (1972), 3 February 2000.

Oleg Cassini, 92, fashion designer, name attached to many products, designed wardrobe for Jacqueline Kennedy (1960s), created trim package for AMC Matador automobile (1974–1975), 17 March 2006.

Dorothea T. Church, 83, fashion model, one of the first African American models to work in Paris in the 1950s, 7 July 2006.

Liz Claiborne, 78, fashion designer, opened company in 1976, created affordable clothes for professional women, 26 June 2007.

Boyd Coddington, 63, hot-rod designer, mentor to car designers, inducted into the Grand National Roadster Show Hall of Fame and the National Rod & Custom Hall of Fame Museum, 27 February 2008.

John Z. DeLorean, 80, engineer, developed the Pontiac GTO muscle car, Pontiac Firebird, Pontiac Fiero, and DeLorean DMC-12 sports car, which was featured in the movie *Back to the Future* (1985), 19 March 2005.

Philip S. Egan, 88, industrial designer, created the Tucker '48 sedan, 26 December 2008.

Gerard William "Jerry" Ford, 83, businessman, founded Ford Modeling Agency, 24 August 2008.

Suzie Frankfurt, 73, interior decorator, popularized use of Russian furniture, worked with Andy Warhol, 7 January 2005.

Herbert Gallen, 92, founder of women's clothing line Ellen Tracy, 22 September 2007.

Charles Gwathmey, 71, high modernist architect, founded Gwathmey Siegel & Associates with Robert Siegel (1968), designed homes for wealthy clients, designed addition to Frank Lloyd Wright's Guggenheim Museum (1992), 3 August 2009.

Lawrence Halprin, 93, landscape architect, designed Franklin D. Roosevelt Memorial in Washington, D.C., Ghirardelli Square in San Francisco, walkway overlooking the Old City of Jerusalem, urban spaces in Oregon and California, 25 October 2009.

Edna Hipps Hamrick, 89, cofounder of clothing-store chain Hamrick's, 17 September 2007.

Ruth Handler, 85, created the Barbie doll (at Mattel) in 1959, 27 April 2002.

Robert Isabell, 57, floral designer and event planner (including the weddings of Caroline Kennedy and John

F. Kennedy Jr., as well as the funeral of Jacqueline Kennedy Onassis), 8 July 2009.

Philip Johnson, 98, architect, influential in establishing Modernist architecture; designed the Glass House (1949), sculpture garden of the Museum of Modern Art, and pre-Columbian gallery at Dumbarton Oaks in Washington (considered "architectural masterworks"), 25 January 2005.

Denis G. Kuhn, 65, architect, supervised development of Smithsonian's National Museum of the American Indian, 10 May 2007.

Estée Lauder, 97, business owner, created cosmetics empire, 24 April 2004.

Dorian Leigh, 91, fashion model, appeared on the cover of magazines such as *Vogue, Harper's Bazaar, Paris Match, LIFE,* and *Elle,* became the face of Revlon (1944), 7 July 2008.

Charles "Mask" Lewis Jr., 46, businessman, along with two friends cofounded TapouT (a clothing line associated with mixed martial arts and aimed at young male buyers), 11 March 2009.

Samuel "Sambo" Mockbee, 57, architect, designed housing for rural Alabama, taught students to provide service to the community as well as creativity in design, 30 December 2001.

Nonnie Moore, 87, fashion editor, worked for such magazines as *Mademoiselle, Harper's Bazaar,* and *GQ,* 19 February 2009.

Suzy Parker, 69, model, glamorous redhead who modeled one of the first bikini bathing suits, 3 May 2003.

Jean Patchett, 75, model during the 1950s, 22 January 2002.

Irving Penn, 92, fashion photographer, long associated with *Vogue,* 7 October 2009.

Robert Riley, 90, curator, design expert who was director of Fashion Institute of Technology, developed several collections of fashions, 6 October 2001.

Mary Jane Russell, 77, fashion model, popular print model in 1940s and 1950s, Revlon spokesperson, 20 November 2003.

Kalman Ruttenstein, 69, retailer, senior vice president of fashion design for Bloomingdale's, 8 December 2005.

Richard Sylvan Selzer (Mr. Blackwell), 86, fashion critic, skewered Hollywood elite for fashion missteps, 19 October 2008.

Alfred Shaheen, 86, designer of Hawaiian shirts, 22 December 2008.

Naomi Sims, 61, model, known as the "first black supermodel," appeared on cover of *Ladies' Home Journal* (1968), after modeling career headed successful wigmaking business, 1 August 2009.

Luke Smalley, 53, photographer, best known for pictures of men's fashion, 17 May 2009.

Amy M. Spindler, 40, fashion critic, style editor with *The New York Times Magazine,* 27 February 2004.

Stephen Sprouse, 50, fashion designer, known for graffiti-printed collections, 4 March 2004.

Pauline Trigère, 93, French-born designer, promoter of "American Style," 13 February 2002.

Jack Arnold Weil, 107, creator of western-style shirts and fashions, 13 August 2008.

Stephan Weiss, 62, artist, helped found design house with his wife Donna Karan, 10 June 2001.

Jenny Bechtel Whyte, 75, designer, used African textiles and patterns in her work, 1 September 2002.

Christa Worthington, 46, fashion writer for *Women's Wear Daily* and *Elle,* murdered in Truro, Massachusetts, 6 January 2002.

PUBLICATIONS

Cey Adams and Bill Adler, *Definition: The Art and Design of Hip-Hop* (New York: Collins Design, 2008);

Victoria Beckham, *That Extra Half an Inch: Hair, Heels, and Everything in Between* (New York: HarperCollins, 2007);

Sandy Black, *Eco-Chic: The Fashion Paradox* (London: Black Dog, 2008);

J. E. Bright, *America's Next Top Model: Fierce Guide to Life: The Ultimate Source of Beauty, Fashion, and Model Behavior* (New York: Universe, 2009);

Francis D. K. Ching, *Architecture: Form, Space, and Order,* third edition (Hoboken, N.J.: Wiley, 2007);

Kimberly Elam, *Geometry of Design: Studies in Proportion and Composition,* second edition (New York: Princeton Architectural Press, 2001);

Kate Fletcher, *Sustainable Fashion and Textiles: Design Journeys* (London & Sterling, Va.: Earthscan, 2008);

Bridget Foley, *Marc Jacobs (Memoirs)* (New York: Assouline, 2004);

Foley, *Tom Ford* (New York: Rizzoli, 2004);

Hadley Freeman, *The Meaning of Sunglasses: And a Guide to Almost All Things Fashionable* (New York: Viking, 2008);

Nina Garcia, *The Little Black Book of Style* (New York: HarperCollins, 2007);

Garcia, *The Style Strategy: A Less-is-More Approach to Staying Chic and Shopping Smart* (New York: HarperCollins, 2009);

Joseph Hancock, *Brand/Story: Ralph, Vera, Johnny, Billy, and Other Adventures in Fashion Branding* (New York: Fairchild, 2009);

Gail Greet Hannah, *Elements of Design: Rowena Reed Kostellow and the Structure of Visual Relationships* (New York: Princeton Architectural Press, 2002);

Harold Koda and Kohle Yohannon, *The Model as Muse: Embodying Fashion* (New York: Metropolitan Museum of Art; New Haven, Conn.: Yale University Press, 2009);

Alla Myzelev and John Potvin, *Fashion, Interior Design, and the Contours of Modern Identity* (Burlington, Vt.: Ashgate, 2010);

Mandi Norwood, *Michelle Style: Celebrating the First Lady of Fashion* (New York: Morrow, 2009);

Alberto Oliva and Norberto Angletti, *In Vogue: The Illustrated History of the World's Most Famous Fashion Magazine* (New York: Rizzoli, 2006);

Marna Owen, *Animal Rights: Noble Cause or Needless Effort?* (Minneapolis: Twenty-First Century Books, 2010);

Brenda Polan and Roger Tredre, *The Great Fashion Designers* (New York: Berg, 2009);

Scott Schuman, *The Sartorialist* (New York: Penguin, 2009);

Todd Selby, *The Selby Is in Your Place* (New York: Abrams, 2010);

Sharon Lee Tate, *Inside Fashion Design,* fifth edition (Upper Saddle River, N.J.: Prentice Hall, 2004);

The Teen Vogue Handbook: An Insider's Guide to Careers in Fashion (New York: Razorbill, 2009);

Linda Watson, *Vogue Fashion: Over 100 Years of Style by Decade and Designer* (New York: Firefly, 2008);

Rachel Zoe and Rose Apodaca, *Style A to Zoe: The Art of Fashion, Beauty, & Everything Glamour* (Buffalo, N.Y.: Grand Central, 2007);

Allure, periodical;

Architectural Digest, periodical;

Architectural Record, periodical;

Architecture, periodical;

Elle, periodical;

Esquire, periodical;

GQ, periodical;

Interior Design, periodical;

Interiors, periodical;

Marie Claire, periodical;

Seventeen, periodical;

Vanity Fair, periodical;

Vogue, periodical;

W, periodical.

Vogue editor in chief Anna Wintour (second from right) watches from the front row along with tennis star Roger Federer and other *Vogue* editors during Oscar de la Renta's 2008 spring/summer collection at New York's fashion week, 10 September 2007 (AP Photo/Dima Gavrysh)

GOVERNMENT
AND POLITICS

by MEEGHAN KANE

CONTENTS

Sidebars and tables are listed in italics.

2000

22 Apr.   Elián González, the young survivor of a tragic attempt to emigrate from Cuba to the United States in November 1999, is taken from his late mother's family in Miami. He is returned to Cuba to live with his father on 28 June. The controversial decision to return González sparks tensions between Cuban immigrants and the federal government.

12 Oct.   Al Qaeda terrorists attack the USS *Cole* at port in Yemen, killing seventeen U.S. sailors.

7 Nov.   In the presidential election between Democrat Al Gore and Republican George W. Bush, the popular vote goes to Gore, but the electoral college tally is too close to call.

9 Nov.   With the incomplete count giving Bush a lead of fewer than two thousand votes in Florida, a mandatory recount is ordered.

12 Dec.   The U.S. Supreme Court decides in favor of Bush, overturning the Florida Supreme Court's decision to continue the recount of disputed ballots in Florida.

13 Dec.   Gore concedes the election to Bush.

2001

20 Jan.   Bush is inaugurated as the forty-second president of the United States.

26 May   Congress passes a major tax-relief bill in favor of large corporations.

11 Sept.   Terrorists hijack four American airliners. Both towers of the World Trade Center and the Pentagon are hit, and the fourth plane crashes in a field south of Pittsburgh, Pennsylvania.

Mid Sept. –Nov.   For several weeks anthrax spores are mailed to media centers in Florida and New York and congressional offices in Washington, D.C. Five people die as a result of the attacks. After a long and exhaustive investigation, the Federal Bureau of Investigation (FBI) traces the attacks to Dr. Bruce Edwards Ivins, a former biodefense scientist for the federal government, who kills himself in 2008 before charges can be filed.

20 Sept.   Bush outlines his plan to confront worldwide terrorism.

7 Oct.   U.S. and British forces begin air strikes (Operation Enduring Freedom) in Afghanistan. Hours after U.S. forces strike, Osama bin Laden releases a video praising the terrorist attacks on 11 September, though he does not take credit for them.

26 Oct.   Bush signs the Uniting and Strengthening America by Providing Appropriate Tools Required to Intercept and Obstruct Terrorism Act (USA PATRIOT Act), commonly known as the Patriot Act, into law, which expands the ability of law enforcement agencies to surveil private communication.

13 Nov.   Bush signs an executive order authorizing military tribunals for terror suspects.

25 Nov.   The first American casualty during hostilities in Operation Enduring Freedom is Central Intelligence Agency (CIA) agent John Micheal Spann, killed in a Taliban prisoner uprising in Afghanistan. American John Walker Lindh is among the prisoners.

2 Dec.   The giant energy corporation Enron files for Chapter 11 bankruptcy, the largest filing in U.S. history.

9 Dec.   U.S. forces capture Kandahar, a symbol of Taliban power.

18 Dec. Congress passes No Child Left Behind, Bush's education proposal to develop standardized tests to chart student development in all grades. Bush signs the act into law on 8 January 2002.

22 Dec. British citizen Richard Reid attempts to ignite a bomb packed in his shoes on board a flight from Paris, France, to Miami, Florida. The smell of a burning match alerts passengers and flight personnel, and the plane is diverted to Boston where Reid is arrested. Labeled the "Shoebomber," Reid admits to being a member of al Qaeda.

30 Dec. At Ground Zero, site of the fallen World Trade Center towers, a viewing platform opens for the public. Tickets are issued for crowd control.

2002

11 Jan. The first twenty detainees arrive at the detainment facility established on the U.S. Naval Base in Guantanamo Bay, Cuba. Labeled "enemy combatants" by Defense Secretary Donald Rumsfeld, these prisoners have no rights under the Geneva Convention.

29 Jan. Bush labels Iran, North Korea, and Iraq an "axis of evil" in his State of the Union address.

21 Feb. A video of the beheading of *Wall Street Journal* reporter Daniel Pearl, who had traveled to Pakistan to investigate the links between "Shoebomber" Richard Reid and al Qaeda, is released to the media.

1 June In a speech at West Point, Bush clarifies the Bush Doctrine, his administration's case for preemptive war against terrorists and those countries that harbor them.

13 June The United States withdraws from the thirty-year-old Anti-Ballistic Missile Treaty with Russia.

30 July Bush signs corporate reform law creating a federal accounting board.

16 Oct. The Iraq War Resolution is passed, granting the Bush administration authorization to use military force in Iraq if diplomatic efforts fail.

5 Nov. In the midterm elections, Republicans win the Senate and expand their majority in the House.

25 Nov. The Department of Homeland Security is established. Pennsylvania governor Tom Ridge is tapped as the agency's first secretary.

5 Dec. At longtime senator Strom Thurmond's one-hundredth birthday celebration, Republican Senate majority leader Trent Lott observes that his state of Mississippi had proudly backed Thurmond's 1948 bid for the presidency. Running as a nominee of the States' Rights Party, Thurmond of South Carolina and a majority of southern congressmen had left the Democratic Party, pledging to maintain segregation. Lott later apologizes for the insensitive nature of his remarks.

2003

5 Feb. Secretary of State Colin Powell addresses the United Nations to plead the U.S. case for an invasion in Iraq. Powell insists that evidence confirms biological and chemical weapons in Iraq.

20 Mar. The invasion of Iraq begins with the bombing of Baghdad's planning ministry.

1 Apr.   Private First Class Jessica Lynch is rescued by U.S. Special Forces from a hospital in Iraq. Members of the Iraqi military had taken Lynch after nine of her fellow soldiers were killed in an ambush. Her rescue is videotaped by a military cameraman and edited footage is released to the media, portraying Lynch as a heroic prisoner of war. However, Lynch later testifies that she had not fought back when captured and accused the Pentagon of fabricating a story for war propaganda.

12 Apr.   Congress approves $79 billion for military spending in Iraq, Homeland Security costs, and to provide aid to allies in the war on terrorism.

14 Apr.   The Pentagon declares victory in Iraq.

1 May   Bush holds a press conference on the USS *Abraham Lincoln,* declaring an end to major military operations in Iraq. He stands before a banner that reads "Mission Accomplished." As violence escalates in Iraq, Bush is criticized for declaring the end to what could be a much longer war. In 2009 the president admits that the banner was a "mistake."

28 May   Bush signs a $350 billion tax cut, the third largest in American history.

2 June   In a three-to-two vote along political party lines, Republican commissioners of the Federal Communications Commission remove many restrictions that limit ownership of media within a local area, allowing for increased corporate media consolidation.

3 July   Responding to a reporter's questions about increasing U.S. casualties in Iraq, Bush says, "There are some who feel like—that the conditions are such that they can attack us there. My answer is, bring 'em on. We've got the force necessary to deal with the security situation." Critics call the comments irresponsible.

14 July   In his *Washington Post* column, Robert Novak exposes Valerie Plame as an undercover CIA operative. The scandal surrounding the leak of Plame's identity to Novak reaches the office of Vice President Dick Cheney.

7 Oct.   Former action-movie star Arnold Schwarzenegger is elected governor of California after Gray Davis is recalled.

5 Nov.   Bush signs the Partial-Birth Abortion Ban Act.

8 Dec.   Bush signs the Medicare Modernization bill into law, adding prescription benefits to the program, allowing for billions of dollars in subsidies to health-care and insurance providers and opening up competition from private plans.

14 Dec.   After months of eluding U.S. troops, Saddam Hussein is discovered in a bunker on a farm near the Iraqi city of Tikrit.

2004

19 Jan.   Presumed Democratic front-runner for the presidential nomination, Vermont governor Howard Dean loses the Iowa primary, finishing third behind Massachusetts senator John Kerry and North Carolina senator John Edwards. During his concession speech, Dean screams loudly, delivering a passionate plea to his supporters. His flushed face and zeal make him a target for political pundits who criticize his speech as being too emotional. His campaign never recovers.

31 Mar.   A crowd of Iraqis chanting anti-American slogans drag the burnt and mutilated bodies of four contractors employed by the U.S.-led coalition through the streets of Al Fallujah.

1 Apr.   Bush signs the Unborn Victims of Violence bill into law. The law recognizes an unborn child, in any state of development, as a legal victim if injured or killed.

22 Apr.	Patrick Daniel "Pat" Tillman, football star and Army Ranger, is killed in combat in Afghanistan. His death becomes an embarrassing scandal for the U.S. Army when it is revealed that military officials covered up his death by friendly fire in order to avoid bad publicity. He is posthumously awarded the Silver Star citation for valor by Lieutenant General Stanley McChrystal.
Apr.–May	*New Yorker* journalist Seymour M. Hersh publishes articles revealing the Abu Ghraib prisoner-abuse scandal. Seventeen soldiers in Iraq are removed from duty for mistreating Iraqi prisoners after photographs of sexual, physical, and emotional abuse emerge.
5 June	Former president Ronald Reagan dies at his home in Bel Air, California, at the age of ninety-three.
9 July	A Senate panel criticizes U.S. intelligence efforts preceding the war in Iraq.
22 July	The 9/11 Commission Report, formally the *Final Report of the National Commission on Terrorist Attacks upon the United States,* is released. The report, a nationwide best seller, is the conclusion of a much-publicized and politicized investigation of the attacks.
12 Aug.	New Jersey governor Jim McGreevey declares that he is gay and has had an extramarital affair, and announces he will resign from office on 15 November.
3 Nov.	Bush is reelected to the presidency.

2005

20 Jan.	Bush is sworn in for his second term as president.
2 Feb.	In his State of the Union address, Bush calls for changes in the Social Security system, which he claims is headed for bankruptcy. Bush suggests that employees would benefit from private accounts that could be invested in the stock market.
17 Mar.	Congress holds hearings on steroid use in baseball, hoping to prevent abuse and encourage more-stringent testing policies. Prominent players, including Jose Canseco and Mark McGwire, provide revealing testimony that suggests widespread abuse.
31 Mar.	After a lengthy court battle and a passionate political debate, Terri Schiavo dies in hospice care at the age of forty-one. Schiavo became the center of national media attention when her husband successfully petitioned to have her feeding tube removed. Her parents appealed the decision and attracted the support of prominent politicians. However, when the federal appeals were exhausted, Schiavo's feeding tube was removed and she died of dehydration.
7 July	In a series of coordinated suicide bombings, terrorists affiliated with al Qaeda attack London's transit system, killing fifty-two civilians and wounding seven hundred. The bombers claimed to be reacting to Britain's involvement in the U.S.-led war against Iraq.
28 July	The House narrowly passes the Central America Free Trade Agreement.
29 Aug.	Hurricane Katrina strikes New Orleans. The storm and its aftermath devastates coastal regions in Louisiana, Mississippi, Alabama, and the Panhandle of Florida, killing 1,833 people and displacing hundreds of thousands. The Bush administration is severely criticized for perceived tardiness and ineptitude in responding to the catastrophe.
3 Sept.	Chief Justice William Hubbs Rehnquist dies after serving on the Supreme Court for thirty-three years.

28 Sept.   A Texas grand jury indicts House Majority Leader Republican Tom DeLay on charges of criminal conspiracy relating to the scandal associated with powerful Washington lobbyist Jack Abramoff. DeLay announces his resignation from Congress on 4 April 2006.

27 Oct.   The Bush administration pulls back the nomination of Harriet Miers, White House legal counsel, to the vacant seat on the Supreme Court.

29 Oct.   John Glover Roberts Jr. becomes the seventeenth chief justice of the U.S. Supreme Court.

2006

3 Jan.   Abramoff pleads guilty to felony charges of corruption. A broad investigation reveals that he had defrauded his Native American clients with the help of several White House officials. He is also found guilty of trading expensive gifts, including trips and meals, for political favors. The scale of Abramoff's corruption rallies reformers in Congress against the influence of lobbyists in Washington, D.C.

3 May   Zacarias Moussaoui is sentenced to life in prison by a federal jury for conspiring to kill U.S. citizens in the September 11 terrorist attacks. He denies involvement, claiming that he belonged to a separate al Qaeda cell.

25 May   Kenneth Lay and Jeffrey Skilling, former Enron executives, are convicted of securities and wire fraud.

31 May   Former FBI associate director W. Mark Felt Sr. admits that he is "Deep Throat," the key informant to *Washington Post* reporters Bob Woodward and Carl Bernstein, whose investigative journalism uncovered the Watergate scandal.

29 June   In a five-to-four decision, the Supreme Court rejects military tribunals for terrorism suspects, a significant component of Bush's war on terrorism. The ruling finds the tribunals to be in conflict with federal law and the rules of war established by the Geneva Convention.

19 July   Bush vetoes embryonic stem-cell research bill.

7 Nov.   In a major political shift, elections allow Democrats take the House of Representatives, the Senate, and a majority of governorships.

26 Dec.   Gerald R. Ford, the thirty-eighth president of the United States, dies.

30 Dec.   Saddam Hussein, after a much publicized 2004 trial, a conviction of crimes against humanity, and a death sentence, is hanged.

2007

4 Jan.   Democratic representative Nancy Pelosi of California is elected the first female Speaker of the House.

10 Jan.   Bush announces an escalation of troop deployment in Iraq. Later known as the "surge," the increase of military personnel becomes a hotly contested foreign-policy decision for the White House. By 2008 many pundits agree that the surge, along with growing support from Iraqis, had decreased violence.

20 Jan.   New York Democratic senator Hillary Clinton announces her 2008 presidential candidacy, stating, "I'm in, and I'm in to win."

10 Feb.   Illinois Democratic senator Barack Obama formally announces his 2008 presidential candidacy.

6 Mar.   Vice President Cheney's former chief of staff Irving Lewis "Scooter" Libby is convicted of perjury and obstruction of justice in the Valerie Plame case. He is sentenced to thirty months in jail. Bush later commutes Libby's sentence.

18 Apr.   In a five-to-four decision, the Supreme Court upholds a partial-birth abortion ban.

9 May   Bush signs the National Security and Homeland Security Presidential Directive that gives the president the power to direct all three branches of the government in case of a catastrophic disaster.

27 Aug.   U.S. attorney general Alberto R. Gonzales resigns amid accusations of perjury before Congress, related to his testimony about the improper or illegal use of the Patriot Act to expose information about citizens.

31 Aug.   A key advisor and close confidant of Bush, Karl Rove resigns from his post as White House deputy chief of staff.

6 Dec.   Mortgage lenders reach an agreement with the Bush administration to freeze interest rates on subprime mortgages, high-interest home loans that were considered risky. While criticized by Democrats for not going far enough, the White House hopes to mitigate an increasingly dire mortgage crisis.

12 Dec.   Bush vetoes Child Health Care Bill, legislation that would have expanded the State Children's Health Insurance program by $35 billion.

2008

14 Jan.   Bush proposes a $145 billion stimulus package focused on tax breaks for consumers and businesses, in order to spur economic recovery in the face of increasing unemployment and home foreclosures.

8 Mar.   Bush vetoes a bill that would ban the CIA from harsh interrogation tactics, including waterboarding.

12 Mar.   New York Democratic governor Eliot Spitzer resigns in disgrace amid a sex scandal.

24 Mar.   The death toll for American soldiers in Iraq reaches four thousand.

3 June   Having won a majority of primary delegates, Obama becomes the presumptive Democratic nominee. Clinton ends her competitive run for the nomination.

27 June   The Supreme Court rejects a Washington, D.C., ban on handgun possession. The decision marks the first time in U.S. history that the Second Amendment is interpreted to affirm an individual's right to gun ownership.

10 July   Bush signs the Foreign Intelligence Surveillance Amendments Act (FISA), which loosens federal wiretapping restrictions regarding civilian surveillance involving terrorism and espionage.

14 July   Bush lifts the offshore oil drilling ban for the outer continental shelf, legislation implemented by his father, President George H. W. Bush.

8 Aug.   John Edwards confesses to having had an extramarital affair with campaign photojournalist Rielle Hunter.

29 Aug.   Republican presidential nominee John McCain chooses Alaska governor Sarah Palin as his running mate. She is the first woman on a Republican presidential ticket and proves to be an energizing force within the party.

15 Sept.   Lending giant Lehman Brothers Holdings Inc. files for Chapter 11 bankruptcy protection, becoming the largest bankruptcy filing in U.S. history.

29 Sept.   The Dow Jones Industrial Average drops nearly 800 points, the biggest single-day point loss in stock market history. The loss marks the beginning of a long and damaging economic recession in the United States.

3 Oct.   Bush signs the Emergency Economic Stabilization Act, a $700 billion bailout of the U.S. financial system, which establishes the Troubled Asset Relief Program (TARP).

4 Nov.   Obama wins the presidential election.

19 Dec.   Bush announces a $17.4 billion auto-industry rescue, with $13.4 billion in emergency loans to prevent General Motors and Chrysler from collapsing.

2009

20 Jan.   Obama is inaugurated as the forty-fourth president of the United States.

29 Jan.   Obama signs the Lilly Ledbetter Fair Pay Act, which supports equal pay regardless of race, sex, or age.

27 Feb.   Tea (Taxed Enough Already) Party groups gather across the United States to protest TARP.

13 Apr.   Obama signs a presidential memorandum removing restrictions that prevent Cuban Americans from visiting relatives in Cuba and sending remittances.

31 May   Physician George Tiller is gunned down while serving as an usher during Sunday services at the Reformation Lutheran Church in Wichita, Kansas. The gunman, Scott Roeder, is an antiabortion activist, targeting Tiller for administering late-term abortions.

4 June   Obama gives a speech in Cairo, Egypt, reaching out to the Muslim world, thought to signal a dramatic shift in U.S. diplomacy.

24 June   South Carolina Republican governor Mark Sanford admits to and apologizes for an affair with an Argentine woman, during which time he disappeared from the country while his staff, based on Sanford's communication with them, claimed he was hiking in the Appalachian Mountains. Despite calls for his removal, he serves out his term.

6 Aug.   Sonia Sotomayor is confirmed the first Hispanic woman on the Supreme Court.

25 Aug.   Massachusetts Democratic senator Edward M. "Ted" Kennedy dies.

5 Nov.   U.S. Army major Nidal Malik Hasan kills twelve fellow soldiers and a civilian in a shooting rampage at Fort Hood, Kansas.

1 Dec.   Obama announces an escalation of 30,000 troops in Afghanistan. The effort is designed to combat increased activity of Taliban fighters.

10 Dec.   Obama is awarded the Nobel Peace Prize. Critics declare the award premature.

OVERVIEW

Contentious Decade. The decade of the 2000s was marked by war, tragedy, and economic collapse. The U.S. role as a global leader faltered and terrorists became elusive enemies. The United States waged preemptive wars in Afghanistan and Iraq to destroy terrorist cells and promote democracy, but these attempts were marred by mismanagement, misunderstanding, persistent instability, and civil war. Other industrialized nations became distrustful of American intentions and suspicious of its methods. U.S. politicians, however, embraced a vast expansion of the federal government to meet these new dangers. At home, politics shifted to the Right—deregulation, tax cuts, and social conservatism dominated domestic policy, though not without considerable dissent. The emergence of a new breed of political celebrity in the news media coincided with a fractious divide separating society between "red (Republican) states" and "blue (Democrat) states." Cable-news journalists divided into conservative and liberal camps with clear political allegiances, and comedians mocked the fevered pitch of political discourse.

Red States and Blue States. The 2000 election split the nation almost equally into two deeply divided political camps. The popular vote narrowly went to Vice President Al Gore over Texas governor George W. Bush, but the Supreme Court ruled to halt a recount of Florida votes and declared Bush the winner of the electoral vote. The media relegated constituents in that election to red (Republican) or blue (Democrat) states according to votes along party lines. While red states went for Bush and blue states for Gore, the coveted swing states, including Florida, Ohio, and Michigan, became deeply contested battlegrounds. This pattern of dividing the nation geographically continued throughout the decade and became a simplistic if useful map for charting the poles of American politics. Taking cues from their constituents, Republicans sharpened their image as the representatives of social conservatism, alongside their more traditional affiliation with fiscal conservatism. Following a pattern begun in the 1960s and 1970s, the Solid South fully transformed from a Democratic region to a Republican one by the 2000 election, forming a loyal and conservative voting bloc for the Republican Party, along with the Midwest and Rocky Mountain states. These red states embraced political platforms that opposed abortion and gay rights, promoted faith-based initiatives and defense spending, and called for a smaller federal government. The Democrats, on the other hand, tried to widen their political platform to appeal to moderate-to-conservative voters beyond their typical bases, New England and California. Purple states popped up on election maps by the 2006 midterms, defying neat labels. In 2008 the "fifty-state strategy" for the Democrats brought some conservatives into the fold, helped elect Barack Obama as president, and fueled an overwhelming Democratic victory in Congress. Yet, the overall effect of putting cultural issues at the center of politics precipitated a broad move to the Right in both parties that alienated moderate Republicans and liberal Democrats.

War on Terrorism. Though the bombing in late 2000 of the destroyer USS *Cole* in Yemen provoked outrage, the tragedy of the September 11 terrorist attacks signaled a new era of national defense and global awareness. The specter of terrorism hung heavy over the decade. Osama bin Laden, Islamic fundamentalist and head of al Qaeda, became the principal face of terrorism for Americans. But President George W. Bush quickly broadened his list of enemies to include Iraq, North Korea, and Iran, labeling them the "Axis of Evil." His administration targeted Iraqi leader Saddam Hussein for allegedly harboring terrorists and developing weapons of mass destruction. Two years after 9/11, the United States was engaged in wars against ill-defined enemies. American troops fought the Taliban and al Qaeda in Afghanistan and Hussein's supporters in Iraq, but the lines of battle were blurred as conditions worsened in the two countries. The Americans labored to reach a fragile political balance, secure democratic institutions, and introduce economic reforms. Yet, unstable and ineffective elections led to violence, and U.S.-backed leaders were accused of corruption. Many Afghans and Iraqis resented military occupation. In the United States, debate over these distant wars became the central focus of two presidential elections. The threat of terrorism generated a vast bureaucracy, with oversight by the Department of Homeland Security (established by the Bush administration), which heavily influenced foreign and domestic policy.

TOPICS IN THE NEWS

BUSH ELECTED—2000

Time for a New President. The political campaign to replace outgoing two-term Democratic president Bill Clinton was a close contest that reflected both a desire for new leadership and the shifting social and cultural changes of the nation. Despite his alleged moral failings while in office, as well as a vocal opposition from the Right, Clinton left office with favorable polling figures (a percentage approval rating in the mid 60s) and broad support. Although he had been only the second president to face impeachment, he completed his term. His administration had signed trade pacts with more than 250 countries, engaged in active foreign diplomacy (though efforts to broker peace in the Middle East had failed), and benefited from a strong economy. A slight recession affected the country, and unemployment rates stood at around 4 percent. The federal budget had a surplus of $227 billion, although the national debt continued to grow.

Republican Candidates. Texas governor George W. Bush's win in the Iowa caucus in January 2000 confirmed him as the early front-runner in the Republican primary. However, his awkward on-screen presence and scripted talking points during debates became a problem for the Bush team. As Bush's advisers crafted his media responses and prepared him for the long run, Arizona senator John McCain, who considered himself a long shot and moderate, became a serious challenger when he soundly defeated Bush in the New Hampshire primary on 1 February. At the helm of his "Straight Talk Express" bus, McCain was a media favorite, offering reporters near-unfettered access as he explained his ideas on reforming the Republican Party and federal government. Karl Rove, Bush's political director, increased spending on advertising and Bush amped up his conservative rhetoric, focusing on cutting taxes and education, and moving away from the earlier pleas for "compassionate conservatism." McCain, whose initial focus was campaign finance reform, called tax cuts for the wealthy a risky proposition. Bush labeled McCain a complacent Washington insider. Channeling his father George H. W. Bush's campaign promises of "no new taxes" nearly a decade earlier, Bush declared there would be no new tax cuts.

A Broward County canvassing board member examines disputed ballots in Florida during the recount in the controversial 2000 election of George W. Bush (AP Photo/Alan Diaz).

South Carolina Primary. In the run-up to the South Carolina primary (19 February), both McCain and Bush claimed to represent the values and new direction of the Republican Party. Bush resonated with evangelical Christians and made a campaign appearance at Bob Jones University, an institution that banned interracial dating and

As the polls tightened between the two candidates, Gore was forced to contend with a third-party candidate who was gaining momentum. Green Party candidate Ralph Nader was polling at 6 percent of the national vote by the end of the Democratic National Convention. Modeled after Germany's Green Party, an antinuclear and environmentalist party that gained traction in the 1980s, America's Green Party ran a quiet presidential campaign for Nader in 1996, spending less than $5,000 and appearing on ballots in only a few dozen states. In 2000, however, Nader campaigned in all fifty states and drew left-wing voters away from the Democratic Party. In liberal strongholds in the western states, Nader polled at 10 percent. With both George W. Bush and Al Gore attempting to remain politically moderate, Nader's supporters argued that these candidates were equally unappealing. At the launch of his campaign in July 2000, Nader explained the need for a third-party candidate, "The other two parties are overwhelmed with arrogance and complacency. They are the same corporate party wearing two heads with different makeup." Many on Gore's staff feared potential votes for Nader but were hopeful that Green Party activists were safely ensconced in overwhelmingly Democratic regions and would not affect final tallies. Some were solaced by the fact that the Green Party and Nader were often ideologically and strategically at odds. A consumer activist interested in the legal side of reform, Nader refused to pander to identity politics, which for decades had remained a passionate motivation for activism on the Left. However, the alliance of Nader's following with Green Party supporters, along with many leftist Democrats who had long felt neglected by their party, threatened to put a dent in Gore's electoral victories. In addition, the GOP faced no such challenge from the Right; Pat Buchanan and the Reform Party never gained the same momentum as Nader's run. As Election Day approached, Nader's Green Party threatened to upend Gore's bid for the presidency. Brushing off calls to end his campaign for the sake of the Democratic Party, Nader declared, "The only difference between Al Gore and George W. Bush is the velocity with which their knees hit the floor when the corporations knock." Nader attracted die-hard liberals and swing voters, critics of global markets, environmentalists, union members, and a few former John McCain supporters who railed against campaign-finance corruption. Nader could not win, but he tilted the race in Bush's favor. After the close vote tallies and controversial Supreme Court ruling that gave Bush the presidency, Nader was demonized by Democrats for throwing the election.

Sources: Jonathan Alter, "What Presidents Are For," *Newsweek* (23 October 2000);

Mathew Cooper, "Watching a Gadfly Create a Buzz," *Time* (3 July 2000);

Frank Pellegrini, "To Gore, He's Darth Nader—and Dangerous," *Time* (23 October 2000);

Eric Pooley and others, "Campaign 2000: Chasing the Undecided: The Swing Set," *Time* (2 October 2000);

Tom Squitieri, "Green Party Puts Its 'Dreams on Wheels' with Nader Third-Party Nominee Could Become Spoiler in Presidential Race," *USA Today*, 26 July 2000.

had taken a public anti-Catholic stance. McCain appeared to be a threat to traditional GOP standards, such as cutting taxes and pandering to the far Right. McCain reached out to conservative Democrats and independents, attacking evangelical Christian leaders Pat Robertson and Jerry Falwell as "agents of intolerance." In South Carolina, Bush and his surrogates launched a devastating campaign against McCain. Alongside Bush on the campaign trail, a former Green Beret, Ted Sampley, accused McCain of betraying veterans, and a Bob Jones University professor, Richard Hand, sent out a mass email suggesting that McCain had fathered a child out of wedlock with an African American woman, a smear that played upon racial tensions and twisted the facts regarding the McCain family's adoption of a child from Bangladesh. At the same time, push polls—partisan attacks disguised as polls—helped spread false rumors about McCain's wife's drug addiction, while several right-wing religious groups claimed that McCain had been brainwashed by his captors during his time as a prisoner of war during the Vietnam War. In the end, McCain's loss in the South Carolina primary proved his vulnerability among conservative Republicans and southern constituents, and marked the sharp ideological shift of the GOP further toward the political Right. McCain failed to regain his footing and left the race after a resounding defeat on Super Tuesday (7 March).

Democratic Candidates. In the Democratic primary, Vice President Al Gore faced New Jersey senator and former professional basketball star Bill Bradley. Early on, Bradley showed promise, matching Gore in fund-raising, attracting key endorsements (one from popular basketball celebrity Michael Jordan), and benefiting from savvy campaign ads from movie director Spike Lee. But lacking Gore's political capital, Bradley's team organized a campaign that challenged politics as usual. Bradley insisted that he was engaging in a "new politics" and condemned the Gore team for relying on image and a traditional political style that no longer appealed to voters. While the two candidates agreed on many issues, often varying only by degrees on key Democratic themes (such as the environment, education, and health care), Gore stayed closer to the political center and Bradley attempted to attract more-liberal voters. As Bradley's attacks became sharper, Gore tried to usurp the underdog position and painted himself as a Washington outsider, digging up Bradley's legislative record and accusing him of capitulating to former president Ronald Reagan's conservative policies on welfare reform. In the end, Gore handily defeated Bradley, winning twenty primaries before Bradley conceded after a Super Tuesday sweep in Gore's favor. After a bitterly personal primary race, Democratic supporters feared the animosity between Gore and Bradley would linger. However, quoting former Green Bay Packers head coach Vince Lombardi in a speech endorsing Gore, Bradley declared months after his defeat, "Winning is a team sport."

Candidate Bush. Despite the overwhelming primary win, the Bush campaign faced a tough and politically savvy opponent in Gore, and they worried that the South Carolina primary had painted their candidate as too socially conservative for the rest of the nation's voters. Bush was forced to contend with his appearance at Bob Jones University, tax-cut proposals, and support for concealed-weapon permits in Texas. The campaign also had to weather a few controversies. His alleged drug use as a young man became a brief but intense focus for reporters when he was asked whether he could clear a Federal Bureau of Investigation (FBI) background check. His response seemed to verify the contention that he had indeed indulged in illegal drugs in his past. Bush's team denied the press a definitive answer but insisted that he had been able to pass the check since 1974 when his father became vice president. With his trusted adviser Karen Hughes, Bush labored over his acceptance speech for the Republican convention that successfully struck a new tone of openness and moderation for the Republican Party. But these moments were overshadowed when Bush was unexpectedly caught on microphone calling a *New York Times* reporter a "major league asshole." *Vanity Fair* ran an article claiming that Bush was dyslexic, and, despite ads stating the contrary, many felt that Bush was afraid to debate Gore. Bush's team avoided reading the bad press and lightened the candidate's schedule in order to fully prepare for the debates, a persistent concern for his advisers. For five months, Bush's strategists staged mock debates to hone his movements and talking points, readying themselves for what they considered to be Bush's biggest hurdle.

Candidate Gore. The Gore campaign fought the pervasive image of their candidate as a stiff, academic, Beltway-based politician. The media reveled in comparisons between President Clinton and his vice president, repeatedly questioning whether Gore could compete with Clinton's charisma. As Gore entered the primaries, he was careful to distance himself from Clinton, even condemning the president for his affair with Monica Lewinsky. But as Gore faced Bush in the national race, Democrats debated whether or not to actively use Clinton on the campaign trail. Some argued that the charismatic president would outshine Gore, while others claimed that Clinton's over-

whelming popularity among Democrats could only help win the White House. Many among the Democratic leadership, however, felt the country was weary of Clinton—his infidelities, the impeachment scandal, and charges of campaign finance corruption. Bush claimed West Texas roots, and Clinton had been the man from Hope, Arkansas, but Gore remained in Washington with a separate, though largely nominal, headquarters in Nashville. Gore struggled to develop a popular image—was he the son of a Tennessee tobacco grower or a political scion? His advisers hired feminist writer Naomi Wolf to spice up Gore's straitlaced persona and make him more appealing to voters. Wolf was paid $15,000 a month to provide running commentary on minute details and important decisions, from wardrobe choices to political themes for the campaign, including keeping Clinton at bay and encouraging Gore's wife Tipper to discuss his sexiness. Soon the media seized on the story and the feminist adviser became fodder for the late-night shows. Campaign morale slumped; a lackluster national tour left the media cold and Gore's team looking for an entirely new direction.

Final Campaign Push. In the final weeks of the race, polls revealed little but statistical ties, the closest presidential race in decades. The candidates campaigned hard in swing states, battling for undecided voters and clogging the airwaves with political advertisements. Both Bush and Gore spent massive amounts of money and precious time in the Midwest, Northwest, and Florida. Gore stumped for working-class support, focusing on the employment and health-care worries of industrial workers, while Bush defended his plan for young people to invest a portion of their social-security taxes in the stock market. Florida became a major target for both camps. Between the debates and Election Day, Gore visited Florida thirteen times and Bush took nine trips to the Sunshine State. Both candidates focused their resources on voter turnout, investing heavily in advertisements attacking their opponent's views on Medicare, tax cuts, and Social Security. Amid the election chaos, a tragedy a hemisphere away highlighted differences between Gore and Bush on foreign-policy issues. On 12 October a terrorist bomb killed seventeen American sailors on the destroyer USS *Cole* in Yemen. While the Bush team touted its commitment to an antiballistic missile system, the campaign also felt obligated to once again defend his lack of foreign-policy experience. Gore, on the other hand, had been the most active vice president regarding diplomacy. On 7 November, Bush and Gore settled into their respective headquarters to wait for election results. Early returns suggested that Bush had benefited from his moderate stance, gaining some votes that had previously gone to the Democrats. While the majority of low- to middle-income voters, Hispanics, young people, and Catholics supported Gore, a substantial number of these constituencies voted for Bush. Gore was winning key states, including swing-state Pennsylvania and California, usually a Democratic stronghold in presidential races that

Democratic presidential candidate Vice President Al Gore at a campaign rally in Nashville, Tennessee, on 7 March 2000 after his Super Tuesday victories (AP Photo/Amy Sancetta)

Bush had hoped to capture. As the results came back, the race remained very close.

Too Close to Call. The media focused on Florida. With twenty-five electoral votes, Florida was among the biggest and most hotly contested swing states. Therefore, at 7:50 P.M., when MSNBC projected Florida would go to Gore, the Bush team was devastated. Bush's father and brother, Jeb, consoled him. Bush's twin daughters, Jenna and Barbara, began to cry, hugging their father. Michigan, another coveted swing state, was soon called for Gore, as well. In Austin, Bush's campaign strategist Karl Rove was concerned that MSNBC had called the Florida vote too early, before the polls had even closed in the predominantly Republican Panhandle. By 9:30 P.M. the once-jubilant Gore campaign was silenced as the networks again placed Florida in the "too close to call" category. As the networks confirmed definitive winners in the rest of the states, it became clear that Florida would decide the election. Both campaigns watched the results come in, precinct by precinct. Bush commented to his brother, "I can't believe this is happening. This is like running for a city council seat." At 2:15 A.M., Fox News called Florida and the presidential election for Bush, and other networks soon followed. In Nashville, Gore showed little emotion, thanked his staff,

spent a few minutes alone with his family, and immediately called Bush to concede the race. But minutes later, as Gore's motorcade drove toward its final rally, Nashville's airwaves were jammed with frantic calls that Gore was still gaining votes in Florida. One Gore adviser received word that Bush's lead had shrunk from 50,000 votes with 98 percent of precincts reporting to 500 with 99.5 percent. A recount was imminent if the margin remained less than one percent. Bush responded incredulously when Gore called him to retract his concession.

Recount. The next day, it was clear that Gore had won the popular vote. He was leading by more than 250,000 votes (twice the margin of the close race between John F. Kennedy and Richard M. Nixon in 1960), but the electoral vote was still up in the air. With a recount looming, Gore's advisers gathered a team under former secretary of state Warren Christopher to handle any legal challenges. While the Gore team used the popular-vote victory to pad their argument for a recount, Rove looked for film footage of Gore extolling the function of the Electoral College. The Bush campaign insisted that a recount would be a formality if needed. As more counties reported final tallies, the margin dropped below two hundred votes. Bush's team eagerly awaited absentee ballots—many from servicemen and women stationed overseas, who had generally supported Bush. Yet, Gore's advisers claimed that many of the absentee ballots were from Democratic-leaning South Florida Jews, traveling or living in Israel. By 9 November, with Bush ahead by one-third of one percent and Gore ahead in the electoral college vote 260 to 246, the Florida recount began in Volusia, Miami-Dade, Broward, and Palm Beach Counties. The Bush team filed injunctions against the recount, while Gore's lawyers asked election officials to withhold certifying the results until the hand recount was completed. Furthermore, the National Association for the Advancement of Colored People (NAACP) reported incidents of racial discrimination at polling stations. In Palm Beach County, around 19,000 punch-card ballots were thrown out because more than one candidate was chosen. In Broward County "hanging chads"—where the punch was incomplete, leaving a hanging piece of paper—caused 6,700 ballots to be discounted because the vote was not counted mechanically.

Bush v. Gore. For a month, legal battles were fought in nearly every forum possible, on the local, state, and federal levels. Gore's supporters, who knew that thousands of ballots were rejected by voting machines and had not yet been examined by hand, argued for a continuation of the recount. Bush maintained a small lead, however, and was intent on keeping it. The onus was on Gore to keep the recount going by convincing judges and American voters, while Bush's legal team pressed for a decision and an end to the election. In early December the Florida Supreme Court ordered sixty-seven counties to inspect their ballots under the supervision of Florida district court judge Terry Lewis in Tallahassee. In effect, Lewis was charged with the delicate task of deciphering the intent of voters and determining the forty-third president of the United States. Yet, within hours, the U.S. Supreme Court stopped the recount. The stakes had become too high to rest in the hands of one Florida judge. Despite Gore's argument for a continuance and his conviction that every voter deserved their vote to be counted, the Supreme Court decided in a five-to-four decision to end the recount and, therefore, grant Bush the presidency. The recount controversy haunted the Bush administration throughout its first term, and became one of a series of debates about the efficiency and function of the government.

Sources:
Matt Bai, "Bill Bradley's Last Stand," *Newsweek* (6 March 2000);

Caryn Baird, "The Fight for Florida: So Far," *St. Petersburg Times*, 13 November 2000;

Dan Balz, "The Story So Far; Presidential Underdogs Face Five Week Gauntlet," *Washington Post*, 24 December 1999;

"Bush's Dirty Politcking," *St. Petersburg Times*, 19 February 2000;

Andrew Cain, "Bush and Gore Rule Super Tuesday," *Washington Times*, 8 March 2000;

James Carney and others, "Campaign 2000: Bush Bears Down," *Time*, 155 (24 January 2000);

Gail Russell Chaddock, "After the Conventions, Gore Works the Third Party Math," *Christian Science Monitor* (15 August 2000);

Adam Clymer, "The 2000 Campaign: The Democrats; Two Democrats Fire Broadsides in Testy Debate," *New York Times*, 27 January 2000;

Richard Cohen, "Farewell to a Long Shot," *Washington Post*, 9 March 2000;

James Dao, "Democrats Seeking Some Clinton Magic for Gore in the Fall," *New York Times*, 16 July 2000;

Michael Duffy and others, "Election 2000: What It Took," *Time* (20 November 2000);

Thomas B. Edsall, "Bush Cuts Deeply into Democratic Coalition: But Gore's Base Kept Contest Competitive," *Washington Post*, 8 November 2000;

Susan Estrich, "Gore Can't Afford to Distance Self from Clinton," *Dallas Morning News*, 6 July 1999;

Linda Feldmann, "Gore versus Bradley: How Would They Lead," *Christian Science Monitor* (7 January 2000);

Nancy Gibbs, "Reversal of Fortune," *Time* (11 November 2000);

"Long Road to the White House," *St. Petersburg Times*, 7 November 2000;

Tim Nickens, "State of Confusion; Recount Begins as World Watches," *St. Petersburg Times*, 9 November 2000;

Frank Pellegrini and Jessica Reaves, "The Final Tally: Bush Wins. Or Does He?" *Time* (7 November 2000);

Dick Polman, "Bradley's Lonely Battle as Bradley's Campaign Falters," *Philadelphia Inquirer*, 6 February 2000;

Evan Thomas, Peter Goldman, and others, "What a Long, Strange Trip," *Newsweek* (20 November 2000);

David Von Drehle, "2000: A Nation Divided," *Time* (24 November 2010).

BUSH-KERRY—ELECTION 2004

Partisan Divide. By the 2004 presidential election, the national unity that followed 9/11 was replaced with divisive partisan politics. Bush's approval ratings had plummeted, reaching just below 50 percent, and many of his supporters and critics were equally vocal and unwavering in their opinions. There were bumper stickers that read "He's Not My President," while action figures of Bush in an aviator's uniform set records in toy sales. Though strong candidates emerged in the Democratic Party to challenge Bush, the president's policies and personality dominated debates and discussions. Voters and pundits argued whether he was decisive or arrogant, assertive or reckless, fearless or stubborn. Some hated his policies, but liked his dedication and resolve. Many claimed to relate to Bush on a personal level; he seemed compassionate and straightforward. A grim minority of voters angrily protested the Bush administration. But Bush conceded little to his critics, instead, maintaining an agenda that portrayed a world of good vs. evil. For voters, their decision would ultimately be a referendum on this agenda.

Courting "Values Voters." Contending with a first-term legacy that included devastating terrorist attacks on American soil, two wars, and a broad swath of controversial domestic initiatives, Bush's reelection team shaped the campaign to suit a major conservative base of support, so-called values voters who were motivated to vote in support of socially conservative policies. As a vocal defender of his faith, Bush brought religion to the forefront of his political agenda and activated the once-diminishing evangelical vote. He proposed a constitutional amendment against gay marriage, withheld funding to international organizations that supported abortion, and banned partial-birth abor-

President George W. Bush, left, and Democratic candidate Senator John Kerry during their second presidential debate at Washington University in St. Louis, Missouri, on 8 October 2004 (AP Photo/Charlie Riedel)

tions. His staunch opposition to stem-cell research, the use of embryonic cells in medical studies, received praise from antiabortion protesters, Catholics, and evangelicals. However, critics, including some Republican congressmen, claimed that his policy was shortsighted and hindered research on illnesses, such as Alzheimer's disease and diabetes, and sent important medical funding abroad. His economic policies also faced tough criticism. When charged with making careless allowances to big corporations and wealthiest citizens, Bush's supporters countered that his tax cuts had revived a flagging post-9/11 economy and his concessions to business interests had helped build investor confidence.

Politics of War. The attacks on 11 September and the wars in Afghanistan and Iraq became prominent themes in the campaign, but not without scrutiny. Early on, the Bush campaign weathered biting criticism from Democrats for using 9/11 as a campaign tool, after airing ads featuring actual footage from the chaos at Ground Zero. Further, Bush was forced to defend his foreign-policy decisions. To critics of the Bush Doctrine, he insisted that his policy of preemptive war had compelled otherwise rogue states to cooperate with the United States. In answering calls for an investigation into intelligence used to support the war against Iraq, Bush maintained that the conflict was "a war of necessity." The principal campaign tactic for Karl Rove, Bush's chief strategist, was to rally voters around their president. No wartime president had ever lost an election.

Democratic Primaries. While Bush's nomination was a foregone conclusion, Democrats from across the political spectrum lined up for their chance to take on the incumbent. Among the top contenders in the primary race were Senator John Kerry of Massachusetts, Senator John Edwards of North Carolina, Senator Joseph Lieberman of Connecticut, and retired General Wesley Clark. But it was Vermont governor Howard Dean who leaped ahead in the polls and emerged as a formidable challenger. An antiwar Washington outsider, medical doctor, and Christian, he was an acerbic critic of Bush's policies on everything from health care to the Iraq War. Dean's zeal was only surpassed by the overwhelming support of an army of devoted liberal followers on the Internet, playfully called Deaniacs. He tapped into the discontent and eagerness for change expressed by many progressive Democrats angry that their party had capitulated to what they saw as the Bush administration's overreaching policies. Dean's enthusiasm and ability to attract new voters and raise campaign funds impressed Democrats and worried the Bush campaign. After a key endorsement from Al Gore, Dean became the front-runner. However, as Dean attempted to win over the Democratic establishment, other hopefuls argued that while Dean had galvanized the party, he was a political liability, because he was too liberal, impassioned, inexperienced, and inconsistent to stand a chance against Bush in the general election. While many still believed that Dean had the nomination before a single vote had been cast, he

The rapid rise of Howard Dean in national politics during the 2004 Democratic primary owed much to the increased role of the Internet in political organizing. Though only a small-state governor with little name recognition before the primaries, Dean was propelled to the top of the slate of candidates and led in early fund-raising due to savvy use of the Internet. After taking a firm stance against the Iraq War and encouraging Democrats to become more vocal in opposition to Bush administration policies during the early debates, grassroots supporters began using the social networking website meetup.org to organize rallies and campaign activities at the local level. Through the site, like-minded Dean supporters could plan and schedule actual meetings with one another. With very little effort on the part of campaign workers, supporters were organizing and holding hundreds of monthly meetings across the country by the summer of 2003. Dean supporters became known as "Deaniacs," for their devotion to the candidate, a loyalty that owed in large part to the feeling that they held a personal stake in the campaign. Decentralization had its pitfalls, however, and despite shattering early fund-raising records, the Dean campaign had a difficult time translating the fervor of its online supporters into actual votes in the primary states. After losing the early Iowa caucuses (a contest he was expected to win), Dean began to slide in the polls. Despite his failure to garner the nomination, however, the work of Dean and his innovative campaign manager, Joe Trippi, helped redefine the way modern campaigns could utilize Internet technology.

Source: *Wired.com.*

landed in a disappointing third place behind Kerry and Edwards in the first Democratic primary, the Iowa caucus. After screaming and fist-pumping his way through a concession speech, Dean's emotional pleas to his supporters to keep fighting instantly became the joke of the political season, comedic fodder of the late-night talk-show circuit, and featured in loops on the political networks. The next day, pundits wrote his political obituary. Dean stayed on the ballots, but he trailed far behind Kerry, who moved to the top of the polls. Still, Dean remained a vital force in the primary, having shaken up a complacent Democratic Party struggling to find a decisive voice against the Bush administration.

John Kerry. As the presumptive nominee, Kerry shifted his focus to the wartime president's foreign policy, claiming that Bush's reliance on military action over diplomacy had created an entire generation of anti-American sentiment in the Middle East. Further, Kerry insisted that the president had yet to answer critical questions about the intelligence that led America to war in Iraq. But the wars in Afghanistan and Iraq were precarious political tools for both parties. When Iraqi leader Saddam Hussein was captured in December 2003, Dean, then a front-runner, had been forced to rework his antiwar stance, fending off attacks from fellow primary candidates. From the bottom of the polls, Lieberman chided Dean, "If Howard Dean has his way, Saddam Hussein would still be in power today, not in prison, and the world would be a much more dangerous place." Yet, Rove worried that the Bush campaign's strategy of showcasing the commander in chief would be threatened by Dean's relentless arguments against the war. With violence escalating in Iraq throughout the spring, Rove welcomed Kerry as Bush's likely opponent. For Rove, Kerry's long tenure in Congress made him vulnerable as both an antiwar crusader and hawkish patriot. The Bush team was quick to point out Kerry's initial vote to authorize the Iraq invasion, and compiled a lengthy history of Kerry's record on Iraq, condemning Hussein and the Iraqi leader's dismissal of UN weapons inspectors, and accusing Hussein of possessing weapons of mass destruction. But Iraq remained a needling issue for the Bush team, particularly after CBS news program *60 Minutes II*, in late spring, broadcast disturbing photographs exposing prisoner abuse by U.S. soldiers at Abu Ghraib detention center in Iraq. The photographs depicted soldiers humiliating and degrading prisoners—sexually, physically, and emotionally. Bush was forced to address the nation, declaring his own outrage and disgust, but he insisted that those soldiers were not representative of the armed forces stationed in Iraq.

Military Credentials. The Kerry and Bush campaigns also battled over a more distant conflict in American memory. Arguments about patriotism, sacrifice, and the use of a military record for political purposes focused attention on the Vietnam War. Early in the primary, Kerry, a decorated naval officer who served in Vietnam, received support from veterans at campaign stops, particularly Jim Rassmann, a Green Beret whose life Kerry saved in 1969. Also, historian Douglas Brinkley published a timely authorized biography of Kerry's war service, *Tour of Duty: John Kerry and the Vietnam War* (2004). Tamping down Kerry's military credentials, the Bush campaign, hoping to paint Kerry as a left-wing liberal, called attention to his participation in a Vietnam Veterans against the War protest in Washington, D.C., where the future senator along with other veterans threw away ribbons and medals received during combat. In order to escape the potentially damaging liberal mantle, Kerry launched the most expensive presidential ad campaign in history, spending $25 million in nineteen states to promote his military service. Further, Kerry, who had volunteered for the navy, derided the president and his closest advisers, Vice President Dick Cheney and Rove, for avoiding their calls to war. Both Cheney and Rove had received college deferments, and, after he was drafted, Bush spent the war

Political cartoon by Jack Ohman showing how the claims of the anti-Kerry political group "Swift Boat Veterans for Truth," formed by Vietnam War veterans, could not "hold water" (*U.S. News & World Report*).

stateside in the Air National Guard in Texas. In a more pointed jibe, Kerry, referring to Bush's "Mission Accomplished" moment, when the president prematurely declared victory in Iraq, teased, "I know something about aircraft carriers for real." Investigative journalists revealed holes in Bush's military record, reporting that Bush had left his National Guard unit two years before his tour was up, transferring to Alabama to help with a friend's senate campaign. Yet, Bush never showed up for duty. Soon after, he was honorably discharged eight months early, immediately before attending Harvard Business School.

Swift Boat Veterans for Truth. Throughout the summer, the attacks intensified and questions about both candidates' military service persisted. By August, the Kerry campaign faced a full assault on their candidate's war record. Swift Boat Veterans for Truth aired ads featuring Kerry's 1971 testimony protesting the Vietnam War before the Senate Foreign Relations Committee. In other ads, the group accused Kerry of lying in order to receive medals and complained that he had betrayed his brothers in arms by calling them war criminals. While publicly calling the ads unfair and a blatant distortion of the truth, Kerry's advisers cautioned the candidate and his newly chosen running mate, Senator John Edwards, against fighting back, arguing that Kerry may appear too angry or bitter. Some media pundits shook their heads in disbelief, wondering why Kerry would leave his war record at the mercy of the news cycle. Funded by a devoted Bush supporter, the Swift Boat Veterans only invested several thousand dollars, but their

ads played relentlessly on cable-news shows. After a campaign stop where dozens of veterans urged Kerry to defend himself, he delivered a speech that recalled his service and injuries, and defiantly challenged anyone to doubt his commitment.

***60 Minutes* Scandal.** President Bush, on the other hand, watched the scandal regarding his military service die down until *60 Minutes II* reported that they had uncovered documents written by Bush's superior officer in the Texas Air National Guard that claimed Bush had not fulfilled his duties. Bush was skeptical of their validity, but admitted to shirking some of his duties. The Bush team, already wary of the television program for its report on Abu Ghraib, went on the offensive, insisting that the documents were falsified, and accusing the network, *60 Minutes II*, and veteran CBS anchor Dan Rather of being biased. The campaign's attack set the tone for the media frenzy that followed, shifting the focus of the report from its content to Rather's alleged shoddy journalism. In the end, Rather and CBS admitted that the documents and their source, retired Texas Air National Guard officer, Bill Burkett, were suspect. The network admitted that the documents could not be authenticated and Rather's reputation was irrevocably tarnished, while any further investigations into Bush's National Guard service were ignored or abandoned. Both the Swift Boat ads and the *60 Minutes II* report highlighted the intense media spotlight on the 2004 election. The more media-savvy the campaign, the better press it received, but the Bush campaign also showed the potential payoff in guiding the news. Increasingly, networks and cable-news channels were accused of bias, with Democrats crying foul against Fox News and Republicans complaining about mainstream journalism, particularly, in this case, CBS.

Tough Campaigning. Following the national conventions, where Kerry burnished his image as a credible commander in chief and Bush touted his leadership after 9/11, the candidates sharpened their attacks and chased headlines on the Iraq War, ready to pry out any advantage they could. Kerry continued hammering Bush with questions about Iraq: Where were the weapons of mass destruction? Why had Bush rushed to war? Had all diplomatic channels been exhausted? Deflecting Kerry's attacks, Rove pulled an excerpt from a Kerry campaign speech when the Democratic nominee said, "I actually did vote for the $87 billion before I voted against it." Kerry tried to explain his reasons for voting against a bill for supplemental funding for troops in Iraq, which he had voted for in the Senate when the Democratic bill included a repeal of Bush's tax cuts to people earning more than $300,000 a year, but he voted against the bill when that tax measure was omitted. Rove branded Kerry indecisive and lacking confidence, a "flip-flopper." An unfortunate euphemism that stayed with Kerry in the form of protesters in flip-flop costumes at speaking events and near constant references in the media, "flip-flopping" became a part of the political lexicon in 2004. Kerry fought back, declaring, "I will not have my commitment to defend this country questioned by those who refused to serve when they could have and who misled America into Iraq." But with Kerry's votes on the conflict hopelessly complicated, he attempted to divert attention away from his Senate record and redirect the focus back to Bush. Kerry began to hit the president on Afghanistan, condemning him for starting another war when he had yet to find Osama bin Laden.

Bush Reelected. On 3 November, Bush achieved an unquestionable victory and the popular vote that had eluded him in 2000, but he won by the smallest margin of any incumbent president since Democrat Woodrow Wilson. The dueling campaigns spent enormous sums of money, making this presidential election the first where candidates spent more than a billion dollars. Close results in several swing states suggested that voters were just as polarized as they had been four years earlier, presenting a renewed leadership challenge for Bush. Rove had been correct in his prediction that Ohio's twenty electoral votes would decide the election. Kerry kept returning to the historically Republican state, which had suffered economically more than most during the Bush years and had voted for Clinton in 1992 and 1996, visiting Ohio twenty-seven times compared to Bush's eighteen campaign stops. But Bush won Ohioans over in the end, perhaps convincing them that he was the best leader to continue the war on terrorism and revive the economy. In a sign that the culture wars were far from over, driving Bush's supporters to the polls in Ohio and other states were ballot initiatives calling for state constitutional bans against gay marriage. For many

Americans, however, voting for the president in office during the 9/11 attacks was the deciding factor. Record turnouts and exit polling suggested that the election had been about Iraq, and the majority opted to stay the course with Bush.

Sources:

Randal C. Archibold, "Dean Faces New Attack, This One on Tax Policy," *New York Times*, 13 December 2003;

Perry Bacon Jr., "The Spirit of Howard Dean," *Time* (13 June 2006);

Holly Bailey and others, "The Vets Attack," *Newsweek* (15 November 2004);

Julian Borger, "Bush Launches Campaign with Gung-Ho Address," *Irish Times*, 21 January 2004;

"Come Back, Little Deaniacs," *New York Times*, 1 February 2004;

David T. Cook, "Hanging in the Balance in Ohio," *Christian Science Monitor* (4 November 2004);

John F. Dickerson and others, "2004 Election: Inside the War Rooms," *Time* (15 November 2004);

Dickerson and others, "The Love Him, Hate Him President," *Time* (1 December 2003);

Linda Feldmann, "With Ads, Bush Joins Fray," *Christian Science Monitor* (25 November 2003);

Howard Fineman, "Having a Gay Old Time," *Newsweek* (5 May 2003);

Fineman and others, "A Sweet Victory . . . And a Tough Loss," *Newsweek* (15 November 2004);

Philip Gailey, "Warts and All, Dean Would Be Missed," *St. Petersburg Times*, 25 January 2004;

David R. Guarino and Andrew Miga, "Democratic National Convention; Beantown Blowout," *Boston Herald*, 27 July 2004;

David M. Halbfinger, "Kerry Says Dean Lacks Presidential Traits," *New York Times*, 17 December 2003;

Mimi Hall and Judy Keen, "President Defends Iraq War Decision," *USA Today*, 8 February 2004;

William Hershey, "Republicans Solidified Grip on State," *Dayton Daily News*, 7 November 2004;

Deborah Kalb, "The Vietnam Effect in 2004," *The Hill*, 26 January 2004;

Howard Kurtz, "Rather Admits 'Mistake in Judgment;' CBS Was Misled about Bush National Guard Documents, Anchor Says," *Washington Post*, 21 September 2004;

Gebe Martinez, "Election 2004; U.S. Vote Essentially Was Decided in Iraq," *Houston Chronicle*, 3 November 2004;

Miga, "Saddam Captured; Kerry, Lieberman Blast Anti-War Leader Dean," *Boston Herald*, 15 December 2003;

Vincent Morris, "Bush Evokes 9/11 in Re-Election Ads," *New York Post*, 4 March 2004;

Robert B. Reich, "Vietnam Remembered," *American Prospect* (5 March 2004);

Bennett Roth, "2004 Republican Convention; Bush Pledges a 'Safer World,'" *Houston Chronicle*, 3 September 2004;

Jim Rutenberg and James Dao, "1971 Tape Adds to Debate Over Kerry's Medal Protest," *New York Times*, 26 April 2004;

Andrea Sachs and James Poniewozik, "2004 Election: Bush vs. Kerry vs. the Media," *Time* (15 November 2004);

Scott Shepard, "Kerry Launches Record $25 Million Ad Campaign," *Atlanta Journal-Constitution*, 4 May 2004;

Andrew Stephen, "The Boy Genius Behind Bush," *New Statesman* (15 November 2004);

Richard W. Stevenson, "Bush's Advisors Focus on Dean As Likely Opponent Next Year," *New York Times*, 11 December 2003;

Sheryl Gay Stolberg, "Limits on Stem-Cell Research Re-emerge as Political Issue," *New York Times*, 6 May 2004;

Evan Thomas, "How Bush Did It," *Newsweek* (15 November 2004);

"Vietnam Is the Past," *Austin American-Statesman*, 5 February 2004;

"A War of Words Erupts over Vietnam," *Dallas Morning News,* 12 February 2004;

Jodi Wilgoren, "Kerry Attacks Bush Officials Who Received Draft Deferrals," *New York Times,* 17 April 2004;

Bob Woodward, "Rove Revels in Democrat Kerry's Lead," *Washington Post,* 18 April 2004.

DEMOCRATIC RESURGENCE: OBAMA WINS

A Fresh Slate. The 2008 presidential election was the first in more than fifty years that did not feature either an incumbent or vice president as candidates. After eight tumultuous years of the Bush administration, the race for the Republican nomination was wide open with no clear front-runner leading up to the primaries. No contenders from Bush's inner circle stepped forward and Bush's approval ratings had plunged to new depths. Instead, a few strong candidates with vastly different conservative credentials emerged. Early polling suggested that three men were among Republicans' top choices: Governor Mike Huckabee of Arkansas, a southerner and former Baptist minister; first-term Massachusetts governor Mitt Romney, a Mormon and a wealthy, fiscal conservative; and Rudolph Giuliani, the former mayor of New York City who took a controversial hard line in cleaning up New York and famously led the city through the aftermath of 9/11. Senator John McCain of Arizona, a former presidential contender in 2000, known for his bipartisan political approach and his heroism as a POW during the Vietnam War, was once again considered an underdog in 2008. His campaign had capsized by August 2007, with staffers resigning and his war chest nearly empty, but McCain was steadily rebuilding. Media pundits saw an ailing party that refused to expand or change its policies to embrace new voters. The Republican Party seemed out of step with the majority of voters on controversial domestic issues, including Bush's proposal for a constitutional ban on gay marriage, overturning *Roe* v. *Wade,* and banning stem-cell research. Further, Bush's disastrous handling of the devastation left in the wake of Hurricane Katrina, the scandals surrounding private military contracts, and the vicissitudes of two wars damaged the party's image regarding other fundamental Republican concerns. In comments regarding his party, Republican governor of South Carolina Mark Sanford said, "We've lost, clearly, some of the moral high ground on the larger issues of taxing and spending."

John McCain. As voters went to the polls in the Republican primary, McCain was the victor in enough key races to force both Romney and Giuliani to concede. Huckabee remained in the race longer, buoyed by the support of southern states where social conservatives and evangelical Christians held sway, but he too left the primary by March. McCain's wins, particularly in South Carolina, made him the clear winner and confounded his right-wing critics. Detractors, such as ultraconservative talk-radio host Rush Limbaugh and right-to-life groups, condemned McCain's record of supporting stem-cell research, campaign-

FIFTY-STATE STRATEGY

As Democratic national chairman, Howard Dean turned the lesson he learned in his failed 2004 presidential bid into a broad political strategy for the party in the 2008 election. In his campaign for president, Dean had attempted to expand the Democratic base with a fifty-state strategy rather than stick to the safer, blue states, with an exhaustive travel schedule and an intense Internet-driven campaign. By the 2006 midterm elections, Dean, as chairman, had provided party leaders in each state with enough funding to begin to implement that strategy. Dean argued that Democrats had left behind important and historically Democratic supporters, such as Catholics and working-class voters who were socially conservative but liberal on economic issues. In mapping the future of the party, Dean also insisted that Democrats needed to welcome a broad swath of Americans, from evangelicals and fiscal conservatives to antiabortionists and national security hawks. Many in his party bitterly disagreed with Dean, but his plan paid off in 2006, with Democrats winning a majority in both the House and Senate. In a few close races, Democrats won congressional seats in solid Republican territory. Dean, who had claimed that it would be years before seeing his plan's dividends, was encouraged by the midterm elections and continued to lay the groundwork for an expansive fifty-state presidential campaign in 2008.

Sources: Perry Bacon Jr., "Dean Leaves No State Behind," *Time* (23 October 2006);

Jeffrey Goldberg, "Central Casting: The Democrats Think about Who Can Win in the Midterms and 2008," *New Yorker* (29 May 2006);

Martin Kasindorf and Tom Kenworthy, "Behind Democrats' Climb in Mountain West," *USA Today,* 21 November 2006;

Jeff Zeleny, "Democratic Leader Reminds Party that Victory Is No Mandate," *New York Times,* 3 December 2006.

finance reform, and a path to citizenship for illegal aliens. McCain's supporters, who championed character and national security as their top concerns in polls, created a new and tentative coalition of Republicans, along with moderate, near-right, and left-leaning members of the party. Despite McCain's insistence that he had a conservative record in the Senate and was opposed to abortion, the far Right of the GOP kept a cool distance during the primary. Some suggested that a fractured evangelical community, unwilling to fall in line behind McCain, signaled an internal battle born of the frustration in losing a vocal supporter in Bush. McCain attempted to keep his head above the fray, focusing on his strengths: his reputation, though not undisputed, as tough on lobbyists and as a campaign-finance reformer. He also enjoyed a warm relationship with the press, freely extending hospitality and frank perspective to reporters aboard his campaign bus, the Straight Talk Express. Some questioned, however, if McCain's popularity

Saddleback Civil Forum On
THE PRESIDENCY
SATURDAY, AUGUST 16, 2008 • 5 - 7 P.M.

Senator **JOHN McCAIN** AND *Senator* **BARACK OBAMA**

MODERATED BY
Pastor **RICK WARREN**

FOR MORE INFORMATION VISIT SADDLEBACKCIVILFORUM.COM

Poster for a debate between presidential candidates John McCain and Barack Obama
(www.saddlebackcivilforum.com>)

with the media would wither if Illinois senator Barack Obama, a media darling, won the Democratic nomination. Another potential pitfall going into the general election was McCain's staunch support of the Iraq War. With 90 percent of Democrats and a third of Republicans hoping for an end to that conflict, McCain, who largely benefited from his experience in national-security issues, argued that the troop surge he had supported was working to quell violence and could mean a withdrawal from Iraq in the near future.

Democratic Candidates. Despite a strong campaign early on from Senator John Edwards of North Carolina, Senators Hillary Clinton of New York and Barack Obama of Illinois quickly became the two principal contenders in the Democratic primary. As a tough candidate, party stalwart, and prodigious fund-raiser, Clinton seemed a practical choice for Democrats. She was a popular senator and a veteran of moderate Democratic politics, who as First Lady had actively lobbied for legislative platforms from the executive office. Yet, Clinton was nonetheless a polarizing figure. She struggled with issues of likability and her husband

Bill Clinton's legacy—including scandals, political battles with Republican congressmen, and general fatigue felt within the party following his presidency. But Hillary successfully ignited the passions of many voters, as an experienced candidate with a wide range of foreign and domestic policy credentials and, potentially, the first woman to be elected president of the United States. Surpassing fund-raising expectations through media buzz and innovative Internet marketing, Obama made up in moving speeches and campaign promises for change for what he lacked in experience as a junior senator. The Obama campaign also enlisted an army of supporters for a grassroots campaign that broadened the reach of the candidate's message beyond established Democratic Party channels. Obama's youth inspired many voters, as did the possibility of his becoming the first African American president. As McCain swept the Republican primaries, many Democratic voters doubted Obama's chances against McCain in the general election and worried that latent racism in the United States or his short political career would make him a liability. At the

The Tea Party gathered strength following the historic election of Democrat Barack Obama in 2008, the first African American president of the United States. Obama's presidency was accompanied by an equally historic Democratic takeover in both houses of Congress. With a mandate for change and in the midst of a deep recession, the Obama administration along with a friendly Congress, passed economic relief legislation to keep banking giants afloat, housing legislation to slow foreclosures in a plummeting real-estate market, and tax cuts to ease middle- and working-class suffering as unemployment reached new heights. The following year, the White House with the help of House and Senate majority leaders, Nancy Pelosi of California and Harry Reid of Nevada, respectively, passed landmark health-care reform in a grueling congressional battle that left a watered down but significant bill, highlighting consumer rights and increasing regulations and restrictions on health-care providers. As the recession dragged on and propaganda surrounding health-care reform led to misguided headlines suggesting, for example that "death panels" would decide the fate of elderly Americans, the reforms alarmed conservatives. The Tea Party became the loudest voice of dissent, challenging Democrats and the Republican establishment from within its ranks, and emerging as a populist movement combining loosely organized insurgent conservatives across the nation, though the speeches and rallies were often organized and funded by wealthy donors. They accused both parties of allowing a mounting deficit to weaken the United States. Though a coherent political platform never materialized, the Tea Party focused on eliminating taxes and lessening the reach of the federal government. Members were socially conservative and deeply distrustful of the federal government, and they served as a rebuke to elitism in politics. A coterie of plainspoken politicians, primarily affiliated with the Republican Party, railed against the excesses of both parties. Their first political victory came in support of Republican Scott Brown, who replaced the late Edward Kennedy of Massachusetts in the Senate. It was a stunning upset for a Republican to win a historically Democratic seat. Rising stars included former Republican vice-presidential candidate Sarah Palin, who was adored for her sometimes vitriolic rhetoric against Obama and her accusations that health-care reform was a socialist takeover of American medical care. Problems within the Tea Party, however, stemmed from a lack of structure. The absence of a clear platform turned the movement into a cacophony at times. As a Republican candidate in the Kentucky senate race, Rand Paul claimed to embody the values of the Tea Party and called for tax cuts and the scaling back of federal entitlement programs, including national security and Social Security. In a television interview, Paul incurred the wrath of civil-rights advocates and progressives when he said that he would repeal the Civil Rights Act of 1964 because it allowed the federal government too much influence in private enterprise. Christine O'Donnell, Republican senatorial candidate of Delaware, also campaigned for smaller government, but her deeply conservative views on evolution, abortion rights, and gay marriage alarmed both moderates and liberals. O'Donnell was ridiculed for her shaky debate performances and her earlier activism in an antimasturbation drive. Even Palin struggled to move beyond slogans and platitudes in describing the movement's tenets. Tea Party rallies combined a broad swath of conservative Americans. Signs held by demonstrators became the topic of intense criticism, regularly featuring images of Obama as Hitler, and accusations of racism put Tea Party activists on the defensive.

Sources: "Doubting Sarah," *salon.com*;

"Tea Party Supporters: Who They Are and What They Believe," *cbsnews.com*.

same time, Clinton's supporters maintained that her drive and experience were key assets against a political veteran such as McCain.

Historic Primary Battle. The Democratic primary was both bruising and exhausting, with the two candidates in a tight race for months, splitting voters. Both Clinton and Obama held similar views on many domestic issues, including funding for social programs, increasing taxes on wealthy Americans, withdrawing troops from Iraq, encouraging diplomacy over military action, and establishing a universal health-care system, though the candidates meticulously debated the finer points of their respective platforms. Clinton focused on her experience, arguing that she, along with her husband, ran two successful presidential campaigns. She pointed out that she had served creatively and diligently as First Lady and senator of New York. Obama, quoting Bill Clinton in his 1992 presidential bid against George H. W. Bush, claimed that his "real world" experience trumped a long and storied career as a Washington insider. Each candidate drew support from different corners of the Democratic Party base. Clinton's campaign attracted women, seniors, Hispanics, and working-class white voters. She initially benefited from the support of African Americans and important black political leaders. But as Obama continued to win primaries, Clinton lost some key endorsements, including civil-rights veteran Congressman John Lewis of Georgia. Obama garnered much of the African American vote, and he consistently polled favorably among young voters, affluent Democrats, and new voters. Obama's campaign touting hope and change inspired media-savvy supporters who launched viral Internet and print campaigns. Obama appeared to signal a shift in American politics, with more voters seemingly persuaded by his pleas for leaving behind the old divisions between Right and Left and the culture wars born of the 1960s. Clinton fought the old polarities as well, reminding voters of her practical approach to politics. But by early June, despite Clinton's tenacity, Obama's promise of change defeated her campaign, ending a grueling and often bitter nomination race. After conceding, Clinton quickly endorsed Obama, but Democratic leaders worried that deeper animosities held by her supporters might prevent a united party from taking on McCain in the general election.

Vice-Presidential Picks. Though they had secured the nominations, both McCain and Obama faced divided parties. Each candidate attempted to broaden his appeal and reach out to independent voters. But as Obama smoothed the edges of positions that had attracted left-leaning voters, his base began to worry about his commitment. Some criticized his reluctant backing of a foreign-surveillance bill. Veteran activist and Democratic California representative Tom Hayden, doubted Obama's antiwar rhetoric and demanded that the candidate represent his peaceful supporters, not only the national-security hawks. However, Obama gambled on a broader spectrum of voters, appealing to conservative voters and evangelicals on divisive issues, including the Afghanistan War and gay marriage. Despite rumors that he would choose Clinton, Obama placated some among the Democratic base by naming Joe Biden, a longtime senator from Delaware and a Catholic with a solid working-class background, as his running mate. McCain struggled to unify his party and return to the fold Christian evangelists and those Republicans who disliked his stance against Bush's tax cuts. But McCain's broader problem was a lack of energy and enthusiasm from Republicans. Compared to the grassroots passion of Obama's supporters, McCain's campaign seemed lackluster and out of touch. In an explosive moment in presidential politics, McCain managed to electrify his party, introduce a relatively unknown governor to Americans, and make history by nominating the first woman as a Republican vice-presidential candidate. McCain surprised nearly everyone outside of his own tight circle of advisers when he tapped Alaska governor Sarah Palin as his running mate. Amidst deafening applause following Palin's introduction at the Republican National Convention, NBC's political pundit Chuck Todd announced that "Conservatives have found their Obama."

Sharpening the Differences. While introducing new faces and hammering home party unity, the conventions also highlighted the direction of the campaigns for the final months leading up to the election. With his new and popular running mate, McCain confidently closed the Republican convention, declaring that the troop surge in Iraq was a success; offshore drilling would soothe the energy woes; and higher taxes on the wealthy were not the answer. Battling criticism that her thin résumé and ultraconservative connections made her a liability, Palin claimed that her relatively short political career was clear of influence from lobbyists and special interests. She demanded that the rest of the country needed to follow Alaska's lead, diminish its reliance on foreign oil, and "Drill, Baby, Drill!" She derided Obama for his past acquaintances, particularly William Ayers, a college professor and former member of the small but radical and violent Vietnam-era protest group the Weather Underground. Both Ayers and Obama lived in an upper-class enclave in Chicago, and they had briefly met during a committee meeting. For his part, Obama promised Americans change and increasingly insisted that McCain and Bush were one and the same, both on foreign and domestic issues. As the economy careened toward disaster, gas prices soared, and U.S. troops battled in two wars, Obama vowed that McCain and the Republican Party would continue the policies of the Bush administration. Both McCain and Palin countered that they were "mavericks" of the Republican Party and would set a new and prosperous course for the country.

Personal Narratives. Obama and McCain disagreed bitterly on most policy issues, but voters also considered each man's personal narrative. Indeed, all four candidates represented different segments of the population. Both an asset and a burden, their biographies attracted some voters and repelled others. The differences between the presidential candidates were striking. Obama, with a white mother from the Midwest and a black father from Kenya, grew up in Hawaii and Indonesia and was Harvard educated. The changing demographics of the United States seemed to suggest that the country was ready, even eager, for a man of Obama's diverse background. McCain, a Vietnam POW and the son of elite naval officers, had served for decades in politics, styling himself after his adopted home state's conservative son and maverick politician, Barry Goldwater. McCain's military background and conservative upbringing recalled, for many, a national ideal. Obama, age forty-seven, and McCain, age seventy-two, represented the largest age gap between presidential opponents in American history, one that mirrored generational differences among the candidates' supporters, as well as McCain's message of experience versus Obama's of change. The vice-presidential candidates were chosen, in part, for their personal stories. White working-class Americans, particularly Catholics, in the ailing cities and aging suburbs identified with Biden's background. Palin appealed to evangelical Christians, working and homemaking women, and plain rural folks.

Obama Elected. After a dynamic and historic election season, with unprecedented twists and devastating disappointments, Obama became the first African American and forty-fourth president of the United States. His victory was decisive, though not a landslide, and highlighted Americans' desire for change. Most political analysts ascribed the victory to his steady and sharp campaign, grassroots support, and promise of change. But pundits also agreed that eight years of Republican leadership under the Bush administration had done the most damage to McCain's campaign. Recession, war, and a long legacy of secrecy and missteps in the Bush presidency—from failure to locate weapons of mass destruction to torture mandates—prevented many Americans from choosing another Republican president. The United States and the world seemed ready to turn the page on American politics. Seventy thousand Obama fans celebrated in Chicago at the largest campaign victory party in American history, while many around the world rejoiced as well. Less than half a century after the end of Jim Crow segregation, Americans had elected a black president and people everywhere felt a renewed connection to the United States. Citizens of multicultural countries, including France, Brazil, South Africa, and India, expressed hope that such a powerful and wealthy country had a new perspective that would lead to a more inclusive attitude toward the rest of the world.

Sources:

Jonathan Alter, "Scoping Out Obama vs. McCain," *Newsweek* (25 February 2008);

Alter, "Twilight of the Baby Boom: A Generational Struggle Is Underway," *Newsweek* (2 February 2008);

Perry Bacon Jr., "Dean Leaves No State Behind," *Time* (23 October 2006);

Bacon, "Huckabee Not Ruling Out Number 2 Spot on Ballot," *Washington Post*, 6 March 2008;

Michael Barone, "The Battle of the Party Themes," *U.S. News & World Report* (6 September 2008);

Sharon Begley, "Heard Any Good Stories Lately?: A Candidate's Personal Narrative Might Sway More Voters than Experience, Positions on Issues, and Policy Proposals," *Newsweek* (13 September 2008);

"Biden is Safe, Solid Choice for Obama," *St. Petersburg Times*, 26 August 2008;

"The Big Remaining Question," *Economist* (10 May 2008);

"The Choice," *New Yorker* (13 October 2008);

Michael Cooper and Elisabeth Bumiller, "Alaska Is McCain's Choice; First Woman on GOP Ticket," *New York Times*, 29 August 2008;

Michael Duffy, "The GOP Race: None of the Above," *Time* (13 December 2007);

Bonnie Erbe, "Barack Obama and John McCain: Both Struggle with How to Deal with their Base," *U.S. News & World Report* (7 July 2008);

Jeffrey Goldberg, "Central Casting: The Democrats Think about Who Can Win in the Midterms—and 2008," *New Yorker* (29 May 2006);

Michael Grunwald, "Barack Obama Elected President with Mandate for Change," *Time* (4 November 2008);

Liz Halloran, "The Leader of the Pack," *U.S. News & World Report* (18 February 2008);

Stephen Hayes, "The Enthusiasm Gap: Part II," *Weekly Standard* (21 July 2008);

John Heilemann, "The Sixty-Day War: With One Hastily Made Decision, John McCain Upended the Race," *New York Magazine* (5 September 2008);

Martin Kasindorf and Tom Kenworthy, "Behind Democrats' Climb in Mountain West," *USA Today*, 20 November 2006;

Joe Klein, "What Hillary Believes," *Time* (7 November 2007);

Adam Nagourney and Jeff Zeleny, "Clinton Ready to End Bid and Endorse Obama," *New York Times*, 5 June 2008;

Jay Newton-Small, "Can Hillary Readjust to the Senate?" *Time* (27 May 2008);

"No Country for Old Men: John McCain's Obstacles," *Economist* (28 February 2008);

Emma Schwartz, "Huckabee's Long Shot Candidacy Helps Define the Race," *U.S. News & World Report* (18 February 2008);

Kevin Sullivan, "U.S. Again Hailed as 'Country of Dreams': Around the World, Obama's Victory Is Seen as a Renewal of American Ideals and Aspirations," *Washington Post*, 6 November 2008;

Karen Tumulty, "Obama's Viral Marketing Campaign," *Time* (5 July 2007);

Kenneth T. Walsh, "And the Race Goes On and On," *U.S. News & World Report* (18 February 2008);

Jeff Zeleny, "Democratic Leader Reminds Party that Victory Is No Mandate," *New York Times*, 3 December 2006.

GOVERNMENT SCANDALS

Political Embarrassments. Throughout the decade, scandals took their toll on American voters, who weathered political storms that exposed corruption, infidelity, and corporate collusion. Sex scandals, in particular, ended the careers of several politicians and raised lingering suspicions about others. Republican senator Larry Craig of Idaho was arrested in 2008 for engaging in sexual behavior with an undercover police officer in the Minnesota-St. Paul International Airport's men's bathroom. Accused of tapping the officer's foot and waving his hand beneath the stall, allegedly a signal of sexual intent, Craig denied any misconduct, claiming his actions were innocent and misunderstood. He was fined $500 and given a year of unsupervised probation. A conservative politician who publicly opposed gay-rights

Republican senator Larry Craig of Idaho
(U.S. Senate Photo)

Valerie Plame became the center of a political leak scandal that called into question the legitimacy of the U.S. invasion of Iraq, laid bare deep political divisions surrounding the Iraq War, and tested the limits of journalistic integrity. On 6 July 2003, four months after war had been declared against Iraq, former ambassador Joe Wilson wrote in *The New York Times* that the Bush administration had exaggerated evidence when presenting its case for war. An Africa expert, Wilson claimed that in 2002 Vice President Dick Cheney's office had hired him to investigate the alleged sale of yellowcake uranium from Niger to Iraq. Wilson insisted that he had come up with nothing to authenticate the sale, but the White House ignored his findings and proceeded with war preparations, going so far as to use the discredited yellowcake evidence in their presentation to the United Nations. *The New York Times* article wreaked chaos in Washington, D.C. Days after its publication, a memo from the State Department to Secretary of State Colin Powell identified Wilson's wife, Valerie Plame, as a CIA operative and noted her recommendation of Wilson for the Niger mission. By 11 July, Karl Rove, Bush adviser and powerful media liaison, received a call from *Time*'s Washington correspondent, Matthew Cooper. Rove accused Wilson of distorting his duties in Niger and denied having approved his involvement. Cooper later testified that Rove maintained that Plame, a weapons-of-mass-destruction expert, had authorized the trip. Cooper then gave this information to political columnist Robert Novak, who reported Wilson's connection to Plame and the CIA. Plame's position was compromised, and she was pulled from her assignment. At issue in the federal investigation that followed was how

Rove and vice-presidential chief of staff I. Lewis "Scooter" Libby obtained information regarding Plame's identity, how it was leaked to the press, and why. Both Libby and Rove claimed that they had never seen the State Department memo, but heard about Plame from other reporters. They further argued that the leak had done no damage, since Plame had not been an active spy for years. Critics worried that a growing rift between the CIA and White House had led to the leak. The CIA had protested the use of some uncertain evidence against Iraq, while the White House complained of poor quality findings from the agency. Was it a case of revenge against the CIA or against Wilson? Pundits suggested that Rove had revealed Plame's identity and exaggerated her role in order to discredit Wilson's findings. The federal investigation discovered that several reporters and journalists, including NBC's Tim Russert and *New York Times* reporter Judith Miller, knew Plame's connection. In a dramatic showdown, Miller refused to reveal her source and was jailed. Revealing Plame's identity put her at risk and, ultimately, changed her role in the CIA. The most damaging revelation was that the White House, in a rush to go to war in Iraq, had either willingly or mistakenly disregarded evidence. Libby was found guilty of perjury, obstruction of justice, and making false statements, though President George W. Bush commuted his thirty-month prison sentence.

Sources: Dan Eggen, "White House Blocks Release of FBI Files, *Washington Post*, 17 July 2008;

Dafna Linzer, "In Memoir, Ex-Spy Tells Her Side of CIA Leak Case," *Washington Post*, 20 October 2007;

Jeffrey R. Smith, "Judge Questions Justice Dept. Effort to Keep Cheney Remarks Secret," *Washington Post*, 19 June 2009.

measures, he served out his term, but he was increasingly abandoned by fellow Republicans and targeted by gay-rights groups who publicized accusations that he had engaged in homosexual acts. In 2004, New Jersey Democratic governor James McGreevy declared that he was gay and resigned from office, amid accusations that he had engaged in a sexual relationship with a male aide. Florida Republican representative Mark Foley resigned in 2006 after allegations that he sent teenage male congressional pages sexually explicit emails and instant messages. The congressman later checked into a rehabilitation facility for alcoholism and admitted that he was gay.

Prostitution. A federal investigation in Washington, D.C., uncovered a far-reaching prostitution ring that implicated several leading lawmakers. Louisiana Republican senator David Vitter's cell-phone number appeared in a call log that linked him to an elite call-girl service.

Although he had campaigned on family values, Vitter admitted vaguely that he had committed a "serious sin" and later won his party's nomination for the Senate in 2010. New York Democratic governor Eliot Spitzer was also tied to the investigation. Within days of being caught on a federal wiretap soliciting a prostitute, Spitzer resigned from office, claiming that he intended to take responsibility for his actions. As a politician who campaigned on ethics reform, Spitzer faced bitter criticism from state legislators who welcomed his replacement, Lieutenant Governor David Paterson.

Southern Shenanigans. The most sensational sex scandals involved Democratic presidential hopeful Senator John Edwards of North Carolina and Republican governor Mark Sanford of South Carolina. During Edwards's run for the Democratic presidential nomination in 2008, reports surfaced that he had fathered a child with Rielle Hunter, owner of a media consulting firm that had worked with the campaign. After Edwards left the race, he admitted that he had had an affair with Hunter, though he denied being the father of her child. His wife, Elizabeth Edwards, who suffered from cancer, divorced the senator soon after. In 2009, Governor Sanford, a prominent Republican and rumored 2012 presidential candidate, alarmed the South Carolina capital city of Columbia when reports surfaced that his aides did not know where he was. They eventually claimed, based on Sanford's communication with them, that he had taken some personal time to hike the Appalachian Trail, but reporters discovered that he had traveled to Buenos Aires. In a bizarrely public and effusive admission, Sanford contacted the Associated Press to confess his yearlong extramarital affair with an Argentine woman whom he first met in Uraguay in 2001 and began an affair with during a taxpayer-funded trip to Argentina in 2008. The state legislature followed up with an ethics investigation, censuring Sanford and charging him with thirty-seven violations that involved misspent state finances. The governor agreed to pay the state of South Carolina $74,000. His wife, Jenny Sanford, filed for divorce.

Political Payoffs. Corruption charges against high-profile lawmakers and Washington insiders were the biggest scandals of the decade. Nevada senator John Ensign involved lobbyists, corporate colleagues, and fellow senators in his attempts to calm the waters following his affair with a campaign aide. He used his influence to secure a job for an aide's husband, allegedly violating lobbyist restrictions. Ensign denied any wrongdoing but alienated colleagues who felt betrayed and manipulated. Illinois governor Rod Blagojevich was removed from office in January 2009 by the state legislature for abuse of office. A two-term Democrat, Blagojevich was charged with sixteen felonies, including racketeering conspiracy, wire fraud, extortion conspiracy, and making false statements to federal agents. Among the many crimes he was accused of committing, the former governor was charged with attempting to sell President Barack Obama's vacated U.S. Senate seat. Between leaving office and being convicted of making false statements to FBI agents, Blagojevich became a regular on talk shows and even appeared on real-estate mogul Donald Trump's reality-television program, *The Apprentice.*

The Abramoff Scandal. In 2006 lobbyist Jack Abramoff pleaded guilty to felony charges of fraud, corruption, and conspiracy in a testimony that implicated several congressmen, including Republican House majority leader Tom DeLay. Abramoff had lavished gifts on congressional and executive branch officials of President George W. Bush's administration in return for political favors to benefit his clients. Abramoff lied, bribed clients, and evaded taxes. He also swindled Indian tribes out of millions of dollars and referred to his Native American clients as troglodytes in email messages. Abramoff served three and a half years in federal prison. DeLay, tied to the disgraced lobbyist, resigned his leadership post in 2006. The Justice Department dropped federal corruption charges against

Former CIA operative Valerie Plame testifies before the House Committee on Oversight and Government Reform, 16 March 2007 (AP Photo/Susan Walsh).

DeLay, but he faced campaign-finance charges in Texas. Abramoff's testimony led to the convictions of two DeLay aides, Ohio Republican representative Bob Ney, two former White House officials in the Bush administration, and several former congressional aides and lobbyists. In a separate corruption case, Republican representative Randy Cunningham of California was sentenced to eight years in a federal prison for taking more than $2 million in bribes from military contractors in exchange for funneling federal money into specific projects. These scandals had deep repercussions, leading, in part, to the 2006 Democratic takeover of Congress.

Democratic Misdeeds. Democrats also suffered their share of political scandals. In 2006, Louisiana representative William J. Jefferson's office was raided by federal agents investigating bribery charges. The agents found a freezer filled with cash belonging to the congressman. Jefferson was removed from the influential Ways and Means Committee during the investigation, which damaged Democratic campaigns that focused on questionable Republican ethics. The investigation revealed that Jefferson and his relatives profited from overseas ventures that he promoted through his office, and he was convicted in 2009. Democratic representative Charles Rangel of New York was investigated for corruption. The House ethics committee revealed that he had illegally accepted gifts, including corporate-sponsored trips to the Caribbean, and had failed to report or pay taxes on hundreds of thousands of dollars in assets. Rangel refused to admit any fault or wrongdoing and congressional efforts to resolve the investigation stalled.

Sources:

"Blagojevich Fired By Donald Trump," *cbsnews.com* (5 April 2010);

Gregory Bryce, "Former LA Congressman William J. Jefferson Is Sentenced to 13 Years in Prison," *New Orleans Progressive Examiner* (14 November 2009);

Ana Campoy, "DeLay's Guilty Verdict Could Reverberate in Other States," *Wall Street Journal*, 26 November 2010;

Chris Cillizza, "The Fix: S.C. Governor Mark Sanford Admits Affair," *Washington Post*, 24 June 2009;

Jeff Coen and others, "Illinois Gov. Rod Blagojevich Arrested on Federal Charges," *Chicago Tribune*, 10 December 2008;

"Congressman Resigns After Bribery Plea," *cnn.com* (28 November 2005);

Lou Dubose, "The Verdict on DeLay: Guilty," *texasobserver.org* (24 November 2010);

"Edwards: I Fathered a Child Out of Wedlock," *cbsnews.com* (21 January 2010);

"GOP Seeks Distance, Dems Pounce after Ney's Guilty Plea," *cnn.com* (14 October 2006);

Danny Hakim and William K. Rashbaum, "Spitzer Is Linked to Prostitution Ring," *New York Times*, 10 March 2008;

Carl Hulse, "Senate Ethics Committee Admonishes Larry Craig," *New York Times*, 14 February 2008;

Paul Kane and Cillizza, "Sen. Ensign Acknowledges an Extramarital Affair," *Washington Post*, 17 June 2009;

David Kocieniewski, "House Panel Finds Rangel Guilty," *New York Times*, 16 November 2010;

Brad Larosa and Lauren Sher, "Jenny Sanford Files for Divorce from Husband Gov. Mark Sanford after Affair," *abcnews.go.com* (11 December 2009);

"Members of Congress Charged with Crimes," *usatoday.com* (4 June 2007);

"New Jersey Governor Quits, Comes Out as Gay," *cnn.com* (13 August 2004);

Joel Roberts, "Senator Caught in 'D.C. Madam' Scandal," *cbsnews.com* (10 July 2007);

Jim Rutenberg, "Sanford Case a New Dose of Bad News for Republicans," *New York Times*, 24 June 2009;

Rutenberg, "A Senator, an Affair, a Demand for Money," *New York Times*, 19 June 2009;

"S.C. Gov. Sanford Dishes Details of Meetings with Mistress," *abcnews.com* (30 June 2009);

Michael Scherer, "Governor Gone Wild: The Blagojevich Scandal," *Time* (11 December 2008);

Susan Schmidt and James V. Grimaldi, "Abramoff Pleads Guilty to 3 Counts," *Washington Post*, 4 January 2006;

Kate Zernike and Abby Goodnough, "Lawmaker Quits Over Messages Sent to Teenage Pages," *New York Times*, 30 September 2006.

HURRICANE KATRINA

Landfall. On Monday morning, 29 August 2005, Katrina, a category-three hurricane, slammed into America's Gulf Coast, wreaking havoc from Louisiana to Florida. Initial reports revealed a devastating storm that claimed more than one hundred lives and caused billions of dollars in property damage. The region's economy ground to a halt as cleanup efforts began. Highways were destroyed; homes were flooded; shuttered oil rigs raised gas prices; and coastal casinos were gutted. In New Orleans, for the first time since the Civil War, an entire city had been ordered to evacuate and abandon homes and businesses. New Orleans officials feared the worst in a city resting below sea level, protected by an aging system of levees. But after the storm passed by, many people of New Orleans—those who had fled, had stayed in their homes, or sought shelter—felt that they had escaped disaster. However, the following day, a major levee

Technical Sergeant Lem Torres surveys houses in New Orleans on 2 September 2005 looking for victims of Hurricane Katrina (U.S. Air Force photograph by Staff Sergeant Manuel J. Martinez).

Air National Guard members deliver water and food to stranded citizens of New Orleans after the city was devastated by Hurricane Katrina (U.S. Navy photograph by Photographer's Mate First Class Brien Aho).

was breached, sending the muddy water from Lake Pontchartrain flooding into the city. Eighty percent of the city was submerged, leaving more than 100,000 people stranded.

Citywide Disaster. In New Orleans, where many vulnerable citizens had attempted to weather the storm in homes or designated shelters such as the Superdome or convention center, more than 25,000 people spent six terrifying days in the Superdome. Most of them were old, sick, or simply too poor to leave the city. Days went by without

electricity. The generators ran out of fuel, and the Superdome became sweltering, dark, and dangerous. Deaths and incidents of rape occurred while people waited to evacuate. Hospitals, too, lost power, and nurses and doctors attempted to keep patients alive with hand ventilators, food from vending machines, and dwindling supplies of bottled water. New Orleans's streets became rivers filled with sewage, chemicals, and debris. In some cases, people were forced to tear through their roofs hoping to be spotted by passing helicopters. Across the city, looters broke into stores and restaurants, some in desperate search for food and supplies, while others seized an opportunity to steal merchandise. At the same time, millions watched the horrific events unfold and wondered how camera crews and news commentators had reached the city while federal and state relief organizations failed to bring assistance. Former Louisiana senator John Breaux labeled the city "Baghdad under water." In hospitals, homes, shelters, and the streets, corpses began to pile up.

Dealing with the Damage. Rescue efforts were stymied by miscommunication, procedural red tape, and lack of preparation and resources. Mayor C. Ray Nagin of New Orleans, in a radio interview, blasted the federal government for its slow response, though the city's evacuation plans and state-level response had also been woefully inadequate. Nagin commanded the police force to abandon rescue missions and devote their time to stopping looters. Five hundred poorly trained National Guardsmen had maintained tenuous order with irresponsible threats at the shelters. Anger and resentment grew as people began to feel forgotten and abused. In Washington, D.C., Secretary of Defense Donald Rumsfeld was hesitant to take the lead on disaster relief, something that was typically left to the National Guard and Federal Emergency Management Agency (FEMA). The Bush administration debated the legalities of who was in charge for days, while circumstances in New Orleans and the broader Gulf Coast region deteriorated. By the end of the week, a fleet of helicopters began to rescue survivors and drop off supplies, guardsmen brought food and water, and FEMA attempted to orchestrate transportation, but a centralized effort would not become apparent for several more days. Incredulous pundits questioned how a country that had taken pride in a new sense of preparedness following 9/11 had failed to mobilize after the storm. Further complicating the relief effort, more than 500,000 people had left the city. More people were displaced in a matter of days than had fled the Dust Bowl in the 1930s, and many had little hope of returning in the near future.

Relief Efforts. A week after the storm hit, troops and supplies, at last, poured into the city. The Superdome and the convention center, symbols of the city's desperation, were emptied, and survivors were bused out of New Orleans. A central command station and medical triage were set up at the airport. With relief underway, politicians argued over whom to blame. Some critics accused Bush of callously allowing New Orleans to drown, pointing out that he had flown over the city on an unrelated trip and had failed to visit the city for five days. Both Democrats and Republicans expressed shock that Bush's senior staff had been unavailable, absent, or on holiday, and that Bush had remained aloof. Further, FEMA head Michael Brown offered little plausible explanation in defending the agency's slow and muddled response, while struggling nations—including Cuba, Sri Lanka, and Iran—had mobilized teams of doctors with food and medical supplies. Criticism of FEMA deepened when Homeland Security chief Michael Chertoff appeared on television claiming that he was unaware of people stranded at the Superdome, and reports revealed that Brown was ill-suited and unqualified for his position. The administration claimed that Hurricane Katrina was an unprecedented disaster that required a multifaceted and calculated response. Bush admonished attempts to politicize the tragedy, though he admitted that the government's relief efforts had been "unacceptable." His administration, however, maintained that state and local operations had failed and the federal government was merely helping to straighten out the mess.

Criticism of the Response. The storm shook the faith of many Americans who waited in terror to be rescued or who helplessly watched thousands of people in New Orleans run out of safe water and food. A reported 1,600 people died. Many critics insisted that the government had failed to protect its citizens and began to ask why. For more than a century, the Army Corps of Engineers had shaped and reshaped the Mississippi River for commerce and constructed levees to protect from flooding. While conspiracy theories circulated that the Corps purposefully breached one levee in order to save New Orleans's wealthier enclaves, most agreed that inadequate funding and poor planning had crippled the city's flood protection. After 9/11, funds had overwhelmingly been redirected to national security. The worst flooding had disproportionately affected poor neighborhoods, just as the poor, elderly, and sick had suffered while others escaped. For New Orleans, like many American cities, the poorest citizens were also African American. Outraged critics claimed that racial discrimination had skewed media coverage and hampered rescue efforts. They argued that America's image had been weakened by the inequality exposed by the tragedy and called for efforts to reexamine racism. In all, 1.5 million people left New Orleans, sparking a massive demographic shift, largely absorbed by cities such as nearby Houston and Baton Rouge. New Orleans faced years of rebuilding its infrastructure and experimenting with environmental, cultural, and social policies. Other cities and states that sustained terrible damage bristled at the attention that New Orleans received. The impact of Hurricane Katrina continued to be felt in politics, sparking debates on race relations and discrimination, poverty, education, the effectiveness of federal and state emergency operations, and the difference between man-made and natural disasters.

Sources:
"4 Places Where the System Broke Down," *Time* (11 September 2005);

Nancy Gibbs, "The Aftermath," *Time* (4 September 2005);

Michael Grunwald, "Hurricane Katrina—Two Years Later: The Threatening Storm," *Time* (2 August 2007);

"Hurricane Katrina: The Shaming of America," *Economist* (8 September 2005);

Julie Mason, "White House Watch: Seeking Own Relief, Bush Blames Politics," *Houston Chronicle*, 4 September 2005;

Tim Padgett, "Katrina: Five Years After," *Time* (27 August 2010);

Padgett, "New Orleans, 2005–2010," *Time* (6 September 2010);

Amanda Ripley, "How Did This Happen?" *Time* (4 September 2005);

Evan Thomas, "The Lost City," *Newsweek* (12 September 2005);

Joseph P. Treaster and Kate Zernike, "Hurricane Katrina Slams into Gulf Coast; Dozens Are Dead," *New York Times*, 30 August 2005;

David Von Drehle and Jacqueline Salmon, "Displacement of Historic Proportions," *Washington Post*, 2 September 2005;

"When Government Fails—Katrina's Aftermath," *Economist* (8 September 2005).

MISDEEDS AT ENRON

Bankruptcy. In early 2002, energy giant Enron declared bankruptcy. Overnight, their stock became worthless and hundreds of employees, investors, and pensioners lost billions of dollars in savings and retirement funds. During the 1990s, Enron epitomized the success of Wall Street trading, weathering economic downturns, and encouraging the privatization of pensions. The Houston-based company's sudden collapse exposed it as a hollow and corrupt structure buoyed by speculation and congressional collusion. As Enron's ties to President George W. Bush's administration and the depth of desperate lobbying that had kept it running were revealed, the corporate label, a slanted *E,* became synonymous with excess and greed.

Investigation. The ensuing federal investigation fueled criticism of the Republican Party, long dogged by accusations of corporate influence and dubious ties to wealthy investors. Bush gave former Enron executives prominent positions in his administration, including army secretary and trade representative, and some ex-Enron chiefs assumed places in Bush's inner circle, where they shaped energy policies. The corporation's demise had a far-reaching impact, badly damaging the U.S. economy and shaking investor confidence. Several Enron employees faced fraud and corruption charges. One executive, J. Clifford Baxter, was found dead—an apparent suicide—in his car. Company founder Kenneth Lay was convicted on fraud and conspiracy charges, though he died of a heart attack before sentencing. Former chief executive Jeffrey Skilling was convicted of fraud, conspiracy, and insider trading. Critics from the Democratic Party used populist rhetoric to accuse the Bush administration and Republican congressmen of accepting campaign contributions from Enron in return for legislative favors. Campaign-finance reform found new congressional support, and Bush's high approval ratings in the wake of 9/11 dropped as voters sensed an ethics dilemma in the White House. Many sensed that a slumping economy that had been blamed on the September terrorist attacks was part of a broader problem on Wall Street. Enron temporarily shattered Americans' persistent trust in stock trading. By the end of the decade, as markets began to recover, the relaxed regulatory measures, a hallmark of Republican economic policies devised to encourage market confidence, triggered a housing market crisis that sent the country into a deep recession.

Source:
"The Fall of Enron," *businessweek.com* (17 December 2001).

RECESSION

Economic Instability. Though the economic recession seemed to hit the nation with a sudden fury in 2008, the storm had been gathering force for years. Deregulation and stability had afforded Wall Street traders a self-confidence that encouraged them to take significant risks, many centered on America's growing number of homeowners, who took advantage of relaxed credit restrictions and a market

---

TEA PARTY BY THE NUMBERS

Who they are

Seven demographic characteristics of Tea Party supporters:

78%	are Republicans or independents who lean Republican.
77%	are non-Hispanic whites.
69%	are conservatives.
62%	are married.
56%	are men.
47%	are 55 or older.
23%	are under 35.

What they believe

Seven defining attitudes of Tea Party supporters:

92%	believe the federal government debt is a very serious/extremely serious threat to the nation's future well-being.
90%	believe terrorism is a very/extremely serious threat to the nation's future well-being.
90%	are dissatisfied with the way things are going in this country.
87%	disapprove of the job congressional Democrats are doing.
85%	believe the size and power of the federal government are very/extremely serious threats to the nation's future well-being.
83%	say most members of Congress don't deserve re-election.
83%	say President Obama doesn't deserve reelection.

Source: *usatoday.com* (8 July 2010).

---

wide open to lending. Subprime mortgages (high-risk home loans) began to take their toll on the economy as homeowners defaulted or fell behind on payments. When Henry Paulson reluctantly accepted the position of secretary of the treasury in 2006, he immediately began to reach out for economic reform. Paulson initially focused on Fannie Mae (Federal National Mortgage Association) and Freddie Mac (Federal Home Loan Mortgage Corporation), two government-sponsored mortgage institutions responsible, either directly or indirectly, for nearly one-half of the nation's $12 trillion in mortgages. Facing a war of economic ideology between a Democratic Congress and a conservative White House, Paulson failed to achieve a compromise to address concerns about Fannie Mae and Freddie Mac's continued viability and, more broadly, the volatility of subprime mortgages.

Full-Blown Crisis. In the summer of 2008, both institutions were on the verge of collapse. A $300 billion credit line was extended to stabilize Fannie Mae and Freddie Mac, but ten days later Lehman Brothers, an international financing firm, declared bankruptcy, the largest in U.S. history. The next day, the federal government authorized an $85 billion buyout of A.I.G. Financial Products, an insurance group closely related to Goldman Sachs, another financial behemoth specializing in investments. Citigroup, Merrill Lynch, and other companies teetered on the brink of bankruptcy and were forced to radically restructure. A general alarm sounded as the healthy financial institutions shut down credit lines and less-fortunate companies scrambled for economic security through mergers, buyouts, and federal bailouts. By late September, the Bush administration began lobbying for a massive bailout of Wall Street firms. The crisis hijacked the 2008 presidential election as both candidates, Republican senator John McCain and Democratic senator Barack Obama, flew back to Washington, D.C., to attend an emergency meeting at the White House. Despite the hysteria of bipartisan fights, with Republicans blocking legislation and McCain suspending his campaign, Bush signed the Troubled Asset Relief Program (TARP) on 3 October, authorizing $700 billion in rescue funds to beleaguered banking firms. More than $17 billion was carved out to save the auto industry.

Stimulus. The political fallout was immediate, but the recession continued to deepen, provoking further federal action. While fiscal conservatives condemned the bailouts for using taxpayer money to rescue corrupt or incompetent companies, the newly elected Obama administration stepped in with a federal stimulus package to save failing state governments that were struggling to meet payrolls and to continue welfare and unemployment programs. In February 2009, the American Recovery and Reinvestment Act offered $787 billion in federal funds for domestic spending to help struggling homeowners and state and local governments. A month later, news reports revealed that parting CEOs from Wall Street firms that had benefited from bailouts received shocking severance packages. These "golden parachutes," as they were labeled in the media, along with Obama's stimulus package, elicited a mammoth response from conservatives and liberals alike. In particular, a new group of activists, the Tea Party, organized against federal spending. A series of conservative governors tried to block their states' access to the stimulus. By early 2010 the economy had stabilized, but unemployment remained high. The Tea Party widened its platform to become the anti-government party, distancing itself from earlier attacks on CEOs and even endorsing golden-parachute recipient Carly Fiorina, former CEO of Hewlett-Packard, in the Senate race in California.

Sources:
Daniel Gross, "Timothy Geithner: The Treasury Secretary Was Largely Responsible for Directing the Government's Response to the Financial Crisis," *Newsweek* (4 January 2010);

A Tea Party protester dressed as the Statue of Liberty bound in chains that represent the national debt at a Tax Day protest in Pleasanton, California, 15 April 2009 (AP Photo/Paul Sakuma)

President George W. Bush signs the Patriot Act into law in the East Room of the White House on 26 October 2001 (White House photograph by Eric Draper).

Ryan Lizza, "Inside the Crisis: Larry Summers and the White House Economic Team," *New Yorker* (12 October 2009);

Todd S. Purdum, "Henry Paulson's Longest Night," *Vanity Fair* (October 2009);

Bill Saporito, "How AIG Became Too Big to Fail," *Time* (19 March 2009);

Andy Serwer and Allan Sloan, "How Financial Madness Overtook Wall Street," *Time* (18 September 2008).

SEPTEMBER 11, 2001: A WAR ON TERROR

The Attacks. On 11 September 2001 the United States suffered its first large-scale attack on native soil since Japan's bombing raid on Pearl Harbor in December 1941. At 8:46 A.M., a commercial airliner out of Boston flew into one of the World Trade Center towers in New York City. As the nation watched the smoldering top floors of the building and media outlets argued over the implications, another airliner from Boston flew into the second tower. New York City officials shut down the ports and bridges, and President George W. Bush broke away from a speaking engagement in Florida to declare that the country had been attacked. At 9:37 A.M., a plane hit the Pentagon in Washington, D.C. The White House, State and Justice Departments, United Nations buildings, and World Bank were evacuated. Finally, a fourth plane crashed in a field in Somerset County, Pennsylvania, southeast of Pittsburgh. Bush was flown from Florida to Barksdale Air Force Base in Louisiana where he declared, "Make no mistake, the United States will hunt down and punish those responsible for these cowardly acts." He then left aboard Air Force One for Nebraska, while the navy gathered warships along the East Coast. Airports in Los Angeles and San Francisco (destinations of the hijacked planes) were shut down. By this time, the twin towers of the World Trade Center had fallen, sending a smoky cloud of debris throughout lower Manhattan, and a portion of the Pentagon had buckled and collapsed. Across the globe, people watched the events unfold, with network anchors and reporters logging record hours in their attempts to make sense of the tragedy. The next day, leaders around the world joined Bush in condemning the attacks and mourning the thousands of people who lost their lives. However, the realization that a dangerous enemy had carried out a terrorist plot against Washington, D.C., and one of the world's great cities, New York, cast a long shadow.

Aftermath. In the wake of the attacks, the United States entered a painful period of fear, sorrow, and anger; aggressive foreign policy; and heightened patriotism. The human toll was staggering: 2,819 men and women died from the attacks. Citizens of the New York City metropolitan area suffered the most devastating casualties. More than two thousand employees at the World Trade Center and hundreds of rescue workers—including firemen, paramedics, and police officers—died. More than 400,000 New Yorkers were ultimately diagnosed with posttraumatic stress disorder related to the attacks. Furthermore, the glaring absence of the towers from the skyline became a constant reminder of the massive loss of life. Indeed, the site of the fallen twin towers, later labeled Ground Zero, became a troubling symbol of the deep social and political changes of a post-9/11 America. As crews searched for survivors in the rubble and recovered remains, the country grappled with grief and anxiety triggered by the tragedy. Patriotic sentiment surged, manifesting itself in feelings of not only pride and unity but also fear and anger. Retailer giant Wal-Mart reported a nearly 2,000 percent increase in the sale of American flags and a 100 percent rise in ammunition sales.

Bin Laden. On 15 September, President Bush declared, "We're at war," and pointed to the Islamic fundamentalist group al Qaeda and its leader, Saudi fugitive and millionaire militant Osama bin Laden, as the culprits behind the terrorist attacks. Bin Laden, a prime suspect in a series of international terrorist plots, including the 1993 World Trade Center bombing, had for years eluded efforts to bring him to justice. He was already an established villain, rumored to have circulated a poem via video congratulating the perpetrators of the USS *Cole* bombing. Intelligence reports suggested that bin Laden had been planning to attack the United States for its support of Israel. A military response was a priority for the Bush administration, but "who to target" and "where to strike" remained important questions. As investigations eventually revealed, the nineteen men who hijacked the planes were jihadists of varying origins within the Middle East, trained in far-flung terrorist cells. However, bin Laden's global terrorist network, al Qaeda, linked them together. For Bush, the goal was not simply a war against bin Laden, but a war against terrorism and those countries suspected of harboring terrorists. His administration intended to target al Qaeda, but also the Taliban, a powerful Islamic fundamentalist sect in Afghanistan, accused of protecting bin Laden. Yet, as Bush eyed the troubled country of Afghanistan to challenge the Taliban and root out al Qaeda, he delivered a message to the rest of the world, as well, "Every nation in every region now has a decision to make: Either you are with us, or you are with the terrorists." Bush also took pains to assure Muslims around the world that the United States intended to wage war on terrorists not Islam.

War on Terror. Congress quickly authorized military force to fight terrorism in a sweeping resolution that expanded the president's authority. When the Taliban refused to assist the United States and hand over bin Laden, Afghanistan became the first military target. Officials insisted that a military strike against Afghanistan would loosen the Taliban's hold on Afghan citizens, end bin Laden's powerful influence, and serve as a definitive warning to other countries protecting suspected terrorists. The Bush administration launched a campaign to construct a global coalition to combat terrorism, encouraging nations

Director of Homeland Security Tom Ridge unveils the Homeland Security Advisory System to the media on 12 March 2002 (White House photograph by Paul Moore).

President Bush delivered the commencement address at West Point on 1 June 2002. In his speech, excerpted below, he clarified his administration's position in the war on terror and expounded upon the principles that became known as the Bush Doctrine:

For much of the last century America's defense relied on the cold war doctrines of deterrence and containment. In some cases those strategies still apply. But new threats also require new thinking.

Deterrence, the promise of massive retaliation against nations, means nothing against shadowy terrorist networks with no nation or citizens to defend. Containment is not possible when unbalanced dictators with weapons of mass destruction can deliver those weapons on missiles or secretly provide them to terrorist allies.

We cannot defend America and our friends by hoping for the best. We cannot put our faith in the word of tyrants who solemnly sign nonproliferation treaties and then systematically break them. If we wait for threats to fully materialize we will have waited too long.

Homeland defense and missile defense are part of a stronger security. They're essential priorities for America.

Yet the war on terror will not be won on the defensive. We must take the battle to the enemy, disrupt his plans and confront the worst threats before they emerge.

In the world we have entered the only path to safety is the path of action. And this nation will act.

Our security will require the best intelligence to reveal threats hidden in caves and growing in laboratories. Our security will require modernizing domestic agencies, such as the FBI, so they are prepared to act and act quickly against danger. Our security will require transforming the military you will lead. A military that must be ready to strike at a moment's notice in any dark corner of the world. And our security will require all Americans to be forward looking and resolute, to be ready for preemptive action when necessary to defend our liberty and to defend our lives.

The work ahead is difficult. The choices we will face are complex. We must uncover terrorist cells in sixty or more countries using every tool of finance, intelligence and law enforcement.

Along with our friends and allies we must oppose proliferation and confront regimes that sponsor terror as each case requires. Some nations need military training to fight terror and we will provide it. Other nations oppose terror but tolerate the hatred that leads to terror and that must change.

We will send diplomats where they are needed. And we will send you, our soldiers, where you're needed.

All nations that decide for aggression and terror will pay a price. We will not leave the safety of America and the peace of the planet at the mercy of a few mad terrorists and tyrants. We will lift this dark threat from our country and from the world.

Because the war on terror will require resolve and patience, it will also require firm moral purpose. In this way our struggle is similar to the cold war. Now, as then, our enemies are totalitarians, holding a creed of power with no place for human dignity. Now, as then, they seek to impose a joyless conformity, to control every life and all of life.

America confronted imperial communism in many different ways: diplomatic, economic and military. Yet moral clarity was essential to our victory in the cold war.

When leaders like John F. Kennedy and Ronald Reagan refused to gloss over the brutality of tyrants they gave hope to prisoners and dissidents and exiles and rallied free nations to a great cause.

Some worry that it is somehow undiplomatic or impolite to speak the language of right and wrong. I disagree. Different circumstances require different methods but not different moralities. Moral truth is the same in every culture, in every time and in every place. Targeting innocent civilians for murder is always and everywhere wrong. Brutality against women is always and everywhere wrong.

There can be no neutrality between justice and cruelty, between the innocent and the guilty. We are in a conflict between good and evil. And America will call evil by its name.

By confronting evil and lawless regimes we do not create a problem, we reveal a problem. And we will lead the world in opposing it.

Source: *nytimes.com.*

to denounce the Taliban, cut ties with Afghanistan, and help the United States militarily. In addition to the military commitment promised by industrialized nations—including Germany, France, and Great Britain—Japan pledged humanitarian assistance, former Soviet satellite Kyrgyzstan offered air space, and Saudi Arabia broke diplomatic and economic ties with Afghanistan. Meanwhile, Bush attempted to garner support among Afghan citizens with promises of $320 million in food and medical supplies. By 7 October the United States, with British forces and broad international support, initiated air strikes in the Afghan capital Kabul, marking the beginning of Operation Enduring Freedom. Within hours of the strikes, bin Laden, in his first public acknowledgment of the 9/11 attacks, praised the hijackers and connected his cause to theirs, calling Americans "the cowards of the age" and Bush "the head of the infidels worldwide."

Bush Doctrine. American military actions in Afghanistan were among many far-reaching escalations in U.S. foreign and domestic policy, aimed at heightening security and protecting U.S. interests. Within days of the invasion of Afghanistan, the White House issued rules of engagement guiding the war on terrorism. Labeled the Bush Doctrine, the policy demanded that the world choose sides, and those countries that did not line up beside the United States could suffer military consequences. In effect, any nation suspected of harboring terrorists would be considered a target for preemptive strike. Expanding the scope of their rhetoric to reach beyond bin Laden and al Qaeda, the Bush administration included Iraq on their list of seven states that sponsored terrorism, labeling three the "axis of evil"—North Korea, Iran, and Iraq. A little over a year later, Bush declared war on Iraq.

Unlawful Combatants. The war on terrorism inevitably led to captured militants and suspected terrorists allegedly associated with the Taliban and al Qaeda. When Defense Secretary Donald Rumsfeld announced that the United States would hold these prisoners at a naval base in Guantanamo Bay, Cuba, questions quickly arose about the status of the detainees. The war on terror did not have physical boundaries and Rumsfeld, along with other members of the Bush administration, claimed that international rules of war stated in the Geneva Convention simply did not apply. Secretary of State Colin Powell defied some in the administration, voicing his concerns that circumventing the protections afforded prisoners of war would forever muddy the waters of diplomacy. He argued that using the status of "unlawful combatants" for those held at Guantanamo threatened policies that sought to preserve integrity and sovereignty during times of war. Rumsfeld, on the other hand, insisted that unlawful combatants who targeted civilians and held no national allegiances presented new challenges. He emphasized the need to interrogate detainees, an imperative that the White House did not want complicated by the Geneva Convention. Military tribunals, with officers as judges, were organized to try combatants. But the existence of the detention center, combined with the use of extralegal proceedings,

began to raise red flags. Critics claimed that the search for terrorists undermined the freedoms that the Bush administration promised to protect and preserve.

Protecting the Home Front. As the White House increased efforts to combat terrorism abroad, plans to eliminate security threats on the home front faced scrutiny. The Bush administration introduced initiatives that loosened restrictions on the federal government, opened new intelligence channels, and expanded the reach of law-enforcement agencies. The federal government gained access to conversations between attorneys and terror suspects, detained hundreds of people domestically without releasing their identities, and interrogated thousands of Arab Americans and Muslim Americans. On 26 October, Bush signed the Uniting and Strengthening America by Providing Appropriate Tools Required to Intercept and Obstruct Terrorism Act (USA PATRIOT Act), commonly known as the Patriot Act, into law. At the urging of Attorney General John Ashcroft and with overwhelming support from Congress, the antiterrorism legislation was passed quickly to give the federal government and executive branch, in particular, unprecedented powers of surveillance and law enforcement. Civil-liberties advocates decried the Patriot Act for giving the government free rein in accessing emails of suspected terrorists, wiretapping, and the sharing of information. Some critics compared the legislation to past civil-liberties abuses during wartime, including the internment of Japanese Americans during World War II and Abraham Lincoln's suspension of habeas corpus during the Civil War. However, the White House claimed that it was creating a stronger infrastructure to suit dangerous times. When in early October, anthrax traced from a mailbox in New Jersey showed up in Florida, New York City, and several U.S. senators' offices in Washington, D.C., the need for an enhanced security network became more pressing for the White House.

Department of Homeland Security. On 8 October 2001, President Bush issued an executive order establishing the Office of Homeland Security. Initially an entity within the White House, the new office was created to protect the United States from domestic terrorism. Bush appointed Pennsylvania governor Tom Ridge to head the agency. While prior to the attacks, forty federal agencies had managed homeland security, Ridge's role was to centralize the effort to combat terrorism. By November of the following year, Homeland Security became a cabinet-level department and was expanded to include the Federal Emergency Management Agency (FEMA), Transportation Security Administration (TSA), Coast Guard, Customs Service, and United States Secret Service. It eventually constituted twenty-two government agencies. The department inflated the security industry, as well, with lobbyists, law firms, and technology companies flocking to Washington, D.C., to bid for federal dollars. Notably, the Department of Homeland Security did not include the FBI or CIA and critics claimed that rather than create another separate intelligence agency, the nation needed more collaboration between its existing departments. Still others worried that

In May 2006 a Zogby poll revealed that 42 percent of Americans believed the 9/11 Commission or the federal government had "concealed or refused to investigate critical evidence that contradicts their official explanation" of the attacks. Conspiracy theorists asked: Had the government hindered the reaction of the air force to ensure an attack that would trigger a war against Islam? Was the World Trade Center professionally demolished? Was the fourth plane shot down by the air force over Pennsylvania? The 9/11 myths have largely been debunked, but for critics the troubling legacy of 9/11 continues to be seen in the wars, military occupations, civil-rights abuses, and heightened security of a nation struggling to feel secure again.

The following is an excerpt from the Executive Summary of the 9/11 Commission Report:

A NATION TRANSFORMED

At 8:46 on the morning of September 11, 2001, the United States became a nation transformed.

An airliner traveling at hundreds of miles per hour and carrying some 10,000 gallons of jet fuel plowed into the North Tower of the World Trade Center in Lower Manhattan. At 9:03, a second airliner hit the South Tower. Fire and smoke billowed upward. Steel, glass, ash, and bodies fell below. The Twin Towers, where up to 50,000 people worked each day, both collapsed less than 90 minutes later.

At 9:37 that same morning, a third airliner slammed into the western face of the Pentagon. At 10:03, a fourth airliner crashed in a field in southern Pennsylvania. It had been aimed at the United States Capitol or the White House, and was forced down by heroic passengers armed with the knowledge that America was under attack.

More than 2,600 people died at the World Trade Center; 125 died at the Pentagon; 256 died on the four planes. The death toll surpassed that at Pearl Harbor in December 1941.

This immeasurable pain was inflicted by 19 young Arabs acting at the behest of Islamist extremists headquartered in distant Afghanistan. Some had been in the United States for more than a year, mixing with the rest of the population. Though four had training as pilots, most were not well-educated. Most spoke English poorly, some hardly at all. In groups of four or five, carrying with them only small knives, box cutters, and cans of Mace or pepper spray, they had hijacked the four planes and turned them into deadly guided missiles.

Sources: Richard A. Clarke, "Conspiracy Theories," *Time* (July 2009);

Richard A. Falkenrath, "The 9/11 Commission Report; A Review Essay," *International Security* (2004 Winter/2005 Winter);

9-11commission.gov;

"The Truth about 9/11 Revealed," *Popular Mechanics* (1 September 2006).

the size and scope of the department made management a problem, leaving the largest security agency in the United States impervious to federal oversight.

Political Fallout. The attacks on 9/11 sparked a seismic shift in the American political landscape. Invoking the Bush Doctrine, the United States waged preemptive wars against al Qaeda and the Taliban in Afghanistan and Saddam Hussein in Iraq. In both countries, long American occupations laid bare bitter ethnic rivalries. But investigations on the home front became a priority as victims' families appealed to the federal government for answers. The 9/11 Commission, an independent congressional committee organized to investigate the attacks and the aftermath, attempted to provide a narrative of the events and to evaluate the federal government's and, more specifically, the Bush administration's response. Dramatic moments of the investigation included successfully gaining unprecedented access to Bush's cabinet for interviews, particularly Secretary of State Condoleezza Rice. She along with former assistant secretary of state Richard Alan Clarke, another interviewee, publicly accused the Bush administration of undermining the war on terrorism by invading Iraq. The report was published to surreal fanfare for a committee report and became a best seller, largely due to its account of the tragic days. The commission's findings were notable for their judgments regarding the federal government's failings before the attacks, chiefly a lack of communication among intelligence agencies, though it refrained from blaming either the Bush or Clinton administrations. The commission also argued that the United States could have been more vigilant and more imaginative in its preparations against such an attack. However, the report's official recommendations fell short. The investigative mandate ended on 20 September 2001, leaving little opportunity for committee members to suggest a new course for the war on terror.

Sources:
Julian Borger, "President Broadens War on Terrorism," *Guardian*, 31 January 2002;

"Brief Documentary History of the Department of Homeland Security: 2001–2008," Department of Homeland Security, *dhs.gov* (2008);

"Bush's Coalition Falls into Line," *St. Petersburg Times*, 26 September 2001;

"Chronology of Terror," *cnn.com;*

Adam Cohen and others, "The Law: Rough Justice," *Time* (10 December 2001);

Dan Eggen and Vernon Loeb, "U.S. Intelligence Points to Bin Laden Network," *Washington Post*, 12 September 2001;

Richard A. Falkenrath, "The 9/11 Commission Report: A Review Essay," *International Security*, 29 (Winter 2004/2005): 170–190;

Jack A. Goldstone, "Homeland Security's Secret for Success," *Christian Science Monitor* (21 June 2002);

Michael R. Gordon, "After the Attacks: The Strategy; A New War and Its Scale," *New York Times*, 17 September 2001;

Jill Lawrence, "Suspected Mastermind Salutes Hijackers on Video," *USA Today*, 8 October 2001;

Laurence McQuillan, "'Bush Doctrine' Sets Up Rules of Engagement," *USA Today*, 9 October 2001;

Martin Merzer, "U.S. Wants Him Dead or Alive," *Philadelphia Inquirer*, 18 September 2001;

"9/11 by the Numbers: Death, Destruction, Charity, Salvation, War, Money, Real Estate, Spouses, Babies and Other September 11 Statistics," *New York Magazine, nymag.com;*

"9/11 Timeline," *Christian Science Monitor* (11 March 2002);

Tim Padgett, "Are They POWs or Terrorists?" *Time* (28 January 2002);

Frank Pellegrini, "The Bush Speech: How to Rally a Nation," *Time* (21 September 2001);

Jessica Reaves, "Tom Ridge Has the Biggest Job in Washington," *Time* (21 September 2001);

Reaves, "Why the Anthrax Scare Isn't as Bad as You May Think," *Time* (19 October 2001);

Judy Sarasohn, "Explosion in Homeland Security Field," *Washington Post*, 12 December 2002;

Katharine Q. Seelye, "A Nation Challenged: The Detention Camp; US to Hold Taliban Detainees in 'the Least Worst Place,'" *New York Times*, 28 December 2001;

Elaine Shannon and Amanda Ripley, "Osama's Trail: Soft Evidence," *Time* (1 October 2001);

"Timeline: A Day-by-Day Look at the Attacks, Response," *USA Today*, 8 October 2001;

Robin Toner and Neil A. Lewis, "A Nation Challenged: Congress; House Passes Terrorism Bill," *New York Times*, 13 October 2001.

WAR IN AFGHANISTAN

War Begins. Following the attacks on 11 September 2001, President George W. Bush targeted Osama bin Laden and the terrorist group al Qaeda for retaliation. Tracking bin Laden to the mountains of Afghanistan, U.S. officials attempted to persuade the Taliban, the ruling regime, to hand him over or face a military assault. The Taliban resisted and instead offered to try bin Laden in an Afghan court if the United States provided evidence. Citing the Bush Doctrine, a war plan that did not distinguish between terrorists and the countries that harbored them, the Americans refused to negotiate and joined with British forces to begin air strikes on 7 October, launching Operation Enduring Freedom. As the bombs dropped, the Americans reached out to anti-Taliban rebels, particularly Afghanistan's Northern Alliance, while cargo planes distributed food aid and medicine to Afghan civilians.

Complications on the Ground. But the political situation on the ground prevented the air campaign from being entirely successful. The United States refrained from hitting Taliban forces outside of Kabul, fearing that the Northern Alliance would conquer the capital city and take control of the country. Instead, the Americans hoped to build a broad coalition of Afghan forces, one that would not threaten diplomacy with the Pakistanis, who refused to cooperate with U.S. forces if the Northern Alliance seized

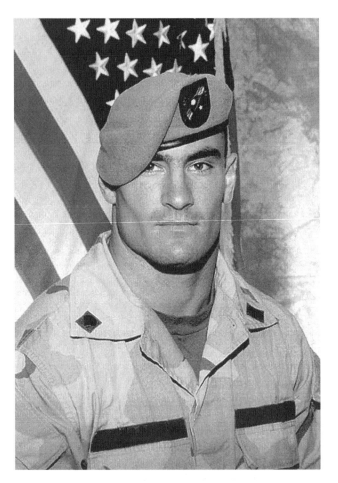

Corporal Patrick Tillman, Army Ranger, who retired from The National Football League to serve in Afghanistan. He was killed by friendly fire on 22 April 2004 (photograph by Department of Army).

Kabul. By December, ground troops along with air strikes had routed al Qaeda forces in the mountainous regions and deposed Taliban leaders in Kabul and Kandahar, two major cities. Yet, bin Laden and many top Taliban leaders had eluded capture. As if to punctuate the complicated nature of a war against terrorist enemies from varying backgrounds and nationalities, young American John Walker Lindh, a former suburban teenager from California who turned radical Muslim while studying in Yemen, was found filthy and wounded among a group of captured Taliban fighters in early December. Walker had left Yemen for Pakistan, following the USS *Cole* bombing in 2000, where he met Taliban fighters who urged him to join an al Qaeda training camp.

Regime Change. With bin Laden still at large and the Taliban proving difficult to eliminate, Bush warned Americans that the war on terrorism was far from over. Polling suggested that an overwhelming majority of Americans supported the president; his approval ratings remained at 90 percent in the first months of the war. But as Bush began to press other nations to assist in U.S. efforts and expanded his list of nations that posed a threat to American security, he faced political opposition at home, with a recession threatening to derail his domestic agenda. At the same

A U.S. Army medic examines the chest of an Afghan man during a medical assistance operation in Kharghar, Afghanistan, 15 December 2004 (Department of Defense photograph by Sergeant J. Antonio Francis, U.S. Army).

time, coalition forces, including U.S., British, and Afghan soldiers, continued to fight in Afghanistan, and a UN panel tapped Hamid Karzai, an Afghan politician who had experience working with both the Taliban and former mujahideen factions, as interim prime minister. Karzai faced a long road in rebuilding Afghanistan's infrastructure and government. He dealt with tough opposition from other anti-Taliban groups, most of whom had resisted American requests for a cooperative force, but he enjoyed the support of neighboring Pakistan. Karzai's most difficult challenge was negotiating with the remaining Taliban soldiers to persuade them to lay down their weapons and surrender. With a massive rebuilding effort on the horizon in Afghanistan, the Bush administration hoped that Karzai would guide Afghan progress, leaving the White House to further implement the Bush Doctrine and broaden the scope of the war on terrorism.

Distractions? By the end of 2001, American-led coalition forces had unseated the Taliban and uprooted al Qaeda. Bush immediately turned his attention to the "axis of evil" (North Korea, Iraq, and Iran), which he maintained posed significant threats for a chemical, biological, or nuclear attack against the United States. The Bush administration first focused on Iraq, gathering evidence against Saddam Hussein. In early 2002, troops were

pulled from Afghanistan and redeployed to prepare for action in Iraq. At the same, Bush stressed the importance of staying the course in Afghanistan and finding bin Laden. Avoiding the term "nation-building," Bush invoked the Marshall Plan, the post–World War II rebuilding effort in Europe, to describe his hopes for an American role in Afghanistan. He claimed that promoting democracy, education, and prosperity were his top priorities, not military occupation. But as the White House stoked the fires of war against Iraq, U.S. military officials in Afghanistan watched uneasily as their resources were redirected. Critics condemned Bush's plans against Iraq, claiming it was irresponsible to start another war without finding bin Laden. Some worried that war in Iraq would make an incomplete job of Afghanistan, threaten the fragile Karzai administration, and allow the Taliban to reestablish control, or perhaps destabilize the entire region. Yet, despite the risks of fighting two wars, by early 2003, the Bush administration readied troops for action in Iraq, while assuring the Afghan people that they would not forget them.

Ongoing War. The war in Iraq took center stage in the Bush administration's war on terrorism, pushing from the headlines military efforts in Afghanistan, where tribal leadership superseded Karzai's mandates from Kabul. Karzai struggled to build a national government with limited funds and a military balkanized by allegiances to local warlords, all of whom were former mujahideen commanders who had fought against the Soviets. Indeed, warlords throughout Afghanistan defied national leadership and instead headed their own provinces, controlling trade and revenues. A spark in trade was precipitated by the return of a lucrative opium crop. Opium had been banned by the Taliban in 2000, but as former mujahideen reestablished control, poppy cultivation in Afghanistan overwhelmed the world's heroin market. The United States tolerated the warlords, who initially provided military assistance with hopes of receiving land and power. Perhaps more troubling, however, the Taliban took advantage of Karzai's weaknesses, slowly regrouping and reestablishing control. By spring 2004 critics began to scrutinize the Bush administration's swift victories in Afghanistan and Iraq, as the Americans faced years of occupation and political maneuvering. By March 2004, 130,000 American troops were stationed in Iraq and the United States was spending $4 billion a month there, while Afghanistan languished with 20,000 foreign peacekeepers (including 11,000 U.S. troops) on $900 million a month. With the first free elections approaching, Afghan and U.S. officials urged the White House to commit more troops and resources.

2004 Election. The war in Afghanistan emerged as a hot political issue during the 2004 presidential campaign. President Bush's approval ratings fell below 50 percent, largely due to his handling of Iraq. Democratic nominee Senator John Kerry of Massachusetts attacked Bush for invading Iraq rather than committing more U.S. troops to finding bin Laden and defeating al Qaeda. Kerry argued that Iraq had been a mistake without international support, while Afghanistan was key to winning the war on terrorism. Bush countered that even though the United States had not located bin Laden, the world was a safer place, minus a substantial number of al Qaeda operatives and Hussein, who had posed a significant threat. In November Bush was reelected, voters perhaps agreeing that the nation should not change course while immersed in two wars. A month later, Karzai was elected prime minister in Afghanistan, which supporters offered as evidence that Bush's plans were working. By 2005, with investigations revealing prisoner-abuse scandals at Bagram Air Base north of Kabul, Guantanamo Bay, and Iraq's Abu Ghraib Prison, Karzai demanded that the United States turn over Afghan prisoners to his gov-

Two U.S. Air Force personnel stand atop "Lion Hill" behind their Forward Operating Base in Afghanistan on 24 May 2009. The Afghanistan hills proved to be a difficult and dangerous terrain for military operations (U.S. Air Force photograph by Captain Stacie N. Shafran).

ernment. Karzai also asked Bush for help in creating economic opportunities outside of opium cultivation, which had skyrocketed to between 40 and 60 percent of the Afghan economy. Critics claimed that Bush remained aloof to these requests while basking in Karzai's political accomplishments. At a press conference, Bush proclaimed, "I am honored to stand by the first democratically elected leader in the 5,000 year history of Afghanistan." By 2006, Bush was forced to address renewed political turmoil and violence in Afghanistan. It became clear to U.S. officials that Afghan forces lacked the training and funding to effectively take over operations against the Taliban, ensuring a prolonged U.S. presence. The return of the Taliban was a particularly pressing problem. Opium production had reached a critical point, providing funding for the once-disapproving Taliban. The United States was left with few options: turn a blind eye or face an angry local population who benefited immensely from the booming heroin trade. Faced with a rapidly deteriorating situation, the U.S. military pressed Bush to redirect troops from Iraq to Afghanistan. While violence had largely diminished in Iraq, a resurgent Taliban intensified their attacks, operating from bases inside Pakistan.

2008 Election. In 2007 approximately 26,000 American troops alongside 28,000 North Atlantic Treaty Organization (NATO) forces (consisting predominantly of Canadian, Australian, British, and Dutch soldiers), battled a growing number of insurgents and fought for the hearts and minds of Afghan civilians who were still suffering from poverty, corruption, a crumbling infrastructure, and violence. Coalition forces this year suffered the highest casualties in Afghanistan since 2001, and casualties among Afghan civilians rose as well. Bush defended his actions in Afghanistan, emphasizing improvements in education, women's rights, and voting. But as presidential candidates Senators John McCain of Arizona and Barack Obama of Illinois debated over the proper course to take in the war on terror, Bush promised to provide additional troops in Afghanistan and remove soldiers from Iraq, and announced plans to double the size of the Afghan army. Obama praised this new direction, claiming Bush had, at last, chosen the right strategy: pulling back from Iraq and tackling terrorism at its source in Afghanistan. But Obama faulted Bush for not committing enough troops sooner. McCain argued that the United States needed to remain faithfully engaged in both countries, or risk destabilizing the entire Middle East region.

New Commander in Chief. As victor in the 2008 presidential election, Obama inherited both wars. Stating his plans to slowly disengage from Iraq, Obama declared that he would escalate U.S. involvement in Afghanistan. A month before his inauguration, *Time* magazine deemed the war in Afghanistan a "slow bleed" and an "aimless absurdity." At its outset, the war had been a search-and-destroy mission: finding bin Laden and ridding Afghanistan of Taliban leadership. Both aims were lost in nearly a decade of conflict. A secondary goal of the Bush administration,

establishing democracy and prosperity, had been a restive process with accusations of corruption and vice plaguing rebuilding efforts. Among Obama's first actions was to pledge 30,000 additional troops for military operations in Afghanistan and defend the right of the United States to attack al Qaeda forces in Pakistan. But Obama also promised to begin withdrawing troops by mid 2011, insisting that the United States would no longer commit to endless war. Confronting many of the same problems that hindered Bush, Obama's strategy for a troop surge contended with a persistent and persuasive Taliban, a weak Afghan militia, and weary, frightened Afghan civilians. Rumors of scandal and corruption surrounded the Karzai administration, which critics claimed had nurtured deep connections to both the opium trade and the Taliban.

Sources:
Michael Abramowitz and Peter Baker, "Bush Faces Pressure to Shift War Priorities," *Washington Post*, 17 December 2007;

Mike Allen, "Bush Resumes Case against Iraq; Democratic Countries Must Confront 'Axis of Evil,' President Tells VMI Cadets," *Washington Post*, 18 April 2002;

Aryn Baker, "The Warlords of Afghanistan," *Time* (12 February 2009);

Peter Baker, "In Afghanistan, for Better or Worse," *Washington Post*, 11 February 2008;

John F. Burns, "A Nation Challenged: Strategy," *New York Times*, 12 October 2001;

James Carney and John F. Dickerson, "The War at Home," *Time* (14 January 2002);

Michael Duffy and others, "Iraq: Moment of Reckoning: Collateral Damage," *Time* (24 May 2004);

Dan Eggen, "Focus Is on Afghanistan as Bush Lays Out Plans," *Washington Post*, 10 September 2008;

"Further into Taliban Country," *Economist* (26 March 2009);

"The Future of Afghanistan," *New York Times*, 15 October 2001;

Bradley Graham, "As an Issue, War Is Risky for Both Sides," *Washington Post*, 2 October 2004;

"The Hunt for Osama bin Laden," *New York Times*, 18 December 2001;

Joe Klein, "The Aimless War: Why Are We in Afghanistan?" *Time* (11 December 2008);

J. F. O. McAllister, "Remember This War?" *Time* (27 August 2006);

Tim McGirk, "Remember Afghanistan?" *Time* (8 March 2004);

McGirk and others, "The Great New Afghan Hope," *Time* (17 December 2001);

Ron Moreau, "Reining in the Warlords," *Newsweek* (28 April 2003);

David Rohde, "The Afghanistan Triangle," *New York Times*, 1 October 2006;

"Safe at Home; Candidates Have Different Views on How to Combat Terrorism," *Washington Post*, 28 October 2004;

David E. Sanger, "Bush Deflects Afghan's Request for Return of Prisoners," *New York Times*, 24 May 2005;

Sanger, "News Analysis: The Commonalities of Two Surges Mask Their Crucial Differences," *New York Times*, 4 December 2009;

Sheryl Gay Stolberg and Helene Cooper, "Obama Speeds Troops to Afghanistan; Vows to Begin U.S. Withdrawal in 2011," *New York Times*, 1 December 2009;

Dick Thompson and Gerald Bourke, "Afghanistan: Death of a City," *Time* (24 June 1996);

Mark Thompson, "The Soviets in Afghanistan: Obama's Déjà vu?" *Time* (19 October 2009);

Josh Tyrangiel, "The Taliban Next Door," *Time* (9 December 2001);

Scott Wilson and Rajiv Chandrasekaran, "President Obama and President Karzai," *Washington Post*, 9 May 2010.

Hussein's Iraq. Following the first strikes in the war on terrorism in Afghanistan in October 2001, the Bush administration quickly began gathering evidence against President Saddam Hussein of Iraq, whom they suspected of possessing biological, chemical, or nuclear weapons. Hussein was a personal target for President George W. Bush. As president of Iraq since 1979, Hussein's relationship with the United States had changed dramatically. In 1980, when Iraq invaded Iran, weakened by revolution, the United States was wary of Iraq, which had for decades received military support from the Soviets. But the United States, threatened more by Iran's new Islamic fundamentalist regime, chose to supply intelligence and technology to Iraq, though the Reagan administration was accused of secretly selling weapons to both nations. Dragging on for eight years, the Iran-Iraq War ended bitterly with the United Nations charging Iraq with using chemical weapons against Iranian soldiers, civilians, and Kurdish rebels in northern Iraq. Two years later, when Hussein invaded Kuwait over an oil-revenue dispute, the United States mobilized against Iraq with a broad coalition backed by the United Nations that included Arab forces. President George H. W. Bush quickly and suc-cessfully drove Hussein's forces out of Kuwait, though his commander in Iraq, General Norman Schwarzkopf, Chairman of the Joint Chiefs of Staff Colin Powell, and Secretary of Defense Dick Cheney, stopped short of sending troops to Baghdad and removing Hussein from power. Relations remained tense between the two countries (Hussein even authorized an assassination attempt on the former president when Bush visited Kuwait in 1993), and the United Nations kept sanctions in place against Iraq, keeping a close eye on Hussein's weapons' production. A little over a decade later, the United States once again mobilized against Hussein. But unlike his father's military operation, President George W. Bush launched an attack without international support.

New Target. Following the events of 9/11, much of the world rallied in support of Bush's offensive in Afghanistan and his attempt to find Osama bin Laden and wipe out al Qaeda. The rest of the world, however, was less eager for another preemptive war in the Middle East. But the president and his advisers were convinced that Hussein posed a significant threat to American national security and insisted that diplomacy with the dictator had failed. By early 2002 the Bush administration intensified efforts to collect intelligence exposing Hussein. The president and his advisers anticipated a link between Iraq and the 9/11

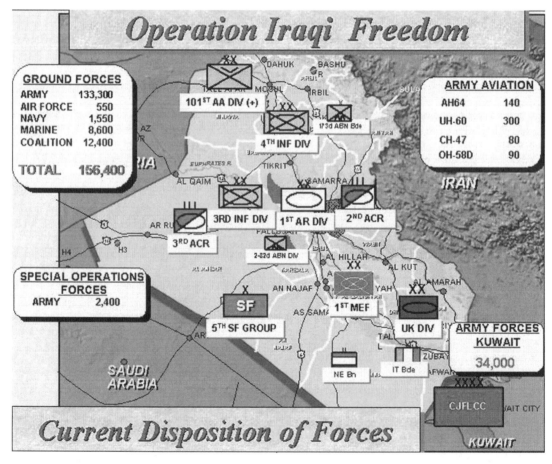

Map showing the strategic locations of various forces involved in the invasion of Iraq (<www.army.mil>)

U.S. soldiers and Iraqi civilians watch as the statue of Saddam Hussein is toppled in Firdous Square, in downtown Bagdhad, on 9 April 2003 (AP Photo/Jerome Delay).

attacks and al Qaeda. They felt certain that Hussein, who had expelled UN weapons inspectors in 1998, had illegally produced chemical, biological, or nuclear weapons, soon termed "weapons of mass destruction" (WMD) by the administration. While Bush amped up his rhetoric against Iraq, labeling that country, along with North Korea and Iran, the "axis of evil," Bush's inner circle, particularly National Security Advisor Condoleezza Rice and Vice President Dick Cheney, compiled evidence to legitimatize U.S. military action to remove Hussein from power and destroy illegal weapons. By October 2002, Bush secured congressional approval for the use of military force to depose Hussein, but he relented to Secretary of State Colin Powell's requests to argue the U.S. case before the UN Security Council. Powell hoped to build a coalition, much like Operation Desert Storm.

Case Against Iraq. President Bush enjoyed hard-won congressional support at home. Yet, he faced an ambivalent public and a wary UN Security Council. Many Americans agreed that Hussein was a brutal dictator guilty of human-rights atrocities, but remained skeptical of his threat to the United States. Others agreed with the Bush administration: evidence of WMD and al Qaeda ties to Iraq were a terrifying prospect, and Hussein needed to be removed from power. The UN Security

Council proceeded carefully, passing Resolution 1441 that demanded Iraq allow weapons inspectors to find and destroy WMD, as well as suggesting vague but threatening consequences if there was no compliance. Hussein responded angrily, denying the existence of WMD, but quickly agreed to allow inspectors back in. Bush, on the other hand, expressed his doubts about the Iraqi leader's sincerity in reopening Iraq to thorough inspections. By February 2003, the Bush administration sent Powell to the Security Council for a second resolution, this time for war. With evidence from U.S. and British sources, Powell claimed that valuable "human intelligence" proved that Iraq was a security threat, with stockpiles of anthrax, dangerous ties to al Qaeda terrorists, mobile biological weapons labs, and proof that Iraq had obtained uranium from Niger. However, chief UN weapons inspector Hans Blix's report contradicted Powell's evidence and conclusions. Buoyed by Blix's information, France led the dissent against the second resolution, garnering strong support. Bush sensed defeat in a Security Council vote for war and withdrew the second resolution, insisting that the United States and Britain had proven that Iraq had WMD regardless of UN inspectors' findings. Both Bush and British prime minister Tony Blair maintained that Resolution 1441 left ample room for a legal invasion.

Eve of War. Bush issued a final ultimatum to Hussein, demanding he step down and leave Iraq. Instead, as U.S. troops poured into the region and Iraqis braced for an invasion, Hussein televised a mocking rejection of Bush's ultimatum, effectively eliminating any hope for peace. Immediately, Bush readied for war and finalized invasion plans with Central Command leader General Thomas Franks. Win Without War, a broad coalition of organizations including NAACP, Sierra Club, Oxfam America, and National Council of Churches, opposed the invasion. They organized a "virtual march" in February, encouraging supporters to voice their dissent by calling and faxing congressmen. With war on the horizon, they called protesters to gather in Washington, D.C., for a global vigil for peace. More-militant antiwar groups coordinated acts of civil disobedience across the United States. Congressmen, however, gathered together in a show of bipartisan unity behind the president, and many more Americans simply hoped for a swift end to the war with minimal casualties.

Invasion. On 19 March 2003, Operation Iraqi Freedom began with British and American forces collaborating in a U.S.-led military invasion of Iraq. Air strikes followed by a comprehensive ground invasion (20 March) devastated Iraqi forces. Within a few weeks, coalition troops reached Baghdad. While news reports featured staged footage of Iraqis toppling a giant statue of Hussein, the leader himself escaped the city amid the firefights, bombings, and lootings. Throughout Baghdad, U.S. troops faced fierce resistance from Hussein loyalists and guerrilla fighters, and hospitals struggled to treat thousands of civilians injured during the bombings. Yet, it seemed a clear victory for the United States. On 1 May, less than two months after the

initial invasion, Bush landed on the aircraft carrier USS *Abraham Lincoln* and delivered a stirring address declaring an end to major combat operations in Iraq. The first president to speak to his constituents aboard a warship at sea, Bush arrived in a flight suit and later spoke before a banner proclaiming: "Mission Accomplished." He expressed his gratitude to U.S. and British troops and the families of soldiers who had died. He invoked the memory of 11 September, reassuring Americans that the cause in Iraq was just. Bush insisted that the victory in Iraq was one against terrorism: "We removed an ally of al Qaeda and cut off a source of terrorist funding."

Domestic Politics. As the 2004 presidential election campaign kicked off in the summer of 2003, Iraq became a central issue. Despite an easy victory, U.S. troops faced a counterinsurgency operation against Hussein loyalists and guerilla fighters among Iraq's Sunni Muslim population. Unable to directly take on U.S. forces, insurgents conducted hit-and-run attacks while staying ensconced in civilian areas, aggravating American efforts to target enemy fighters while keeping civilians safe. Politically, Bush suffered from the continued violence in Iraq, but more damaging were reports that began to emerge, disputing his reasons for declaring war. U.S. officials were forced to admit that evidence that the Iraqi government had obtained uranium in Niger was likely inaccurate and incomplete, and the 9/11 Commission, a congressional committee charged with investigating the 2001 terrorist attacks, found no connection between Hussein and al Qaeda. But Bush, buoyed by a historical pattern of two-term wartime presidents and solid support of his party, also benefited from a divided Democratic Party that argued bit-

Bush aboard the USS *Abraham Lincoln* aircraft carrier after giving his "Mission Accomplished" speech on 1 May 2003 in which he prematurely declared an end to major combat in Iraq (AP Photo/J. Scott Applewhite)

A bombed restaurant in the Shula neighborhood of Baghdad remains in ruins in 2009, showing the devastation of the war on the city (U.S. Navy photograph by Mass Communication Specialist Sec. Class Robert J. Whelan).

terly over their own reasons for supporting the war and plans for reconstructing Iraq. By the end of 2003, while Democrats struggled to unite behind a central message, Bush scored a political victory when Hussein was found in a basement beneath a rural farmhouse near his hometown of Tikrit. The war in Iraq nonetheless became the most divisive military operation to affect American politics since the Vietnam War. Battling Democratic nominee John Kerry in the general election, Bush made clear that, regardless of the validity of the supporting evidence, his decision to go to war had removed a dangerous dictator from power and represented a decisive move against global terrorism. Kerry, however, charged that the war in Iraq had been a disastrous diversion that had taken much-needed resources away from a clear-cut fight in Afghanistan where bin Laden was yet to be found. But by calling the war a mistake, Kerry left himself open to repeated criticisms from Bush, who insisted that Kerry thought the world was better off with Hussein in power. As the candidates fought to define the war in Iraq, increased violence, suicide bombings, civilian deaths, troop casualties, and the beheading of military contractors dominated headlines and fueled debates. Bush held fast to his convictions that both U.S.-led wars in the Middle East represented steps toward bringing democracy to the region and protecting

Americans from terrorists. Kerry, on the other hand, pledged to ease troops out of Iraq and hand over power to Iraqis, while bolstering U.S.-trained Iraqi security forces. On 4 November, Bush won a clear majority of American voters, who trusted the Bush Doctrine and the administration's strategy.

Fighting the Insurgency. Following the election, Bush's political fortunes remained tied to events in Iraq, where despite efforts to create a sustained central government and obtain high voter turnout, bitter religious rivalries dominated elections and persistent sectarian violence dimmed hopes for democracy. While there was no sign of al Qaeda operatives at the beginning of Operation Iraqi Freedom, the terrorist group had increasingly become a problem as conditions worsened. A report in 2006 claimed that the death toll in Iraq since the invasion had reached more than 650,000. Criticizing the validity of these high numbers, the Bush administration defended its military operations, insisting that insurgent tactics put civilians in danger and that U.S. troops protected Iraqi citizens to the best of their ability. But a Democratic takeover in Congress during the 2006 midterm elections indicated that Americans were growing weary of U.S. involvement in Iraq. By January 2007, with another presidential election on the horizon and conditions deteriorating in Iraq, the Bush administration shifted their military strategy. In order to stabilize the country and give Iraq's new administration the opportunity to govern, Bush committed an additional 20,000 troops, adding that his support was "open-ended," providing that the Iraqi government met political guidelines. Bush also allocated $1 billion to reconstruction and infrastructure projects. The decision initially provoked condemnation. Polls suggested that more than 60 percent of Americans disapproved of sending additional troops. Democrats pounced on Bush's declining poll numbers, but by the end of summer 2007 violence in Iraq began to subside. Increasing troops in and around Baghdad, along with General David H. Petraeus's counterinsurgency plan, had stemmed attacks. Some factored in a major shift in sectarian politics with the "Anbar Awakening," when many Iraqi Sunnis rejected al Qaeda and instead joined U.S. efforts. Regardless, the Bush administration claimed a victory.

Election. In 2008, Democratic presidential nominee Barack Obama insisted that he had always been against U.S. intervention in Iraq. He claimed he had correctly predicted a prolonged occupation, provoking violence and political chaos. Public opinion polls showed that a majority of Americans felt the war was going badly, which hurt Republican candidate John McCain, a longtime supporter of the war. But with violence down 80 percent, Obama was forced to defend his attempts to block Bush's troop surge, while McCain touted his three-year effort to implement the surge. Yet, McCain remained saddled with Bush's legacy and accusations that a McCain presidency would be the equivalent of a third term for Bush. As the election approached, the U.S. economy crashed, diverting attention away from war but heaping further blame on Bush's presidency. The elections were a watershed moment for Democrats, who took the White House and strengthened their majorities in the House of Representatives and the Senate. While McCain's loss cannot be entirely attributed to his views on Iraq, many Americans were persuaded by Obama's disapproval of the war and his calls for a timeline for U.S. withdrawal.

Obama and Iraq. A major shift in the broader political landscape in the United States created an opening for dramatic policy changes. With the economy in shambles and promises of health-care reform to keep, domestic issues determined Obama's agenda during his first year in office. The administration's foreign-policy decisions were dominated by the troop surge in Afghanistan, which had been a campaign pledge. Reprioritizing American military operations, the United States focused its attention on fighting al Qaeda and the Taliban in Afghanistan and Pakistan, relying more heavily on the Iraqi government to maintain stability in that country. In early 2009, renewed violence in Iraq suggested that there were limits to the political alliances that had aided the troop surge. For most Americans, however, the war in Iraq remained an expensive problem that hampered economic recovery. After six years, the United States had spent nearly $700 billion and lost more than 4,000 military personnel. The war proved to be the most divisive political issue Americans had dealt with in decades. In February 2009, on a trip to visit U.S. forces in Iraq, Obama

ABU GHRAIB

By 2007 a growing number of Americans opposed the Iraq War. Early that year, the politics intensified when CBS news program *60 Minutes II* aired photographs exposing prisoner abuse in Abu Ghraib, a U.S. detention center in Iraq. Amid increasing reports of brutal violence and abuse by U.S. troops in Iraq, the photographs were particularly shocking to Americans. The Arab world was outraged. Along with the photos revealing startling sexual, physical, and emotional abuse, interviews with detainees uncovered the extent of the cruelty. One prisoner spent nine months at Abu Ghraib without being charged or interrogated. Four months in, American guards led him and other detainees into a large cell block, stripped them of their clothes, and commanded them to pose in degrading positions while the guards took photographs. The images included prisoners simulating oral sex and a female guard pointing at a prisoner's genitals and smiling. An investigation discovered a deplorable pattern of abuse at Abu Ghraib. The White House struggled to find an appropriate response. President George W. Bush called the acts "abhorrent" and suggested that they were isolated, but mounting evidence suggested otherwise. Seven soldiers directly involved with the leaked photographs were charged with conspiracy, maltreatment, and indecent acts. Six other soldiers were severely reprimanded. Secretary of Defense Donald Rumsfeld faced intense criticism from the media and was forced to admit that he had known about the abuse. In leaks to the press, the White House let it be known that they had chastised Rumsfeld for failing to let them know the extent of the problem. In a congressional hearing, the secretary acknowledged his error in judgment.

Source: "Abuses at Abu Ghraib," *New York Times*, 1 May 2004.

declared, "Let me say this as plainly as I can. By August 31, 2010, our combat mission in Iraq will end." A little more than a year later, he fulfilled that promise. While admitting that Iraqi politics were far from stable and violence still persisted, Obama removed all but 50,000 troops from Iraq and guaranteed that the remaining soldiers would leave by the end of 2011. Although insurgent attacks escalated and the Iraqi government remained in a political stalemate, most Iraqis looked forward to the end of U.S. occupation. Obama faced little opposition at home, though some Republicans accused him of taking credit when Bush's surge had made withdrawal possible. Other critics, however, worried that Iraq's political standoff would become a vacuum filled by a growing insurgency or a battleground for regional tensions.

Sources:

Michael Abramowitz and Robin Wright, "Bush to Add 21,500 Troops In an Effort to Stabilize Iraq," *Washington Post*, 11 January 2007;

"Antiwar Coalition Plans a Global Vigil," *Philadelphia Inquirer*, 20 March 2003;

Peter Baker, "In Announcing Withdrawal Plan, Obama Marks Beginning of Iraq War's End," *New York Times*, 28 February 2009;

Donald L. Barlett and James B. Steele, "The Oily Americans," *Time* (19 March 2003);

Shashank Bengali and Mohammed al Dulaimy, "Insurgents Exploit Iraq's Power Vacuum," *Christian Science Monitor* (20 September 2010);

Sarah Boseley, "One in 40 Iraqis Killed since Invasion," *Guardian*, 12 October 2006;

Bryan Burrough, "The Path to War," *Vanity Fair* (May 2004);

Andrew Lee Butters, "A Tale of Two Wars: Iraq," *Time* (31 October 2008);

Frank Davies and Patrick Stack, "Dialing Up Anti-War Protests," *Time* (26 February 2003);

Michael Elliot and James Carney, "First Stop, Iraq," *Time* (31 March 2003);

Howard Fineman, "A Sweet Victory . . . And a Tough Loss," *Newsweek* (15 November 2004);

Peter Grier, Peter Ford, and Josh Burek, "US Attacks Iraq," *Christian Science Monitor* (25 March 2003);

Ted Gup, "History a Man You Could Do Business With," *Time* (11 March 1991);

"Iraq's Election Result," *Washington Post*, 22 December 2005;

Tony Karon, "America's New War in Iraq," *Time* (19 June 2003);

Karon, "Baghdad Falls," *Time* (9 April 2003);

Karon, "A War No Longer on Autopilot: What if Iraq Unravels?" *Time* (5 May 2009);

Karon, "What the U.S. Leaves Behind: An Unstable, Vulnerable Iraq," *Time* (1 September 2010);

Nicholas Lemann, "How It Came to War: When Did Bush Decide that He Had To Fight Saddam?" *New Yorker* (31 March 2003);

"Mission Truncated: The Iraq War," *Economist* (4 September 2010);

Chris Mondics and Chris Gray, "On Eve of War, Congress Rallies Behind Bush," *Philadelphia Inquirer*, 19 March 2003;

Rick Montgomery, "Hussein Has a Long History of Survival," *Philadelphia Inquirer*, 15 December 2003;

"Obama Declares an End to Iraq Combat Mission," *New York Times*, 1 September 2010;

David E. Sanger, "Threats and Responses: The White House," *New York Times*, 14 November 2004;

Sanger, "When Goals Meet Reality," *New York Times*, 31 March 2004;

Anthony Shadid, "Hussein Scorns Ultimatum as War Nears," *Washington Post*, 19 March 2003;

Tom Shales, "Aboard the Lincoln, a White House Spectacular," *Washington Post*, 2 May 2003;

Jim VandeHei and Juliet Eilperin, "Congress Passes Iraq Resolution," *Washington Post*, 11 October 2002;

Jeevan Vasagar, "Threat of War: Reliability of Defectors Questioned," *Guardian*, 6 February 2003;

"The War for the White House: The American Election and Iraq," *Economist* (14 June 2008);

Kevin Whitelaw and Julian E. Barnes, "The Great Iraq Debate," *U.S. News & World Report* (4 October 2004);

Bob Woodward, "Why Did Violence Plummet? It Wasn't Just the Surge," *Washington Post*, 8 September 2008.

HEADLINE MAKERS

GEORGE W. BUSH

1946–

PRESIDENT OF THE UNITED STATES

Background. As the eldest son of former president George H. W. Bush, George W. Bush enjoyed a privileged upbringing and a prestigious family name. He and his brother, Jeb, both seemed destined for politics and their father encouraged an interest in governing, while hoping to establish a political dynasty. Though he was the only Bush child not to be born in Texas, George W. nevertheless spent his formative years in Midland, the oil capital of West Texas, and later began his business career there. After a brief stint in the Texas Air National Guard and earning an M.B.A. from Harvard Business School, Bush returned to West Texas and worked in the oil industry, eventually becoming part owner of the Texas Rangers baseball team. His return to Texas was rocky and was marked by failures in business, as well as alcohol abuse. In the late 1970s, Bush met and married Laura Welch, a schoolteacher and librarian, and launched a campaign for a West Texas congressional seat, though he lost in the Republican primary. In the early 1980s, his oil ventures were plagued by dropping prices and fraud investigations. Still, Bush's investments and leadership positions in oil companies made him wealthy and independent from his family's money. By 1986 he committed himself to sobriety, embraced Christianity, and supported his father's presidential campaign. Bush insisted that his temperament and impulsive nature were attributable to time spent in West Texas, traits that ultimately shaped his political persona and ideology.

Governor. In 1994 Bush ran for the governorship of Texas. He took advantage of the vast fund-raising network that he had helped to build during his father's campaign. Bush was also a committed conservative politician and capitalized on many Texans' disapproval of Democratic president Bill Clinton. His campaign promised to tackle juvenile crime, lengthen jail sentences, and expand the prison system. Bush opposed gay rights and abortion, and he railed against the excesses of state and federal governments, claiming that he would leave school systems to their communities and limit welfare payments. In a stunning upset, Bush won the election by a significant margin and became only the second Republican governor of Texas in the twentieth century. Although his brother's loss to Governor Lawton Chiles in Florida dampened the mood, Bush declared his intention to work with the predominantly Democratic state legislature to bring Texans the changes for which they had voted. By 1998 he had largely kept his promise to work with Democrats in Texas, and proudly called himself a "unifier, not a divider." But Bush had crossed Texas Republicans in his attempts to restructure the state's tax base to improve schools in poorer districts, funded by increasing tax burdens on large industries. Some Republicans chided Bush for funding new reading programs in high schools and his unwillingness to formally denounce gay rights. While the state GOP platform rejected abortion under most circumstances, Bush insisted that, though he was prolife and against abortion, the matter had been settled by the Supreme Court. But the governor maintained his popularity among conservatives and appealed to Hispanics, women, and moderate voters. He won a historic victory in 1998, becoming the only governor in Texas to win consecutive four-year terms. During his second term, he assuaged conservative concerns by focusing on faith-based initiatives and declared 10 June "Jesus Day" in Texas in 2000. As a politician with broad appeal and an eye toward the presidency, Bush hoped to calm Republicans' fears regarding his role as a social and fiscal conservative leader. But, according to polls, his persisting popularity seemed to be a matter of personality; voters found him likable.

Presidential Candidacy. When Bush announced his candidacy for president in June 1999, few were surprised though many wondered why he had waited so long. A wide range of candidates emerged, particularly among Republicans. Though he successfully raised a war chest through early fund-raising and received several key endorsements, Bush's campaign went up against a bevy of nationally known politicians, including Pat Buchanan, John McCain, and Elizabeth Dole. But Republicans flocked to Bush, despite his short résumé. His tenure as governor of Texas proved that he could attract conservative and moderate voters; he was a quick and enthusiastic fund-raiser; and his

personality softened the Republican Party's moralistic, stodgy image. Though he stumbled in the New Hampshire primary, Bush ignobly routed McCain in South Carolina and won the nomination. He soon gained a powerful ally in running mate and veteran Washington insider, Dick Cheney, and turned his attention to Democratic candidate Vice President Al Gore.

Early Presidency. With a hard-fought but disputed win in 2000, Bush lacked a clear mandate when elected. To ease the transition and appeal to all voters, Bush expressed an eagerness to bridge the sharp split and build a bipartisan coalition. He toned down his stand against gay rights and reached out to minorities. Bush scheduled meetings with Democratic legislators to discuss education reform in December 2000 and began working closely with Democratic senators Edward Kennedy and George Miller. By the spring of 2001, Bush and Kennedy worked together to pass a sweeping education bill, No Child Left Behind, with overwhelming support from both parties. Yet, Bush alienated some voters and Democratic congressmen with his terse rejection of an international agreement to manage global warming through the Kyoto Protocol, his plan to deregulate energy industries, and a $1.35 trillion tax cut that was ostensibly designed to head off a recession. The Bush administration led the way in diminishing workplace-safety regulations and halting environmental restrictions on road building in wilderness areas and arsenic pollution. By fall 2001 much of the budget surplus left by Clinton had evaporated, making a worsening economic slump more alarming and sending Bush's approval ratings spiraling downward.

Terrorism. The terrorist attacks on 11 September 2001 radically altered Bush's agenda, shifting his focus to national security but empowering him to make unilateral decisions on domestic policy, as well. His leadership in the immediate aftermath of 9/11 was lauded around the world, and Bush's approval ratings skyrocketed as his administration prepared a far-reaching response. Bipartisan support buoyed Bush's initial military operation against Afghanistan and his rapid expansion of the federal government to address terrorist threats against the United States. Within months, Bush introduced sweeping legislation, including the Patriot Act, and created the Department of Homeland Security to address the problems of communications and security across federal agencies. Through controversial "signing statements" and executive orders, Bush dramatically changed the political landscape, giving the president unprecedented power over policy making. The Bush administration dodged Congress in making energy deals, authorizing military tribunals, masking the real costs of Medicare reform, and stymieing investigations of poor intelligence. A clear breaking point came when the White House pushed for war against Iraq. Though it received initial support from Congress, the U.S.-led invasion of Iraq in 2003 troubled many Americans, as reports revealed intelligence failures regarding the existence of weapons of mass destruction

(WMD), the principal reason given for the war. Support further deteriorated as conditions in Iraq worsened and Bush's triumphant and hubristic speech prematurely announced an end to military operations.

Final Term. In 2004, despite declining approval ratings and two divisive wars, Bush won a second term. Americans chose to stay the course with Bush, though a close victory over Democratic nominee John Kerry and the harsh rhetoric of Kerry's supporters signaled an intense opposition to Bush's leadership. The election highlighted weaknesses of Bush's policies. Osama bin Laden remained at large and the Iraq War diverted much-needed resources away from Afghanistan. Support for the war had dropped to 38 percent. The economy still flagged; No Child Left Behind struggled with underfunding and mismanagement; and Bush's expensive Medicare prescription-drug program wreaked havoc on an already convoluted system of elder care. When the White House botched their response in the horrific aftermath of Hurricane Katrina, Democrats pounced, and Republican congressmen began to distance themselves from the Bush administration. Leading up to midterm elections in 2006, Democratic leaders railed against the president for his questionable corporate ties. They drew attention to the administration's links to failed energy giant Enron and disgraced lobbyist Jack Abramoff, as well as Vice President Cheney's former association with military contractor Halliburton. The Democrats took over the House and Senate in 2006 with a broad platform of change, but Americans were most concerned with the direction of the Iraq War. Still, Bush retained an enthusiastic base of support, regardless of the overhaul in Congress. The 2004 election may have exposed some failings, but it also rallied social conservatives to his cause. Bush worked hard to bring his own brand of morality to policy making and wore his faith on his sleeve. Evangelical Christians and Catholics stepped into the political spotlight to defend his crusade to end partial-birth abortions and his rejection of federal funding for stem-cell research. Bush's support of a constitutional ban on gay marriage was a condition for many conservative Christians' endorsement. A general rightward shift among Republicans was apparent; religious groups emerged as powerful lobbyists. Conservative values became the cornerstone of Republican policy and a near prerequisite for party membership. But as the Democrats gained traction in Congress, even the seemingly monolithic voting bloc of conservative evangelicals bore the cracks of dissent. Within their ranks, evangelicals disagreed over the politics of abortion and gay marriage, particularly among young voters. By 2008, both presidential candidates, Senators John McCain and Barack Obama, sidestepped most of the pitfalls of social conservatism that had swayed voters in the 2004 election.

Final Days in Office. Though Bush's approval ratings had plummeted to new lows, he claimed that history would absolve him. He maintained that his decision to send more troops to Iraq in 2007, despite being politically unpopular,

had helped decrease violence and pave the way for an end to the war. Media interviews with key administration figures revealed a coordinated effort to paint Bush as a reformer, pointing out his work to revamp immigration laws, offer immigrants a path to citizenship, and privatize Social Security. His war on terror remained highly controversial. Bush insisted that his policies had prevented another terrorist attack in the United States, but critics condemned the sanctioning of torture techniques in the pursuit of intelligence, the detainment of prisoners at Guantánamo Bay, and the loss of thousands of U.S. troops who had died in Iraq and Afghanistan. Yet, for all the contentious issues that shaped Bush's presidency, the struggling economy plagued both of his terms in office. In 2008, with powerful banking institutions declaring bankruptcy and other industries careening toward collapse, Bush signed the Troubled Asset Relief Program (TARP), authorizing more than $700 billion in federal funds to bail out Wall Street and save the auto industry.

Legacy. Bush devoted his presidency to building a strong and enduring Republican leadership and promised to work with Democrats. But by the end of his presidency, his party suffered from disillusionment and lacked clear direction. Fiscal conservatives claimed that Bush had recklessly spent the budget surplus and expanded the federal government, while social conservatives complained that their influence had waned toward the end of Bush's second term. Liberal critics found little to praise in Bush. They attacked his human-rights record, social policies, and handling of the economy. Furthermore, the Bush administration's scorched-earth strategy in dealing with its opponents left a bitterly divided political terrain.

Sources:
Sam Attlesey, "Bush Eager to Begin Mandate for Change," *Dallas Morning News,* 10 November 1994;

Justin Ewers, "Shunning the Culture Wars," *U.S. News & World Report* (1 September 2008);

Linda Feldmann, "For Bush, Timing Is Everything," *Christian Science Monitor* (11 May 1999);

Feldmann, "How Will History Judge Bush?" *Christian Science Monitor* (13 January 2009);

Feldmann, "Social Issues Stir Passions," *Christian Science Monitor* (27 October 2004);

Howard Fineman, "Praying to Win," *Newsweek* (21 August 2000);

S. C. Gwyn, "The Sons Also Rise," *Time* (26 September 1994);

Liz Halloran, "A Brewing Fight on the Right," *U.S. News & World Report* (22 October 2007);

"Je ne regrette rien—Je ne regretted rien, The Bush Presidency," *Economist* (28 August 2004);

Jill Lawrence, "Why the Rush to Bush?" *USA Today,* 8 March 1999;

David Maraniss, "The Bush Bunch," *Washington Post,* 22 January 1989;

Karen Tumulty, "Bush's Lonely Election Season," *Time* (29 October 2006);

Sam Howe Verhovek, "Is There Room on a Republican Ticket for Another Bush?" *New York Times,* 13 September 1998;

Douglas Waller and others, "Inside the Mind of George Bush," *Time* (6 September 2004);

"You Ain't Seen Nothing Yet: America's Religious Right," *Economist* (25 June 2005).

JOHN MCCAIN

1936–

MILITARY HERO, SENATOR, AND PRESIDENTIAL CANDIDATE

Military Roots. Republican politician John Sidney McCain III's longtime reign in the Senate made him an influential power-broker in Washington, D.C, but his political acumen and trademark candor combined with compelling personal narrative propelled him into the national spotlight. McCain was born into a military family on 29 August 1936. His grandfather commanded a carrier fleet against Japan during World War II, while his father commanded a submarine in the Pacific. His father later served as commander of Pacific forces during the Vietnam War. McCain attended the U.S. Naval Academy, where he studied naval aviation and earned a reputation as a rebellious daredevil and an average pilot. In 1967 he entered combat duty in Vietnam and was shot down on his twenty-third mission. After parachuting into Hanoi, capital of North Vietnam, McCain was attacked by a North Vietnamese guard who broke McCain's shoulder with a rifle butt and stabbed his ankle and groin with a bayonet. McCain spent more than a year in solitary confinement, though he was able to communicate with other prisoners by tapping on the walls. Labeled the "Crown Prince" because of his father's position, McCain was offered early release, but he chose to remain with his fellow prisoners of war. He endured five years of physical, mental, and emotional torture before he was freed owing to the 1973 Peace Accords. McCain came back to the United States a war hero and returned to the navy as a field instructor. By 1981, the year McCain's father died, he left the military for a career in politics and was elected Republican representative of Arizona's First District in 1982. In the House of Representatives, McCain actively engaged in foreign-policy debates, though he resisted party politics. He advocated alongside President Ronald Reagan's supporters for aid to contras in Nicaragua, but strongly opposed the proposal to keep U.S. Marines in Lebanon.

Senate. After winning Barry Goldwater's vacated Senate seat in 1986, McCain quickly became a leading voice on national security and foreign policy, but McCain suffered a major blow when he was implicated in the Keating Five controversy, a congressional scandal that linked congressmen to disgraced savings-and-loan financier Charles Keating. Accused of "poor judgment" by the Senate Ethics Committee, though largely exonerated of any wrongdoing, McCain was stung by the damage to his reputation. He later credited the scandal with changing his approach to

politics. By 1994 he reached out to Democratic senator Russ Feingold of Wisconsin with a proposal to restructure campaign financing and make politicians and politics more transparent. Reaching across the aisle and rejecting powerful lobbyists who influenced Washington, McCain shifted his identity, retaining the mystique of his heroic past but, at the same time, cultivating the image of a political maverick. He emerged as a singular figure in the Senate, willing to cross party lines but devoted to the tenets of Republican conservatism. Just as significant, however, were McCain's antics and temper as a senator. He became known for his volatility and obscenities in debating policy and appeared to have made as many enemies as friends.

2000 Election. When McCain announced his run for the Republican nomination in the 2000 presidential election, his maverick status earned him the role of political outsider despite his long tenure in Congress. But McCain was also considered a party stalwart and an emerging political celebrity. In 1996 McCain was given the honor of nominating fellow veteran Bob Dole as the Republican presidential candidate, and, in 1999 he published a best-selling memoir detailing his ordeal in Vietnam to coincide with the announcement of his intention to run for president. In Republican debates, McCain established himself as the choice for moderate Republicans and Independent voters, touting his cooperative legislative victories and difficult but principled stands, highlighting his long fight for campaign-finance reform. Outspent by his chief rival George W. Bush, McCain won a remarkable victory in the New Hampshire primary and favorable press from journalists who enjoyed his blunt and opinionated views aboard his campaign bus, the Straight Talk Express. But the South Carolina primary was McCain's last stand. There, he was unable to prove his conservative credentials, as he stumbled through issues ranging from the states flying the Confederate flag to Christian fundamentalism. Perhaps more damaging were the Bush campaign's authorization of a barrage of leaflets and phone calls that falsely accused McCain, in part, of giving his wife a crippling venereal disease, fathering a child by an African American prostitute (a reference to his adopted Bangladeshi daughter), and committing treason while a prisoner of war. McCain, predicting a loss, pulled all negative ads, and told his campaign staff that he would go out honorably. The McCain camp remained bitter about the hollow and sordid attacks, but, in the end, McCain offered his endorsement to Bush in a show of party solidarity. Although McCain lost the nomination and the right wing of the Republican Party remained suspicious of him, he enjoyed broad appeal that made him an asset to both Republicans and Democrats. After endorsing Bush, McCain launched an exhaustive campaign to endorse more than fifty Republican candidates, particularly in states where the GOP struggled to gain a foothold. By 2000 the party enjoyed solid support in the South and Mountain States but continued to lose ground on the West Coast, Northeast, and upper Midwest. With stump speeches and personal appearances, McCain solidified his bipartisan popularity, helped Republicans make significant gains in Congress, and shored up support for his campaign-finance legislation.

Independent. As a senator during Bush's tenure in office, McCain rarely toed party lines. He opposed Bush's tax cuts and finally pushed through campaign-finance reform despite reservations from the White House. McCain threw his support behind the president after 9/11 and endorsed Bush's decision to go to war with Iraq. But as the conditions in Iraq deteriorated, McCain began to doubt Bush's handling of the war. In 2004 McCain even briefly discussed sharing the 2004 Democratic presidential ticket with Massachusetts senator John Kerry, a harsh critic of the Iraq War. Instead, McCain again backed Bush, rigorously campaigning for the president's reelection. During Bush's second term, McCain, looking ahead to another run at the presidency in 2008, softened his approach toward the White House. He studied Bush's political organization, hired Bush strategists and fund-raisers, and shifted to the Right. Yet, McCain remained conflicted about the president's policies. He changed course and supported the administration's tax cuts, but became increasingly critical of the direction of the war and Bush's stance on the detention and torture of prisoners of war.

Republican Nominee. McCain's 2008 presidential race revealed the limits of his political independence. After a near-devastating crisis of money and organization in mid 2007, the campaign righted itself. McCain surrounded himself with political tacticians, some of whom had worked closely with Bush, notably Tucker Eskew, who worked against McCain during the 2000 South Carolina primary, and Steve Schmidt, a disciple of Karl Rove. While Mark Salter, McCain's longtime friend and adviser, and coauthor of his memoir, took a backseat, McCain built a new political organization of conservatives and honed his message to attract all corners of the Republican Party. The media accused him of abandoning his former style, but McCain frequently referred to himself as a "maverick." He insisted that the scale of the campaign and intensity of the twenty-four-hour news cycle prevented access he had formerly given to journalists, thus provoking the media's criticism. But McCain was forced to move to the Right, economically and socially. His platform included making Bush's tax cuts permanent and revoking the estate tax (a policy he once championed). He reversed his position on his own immigration reform bill, offshore drilling, and the use of torture during interrogation. In McCain's battle against Democratic candidate Barack Obama, some pundits felt that he had allowed the character assaults against Obama to go too far.

After the Election. When McCain lost the race, it seemed to change his political outlook. His decision to make Alaska governor Sarah Palin his running mate had initially energized the Republican Party, particularly those on the far Right who had shown little enthusiasm for McCain. But the choice quickly became a liability, when critics found Palin lacking in experience and knowledge

expected in a candidate. Some felt the choice was surprisingly cynical. Yet, her popularity eclipsed McCain's, a reality that carried over into his postelection career. In 2010 the ultraconservative Tea Party, inspired by Palin's rhetoric, threatened McCain's run for Senate in Arizona. In a requiem to their failed bid for control of the White House, Palin salted wounds by accusing the McCain camp of silencing her on the campaign trail and editing her populist message. The political tide continued to change after Obama's election. McCain, once revered for his independence and bipartisan approach, was now accused of being soft on immigration and national security by the far Right of the Republican Party and the growing ranks of the Tea Party.

Sources:
Peter Baker, "The Final Days," *New York Times*, 31 August 2008;

Nancy Gibbs and John F. Dickerson, "Campaign 2000: The Power and the Story," *Time* (13 December 1999);

David Grann, "The Fall: John McCain's Choices," *New Yorker* (17 November 2008);

Nicholas Lemann, "The McCain Code: From Airport Security to Enron," *New Yorker* (4 February 2002);

Joshua Micah Marshall, "The Other Republican," *American Prospect* (18 December 2000);

Susan Rasky, "Washington Talk: Working Profile: Senator John McCain," *New York Times*, 9 August 1988;

Evan Thomas and others, "What These Eyes Have Seen," *Newsweek* (11 February 2008).

BARACK OBAMA

1961–

PRESIDENT OF THE UNITED STATES

Background. Barack Hussein Obama's powerful personal narrative, covered in two memoirs, *Dreams of My Father* and *The Audacity of Hope*, highlighted his unique upbringing and gave the media no shortage of material in countless biographical essays that followed his ascent into politics. Obama's mother was a white woman from Kansas, who met Obama's father, a Kenyan exchange student, while they were both studying at the University of Hawaii. They married, but when Obama was two years old, his father left for Harvard to study economics and then returned to Kenya where he already had another family. His mother married an Indonesian and moved to Jakarta, where Obama lived from age six to ten. He returned to live with his grandparents in Hawaii; his mother, after separating from her husband, moved back as well. One of only a few black students, Obama finished high school in Honolulu. After two years at Occidental

College in Los Angeles, he graduated from Columbia University in New York City and worked as a community organizer in Chicago. In 1990 he attended Harvard Law School and became the first African American president of the Harvard Law Review. Obama returned to Chicago and married fellow Harvard Law graduate, Michelle Robinson, a native of Chicago's South Side. He practiced civil-rights law for a small public-interest firm, representing victims of employment and housing discrimination, and taught classes at the University of Chicago's law school. But Obama was waiting for an opportunity to become involved in politics. In 1992 he was a political asset to the Democratic Party, organizing a voter-registration drive and adding 150,000 voters who helped Bill Clinton carry Illinois in his presidential race against George H. W. Bush.

Into Politics. Obama ran for state senate and won in 1996, though he lost a 2000 bid for a U.S. House seat to former Black Panther Bobby Rush, who labeled Obama an opportunist, Harvard elitist, and an outsider who did not understand the challenges facing African Americans of the South Side. Yet, Obama was a popular state legislator and successfully fought for death-penalty reforms and health care for poor children. Obama won over the more-liberal wing of the Democratic Party when he gave a rousing speech at a 2002 antiwar rally, opposing U.S. intervention in Iraq. In 2003 Obama launched a campaign for the U.S. Senate for Illinois. He handily beat his opponent, millionaire Brian Hull, in the Democratic primary after the media revealed that Hull's former wife had issued a restraining order against him. Jack Ryan, Obama's Republican challenger, withdrew from the race when reporters discovered that his former wife had complained of his sexual fetishes during their divorce proceedings. Ryan's replacement, Alan Keyes, was a powerful politician, but most voters abandoned him following his strange attacks on gays, calling homosexuality "selfish hedonism," and other bizarre antics. At the 2004 Democratic National Convention, Obama gave an electrifying opening speech, catapulting his Senate race to the national spotlight. He claimed to embody the American Dream, living in a nation where a "skinny kid with a funny name" could work hard and succeed: "In no other country on earth is my story even possible." He presented a version of America many voters wanted to see, a country that could transcend racial tensions, economic inequality, social injustice, and corruption. Both Democrats and Republicans rushed to claim Obama after the speech. He easily won the election, becoming the only African American in the U.S. Senate and only the third black senator in more than one hundred years.

Hope and Change. Obama's ability to bridge political and social divides, combined with his new celebrity, captivated voters and made him an early favorite for the Democratic nomination for president in 2008. Though he had the most liberal voting record in the Senate, he worked effectively with conservatives. Obama gained a reputation for having a cool temperament and self-confidence that colleagues respected. His candidacy was based on transcending deep conflicts in American politics and he charmed voters with eloquent, impassioned speeches, promising change and cooperation. He campaigned on health-care reform, ending the war in Iraq, and reviving the economy. But he faced tough competition from fellow Democratic senator Hillary Clinton, whose campaign attacked Obama for his relative inexperience and derided his hopes for bipartisanship as naive. His slogans of "Yes, We Can," "Hope," and "Change" were disparaged as hollow and unrealistic. Although Clinton repeatedly warned that he was not ready for the presidency, Obama won over Democratic voters.

2008 Election. Similar criticisms were leveled against Obama in the general election, but Republican attacks ran deeper. Republican nominee John McCain and his running mate Sarah Palin attempted to turn Obama's carefully constructed narrative against him. In particular, Palin drew attention to his background, tenure as community activist and law teacher in Chicago, and stand against the Iraq War. She focused on his left-wing allegiances as far outside the American mainstream. McCain's surrogates accused Obama of being a Muslim born in Kenya, despite his long-time devotion to Christianity and his birth in Hawaii. But after eight years of war and economic instability with a Republican White House, Americans were as unsympathetic to Republican appeals as they were hopeful of Obama's promises of change. In November 2008, Obama's presidential win and a wave of Democratic congressional victories signaled a deep dissatisfaction with the Bush administration.

First African American President. Obama's historic inauguration as the first black president attracted millions of people to Washington, D.C., and was celebrated globally. Many in the media lavished Obama with premature praise and applauded Americans for moving beyond the politics of race and embracing a promising, young politician. Approval of the United States abroad skyrocketed. Obama's Ivy League education and cosmopolitan upbringing seemed to indicate a new era of American compassion for Muslim nations and developing countries. Within months of entering the Oval Office in 2009, Obama was awarded the Nobel Prize for Peace, only the third sitting president to receive that honor.

Presidency. Despite a mandate for change, Obama inherited two wars, the worst recession since the Great Depression, and a massive federal deficit. The Obama administration faced entrenched opposition from Republicans. As the recession deepened, the Obama administration put forth a $787 billion federal stimulus package, the American Recovery and Reinvestment Act, to jump-start the economy and spur job creation, investment, and consumer spending. Conservatives railed against the measure, resisting deficit spending despite the economic crisis. Republican governors in several states attempted to block the funding. Self-proclaimed Tea Party activists rose to prominence, protesting the federal bailout of state governments and extensions of welfare and unemployment payments. Further, regulatory measures to rein in the Wall Street trading and mortgage lending were met with stiff opposition. In foreign policy, Obama was committed to timelines for troop withdrawals in Iraq and Afghanistan, and continued assaults on terrorist cells in Pakistan. As his approval ratings began to slide, Republican congressmen fought Obama's second major legislative effort, health-care reform. Democratic congressional leadership lobbied hard for universal health care, arguing that it was the government's duty to protect Americans' health. Republicans countered that expanding the federal role would only increase bureaucratic excess, raise costs and premiums, and create an inefficient system. A compromise bill passed in the spring of 2010 despite conservative protests. The Patient Protection and Affordable Care Act included mandatory health coverage and subsidies for poor Americans and prevented insurance providers from denying coverage based on preexisting conditions or capping the amount of care for which a consumer is eligible. The Children's Health Insurance Reauthorization Act granted coverage to eleven million children, four million of whom were previously uninsured. In his second year as president, Obama strained to preserve the enthusiasm and excitement that followed him into office. His administration and Democrats in Congress paid a heavy political price in passing economic and health-care reforms, and Obama's progressive support began to wane. Rumors circulated by "Birthers," those who claimed Obama was born in Kenya and was thus unqualified to be president, persisted and gathered strength leading up to the midterm elections. Critics from the Left attacked Obama for propping up corrupt and reckless financial institutions, allowing enemy combatants to remain at Guantánamo Bay, coming up short on global climate-change laws, and tepidly approaching gay rights. But many pundits pointed out that the president had had far more successes than failures, though he had been slow to capitalize on them politically. The economy stabilized, and imperfect but comprehensive health-care legislation was a significant achievement. Among his underreported legislative accomplishments, Obama instituted the enforcement of equal pay for women, ended the media blackout on war casualties and the return of fallen soldiers, closed offshore tax havens, lowered drug costs for seniors, and increased Pell Grants available to college students. He eased travel restrictions to Cuba to allow Americans to visit Cuban relatives. Obama negotiated a landmark weapons-reduction treaty with Russia, laid the foundations for mending diplomatic relations with Iran, launched an effective assault against terrorist cells in Pakistan, and announced an end to military operations in Iraq. Further, he endorsed a timeline for an end to the war in Afghanistan. For soldiers and military personnel, Obama improved conditions at Walter Reed and other military hospitals, increased pay and benefits, and provided better quality equipment.

Sources:

Peter Baker, "Obama's War Over Terror," *New York Times*, 17 January 2010;

"Explaining the Riddle: Barack Obama," *Economist* (23 August 2008);

William Finnegan, "The Candidate: How the Son of a Kenyan Economist Became the Illinois Everyman," *New Yorker* (31 May 2004);

Larissa Macfarquhar, "The Conciliator: Where is Barack Obama Coming From?" *New Yorker* (7 May 2007);

Jon Meacham, "On His Own: Cerebral and Cool, Obama Is Also Steely," *Newsweek* (1 September 2008);

"Reality Bites: Barack Obama's First Year," *Economist* (16 January 2010);

Amanda Ripley and others, "2004 Election: Obama's Ascent," *Time* (15 November 2004);

David Von Drehle, "The Five Faces of Barack Obama," *Time* (21 August 2008).

SARAH PALIN

1964–

GOVERNOR OF ALASKA AND REPUBLICAN CANDIDATE FOR VICE PRESIDENT

Background. Sarah Palin slowly worked her way into local Alaska politics, from a community activist to a city councilwoman. In 1996 she won her first major race to become mayor of Wasilla with 616 votes. She ran against John Stein, the incumbent mayor who helped Palin with her early political ambitions. Palin ran a strikingly tough and broad campaign, surprising her opponent and dividing the town. She capitalized on the shift that began to define Wasilla politics, with traditional libertarian voters replaced by social conservatives and Christian fundamentalists. She attracted out-of-state donors and galvanized voters with national issues, including gun control and abortion rights, while Stein focused on local issues that centered on an increased tax base and expanded civic programs. After becoming mayor, Palin replaced Stein's appointments, creating her own powerful political network, though she alienated some former supporters, including the former police chief, who filed suit against Palin because she had dismissed him at the behest of the National Rifle Association. She fired the city's librarian and local museum director. Despite some bad feelings, Palin became a popular mayor, hired a lobbyist firm to attract millions of dollars to Wasilla, promoted conservative values, and left office only after she met her term limit in 2002.

Statewide Politics. That year, Palin turned to state politics. She lost her bid for lieutenant governor of Alaska, but was tapped to head the state's energy commission by Governor Frank Murkowski. Her new appointment, however, was short-lived. Palin quit in protest, claiming that she could not support an administration that embodied the cronyism and corruption that had long ruled state politics. This theme proved vital for her gubernatorial race in 2006, when she boldly took on the state's leadership regarding oil revenues, winning over the electorate. As governor, Palin challenged entrenched political organizations, forging new corporate oil ties and championing resources for Alaskans, who benefited from invasive oil drilling as collective owners of the natural resources, receiving dividends in the form of individual annual payments. During Palin's tenure as governor, high oil prices resulted in record-breaking dividends. In effect, Palin scored against the oil companies, who were deeply unpopular, and returned an unprecedented amount of money to Alaskans. She focused on her role as a maverick reformer while downplaying social issues that defined her tenure as mayor, but always remained open to the concerns of everyday citizens. By 2008 her approval ratings hovered around 80 percent.

Vice-Presidential Candidate. As a fellow maverick politician who embraced the conservative values of many Republicans, Palin was picked to run alongside John McCain in his 2008 bid for the presidency. McCain's campaign gambled on Palin, a relatively unknown though ambitious politician, hoping to electrify social conservatives and right-wing Christians of the Republican base—those who had been slow to support McCain. Palin transformed the race, from her dramatic introduction to thunderous applause at the Republican National Convention to addresses to packed auditoriums. Her success in combining her role as an outspoken political reformer with that of a dedicated mother of five, including a developmentally disabled infant, inspired many women voters. But it was Palin's fierce and pointed attacks against Democratic presidential nominee Barack Obama that captivated her supporters. She proved useful in the role of heavy for the McCain campaign. She accused Obama of associating with terrorists, referring to William Ayers, former Weather Underground activist who briefly shared a citizens' committee with Obama in Chicago. Palin stressed the Democratic nominee's middle name, Hussein, when speaking about him, intending to associate Obama with Saddam Hussein or draw attention to the Muslim name. She cried, "Drill, Baby, Drill" to support offshore drilling, advocated gun rights, spoke passionately about her Christian beliefs, and campaigned with her family in tow. Conservative radio personality Rush Limbaugh, who had been a critic of McCain, lavished praise on Palin, writing, "Palin=Guns, Babies, Jesus. Home f***ing run."

Controversy. But Palin also became a lightning rod for controversy. Immediately following McCain's announcement, it was revealed that Palin's sixteen-year-old daughter Bristol was pregnant. As pundits argued the political fallout of teenage pregnancy, Palin proudly defended her daughter while admitting the difficulties of personal family matters writ large in a national political campaign. Embracing the media spotlight, Palin invited the father of Bristol's child, Levi Johnston, to accompany the family to the Republican National Convention. Rumors began to circulate that Palin's infant child, Trig, who suffers from Down's syndrome, was actually Bristol's child. Palin maintained that she had kept the pregnancy a secret to avoid criticism. The McCain campaign castigated the press for violating the Palins' privacy and insisted that they embodied the Christian values of American voters.

Ready for Office? Critics claimed that Palin lacked experience and that she struggled during key interviews. As a one-term mayor and a recently elected governor, she had a limited record, though a few policies came under intense scrutiny. In what became known as "Troopergate," the Alaskan state legislature investigated accusations that Palin had abused her power as governor to have her former brother-in-law, state trooper Mike Wooten, fired. Palin's support of aerial wolf shooting, her lawsuit against the federal government to keep polar bears off the endangered-species list, and her denial of the existence of global warming drew the ire of environmentalists. To these criticisms, Palin claimed that hunting and oil were a fact of life in Alaska, and she was protecting her state's residents from the overreaching policies of the federal government. In interviews, Palin appeared unable to effectively articulate her views and while speaking to CBS anchor Katie Couric, Palin failed to name a single newspaper that she regularly read. Further, Palin insisted that her foreign-policy experience was boosted by Alaska's proximity to Russia and winked through debates. The McCain campaign attempted to coach Palin and then, increasingly, censored her.

Election of 2008. Despite Palin's popularity, some blamed McCain's loss to Obama on Palin's polarizing views and political missteps. While McCain failed to energize the Republican base, Palin divided conservative voters, many of whom felt that she was not ready to lead the nation and that her views were too far to the Right. Yet, Palin capitalized on her new fame. In May 2009 she signed a book deal with HarperCollins to write her autobiography and by July she announced her intentions to step down as governor. After publication of *Going Rogue*, which explored her maverick approach to politics and revealed the tensions between her and the McCain campaign, she made millions of dollars selling books and collecting speaking fees. Her celebrity grew as she embraced the conservative Tea Party. Through the political power of Palin's endorsements and incendiary attacks against the Democratic leadership, Tea Party activists ascended to the forefront of American politics. The movement, with Palin as its chief proponent, threatened Democrats and Republicans alike, as she railed against elitism and establishment politics. Palin's populist rhetoric in the wake of the far-reaching reforms of the Obama administration made her one of the rumored front-runners for Republican nomination for president in 2012.

Sources:

Nancy Gibbs, "Person of the Year 2008: Runner Up," *Time* (17 December 2008);

Philip Gourevitch, "The State of Sarah Palin," *New Yorker* (22 September 2008);

Gabriel Sherman, "The Revolution Will Be Commercialized: Sarah Palin Is Already President and It's a Position with a Very Big Salary," *New York Magazine* (3 May 2010);

Nathan Thornburgh, "How Sarah Palin Mastered Politics," *Time* (4 September 2008).

PEOPLE IN THE NEWS

Samuel Alito was sworn in as the 110th Supreme Court justice in 2006, despite a deeply divided confirmation that split along party lines. Nominated by Bush, Alito succeeded Sandra Day O'Connor and was expected to lean to the Right on partisan issues ranging from affirmative action to the death penalty. Indeed, along with the nomination of John Roberts as chief justice, Alito has helped make the court the most conservative in decades.

In 2000, after **John Ashcroft** lost his Senate candidacy to recently deceased governor Mel Carnahan (who had died the October prior to the election; his widow, Jean, was appointed to his seat), the Missouri Republican was tapped by newly elected President George W. Bush to head the Justice Department. As attorney general, Ashcroft played a significant role in expanding executive power during the Bush administration's war on terror. He resigned in 2005.

Joseph R. Biden served as a Democratic senator from Delaware beginning in 1972 until he joined Barack Obama on the Democratic presidential ticket in 2008. As vice president, Biden has been an unwavering supporter and integral part of the Obama administration, charged with overseeing the distribution of the federal stimulus package in 2008 and diplomacy in Afghanistan. He is known as an impulsive though direct politician and a foreign-policy expert, having served as chairman of the Senate Foreign Relations Committee.

John Boehner rose steadily through the ranks of Republican leadership as a representative from Ohio. Elected in 1990, he served as the calming influence to House speaker Newt Gingrich's divisive antics after the Republican Revolution of 1994 and later as a key GOP component of the bipartisan effort to reform education with Bush's No Child Left Behind. In 2006 he won the minority leadership position and became a fierce opponent of the Democrats who took over Congress. Boehner is well known as a consummate country-club politician who counts lobbyists among his good friends, legislates on the golf course, and frequently flies on corporate jets, but his colleagues maintain that he is a committed conservative who remains devoted to tax cuts and

small government. In 2010 Boehner was poised to assume the position of Speaker of the House, following the election of a Republican majority.

Jeb Bush was elected as Republican governor of Florida in 1999. As a politician and younger brother of George W. Bush, he was a controversial figure during the recount of Florida votes in the 2000 presidential election. As governor, Jeb remained fairly popular, with approval ratings in excess of 50 percent in a sharply divided state. An ideological conservative, Bush attempted to decrease state spending and reform education through vouchers and merit pay for teachers. While he has remained dismissive of supporters' calls for a presidential run and declined to run for Senator Mel Martinez's vacated seat in 2010, Bush is considered a political asset to the Republican Party and hailed as the next Bush to carry on the family's political dynasty.

Eric Cantor was elected as a Republican representative from Virginia in 2000. He has served as a vital fundraiser for the Republican National Committee and a bitter critic of Democrats in Congress. As minority whip, Cantor successfully kept all Republicans in the House from supporting the stimulus bill in 2008. Cantor recruited new and up-and-coming conservatives and introduced a rigid structure to the Republican Party, insisting that members aggressively raise money. He also encouraged "guerilla tactics" against Democratic congressmen, chasing them down and making them explain their votes and positions. As his party again took over Congress in 2010, Cantor became the primary candidate for majority leader, representing the hard-line partisan stand of the GOP. As of 2010, Cantor was the only Jewish Republican in Congress.

Dick Cheney served as President Bush's vice president and has been viewed as a powerful and principal adviser on foreign-policy decisions following the 11 September 2001 attacks. A prominent politician in the Republican Party for decades, Cheney became an aggressive hawk in U.S. invasions of Afghanistan and Iraq. He was heavily criticized for secret meetings concerning energy policy with oil-company leaders and for allegedly helping his former company, Halliburton, gain privileged access to wartime contracts. In the final years of the Bush presidency, Cheney's more forceful approach was increasingly disregarded in favor of diplomacy, including negotiations with North Korea. Cheney remained a loyal defender of Bush's legacy despite a split when the president decided not to pardon Cheney's chief of staff I. Lewis Libby in the aftermath of the Valerie Plame scandal.

During Al Gore's 2000 presidential bid President **Bill Clinton** was kept at arm's length. Gore even chose Senator Joseph Lieberman of Connecticut, a vocal critic of Clinton's affair with Monica Lewinsky, as his running mate. After Clinton's official political career ended, however, he continued to influence the Democratic Party as an elder statesman, offering endorsements and galvanizing the fund-raising base. During his wife's race for the presidential nomination, Clinton became a divisive figure. Pundits speculated that his legacy may have overpowered her campaign. When Hillary became secretary of state in the Obama administration, Clinton devoted time to traveling in support of charitable organizations and for paid speaking engagements. In 2009, Clinton met with reclusive North Korean leader Kim Jong-il and successfully negotiated the release of two imprisoned American journalists.

Hillary Clinton's political career spans decades, from her important supporting role to husband Bill Clinton's tenure as Arkansas governor and U.S. president to her own historic run for the presidency in 2008. While she fell short of the Democratic nomination, losing to Obama, she served as a U.S. senator from New York and was later appointed secretary of state by the Obama administration. She has been a strong and effective envoy for American interests abroad and a tough negotiator.

U.S. congressman **James Clyburn** of South Carolina served as the House Majority Whip from 2007 to 2010, only the second African American to hold the position.

Former governor of Vermont **Howard Dean** became a galvanizing figure in the 2004 Democratic presidential primary and effectively mobilized the left wing that disagreed with Bush's policies on Iraq and domestic issues, including gay rights and stem-cell research. Dean used the Internet to bring new and young voters into politics and provided a blueprint for grassroots organizers. Although he failed to win the nomination, he headed the Democratic National Committee, instituting a broad fifty-state strategy that reached out to traditionally Republican-leaning states and is credited with electing a Democratic Congress in 2006 and energizing the party base for the 2008 presidential election.

John Edwards, single-term senator from North Carolina and vice-presidential candidate on Senator John Kerry's Democratic ticket in 2004 against Republican president George W. Bush, was a pragmatic choice, offering a youthful and moderate perspective and proving formidable in debates against Dick Cheney. In 2008 Edwards

ran for the Democratic presidential nomination. Although a strong candidate, he was quickly overshadowed by establishment candidate Hillary Clinton and progressive Barack Obama. Edwards lost momentum amid rumors that he had fathered a child in an extramarital affair with a media consultant named Rielle Hunter. In March 2009 he confessed to being the father of Hunter's child.

Rudolph W. Giuliani worked as a prosecutor and Justice Department official, and served as New York City mayor for eight years before becoming a national figure in the aftermath of the 11 September terrorist attacks. When the World Trade Center towers fell, Giuliani led the city through the tragic loss, exhaustive search for survivors, and divisive compensation process for first responders' and victims' families. He turned the ensuing celebrity in 2008 into a run for the Republican presidential nomination, campaigning on strong national security and fiscal conservatism. However, he remained liberal on many social issues, including gay rights and abortion, though later reversals on these positions failed to convince conservative Republicans, and he lost the primary to Senator John McCain.

Alberto R. Gonzales served as Bush's attorney general for two and a half years before resigning in 2007 amid scandals over his part in a National Security Agency wiretapping program and the firing of nine U.S. attorneys. Gonzales began working for Texas governor Bush as general counsel and became chief White House counsel in 2001. Gonzales promoted Bush administration programs and defended the interests of the White House. Gonzales's independence was questioned when evidence surfaced that the firings were politically motivated and originated in the White House. Gonzales was also accused of coercing his predecessor John Ashcroft into approving a surveillance program that had been rejected by the Justice Department.

Albert Arnold Gore Jr. ran for president as the Democratic nominee in 2000, after serving as President Clinton's vice president for eight years. The race revealed deep political divisions in the United States. The disputed election resulted in a politically charged recount of votes in Florida. Gore lost his bid for president after the *Bush v. Gore* decision gave Bush an electoral college victory, even though Gore had clearly won the popular vote. Gore became an elder statesman of the Democratic Party, providing influential commentary and support, and was an outspoken environmental activist on global warming and climate-change issues, producing and narrating the Academy Award–winning documentary *An Inconvenient Truth* (2006). In 2007 he was cowinner, with the Intergovernmental Panel on Climate Change, of the Nobel Peace Prize.

Mike Huckabee channeled a Southern folksiness that made him a popular choice for the Republican presidential nominee in 2008. A self-proclaimed political outsider, Huckabee served two terms as governor of Arkansas and was able to work with both Democrats and Republicans in the state legislature. Huckabee invoked his commitment to bipartisan leadership, along with his conservative Christian evangelism, and proved a popular candidate in the South. After losing the nomination to McCain, Huckabee became a commentator and talk-show host for the conservative FoxNews Network.

Bobby Jindal made history in 2007 when he won Louisiana's gubernatorial election, becoming the first Indian American governor. Jindal represents an emerging group of powerful, youthful, reform-oriented, and fiscally conservative Republicans. In his race against incumbent governor Kathleen Blanco, Jindal benefited from her mishandling of the aftermath of Hurricane Katrina and the general dissatisfaction with economic woes and racial inequalities. Jindal took advantage of the mood for change, along with record-high oil prices, to enact economic reforms, which made him popular in the national Republican Party. But, even after the country plunged into a recession and oil prices crashed, Jindal remained a committed fiscal conservative, refusing some funds from the federal stimulus package, and was chosen by fellow Republicans to deliver the televised rebuke to Obama's policy speech.

Senator **John Kerry** of Massachusetts was the 2004 Democratic presidential nominee in a bruising race against incumbent George W. Bush. He lost his bid but remained a powerful force on the Foreign Relations Committee and lobbied to become secretary of state in Obama's administration, though the post went to Hillary Clinton. As a Vietnam veteran, Kerry became an outspoken antiwar activist and served as an authority on foreign policy. Obama gave Kerry influential diplomatic duties in Afghanistan in negotiating with President Hamid Karzai.

I. Lewis "Scooter" Libby Jr. served as Vice President Cheney's chief of staff. In 2007 Libby was convicted of obstruction of justice, perjury, and lying to investigators in a federal investigation dealing with the leak of Valerie Plame's employment with the CIA.

Joe Lieberman became a national figure when, as a senator from Connecticut, he was the lone Democrat to criticize President Clinton during the Lewinsky scandal. In 2000, Al Gore tapped Lieberman to be his running mate, the first Jewish vice-presidential candidate. Considered a moderate Democrat who rarely toed party lines, Lieberman pursued a failed bid for the Democratic presidential nomination in 2004. Following his loss, Lieberman increasingly upset fellow Democrats with his persistent support for the Iraq War. Although he lost the primary race for reelection in 2006, he ran under his own party, Connecticut for Lieberman, and easily won the general election. As an independent force in the Senate, Lieberman distanced himself from the

Democratic Party, backing Republican John McCain for president in 2008 and threatening to filibuster, alongside other conservatives, any government-run health-care plan or public option.

Trent Lott was among the first wave of Republicans to be elected to Congress from previously solid Democratic Southern states during Richard Nixon's reelection bid in 1972. As a representative from Mississippi, Lott served as House Minority Whip in 1981. He was elected senator in 1988 and became majority leader when Kansas senator Robert Dole resigned to run for president. A powerful politician, Lott's popularity plummeted after he attended veteran South Carolina senator Strom Thurmond's centennial birthday party, fondly recalling his state's endorsement of Thurmond's 1948 presidential run with the States' Rights Party (Dixiecrats), which included many prominent Southern politicians who briefly abandoned the Democratic Party when President Harry Truman introduced a modest civil-rights platform. Lott worked his way back into Republican favor and became minority whip before suddenly announcing his retirement in 2007.

C. Ray Nagin was mayor of New Orleans when Hurricane Katrina struck the city in 2006. After several days of waiting for help, Nagin made headlines when he appeared on national television, pleading for assistance and condemning federal and state agencies for their lack of preparation. Nagin won another term as mayor, campaigning on his strong advocacy for his "chocolate city," referring to the many African American citizens of New Orleans. However, by 2008, Nagin's municipal career was halted by term limits and general apathy among voters.

Michelle Obama became the first African American First Lady in 2009, when her husband was inaugurated. She served a vital role as Obama's surrogate on such issues as childhood obesity, nutritional standards, federal financing of health clinics, and disaster relief.

Republican representative **Ron Paul** of Texas ran for president in 1988 and became a leading spokesman for libertarians who supported fiscal discipline and small government. In his 2008 primary race for the Republican presidential nomination, Paul proved to be a successful grassroots politician, harnessing the Internet for fund-raising and support. Particularly popular among young conservative voters, Paul's platform included opting out of Social Security, auditing the national gold reserves at Fort Knox, and ending the war in Iraq. Though he lost the nomination, Paul's movement remained strong in conservative politics and represented the base of the insurgent Tea Party movement that helped his son Rand win a Senate seat in Kentucky in 2010.

Journalist **Daniel Pearl** traveled to Pakistan in 2002 to investigate Richard Reid, the would-be terrorist who attempted to ignite a bomb in his shoe while aboard a plane in a Chicago airport. Pearl was abducted in Karachi, Pakistan; held six days; and then murdered, the event caught on videotape. It is believed that radical Muslims who held him were enraged by news during his captivity that included stories about Palestinian homes being razed by Israelis, images of Guantanamo Bay detainees, and a report revealing that Pearl was Jewish.

Nancy Pelosi was first elected as a Democratic representative from California in 1987. She became minority whip in 2001 and minority leader in 2002. Each time, she was the first woman to assume these leadership roles in Congress. When Democrats took control of Congress in 2006, she became the first female majority leader. Under her leadership, Democrats made historic gains in the House in 2008, and Pelosi enjoyed the cooperation of a Democratic White House. She bore the brunt of the conservative backlash to health-care reform, federal stimulus package, and bank- and auto-industry bailouts (which Republicans called wasteful and irresponsible spending).

Colin L. Powell achieved remarkable popularity as the first African American to serve as national security adviser, chairman of the Joint Chiefs of Staff, and secretary of state, the latter under President Bush. Born in Harlem to Jamaican immigrants and raised in South Bronx, Powell seemed to embody the American dream. His supporters encouraged him to run for president after a long tenure in the 1990s as a pragmatic and compassionate military and political adviser. However, he felt his tenure as secretary of state tarnished his record. Evidence that he presented to the United Nations in support for the war against Iraq in 2003 was disputed and later discredited. An independent, though officially Republican, politician throughout most of his career, Powell endorsed Democratic presidential nominee Obama in 2008.

Erik Prince, former Navy Seal and heir to a Michigan auto-parts fortune, was the head of Blackwater Worldwide. A private security contractor, Blackwater was founded in 1997 and expanded quickly, gaining contracts through the State Department, CIA, and Defense Department. Prince's company became a well-known brand during the Iraq War, largely due to Blackwater's reputation of working outside the boundaries of U.S. military rules. In late 2007, Blackwater guards opened fire with machine guns in Nisoor Square in Baghdad, killing seventeen Iraqi civilians. An investigation by the State Department ended its contract, and the Justice Department launched its own investigation into allegations that Blackwater bribed Iraqi officials. Prince left Iraq amid mounting criminal and congressional investigations, and changed the name of his company to Xe Services.

Nevada senator **Harry Reid** represents the more-conservative wing of the Democratic Party. A powerful majority leader, the first Mormon in the position, Reid enjoyed a warm relationship with Obama. However, he was known for his personal disdain for President Bush and partisanship in the Senate, despite voting against many liberal measures (including gun control, partial-birth abortion, and environmental issues). Along with Pelosi, Reid suffered vehement Republican attacks for his success in pushing for comprehensive health-care reform, among other legislation in cooperation with the Obama White House.

Tom Ridge was governor of Pennsylvania and a moderate Republican when he was tapped by President Bush to head the Office of Homeland Security in 2001. Ridge gained a cabinet-level position when the office became a department. He oversaw one of the largest government reorganizational projects since World War II, coordinating the efforts of various agencies, including the CIA and FBI, in an effort to facilitate smoother and broader communications to protect against terrorism and prepare for national emergencies. He created a color-coded alert system. Although he stepped down in 2005, before the federal mishandling of relief efforts following Hurricanes Katrina and Rita in 2006, the preparedness and efficiency of his system were called into question.

John Roberts was originally nominated to replace Sandra Day O'Connor as an associate Supreme Court justice, but when Chief Justice William Rehnquist announced his resignation in 2006, President Bush tapped Roberts to replace him. In his confirmation hearing, Roberts claimed his judicial approach focused on modesty and precedent. Roberts has led the court to the Right, limiting the reach of the federal government and siding with conservatives on social issues.

Mitt Romney was elected as governor of Massachusetts in 2002. A Republican in a liberal state, he campaigned on his skill as a corporate problem solver and on his family values as a devout Mormon, but he took moderate stances on important social issues, supporting gay rights (though he was a vocal opponent of gay marriage) and abortion. As governor, he implemented a state mandatory health-care law. When he ran for president in the Republican primary, Romney disavowed his earlier stance on abortion rights but was unable to overcome conservative voters' skepticism about his views and his Mormon background.

Karl Rove was a trusted adviser of the Bush family and worked closely with George W. throughout his political career. Rove was instrumental in shaping Bush's political strategy, focusing on discipline, pointed attacks, and expansion of the conservative base. Coordinating a coalition of wealthy donors, influential corporate collaborators, and energized social conservatives, Rove consolidated a broad and dedicated force of supporters. He was bitterly criticized by Democrats, who claimed he manipulated voters with isolated sound bites and, at times, outright lies. His behind-the-scenes maneuvers ran afoul of some Republicans when Rove fell short in his plans to overhaul Social Security and immigration reform. Rove left the White House in 2007 and served as an analyst for Fox News Channel and columnist for the *Wall Street Journal*. He was a critic of Tea Party activists, a vocal and growing force within the Republican Party.

Donald H. Rumsfeld served as President Bush's secretary of defense and was considered the most powerful secretary since Robert S. McNamara. He is credited with returning civilian control to the Pentagon and transforming military culture, particularly after the September 11 terrorist attacks, when he managed the war on terror. Rumsfeld was a longtime political insider and architect of the entrenched war in Iraq, which was labeled an unwinnable "quagmire" by his opponents. As public opinion turned against the war and Rumsfeld seemed unwilling to authorize new tactics, Bush asked him to step down in 2006. Rumsfeld refused to admit any wrong course of action and insisted that he was a scapegoat for critics against the war.

Arnold Schwarzenegger was elected governor of California in 2003 in a recall election against incumbent Gray Davis. As a popular actor, former bodybuilder (Mr. Universe, 1967–1970; Mr. Olympia, 1970–1975, 1980), and newly minted Republican politician, Schwarzenegger promised fiscal reform as his state faced unprecedented deficits. He struggled to balance the budget because of its expansive and unionized bureaucracy and instituted unpopular cuts to the university system, prisons, and public schools. Schwarzenegger faced student protests and vitriolic rhetoric from the political Left.

Sonia Sotomayor is the first Hispanic Supreme Court justice, nominated by President Obama, his first appointment, to replace Justice David H. Souter. While some Republicans claimed she was a liberal activist judge, she was generally considered a mainstream jurist with liberal leanings on her decisions determining employment dis-crimination and free speech. She was sworn in by Chief Justice John Roberts on 8 August 2009.

First elected in 1980, Republican senator **Arlen Specter** of Pennsylvania lost his bid for a sixth term in 2010. After he voted for a federal stimulus package, Specter lost Republican support and switched to the Democratic Party in 2009. Specter split the Bush administration when he championed stem-cell research, called for an investigation of prisoner treatment at Guantanamo Bay, and introduced a bill with California Democratic senator Dianne Feinstein to regulate civilian surveillance in the Patriot Act. Although a Democrat, he tried to retain Republican support by opposing President Obama's nominee for the Supreme Court Elena Kagan.

On 22 April 2004 army ranger and former professional football player **Pat Tillman** was killed in Afghanistan. Tillman had enlisted in response to the 9/11 attacks, and his death by friendly fire was initially covered up by the military and revealed only after investigative efforts by his family. Tillman's service was a public and tragic illustration of both American patriotism, rejuvenated by 9/11, and growing public criticism of the wars in Iraq and Afghanistan.

John Yoo served as assistant attorney general in the Justice Department under President Bush in 2002. While not a major White House appointment, Yoo's focus on executive power over international law became a touchstone for the administration's foreign policy. Yoo authorized torture of enemy combatants in Bush's war against terrorism, claiming the Geneva Convention did not apply. He backed a secret program of surveillance, eavesdropping without federal warrants on communications between Americans and foreigners. After leaving the Justice Department in 2003, an internal investigation admonished Yoo for lack of judgment in authorizing the use of harsh interrogation techniques.

DEATHS

Victoria Gray Adams, 79, civil-rights activist, key organizer of the Mississippi Freedom Democratic Party that challenged the all-white Democratic Party, first woman to run for a U.S. senate seat in Mississippi, traveled to 1964 Democratic National Convention to draw attention to the cause of African American voting rights in the South, 12 August 2006.

Carl Bert Albert, 91, representative (D) from Oklahoma (1947–1977), House majority leader (1962–1971), Speaker of the House (1971–1977), nicknamed the "Little Giant from Little Dixie," publicly supported President Lyndon Johnson's civil-rights legislation and the Vietnam War, 4 February 2000.

Stew Albert, 66, political activist, cofounder of the Yippie Party, an antiestablishment, loosely defined organization that protested the Vietnam War, arrested while nominating a pig, Pigasus, for president at the 1968 Democratic National Convention in Chicago, 30 January 2006.

Stephen E. Ambrose, 66, historian and biographer, founder of the National D-Day Museum in New Orleans, 13 October 2002.

Elmer L. Andersen, 95, governor (R) of Minnesota (1961–1963), human-rights advocate, helped establish Voyageurs National Park along the Canadian border, 15 November 2004.

Anne Armstrong, 80, cochair of the Republican National Committee (1971–1973), presidential adviser to Richard Nixon and Gerald R. Ford, U.S. ambassador to the United Kingdom (1976–1977), first woman named to cabinet position, created White House Office of Women's Programs, keynote speaker at 1972 Republican National Convention, chair of Ronald Reagan's 1980 presidential campaign, awarded Presidential Medal of Freedom (1987), 30 July 2008.

Aaron Bank, 101, U.S. Army colonel, served in the Office of Strategic Service, precursor to the CIA, founded U.S. Special Forces (Green Berets) during the Kennedy administration, 1 April 2004.

Lloyd Millard Bentsen Jr., 85, Democratic representative (1948–1955) and senator from Texas (1971–1993), secretary of the treasury in the Clinton administration (1993–1994), moderate who supported abortion rights, Equal Rights Amendment, and civil rights, but also endorsed school prayer and tax cuts; unsuccessful vice presidential candidate alongside Michael Dukakis (D) in 1988, 23 May 2006.

Phillip Berrigan, 79, militant-pacifist activist, former Catholic priest, led anti–Vietnam War protests, broke into draft board buildings and burned draft cards, 6 December 2002.

James L. Bevel, 72, civil-rights activist, close adviser to Martin Luther King Jr., controversial leader of Southern Christian Leadership Conference (SCLC) projects, notably Project C (Birmingham, Alabama, children's campaign, 1964), present when King was assassinated in Memphis, Tennessee, 19 December 2008.

David McClure Brinkley, 82, newscaster and commentator, reported for NBC for nearly four decades, left in 1981 for ABC to anchor "The Week with David Brinkley," received Presidential Medal of Honor (1992), covered presidential elections from Stevenson-Eisenhower (1956) to Clinton-Dole (1996), 11 June 2003.

William F. Buckley Jr., 82, political commentator and writer, conservative pundit who targeted New Deal liberals, gained following during Barry Goldwater (R) presidential race (1964), started *National Review* (1955), denounced the John Birch Society, 27 February 2008.

George Dekle Busbee, 76, governor (D) of Georgia (1975–1983), 16 July 2004.

Carroll Campbell Jr., 65, governor of South Carolina (1987–1995), helped George W. Bush win pivotal 2000 state Republican presidential primary, 7 December 2005.

Mel Carnahan, 66, governor (D) of Missouri (1993–2000), backed tax increases for public education, increased number of prison beds, and expanded health insurance for children, elected posthumously during 2000 Senate campaign against incumbent John Ashcroft (R), 16 October 2000.

Elbert N. Carvel, 94, two-time governor of Delaware (1949–1953, 1961–1965), fought for civil rights, 6 February 2005.

Robert P. Casey, 68, governor (D) of Pennsylvania (1987–1994), outspoken opponent of abortion, supported *Planned Parenthood* v. *Casey*, brought national attention to issue of organ donation, 30 May 2000.

Helen Chenoweth-Hage, 68, representative (R) from Idaho, conservative politician who campaigned for a smaller federal government and states' rights, mocked the Endangered Species Act, and called for the dissolution of the Departments of Education, Energy, Commerce and Housing, left office after serving three terms, in accordance with a conservative pledge for term limits as stated in the Contract with America, 2 October 2006.

Shirley Chisholm, 80, congresswoman (D) from New York (1969–1983), first black woman to serve in Congress and first woman to seek Democratic presidential nomination (1972), with the slogan "Unbought and Unbossed," she became a leading voice in liberal politics in the 1960s and 1970s, 1 January 2005.

George Christian, 75, press secretary for President Lyndon Johnson (1966–1969), served the president while Johnson struggled with his response to riots following Martin Luther King's assassination and the antiwar protests, 27 November 2002.

William Sloane Coffin, 81, activist, Presbyterian minister, advocated for social change and civil rights through civil disobedience, arrested as a Freedom Rider in 1961, campaigned against the Vietnam War, 12 April 2006.

Alan Cranston, 86, senator (D) from California (1969–1992), served as majority or minority whip (1977–1991), during which he worked to end the Vietnam War and control nuclear proliferation, was rebuked by the Senate (1991) for his intervention in federal investigations on behalf of savings-and-loan financier Charles Keating, founded the Global Security Institute (a nonprofit that advocates abolishing nuclear weapons), 31 December 2000.

Walter Cronkite, 92, broadcast journalist and anchorman, known as the most trusted man in America because of decades of nightly news broadcasts on *CBS Evening News,* famously broke into tears while reporting John F. Kennedy's assassination (1963) and deemed the Vietnam War unwinnable (1968), 17 July 2009.

Benjamin O. Davis Jr., 89, U.S. Army general, son of the first black army general, first twentieth-century black cadet to graduate from West Point, among the first black pilots (Tuskegee Airmen) to serve the United States in combat during World War II, 4 July 2002.

Jimmie H. Davis, approximately 101, twice governor (D) of Louisiana (1944–1948 and 1960–1964), sharecropper's son, developed successful singing career, wrote "You Are My Sunshine" (1940), brought drivers' licenses to Louisiana in the 1940s, passed segregation laws in the 1960s but was never considered a demagogue or race baiter, 5 November 2000.

Carmine DeSapio, 95, considered the last political boss of powerful Manhattan Democratic Party organization Tammany Hall, was rumored to have handpicked New York City mayor Robert F. Wagner Jr. and New York governor W. Averill Harriman, 27 July 2004.

Desmond T. Doss, 87, activist, pacifist, served as an unarmed army medic in World War II, became the first conscientious objector to win the Medal of Honor, 23 March 2006.

Lee Sherman Dreyfus, 81, governor (R) of Wisconsin (1979–1983), fiscal conservative and social moderate who signed his state's first civil-rights legislation into law, making housing and employment discrimination against gays and lesbians illegal, 2 January 2008.

Robert F. Drinan, 86, representative (D) from Massachusetts (1971–1981), first Catholic priest to serve as voting member of Congress, first congressman to call for President Nixon's impeachment after Watergate scandal, supported human rights and abortion rights, opposed the Vietnam War and worked to abolish the House Internal Security Commission (previously the House Un-American Activities Committee), was asked to step down by Pope John Paul II (who claimed to be enacting canonical law forbidding priests to hold elective office), 28 January 2007.

Jennifer Dunn, 66, representative (R) from Washington (1993–2005), unsuccessfully challenged Dick Armey for majority leadership position, fiscal and foreign-policy conservative, voted as a moderate on cultural and social issues, 5 September 2007.

Thomas F. Eagleton, 77, senator (D) from Missouri (1968–1987), briefly George McGovern's vice-presidential running mate until press reports revealed he been hospitalized and given shock treatment for depression, led call to stop U.S. bombing in Cambodia, 4 March 2007.

Rowland Evans, 79, television host and conservative columnist who targeted liberal politicians, along with columnist Robert Novak was at forefront of opinion journalism on television, hosted *Evans & Novak* on CNN, coauthored "Inside Report" column, 23 March 2001.

W. Mark Felt, 95, associate director of the FBI, key source ("Deep Throat") to *Washington Post* reporters Bob Woodward and Carl Bernstein, linked President Nixon to a break-in at the Democratic Party National Headquarters in the Watergate Hotel, kept silent about his involvement until 2005, 18 December 2008.

Thomas M. Foglietta, 75, representative (D, I) from Pennsylvania (1981–1997), U.S. ambassador to Italy, known for his human-rights work in South Korea, assaulted by Seoul police in 1985 while traveling with South Korean dissident Kim Dae Jung, 13 November 2004.

Hiram L. Fong, 97, senator (R) from Hawaii (1959–1977), first Asian American senator, amended civil-rights bill to require polling sites to be audited to protect minority-voting rights, cosponsored bill that allowed Asians to the immigrate to the United States in the same numbers as people from other countries, 18 August 2004.

Gerald R. Ford Jr., 93, representative (R) from Michigan (1948–1974), vice president (1973–1974), and thirty-eighth president of the United States (1974–1977), popular minority leader, appointed to Warren Commission by Lyndon Johnson to investigate John F. Kennedy's assassination, named by Nixon to replace Spiro Agnew as vice president, pardoned Nixon, faced rising inflation and unemployment, narrowly won nomination for the presidency in 1976, lost to Jimmy Carter (D), 26 December 2006.

James Forman, 76, civil-rights activist, leader in Student Nonviolent Coordinating Committee (SNCC), participated as Freedom Rider, organized volunteers for a voting-rights campaign during Mississippi Freedom Summer (1964), active in Black Panther Party and International Black Workers Congress, 10 January 2005.

Joe (Joseph Jacob) Foss, 87, governor (R) of South Dakota (1955–1959), awarded the Medal of Honor as a marine fighter pilot during World War II, early commissioner of the American Football League (AFL), headed the National Rifle Association (NRA), 1 January 2003.

John Hope Franklin, 94, historian, African American scholar, worked with Thurgood Marshall as a researcher on *Brown* v. *Board of Education* (1954), reshaped American thought on the history of race relations, 25 March 2009.

Orville L. Freeman, 84, governor (D) of Minnesota (1954–1960), helped found Minnesota Democratic-Farmer-Labor Party, U.S. secretary of agriculture (1961–1969), established food stamps and school-breakfast programs, advocated for farmers, expanded global markets, helped bring water and sewer systems to rural areas, pressured Congress to increase food-safety protections, 20 February 2003.

Betty Friedan, 85, activist, author, wrote *The Feminine Mystique* (1963), leader in women's rights movement of the 1960s, helped found the National Organization of Women (NOW) in 1966 and National Women's Political Caucus in 1971, 4 February 2006.

John Kenneth Galbraith, 97, liberal economist, presidential adviser, diplomat, served in presidential administrations from Franklin D. Roosevelt to Lyndon Johnson, wrote *The Affluent Society* (1958), criticized "irresponsible" spending of American consumers who ignored civic needs and the impoverished, argued that post–World War II consumer culture of overproduction and overextension of credit led to inflation and recession, cautioned

against growing oligarchy in politics, awarded Medal of Freedom (2000) by President Clinton, 29 April 2006.

Paul E. Gillmor, 68, representative (R) from Ohio (1989–2007), considered a moderate, demanded that Attorney General Alberto R. Gonzales be dismissed for firing Department of Justice attorneys for political reasons, died 5 September 2007.

Vance Hartke, 84, senator (D) from Indiana (1959–1977), supported civil-rights and health-care reform (including Civil Rights Act of 1964 and Voting Rights Act of 1965), forceful opponent of the Vietnam War, unsuccessfully sought presidential nomination (1972), 27 July 2003.

Stanley K. Hathaway, 81, governor (R) of Wyoming (1967–1975), U.S. secretary of the interior (1975), implemented environmental laws, reorganized state government, created arts council, addressed Native American welfare issues on reservations, advocated for expansion of federal coal leasing, 4 October 2005.

Bob Hattoy, 56, political aide to President Clinton (1993–1999), national voice for gay rights, spoke about the tragic effects of the AIDS epidemic at 1992 Democratic convention, 4 March 2007.

Augustus F. Hawkins, 100, representative (D) from California (1963–1991), first black representative from California, served in the California Assembly (1934–1962), civil-rights activist, helped found Congressional Black Caucus (1970), 10 November 2007.

Harry Hay, 90, activist, early advocate for gay rights, founded Mattachine Society (1950, a secret organization in Los Angeles that helped spark gay-rights movement), 24 October 2002.

Jesse Helms, 86, senator (R) from North Carolina, leader of Christian Right in Republican politics, gained nickname "Senator No" (for railing against the National Endowment for the Arts, federal funding for AIDS research, gay rights, feminism, civil rights, disability rights, and the liberal bias of the national media in America), supported Ronald Reagan, 4 July 2008.

Don Hewitt, 86, television producer, worked at CBS for more than fifty years, oversaw the first presidential debate between Kennedy and Nixon, pioneered the televised news magazine, created CBS's *60 Minutes* (1968), credited with helping develop celebrity television journalists (such as Walter Cronkite, Dan Rather, and Mike Wallace), 19 August 2009.

Brenda Howard, 58, activist, protested against the Vietnam War and for feminist causes, leader of the Gay Liberation Front, organized first commemoration of the Stonewall Rebellion, considered mother of modern Lesbian Gay Bisexual Transgender (LGBT) rights movement, 28 June 2005.

E. Howard Hunt, CIA agent (1949–1970), organized failed break-in of the Democratic Party National Headquarters at the Watergate Hotel, 23 January 2007.

Henry J. Hyde, 83, representative (R) from Illinois (1975–2007), helped end federal funding for abortions, led impeachment proceedings against President Clinton, supported extension of Voting Rights Act (1981) and ban on assault weapons, but backed aid to Nicaraguan contras and constitutional amendments prohibiting flag-burning and same-sex marriages, 29 November 2007.

Molly Ivins, 62, newspaper columnist, wrote syndicated column featuring wry and pointed attacks against politicians, campaigned against President George W. Bush and against the Iraq War, called for Bush's impeachment, 31 January 2007.

Peter Jennings, 67, ABC *World News Tonight* anchor, served as foreign correspondent, established Middle East bureau in Beirut, Lebanon (first American news bureau in Arab world), known for marathon coverage of events, followed September 11, 2001 attacks as anchor for seventeen hours, 7 August 2005.

Stephanie Tubbs Jones, 58, representative (D) from Ohio (1999–2008), liberal, first African American representative from Ohio, cosponsored health-care legislation for lower- and middle-class people and rehabilitation programs for convicts, wrote legislation requiring certification for mortgage brokers and stricter penalties for predatory lenders, opposed Iraq War, along with California senator Barbara Boxer protested Ohio's twenty electoral votes going to George W. Bush (2004), 20 August 2008.

Jack Kemp, 73, representative (R) from New York (1971–1989), U.S. secretary of housing and development (1989–1993), ran for vice president alongside Senator Bob Dole (1996), former all-star quarterback for the Buffalo Bills, fervent fiscal conservative who shaped modern Republican economic philosophy, 2 May 2009.

George F. Kennan, 101, diplomat, had powerful influence on Cold War policy, U.S. envoy to the Soviet Union, architect of post–World War II policy of containment (political and economic policies to contain communism in Europe), 17 March 2005.

Edward Kennedy, 77, senator (D) from Massachusetts (1962–2009), lost two brothers to political assassinations, was critically injured in a plane crash, became center of a scandal when he emerged from a car crash (while his female companion died) in which his wealth and influence were rumored to allow him to escape prosecution, ran unsuccessfully for presidential nomination (1980), dedicated reformer and champion of liberal issues (Voting Rights Act, Fair Housing Law, and Americans with Disabilities Act), helped create the Occupational Safety and Health Administration (OSHA), worked to direct federal funds (community centers, cancer research, Meals on Wheels programs, and nutritional programs for pregnant women and infants), supported Senator John McCain's immigration bill and President George W. Bush's education reform (No Child Left Behind), advocated for federal health care, 25 August 2009.

Coretta Scott King, 78, civil-rights activist, widow of Martin Luther King Jr., supported nonviolent protest for social justice and equal rights, 30 January 2006.

Edward J. King, 81, governor (D) of Massachusetts (1979–1983), conservative Roman Catholic politician who beat future presidential nominee Michael Dukakis in 1978 Democratic gubernatorial primary, but lost to Dukakis in 1982, switched to the Republican Party in 1986, 18 September 2006.

Richard G. Kleindienst, 76, U.S. Attorney General (1972–1983), served in Arizona state legislature, epitomized President Nixon's campaign promise of "law and order," authorized wiretapping in organized crime and national-security cases, supported the mass arrests of Vietnam protesters, supported civil rights, advocated for black lawyers in the Justice Department, 3 February 2000.

John V. Lindsay, 79, representative (R) from New York (1959–1965), mayor of New York City (1966–1973), celebrity politician who managed New York City during racial and civil unrest, unsuccessful candidate for 1972 Democratic presidential nomination, 19 December 2000.

Russell B. Long, 84, senator (D) from Louisiana (1948–1987), son of famous Louisiana politician Huey P. Long, continued his father's populist legacy, expanded Social Security and reshaped income-tax laws, served as whip during President Johnson's administration, 9 May 2003.

Lester Maddox, 87, governor (D) of Georgia (1967–1971), segregationist who exploited his celebrity as an intolerant Atlanta restaurant owner who refused to serve black patrons, 25 June 2003.

Woodrow Mann, 85, mayor of Little Rock, Arkansas, reformer, instituted integrated bus system, overturning Jim Crow laws, disagreed with Supreme Court's decision to desegregate schools in *Brown* v. *Board of Education* (1954), asked for National Guard troops from Arkansas governor Orval Faubus to prevent mob disruption of integration of Little Rock Central High School (1957), helped force President Dwight Eisenhower to intervene (setting a precedent for federal intervention in the civil-rights movement), 6 August 2002.

Mike J. Mansfield, 98, Democratic representative (1943–1953) and senator from Montana (1953–1977), longest-serving Senate majority leader (1961–1977), powerbroker during Johnson administration, shepherded legislation (civil rights, health care, antipoverty, and education), 5 October 2001.

Robert Bruce "Bob" Mathias, 75, representative (R) from California (1967–1975), decathlete, won two Olympic gold medals, officer in the U.S. Marines, 2 September 2006.

Robert Takeo Matsui, 63, representative (D) from California (1993–2005), instrumental in passing the Japanese-American Redress Act (1988), which included an official apology from the federal government for the internment of Japanese immigrants and Japanese Americans during World War II, obtained national historic landmark status for Manzanar internment camp, 1 January 2005.

Nicholas Mavroules, 74, representative (D) from Massachusetts (1979–1993), chairman of the House committee of investigations (navy spending, 1983 bombing of marine barracks in Beirut, 1989 battleship USS *Iowa* explosion), opposed nuclear proliferation and President Reagan's missile-defense shield program, was voted out of office amid a corruption scandal, served time in prison on charges relating to bribery and racketeering, 25 December 2003.

Eugene J. McCarthy, 89, Democratic representative (1949–1959) and senator from Minnesota (1959–1971), insurgent antiwar candidate for Democratic presidential nomination whose campaign led to President Johnson's decision not to run for reelection, became popular choice for young Americans (disillusioned by politics, against the Vietnam War, and shocked by the assassinations of Robert Kennedy and Martin Luther King Jr. in 1968), defeated by Hubert Humphrey, remained an outsider railing against established party politics, 10 December 2005.

Mary McGrory, 85, liberal journalist and columnist, covered American politics for more than fifty years, awarded Pulitzer Prize for commentary (1975), 20 April 2004.

Sid McMath, 91, governor (D) of Arkansas (1949–1953), opposed Southern politicians who left the Democratic Party in 1948 when President Harry Truman introduced a modest civil-rights platform, oversaw many programs (building of the University of Arkansas's medical school, bank regulation, voting- and civil-rights reform, expansion of highway system), 4 October 2004.

Robert S. McNamara, 93, U.S. secretary of defense (1961–1968), expanded role of defense secretary, engaged foreign diplomacy and troop deployment for domestic civil-rights crises, "architect" of the Vietnam War, policies featured in Oscar-winning documentary *The Fog of War* (2004), 6 July 2009.

Warren J. Mitofsky, 71, pollster, innovator of the random-digit dialing system of polling, devised exit polling (1967), 1 September 2006.

Joe Moakley, 74, representative (D) from Massachusetts (1973–2001), proud South Boston Irish Democrat, instrumental in Boston Harbor cleanup and construction of a Boston highway tunnel (one of the largest public works projects in U.S. history), 28 May 2001.

Frank Moss, 91, senator (D) from Utah (1959–1977), liberal reformer, opponent of Vietnam War, advocated ban on cigarette advertising on radio and television, sponsored early Medicaid legislation, supporter of conservation, helped establish national parks and recreation areas, 29 January 2003.

Daniel Patrick Moynihan, 76, senator (D) from New York (1977–2001), presidential adviser to four administrations from John F. Kennedy to Gerald Ford, advocated innovative and controversial approaches to mass transportation, urban blight, and effects of racism, remembered for Labor Department research commonly referred to as the *Moynihan Report* (in which he argued that the legacy of slavery made African Americans dependent on the government), claimed his research advocated affirmative action in overcoming the effects of slavery and discrimination, 26 March 2003.

Gaylord Nelson, 89, Democratic governor (1959–1963) and senator (1963–1981) from Wisconsin, founded Earth Day and helped launch the modern environmental movement, 3 July 2005.

Charlie (Charles W.) Norwood Jr., 65, representative (R) from Georgia (1995–2007), advocated for gun rights and a "patient's bill of rights" (allowing consumers easier access to health care and more information in order to take legal action), 13 February 2007.

Robert Novak, 78, political columnist and cable-news commentator, coauthor, with Rowland Evans, of popular syndicated column, "Inside Report," drawn into center of political scandal that resulted in conviction of Vice President Cheney's chief of staff I. Lewis Libby for publishing name of CIA operative Valerie Plame, 18 August 2009.

Frank L. O'Bannon, 73, governor (D) of Indiana (1997–2003), conservative who supported the death penalty and lobbied for stone tablets emblazoned with the Ten Commandments to be placed on the state capitol grounds (blocked by Supreme Court decision), 13 September 2003.

Rosa Parks, 92, civil-rights activist, longtime NAACP activist, pioneered direct-action civil-rights protests in the South, triggered Montgomery Bus Boycott (1956) by refusing to give up her seat to a white passenger, 24 October 2005.

Claiborne Pell, 90, senator (D) from Rhode Island (1961–1997), sponsored federal funding for financially needy college students in the push for Basic Educational Opportunity Grants (Pell Grants), authored National Foundation for the Arts and the Humanities Act (1965, later known as National Endowment for the Arts), opposed the Vietnam War, challenged President Reagan's backing of anti-Sandinista guerillas in Nicaragua, 1 January 2009.

Jody Powell, 65, press secretary for President Jimmy Carter (1981), close friend and trusted aide to Carter, 14 September 2009.

William A. Price, 94, reporter for *New York Daily News* who refused to answer questions before a Senate panel about alleged Communist ties (invoked First Amendment protection for the freedom of the press instead of the Fifth which protects defendants from self-incrimination), was found in contempt of court, phone wiretapping (1972) by FBI agents (who thought he was in contact with radical 1960s protest group the Weather Underground) led to successful lawsuit against the agency (1981), 29 April 2009.

William Proxmire, 90, senator (D) from Wisconsin (1957–1989), maverick politician, first elected to fill remainder of Joseph McCarthy's term, announced monthly winners of Golden Fleece Awards (to draw attention to irresponsible government spending), 15 December 2005.

Ronald Reagan, 93, Republican governor of California (1967–1975), fortieth president of the United States (1981–1989), began political career as anticommunist activist and social conservative, ushered in era of optimism and confidence in the Republican Party (with an easy and persuasive demeanor and a political coalition that included Christian fundamentalists, national-security hawks, fiscal conservatives, and Democrats wary of the expansive social programs), enjoyed widespread popularity and led the United States through the end of the Cold War (with the collapse of the Soviet Union and destruction of the Berlin Wall), reputation was tarnished by the Iran-Contra scandal, 5 June 2004.

James A. Rhodes, 91, governor (R) of Ohio (1963–1971 and 1975–1983), popular for bringing federal funds for highways and vocational education, called in the National Guard (1969) to manage anti–Vietnam War protests at Kent State University that resulted in guardsmen opening fire and killing four students, 4 March 2001.

Ann Richards, 73, governor (D) of Texas (1991–1995), outspoken and popular supporter of civil rights (for gay men and lesbians, minorities, and women), lost bid for a second term to future president George W. Bush, 13 September 2006.

Peter W. Rodino, 95, representative (D) from New Jersey (1949–1989), advocate for immigration reform and civil rights, fair but firm chairman of President Nixon's impeachment proceedings, 7 May 2005.

William P. Rogers, 87, U.S. attorney general (1957–1961), secretary of state (1969–1973), served on two UN panels that studied global prison conditions (1955) and problems in Africa (1967), personal and foreign-policy adviser to President Nixon, 2 January 2001.

Michael Rossman, 68, activist, author, organizer of the Free Speech Movement on the University of California's Berkeley campus (1964) to protest for political and social causes, 12 May 2008.

Walt Whitman Rostow, 86, economic historian, National Security Advisor to President Lyndon Johnson (1966–1969), White House and State Department aide during Kennedy administration, defender of the Vietnam War, 13 February 2003.

William V. Roth Jr., 82, senator (R) from Delaware (1971–2001), legislated steep tax cuts during President Reagan's administration and introduced tax-sheltered retirement accounts (Roth I.R.As), 13 December 2003.

Tim Russert, 58, television journalist and moderator of *Meet the Press,* former anchor of NBC *Nightly News,* served as Washington bureau chief and senior vice president of NBC News, during 2000 presidential election provided lasting image of recount controversy when he noted "Florida, Florida, Florida" and popularized the terms "red state" and "blue state," 13 June 2008.

William Safire, 79, speechwriter for President Richard Nixon, political columnist, won 1978 Pulitzer Prize for commentary for *The New York Times,* received Presidential Medal of Freedom (2006), 27 September 2009.

George Edward Sangmeister, 76, representative (D) from Illinois (1989–1995), 7 October 2007.

Richard M. Scammon, 85, political scientist and director of the Census Bureau, founded nonprofit Elections Research Center, influenced political polling and census data for politicians and journalists, 27 April 2001.

Arthur M. Schlesinger Jr., 89, historian, biographer, liberal, argued that powerful presidents had a dramatic impact on American history, campaigned for both President Kennedy and presidential candidate Senator Robert Kennedy, 28 February 2007.

Robert Walter Scott, 79, governor (D) of North Carolina (1969–1973), served during violent campus protest at the predominately black North Carolina Agricultural & Technical State University, credited for historical preservation efforts with the state archives, 23 January 2009.

Harry L. Sears, 82, senator (R) in the New Jersey legislature (1967–1971), delivered briefcase containing $200,000 from client financier Robert Vesco to Richard Nixon's reelection campaign (1972), indicted on charges of helping Vesco to evade a Securities and Exchange Commission investigation, 17 May 2002.

Raymond P. Shafer, 89, governor (R) of Pennsylvania (1967–1971), headed President Nixon's National Commission on Marijuana and Drug Use (Shafer Commission) which recommended that marijuana remain illegal but decriminalized for personal use (which stunned Nixon who denounced the findings), 12 December 2006.

Eunice Kennedy Shriver, 88, sister of John F. Kennedy, Robert Kennedy, and Edward Kennedy, close relationship with developmentally challenged sister Rosemary drove her political activism, instrumental in the development of the National Institute of Child Health and Human Development, helped create network of mental retardation research centers and two medical ethics centers, founded Special Olympics (1968), 11 August 2009.

Paul Simon, 75, Democratic representative (1975–1983) and senator (1985–1977) from Illinois, committed liberal who provided conservative leadership by facilitating bipartisan support for controversial legislation, including the North American Free Trade Agreement and a balanced budget amendment, 9 December 2003.

George Smathers, 93, senator (D) from Florida (1951–1969), influenced John F. Kennedy and Lyndon Johnson, accused political foes of being communist sympathizers at the height of the Cold War (particularly political foe Democratic congressman Claude Pepper), early critic of Cuban leader Fidel Castro, 20 January 2007.

Howard K. Smith, 87, broadcast journalist, member of Edward R. Murrow's radio broadcast team during World War II and the Nuremburg trials, reported for CBS and ABC (civil-rights movement, Vietnam War, Watergate scandal), often battled executives and producers to cover events with his own commentary, condemned racism and corruption, 15 February 2002.

Preston E. Smith, 91, governor (D) of Texas (1969–1973), advocated first comprehensive drug-abuse program in Texas and first minimum wage law, longtime supporter and fund-raiser for Texas Tech, 18 October 2003.

Harold E. Stassen, 93, governor (R) of Minnesota (1939–1943), unsuccessful candidate to gain nomination for president nine times, most notably against Thomas Dewey (1948) and against Dwight Eisenhower (1952), served as president of the University of Pennsylvania (1948–1953), 4 March 2001.

Gerry Studds, 69, representative (D) from Massachusetts (1973–1997), first openly gay member of Congress, supported New England fishermen, gay rights, and AIDS research and treatment, 14 October 2006.

Bob Stump, 76, representative (R) from Arizona (1977–2003), advocated for increased health benefits and expanded college assistance for veterans as chairman of committees on Armed Services and Veterans Affairs, 20 June 2003.

Percy E. Sutton, 89, lawyer and politician, civil-rights activist who was arrested as a Freedom Rider in Mississippi and Alabama (1961) and at a rally supporting Malcolm X, longest-serving Manhattan borough president (1966–1977), member of influential group of black New York City politicians (Gang of Four), 26 December 2009.

Herman Talmadge, 88, Democratic governor (1948–1955) and senator (1957–1981) from Georgia, denounced school desegregation but legislated equal pay for African American teachers, advocated for the poor, expanded school lunch and food-stamp programs, built roads and schools, promoted jobs and infrastructure projects in rural areas, lost his fifth Senate run in 1980 (after a bitter divorce, public battle with alcoholism, and ethics investigation regarding official finances), 21 March 2002.

Craig Thomas, 74, Republican representative (1989–1995) and senator (1995–2007) from Wyoming, took Dick Cheney's seat, conservative, supported small businesses and tax cuts, opposed abortion and environmental legislation, 4 June 2007.

James Strom Thurmond, 100, Democratic governor (1947–1951), Democratic senator (1953–1962), and Republican senator (1963–2003) from South Carolina, formed the States' Rights Party (southern Democrats called Dixiecrats who opposed integration), ran as States' Rights candidate for president (1948), led exodus of southern Democrats to the Republican Party when he switched parties to support Barry Goldwater (1964), sparked massive realignment in postwar politics, vocal opponent of civil-rights movement and rallied white southerners to support Richard Nixon's candidacies for president (1968 and 1972), had a biracial daughter with his family's former maid who was never publicly acknowledged until after his death, 26 June 2003.

James Tobin, 84, economist, presidential adviser, advocated Keynesian economics during Kennedy's administration, encouraged government intervention in the economy, received Nobel Prize in economics (1981), 11 March 2002.

Robin Toner, 54, journalist, first woman to work as a national political correspondent for *The New York Times*, 12 December 2008.

Cecil H. Underwood, 86, governor (R) from West Virginia (1957–1961 and 1997–2001), youngest governor in state history at age of 34 and oldest at 74, 24 November 2008.

Charles Vanik, 94, representative (D) from Ohio (1955–1981), liberal politician from Cleveland, who advocated for the immigration of Jews to the United States and successfully passed the Jackson-Vanik amendment to the Trade Act of 1974 that penalized the Soviet Union for not allowing Jewish emigration, 30 August 2007.

Richard Wade, 87, urban historian, political strategist, pioneer of urban studies, challenged Frederick Jackson Turner's thesis of westward expansion, adviser for Democratic presidential candidates (Adlai Stevenson, Robert Kennedy, and George McGovern), 18 July 2008.

Caspar W. Weinberger, 88, secretary of defense (1981–1987) and secretary of health, education, and welfare (1973–1975), supported nuclear-arms proliferation and a military buildup as a Cold War defense against the Soviet Union, key sponsor for the Strategic Defense Initiative (better known as Star Wars), indicted for felony perjury and obstruction of justice for his testimony during the Iran-Contra hearings (an investigation into the covert selling of arms to Iran in order to fund Nicaraguan guerilla fighters), 28 March 2006.

William C. Westmoreland, 91, U.S. Army general, Army Chief of Staff (1968–1972), commanded U.S. troops in Vietnam (1964–1968), oversaw a dramatic increase of troops from 16,000 to 500,000, criticized President Johnson's decision to replace him as political and not tactical, faced antiwar protesters and bitter criticism when he spoke at college campuses, led Vietnam veter-ans in a march to their war memorial in Washington, D.C. (1982), 18 July 2005.

Harriett Woods, 79, activist, lieutenant governor (D) of Missouri (1985–1989), president of National Women's Caucus (1991–1995), first woman elected to statewide office and lieutenant governor of Missouri, ran several failed attempts to win congressional seat, national leader for women seeking political office, founded Emily's List (a political-action group that supported Democratic women candidates), 8 February 2007.

Rose Mary Woods, 87, secretary of President Richard M. Nixon, accidentally erased a Watergate tape from 20 June 1972 that could have determined if Nixon knew about break-in at the Democrat headquarters, 22 January 2005.

PUBLICATIONS

Ari Berman, *Herding Donkeys: The Fight to Rebuild the Democratic Party and Reshape American Politics* (New York: Farrar, Straus & Giroux, 2010);

Carl Bernstein, *A Woman in Charge: The Life of Hillary Rodham Clinton* (New York: Knopf, 2007);

Douglas Brinkley, *The Great Deluge: Hurricane Katrina, New Orleans, and the Mississippi Gulf Coast* (New York: Morrow, 2006);

George W. Bush, *Decision Points* (New York: Crown, 2010);

Richard Clarke, *Against All Enemies: Inside America's War on Terror* (New York: Free Press, 2004);

Steve Coll, *Ghost Wars: The Secret History of the CIA, Afghanistan, and bin Laden, from the Soviet Invasion to September 10, 2001* (New York: Penguin, 2004);

Howard Dean and Judith Warner, *You Have the Power: How to Take Back Our Country and Restore Democracy in America* (New York: Simon & Schuster, 2004);

Robert Draper, *Dead Certain: The Presidency of George W. Bush* (New York: Free Press, 2007);

Dexter Filkins, *The Forever War.* (New York: Knopf, 2008);

Thomas Frank, *What's the Matter with Kansas?: How Conservatives Won the Heart of America* (New York: Metropolitan, 2004);

John Heilemann and Mark Halperin, *Game Change: Obama and the Clintons, McCain and Palin, and the Race of a Lifetime* (New York: Harper Perennial, 2010);

Jed Horne, *Breach of Faith: Hurricane Katrina and the Near Death of a Great American City* (New York: Random House, 2006);

Seth G. Jones, *In the Graveyard of Empires: America's War in Afghanistan* (New York: Norton, 2009);

Jill Lepore, *The Whites of Their Eyes: The Tea Party's Revolution and the Battle over American History* (Princeton, N.J.: Princeton University Press, 2010);

Michael Lewis, *The Big Short: Inside the Doomsday Machine* (New York: Norton, 2010);

Jane Mayer, *The Dark Side: The Inside Story of How the War on Terror Turned into a War on American Ideals* (New York: Doubleday, 2008);

Bethany McLean and Peter Elkind, *The Smartest Guys in the Room: The Amazing Rise and Scandalous Fall of Enron* (New York: Portfolio, 2003);

National Commission on Terrorist Attacks upon the United States, *The 9/11 Commission Report: Final Report of the National Commission on Terrorist Attacks upon the United States* (New York: Norton, 2004);

Barack Obama, *The Audacity of Hope: Thoughts on Reclaiming the American Dream* (New York: Crown, 2006);

George Packer, *The Assassins' Gate: America in Iraq* (New York: Farrar, Straus & Giroux, 2006);

Sarah Palin, *Going Rogue: An American Life* (New York: HarperCollins, 2009);

David Remnick, *The Bridge: The Life and Rise of Barack Obama* (New York: Knopf, 2010);

Thomas E. Ricks, *Fiasco: The American Military Adventure in Iraq* (New York: Penguin, 2006);

Karl Rove, *Courage and Consequence: My Life as a Conservative in the Fight* (New York: Simon & Schuster, 2010);

Larry J. Sabato, ed., *Divided States of America: The Slash and Burn Politics of the 2004 Presidential Election* (New York: Pearson-Longman, 2006);

Jeremy Scahill, *Blackwater: The Rise of the World's Most Powerful Mercenary Army* (New York: Nation, 2007);

Andrew Ross Sorkin, *Too Big to Fail: The Inside Story of How Wall Street and Washington Fought to Save the Financial System—and Themselves* (New York: Viking, 2009);

Andrew Sullivan, *The Conservative Soul: How We Lost It, How to Get it Back* (New York: HarperCollins, 2006);

Jeffrey Toobin, *Too Close to Call: The Thirty-Six-Day Battle to Decide the 2000 Election* (New York: Random House, 2002);

Rebecca Traister, *Big Girls Don't Cry: The Election that Changed Everything for American Women* (New York: Free Press, 2010);

Bob Woodward, *Bush at War* (New York: Simon & Schuster, 2002).

Barack Obama being sworn in as the forty-fourth president of the United States by Chief Justice of the United States John G. Roberts Jr. in Washington, D.C., 20 January 2009 (Department of Defense photo by Master Sergeant Cecilio Ricardo, U.S. Air Force)

LAW AND JUSTICE

by ERIC BARGERON

CONTENTS

Sidebars and tables are listed in italics.

2000

21 Mar.   In *FDA* v. *Brown & Williamson Tobacco Corp.* the U.S. Supreme Court rules 5-4 that the Food and Drug Administration does not have jurisdiction to regulate tobacco as a drug.

22 Apr.   Federal agents seize six-year-old Cuban refugee Elian González from the home of relatives in Miami.

26 Apr.   Following two rulings earlier in the week, the U.S. Supreme Court tells lower courts to increase opportunities for convicts to appeal their convictions.

7 June   U.S. District Court judge Thomas Penfield Jackson, who on 3 April had found software manufacturer Microsoft in violation of the nation's antitrust laws, orders the firm broken up into separate and competing companies—one for its Windows operating system and one for its other computer programs and Internet businesses.

19 June   Prayers at school-sponsored extracurricular activities are deemed unconstitutional by the U.S. Supreme Court in *Santa Fe School District* v. *Doe*.

28 June   In *Mitchell* v. *Helms* the U.S. Supreme Court rules 6-1 that the Education Consolidation and Improvement Act (1981) allows federal monies to be used to provide computers and other equipment to private schools.

28 June   The U.S. Supreme Court rules in *Boy Scouts of America* v. *Dale* that the Boy Scouts did not discriminate by choosing to "forbid membership to homosexuals."

28 June   Elian González returns to Cuba with his father, Juan Miguel.

1 Oct.   Former president Bill Clinton is suspended from practice before the U.S. Supreme Court because of perjury he committed during the Monica Lewinsky affair; he resigns from the high-court bar in November.

12 Dec.   In the controversial *Bush* v. *Gore* decision the U.S. Supreme Court orders an end to the recount of votes in Florida for the 2000 presidential election, handing the presidency to George W. Bush.

2001

20 Jan.   Bush is inaugurated as the forty-third president of the United States.

2 Feb.   Former U.S. senator John David Ashcroft (R-Missouri) is sworn in as attorney general of the United States.

18 Feb.   Robert Hanssen, a Federal Bureau of Investigation (FBI) agent, is charged with spying for the Soviet Union.

27 Feb.   The U.S. Supreme Court unanimously rules that the Environmental Protection Agency has the power to set air-quality standards.

21 Mar.   In *Ferguson* v. *Charleston* the U.S. Supreme Court rules that involuntary drug testing of women violates the Fourth Amendment protection against unreasonable search and seizure.

14 May   The U.S. Supreme Court rules in *United States* v. *Oakland Cannabis Buyers' Cooperative* that marijuana cannot be legally used for medical purposes.

11 June   The U.S. Supreme Court rules in *Good News Club, Inc.* v. *Milford Central School* that public schools must allow religious groups access to facilities for after-school activities.

11 June   Timothy McVeigh is executed for his role in the 19 April 1995 bombing of the Alfred P. Murrah Federal Building in Oklahoma City.

6 Sept.   The U.S. Department of Justice drops its bid to break up Microsoft.

25 Sept.   Deputy Assistant Attorney General John C. Yoo of the Office of Legal Counsel writes a memo that the White House uses to justify eavesdropping without warrants in the fight against terrorism.

23 Oct.   Yoo and special counsel Robert J. Delahunty write a memo to White House counsel Alberto R. Gonzales defending the use of military forces to fight terrorism domestically.

26 Oct.   The Uniting and Strengthening America by Providing Appropriate Tools Required to Intercept and Obstruct Terrorism (USA PATRIOT) Act is signed into law by President Bush.

13 Nov.   President Bush orders that foreigners suspected of involvement in terrorism against the United States be tried by military tribunals if captured.

30 Nov.   Gary Ridgway, the "Green River Killer," is arrested. He later confesses to the murders of more than forty women.

11 Dec.   Zacarias Moussaoui, a French citizen, is indicted for his alleged role in the September 11 terrorist attacks.

2002

Jan.   The Justice Department begins its investigation of criminal proceedings at the failed energy conglomerate Enron.

8 Jan.   The No Child Left Behind Act, an education-reform law, is signed by President Bush.

12 Mar.   After a highly publicized trial, Andrea Yates of Houston, Texas, is found guilty of three counts of murder in the drownings of her five children. She is later sentenced to life in prison.

16 Apr.   In a 6-3 decision, the U.S. Supreme Court strikes down the Child Pornography Prevention Act (1996) as a violation of the First Amendment.

10 May   Hanssen is sentenced to life in prison after he is found guilty of spying for the Soviet Union.

22 May   Former Klu Klux Klan member Bobby Frank Cherry is convicted of murder for his role in the 1963 16th Street Baptist Church bombing in Birmingham, Alabama, which killed four young girls who were attending Sunday School classes. The bombing was a major catalyst for federal intervention on civil rights.

20 June   The U.S. Supreme Court rules in *Atkins* v. *Virginia* that the execution of mentally handicapped convicts is cruel and unusual punishment.

27 June   In a 5-4 decision the U.S. Supreme Court approves random drug testing of public-school students as a prerequisite for participation in extracurricular interscholastic competitions.

24 Oct.   After thirteen attacks (ten fatal) carried out over a twenty-two-day shooting spree in Washington, D.C., Maryland, and Virginia, the "Beltway Snipers" John Allen Muhammad and Lee Boyd Malvo are arrested.

25 Nov.   The Homeland Security Act is signed into law, creating the cabinet-level Department of Homeland Security.

2003

21 Jan. The U.S. Supreme Court rules that individuals can be charged with conspiracy even if their arrests prevented the conspiracy from being carried out.

5 Mar. The U.S. Supreme Court rules 6-3 that states can continue to post the names and pictures of convicted sex offenders on the Internet.

7 Apr. The U.S. Supreme Court rules that cross burning with the intent of intimidation is not protected by the First Amendment, and that more than simply carrying out the act is needed to prosecute.

31 May Fugitive Eric Robert Rudolph, a suspect in the 1996 Centennial Olympic Park bombing in Atlanta, Georgia, is arrested in the mountain community of Murphy, North Carolina.

4 June Lifestyle guru Martha Stewart and her former stockbroker are indicted by a federal grand jury in New York City for allegedly lying to investigators in an insider-trading case.

23 June In *Grutter* v. *Bollinger* the U.S. Supreme Court upholds (5-4) the University of Michigan Law School's affirmative-action admissions policy because it is narrowly tailored to promote diversity. On the same day, in *Gratz* v. *Bollinger* the court strikes down (6-3) the university's undergraduate affirmative-action policy, which awards twenty points to blacks, Hispanics, and Native Americans on an admissions rating scale.

23 June The U.S. Supreme Court rules that libraries can install software that protects patrons, especially children, from gaining access to pornographic Internet websites.

26 June The U.S. Supreme Court declares sodomy laws unconstitutional in *Lawrence* v. *Texas*.

7 Oct. California voters recall Democratic governor Joseph Graham "Gray" Davis Jr. from office and select Austrian-born movie actor and former bodybuilder Arnold Schwarzenegger, a Republican, over 134 other candidates to replace him.

5 Nov. President Bush signs into law the Partial Birth Abortion Ban Act.

12 Nov. Alabama chief justice Roy Moore is forced to step down from the bench for refusing to remove a monument of the Ten Commandments from the state's Judicial Building after it was ruled to violate the establishment clause of the First Amendment to the U.S. Constitution.

10 Dec. The U.S. Supreme Court in *McConnell* v. *Federal Election Commission* bans "soft money" contributions to political parties and overturns provisions restricting those under the age of eighteen from contributing to political campaigns.

2004

12 Feb. The city of San Francisco, California, begins issuing marriage licenses to homosexual couples.

25 Feb. In *Locke* v. *Davey* the U.S. Supreme Court rules 7-2 that states that offer taxpayer-funded scholarships to academically qualified low- and middle-income students do not have to give them to those who wish to study for the ministry.

1 Apr. President Bush signs the Unborn Victims of Violence law, which recognizes an unborn child, in any stage of development, as a legal victim if injured or killed.

19 May U.S. Army Specialist Jeremy Sivits pleads guilty in a court martial to his role in the Abu Ghraib prisoner abuse scandal in Iraq.

26 May Terry Nichols is found guilty of murder for his role in the 1995 Oklahoma City bombing.

14 June	The U.S. Supreme Court rules unanimously in *Elk Grove* v. *Newdow* that the words "under God" in the Pledge of Allegiance do not violate the establishment clause of the First Amendment.
28 June	In *Rasul* v. *Bush* the U.S. Supreme Court rules that foreign nationals captured abroad and detained at Guantánamo Bay naval base in Cuba may challenge their detention in federal courts. In *Hamdi* v. *Rumsfeld* the court asserts that citizens held as enemy combatants have the right to contest their status.
13 Sept.	The Assault Weapons Ban (1994) expires.
2 Nov.	Gay-marriage bans are passed in Arkansas, Georgia, Kentucky, Michigan, Mississippi, Montana, North Dakota, Oklahoma, Ohio, Utah, and Oregon.
9 Nov.	The White House accepts the resignation of Attorney General Ashcroft, who will remain in the position until his replacement is selected.

2005

20 Jan.	George W. Bush is sworn in as president for a second term.
3 Feb.	Alberto Gonzales is appointed U.S. attorney general.
25 Feb.	Dennis Lynn Rader, the "BTK" (Bind-Torture-Kill) serial killer alleged to have murdered ten people, is arrested in Wichita, Kansas.
1 Mar.	In *Roper* v. *Simmons* the U.S. Supreme Court rules that the death penalty may not be imposed upon juvenile offenders.
31 May	Former FBI agent W. Mark Felt reveals that he was "Deep Throat," a key source in the *Washington Post* coverage of the Watergate scandal that led to the resignation of President Richard M. Nixon in 1974.
13 June	The U.S. Supreme Court orders the conviction of Texas death-row inmate Thomas Miller-El thrown out because prosecutors had systematically excluded black jurors.
23 June	The U.S. Supreme Court decides in *Kelo* v. *City of New London, Connecticut* that governments can use eminent-domain laws for the purpose of economic development.
27 June	In *MGM* v. *Grokster* the U.S. Supreme Court rules that companies that actively and intentionally promote the illegal use of their software—in this case, for downloading copyrighted music and videos—could be sued.
27 June	In *McCreary County, Kentucky* v. *American Civil Liberties Union of Kentucky* the U.S. Supreme Court rules 5-4 that courthouse displays of the Ten Commandments are unconstitutional because they lack a primary secular purpose. In *Van Orden* v. *Perry,* however, it decides, also by a 5-4 majority, that a monument on the Texas state capitol grounds that depicts the commandments is permissible.
1 July	Associate Justice Sandra Day O'Connor announces plans to retire from the U.S. Supreme Court.
3 Sept.	Chief Justice William H. Rehnquist dies.
26 Sept.	Army reservist Lynndie England is convicted for her role in the Abu Ghraib prisoner-abuse scandal.
28 Sept.	House majority leader Tom DeLay (R-Texas) is charged with criminal conspiracy for illegal campaign finance practices.

29 Sept.	John G. Roberts Jr. is sworn in as the seventeenth chief justice of the U.S. Supreme Court.
3 Oct.	President Bush nominates former White House deputy chief of staff Harriet Miers for the U.S. Supreme Court.
27 Oct.	Miers withdraws from the Supreme Court nomination process after questions are raised about her qualifications for the post.
31 Oct.	President Bush nominates Samuel Alito for the Supreme Court.
20 Dec.	U.S. District Judge John E. Jones III rules that teaching intelligent design in the classroom equates to teaching religion.

2006

17 Jan.	In *Gonzales* v. *Oregon* the U.S. Supreme Court upholds the Oregon Death with Dignity Act (1997).
20 Jan.	A state court rules Maryland's gay-marriage ban unconstitutional.
31 Jan.	Alito is sworn in as an associate justice of the Supreme Court.
6 Mar.	In *Rumsfeld* v. *Forum for Academic and Institutional Freedom* the U.S. Supreme Court decides that law schools must provide military recruiters with equal access to students on campuses.
22 May	The U.S. Supreme Court rules that police officers do not need a warrant to enter a home when individuals are fighting or someone is threatened with attack.
23 June	The "Liberty City Seven," members of the radical religious group Seeds of David, are arrested by FBI agents in Miami, Florida, for plotting to destroy the Sears Tower in Chicago.
29 June	The U.S. Supreme Court rejects military tribunals for terrorist suspects, finding the tribunals in conflict with federal law and the rules of war established by the Geneva Conventions.
20 Oct.	In *Purcell* v. *Gonzalez* the U.S. Supreme Court unanimously overturns a lower court's injunction against an Arizona law requiring voters to provide proof of citizenship when they register and to present identification when they vote.
7 Dec.	The Ohio ban against smoking in indoor public places goes into effect.
7 Dec.	Seven U.S. attorneys are fired by the Republican Bush administration, allegedly because they had failed to pursue investigations of Democratic officeholders. By mid 2007 many upper-level Justice Department officials, including Attorney General Gonzales, will resign their posts.

2007

4 Jan.	White House legal counsel Harriet Miers announces her resignation, effective at the end of the month. She is replaced by Fred Fielding.
6 Feb.	Deputy Attorney General Paul McNulty testifies before the Senate Judiciary Committee that the attorneys fired in 2006 were not relieved of their posts for political reasons. He later claims that he had been misled as to the reasons for the dismissals, because almost all of the attorneys had received high marks on job-performance evaluations.
12 Feb.	Five people are killed by a shooter at the Trolley Square Mall in Salt Lake City, Utah.

16 Apr.	Student Seung-Hui Cho shoots and kills thirty-two people and wounds dozens of others on the Virginia Tech campus before fatally shooting himself.
18 Apr.	The U.S. Supreme Court upholds a partial-birth abortion ban.
25 Apr.	Ohio congressman Dennis Kucinich attempts to introduce articles of impeachment against Vice President Dick Cheney.
29 May	In *Ledbetter* v. *Goodyear Tire and Rubber Company* the U.S. Supreme Court rules 5-4 that employees filing pay-discrimination complaints under Title VII of the Civil Rights Act must do so within 180 days of the adverse pay decision, even if they were not privy to information about their colleagues' compensation.
25 June	The U.S. Supreme Court rules in *Morse* v. *Frederick* that school administrators can prohibit students from displaying pro-drug-use messages.
27 Aug.	Gonzales announces his resignation as U.S attorney general, effective 17 September.
9 Nov.	Michael B. Mukasey is installed as U.S. attorney general.
5 Dec.	Gunman Robert A. Hawkins kills eight at the Westroads Mall in Omaha, Nebraska, before committing suicide.
10 Dec.	The U.S. Supreme Court decides in two cases that federal district court judges have latitude in determining sentences, instead of being forced to accept legislative standards.

2008

15 Jan.	The Food and Drug Administration rules that food processed from cloned livestock is safe to eat.
16 Apr.	The U.S. Supreme Court rules that states can continue to use lethal injection as their method of execution.
15 May	The California Supreme Court rules that the state's gay-marriage ban is unconstitutional.
25 June	In *Kennedy* v. *Louisiana* the U.S. Supreme Court rules that a sentence of death in cases of child rape is not proportional to a crime that leaves the victim alive. Part of their reasoning is that knowledge of a possible death sentence might push a rapist to kill his victim rather than leave a witness.
27 Jun.	The U.S. Supreme Court rejects a Washington, D.C., ban on handgun possession, although it allows the district to ban certain individuals (criminals and the mentally ill) and weaponry (machine guns).
3 Oct.	The Emergency Economic Stabilization Act is signed into law, appropriating funds for the Treasury Department to bail out failing banks.
4 Nov.	Barack Obama is elected the forty-fourth president of the United States.
19 Nov.	Judge Richard J. Leon of the federal district court in Washington, D.C., orders the release of five Algerian terrorist suspects who have been held at Guantánamo Bay for seven years because the government's secret evidence in the case was weak.

2009

20 Jan.	Barack Obama is inaugurated as president; Chief Justice Roberts mistakenly rearranges the wording of the oath of office, and the oath is readministered two days later.

22 Jan.	President Obama issues an executive order to close the detention camp at Guantánamo Bay within one year.
29 Jan.	Illinois governor Rod Blagojevich, impeached by the state House of Representatives on corruption charges on 9 January, is unanimously convicted by the Senate and removed from office.
3 Feb.	Eric Himpton Holder Jr. is sworn in as U.S. attorney general.
25 Feb.	The U.S. Supreme Court rules unanimously in *Pleasant Grove City* v. *Summum* that a Utah city did not restrict the free speech of a religious sect when it did not allow the group to place a monument in a public park.
9 Mar.	President Obama signs an executive order overturning the Bush-era ban on federal funding of research on embryonic stem-cell lines that were not in existence as of 9 August 2001.
3 Apr.	The Iowa Supreme Court rules that a ban on gay marriage is unconstitutional.
19 May	President Obama implements stricter federal requirements for vehicle emissions and gas mileage.
3 June	New Hampshire legalizes gay marriage.
25 June	In *Safford Unified School Dist. #1* v. *Redding* the U.S. Supreme Court rules 8-1 that a strip search of a public middle-school student suspected of distributing a prescription drug on campus violated her Fourth Amendment right to freedom from an unreasonable search.
29 June	In *Ricci* v. *DeStefano* the U.S. Supreme Court rules that New Haven, Connecticut, erred in throwing out the results of a firefighter promotion test because African American and Latino candidates had not performed as well as white candidates, arguing that race-conscious policies could only be used in cases of disparate-impact discrimination.
3 July	Alaska governor and former vice-presidential nominee Sarah Palin announces her resignation, citing "frivolous" ethics investigations.
8 Aug.	Sonia Sotomayor is sworn in as associate justice, becoming the third woman to serve on the U.S. Supreme Court.
2 Sept.	Pharmaceutical giant Pfizer announces that it has finalized a $2.3 billion settlement over marketing its arthritis drug Bextra for unapproved uses and that its Pharmacia & Upjohn unit would plead guilty to one criminal count of violating the Food, Drug, and Cosmetic Act.
27 Sept.	Film director Roman Polanski is arrested in Switzerland on an outstanding U.S. warrant on statutory rape charges.
28 Oct.	The Matthew Shepard and James Byrd Jr. Hate Crimes Prevention Act is signed into law. The provision extends federal hate-crimes law to include sexual orientation, gender identity, and disability.
6 Nov.	The South Carolina Supreme Court orders a report by the State Ethics Commission into publicly funded travel by Governor Mark Sanford during an alleged affair with an Argentine woman be made public.
10 Nov.	Convicted gunman John Allen Muhammad is executed for his role in the 2002 "Beltway Sniper" attacks.
1 Dec.	Virginia's public-smoking ban is implemented.

OVERVIEW

The War on Terror. No single event shaped the American approach to law and justice in the 2000s more than the terrorist attacks of 11 September 2001. As the United States struggled to comprehend the new threat of spectacular violence, the administration of President George W. Bush undertook a large-scale expansion of the nation's domestic security apparatus, strengthening the law enforcement tools of the Justice Department, authorizing the National Security Agency to conduct warrantless wiretapping, and creating a cabinet-level Department of Homeland Security. Perhaps no other piece of legislation commanded more public attention in the decade than the USA PATRIOT (Uniting and Strengthening America by Providing Appropriate Tools Required to Intercept and Obstruct Terrorism) Act, first as a measure of the government's resolve to take unprecedented bold steps to prevent future terrorist attacks and later as a symbol of the Bush administration's alleged disregard for civil liberties. The creation of the detention center at the American naval base at Guantánamo Bay, Cuba, inaugurated a discussion of the limits of executive power and the exercise of military justice with regard to international law.

An Evolving Court. The U.S. Supreme Court underwent major changes in the decade as John G. Roberts replaced William H. Rehnquist as chief justice. Observers noted a rightward shift in the middle of the decade as the stalwart moderate Justice Sandra Day O'Connor, a longtime swing vote in favor of abortion rights and other typically closely decided issues, was replaced by the more conservative Justice Samuel Alito. Even after the addition of two of his appointees to the Court, President Bush suffered setbacks as justices rejected his broad interpretation of executive power under law. In other areas, however, conservatives could mark signal victories as the Roberts court expanded gun rights, limited Affirmative Action, and invalidated campaign-finance regulations. President Barack Obama made a mark on the court's composition by nominating Sonia Sotomayor, the court's third woman and first Hispanic, to replace outgoing justice David Souter.

Celebrity Trials. Public interest in celebrity misdeeds continued to rise, and high-profile cases dominated media coverage throughout the decade. The growth of twenty-four-hour cable news outlets fed the trend as networks such as CNN, MSNBC, and Fox News inaugurated programs focused on legal issues. The most-followed celebrity case by far was the child-molestation trial of pop star Michael Jackson, whose unconventional lifestyle and behavior only added to the intrigue. Other celebrities on trial included actor Robert Blake and legendary record producer Phil Spector, both charged with murdering women. Basketball superstar Kobe Bryant was accused of sexual assault in a case that was settled out of court. Polish-French filmmaker Roman Polanski was arrested in Switzerland on a decades-old U.S. warrant stemming from statutory rape charges.

Gay Rights. The 2003 *Lawrence* v. *Texas* decision invalidated state sodomy laws regulating intimate relations between consenting adults, which were increasingly seen as outdated and discriminatory toward homosexuals. The major legal focus of the gay rights movement, however, was the struggle for the recognition of same-sex marriage. The Massachusetts Supreme Court handed advocates of gay marriage a victory when it ruled that the state could not legally bar same-sex couples from marrying. The decision sparked a nationwide backlash, however, and many state lawmakers rushed to amend their constitutions to eliminate any opportunity for similar rulings in their own states. Many were disappointed by what was seen as the slow pace of the new Obama administration in making good on its campaign promises to promote gay rights, especially on the controversial "Don't Ask, Don't Tell" policy, under which gays could not openly serve in the military. Still, on 28 October 2009 President Obama signed into law the Matthew Shepard and James Byrd Jr. Hate Crimes Prevention Act, which extended federal hate-crimes law to include violent acts motivated by perpetrators' bias against the victim's actual or perceived race, color, religion, national origin, gender, sexual orientation, gender identity, or disability.

Justice on Television. Americans' appetite for crime and punishment in prime time continued to grow in the 2000s. The long-running *Law and Order* series spawned spin-offs and video games, while other programs, such as

CSI: Crime Scene Investigation (which also had spin-off series), *Cold Case*, and *The Shield* proved the longevity of the police procedural television drama. Real-life criminal cases drew large followings, as well, as cable-news hosts such as Nancy Grace and Greta Van Susteren devoted huge amounts of airtime to teenage abduction cases and other sensational stories. By far the biggest of these cases was that of Natalee Holloway, a recent high-school graduate who went missing while on vacation in Aruba; viewers were glued to every twist and turn in the coverage as months passed in the search for the missing teen. Critics charged that media outlets were cherry-picking the crimes they chose to follow and that they showed an overwhelming proclivity toward young white women, while cases in which minorities were the victims went largely unnoticed.

TOPICS IN THE NEWS

ABORTION AND END-OF-LIFE ISSUES

Partial-Birth Abortion Ban. Three decades after the *Roe* v. *Wade* decision, the right of women to obtain abortions remained one of the most contentious legal issues in America. Opponents of abortion focused much of their attention in the decade on a procedure that was technically known as "intact dilation and extraction" but was often called "partial-birth abortion." The phrase "partial-birth abortion" came to represent any procedure that involved the destruction of a viable fetus, usually in the second or third trimester, after its partial extraction from the mother. Definitional problems often plagued legislative attempts to curb the procedures. Indeed, in the 2000 *Stenberg* v. *Carhart* decision, the U.S. Supreme Court ruled 5-4 that a Nebraska law banning such operations not only placed an undue burden on a woman's ability to choose an abortion and lacked an exception for cases that risked the health of the mother but was also overly vague in its definition of the procedure. In forming their approach to the ban on the federal level, abortion foes drew lessons from the majority's language in the *Stenberg* decision, drafting legislation that provided a clearer definition of what was meant by a partial-birth abortion; the Senate version of what became the Partial Birth Abortion Ban Act included an amendment by Senator Tom Harkin (D-Iowa) that added an exception to the ban for pregnancies that jeopardized the health of the mother. The Harkin amendment was dropped from the final version of the bill, and President Bush signed it into law on 5 November 2003. After immediate challenges by Planned Parenthood and others, the law was ruled unconstitutional in the lower courts. These decisions were appealed by the Bush Justice Department, and in November 2006 the Supreme Court heard arguments in *Gonzales* v. *Carhart*. Proponents of the law were heartened by the apparent rightward shift of the court on the issue, as Justice Sandra Day O'Connor, who had long voted to uphold abortion rights, had been replaced by Bush appointee Samuel Alito. In a 5-4 decision the court upheld the law in April 2007, noting that the legislation differed significantly from the Nebraska law considered in the *Stenberg* decision by providing a more complete definition of the procedure in question. The ruling was hailed as a signature victory for the prolife movement, while prochoice advocates complained that it represented a radical shift away from settled abortion case law.

State Challenges. Emboldened by fresh federal action limiting abortion, as well as the retirement of Justice O'Connor, opponents of abortion went on the attack at the state level. In 2006 lawmakers in fourteen states proposed bans of one form or another. In March, Governor Mike Rounds of South Dakota signed into law a bill that directly challenged Supreme Court precedent in *Roe* v. *Wade* by banning most abortions; in June, Louisiana passed a law that would immediately ban abortion should *Roe* v. *Wade* be overturned. The South Dakota law, dubbed the Women's Health and Human Life Protection Act, provided no exceptions for cases of rape or incest and allowed doctors to perform the procedure only when it was deemed necessary to save the life of the mother. In passing the law, legislators had been forthright in their intention to capitalize on the perceived shift on the Supreme Court and to overturn *Roe* v. *Wade*. There was immediate outcry from prochoice advocates in the state, who set to work gathering signatures in an eventually successful effort to petition the legislature for a statewide referendum on the law. As the November election approached, South Dakota became a battleground in the fight over abortion rights. Prochoice advocates focused their campaign on the allegedly radical nature of the law, in that it lacked rape or incest

Protesters gather outside of Woodside Hospice in Pinellas Park, Florida, on 25 March 2005 in support of keeping Terri Schiavo on life support (photograph by Teresa Fritz).

exceptions. On 7 November, 56 percent of South Dakota voters opted for repeal, and the law never took effect. In July 2008 a law went into effect that required doctors to ask women if they wanted to see ultrasound pictures of their fetuses before having an abortion, and enforcement began of a 2005 law that required doctors to tell women seeking abortions that the procedure ends a human life. The November 2008 ballot in South Dakota included Measure 11, a proposed constitutional amendment that would have banned all abortions in the state except for those performed because of rape or incest or to protect the woman's health. Doctors who performed abortions in violation of the provisions could have been charged with a Class 4 felony, which carried a maximum punishment of ten years in prison and a $20,000 fine. The initiative lost, with 55 percent voting against it.

Terri Schiavo. The most widely reported and sensational case involving end-of-life issues involved Terri Schiavo, a Florida woman who fell into a persistent vegetative state after suffering brain damage in 1990. In 1998, after doctors had failed in multiple attempts over several years to restore Schiavo to normal brain function, her husband, Michael Schiavo, petitioned to have her feeding tube removed so that she could be allowed to die. Terri Schiavo's parents, Robert and Mary Schindler, believed that she had a chance to recover and sued to gain legal guardianship of their daughter. After years of legal wrangling, doctors removed the tube on 24 April 2001; but the Schindlers appealed, and she was placed back on life support two days later. A two-year court battle over the right to make life decisions for Schiavo ensued, ending in the Sixth Judicial Circuit's dismissal

On 17 March 2005, Senator Bill Frist (R-Tennessee) spoke on The Senate Floor about the Terri Schiavo case. Critics accused him of attempting to diagnose a medical condition he knew little about for political gain.

I close this evening speaking more as a physician than as a U.S. Senator and speak to my involvement as a physician and as a Senator and as a leader in the Senate in what has been a fascinating course of events for us over the last 48 hours, a saga which has not ended but one which we took major steps toward tonight in seeing that this woman is not starved to death tomorrow beginning at 1 o'clock, about 13 hours from now.

When I first heard about the situation facing Terri Schiavo, I immediately wanted to know more about the case from a medical standpoint. I asked myself, just looking at the newspaper reports, is Terri clearly in this diagnosis called persistent vegetative state? I was interested in it in part because it is a very difficult diagnosis to make and I have been in a situation many times before as a transplant surgeon. . . .

Persistent vegetative state, which is what the court has ruled, I say that I question it, and I question it based on a review of the video footage which I spent an hour or so looking at last night in my office here in the Capitol. And that footage, to me, depicted something very different than persistent vegetative state. . . .

Source: *Congressional Record—Senate* (17 March 2005), pp. 3090–3091.

of the Schindlers' final appeal on 10 October 2003. Five days later, at the request of Michael Schiavo, Terri's feeding tube was once again removed. In response, the Florida legislature passed "Terri's Law" on 21 October, granting Governor Jeb Bush authority to intervene in the case. Bush immediately ordered the tube reinserted. In September 2004 the Florida Supreme Court affirmed a lower court ruling that Terri's Law was unconstitutional, and after the U.S. Supreme Court refused to hear the case, a Florida circuit court judge ordered on 25 February 2005 that the feeding tube be removed on 18 March. The case, which had been garnering increasing media attention, became a national issue when several Republican federal lawmakers sought to intervene. At issue, in particular, was brief video footage, shot by the Schindlers, that appeared to show Terri responding to stimulation and verbal prompts, despite overwhelming evidence presented by her doctors that her brain damage was too severe for any hope of recovery and claims that the video had been heavily edited. In a last-ditch effort to keep her on life support, Senator Bill Frist (R-Tennessee), a physician, issued a subpoena for Schiavo to testify before the U.S. Senate committee on Health, Education, Labor, and Pensions one day before the scheduled removal of the feeding tube; the purpose was to grant her protection as a witness. The subpoena was quickly ruled unconstitutional, and the removal continued as scheduled. As a result Congress passed the Act for the Relief of the Parents of Theresa Marie Schiavo, a measure known as the "Palm Sunday Compromise," which provided for the transfer of the case to federal court. Despite widespread consensus that the bill was unconstitutional for, among other problems, violating the separation of powers, President George W. Bush signed it into law on 21 March. Even after the passage of the law, all further appeals were denied, and forty-one-year-old Terri Schiavo died on 31 March. An autopsy concluded that she suffered from massive brain damage and would have had no prospect of returning to anything like a normal life.

Assisted Suicide. In November 2008 voters in the state of Washington approved the Washington Death with Dignity Act. The law granted terminally ill patients the right to request lethal doses of medication if they were determined by doctors to be within six months of death, so long as they were also deemed mentally competent to make personal medical decisions. Washington was the second state to allow so-called physician-assisted suicide after Oregon, which had passed a similar law in 1994. Linda Fleming, a sixty-six-year-old woman from Sequim, became the first person to receive a fatal dosage under the law in May 2009, citing unbearable pain as her pancreatic cancer spread. By the end of the decade 150 Washingtonians had opted for physician-assisted suicide under the law.

Sources:

Jeremy Alford, "Louisiana Governor Plans to Sign Anti-Abortion Law," *New York Times*, 7 June 2006, p. A18;

Don Colburn, "First Death under Washington Death with Dignity Law," *Oregonian*, 22 May 2009;

Jennifer Frey, "Terri Schiavo's Unstudied Life: The Woman Who Is Now a Symbol and a Cause Hated the Spotlight," *Washington Post*, 25 March 2005, p. C1;

"Frist Responds on Schiavo," *New York Times*, 17 June 2005, p. A22;

Linda Greenhouse, "Justices Appear Set to Reject Law Banning Late Abortion," *New York Times*, 26 April 2000, p. A1;

John Holusha, "South Dakota Governor Signs Abortion Ban," *New York Times*, 6 March 2006;

Mary Snow, "Medical Examiner Releases Terri Schiavo Autopsy Report," *cnn.com* (15 June 2005);

"South Dakota Abortion Ban Rejected" *USA Today*, 8 November 2006;

Sheryl Gay Stolberg, "The Schiavo Case: Doctor-Politicians; Drawing Some Criticism, Legislators with Medical Degrees Offer Opinions on Schiavo Case," *New York Times*, 23 March 2005, p. A14;

"Terri Schiavo Timeline," *abcnews.com* (6 January 2006);

Janet I. Tu, "'Death with Dignity' Act Passes," *Seattle Times*, 5 November 2008, p. 1;

Wayne Washington and Lyle Denniston, "Law Bans Late-Term Abortion Procedure: U.S. Judge Limits Its Application," *Boston Globe*, 6 November 2003;

Kate Zernike, "30 Years after Abortion Ruling, New Trends but the Old Debate," *New York Times*, 20 January 2003, p. A1.

Frank Ricci, left, and Ben Vargas testifying on Capitol Hill before Supreme Court nominee Sonia Sotomayor in the *Ricci* v. *DeStefano* trial on 16 July 2009 (AP Photo/Charles Dharapak)

CIVIL RIGHTS

Affirmative Action in Higher Education. The legal status of affirmative-action laws was challenged by twin cases involving admissions policies at the University of Michigan in 2003. In *Grutter* v. *Bollinger* a white Michigan resident, Barbara Grutter, alleged that the University of Michigan School of Law had discriminated against her on the basis of race when she was denied admission, since similarly qualified minority candidates had received preference on the basis of race. The school's policy, according to Grutter's lawyers, was in violation of the guidelines set by the U.S. Supreme Court's 1978 *Regents of the University of California* v. *Bakke* decision, which found that affirmative-action policies in higher education must be "narrowly tailored" and could not include quotas. On 23 June the Supreme Court ruled that the school had not violated *Bakke* guidelines, since race was only one factor among many considered in admissions, and that the university had a justifiable interest in creating a diverse student body. In a case heard concurrently, two white applicants for undergraduate admission at the University of Michigan, Jennifer Gratz and Patrick Hamacher, argued that the school's 150-point ranking scale was unconstitutional since it awarded minorities an automatic twenty points. In *Gratz* v. *Bollinger*

the Supreme Court held that the automatic granting of points was unconstitutional because it failed to meet the "narrowly tailored" standard. The two Michigan rulings, handed down on the same day, upheld affirmative-action policies but also continued the court's trend of limiting their scope. Justice Sandra Day O'Connor remarked in the *Grutter* opinion that such policies might not be necessary in twenty-five years.

Affirmative Action in Primary Education. Three years after the University of Michigan decisions, two cases involving affirmative action in primary education further clarified the court's developing stance on the issue. In *Parents Involved in Community Schools* v. *Seattle School District No. 1* and *Meredith* v. *Jefferson County [Kentucky] Board of Education*, which were decided concurrently, the justices ruled 5-4 that the school districts' use of race as the sole determining factor in maintaining a numerically predetermined level of racial diversity was unconstitutional. Though the decision did not rule out the possibility that certain programs designed to achieve diversity could be constitutional, many school districts complained that the sweeping ruling made these goals much more difficult to reach.

Workplace Discrimination. *Ricci* v. *DeStefano* was a case heard by the U.S. Supreme Court in which white and Hispanic firefighters employed by the city of New Haven, Connecticut, alleged that they had been discriminated against on the basis of race when they were passed over for management positions. The seventeen men, who filed suit against the city in 2004, had all passed the test given to candidates for promotion to lieutenant or captain, but the city had thrown out the results when it discovered that no African American firefighters had passed. City officials claimed that they simply wanted to avoid the implication of racial bias in the testing and hiring process, as well as to avoid a potential lawsuit by African American firefighters. In a 5-4 decision on 29 June 2009 the court agreed with the plaintiffs that the actions taken by the city of New Haven represented discrimination on the basis of race.

Homosexuality and the Boy Scouts. In 1990 James Dale, a student at Rutgers University, was fired as an assistant scoutmaster after officials of the Boy Scouts of America read a newspaper interview in which he revealed that he was gay. Dale had been a member of his troop since age eight and had attained the rank of Eagle Scout, the organization's highest level of achievement; but according to the Boy Scouts, homosexuality was inconsistent with Scout values, and Dale was, therefore, unfit to serve in a leadership role. Dale filed suit in the New Jersey Superior Court, claiming that his termination violated state law banning discrimination on the basis of sexual orientation. The court found in his favor, and the Boy Scouts appealed the decision to the U.S. Supreme Court. On 28 June 2000, by a 5-4 vote, the Supreme Court reversed the lower court's decision. The majority held that the First Amendment guarantee of free association meant that the Boy Scouts could not be forced "to accept members where such acceptance would derogate from the organization's expressive message." Justice John Paul Stevens was among the dissenters, writing that "the only apparent explanation for the majority's holding . . . is that homosexuals are simply so different from the rest of society that their presence alone . . . should be singled out for special first amendment treatment."

Gay Marriage. The debate over gay marriage was a central front in the struggle for gay rights, as well as one of the most contentious legal issues of the decade. Massachusetts became the first state to allow same-sex marriage after the Supreme Judicial Court ruled in *Goodridge* v. *Department of Health* on 18 November 2003 that barring gay couples from marrying was in violation of the Massachusetts constitution. The ruling generated huge political controversy in the state and across the country. On 4 February 2004 the court clarified its position in an advisory opinion requested by the state senate, noting that a proposed civil-union bill would not pass constitutional muster. In May 2004, although the legislature had failed to change the state's marriage law, Governor Mitt Romney ordered municipalities to begin issuing marriage licenses to same-sex couples in accordance with the court ruling. The city of Cambridge became the

first to issue licenses to same-sex couples, beginning just after midnight on the day of the order's implementation. Despite many attempts by gay-marriage foes to work around the court's ruling, including the convening of two separate constitutional conventions, same-sex marriage remained legal in Massachusetts. Under the terms of the 1996 Defense of Marriage Act, however, gay couples married under Massachusetts law were not recognized as legally married by the federal government. In 2008 Connecticut became the second state to allow gay marriage, followed by Iowa and Vermont in 2009.

State Bans. In the wake of the controversy surrounding the *Goodridge* decision, many states undertook to institute outright bans on gay marriage. Socially conservative lawmakers sought to avoid the situation that Massachusetts faced by preempting the courts and putting the issue up for a vote as amendments to their state constitutions. In the November 2004 elections the measures passed easily in the conservative Southern states Arkansas, Georgia, Kentucky, and Mississippi. Even in swing-state Ohio, however, a constitutional ban passed by a 3-2 margin. Other states enacting bans included Michigan, Montana, North Dakota, Oklahoma, Utah, and Oregon. Critics claimed that the ballot initiatives were designed to boost Republican chances in the 2004 election by drawing socially conservative voters to the polls.

Sodomy Laws. For much of the nation's history, statutes known as sodomy laws made a range of sexual acts illegal as a means of enforcing the practice of mainstream heterosexuality and discouraging sexual behavior traditionally thought by some to be immoral. By 2000 only fourteen states still had such laws on the books; most had either repealed them or seen them invalidated by state courts. The states that retained sodomy laws rarely enforced them, since they dealt primarily with private relations between consenting adults. Still, the remaining presence of these statutes was a clear symbol of historical discrimination against homosexuals, whose sexual lives were often implicitly or explicitly the target of their regulation. Four states (Kansas, Missouri, Oklahoma, and Texas) maintained sodomy laws that specifically targeted homosexual behavior. In 2003 the U.S. Supreme Court heard arguments in *Lawrence* v. *Texas,* a case that challenged the validity of Texas's law. John Lawrence and Tyron Garner had been arrested in 1998 when a police officer responding to a domestic-disturbance call entered Lawrence's apartment and witnessed the couple engaging in a sexual act. The two challenged the conviction on the grounds that the law in question violated the Fourteenth Amendment. In a 6-3 decision on 26 June 2003 the court agreed, holding that "the Texas statute making it a crime for two persons of the same sex to engage in certain intimate sexual conduct violates the Due Process Clause." The ruling had the effect of invalidating all remaining state sodomy laws and was hailed as an important legal step forward in the struggle for gay rights.

Sources:

Pam Belluck, "Gays Elsewhere Eye Marriage Massachusetts Style," *New York Times*, 14 May 2004;

Belluck, "Massachusetts Rejects Bill to Eliminate Gay Marriage," *New York Times*, 15 September 2005, p. A14;

Dale Carpenter, "How the Law Accepted Gays," *New York Times*, 28 April 2011;

Linda Greenhouse, "Justices Reject Diversity Plans in Two Districts," *New York Times*, 28 June 2007;

Greenhouse, "Supreme Court Backs Boy Scouts in Ban of Gays from Membership," *New York Times*, 29 June 2000, p. A1;

Glenn Greenwald, "The Supreme Court's Ricci Decision," *salon.com* (29 June 2009);

Frank Phillips and Raphael Lewis, "Legislature Considers Constitutional Ban on Same-Sex Marriages," *Boston Globe*, 11 February 2004;

Warren Richey, "US Supreme Court Takes up 'Reverse Discrimination' Case," *Christian Science Monitor*, 9 January 2009;

Joel Roberts, "11 States Ban Same-Sex Marriage," *cbsnews.com* (2 November 2004);

"Split Ruling on Affirmative Action," *npr.org* (23 June 2003);

Supreme Court of the United States, *Lawrence* v. *Texas*, 539 U.S. 558 (2003).

MAJOR SUPREME COURT DECISIONS

Bush v. *Gore.* A close and contentious race between Republican George W. Bush and Democrat Al Gore in the 2000 presidential election ended with a legal stalemate that resulted in the U.S. Supreme Court intervening in the contest. As returns came in on election night, some television networks called the election for Gore on the basis of exit polls that showed him carrying the state of Florida. The actual vote count, however, proved much closer, and in the early hours of the following morning the final tally showed Bush leading by approximately two thousand votes—a margin slim enough to trigger an automatic recount. By this time Florida's twenty-five electoral votes had taken on huge significance: the candidate who won them would be the next president. As the confusion over the outcome of the election forced the networks to hold off on their projections, NBC Washington bureau chief Tim Russert simplified the matter for viewers at home, holding up a whiteboard on which he had scribbled "Florida! Florida! Florida!" For the next several weeks, the two campaigns shifted from a political fight into a legal battle over the question of recounts. The Gore campaign requested recounts in four Florida counties: Broward, Miami-Dade, Palm Beach, and Volusia. These counties were traditionally Democratic-leaning areas that had also experienced widespread complaints of irregularities in the voting booth. The punch-card voting system had proved confusing for some voters, causing them to miscast their votes; in other cases, voters reported that ballots improperly recorded their selections. Interpreting the ballot intentions of the voters also proved difficult for poll workers, and before the manual recounts were finished, Secretary of State Katherine Harris (a Bush campaign cochair) certified the election for Bush on 26 November. After a legal challenge of the certification by the Gore campaign, the Florida Supreme Court ordered a statewide manual recount on 8 December. The decision was appealed to the U.S. Supreme Court. With uncommon

speed, the high court heard arguments on 11 December and handed down its ruling the following day. In the 5-4 *Bush* v. *Gore* decision, the majority held that the statewide recount would violate the equal protection clause of the Fourteenth Amendment because there was insufficient time under the Florida vote-certification deadline to recount all votes under a single, clear standard. By stopping the recount, the court sealed Bush's victory in the Electoral College. Critics of the decision condemned what was perceived as partisan bias behind the veil of legal jargon: all Republican appointees on the court voted to stop the recount with the exception of David Souter, a George H.W. Bush appointee long considered an unexpectedly liberal presence on the court. In his dissent, Associate Justice John Paul Stevens leveled a stinging critique: "Although we may never know with complete certainty the identity of the winner of this year's Presidential election, the identity of the loser is perfectly clear. It is the Nation's confidence in the judge as an impartial guardian of the rule of law."

Kelo v. *City of New London.* In 2005 the U.S. Supreme Court weighed in on the issue of property rights in a decision that strengthened the hand of city governments. In *Kelo* v. *City of New London* the court held that the city of New London, Connecticut, had the right to use the power of eminent domain to take possession of

HARRIET MIERS

President George W. Bush's first choice to replace retiring Justice Sandra Day O'Connor in the summer of 2005 was John G. Roberts, but Roberts was, instead, tapped to fill the role of chief justice on the unexpected death of William Rehnquist. On 3 October, Bush announced that he would instead nominate Harriet Miers, his White House counsel and longtime confidante. The reaction to her nomination was swift, and even the president's allies questioned the wisdom of nominating someone who seemed so unqualified for the position. Since others were available who had more prestigious backgrounds and greater judicial experience, many assumed that Bush had chosen Miers because he could expect loyalty from her. Many conservatives, hoping for a shift in the ideological composition of the court, were frustrated that Miers's past pointed toward a moderate-to-liberal approach. Right-wing author and provocateur Ann Coulter joked, "I eagerly await the announcement of President Bush's real nominee to the Supreme Court." Coulter did not have to wait long: after weeks of criticism, Miers withdrew her name from consideration on 27 October.

Sources: Ann Coulter, "This Is What 'Advice and Consent' Means," *anncoulter.com* (5 October 2005);

Michael Fletcher and Charles Babington, "Miers, under Fire from Right, Withdraws as Court Nominee," *Washington Post*, 28 October 2005.

The United States Supreme Court in 2009; top row (left to right): Samuel A. Alito, Ruth Bader Ginsburg, Stephen G. Breyer, and Sonia Sotomayor; bottom row: Anthony M. Kennedy, John Paul Stevens, John G. Roberts, Antonin G. Scalia, and Clarence Thomas (photograph by Steve Petteway, staff photographer of the Supreme Court)

private property not only for public purposes such as parks or roads but also to benefit commercial interests, as long as the goal was the economic development of the community. The appellants—owners of fifteen parcels who had refused to sell their property to the city, some of whom had lived in their homes all their lives—had argued that "economic development" was too vague and subjective a ground for the use of such power, but the five-justice majority found that the Fifth Amendment granted local governments the right. Libertarian groups were joined in their negative reaction to the decision by such organizations as the American Association of Retired Persons (AARP) and the National Association for the Advancement of Colored People (NAACP). Many states subsequently enacted laws prohibiting the use of eminent domain to acquire property for commercial redevelopment.

District of Columbia* v. *Heller. A 2008 case challenging the 1975 Firearms Control Regulations act of the District of Columbia resulted in a landmark innovation in the U.S. Supreme Court's approach to the right to bear arms. In *District of Columbia* v. *Heller* the majority held that the district's regulation of gun ownership violated the Second Amendment to the constitution. Dick Anthony Heller, a Washington, D.C., resident, sued the district for its ban on handgun ownership and its requirement that firearms be outfitted with trigger locks in the home, claiming that the locks invalidated the

guns' purpose of protection. In siding with Heller, the court for the first time affirmed that the Second Amendment protected an individual's right to gun ownership not contingent on his or her membership in what the amendment calls a "well regulated militia." The case was hailed as a major victory for gun-rights groups such as the National Rifle Association, which had long lobbied for such an interpretation of the Second Amendment. Some law-enforcement organizations lamented the potential problems that could arise if local govern-

U.S. INMATE POPULATION, 2008

Federal Prisons	189,770
Privately Operated Facilities	24,518
Community Corrections Centers	8,644
State Prisons	1,320,145
Local Jails	785,556
Total	2,328,633

Source: U.S. Department of Justice, Bureau of Justice Statistics.

. . . After September the 11th, we needed to move quickly, and so I appointed Tom Ridge as my Homeland Security Advisor. As Governor Ridge has worked with all levels of government to prepare a national strategy, and as we have learned more about the plans and capabilities of the terrorist network, we have concluded that our government must be reorganized to deal more effectively with the new threats of the 21st century. So tonight, I ask the Congress to join me in creating a single, permanent department with an overriding and urgent mission: securing the homeland of America, and protecting the American people.
Right now, as many as a hundred different government agencies have some responsibilities for homeland security. And no one has final accountability. . . .

Tonight, I propose a permanent Cabinet-level Department of Homeland Security to unite essential agencies that must work more closely together: among them the Coast Guard, the Border Patrol, the Customs Service, Immigration officials, the Transportation Security Administration, and the Federal Emergency Management Agency. Employees of this new agency will come to work every morning knowing their most important job is to protect their fellow citizens.

The Department of Homeland Security will be charged with four primary tasks. This new agency will control our borders and prevent terrorists and explosives from entering our country. It will work with state and local authorities to respond quickly and effectively to emergencies. It will bring together our best scientists to develop technologies that detect biological,

chemical, and nuclear weapons—and to discover the drugs and treatments to best protect our citizens. And this new department will review intelligence and law enforcement information from all agencies of government, and produce a single daily picture of threats against our homeland. Analysts will be responsible for imagining the worst—and planning to counter it.

The reason to create this department is not to increase the size of government, but to increase its focus and effectiveness. The staff of this new department will be largely drawn from the agencies we are combining. By ending duplication and overlap, we will spend less on overhead, and more on protecting America. This reorganization will give the good people of our government their best opportunity to succeed by organizing our resources in a way that is thorough and unified. . . .

Only the United States Congress can create a new department of government. So tonight, I ask for your help in encouraging your representatives to support my plan. We face an urgent need, and we must move quickly, this year, before the end of the congressional session.

All in our government have learned a great deal since September the 11th, and we must act on every lesson. We are stronger and better prepared tonight than we were on that terrible morning — and with your help, and the support of Congress, we will be stronger still. . . .

Source: "Bush: New Agency to Secure 'American Homeland,'" *cnn.com* (6 June 2002).

---

ments were handicapped in their ability to regulate firearms. While the court made clear that long-standing proscriptions of gun ownership by felons and the mentally ill were not affected by its decision, it ruled that trigger locks and handgun bans were violations of the Second Amendment. By limiting its scope to the federal territory of the District of Columbia, the court did not explicitly extend the ruling to the states.

Sources:

Alex Altman, "The Future of Gun Control," *time.com* (26 June 2008);

Robert Barnes, "Supreme Court Affirms Gun Rights," *Boston Globe*, 27 June 2008;

John M. Broder, "States Curbing Right to Seize Private Homes," *New York Times*, 21 February 2006, p. A1;

Brian Knowlton, "Gore Suspends Recount Effort as Texas Governor Savors His Victory," *New York Times*, 14 December 2000;

Charles Lane, "Justices Affirm Property Seizures," *Washington Post*, 24 June 2005, p. A1;

Supreme Court of the United States, *Bush v. Gore*, 531 U.S. 98 (2000);

Jeffrey Toobin, "Precedent and Prologue," *New Yorker*, 86 (6 December 2010).

THE WAR ON TERROR

Patriot Act. The Bush administration's response to the terrorist attacks of 11 September 2001 included a wide range of legal measures intended to strengthen national security by granting new tools to law enforcement, as well as strengthening existing ones. The Uniting and Strengthening America by Providing Appropriate Tools Required to Intercept and Obstruct Terrorism (USA PATRIOT) Act of 2001 was the first and most widely discussed of these measures, and it became a signature element of the government's aggressive new legal approach to counterterrorism. In particular, it expanded the ability of law-enforcement agencies to conduct domestic wiretapping, giving them access to emails, telephone conversations, and other communications, as well as financial and medical records. The Patriot Act was passed with wide support on 26 October 2001, in the frenzied aftermath of the 9/11 attacks. After its enactment, however, many began to criticize the reach and scope of the law, claiming especially that

. . . On the first day we had been taking detainees from the in-processing center to their cages for quite a while when myself and the guy that was my escorting partner grabbed the next detainee to be taken. He was an older man. Probably in his mid to late 50s—short and kind of a husky build. I remember grabbing him and then starting to walk first through the rocks and then through the sally port (a long walkway with gates on both sides) heading towards Alpha Block. Then I noticed he was really tense, shaking really bad, and not wanting to walk or move without being forced to do so. We made our way to Alpha Block to the cage he would be placed in. He was instructed to go to his knees, which he did. My partner then went down and took off his leg shackles. I still had control of his upper body, and I could still feel him tensing up. Once the shackles were off my partner started to take off the hand cuffs. The detainee got really tense and started to pull away. We yelled at him a couple times "Stop moving!" Over and over. Then he stopped moving, and when my partner went to put the key in that first handcuff, the detainee jerked hard to the left towards me. Before I knew it, I threw the detainee to the ground and was on top of him holding his face to the cement floor.

At this time my partner had left the cage. The block NCOIC (or Non-Commissioned Officer in Charge) was on the radio yelling code red which meant emergency on the block. Before I knew, I was being grabbed from behind and pulled out of the cage by the IRF [Immediate Reaction Force] team. They grabbed this man and hog-tied him. He laid there like that for hours that day before he was released from that position.

A couple days later I found out from a detainee who was on that block that the older detainee was just scared and that when we placed him on his knees he thought he was going to be executed. He then went on to tell me that this man had seen some of his friends and family members executed on their knees. I can remember guys coming up to me after it was over that night and said "Man, that was a good job; you got you some."

I did not feel good about what I did. It felt wrong. This man was old enough to be my father, and I had just beaten up on him. I still to this day don't know who was more scared before and during this incident me or the detainee.

I remember seeing him the next day when I walked into camp. His face was all bruised and scraped up. I was young and didn't question anything back then. As I do nowadays. But even then, when I was as pissed off as anyone there, I felt ashamed of what I did. As the years have went on and the more I learn the more guilt I feel. This is one of the incidents from my time at Guantánamo that haunts me. . . .

Source: UC Davis Center for the Study of Human Rights in the Americas, www.humanrights.ucdavis.edu (29 October 2009).

it violated Americans' privacy and gave the government too much power to engage in domestic spying. Particularly galling to some was Section 215, which granted law-enforcement agents the authority to access, secretly and without a warrant, the records of library patrons. Roving wiretaps, which used computer technology to monitor the communications of millions of Americans without a warrant, was also controversial. After a 2004 lawsuit brought by the American Civil Liberties Union (ACLU), U.S. District Judge Victor Marrero ruled in 2007 that the FBI could not demand personal information about subscribers from Internet service providers, since doing so represented prior restraint of speech. The law was intended in many ways as an emergency measure, crafted to meet specific law-enforcement needs in the early days of the war on terrorism, and most of its provisions were set to expire in 2005. Nearly all of them, however, were reauthorized in 2005 and made permanent in 2006.

Guantánamo Bay. The U.S. war in Afghanistan was launched in October 2001 to overthrow that country's ruling Taliban regime and to capture or kill associates of al Qaeda, the international terrorist organization responsible for the 9-11 attacks. As fighting in Afghanistan became the central front in the war on terror, it was unclear what to do with those who were captured and were deemed a terrorist threat to the United States. Since associates of al Qaeda were not typical soldiers and did not necessarily fight out of allegiance to any particular country, they fell into a gray area of international law. In the fear-ridden aftermath of 9/11, it was considered too dangerous to maintain prison camps within American borders. As a result, the Bush administration authorized the creation of a detention center at the U.S. naval base at Guantánamo Bay, Cuba, where captives could be housed as "enemy combatants" rather than as prisoners of war who were entitled to the protections of the Geneva Conventions. The first detainees arrived in January 2002. Since they were being housed outside of U.S. legal jurisdiction, the Bush administration maintained that they did not fall under the protections of the U.S. Constitution. As the decade progressed, more than seven hundred detainees were brought to the Guantánamo Bay detention center; most of them had been

Detainees are held for in-processing at U.S. naval base Guantánamo Bay, Cuba, on 11 January 2002 (Department of Defense photograph by Petty Officer 1st Class Shane T. McCoy, U.S. Navy).

captured in Afghanistan or in Iraq, which the United States invaded on 19 March 2003. While for some the prison camp represented a reassuring sign of the administration's forceful and decisive action in combating global terrorism, others began to criticize the fact that the United States was taking prisoners and holding them indefinitely, without due process and without respecting the conditions laid down by the Geneva Conventions. Yaser Hamdi, who was captured in Afghanistan and accused of fighting for the Taliban, was held at Guantánamo Bay until it was discovered that he had been born in the United States and was, therefore, an American citizen. He was then transferred to a naval brig in Charleston Harbor in South Carolina. In the case of *Hamdi* v. *Rumsfeld* (2004) the U.S. Supreme Court ruled that the Bush administration could not, as it claimed, simply designate Hamdi, an American citizen, as an illegal enemy combatant and detain him without judicial due process. In *Hamdan* v. *Rumsfeld* (2006), involving Yemeni citizen Salim Ahmed Hamdan, who had been employed as al Qaeda leader Osama bin Laden's driver and had been captured during the U.S. invasion of Afghanistan in November 2001, the Supreme Court dealt another blow

to the Bush administration's position by ruling that the executive branch did not have the authority to create, unilaterally, military tribunals outside the protection of the Geneva Conventions or the Uniform Code of Military Justice. In essence, the court held, the president was seeking not only to avoid the accepted standards of justice for those captured in war but also to avoid domestic protections by housing the detainees outside of the United States. The final blow to the administration's position was the Supreme Court's ruling in the case of *Boumediene* v. *Bush*, where the court held that despite Bush's claim that the Guantánamo naval base was ultimately under Cuban sovereignty—the United States holds a lease on the property—detainees at the prison camp have a habeas corpus right to challenge their detention under the U.S. Constitution. The court's evolving antagonism toward the Bush administration's Guantánamo policy coincided with growing public suspicion. In November 2008 Barack Obama was elected president after having campaigned on a promise to close the Guantánamo Bay detention center. One of his first actions as president was to issue an executive order on 22 January 2009 that the camp should be shut down within a year.

A pay phone with a sticker referring to the U.S. Patriot Act of 2001 (photograph by David Drexler)

Warrantless Wiretapping. Shortly after the 9/11 terrorist attacks, President Bush authorized the National Security Agency (NSA) to conduct wiretaps without warrants on telephone calls and emails suspected of involving foreign terrorist agents, even if the call originated or was received domestically. The surveillance program continued in secret until it was revealed by a whistleblower in 2005. In addition to wide public dissatisfaction with the idea of secret domestic spying, there was also a potential legal problem: the administration had improperly bypassed the 1978 Foreign Intelligence Surveillance Act (FISA), which established protocols for the secret wiretapping of American citizens. Created to allow greater legal flexibility for government agencies tracking "foreign powers" and the "agents of foreign powers," FISA established the Foreign Intelligence Surveillance Court, which operated behind closed doors and reviewed requests for wiretap warrants that, for national-security reasons, had to be obtained quickly and remain secret. The Bush administration claimed that the congressional resolution authorizing it to wage war on al Qaeda granted it broad powers to pursue terrorists domestically—powers that included the right to bypass FISA. Public outrage led to congressional hearings and the passage in August 2007 of the Protect America Act, which revised FISA to create new procedures and some judicial oversight of domestic wiretapping of individuals believed to be involved in terrorist activities. A revised version of the act, which was signed into law on 9 July 2008, contained a controversial provision granting retroactive immunity to telecommunications providers who had assisted in the NSA warrantless-wiretapping program.

Sources:

Asthana Anushka and Karen DeYoung, "Bush Calls for Greater Wiretap Authority," *Washington Post,* 8 September 2006, p. A1;

Joan Biskupic and Laura Parker, "Justices Reject Guantánamo Tribunals," *USA Today,* 30 June 2006;

Neil Lewis, "Judge Extends Legal Rights for Guantánamo Detainees," *New York Times,* 1 February 2005, p. A12;

Eric Lichtblau, "Congress Strikes Deal to Overhaul Wiretap Law," *New York Times,* 20 June 2008, p. A1;

Lichtblau, "Judge Rejects Bush's View on Wiretaps," *New York Times,* 3 July 2008, p. A17;

Toni Locy, "ACLU Sues over Patriot Act Seizures Provision," *USA Today,* 30 July 2003;

Jerry Markon, "US to Free Hamdi, Send Him Home," *Washington Post,* 23 September 2004, p. A1;

Ann McFeatters, "Bush Signs Anti-Terror Bill; Says Tough Law Will Preserve Constitutional Rights," *Pittsburgh Post-Gazette,* 27 October 2001, p. A6;

Julia Preston, "Judge Strikes down Section of Patriot Act Allowing Secret Subpoenas of Internet Data," *New York Times,* 30 September 2004, p. A26;

James Risen and Eric Lichtblau, "Bush Lets U.S. Spy on Callers without Courts," *New York Times,* 16 December 2005, p. A1;

David E. Sanger and Scott Shane, "Court's Ruling Is Likely to Force Negotiations over Presidential Power," *New York Times,* 30 June 2006, p. A21.

HEADLINE MAKERS

JOHN ASHCROFT

1942–

SENATOR, ATTORNEY GENERAL

Early Life. The son of a Christian minister, John Ashcroft was born in Chicago on 9 May 1942. He attended Yale University and received his law degree from the University of Chicago in 1967. After an unsuccessful 1972 bid to represent Missouri in the House of Representatives, he served as state auditor before being elected state attorney general. He was elected governor of Missouri in 1984 and served two terms. In 1994 Ashcroft was elected to the U.S. Senate, where he developed a reputation as a strong social conservative by promoting prolife policies.

Attorney General. In 2000 Ashcroft lost his Senate reelection bid to Governor Mel Carnahan, who had died two weeks earlier in a plane crash but whose name remained on the ballot. Lieutenant Governor Roger Wilson had announced before the election that he would name Carnahan's widow to the open Senate seat, should he win. Ashcroft was nominated to be the seventy-ninth U.S. attorney general by President George W. Bush in early 2001. In a contentious confirmation hearing, Democratic senators questioned Ashcroft's role as Missouri governor in opposing desegregation efforts. In the end he was confirmed by the Senate 58-42. Known for his deeply held religious beliefs, Ashcroft convened regular prayer meetings at the Department of Justice. He was lampooned in the media as a prude after reportedly ordering that a nude statue representing "the spirit of justice" in female form be shrouded by a curtain. During his tenure as attorney general, Ashcroft oversaw a robust expansion of the government's domestic surveillance activities in the war on terror, and he was a staunch defender of the administration's approach to such con-

troversial issues as the legal status of Guantánamo Bay detainees, the Patriot Act, and the National Security Administration wiretapping program. As such, he became a symbol of many of the most contentious elements of the administration's policy, and he remained a politically divisive figure throughout his tenure as attorney general.

Retirement. Ashcroft announced his resignation as head of the Justice Department in November 2004. He was succeeded by Alberto Gonzales. After stepping down he began a consulting and lobbying firm, the Ashcroft Group. He also taught at Regent University in Virginia and wrote several books, including *Never Again: Securing America and Restoring Justice* (2006).

Sources:

Joe Conason, "From John Ashcroft's Justice Department to Abu Ghraib," *salon.com* (22 May 2004);

"John David Ashcroft," *bioguide.congress.gov;*

Jeffrey Toobin, "Ashcroft's Ascent," *New Yorker,* 15 April 2002.

JOHN GLOVER ROBERTS

1955–

CHIEF JUSTICE OF THE SUPREME COURT

Origins. John Glover Roberts was born in Buffalo, New York, on 27 January 1955. His family later moved to Long Beach, Indiana, where Roberts attended high school; he was captain of the football team and valedictorian of the graduating class. He attended Harvard University, where he studied history before enrolling in Harvard Law School. There he became managing editor of the prestigious *Harvard Law Review.*

Early Career. After graduating in 1979, Roberts clerked for one year under Judge Henry Friendly of the

Second Circuit Court of Appeals. He later served in the White House as associate counsel to President Ronald Reagan. After briefly entering private practice, Roberts returned to public life, serving as deputy solicitor general from 1989 to 1993 under President George H. W. Bush. He was named to the U.S. Court of Appeals for the District of Columbia Circuit by George W. Bush and was confirmed on 8 May 2003. On the circuit court he established a reputation as a conservative jurist. He affirmed the dismissal of the case of *Hedgepeth* v. *Washington Metropolitan Area Transit Authority*, a suit brought by the parents of a twelve-year-old girl who had been arrested, handcuffed, and detained at a police station after violating a Washington Metro station's zero-tolerance "no eating" policy. In the case of *Hamdan* v. *Rumsfeld* Roberts upheld the Bush administration's right to establish military tribunals for detainees at Guantánamo Bay, a decision that was later overturned by the U.S. Supreme Court.

Supreme Court. Roberts was first nominated to the Supreme Court to fill the vacancy left by the impending retirement of Justice Sandra Day O'Connor, who announced that she would step down from the bench on 1 July 2005. President Bush announced the nomination on 18 July; but while the Roberts confirmation hearings were pending, Chief Justice William H. Rehnquist died on 3 September, leaving vacant the position of chief justice. Two days later, Bush withdrew the earlier nomination and named Roberts to head the court. Roberts's confirmation hearings went smoothly; he charmed senators, likening his judicial role to that of a baseball umpire. After being confirmed by the Senate, he was sworn in on 29 September as the seventeenth chief justice of the United States.

The Roberts Court. Under Chief Justice Roberts the Supreme Court took a more conservative judicial approach. O'Connor, who had been a moderate swing vote on the Rehnquist court, was replaced in 2006 by Samuel A. Alito, a more reliably conservative jurist. The Roberts court handed down major decisions limiting the scope of affirmative-action policies, striking down campaign-finance regulations, and, for the first time in the Supreme Court's history, asserting an individual's right to bear arms under the Second Amendment. Roberts suffered a mild embarrassment in January 2009 when, at the inauguration of President Barack Obama, he flubbed his lines while administering the Oath of Office. The oath was correctly readministered a few days later in a private White House ceremony.

Sources:

Peter Baker, "Unraveling the Twists and Turns of the Path to a Nominee," *Washington Post,* 25 July 2005;

Linda Greenhouse, "In the Confirmation Dance, the Past But Rarely the Prologue," *New York Times,* 24 July 2005;

"Justice John G. Roberts, Jr.," *oyez.org.*

SONIA SOTOMAYOR

1954–

ASSOCIATE JUSTICE OF THE SUPREME COURT

Early Life. Sonia Sotomayor was raised by her widowed mother in a housing project in the Bronx, New York. Despite growing up without many of the benefits other children enjoyed, she excelled in her studies and earned admission to Princeton University. After graduating summa cum laude, she attended Yale Law School, where she was an editor of the *Yale Law Journal*. She was an assistant district attorney in New York from 1979 to 1983; working under longtime New York District Attorney Robert Morgenthau, she successfully prosecuted several high-profile cases, including that of Richard Maddicks, the "Tarzan murderer." She entered private practice in 1984 and served in several public-service roles in the late 1980s, including the State of New York Mortgage Agency and the Puerto Rican Legal Defense and Education Fund.

Federal Court Judge. In 1991 Sotomayor was nominated by President George H. W. Bush to a seat on the U.S. District Court for the Southern District of New York. Her confirmation to the bench broke new ground, as she was the first woman of Puerto Rican descent to serve as a federal court judge and New York State's first Hispanic woman to become a federal judge. Perhaps the most widely publicized ruling during her tenure on the district court was in *Silverman* v. *Major League Baseball Player Relations Committee, Inc.,* which ended the 1994 baseball players' strike just in time for the season to begin. In June 1997 she was nominated by President Bill Clinton to a seat on the U.S. Court of Appeals for the Second Circuit. After a contentious process, Sotomayor was confirmed by the Senate on 2 October 1998. Her highest-profile case as an appeals court judge was *Ricci* v. *DeStefano* (2008), in which she sided with the city of New Haven, Connecticut, in approving the lower court's dismissal of a lawsuit brought by white firefighters who claimed that the city discriminated against them when it threw out their scores on a promotion test that no black firefighter passed.

Supreme Court Justice. After Justice David Souter's retirement plans became publicly known in April 2009, President Obama tapped Sotomayor to fill the vacancy; he announced her nomination on 26 May 2009. In promoting its nominee, the Obama administration emphasized not only Sotomayor's experience in public service and the fact that she was nominated to federal judgeships by both Republican and Democratic presidents but also the inspiring story of her rise from humble beginnings to the pinnacle of the legal profession. Critics of the nomination, particularly conservative pundits, centered their campaign against the confirmation on her 2001 remark that a "wise Latina woman with the richness of her experiences would more often than not reach a better conclusion than a white male who hasn't lived that life." Though the surfacing of the remark did some political damage, Sotomayor explained that the quotation was taken out of context and that she meant only to emphasize the importance of life experience. She was eventually confirmed 68–31, with the support of nine Republicans. On being sworn in as associate justice on 8 August 2009, she became the first Hispanic to serve on the Supreme Court.

Sources:
Michael Fletcher, "A Compelling Biography is no Guarantee of a Smooth Confirmation," *Washington Post,* 30 May 2009;
"Who is Sonia Sotomayor?" *cnn.com* (26 May 2009).

PEOPLE IN THE NEWS

On 31 January 2006 **Samuel A. Alito** was sworn in as associate justice of the U.S. Supreme Court. A noted judicial conservative, Alito had served as U.S. attorney for the district of New Jersey and on the Third Circuit of the U.S. Court of Appeals before being nominated to the Supreme Court by President George W. Bush.

On 11 December 2000 noted attorney **David Boies** provided oral arguments before the U.S. Supreme Court on behalf of Al Gore in the case of *Bush* v. *Gore.*

In 2004 former U.S. attorney general **Ramsey Clark** joined the defense team of former Iraqi president Saddam Hussein. Known for his often radical positions on U.S. foreign policy, Clark was at one point ejected from the Iraqi Special Tribunal trial of Hussein for claiming that the court was making a mockery of justice.

In 2006 the University of Alabama School of Law honored Southern Poverty Law Center founder **Morris Dees** by creating the Morris Dees Justice Award. The award recognizes a career spent in the pursuit of justice and the public interest.

On 28 September 2005 a Travis County, Texas, grand jury indicted Republican House Majority Leader **Tom DeLay** on charges of conspiracy to violate election law. District Attorney **Ronnie Earle** charged that DeLay, through his involvement in the political action committee Texans for a Republican Majority, had illegally directed corporate donations to statewide races.

In 2008 Missouri mother and businesswoman **Lori Drew** was indicted for having created a fictitious MySpace character that allegedly harassed a young woman, a rival of Drew's daughter, to the point of committing suicide. Although she was convicted on a misdemeanor for violating terms of usage of the computer, she was later acquitted. Missouri later passed stronger legislation against so-called cyberbullying.

On 31 May 2005 former FBI associate director **W. Mark Felt** revealed himself to be the Watergate whistleblower known as "Deep Throat." Felt's identity as a source had been closely guarded by *Washington Post* journalists **Bob Woodward** and **Carl Bernstein,** to whom he had provided information crucial to their coverage of the scandal.

On 6 April 2007 **Monica M. Goodling,** aide to U.S. Attorney General **Alberto R. Gonzales,** resigned from her position after she refused to appear before a Senate committee investigating the firings of eight U.S. attorneys by the Bush administration. After being granted immunity, she admitted offering political favors in return for the dismissal of the federal prosecutors, who were deemed insufficiently supportive of Republican goals.

Beginning in 2000 **George Greer,** a Pinellas-Pasco County, Florida, circuit court judge, played a central role in the case of the comatose **Terri Schiavo,** which became a cause célèbre for prolife advocates. Judge Greer ordered that Schiavo's feeding tube be removed in accordance with the wishes of her husband.

On 30 May 2005 teenager **Natalee Holloway** went missing while on vacation in Aruba. The ultimately unsuccessful attempts to locate her attracted widespread media attention, especially on twenty-four-hour cable-news networks.

In May 2007 radio "shock jock" **Don Imus** filed suit against CBS for wrongful termination after he was fired for inflammatory comments about the Rutgers University women's basketball team. Imus hired attorney **Martin Garbus,** known for freedom of speech cases. Imus and CBS reached a settlement in the case on undisclosed terms in August 2007.

In 2005 **Thomas Mesereau** served as lead trial counsel for **Michael Jackson** in the pop star's high-profile child-molestation case. A highly regarded trial lawyer, Mesereau also served briefly as counsel in the 2004 Robert Blake murder trial. After a five-month trial in the Jackson case, Mesereau and his team obtained a verdict of not guilty on all counts.

In 2004 San Francisco mayor **Gavin Newsom** instructed his city clerk to begin issuing marriage licenses to same-sex couples who filed for them, despite state law prohibiting such action. The California Supreme Court later invalidated all marriages performed under Newsom's directive.

The botched execution by lethal injection of **Christopher J. Newton** at the Southern Ohio Correctional Institution on 24 May 2007 raised anger and concern over the death penalty and how it was carried out. The process took two hours and included at least ten tries to install the tubes for administration of the drugs.

On 1 July 2005 Justice **Sandra Day O'Connor** announced her intention to retire from the U.S. Supreme Court as soon as a successor could be confirmed. Nominated by President Ronald Reagan in 1981, O'Connor was the court's first female justice and for decades provided a crucial swing vote in favor of abortion rights. On 12 August 2009 she was awarded the Presidential Medal of Freedom by President Barack Obama.

Former assistant attorney general **Theodore Olson** represented George W. Bush in the case of *Bush* v. *Gore* before the U.S. Supreme Court on 11 December 2000. Olson argued succesfully that the Gore campaign's call for vote recounts violated the equal protection clause of the Fourteenth Amendment. He was later named to the position of solicitor general by President Bush.

On 11 January 2007 **Charles D. "Cully" Stimson,** deputy assistant secretary of defense for detainee affairs, raised controversy by criticizing, on the radio, law firms that provided legal assistance to detainees at Guantánamo Bay. He later apologized and resigned his position.

Navy Lieutenant Commander **Charles D. Swift,** a lawyer with the Judge Advocate General Corps, successfully defended Guantánamo detainee **Salim Ahmed Hamdan,** a former driver for **Osama bin Laden** in Afghanistan, against charges of terrorism in the U.S. Supreme Court case *Hamdan* v. *Rumsfeld* (2006). For doing his job, he was passed over for promotion and forced to retire from the navy.

In 2000 ABC legal analyst **Jeffrey Toobin** received an Emmy award for his coverage of the Elian González custody battle. Toobin joined CNN in 2002 and covered high-profile legal cases for the network throughout the rest of the decade.

Former criminal defense lawyer and CNN legal analyst **Greta Van Susteren** joined the Fox News network as host of *On the Record*, a current-affairs program with an emphasis on criminal cases. The show experienced high ratings during its extensive coverage of the 2005 **Natalee Holloway** affair, which involved the search for an American teenager who went missing during a vacation trip to Aruba.

AWARDS

AMERICAN BAR ASSOCIATION
Robert F. Drinan Award For Distinguished Service

Recognizes those who have "advanced its mission of providing leadership to the legal profession in protecting and advancing human rights, civil liberties, and social justice."

2001: Robert F. Drinan

2002: John H. Pickering

2003: John J. Curtin Jr.

2004: Marna S. Tucker

2005: Cruz Reynoso

2006: Jerome J. Shestack

2007: Talbot D'Alemberte

2008: Martha Barnett

2009: Michael S. Greco

Thurgood Marshall Award

Recognizes those who "exemplified Justice Marshall's commitment to the causes of civil and human rights."

2000: Revius Q. Ortique Jr.

2001: William Wayne Justice

2002: Don Edwards

2003: Dale Minami

2004: Fred D. Gray

2005: Abner J. Mikva

2006: Julius Chambers

2007: Matthew J. Perry Jr.

2008: Nancy Gertner

2009: Janet Reno

AMERICAN COLLEGE OF TRIAL LAWYERS
Griffin Bell Award for Courageous Advocacy

2000: Nickolas C. Murnion

2001: Oliver W. Hill

2004: Bryan A. Stevenson

DEATHS

Albert Armendariz, 88, judge, helped found the Mexican American Legal Defense and Educational Fund, 4 October 2007.

Edward R. Becker, 73, chief judge of the 3rd U.S. Circuit Court of Appeals, 19 May 2006.

Hugo Black III, 54, lawyer, assistant U.S. attorney in Florida, 29 September 2007.

Jane Bolin, 98, judge, first African American female judge in the United States, first black woman to graduate from Yale Law School, 8 January 2007.

James Butler, 84, lawyer, won famous thalidomide (chemical which caused birth defects) case (1971) against drug company Richardson-Merrell, 26 May 2005.

William Matthew Byrne Jr., 75, federal judge, served on President Richard M. Nixon's Commission on Campus Unrest; presided over trial of military analyst Daniel Ellsberg, 12 January 2006.

David Carliner, 89, lawyer, founded Washington, D.C., chapter of the American Civil Liberties Union, 19 September 2007.

Richard Conway Casey, 74, federal judge, served while legally blind; nominated by President Bill Clinton (1997), 22 March 2007.

Jim Clark, 84, Alabama sheriff, violently blocked voting-rights marches in Selma, Alabama (1965); attacked marchers on the Edmund Pettus Bridge ("Bloody Sunday"), 4 June 2007.

Johnnie L. Cochran Jr., 67, defense attorney, defended O. J. Simpson against murder charges (1995), 29 March 2005.

David Conn, 56, lawyer, prosecuted Erik and Lyle Menendez murder case (1996), 24 October 2006.

Lloyd Cutler, 87, lawyer, White House counsel to Presidents Jimmy Carter and Bill Clinton; served on the commission investigating flawed intelligence on weapons of mass destruction in Iraq, 8 May 2005.

Samuel Alexander Garrison III, 65, lawyer, defended President Richard M. Nixon in impeachment hearings (1974); gay activist, 27 May 2007.

Truman K. Gibson Jr., 93, lawyer, fought racial discrimination during World War II while adviser with the War Department; represented heavyweight champion boxer Joe Louis, 23 December 2005.

Morris P. Glushien, 96, general counsel for the International Ladies Garment Workers Union, 19 May 2006.

Roger D. Groot, 63, law professor, taught at Washington & Lee University; assisted in defense of sniper Lee Boyd Malvo, 12 November 2005.

Douglas W. Hillman, 84, federal district judge, appointed to the bench by Jimmy Carter (1979), 1 February 2007.

Nat H. Hentel, 87, New York district attorney and State Supreme Court justice (1987–1992), 31 January 2007.

Odell Horton, 77, federal judge, first African American to sit on federal bench in Tennessee since Reconstruction, nominated by President Jimmy Carter (1980), 22 February 2006.

George Howard Jr., 82, federal judge, presided over trials of James and Susan McDougal and former Arkansas governor Jim Guy Tucker (Whitewater), 21 April 2007.

William G. Hundley, 80, lawyer, served in Eisenhower and Kennedy administrations, 11 June 2006.

Robert E. Keeton, 87, federal judge, Harvard law professor, appointed by President Jimmy Carter (1979), 1 July 2007.

John T. Kramer, 68, legal scholar, civil rights and poverty specialist, executive director of National Council on Hunger and Malnutrition in 1960s and 1970s, 8 March 2006.

Ray Kurtzman, 79, entertainment lawyer, worked for Creative Artists Agency, 23 April 2007.

Anthony A. Lapham, 70, lawyer, served as counsel for the Central Intelligence Agency in the 1970s, 11 November 2006.

Donald P. Lay, 80, federal judge, served on U.S. Court of Appeals for the 8th Circuit, 29 April 2007.

Leonard W. Levy, 83, constitutional historian, wrote *Origins of the Fifth Amendment* (1968), 24 August 2006.

Carlene Lewis, 51, lawyer, litigated against Vioxx maker, Merck; won 1969 Pulitzer Prize for History; 5 June 2006.

Michele Maxian, 55, lawyer, fought for arraignment of suspects within twenty-four hours, 14 November 2006.

Theodore McMillian, 86, federal judge, first black judge on the 8th U.S. Circuit Court of Appeals (Missouri), 18 January 2006.

John McTernan, 94, lawyer, active in civil rights and labor cases; defended witnesses at House Un-American Activities Committee, 28 March 2005.

Bernard D. Meltzer, 92, lawyer and scholar, helped draft United Nations charter; prosecutor at the Nuremberg trials of Nazi criminals, 4 January 2007.

Pamela Minzner, 63, judge, chief justice on New Mexico's Supreme Court (1999–2000), 31 August 2007.

William B. (Bill) Moffitt, 60, lawyer, past president of the National Association of Criminal Defense Lawyers, 24 April 2009.

Charles Older, 88, judge, presided over Charles Manson murder trial, 17 June 2006.

John Garrett Penn, 75, federal judge, appointed by President Jimmy Carter (1979), 9 September 2007.

Catherine Roraback, 87, lawyer, won *Griswold* v. *Connecticut* (1965), which established the right to privacy and the use of contraception, 17 October 2007.

Stanley Rothenberg, 76, lawyer, specialist in copyright law, 3 November 2006.

Elsijane Trimble Roy, 90, judge, first woman to serve on 8th U.S. Circuit and Arkansas Supreme Court, 23 January 2007.

Mel A. Sachs, 60, defense attorney, defended famous celebrity clients, 30 August 2006.

Jack Tanner, 86, U.S. District judge, first black judge in Washington state, nominated by President Jimmy Carter (1978), 10 January 2006.

PUBLICATIONS

Michelle Alexander, *The New Jim Crow: Mass Incarceration in the Age of Colorblindness* (New York: New Press, 2010);

Akhil Reed Amar, *America's Constitution: A Biography* (New York: Random House, 2005);

Bill Barnhart and Gene Schlickman, *John Paul Stevens: An Independent Life* (Dekalb: Northern Illinois University Press, 2010);

Seyla Benhabib, *The Rights of Others: Aliens, Residents, and Citizens* (Cambridge & New York: Cambridge University Press, 2004);

Sarah A. Binder and Forrest Maltzman, *Advice & Dissent: The Struggle to Shape the Federal Judiciary* (Washington, D.C.: Brookings Institution Press, 2009);

George Chauncey, *Why Marriage?: The History Shaping Today's Debate over Gay Equality* (New York: Basic Books, 2004);

Erwin Chemerinsky, *The Conservative Assault on the Constitution* (New York: Simon & Schuster, 2010);

John Dean, *The Rehnquist Choice: The Untold Story of the Nixon Appointment that Redefined the Supreme Court* (New York: Touchstone, 2001);

Lee Epstein and Jeffrey A. Segal, *Advice and Consent: The Politics of Judicial Appointments* (Oxford & New York: Oxford University Press, 2005);

Christopher M. Finan, *From the Palmer Raids to the Patriot Act: A History of the Fight for Free Speech in America* (Boston: Beacon, 2007);

Lawrence M. Friedman, *A History of American Law*, third edition (New York: Simon & Schuster, 2005);

David Garland, *Peculiar Institution: America's Death Penalty in an Age of Abolition* (Cambridge, Mass.: Belknap Press of Harvard University Press, 2010);

Garret M. Graff, *The Threat Matrix: The FBI in the Age of Global Terror* (New York: Little, Brown, 2011);

Kermit L. Hall, ed., *The Oxford Companion to the Supreme Court of the United States*, second edition (Oxford & New York: Oxford University Press, 2005);

Michael Lewis and others, *The War on Terror and the Laws of War: A Military Perspective* (Oxford & New York: Oxford University Press, 2009);

Thomas R. Marshall, *Public Opinion and the Rehnquist Court* (Albany: SUNY Press, 2008);

Sandra Day O'Connor, *The Majesty of the Law: Reflections of a Supreme Court Justice,* edited by Craig Joyce (New York: Random House, 2003);

O'Connor and H. Alan Davis, *Lazy B: Growing Up on a Cattle Ranch in the American Southwest* (New York: Random House, 2002);

Robert Perkinson, *Texas Tough: The Rise of America's Prison Empire* (New York: Metropolitan Books, 2010);

Richard M. Pious, *The War on Terrorism and the Rule of Law* (Los Angeles: Roxbury, 2006);

Lucas A. Powe Jr., *The Supreme Court and the American Elite, 1798–2008* (Cambridge, Mass.: Harvard University Press, 2009);

David A. J. Richards, *The Sodomy Cases: Bowers v. Hardwick and Lawrence v. Texas* (Lawrence: University Press of Kansas, 2009);

Jeffrey Rosen, *The Supreme Court: The Personalities and Rivalries that Defined America* (New York: Times Books, 2006);

Gary D. Solis, *The Law of Armed Conflict: International Humanitarian Law in War* (Cambridge & New York: Cambridge University Press, 2010);

Geoffrey R. Stone, *Perilous Times: Free Speech in Wartime: from the Sedition Act of 1798 to the War on Terrorism* (New York: Norton, 2004);

Fred Strebeigh, *Equal: Women Reshape American Law* (New York: Norton, 2009);

Clarence Thomas, *My Grandfather's Son: A Memoir* (New York: Harper, 2007);

Scott Turow, *Ultimate Punishment: A Lawyer's Reflections on Dealing with the Death Penalty* (New York: Farrar, Straus, and Giroux, 2003);

Elizabeth Vrato, *The Counselors: Conversations with 18 Courageous Women Who Have Changed the World* (Philadelphia: Running Press, 2002);

Benjamin Wittes, *Law and the Long War: The Future of Justice in the Age of Terror* (New York: Penguin, 2008);

ABA Journal, periodical;

American Lawyer, periodical;

The Federal Lawyer, periodical;

National Law Journal, periodical.

C H A P T E R   E I G H T

LIFESTYLES AND SOCIAL TRENDS

by TRACY BEALER

CONTENTS

Sidebars and tables are listed in italics.

2000

- Toyota introduces its hybrid-model, Prius, as a 2001 model year in the United States and immediately generates long waiting lists, evidence of evolving interest in eco-consciousness and climate change.

1 Jan. The so-called Y2K bug does not result in widespread computer malfunctions, inaugurating a decade dominated by digital technology.

10 Mar. The Nasdaq closes at a record high in the frenzy surrounding the Internet bubble. The next day the financial success of Internet start-up companies takes a significant downturn, in what the media call the "dot com bust."

3 Apr. The Supreme Court fines Microsoft Corporation under antitrust laws in a ruling some critics warn might set the precedent for more regulation of the Internet.

16 Apr. Discovery Channel's broadcast of the British series *Walking with Dinosaurs* becomes the most-watched documentary show in cable history.

19 Apr. Oprah Winfrey debuts *O: The Oprah Magazine*.

26 Oct. Sony launches its popular PlayStation 2 video-game console.

7 Nov. The presidential election is too close to call, leading to an extended recount in Florida and a Supreme Court decision (12 December) awarding the office to George W. Bush.

2001

- Bratz, a line of ten-inch multicultural dolls with enlarged heads and modern clothing and makeup, is released in the United States and becomes a favorite toy for young girls. Annual sales reach $500 million in 2008.

- Valerie Gibson publishes *Cougar: A Guide for Older Women Dating Younger Men*, popularizing the use of the word "cougar."

15 Jan. The online encyclopedia Wikipedia is launched with completely user-generated content.

June The Nintendo handheld gaming system, Game Boy Advance, is released for sale in the United States.

11 June Comedian Joe Rogan hosts the reality-competition series *Fear Factor*.

25 Aug. Popular R&B singer and actress Aaliyah dies in a plane crash in the Bahamas.

11 Sept. Suicide bombers hijack four airplanes, crashing two of them into New York City's World Trade Center and one into the Pentagon. The fourth plane crashes in Shanksville, Pennsylvania, killing all forty passengers and airflight crew and the four hijackers aboard.

23 Oct. Apple debuts its handheld MP3 music-file-storing device, the iPod, which quickly becomes one of the most sought-after personal electronic devices.

2002

- Media attention turns to allegations of widespread sexual abuse in the Catholic Church, sparking a crisis that reverberates throughout the decade.

- The BlackBerry smartphone hits the market.

8 Jan. President Bush signs the No Child Left Behind Act.

Feb. Merchandise featuring Disney character Lizzie McGuire (played by Hilary Duff) is heavily marketed to pre- and early-teen girls.

8–24 Feb. The Olympic Winter Games are held in Salt Lake City, Utah, and extreme-sports stars such as snowboarders compete for the first time.

19 May   The popular science-fiction/thriller series *The X-Files* broadcasts its final episode.

11 June   The first season of *American Idol* premieres; the season ends with Kelly Clarkson winning the title in September.

21 Oct.   The U.S. Department of Agriculture (USDA) organic label is issued.

2003

Mar.   The World Health Organization releases a warning on the respiratory disease SARS (Severe Acute Respiratory Syndrome), sparking worldwide concern and an increase in the use of surgical masks.

Apr.   Apple opens its online music-downloading service, iTunes.

May   The first "flash mob" occurs in Manhattan; groups of individuals gather suddenly at a location and perform a song or dance, often captured on video, and then the participants quickly disperse.

15 July   *Queer Eye for the Straight Guy* premieres on cable network Bravo.

10 Oct.   Popular conservative talk-radio host Rush Limbaugh admits he has an addiction to painkillers.

18 Nov.   The Massachusetts Supreme Court rules anti-same-sex marriage laws unconstitutional; the state legalizes gay marriage in 2004.

2004

Feb.   The online social-networking site Facebook debuts.

29 Apr.   The World War II Memorial opens on the National Mall. "Honor Flights" are commissioned to enable veterans to attend the dedication, held on 29 May.

July–Aug.   The major party conventions offer press credentials to bloggers, demonstrating the growing presence of amateur online journalism in mainstream politics.

22 Sept.   ABC airs the pilot of *Lost*, which generates devoted followers and demonstrates how television can employ the Internet by linking viewers to several sites related to a program.

21 Nov.   The handheld Nintendo DS gaming system is released for sale in the United States.

4 Nov.   Eleven states ban gay marriage in local elections as voters report in exit polls that "moral values" are the most important issue on the ballot. President Bush wins reelection, defeating Democratic candidate John Kerry.

2005

- A wave of online identity theft plagues Internet users, exposing the danger posed to privacy by the ubiquity of the Internet.

- The Sony PlayStation Portable (PSP) handheld gaming system is released for sale in North America.

16 Feb.   The Kyoto Protocol, an international agreement aimed at fighting climate change, goes into effect without the support of the United States.

Mar.   YouTube, a video-sharing website, is launched.

3 Mar.	Millionaire Steve Fossett completes a nonstop solo flight around the globe, breaking a world record.
May	The political blog and news aggregator, *The Huffington Post*, is launched.
19 May	The final installment of the six-movie *Star Wars* series, *Revenge of the Sith*, opens.
2 July	A series of ten simultaneous concerts, known as Live 8, takes place across the world, including one in Philadelphia, to call attention to global poverty.
29 Aug.	Hurricane Katrina makes landfall in New Orleans, Louisiana, resulting in a massive storm surge that overcomes the city's levees, leaving much of the town underwater for weeks. Portions of Mississippi and Alabama are also devastated.

2006

- A national survey reveals that nearly one out of every four American adults from the age of eighteen to fifty has at least one tattoo.

- Bakugan Battle Brawlers, a game (based on a Japanese anime series) that employs cards and little magnet-embedded spheres that pop open, becomes popular, especially with young boys.

24 Jan.	*An Inconvenient Truth* opens at the Sundance Film Festival. The documentary featuring Al Gore and his mission to educate the American public about climate change becomes one of the most popular documentaries of all time.
24 Mar.	The Disney Channel debuts the *Hannah Montana* series, featuring Miley Cyrus in the lead role. The show influences music and style choices of children.
10 Apr.	Massive protests take place in cities across the country, protesting proposed changes in immigration policy that would make aiding and abetting illegal immigration a felony and rallying for a comprehensive immigration reform.
July	Microblogging platform Twitter is launched. "Tweeting" quickly becomes a trendy way to publicize events, keep up with celebrities, and break and follow news stories before major media outlets arrive at the scene.
Aug.	A major transatlantic terrorist highjacking plot is foiled, leading to new policies for airline passengers, including a ban on bringing liquids through security.
Nov.	Democrats gain a majority in Congress, reflecting frustration with the war in Iraq, the mishandling of Hurricane Katrina, and a series of scandals involving Republican politicians.
20 Nov.	Comedian Michael Richards, best known for his role as "Kramer" on *Seinfeld*, makes racist comments during a stand-up routine and is heavily criticized in the media. He later apologizes.

2007

- Many items made in China—including children's toys, pet food, and makeup—are pulled from U.S. shelves because of health and safety concerns.

Jan.	Apple enters the smartphone market with the debut of the iPhone, which quickly becomes the trendsetter in cell-phone design and technology.
Mar.	Comic character Captain America, who first appeared in print during World War II, is killed off in a story line by Marvel Comics.

4 Apr.   Radio personality Don Imus makes a racial slur against members of the Rutgers University women's basketball team; he is later fired.

16 Apr.   A disturbed student at Virginia Tech goes on a shooting rampage, killing thirty-two people and injuring twenty in the deadliest campus shooting incident in U.S. history. The tragedy leads to upgraded security measures on college campuses nationwide, a close look at mental-health services and safeguards for students, and questions about gun regulation.

19 July   The cable drama *Mad Men* premieres. The popularity of the program prompts a resurgence in 1960s-era style in clothing and accessories.

20 Sept.   Thousands travel to Jena, Louisiana, to protest what they feel is the unfair arrest and harsh sentencing of six young black men for assault in an incident stoked by racial animosity following the display of a noose from a tree in front of the Jena High School.

Nov.   The first signs of a major meltdown in the previously robust housing market emerge. The real-estate bust sparks the economic downturn of the latter part of the decade.

19 Nov.   The Amazon Kindle ereader debuts. It is soon followed by handheld reading devices designed by Sony, Barnes & Noble, and Apple.

2008

•   Rising gas prices lead many Americans to consider trading large vehicles for fuel-efficient or hybrid models, and to make use of public transportation and car-pooling.

30 Apr.   The independent Dutton's Bookstore in Los Angeles closes.

May   More than six million copies of the video game *Grand Theft Auto IV* are sold in one week.

June   California courts legalize same-sex marriage; voters repeal the law in the November elections.

July   YouTube cohosts with CNN a two-part presidential debate.

1 July   California orders that phone devices in cars must be hands-free. Many states and localities struggle with the phenomena of drivers making cell-phone calls or texting while on the road.

12 July   The Harley-Davidson Museum, honoring the motorcycle company that was founded 105 years previously, opens in Milwaukee, Wisconsin.

13 Sept.   Comedian Tina Fey spoofs Republican vice-presidential candidate Sarah Palin on *Saturday Night Live*.

4 Nov.   America elects its first African American president, Barack Obama.

13 Nov.   Millions of fans of the online game *World of Warcraft* line up to buy the latest update.

21 Nov.   The Smithsonian Institution's National Museum of American History reopens after a two-year renovation, including a permanent display of the restored Star Spangled Banner.

2009

Feb.   The final installment in Neil Gaiman's graphic novel series, *Sandman*, is published.

11 June	H1N1 flu, popularly known as "swine flu," is declared a pandemic, putting a high demand on vaccines and leading to the proliferation of hand-sanitizing products in schools and businesses.
25 June	Pop icon Michael Jackson dies at his home in Los Angeles.
July	A national debate over racial profiling is provoked when Harvard English professor Henry Louis Gates Jr. is accused of breaking into a house (which turns out to be his own home) by a white Cambridge, Massachusetts, police officer. President Obama, who initially criticized the officer, invites both men to the White House for a "beer summit" on 30 July to discuss the issue informally, an incident that tests the "post-racial" climate some hoped the election of an African American president signaled.
4 July	Radio personality Casey Kasem, host of *American Top Forty*, signs off the air for his last broadcast.
9 Sept.	President Obama addresses Congress on the topic of health care, making health-care reform a major element of his domestic agenda and laying the groundwork to transform the way insurance and health care operate.
13 Sept.	Rapper Kanye West interrupts singer Taylor Swift while she is giving an acceptance speech at the MTV Video Music Awards ceremony, grabbing the microphone to proclaim that Beyonce Knowles should have won the best female music video award.
Oct.	Major retailers Wal-Mart, Target, and online-store Amazon engage in a major price war over best-selling holiday books, indicating the predominance of online shopping.
15 Oct.	A Colorado couple stages a hoax in which they claim one of their sons has drifted off attached to a helium balloon. They will plead guilty in November to charges stemming from the incident.
Nov.	*Gourmet* magazine publishes its final issue.
24 Nov.	Tareq and Michaela Salahi "crash" a White House dinner and pose for pictures with President Obama and other attendees.

OVERVIEW

Person of the Year: You. The cover of *Time*'s annual "Person of the Year" issue in 2006 featured a computer monitor with the typed caption "You." The magazine was responding to a democratizing trend in news, entertainment, and lifestyle that had emerged owing to the growing predominance of the Internet in the lives of most Americans. Blogs created, written, and edited by both professional and amateur journalists were supplanting newspapers as the primary source for information about the world. Social-networking sites such as Facebook and MySpace allowed millions of individuals to carve out a space for themselves on the World Wide Web and employ its increasing speed and reach to connect with other users across the globe to play games, share experiences, and fall in love. YouTube, a video file-sharing site, offered more than one million selections by the end of the decade, with everything from home movies to creative reinterpretations of popular movies and songs to original web series. Apple's iTunes software made digital downloading of individual songs convenient and legal. The "digital democracy" used its voting power to reshape the social, personal, and public lifestyles of Americans during the decade.

Culture Wars. Three presidential elections seemed to foster the perception that there were two Americas: "Red states" and "Blue states." Color coding used by networks to indicate whether an individual state voted Republican or Democratic was expanded to connote a corresponding set of values. Red-state Americans were on the whole considered to be religious, socially conservative, and suspicious of federal government initiatives. Blue-state citizens trended toward support of secular schools and were socially liberal, supporting gay marriage and prochoice policies. The designation became familiar during the contested election of 2000 and remained a handy way for social scientists to study and predict the way certain groups were going to behave economically, socially, or politically. Political scientist Andrew Gelman wrote *Red State, Blue State, Rich State, Poor State: Why Americans Vote the Way They Do* (2008), which used electoral results to investigate personal finance; an opinion piece in *The New York Times* used the title "Red Family, Blue Family" to discuss changing trends in the American nuclear family. The election of Barack Obama,

an African American Democrat, in 2008 led some commentators to speculate whether the culture wars had come to an end and America had entered a "post-racial" era wherein issues such as race, gender, and sexuality would be less polarizing across the national landscape.

Love and Marriage. The decade was marked by changing and contested definitions of personal relationships. Internet use for social relationships extended into the dating realm, with some sites organized by religious affiliation, nationality, and even popular-culture preference. The popularity of these sites was confirmed by studies revealing that an estimated $900 million had been spent on online dating services, and the revenue from the industry was projected to be over $1 billion by the next decade. Along with dating, marriage was a hot topic because of the controversy over the rights of homosexuals to marry. As the constitutional battle was fought in courts and voting booths, gay couples chose to express their commitment to each other publicly in spite of the contested legality of the union and participated in elaborate commitment ceremonies to a greater degree than ever before.

Children and Teens. Novels, films, and products aimed at boys and girls aged nine to fourteen—so-called tweens, between childhood and adolescence—enjoyed enormous popularity, even among adults. The *Harry Potter* and *Twilight* novels and films, the ubiquitous Nickelodeon network star "Hannah Montana," and boutiques aimed at preteen girls all achieved widespread success during the decade. Some commentators wondered if the buying power and heightened consumerism of tweens might be leading them to experiment with other aspects of adult culture they might lack the maturity to handle. Some bemoaned the proliferation of push-up bras and "Nitwit wear" marketed toward young girls, and many parents reported newfound concern that their Internet-savvy tweens were using Facebook and texting to bully or flirt with other children, often in an unsupervised manner.

Green Living. Many factors combined to make eco-consciousness a predominant social trend during the 2000s. Skyrocketing gas prices, a sustained economic recession, and growing awareness of global climate change all led Americans to begin to consider the environmental impact of the cars they drove, appliances they used, and food they ate. This development in lifestyles led to hybrid cars such as the Toyota Prius becoming a trendy status symbol. The number of local farmers' markets surged, as did the availability of organic foods in supermarkets. By the end of the decade, reusable shopping bags and recycle bins became the norm for many American households.

Social Networks. In 2000 sociologist Robert D. Putnam wrote a revelatory study on American lifestyles called *Bowling Alone: The Collapse and Revival of American Community.* Putnam argued that the social networks that sustained Baby Boomers, such as neighborhood bowling leagues and community bridge games, were nearly obsolete in the late twentieth century, resulting in Americans being more lonely and dependent on the nuclear family for the bulk of their emotional needs. Additionally, fewer Americans were getting married, or were waiting until later in life to do so. By the end of the decade, more than 25 percent of Americans lived alone. The twenty-first century, however, introduced some new coping strategies for the dissolution of traditional social networks. The number of household pets steadily increased, as did the availability and range of services and products to care for them. In addition to canine and feline companionship, Americans used the Internet to create communal bonds in new and numerous ways. The social-networking site Facebook made a verb of the word "friend," and users built vast online networks of hundreds or thousands of friends. Though the benefits of social networks included easy contact with friends and family across the country and the ability to reconnect with old acquaintances, scholars and social critics began to question the impact of the Internet on interpersonal social skills. As Martin Bailey, senior fellow at the Brookings Institution, described in *The New York Times,* "the minuses are that some people become addicted to life on the computer screen, and withdraw from personal contact—it's a long way from people sitting on the porch and talking to friends and neighbors."

The Great Recession. The economic downturn that began in 2007 and lasted until the end of the decade had a profound impact on the way Americans lived, worked, and played. The collapse of the housing market had a ripple effect on all sectors of the economy, resulting in bank bailouts and numerous layoffs. Though jobs in technological fields continued to be a relatively safe career choice, even previously "recession proof" careers such as teaching were hit with layoffs and forced furloughs. The unemployment rate in the United States doubled from 2006 to 2009. Americans responded by tightening their belts, staying at home rather than going on vacation, and expressing outrage over their government's handling of the crisis. A Pew poll found that eight in ten Americans cut back on their spending in some way in 2009, and more than half of the respondents reported being adversely affected by the economic downturn. Birthrates fell; involvement in community activities declined; and many unemployed complained of anxiety and depression. Fewer than half of the parents polled by Pew expected their children to have better lives than their own. However, the economic downturn also had an effect on the way mothers and fathers lived and worked in ways that were not solely negative but also transformative. Because job markets traditionally staffed by women, such as nursing, fared relatively better, some families saw laid-off fathers staying at home with the children while mothers became the sole breadwinners. Children of doting parents who were accustomed to an overabundance of extracurricular activities saw their schedules sharply curtailed, an effect some experts in child care saw as beneficial.

Health and Fitness. The overall health and fitness of Americans worsened in the decade. Despite Surgeon General David Satcher's 2001 "call to action" on obesity, the numbers on the national scale continued to climb. Between 2007 and 2009, 2.4 million adult Americans became obese, bringing the national total to 75 million. Men and women tried to combat the problem with rising gym memberships and low-carb diets. First Lady Michelle Obama declared a war on childhood obesity in 2009, and encouraged parents and schools to provide more fresh fruits and vegetables for young people, the fastest growing segment of overweight Americans. Studies found that unhealthy eating, combined with record amounts of television viewing and video-game playing, contributed to childhood obesity. A 2009 study by the Kaiser Family Foundation found that children spent an average of 7.5 hours a day in front of a television or computer screen and that heavy users of media reported having lower grades in school. Doctors encouraged an increase in physical activity for both children and adults, and some schools brought back outside recess time while parents dabbled with spin and yoga classes at the gym. Companies such as Nintendo sought to marry the need for activity with the desire for entertainment. The Wii Fit video game, designed to operate on the company's popular Wii console, came with a balance board and preloaded activities that simulated bike riding, aerobics, and yoga. By the end of the decade, it was the third-best-selling console game in history, with more than 22 million copies sold.

TOPICS IN THE NEWS

CYBERSPACE CULTURE

File Sharing. The late 1990s saw an explosion in the sharing of music, movies, and software across peer-to-peer or "P2P" networks. The legal and cultural ramifications of file sharing continued to be felt well into the 2000s, as online file-sharing sites responded to court rulings and popular tastes created new and better ways for ordinary Americans to share and access entertainment. Napster, which went online in 1999, allowed users to swap copyrighted MP3 music files for no charge. Major record labels sued the site in 2000, and the court case and subsequent appeals captured popular attention as artists such as Metallica, Dr. Dre, and Madonna weighed in against the file-sharing giant. The public debated as to whether those who downloaded music illegally were negligent criminals or cunning "pirates" subverting corporate giants. Despite defenders such as Chuck D, who argued such sites would "expose more music to more people," the recording industry eventually won, resulting in Napster declaring bankruptcy in 2002. The scope of file sharing broadened from music to film in the early part of the decade. In 2002 Motion Picture Association of America (MPAA) president Jack Valenti infamously termed his organization's attempts to combat illegal downloads as "fighting our own terrorist war." Two years later the MPAA claimed up to 600,000 movies were being illegally downloaded every day. In 2005 the Supreme Court ruled in favor of the MPAA, agreeing that file-sharing sites that enable easy access to illegally downloaded files could be prosecuted. The question then became whether and how stringently to punish the millions of Americans who had illegally downloaded music or movie files. In 2003 a bill had come before Congress making it a felony to share a single illegally downloaded file with one other person. Over the second half of the decade, however, the Recording Industry Association of America (RIAA) phased out litigation against individuals, largely because of changes in the online music marketplace. Then, the International Federation of the Phonographic Industry in 2009 made headlines by reporting that 95 percent of all music downloads were illegal, and the MPAA claimed that it lost $6.1 billion from online piracy in 2006. In 2005 *Star Wars: Episode III* was uploaded the day before its theatrical release, and in 2009 *X-Men Origins: Wolverine* found its

Napster Inc. founder Shawn Fanning, left, and CEO Hank Barry, leaving a federal courthouse in San Francisco, 2 March 2001. Napster promised the court it would unveil a screening system within two days that could block users from trading up to one million titles of pirated music (AP Photo/Paul Sakuma).

way online a full month early, where it was downloaded more than a million times.

YouTube. However, not all file-sharing sites openly challenged copyright law. As digital cameras became more popular and prominent, Internet sites were created to facilitate sharing digital media with family, friends, or the Internet community at large. YouTube, a file-sharing site that appeared in 2005 and gained massive popularity during the second half of the decade, largely escaped the legal quagmire epitomized by Napster. The site was designed to provide an easy way to upload and share digital videos that were becoming more prevalent owing to cell phones and computers equipped with cameras. The content of the site broadened from amateur home videos to more-creative offerings, such as homemade "mashups" of scenes from movies and television shows and music videos from emerging artists. When one of these videos achieved widespread Internet popularity, it was said to have "gone viral." Cofounder and company CEO Chad Hurley said he wanted to "democratize the entertainment process," and his venture found immediate and lasting success. A year after its inception, the site had 34 million monthly users. By 2009 YouTube was the third-biggest site on the Internet, with 426 million monthly visitors uploading twenty hours of video every minute. As the site developed, it responded to copyright infringements by quickly taking down material that was bootlegged or objected to by rights holders such as RIAA and MPAA. The site's demographics were indicative of the youth-dominated culture of online file sharing, with about half of registered YouTube users under the age of twenty. The site's national impact was confirmed when it cohosted a 2008 presidential debate, enabling average voters to upload videos of themselves asking questions directly to the candidates. The explosion of file-sharing sites online revealed the increasing capacity of the Internet to serve as a multimedia communications tool.

Blogs and Online News. Another trend in Internet culture was a sharp increase in the number of Americans writing blogs and reading news online. One host of individual weblogs recorded 41,000 people creating new accounts in January of 2002. Evan Williams, who ran one of the most popular blogging sites, noted that in the early part of the decade, blogs transitioned from a "self-contained community" to an Internet-wide phenomenon with "a million different kinds of weblogs." By July 2006 approximately 175,000 new blogs were created each day, according to Technocrati, an online data collection company. Not only were Americans writing blogs, they were also reading them at an unprecedented rate. In 2005 a web-hosting company conducted a survey of the general public that revealed that 30 percent of their sample had visited a blog recently. The upward trend continued through the decade, with 126 million blogs active in 2009. As one anonymous blogger put it, blogs were a way "to provide a digital foundation on which individuals, who frequently feel increasingly divorced from society, can build their relationship to the rest of the world." CEOs of corporations such as Whole Foods started blogs to promote and personalize their companies; politicians such as Ralph Nader and Howard Dean maintained blogs to campaign; and popular musicians such as Radiohead and John Mayer used blogs to communicate with fans and boost ticket and record sales. As blogs became a more popular source of information for entertainment news, some bloggers became celebrities in their own right. Journalist Perez Hilton began his Hollywood gossip blog in 2004 and quickly gained notoriety both for his scoops and negative commentary about celebrities he fea-

TWITTER

The twin trends of blogging and social networking found a perfect marriage in the microblogging site Twitter. Created in 2006, Twitter attracted a 1,500 percent increase in registered users over four years. Twitter allowed users to post brief status updates, or "tweets," from their computers or mobile devices, that were then instantly distributed to those who "follow" the user by joining his or her extended social network. The site was embraced by average Americans, celebrities, and politicians alike, who found its 140-character maximum not a limitation but an invitation for succinct creativity. During the second half of the decade, national disasters transformed Twitter into an emergency alert system and everyday Twitter users into reporters and aid workers. During Hurricane Gustav in 2008, local New Orleans blogger Sheila Moragas remarked that Twitter compensated for the holes in major network news coverage, becoming an "online neighborhood" for locals to receive and share information about the storm's progress, shelters, and evacuation. Business writer Steven Johnson asserted that the ease and speed with which the Twitter network allows information to be shared will result in "every major channel of information being Twitterfied in one way or another in the coming years."

Sources: Ki Mae Heussner, "Social Media Proves Itself as Emergency Tool," *abcnews.com* (2 September 2008);

Steven Johnson, "How Twitter Will Change the Way We Live," *Time* (5 June 2009).

tured, leading one television newsmagazine to dub his blog "Hollywood's Most-Hated Website." Hilton became as well known as the stars he wrote about, appearing on his own reality show and cohosting several awards programs. Americans increasingly put down their daily newspapers and consulted blogs for serious news. Author and political doyenne Arianna Huffington launched an aggregated blog called *The Huffington Post,* designed to cover political news and commentary, in 2005; it quickly gained a large readership and contributions from high-profile figures such as Barack Obama, Hillary Clinton, and Nancy Pelosi. The one million comments per month posted to the site attested to its relevance for Internet users. Hilton and Huffington epitomized the way blogs transitioned from online diaries written by everyday Americans to sites Internet users visited to get the latest news, gossip, and cultural commentary from a variety of perspectives. Because blogs could disseminate stories almost in real time, coupled with the growing number of devices for accessing the Internet, online news sites began seriously challenging print journalism for readership and advertising. The decline in newspaper circulation accelerated, with only a third of Americans reading a newspaper during the week by 2009, and demographics suggest the downward trend will con-

Facebook product manager Mark Slee demonstrating the new look of Facebook during a product-announcement meeting at the company headquarters in Palo Alto, California, 21 May 2008 (AP Photo/Paul Sakuma)

tinue. Only 23 percent of young people read newspapers daily, according to the Kaiser Family Foundation. Rick Edmonds, a media analyst and journalism professor at the Poynter Institute, speculated that newspapers would eventually go out of business due to an increasing preference for online media.

Social Networking. Internet social-networking sites redefined the way Americans understood and managed personal relationships. Online communities and chat rooms of the previous decade developed more-personalized and advanced methods for people to find and stay in touch with friends and family. Early versions of these sites—such as Friendster (2002), MySpace (2003), and Facebook (2004)—allowed users to set up individual profile pages, taking advantage of web software that made online design more accessible and easy to use. Profile pages publicized information about preferences in music, books, movies, political affiliation, and personal life. Users could then add individuals to their networks, allowing these "friends" to make comments on profile pages, enabling complete conversations, and in some cases, entire relationships, to exist exclusively in cyberspace. These sites were designed in part to provide younger Internet users with a safe way to connect with others online. Facebook, which emerged as the most popular social-networking site by the end of the decade, claimed more than 400 million active users, half of whom logged on every day. It was created by a group of Harvard computer-science students in their dorm room. The demographics of social networkers quickly expanded

to include older users. From 2005 to 2008 the number of adults who maintained a profile on a social-networking site quadrupled from 8 percent to 35 percent. By 2009 there were more than 215 million active users of social networks. The widespread popularity of these sites resulted in the creation of a new lexicon in American popular culture, including the verb "to friend" indicating adding a new contact to one's network. Facebook cofounder Mark Zuckerberg seemingly achieved his goal of "making the world more open and connected." However, with this openness came new concerns about privacy, particularly for young adults. Parents became increasingly concerned about the online presence of their children. Because young adults in particular were living their lives in large part "online," not only publicizing their likes and dislikes but also near real-time accounts of where they were, what they were doing, and how they were feeling, the line between public and private was increasingly blurred and redefined. A 2006 study found that more than half of Facebook users underestimated the number of people who could access at least some portion of their profile. Because intimate personal information was routinely shared, and online activity could easily be kept secret, unwanted online attention sometimes had real-life consequences. Several high-profile cases of Internet stalking and bullying gained media attention. So-called cyberstalkers were arrested for assaulting young women they had initially contacted through social-networking sites, and many students suffered online attacks from classmates in a phenomenon termed "cyberbullying." A 2009 study by the

Cyberbullying Research Center found that one in five middle-school students were victims of online harassment. Despite the hazards, the benefits of online social networking attracted regular and dedicated participants. By December of 2009, more than 300 million social networkers were spending an average of six hours per month on the sites.

Sources:
Dan Fletcher, "How Facebook Is Redefining Privacy," *Time* (20 May 2010);

Jan Hoffman, "Online Bullies Pull Schools into the Fray," *New York Times,* 28 June 2010;

Amanda Lenhart, "Adults and Social Network Websites," *pewinternet.org* (14 January 2009);

Steven Levy, "Pirates of the Internet," *Newsweek* (4 August 2003): 48;

Daniel Lyons, "Watch the Funny Kittens," *Newsweek* (9 July 2009);

Ben McGrath, "It Should Happen to You: The Anxieties of YouTube Fame," *New Yorker* (16 October 2006): 86–95;

Fred Vogelstein, "Is It Sharing or Stealing?" *U.S. News & World Report* (12 June 2000): 38;

Pete Williams, "MySpace, Facebook Attract Online Predators," *msnbc.com* (3 February 2006).

EDUCATION

Homeschooling. One lifestyle trend in education that gained mainstream popularity during the 2000s was homeschooling. *Time* featured a cover story in 2001 that posed the question "Is Home Schooling Good for America?" and a growing number of parents believed the answer to be yes. The practice of homeschooling transcended its reputation of being a haven for ultraconservative religious families to becoming a viable choice for many American families. Parents whose occupations included university professors, stay-at-home moms, writers, and attorneys opted to "opt out" of the traditional public or private school system and "unschool" their children at home. The circumstances that led parents to choose this unconventional method of education varied from frustration with the shortcomings of the public-school system, children ill-suited to traditional pedagogical styles, or simply the perceived need for more time to bond as a family. Memoirs by parents who chose to homeschool their children appeared late in the decade, highlighting the different paths that led to homeschooling. *The Film Club: A Memoir* (2008) follows a father's decision to allow his fifteen-year-old son, who was failing high school and experimenting with drugs, to officially drop out on the condition that he continue his education through watching movies. *Homeschooling: A Family's Journey* (2008) chronicles the challenges of homeschooling six children whose only other options for education would be a failing public school or a dogmatic religious academy. Another parent noted the increasingly crowded classrooms, remarking, "With 30 students in one room, the teacher doesn't have time for each kid." In 2007 there were more than 1.5 million children homeschooled in the United States, up from 850,000 in 1999. That number grew to 2 million in 2008, and some analysts predict 3 million homeschooled children by 2011. Parents could select curricula from a wide variety of publishers and philosophical perspectives, read about the latest innovations in *Homeschooling Today* and

"BRAINY BABIES"

One educational trend that gained popularity during the 2000s was the newfound interest in giving children as young as three months an advantage in education. Though "classes" for infants and toddlers in activities such as gymnastics, swimming, and even learning a second language were popular as early as the 1980s, the prevalence of technology produced a new trend in preschool education. A series of videos aimed at parents of infants carried titles such as "Baby Einstein" and "Brainy Babies," and claimed to instill language and reading skills at an accelerated pace in children from newborn to three years of age. One line of smart baby products took this trend to the extreme by touting itself as a "prenatal education system" with the slogan "Your womb . . . the perfect classroom." Scientific studies, however, introduced a note of skepticism into the claims of these products. Toddlers who had been exposed to the DVDs, CDs, and games showed no more discernible advantages in reading and speaking than babies who had not, and in some cases actually scored lower in vocabulary skills. As a professor of pediatrics explained, "Babies require face-to-face interaction to learn. They don't get that interaction from watching TV or videos. In fact, the watching probably interferes with the crucial wiring being laid down in their brains during early development."

Sources: Alice Park, "Baby Einsteins: Not So Smart After All," *Time* (6 August 2007);

David Wright and Hana Karar, "Prenatal Learning Products Draw Expert Skepticism," *abcnews.com* (12 January 2010).

Homeschooling Parent, and share tips and anecdotes with other parents on hundreds of blogs. Analysis of test scores seemed to support the choice of the thousands of families that chose homeschooling. The National Home Education Research Institute found in 2009 that homeschooled children scored an average of 34 to 39 percent higher on standardized tests than students from more-conventional academic backgrounds, and outranked the national average consistently in reading, math, social studies, and the language arts. In 2007 a homeschooled thirteen-year-old won the Scripps National Spelling Bee.

Charter Schools. Another trend in unconventional schooling that gained attention during the 2000s was the increasing popularity of and interest in charter schools. Growing frustration with the American public-school system spawned a trend to support schools that were publicly financed but run independently of national curricula and therefore free to experiment with novel and cutting-edge trends in education. By 2009 there were five thousand charter schools in the nation, and many were organized around an inventive educational philosophy. The critically acclaimed documentary *The Lottery* (2010) highlighted the desperation of four underprivileged families that entered their children in New York City's annual lottery for a chance to win a spot at the Harlem Success Academy. Director Madeleine Sackler was searching for the impetus behind the trend in charter schools, explaining, "I was blown away by the number of parents that were [participating in the lottery]. I wanted to know why so many parents were entering their kids in the lottery and what it would mean for them." The filmmaker discovered a tendentious political debate about the real benefits of this educational trend. By the end of the decade, studies were beginning to challenge the results of charter schools. A report by the Center for Research on Academic Outcomes found that about half of charter schools produced students that performed equivalently to children educated in public schools, and a third performed worse.

Technology in the Classroom. Advancements in technology also found their way into schools and colleges, transforming the way American students learned. From kindergarten to college, technology began to infuse every aspect of the academic experience. Computers moved from the marginalized "computer lab" of the previous decade to the center of the classroom, where interactive games taught reading and math, and Internet access provided instant information. Some universities began to issue laptops to incoming freshmen; a greater number of college classrooms were connected to the Internet; and students began buying electronic versions of textbooks to download onto ereaders. The developments were designed to more fully integrate the college experience into students' technology-centered lives. One faculty member observed, "A lot of people my age see technology as a tool to check e-mail and do grades. But for kids, the technology is just the environment that they know." As handheld electronic devices, cell phones, and laptops became more common in the classroom, high-tech cheating became a trend that educators had to combat creatively. The large memory capacity of common electronic accessories allowed students to cram a semester's worth of notes into a device that fit in the palm of their hand. Even MP3 players could be programmed with files that contained a playlist of facts likely to show up on an exam. A group of students even got caught using their cell-phone cameras to take a photo of a test and email it to friends who had a later class time. Teachers responded by banning cell phones and MP3 players in the classroom, disabling Internet access during exams, and employing antiplagiarism software.

Sources:

John Cloud and Jodie Morse, "Home Sweet School," *Time* (27 August 2001);

Trip Gabriel, "Despite Push, Success at Charter Schools Is Mixed," *New York Times*, 1 May 2010;

David Gilmour, *The Film Club: A Memoir* (New York: Twelve, 2008);

Kathleen Gray and Robin Erb, "College technology 'catching up' with students," *USA Today*, 5 October 2009;

Penelope Green, "The Anti-Schoolers," *New York Times*, 16 October 2008;

"Home-Schooled Student Wins Spelling Bee," *npr.org* (1 June 2007);

Andrew Kantor, "Cheating goes high-tech with commonplace tools," *USA Today*, 21 May 2004;

Lila King, "Put your feet up, it's time for school," *cnn.com* (16 August 2004);

Gregory Millman and Martine Millman, *Homeschooling: A Family's Memoir* (New York: Penguin, 2008);

National Home Education Research Institute (1 August 2010);

Michael Van Beek, "High-Flying Home-Schoolers," *Mackinac Center for Public Policy* (18 December 2009);

Bari Weiss, "Storming the School Barricades," *Wall Street Journal*, 5 June 2010.

THE ENVIRONMENT

Eco-Consciousness. Several factors contributing to a new interest in environmentalism amongst many Americans during the first decade of the twenty-first century resulted in ideas of sustainable living becoming mainstream and fashionable. Popular media sources, including *The New York Times, Vanity Fair, Time,* and *The Washington Post* debuted "green issues," in which every article addressed some aspect of eco-consciousness. Though *Vanity Fair* editor Graydon Carter explained the inaugural green issue's main point to be "reporting on the threat to our precious environment," articles on environmentally friendly sports cars, "Eco TVs," and "greener" pets were also featured throughout the decade. As well as a social movement, eco-consciousness was clearly incorporated into many other, more-commercial, aspects of modern life.

Global Warming. One environmental issue that straddled the line between policy debate and mainstream popularity was global warming. Thanks to the advocacy of former vice president Al Gore, climate change was put front and center in the minds of many Americans. Gore was able to make the most of his message through the documentary *An Inconvenient Truth* (2006), which debuted at the Sundance Film Festival. It combined the relatively low-tech one-man slideshow and lecture Gore had given since the 1980s and a more-conventional documentary about his ongoing campaign to educate Americans about global warming. The movie was an instant success, earning an Academy Award for Best Documentary Feature in 2007 and becoming the fifth-highest-grossing documentary in U.S. history. Gore explained the concept of a "carbon footprint"—the amount of electricity and fossil fuel consumed by an individual through his or her activities. This phrase helped Americans visualize and personalize their own environmental impact. According to a Nielsen survey, 89 percent of viewers said watching the film made them more aware of global warming, and three out of four claimed they had changed their energy-consumption habits because of its message. As a senior fellow at the University of Oxford observed, "*An Inconvenient Truth* has pushed Al Gore and the message of concern for climate change up the public agenda."

Oil. An environmental development that gained more attention during the 2000s because of its direct effect on the pocketbooks of millions was the escalating price of oil. In 1998 a gallon of gas averaged $1.02, but by 2008 the cost had

In response to growing eco-consciousness, some citizens took green living to the extreme, and turned their experiences into lucrative book and movie contracts. In an attempt to eliminate their carbon footprint, one American family committed to a yearlong experiment in zero environmental impact. Colin Beavan, along with his wife and two-year-old daughter, bought nothing new (including toilet paper), consumed no food produced outside a twenty-five-mile radius of their New York City home, and used no carbon-fueled transportation. The self-proclaimed "No Impact Man" wrote a book, filmed a documentary, and maintained a blog about the experience. Beavan explained his radical lifestyle change in terms of incorporating eco-consciousness into modern standards of living, observing, "That's the thing about this current wave of environmentalism. It's not about, how do we protect some abstract pristine space? It's about what real people do in their home or office." Some other eco-experiments in extreme green living documented on American bookshelves were a cross-country road trip in a vehicle that used only cooking oil for fuel and a journalist and "regular American" who "tries to kick oil, live locally, and keep his goats out of the rose bushes" as ranchers in New Mexico.

Sources: Colin Beavan, *No Impact Man: The Adventures of a Guilty Liberal Who Attempted to Save the Planet and the Discoveries He Makes about Himself and Our Way of Life in the Process* (New York: Farrar, Straus & Giroux, 2009);

Doug Fine, *Farewell, My Subaru: An Epic Adventure in Local Living* (New York: Villard, 2008);

Penelope Green, "The Year without Toilet Paper," *New York Times,* 22 March 2007;

Elizabeth Kolbert, "Green Like Me," *New Yorker* (31 August 2009).

increased 294 percent to just over $4. Whereas other environmental issues such as water shortages and nuclear energy could seem abstract to everyday Americans, skyrocketing gas prices caused many individuals to quickly and radically adjust their lifestyles. In the 1990s, large, fuel-inefficient sport utility vehicles (SUVs), were popular, but a decade later Americans were buying cars that got better gas mileage, not traveling as much by road, and turning toward public transportation and bicycles. The Transportation Department marked its largest month-on-month percentage decline in the number of miles driven by Americans from March 2007 to March 2008. As one economist noted, "The psychology has changed. People have recognized that prices are not going down and are adapting to higher energy costs. It's a capitulation." One adaptation that remained in keeping with the culture of car dependency in America was the newfound cachet of driving a gas-electric hybrid car. The make and model that captured the buying public's imagination most completely was the Prius. By 2007 Toyota had sold more than 400,000 cars in the United States, leading one reporter to claim that "The Prius has become . . .

the four-wheel equivalent of those popular rubber 'issue bracelets' . . . it shows the world that its owner cares." The popularity of the Prius confirmed that environmental consciousness had become a trendy lifestyle choice. Movie stars, talk-show hosts, and musicians were photographed driving them, and many auto dealerships reported waiting lists of customers who wanted to purchase one. According to one survey, more than half of Prius owners in 2007 bought the car not for its innovative technology or fuel economy, but because "it makes a statement about me."

Eco-Chic. The blend of sustainable living and consumerism extended beyond the areas of auto market to fashion, technology, and home decor. The phrase "eco-chic" began to spring up in blogs, books, and news articles to describe the new blend between trendiness and eco-consciousness. As fashion writer Suzanne D'Amato put it, "green is indeed the new black." Green fashion underwent a complete turnaround from its previous reputation as shapeless clothing in boring colors worn by "tree huggers" to cutting-edge style. Designers used sustainable fabrics and fair trade practices to create clothing worn on runways and red carpets. And the trend was not limited to high-end boutiques or specialty shops. Popular stores known for their wide appeal and discounted prices such as Wal-Mart and American Apparel came out with "green" clothing lines made from organic and earth-friendly fabrics. Much like the cultural trendiness of driving a hybrid car, clothing was also designed to make the wearer's environmental consciousness apparent without a need to check the label. Discount retailer Old Navy offered a T-shirt proclaiming "It's easy being green!" and Gap's line of infant clothing designed organic cotton onesies with eco-conscious slogans such as "solar powered" and "conserve energy . . . take a nap." Through more environmentally friendly design and manufacturing practices and clever advertising, the fashion industry responded to the American consumer's new taste for green living. In addition to clothing, a variety of other "green" gadgets and appliances became widely available and popular. From toasters to refrigerators, electronic devices bearing the Energy Star certification promised consumers that they were making an energy efficient choice. The government program, founded in 1992 by the Environmental Protection Agency (EPA), offered tax incentives for buying green, and by 2009, Americans had purchased more than 2.5 billion products bearing the certification. Apple also launched a line of laptop computers promising to be the "world's greenest lineup of notebooks . . . designed with the environment in mind." By the end of the decade, Sony marketed a laptop computer partly constructed from recycled CDs that was pale green in color. Consumers could also choose eco-friendly furniture and accents from stores ranging from the high-end Pottery Barn to the discount outlet Target. Eco-consciousness was a dominant force in the American marketplace and marketing executives took note. Because environmental consciousness became so trendy, several corporations not known for green practices changed their logos and advertising strategies to be more in

CELL PHONES IN THE AUDIENCE

As cell phones became predominant in American culture their uses expanded well beyond placing and receiving telephone calls. In addition to using mobiles to text message friends, access the Internet, and read ebooks, the devices were also put to less practical and more creative uses. One unexpected use for cell phones occurred at sporting events and concerts. The sight of thousands of arms holding up cell phones to capture an exciting performance on camera or video, or to share audio with a friend online, became commonplace. Additionally, the lighted LED screen featured on most models began to take the place of cigarette lighters during power ballads at rock concerts. As smoking and smoker-friendly environments declined during the 2000s, cell phones became the concert prop of choice to indicate crowd approval. As Michael Marion, general manager of Alltel Arena in Arkansas, notes, "At concerts, you don't have cigarette lighters like you used to. It's dark, except for the cell phones." The trend became so popular that Bic and Zippo, corporations that manufacture lighters, offered iPhone applications that replicated the look and sound of a conventional lighter on the screen. The ubiquity of cell phones at concerts and public performances led to many theaters imposing strict policies banning the use of cell phones that were not always obeyed. During a Broadway performance, actor Hugh Jackman interrupted the play to berate an audience member for refusing to silence his cell phone.

Sources: Douglas Quenqua, "As the Rudes Get Ruder, the Scolds Get Scoldier," *New York Times*, 15 November 2009;

Neil Strauss, "A Concert Communion with Cell Phones; Press 1 to Share Song, 2 for Encore, 3 for Diversion, 4 to Schmooze," *New York Times*, 9 December 1998.

Don Hinrichsen and Bryant Robey, "Population and the Environment: The Global Challenge," *actionbioscience.org* (October 2000);

"Inflation Adjusted Average Annual Gasoline Prices 1918–2009," *inflationdata.com* (21 July 2010);

Micheline Maynard, "Say 'Hybrid' and Many People Will Hear 'Prius,'" *New York Times*, 4 July 2007;

Jad Mouawad and Mireya Navarro, "Teeth Gritted, Drivers Adjust to $4 Gasoline," *New York Times*, 24 May 2008;

Brian Murphy, "Green Gospels: Environmental movement aims for religious mainstream," *USA Today*, 7 June 2006;

Fred Pearce, "Greenwash: Why 'clean coal' is the ultimate climate change oxymoron,'" *guardian.co.uk* (26 February 2009);

Eve Tahmincioglu, "The quiet revolution: telecommuting," *msnbc.com* (5 October 2007);

Stephen Williams, "Sony's Green Laptop (Literally)," *New York Times*, 7 January 2010.

FAR-REACHING NEW TECHNOLOGIES

Cell Phones. In the 2000s cellular telephones became a necessary communication device for Americans of all ages. Though cell phones (also referred to as mobile phones or cells) were in use as early as the 1980s, technological advances made smaller phones more prominent and affordable, and network expansion made calls clearer and more reliable. From 2002 to 2009, Americans who owned cell phones ballooned from 140 million to 250 million, more than 82 percent of the population. The mobility and convenience reached new heights with Bluetooth technology, which allowed users to talk on their phones completely hands-free, speaking and listening through a small device that fit directly in the ear. An even more telling indication that cell-phone use had become an indelible part of the American lifestyle was the growing number of citizens who used cells as their only means of telephonic communication. By 2009, 20 percent of the population lived in cell-phone-only households. Because of the ubiquity and convenience of wireless devices, talking on the phone while driving became a common practice, and one that generated much controversy for the danger it potentially posed. By 2009, twenty-nine states had passed legislations banning some or all use of wireless devices while driving.

Diverse Communications. In addition to the new-found mobility cell phones afforded Americans, the devices themselves offered features beyond placing and receiving telephone calls. The first innovation was text messaging, or texting, which allowed users to send short, text-only messages from one mobile device to another. The new development was quickly embraced by young adult users, resulting in a shift in the preferred method of communication from telephone conversations to texts. A 2009 Pew Research study found that 88 percent of cell-phone users ages twelve to seventeen used text messaging, and one in three teens sent more than one hundred text messages a day. The popularity of text messaging also began to influence American slang. The preference for brevity in texting led to the widespread popularization of certain abbreviations, such as "LOL" (laugh out loud) or "OMG" (Oh, my God). The language of text messaging found its way into formal writing as well. A 2008 study found that 64 percent of teenagers

step with consumer sentiment, a practice that became known as "greenwashing." Some examples were the "clean coal" campaign, which commentator Fred Pearce called "the ultimate climate change oxymoron," and oil conglomerate BP's corporate rebranding from British Petroleum to "Beyond Petroleum," accompanied by a bright green flower logo.

Sources:
Apple MacBook Pro (advertisement page), *apple.com/macbookpro/environment*;

Graydon Carter, "Green is the New Black," *Vanity Fair* (May 2006);

Suzanne D'Amato, "The Look," *Washington Post*, 6 August 2006;

Energy Star, *energystar.gov*;

"Global Consumers Vote Al Gore, Oprah Winfrey, and Kofi Annan Most Influential to Champion Global Warming," *Nielsen* (2 July 2007);

Al Gore, *An Inconvenient Truth: The Planetary Emergence of Global Warming and What We Can Do About It* (Emmaus, Pa.: Rodale Books, 2006);

John Heilemann, "The Come-Back Kid," *New York Magazine* (29 May 2006);

	All adults	White, non-Hispanic	Black, non-Hispanic	Hispanic (English-speaking)
Own a cell phone	82%	80%	87%*	87%*
% of cell owners within each group who do the following on their phones				
Take a picture	76	75	76	83*
Send/receive text messages	72	68	79*	83*
Access the internet	38	33	46*	51*
Send/receive email	34	30	41*	47*
Play a game	34	29	51*	46*
Record a video	34	29	48*	45*
Play music	33	26	52*	49*
Send/receive instant messages	30	23	44*	49*
Use a social networking site	23	19	33*	36*
Watch a video	20	15	27*	33*
Post a photo or video online	15	13	20*	25*
Purchase a product	11	10	13	18
Use a status update service	10	8	13	15
Mean number of cell activities	4.3	3.8	5.4	5.8

Graph illustrating use frequency of cell-phone features among various groups; Pew Research Center's Internet & American Life Project, 29 April–30 May 2010 Tracking Survey. N= 2,252 adults 18 and older, including 1,917 cell-phone users * = statistically significant difference compared with whites (<www.qwasi.com>)

admitted to using texting symbols and shorthand in their academic assignments. Cell phones also began to come equipped with cameras, allowing users to capture, store, and share snapshots and short videos directly from their phones. In addition to text messaging and camera and video capability, emergent technology allowed cell phones to access the Internet, enabling users to check their email and surf the Web directly. The first device to capture the market for Internet-savvy cell-phone users was the BlackBerry "smartphone," introduced in 2002. The phone featured a small keyboard that users could manipulate with their thumbs. BlackBerries were embraced by people who sought to be perpetually "plugged in," earning the nickname "crackberries" to indicate the fervency with which users depended on the devices to maintain personal and professional connections. President Barack Obama became the most famous of the twenty-one million BlackBerry devotees in 2008, when he revealed shortly after his election that he had "won the fight" to continue to use his phone in the Oval Office. The BlackBerry dominated the smartphone market until the debut of Apple's iPhone in early 2007. The device quickly made its mark on American lifestyles. Technology writer David Pogue called the phone "the most sophisticated, out-look challenging piece of electronics to come along in years." In addition to the iPhone's multitouchscreen and virtual keyboard, the device's ability to access third-party applications, or "apps," transformed the way smartphones were designed. The apps were extraordinarily diverse in design, allowing users to play games, map their locations using global positioning software, and even access social-networking sites directly from their phones. As of 2009 there were more than 200,000 apps available for downloading onto the iPhone.

Entertainment. Developments in technology introduced new ways for Americans to listen to music, watch television and movies, and read books. Access to entertainment became increasingly integrated with the Internet. The MP3 music files of individual songs that became popular during the early part of the decade found their technological counterpart in the debut of Apple's iPod in 2001. Though the iPod was not the only digital music storage device on the market, it quickly became the most popular, selling two million units in just over six months. The product was lauded for its sleek design and previously unheard-of memory capacity. The first-generation iPod could hold more than 1,000 songs, and by 2009 that number had skyrocketed to more than 30,000. The devices allowed users to compile their own playlists, which made individual songs more marketable for musicians than albums and CDs. Songs consumers chose to download onto their iPods became a trendy way of communicating individual personality, much like social-networking profile pages. The evolving individualization of entertainment was also apparent in the development of digital video recorders (DVRs) that enabled individuals to record television programs onto a hard disc and watch them later, commercial-free, at their leisure. DVRs could hold many more hours of programming than VHS tapes, allowed for the recording of multiple programs at once, and also used software to suggest and automatically record programs the viewer might enjoy based on what had been selected for saving. The most popular of these devices was the TiVo, which was introduced in 1999 and had 1.6 million subscribers by 2009. The devices gave consumers the capacity to arrange their television viewing according to their individual schedules, which could be a significant advantage for a population that averaged 151 hours in front of the television a month in 2009. In a 2004 *New York Times* article one satisfied customer explained: "Before we got TiVo, my son was getting C's and D's in school because he was staying up late to watch his shows . . . Now we watch TV together as a family after dinner, and my son even has enough time to get a job. So it's improved his sense of the value of time. And it's improved my relationship with him." The convenience of DVRs dovetailed with another trend in how Americans accessed entertainment: mail-order home-video rental. The inauguration of Netflix's subscription service in 1999 transformed the home-video market. Rather than visit brick and mortar stores, movie fans embraced the convenience of home delivery, a flat monthly rate for unlimited rentals, and a larger catalogue of available titles than any one store could hope to offer. Late in the decade, online rental sites offered movies that could be streamed directly to the subscriber's television on demand. This service, along with improvements in home-theatre systems, resulted in fewer Americans going to the movies. In the latter half of the decade, movie attendance declined due to rising ticket prices and the convenience of home rental services.

Telecommuting. The relative affordability of home computers, coupled with the expanding availability of high-speed Internet access across the country, made working from home, or telecommuting, a widespread phenomenon in the American workplace during the 2000s. "Mobile workers" saved their employers the overhead costs of office space and supplies, and gained the freedom to work from their homes while watching their children, in coffee shops, or on vacation. An analyst who studied trends in telecommuting called the increase in remote employees a "quiet revolution" in the way business was done in America. The number of workers who connected to their offices electronically more than doubled during the decade, growing from six million in 2000 to fourteen million in 2009. Videoconferencing through webcams also bolstered the trend by restoring face-to-face interactions. The flexibility and balance between home and work that telecommuting offered to employees was equally well-suited to the new generation of young workers who grew up using email and social-networking sites, and to older workers transitioning into retirement. Banks made online bill paying easy,

convenient, and cheap, which, along with the continued popularity of email, made the post office and "snail mail" increasingly underused. The United States Post Office took a significant financial hit, as evidenced by rate hikes on stamps and discussion of canceling Saturday mail service.

Sources:
Sharon Begley, "Will the BlackBerry Sink the Presidency?" *newsweek.com* (7 February 2009);

Mark Floyd, "Cell Phones, Driving Don't Mix," *EurekAlert!* (9 December 2005);

Amanda Lenhart, "Teens, Cell Phones, and Texting," *Pewresearch* (20 April 2010);

Rich Ling, *The Mobile Connection: The Cell Phone's Impact on Society* (San Francisco: Morgan Kaufman, 2004);

John Markoff, "The Cellphone, Navigating Our Lives," *New York Times,* 17 February 2009;

Claire Cain Miller, "E-Books Top Hardcovers at Amazon," *New York Times,* 20 July 2010;

Tom Peters, "As the book changes form, the library must champion its own power base," *Library Journal* (1 November 2009);

David Pogue, "The iPhone Matches Most of Its Hype," *New York Times,* 27 July 2007;

Eric A. Taub, "How Do I Love Thee, TiVo?" *New York Times,* 18 March 2004;

"TV, Internet and Mobile Usage in U.S. Continues to Rise," *Nielsenwire* (23 February 2009);

University of Alabama Computers and Applied Technology Program, *Technology Education: A Series of Case Studies* (2009);

Jose Antonio Vargas, "The iPod: A Love Story Between Man, Machine," *Washington Post,* 17 August 2005.

FOOD AND DRINK

Sustainable Eating. The growing trend toward eco-consciousness that manifested during the 2000s was equally evident in food and drink. Consumers began to think about where and how their food was produced, and the market responded by offering more sustainable and health-oriented options. Informed by books such as *Fast Food Nation: The Dark Side of the All-American Meal* (2001) and the documentary *Supersize Me* (2004), Americans became concerned about the political, social, and medical implications of the food on their tables. As Michael Pollan wrote in *The Omnivore's Dilemma: A Natural History of Four Meals* (2006), "Eating . . . is an ecological act, and a political act, too. Though much has been done to obscure this simple fact, how and what we eat determines to a great extent the use we make of the world, and what is to become of it." A growing segment of the population chose to explore what one writer termed "the ethics of eating." Eating sustainably involved choosing food that was locally grown, organically produced, and humanely treated. The focus on local goods emerged out of a growing awareness of the energy required to bring out-of-season fruits and vegetables to supermarkets year-round, as well as the corporatization of food production, which often coincided with questionable labor practices. Buying locally grown food cut down on one's carbon footprint and supported community-based farmers, as well as encouraged a more varied diet.

Organic Foods. The label "locavore" was coined to describe ethical eaters who committed themselves to con-

Environmental Working Group's

SHOPPER'S GUIDE TO

PESTICIDES
in PRODUCE

DIRTY DOZEN CLEANEST 12
Buy These Organic   Lowest in Pesticides

WORST			BEST
	Peaches	Onions	
	Apples	Avocado	
	Sweet Bell Peppers	Sweet Corn (Frozen)	
	Celery	Pineapples	
	Nectarines	Mango	
	Strawberries	Sweet Peas (Frozen)	
	Cherries	Asparagus	
	Lettuce	Kiwi	
	Grapes (Imported)	Bananas	
	Pears	Cabbage	
	Spinach	Broccoli	
	Potatoes	Eggplant	

Don't see your favorites? Get the full results at www.foodnews.org
& support EWG research with an online gift.

ENVIRONMENTAL WORKING GROUP

Consumer guide to items of produce containing the
highest and lowest levels of pesticides
(<http://spectrumwellness.net>)

suming only food grown or raised within close proximity to their homes. In response to this trend, local farmers' markets became more numerous and popular; from 2000 to 2009 the number of farmers' markets grew from 3,000 to more than 5,000. The "organic" label in mainstream and specialty grocery stores also became a major marketing tool during this decade. Though consumers had been concerned about pesticides and food-safety issues for decades, it was not until the 2000s that organic agricultural practices were codified and regulated by the U.S. government. In October 2002 the first products bearing the U.S. Department of Agriculture (USDA)'s "Organic" label were stocked on grocery-store shelves. In order to qualify for this label, foods had to be free of synthetic pesticides, irradiation, and genetic modification, and livestock had to be raised "humanely," which meant that animals had pasture access, organic feed, and were free from growth hormones and antibiotics. The organic food market quickly became a widespread phenomenon, with Americans spending $23 billion on organic food in 2008. Specialty health-food stores such as Whole Foods Market and Earth Fare experienced booming business, while discount grocers such as Wal-Mart and Costco began offering organic options. One of the more extreme trends in ethical eating was "raw food." Adherents believed that cooking food robbed it of its nutrients, and therefore consumed uncooked, unprocessed

foods for a large portion of their diet. Though a declining economy and emerging skepticism about the benefits of eating organic caused a slight downturn in the market, by 2009 U.S. farmers had dedicated more than 4.8 million acres of farmland to organic food production, and more than 11.4 percent of the fruits and vegetables sold in the United States carried the organic label. Consumption of organic foods increased fivefold from the previous decade.

Trendy Foods. The term "foodie culture," coined in the early 1980s to describe aficionados of fine food and drink outside the professional food industry, remained a catch-all phrase to describe the various trends in food and drink that enjoyed popularity in America during the 2000s. Several trends in foodie culture were made even more widespread by the growing popularity of the Food Network on basic cable. The channel, running food- and entertainment-themed programming twenty-four hours a day, first aired in the early 1990s, and gained increased cultural visibility through "name brand" chefs such as Emeril Lagasse, Mario Batali, and Rachael Ray. The latter in particular gained a loyal audience, and her "30 Minute Meals," designed for amateur cooks, led to a series of cookbooks, a magazine, and a daily talk show. By 2007 the network had an average prime-time audience of more than 700,000. Several food crazes got their start from a trendsetting series on another cable network, *Sex and the City,* which premiered in 1998 and ran for six seasons. Though better known for its impact on fashion, the series, which followed a quartet of female friends dating their way across Manhattan, also boosted trends in food and drink. Women began throwing *Sex and the City*–themed parties and served foods and drinks featured on the hit show. The show's influence could be noted everywhere from the ubiquity of pink cosmopolitan cocktails to the demystification of sushi. After the women were featured frequenting a Manhattan cupcake shop in 2000, the treat went from a children's birthday party staple to the "it dessert" of 2001. *Publishers Weekly* reported a "deluge" of new cupcake cookbooks, and local cupcake-only bakeries appeared across the country.

Beverages. Perhaps the most visible trend in what Americans were eating and drinking during the 2000s was epitomized by a white cup, green logo, and a brown cardboard sleeve. The Starbucks coffee-shop franchise, which grew from a single store in Seattle, Washington, was the largest coffeehouse chain in the world by the end of the decade. Though the coffee itself was at times pilloried by food critics and consumers alike—the chain's brew lost to McDonald's in a 2007 taste test—the brand kept customers returning to its ever-increasing number of stores. The chain bolstered its desirability by creating idiosyncratic names for beverage sizes (tall, grande, venti), and encouraging customers to personalize their drinks using lingo that seemed indecipherable to the uninitiated. Several websites appeared that were dedicated to tips for ordering at Starbucks, and one blog in Seattle started a thread dedicated to finding "the most complicated Starbucks order ever." Another beverage that enjoyed popularity was a less conventional choice. So-called energy drinks were introduced into the U.S. market in the late 1990s, and by the middle of the 2000s they were generating $3 billion a year in the beverage market; by 2008 "the market has blossomed and there's literally hundreds of energy drinks available." Corporations such as Coca-Cola and Pepsi came out with their own brands after the Austrian manufacturer Red Bull inaugurated the trend in America. The canned beverages contained as much as three times the amount of caffeine as soda, and also large quantities of sugar and "natural ingredients" that promised to deliver more vitality. These claims were bolstered by brand names such as "Rockstar," "Monster," and "No Fear." The drinks were largely marketed to teens and young adults, and their ingredients prompted warnings from the medical community concerning the risks of imbibing so much caffeine and sugar. New cocktails created by mixing energy drinks with alcohol also caught the attention of concerned medical professionals, who published studies showing that using energy drinks as a mixer carried health risks including inhibited respiration, dizziness, disorientation, and impaired decision-making skills.

Frugality. The downward trend in the global economy in the late 2000s affected every aspect of most Americans' lives. More consumers chose generic brands over pricier brand-name products, and membership in warehouse-style stores that offered deep discounts on groceries experienced exceptional growth. One cost-cutting measure that dovetailed with the trendy appeal of local and sustainable eating was a resurgence in home gardening. During the 1940s, so-called Victory Gardens were a popular way every American could support the war effort. In the 2000s, home gardening was seen as a way to save money, fight inflation, and encourage the kind of local eating that benefited the environment and individual health. By the end of the decade, there were almost one million community gardeners growing vegetables in parks and backyards across the country. The trend's momentum was bolstered by Michele Obama's decision to plant the first vegetable garden at the White House since Eleanor Roosevelt's tenure as first lady, and the first ever to follow organic gardening procedures. Obama had embraced local foods as a young mother in Chicago because of the health, environmental, and economic benefits. In an interview, she explained, "I wanted to be able to bring what I had learned to a broader base of people. And what better way to do it than to plant a vegetable garden in the South Lawn of the White House?"

Belt-Tightening. Less money for luxuries also changed where Americans dined. Restaurants, particularly those billed as "fine-dining establishments," experienced a significant downturn in business. Not only were Americans eating at home, they were drinking alcohol at home in record numbers. Though alcohol consumption increased during the decade, sales of beer, wine, and liquor at restaurants decreased. On average, 10 drinks a month were consumed at home, as compared with 5.7 at bars and restaurants. In addition to bolstering sales of cheaper brands of wine and beer at discount stores, the inclination toward frugality in

THEME RESTAURANTS

During the 2000s, several restaurants across the country made headlines for the specificity or oddity of their concept rather than their exceptional food and drink. Joining chains that created an identity by replicating the diners popular in the 1950s or promising creative insults from servers, several high-end theme restaurants gained notoriety. Ninja New York was designed to resemble a feudal Japanese village, and the athletic wait staff were trained to stalk and ambush the diners. One dining experience extreme enough to merit a pop-culture parody was "dark dining." The concept involved diners eating in total darkness while waitstaff in infrared goggles negotiated the pitch-black space. Such sensory deprivation was meant to encourage diners to engage only their taste buds, thereby gaining a more subtle and intense appreciation for the food. However, the idea was also rife with comic possibilities, as in the romantic comedy film *When in Rome* (2010) in which diners run into tables, accidentally touch each other's food, and are menaced by the waiters who ominously intone "you can't see us, but we can see you."

Sources: Frank Bruni, "Yelping Warriors, and Rocks in the Broth," *New York Times*, 26 October 2005;

Caitlin A. Johnson, "Dining in the Dark—On Purpose," *cbsnews.com* (3 December 2006).

alcohol consumption connected with a trend that favored local food production and consumption to make the illegal distilled spirit known as moonshine popular toward the end of the decade. The cultural connotations of the highly concentrated alcoholic beverage transformed from a poisonous brew made by bootleggers and favored by backwoodsmen to an artisanal white whiskey made and tasted by "moonshine geeks." One food writer accounted for the newfound popularity of white lightning this way: "Because it's delicious. Because it's illegal. And because it's cool."

Sources:
Melly Alazraki, "Stocks in the News: Costco, BP, J&J," *dailyfinance.com* (27 May 2010);

Allison Aubrey, "The Buzz over Energy Drinks," *npr.org* (4 January 2007);

Drake Bennett, "The localvore's dilemma," *Boston Globe*, 22 July 2007;

Marian Burros, "Obamas to Plant Vegetable Garden at White House," *New York Times*, 20 March 2009;

"Farmers Market Growth: 1994–2009," *Agricultural Marketing Service: United States Department of Agriculture* (5 October 2009);

Steven Gray, "Fighting to Keep Organic Foods Pure," *Time* (30 August 2007);

Monica Guzman, "The Most Complicated Starbucks Order Ever," *SeattlePI* (28 March 2008);

Ray Isle, "Sushi in America," *Food & Wine* (September 2005);

Elizabeth Jensen, "Changing Courses at the Food Network," *New York Times*, 17 December 2007;

Mary MacVean, "Tackling the ethics of eating," *Los Angeles Times*, 22 April 2009;

Janet Morrissey, "In Recession, Drinking Moves from Bars to Home," *Time* (3 August 2010);

Josh Ozersky, "White Dog Rising: Moonshine's Moment," *Time* (18 May 2010);

Nick Paumgarten, "Food Fighter," *New Yorker* (4 January 2010);

Michael Pollan, *The Omnivore's Dilemma: A Natural History of Four Meals* (New York: Penguin, 2006);

Nancy Rodriguez, "Red Bull Not the Best Mixer," *abcnews.com* (30 December 2006);

Andrea Sachs, "How the Petite Eat," *Time* (20 January 2005);

Denise Shoukas, "The Exploding American Palate: Ethnic Flavors Spice Up the Mix," *Specialty Food Magazine* (April 2009);

Jerry Shriver, "Sushi takes on an international flavor," *USA Today*, 30 August 2007;

"Starbucks Wars," *Consumer Reports* (March 2007);

Melanie Warner, "A Jolt of Caffeine, by the Can," *New York Times*, 23 November 2005;

Philip S. Wenz, "Bring back the WWII-era victory garden," *San Francisco Chronicle*, 12 April 2008;

Bonnie Wolf, "Dishing Up Comfort Food for Hard Times," *npr.org* (23 October 2005).

GAY CULTURE

Same-Sex Parents. Political, social, and cultural evidence was produced in the 2000s that family structures that included homosexual partnerships were becoming more mainstream. Many states enacted domestic-partnership laws and began performing civil unions. By the end of the decade, same-sex couples were issued licenses to marry in several states. Though the exact legal status of gay marriage remained undecided, the cultural recognition of homosexual partnerships and parenting increased. Popular network television shows such as *Friends* and *Buffy the Vampire Slayer* and blockbuster films such as *The Hours* (2002) portrayed same-sex couples as typical romantic couples, not as scandalous or exotic partnerships. The onscreen wedding of a lesbian couple on *Friends* in 1996 was television's first, but same-sex commitment ceremonies became much more prominent in the 2000s. The cable network Bravo debuted *Gay Weddings* in 2002, a reality show that followed several same-sex couples as they planned their ceremonies. The surge in gay unions was answered by an expansion of the wedding industry to accommodate adjustments in invitations, cake toppers, and gay-friendly vendors for the service and reception. Outvite.com, an invitation service for gay couples, was launched in 2003, and several websites catering to couples planning a commitment ceremony saw their businesses expand exponentially. One owner of a site offering gay-themed wedding products remarked, "There has been a shift of consciousness in the community. . . . People say, 'We don't have to wait for it to be legal, we can have a ceremony that honors our commitment now.'" Committed homosexual partners raising children also became more culturally visible and accepted. A Pew Center poll found that support for gay adoption rose 38 percent from 1999 to 2007. Dozens of books and hundreds of blogs are devoted to the experience of raising children in a household with same-sex parents, and *Gay Parent* magazine enjoyed a circulation of 60,000 copies by the end of the decade. The difficulty in finding socially sanctioned ceremonies and celebrations for families comprised of

COMING OUT

The phrase "coming out of the closet" to describe the public declaration of homosexuality dates back to the early twentieth century. However, in the twenty-first century, the increasing acceptance of homosexuality led to a transformation in the manner and timing with which men and women discussed their sexual preference openly for the first time. Ellen DeGeneres's confirmation of her lesbianism on the *Oprah Winfrey Show* and on a cover of *Time* (bearing the headline, "Yep, I'm gay") was a significant news event of 1997. By the 2000s, "coming out" was happening earlier and with considerably less fanfare. Due to a less hostile social environment, boys and girls began informing their friends and family of their homosexuality as early as middle school. Writing about the trend in *The New York Times Magazine*, Benoit Denizet-Lewis wrote that the vast majority of gay men and women just a generation older waited until college to come out, but "a new kind of gay adolescent appearing . . . proud, resilient, even *happy*" typified the early 2000s. A celebrity or public figure coming out still attracted press attention, but the backlash experienced by DeGeneres had largely evaporated. Actors and musicians even coordinated their statements with public-relations campaigns, using the resultant media blitz to promote a book, album, or project. As the decade drew to a close, social media became increasingly involved in the coming-out process, with gossip blogger Perez Hilton prompting confirmations from actor Neil Patrick Harris and singer Lance Bass. Musician Ricky Martin shared his homosexuality on his personal website.

Sources: Benoit Denizet-Lewis, "Coming Out in Middle School," *New York Times Magazine*, 23 September 2009;

Lisa Respers France, "When the stars 'come out,'" *cnn.com* (5 May 2010).

same-sex parents lamented by father Jesse Green in his article "The Day that Hallmark Forgot," was partially addressed by children's clothing websites that offered "I love my daddies" bibs and greeting-card companies that wished a "Happy Mothers Day to my two moms."

Pop Culture and Fashion. Television shows, movies, and music also contributed to normalizing gay identities, sometimes to a controversial degree. The representation of gay culture as a hip trend was both comforting and disturbing for gay-rights advocates and the gay community at large. Though more television shows and films presented homosexuality as a legitimate and conventional identity, some representations of gay life translated sexual preference into pop-culture stereotype. The show that most captured the increasing acceptance of gay culture was *Queer Eye for the Straight Guy*. The show premiered in 2003 and quickly became the most talked-about new program of the year. Ratings reached as high as 3.34 million viewers an episode, extraordinarily high for a show on basic cable. The reality program followed five gay men as they transformed a heterosexual man's hairstyle, wardrobe, home, and relationship skills to be more in line with the superior sense of style and personal sensitivity that gay men were stereotypically assumed to possess. Part of the show's appeal derived from the conceit that straight men could borrow the more superficial, and sexually desirable, surface qualities from gay male culture and still maintain their sense of masculinity.

Metrosexuality. The show was a catalyst for a larger trend in men's personal style that gained traction during the 2000s: metrosexuality. The 2003 essay "Just Gay Enough" defined the typical metrosexual as a man who "gets manicures and pedicures on Saturday nights; he shops till he drops; he conditions his curls, and he watches 'Queer Eye for the Straight Guy' . . . and actually picks up its tips." Cultural commentator Malcolm Beith noted that formerly female-identified behaviors—care in personal grooming, shopping—became more acceptable for straight men. Skin-care products available for men expanded beyond shaving cream. Salons began offering facials and waxing treatments specifically marketed to men, and skin-care lines such as The Body Shop and Nivea offered face scrubs, moisturizers, and masks exclusively that came in muted, presumably more masculine, packaging. An online editor of *GQ* noted in 2007 that "men are spending more on grooming products than ever before," and marketing data confirmed that body washes and shower gels aimed exclusively at men nearly doubled in number in the early part of the decade.

Lesbian Chic. For some women, gay culture became an outlet for experimenting with taboo-breaking behaviors, usually in a relatively benign environment—a trend dubbed "lesbian chic." The trend seemed to center around the explosive popularity of Katy Perry's single "I Kissed A Girl" (2008). The song prompted a flurry of editorials decrying "heteroflexibility," particularly in young women. In other areas of pop culture, the spectacle of straight women sharing a kiss had been exploited by the opening performance of the 2007 *MTV Video Music Awards,* in which the legendary iconoclast Madonna kissed young protégé Britney Spears. Some argued that, more than simply a lurid marketing opportunity, lesbian chic became a testing ground for women to explore sexual expression in subversive ways. The growing tolerance of homosexuality as an acceptable identity was reflected in the decade's increasing commercialization of heterosexual appropriation of gay culture and behavior as a social trend, though the uncertain legal status of long-term homosexual relationships indicated that full social recognition of gay men and women was still a work in progress.

Sources:

Malcolm Beith, "Letter from New York: Just Gay Enough," *Newsweek* (27 October 2003);

Jesse Green, "The Day that Hallmark Forgot," *Parents* (21 October 2009);

Claire Hoffman, "Joe Francis: 'Baby, give me a kiss,'" *Los Angeles Times,* 6 August 2006;

Logan Levkoff, "Girls Kissing Girls: In Vogue or Old News?" *Huffington Post* (19 September 2008);

Tim Padgett, "Gay Family Values," *Time* (5 July 2007);

Cast members from *Queer Eye for the Straight Guy* pose in the press-room during the MTV Video Music Awards at New York's Radio City Music Hall, 28 August 2003 (AP Photo/Mary Altaffer).

Laura Petrecca, "Soap sellers steer men with sexy promises," *USA Today,* 15 March 2007;

Maria Puente, "Much ado about gay commitment ceremonies," *USA Today,* 16 May 2004;

Katherine Sender, "Dualcasting: Bravo's Gay Programming and the Quest for Women Audiences," *Cable Visions: Television beyond Broadcasting,* edited by C. Chris and A. Freitas (New York: New York University Press, 2007), pp. 302–318;

Adam B. Vary, "Pride, Patriotism, and Queer Eye," *Advocate* (22 June 2004): 120–136.

HEALTH AND FITNESS

Trendy Diets. By 2000, America was suffering from what doctors called an "obesity crisis." In 2004 two-thirds of Americans were officially overweight, with one in six children also fitting that designation. The Centers for Disease Control and the American Heart Association routinely published studies that warned of the dire consequences for overweight or obese men, women, and children, including increased risk of heart disease, stroke, diabetes, and cancer. The concern Americans felt about the obesity epidemic was reflected in a TIME/ABC poll that found that nearly 60 percent of citizens would like to lose weight. The strategies for achieving that elusive goal evolved, which saw many trends in dieting wax and wane in popularity. One strategy that attracted a substantial number of adherents was the low-carb or no-carb diet. The most prominent source that suggested reducing or eliminating carbohydrates to lose weight was the Atkins diet, first introduced in the 1970s. It was rediscovered in the early 2000s, and "going on Atkins" became common parlance for skipping breads, bagels, and sugar and doubling up on proteins and fats. The appeal of a diet that permitted bacon and butter proved widespread, and more than 9 percent of the country followed some form of low-carb eating in 2004. The trend became so predominant by the middle of the decade that Coca-Cola premiered a low-carb soda; beers proclaimed their low-carb counts as an advertising strategy; and celebrities such as actor Jennifer Aniston and comedian Drew Carey could be seen ordering their hamburgers without the bun. Corporations that produced pasta and doughnuts suffered, and responded by offering low-carb versions of their products, with more than 3,000 new "Atkinized" products on the shelves from 2002 to 2004. Though the diet produced noticeable effects quickly, many Americans had a difficult time sustaining its limitations, and gained weight after resuming typical eating habits. Additionally, some doctors expressed concern about the advisability of consuming a high amount of saturated fats found in meat products. Former U.S. surgeon general C. Everett Koop was quoted as saying, "People need to wake up to the reality that diets that restrict the consumption of entire food groups—especially essential carbohydrates like fruit and vegetables—are unhealthy and can be dangerous." Though the overwhelming popularity of low-carb diets was largely on the decline by the end of the 2000s, some remnants of the Atkins craze could still be detected in restaurants that offered their meat dishes "naked"—without the

MESSAGE BRACELETS

In 1996 world-champion cyclist Lance Armstrong was diagnosed with an aggressive form of testicular cancer. He beat the disease, and began "Livestrong," a foundation to fund research and advocate for Americans living with cancer. In 2004 Livestrong began selling yellow rubber bracelets emblazoned with the foundation's name (for $1.00). They became ubiquitous accessories among Americans of all ages, and more than seventy million were sold by the end of the decade. The popularity and success of Livestrong's fund-raising effort spawned other "accessories-with-a-message," including pink bracelets for breast cancer, red bracelets for AIDS awareness, and green bracelets to raise awareness of the atrocities in Darfur. During the 2008 presidential campaign, both candidates wore black bracelets embossed with the name of a soldier who had died in Iraq. Online stores offered personalized silicone bracelets that could be imprinted with a cause, team, or message of the consumer's choice. As one reporter put it, "the rubbery adornment has become this generation's AIDS ribbon."

Sources: *livestrong.org;*

Claire Suddath, "Bracelets," *Time* (2 October 2008).

bun or tortilla. Low-carb diets were not the only trendy strategy for losing weight. Some of the more bizarre and short-lived crazes included the Paleo diet, which encouraged adherents to eat like their Paleolithic ancestors; the Dietary Approaches to Stop Hypertension (DASH) diet—the anti-Atkins—advising grains and plant-based proteins over meat; and *The New York Times* best-selling Blood Type Diet, which argued that blood types processed food into fat differently. Talk-show host Oprah Winfrey, who made her lifelong struggle with weight a regular topic on her program, used her enormous popularity and influence to promote several weight-loss strategies. She teamed up with personal trainer Bob Greene to create the Best Life diet, which had a tie-in book, blog, and online journal. The cookbook became a *New York Times* best seller. Though Americans showed a desire to lose weight through their buying habits, the end of the decade still showed increasing percentages of overweight and obese men and women in the population.

Medical Procedures. The national obsession with staying young and thin resulted in an increase in surgical procedures that promised to erase the signs of aging and aid in weight loss. Among the most prominent of the trendy cosmetic treatments to emerge was Botox. During the late 1990s, doctors discovered that the same toxin that caused botulism also smoothed skin with relatively few side effects when injected directly into the face. One plastic surgeon marveled, "Advertisers can present this as a face-lift in a bottle. This is a true miracle drug." Millions of Americans

Advertisement promoting the full range of services offered by a Michigan cosmetic-surgery provider, including pedicure, massage, Botox injections, and liposuction (<www.plasticsurgeryarts.com>)

agreed, and by 2002, Botox was the most popular cosmetic procedure in America. The number of injections administered increased 500 percent over the decade, and more than two million people tried it in 2008. Early enthusiasts were celebrities and wealthy beauty-treatment adherents, but soon average Americans were hosting Botox parties where professionals would travel to a home or hotel and inject partygoers in a casual social situation. Though the vast majority of Botox users were women, some men also lauded the benefits of the age-erasing injection, claiming friends told them, "it makes you look ten years younger!" Not all popular medical procedures, however, were as portable as the muscle-paralyzing "face-lift in a bottle." Celebrities who had undergone gastric-bypass surgery and achieved quick and dramatic weight loss prompted many Americans to try the stomach-reduction technique. Singer Carnie Wilson was an early proponent of the procedure, appearing on magazine covers and hosting an infomercial that described her weight loss from 300 to 150 pounds after surgery that reduced her stomach to the size of an egg. By 2005, thirty-five thousand stomach-reduction surgeries had been performed, including an increasing number on children. Celebrities such as author Anne Rice, comedian

Roseanne Barr, and TV weatherman Al Roker publicly discussed their decision to have the surgery, and their visibly thinner bodies fueled the procedure's popularity.

Trends in Exercising. Despite the popularity of simpler measures, doctors continued to advise patients that regular exercise was the best method of weight loss. One exercise trend that became popular used a piece of equipment that had been around since the 1960s: the stationary exercise bike. So-called spin classes allowed a group of cyclers to pedal in time to music, and adjust the resistance on their bikes to mimic the hills and flats of outdoor cycling in a temperature-controlled (and automobile-free) environment. The high-impact classes usually took place in a darkened room led by instructors who set the tempo and monitored participants' revolutions per minute. By the end of the decade, spin classes were a staple in most gyms, and characters in films and television shows were featured attending classes. Other trends that were lower impact than a fifty-minute spin class, like mat-based stretching and strengthening exercises Pilates and yoga, were embraced. The slower pace and breathing common to both activities appealed to some technology-saturated and recession-weary Americans. Pilates appeared on the 2008 and 2009 American College of

Group fitness department manager Andrea Porter, left, leads a power-yoga group at the Summit Athletic Club in Altoona, Pennsylvania, 19 December 2006 (AP Photo/*The Mirror*, J. D. Cavrich).

Sports Medicine Top Fitness Trends lists, and gained a pop-culture presence. Celebrities as diverse as Jennifer Aniston, Gwyneth Paltrow, and the San Francisco 49ers football team credited the series of stretches and crunches for providing strength, flexibility, and balance. Yoga promised the same benefits, along with a soothing atmosphere and quieted mind. Though most of the 15.8 million Americans who were taking yoga eschewed the Eastern philosophy behind the practice and embraced the physical benefits alone, it became an undeniable presence on the American fitness landscape. Practitioners spent $5.7 billion a year on yoga accessories and vacations, leading some yogis to complain that Americans might be missing the point of the ancient practice based partly on self-denial. Nonetheless, many varieties of yoga became common throughout the decade, including mixing the series of poses with elevated temperatures ("hot yoga"); food (classes followed by a multicourse dinner); and even pets ("doga" classes attended by humans and their canine companions). Perhaps the most unconventional calorie-burning activity was so-called strip aerobics, which gained notoriety after being presented on the *Oprah Winfrey Show* and *The View*. The classes encouraged women to get exercise and embrace their inner sex kitten by combining moves found in strip clubs with aerobics, dance, and Pilates. One major proponent of the trend, actor and mother Sheila Kelley, who discovered the activity while trying to lose pregnancy weight, touts the inner as well as outer benefits for women who participate in the routine, promising "When you do this, you fall in love with yourself, no matter what size you are."

Sources:
Jennifer Barrett, "Extreme Measures," *Newsweek* (6 January 2005);

Richard Corliss, "Smile—You're on Botox!" *Time* (10 February 2002);

Hilary Howard, "Spinning Goes Boutique," *New York Times*, 8 July 2010;

Jean Lawrence, "Cardio Striptease: Take It Off," *medicinenet.com* (11 February 2004);

Michael D. Lemonick, "How We Grew So Big," *Time* (7 June 2004);

Julia Moskin, "When Chocolate and Chakras Collide," *New York Times*, 26 January 2010;

Christy Oglesby, "What's behind the curb-your-carbs craze?" *cnn.com* (18 June 2004);

Melanie Warner, "Is the Low-Carb Boom Over?" *New York Times*, 5 December 2004;

"Worldwide Survey Reveals Fitness Trends," *ACSM's Health and Fitness Journal*, 13 (November/December 2009): 9–16;

"Yoga in America," *Yoga Journal* (26 February 2008);

Rachel Zavala, "Deserving a Better Spin," *Washington Post*, 3 April 2007.

PARENTING

Stay-at-Home Dads. Several factors contributed to the increasing prevalence and acceptance of fathers staying at home to be primary caregivers while mothers worked outside of the home. The late-decade recession resulted in high numbers of layoffs in professions traditionally held by men, such as construction and manufacturing. Men lost 3 million jobs in these sectors alone, and 4.75 million jobs overall. Professions traditionally staffed by women, such as health care, education, and government, were not as badly hit, and women lost only 1.66 million jobs during the same time period. The effects of this trend on families with children were often that unemployed men, either temporarily or permanently, stayed home with the children while women were the sole breadwinners. In addition to the economic factors, gender roles in general became less rigid in terms of child care. The evolution of family dynamics began to lessen the stigma of men staying at home, and diminished the maternal slant previously associated with child care. Other fathers made the decision to stay at home based on their wives' better-paying jobs, or simply a desire to experience a closer relationship with their children. In 2007 the U.S. Census Bureau found that the number of stay-at-home dads had tripled over the decade, numbering more than 159,000 fathers. Websites, blogs, and products aimed at this growing demographic became more prominent. The At-Home Dad's Annual Convention held its fourteenth meeting in 2009 in Omaha, Nebraska, and men's public restrooms began to include diaper-changing tables. This transformation was also apparent in the media. Popular films such as *Signs* (2002) and the critically acclaimed *The Ballad of Jack and Rose* (2005) featured fathers as the sole caregivers for their children. The movie *Daddy Day Care* (2003) mined for comic potential the phenomenon of unemployed fathers learning child care. However, some fathers complained of being stigmatized both by other men and mothers for their decision to stay at home. After quitting his job to work from home as a consultant and care for his children, one father recalled, "My friends asked me if I got fired. You don't stay home from a good job to be with your kids." Other men reported being excluded from mothers' groups or being eyed suspiciously as a lone man at a playground. However, the social stigma of being a stay-at-home dad greatly lessened, as more men became primary caregivers.

The Mommy Wars. Whereas men challenged and partly overcame social skepticism for choosing or embracing not working, mothers who worked outside the home full- or part-time continued to encounter personal and public reservations about their choice. The social acceptance of women achieving power in the workplace became a more fraught question when motherhood was involved. The controversy concerning women who tried to balance career and family became widespread and socially prominent during the 1980s when women who had no financial need to do so, chose to return to their careers after having children. The variation in lifestyle choices made by women for different reasons was posed in the media as a battle between women who chose to stay home with their children and those who relied on daycare, babysitters, or school to care for their children while they worked. The issue evolved from an economic choice to an ethical judgment. Are women who stay at home "better" parents? Are women who work "more feminist"? The prevalence and difficulty of the issue was described by one mother as "Every other week there's an article saying that if you don't work, you're in trouble financially, and if you do work, your child is at risk."

Opt-Out Revolution. The newfound interest in women who were highly educated and accomplished, but chose to forego their careers and raise children was highlighted by a 2003 cover story in *The New York Times Magazine* that featured eight Ivy League graduates who left jobs as attorneys,

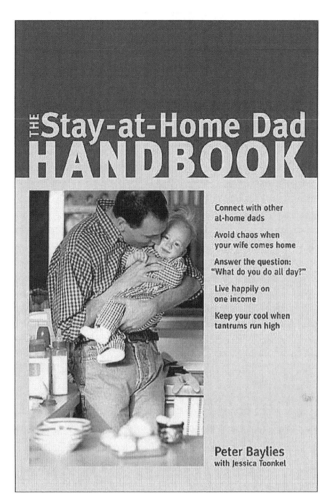

A 2004 guidebook offers advice to the growing number of "stay-at-home" dads (<www.amazon.com>).

university professors, and corporate executives to parent their children full-time. Author Lisa Belkin termed the phenomenon "The Opt-Out Revolution," and investigated why even though many of the institutionalized forms of sexism that prevented women from achieving professional success had been dismantled, large groups of educated, high-income women chose not to work. The piece generated a huge response, becoming the *Times*'s most emailed article of the year, highlighting how contentious the issue of working or not working remained for many mothers. The discussion reached its apex near the end of the decade, with talk-show hosts Dr. Phil McGraw and Oprah Winfrey airing programs featuring women debating the issue, and the publication of a collection of essays titled *Mommy Wars: Stay-at-Home and Career Moms Face Off on Their Choices, Their Lives, Their Families* (2006).

Helicopter Parenting Backlash. During the 2000s, a concern about the effects of the previous decade's trend toward overparenting, either through excessive attempts to protect a child's health, overscheduling extracurricular activities, or taking an intense interest in micromanaging a child's life, led some teachers to coin the phrase "helicopter parenting." The term was meant to invoke the omnipresent hovering of these overinvolved mothers and fathers. One social trend that reflected possible overparenting was an extreme effort on the part of some parents to protect their children from real or imagined threats. Even though kidnapping rates remained stable, ominous and ubiquitous media reports of some high-profile cases of missing children led some parents to avoid giving their children any time unsupervised by an adult. Only 13 percent of children walked or rode their bikes to school in 2001, down from 49 percent in the mid twentieth century. "Stranger danger" was joined by concern about possible injuries that might result from "free play" on school jungle gyms and hypervigilance about germs and allergies. Another manifestation of helicopter parenting was identified by parents who enrolled their children in sporting, academic, or artistic activities that completely encompassed a child's day from the time of waking up to going to bed. A child psychiatrist and author of *The Over-Scheduled Child: Avoiding the Hyper-Parenting Trap* (2001) diagnosed the phenomenon as arising from parental guilt, "Overscheduling our children is not only a widespread phenomenon, it's how we parent today. Parents feel remiss that they're not being good parents if their kids aren't in all kinds of activities. Children are under pressure to achieve, to be competitive." A 2009 cover story in *Time* described the causes of a widespread social "backlash" against the trend of overparenting. The worsening economy demanded that some parents cut back dramatically on expensive extracurricular activities such as team sports with pricey equipment and private music lessons. In the second half of the decade, a third of parents downsized their children's extracurricular schedules. In addition to economic factors, a flurry of studies reported on the psychological danger of micromanaging a child's life rather than letting him or her make personal decisions and mistakes. One study found that older children who had been helicopter parented were much more likely to be dependent, neurotic, and unwilling to try new experiences than those who were less managed. Another study commissioned by the Centers for Disease Control even found that wildly popular antibacterial house products actually resulted in a higher instance of allergies. New trends emerged that countered a parent's impulse to overinvest in their children. Proponents of this style of parenting called the method "slow parenting" or "simplicity parenting," and encouraged time for unstructured play rather than an abundance of extracurricular activities, letting children reach developmental and academic milestones on their own schedules, and avoiding making decisions for their children. The movement inspired a media and lifestyle industry, spawning seminars, books such as *The Dangerous Book for Boys* (2006) that advocated hands-on, unstructured play, and even lifestyle coaches who visited individual homes and gave children's rooms and schedules a "simplicity parenting" makeover.

Sources:

Lisa Belkin, "The Opt-Out Revolution," *New York Times Magazine,* 26 October 2003;

Dennis Cauchon, "Women gain as men lose jobs," *USA Today,* 2 September 2009;

Nancy Gibbs, "The Growing Backlash Against Overparenting," *Time* (20 November 2009);

E. J. Graff, "The Mommy War Machine," *Washington Post,* 29 April 2007;

Conn Iggulden and Hal Iggulden, *The Dangerous Book for Boys* (London: HarperCollins, 2006);

Donna Krache, "How to ground a 'helicopter parent,'" *cnn.com* (13 August 2008);

Stuart B. Levy, "Antibacterial House Products: Cause for Concern," *Centers for Disease Control and Prevention,* 7, 3 (June 2001);

Alvin Rosenfeld and Nicole Wise, *The Over-Scheduled Child: Avoiding the Hyper-Parenting Trap* (New York: St. Martin's Griffin, 2001);

Katherine Shaver, "Stay-at-Home Dads Forge New Identities, Roles," *Washington Post,* 17 June 2007.

PATRIOTISM

Post-9/11 Patriotic Displays. After the 11 September 2001 terrorist attacks on New York City and Washington, D.C., Americans experienced a resurgence of open displays of patriotic feeling to commemorate the loss of life and demonstrate solidarity in the face of a new kind of war. The trend, termed the "politics of display" by some cultural commentators, was a long-lasting cultural effect of the attacks. A poll conducted in 2005 found that 81 percent of Americans considered patriotism to be an important component of their individual identities. Analysts noted, "We tracked patriotism, spirituality and religion, and giving to charities and volunteerism right after 9/11. All three popped up. Within about nine months volunteering was down and so was religion, but what has stayed with us is

FREEDOM FRIES

The fervency with which Americans embraced patriotic feeling in the years following the 9/11 attacks became more politicized owing to the prospect of war with Iraq in 2003. The run-up to the American invasion generated heated domestic and international debate, and the response of some conservative politicians was to demonize those opposed to the war as un-American. This impulse was encapsulated by the Republican lawmakers who officially changed the menu items "French fries" and "French toast" to "Freedom fries" and "Freedom toast" in three government office buildings to express displeasure with France's opposition to an American invasion. The confluence between anti-French sentiment and public displays of patriotism was not confined to the U.S. House of Representatives cafeteria. Sports bars and cafés across the nation also adopted the change, and popular mustard company French's launched a public-relations campaign proclaiming, "The only thing French about French's Mustard is the name." Though the trend was short-lived, it was a full three years before French fries were back on the menu at the U.S. Capitol.

Sources: Jennifer Duck, "No More 'Freedom' for Your Fries," *abcnews.com* (3 August 2006);

"French's mustard denies French connection," *cbcnews.com* (27 March 2003);

Sean Loughlin, "House cafeterias change names for 'french' fries and 'french' toast," *cnn.com* (12 March 2003).

The end of the Black Hills motorcycle run through Rapid City, South Dakota, 22 September 2007, in memory of the 343 firefighters who died in the 11 September 2001 attacks on the World Trade Center in New York City (AP Photo/*Rapid City Journal*, Steve McEnroe)

patriotism." A popular way to express the patriotic feelings was to publicly display the American flag, sometimes in unconventional ways. Historian Phillip M. Bratta reported, "American flags were hung not only from windows and porches. They also appeared bound on automobile bumpers, tattooed on various body parts, as a wallpaper screen on cell phones, on all types of attire from boxers and socks to winter coats, collectibles, pins, and many more." One manufacturer sold more than 31 million flag decals during a three-month period in 2001, and sales and production of items featuring the flag, the World Trade Center towers, or a red, white, and blue color scheme, soared. A related trend in apparel was the popularity of attire bearing the FDNY and NYPD insignia to show support for the losses sustained by the New York City fire and police departments while responding to the attacks. As the nation went to war against Afghanistan (2001) and then Iraq (2003), individual patriotic displays also included yellow-ribbon decals to express support for troops overseas. The trend toward patriotic display also entered the political arena, as American flag lapel pins became required accessories for politicians, particularly those running for office. Democratic presidential candidate Barack Obama was compelled to address his decision not to wear an American flag pin on the campaign trail in 2007. The senator argued that the trend had become an empty gesture, explaining, "My attitude is that I'm less concerned about what you're wearing

on your lapel than what's in your heart. You show your patriotism by how you treat your fellow Americans, especially those who served." However, the cultural power proved overwhelming, and by May of election year, the flag pin reappeared on Obama's lapel.

Sources:

Phillip M. Bratta, "Flag Display Post-9/11: A Discourse on American Nationalism," *Journal of American Culture,* 32 (9 September 2009): 232–243;

Anthony Faiola, "'Buy American' Rider Sparks Trade Debate," *Washington Post,* 29 January 2009;

Allison Linn, "The resurgence of 'pocketbook patriotism,'" *msnbc.com* (20 May 2008);

Michael E. Ross, "Poll: U.S. patriotism continues to soar," *msnbc.com* (4 July 2005);

Jeff Zeleny, "The Politician and the Absent American Flag Pin," *New York Times,* 5 October 2007.

TRENDS IN LEISURE

Games and Technology. The growing prevalence of computers and Internet access during the 2000s affected how Americans played as well as worked. As computer speeds and memory increased, higher quality gaming experiences were available to a wider segment of the population. Though electronic games had been popular among children and adults for decades, the Internet made massive multiplayer online games (MMOs), a new experience. The games evolved from tabletop role-playing

Nintendo advertisement demonstrating the interactive features of the Wii gaming console (<http://limelight.es>)

games and allowed a large number of players from remote locations to team up and compete against other gamers from around the world in strategy and battle. By 2008 the MMO *World of Warcraft* boasted eleven million subscribers. During the decade, the games became more mainstream and appealed to a wider variety of Americans as the design evolved from strictly fantastic or combat scenarios. Many popular films, such as *Lord of the Rings* trilogy (2001–2003), *Iron Man* (2008), and the *Harry Potter* series (2001–2009) inspired video games featuring the characters and based on the sets. Conversely, several video-game franchises were turned into movies, such as *Lara Croft: Tomb Raider* (2001), *Pitch Black* (2000), and *Resident Evil* (2002). Another technological development that encouraged the mainstreaming of video games was the debut of several popular and user-friendly gaming consoles. Three highly anticipated releases of new consoles arrived from the biggest names in gaming: Sony's PlayStation 2, Nintendo's GameCube, and Microsoft's XBox. These systems offered new features such as the capacity to play DVDs, Ethernet ports to allow for high-speed online gaming, and superior graphics. Consoles continued to become more technologically advanced, with the so-called seventh generation of machines appearing in the middle of the decade, offering wireless capacity, faster Internet connections, and larger hard drives. The popularity of these consoles

STAYCATIONS

The economic instability of the 2000s prompted many Americans to rethink the way they spent time and money on leisure activities. As a result of national and international travel becoming even pricier because of rising oil and food prices, the decline of the dollar overseas, and high unemployment and layoffs leading to tighter budgets, some working families became more creative in the ways they enjoyed time off from work. Traditional destination vacation spots such as the beach, amusement parks, or European tours were foregone for "staycations": time spent off work but at or close to home. One businessman felt he got "the most bang for my buck" by relaxing with friends and family and remodeling his home during paid leave from his job. Other staycationers appreciated the environmental benefits of reducing their carbon footprint by avoiding airline travel and instead exploring their cities, eating homecooked meals, and spending time with their families without the hassle and pressure of an overbooked and overpriced family vacation.

Sources: Debra Alban, "Staycations: Alternative to pricey, stressful travel," *cnn.com* (12 June 2008);

Jeff Brown, "Avoiding high gas prices with a 'staycation,'" *msnbc.com* (29 May 2008).

Promotional photograph for the World Series of Poker showcasing the large cash prize for winners of the tournament
(<http://govegas.about.com>)

prompted a major newspaper to print an article offering the best strategies for acquiring a console on the day of its release. The author advised gamers to anticipate long lines and to consider camping out days ahead of time. In a phenomenon called "console wars," the producers of the consoles tended to premiere systems at roughly the same time and usually around the Christmas season, ensuring massive sales numbers and high demand. The debut of Sony's PlayStation 3 in 2006 resulted in store employees having to pepper spray a stampeding crowd trying to make its way to the machines, which sold out nationwide hours after they became available. By the end of the decade, more than 200 million units had been sold in the United States. Though second with 30 million units sold, the Nintendo Wii (2006) was the trendiest console for average Americans outside the gaming community. The Wii aimed to dismantle the divide between gamers and nongamers by changing the game's interface. The device's controller was a small wireless remote that the player manipulated with broad body movements rather than the thumbs. One of the designers explained the experience of playing video football: "You're basically playing football in your living room. . . . No buttons to press, just gesture a hiking motion, and the ball's in the hands of the QB. . . . It truly plays like nothing you've ever experienced." The device's novelty quickly captured the imagination of Americans of all ages, from children who played G-rated games that simulated raising and training a puppy to senior citizens who used the console's Wii Fit accessories to stay physi-

cally strong and balanced. The Wii console achieved its designer's goal "to come up with games that would attract people who don't play games."

Trendy Games. Another popular game that surfaced during the technology-saturated 2000s was one that did not require any opponents at all. Many office workers found online solitary games to be particularly addictive. Downloadable or preinstalled solitaire programs such as Spider Solitaire and FreeCell Solitaire found their way onto many office computers. Computer Solitaire's status as "one of the more common, if stealthy, ways of passing time in the modern office" was solidified when a government worker was fired by New York City mayor Michael Bloomberg for having a game open on his desktop, and the popular television series lampooning cubicle life, *The Office,* featured a character discussing how much she liked Spider Solitaire. Americans also embraced games that required nothing more than pen and paper or a deck of cards. In 2005 a Japanese logic puzzle began appearing in American newspapers alongside the crossword puzzle and jumble. Sudoku, which translates to "single number" in Japanese, presents the player with a grid of eighty-one boxes. The objective is to ensure that each row, column, and square ultimately contains the digits one through nine. The puzzles were embraced by commuters, vacationers, and doctors, who recommended the exercise for sharpening memory and logic skills. In the summer of 2005, six of *USA Today's* 150 top-selling books were Sudoku themed. More high-tech media soon followed suit, with computer programs and smartphone applications that replicated the infamous grid. Another trend in games was a new-found interest in poker. The card game, particularly a variant called Texas Hold'em, was embraced by a new generation of enthusiasts. The trend was spurred on by televised poker tournaments that made celebrities of professional players, and reality shows such as *Celebrity Poker Showdown*. The 2006 World Series of Poker, televised on sports network ESPN, had more than one million viewers. Celebrities such as Ben Affleck, Jennifer Tilly, and James Woods played in professional and amateur tournaments and took home substantial winnings. Amateur gamblers of all ages also put on their poker faces at home games, small tournaments, and online. One math professor at Emory University used his students' enthusiasm for the game to teach probability. Some players, however, got into serious financial trouble because of what psychologists diagnosed as a pathological addiction to gambling. The ease and twenty-four-hour availability of playing poker online was tempting for some players, especially college students away from home and parental supervision for the first time. A *New York Times* study found that college students, inspired by the legend of Chris Moneymaker (who made $2.5 million), were depositing more than $2 billion in online gambling. In 2005 more than one million students admitted to gambling online, and some lost thousands of dollars. Even participating in small tournaments could cross the line between having fun and committing a crime. A number of these tournaments were technically illegal according to some states' antigambling laws. However, the transgression only seemed to add to the thrill for some players. An enthusiast interviewed for an article on increasing crackdowns on poker players observed, "This secret world of card players is a little bit of a thrill."

Sources:

Sarah Bailey, "It's just logical: Sudoku books fuel the craze," *USA Today*, 24 August 2005;

Lev Grossman, "A Game for All Ages," *Time* (8 May 2006);

Winnie Hu, "Solitaire Costs Man His City Job after Bloomberg Sees Computer," *New York Times*, 10 February 2006;

Charisse Jones, "National poker craze drawing attention of law enforcement," *USA Today*, 17 January 2006;

Josh Levin, "Solitaire-y Confinement," *slate.com* (16 May 2008);

Mike Musgrove, "Video Game Console's Debut Sparks Violence," *Washington Post*, 18 November 2006;

Mattathias Schwartz, "The Hold-'Em Holdup," *New York Times Magazine*, 11 June 2006;

Mike Snider, "Looking for a new video game system?" *USA Today*, 10 November 2006;

Nathan Thornburgh, "Parents for Poker," *Time* (25 September 2006).

HEADLINE MAKERS

GLENN BECK

1964–

CONSERVATIVE TALK SHOW HOST

Culture Warrior. The 2000s were marked by a polarizing trend in politics that was echoed in American lifestyles. As news media became more diffuse and ubiquitous through blogs, talk radio, and twenty-four-hour networks, people could immerse themselves in political commentary, which some argued only furthered the divide between "Red State" and "Blue State" Americans. One political pundit who exploited the new media to appeal to an increasingly vocal conservative strain was Glenn Beck. Through his television program, radio show, and best-selling books, Beck straddled the line between commentator and celebrity, and recast conservative Americans as an alienated and marginalized subgroup in a liberal social landscape. Beck's fiery rhetoric bemoaning increased secularism in America touched a nerve, as the two million viewers of his television show and five million visitors to his blog could attest. Beck reached *The New York Times* best-seller list in four categories at the end of the decade, with both his political rhetoric and his sentimental fiction finding a large reading audience.

Tea Parties and 9/12. Beck's brand of conservatism appealed to those Americans who felt the resurgence in national patriotism after the 9/11 attacks had diminished unacceptably in the latter years of the decade. He inaugurated the 9/12 project in 2009 to reclaim a country that, as Beck alleged, had ceased to stand up for "the little guy." Beck appealed to the spirit of the Founding Fathers explicitly with his popular screed *Glenn Beck's Common Sense: The Case against an Out-of-Control Government, Inspired by Thomas Paine* (2009), in which he argued that federal programs to redistribute wealth, especially during a recession, were unjust and un-American. Beck's rhetoric of underdog politics dovetailed with the frustration and anger many Americans were feeling over the grim economic situation during the latter half of the decade. Beck organized a massive march on Washington in March of 2009 to protest overtaxing. This event is widely credited as contributing to the birth of the "Tea Party" (Taxed Enough Already) movement that became an increasingly trendy political affiliation. Beck is a figure who encapsulates how the culture wars were both reflected in and shaped by a media-saturated landscape.

Sources:
Matthew Continetti, "Rick Santelli, Glenn Beck, and the future of the populist insurgency," *Weekly Standard,* 15 (28 June 2010);

Brian Stelter and Bill Carter, "Fox News's Mad, Apocalyptic, Tearful Rising Star," *New York Times,* 29 March 2009.

ELLEN DEGENERES

1958–

COMEDIAN, TALK-SHOW HOST, ACTOR

Young Comic. With her gentle humor and affable personality, Ellen DeGeneres helped to advance public acceptance of homosexuality in the first decade of the twenty-first century. Born in Metairie, Louisiana, she moved with her mother and her mother's second husband to Atlanta, Texas, as a teenager. She dropped out of the University of New Orleans after one semester to work on her standup comedy act. The death of her first serious love, poet Kathy Perkoff, in a car accident in 1980 inspired DeGeneres's "Phone Call to God" routine about mortality, which won her the designation of Showtime's Funniest Person in America in 1982. She performed the monologue during her debut on *The Tonight Show with Johnny Carson* in 1986; when she finished her act, Carson called her over to sit on the couch next to his desk and chat. Carson only extended such invitations to comics who particularly impressed him, and DeGeneres was the first female to receive one.

Coming Out. In 1994 DeGeneres starred in the ABC situation comedy *These Friends of Mine,* an ensemble show designed to capitalize on the success of NBC's *Seinfeld.* It did poorly in the ratings but became successful after being retooled as *Ellen* for the second season. DeGeneres played neurotic bookshop manager Ellen Morgan, who was presumably heterosexual but had little success with men. By 1997 the ratings were again flagging. Then, DeGeneres announced on *The Oprah Winfrey Show* and in a *Time* magazine interview that she was gay; and in a one-hour episode of *Ellen* broadcast on 30 April, Ellen Morgan came to the realization that she, too, was a lesbian. The show attracted a viewership of forty-two million and stirred up an enormous controversy; some sponsors withdrew from the program, and religious groups protested it. The episode marked a milestone: gay regular characters played by gay actors had already appeared on network television series such as *NYPD Blue* and *Spin City,* but never in the leading roles. (Tony Randall had starred as a gay man in the 1981–1982 sitcom *Love, Sidney,* but the character's sexuality had been downplayed to the point of invisibility, and Randall himself was straight.) *Ellen* emphasized gay themes from that point onward and was cancelled at the end of the next season.

Talk-Show Success. In November 2001 DeGeneres emceed the Fifty-Third Annual Primetime Emmy Awards show, which had been postponed because of the September 11 terrorist attacks; she opened it by asking, "What would bug the Taliban more than seeing a gay woman in a suit surrounded by Jews?" She played another lesbian character, Ellen Richmond, in the short-lived CBS sitcom *The Ellen Show* (2001–2002) before finding success as the host of the syndicated daytime talk program *The Ellen DeGeneres Show* beginning in 2003. The show featured interviews with celebrities, musical acts, audience participation, and segments on noncelebrities with interesting stories or unusual talents. It won Daytime Emmy Awards as Outstanding Talk Show in 2004, 2006, and 2007; DeGeneres won as Outstanding Talk Show Host in 2005, 2006, 2007, and 2008.

Relationships and Marriage. After coming out in 1997, DeGeneres had a high-profile romance with actor Anne Heche, whose previous involvements (including one with comedian Steve Martin) had been heterosexual. That relationship ended in a well-publicized breakup in August 2000. In 2004 DeGeneres left her girlfriend of four years, photographer/director Alexandra Hedison, for actor Portia de Rossi, who was then appearing in the Fox Television sitcom *Arrested Development.* The California Supreme Court ruled the state's ban on same-sex marriage unconstitutional in May 2008, and DeGeneres and de Rossi were married on 16 August of that year. In November, however, California voters passed Proposition 8, which amended the state constitution and reinstituted the ban. On 26 May 2009 the California Supreme Court ruled that the amendment was not retroactive; therefore, same-sex couples such as DeGeneres and de Rossi who had been legally married before the passage of Proposition 8 were still married afterward.

Sources:
"Ellen DeGeneres," *people.com;*

"Ellen Steps Out," *newsweek.com* (14 April 1997);

Bruce Handy, Elizabeth L. Bland, William Tynan, and Jeffrey Ressner, "Television: Roll Over, Ward Cleaver," *time.com* (14 April 1997);

Paul W. Thorndal, "Are We Still Married? Same-Sex Marriage FAQ," waldlaw.net.

RACHAEL RAY

1968–

CELEBRITY CHEF, TELEVISION PERSONALITY

"Yum-o!" In November of 2001, Rachael Ray's cooking series *30 Minute Meals* debuted on the Food Network. By the end of the decade, the perky chef from New York had her own magazine, hosted a talk show that won the 2008 and 2009 Emmy Awards, and had been named the seventy-ninth most powerful celebrity in the world by *Forbes* magazine. As fellow celebrity chef Mario Batali put it in a 2006 *Time* profile of Ray, "In fewer than five years, Rachael Ray has radically changed the way America cooks dinner." Ray's show contributed to the trends toward comfort foods, affordable eating, and health consciousness that were dominant in American cooking during the 2000s. Ray's meals included familiar and affordable ingredients, healthy components, and easy preparation. She also infused the program with her easygoing and accessible personality, indoctrinating the catchphrases "Yum-o!"; "G.B." ("garbage bowl," a countertop repository for food scraps that Ray designed for a line of cookware); and "EVOO," an abbreviation for extra-virgin olive oil that the *Oxford American College Dictionary* included in its 2007 edition.

Media Maven. As Ray's Food Network programs grew in popularity, she began to expand her influence beyond the kitchen into American living rooms. After numerous appearances on the *Oprah Winfrey Show*, Ray's own syndicated talk show debuted in 2006. During the hour-long program, Ray shared personal anecdotes, interviewed celebrity guests, and shared housekeeping tips from viewers. The popularity of the show was matched by her magazine, *Everyday with Rachael Ray*, which had a circulation of 1.7 million by the end of the decade. This "down-market Martha Stewart" was the perfect fit for a time-strapped and recession-weary public looking for ways to downsize their lifestyles while still feathering their nests.

Sources:
"Adding a Little EVOO . . . to the Dictionary!" *rachaelray.com* (11 June 2007);

Mario Batali, "Rachael Ray," *Time* (30 April 2006);

Alessandra Stanley, "Beyond the Kitchen, Breaking Bread with America," *New York Times*, 19 September 2006.

MARK ZUCKERBERG

1984–

SOCIAL-MEDIA INNOVATOR

"Just a Harvard Thing." In 2004 Mark Zuckerberg and a group of his classmates at Harvard were looking for a way to help fellow students stay in touch and make friends online. They decided to replicate a student directory online, including photos, ways to connect electronically, and a forum for individual self-expression. Their dorm-room invention, called "Facebook," soon expanded beyond Harvard and took college campuses across the country by storm. By 2009 Facebook had 400 million members of all ages, and had changed the way people understood social relationships and privacy.

Accidental Billionaire. With the phenomenal popularity of Facebook came a large amount of money, as well as a lot of attention directed toward Zuckerberg's personal and professional reputation. Though Facebook was founded by a group of four students, Zuckerberg quickly became the face of Facebook and the CEO of the multi-billion-dollar corporation. In 2009 he was named one of *Time*'s most influential people, and at twenty-six, was the youngest billionaire in the world. However, Zuckerberg also experienced legal and personal attacks. He was accused of stealing the idea for the social-networking site, lying to his friends and cofounders, and living the life of a spoiled playboy. Though Zuckerberg was quoted as wanting to be thought of as a "good guy," the movie *The Social Network* (2010) depicted his part in Facebook's founding and the messy aftermath, focusing on Zuckerberg's ego rather than his innovation.

Sources:
Dan Lyons, "The Father of Social Networking," *Newsweek* (22 July 2009);

Janet Maslin, "Harvard Pals Grow Rich: Chronicling Facebook without Face Time," *New York Times*, 19 July 2009;

Craig Newmark, "Mark Zuckerberg," *Time* (30 April 2009).

PEOPLE IN THE NEWS

On 29 June 2008 **Thomas Beatie,** already immortalized as the "pregnant man," gave birth to a daughter. The transgendered father, who made the choice to live as a man without surgically removing his female sex organs, was a highly visible example of the ways nontraditional families were becoming more acceptable.

In April 2004 photos documenting American soldiers torturing and humiliating Iraqi prisoners in the Abu Ghraib prison shocked the nation. **Lynndie England** and **Charles A. Graner** were convicted in 2005 trials, though many were convinced that the responsibility for the atrocities reached higher in the chain of command. The photos led some Americans to question the war in Iraq and the culture of the military.

In September of 2005 **Oprah Winfrey** selected *A Million Little Pieces* by **James Frey** as the next selection in her phenomenally popular Book Club. After large portions of the book were revealed to be fictional, Winfrey summoned the author to her show for a public scolding. Frey's was not the only memoir to be debunked as the American public's appetite for salacious "real-life" stories prompted some authors to bend the truth for a lucrative book contract.

In June of 2000 Cuban immigrant **Elian Gonzalez** was returned to Cuba to live with his father after spending the previous months with the family of his deceased mother. The photograph of a terrified Gonzalez being taken from his family at gunpoint was a seminal image of the immigration debate in America.

The devastating attacks on New York City and Washington, D.C., on 11 September 2001 resulted in an upswell of nationwide mourning and a resurgence in patriotism. New York City mayor **Rudolph Guliani** was lauded for his coolheaded and compassionate response in the immediate aftermath of the collapse of the Twin Towers and became known as "America's Mayor."

Megachurch preacher **Ted Haggard** was forced from the pulpit in November 2006 resulting from allegations of sexual misconduct and drug use. The married father of five went into intensive counseling designed to rid him of homosexual impulses.

On 15 October 2009 the country was momentarily held rapt by a seemingly gut-wrenching drama: a six-year-old boy was trapped in a runaway helium balloon. After the boy's "recovery," it was quickly discovered that the **Heene Family** had duped the twenty-four-hour news cycle and orchestrated the hoax to try to land a reality television series.

In 2004 Mario Armando Lavandeira Jr., known to the world as **Perez Hilton,** launched his gossip blog.

On 9 May 2005 political doyenne **Arianna Huffington** took *The Huffington Post* live. The blog was an aggregate of political news, gossip, and cultural commentary, and it was meant to offer a more progressive alternative to conservative-dominated talk radio. *The Huffington Post* attained widespread popularity and included guest bloggers such as **Madeleine Albright, Jamie Lee Curtis,** and **Madonna.**

In February of 2005 **Chad Hurley, Steve Chen,** and **Jawed Karim,** a group of computer programmers, founded YouTube, a peer-to-peer video-sharing site that soon became one of the most influential sites in online culture.

In November 2002 former governor of New Jersey **Thomas Keane** (Republican) was named chairman of the 9/11 Commission. Comprising five Democrats and five Republicans, the commission was charged with compiling a report that detailed the lead-up to and aftermath from the 11 September attacks. The report, released in July 2004, became a *New York Times* best seller.

In the spring and summer of 2001, Americans were transfixed by the disappearance in May of Washington, D.C., intern **Chandra Levy** and the allegations of her extramarital affair with Representative **Gary Condit** (D-Cal.), who was briefly named a suspect in the case. Her skeletal remains were located in a park in 2002; her alleged murderer was arrested in 2009.

On 15 November 2004 New Jersey governor **James E. McGreevey** (D) officially resigned from office and announced in a press conference that he was a "gay American."

In 2005 *Twilight* by **Stephenie Meyer** was published and soon became one of the best-selling books of the decade. The popularity of the four-volume series and film adaptations highlighted the power of tweens to affect the cultural and media marketplace.

In November 2008 **Barack Obama** won the presidential election, making him the first African American president in U.S. history. Obama's election was used as evidence by some as a "postracial" turn in American society, indicating that the racial divide was no longer as influential as it had been in past decades.

In 2005 *You: The Owner's Manual: An Insider's Guide to the Body That Will Make You Healthier and Younger,* by **Oprah Winfrey**–endorsed physicians **Mehmet C. Oz** and **Michael F. Roizen,** was published. The book's common-sense advice about health and well-being struck a nerve with increasingly health-conscious, yet overweight, Americans.

In September 2008 **Bristol Palin,** the daughter of GOP vice-presidential candidate **Sarah Palin,** confirmed she was five months pregnant. Seventeen years old and unmarried, Bristol was the public face of the increasing number of young, unmarried mothers during the 2000s.

In February 2009 pop singer **Rihanna** was assaulted by her boyfriend, R&B star **Chris Brown.** Police photos of the star's battered face prompted a national conversation on the prevalence of domestic violence.

In July 2007 British author **J. K. Rowling** released the seventh and last installment in her phenomenally popular Harry Potter young-adult fantasy series. Over the span of the decade, the books had sold more than 400 million copies, and movies based on the series consistently broke box-office records during the 2000s.

In March 2005 the feeding tube was removed from brain-damaged **Terri Schiavo** after a prolonged court battle between her husband and her parents. The notoriety of the case and the federal government's involvement prompted many Americans to think about end-of-life issues.

On 8 August 2009 **Sonia Sotomayor** was sworn in as the first Hispanic justice on the Supreme Court, and the third woman in the Court's history.

In August of 2003 **Britney Spears** and **Madonna** shared an infamous kiss during the MTV Video Music Awards.

In October of 2004 domestic diva and media queen **Martha Stewart** began her five-month prison term for lying in court. True to form, she left the minimum-security prison in March of 2005 sporting a hand-made poncho, knitted by a fellow inmate. Top yarn companies were soon offering the pattern to homemakers.

In January 2009 **Nadya Suleman,** already a mother to six young children, gave birth to octuplets. Along with the tabloid fodder, the story of the "Octomom" raised ethical questions about multiple births and artificial insemination.

In August 2007 professional football player **Michael Vick** was arrested and charged with animal cruelty for his part in running a dog-fighting ring; Vick served twenty-three months in prison.

In May of 2005 **Antonio Villaraigosa,** the son of Mexican immigrants, was elected the first Hispanic mayor of Los Angeles.

DEATHS

Brooke Astor, 105, socialite, philanthropist, and author, 13 August 2007.

Susan Atkins, 61, convicted murderer and member of the "Manson Family," a group led by Charles Manson who committed nine murders in the summer of 1969, 24 September 2009.

Joseph Barbera, 85, cartoon pioneer, cofounder of animation studio Hanna-Barbera, 18 December 2006.

James Brown, 73, prolific musician dubbed the "Godfather of Soul," 25 December 2006.

Johnny Carson, 79, host of late-night's popular *The Tonight Show* for nearly 30 years, 23 January 2005.

Johnny Cash, 71, singer-songwriter, country legend, known as "The Man in Black," 12 September 2003.

Ivan Combe, 88, inventor of popular acne cream Clearasil, 11 January 2000.

Walter Cronkite, 92, journalist and anchorman for *CBS Evening News* from 1962 to 1981. Cronkite reported such landmark events as the Vietnam War, the assassination of President John F. Kennedy, and the NASA moon landing, 17 July 2009.

Bo Diddley, 79, guitarist and rock-and-roll pioneer, 2 June 2008.

Dolly the Sheep, 6, first mammal to be cloned from an adult cell, 14 February 2003.

Dale Earnhardt Sr., 49, race-car driver and seven-time NASCAR Winston Cup champion, during the Daytona 500, 18 February 2001.

William Mark Felt Sr., 95, Nixon-era associate director of the FBI. In 2005, Felt revealed himself to be "Deep Throat," the inside source who aided reporters Bob Woodward and Carl Bernstein in exposing the Watergate scandal, 18 December 2008.

Gerald R. Ford, 93, sworn in as thirty-eighth president (1974–1977) of the United States after the resignation of Richard M. Nixon, 26 December 2006.

Ernest Gallo, 97, cofounder of E&J Gallo winery, 6 March 2007.

William Hanna, 90, cartoon pioneer, cofounder of animation studio Hanna-Barbera, 22 March 2001.

George Harrison, 58, singer-songwriter, member of The Beatles, 29 November 2001.

Jesse Alexander Helms Jr., 86, five-term U.S. senator from North Carolina (Republican), one of the major figures of the modern conservative movement, 4 July 2008.

Charlton Heston, 84, film star, chairman of the National Rifle Association, 5 April 2008.

Bob Hope, 100, comedian, film star, and humanitarian, 27 July 2003.

Mark R. Hughes, 44, founder and CEO of nutritional company Herbalife, 21 May 2000.

Steve Irwin, 44, environmentalist, "Crocodile Hunter," and reality-television star, 4 September 2006.

Michael Jackson, 50, singer known as the "King of Pop" who battled legal, financial, and health challenges after early success with the Jackson 5, 25 June 2009.

Lady Bird Johnson, 94, former first lady and environmental advocate, 11 July 2007.

Estée Lauder, 95, cosmetics mogul, 24 April 2004.

Lisa "Left Eye" Lopes, 30, member of the R&B group TLC, 25 April 2002.

Robert Ludlum, 73, popular author of spy novels including the *Bourne* series, 12 March 2001.

Jeff MacNelly, 51, three-time Pulitzer Prize–winning political cartoonist, 8 June 2000.

Tammy Faye Messner, 65, televangelist and talk-show host; was known for her heavy makeup and for her involvement in the financial mismanagement of PTL, 20 July 2007.

Henry Nicols, 26, first AIDS patient to disclose his medical status in an American school, 8 May 2000.

Rosa Parks, 92, civil-rights icon who refused to give up her seat on a segregated bus, thereby sparking the modern civil-rights movement, 24 October 2005.

Richard Pryor, 65, groundbreaking comedian and actor, 10 December 2005.

Ronald Reagan, 93, fortieth president of the United States, set the cultural and economic tone for the 1980s, 5 June 2004.

Fred Rogers, 74, host of beloved children's television series *Mr. Rogers' Neighborhood*, 27 February 2003.

Tim Russert, 58, journalist and moderator of *Meet the Press*, 13 June 2008.

Charles M. Schulz, 77, cartoonist and creator of "Peanuts," 12 February 2000.

Anna Nicole Smith, 39, former *Playboy* centerfold and reality-television star, 8 February 2007.

Aaron Spelling, 83, television producer, creator of *The Love Boat, Charlie's Angels,* and *Beverly Hills 90210,* 23 June 2006.

Dave Thomas, 69, founder and CEO of popular fast-food chain Wendy's, philanthropist, 8 January 2002.

PUBLICATIONS

Stuart Allan, *Online News: Journalism and the Internet* (New York: Open University Press, 2006);

Ted Allen, Kyan Douglas, Thom Filicia, Carson Kressley, and Jai Rodriguez, *Queer Eye for the Straight Guy: The Fab 5's Guide to Looking Better, Cooking Better, Dressing Better, Behaving Better, and Living Better* (New York: Clarkson Potter, 2004);

James Bradley and Ron Powers, *Flags of Our Fathers* (New York: Bantam, 2000);

Hillary Rodham Clinton, *Living History* (New York: Simon & Schuster, 2003);

David Crystal, *Txtng: The Gr8 Db8* (New York: Oxford University Press, 2008);

Doug Fine, *Farewell, My Subaru: An Epic Adventure in Local Living* (New York: Villard, 2008);

Thomas L. Friedman, *Hot, Flat, and Crowded: Why We Need a Green Revolution—and How It Can Renew America* (New York: Farrar, Straus & Giroux, 2008);

David Gilmour, *The Film Club: A Memoir* (New York: Twelve, 2008);

Al Gore, *An Inconvenient Truth: The Planetary Emergency of Global Warming and What We Can Do About It* (Emmaus, Pa.: Rodale Books, 2006);

Conn Iggulden and Hal Iggulden, *The Dangerous Book for Boys* (London: HarperCollins, 2006);

Jon Krakauer, *Where Men Win Glory: The Odyssey of Pat Tillman* (New York: Doubleday, 2009);

Steven D. Levitt and Stephen J. Dubner, *Freakonomics: A Rogue Economist Explains the Hidden Side of Everything* (New York: Morrow, 2005);

Rich Ling, *The Mobile Connection: The Cell Phone's Impact on Society* (San Francisco: Morgan Kaufman, 2004);

Joseph Menn, *All The Rave: The Rise and Fall of Shawn Fanning's Napster* (New York: Crown Business, 2003);

Ben Mezrich, *The Accidental Billionaires: The Founding of Facebook: A Tale of Sex, Money, Genius, and Betrayal* (New York: Doubleday, 2009);

Barack Obama, *The Audacity of Hope: Thoughts on Reclaiming the American Dream* (New York: Crown, 2006);

Bill O'Reilly, *Culture Warrior* (New York: Broadway Books, 2006);

Michael Pollan, *The Omnivore's Dilemma: A Natural History of Four Meals* (New York: Penguin, 2006);

William Powers, *Hamlet's BlackBerry: A Practical Philosophy for Building a Good Life in the Digital Age* (New York: Harper, 2010);

Eric Schlosser, *Fast Food Nation: The Dark Side of the All-American Meal* (New York: Houghton Mifflin, 2001);

Bryant Simon, *Everything but the Coffee: Learning about America from Starbucks* (Berkeley: University of California Press, 2009);

Leslie Morgan Steiner, ed., *The Mommy Wars: Stay-at-Home and Career Moms Face Off on Their Choices, Their Lives, Their Families* (New York: Random House, 2006);

Michael Strangelove, *The Empire of the Mind: Digital Piracy and the Anti-Capitalist Movement* (Toronto: University of Toronto Press, 2005);

Morley Winograd and Michael D. Hais, *Millennial Makeover: MySpace, YouTube, and the Future of American Politics* (New Brunswick, N.J.: Rutgers University Press, 2008);

Body + Soul, periodical;

Everyday with Rachael Ray, periodical;

The New Yorker, periodical;

Newsweek, periodical;

O: The Oprah Magazine, periodical;

Rolling Stone, periodical;

Time, periodical;

Vanity Fair, periodical.

MEDIA

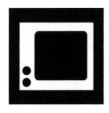

by RACHEL LURIA

CONTENTS

Sidebars and tables are listed in italics.

2000

- Nightly network news attracts fewer than 30 million regular viewers, down almost half since 1980. More people are turning to the Internet and cable news programs.

2 Feb. *The Daily Show* on Comedy Central begins its popular satirical election coverage with a series of episodes titled "Indecision 2000," focusing on the primary in New Hampshire.

13 Mar. The Tribune Company announces it will purchase the *Los Angeles Times, Baltimore Sun, Newsday,* and several other media outlets.

19 Apr. *O: The Oprah Magazine,* headed by Oprah Winfrey, is launched.

31 May *Survivor* (Borneo), a competition reality program, premieres on CBS.

11 June A Pew Research Center report notes that one-third of Americans use the Internet for news, while viewership of national news broadcasts falls.

5 July CBS debuts the competition reality series *Big Brother.*

6 Oct. CBS's *CSI: Crime Scene Investigation* debuts; the forensics-based crime show will spawn similar programs on this and other networks.

3 Dec. Showtime's *Queer as Folk* debuts; the drama, based on an earlier British series, follows the lives of five gay men in Pittsburgh and quickly becomes one of Showtime's most-watched programs.

14 Dec. AOL and Time Warner merge.

2001

- *The New Yorker* launches *newyorker.com,* an editorial website.

- More than half of U.S. households use at least one cell phone.

15 Jan. The online encyclopedia site Wikipedia debuts.

Mar. *George,* a magazine founded by John F. Kennedy Jr. (who died in a plane crash in 1999), ends publication.

5 Mar. Bethany McLean's article for *Fortune* questioning Enron's stock price ultimately leads to the unmasking of illegal business dealings and the collapse of the company.

3 Apr. Comedian and talk-show host Rosie O'Donnell's magazine *Rosie* hits newsstands.

25 June The Supreme Court rules that publishers must obtain copyright consent before posting freelancers' work online.

11 Sept. Viewers watch in horror as the World Trade Center towers collapse on live television after terrorist attacks.

17 Sept. Bill Maher, comedian and political pundit, as host of ABC's *Politically Incorrect* says that the World Trade Center terrorists were not "cowards"; he is fired in 2002, but reemerges on HBO with a program with a similar format.

24 Sept. The XM Satellite Radio service is launched, providing news, music, and other entertainment.

23 Oct. Apple releases the iPod.

6 Nov. The television program *24* premieres on the Fox network.

6 Nov. More than 400 million people regularly use the Internet.

2002

1 Jan. The term "blogosphere" (first coined by Brad Graham in 1999) is popularized by William Quick when he uses it on his blog "Daily Pundit" to describe the rise in blogging.

21 Jan. Tina Brown's *Talk* magazine folds.

22 Jan. AOL/Time Warner launch an antitrust lawsuit against Microsoft.

23 Jan. *Wall Street Journal* reporter Daniel Pearl is kidnapped in Karachi, Pakistan. He is murdered by al-Qaeda on 1 February.

Mar. The social network Friendster is founded; membership is strongest in Asian countries.

25 Mar. ABC debuts the romance reality show, *The Bachelor.*

11 June *American Idol*, a talent-competition show, premieres on Fox.

1 July The satellite radio service Sirius is launched, providing uncensored, twenty-four-hour news, sports, music, and other entertainment.

2003

Feb. *Teen Vogue*, a fashion magazine aimed at young girls, begins publication.

Mar. The social-networking website MySpace launches.

20 Mar. The invasion of Iraq begins; hundreds of journalists have been "embedded" with individual units in the field.

3 Apr. Michael Kelly of the *Washington Post* is the first American reporter killed in Iraq.

9 Apr. Images of Iraqis toppling the statue of Saddam Hussein make international news.

11 May *The New York Times* publishes an explanation and apology for the plagiarism and fabricated stories of reporter Jayson Blair.

20 May Supermodel Tyra Banks hosts the first episode of the reality competition show, *America's Next Top Model.*

Oct. *The New York Times* names Daniel Okrent its first public editor (an ombudsman tasked with being a watchdog on reporting by the paper).

2004

8 Jan. Real-estate mogul Donald Trump debuts his reality show, *The Apprentice.*

23 Jan. Robert Keeshan, better known from 1955 to 1984 as Captain Kangaroo (as well as Clarabel the Clown on the *Howdy Doody Show*, 1948–1953), dies.

Feb. Photo-sharing website Flickr is launched.

1 Feb. Viewers of the Superbowl Halftime Show witness Janet Jackson's "Wardrobe Malfunction," in which a portion of her costume is ripped off by fellow performer Justin Timberlake and her breast is exposed. The Federal Communications Commission later fines Viacom $27,500 for each of the twenty CBS-owned television stations for a total of $550,000.

4 Feb. Social-networking site Facebook is launched for Harvard students only.

22 Feb. HBO's popular television series *Sex and the City*, which began in 1998, comes to an end.

21 Mar. *Deadwood*, a historical drama about a late-nineteenth-century South Dakota town, premieres on HBO.

10 May *New Yorker* investigative reporter Seymour Hersh publishes article on abuses of prisoners by U.S. troops at Abu Ghraib in Iraq.

2 June Ken Jennings begins his record-setting winning streak on *Jeopardy!*

22 Sept. Television program *Lost* premieres on ABC.

6 Oct. Radio "shock jock" Howard Stern signs a five-year, $500 million deal with Sirius satellite radio.

8 Oct. Martha Stewart begins serving a five-month prison sentence for conspiracy, obstruction of justice, and making false statements.

19 Oct. *The Biggest Loser*, a reality show based on weight loss, debuts.

2 Nov. Bloggers post early results from the polling stations in the national election.

9 Nov. The Mozilla Firefox web browser, an open source, free alternative to Internet Explorer, is released.

30 Nov. Jennings ends his winning streak on *Jeopardy!*, the longest-running in program history. He competed in seventy-four episodes and won more than $2.5 million.

1 Dec. Longtime *NBC Nightly News* anchorman Tom Brokaw retires.

14 Dec. Google announces it will scan and post books in the public domain from five major libraries.

2005

15 Jan. *Tsunami Aid: A Concert of Hope*, a telethon organized to provide relief for victims of the 26 December Indonesian tsunami, airs on NBC and affiliate networks.

15 Feb. YouTube, a video-sharing website, launches.

24 Mar. The U.S. version of the British situation comedy *The Office* premieres on NBC.

23 Apr. The first YouTube video is uploaded.

9 May The progressive news and blogging website Huffington Post debuts.

31 May NBC launches the blog *The Daily Nightly*.

1 June ABC debuts *Dancing With the Stars*, a competition show that pairs professional ballroom dancers with celebrities.

28 June The three-dimensional mapping site Google Earth is launched.

July *Vanity Fair* reveals that Mark Felt was "Deep Throat," the FBI officer who helped reporters uncover the Watergate affair and President Richard Nixon's involvement.

12 Sept. CBS News launches its blog *Public Eye*.

2006

3 Jan. *ABC World News Tonight* launches a blog, *The World Newser*.

Mar. Twitter, a messaging and social-networking website, is launched.

Mar. The McClatchy Company purchases Knight Ridder, making it the second largest newspaper corporation in the United States.

21 June	NBC debuts its challenge to Fox's *American Idol,* with *America's Got Talent.*
Aug.	Twitter is made available to the public.
31 Aug.	The documentary film *An Inconvenient Truth,* featuring Al Gore, is released, bolstering the growing green trend in the United States.
Sept.	Sony Corporation issues its first portable tablet ebook device, the Sony Reader.
5 Sept.	Katie Couric joins *CBS Evening News* as the first solo female evening anchor. The network also begins simulcasting the show on the World Wide Web.
26 Sept.	Facebook is made available to users over the age of thirteen with a valid email address.
28 Sept.	The popular comedy *Ugly Betty* premieres on ABC.
4 Oct.	Wikileaks, a website created to reveal secret government documents, debuts.
9 Oct.	Google buys YouTube for $1.65 billion.
11 Oct.	Tina Fey's situation comedy *30 Rock,* about running a late-night comedy show, premieres on NBC.

2007

9 Jan.	Apple unveils the iPhone. It will officially be released to the public in June.
11 Apr.	CBS fires popular radio host Don Imus after he makes a racist comment about the Rutgers University women's basketball team.
10 June	HBO's hit drama *The Sopranos,* which began in 1999, airs its controversial series finale.
19 July	AMC's period drama *Mad Men,* about Madison Avenue advertising executives in the 1960s, premieres.
23 July	CNN and YouTube jointly host a presidential debate.
5 Nov.	A Writers Guild of America strike halts production of scripted television and leads to a rise in "reality television" shows.
19 Nov.	Amazon releases the Kindle, which allows users to purchase and read digital versions of books and magazines.

2008

Jan.	The White House begins a blog.
5 Jan.	ABC and Facebook cosponsor presidential debates.
8 Feb.	Negotiations with the Writers Guild of America are successfully completed, ending the Hollywood writers' strike.
Aug.	More than 100 million people use Facebook.
16 Dec.	The *Detroit Free Press* and *Detroit News* announce that they will end home delivery except on Thursdays, Fridays, and Sundays.

2009

15 Jan.	Pilot Chesley "Sully" Sullenberger safely lands U.S. Airways flight 1549 on the Hudson River after the plane is critically damaged by a bird strike. Media outlets dub the event "Miracle on the Hudson."

27 Mar.	The *Christian Science Monitor* shifts its efforts to the Internet and publishes its last paper edition.
19 May	Fox's television musical *Glee*, which follows a group of glee-club misfits, premieres after *American Idol.*
12 June	All television stations are required to shift from analog to digital broadcasting.
17 July	"The most trusted man in America," news anchor Walter Cronkite, dies at age 92.
14 Sept.	Jay Leno leaves the *Tonight Show* but remains with NBC for a five-nights-a-week 10:00 P.M. program, which lasts for only ninety-five episodes.
19 Oct.	*The New York Times* announces it will cut one hundred newsroom jobs.
Nov.	The final issue of *Gourmet,* a magazine for food lovers, is released.
20 Nov.	Oprah announces her retirement (to occur in 2011) from the *Oprah Winfrey Show.*
Dec.	A consortium of large American newspaper and magazine publishers announce plans to build a new Internet platform to allow future devices to access their products.
3 Dec.	GE announces the sale of NBC to Comcast.
18 Dec.	The Sony eReader allows subscribers to get the *Wall Street Journal* and *New York Post.*

OVERVIEW

Technology and Transition. The first decade of the new millennium was marked by far-reaching changes in the way Americans received their news, entertained themselves, and communicated with one another. Evolving Internet and cell-phone technologies made information more easily accessible than ever before. Media outlets updated stories as they developed and connected with audiences in more personal and immediate ways, such as through online polls, Twitter feeds, and Facebook pages. Audience demand for information grew, but the ways Americans accessed their information brought changes in the style and format of news. Older print newspapers and magazines launched online versions, but often free online content came at the expense of operating budgets. If you could access all the news free on your computer, why pay for a paper subscription? Some media providers met this challenge by charging an online subscription fee, others covered the costs with more advertising, while many others drastically cut budgets and reduced staff. For example, in 2008, The *Detroit Free Press* and *Detroit News* ended home delivery on all days but Thursdays, Fridays, and Sundays to cut costs; in 2009 *The New York Times* announced that it would be cutting one hundred newsroom jobs. The media both embraced changing technology and struggled to adapt.

Speed of Political Coverage. The sheer speed with which audiences could access and spread breaking news changed the shape of news coverage. The presidency of George W. Bush took place entirely within this new media environment of constant scrutiny and feedback. For example, in 2001 the president squirmed under intense media attention in the wake of the 11 September attacks, as many questioned the speed of his reaction. After the successful invasion of Iraq, Bush's 1 May 2003 appearance on the USS *Abraham Lincoln* aircraft carrier wearing a flight suit and giving a speech in front of a large "Mission Accomplished" banner seemed a savvy and well-orchestrated media moment. As conditions on the ground in Iraq continued to worsen, however, Bush's photo-op became fodder for late-night television jokes and Internet satire. In 2008 the candidacy of Barack Obama appealed especially to young voters who helped campaign videos "go viral" (that is, to receive extremely large number of "hits," or times

viewed) and rallied on social-networking sites such as Facebook. Though others had used the Internet as a political organizing tool in the past, Obama harnessed its power to reach new heights in communication, fund-raising, and get-out-the-vote efforts. Obama got another major boost when media giant Oprah Winfrey came out in support of his campaign—the first time she had ever publicly supported a candidate. The perceived favoritism shown to the Obama campaign by the media, however, fueled continued concerns among conservatives that there was a liberal bias in news reporting and led to continued growth in conservative news outlets.

Bursting Bubbles. The decade began and ended with two enormous financial crises: the bursting of the dotcom bubble, coupled with the fallout from the 11 September terrorist attacks, and the crash of the subprime housing market. Still, much of the early half of the decade featured a media obsession with opulence and celebrity lifestyles, as programs such as *MTV Cribs* and the Bravo network's *Real Housewives* treated audiences to a peek inside the extravagant lifestyles of the very wealthy. By the end of the decade, however, the dominant media trend was a turn toward themes of economic hardship, with stories of foreclosures and rising joblessness after the housing crash of 2007–2008. Sitcoms increasingly featured families enduring changes in circumstances due to the economic downturn. Programs such as NPR's *This American Life* documented the rise and fall of the housing market, which led to the worst recession in U.S. history since the Great Depression. Financial scandals also demanded media attention. Many of the corporate culprits became stock villains in media coverage. The book *Enron: The Smartest Guys in the Room: The Amazing Rise and Scandalous Fall of Enron* (2003) and documentary movie *Enron: The Smartest Guys in the Room* (2005) chronicled the 2001 fall of corporate giant Enron and the financial disaster that followed in its wake. Bernard Madoff's billion-dollar defrauding of investors (capped by his arrest in 2008 and conviction in 2009) became a symbol of Wall Street greed.

Going Green. Al Gore's Oscar-winning 2006 documentary *An Inconvenient Truth* set off a national fascination with and a storm of media coverage on environmental issues and even inspired some networks to attempt to "go green," a term frequently used during the decade to refer to environmentally friendly behavior. In 2007 NBC started its own Go Green campaign, making its facilities more eco-friendly and airing green-themed episodes such as *30 Rock*'s episode "Greenzo," which featured an appearance by Gore. The network even temporarily changed their multicolored peacock logo to all green for the occasion. While many celebrities continued to parade the media spotlight in extravagant, gas-guzzling vehicles, and reside in out-sized homes, others sought to use their prominence to promote green choices. Some, like Larry David—star of the HBO comedy *Curb Your Enthusiasm*—did so by driving a Toyota Prius hybrid car both on and off screen. The reality-television program *Living With Ed* featured the low-environmental impact lifestyle of Ed Begley Jr., who even went as far as using electricity generated by a stationary bicycle to power small appliances in his home.

TOPICS IN THE NEWS

CABLE SHOWS

The Sopranos. Home Box Office (HBO)'s series about the life of a depressed New Jersey mafia boss debuted in 1999 and ran six seasons before concluding in 2007. James Gandolfini portrayed Tony Soprano, a violent and volatile but endearing father who struggles to hold his home life and mental health together while rising to the top of his organized crime "family." Creator David Chase struck a balance between drama and humor, making *The Sopranos* HBO's most popular and profitable series. The show's success spawned a renaissance in television drama, not only on HBO but other cable channels such as Showtime and AMC. In addition to being wildly popular, *The Sopranos* was a critical favorite, garnering twenty-one Emmys and five Golden Globes.

Six Feet Under. Building on the success of *The Sopranos*, HBO found another hit in the dark drama *Six Feet Under*, which followed the lives of a family running a funeral home. The series, which ran from 2001 to 2005, dealt frankly with death—with many characters engaging in imagined conversations with the deceased—and with the modern problems of an unconventional family. Though the program was often funny, its tone matched the grim setting and focus on mortality. *Six Feet Under* ran for only sixty-three episodes, but won nine Emmys and three Golden Globes.

Weeds. The Showtime network joined the growing trend of quality television on premium cable with its dark comedy *Weeds*, which debuted in 2005. The show featured Mary-Louise Parker, who played Nancy Botwin, an upper-middle-class widow struggling to maintain her family's lifestyle after the death of her husband. In order to make

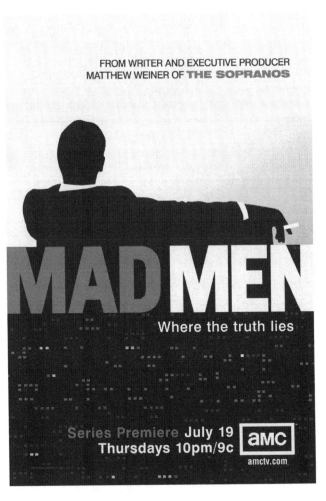

Advertisement for the first season
(<www.impawards.com>)

Advertisement for the HBO comedy series starring Larry David (<www.picasaweb.google.com>)

ends meet, Nancy begins selling marijuana and quickly becomes a major drug distributor. Though structurally similar to *The Sopranos,* in showcasing the main character's struggle to hold together two radically opposed halves of her life, *Weeds* struck a lighter, more comedic tone. The series was Showtime's most highly watched program, and garnered multiple Emmy (one win in 2009) and Golden Globe nominations.

Curb Your Enthusiasm. Larry David, best known for being the cocreator of the 1990s hit *Seinfeld,* became a television star in his own right with HBO's faux-reality comedy *Curb Your Enthusiasm.* The series, which debuted in 2000, followed the day-to-day life of David, who played an exaggerated version of himself. Reviving *Seinfeld*'s winning formula, *Curb Your Enthusiasm* highlighted David's basic inability to deal with the annoying and sometimes excruciating minutiae of everyday life. His loveable misanthropic portrayal often drew on his own life experiences. Season six, for example, revolved around the story line of onscreen marital troubles and divorce, even as the real-life David's marriage was crumbling.

Dexter. Showtime's campy drama *Dexter,* about the life of a justice-minded serial killer, debuted in 2006. Michael C. Hall portrayed Dexter Morgan, whose daytime job as a blood-splatter analyst for the Miami Police Department fit disconcertingly well with his darker alter ego as a killer who targeted criminals. It was revealed that Dexter had witnessed the brutal murder of his mother as a young child, an experience that created in him an undeniable urge to kill. But Dexter was no ordinary sociopath: trained by his adopted policeman father to channel his murderous tendencies, he chose victims carefully and murdered only those whom he deemed to be truly guilty (but who had escaped punishment through traditional channels). Based on a popular series of novels by Jeff Lindsay, *Dexter* was a hit and received multiple awards and nominations.

Mad Men. American Movie Classics (AMC), a network known principally for airing old movies, became a serious television contender with its popular period drama *Mad Men,* which premiered in 2007 and revolved around a Madison Avenue advertising firm in the 1960s. In addition to its critically acclaimed acting and story lines, the show attracted attention for its high production values, especially its period-correct fashion and set design. While the 2009 season's audience of 2.9 million viewers remained relatively small in comparison with major network dramas, the show was a runaway hit with critics, and its stylized portrayal of 1960s modern chic seeped into the culture, spawning *Saturday Night Live* spoofs and a growth of interest in vintage fashion.

Additional Shows. Premium-cable shows, many of which were controversial or pushed the limits of cultural acceptance, provided dramatic entertainment and garnered critical acclaim. HBO produced *Big Love* (2006–), on a polygamous family; *Carnivale* (2003–2005), about a Depression-era carnival troupe; *Deadwood* (2004–2006), a western situated in a nineteenth-century mining town in the Dakota Territory; *Entourage* (2004–), about a popular actor and his group of hangers-on; *True Blood* (2008–), featuring vampires and other fantasy characters living in Louisiana; *Rome* (2005–2007); and *The Wire* (2002–2008), about undercover police in Baltimore, Maryland. Showtime countered with *Californication* (2007–), about a struggling writer; *The L Word* (2004–) on the lesbian lifestyle; *Nurse Jackie* (2009–), about an addicted but strong-willed nurse; *Queer as Folk* (2000–2005), about gay men in Pittsburgh; and *The Tudors* (2007–2010). AMC offered *Breaking Bad* (2008–), about a chemistry teacher selling crystal meth.

Sources:
American Movie Classics, *amc.com;*

Home Box Office, *hbo.com;*

International Movie Database, *imdb.com;*

Showtime, *showtime.com.*

COMEDY AND THE NEWS

The Daily Show. *The Daily Show with Jon Stewart* premiered on the Comedy Central network in 1996 and was first hosted by former sports newscaster Craig Kilborn. The show's original incarnation focused on popular culture but shifted to politics and journalism when Jon Stewart took the helm in 1999. A self-professed "fake news program," the show imitated "real" news shows, but with an absurd and satirical twist, taking inspiration from programs such as David Frost's *That Was the Week That Was* and *Saturday Night Live*'s "Weekend Update" feature. The show included a regular cast of correspondents reporting from the field and often covered the same headlines as mainstream media. Stewart and company, however, found ways to subtly editorialize through their humorous takes on these topics. A favorite target was the self-importance of many Washington figures. For example, in a 15 January 2007 episode, footage of Democratic senators expressing outrage at the Bush administration was intercut with footage from *The Breakfast Club* (1985) and *Willy Wonka and the Chocolate Factory* (1971); in a 2002 clip covering potential changes after the election, a picture of the new Congress included the animated character Shrek. Despite its humorous angle, *The Daily Show* regularly attracted major politi-

Stephen Colbert, host of comedy-news program *The Colbert Report,* interviewing Army General Ray Odierno during a taping of the show in Iraq (U.S. Army photograph)

cal and media stars as guests. As the importance of the program in American culture continued to rise, Stewart interviewed former presidents Bill Clinton and Jimmy Carter, international leaders such as British prime minister Tony Blair, and veteran journalists Tom Brokaw and Dan Rather. *The Daily Show*'s first presidential election coverage, dubbed "Indecision 2000," covered the primaries and general election contest between George W. Bush and Al Gore. The special segments proved to be immensely popular (and thus they returned for the 2004 and 2008 elections), and the title proved to be eerily prescient in 2000, as for weeks the final vote in Florida was counted and recounted. In 2004 Stewart and other *Daily Show* writers published a satirical nonfiction book about politics, *America (The Book)*. Written in the style of a high-school civics textbook (including discussion questions and classroom activities), it poked fun at such things as the 2000 election and increased cynicism of the media. In 2007 Stewart was ranked as the fourth-most admired journalist in America in a Pew Research Center poll, tied with "serious" anchormen Brokaw, Rather, Brian Williams, and Anderson Cooper. A 2009 *Time* poll found that Stewart had inherited Walter Cronkite's crown as the "Most Trusted Newscaster in America."

In Pursuit of "Truthiness." Stephen Colbert began his rise to fame on Comedy Central as a *Daily Show* correspondent in 1997. His over-the-top Bill O'Reilly-esque persona proved so popular that he was given his own Comedy Central show in 2005, *The Colbert Report*, which mocked right-wing punditry and, like *The Daily Show*, included commentary and interviews with politicians, media personalities, and noted authors. One feature was "The Word," in which Colbert defined a word that captured the zeitgeist of the moment. In the 2005 pilot he coined the term "truthiness," defining it as a "truth" that one knows "from the gut" despite a lack of evidence, logic, or factual support. The word gained such a foothold it was named the Word of the Year by the American Dialect Society (2005) and Merriam-Webster (2006). Colbert's cultural influence was also felt when in 2006 he convinced viewers to highlight the limitations of the user-generated content of online encyclopedia Wikipedia. At his urging, viewers flooded the Wikipedia entry on elephants with humorous and absurd content, changing the African elephant page to read that the population had tripled in the past six months, and altering the entry on Dumbo to say "sadly, Dumbo died after tripling in size and exploding." Colbert also caused a stir in 2006 when he was featured speaker at the White House Correspondents' Association Dinner. He delivered a blistering satire of George W. Bush and his administration that was not particularly well received by the correspondents or the mainstream media but was celebrated by the public when a video of the speech circulated on the Internet.

The Onion. Founded in 1988 at the University of Wisconsin-Madison, *The Onion* was a satirical newspaper that found new life and audiences in the digital media. By 2009 it boasted a print circulation of 690,000. In 2007 *The Onion* launched a daily web video broadcast called *The Onion News Network* and in 2008 released a direct-to-DVD film titled *The Onion Movie*. *The Onion* featured realistic-sounding stories that were nevertheless pure satire. For example, the regular "In the News" feature offers fictional headlines such as "The Thinkable Happens to Local Man" and "First Generation American's Job Taken by His Father." The satire was so good that some failed to recognize the joke. In 2002 the *Beijing Evening News* republished an *Onion* story "Congress Threatens to Leave D.C. Unless New Capitol Is Built" as serious news in their international section. In 2004 Deborah Norville presented "Study: 58 Percent of U.S. Exercise Televised" as genuine news on her MSNBC show, and in 2009 three international outlets reprinted *Onion* stories as actual news. The quality of *The Onion*'s satire was recognized with a Peabody Award in 2009.

Sources:

comedycentral.com;

"Journalism, Satire or Just Laughs? 'The Daily Show with Jon Stewart,' Examined," Pew Center's Project for Excellence in Journalism (8 May 2008), *journalism.org*;

"2006 Media Person of the Year: Stephen Colbert," *iwantmedia.com*.

COVERING TERROR

Images of Disaster. As one of the greatest domestic disasters in American history, the September 11 terrorist attacks were the subject of an unprecedented level of media coverage. The proliferation of recording technologies and ease with which images and video could be spread via the Internet shaped the coverage of and the reaction to the event. Viewers watched on television as images, video, and audio of the tragedy were transmitted in real time, making the shared experience of 9/11 all the more shocking, intimate, and harrowing.

Terror Alert. As the new Department of Homeland Security's terror alert system encouraged Americans to remain in a state of watchfulness, media outlets reported one terrorist threat after another. Americans seemed to have plenty to fear. In the immediate wake of the September 11 attacks, envelopes containing the anthrax virus were mailed to the offices of several congressmen and news outlets, a crime that was later attributed to Bruce Ivins. On 22 December 2001, Richard Reid, the so-called shoe bomber, unsuccessfully attempted to blow up a passenger flight by igniting a bomb in his shoe. John Allen Muhammad and Lee Boyd Malvo, the D.C. snipers (October 2002), terrorized Washington and surrounding areas with random shootings that left three people dead. In 2007 Seung-Hui Cho, a student at Virginia Tech, killed thirty-two people in a shooting rampage on that campus. The media-rich environment only amplified the terrifying impact of these events.

Changing Focus. The September 11 attacks had a profound impact on the nature of what was covered by news outlets. A study conducted by the Pew Research Center's

Radio shock jock Don Imus made a living by being controversial, but in 2007 he went too far. Referring to the African American members of the Rutgers University women's basketball team, who had just won the NCAA women's basketball championship, as "nappy-headed hos," Imus found himself at the center of antiracist protests, and his CBS radio broadcast was suspended. MSNBC also decided to no longer simulcast his Imus in the Morning program, despite Imus's attempts to make amends, including an on-air apology and discussion with civil-rights activist Al Sharpton on his radio program Keepin' It Real. Critics charged that Imus's comments were only the latest in a long chain of racially insensitive pronouncements from the radio personality, and that Bernard McGuirk, a producer on the show, specialized in racist on-air humor. As media outlets began poring over decades of transcripts, they found multiple examples of racist, sexist, or homophobic material. When he returned to the air, Imus sought to show contrition for his comments and demonstrate racial sensitivity, hiring an African American comedian for feature segments. In 2009 he signed a multiyear deal with Fox Business Channel to simulcast his show on television.

Sources: Bill Carter and Jacques Steinberg, "Off the Air: The Light Goes Out for Don Imus," *New York Times*, 13 April 2007;

"Imus called Women's Basketball Team 'nappy-headed hos,'" Media Matters for America (4 April 2007), *mediamatters.org*.

Project for Excellence in Journalism found that in the five years following the attacks, coverage of terrorism and foreign policy more than doubled while coverage of other domestic issues fell. Major networks (ABC, CBS, and NBC) shifted their "hard news" focus, yet still found time for "softer" personal-interest stories. Katie Couric's debut newscast (5 September 2006) on *CBS Nightly News* as the nation's first female solo anchor was cited by the study as typical: "After leading with a disquieting story about the resurgence of the Taliban in Afghanistan, the broadcast moved to an interview with columnist Tom Friedman, the first pictures of baby Suri Cruise, a soapbox-style speech by filmmaker Morgan Spurlock and a heart-warming story about Nicaraguan orphans."

Source:
"How 9-11 Changed the Evening News," Pew Center's Project for Excellence in Journalism (11 September 2006), *journalism.org*.

NEWS IN THE NEWS

Changes in Television Journalism. The explosive growth of television coverage changed the shape of television reporting as a proliferation of cable-news outlets provided Americans not only around-the-clock access but also multiple options. The launch of Fox News Network and MSNBC in 1996 brought competition for CNN, which revamped its Headline News Channel in 2003 to provide brief, repetitive summaries of news items. A bounty of slots provided opportunities for new celebrity journalists, many of whom rivaled politicians for airtime. Fox News led the way, showcasing the ideological divide between conservatives and liberals, featuring conservative commentators

Radio and television personality Don Imus speaks with civil-rights activist Al Sharpton about Imus's racially charged comments about the Rutgers women's basketball team on 9 April 2007 (AP Photo/Richard Drew).

(including Bill O'Reilly, Sean Hannity, and Glenn Beck) who railed against a perceived liberal bias in the media and became the Bush administration's most ardent supporters. Fox News wielded considerable influence in shaping debates and gave Republican politicians and activists a forum to develop and disseminate party platforms. MSNBC's Keith Olbermann and Rachel Maddow rivaled Fox News as cable news's liberal counterparts. Critics of this trend bemoaned the need to sensationalize politics and the loss of objectivity. Still, audiences gravitated to these networks, which cut into the ratings of the big three nightly broadcasts (ABC, NBC, and CBS), and cable news pioneer, CNN.

BALLOON BOY

On 15 October 2009, in a bid to land his family its own reality show, Richard Heene launched a home-made weather balloon and claimed that his six-year-old son, Falcon, was trapped inside. Authorities spent the day tracking the balloon and searching for the boy. When it landed twelve hours and more than fifty miles later, Falcon was nowhere to be found. Still believing the Heenes' story, police continued their search, fearing the boy may have fallen out. Later that afternoon, Heene reported discovering his son hiding in the attic, where he had apparently been all along. While the media and public initially accepted this story, suspicions were raised after the family's appearances on national television. On 16 October the family was interviewed by Wolf Blitzer on CNN's *Larry King Live.* When the boy was asked why he hid in the attic, he replied, "We did it for the show." If that were not incriminating enough, the clearly distraught boy vomited after interviewers on ABC's *Good Morning America* and NBC's *The Today Show* asked him to explain his comment. Suspicions of a hoax were confirmed after investigators uncovered evidence that the entire incident was a ploy to get publicity and, ultimately, a reality show—including reports from researcher Robert Thomas who allegedly helped Heene build the balloon and plan the stunt. Heene and his wife, Mayumi, eventually admitted to the hoax and pled guilty to charges of falsely influencing authorities and filing a false report. Heene was sentenced to ninety days in jail and home detention, while his wife was sentenced to community service. The fame-hungry family had previously twice appeared in episodes of the ABC reality show *Wife Swap.*

Sources: Trever Hughes, "'Balloon Boy' Family Moves to Florida," *USA Today,* 3 September 2010;

Nate Taylor and Emily Bazar, "Balloon Boy Saga Captivates Nation," *USA Today,* 16 October 2009.

Arianna Huffington, cofounder of the liberal news website *The Huffington Post* (photograph by David Shankbone)

Minor News. As cable news providers competed for viewers, even the nature of what was covered changed with no story too small to report. Cable networks sought to break the monotony of news programming by cutting away to such sensational stories as live coverage of police automobile chases. Viewer taste for coverage and analysis of high-profile murder and abduction cases grew, as networks devoted increasing time to stories such as that of Natalee Holloway, a young woman who disappeared and was allegedly murdered while on vacation in Aruba. Critics charged that these crime stories typically only garnered lavish media attention when the victim was white, with little coverage devoted to minority victims of violent crime. Seemingly harmless gestures became national news as when President Barack Obama swatted a fly during a 17 June 2009 television interview on CNBC, prompting a rebuke from the activist group, People for the Ethical Treatment of Animals (PETA). Media outlets then rushed to cover the mini-controversy. The incident was joked about on late-night talk shows such as *Late Night with Conan O'Brien* and *Late Night with Jimmy Fallon,* and a video of the interview went viral when it was posted to YouTube, getting more than 750,000 views.

Online News. The sheer quantity of media content available on the web could prove daunting as users sought news and information. New websites emerged that were designed not to generate original content but to guide readers to articles and features scattered across the web. *The Huffington Post* was founded in 2005 by Arianna Huffington, Kenneth Lerer, and Jonah Peretti as an openly liberal news website. The venture included coverage of politics, media, business, entertainment, and other topics. *The Huffington Post* was primarily a news aggregator, a site that collected articles from other outlets rather than generating original content. Leonard Downie, former executive editor of the *Washington Post,* called the site a news parasite. The site did include original content by contributors such as Harry Shearer and Rosie O'Donnell, as well as many others, in the form of editorial blog entries. *The Huffington Post* was seen mainly as a liberal challenger to the popular conservative site *Drudge Report.* Matt Drudge founded the *Drudge Report* in 1996 as an e-mail dispatch but created his own website in 1997. Originally it covered only Washington, D.C., gossip but quickly became a pioneer in news aggrega-

DROPPING DAILY NEWSPAPER CIRCULATION		
YEAR	NO. OF NEWSPAPERS	CIRCULATION (IN THOUSANDS)
2000	1,480	55,773
2001	1,468	55,578
2002	1,457	55,186
2003	1,456	55,185
2004	1,457	54,626
2005	1,452	53,345
2006	1,437	52,329
2007	1,422	50,742
2008	1,408	48,597
2009	1,387	45,653

Source: "Total Paid Circulation: Newspaper Circulation Volume," *Newspaper Association of America.*

MATTHEWS GETS A THRILL

Chris Matthews, the longtime host of MSNBC's political news program *Hardball,* became both the butt of jokes and a symbol for a perceived media bias toward Illinois senator Barack Obama (D) in the 2008 election when he relayed his intimately physical reaction to the candidate's speech live on air on 12 February 2008. Matthews gushed, "I have to tell you, you know, it's part of reporting this case, this election, the feeling most people get when they hear Barack Obama's speech. My, I felt this thrill going up my leg. I mean, I don't have that too often." The next day on MSNBC's *Morning Joe* program, cohost Joe Scarborough joked that "if I were running Hillary Clinton's campaign right now . . . I might actually have a feeling running *down* my leg." Republican candidate Arizona senator John McCain's campaign took advantage of the moment to create an ad meant to highlight the alleged pro-Obama bias, which featured clips of Matthews and others speaking positively about Obama over the song "Can't Take My Eyes Off of You," and ending with the tagline "Do You Feel That Thrill Running Up Your Leg Yet?" Matthews laughed about the incident and defended himself in an interview with Jay Leno on the *Tonight Show,* saying "I'd rather be honest and say what I feel than sit there like some kind of statue. . . . I'm a frickin' American. I do have a reaction to things," adding "I report all senses."

Sources: "Chris Matthews Jokes about 'Thrill Up My Leg' Comment on Leno," *huffingtonpost.com* (22 July 2008);

"John McCain Hits Back with 'Obama Love' Video," *The Telegraph* (23 July 2008), *telegraph.co.uk;*

Mark Steyn, "Obama, Political Viagra," *National Review Online* (7 June 2008), *nationalreview.com.*

tion, providing links to stories and editorials deemed relevant to conservatives. The *Drudge Report*'s freewheeling conservative editorial outlook was coupled with a minimalistic style that allowed Drudge to focus the attention of his readership on a single issue or concept. In 2008, for example, the *Drudge Report* fueled speculation about Obama's nationality by publishing a photo of the candidate in Somali tribal dress. In 2008 former *New Yorker* and *Vanity Fair* editor Tina Brown founded *The Daily Beast,* which offered opinion, news aggregation, and original reporting. The site quickly became an important destination for World Wide Web cognoscenti. Describing her site, Brown called it "a speedy, smart edit of the web. . . . the omnivorous friend who hears about the best stuff and forwards it to you with a twist."

Sources:
Rob Considine, "Journalist Claims to Crack Natalee Holloway Case," *msnbc.com* (1 February 2008);

Jimmy Orr, "PETA Condemns Obama for Murdering Innocent Fly," *Christian Science Monitor* (18 June 2009);

Maria Russo, "Tina Brown's Daily Beast, the Glitziest Web Filter in Town," *latimes.com* (7 October 2008);

Richard Siklos, "More: Online, Arianna Huffington Reigns Supreme," *cnnmoney.com* (29 October 2007);

"US Media Prepares for Ratings War," *independent.co.uk* (3 November 2008).

RADIO IN FLUX

Broadcasting Milestone. National Public Radio (NPR) celebrated its thirtieth anniversary in 2001. Created in 1970, it was a nonprofit membership organization that received some federal funding, but came to rely over time on private financing. The first broadcasts aired in April 1971. NPR expanded greatly, opening a West Coast production facility in Culver City, California, in 2002. A $200 million bequest in 2003 from the estate of billionaire Joan Kroc, the largest ever to a cultural institution, allowed NPR to increase its annual budget by 50 percent and prompted a review of programming, with an eye toward freshening the content and attracting new lis-

Logo for National Public Radio
(<www.npr.org>)

teners. One casualty of these changes was veteran *Morning Edition* reporter Bob Edwards, who had hosted the popular news program from its first broadcast. In 2004 he was replaced with Steve Inskeep and Renée Montagne, a move that prompted thousands of complaints from loyal listeners. Edwards refused to stay on as a "special correspondent," and soon began hosting his own interview program, *The Bob Edwards Show,* on XM Satellite radio. In February 2000 NPR created *All Songs Considered,* a web-only program that presented samples of the vast and diverse collection of music featured on NPR shows. Hosted by *All Things Considered* director Bob Boilen, the program also began a free podcast in August 2005. NPR began offering much of its content for free online, either through podcast or streaming audio. In the late 2000s, followers with smartphones or tablets could download an NPR application that allowed them to listen to individual programs or stories from anywhere.

Satellite Radio Wars. Satellite radio technology emerged in the 1990s and entered the mainstream in the 2000s. The service held many advantages over traditional AM/FM broadcasts, notably in the number of channels and clarity of sound. Proximity to broadcast stations was no longer an issue with satellite radio, and listeners could hear national broadcasts anywhere their receivers could pick up a signal. In the first half of the decade two major

Bob Edwards, who was replaced as a reporter for the NPR program *Morning Edition* and went on to start the XM Satellite Radio program *The Bob Edwards Show* (photograph by Jared Benedict)

satellite radio providers, XM and Sirius, battled for control of the burgeoning market. Sirius generated huge interest in its service with the October 2004 announcement that it had signed shock jock Howard Stern, who was rewarded handsomely for making the switch, garnering $500 million for a five-year contract. Sirius's investment in Stern paid off, however, and the controversial host was given a multi-million-dollar bonus in 2005 for exceeding subscriber goals. XM also raised its profile in October 2004 when it announced an eleven-year $650 million deal to become the official satellite-radio provider of Major League Baseball. In February 2007 the two companies announced that they would merge, a decision that reflected the industry's difficulties competing with broadcast radio. After months of debate, the Federal Communications Commission approved the merger in July 2008, allowing Sirius XM radio to go forward. At the end of 2009, Sirius XM reported having more than 18 million subscribers.

Sources:
Alex Beam, "Where Did NPR's Burger Money Go?" *Boston Globe,* 20 September 2006;

"Bob Edwards Leaving NPR," *npr.org* (2 April 2004);

Olga Kharif, "The FCC Approves the XM-Sirius Merger," *Business Week* (25 July 2008), *businessweek.com.*

NUMBER OF STATIONS OWNED BY TOP BROADCASTING COMPANIES (DECEMBER 2008)	
BROADCAST COMPANY	STATIONS OWNED
Clear Channel	833
Cumulus	346
Citadel Communications	230
CBS Radio	140
Entercom	111
Salem Communications Corporation	92
Saga Communications Inc.	92
Cox Radio Inc.	85
Univision	69

Source: "The State of the News Media: An Annual Report on American Journalism: Audio: Ownership," Pew Project for Excellence in Journalism (2009), *journalism.org.*

Survivor. The concept for CBS's *Survivor*, which premiered on 31 May 2000, was adapted from a hit Swedish show and involved a cast of ordinary people living on an island and competing in a series of physical and mental challenges. The contestants were further pitted against one another in weekly meetings called "Tribal Council" where one cast member was voted off each week. The format encouraged scheming, alliances, and double crosses—gripping psychological drama that made *Survivor* as much a melodrama as a competitive game show. Though shows such as MTV's *The Real World*, which first aired in 1992, introduced the idea that unscripted interactions of ordinary people could make for compelling drama, *Survivor* blended drama with competition and made reality TV a mainstream media sensation in the United States. Richard Hatch was the first winner of *Survivor*, making him a millionaire and one of the first reality-television celebrities. Soon other European imports, particularly from England, were adapted for American television and flooded the airwaves. Shows that focused purely on competition, such as *Who Wants to be a Millionaire?*, *America's Got Talent*, and *Dancing With the Stars*, were popular as were those that combined personal drama with competition, such as *Big Brother*, *Temptation Island*, *Paradise Hotel*, *America's Next Top Model*, *Beauty and the Geek*, and *High School Reunion*.

Talent Sensation. *American Idol*, a talent show that debuted in 2002 (inspired by the British *Pop Idol*) held open casting calls in search of singers who held the promise of popular appeal. The early rounds quickly became famous for showcasing the wackiest and most deluded musical hopefuls. One such contestant, William Hung, actually enjoyed some fame as a result of his ear-battering audition. His performance of the pop song "She Bangs" was so mesmerizingly bad it led to repeat performances on several talk shows and eventually to a record deal. Many truly promising singers, however, were discovered and sent to the next round of eliminations with the words "You're Going to Hollywood." *American Idol* judges were a panel of industry experts (former pop star Paula Abdul, and award-winning record producers Randy Jackson and Simon Cowell), who had disparate tastes in music and approaches to judging—Abdul the most forgiving and Cowell the least—and on-screen bickering among judges proved to be almost as popular as the singing competitions. Contestants were eliminated weekly, first by the judges and then by viewer votes. The winner was awarded a record deal meant to provide an opening into the industry. Winners occasionally enjoyed lasting success and fame: for instance, Kelly Clarkson (season one) and Carrie Underwood (season four). Just as often, however, second-place or lower finishers achieved real commercial success—the most striking cases being the immense popularity of season-two runner-up Clay Aiken, whose 2003 debut

Kelly Clarkson, the winner of the first season of the television talent show *American Idol* in 2002 (U.S. Navy photograph by Chief Photographer's Mate Eric A. Clement)

album went platinum, and Jennifer Hudson, who was voted off the show early in its third season but went on to a successful recording career and won an Oscar for her role in *Dreamgirls* (2006) and a Grammy in 2009.

The Bachelor. What began in 2002 as a new twist on the old dating-show format turned into a reality-TV institution and the template for a new brand of elimination-style program. The premise of *The Bachelor* was simple: a single man sought true love by choosing from a pool of young, attractive, single female applicants. The bachelor combined physical attractiveness with an impressive resume (some were doctors, pilots, professional athletes, and business moguls), and he tried to make a connection with one of the contestants, all of whom were housed together in a mansion. As the season progressed, the bachelor went on dates with the contestants—sometimes one-on-one, sometimes in groups. Each episode ended with a "rose ceremony," a highly dramatized segment in which the bachelor eliminated one contestant by giving a rose to the luckier candidates. The last woman standing was offered a proposal of marriage. A spin-off, *The Bachelorette*, debuted in 2003 and

BIGGEST MEDIA COMPANIES

COMPANY	2009 REVENUES	HOLDINGS INCLUDE
General Electric	$157 billion	NBC, Telemundo, Universal Pictures, MSNBC, Bravo, Sci Fi Channel.
Walt Disney	$36.1 billion	ABC, ESPN, the Disney Channel, A&E, Lifetime, Touchstone, Miramax, Pixar, Walt Disney Pictures.
News Corp.	$30.4 billion	Fox Broadcasting Company, Fox News Channel, Fox Business Channel, National Geographic, FX, Wall Street Journal, New York Post, TVGuide, Barron's, SmartMoney, HarperCollins, 20th Century-Fox, Fox Searchlight Pictures.
Time Warner	$25.8 billion	CNN, the CW, HBO, Cinemax, TBS, TNT, America Online, Warner Bros., New Line Cinema, Time, Sports Illustrated, Fortune, Marie Claire, People.
Viacom	$13.6 billion	MTV, Nickelodeon, VH1, BET, Comedy Central, Paramount Pictures.
CBS	$13 billion	CBS Television Network, Showtime, Simon & Schuster, CBS Radio, Inc.

Source: "Ownership Chart: The Big Six," *Free Press* (n.d.), *freepress.net.*

starred Trista Rehn who was introduced to viewers during the first season of *The Bachelor*, when she made it to the final round but was rejected for her competitor, Amanda Marsh. The bachelorette chose Ryan Sutter, whom she later married and with whom she is raising two children; five subsequent bachelorettes fared worse, as all failed to fulfill their romantic dreams.

Source:
imdb.com.

TELEVISION TECHNOLOGY

High Definition. High Definition Television (HDTV), which delivered video digitally with a higher pixel resolution and a wide-screen aspect ratio, had been available for decades, but only in 2003 did all public channels have to switch to digital high-def transmitters. It was not until 2009 that all channels, even basic and premium cable channels, had to make the transition. The sharper image and wider aspect ratio made the image more accurately resemble what was seen in real life. This clarity not only created problems for makeup artists charged with disguising celebrity blemishes but also created a more vivid and immersive viewing experience. The digital transition brought with it a commensurate upgrade in television technology.

Better Televisions. Flat-screen technology found a wide audience in the 2000s. Plasma screens, televisions that used plasma cells rather than cathode rays, were first developed in the 1960s but did not become commercially available for home use until 1997. In addition to taking up far

less space to provide a large, clear picture, plasma screens had some technical challenges, such as images burning into the screen and leaving ghostly apparitions. Plasma televisions were quickly replaced in popularity by the Liquid Crystal Display (LCD) televisions. Both types of televisions were able to display images in high definition. The sharp picture and intense colors proved popular with viewers. Again, television performers struggled to keep up appearances under the microscope of enhanced screen resolution, in which even the smallest imperfection became highly visible. Makeup artists and cosmetic companies developed new products and strategies to keep actors camera-ready.

Replays. TiVo was the brand name of a digital video-recording device that was launched in the 1990s but became a household name in the 2000s. Much like Xerox went from a brand name to a verb (meaning to "photocopy"), "tivo" became a verb signifying "to digitally record live television in the home." Marking an improvement in quality and ease of use over VCR technology, TiVo and other digital video recorders (DVRs) record high-quality images and hold more information. Perhaps the most popular innovation, however, was the ability to pause live television. By using a hard drive similar to those found in computers, TiVo was able to record and broadcast content at the same time, allowing viewers to pause a live broadcast while they were otherwise distracted. Viewers could then fast-forward through commercials and other content and either catch up to the live broadcast or remain in delay.

TiVo was first to market this technology, but satellite and cable providers quickly caught up and offered DVRs as part of their services.

On Demand. Once DVRs became commonplace, the next development in technology was "On Demand" content. Cable companies and television networks partnered to bring video on demand to subscribers. Archives of new and classic television and film content could be accessed directly from the television screen for no additional charge. Some independent film distributors such as Magnolia and IFC began releasing products On Demand and in theaters on the same day—thus expanding their viewing audience to cities where the movie did not have a theatrical release. Though this technology was eagerly embraced by cable subscribers, DVRs and On Demand caused some complications for networks and video-rental companies such as Blockbuster. For networks, the problem became attracting sponsors—if subscribers could watch single episodes or use their DVR to automatically record programs, how could networks ensure that viewers would watch commercials? This issue was partially resolved with a compromise: limited commercial interruptions in On Demand programs.

Streaming. Apple's iTunes software had made television content available for download for a charge since 2001, but streaming allowed consumers to watch programs on demand through a cell phone or computer. Online archives such as *Hulu.com* began offering new and classic content via streaming; *Amazon.com* and *Netflix.com* quickly offered their own streaming content, as did cable providers and television networks. In fact, by the end of the decade nearly every cable and network channel had websites with streaming content available that offered archives of recently aired shows as well as specialty content created especially for the web—mini episodes called Webisodes. In addition to operating their own websites, CBS streams on *TV.com*, while NBC and ABC (as well as several other networks) stream on *Hulu.com*.

Sources:
"DirecTV and Tivo History," *tivopedia.com* (n.d);

Sam Grobart, "Beyond Flat Panels: A New Generation of TV Sets," *nytimes.com* (10 June 2010).

VAMPIRES

Dawn of a Craze. Though vampires had been a fiction staple for hundreds of years, never before did they dominate the airwaves. Aside from the cult favorite *Buffy the Vampire Slayer*, which aired from 1997 to 2003, vampires were not a major part of television programming until the skyrocketing popularity of Stephenie Meyer's *Twilight* series, which included the teen novels *Twilight*, *New Moon*, *Eclipse*, and *Breaking Dawn*. The books modernized old vampire themes and placed the familiar monsters in new situations, highlighting especially teen angst over status and sexuality. After the success of those books, networks eagerly capitalized on the craze. The television network Spike brought the comic *Blade* to the small screen in 2006; CBS premiered *Moonlight*, a mystery show about a vampire

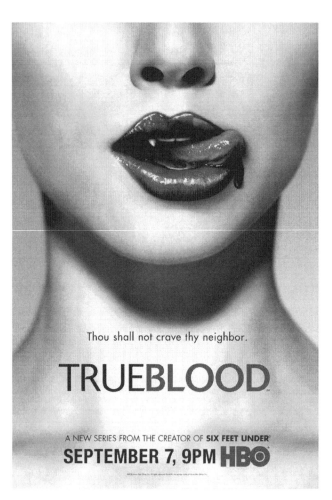

Thou shall not crave thy neighbor.

TRUEBLOOD.

A NEW SERIES FROM THE CREATOR OF **SIX FEET UNDER**
SEPTEMBER 7, 9PM HBO

Advertisement for the first season of the HBO vampire series (<www.impawards.com>)

detective, in 2007; Lifetime network brought *Blood Ties*, a show that also featured a vampire detective. NBC's hit comedy *The Office* featured a vampire-themed episode in 2007 titled "Business School."

True Blood. In 2008 HBO found a new hit series in *True Blood*, a campy soap opera based on the *Southern Vampire* series written by Charlaine Harris. The show starred Anna Paquin as Sookie Stackhouse, a telepathic waitress living in the fictional Louisiana town of Bon Temps. The show chronicled her rocky romance with southern gentleman and vampire Bill Compton, played by British actor Stephen Moyer, as they battle a variety of supernatural and human foes. The show was created by Alan Ball, award-winning writer of the movie *American Beauty* (1999) and creator of the previously successful HBO series *Six Feet Under* (2001–2005). Like his other works, *True Blood* took a dark, though often comical, look at American culture and politics. Here viewers found vampires standing in for oppressed minorities such as homosexuals and African Americans. *True Blood*'s story line begins shortly after vampires have "come out of the coffin" and have revealed themselves to their human neighbors. They face discrimination and mistrust, especially in the South, as fearful humans chanted

"God hates fangs," echoing the hate cries of real-life radical antigay activists who claimed "God hates fags." Though the show was not afraid to tackle such heavy topics, its focus remained on romantic plots and supernatural elements. The popularity of *True Blood* and its vampire hunks gave rise to a slang phrase used to apply to anyone with an obsession with vampires: fangbanger.

The Vampire Diaries. The CW network premiered *The Vampire Diaries,* based on the young-adult books by L. J. Smith, in 2009. Though far less politically ambitious, *The Vampire Diaries* took up the campy, romantic focus of *True Blood.* The series focused on the supernatural adventures and romantic yearnings of the Salvatore brothers, Stefan and Damon, who had been turned into vampires over a century before. The brothers were portrayed by Paul Wesley and Ian Somerhalder, both veterans of the supernatural genre: Somerhalder played Boone on ABC's enigmatic hit series *Lost* (2004–2010), and Wesley played a werewolf on CBS's short-lived *Wolf Lake* (2001–2002). The love-struck vampires vie for the affections of Elena Gilbert, played by Nina Dobrev, while also battling vengeful witches and rival vampires. The series won seven Teen Choice Awards, and its actors appeared on many magazine covers, cementing its status as another vampire-themed hit.

Sources:

"Fans Sink Teeth into Vampire Tales," *cbs.com* (24 August 2009);

imdb.com;

Choire Sicha, "Inside the Vampire Diaries Craze," *cnn.com.*

WEB 2.0

Rise of Social Media. The term "web 2.0" refers to the growing focus on collaborative, interconnected, user-generated content that distinctly altered the way Internet users spent time on the World Wide Web. Increased bandwidth meant that sharing songs, videos, and other content was much easier and faster than ever before. Sites such as *myspace.com* and *facebook.com,* which allowed users to create individualized profiles as a part of a network of friends and contacts, also effectively became file-sharing outlets. Videos uploaded to the file-sharing site *youtube.com* could be easily posted on Facebook or Myspace and shared among friends. Copyright issues remained cloudy: YouTube claimed limited ability to oversee the content uploaded by users. While some media companies sued for copyright infringement, others sought to utilize social media as a means to promote their content. The hit NBC show *The Office,* for example, created special web extras that could only be found online.

Going Viral. Web and television content merged as websites streamed television programs and television shows developed around Internet sensations known as "viral videos." To go "viral," a web video had to spread quickly, being sent from person to person, until thousands, and often millions, of people had seen the video. Whether professionally produced or the work of amateurs, a viral video is often humorous—intentionally or unintentionally, adorable, disgusting, or otherwise remarkable. Viral videos made stars,

and household names, of ordinary people such as The Star Wars Kid, who taped himself reenacting a lightsaber fight from *Star Wars* using only his imagination and a stick, and the Numa Numa kid, whose lip synching to European pop hit *Dragostea din tei* went viral. But videos of sleeping kittens and laughing babies were just as likely to go viral. Sensing an appetite for this content, networks happily built a bridge between the Internet and television, giving viewers programs such as cable network G4's *Web Soup,* which began in June 2009, in which host Chris Hardwick aired videos culled from the web and made sarcastic remarks about them. This format also proved successful for Daniel Tosh of Comedy Central's *Tosh.0,* which debuted in June 2009. Tosh added a new spin, however, by offering "Web Redemptions," in which people humiliated in a video were given the chance, under his sarcastic guidance, to reenact the embarrassing events with a more successful outcome. For example, "AfroNinja," known for his hairstyle and attempt at performing martial arts (he tried to do a back flip and landed directly on his face), was given the chance to redeem himself.

Sources:

Anne Broache and Greg Sandoval, "Viacom Sues Google over YouTube Clips," *cnet.com* (13 March 2007);

Jano Gibson, "Star Wars Kid Tops Viral Video Rankings," *The Age* (28 November 2006), *theage.com;*

Michael Malone, "The First Amendment vs. Patents in Web 2.0," ABC News (3 May 2007), *abcnews.com.*

WOMEN IN MEDIA

Hillary Clinton. Former first lady and New York senator Hillary Clinton became the nation's first serious female presidential candidate in 2008. She defeated six other contenders in the Democratic nomination contest, leaving her in a tight primary battle with eventual winner Illinois senator Barack Obama. Her campaign had early support and significant media coverage—garnering 17 percent of media coverage in 2007, according to the Project for Excellence in Journalism and Joan Shorenstein Center on the Press, Politics, and Policy. She won 1,923 delegates. Many blamed Clinton's narrow loss on her on-camera demeanor, saying she appeared cold and calculating, while others blamed an unfairly critical media. In a January 2008 poll conducted by *The New York Times* and CBS News, 51 percent of Democratic primary voters "thought the media had been harder on Clinton than on the other candidates." Though she failed to win, she earned a place in the new president's administration as secretary of state.

Sarah Palin. In August 2008 Republican presidential nominee Arizona senator John McCain named Alaska governor Sarah Palin as his running mate. Palin was popular with conservative voters because of her positions on issues concerning "family values" and small government. She was also a camera-ready candidate whose plainspoken ways appealed to those who related to her "hockey mom" persona. A former Miss Alaska, Palin maintained a folksy, down-to-earth image while remaining stylish and attractive. Media commentary often focused as much on her

The women of ABC's daytime talk show *The View*—from left, Whoopi Goldberg, Barbara Walters, Joy Behar, Sherri Shepherd, and Elisabeth Hasselbeck—interview President Barack Obama (official White House photograph by Pete Souza).

wardrobe as on her policies. The $150,000 price tag for her campaign wardrobe, including suits from Neiman Marcus and Saks Fifth Avenue, caused a stir and garnered intense coverage. A bigger controversy, however, was Palin's interview presence. In the most infamous occasion—the 24 September 2008 interview with CBS anchorwoman Katie Couric—Palin flubbed her answers to even softball questions such as "What magazines do you read?" When pressed, Palin was unable to name a single magazine, instead claiming she read "all of them." Though her unsophisticated, homespun way of communicating was a major part of Palin's appeal, the disastrous interview made many question her readiness to fill the office of vice president. She became the target of ridicule by look-alike comedian Tina Fey, who performed two remarkable imitations of her on the comedy program *Saturday Night Live*. Palin seemed to take the joke in stride, even appearing alongside Fey in an 18 October 2008 episode. Even though her ticket lost the election, Palin remained in the spotlight. In 2009 Palin resigned from her post as Alaska governor eighteen months before the end of her term, citing distractions due to partisan ethics investigations that arose after her selection as McCain's running mate, and released a memoir, *Going Rogue: An American Life*.

The View. The ABC daytime talk show *The View* debuted in 1997 but became a major media influence in

the 2000s. In 2009 *Forbes* listed the hosts at number eleven on their list of most influential women in the media. Show creator Barbara Walters was the star of the program, and her status as a news legend helped bring in viewers, as well as celebrity and political guests. Walters shared the stage with a rotating cast of cohosts, including comedian Joy Behar and reality-television star Elisabeth Hasselbeck. In the early years, former prosecuting attorney Star Jones shared hosting duties, before leaving to pursue her own show on the truTV network. *The View*'s most controversial cohost, however, was Rosie O'Donnell, who joined the cast in September 2006. Though O'Donnell was known as the "Queen of Nice" when she hosted her own daytime talk show, she earned a different reputation on *The View*. The politically outspoken O'Donnell found herself embroiled in several on-air feuds with other media personalities, including Hasselbeck. On 23 May 2007, O'Donnell and Hasselbeck argued over the U.S. invasion of Iraq. O'Donnell felt Hasselbeck should have been more outspoken against the invasion and should have at least defended her right to criticize, calling Hasselbeck cowardly. This fight proved to be the breaking point for O'Donnell, who had also experienced off-air problems with Walters, and she soon asked to be released from her contract. Though O'Donnell's outspoken personality certainly

Suffering from severe postpartum depression, a Texas woman named Andrea Yates drowned her five young children on 20 June 2001. The oldest child, Noah, was seven years old, and the youngest, Mary, was six months old. Yates was initially convicted of capital murder in 2002, but that conviction was overturned on 26 July 2006 when a jury found her not guilty by reason of insanity. Yates was committed to the North Texas State Hospital in Vernon where she received treatment until January 2007, when she was moved to a low-security state mental hospital in Kerrville. The Yates trial was one of many high-profile trials that not only captured the attention of Americans and focused on postpartum depression, but also fueled a growing fascination for spectacular murder cases.

Sources: Melissa McNamara, "Andrea Yates Found Not Guilty," *cbsnews.com* (26 July 2006);

"Opening Statements in Andrea Yates Trial, Reactions," *cnn.com* (18 February 2002).

brought in viewers, the show continued to be a strong media presence after her departure. O'Donnell was replaced by comedian Whoopi Goldberg.

Mega Moms. Women in the media tackled new roles and broke barriers, but many women received attention for maintaining traditional roles, albeit in sensationalized ways. As reality-television stars and mothers of extra-large families, these women were dubbed "mega moms." The first and most famous of these mega moms was Kate Gosselin, who rose to fame with the reality program *Jon & Kate Plus 8*, which aired on cable network The Learning Channel (TLC) from 2007 to 2009. The "plus 8" referred to Gosselin's eight children with husband Jon. Using fertility treatments, the Gosselins had twins Cara and Mady in 2000. Kate then gave birth to sextuplets, again with the help of fertility treatments, in 2004. The family was the subject of two TLC specials before being tapped for the weekly series. The show followed the ups and downs of raising such a large family and was a hit with viewers. The Gosselins became gossip favorites in 2009 as they went through a contentious and public divorce. Kate and the children remained on television, and TLC's *Jon & Kate Plus 8* was renamed *Kate Plus 8*. Gosselin was not the only mega mom capturing the spotlight, however. Nadya Suleman grabbed headlines when she gave birth to octuplets in 2009 and was quickly dubbed "Octomom." Suleman already had six children when she conceived the octuplets via in vitro fertilization. While the public was initially fascinated, opinion quickly turned negative as news broke that Suleman was unemployed and could not provide sufficient explanation as to how she intended to pay for her childrens' upbringing. Her case also raised questions about medical ethics surrounding fertility treatments. Eventually, Suleman shrank to the margins of media coverage, but the press had another controversial mega mom to follow: Angelina Jolie, who stirred controversy when she became involved in 2005 with her *Mr. & Mrs. Smith* costar Brad Pitt, who at the time was married to actor Jennifer Aniston. Jolie already had two adopted children: son Maddox and daughter Zahara. After she and Pitt became committed partners, they expanded the family with the addition of three biological children (daughter Shiloh, followed by twins Knox and Vivienne), and another adopted son, Pax. The mega family was frequently featured in gossip magazines.

Sources:
Taryn Winter Brill, "'No Kate Plus Eight' Without Jon?" *abcnews.com* (2 October 2009);

Ted Casablanca and Taryn Rider, "Jolie: More Kids with Pitt but No Mr. and Mrs. Smith 2," *eonline.com* (11 August 2009);

Matthew Daly, "Sarah Palin Steps Down as Alaska Governor," *Seattle Times*, 27 July 2009;

Robin Givhan, "After a $150,000 makeover, Sarah Palin has an Image Problem," *Washington Post*, 23 October 2008;

Kristen Mascia, "Nadya Suleman Shares Details about Octuplets' Dad," *People* (21 March 2009);

Maureen Ryan, "Tina Fey out-Palined Sarah Palin on 'SNL'," *Chicago Tribune*, 15 September 2008;

Ben Smith, "As Campaign Ends, Was Clinton to Blame?" *politico.com* (7 June 2008).

HEADLINE MAKERS

KATIE COURIC

1957–

JOURNALIST AND NEWS ANCHOR

Background. Katherine Anne "Katie" Couric was born in Arlington, Virginia, on 7 January 1957. Her father was a newspaper reporter. She attended Yorktown High School and earned a B.A. at the University of Virginia. She began her career at ABC and then worked as a reporter for CNN. After working at some local stations, she was hired by NBC in 1989.

Fight against Colon Cancer. Katie Couric rose to fame as "America's sweetheart" on NBC's morning news program *The Today Show,* which she joined as a cohost in 1991. She was such a well-liked figure that audiences were willing to follow her anywhere—even into the operating room. Couric lost her husband, Jay Monahan, to colon cancer in 1998, as well as her sister to pancreatic cancer in 2001, and used her status as a public figure to raise awareness of the often ignored disease. In 2000 Couric allowed television cameras to record as she received an on-air colonoscopy. The strategy proved effective, as more people sought to receive the potentially lifesaving procedure. Couric again advocated for cancer awareness by televising her mammogram.

CBS Nightly News. Couric was beloved for her candor and bright personality in the lighthearted morning news format, so it came as a shock when she announced her departure from *The Today Show* on 5 April 2006. On 5 September 2006 she joined *CBS Nightly News* as the nation's first female solo anchor. The adjustment was rocky, and initial ratings were low. The network stuck with her, however, and ratings improved. Memorable moments, such as her interview of 2008 vice-presidential candidate Sarah Palin, helped boost her appeal. Couric's ratings still fluctu-

ated—sometimes hitting historic lows—but CBS remained faithful. As of 2009, Couric remained at the helm of the program and had won several significant awards, such as the Edward R. Murrow Award for best news broadcast.

Sources:

Michelle Healy, "Katie Couric Effect Boosts Colonoscopy Rates," *USA Today,* 14 July 2003;

Rachael A. Koestler-Grack, *Katie Couric: Groundbreaking TV Journalist* (New York: Gareth Stevens, 2009);

Sherry Beck Paprocki, *Katie Couric* (New York: Chelsea House, 2001);

Tom Shales, "Katie Couric, CBS Anchor? It's Like Night and 'Today,'" *Washington Post,* 20 January 2005.

TINA FEY

1970–

COMEDY WRITER AND ACTOR

Background. Elizabeth Stamatina "Tina" Fey was born in Upper Darby Township, Pennsylvania, on 18 May 1970. A good student, she realized in middle school that she had a talent for making people laugh. She graduated from the University of Virginia and decided on a career in comedy. The bespectacled comedian got her start in Chicago's improvisational comedy troupe, *Second City,* but it was when she joined the writing staff of *Saturday Night Live (SNL)* in 1997 that she started on the road to becoming a well-known celebrity. Promoted to head writer in 1999, making her *SNL's* first female head writer, she won seven Emmy Awards, three Golden Globes, four Screen Actors Guild Awards, and four Writers Guild of America Awards. She was named Associated Press Entertainer of the Year in 2008. Her movie *Mean Girls* (2004), which she wrote and costarred in, earned critical acclaim and grossed more than $86 million.

Weekend Update. Fey moved from behind the scenes in 2000 when she began acting in *SNL* sketches and cohosting the show's regular "Weekend Update" segment with Jimmy Fallon. She had to audition, but producer Lorne Michael recognized her talent and chemistry with Fallon. While most "Weekend Update" anchors create a signature sign-off, Fey chose to give a nod to predecessors Chevy Chase and Jane Curtin and end with "Goodnight and have a pleasant tomorrow." Fey and Fallon cohosted until 2004 when Fallon left to pursue a movie career. He was replaced by Amy Poehler, who, with Fey, became the first female duo to host the segment. Fey later collaborated with Poehler in the comedy *Baby Mama* (2008). Fey left *SNL* in 2006 to develop her sitcom *30 Rock.*

30 Rock. Fey created the thirty-minute sitcom about a group of writers and actors struggling to put on a weekly sketch-comedy show that premiered on NBC on 11 October 2006. The show was inspired by Fey's experiences as a writer and performer on *SNL* and has been a critical success from the start. Fey portrays Liz Lemon, head writer for *TGS with Tracy Jordan.* The comedy follows Lemon's romantic foibles as well as her difficulties dealing with the high-maintenance stars and staff. The program is named for the address where *SNL* is filmed: 30 Rockefeller Plaza in New York. Many A-list celebrities have made guest appearances, including Jerry Seinfeld, Oprah Winfrey, Salma Hayek, and Julianne Moore. By 2006 the show was named to several "best of" lists including *The New York Times, Chicago Sun Times,* and *Entertainment Weekly.* In 2009 *Newsweek* called *30 Rock* the decade's best comedy on television. Further accolades include thirty-eight Emmy nominations and ten wins, including Outstanding Writing for a Comedy Series (2009) and Outstanding Comedy Series (2007–2008).

"I Can See Russia from My House." With these words while spoofing vice-presidential candidate and Alaska governor Sarah Palin, Fey solidified her status as a cultural icon. Her spot-on impression was so popular that even Palin admitted she liked it. Fey uttered this memorable phrase during a guest appearance on *SNL* on 13 September 2008 with Poehler, who was playing presidential hopeful Hillary Clinton. The performance became NBC's most watched video: 5.7 million viewers on *NBC.com* in less than a week. Fey reprised her impression on 18 October 2008, when she was joined by Palin herself, and won an Emmy for Outstanding Guest Actress in a Comedy Series.

Sources:

Hal Bodeker, "Tina Fey Rocks on Witty '30 Rock,'" *Orlando Sentinel,* 26 October 2008;

Julie Bosman, "On 'SNL,' Fey as Palin, and Palin as Palin," *New York Times,* 19 October 2008;

"30 Rock," and "Tina Fey," Internet Movie Database, *imdb.com;*

"Tina Fey," *New York Times, nytimes.com;*

Aidin Vaziri, "Tina Fey Takes on Pregnancy in Baby Mama," *San Francisco Chronicle,* 24 April 2008.

JAY LENO

1950–

COMEDIAN AND TALK-SHOW HOST

Background. James Douglas Muir Leno, the son of an Italian father and Scottish mother, was born on 28 April 1950 in New Rochelle, New York, but was raised mostly in Massachusetts. He earned a B.A. at Emerson College in Boston. He began his career as a well-traveled stand-up comic, although he worked many other jobs, including as an auto mechanic. In 1974 he moved to California, and by 1977 had made a guest appearance on NBC's venerable *The Tonight Show;* he took over the show as host in 1992, after Johnny Carson retired.

Tonight Show. By 2009 Jay Leno was in his seventeenth season as host of *The Tonight Show with Jay Leno,* with over three thousand episodes. Notable guests in the 2000s included future California governor Arnold Schwarzenegger, who announced his candidacy on the show; actor Colin Farrell, who was accosted by his stalker during his interview; and President Barack Obama, the first sitting president to appear on a late-night talk show. Obama caused controversy when he made a joke comparing his bowling abilities to those of participants in the Special Olympics. When the Writers Guild of America (WGA) went on strike in 2007, Leno, a guild member, was accused of violating WGA guidelines by writing his own monologues. Initially, Leno claimed he had had permission from the guild's president, but by November Leno relented and the show went into reruns. When the strike ended on 12 February 2008, Leno returned to writing his material. Leno announced he would be leaving the show in 2009, stepping down to host a prime-time comedy hour on NBC titled *The Jay Leno Show.* Conan O'Brien of NBC's *Late Night with Conan O'Brien* took over hosting duties for *The Tonight Show.*

Prime Time. Leno's prime-time show had much in common with *The Tonight Show,* and included celebrity guests such as Jerry Seinfeld, who appeared on the 14 September debut, and controversial rapper Kanye West, who appeared fresh from his *MTV Video Music Awards* scandal in which he hijacked singer Taylor Swift's acceptance speech (even Obama had weighed in on the incident, calling West a "jackass"). Although the show included popular comedy bits such as "Jay Walking," in which Leno stopped people on the street, quizzed them about current events, and chuckled at their baffling responses, viewers felt he was not as biting or sarcastic as host of *The Tonight Show.* The show struggled to find an audience. In January 2010 NBC attempted to move Leno back to late night, shortening his show, airing it at 11:35 P.M., and pushing Conan O'Brien's *The Tonight Show* back to 12:05 A.M. O'Brien refused to go along with the rescheduling move and after several tense weeks of negotiation agreed to step down and allow Jay Leno to return as host of *The Tonight Show.* Many viewed Leno's role in the affair as underhanded, and supporters rallied to O'Brien's cause, but with Leno back at the helm *The Tonight Show* returned to the top spot in the late-night programming race.

Sources:

Jay Leno and Bill Zehme, *Leading With My Chin* (New York: Harper-Collins, 1996);

"Jay Leno," Internet Movie Database, *imdb.com.*

WILL.I.AM

1975–

MUSICIAN AND ACTIVIST

Yes We Can. Jamaican American rapper William James Adams Jr., born on 15 March 1975 in Los Angeles, California, first rose to fame as Will.i.am, a member of the musical group the Black Eyed Peas, but he became a household name during the 2008 presidential election. Taking Barack Obama's 8 January 2008 New Hampshire primary speech and setting it to music, Will.i.am created a web video that spoke to the political beliefs of many young Americans. The video, directed by Dan Fletcher, was shot in black and white and featured notable celebrities such as John Legend, Kareem Abdul-Jabbar, Nicole Scherzinger of The Pussycat Dolls, and Scarlett Johansson. As video footage of Obama reciting his speech played, a chorus of celebrities sang the words over a melody composed by Will.i.am. The video debuted on 2 February 2008 on *Dipdive.com* and *YouTube.com* and was viewed more than 21 million times. It won a Creative Arts and Entertainment Daytime Emmy (2008) for New Approaches in Daytime Entertainment. Though it became the unofficial theme song of the Obama campaign, the motivation for the video's creation was not initially political. Will.i.am was moved by the speech and hoped it would one day be taught in schools the way the words of past American political figures such as Abraham Lincoln and Martin Luther King Jr. had. He hoped that, by setting the speech to a melody, he could provide an instructional tool for generations of schoolchildren to learn and recite the words.

CNN's First "Hologram." After the success of the video, Will.i.am became an important player in election coverage. CNN debuted new technology on election night (4 November 2008) that included an interview with a holographic image of Will.i.am. The pop star was "beamed in" from Grant Park to discuss his *Yes We Can* video and hopes for postelection America. The image was not truly a hologram but was inserted digitally to appear that Will.i.am and Jessica Yellin, another interviewee, were in the studio. Nevertheless, the technology represented a significant advance in remote communication and was a mark of Will.i.am's cultural and political significance. In the interview with Anderson Cooper, Will.i.am explained his motivation for creating the *Yes We Can* video. CNN had more than 12 million viewers tune in for the hologram interviews and election coverage.

A New Day. Will.i.am continued to actively support Obama and his relationship with CNN. He composed "It's a New Day." In an article on *The Huffington Post*, he noted that it "was inspired by America. It's about Obama winning, and really paying tribute to those people who are responsible for that happening, and that's the American people." The video debuted on 7 November 2008 on the *Oprah Winfrey Show* and featured footage from the campaign trail and election night. He composed the Obama-inspired "America's Song," which also debuted on the *Oprah Winfrey Show* on 19 January 2009. After the success of this follow-up song and video, CNN once again turned to Will.i.am for discussion of the election. At CNN's request, the Black Eyed Peas' front man created a short film titled *New Day* that depicted his experiences at Obama's inauguration, which debuted 25 January 2009. Will.i.am hoped the video would be "a visual backdrop of his reflections at the inauguration and his thoughts on where we need to go next as a country."

Sources:

"Will.i.am," Internet Movie Database, *imdb.com;*

Will.i.am.com;

"Will.i.am's Hope for the Future with Obama," *cnn.com* (25 January 2008).

PEOPLE IN THE NEWS

Once a Google ad executive, **Tim Armstrong** became chief executive of AOL in March 2009, after the dissolution of the AOL/Time Warner merger. Armstrong was charged with managing the Time Warner Internet unit once it separated from its parent company.

In the fall of 2006, **Dean Baquet** resigned as editor of the *Los Angeles Times* rather than make enormous staff and budget cuts. He joined the staff of *The New York Times* in 2007 as their Washington bureau chief.

Radio and television personality **Glenn Beck,** a self-proclaimed conservative on the Fox News Channel program *Glenn Beck,* became famous for inciting controversy when he called Barack Obama a racist. In 2009 he was named one of the most powerful "voices for American conservative populist anger" by I Want Media, an online media news resource.

In May 2003 *The New York Times* revealed that promising reporter **Jayson Blair** had plagiarized articles as well as fabricated details of his stories, including ones he wrote about such sensational events as the Washington, D.C., sniper attacks. *The New York Times* revealed his misdeeds and apologized for the betrayal of public trust.

Mark Burnett led the British television invasion, importing popular competition-based reality programming to the United States. Launching a decade's long (and counting) fascination with such programs, Burnett brought *Survivor* to CBS in 2000 and has produced several more popular reality shows, including *The Apprentice* (2004), *Are You Smarter Than a 5th Grader?* (2007), and *Shark Tank* (2009).

After making a name for himself as a correspondent for ABC News, in 2001 **Anderson Cooper** became co-anchor of CNN's *American Morning* and was the weekend prime-time anchor before getting his own show, *Anderson Cooper 360,* in September 2003; in 2005 he was voted Media Person of the Year by *iwantmedia.com*'s readers.

Nick Denton founded Gawker Media in 2003. Its flagship blog, *Gawker.com,* reported on Hollywood and political news and gossip, and expanded into a network of popular blogs including Jezebel, Gizmodo, and others.

Financial reporter **Lou Dobbs,** who became host of CNN's *Lou Dobbs Tonight* in 2001, was criticized for using his program as a platform for conservative viewpoints, notably on the issue of immigration. He resigned from CNN in November 2009.

As the cofounders of Twitter, **Jack Dorsey, Biz Stone,** and **Evan Williams** were named the Media Person(s) of the Year in 2009 by *iwantmedia.com*.

Celebrity gossip blogger **Perez Hilton** (born Mario Lavandeira) posted unflattering pictures of celebrities and added acerbic comments and illustrations; with more than 30 million page hits, Hilton became the celebrity-gossip standard and set the tone for similar coverage. In 2007 he took his sarcastic comments to the airwaves with VH1's *What Perez Sez.*

Cofounder and CEO of YouTube, founded in 2005, **Chad Hurley** gave millions of Americans a venue to share videos online; in 2006 Hurley and cofounder **Steve Chen** sold the site to Google for $1.65 billion.

In 2008 **Mel Karmazin** became the CEO of Sirius XM Radio, formed by the merger of Sirius and XM satellite radio services, which faced serious financial troubles and competition from Internet radio channels.

On 3 April 2003 *Washington Post* reporter **Michael Kelly** became the first American journalist killed in Iraq.

Late-night talk-show host **David Letterman** shocked viewers in 2009 when he admitted on air to sleeping with female employees of his *Late Show with David Letterman,* which aired on CBS. The confession was prompted by a threat from an extortionist. Letterman's dalliances did little to tarnish his reputation, however, as viewers turned out in even greater numbers after the confession.

MSNBC commentator **Rachel Maddow** switched from radio to television in September 2008 and proved she had a loyal following; despite initial concern that Maddow, an open lesbian, might be too controversial for mainstream viewers, her show experienced great success. MarketWatch's Jon Friedman called her the "future of MSNBC."

In January 2006 **Leslie Moonves** took the helm of CBS Corporation as president and CEO. He had previously served as chairman and CEO of CBS Broadcasting and president of CBS Entertainment, bringing such successful franchises as *CSI* and *Survivor*, but it was not until he took over all control of operations that CBS found new life and ratings success.

The successful host of the NBC late-night program, *Late Night*, **Conan O'Brien** was tapped to replace Jay Leno as host of *The Tonight Show*, taking over hosting duties on 1 June 2009.

Comedian and daytime talk-show host **Rosie O'Donnell,** once the "Queen of Nice," earns a new reputation in 2006 after joining the cast of *The View*, following on-air feuds with cohost Elisabeth Hasselbeck and guest Donald Trump; she left *The View* in 2007, but continued to attract the spotlight with her memoir *Celebrity Detox* and her Sirius XM Radio show *Rosie Radio*, which premiered in November 2009.

Google CEO **Eric Schmidt** made the search engine a media giant; in 2008 Google was named number twelve on *Advertising Age*'s top 100 Leading Media Companies and collaborated with media outlets such as NBC and *Life* magazine. Google also worked with print newspapers to make their content more searchable.

On 6 October 2004 controversial radio personality **Howard Stern** announced a five-year $500 million deal with Sirius, a satellite radio provider.

Jeff Zucker was named NBC Entertainment president (2000), president of NBC Television Group (2004), and CEO of NBC Universal (2005). His climb to the top of the NBC corporate ladder was due to successful management of programming and making popular NBC-owned channels such as Bravo and SyFy (formerly SciFi). In 2009 Zucker faced the difficult task of managing the shift of control from General Electric to Comcast.

AWARDS

EMMY AWARDS

2000

Outstanding Comedy Series: *Will & Grace* (NBC)

Outstanding Drama Series: *The West Wing* (NBC)

Outstanding Non-Fiction Series: *American Masters: Hitchcock, Selznick and the End of Hollywood* (PBS)

2001

Outstanding Comedy Series: *Sex and the City* (HBO)

Outstanding Drama Series: *The West Wing* (NBC)

Outstanding Non-Fiction Program (Reality): *American High* (Fox)

Outstanding Non-Fiction Series: *American Masters: Finding Lucy* (PBS)

Outstanding Variety, Music, or Comedy Series: *The Late Show with David Letterman* (CBS)

2002

Outstanding Comedy Series: *Friends* (NBC)

Outstanding Drama Series: *The West Wing* (NBC)

Outstanding Non-Fiction Program (Reality): *The Osbournes* (MTV)

Outstanding Non-Fiction Series (Informational): *Biography* (A&E)

Outstanding Variety, Music, or Comedy Series: *The Late Show with David Letterman* (CBS)

2003

Outstanding Comedy Series: *Everybody Loves Raymond* (CBS)

Outstanding Drama Series: *The West Wing* (NBC)

Outstanding Non-Fiction Program (Alternative): *Cirque du Soleil: Fire Within* (Bravo)

Outstanding Non-Fiction Series (Traditional): *American Masters* (PBS)

Outstanding Reality Competition: *The Amazing Race* (CBS)

Outstanding Variety, Music, or Comedy Series: *The Daily Show with Jon Stewart* (Comedy Central)

2004

Outstanding Comedy Series: *Arrested Development* (Fox)

Outstanding Drama Series: *The Sopranos* (HBO)

Outstanding Non-Fiction Series: *American Masters* (PBS)

Outstanding Reality Competition Program: *The Amazing Race* (CBS)

Outstanding Reality Program: *Queer Eye for the Straight Guy* (Bravo)

Outstanding Variety, Music, or Comedy Series: *The Daily Show with Jon Stewart* (Comedy Central)

2005

Outstanding Comedy Series: *Everybody Loves Raymond* (CBS)

Outstanding Drama Series: *Lost* (ABC)

Outstanding Non-Fiction Series: *Broadway: The American Musical* (PBS)

Outstanding Reality Competition Program: *The Amazing Race* (CBS)

Outstanding Reality Program: *Extreme Makeover: Home Edition* (ABC)

Outstanding Variety, Music, or Comedy Series: *The Daily Show with Jon Stewart* (Comedy Central)

2006

Outstanding Comedy Series: *The Office* (NBC)

Outstanding Drama Series: *24* (Fox)

Outstanding Non-Fiction Series: *Ten Days That Unexpectedly Changed America* (The History Channel)

Outstanding Reality Program: *Extreme Makeover: Home Edition* (ABC)

Outstanding Reality Competition Program: *The Amazing Race* (CBS)

Outstanding Variety, Music, or Comedy Series: *The Daily Show with Jon Stewart* (Comedy Central)

2007

Outstanding Comedy Series: *30 Rock* (NBC)

Outstanding Drama Series: *The Sopranos* (HBO)

Outstanding Non-Fiction Series: *Planet Earth* (Discovery Channel)

Outstanding Reality Program: *Kathy Griffin: My Life on the D–List* (Bravo)

Outstanding Reality Competition Program: *The Amazing Race* (CBS)

Outstanding Variety, Music, or Comedy Series: *The Daily Show with Jon Stewart* (Comedy Central)

2008

Outstanding Comedy Series: *30 Rock* (NBC)

Outstanding Drama Series: *Mad Men* (AMC)

Outstanding Non-Fiction Series: *American Masters* (PBS) and *This American Life* (Showtime)

Outstanding Reality Program: *Kathy Griffin: My Life on the D–List* (Bravo)

Outstanding Reality Competition Program: *The Amazing Race* (CBS)

Outstanding Variety, Music, or Comedy Series: *The Daily Show with Jon Stewart* (Comedy Central)

2009

Outstanding Comedy Series: *30 Rock* (NBC)

Outstanding Drama Series: *Mad Men* (AMC)

Outstanding Non-Fiction Series: *American Masters* (PBS)

Outstanding Reality Program: *Intervention* (A&E)

Outstanding Reality Competition Program: *The Amazing Race* (CBS)

Outstanding Variety, Music, or Comedy Series: *The Daily Show with Jon Stewart* (Comedy Central)

Sources:
Academy of Television Arts and Sciences;
Internet Movie Database, *imdb.com.*

PULITZER PRIZE: JOURNALISM
2000

Breaking News Reporting: *Denver Post,* "for its clear and balanced coverage of the student massacre at Columbine High School."

Breaking News Photography: *Rocky Mountain News,* "for its powerful collection of emotional images taken after the student shootings at Columbine High School."

Editorial Cartooning: Joel Pett, *Lexington* (Ky.) *Herald-Leader.*

Editorial Writing: John C. Bersia, *Orlando Sentinel*, "for his passionate editorial campaign attacking predatory lending practices in the state, which prompted changes in local lending regulations."

International Reporting: Mark Schoofs, *Village Voice,* "for his provocative and enlightening series on the AIDS crisis in Africa."

National Reporting: Staff of *Wall Street Journal,* "for its revealing stories that question U.S. defense spending and military deployment in the post–Cold War era and offer alternatives for the future."

Public Service: *Washington Post,* "notably for the work of Katherine Boo that disclosed wretched neglect and abuse in the city's group homes for the mentally retarded, which forced officials to acknowledge the conditions and begin reforms."

2001

Breaking News: *Miami Herald,* "for its balanced and gripping on-the-scene coverage of the pre-dawn raid by federal agents that took the Cuban boy Elián González from his Miami relatives and reunited him with his Cuban father."

Breaking News Photography: Alan Diaz, Associated Press, "for his photograph of armed U.S. federal agents seizing the Cuban boy Elián González from his relatives' Miami home."

Editorial Cartooning: Ann Telnaes, Tribune Media Services.

Editorial Writing: David Moats, *Rutland* (Vt.) *Herald*, "for his even-handed and influential series of editorials commenting on the divisive issues arising from civil unions for same-sex couples."

International Reporting: Ian Johnson, *Wall Street Journal*, "for his revealing stories from China about victims of the government's often brutal suppression of the Falun Gong movement and the implications of that campaign for the future"; and Paul Salopek, *Chicago Tribune*, "for his reporting on the political strife and disease epidemics ravaging Africa, witnessed firsthand as he traveled, sometimes by canoe, through rebel-controlled regions of the Congo."

National Reporting: *The New York Times*, "for its compelling and memorable series exploring racial experiences and attitudes across contemporary America."

Public Service: *Portland Oregonian*, "for its detailed and unflinching examination of systematic problems within the U.S. Immigration and Naturalization Service, including harsh treatment of foreign nationals and other widespread abuses, which prompted various reforms."

2002

Breaking News Reporting: *Wall Street Journal*, "for its comprehensive and insightful coverage, executed under the most difficult circumstances, of the terrorist attack on New York City, which recounted the day's events and their implications for the future."

Breaking News Photography: *The New York Times*, "for its consistently outstanding photographic coverage of the terrorist attack on New York City and its aftermath."

Editorial Cartooning: Clay Bennett, *Christian Science Monitor*.

Editorial Writing: Alex Raksin and Bob Sipchen, *Los Angeles Times*, "for their comprehensive and powerfully written editorials exploring the issues and dilemmas provoked by mentally ill people dwelling on the streets."

International Reporting: Barry Bearak, *The New York Times*, "for his deeply affecting and illuminating coverage of daily life in war-torn Afghanistan."

National Reporting: *Washington Post*, "for its comprehensive coverage of America's war on terrorism, which regularly brought forth new information together with skilled analysis of unfolding developments."

Public Service: *The New York Times*, "for 'A Nation Challenged,' a special section published regularly after the September 11th terrorist attacks on America, which coherently and comprehensively covered the tragic

events, profiled the victims, and tracked the developing story, locally and globally."

2003

Breaking News Reporting: *Lawrence* (Mass.) *Eagle-Tribune*, "for its detailed, well-crafted stories on the accidental drowning of four boys in the Merrimack River."

Breaking News Photography: *Rocky Mountain News*, "for its powerful, imaginative coverage of Colorado's raging forest fires."

Editorial Cartooning: David Horsey, *Seattle Post-Intelligencer*, "for his perceptive cartoons executed with a distinctive style and sense of humor."

Editorial Writing: Cornelia Grumman, *Chicago Tribune*, "for her powerful, freshly challenging editorials on reform of the death penalty."

International Reporting: Kevin Sullivan and Mary Jordan, *Washington Post*, "for their exposure of horrific conditions in Mexico's criminal justice system and how they affect the daily lives of people."

National Reporting: Alan Miller and Kevin Sack, *Los Angeles Times*, "for their revelatory and moving examination of a military aircraft, nicknamed 'The Widow Maker,' that was linked to the deaths of 45 pilots."

Public Service: *Boston Globe*, "for its courageous, comprehensive coverage of sexual abuse by priests, an effort that pierced secrecy, stirred local, national and international reaction, and produced changes in the Roman Catholic Church."

2004

Breaking News Reporting: *Los Angeles Times*, "for its compelling and comprehensive coverage of the massive wildfires that imperiled a populated region of southern California."

Breaking News Photography: David Leeson and Cheryl Diaz Meyer, *Dallas Morning News*, "for their eloquent photographs depicting both the violence and poignancy of the war with Iraq."

Editorial Cartooning: Matt Davies, *Journal News*, "for his piercing cartoons on an array of topics, drawn with a fresh, original style."

Editorial Writing: William R. Stall, *Los Angeles Times*, "for his incisive editorials that analyzed California's troubled state government, prescribed remedies, and served as a model for addressing complex state issues."

International Reporting: Anthony Shadid, *Washington Post*, "for his extraordinary ability to capture, at personal peril, the voices and emotions of Iraqis as their country was invaded, their leader toppled, and their way of life upended."

National Reporting: *Los Angeles Times*, "for its engrossing examination of the tactics that have made Wal-Mart the largest company in the world with cascading effects across American towns and developing countries."

Public Service: *The New York Times*, "for the work of David Barstow and Lowell Bergman that relentlessly examined death and injury among American workers and exposed employers who break basic safety rules."

2005

Breaking News Reporting: *Newark* (N.J.) *Star-Ledger*, "for its comprehensive, clear-headed coverage of the resignation of New Jersey's governor after he announced he was gay and confessed to adultery with a male lover."

Breaking News Photography: Associated Press, "for its stunning series of photographs of bloody yearlong combat inside Iraqi cities."

Editorial Cartooning: Nick Anderson, *Louisville* (Ky.) *Courier-Journal*, "for his unusual graphic style that produced extraordinarily thoughtful and powerful messages."

Editorial Writing: Tom Philp, *Sacramento Bee*, "for his deeply researched editorials on reclaiming California's flooded Hetch Hetchy Valley that stirred action."

International Reporting: Kim Murphy, *Los Angeles Times*, "for her eloquent, wide-ranging coverage of Russia's struggle to cope with terrorism, improve the economy and make democracy work"; (and) Dele Olojede, *Long Island* (N.Y.) *Newsday*, "for his fresh, haunting look at Rwanda a decade after rape and genocidal slaughter had ravaged the Tutsi tribe."

National Reporting: Walt Bogdanich, *The New York Times*, "for his heavily documented stories about the corporate cover-up of responsibility for fatal accidents at railway crossings."

Public Service: *Los Angeles Times*, "for its courageous, exhaustively researched series exposing deadly medical problems and racial injustice at a major public hospital."

2006

Breaking News Reporting: *New Orleans Times-Picayune*, "for its courageous and aggressive coverage of Hurricane Katrina, overcoming desperate conditions facing the city and the newspaper."

Breaking News Photography: Staff of the *Dallas Morning News*, "for its vivid photographs depicting the chaos and pain after Hurricane Katrina engulfed New Orleans."

Editorial Cartooning: Mike Luckovich, *Atlanta Journal-Constitution*, "for his powerful cartoons on an array of issues, drawn with a simple but piercing style."

Editorial Writing: Rick Attig and Doug Bates, *Portland Oregonian*, "for their persuasive, richly reported editorials on abuses inside a forgotten Oregon mental hospital."

International Reporting: Joseph Kahn and Jim Yardley, *The New York Times*, "for their ambitious stories on ragged

justice in China as the booming nation's legal system evolves."

National Reporting: James Risen and Eric Lichtblau, *The New York Times*, "for their carefully sourced stories on secret domestic eavesdropping that stirred a national debate on the boundary line between fighting terrorism and protecting civil liberty"; (and) *San Diego Union-Tribune* and Copley News Service, "with notable work by Marcus Stern and Jerry Kammer for their disclosure of bribe-taking that sent former Rep. Randy Cunningham to prison in disgrace."

Public Service: *New Orleans Times-Picayune*, "for its heroic, multi-faceted coverage of Hurricane Katrina and its aftermath, making exceptional use of the newspaper's resources to serve an inundated city even after evacuation of the newspaper plant"; (and) *Biloxi-Gulfport* (Miss.) *Sun Herald*, "for its valorous and comprehensive coverage of Hurricane Katrina, providing a lifeline for devastated readers, in print and online, during their time of greatest need."

2007

Breaking News Reporting: *Portland Oregonian*, "for its skillful and tenacious coverage of a family missing in the Oregon mountains, telling the tragic story both in print and online."

Breaking News Photography: Oded Balilty, Associated Press, "for his powerful photograph of a lone Jewish woman defying Israeli security forces as they remove illegal settlers in the West Bank."

Editorial Cartooning: Walt Handelsman, *Long Island* (N.Y.) *Newsday*, "for his stark, sophisticated cartoons and his impressive use of zany animation."

Editorial Writing: Arthur Browne, Beverly Weintraub, and Heidi Evans, *New York Daily News*, "for their compassionate and compelling editorials on behalf of Ground Zero workers whose health problems were neglected by the city and the nation."

International Reporting: *Wall Street Journal*, "for its sharply edged reports on the adverse impact of China's booming capitalism on conditions ranging from inequality to pollution."

National Reporting: Charlie Savage, *Boston Globe*, "for his revelations that President Bush often used 'signing statements' to assert his controversial right to bypass provisions of new laws."

Public Service: *Wall Street Journal*, "for its creative and comprehensive probe into backdated stock options for business executives that triggered investigations, the ouster of top officials, and widespread change in corporate America."

2008

Breaking News Reporting: *Washington Post*, "for its exceptional, multi-faceted coverage of the deadly shooting rampage at Virginia Tech, telling the developing story in print and online."

Breaking News Photography: Adrees Latif, Reuters, "for his dramatic photograph of a Japanese videographer, sprawled on the pavement, fatally wounded during a street demonstration in Myanmar."

Editorial Cartooning: Michael Ramirez, *Investor's Business Daily*, "for his provocative cartoons that rely on originality, humor, and detailed artistry."

Editorial Writing: No Award.

International Reporting: Steve Fainaru, *Washington Post*, "for his heavily reported series on private security contractors in Iraq that operate outside most of the laws governing American forces."

National Reporting: Jo Becker and Barton Gellman, *Washington Post*, "for their lucid exploration of Vice President Dick Cheney and his powerful yet sometimes disguised influence on national policy."

Public Service: *Washington Post*, "for the work of Dana Priest, Anne Hull, and photographer Michel du Cille in exposing mistreatment of wounded veterans at Walter Reed Hospital, evoking a national outcry and producing reforms by federal officials."

2009

Breaking News Reporting: *The New York Times*, "for its swift and sweeping coverage of a sex scandal that resulted in the resignation of Gov. Eliot Spitzer, breaking the story on its website, and then developing it with authoritative, rapid-fire reports."

Breaking News Photography: Patrick Farrell, *Miami Herald*, "for his provocative, impeccably composed images of despair after Hurricane Ike and other lethal storms caused a humanitarian disaster in Haiti."

Editorial Cartooning: Steve Breen, *San Diego Union-Tribune*, "for his agile use of a classic style to produce wide-ranging cartoons that engage readers with power, clarity, and humor."

Editorial Writing: Mark Mahoney, *Glens Falls* (N.Y.) *Post-Star*, "for his relentless, down-to-earth editorials on the perils of local government secrecy, effectively admonishing citizens to uphold their right to know."

International Reporting: *The New York Times*, "for its masterful, groundbreaking coverage of America's deepening military and political challenges in Afghanistan and Pakistan, reporting frequently done under perilous conditions."

National Reporting: *St. Petersburg Times*, "for 'PolitiFact,' its fact-checking initiative during the 2008 presidential campaign that used probing reporters and the power of the World Wide Web to examine more than 750 political claims, separating rhetoric from truth to enlighten voters."

Public Service: *Las Vegas Sun*, "and notably the courageous reporting by Alexandra Berzon, for the exposure of the high death rate among construction workers on the Las Vegas Strip amid lax enforcement of regulations, leading to changes in policy and improved safety conditions."

Source: The Pulitzer Prizes, *pulitzer.org*.

DEATHS

Elie Abel, 83, journalist, worked at NBC (1961–1969) with Chet Huntley and David Brinkley, 22 July 2004.

Eddie Adams, 71, photojournalist, won Pulitzer Prize for a photograph of a Communist guerilla being executed in Saigon during the Vietnam War, 19 September 2004.

Army Archerd, 87, actor turned Hollywood reporter, columnist (1953–2005) for *Daily Variety*, 8 September 2009.

Bea Arthur, 86, actor and comedian, best known for her work on *Maude* and *The Golden Girls*, famous for dry wit and biting delivery, 25 April 2009.

Richard Avedon, 81, photographer, whose work appeared in many magazines, including the *New Yorker*, 1 October 2004.

Frank Batten Sr., 82, founded the Weather Channel, 10 September 2009.

David Bloom, 39, reporter for NBC's *Today*, collapsed and died while reporting on war in Iraq, 6 April 2003.

Les Brownlee, 90, journalist, first black reporter for the *Chicago Daily News*, 21 November 2005.

Art Buchwald, 81, columnist and author, won Pulitzer Prize, 17 January 2007.

George Carlin, 71, comedian and actor, made a name for himself with oft-quoted "The 7 Words You Can't Say on Television" routine, 22 June 2008.

Lucien Carr, 79, journalist, early Beat Generation writer, friend of Allen Ginsberg, William S. Burroughs, and Jack Kerouac, editor for United Press International, 28 January 2005.

David Carradine, 72, actor, famous for role on television program *Kung Fu* (1972–1975), played title role in Quentin Tarantino films *Kill Bill: Vol. 1* (2003) and *Kill Bill: Vol. 2* (2004), 3 June 2009.

Johnny Carson, 79, comedian and television host of NBC's *The Tonight Show* (1962–1992), 23 January 2005.

W. Horace Carter, 88, North Carolina newspaper publisher and editor who challenged the Ku Klux Klan, won Pulitzer Prize in 1953, 16 September 2009.

Claudia Cohen, 56, gossip columnist, 15 June 2007.

Edward R. Cony, 76, won Pulitzer Prize (1961) for reporting at *Wall Street Journal,* 12 January 2000.

Walter Cronkite, 92, broadcast journalist and anchorman, hosted *CBS Evening News* (1962–1981), 17 July 2009.

Elizabeth Crow, 58, editor of *Parents* (1978–1988) magazine, 4 April 2005.

William J. Eaton, 74, reporter, foreign correspondent, won Pulitzer Prize for work on unsuccessful Clement Haynesworth appointment to the Supreme Court (1970), 23 August 2005.

Ralph Edwards, 92, host of television show *This Is Your Life,* produced shows such as *Name That Tune* (1954–1957) and *The People's Court* (1981–1993), 16 November 2005.

William A. Emerson Jr., reporter for *Newsweek* during civil rights era, editor of *The Saturday Evening Post,* 25 August 2009.

Farrah Fawcett, 62, actor, sex symbol, and star of *Charlie's Angels* (1976–1980), 25 June 2009.

Clay Felker, 82, founded or helped start such magazines as *Ms., New York Magazine, Sports Illustrated,* editor in chief of *Village Voice* (1974), published Tom Wolfe and Gloria Steinem, 1 July 2008.

Will Fowler, 81, Los Angeles crime reporter, famous for being first reporter at Black Dahlia (January 1947) murder scene, 13 April 2004.

Sylvan Fox, 79, journalist, won Pulitzer Prize for rewrites about 1962 airline crash, 22 December 2007.

Edward Lewis Gaylord, 83, publisher of the *Daily Oklahoman,* 27 April 2003.

Merv Griffin, 82, singer, television talk-show host, game-show creator, hosted *The Merv Griffin Show* (1962–1986), created *Jeopardy!* and *Wheel of Fortune,* 12 August 2007.

David Halberstam, 73, reporter, historian, won Pulitzer Prize for coverage during Vietnam War, wrote *The Best and the Brightest* (1972), 23 April 2007.

Radie Harris, 96, Broadway columnist for *Hollywood Reporter* for fifty years, 22 February 2001.

Paul Harvey, 90, popular radio news commentator, 28 February 2009.

George Herman, 85, CBS correspondent, moderated *Face the Nation,* 8 February 2005.

Don Hewitt, 86, created television news show *60 Minutes,* 19 August 2009.

Molly Ivins, 62, author and columnist, critic of George W. Bush administration, 31 January 2007.

Peter Jennings, 67, journalist, anchor for ABC's *World News Tonight* (1978–2000), 7 August 2005.

Tichi Wilkerson Kassel, 77, editor and publisher of the *Hollywood Reporter,* 8 March 2004.

Bob Keeshan, 76, best known for host role on *Captain Kangaroo* children's program on CBS (1955–1984), 23 January 2004.

Don Knotts, 81, comedic actor, best known as character Deputy Barney Fife on *The Andy Griffith Show* (1960–1968) and Ralph Furley on *Three's Company* (1979–1984), 24 February 2006.

Harry W. Lawton, 77, journalist, author of *Willie Boy: A Desert Manhunt* (1960), which inspired the movie *Tell Them Willie Boy Is Here* (1969), 20 November 2005.

Irving R. Levine, 86, foreign correspondent and business reporter for *NBC News,* 27 March 2009.

Al Lewis, 82, actor, best known as character Grandpa Munster on television series *The Munsters* (1964–1966) and for role as Officer Leo Schnauser on *Car 54, Where Are You?* (1961–1963), 3 February 2006.

Malcolm MacPherson, 65, reporter, novelist, war correspondent for *Newsweek,* 17 January 2009.

Billy Mays, 50, pitchman for OxyClean and other products, along with Anthony "Sully" Sullivan hosted reality show *Pitchmen* (2009) for the Discovery Channel, 28 June 2009.

Darren McGavin, 83, actor, best known for title role in *Kolchak: The Night Stalker* (1974–1975) and the classic movie *A Christmas Story* (1983), 25 February 2006.

Ed McMahon, 86, television announcer and cohost, best known as loyal sidekick to Johnny Carson on *The Tonight Show,* spokesman for Publishers Clearinghouse, 23 June 2009.

J. Edward Murray, 90, journalist and foreign correspondent for United Press International, president of the Associated Press Managing Editors Association, won John Zenger Award for service to freedom of the press, 2 November 2005.

Jack Nelson, 80, Pulitzer Prize–winning investigative journalist, reported on the Orangeburg Massacre (8 February 1968), 21 October 2009.

Robert D. Novak, 78, political reporter, columnist, worked with Rowland Evans on long-running syndicated column, 18 August 2009.

Carroll O'Connor, 76, actor famous for role as grouchy patriarch Archie Bunker of *All in the Family* (1968–1979), starred in *In the Heat of the Night* (1988–1995), 21 June 2001.

Joe O'Donnell, 85, government news photographer, took pictures of aftermath at Hiroshima bombing, took pictures of presidents ranging from Harry Truman to Lyndon B. Johnson, 9 August 2007.

Daniel Pearl, 38, journalist for the *Wall Street Journal* whose death became international news after he was kidnapped and beheaded in Karachi, Pakistan, 1 February 2002.

William A. Price, 94, invoked First Amendment in Senate hearings on communism in newspapers (1956), 29 April 2009.

Whitelaw Reid, 95, war correspondent, editor, and president of *New York Herald Tribune,* 18 April 2009.

Charles Nelson Reilly, 76, comic actor, best known for appearances on television show *Hollywood Squares* and the *Tonight Show* with Johnny Carson, 25 May 2007.

John Ritter, 54, actor best known for his work on television programs *Three's Company* (1976–1984) and *8 Simple Rules* (2002–2003), 11 September 2003.

Nan C. Robertson, 83, journalist, won Pulitzer Prize (1983) while at *The New York Times,* 13 October 2009.

Fred Rogers, 74, better known as Mr. Rogers, host of long-running and much-beloved PBS children's program *Mr. Rogers' Neighborhood* (1968–2001), 27 February 2003.

Judd Rose, 45, reporter and co-anchor on ABC's *Prime Time Live,* 10 June 2000.

Tim Russert, 58, journalist, anchor of *Meet the Press* (1991–2008), 13 June 2008.

William Safire, 79, political columnist, speechwriter for President Richard M. Nixon, won Pulitzer Prize (1978), 27 September 2009.

Charles M. Schulz, 77, cartoonist for long-running *Peanuts* comic strip, died of colon cancer the day before final original strip appeared in Sunday newspapers, 12 February 2000.

Charles E. Scripps, 87, chairman of the Scripps media company, 3 February 2007.

Billy Shadel, 96, journalist, covered D-Day in World War II, ABC-TV anchor, 29 January 2005.

Anna Nicole Smith, 39, model, actor, best known for her appearances in *Playboy* and advertisements for clothing line *Guess,* starred in reality program on the E! channel, *The Anna Nicole Show* (2002), 8 February 2007.

Helen Smith, 84, press secretary (1973–1974) for First Lady Pat Nixon, 9 April 2004.

Tony Snow, 53, press secretary (2006–2007) to President George W. Bush, 12 July 2008.

Aaron Spelling, 83, legendary producer of such television hits as *Charlie's Angels* (1976–1981), *The Love Boat* (1977–1987), *Fantasy Island* (1978–1984), *Dynasty* (1981–1989), *Beverly Hills 90210* (1990–2000), *Melrose Place* (1992–1999), *7th Heaven* (1996–2006), and *Charmed* (1998–2006), 23 June 2006.

Ron Ziegler, 63, press secretary to President Richard M. Nixon (1969–1974), 10 February 2003.

PUBLICATIONS

Sumbul Ali-Karamali, *The Muslim Next Door: The Qur'an, the Media, and That Veil Thing* (Ashland, Ore.: White Cloud, 2008);

Eric Alterman, *What Liberal Media?: The Truth about Bias and the News* (New York: Basic Books, 2003);

Robin Andersen, *A Century of Media, a Century of War* (New York: Peter Lang, 2006);

Ben H. Bagdikian, *The New Media Monopoly* (Boston: Beacon, 2004);

Steve Michael Barkin, *American Television News: The Media Marketplace and the Public Interest* (Armonk, N.Y.: M. E. Sharpe, 2002);

Joel Best, *Damned Lies and Statistics: Untangling Numbers from the Media, Politicians, and Activists* (Berkeley: University of California Press, 2001);

Eric Boehlert, *Lapdogs: How the Press Rolled Over for Bush* (New York: Free Press, 2006);

David Brock and Paul Waldman, *Free Ride: John McCain and the Media* (New York: Anchor, 2008);

Jeff Chester, *Digital Destiny: New Media and the Future of Democracy* (New York: New Press, 2007);

Lynn Schofield Clark, ed., *Religion, Media, and the Marketplace* (Rutgers, N.J.: Rutgers University Press, 2007);

Elliot D. Cohen and Bruce W. Fraser, *The Last Days of Democracy: How Big Media and Power-Hungry Government are Turning America into a Dictatorship* (Amherst, N.Y.: Prometheus, 2007);

Stuart Croft, *Culture, Crisis and America's War on Terror* (Cambridge & New York: Cambridge University Press, 2006);

David Croteau and William Hoynes, *The Business of Media: Corporate Media and the Public Interest* (Newbury Park, Cal.: Pine Forge, 2001);

Thomas De Zengotita, *Mediated: How the Media Shapes Our World and the Way We Live* (New York: Bloomsbury, 2005);

Karen E. Dill, *How Fantasy Becomes Reality: Seeing through Media Influence* (Oxford & New York: Oxford University Press, 2009);

Meenakshi Gigi Durham and Douglas Kellner, *Media and Cultural Studies: Keyworks* (Malden, Mass.: Blackwell, 2001);

Susan Faludi, *The Terror Dream: Fear and Fantasy in Post-9/11 America* (New York: Metropolitan, 2007);

Anthony R. Fellow and John Tebbel, *American Media History* (Belmont, Cal.: Thomson/Wadsworth, 2005);

Al Franken, *Lies (and the Lying Liars Who Tell Them): A Fair and Balanced Look at the Right* (New York: Dutton, 2003);

Ben Fritz, Bryan Keefer, and Brendan Nyhan, *All the President's Spin: George W. Bush, the Media, and the Truth* (New York: Simon & Schuster, 2004);

David Gauntlett, *Media, Gender and Identity: An Introduction* (London & New York: Routledge, 2002);

John Gibson, *How the Left Swiftboated America: The Liberal Media Conspiracy to Make You Think George Bush Was the Worst President in History* (New York: Harper, 2009);

Rosalind Gill, *Gender and the Media* (Cambridge & Malden, Mass.: Polity, 2007);

Dan Gillmor, *We the Media: Grassroots Journalism by the People, for the People* (Sebastopol, Cal.: O'Reilly, 2004);

Todd Gitlin, *Media Unlimited: How the Torrent of Images and Sounds Overwhelms Our Lives* (New York: Metropolitan, 2001);

Bernard Goldberg, *Bias: A CBS Insider Exposes How the Media Distort the News* (Washington, D.C.: Regnery, 2001);

Amy Goodman and David Goodman, *The Exception to the Rulers: Exposing Oily Politicians, War Profiteers, and the Media that Love Them* (New York: Hyperion, 2004);

Goodman and Goodman, *Static: Government Liars, Media Cheerleaders, and the People Who Fight Back* (New York: Hyperion, 2006);

Richard Gunther and Anthony Mughan, *Democracy and the Media: A Comparative Perspective* (Cambridge & New York: Cambridge University Press, 2000);

Theodore Hamm, *The New Blue Media: How Michael Moore, MoveOn.org, Jon Stewart and Company are Transforming Progressive Politics* (New York: New Press, 2008);

Mark B. N. Hansen, *New Philosophy for New Media* (Cambridge, Mass.: MIT Press, 2004);

Rahaf Harfoush, *Yes We Did: An Inside Look at How Social Media Built the Obama Brand* (Berkeley, Cal.: New Riders, 2009);

John Harrison and Martin Hirst, *Communication and New Media: From Broadcast to Narrowcast* (New York: Oxford University Press, 2007);

David Henderson, *Making News: A Straight-Shooting Guide to Media Relations* (Lincoln, Neb.: iUniverse Star, 2006);

Stephen Hess and Marvin L. Kalb, eds., *The Media and the War on Terrorism* (Washington, D.C.: Brookings Institution Press, 2003);

Thomas A. Hollihan, *Uncivil Wars: Political Campaigns in a Media Age* (Boston, Mass.: St. Martin's Press, 2001);

Gary Indiana, *Schwarzenegger Syndrome: Politics and Celebrity in the Age of Contempt* (New York: New Press, 2005);

Mizuko Ito and others, *Living and Learning with New Media: Summary of Findings from the Digital Youth Project* (Cambridge, Mass.: MIT Press, 2009);

Shanto Iyengar and Jennifer McGrady, *Media Politics: A Citizen's Guide* (New York: Norton, 2007);

Carrie James, *Young People, Ethics, and the New Digital Media: A Synthesis from the Good Play Project* (Cambridge, Mass.: MIT Press, 2009);

Henry Jenkins, *Convergence Culture: Where Old and New Media Collide* (New York: NYU Press, 2006);

Bill Katovsky and Timothy Carlson, eds., *Embedded: The Media at War in Iraq—An Oral History* (Guilford, Conn.: Lyons, 2003);

Eric Klinenburg, *Fighting for Air: The Battle to Control America's Media* (New York: Metropolitan, 2007);

Jonathan A. Knee, Bruce C. Greenwald, and Ava Seave, *The Curse of the Mogul: What's Wrong with the World's Leading Media Companies* (New York: Portfolio, 2009);

Paul Levinson, *New New Media* (Boston: Allyn & Bacon, 2009);

Rebecca Ann Lind, ed., *Race/Gender/Media; Considering Diversity Across Audience, Content, and Producers* (Boston: Allyn & Bacon, 2004);

Neil MacFarquhar, *The Media Relations Department of Hizbollah Wishes You a Happy Birthday: Unexpected Encounters in the Changing Middle East* (New York: PublicAffairs, 2009);

Lev Manovich, *The Language of New Media* (Cambridge, Mass.: MIT Press, 2001);

Jeremy D. Mayer, *American Media Politics in Transition* (Boston, Mass.: McGraw-Hill, 2007);

Robert W. McChesney, *The Problem of the Media: U.S. Communication Politics in the Twenty-First Century* (New York: Monthly Review, 2004);

Norman J. Medoff and Barbara Kaye, *Electronic Media: Then, Now, and Later* (Boston: Allyn & Bacon, 2004);

Bill Moyers, *Moyers on America: A Journalist and His Times*, edited by Julie Leininger Pycior (New York: New Press, 2004);

James E. Mueller, *Towel Snapping the Press: Bush's Journey from Locker-room Antics to Message Control* (Lanham, Md.: Rowman & Littlefield, 2006);

John Nichols and McChesney, *Tragedy and Farce: How the American Media Sell Wars, Spin Elections, and Destroy Democracy* (New York: New Press, 2005);

Tim O'Reilly and Sarah Milstein, *The Twitter Book* (Sebastopol, Cal.: O'Reilly, 2009);

W. James Potter, *11 Myths of Media Violence* (Thousand Oaks, Cal.: Sage, 2003);

Erik Qualman, *Socialnomics: How Social Media Transforms the Way We Live and Do Business* (Hoboken, N.J.: Wiley, 2009);

Benjamin Radford, *Media Mythmakers: How Journalists, Activists, and Advertisers Mislead Us* (Amherst, N.Y.: Prometheus, 2003);

Karen Ross, *Gendered Media: Women, Men, and Identity Politics* (Lanham, Md.: Rowman & Littlefield, 2010);

Mark J. Rozell, ed., *Media Power, Media Politics* (Lanham, Md.: Rowman & Littlefield, 2003);

Catherine R. Squires, *African Americans and the Media* (Cambridge & Malden, Mass.: Polity, 2009);

Federico Subervi-Velez, ed., *The Mass Media and Latino Politics: Studies of U.S. Media Content, Campaign Strategies and Survey Research: 1984–2004* (New York: Routledge, 2008);

Darrell M. West, *The Rise and Fall of the Media Establishment* (Boston: St. Martin's Press, 2001);

Marcy Wheeler, *Anatomy of Deceit: How the Bush Administration Used the Media to Sell the Iraq War and Out a Spy* (Berkeley, Cal.: Vaster, 2007);

James Wolcott, *Attack Poodles and Other Media Mutants: The Looting of the News in a Time of Terror* (New York: Miramax, 2004).

CHAPTER TEN

MEDICINE AND HEALTH

by ROBERT J. WILENSKY

CONTENTS

Sidebars and tables are listed in italics.

2000

17 Jan.   The Clinton administration calls for Food and Drug Administration (FDA) regulation of online pharmaceutical sales.

18 Jan.   Michael J. Fox announces his retirement as an actor from the hit television series *Spin City* due to the effects of Parkinson's disease, a condition that he had disclosed to the press in 1998. He will continue to appear in guest roles and launches the Michael J. Fox Foundation for Parkinson's Research.

21 Jan.   The FDA closes down gene-therapy experiments at the University of Pennsylvania following the death of patient Jesse Gelsinger on 17 September 1999. The FDA discovered that federal guidelines were not being followed.

17 Feb.   The University of Pennsylvania fires medical school dean William Kelley.

7 Mar.   Katie Couric, television news personality and cohost of *Today*, undergoes a colonoscopy procedure live on television.

19 Apr.   Ten-year-old North Carolinian Candace Newmaker, diagnosed with mental health and learning problems, dies in Colorado one day after undergoing a "rebirthing" program of intense breathing exercises (meant to be therapeutic and to foster a bond with her adoptive mother). Charges are brought against her mother and the therapists.

24 Apr.   Adam David Litwin is discovered to be impersonating a resident in surgery after nearly six months at UCLA Medical Center. The incident highlights security concerns at this and other medical facilities.

27 Apr.   Mayor Rudolph Giuliani of New York City announces he is undergoing treatment for prostate cancer, and later decides not to challenge Hillary Clinton for the New York senate seat.

11 May   The FDA approves use of saline-filled breast implants.

15 May   The San Francisco Department of Public Health offers free Tower Records gift certificates and condoms to individuals who agree to be tested for gonorrhea and chlamydia while at the Cat Club in an effort to combat the spread of sexually transmitted diseases.

22 May   Two U.S. drug companies (Merck and Bristol-Myers Squibb) and three European drug companies announce they will provide AIDS drugs to poor nations at deep discounts, following intense pressure from the World Health Organization (WHO) and the Clinton administration.

7 Aug.   The West Nile virus is reported in Boston, and alerts soon spread to seventeen states.

2001

- At the Rehabilitation Institute of Chicago a new nerve-cell operation allows a double amputee to control his robotic arms.

11 Jan.   The Oregon Regional Primate Research Center announces the creation of the first genetically altered primate, a rhesus monkey named ANDi. It is hoped this will be useful in research into diseases such as Alzheimer's.

13 Jan.   Former president Ronald Reagan, who is eighty-nine and suffers from Alzheimer's disease, undergoes surgery to repair a broken right hip.

2 Feb.   Former Wisconsin governor Tommy Thompson takes over as secretary of the Department of Health and Human Services (HHS), replacing Donna Shalala.

21 Mar.   The Supreme Court rules in *Ferguson* v. *Charleston* that involuntary drug testing of women violates Fourth Amendment protection against unreasonable search and seizure because of the right to privacy.

25 Apr.   A National Institute of Child Health and Human Development report cited in the *Journal of the American Medical Association* claims that 16 percent of schoolchildren experience bullying.

30 Apr.   Psychological therapist Connell Watkins and associate Julie Ponder are convicted of reckless child abuse in the death of Candace Newmaker and are given sixteen-year sentences; the mother and two assistant therapists are sentenced to probation. The governor of Colorado, Bill Owens, signs a bill banning the so-called rebirthing breathing therapy that led to the death.

14 May   The Supreme Court rules unanimously in *United States* v. *Oakland Cannabis Buyers' Cooperative* that marijuana cannot be legally used for medical purposes.

29 May   Disabled golfer Casey Martin, suffering from Klippel-Trenaunay-Weber Syndrome, a progressive and untreatable circulatory disorder in his right leg, wins a ruling by the Supreme Court that he can participate on the professional tour using a motorized cart.

2 July   Robert Tools, fifty-nine, receives the first fully implantable, battery-powered artificial heart, at Jewish Hospital in Louisville, Kentucky. The surgery is performed by Laman A. Gray Jr. and Robert D. Dowling.

Aug.   President Bush restricts federal support of stem-cell research on surplus embryos obtained from fertility clinics.

1 Aug.   Minnesota Vikings offensive lineman Korey Stringer dies from heatstroke during practice; his death leads to discussions and changes in athletic practices held during periods of extreme heat.

6 Nov.   Attorney General John Ashcroft issues a directive that physicians prescribing controlled substances for use in the Oregon Death with Dignity Act are in violation of the Controlled Substances Act (1970). The U.S. District Court quickly issues an injunction against Ashcroft's directive.

27 Nov.   The National Cancer Institute announces that cigarettes labeled as "light" or "mild" are no safer than regular cigarettes.

2002

•   Nearly 4,200 cases of West Nile virus infection are reported during the year; 284 people die from the disease.

28 Feb.   The FDA approves new cost-effective plasma-screening tests to protect the nation's blood supply from AIDS and hepatitis.

26 Mar.   Elias A. Zerhouni is appointed head of the National Institutes of Health (NIH).

18 July   The California Supreme Court upholds Proposition 215, which allows the use of medical marijuana for seriously ill patients.

5 Aug.   Richard H. Carmona becomes the seventeenth surgeon general of the United States, replacing acting-general Kenneth P. Moritsugu (who later serves again in the acting position from 2006 to 2007).

29 Oct.   The San Francisco federal court of appeals rules that doctors cannot have their licenses revoked for prescribing marijuana.

2003

- Nearly 9,900 cases of West Nile virus infection are reported during the year; 264 people die from the disease.

Jan. The FDA bans gene-therapy research involving retroviral vectors in blood stem cells. The ban will be relaxed in April.

22 Jan. Federal Judge Robert Sweet dismisses a suit brought by Samuel Hirsch against McDonald's fast-food restaurants on behalf of obese teenagers.

17 Feb. Baltimore Orioles pitcher Steve Bechler dies in Florida of heatstroke. He had been taking the weight-loss pill Xenadrine RFA-1 (containing ephedra).

July Beaches in New Jersey are closed after medical waste (vials and syringes) wash up onshore.

9 July The FDA announces it will begin requiring makers of snack foods to indicate levels of trans fats on nutritional labels.

14 July The *Archives of Internal Medicine* publishes a report that notes the beneficial effects that Katie Couric's 2000 live television colonoscopy and colon-cancer awareness effort has had in increasing testing and early detection.

21 Oct. The U.S. Senate passes legislation banning "partial-birth" abortions; President Bush signs the legislation on 5 November.

8 Dec. President Bush signs the Medicare Prescription Drug Improvement and Modernization Act into law.

30 Dec. The FDA bans dietary supplements that include ephedra.

2004

- The bodies of servicemen and -women killed in Afghanistan or Iraq are autopsied and given full CAT scans in order to build databases used in developing new techniques, procedures, and equipment to save lives in the future. One immediate change is lengthening the tube used to reinflate collapsed lungs.

29–30 Mar. The NIH holds the first National Sleep Conference to address sleep disorders.

12 Apr. The FDA bans dietary supplements containing ephedrine alkaloids.

5 June Former president Ronald Reagan dies after deteriorating health due to Alzheimer's disease. His family publicly supports stem-cell research as an avenue for potential cures.

2 Aug. President Bush signs the Food Allergen Labeling and Consumer Protection Act, which requires food labels to list potential allergens for consumers.

8 Oct. Congress passes the Anabolic Steroid Control Act, which reclassifies some performance-enhancing drugs as controlled substances and stiffens penalties for companies trying to work around steroid laws.

2005

26 Jan. Tommy Thompson is replaced as head of HHS by Mike Leavitt, former Utah governor and administrator with the Environmental Protection Agency.

Feb. University of Michigan researchers make advances in registering sound by delivering genes to guinea pigs that promote growth of hair cells in the cochlea.

Feb. The U.S. Supreme Court refuses to hear a case brought by Norma McCorvey (the "Jane Roe" of the 1973 *Roe* v. *Wade* decision) to overturn the original ruling.

18 Mar. In Florida, patient Terri Schiavo's feeding tube is removed, following approval from the U.S. Supreme Court. Schiavo, who suffered from severe brain damage, was in a coma for fifteen years, and dies on 31 March.

31 Aug. Emergency-power generators fail at Memorial Medical Center in New Orleans, as floodwaters caused by damage inflicted by Hurricane Katrina (which hit the city forty-eight hours earlier) inundate the lower floors, trapping patients and staff in the stifling-hot building (temperatures remained above 100 degrees for ten days). Critically ill patients with the least chance of survival were placed last on the evacuation list. Some patients on ventilators begin to die. On 1 September hospital staff administer drugs to patients deemed beyond saving and leave the facility. On 11 September forty-five bodies were removed from the shuttered hospital.

2006

17 Jan. The Supreme Court rules in *Gonzales* v. *Oregon* that the Controlled Substances Act does not authorize the U.S. attorney general to regulate state standards of practice for medicine or allow the attorney general to declare a medical practice authorized under state law to be illegal. The ruling means that the Oregon Death with Dignity Act (1997) stands.

16 Feb. The last Mobile Army Surgical Hospital (MASH) is decommissioned, as mobile combat medical units are deployed in war zones.

Mar. Gene therapy proves effective in treating two adult patients with blood myeloid disorders.

8 June The FDA approves Gardasil, touted as the first-ever cervical-cancer vaccine, for blocking infections associated with the human papillomavirus.

17 July Anna Pou and two nurses are arrested for their part in hastening the deaths of patients trapped in Memorial Medical Center in New Orleans during Hurricane Katrina.

Aug. Seventeen patients under the care of the National Cancer Institute show regression of advanced melanoma due to the use of genetically engineered white blood cells.

24 Aug. The FDA approves nonprescription use of the Plan B "morning-after pill," which is taken within seventy-two hours after intercourse to prevent pregnancy.

5 Dec. New York City becomes the first major city to ban the use of trans fats in restaurants.

8 Dec. Researchers at the University of Michigan announce the development of a bioengineered heart muscle.

19 Dec. President Bush signs a bill promoting public awareness of autism and funding research into the condition.

2007

15 Jan. The University of Texas M. D. Anderson Cancer Center and Southwestern Medical Center announce that tumor-suppressing genes with lipid-based nanoparticles have reduced the number and size of human lung-cancer tumors in test mice.

9 Apr. New Mexico legalizes medical marijuana; the state will oversee production and distribution.

12–28 May	Attorney Andrew Speaker flies to Europe on his honeymoon and then back to the United States via Canada, with "extremely drug-resistant tuberculosis (XDR-TB)," claiming he was never told he could not fly but was simply "advised" not to do so.
1 June	Right-to-death advocate Dr. Jack Kevorkian, who was serving a ten-to-twenty-five-year sentence for a 1999 second-degree murder conviction for assisting in a suicide, is released from prison on parole.
24 July	A grand jury refuses to indict Pou on any of the charges stemming from the deaths of hospital patients during Hurricane Katrina.

2008

May	Senator Edward M. "Ted" Kennedy (D-Mass.) is diagnosed with brain cancer.
Dec.	Cleveland (Ohio) Clinic doctors perform the world's first near-total facial transplant surgery.

2009

26 Jan.	Nadya Suleman (known derisively in the media as "Octomom"), an unemployed single mother, gives birth to eight children after fertility treatments (she already had six). She is accused of wishing to become famous, misusing fertility treatments, and wanting to "cash in" on the birth of her children.
Mar.	New York City establishes a Bedbug Advisory Board to deal with an infestation of the pests.
9 Mar.	President Barack Obama overturns his predecessor's stem-cell policy and allows the National Institutes of Health to fund research on embryonic stem cells beyond previous restrictions.
28 Apr.	Kathleen Sebelius is sworn in as secretary of HHS.
29 Apr.	Speaker is informed that his initial diagnosis was incorrect, and files suit against the Centers for Disease Control and Prevention (CDC).
22 June	President Obama signs the Family Smoking Prevention and Tobacco Control Act; it seeks to protect children by banning flavored cigarettes, advertisement near playgrounds and on sporting logos, and the use of terms "light," "low tar," or "mild."
24 Oct.	President Obama declares the swine-flu pandemic (H1N1) a national emergency.
3 Nov.	Regina Benjamin becomes the eighteenth surgeon general of the United States.
Dec.	Federal health officials estimate that approximately ten thousand Americans have died since April from the recent swine-flu outbreak.

OVERVIEW

Pressures. During the 2000s there were significant technological and scientific advances in medicine, including the development of advanced prosthetics and the introduction of robotic surgery; there was also an intense focus on the means of providing cost-efficient health care for everyone. Medical costs rose significantly and were scrutinized closely. Legislation affected how physicians, nurses, hospitals, and others interacted with patients. Economic pressures led employers to reexamine providing health-care coverage to their employees, causing millions to worry about losing their health coverage. Uninsured individuals incurred large nonreimbursed expenditures by institutions delivering care to them. Anxiety grew especially toward the end of the decade as the economy went into a downturn and job losses accelerated. Conflict emerged over the rights of patients to purchase less-expensive drugs from overseas and over the Internet.

Political Responses. Politics frequently influenced health-care choices, from restrictions placed on stem-cell research and abortion rights to expanding health-care coverage to all Americans. Politicians debated expanding coverage and how to pay for it, the role of state versus federal government involvement, and whether individuals should be permitted to make their own decisions in regard to insurance. Conservatives claimed that the government was infringing on the right of people and doctors to control medical decisions, while those with insurance (some 85 percent of the population) bridled at paying for those without it. Others argued that no one in the richest country in the world should be without health coverage.

Ethics. The medical profession struggled with several questions as ethical standards continued to evolve. Increased attention was paid to the relationship between physicians and hospitals and pharmaceutical companies, which impacted how physicians obtain information about drugs and affected research projects. There was renewed interest in the financial connections between researchers and scientific authors concerning drug producers and manufacturers of medical devices. In 2006 the *Journal of the American Medical Association* learned after the fact that the authors of three articles had not disclosed financial ties to companies with a stake in their findings. The deaths of critically ill patients in a New Orleans hospital hit hard by the ravages of Hurricane Katrina raised questions about ethical decisions made by some of the staff. Elsewhere, the actions of some doctors, such as one who allowed an unemployed woman with six children to receive fertility treatments that resulted in the birth of octuplets, also raised concerns about social responsibility in medicine. The overuse of cosmetic surgery and botox injections also came into question.

Administrative Changes. In hospitals the role of chief medical officer increased. Critics realized that care given in institutions had not been as safe as it should be, and widespread efforts were instituted to rectify this situation. Physician acceptance of protocols or pathways increased. Multidisciplinary teams were developed, crossing specialties and incorporating such nonphysician health personnel as nurses, social workers, ethicists, and pharmacists to deal with complex issues such as organ transplantation.

Health Issues. Public-health concerns also were prominent during the decade. Reducing childhood obesity by promoting healthy diets and exercise concerned everyone from the doctor's office to the White House. Communities placed greater restrictions on smoking and sought options to regulate fast food and sodas. Chemicals encountered in everyday life came under scrutiny, such as Bisphenol A (BPA), used in many plastic products as a strengthener; phthalates (also used in plastics); and brominated flame retardants (PBDEs), used in fabrics, mattresses, and computer circuit boards and casings. Laboratory studies revealed abnormalities developing with exposure to these chemicals, alone or in combination. Dangerous chemicals were found in the umbilical-cord blood of newborns, for instance, and manufacturers were forced by market pressures to produce such products as baby bottles free of damaging chemicals, even though the Food and Drug Administration considered them safe. The public was increasingly aware, as well, of the dangers of biological terrorist attacks (highlighted by the anthrax scare of 2001) and the effects on emergency responders to destroyed buildings. Also prominent in the minds of many Americans were the continuing AIDS epidemic; outbreaks of West Nile virus and H1N1 influenza; and the continuing fights against cancer, autism, muscular dystrophy, and a host of other ailments.

TOPICS IN THE NEWS

AIDS

Continuing Crisis. By 2006, 25 million people had died from Human Immunodeficiency Virus / Acquired Immune Deficiency Syndrome (HIV/AIDS) and an estimated 40+ million more were infected worldwide. For many sufferers, the disease became a chronic condition rather than leading to a rapid death. For those who could afford them, drugs were widely available to control the progression of the disease. However, this ability to manage the disease led in some cases to a recurrence of risky behavior. Though it was widely known how to limit the spread of the disease, doing so required a modification in behavior that was difficult to achieve. As Jonathan Mann, former head of the World Health Organization's Global AIDS program, said, "We know how to stop the spread of AIDS, people just don't like that answer and want another one."

Inhibitors. Antiretroviral drugs, which inhibit the growth and spread of viruses within the body, had been in limited use since the 1980s. In the 1990s doctors came increasingly to rely on a mixed approach of prescribing multiple antiretrovirals, known as Highly Active Antiretroviral Therapy (HAART). Since the introduction of HAART in 1996 the annual rate of infection by 2009 had fallen by 52 percent. During this period the number of people receiving such treatment increased by 547 percent. There was a 17 percent fall in the rate of new HIV infections between 2001 and 2008, and the cost of treatment dropped from $10,000 a year in 1995 to $100 or less by 2010.

Minority Communities. Traditionally, with less access to primary health care, minority communities have been disproportionately affected by HIV/AIDS. A study in five major U.S. cities found that among gay and bisexual men infected with HIV, 46 percent were black, compared with 21 percent white and 15 percent Latino. AIDS was the leading cause of death for African American women between the ages of twenty-five and thirty. Black women accounted for the largest share of new HIV infections among women (61 percent in 2006), and the incidence rate for them was nearly fifteen times the rate for white women. Black women were most likely to be infected through heterosexual transmission, white women through drug injection. Of the 1.1 million people in the United States with HIV/AIDS, some 200,000 were Latinos,

who had more difficulty than whites obtaining care. Latinos were the largest- and fastest-growing minority group in the United States (15 percent of the population), a significant statistic because the percentage of HIV/AIDS patients who were Latino was 18 percent (2006), and they were 19 percent of all new cases (2007). Their AIDS case rate per 100,000 was about three times that of whites, but only one-third that of blacks. Heterosexual transmission accounts for a greater share of infections among Latinos than among whites.

Sources:
Centers for Disease Control and Prevention, Department of Health and Human Resources, *HIV/AIDS among Men Who Have Sex with Men* (September 2010);

Henry J. Kaiser Family Foundation, "Fact Sheet: Latinos and HIV/AIDS" (September 2009);

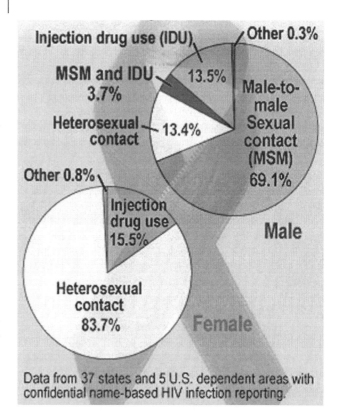

Centers for Disease Control chart showing HIV diagnoses and methods of contraction among adult and adolescent Latinos in 2008 (<www.cdc.gov>)

David J. Jefferson, "How AIDS Changed America," *Newsweek*, 147 (15 May 2006): 27–34;

"Waltzing with Death (The XVIII International AIDS Society Meeting)," *Economist*, 396 (22 July 2010): 77–78.

BARIATRIC SURGERY

Morbid Obesity. Clinically severe obesity is a disease of excess energy stored in the form of fat. It correlates with a Body Mass Index (BMI) of 40 kg/m2, or being one hundred pounds overweight. Being overweight has significant health consequences, the most severe of which is an increased mortality rate. Men 50 percent above average weight have a twofold increase in mortality and a fivefold increase in diabetes. The National Heart, Lung, and Blood Institute (NHLBI)'s Framingham Heart Study noted that the first cohort to terminate because of the demise of all participants was that of the morbidly obese. None of the individuals listed in the *Guinness Book of World Records* for their high weight lived beyond the age of forty. Obesity is a danger to health due to high blood pressure, high blood sugar, high levels of triglycerides in the blood, excess levels of insulin, and low levels of HDL cholesterol (beneficial cholesterol that cleans blood vessels). Consequences of obesity include cardiac dysfunction, pulmonary problems, digestive disease, and endocrine disorders as well as obstetric, orthopedic, and dermatologic complications. Thus, the dangers of being overweight are manifest and well known. Due to rising concerns over the problem, bariatric surgical procedures increased from 12,480 in 1998 to 113,500 in 2005.

Gastric Bypass. Surgical treatment for clinically severe obesity was not a cosmetic procedure and increasingly came to be covered by insurance plans. Patients whose BMI exceeded 40 were potential candidates for surgery. The procedure included many risks: morbidity in the immediate postoperative period with wound infections, dehiscence (bursting of a wound), leaks from staple breakdown, stomal stenosis (narrowing of the connection between stomach and lower intestine), marginal ulcers, pulmonary problems, and deep-vein thrombophlebitis (swelling caused by a blood clot). Weight loss usually reached a maximum between eighteen and twenty-four months postoperatively. The average weight loss after five years ranged from 48 to 74 percent. Procedures that bypassed parts of the intestinal tract (duodenum and proximal jejunum) put the patient at risk for iron and vitamin deficiencies. Lifelong replacement of iron, vitamin B12, vitamin D, and calcium was often necessary. Also, after achieving the desired level of weight loss, additional surgery was often required to deal with excess skin left behind. Alan Matarasso, senior scientific editor of *The Aesthetic Surgery Journal*, termed this "new" field "bariatric plastic surgery." He advocated a team approach to the problem, with weight-loss specialists,

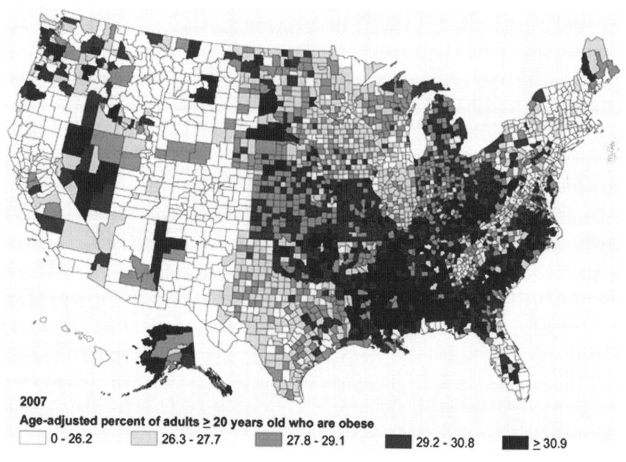

2007
Age-adjusted percent of adults ≥ 20 years old who are obese
0 - 26.2   26.3 - 27.7   27.8 - 29.1   29.2 - 30.8   ≥ 30.9

A county-level map of the percentages of obese adults in the United States in 2007 (<www.cdc.gov>)

dietitians, psychiatrists, bariatric surgeons, plastic surgeons, and geneticists. Together the integrated fields of bariatric medicine and surgery may provide both lifesaving treatment and increased quality of life. Several famous celebrities had the surgery. *American Idol* judge Randy Jackson lost more than one hundred pounds in 2003; talk-show host Star Jones dropped more than one hundred and fifty pounds in 2007; other celebrities who used the procedure were weatherman Al Roker, coach Charlie Weis, and opera singer Deborah Voight.

Sources:
American Society for Metabolic and Bariatric Surgery, *www.asmbs.com*;

M. A. Maggard and others, "Pregnancy and Fertility Following Bariatric Surgery," *JAMA*, 300 (2008): 2286–2289;

Alan Matarasso, "Bariatric Plastic Surgery," *Aesthetic Surgery Journal* (May 2003): 188–189;

National Institutes of Health, *NHLBI's Framingham Heart Study Finds Strong Link between Overweight/Obesity and Risk for Heart Failure* (31 July 2002).

BIONICS

Artificial Heart. Advances in bionics included a totally contained artificial heart that was developed and first used at Jewish Hospital in Louisville, Kentucky, in June 2001. Previous artificial hearts had required external power sources. The patient, a fifty-nine-year-old man whose heart was on the verge of failure, survived for five months with the new device, which was longer than the two-month period the Food and Drug Administration (FDA) required before authorizing larger trials on patients who were not near death.

SEWN-IN TOWEL

Bonnie Valle, who underwent surgery for emphysema in 1995, died in 2002 and donated her remains to science. While dissecting her body, a faculty member at the Northeastern Ohio College of Medicine was surprised to discover a large piece of surgical cloth behind her left lung. In the years following the surgery, her family claimed she had often complained of a strange feeling in her chest and that something was putting pressure on her lung. Indeed, surgeons had left the cloth inside her chest after her surgery, and she had lived with it for seven years. After the discovery, Valle's family sued, claiming that the forgotten towel had caused discomfort and created complications that eventually led to her death. The Cleveland Clinic, where the surgery was performed, argued that her death was due only to the advanced emphysema for which the surgery was performed and that she had lived as long as could be expected under the conditions. The clinic eventually settled the lawsuit out of court.

Source: Raksha Shetty, "Towel Found in Dead Woman's Body," *cbsnews.com* (6 August 2004).

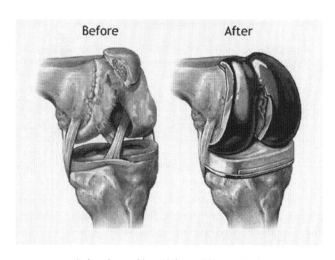

A deteriorated knee joint and its prosthetic replacement (U.S. National Library of Medicine, National Institutes of Health <www.nlm.nih.gov>)

Joint Replacement. In the 2000s joint replacement became nearly routine. More than 450,000 knee replacements and 208,000 hip replacements were performed each year. It was expected that those numbers would rise as the baby-boomer generation aged: running and jogging have been hard on their joints, and they wish to be able to continue to be physically active. Shoulder, elbow, and ankle replacements were also on the rise. Three-dimensional joint-viewing systems can be used to select the most appropriate replacement device.

Sources:
"Artificial Heart Recipient Meets the World," *abcnews.com* (21 August 2001);

Brie Zeltner, "Joint Replacements More Common as Boomers Age and an Overweight Population Wears Out Early," *Cleveland Plain Dealer*, 22 February 2011.

CANCER

Targeted Therapy. The most significant advance in cancer research in the 2000s was in targeted therapy. Unlike chemotherapy, which destroys all rapidly dividing cells, targeted therapy focuses on proteins found in cancer cells. This approach promises not only a more effective treatment but also relief from typical side effects of chemotherapy, such as hair loss and anemia. The science of targeted cancer therapy remained in its infancy, however, with many ongoing drug trials.

Breast Cancer. Approximately 200,000 new cases of breast cancer occurred each year. The causes of breast cancer were varied and often unclear. Women using hormone replacement therapy for relief of menopausal symptoms were at higher risk for breast cancer in cases where only estrogen was used. There was also a hereditary risk for the disease, and it was estimated that between one in 300 and one in 800 women carried these mutations. In these women, cancers tended to occur in both breasts and at an earlier age than normally seen, as well as in family groups. In terms of prevention, it appeared that exercise could

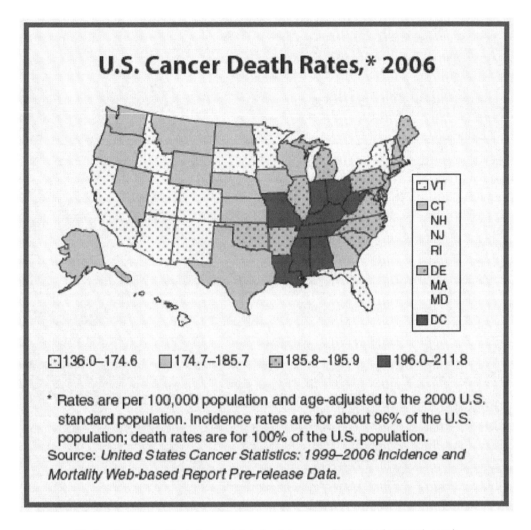

U.S. Cancer Death Rates,* 2006

VT
CT
NH
NJ
RI
DE
MA
MD
DC

136.0–174.6   174.7–185.7   185.8–195.9   196.0–211.8

* Rates are per 100,000 population and age-adjusted to the 2000 U.S. standard population. Incidence rates are for about 96% of the U.S. population; death rates are for 100% of the U.S. population.
Source: *United States Cancer Statistics: 1999–2006 Incidence and Mortality Web-based Report Pre-release Data.*

Centers for Disease Control map of state-by-state cancer death rates (<www.cdc.gov>)

decrease the risk of breast cancer. Two-thirds of all breast cancers are estrogen positive, meaning that estrogen fuels their growth. Exercise lowers levels of estrogen. It also aids in the loss of excess fat tissue, which is hormonally active and converts androgens into estrogen. In a study reported in July 2006 from Boston's Brigham and Women's Hospital, a correlation was noted between weight gain and breast cancer. Women who had never used hormone replacement therapy and had gained fifty-five pounds since the age of eighteen had double the risk of women who maintained their weight.

Ovarian Cancer. Responsible for some 15,000 deaths in 2008, ovarian cancer remained the most lethal of all gynecologic malignancies. The majority of cases were diagnosed late, with 70 percent in an advanced stage of the disease. Early diagnosis remained difficult in the majority of cases, as symptoms tend to be nonspecific. There was no reliable screening test. Oncofertility emerged as a new field devoted to maintaining fertility in those receiving treatment for cancer. Of the 125,000 women under the age of forty-five who had cancer, most received treatments that affected their fertility. Harvesting eggs or an ovary before the onset

of chemotherapy and freezing them for future use proved to be feasible and effective in maintaining reproductive options for patients.

Recurrence. Doctors and researchers increasingly focused on methods of reducing the level of cancer recurrence in patients after treatment. In the face of mounting evidence that anesthesia used during surgery played a role in recurrence and metastasis (spread) of cancer, doctors began the intraoperative administration of the nonsteroidal anti-inflammatory drug ketorolac to decrease cancer recurrence. The use of this new drug compared favorably with other, more widely used analgesics. The use of inhaled anesthetic agents was also thought to contribute to metastasis after surgery. Opiates, too, can promote the dissemination of malignant cells. New research found that blood transfusions may increase the risk of recurrence, perhaps by suppressing the immune system.

Skin Cancer. Melanoma became the second most common cancer among women in their twenties (after thyroid cancer). Rates for basal cell carcinoma (BCC) tripled in women under the age of forty between 1976 and 2003, and the rate for squamous cell carcinoma quadrupled. Most specialists agreed that the advent and popularity of tanning salons was most likely contributing to the rise in skin cancer numbers. Fortunately, the most common skin cancer was BCC, which, though it could be fatal if left untreated, was also the least dangerous. BCC rarely metastasized or spread to another location, a characteristic of the more deadly melanoma. There was no truly effective medical treatment for melanoma. In addition to the widespread use of sunscreen, clothing was developed to reduce ultraviolet (UV) rays. A product known as Rit Sun Guard, when washed into clothing, absorbed 98 percent of UVA and UVB rays.

Sources:
American College of Obstetricians and Gynecologists, "ACOG Practice Bulletin No. 103: Hereditary Breast and Ovarian Cancer Syndrome," *Obstetrics & Gynecology*, 113 (April 2009): 957–966;

James G. Bovill, "Surgery for Cancer: Does Anesthesia Matter?" *Anesthesia & Analgesia*, 110 (June 2010): 1524–1526;

Barbara Kantrowitz, "Health: Reducing Your Risk," *Newsweek*, 148 (24 July 2006): 57.

DENTISTRY

Advances. Major advances in general dentistry included implant therapy, adhesive dentistry, and cone beam computed tomography (CBCT). Dental implants became a widely accepted and preferred therapy for nonrestorable teeth. Osseointegration, the fusion of titanium with surrounding bone, allowed single- or multiple-tooth replacement in patients with severe periodontal disease, high susceptibility to dental cavities, failing root-canal therapy, or teeth missing from birth or trauma. The science greatly reduced the need to maintain teeth with a marginal prognosis.

Resins. Adhesive dentistry with composite materials advanced with the introduction of nanocomposite resins. These fillings displayed superior wear resistance and polishability, allowing dentists to mimic the properties of both enamel and dentin. Adhesive techniques allowed for bonding to surrounding tooth structure, a procedure lacking with more traditional amalgam (silver) restorations. Unlike amalgam restorations, composite resins allowed dentists to prepare minimally invasive sites, removing only decayed tooth structure while salvaging healthy surrounding enamel and dentin. Nanocomposite resins displayed similar expansion and contraction properties when compared to dentin and enamel. This favorable property minimized the risk of cracks and fractures in teeth often seen with traditional amalgam fillings.

Cone Beam Computed Tomography. The introduction of CBCT greatly improved dentists' ability to diagnose and treat oral disease. CBCT was a three-dimensional imaging technology useful in implant therapy and oral pathology diagnosis and treatment and was most often used to inspect bone volume, quality, and quantity prior to dental implants. CBCT-generated surgical guides were also used to direct implant placement. The machines were highly accurate and useful in fully imaging the pathology in three dimensions

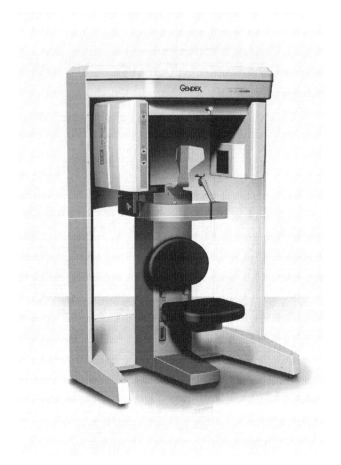

A Cone Beam Computed Tomography device, a technology that has greatly aided dental diagnoses (<www.gendex.com>)

prior to surgery. Useful at the time of operation, they were also helpful in dental implant planning: they could assist in assessing the need for bone grafts or nerve repositioning.

Sources:
Walt Bogdanich and Jo Craven McGinty, "Radiation Worries Rise with 3-D Dental Images," *New York Times*, 23 November 2010;

A. W. G. Walls, "Restorative Dentistry: The Bonding of Composite Resin to Moist Enamel," *British Dental Journal*, 191: 148–150.

DIET AND NUTRITION

Public-Health Issue. In the 2000s the problem of overweight Americans became a public-health issue. More than half of adults were overweight or obese. In 2009 at least 30 percent of adults were obese in nine states; not one state in 2000 had such high obesity rates. According to the Centers for Disease Control and Prevention, medical costs associated with obesity were $147 billion in 2006; medical care for obese people was estimated at $1,429 more per year, or 42 percent higher, than for people of normal weight.

Weight Consciousness. Television advertisements for various weight-loss programs abounded in the decade as the connection between health and weight saturated the media. Celebrities bragged of their weight loss. Fad diets of all kinds came and went. The Atkins diet, which recommended a high-protein, low-sugar, and low-carbohydrate

First Lady Michelle Obama participates in the Healthy Kids Fair on the South Lawn of the White House on 21 October 2009 (<www.whitehouse.gov>).

regimen for weight loss, was particularly popular. The nation watched Oprah Winfrey as she openly and forthrightly struggled with maintaining a healthy weight. Even babies were larger than before. In 2006 *Pediatrics* reported that 280,000 children were too large for their car seats. The obesity rate for children in the two-to-five-year-old range had doubled in the past thirty years. For youth, excess weight was a growing problem. Nearly 15 percent of children between twelve and nineteen were overweight. The number of children with elevated cholesterol or type 2 diabetes tripled in some pediatric practices. As more time was spent in front of television and computer screens and as schools cut back on mandated outdoor recess activities (Virginia was the only state mandating recess as a daily routine), the percentage of overweight teenagers tripled. Fast-food establishments found that the profit they made on "super-sized" portions far exceeded the extra cost to deliver them to their patrons.

Fighting Obesity. As national attention began to focus on the costs of an obese population, various solutions to the epidemic were proposed. Some believed regulation of the fast-food industry was a possible route, while others suggested suing giant corporations such as McDonald's for serving unhealthy meals, especially to vulnerable and impressionable children. Some communities suggested nuisance taxes be placed on soda consumption. In 2004 Morgan Spurlock released the anti-obesity, anti-fast-food-industry documentary *Super Size Me.* The following year the Department of Agriculture released new dietary guidelines, and the Department of Health and Human Services

began offering grants to programs that sought to reduce obesity among African Americans. In March 2009 First Lady Michelle Obama announced that she would take up the cause of fighting obesity in children, promote healthful eating and physical activity, and plant a vegetable garden at the White House.

Sources:

Shelley Hearne, "Obesity: The Pyramid Is Not Enough," *www.npr.org* (19 April 2005);

Elise Soukup, "Child Safety: A Growing Problem. Children Too Large for Child Safety Seats," *Newsweek*, 147 (10 April 2006): 15;

Karen Springen, "Health: Earlier Onsets," *Newsweek*, 145 (10 January 2005): 8.

EDUCATION AND TRAINING

Shorter Hours. A report published in 1999 by the Institute of Medicine indicated that medical error killed between 44,000 and 98,000 patients per year. A 2004 study found that first-year hospital residents working all-night shifts every third night were responsible for more than half of preventable adverse events. In 2003 the American Association of Medical Colleges (AAMC) and the Accreditation Council for Graduate Medical Education (ACGME) instituted rules that regulated the number of hours resident physicians were allowed to work. The limit was set at 80 hours per week, averaged over a four-week period, down from 120 per week. Doctors were to work no more than 30 hours straight, and the Institute of Medicine (IOM) called for an uninterrupted 5-hour nap for every 16-hour shift. From 1985 to 2003 resident physicians worked nearly 65 hours per week; after 2003 this amount decreased to less

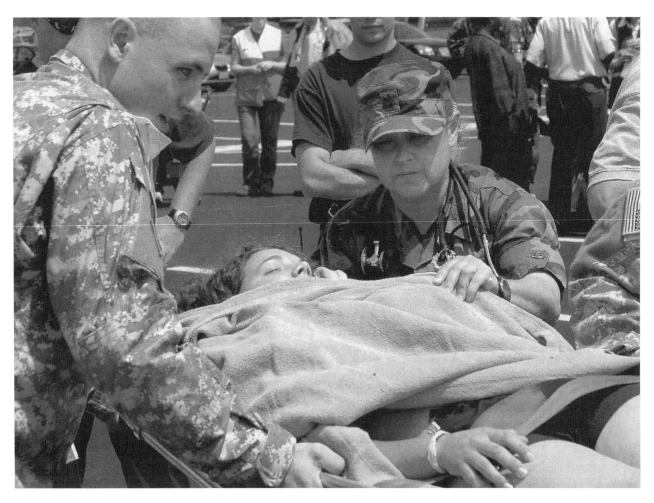

A U.S. Air Force doctor checks on a "victim" of anthrax during a bioterrorism-preparedness exercise at the Pentagon, 16 May 2006 (U.S. Air Force photograph by Staff Sergeant C. Todd Lopez).

than 60 hours per week. Despite these reforms, residents still routinely worked longer hours than nonresident physicians, lawyers, engineers, or nurses.

New Training Technologies. Technology made inroads from the medical-student to the specialist level. At UCLA medical students took part in emergency simulations with dummies that could be monitored by their professors. The simulators allowed students to learn correct procedures without endangering real patients. At the specialty level, new catheterization techniques for blood vessels and the heart were taught using a simulator in which the physician could practice the procedure in a system similar to the flight simulators utilized in pilot training. The use of this technology meant that doctors could receive intense training on difficult procedures and practice them before ever entering the operating room.

Sources:
Linda T. Kohn, Janet M. Corrigan, and Molla S. Donaldson, eds., *To Err is Human: Building a Safer Health System* (Washington, D.C.: National Academy Press, 2000);

David Noonan, "Wiring the New Docs," *Newsweek*, 139 (24 June 2002): 58;

Susan S. Wang, "New Rx for Young Doctors: Shorter Work Day," *Washington Post*, 24 June 2010.

ALLERGIES

In the 2000s there was extraordinary progress in understanding the immune system and significant improvement in treating allergic diseases. Food allergies became an increasing public-health problem, especially in schools. An estimated 11 million Americans suffered from food allergies, with 90 percent of all adverse food reactions attributed to milk, eggs, peanuts, tree nuts, fish, shellfish, soy, and wheat. Though no distinct cure was discovered, studies of desensitization to food antigens, especially in treating peanut allergies (common in the school-age population), have shown promise. Under the Food Allergen Labeling and Consumer Protection Act, any product labeled after 1 January 2006 had to state if it contained any of the eight potential allergens listed above.

Sources: Jennifer Barrett, "Allergies: Read It and Eat," *Newsweek*, 147 (9 January 2006): 12;

S. M. Jones and others, "Clinical Efficacy and Immune Regulation with Peanut Oral Immunotherapy," *Journal of Allergy and Clinical Immunology*, 124 (August 2009): 292–300.

LEGISLATION AND HEALTH POLICY

Rising Costs. Medical care in the United States faced rising costs and an expanding percentage of the nation's gross national product devoted to health care. Expenditures were due to higher prices for services and their aggressive use, advances in expensive technology, the production of new and costly drugs, and an aging population. Much of the spending was devoted to catastrophic care (frequently used for the terminally ill). Twenty-eight percent of all Medicare spending was for the 5 percent of patients who were in their final twelve months of life. Despite widespread awareness of the problem, there was little political will to tackle Medicare reform. The program was popular with the elderly, who typically voted in high numbers. Proposals to restrict access, limit funding, cap expenditures, or raise the age of eligibility garnered little support in Congress.

Prescription Drug Benefit. On 8 December 2003 President George W. Bush signed into law the Medicare Prescription Drug Improvement and Modernization Act. It created Medicare Part D, which provided drug coverage for senior citizens beginning on 1 January 2006 through private companies. The act also provided a subsidy for large employers to discourage them from eliminating private prescription-coverage plans for retired workers and prohibited the federal government from negotiating discounts with drug companies and from establishing a drug formulary. Seniors could enroll in a drug plan or provide documentation of a suitable approved alternative plan under their existing insurance. Seniors who failed to do either would pay a penalty if they sought to enroll in the coverage at a later time. Other provisions renamed "Medicare+Choice" (the private plan options available in place of traditional Medicare) as "Medicare Advantage," with increases in payments to health plans beginning in 2004. The Part B (medical insurance) deductible rose from $100 to $110 in 2004 and was indexed to spending increases starting in 2005. Starting in 2007 high-income beneficiaries (above $80,000) would pay up to 80 percent of their Part B premium's cost, as opposed to the 25 percent requirement for lower-income recipients. Seniors with incomes less than 150 percent of the federal poverty line were not required to pay Part D premiums or deductibles and would pay no more than $2 for generic drugs and $5 for brand-name drug prescriptions.

Health Savings. Health Savings Accounts (HSAs) were established in 2004 as tax-advantaged savings accounts to cover medical expenses in combination with high-deductible insurance plans. HSAs could either be employer- or self-funded. The changes also included increased Medicare payments to rural providers and hospitals and physician payment adjustments. Another option available to help with medical expenses for companies seeking tax advantages was Health Reimbursement Accounts (HRAs), which allowed employers to reimburse employees for medical expenses by using a third-party manager.

CHIP. In 2007 Congress passed a bipartisan measure to renew and expand the Children's Health Insurance Program (CHIP, originally known as the State Children's

President George W. Bush signing the Medicare Prescription Drug Improvement and Modernization Act, 8 December 2003 (<www.ssa.gov>)

Health Insurance Program), which was created in 1997 through legislation cosponsored by Senators Ted Kennedy (D-Mass.) and Orrin Hatch (R-Utah) to provide health insurance for children after the Clinton health-care initiative failed. Under the program every state had an approved plan that it could tailor to its needs. By federal fiscal year 2006 some 6.6 million children and 670,000 adults were covered. The program was jointly funded by federal and state governments and administered by the states. The 2007 bill called for a budget increase totaling $35 billion, raising total spending to $60 billion over five years. Opposition focused on the cost and the coverage for illegal immigrants. On 3 October 2007 President Bush vetoed the bill, stating he believed it would "federalize health care" and expand the scope of CHIP beyond its original intent. The House of Representatives was unable to overturn the veto. A second bill, H.R. 3963, suffered the same fate. A bill was finally passed extending funding through 31 March 2009, and Bush signed it into law on 21 December 2007. Following the 2008 election of Barack Obama and a Democratic majority in Congress, H.R. 2 was passed 290 to 138 within two weeks of Obama's inauguration on 20 January 2009. It added $32.8 billion to the program to include about 4 million more children. The Senate passed it by 66 to 32, and President Obama signed the law financing CHIP (through 2013) on 4 February 2009.

Stimulus. The American Recovery and Reinvestment Act (ARRA) of 2009, passed with overwhelming support from Democrats in Congress and without significant Republican support, was signed on 17 February 2009. The stimulus package allocated $787 billion for federal tax cuts, expansion of unemployment benefits and other welfare provisions, and domestic spending on health care, education, and infrastructure, including the energy sector. The bill expanded funding for Medicaid, contained new subsidies for the Consolidated Omnibus Budget Reconciliation Act (COBRA), subsidized medical technology updates, and provided funding for comparative effectiveness research. Medicaid funding was increased by $86.8 billion, which aided states that had seen a decrease in their revenue from falling property, sales, and income taxes in the economic downturn.

Sources:
Michael Abramowitz and Jonathan Weisman, "Bush Vetoes Child Health Bill," *Washington Post*, 4 October 2007;

Atul Gawande, "Letting Go: What Should Medicine Do When It Can't Save Your Life?" *New Yorker* (2 August 2010): 36–49;

Gail R. Wilensky, "Early Legislative Wins for Obama," *Healthcare Financial Management*, 63 (April 2009): 32–33.

MILITARY MEDICINE

Civilian Applications. The experiences of military medics in the field benefited medicine for the civilian sector. Innovations such as the new hemostatic dressings that each soldier carried in Iraq and Afghanistan had application in treating civilian trauma. The ability to control blood loss at the workplace or in motor-vehicle accidents promised significant decrease in loss of life and limb. The self-

application of military tourniquets led some EMS teams to use them in cases of automobile accidents and other trauma. Along with better control of blood loss, new blood- and fluid-replacement substances and techniques were developed. The avoidance and prevention of shock syndrome improved both survival and limb salvage and greatly decreased morbidity associated with serious injuries.

Prosthetics. During World War I (1914–1918) 1.2 percent of all wounded in action (WIA) sustained a major limb amputation, with the same rate in World War II (1939–1945). In the Korean War (1950–1953) 1.4 percent of all WIA had such an injury. In Operation Enduring Freedom (OEF, 2001–) in Afghanistan amputations accounted for 2.4 percent of all WIA. This difference may be due to the increased survival rate because of the effectiveness of improved body armor. During Operation Iraqi Freedom (OIF, 2003–) as well as OEF, 35 percent of all

DEVICES

In 2002 Congress passed the Medical Device User Fee and Modernization Act (MDUFMA), which required manufacturers of medical devices to pay for the Food and Drug Administration (FDA) review process for their products. Another provision of MDUFMA was the creation of the Office of Combination Products to help facilitate fair and timely review of "combination products" created by the complexities of emerging technologies. The combination products were therapeutic and diagnostic regimes that combined drugs, devices, and/or biological products. In 2007 the Food and Drug Administration Amendments Act (FDAAA) was passed amid rising concern over FDA oversight. It renewed a modified version of the user-fee program and expanded the clinical-trial registry database previously applicable only to drugs to include medical-device studies. It also included provisions for postmarket surveillance of pediatric uses of devices. The evolution of the act was accompanied by a complex web of dynamic premarket and postmarket regulations, guidance documents, and informal agency policies. Perhaps the most significant initiative was the agency's reevaluation of the premarket notification 510(k) program, the pathway by which the vast majority of medical devices came onto the U.S. market. The goal of the new regulations was to protect consumers against potentially dangerous devices by increasing the FDA's reach in product oversight. Critics claimed that it slowed the process of innovation and kept potentially lifesaving technologies from patients.

Source: Jonathan S. Kahan and Edward C. Wilson Jr., "Medical Devices," in *Food and Drug Law and Regulation*, edited by David G. Adams and others (Washington, D.C.: Food and Drug Law Institute, December 2008), pp. 487–489.

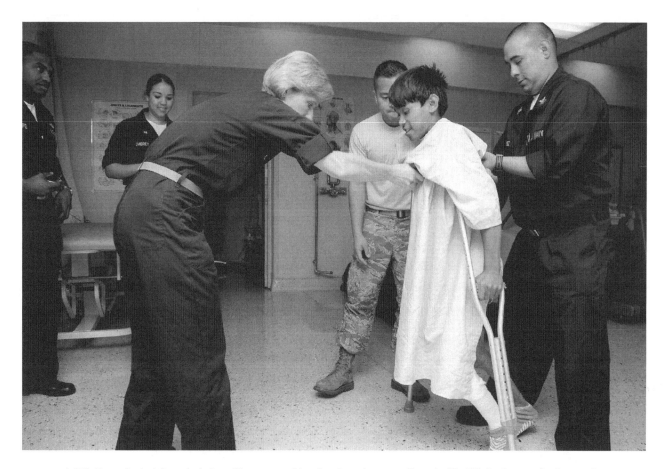

A U.S. Navy physical therapist helps a fifteen-year-old patient learn how to walk again. The Filipino boy received corrective surgery aboard the USNS *Mercy* on 6 June 2008 (Department of Defense photograph by Petty Officer Second Class Joseph Seavey, U.S. Navy).

amputations involved loss of an upper extremity, compared to 5 percent of all amputations in the civilian sector. In December 2001 Lieutenant General James Peake, Surgeon General of the Army, directed the development of an amputee patient-care program. He foresaw the potential for a significant number of amputee patients. As a result, mobile prosthetics were developed to allow those who have lost a limb to remain on active duty and perform in a satisfactory manner. Bionic prostheses that act upon the wishes of the injured were developed, with the potential of restoring patients to a virtually normal existence. DEKA Research and Development Corporation, a New Hampshire company, headed the research under the sponsorship of the Pentagon's Defense Advanced Research Project Agency (DARPA). The aim of the project was to develop a neurally controlled arm and hand prosthesis that would perform, look, and feel like a natural limb. The goal was a prosthesis that would provide touch feedback and enable the user to accomplish normal activities of daily living.

Sources:

David Pope, "DARPA Prosthetics Programs Seek Natural Upper Limb," Neurotech Business Report, *neurotechreports.com;*

Charles Scoville, "Statement to Veterans Affairs Committee," U.S. House of Representatives, Second Session, 108th Congress, Serial No. 108–150 (22 July 2004): 133;

Steve Vogel, "VA Is Testing an Advanced New Prosthetic Arm," *Washington Post,* 3 June 2009.

9/11 AND ITS AFTERMATH

Health Risks of Cleanup. The attack on the World Trade Center in New York City on 11 September 2001 not only caused death and destruction but also was also a major psychic event in the life of the nation. Health issues arose secondary to exposure to the debris and dust of the destroyed buildings. More than 1.2 million tons of rubble had to be removed from the site. New York University Hospital environmental-medicine specialist Max Costa called it the "worst environmental disaster ever inside a city." The U.S. Department of Health and Human Services (HHS) dispatched more than seven hundred experts to the area, including specialists in biohazards, epidemiology, public health, and the environment. Suspected contaminants included asbestos, microscopic carcinogenic fibers, pulverized concrete dust, Freon from air conditioners, and radiation from medical equipment, as well as dioxin and other toxins from cleaning fluids. Some workers initially worked long hours without protective masks and were at high risk for development of asthma and emphysema. World Trade Center Syndrome developed, with symptoms ranging from unrelenting coughs and sinus infections to acute lung trauma. Posttraumatic stress disorder developed in workers and those exposed to the event. Some 40 percent of firefighters developed a cough so persistent that it required medical care, with nearly 4,000 being treated with

Rescue and cleanup workers at the World Trade Center disaster site clear debris and search for survivors on 16 September 2001. Many workers were exposed to harmful contaminates (<www.osha.gov>).

steroids. Some rescue workers claimed they were not told to wear protective clothing and masks. Environment Protection Agency (EPA) head Christine Todd Whitman denied this assertion, saying, "Maybe there was one press release where we didn't say that, but then we said it over and over." Some workers did not wear protective suits as they were heavy, hot, and cumbersome.

Anthrax Scare. Following the attacks, a new terrorist threat arose: anthrax. Individuals in the media and government began receiving letters with white powder in them. Robert Stevens, a photo editor in Boca Raton, Florida, died after inhaling thousands of spores. Erin O'Connor, an NBC News assistant, tested positive for cutaneous anthrax. Letters containing the powder were located in Reno, Nevada, and in offices of the U.S. Senate. New procedures to screen mail were put in place in Washington, D.C. Across the country there was widespread concern, bordering on panic. The antibiotic ciprofloxacin nearly disappeared from pharmacists' shelves as people rushed to stockpile the drug. The Federal Bureau of Investigation (FBI) launched investigations at laboratories doing research with the pathogen, and polygraph tests were administered to scientists working at the U.S. Army research lab at Fort Detrick, Maryland. In August 2002 Attorney General John Ashcroft labeled Steven Hatfill, a

scientist employed at Fort Detrick, a person of interest in the case. His home was searched, and he lost his job. Hatfill sued the FBI, the Department of Justice, Ashcroft, Ashcroft's successor Alberto Gonzales, and others for violating his constitutional rights and the Privacy Act. On 27 June 2008 the Department of Justice announced it would settle the case for $5.8 million. In April 2005 Bruce Ivins, who worked in the anthrax laboratory at Fort Detrick, became the lead suspect. In September 2008 Ivins committed suicide. The FBI identified him as the individual responsible for the attacks, but many of his colleagues expressed doubt as to his culpability.

Sources:
Eleanor Clift and Julie Scelfo, "'Many People Will Die Early,' EPA Attacked for 9/11 Health Concerns," *Newsweek,* 142 (8 September 2003): 8;

David France, "Is Ground Zero Safe?" *msnbc.com* (1 October 2001);

France, "Now, 'WTC Syndrome?'" *Newsweek,* 138 (5 November 2001): 10.

OBSTETRICS AND GYNECOLOGY

Changes in the Field. While there was a marked increase in women working in medicine overall, there was an especially notable increase within the specialty of obstetrics. There was also a rise in the use of nonphysicians to deliver routine labor and delivery care in many institutions.

The use and training in the use of forceps virtually disappeared. Vacuum-assisted vaginal deliveries (VAVD) replaced the use of forceps. Cosmetic gynecology appeared, with practitioners performing liposuction, hair removal, and vaginal rejuvenation procedures. There was also a marked shift to minimally invasive surgery.

Fertility Treatment and Fetal Care. By the 2000s assisted reproductive procedures became so advanced that tubal surgery for infertility was supplanted by in vitro procedures, in which fertilized eggs are planted in the uterus. The value of ultrasound increased as high-definition equipment was developed that could detect sleep cycles in the fetus by picking up eyelid movement and could follow intrauterine development, determine placental status, and diagnose developmental anomalies such as Down's syndrome. In addition, with the manufacture of smaller and less-expensive equipment, ultrasound became an office procedure rather than one requiring a hospital visit. Fetal monitoring became standard in most institutions, with some 85 percent of fetuses assessed. As the number of women in labor undergoing electronic fetal monitoring rose, so did the number of caesarean-section deliveries. By 2004, 30 percent of all deliveries in the United States were by caesarean section. Since many of these babies were perfectly healthy after delivery, some suggested that the practice was overused. However, failure to perform a caesarean delivery if monitors indicated it should be done carried great legal risk for the obstetrician. The issue became so contentious that one specialist, Barry Schifrin (who testified for plaintiffs on many occasions in regard to fetal-monitor misinterpretations), was censured in 2004 by the American College of Obstetricians and Gynecologists (ACOG). He subsequently resigned from the organization.

HPV. The relationship between infection with human papillomavirus (HPV) and both genital warts and cervical cancer—the second most prevalent form of female cancer worldwide—had been recognized for many years. More than one hundred genotypes of HPV were discovered; approximately thirty were found in the genital mucosa, fifteen of which were associated with cervical cancer. With the development and approval of the HPV vaccine Gardasil, doctors hoped for a vast reduction in instances of cervical cancer, even its eradication. The ACOG recommended vaccination of all females aged nine to twenty-six, since the drug was most effective if given before exposure to HPV infection. Disputes arose over whether all girls should be vaccinated, with many maintaining that such action would lead to early sexual activity. Texas governor Rick Perry caused a firestorm with an executive order requiring girls entering the sixth grade to be vaccinated against HPV.

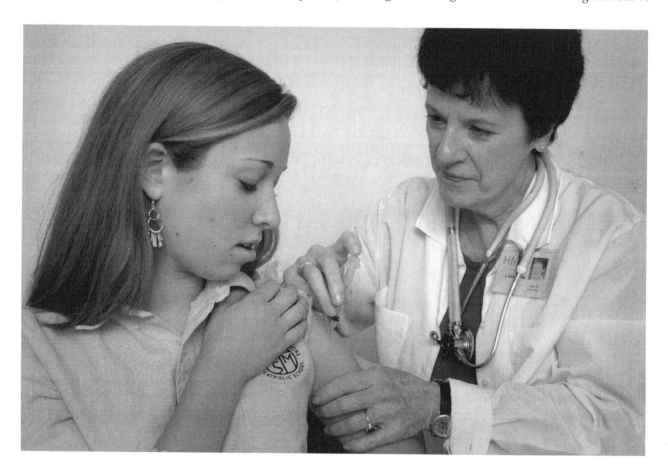

A nurse administers the HPV vaccine to a young woman in 2006 (<www.cdc.gov>).

Some twenty other states and the District of Columbia considered similar rules and legislation. The vaccine became popular on college campuses, for it protected not only against cervical cancer but also against genital warts.

Hormone Replacement. Hormone replacement therapy (HRT) remained controversial throughout the decade. HRT promised relief from such symptoms as hot flashes, night sweats, and vaginal dryness and could even improve sleep, mood, and concentration. It also preserved bone density and protected against fractures. While many internists argued that such procedures amounted to overmedication, gynecologists sought to provide the treatments. Debates over the safety of estrogen replacement and its possible association with the development of diseases such as breast cancer continued.

Medical Abortion. In 2000 the Food and Drug Administration (FDA) approved the sale and use of RU-486 or mifepristone, a pill that induces abortion up to approximately a seven-week gestation age. Though it could result in prolonged bleeding and cramping, studies showed the drug to be 92 to 97 percent effective. The FDA's decision was opposed by abortion foes and cheered by prochoice advocates. Controversy arose when some pharmacists refused to dispense the drug, and in its waning hours the Bush administration's Department of Health and Human Services approved the drug. One report indicated that RU-486 accounted for 14 percent of all abortions nationwide. In 2006 the FDA approved over-the-counter sales of the emergency-contraception or "morning after" pill, Plan B (levonorgestrel), which prevented pregnancy if taken in two doses up to five days after intercourse. Since the drug was only available to those over the age of eighteen, it had to be stocked behind the counter for control purposes. In March 2009 a federal court ordered the FDA to allow seventeen-year-olds to buy Plan B without a prescription. The agency complied on 22 April. On 13 July the FDA approved Plan B One-Step, the first single-dose emergency contraceptive, to replace Plan B.

Sources:
American College of Obstetricians and Gynecologists (ACOG), Committee on Adolescent Health Care, "Committee Opinion No. 344: Human Papillomavirus Vaccination," *Obstetrics & Gynecology*, 108 (September 2006): 699–705;

ACOG, "Practice Bulletin Number 61: Human Papillomavirus," *Obstetrics & Gynecology*, 105 (2005): 905–918;

Jennifer Barrett, "Special Deliveries: Are Doctors Performing Too Many C-Sections?" *Newsweek*, 147 (3 April 2006): 45;

Anna Quindlen, "On Their Own Terms," *Newsweek*, 153 (7 February 2009): 60;

Jessica Ramirez, "Injected Into a Growing Controversy," *Newsweek*, 149 (26 February 2007): 10;

Heather Won Tesoriero, "Doctor Roils Colleagues in Debate on Fetal Monitors," *Wall Street Journal*, 26 October 2007.

RECONSTRUCTIVE AND COSMETIC MEDICINE

Facial Transplant. The field of plastic surgery made advances in both reconstructive and cosmetic arenas. After years of experimentation, the first human-face transplant was performed in France on 27 November 2005. The first such operation in the United States was carried out at the Cleveland Clinic in December 2008. Patients considered for this procedure often suffered from severe burns or had been mauled by animals. Face-transplant surgery carried all the hazards of any other transplant procedure in regard to rejection, infection, or failure. In addition, this particular transplant carried psychological considerations, both on the part of the recipient and the family of the donor. Medical teams taking part in the procedures included not only the normal transplant team but also psychologists and ethicists.

Breast Implants. In the 1990s silicone breast implants were linked to various autoimmune or connective-tissue diseases. In 1992 the FDA banned the use of silicone implants in the United States for cosmetic purposes, but not for reconstructive purposes. Few other countries followed this action. Some viewed the episode as an example of American trial attorneys and media at their worst. In

ROBOTIC SURGERY

The use of robotics in surgery was approved by the Food and Drug Administration (FDA) on 11 July 2000, though its value was disputed; detractors argued it was more costly and led to significantly longer operating times. Most robotic surgery was used in gynecology and urology, though it was also used in cardiac surgery for mitral-valve repair and other procedures. The primary surgeon sat at a console some distance from the patient and controlled the procedure by maneuvering foot pedals and hand controls. Advantages of this technology included three-dimensional visualization with improved depth perception, improved dexterity and instrument articulation secondary to increased freedom of movement, the potential for use in long-distance "telesurgery," and the ability to filter out hand tremors. Disadvantages included high cost (more than $1 million to purchase the system, plus maintenance costs), increased operating time, lack of tactile feedback and sensation, inability to reposition the patient, and bulkiness of robotic systems making it difficult for assistants to maneuver around the patient. Long-distance robotic surgery showed promise for areas where surgeons, and especially specialists, were scarce. A regional center could be established, outfitted, and manned by technicians. Surgery could be performed from afar, or the distant surgeon could assist and advise the surgeon in place.

Sources: American College of Obstetricians and Gynecologists (ACOG), "Technology Assessment No. 6: Robot-Assisted Surgery," *Obstetrics & Gynecology*, 114 (November 2009): 1153–1155;

David Noonan, "The Ultimate Remote Control," *Newsweek*, 137 (25 June 2001): 71–75;

"Robotic-Assisted Laparoscopic Surgery," *Medical Letter on Drugs and Therapeutics*, 52 (14 June 2010): 45.

COSMETIC SURGICAL PROCEDURES	2009	2008	2000	% CHANGE 2009 vs. 2008	% CHANGE 2009 vs. 2000
Breast augmentation (Augmentation mammaplasty)**	**289,328**	**307,230**	**212,500**	-6%	36%
Breast implant removals (Augmentation patients only)	19,857	20,967	40,787	-5%	-51%
Breast lift (Mastopexy)	87,386	92,461	52,836	-5%	65%
Breast reduction in men (Gynecomastia)	17,326	17,902	20,351	-3%	-15%
Buttock implants	799	853	*	-6%	*
Buttock lift	3,143	3,554	1,356	-12%	132%
Calf augmentation	259	247	*	5%	*
Cheek implant (Malar augmentation)	8,789	8,828	10,427	0%	-16%
Chin augmentation (Mentoplasty)	13,110	14,117	26,924	-7%	-51%
Dermabrasion	63,764	78,954	42,218	-19%	51%
Ear surgery (Otoplasty)	27,332	29,434	36,295	-7%	-25%
Eyelid surgery (Blepharoplasty)	**203,309**	**221,398**	**327,514**	-8%	-38%
Facelift (Rhytidectomy)	103,625	112,933	**133,856**	-8%	-23%
Forehead lift	42,365	42,063	120,971	1%	-65%
Hair transplantation	17,787	17,580	44,694	1%	-60%
Lip augmentation (other than injectable materials)	21,651	20,728	18,589	4%	16%
Liposuction	198,251	245,138	**354,015**	-19%	-44%
Lower body lift	8,867	9,286	207	-5%	4184%
Nose reshaping (Rhinoplasty)	**255,972**	**279,218**	**389,155**	-8%	-34%
Pectoral implants	230	1,335	*	-83%	*
Thigh lift	8,563	9,088	5,303	-6%	61%
Tummy tuck (Abdominoplasty)	**115,191**	**121,653**	62,713	-5%	84%
Upper arm lift	14,505	14,059	338	3%	4191%
TOTAL COSMETIC SURGICAL PROCEDURES	**1,521,409**	**1,669,026**	**1,901,049**	-9%	-20%

COSMETIC MINIMALLY-INVASIVE PROCEDURES	2009	2008	2000	% CHANGE 2009 vs. 2008	% CHANGE 2009 vs. 2000
Botulinum Toxin Type A (Botox®, Dysport®)***	**4,795,357**	**5,014,445**	**786,911**	-4%	509%
Cellulite treatment (Velosmooth®, Endermology®)	34,278	36,858	23,952	-7%	43%
Chemical peel	**1,142,949**	**1,048,577**	**1,149,457**	9%	-1%
Intense Pulsed Light (IPL) treatment	429,734	452,352	*	-5%	*
Laser hair removal	**893,054**	**891,712**	**735,996**	0%	21%
Laser skin resurfacing	434,830	400,262	170,951	9%	154%
Ablative	110,931	103,394	*	7%	*
Non-ablative (Fraxel®, etc.)	323,899	296,868	*	9%	*
Laser treatment of leg veins	219,827	222,047	245,424	-1%	-10%
Microdermabrasion	**910,188**	**841,733**	**868,315**	8%	5%
Sclerotherapy	390,341	375,328	**866,555**	4%	-55%
Soft Tissue Fillers	**1,722,054**	**1,613,609**	652,885	7%	164%
Calcium hydroxylapatite (Radiesse®)	192,053	179,489	*	7%	*
Collagen	169,292	178,899	587,615	-5%	-71%
Porcine/bovine-based (Evolence®, Zyderm®, Zyplast®)	36,688	33,563	*	9%	*
Human-based (Cosmoderm®, Cosmoplast®, Cymetra®)	132,604	145,336	*	-9%	*
Fat	50,598	46,218	65,270	9%	-22%
Hyaluronic acid (Juvederm® Ultra, Juvederm® Ultra Plus, Perlane®, Restylane®)	1,209,217	1,109,373	*	9%	*
Polylactic acid (Sculptra®)	85,883	79,653	*	8%	*
Polymethyl-methacrylate microspheres (Artefill®)	15,011	19,977	*	-25%	*
TOTAL COSMETIC MINIMALLY-INVASIVE PROCEDURES	**10,972,592**	**10,896,924**	**5,500,446**	1%	99%
TOTAL COSMETIC PROCEDURES	**12,494,001**	**12,565,950**	**7,401,495**	-1%	69%

Chart of national plastic surgery statistics for 2000, 2008, and 2009 showing cosmetic-procedure trends
(American Society of Plastic Surgeons)

1999 an Institute of Medicine report, "Safety of Silicone Breast Implants," concluded that there was little scientific evidence that silicone implants caused disease problems. In 2000 the FDA granted approval of saline-filled breast implants. In 2003 an FDA panel recommended approval of the use of silicone implants. On 17 November 2006 approval was granted for silicone implants, with long-term patient monitoring. The procedure was popular. By 2001 more than 206,000 breast augmentations were performed each year in the United States, mostly with inflatable or saline-filled implants. In 2007 there were 307,230 such procedures. Nearly one-third of the patients were over the age of forty.

Botox. In 1987 Alastair Carruthers of Vancouver, British Columbia, Canada, first used a dilute solution of botulinum toxin type A to treat wrinkles in the forehead. The medicine had previously been approved for various medical uses, including treatment in imbalance in the muscles of the eye. In 2002 the FDA approved Allergan's patented version, Botox, for cosmetic use. By 2003 the injection of Botox was the most commonly performed cosmetic procedure, with more than 2.2 million applications, a figure that rose to 2.7 million by 2007. This office procedure became a staple in the practices of many plastic surgeons, dermatologists, and ocular plastic surgeons. As a cosmetic procedure, it was not covered by regular insurance. As with many innovations, problems with Botox slowly appeared. Serious reactions, including death, seemed to be related to noncosmetic use, as in cerebral palsy patients. Most reactions in cosmetic cases tended to be local at the injection sites and self-limited. Some early experimental evidence pointed to the possibility that Botox could travel along neural pathways to the brain in rats.

Sources:
Marcia Angell, *Science on Trial: The Clash of Medical Evidence and the Law in the Breast Implant Case* (New York: Norton, 1997);

Jean Carruthers and others, "Introduction to the Consensus Recommendations," *Plastic and Reconstructive Surgery Supplement*, 114 (November 2004): i–iii;

Lisbet Rosenkrantz Hölmich and others, "Breast Implant Rupture and Connective Tissue Disease: A Review of the Literature," *Plastic and Reconstructive Surgery*, 120 (December 2007): 62S–69S;

On 12 November 2008 Sherman Silber of the Infertility Center of St. Louis announced the first child born from a full-ovary transplant. The patient, a German, suffered from premature infertility and underwent the transplant procedure after her twin sister donated an ovary. Though initially intended as a source of relief from early menopause, the transplant led to the patient's naturally conceiving in 2008 (the child was delivered in London, England). Silber, a pioneer in the field, had previously overseen the transplant of ovarian tissue to a woman who subsequently gave birth to the first child resulting from such an operation. The breakthrough offered promise for women suffering from premature infertility due to cancer treatment and other causes.

Source: "Baby Born after Ovary Transplant," *news.bbc.co.uk* (12 November 2008).

Benoit Lengelé and others, "Facing Up Is an Act of Dignity: Lessons in Elegance Addressed to the Polemicists of the First Human Face Transplant," *Plastic and Reconstructive Surgery*, 120 (1 September 2007): 803–806;

Karen Springen, "Health: New Year, New Breasts?" *Newsweek*, 141 (13 January 2003): 65;

Springen, "The Ultimate Transplant," *Newsweek*, 146 (12 December 2005): 60–61.

STEM CELLS

Promise and Controversy. Stem-cell research progressed during the decade amid continued controversy in regard to the ethics of utilizing and possibly destroying human embryos. The topic was entwined with the anti-abortion/prolife movement and various religious groups. Medical researchers often defended their work in arenas totally outside of the laboratory. Embryonic stem cells have two properties that make them valuable: the ability to become any type of specialized cell and the ability to reproduce themselves. Adult stem cells avoid the ethical questions that the use of embryos causes, but they lack the ability to differentiate into specialized cells of a different type. If it were possible to turn adult stem cells into pluripotential (able to transform into different types) cells, they would have the benefits of embryonic stem cells without raising ethical problems. In 2001 Advanced Cell Technology transfered adult DNA into human eggs, hoping to produce stem cells. The experiment failed, and the embryos died; the effort, however, raised the specter of human cloning. If the eggs had survived, would the result be a cloned person?

Embryonic Stem-Cell Ban. In August 2001 President George W. Bush lifted the existing total ban on embryonic stem-cell use for research but in effect placed a ban on the creation of new cell lines by saying that fed-

eral funds could be used for research only on existing lines. This position satisfied almost no one. The majority of Americans (by a three-to-one margin) opposed the ban, including 72 percent of Catholics, according to a *Wall Street Journal*/NBC poll. The prolife movement maintained that it was wrong to use any cell line derived from human embryos. Researchers lamented the inability to create more lines, arguing that those in existence were inadequate.

Research Limitations. In September 2001 the National Institutes of Health (NIH) announced that ten universities, research centers, and companies would control sixty-four human stem-cell lines derived from day-old embryos (blastocysts). Not all of these lines were necessarily suitable for research, and some did not display "markers" indicating they were in fact, stem cells. NIH would only consider grant applications based upon these existing stem-cell lines. Scientists bemoaned the restrictions, feeling that they would inhibit potentially lifesaving research into conditions such as Parkinson's, Alzheimer's, diabetes mellitus, multiple sclerosis, heart disease, and spinal-cord injuries. Former first lady Nancy Reagan opposed the restrictions, noting that Alzheimer's patients (such as her husband, former presi-

Cover for a 2006 leaflet protesting stem-cell research
(<www.youthdefence.ie>)

dent Ronald Reagan) could possibly benefit from the research. The same was true of Andrew Card, President Bush's chief of staff, whose father had died from Parkinson's disease. Prolife conservative senator Orrin Hatch (R-Utah) also opposed the restrictions, as did prolife conservative representative Randall "Duke" Cunningham (R-Cal.).

State Research. In an effort to get around Bush administration restrictions, some states moved ahead on their own. In September 2002 California governor Joseph Graham "Gray" Davis signed legislation promoting stem-cell research. A $3 billion referendum on funding stem-cell research passed in November 2004. Stanford University created the Institute for Stem Cell Biology and Regenerative Medicine with initial funding by an anonymous donor of $12 million. The University of California launched a program with $5 million from Intel chairman Andy S. Grove. In February 2004 New Jersey governor James E. McGreevey announced the creation of the Stem Cell Institute of New Jersey, with $50 million in funding over five years. In November 2004 Wisconsin governor Jim Doyle announced that a $375 million Wisconsin Institute for Discovery would be built on the campus of the University of Wisconsin.

Lifting of the Ban. In July 2006 Bush vetoed a bill that would have permitted surplus embryos from fertility clinics to be used for research, rather than being discarded. In June 2007 he vetoed a bill that would have authorized federal funding for research on surplus frozen embryos. The majority of fertility-clinic clients surveyed indicated they would prefer to have their surplus embryos used in research

rather than simply destroyed. In March 2009 President Barack Obama reversed the Bush directive and permitted federal funding of research on new embryonic stem-cell lines.

Sources:

Sharon Begley and Jamie Reno, "In Search of Stem Cells," *Newsweek,* 138 (10 September 2001): 57;

National Institutes of Health, *Stem Cell Information, stemcells.nih.gov;*

Evan Thomas and Eleanor Clift, "Battle For Bush's Soul," *Newsweek,* 138 (9 July 2001): 28.

TOBACCO AND SMOKING

Fight Against. In announcing his campaign against smoking in 2003, New York City mayor Michael Bloomberg noted that while 14,000 deaths were related to tobacco use each day, little funding went to fight tobacco use and its medical complications. In 2004 the National Cancer Institute spent twice as much on breast cancer as on lung cancer, even though four times as many Americans died from the latter condition. With many U.S. cities banning smoking in public places (such as restaurants, bars, and workplaces), there was a decline in tobacco use. Some companies adopted a more forceful policy: for example, workers at Weyco, a health-benefits administrator in Okemos, Michigan, could be fired for smoking on or off the job. Such businesses noted that smokers had a higher rate of medical complications and missed more work than nonsmokers. They also tended to interrupt the workday for smoking breaks. Professor Linda Sarna and her colleagues reported in *Research in Nursing & Health* in 2005 that nurses who smoked were

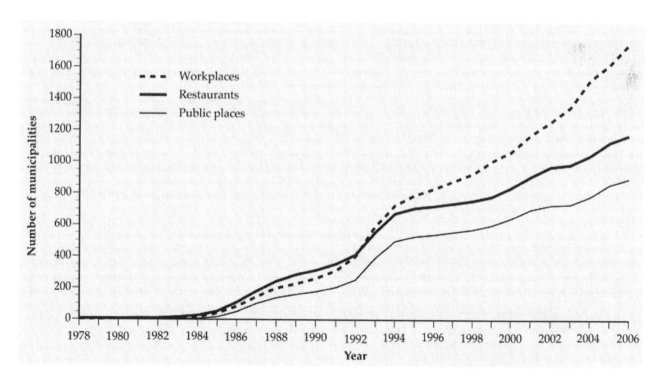

Graph depicting the number of municipalities with local laws against smoking in enclosed public places
(U.S. National Library of Medicine, National Institutes of Health, <www.nlm.nih.gov>)

perceived by colleagues as spending less time with their patients.

Smoking and Lung Cancer. Lung cancer killed more Americans than any other type of malignancy, causing some 160,000 deaths a year during the decade—more than breast, colon, and prostate cancer combined. While some cases of lung cancer occurred in nonsmokers, at least 87 percent were associated with cigarette smoking. The five-year survival rate for those diagnosed with lung cancer was 15 percent. Norman Edelman, chief medical officer of the American Lung Association, put the issue plainly: "If you smoke a pack a day for 20 years or more, you have a 50 per-cent chance of dying from smoke-related disease." There was a distinct correlation between the length of time one smoked and amount one smoked and the long-term health effects. The benefits of quitting smoking were also clear: within ten years of abstinence, half of the cancer vulnerability disappeared.

Sources:

Michael R. Bloomberg, "The Way to Save Millions of Lives is to Prevent Smoking," *Newsweek,* 152 (29 September 2008): 48–50;

Geoffrey Cowley and others, "The Deadliest Cancer," *Newsweek,* 146 (22 August 2005): 42–49;

Linda Sarna and others, "Nurses, Smoking, and the Workplace," *Research in Nursing & Health,* 28 (February 2005): 79–90;

Karen Springen, "Light Up and You May Be Let Go," *Newsweek,* 145 (7 February 2005): 10.

VACCINES AND AUTISM

Causes. In 1998 Andrew Wakefield of the Royal Free Hospital in London, England, stated that autism was caused by the MMR (measles, mumps, and rubella) vaccine. His claim was based on results in eight of twelve children and was published in *Lancet,* a highly respected medical journal. Although scientists noted that they could not prove an association between MMR vaccines and autism, Wakefield condemned use of the vaccine, which led to newspaper headlines and stories that scared the public. Studies were conducted to investigate the connection, as well as the effect of the preservative thimerosal, a mercury-containing compound. By 2003 most childhood vaccines no longer contained thimerosal. By 2004 problems with Wakefield's research began to surface. It appeared some children in his study had autism before they received their vaccines. Also, many were clients of an attorney working against the vaccine makers. The failure of Wakefield to disclose this relationship, and the fact that he had been retained and paid by the lawyer, were clear violations of research ethics. In March 2004 ten of the twelve coauthors of the *Lancet* article retracted their suggestion of a connection between MMR vaccines and autism. Wakefield did not retract. In 2005 Wakefield was charged with professional misconduct by Britain's General Medical Council. On 28 January 2010 his license to practice medicine was revoked. On 2 February 2010, *Lancet* formally retracted the paper from the published record.

Repercussions. In the United States, pending legal cases arguing that MMR vaccines caused autism were

Dr. Andrew Wakefield passes supporters as he arrives to face a disciplinary panel of the General Medical Council in London on 16 July 2007. Wakefield was found guilty of professional misconduct for falsely correlating the MMR vaccination with autism (AP Photo/Sang Tan).

combined to be heard by a special Vaccine Court beginning on 11 June 2007. It issued a ruling on 12 February 2009 that neither thimerosal-containing vaccines nor MMR vaccines caused autism. Many parents and activists remained unconvinced, in spite of a 2004 Institute of Medicine (IOM) study and others debunking a vaccine correlation. The use of MMR and other childhood vaccines fell owing to this controversy; subsequently, there was an increase in diseases such as mumps, measles, whooping cough, and *Haemophilus influenzae* infections in numbers not seen in the United States in decades, including deaths from these diseases.

Sources:

Sharon Begley and Jeneen Interlandi, "Anatomy of a Scare," *Newsweek* (2 March 2009): 42–47;

thelancet.com (2 February 2010);

A. J. Wakefield and others, "Ileal-Lymphoid-Nodular Hyperplasia, Non-Specific Colitis, and Pervasive Developmental Disorder in Children," *Lancet,* 351 (1998): 637–641.

West Nile. In 2000 an epidemic of West Nile virus, spread by mosquitoes, killed birds all along the eastern seaboard from New England to Texas. While only 1 percent of mosquitoes harbored the virus, great anxiety accompanied every dead-bird discovery. Media coverage, in particular, heightened public awareness of and fear over the possibility of outbreak and spread to humans. In reality, the human component was quite mild in almost all cases.

SARS. In 2003 an epidemic of severe acute respiratory syndrome (SARS), a virus related to one that causes the common cold, ranged worldwide. Thought to have originated in animals and spread to humans, it first appeared in China before spreading to six continents via tourists and air travelers. The virus could be spread by coughing and sneezing. In Hanoi, Vietnam, 56 percent of health workers caring for patients with the disease came down with it. Some 810 people died in twenty-nine countries out of about 8,000 cases. More than 96 percent of those infected recovered. Though fears of a possible epidemic fueled intense coverage, incidences in the United States were low.

H1N1. An H1N1 swine-flu strain appeared in 2008–2009 in Mexico and the United States. While this virus had been known for some time, in the spring of 2009 Americans began to die from it. This disease was initially susceptible to treatment with Tamiflu and Relenza, but another strain of H1N1 appeared that was resistant to Tamiflu. Some countries banned the importation of U.S. pork products as a result of the scare. There was a rush to develop a vaccine: by July 2009 more than seventy clinical trials were taking place. In September 2009 the FDA approved four vaccines against H1N1. Availability of the vaccine was limited, however, and demand far outpaced supply. There were great concerns over a pandemic, which did not come to pass. The flu season of 2009 was not remarkably different from those of preceding years.

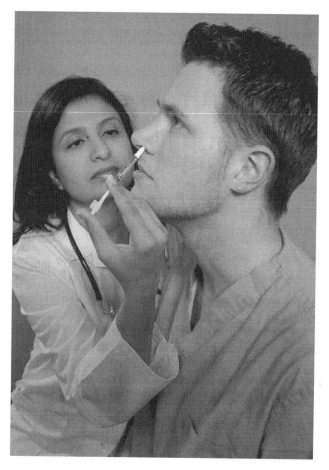

A health-care practitioner administers a nasal-spray flu vaccine for the H1N1 virus to a patient in 2009 (<www.cdc.gov>).

Sources:

Jessica Reaves, "Making Sense of SARS," *time.com* (25 April 2003);

Bryan Walsh, "H1N1 National Emergency: Time for Concern, Not Panic," *time.com* (24 October 2009);

"West Nile Virus Spreading and Killing," *cnn.com* (9 August 2002);

World Health Organization, Initiative for Vaccine Research, "Tables on the Clinical Trials of Pandemic Influenza Prototype Vaccines," *who.int* (July 2009).

HEADLINE MAKERS

RICHARD CARMONA

1949–

SURGEON GENERAL OF THE UNITED STATES, PUBLIC-HEALTH ADMINISTRATOR

Early Life. Richard Carmona was born on 22 November 1949 in New York City of Puerto Rican descent. A high-school dropout, he enlisted in the U.S. Army in 1967, served in combat in Vietnam, earned his Graduate Equivalency Diploma, and trained as a Special Forces medic. He attended college after leaving active duty and earned his M.D. from the University of California Medical School in 1979. His varied career included time as a paramedic, surgeon, professor, and part-time sheriff's deputy in Arizona. He also served as chairman of Arizona's regional emergency medical system.

Surgeon General. President George W. Bush selected Carmona as the seventeenth surgeon general of the United States in 2002, citing the candidate's rich background of experience—particularly in the fields of law enforcement and emergency management, issues that preoccupied the nation following the terrorist attacks of 11 September 2001. In 2006 Carmona issued a landmark report on secondhand smoke and its health effects that dealt with the matter frankly, citing many studies that showed the risks posed by exposure and recommending that indoor smoking bans be enacted in all public places. The danger of so-called passive smoking was known before the report, but Carmona raised the profile of the issue, leading many states and municipalities to enact strict public-smoking bans.

Criticism. After his tenure as surgeon general ended in 2006, Carmona went public with a series of accusations against the Bush administration. In 2007 he joined former surgeon generals testifying before Congress on problems within the office, particularly the issue of political interference. Carmona claimed that he was muzzled by administration officials on many topics, especially those that touched on controversial political issues such as climate change, sex education, and stem-cell research. Even more damning were charges that he had been pressured to water down the findings of his 2006 report on secondhand smoke in the interest of protecting the tobacco industry. "There were many days," he said, "when science gave way to politics."

Sources:

Amy S. Clark, "Ex-Surgeon General: Bush Muzzled Me," *cbsnews.com* (10 July 2007);

Jacquielynn Floyd, "Keep the Smoke to Yourself," *Dallas Morning News,* 30 June 2006;

United States Department of Health and Human Services, "Biography of Vice-Admiral Richard H. Carmona, M.D., M.P.H., F.A.C.S.," *hhs.gov* (10 November 2003).

SANJAY GUPTA

1969–

NEUROSURGEON, MEDIA PERSONALITY

Early Life. Sanjay Gupta was born on 23 October 1969 in a suburb of Detroit. His parents, Subhash and Damyanti Gupta, had immigrated to the United States in the 1960s to work for Ford. He received his M.D. from the University of Michigan in 1993 and specialized in neurosurgery, with an emphasis on treatments for brain and spinal trauma. He was named a White House fellow in 1997, serving as an adviser to First Lady Hillary Clinton on health-care issues. In 2001 he joined the neurosurgery department at Atlanta's Emory University Hospital.

Television Personality. Gupta's proximity to Cable News Network (CNN) headquarters in Atlanta allowed him to both spend time on his medical career and serve as an on-air medical expert. He quickly became a popular figure on news broadcasts. His reporting on the anthrax scare following the 11 September 2001 attacks and his embedded reporting with a naval medical unit in Kuwait during Operation Iraqi Freedom made him a household name. Gupta remained both reporter and doctor, and while embedded with his unit he performed brain surgery in the field five times. His *House Call with Dr. Sanjay Gupta,* a CNN program devoted to medical issues in the news, debuted in 2004. In 2006 he reported from New Orleans on patients left behind at Charity Hospital in the wake of Hurricane Katrina, an effort that earned him a 2006 News & Documentary Emmy Award for Outstanding Feature Story.

Surgeon General Candidate. During the 2008 presidential campaign, Gupta reported often as an expert on one of the season's hottest political topics: health-care reform. In early 2009 president-elect Barack Obama approached Gupta as a potential candidate for surgeon general—the official serves as a spokesperson for the administration's stance on medical issues. It seemed a perfect fit for the medical media star, and many speculated that the move signaled the Obama administration's willingness to make health care a key issue by selecting such a high-profile candidate. Citing an interest in retaining normalcy in his family life however, and surgical career, Gupta turned down the post.

Sources:

"Anchors & Reporters: Sanjay Gupta," *cnn.com;*

Kate Barrett, "Dr. Gupta Withdraws Name for Surgeon General," *abcnews.com* (5 March 2009);

Holly Crenshaw, "Being Dr. Gupta," *Emory Magazine,* 85 (Autumn 2009): 22–25.

FRANK MINYARD

1930–

CORONER, OBSTETRICIAN

Roots. Born and raised in New Orleans, Frank Minyard received his M.D. from the Louisiana State University School of Medicine in 1955. A specialist in obstetrics and gynecology, he taught at Tulane University and LSU. He was active in the U.S. Naval Reserve and served as drug liaison to Admiral Elmo Zumwalt in the early 1970s, retiring at the rank of captain. In addition to his medical practice, Minyard, an accomplished trumpet player, established a foundation called Jazz Roots, which enlists musicians to take part in raising money for local charities.

Coroner during Katrina. Minyard was elected coroner of New Orleans parish in 1974. He received national attention in the wake of Hurricane Katrina, when his office was tasked with handling the large number of bodies left behind after the storm and subsequent flooding ravaged the city. Unable to reach his office during the worst of the flooding, Minyard tried to swim there and found himself stranded for several days before being rescued. The greatest challenge was identifying more than one thousand bodies, a large task for so small an office.

Sources:

Shaila Dewan, "For Trumpet-Playing Coroner, Hurricane Provides Swan Song," *New York Times,* 17 October 2005;

"Frank Minyard, M.D., Coroner," *neworleanscoroner.org.*

PEOPLE IN THE NEWS

Vice Admiral **Regina M. Benjamin** became the eighteenth surgeon general of the United States on 3 November 2009.

President **George W. Bush** signed the Medicare Prescription Drug Improvement and Modernization Act into law on 8 December 2003. The bill included the introduction of a new entitlement under Medicare for prescription drugs through subsidies and tax incentives.

On 13 March 2003 **Johnny Chen,** a Chinese American businessman, died in Hong Kong after exhibiting pneumonia-like symptoms. Chen, who had traveled from Shanghai, China, to Hanoi, Vietnam, before being evacuated to Hong Kong, was diagnosed with severe acute respiratory syndrome (SARS).

On 2 May 2000 **Steven Colvin** and **Eugene Grossi,** New York University Medical Center cardiac surgeons, announced the first successful minimally invasive heart-valve surgery performed using a robotic surgical aid.

In May 2009 **Linda Fleming,** a sixty-six-year-old woman dying of pancreatic cancer, became the first legal assisted suicide carried out in Washington State after the "Death with Dignity" law took effect in March.

Microbiologist **Bruce Edwards Ivins** committed suicide on 29 July 2008. The former army biodefense researcher had been a lead suspect in the 2001 anthrax attacks that killed five people.

In January 2008 **John M. Lasala,** medical director of the Cardiac Catheterization Laboratory at Barnes-Jewish Hospital at Washington University in St. Louis, announced the successful use of a new technique for implanting artificial heart valves. The procedure, which was minimally invasive, offered the possibility of valve replacement for patients too frail to undergo open-heart surgery.

Cardiologist **Conrad Murray** became the focus of police attention following the death of singer Michael Jackson on 25 June 2009; allegations were raised that Murray improperly prescribed the anesthetic drug propofol, delayed contacting emergency medical personnel when Jackson was discovered in distress, and incorrectly administered CPR.

In October 2009 First Lady **Michelle Obama** gave a speech at the Department of Health and Human Services highlighting her campaign to fight the childhood-obesity epidemic through the promotion of healthy eating habits, calling the issue "a major public health threat."

David Drew Pinsky, an internist better known as "Dr. Drew," parlayed a popular radio program into a television series and hundreds of guest appearances and in 2008 began starring in the reality series *Celebrity Rehab with Dr. Drew* on the VH1 cable network.

A New Orleans grand jury in July 2007 refused to indict medical doctor and professor **Anna M. Pou,** who on 1 September 2005 had administered lethal doses of drugs to critically ill patients left to die in a sweltering hospital without electricity after Hurricane Katrina.

In February 2007 billionaire **T. Denny Sanford** gave a $400 million gift to the Sioux Valley Hospitals and Health System in South Dakota, the largest such donation to a hospital in the United States.

Maria Siemienow led a surgical team at the Cleveland Clinic in December 2008 that performed the first partial-face transplant in U.S. history, the fourth worldwide.

In May 2001 **David A. Snowdon,** lead researcher for the "Nun Study," which evaluated the effects of aging on a group of nuns in Michigan, released a report showing that subjects who had written autobiographical essays low in idea density and grammatical complexity in their late teens and early twenties were 80 percent more likely to develop Alzheimer's disease later in life.

Researchers at the J. Craig Venter Institute published the first genome sequence of an individual person in September 2007. **Dr. J. Craig Venter** donated his own genetic material for sequencing.

In March 2002 **Andrea Yates** was found guilty of murder for drowning her five children (20 June 2001) in a case that spotlighted the issue of postpartum depression; a 2006 retrial reversed the decision, declaring her not guilty by reason of insanity, and she was transferred from prison to a state mental hospital.

AWARDS

NOBEL PRIZE WINNERS IN PHYSIOLOGY OR MEDICINE

2000

Eric R. Kandel, Paul Greengard, and Arvid Carlsson (Sweden), "for their discoveries concerning 'signal transduction in the nervous system.'"

2001

No American Winner

2002

Sydney Brenner, H. Robert Horvitz, and John E. Sulston (Great Britain), "for their discoveries concerning 'genetic regulation of organ development and programmed cell death.'"

2003

Paul C. Lauterbur and Peter Mansfield (Great Britain), "for their discoveries concerning magnetic resonance imaging."

2004

Richard Axel and Linda B. Buck, "for their discoveries of odorant receptors and the organization of the olfactory system."

2005

No American Winner

2006

Andrew Z. Fire and Craig C. Mello, "for their discovery of RNA interference-gene silencing by double-stranded RNA."

2007

Mario R. Capecchi, Martin J. Evans (Great Britain), and Oliver Smithies, "for their discovery of principles for introducing specific gene modifications in mice by the use of embryonic stem cells."

2008

No American Winner

2009

Elizabeth H. Blackburn, Carol W. Greider, and Jack W. Szostak, "for the discovery of how chromosomes are protected by telomeres and the enzyme telomerase."

ALBERT LASKER AWARDS

The Albert Lasker Awards are given in honor of medical research or public service of a pioneering nature.

Albert Lasker Basic Medical Research Award

Honors researchers whose work has provided significant advancement toward eliminating the causes of death and disability.

2000

Aaron Ciechanover (Israel), Avram Hershko (Israel), and Alexander Varshavsky, "for the discovery and the recognition of the significance of the ubiquitin system of regulated protein degradation, a fundamental process that influences vital cellular events, including the cell cycle, malignant transformation, and responses to inflammation and immunity."

2001

Mario Capecchi, Martin Evans (Great Britain), and Oliver Smithies, "for the development of a powerful technology for manipulating the mouse genome with exquisite precision which allows the reaction of animal models of human disease."

2002

James Rothman and Randy Schekman, "for discoveries revealing the universal machinery that orchestrates the budding and fusion of membrane vesicles—a process essential to organelle formation, nutrient uptake, and secretion of hormones and neurotransmitters."

2003

Robert Roeder, "for pioneering studies on eukaryotic RNA polymerases and the general transcriptional machinery, which opened gene expression in animal cells to biochemical analysis."

2004

Pierre Chambon (France), Ronald Evans, and Elwood Jensen, "for the discovery of the superfamily of nuclear hormone receptors and elucidation of a unifying mechanism that regulates embryonic development and diverse metabolic pathways."

2005

Ernest McCulloch (Canada) and James Till (Canada), "for ingenious experiments that first identified a stem cell—the blood forming stem cell—which set the stage for all current research on adult and embryonic stem cells."

2006

Elizabeth Blackburn, Carol W. Greider, and Jack W. Szostak, "for the prediction and discovery of telomerase, a remarkable RNA-containing enzyme that synthesizes the ends of chromosomes, protecting them and maintaining the integrity of the genome."

2007

Ralph Steinman, "for the discovery of dendritic cells—the preeminent component of the immune system that initiates and regulates the body's response to foreign antigens."

2008

Victor Ambros, David Baulcombe (Great Britain), and Gary Ruvkun, "for discoveries that revealed an unanticipated world of tiny RNAs that regulate gene function in plants and animals."

2009

John Gurdon (Great Britain) and Shinya Yamanaka (Japan), "for discoveries concerning nuclear reprogramming, the process that instructs specialized adult cells to form early stem cells—creating the potential to become any type of mature cell for experimental or therapeutic purposes."

Lasker-DeBakey Clinical Medical Research Award

Honors researchers whose work has significantly improved clinical treatment.

2000

Harvey Alter and Michael Houghton, "for pioneering work leading to the discovery of the virus that causes hepatitis C and the development of screening methods that reduced the risk of blood-transfusion associated hepatitis in the U.S. from 30 percent in 1970 to virtually zero in 2000."

2001

Robert Edwards (Great Britain), "for the development of in vitro fertilization, a technological advance that has revolutionized the treatment of human infertility."

2002

Willem Kolff and Belding Scribner, "for the development of renal hemodialysis, which changed kidney failure from a fatal to a treatable disease, prolonging the useful lives of millions of patients."

2003

Marc Feldmann (Great Britain) and Ravinder Maini (Great Britain), "for discovery of anti-TNF therapy as an effective treatment for rheumatoid arthritis and other autoimmune diseases."

2004

Charles Kelman, "for revolutionizing the surgical removal of cataracts, turning a 10-day hospital stay into an outpatient procedure and dramatically reducing complications."

2005

Alec Jeffreys (Great Britain) and Edwin Southern (Great Britain), "for development of two powerful technologies—Southern hybridization and DNA fingerprinting—that together revolutionized human genetics and forensic diagnosis."

2006

Aaron Beck, "for the development of cognitive therapy, which has transformed the understanding and treatment of many psychiatric conditions, including depression, generalized anxiety, suicidal behavior, panic attacks and eating disorders."

2007

Alain Carpentier (France) and Albert Starr, "for the development of prosthetic mitral and aortic valves, which have prolonged and enhanced the lives of millions of people with heart disease."

2008

Akira Endo, "for the discovery of statins—drugs with remarkable LDL-cholesterol-lowering properties that have revolutionized the prevention and treatment of coronary heart disease."

2009

Brian Druker, Nicholas Lydon, and Charles Sawyers, "for the development of molecularly-targeted treatments for chronic myeloid leukemia, converting a fatal cancer into a manageable chronic condition."

Lasker-Koshland Special Achievement Award in Medical Science

Honors distinguished careers in medical research and recognizes major research breakthroughs.

2000

Sydney Brenner, "for 50 years of brilliant creativity in biomedical science—exemplified by his legendary work on the genetic code, his daring introduction of the round-worm *Caenorhabditis elegans* as a system for tracing the birth and death of every cell in a living animal; his rational voice in the debate on recombinant DNA, and his trenchant wit."

2002

James E. Darnell Jr., "for an exceptional career in biomedical science during which he opened two fields in biology—RNA processing and cytokine signaling—and fostered the development of many creative scientists."

2004

Matthew Meselson, "for a lifetime career that combines penetrating discovery in molecular biology with creative leadership in the public policy of chemical and biological weapons."

2006

Joseph Gall, "for a distinguished 57-year career—as a founder of modern cell biology and the field of chromosome structure and function; bold experimentalist; inventor of in situ hybridization and early champion of women in science."

2008

Stan Falkow, "for a 51-year career as one of the great microbe hunters of all time—he discovered the molecular nature of antibiotic resistance, revolutionized the way we think about how pathogens cause disease, and mentored more than 100 students, many of whom are now distinguished leaders in the fields of microbiology and infectious diseases."

Mary Woodard Lasker Public Service Award

Honors major achievement in the fields of public health and medical research advocacy.

2000

Betty Ford, "for using her leadership and prestige to bring about lasting progress in research, medicine, and health aimed at drug and alcohol addiction"; Harold Freeman, "for enlightening scientists and the public about the relationship between race, poverty and cancer"; David Mahoney, "for visionary leadership in educating the public and the donor community and a deep commitment about the importance of brain research, and for directing funds for support of neuroscience"; John Edward Porter Jr., "for wise and perceptive leadership on behalf of medical research funding strengthening the science enterprise"; and *Science Times of The New York Times*, "for sustained, comprehensive and high-quality coverage about science, disease and human health."

2001

William Foege, "for his courageous leadership in improving worldwide public health, and his prominent role in the eradication of smallpox."

2003

Christopher Reeve, "for perceptive, sustained, and heroic advocacy for medical research in general, and victims of disability in particular."

2005

Nancy Brinker, "for creating one of the world's great foundations [the Susan J. Komen Foundation] devoted to curing breast cancer and for dramatically increasing public awareness about this devastating disease."

2007

Anthony Fauci, "for his role as the principal architect of two major U.S. government programs, one aimed at AIDS and the other at biodefense."

2009

Michael Bloomberg, "for employing sound science in political decision making setting a world standard for the public's health as an impetus for government action; leading the way to reduce the scourge of tobacco use; and advancing public health through enlightened philanthropy."

AMERICAN MEDICAL ASSOCIATION AWARDS

American Medical Association Foundation Award for Health Education

2000: Ronald A. Arky

2006: Alice A. Tolbert Coombs

2007: Dileep Bal

American Medical Association Benjamin Rush Award for Citizenship and Community

2000: Phil H. Berry Jr.

2003: Kermit L. Newcomer

2005: John A. (Tony) Herring

2006: David F. Der

2009: Manus C. Kraff

American Medical Association Joseph B. Goldberger Award in Clinical Nutrition

2000: M. Molly McMahon

2001: Philip M. Farrell

2004: Bruce R. Bistrian

American Medical Association Distinguished Service Award

2000: Edwin Lawrence Kendig

2001: John G. Wiegenstein

2002: David W. Furnas

2003: Frank A. Riddick Jr., F. Douglas Scutchfield

2004: John E. Chapman

2005: Dennis S. O'Leary

2006: William Craig Vanderwagen

2007: Richard Allen, Portland

2008: James F. Arens, Bayfield

American Medical Association Medal of Valor

2003: David A. Tarantino Jr.

2006: David C. Rutstein

American Medical Association Scientific Achievement Award

2001: Francis S. Collins

2002: David Baltimore

American Medical Association Dr. William Beaumont Award in Medicine

2002: Eric J. Topol

2005: Daniel J. Sucato

2006: Boris D. Lushniak

2007: Kristin Melissa Bell

American Medical Association Isaac Hays, M.D., and John Bell, M.D., Award for Leadership in Medical Ethics and Professionalism

2004: Jay A. Jacobson

2005: Donald E. Saunders Jr.

2006: Frederick R. Abrams

2007: Paul Stuart Appelbaum

American Medical Association Medical Executive Meritorious Achievement Award

2006: Evan H. Jenkins, Sandra B. Mortham, Dave L. Tarver

2007: Arthur R. Ellenberger, Scott Hunt

2009: David A. Cook

AMA MEDICAL EXECUTIVE LIFETIME ACHIEVEMENT AWARD

2006: Jerry Slaughter

2007: William T. Applegate, Richard R. King, Robert K. Seehusen

2009: Jacquelyn T. Coleman, Louis J. Goodman, Palmer P. Jones, Concord, David L. Tarver

AMERICAN COLLEGE OF SURGEONS AWARDS

Distinguished Service Award

2000: Murray F. Brennan

2001: David L. Nahrwold

2002: F. William Blaisdell

2003: J. Roland Folse

2004: Richard B. Reiling

2005: Donald D. Trunkey

2006: Patricia J. Numann

2007: David B. Hoyt

2008: Paul E. Collicott

2009: F. Dean Griffen

Surgeons' Award for Service to Safety

2000: Charles C. Wolferth Jr.

2001: C. James Carrico

2002: Charles Aprahamian

2003: Norman M. Rich

2004: Charles E. Lucas

2005: Lenworth M. Jacobs Jr.

2006: David R. Boyd

AMERICAN COLLEGE OF PHYSICIANS AWARDS

John Phillips Memorial Award for Outstanding Work in Clinical Medicine

2000: John A. Benson Jr.

2001: Marvin H. Sleisenger

2002: David H. Solomon

2003: John C. Beck

2004: Halsted R. Holman

2005: John P. Phair

2006: Myron L. Weisfeldt

2007: Lee Goldman

2008: Brian L. Strom

2009: Robert O. Bonow

JAMES D. BRUCE MEMORIAL AWARD FOR DISTINGUISHED CONTRIBUTIONS TO PREVENTIVE MEDICINE

2000: Nanette K. Wenger

2001: Michael D. Iseman

2003: Pascal James Imperato

2004: Margaret E. Grigsby

2005: John Glenn Morris Jr.

2006: Nancy A. Rigotti

2007: Steven A. Schroeder

2008: Lewis M. Drusin

2009: William Schaffner II

ALFRED STENGEL MEMORIAL AWARD FOR OUTSTANDING SERVICE TO THE AMERICAN COLLEGE OF PHYSICIANS

2000: Gerald E. Thomson

2001: James L. Borland Jr.

2002: Robert B. Copeland

2003: William A. Reynolds

2004: Herbert S. Waxman

2005: Jock Murray

2006: Whitney W. Addington

2007: Rowan K. Zetterman

2008: Mary T. Herald

2009: Sara E. Walker

AWARD FOR OUTSTANDING WORK IN SCIENCE AS RELATED TO MEDICINE

2000: Francois M. Abboud

2001: Julian Solway

2002: Seymour Reichlin

2003: Francis S. Collins

2004: Harvey J. Alter

2005: Janet D. Rowley

2006: Peter C. Agre

2007: Ananda S. Prasad

2008: Robert M. Chanock

2009: Elizabeth G. Nabel, Peter C. Nowell

WILLIAM C. MENNINGER MEMORIAL AWARD FOR DISTINGUISHED CONTRIBUTIONS TO THE SCIENCE OF MENTAL HEALTH

2000: Charles B. Nemeroff

2002: Luther D. Robinson

2003: Timothy E. Quill

2004: Abraham L. Halpern

2006: Glenn Treisman

2007: Aaron T. Beck

2008: David R. Rubinow

2009: Dwight L. Evans

DEATHS

Samuel W. Alderson, 90, inventor of crash-test dummies, 11 February 2005.

Mason Andrews, 87, physician, delivered America's first test-tube baby, 13 October 2006.

Hal O. Anger, 85, electrical engineer, pioneer of nuclear medicine, inventor of the gamma-ray camera, 31 October 2005.

Robert C. Atkins, 72, cardiologist, known for diet books that promoted a high-protein diet with no carbohydrates, 17 April 2003.

Giuseppe Attardi, 84, molecular biologist, pioneered studies in human mitochondrial structure and function, 5 April 2008.

Robert Austrian, 90, epidemiologist, developed a pneumococcal vaccine, 25 March 2007.

Julius Axelrod, 92, biochemist, won Nobel Prize for Physiology and Medicine for research on catecholamine neuroreceptors, 29 December 2004.

Breanna Lynn Bartlett-Stewart, baby girl whose stillbirth cause was first successfully resolved by the Kleihauer-Betke test, 6 September 2000.

Charles R. Baxter, 75, surgeon, one of team of Parkland Memorial Hospital doctors who tried to save President John F. Kennedy (1963) after he was shot, 10 March 2005.

Leonard Berg, 79, neurologist, creator of the clinical dementia rating scale, 15 January 2007.

Ernest Beutler, 80, hematologist, made important discoveries in regard to anemia, Gaucher's disease, disorders of iron metabolism, Tay-Sachs Disease, and bone-marrow transplantation techniques, 5 October 2008.

Stanley H. Biber, 82, physician, pioneer in sex-reassignment surgery, 16 January 2006.

Sidney W. Bijou, 100, child psychologist, began use of behavioral therapy in children, 11 June 2009.

Ira Barrie Black, 64, neuroscientist, advocate of stem-cell research, founder of Stem Cell Institute of New Jersey at the Robert Wood Johnson School of Medicine, 10 January 2006.

Edward A. Boyse, 83, physician and researcher, first to use umbilical-cord blood for hematopoietic reconstitution, advanced the study of odors, 14 July 2007.

Edward N. Brandt Jr., 74, physician, public-health official who directed the initial response to the AIDS epidemic, acting surgeon general (1981–1982), 25 August 2007.

J. Robert Cade, 80, nephrologist, invented Gatorade while at the University of Florida, 27 November 2007.

Bradford Cannon, 98, plastic surgeon, advanced techniques of using grafts for burn victims, past president of American Association of Plastic Surgeons, 20 December 2005.

Mary Elizabeth Carnegie, 91, nurse, fought for racial equality within the profession, 20 February 2008.

William T. Close, 84, surgeon, father of actress Glenn Close, helped stem the first (1976) Ebola virus outbreak in Zaire (Congo), 15 January 2009.

Albert V. Crewe, 82, British-born University of Chicago physicist, invented scanning transmission electronic microscope, 18 November 2009.

George Crikelair, 84, plastic surgeon, advocated fire-resistant coating for children's sleepwear, helped draft Flammable Fabrics Act (1972), 24 February 2005.

Michael DeBakey, 99, cardiovascular surgeon, pioneered bypass surgery, 11 July 2008.

Vincent P. Dole, 93, medical researcher, established that methadone could be used to treat heroin addiction, 1 August 2006.

Howard A. Engle, 89, pediatrician, lead plaintiff in lawsuit against tobacco companies, 22 July 2009.

Harold F. Falls, 96, ophthalmologist, worked on ocular manifestations of genetic syndromes, one of the describers of Nettleship-Falls syndrome occurring in ocular albinism, 27 May 2006.

Jerri Nielsen FitzGerald, 57, physician, diagnosed her own breast cancer while in Antarctica (1999) and began self-treatment, 23 June 2009.

Moses Judah Folkman, 74, cancer researcher, best known for work on tumor angiogenesis, 14 January 2008.

Edward D. Freis, 92, showed the relationship between hypertension and stroke and heart attack, winner of the 1971 Lasker Award, 1 February 2005.

William F. Ganong, 83, neuroendocrinologist, discovered that blood pressure and fluid balance are regulated by hormones of the adrenal glands and kidneys, 23 December 2007.

Norman G. Gaylord, 84, chemist, developed permeable contact lens, 18 September 2007.

Lawrence F. Grey, 51, urologist, pioneer in vasectomy reversal, 29 April 2006.

Thomas Stoltz Harvey, 94, pathologist, performed autopsy (1955) on Albert Einstein and studied his brain, 5 April 2007.

Orvan W. Hess, 96, obstetrician, developed fetal heart monitor, 6 September 2002.

Stephen Heywood, 37, architect, subject of film *So Much, So Fast* about amyotrophic lateral sclerosis (ALS, or Lou Gehrig's Disease), 26 November 2006.

Paul Jennings Hill, 49, antiabortion activist, first person executed for murdering a doctor who performed abortions, 3 September 2003.

Maurice Ralph Hilleman, 85, microbiologist, developed eight of the fourteen recommended vaccines (including measles, mumps, hepatitis A, hepatitis B, chicken pox, meningitis, pneumonia, and *Haemophilus influenza* bacteria), 11 April 2005.

Jane Elizabeth Hodgson, 91, obstetrics and gynecology physician, abortion-rights advocate, only American doctor convicted of performing an abortion in a hospital (1970), 23 October 2006.

Charles Snead Houston, 96, physician, alpine climber, studied high-altitude flying in World War II and pulmonary edema, 27 September 2009.

Mark R. Hughes, 44, founder of Herbalife (a global nutrition, weight-loss, and skin-care company), 21 May 2000.

Charles A. Janeway Jr., 60, physician, immunobiologist, leader in study of T lymphocytes, 12 April 2003.

Murray Jarvik, 84, psychopharmacologist, coinventor of the nicotine patch, 8 May 2008.

Arthur Jones, 80, inventor of the Nautilus exercise machine, 28 August 2007.

Lillian K. Keil, 88, decorated World War II and Korean War flight nurse, 30 June 2005.

Lawrence C. Kolb, 95, psychiatrist, leader in community mental-health movement, 20 October 2006.

Willem J. Kolff, 97, Dutch-born physician, invented first artificial kidney dialysis machine, 11 February 2009.

Paul E. Lacy, 81, research scientist, developed islet-cell transplantation for type 1 diabetes, 15 February 2005.

Alan Landers, 68, smoking model (The Winston Man), later an opponent of cigarettes, of lung and throat cancer, 27 February 2009.

John K. Lattimer, 92, urologist, developed cure for renal tuberculosis, 10 May 2007.

Victor A. McKusick, 86, geneticist, architect of the human genome project, 22 July 2008.

Mary Joan Nielubowicz, 79, rear admiral, head of Navy Nurse Corps (1983–1987), 24 March 2008.

Lorenzo Odone, 30, suffered from adrenoleukodystrophy (ALD), portrayed in movie *Lorenzo's Oil* (1992), 30 May 2008.

Humphry Osmond, 86, psychiatrist, pioneer in LSD experiments, 6 February 2004.

James O. Page, 68, fire chief, founder of modern emergency medical response, 4 September 2004.

Malcolm O. Perry, 80, surgeon, performed tracheotomy on mortally injured John F. Kennedy (1963), died 5 December 2009.

Joseph Ransohoff, 85, neurosurgeon, created first neurosurgical ICU, helped define the fields of pediatric neurosurgery and neuroradiology, 30 January 2001.

Christopher Reeve, 52, actor, advocate for stem-cell research (following his paralysis caused by a horseback-riding accident in 1995), 10 October 2004.

Dana Reeve, 45, actor, widow of Christopher Reeve, activist for stem-cell research, 6 March 2006.

Julius B. Richmond, 91, vice admiral of the Public Health Service and surgeon general (1977–1981), first director of Project Head Start, 27 July 2008.

George Rieveschl, 91, chemical engineer, inventor of Benadryl, 27 September 2007.

Barnett Rosenberg, 82, chemist, discovered cisplatin use in treatment of various cancers, 8 August 2009.

Robert Ross, 86, leader of the Muscular Dystrophy Association (MDA) for forty-four years, persuaded Jerry Lewis to undertake yearly telethon to raise money for research, 5 June 2006.

David C. Sabiston Jr., 84, heart surgeon, worked especially in developing revascularization, 26 January 2009.

Jessica Santillan, 17, heart- and lung-transplant patient whose death made headlines when the Duke University medical team failed to check for compatibility prior to surgery, 22 February 2003.

Albert Schatz, 84, codiscoverer of streptomycin (first antibiotic to treat tuberculosis), 17 January 2005.

Charles L. Schepens, 94, ophthalmologist, "father of retinal surgery," leader in the Nazi resistance movement in Belgium during World War II, 28 March 2006.

Theresa Marie "Terri" Schiavo, 41, coma patient whose feeding tube was removed fifteen years after an accident, case ruled on by U.S. Supreme Court, 31 March 2005.

Eric Schopler, 79, psychologist, known for pioneering work in the treatment of autism, 7 July 2006.

Sheldon J. Segal, 83, embryologist and biochemist, inventor of Norplant, 17 October 2009.

Norman E. Shumway, 83, surgeon, performed first U.S. heart transplant (1968), 10 February 2006.

Harold Snyder, 86, pharmaceuticals magnate and pioneer of generic drugs, 18 December 2008.

James LeVoy Sorenson, 86, inventor of the disposable surgical mask and disposable venous catheter, 20 January 2008.

Herbert Spiegel, 95, psychiatrist, developed use of hypnosis in treatment for "Sybil," a patient with multiple personalities and the basis for the movie of the same name, 15 December 2009.

Irving Sunshine, 90, leader in forensic toxicology, 14 June 2006.

H. J. C. "Jeremy" Swan, 82, cardiologist, coinventor of the Swan-Ganz heart catheter, 7 February 2005.

Gladys Tantaquidgeon, 106, Mohegan Indian medicine woman, wrote books on Native American medical practices, 1 November 2005.

Edward D. Thalmann, 59, physician, navy captain, specialist in diving decompression, developed military and recreational dive tables, 24 July 2004.

George Tiller, 67, physician, abortion provider, killed by antiabortion activist Scott Roeder, 31 May 2009.

Robert Tools, 59, first recipient of a self-contained artificial heart, 30 November 2001.

Susan R. Torres, 26, researcher, brain dead from stage IV melanoma but kept alive on life support until able to deliver daughter, Susan Anne Catherine Torres (who died forty days later of heart failure due to infection after intestinal surgery), 3 August 2005.

Florence S. Wald, 91, nurse and hospice pioneer, 8 November 2008.

Roy Lee Walford, 79, gerontologist, dietitian, author, and pioneer in field of caloric restriction, 27 April 2004.

Joel D. Weisman, 66, physician, pioneer in AIDS detection, 16 July 2009.

Thomas Huckle Weller, 93, virologist, awarded Nobel Prize in 1954 for cultivation of the polio virus in nonnervous tissue, 23 August 2008.

John J. Wild, 95, physician, codeveloper of ultrasound use in cancer detection, 18 September 2009.

Earl H. Wood, 97, physiologist, coinventor of the G suit (pressurized suit for pilots), 18 March 2009.

Xiangzhong "Jerry" Yang, 49, biotechnology researcher, created first American cloned animal (a cow called Amy), 5 February 2009.

Paul C. Zamecnik, 96, molecular biologist, codiscovered transfer RNA, 27 October 2009.

Morris Ziff, 91, physician, rheumatoid specialist, isolated the rheumatoid factor, 22 August 2005.

PUBLICATIONS

Thomas Abraham, *Twenty-First Century Plague: The Story of SARS* (Baltimore: Johns Hopkins University Press, 2005).

Anne Davis Basting, *Forget Memory: Creating Better Lives for People with Dementia* (Baltimore: Johns Hopkins University Press, 2009).

Nancy G. Brinker and Joni Rodgers, *Promise Me: How a Sister's Love Launched the Global Movement to End Breast Cancer* (New York: Crown, 2010).

David Clark, *Germs, Genes & Civilization: How Epidemics Shaped Who We Are Today* (Upper Saddle River, N.J.: FT Press, 2010).

Michael J. Collins, *Hot Lights, Cold Steel: Life, Death and Sleepless Nights in a Surgeon's First Years* (New York: St. Martin's Press, 2005).

Thea Cooper and Arthur Ainsberg, *Breakthrough: Elizabeth Hughes, the Discovery of Insulin, and the Making of a Medical Miracle* (New York: St. Martin's Press, 2010).

Norman Doidge, *The Brain That Changes Itself: Stories of Personal Triumph from the Frontiers of Brain Science* (New York: Viking, 2007).

Madeline Drexler, *Emerging Epidemics: The Menace of New Infections* (New York: Penguin, 2009).

Jonathan Engel, *The Epidemic (A Global History of AIDS)* (Washington, D.C.: Smithsonian, 2006).

Thomas Graboys and Peter Zheutlin, *Life in the Balance: A Physician's Memoir of Life, Love, and Loss with Parkinson's Disease and Dementia* (New York: Union Square, 2008).

Sanjay Gupta, *Cheating Death: The Doctors and Medical Miracles That Are Saving Lives against All Odds* (New York: Wellness Central, 2009).

Susan Whitman Helfgot and William Novak, *The Match: Complete Strangers, a Miracle Face Transplant, Two Lives Transformed* (New York: Simon & Schuster, 2010).

Lawrence R. Jacobs and Theda Skocpol, *Health Care Reform and American Politics* (New York: Oxford University Press, 2010).

Linda T. Kohn, Janet M. Corrigan, and Molla S. Donaldson, eds., *To Err Is Human: Building a Safer Health System* (Washington, D.C.: National Academy Press, 2000).

Joseph LeDoux, *Synaptic Self: How Our Brains Become Who We Are* (New York: Viking, 2002).

Charles R. Morris, *The Surgeons: Life and Death in a Top Heart Center* (New York: Norton, 2007).

Siddhartha Mukherjee, *The Emperor of All Maladies: A Biography of Cancer* (New York: Simon & Schuster, 2010).

Adriana Petryna, *When Experiments Travel: Clinical Trials and the Global Search for Human Subjects* (Princeton: Princeton University Press, 2009).

Michael Pollan, *In Defense of Food: An Eater's Manifesto* (New York: Penguin, 2008).

Pollan, *The Omnivore's Dilemma: A Natural History of Four Meals* (New York: Penguin, 2006).

Matt Ridley, *Genome: The Autobiography of a Species in 23 Chapters,* revised edition (New York: MJF Books, 2011).

John Elder Robison, *Look Me in the Eye: My Life with Asperger's* (New York: Crown, 2007).

Jeffrey M. Schwartz and Sharon Begley, *The Mind and the Brain: Neuroplasticity and the Power of Mental Force* (New York: ReganBooks/HarperCollins, 2002).

David Servan-Schreiber, *Anticancer: A New Way of Life* (New York: Viking, 2008).

Randy Shilts, *And the Band Played On: Politics, People and the AIDS Epidemic, 20th Anniversary Edition* (New York: St. Martin's Press, 2007).

David Snowdon, *Aging with Grace: What the Nun Study Teaches Us about Leading Longer, Healthier, and More Meaningful Lives* (New York: Bantam, 2001).

Jill Bolte Taylor, *My Stroke of Insight: A Brain Scientist's Personal Journey* (New York: Viking, 2008).

J. Craig Venter, *A Life Decoded: My Genome, My Life* (New York: Viking, 2007).

Aesthetic Surgery Journal, periodical;

Anesthesia & Analgesia, periodical;

Journal of Allergy and Clinical Immunology, periodical;

Journal of the American Medical Association, periodical;

Lancet, periodical;

New England Journal of Medicine, periodical;

Obstetrics & Gynecology, periodical;

Research in Nursing & Health, periodical.

RELIGION

by KEVIN KYZER

CONTENTS

Sidebars and tables are listed in italics.

2000

29 Mar. The Central Conference of American Rabbis (Reform Judaism) votes to allow rabbis to perform a marriage ritual between people of the same sex.

19 June The Supreme Court rules 6-3 in *Santa Fe Independent School District* v. *Doe* to disallow student-led prayer, such as in opening invocations, at public school-sanctioned sporting events.

28 June The Supreme Court rules 5-4 in *Boy Scouts of America* v. *Dale* that the Boy Scouts of America was not discriminating by choosing to "forbid membership to homosexuals."

28 June The Supreme Court rules 6-3 in *Mitchell* v. *Helms* that a government-funded program can lend computers to parochial schools.

6 Aug. Democratic presidential candidate Al Gore of Tennessee selects Connecticut senator Joseph Lieberman to be his running mate, the first Jewish candidate to run on a major national presidential ticket.

12 Oct. The USS *Cole* is attacked by al Qaeda operatives in the Yemeni port of Aden. Seventeen sailors are killed and thirty-nine injured.

20 Oct. Former president Jimmy Carter announces that he is renouncing his membership in the Southern Baptist Convention (SBC) because of its increasingly conservative shift.

30 Oct. Delegates at the Baptist General Convention of Texas vote to shift more than $5 million in funding away from SBC and into Texas seminaries.

2001

20 Jan. After contentious recounts and court appeals, George W. Bush is inaugurated as the forty-second president of the United States, having been elected largely with the support of the Christian Coalition and evangelical Christians.

26 Jan. *Left Behind: The Movie*, a Christian film about the "rapture" based on a series of books of the same title by Tim LaHaye and Jerry Jenkins, premieres in select theaters.

29 Jan. President Bush creates the White House Office of Faith-Based and Community Initiatives by executive order, committing tax dollars to social programs led by religious and nonprofit organizations.

12 Mar. Five leaders of the extremist antigovernment Greater Ministries International (Tampa, Florida) are convicted of federal conspiracy and fraud for a Ponzi scheme that amassed more than $500 million, starting in 1993, and swindled nearly 18,000 people.

13 Mar. The Hartford Seminary in Connecticut releases the survey Faith Communities in the United States Today, a study of 14,301 congregations, the largest-ever study of congregational activity up to that point; it concludes that most congregations maintain allegiance to their denominations.

11 June The Supreme Court rules 6-3 in *Good News Club, Inc.* v. *Milford Central School* that public schools must allow religious groups access to facilities for the purpose of after-school activities.

9 Aug. President Bush agrees to allow federal funding for limited stem-cell research on previously extracted embryos but maintains a ban on any new extractions.

11 Aug. Mark S. Hanson is elected presiding bishop of the Evangelical Lutheran Church in America (ELCA).

11 Sept.   Nineteen al Qaeda operatives hijack four planes, committing the largest terrorist attack in U.S. history. Two airplanes, one leaving out of Newark and the other from Boston, were redirected and struck the World Trade Center towers, destroying both. A third was redirected to the Pentagon where it crashed, while the fourth, believed to have been en route to Washington, D.C., was brought down by passengers midflight over Shanksville, Pennsylvania.

22 Oct.   The American Religious Identification Survey is released by the Graduate Center of the City University of New York, a phone survey of 50,281 American households between February and June of 2001. The study is a follow-up to the 1990 National Survey of Religious Identification.

14 Nov.   Aid workers Dayna Curry and Heather Mercer (along with two aid workers from Australia and four from Germany) are freed from the Taliban by troops of the Northern Alliance in Afghanistan after one hundred days of captivity; they were charged with having violated Taliban law by promoting Christianity.

2002

June   The United States Conference of Catholic Bishops releases the *Charter for the Protection of Children & Young People*, a "zero tolerance" policy that ends the former policy of rehabilitation and reassignment of clergy accused of sexual abuse of minors. The body also releases a list of *Essential Norms for Diocesan/Eparchial Policies Dealing with Allegations of Sexual Abuse of Minors by Priests or Deacons*.

27 June   The Supreme Court decides 5-4 in *Zelman* v. *Simmons-Harris* that a Cleveland school district is not in violation of the establishment clause by allowing state-subsidized voucher money to go to private schools run by religious organizations.

1 Nov.   Rick Warren's best seller *The Purpose Driven Life* is published; more than 30 million copies will be sold.

5 Nov.   Spurred by religious conservatives, Republicans gain control of Congress by winning a majority in the Senate and expanding their majority in the House.

13 Dec.   Bernard Francis Law resigns as archbishop of the Catholic Diocese of Boston.

2003

18 Mar.   Dan Brown's novel *The Da Vinci Code* is released in hardback. The book is controversial because it raises questions about the possibility that Jesus had married Mary Magdalene and fathered children.

27 Apr.   After nine seasons on the air, the television series *Touched by an Angel* airs its final episode.

26 June   The Supreme Court rules 6-3 in *Lawrence* v. *Texas* that a ban on sodomy in Texas is unconstitutional.

5 Aug.   The Reverend Gene Robinson, an openly practicing homosexual, is elected bishop of the Episcopal Church in New Hampshire.

23 Aug.   Joseph L. Druce murders defrocked pedophile priest John J. Geoghan, plaintiff in the Boston Catholic Church sex scandal, in his prison cell.

9 Sept.   The Catholic Diocese of Boston settles with victims in the Geoghan sexual-abuse case for $85 million.

26 Sept.   The television series *Joan of Arcadia* premieres on CBS and runs for two seasons.

5 Nov.   President Bush signs a ban on partial-birth abortions, after Congress attempted to pass a similar measure twice under President Bill Clinton, who vetoed it both times.

12 Nov.   An ethics panel removes Chief Justice Roy Moore from office for refusing to remove a monument to the Ten Commandments from Alabama's judicial building after it was ruled to be a violation of the establishment clause of the constitution.

2004

21 Jan.   *Saved!* debuts at the Sundance Film Festival.

Feb.   Bishop Roger Mahoney of the Orange County Diocese in Los Angeles, California, issues the *Report to the People of God: Clergy Sexual Abuse in the Archdiocese of Los Angeles, 1930–2003*. He also begins the *Safeguard the Children* program.

25 Feb.   Mel Gibson's *The Passion of the Christ* is released in theaters.

14 July   The U.S. Senate defeats 50-48 a proposed ban on gay marriage.

Oct.   Joel Osteen's book *Your Best Life Now* is released, and his ministry, Lakewood Church, moves to the Compaq Center, former arena for the NBA's Houston Rockets.

5 Nov.   Phyllis B. Anderson is elected president of Pacific Lutheran Theological Seminary, the first woman to head a Lutheran seminary in the United States.

26 Dec.   A magnitude-nine earthquake erupts in the Indian Ocean, causing a tsunami that eventually kills more than 200,000 in Sri Lanka, India, Indonesia, and Thailand. Relief efforts from people of all faiths around the world pour into the devastated region.

31 Dec.   William Tyndale College, a private Christian school in Michigan, announces it will have to close its doors, citing lack of enrollment.

2005

3 Jan.   The Catholic Diocese of Orange County, California, settles with eighty-seven plaintiffs in a church sexual-abuse case for $100 million.

7 Feb.   *Time* publishes its list of the "25 Most Influential Evangelicals."

11 Feb.   Robert D. Fay, Kelvin Iguabita, Bernard Lane, and Robert Ward are defrocked by the Vatican for their individual involvement in sexual-abuse scandals.

18 Mar.   After years of living in a persistent vegetative state, doctors remove Terri Schiavo's feeding tube after Circuit Judge George Greer rules against last-minute efforts by Florida congressional officials to keep her on life support contrary to the wishes of Schiavo's husband, Michael. The case garnered media attention nationwide and divided people from all across the religious spectrum over the right to life.

2 Apr.   Pope John Paul II dies.

19 Apr.   Cardinal Joseph Ratzinger is elected Pope, taking the name Benedict XVI.

22 June   Billy Graham announces that his three-day event (24–26 June) at Flushing Meadows Corona Park will be his final crusade in America.

27 June   In two similar cases, *McCreary County* v. *ACLU of Kentucky* and *Van Orden* v. *Perry,* the Supreme Court issues seemingly opposing decisions on the display of the Ten Commandments in courthouses.

July	The Antiochian Orthodox Christian Archdiocese of North America leaves the National Council of Churches (NCC) over policies and statements by other NCC denominations regarding homosexuality.
28 July	The Fiqh Council of North America, backed by several other major Muslim organizations, issues a general fatwa against terrorism and extremism.
29 Aug.	Hurricane Katrina, one of the five deadliest hurricanes in U.S. history, strikes the coast of the Gulf of Mexico, causing record destruction in New Orleans, Louisiana. People of all faiths dedicate relief efforts to the region.
17 Sept.	Rick Warren launches his "P.E.A.C.E. Plan," an international missionary effort.
9 Dec.	The movie *The Chronicles of Narnia: The Lion, The Witch, and the Wardrobe*, based on the Christian allegory by C. S. Lewis, is released in theaters.

2006

8 Feb.	Eighty-six leaders of Evangelical churches sign a letter—"Climate Change: An Evangelical Call for Action"—aimed at the National Association of Evangelicals and Congress to address issues of climate change. The letter is part of the larger "Evangelical Climate Initiative."
12 Mar.	The television series *Big Love* premieres on Home Box Office (HBO) and runs for five seasons, winning a Golden Globe, Writer's Guild Award, and BMI Film & Television Award.
6 Apr.	The National Geographic Society announces the translation and release of an ancient Coptic manuscript found in the 1970s that features the "Gospel of Judas." Written by a Gnostic sect of Christianity in the second or third century, the Gospel provides an alternate view of Jesus' crucifixion, in which Christ asks Judas to betray him and gives him prominence among apostles.
29 Apr.	Delegates from the Pacific Southwest region of American Baptist Churches (ABC), USA, vote to withdraw from the ABC, mostly due to differences over the issue of homosexuality.
19 May	The film *The Da Vinci Code*, based on Dan Brown's best-selling novel, is released in theaters.
Oct.	Joel Osteen's *Become a Better You* is published.
2 Nov.	Ted Haggard is accused by prostitute Mike Jones of homosexual relations and drug use. Haggard resigns as head of the National Association of Evangelicals and is subsequently fired from New Life Church in Colorado Springs.
4 Nov.	Katharine Jefferts Schori is invested as presiding bishop of the Episcopal Church.
7 Nov.	Keith Maurice Ellison wins Minnesota's fifth district House seat, becoming the first Muslim (having converted from Catholicism) to serve in Congress in the United States.
6 Dec.	The Committee on Jewish Law and Standards (Conservative Judaism) approves the responsum "Homosexuality, Human Dignity, and Halakha," making it officially legal for a Jewish rabbi to officiate a marriage between same-sex partners.

2007

10 Mar. The Board of Directors of the National Association of Evangelicals affirms its support for Vice President Richard Cizik, responding to a letter signed by Christian conservatives such as James Dobson, Gary Bauer, and Tony Perkins that criticized Cizik's position of "creation care," which supports the view that humans are contributing to global warming.

13 Mar. Toba Spitzer is elected president of the Reconstructionist Rabbinical Assembly; she is the first openly gay person to head a rabbinical organization.

18 Apr. The Supreme Court rules 5-4 in *Gonzales* v. *Carhart* that the Partial-Birth Abortion Ban Act (2003) is constitutional.

31 May The Billy Graham Library is dedicated in Charlotte, North Carolina.

27 July The Mormon Church posts on its website the contents of a new pamphlet, "God Loveth His Children," that addresses the condition of homosexuality. While it maintains the distinction between same-sex attraction and acts, it softens the language used to describe homosexual tendencies, emphasizing a renewed commitment to the church and God.

24 Sept. Four streets in Brooklyn, New York, are plastered with anti-Semitic fliers and graffiti.

25 Sept. Warren Jeffs, leader of the Fundamentalist Church of Jesus Christ of Latter-Day Saints in Salt Lake City, is found guilty on two counts of being an accomplice to rape. He is subsequently sentenced to two consecutive sentences of five years to life in prison.

13 Oct. The declaration "A Common Word between Us and You" is issued from 138 clerics of the Muslim faith in the United States, making a call for open dialogue and mutual understanding between leaders of Islam and Christianity.

23 Nov. Richard Roberts resigns as chancellor of Oral Roberts University over allegations of misuse of university funds.

2008

8 Feb. Thomas S. Monson is named president of the Church of Jesus Christ of Latter-Day Saints, replacing Gordon B. Hinckley, who had died the week before.

25 Feb. The Pew Forum on Religion & Public Life releases the results of its U.S. Religious Landscape Survey, compiled from interviews with more than 35,000 adults from 8 May to 13 August.

14 Mar. In response to media scrutiny of controversial Reverend Jeremiah Wright, then-presidential candidate Barack Obama removes him from his campaign staff and denounces his incendiary statements, while still affirming his support of Wright, who had ministered to Obama at Chicago's Trinity United Church of Christ.

3 Apr. Texas authorities enter the Yearning for Zion Ranch, part of the Fundamentalist Church of Jesus Christ of Latter-Day Saints, in response to an anonymous phone call from a sixteen-year-old girl claiming to have been sexually abused by a fifty-year-old man; officials subsequently remove all 416 children, citing a dangerous environment.

14–19 Apr. Pope Benedict XVI visits the United States, making stops in Washington, D.C., and New York City for open-air masses at Nationals Park and Yankee Stadium, respectively.

15 May In response to a lengthy lawsuit brought forth by gay-marriage advocates against the state, the California Supreme Court rules Proposition 22 (2000), which defines marriage as only being between a man and a woman, unconstitutional.

16 May	*The Chronicles of Narnia: Prince Caspian* is released in theaters.
22 May	Arizona senator John McCain repudiates Reverend John Hagee's endorsement of McCain in the presidential race, in response to the release of a sermon that attributes the Holocaust to God's plan.
29 July	Yale hosts the conference "Loving God and Neighbor in Word and Deed," the first of the "Common Word" meetings aimed at improving dialogue between Muslims and Christians.
16 Aug.	Rick Warren hosts the "Civil Forum on the Presidency" at his Saddleback Church, where presidential candidates Barack Obama and John McCain speak on social issues and faith.
1 Oct.	Bill Maher's documentary *Religulous* (a comedic mocking of organized religion) is released in theaters.
12–15 Oct.	The second "Common Word" conference for Muslim-Christian dialogue is held at Cambridge University, featuring seventeen Muslim and nineteen Christian theologians.
4 Nov.	Voters in California ratify Proposition 8, which repeals California's decision to legalize same-sex marriage. The Mormon Church is credited with the majority of the financial support for Proposition 8 and its subsequent passage.
13 Nov.	Doug Lockhart is appointed president and CEO of International Bible Society and Send the Light (IBS-STL) North America, and Scott Bolinder is appointed president of IBS-STL Global.
17 Nov.	Due to the economic recession, the Christian ministry Focus on the Family announces that it will have to lay off 149 people and cut an additional 53 vacant positions.

2009

20 Jan.	Rick Warren, an opponent of gay marriage, delivers the invocation at President Obama's inauguration, upsetting many gay-rights activists. One week prior to the inauguration, Obama had asked openly homosexual Episcopal bishop Gene Robinson to deliver the invocation at an inaugural celebration in front of the Lincoln Memorial, a move seen as a concession to gay-rights groups.
5 Feb.	At the National Prayer Breakfast, President Obama announces he will continue the White House Office of Faith-Based Initiatives instituted by President Bush, broadening its scope and renaming it the White House Office of Faith-Based and Neighborhood Partnerships.
25 Feb.	The Supreme Court rules unanimously in *Pleasant Grove City* v. *Summum* that a city in Utah did not restrict the free speech of a religious sect (Summum) when they were denied placement of a new monument next to a monument of the Ten Commandments in a public park.
9 Mar.	President Obama lifts the ban on federal funding of stem-cell research.
9 Mar.	Trinity College in Hartford, Connecticut, releases the American Religious Identification Survey 2008, a study of 54,461 Americans carried out between February and November of 2008.
24 June	The Anglican Church of North America, a new province of the Anglican Communion led by conservatives who want to break from the Episcopal Church, installs Reverend Robert Duncan as its first archbishop.

14–15 July The 76th General Convention of the Episcopal Church votes to allow ordination and marriage of homosexuals, further straining relations with its parent body, the Global Anglican Communion.

7 Aug. The American Jewish Congress criticizes conservative commentator Rush Limbaugh for comparing President Obama to Adolf Hitler.

21 Aug. The ELCA votes to allow "monogamous" partners in a committed same-sex relationship to be ordained as ministers. It is the largest mainstream Protestant denomination to make such a decision. One result of the decision is the intent of the Lutheran Coalition for Renewal (CORE), conservative Lutherans who are dissatisfied with the ELCA's decisions on homosexuality, to form the North American Lutheran Church.

1 Sept. Biblica, the publishing company that owns the copyright to the New International Version of the Bible, and Zondervan announce that a new translation will debut in 2011, incorporating changes in English-language use, gender-neutral pronouns, and scholarship on biblical history.

7 Oct. Georgetown University hosts the fourth "Common Word" conference that serves as a forum for interfaith dialogue between Christians and Muslims.

5 Nov. U.S. Army major Nidal Malik Hasan kills thirteen people and injures thirty-one in a shooting spree at Fort Hood, Texas.

OVERVIEW

Nation at War. One of America's most prevalent concerns at the start of the twenty-first century was its relationship with Islam. The implications of the terrorist attacks on 11 September 2001 and the subsequent War on Terror caused many people, some for the first time, to ask "What is Islam?" Terms such as "islamist" and "jihad" increased in public discourse, while attention to the Muslim faith entered public consciousness in a profound way. Was the attack representative of Islam or a distortion of it, and did military action in the Middle East mean war on religion? People of all faiths questioned whether the conflicts in Iraq and Afghanistan were "just" wars. Divisions emerged as a grieving nation sought the right course of action.

Politics. The two most pressing issues regarding religion in the public arena involved the use of public money, space, or facilities for religious purposes and the definition of marriage regarding same-sex partners. The Supreme Court redrew the line between church and state while deciding on issues ranging from private-school vouchers to public displays of religious iconography. President George W. Bush challenged church/state divisions with his Faith-Based Initiative, which evoked strong reaction among both supporters and detractors, as it channeled federal dollars into private social programs run by religious organizations. Many school districts debated whether to complement the teaching of evolution with creationism and intelligent design. The marriage issue was addressed on multiple fronts, both legislatively and within religious bodies. Conservative Christians largely insisted on strict prohibitions, while more moderate and liberal Christians and Jews took steps toward inclusion of homosexuals in leadership and marriage. By the end of the decade these changes took a serious toll, as several church bodies, Episcopalian and Lutheran in particular, experienced fracturing within their ranks. Religious identity remained a critical element in electoral politics. President Bush made frequent mention of his Christian faith and found wide support among evangelicals. Presidential candidate Barack Obama, also a Christian, was beset by rumors that he was secretly a Muslim. Despite evidence to the contrary, many Americans continued to believe the false claim well into his presidency.

Spiritual. America remained a society of believers, but the nature of that belief proved flexible. After a brief increase in attendance at religious services following 11 September, the trend that began during the 1990s in which people claimed they were less "religious" and more "spiritual" continued. Believers who identified themselves as "unaffiliated" increased. Many people left the faith of their upbringing for a different denomination or religion; others joined "megachurches." As old guard Protestant evangelists passed away or retired, charismatic leaders emerged to take their place, part of a nationwide increase in multicampus churches with multiple weekly services and whose congregations numbered in the thousands.

Scandal. As people worldwide mourned the death of Pope John Paul II and welcomed his successor, Pope Benedict XVI, Catholics in the United States wrestled with the fallout from a decades-long sexual-abuse scandal. Increased media coverage of lawsuits against several dioceses inspired more victims to reveal the abuse they had suffered in childhood. Landmark cases in Boston, Los Angeles, and other cities brought record settlements for the victims, as well as fundamental changes within the Catholic hierarchy. Other denominations dealt with scandals as well. Ted Haggard, pastor of New Life Church in Colorado, was discovered engaging in a homosexual relationship, costing him his position with both New Life Church and the National Association of Evangelicals. Richard Roberts, son of evangelist Oral Roberts, was forced to resign as president of Oral Roberts University under suspicion of misuse of funds. Warren Jeffs, president of the Fundamentalist Church of Jesus Christ of Latter-Day Saints, was convicted on two counts of being an accomplice to rape for his role in arranging marriages of men to underage girls.

Growth. Change and growth were some of the challenges facing many religious groups, some of which responded with confidence and a stronger voice. Traditional approaches waned, while newer viewpoints took hold in established religious orders. Some groups fractured, while others grew stronger in conviction as well as numbers. Even atheists and agnostics, often grouped as "nonbelievers," found recognition through the media, signaled by the rise of the "New Atheist." Contentious debate strained relations inside religions and denominations, but overall people found ways to work with each other through the diverse challenges that arose at the outset of the new century.

TOPICS IN THE NEWS

CATHOLIC CHURCH SEX-ABUSE SCANDAL

Brewing Turmoil. Allegations of sexual misconduct by priests had long been discussed within Catholic dioceses in the twentieth century, and extensive official legal proceedings had been conducted, most notably with the Gilbert Gauthe, James Porter, and Rudy Kos cases in the 1980s and 1990s. However, landmark achievements in the public disclosure of official records of sexual misconduct and substantial punitive awards for plaintiffs did not arrive until the first decade of the twenty-first century. Earlier court victories prompted victims to reveal their exploitation by priests, exposing several networks of unresponsive Catholic leadership and spurring proactive measures by the church to address the problem of sexual abuse of minors by clergy.

Boston. The lawsuit brought against John Geoghan in Massachusetts was similar in nature to the prior three high-profile cases, but the scale of alleged abuse was unprecedented. Experts claimed that Geoghan had abused almost eight hundred children over a thirty-three-year period. Two hundred victims filed claims. He was officially counseled several times and reassigned by the diocese of Boston to eight different parishes during his career, evidence of the practice of rehabilitation and reassignment that the church had previously used as its solution for sexual misconduct. Mitchell Garabedian, plaintiffs' attorney for many victims of sexual abuse, successfully reached settlements with the church for $10 million in damages. By 2001 he had amassed a total of eighty-six plaintiffs for a large-scale suit against Geoghan and the archdiocese. Wilson Rogers Jr. had been general counsel for the diocese since 1984 and personal counsel to Cardinal Bernard Law, archbishop of Boston from 1984 to 2002; he refused to settle with the "Geoghan 86." Rogers had succeeded in having the case files from settlements with Garabedian's previous clients sealed permanently. The sealing of such documents was a regular practice. The Geoghan case became a turning point in the handling of sexual misconduct following the *Boston Globe*'s successful lawsuit to obtain documents for its series of stories on clergy misconduct in Boston that won its staff a Pulitzer Prize.

Settlement. Evidence from the case files revealed the decisions by church officials—such as Cardinal Bernard Francis Law—to repeatedly send Geoghan for rehabilitation and then reassign him to a new parish. Law's defense was that in every instance he was assured by "psychiatric or medical assessments" that Geoghan was prepared for reassignment. The diocese quickly settled with all eighty-six plaintiffs for between $15 and $30 million (differing for each individual as they participated in an arbitration process to determine the nature and severity of their individual abuse). The diocese ultimately paid settlements in excess of $120 million to Geoghan victims. Since insurance companies were unwilling to pay, the diocese covered the cost by selling more than sixty-five acres of property to Boston College for $172 million. Geoghan was convicted and sentenced to nine years in prison, but was murdered early in his sentence by a fellow inmate.

Law Resigns. When the church's finance council turned down the settlement agreement, Garabedian deposed Law on 8 May 2002. Law's story changed under oath; he claimed that he had never handled Geoghan's reassignments personally, but instead left the matter to subordinates. The two sides came to a second settlement of $10 million, but damage to the public confidence was perhaps more expensive. Having seen evidence of misconduct and poor handling of the case, the public was indignant at the refusal of the diocese to pay the original settlement amount. Facing public scorn, as well as implication in a report from a comprehensive investigation by Massachusetts attorney general Thomas Reilly, Law resigned as archbishop on 13 December 2002 and fled to Rome for refuge. He was replaced by Archbishop Sean P. O'Malley, who restored public confidence in the church. In the wake of the Geoghan case, 552 people brought suit against the Archdiocese of Boston for sexual abuse. On 9 September 2003 the diocese settled with all victims for $85 million, the largest settlement to date. The success of the settlement was attributed to O'Malley, whom people on both sides regarded as far more trustworthy and honest than Law.

Changes. The impact of the Geoghan case reached beyond the plaintiffs' victory and resulted in substantive change in both Catholic practice and public opinion. It built upon the prior successes of the Gauthe, Porter, and Kos cases but was groundbreaking because sealed files had been opened for public scrutiny. The augmentation of pub-

Former priest John Geoghan is taken into custody by a court officer after being convicted of child sexual abuse in Cambridge, Massachusetts, on 18 January 2002. Geoghan was murdered in prison on 22 February 2003 (AP Photo/Pool, Kevin Wisniewski).

lic discourse resulted in greater numbers of victims speaking out. The public could see documented evidence of the "rehabilitate and reassign" policy that was now perceived as incompetent at best, conspiratorial at worst. Such practices, formerly regarded by the church as temporary solutions, were now regarded as tragically exacerbating.

Nationwide Impact. Reporters began researching cases that had formerly been quietly settled, and other dioceses soon faced legal battles. The press in Los Angeles investigated and reported on a settlement from the late 1990s, focusing on Father Oliver O'Grady, who had abused at least twenty children between 1971 and 1993. A surge of litigation ensued in 2003, aided by California's one-year suspension of the statute of limitations on child-sexual-abuse claims. Eight hundred and fifty civil claims were brought forth, including 560 in Los Angeles. The state also did not place a cap on the amount of damages that could be awarded, a measure that existed in Boston. The Diocese of Orange County settled with eighty-seven victims in January 2005 for $100 million, a single-suit record. In December 2006 the archdiocese settled forty-six more claims for $60 million. All remaining claims were finally settled in July 2007 for $660 million.

Churchwide Documents. Urged to change policy and win back public trust, the United States Conference of Catholic Bishops (USCCB) made ending sexual abuse a top priority in their Dallas meeting in June 2002. They released the *Charter for the Protection of Children & Young People:* a "zero tolerance" policy that ended the former policy of rehabilitation and reassignment. They also created a list of *Essential Norms for Diocesan/Eparchial Policies Dealing with Allegations of Sexual Abuse of Minors by Priests or Deacons.* These efforts established lay review boards for every diocese to address future claims and to make recommendations to the bishop. Whereas past church leaders encouraged victims to forgive their church abusers and move on, now victims' concerns were heard and addressed. Archbishop Roger Mahoney and the USCCB sought to initiate reforms nationwide. The *Report to the People of God: Clergy Sexual Abuse in the Archdiocese of Los Angeles, 1930–2003* was issued by Mahoney in February 2004 and included an apology on behalf of the archdiocese. He also initiated a *Safeguard the Children* program, training more than 26,000 church laity in the prevention and identification of child-sexual abuse.

John Jay Report. A disturbing outcome of the nationwide church sex scandal was the study *The Nature and Scope of Sexual Abuse of Minors by Catholic Priests and Deacons in the United States 1950–2002* performed by the John Jay College of Criminal Justice (referred to as the "John Jay Report"). The study was commissioned by the USCCB National Review Board that was established by *Charter for the Protection of Children & Young People.* It found, "of the 195 dioceses and eparchies that participated in the study, all but seven have reported that allegations of sexual abuse of youths under the age of 18 have been made against at least one priest serving in ecclesiastical ministry in that diocese or eparchy." Approximately 4 percent of priests or deacons serving during the period of the study had allegations of sexual abuse brought against them. It was reported, however, that the percentage of priests alleged to have committed sexual abuse dropped dramatically after the 1980s to a fraction of a percentage by the year 2002. As court cases against offenders became more public and resulted in larger punitive damages, church leadership became more vigilant to prevent and address sexual abuse.

Sources:

"Cash-Strapped Boston Archdiocese Sells Headquarters," *Reuters* (24 May 2007);

Kevin Cullen and Steven Kurkjian, "Church in an $85 Million Accord," *Boston Globe,* 10 September 2003;

David France, *Our Fathers: The Secret Life of the Catholic Church in an Age of Scandal* (New York: Broadway, 2004);

John Jay College of Criminal Justice, *The Nature and Scope of Sexual Abuse of Minors by Catholic Priests and Deacons in the United States 1950–2002* (Washington, D.C.: U.S. Conference of Catholic Bishops, 2004);

Timothy D. Lytton, *Holding Bishops Accountable: How Lawsuits Helped the Catholic Church Confront Clergy Abuse* (Cambridge, Mass.: Harvard University Press, 2008);

Jack Thomas, "Cardinal Law's Attorney, the Low-Profile Wilson Rogers, Faces Some High-Profile Cases," *Boston Globe,* 2 February 2002.

HOMOSEXUALITY AND RELIGIOUS INSTITUTIONS

Divided Church. Following the gains won by the Gay, Lesbian, Bi-Sexual, Transgender, and Queer (GLBTQ) community in the United States in the 1990s, the next decade proved to be equally contentious. Traditional mainstream Christian denominations faced the issue of gay marriage and ordination repeatedly in their national gatherings, sometimes resulting in fractions within their bodies. The more conservative strands maintained their positions regarding homosexuality as incompatible with Christian life, while moderating some of the language used to characterize the lifestyle. No other faiths changed directions on the moral dimensions of sexuality, with the exception of Judaism, which made several alterations in rabbinical law.

New Paths. The Unitarian Universalist Church and United Church of Christ were the two largest Protestant denominations in the United States to allow gay marriage and ordination of homosexual pastors. The Unitarian Universalist Association (UUA) made headlines when two female plaintiffs won a suit against Massachusetts for the right to marry. Hillary and Julie Goodridge were legally married by UUA president William G. Sinkford in May 2004. The United Church of Christ approved the resolution "In the Support of Equal Marriage Rights for All" at its General Synod in June 2005. It guaranteed equal availability to "the rights, protections, and quality of life conferred by the recognition of marriage" and made groundbreaking steps toward inclusion of transgender members as well, welcoming their membership and denouncing violence committed against them.

Lutherans. On 11 August 2001 Mark S. Hanson, having shown concern for homosexuals and the issues they faced in the church, was narrowly elected presiding bishop of the Evangelical Lutheran Church in America (ELCA). In 2003 ELCA produced the booklet *Journey Together Faithfully: The Church and Homosexuality* as a guide to discussion on the issue, the result of a study mandated by the 2001 ELCA Churchwide Assembly on the issue of homosexuality and its impact on the church. Its main conclusion was that a variety of positions exist on the stance regarding homosexuality and that biblical statements ought to be given greater weight; as a result, members should respect the conscience of others when discussing the issue, commit to working together despite differences, and leave matters up to individual pastoral discretion instead of creating overarching policies. On 21 August 2009 the ELCA voted to allow "monogamous" partners in a committed same-sex relationship to be ordained as ministers. The ELCA became the largest mainstream Protestant denomination to make such a decision, leading to a fracture in the body. Missouri Synod Lutherans, the next largest body, voiced its disapproval of the decision. By the end of the decade, dissenting churches began to break away from the ELCA. The North American Lutheran Church was formed as an option for conservative churches that desire to be more "Christ-centered, mission-driven, traditionally grounded and congregationally focused."

Episcopalians. Similar to the ELCA, the Episcopal Church adopted a more progressive position on homosexuality and saw fracturing within its ranks. On 5 August 2003 V. Gene Robinson, an openly practicing homosexual, was elected bishop of the Episcopal Diocese of New Hampshire. He was confirmed by the general convention that summer and in November was consecrated. In response to pressure from the global Anglican Communion, the Episcopal Church's "parent" body, it approved a temporary ban on ordination of gay bishops at the 2006 Episcopal convention. On 14–15 July 2009, however, the Episcopal convention of bishops voted 104-30 to allow ordination of homosexuals and created an option for clergy to perform same-sex unions. The measure stated that "God has called and may call" homosexuals to serve in ministry. The Episcopal Church ordained a second openly gay bishop on 16 May 2010, Canon Mary Glasspool. Many conservative churches disagreed with these decisions and formed the Anglican Church of North America, which contained more than 700 churches and 100,000 members by the end of the decade and sought recognition from the global Anglican Communion.

Julie Goodridge, left, and her spouse, Hillary Goodridge, cross the street from the Unitarian Universalist Church to the State House in Boston after their marriage on 17 May 2004 (AP Photo/Winslow Townson).

Presbyterians. The Presbyterian Church USA (PCUSA) passed an amendment to their "Book of Order" at the 1996 General Assembly stating that "the requirement either to live in fidelity within the covenant of marriage between a man and a woman, or chastity in singleness" would be applied to all clergy. Known as "Amendment B," the amendment was discussed at the 2004 General Assembly and upheld. Then, at the 2006 General Assembly, Amendment B was adopted yet again, but the Assembly also certified a recommendation from the task force on "Peace, Unity, and Purity" (commissioned by the 2001 General Assembly) to allow local presbyteries freedom to ordain whomever they wished, a sign that more LGBTQ persons might potentially be ordained. On 27 June 2008 a motion to have this recommendation removed from the "Book of Order" won in the General Assembly. However, local presbyteries did not muster a majority of approval, so the motion did not carry.

Methodists. The Methodist Church stated clearly its position in the 1990s against ordination and marriage of homosexuals but affirmed that all homosexuals were welcome. At the 2004 General Conference, it amended its social principles to state that "the United Methodist Church does not condone the practice of homosexuality and considers this practice incompatible with Christian teaching. We affirm that God's grace is available to all, and we will seek to live together in Christian community. We implore families and churches not to reject or condemn lesbian and gay members and friends." The 2008 General Conference defeated efforts to allow gay unions and ordination, while condemning homophobia and heterosexism.

Conservatives. Most conservative and evangelical denominations maintained their positions on homosexuality and dedicated much time and money to defeating legislative efforts at equality for homosexuals. Carrie Prejean became a heroine of conservative voices at the 2009 Miss America pageant. When asked by Perez Hilton, an openly practicing homosexual, about whether other states should follow the lead of Massachusetts in legalizing gay marriage, she responded, "[I]n my country, in my family, I think that I believe that a marriage should be between a man and a woman." The Southern Baptist Convention, the largest body of protestant Christians in the United States, urged its members to initiate a nationwide campaign to turn gays into "straights," furthering their belief that homosexuality is a socially determined condition that can be treated through prayer and renewed commitment to a Christian lifestyle. On 27 July 2007 the Mormon Church posted on its website "God Loveth His Children," which maintained the distinction between same-sex attraction and acts, softened the language used to describe such tendencies, and emphasized a renewed commitment to the church and God. The Mormon Church was particularly influential in the campaign to pass California's Proposition 8 that defined marriage as valid only between a man and a woman. The First Presidency of the Mormon Church distributed a letter to all California Mormons encouraging them to advocate for Proposition 8; they accounted for half of the $20 million raised for the group "Yes on 8."

Judaism. In July 2010 more than 150 rabbis signed a "Statement of Principles on the Place of Jews with a Homosexual Orientation in Our Community." While it did not change the Orthodox position against a homosexual serving as a rabbi, the letter treated homosexuals with greater respect and not as a segregated population. The Conservative Committee on Jewish Law and Standards weighed several "responsa" on the issue and adopted three on 6 December 2006, one of which opened the door to ordination and marriage of homosexuals. The responsum "Homosexuality, Human Dignity, and Halakha" argued on the basis of human dignity that rabbis could perform same-sex marriage rituals without fear of censure. It passed by one vote, while the two other responsa maintained prior restrictive views. In effect, rabbis could act according to their views of Jewish law and not be bound by an absolute standard. The Reform movement differed from the orthodox and Conservative movements in that it does not believe Jews are completely bound to Jewish law and should adapt to contemporary viewpoints and attitudes. Reform Jews began to ordain homosexual rabbis in 1990, and in March 2000 the Central Conference of American Rabbis voted to allow rabbis to officiate at same-sex marriages. Reconstructionist Jews became the only rabbinical society to name a gay woman, Toba Spitzer, as president, on 13 March 2007.

Sources:

Peggy Fletcher, "LDS Church Pamphlet Advises on Same-Sex Attraction," *Salt Lake Tribune*, 27 July 2007;

Fletcher, "Prop 8 Involvement a P.R. Fiasco for LDS Church," *Salt Lake Tribune*, 21 November 2008;

"Gays with Partners Can Be Clergy," *St. Paul Pioneer Press*, 22 August 2009;

Laurie Goodstein, "Episcopal Bishops Give Ground on Gay Marriage," *New York Times*, 15 July 2009;

Duke Helfand, "Presbyterians Overturn Ban on Gay Clergy," *Pittsburgh Post-Gazette*, 29 June 2008;

Patrik Jonsson, "Breakaway Episcopalians Install a New Archbishop," *Christian Science Monitor* (25 June 2009);

Charles A. Radin, "A New Voice Among Jewish Leaders," *Boston Globe*, 14 March 2007;

Hanna Rosin, "Reform Rabbis Sanction Gay Unions—Group Recognizes 'Diversity of Opinion,'" *Washington Post*, 30 March 2000;

Jeffrey S. Siker, ed., *Homosexuality and Religion: An Encyclopedia* (Westport, Conn.: Greenwood Press, 2007);

Jeff Strickler, "Lutherans Roll Out Plan for New Denomination," *Minneapolis–St. Paul Star Tribune*, 18 February 2010.

ISLAMIC AMERICANS

Islam. Questions about the nature of Islam concerned many Americans in the wake of the terrorist attacks of 11 September 2001. Right-wing activists insisted that the Islamists were violent by the precepts of their religious faith and that they posed a threat to democracy. Others pointed out that dangerous extremists existed within most organized religion. Heated arguments—and at times, more considered examinations—of passages from the Koran were conducted in public forums in an attempt to understand the history and religious philosophy of Muslim beliefs, as well as their place in a democratic society.

Terrorism. In October 2000 Osama bin Laden's fundamentalist terrorist group al Qaeda bombed the U.S. destroyer *Cole* in the port of Aden off the coast of Yemen. The attack killed seventeen sailors and injured thirty-nine others. Bin Laden remained on the Federal Bureau of Investigation (FBI)'s Most Wanted List, moving to the top on 11 September 2001, after nineteen al Qaeda operatives hijacked four airplanes in coordinated attacks on the World Trade Center towers and Pentagon. A fourth plane was brought down by passengers over Pennsylvania. Americans became familiar with the term "jihad," whose root means "to struggle." Muslims consider jihad an individual's personal struggle with God, but it was appropriated by extremists to be synonymous with a holy war against those whom they believed were a threat to the religion of Islam or Muslims in general.

American Response. President George W. Bush a few days after the 9/11 attacks referred to the War on Terror as a "crusade," a term that historically referred to Christian holy wars against Muslims. He quickly retracted the statement, assuring the world that he had used the term to mean a "broad cause," not to invoke holy war or claim that the United States was conducting a war on Islam. On 17 September 2001 President Bush visited the Islamic Center of Washington to call for tolerance and an end to a surge of violence against Muslim Americans, saying, "The face of terror is not the true face of Islam . . . Islam is peace." Unfortunately, prejudice against Muslim Americans continued. The FBI reported 481 hate crimes against Muslims in 2001, a stark increase from 28 reported in 2000. People of Middle Eastern origin or descent suffered 1,501 hate crimes in 2001, compared with 354 in 2000. Hate crimes against Muslims continually decreased through the rest of the decade, with 107 reported in 2009.

Negative Response. Soon after the attacks, Jerry Falwell and Pat Robertson shocked the country by claiming on *The 700 Club* that part of the blame for the attacks rested with abortionists, homosexuals, the American Civil Liberties Union (ACLU), and other liberal groups. They cited divine retribution as the reason attackers succeeded. President Bush immediately denounced the statements, and both Robertson and Falwell apologized for their insensitivity. Other fundamentalist Christians complicated relations with Muslims by making extreme statements. Franklin Graham, son of Billy Graham, called Islam "a very evil and wicked religion," and Falwell claimed "Muhammad was a terrorist" on *60 Minutes*. Jerry Vines of Jacksonville referred to Mohammed as a "demon-possessed pedophile." Critics pointed out that such incendiary statements increased anti-American sentiment in Muslim nations, already at a dangerously high level.

Fellowship. Despite inflammatory statements from some, most Catholics and Protestants asserted a desire for community with Muslims, drawing a distinction between Islamic faith and fundamentalist extremists. The main criticism from Americans of various religious backgrounds was that moderate Muslims did not do enough to denounce extremism. Muslims believe in a close connection between religious belief and political legislation, whereas Westerners believe in separation between religion and government. Islam has strict requirements of an individual meant to strengthen one's connection to the community of believers, whereas Western culture advocates individual freedom. Westerners claim to be tolerant and respectful of Islam yet insist that Muslims adopt more progressive views on social issues, such as the treatment and dress of women, thus causing tension between the two cultures.

Muslim Response. A letter condemning the September 11 terrorist attacks was sent to President Bush the day of the strike, signed by leaders of the American Muslim Alliance, American Muslim Council, Council on American-Islamic Relations (CAIR), Muslim Public Affairs Council, Muslim American Society, Islamic Society of North America, Islamic Circle of North America, Muslim Alliance in North America, and American Muslims for Jerusalem. CAIR also issued a response to the developing "smear campaign" and harassment of Muslim Americans that began soon after the attacks: "We do not support terrorism in any way, shape or form, whether it is committed by Muslim groups or individuals, or by those who base their violent acts on other religions or philosophies. We condemn by name any individual, group or state that carries out terrorist acts." In July 2005 the Fiqh Council of North America issued a fatwa (religious ruling) against acts of terrorism and extremism on behalf of Islam. Its three main provisions were:

1. All acts of terrorism targeting civilians are haram (forbidden) in Islam.

2. It is haram for a Muslim to cooperate with any individual or group that is involved in any act of terrorism or violence.

3. It is the civic and religious duty of Muslims to cooperate with law enforcement authorities to protect the lives of all civilians.

The fatwa was the most broad-reaching statement made by a body of Muslim leaders in the United States and received endorsement from other major organizations, such as CAIR.

A Common Word. On 13 October 2007 one hundred thirty-eight clerics around the world issued a statement calling for cooperation and understanding between Islam and Christianity. The twenty-nine-page document, "A Common Word between Us and You," explicitly claimed that "the future of the world depends upon peace between Muslims and Christians." It explored several passages from the Koran and Bible that describe the shared responsibilities of adherents of both faiths to honor God and their neighbors. The letter was initiated by the Royal Aal al-Bayt Institute for Islamic Thought in Amman, Jordan, where in 2005 the "Amman Message" was produced, an attempt to ease tensions among different factions of Muslims. The next logical step was to reach out to other faiths. There was an immediate positive response from leaders of Christian bodies, including a letter published in *The New York Times* from more than three hundred leaders of both evangelical and mainstream Christian denominations in the United States. Many saw "A Common Word" as an example of the peaceful denunciation of extremism that other faiths had asked of moderate Muslims. Four distinct "Common Word" conferences were held by Christian institutions in cooperation with the Royal Aal al-Bayt Institute: Cambridge University (October 2008), the Vatican (November 2008), Yale Divinity School (July 2009), and Georgetown University (October 2009). The document also inspired additional conferences, texts, publications, and other forms of interfaith exchange that met the requested call for dialogue among faiths. Unfortunately, near the end of the decade, popular opinion of Islam had turned more negative. According to studies conducted in 2005 by the Pew Forum, 41 percent of respondents had a favorable opinion of Islam and 36 percent had an unfavorable view, with 23 percent undecided. By 2010 only 30 percent had a favorable view with 38 percent having an unfavorable view.

Disenfranchisement. These attitudes had a profound effect on Muslim communities in the United States. Muslims felt that the War on Terror was a war on Islam. In 2007 the Pew Forum reported that 53 percent of Muslims responded that life in the United States had become "more difficult." Fifty-four percent believed that the United States "single[s] out Muslims for extra surveillance." As the profiling of those who "look" Arab increased and travel restrictions became more common, Arab Americans began to fear a "witch hunt" for all Muslims. Public opinion was also influenced by the actions of Army psychiatrist major Nidal Malik Hasan, who on 5 November 2009 using two handguns fired on fellow soldiers at Fort Hood, Texas, killing thirteen and wounding thirty-one. Troubled by conflicts between his faith and his military position, Hasan

Following is a portion of the text from "A Common Word between Us and You" (issued 13 October 2007) from Muslim clerics to people of faith in the United States:

Whilst Islam and Christianity are obviously different religions—and whilst there is no minimising some of their formal differences—it is clear that the *Two Greatest Commandments* are an area of common ground and a link between the Qur'an, the Torah and the New Testament. What prefaces the Two Commandments in the Torah and the New Testament, and what they arise out of, is the Unity of God—that there is only one God. For the *Shema* in the Torah, starts: (Deuteronomy 6:4) *Hear, O Israel: The LORD our God, the LORD is one!* Likewise, Jesus said: (Mark 12:29) *"The first of all the commandments is: 'Hear, O Israel, the LORD our God, the LORD is one."* Likewise, God says in the Holy Qur'an: *Say: He, God, is One. / God, the Self-Sufficient Besought of all.* (*Al-Ikhlas,* 112:1–2). Thus the Unity of God, love of Him, and love of the neighbour form a common ground upon which Islam and Christianity (and Judaism) are founded.

This could not be otherwise since Jesus said: (Matthew 22:40) *"On these two commandments hang all the Law and the Prophets."* Moreover, God confirms in the Holy Qur'an that the Prophet Muhammad brought nothing fundamentally or essentially new: *Naught is said to thee (Muhammad) but what already was said to the messengers before thee* (*Fussilat* 41:43). And: *Say (Muhammad): I am no new thing among the messengers (of God), nor know I what will be done with me or with you. I do but follow that which is Revealed to me, and I am but a plain warner* (*Al-Ahqaf,* 46:9). Thus also God in the Holy Qur'an confirms that the same eternal truths of the Unity of God, of the necessity for total love and devotion to God (and thus shunning false gods), and of the necessity for love of fellow human beings (and thus justice), underlie all true religion:

And verily We have raised in every nation a messenger, (proclaiming): Worship God and shun false gods. Then some of them (there were) whom God guided, and some of them (there were) upon whom error had just hold. Do but travel in the land and see the nature of the consequence for the deniers! (*Al-Nahl,* 16:36)

We verily sent Our messengers with clear proofs, and revealed with them the Scripture and the Balance, that mankind may stand forth in justice.... (*Al-Hadid,* 57:25)

Come to a Common Word!

In the Holy Qur'an, God Most High tells Muslims to issue the following call to Christians (and Jews—the People of the Scripture):

Say: O People of the Scripture! Come to a common word between us and you: that we shall worship none but God, and that we shall ascribe no partner unto Him, and that none of us shall take others for lords beside God. And if they turn away, then say: Bear witness that we are they who have surrendered (unto Him). (*Aal 'Imran* 3:64)

Clearly, the blessed words: *we shall ascribe no partner unto Him* relate to the Unity of God. Clearly also, worshipping *none but God,* relates to being totally devoted to God and hence to the *First and Greatest Commandment.* According to one of the oldest and most authoritative commentaries (*tafsir*) on the Holy Qur'an—the *Jami' Al-Bayan fi Ta'wil Al-Qur'an* of Abu Ja'far Muhammad bin Jarir Al-Tabari (d. 310 A.H. / 923 C.E.)—*that none of us shall take others for lords beside God,* means 'that none of us should obey in disobedience to what God has commanded, nor glorify them by prostrating to them in the same way as they prostrate to God'. In other words, that Muslims, Christians and Jews should be free to each follow what God commanded them, and not have 'to prostrate before kings and the like,' for God says elsewhere in the Holy Qur'an: *Let there be no compulsion in religion....* (*Al-Baqarah,* 2:256). This clearly relates to the Second Commandment and to love of the neighbour of which justice and freedom of religion are a crucial part. God says in the Holy Qur'an:

God forbiddeth you not those who warred not against you on account of religion and drove you not out from your homes, that ye should show them kindness and deal justly with them. Lo! God loveth the just dealers. (*Al-Mumtahinah,* 60:8)

We thus as Muslims invite Christians to remember Jesus's words in the Gospel (Mark 12:29–31):

... the LORD our God, the LORD is one. / And you shall love the LORD your God with all your heart, with all your soul, with all your mind, and with all your strength. This is the first commandment. / And the second, like it, is this: 'You shall love your neighbour as yourself.' There is no other commandment greater than these.

As Muslims, we say to Christians that we are not against them and that Islam is not against them—so long as they do not wage war against Muslims on account of their religion, oppress them and drive them out of their homes, (in accordance with the verse of the Holy Qur'an [*Al-Mumtahinah,* 60:8] quoted above). Moreover, God says in the Holy Qur'an:

They are not all alike. Of the People of the Scripture there is a staunch community who recite the revelations of God in the night season, falling prostrate (before Him). / They believe in God and the Last Day, and enjoin right conduct and forbid indecency, and vie one with another in good works. These are of the righteous. / And whatever good they do, nothing will be rejected of them. God is Aware of those who ward off (evil). (*Aal-'Imran,* 3:113–115)

Is Christianity necessarily against Muslims? In the Gospel Jesus Christ says:

He who is not with me is against me, and he who does not gather with me scatters abroad. (Matthew 12:30)

For he who is not against us is on our side. (Mark 9:40)

… for he who is not against us is on our side. (Luke 9:50)

According to the *Blessed Theophylact's Explanation of the New Testament,* these statements are not contradictions because the first statement (in the actual Greek text of the New Testament) refers to demons, whereas the second and third statements refer to people who recognised Jesus, but were not Christians. Muslims recognize Jesus Christ as the Messiah, not in the same way Christians do (but Christians themselves anyway have never all agreed with each other on Jesus Christ's nature), but in the following way: …. *the Messiah Jesus son of Mary is a Messenger of God and His Word which he cast unto Mary and a Spirit from Him....* (*Al-Nisa',* 4:171). We therefore invite Christians to consider Muslims *not against* and thus *with them,* in accordance with Jesus Christ's words here.

Finally, as Muslims, and in obedience to the Holy Qur'an, we ask Christians to come together with us on the common essentials of our two religions … *that we shall worship none but God, and that we shall ascribe no partner unto Him, and that none of us shall take others for lords beside God …* (*Aal 'Imran,* 3:64).

Let this common ground be the basis of all future interfaith dialogue between us, for our common ground is that on which hangs *all the Law and the Prophets* (Matthew 22:40). God says in the Holy Qur'an:

Say (O Muslims): We believe in God and that which is revealed unto us and that which was revealed unto Abraham, and Ishmael, and Isaac, and Jacob, and the tribes, and that which Moses and Jesus received, and that which the prophets received from their Lord. We make no distinction between any of them, and unto Him we have surrendered. / And if they believe in the like of that which ye believe, then are they rightly guided. But if they turn away, then are they in schism, and God will suffice thee against them. He is the Hearer, the Knower. (*Al-Baqarah,* 2:136-137)

Between Us and You

Finding common ground between Muslims and Christians is not simply a matter for polite ecumenical dialogue between selected religious leaders. Christianity and Islam are the largest and second largest religions in the world and in history. Christians and Muslims reportedly make up over a third and over a fifth of humanity respectively. Together they make up more than 55% of the world's population, making the relationship between these two religious communities the most important factor in contributing to meaningful peace around the world. If Muslims and Christians are not at peace, the world cannot be at peace. With the terrible weaponry of the modern world; with Muslims and Christians intertwined everywhere as never before, no side can unilaterally win a conflict between more than half of the world's inhabitants. Thus our common future is at stake. The very survival of the world itself is perhaps at stake.

And to those who nevertheless relish conflict and destruction for their own sake or reckon that ultimately they stand to gain through them, we say that our very eternal souls are all also at stake if we fail to sincerely make every effort to make peace and come together in harmony. God says in the Holy Qur'an: *Lo! God enjoineth justice and kindness, and giving to kinsfolk, and forbiddeth lewdness and abomination and wickedness. He exhorteth you in order that ye may take heed* (*Al Nahl,* 16:90). Jesus Christ said: *Blessed are the peacemakers …* (Matthew 5:9), and also: *For what profit is it to a man if he gains the whole world and loses his soul?* (Matthew 16:26)

So let our differences not cause hatred and strife between us. Let us vie with each other only in righteousness and good works. Let us respect each other, be fair, just and kind to another and live in sincere peace, harmony and mutual goodwill. God says in the Holy Qur'an:

And unto thee have We revealed the Scripture with the truth, confirming whatever Scripture was before it, and a watcher over it. So judge between them by that which God hath revealed, and follow not their desires away from the truth which hath come unto thee. For each We have appointed a law and a way. Had God willed He could have made you one community. But that He may try you by that which He hath given you (He hath made you as ye are). So vie one with another in good works. Unto God ye will all return, and He will then inform you of that wherein ye differ. (*Al-Ma'idah,* 5:48)

Source: "A Common Word between Us and You," *acommonword.com* (13 October 2007).

Young Islamic Americans in New York City near Ground Zero react against the anti-Muslim sentiment that flourished in the United States after the World Trade Center attacks (photograph by David Shankbone).

allegedly acted out of his own convictions, but many defined his actions as an example of Muslim extremism.

War on Terror. As the United States entered Afghanistan in 2001 and Iraq in March 2003, Americans faced the challenge of reconciling the need for national defense with their personal faiths. In general, evangelical and conservative Christians backed most Bush administration initiatives in the War on Terror, appealing to the "just" war doctrine derived from St. Augustine and Thomas Aquinas. Mainstream Protestant denominations showed more resistance, often questioning the compatibility of military action with Christ's message of forgiveness. In a Pew Forum survey of 1,032 Americans (taken between 13–16 March 2003, one week before the invasion of Iraq), 37 percent said that their clergy had recently spoken on the War on Terror at religious services without taking an explicit position, while 21 percent discerned a particular position advocated by their clergy. Fourteen percent of clergy voiced opposition to the war while 7 percent approved. Those who identified themselves as evangelical heard more approval from the pulpit than disapproval, whereas mainstream Protestants, Catholics, and black Protestants heard messages of opposition.

Church Statements. On 3 October 2002 five evangelical Christian leaders (Richard Land of the Southern Baptist Convention, Chuck Colson of Prison Fellowship Ministries, D. James Kennedy of Coral Ridge Ministries, Bill Bright of Campus Crusade for Christ International, and Carl D. Herbster of the American Association of Christian Schools) sent a letter to President Bush arguing that the decision to invade Iraq qualified as a "just" war. Support also came from Pentecostals and other conservative evangelical groups. On 11 October, however, the heads of more than sixty church bodies in both the United States and Europe wrote to President Bush and British prime minister Tony Blair stating opposition to the proposed invasion, arguing that qualifications for a "just" war had not been sufficiently met. Groups opposing the war included Roman Catholics and most mainstream Protestant and Orthodox denominations. Some Jewish Orthodox groups favored a preemptive strike, while Reform and Conservative Jewish groups remained divided.

Sources:

"'A Common Word': Accomplishments: 2007–2009," *acommonword.com* (November 2009);

Alan Cooperman, "Iraq War Not Justified, Church Leaders Say," *Washington Post,* 12 October 2002;

Federal Bureau of Investigation, "Hate Crime Statistics, 2000," *fbi.com;*

Federal Bureau of Investigation, "Hate Crime Statistics, 2001," *fbi.com;*

Federal Bureau of Investigation, "Hate Crime Statistics, 2009," *fbi.com;*

"Fort Hood Shows There is No 'Army of One,'" *Fort Worth Star-Telegram,* 6 November 2009;

Laurie Goodstein, "Threats and Responses: Religions' Views—Diverse Denominations Oppose the Call to Arms," *New York Times,* 6 March 2003;

"In U.S., Religious Prejudice Stronger Against Muslims," *gallup.com* (21 January 2010);

"'Islamophobic Smear Campaign' Goes Public," *Council on American-Islamic Relations* (November 2001);

Kenneth Jost, "Understanding Islam," *CQ Researcher,* 16 (3 November 2006);

Jane Lampman, "Moderate Muslims Speak—To Christians," *Christian Science Monitor* (15 October 2007);

Dana Milbank and Emily Wax, "Bush Visits Mosque to Forestall Hate Crimes," *Washington Post,* 18 September 2001;

Caryle Murphy and Wax, "Muslims Condemn Acts, Fear Reprisals," *Washington Post,* 12 September 2001;

Mark O'Keefe, "Experts Expect a Backlash from Remarks about Islam," *Houston Chronicle,* 5 October 2002;

Pew Research Center, "Muslim Americans: Middle Class and Mostly Mainstream," *pewresearch.org* (22 May 2007);

"Public Remains Conflicted Over Islam," *Pew Forum on Religion & Public Life* (24 August 2010).

LAW & POLITICS

Public Religion. The two most prevalent issues regarding religion in public life in the 2000s involved the use of public money, space, or facilities for religious purposes and the definition of marriage regarding same-sex partners. The Supreme Court considered many cases that redefined the line between church and state, while the question of how marriage should be defined was addressed on multiple fronts.

Bush's Faith. The campaign season that led up to the 2000 election was framed for many as a "vote on values." After the Bill Clinton/Monica Lewinsky sex scandal hit the White House, many social conservatives rallied behind George W. Bush. The Christian Coalition, "religious right," and "evangelical vote" were all demographic groups who played a large role in Bush gaining enough electoral votes (after lengthy recounts and appeals) to be elected president over former vice president Al Gore. Bush benefited from the same groups in the 2004 election against his Catholic opponent Senator John Kerry. In a poll commissioned by *Time,* 59 percent of those who identified themselves as "very religious" supported Bush, while only 35 percent supported Kerry. In fact, many conservative Catholics called for priests to refuse communion for the liberal Kerry, who supported several causes, such as a prochoice platform, that distanced him and (some say) all liberals from Catholics and evangelical Protestants, the largest group of Christians in the nation. This group served as Bush's base for the eight years of his presidency, as his widely reported reflections on the relationship between his faith and role as president struck a chord with them. The same statements, however, also served to distance him from moderates and liberals, who felt his constant appeals to scripture and faith breached the wall of separation between church and state. Bush's support from Christian congregations and establishments remained strong, even when they were faced with possible loss of tax-exempt status because of their campaign-style advocacy.

Faith-Based Organizations. President Bush's top priority was to create a program to distribute public dollars to faith-based organizations (FBOs), which he had achieved as governor of Texas through the "charitable choice" provision in the 1996 Welfare Reform Act. On 9 January 2001 he created by executive order the White House Office of Faith-Based and Community Initiatives. The initiative was based on the belief that religious groups may be more successful than government-sponsored, secular approaches to solve certain social problems, such as alcoholism and gang-related activity. FBOs could now apply for federal grant money. Concerns from both supporters and opponents included whether faith-based approaches were actually more effective; religious groups required conversion as part of treatment (which violated the Constitution's establishment clause); religious groups could discriminate in the hiring process; support might go to fringe groups, cults, or organizations with goals or methods not in line with the purpose of the initiative; and the government might be able to regulate religious practice by monitoring FBOs. According to a 10 April 2001 poll by the Pew Forum, 59 percent of Americans opposed allowing groups who required religious conversion as part of treatment to compete for federal money. Over three-fourths opposed groups being allowed to hire only people of the same faith. Detractors were also concerned about preferential distribution of funds. Support, however, came from a variety of sources as well. On 27 April 2001 two dozen leading liberal, conservative, and religious leaders sent a letter to the White House supporting government assistance to faith-based groups. The Urban Institute found in a similar study that larger, more theologically liberal, and African American churches were most likely to seek grant money. They concluded that "congregations are more likely to provide short term, small-scale relief of various sorts than to operate ongoing or large-scale programs," which raised the question of whether religious groups offer the appropriate level of service for the needs of the people. To address these concerns, the executive order included safeguards that prevented FBOs from withholding services to people based upon religious preference and using funds for inherently religious activities. However, FBOs were allowed to display material items religious in nature (icons, images, etc.) and maintain the right to hire only employees of their own faith, unless otherwise mandated by their own operating rules or state and local law. Under Title VII of the Civil Rights Act, religious institutions have an exemption from the ruling on hiring discrimination—a contentious issue with some critics, who argued that it could be used as a pretext for discriminating on other grounds (sexual orientation and interracial dating). Other organizations may also be encouraged to discriminate by calling themselves "religious."

Controversial Clergy. The pastors who ministered to the presidential candidates in 2008 played nearly as prominent a role as the candidates themselves. Jeremiah Wright, who preached to then-Senator Barack Obama at Chicago's Trinity United Church of Christ, was caught up in a media storm when footage was released of a controversial sermon he gave after the September 11 attacks. Obama removed Wright from his campaign on 14 March 2008, but continued to support him as a positive and influential church leader. Senator John McCain repudiated the endorsement of John Hagee on 22 May 2008 after Hagee referred to the Holocaust as part of God's plan. Personal faith played a role for Mitt Romney, a Republican candidate and Mormon, in his campaign for the Republican nomination. In a poll conducted by the Pew Forum on Religion & Public Life in December 2007, respondents felt he, above all other candidates, seemed a religious person. However, 25 percent of respondents said they would be less likely to vote for a Mormon. Ultimately, he lost to McCain. At his 2009 inauguration, President Obama made headlines by inviting Rick Warren, pastor of Saddleback Church, to deliver the inaugural invocation and V. Gene Robinson, the first openly homosexual bishop in the Episcopal Church, to deliver the invocation at an inaugural celebration at the Lincoln Memorial. The choice of Warren enraged liberals for his clear and strong opposition to gay marriage. Conversely, the choice of Robinson upset conservatives.

Obama's Faith. Both before and after his election to the presidency, the public debated the question of Obama's religious affiliation. Though he continually attested to practicing Christianity, questions arose about whether he practiced Islam, in part because his biological father Barack Obama Sr. and stepfather Lolo Soetoro were both Muslim. The Pew Forum on Religion and Public Life conducted a survey in March 2008 on the issue of President Obama's religious preference. Forty-seven respondents said "Christian" while 12 percent said "Muslim." The numbers stayed relatively static until August 2010, when in a similar poll 34 percent responded "Christian," and 18 percent responded "Muslim." The Pew Forum observed that opinions were closely linked to positive or negative evaluations of Obama's job performance. The highly contentious healthcare law and struggling economy were strong factors in the change in the public's attitude toward Obama. Despite debate over his beliefs, Obama did not institute any changes other than to rename the agency that former president Bush had created to encourage faith-based organizations in their role as providers of social services. At the National Prayer Breakfast on 5 February 2009 he changed it to the White House Office of Faith-Based and Neighborhood Partnerships. Its main focus would be to fight poverty and help with economic recovery efforts; craft ways to support young mothers and decrease teenage pregnancies; reduce abortions; encourage responsible fatherhood; and foster an international interfaith dialogue.

Court Decisions. One of the most widely publicized decisions by the Supreme Court occurred on 18 April 2007, when in *Gonzales* v. *Carhart* the Court upheld 5-4 the constitutionality of the "Partial-Birth Abortion Ban Act" of 2003. President Bush had signed the act into law in November 2003 after two similar attempts by Congress had been vetoed by President Clinton. It was the first major restriction on abortion since *Roe* v. *Wade* (1973). The line between church and state was also scrutinized by the Supreme Court, as the use of public resources for religious purposes was argued multiple times. On 19 June 2000 the Court ruled 6-3 in *Santa Fe School District* v. *Doe* that the use of the public-address system at school athletic facilities for student-led pregame prayer violated the establishment clause: the grounds, facilities, and event were all government owned, and therefore statements made utilizing those resources were government-endorsed. However, on 28 June 2000 the Court ruled 6-3 in *Mitchell* v. *Helms* that a government-funded program can lend computers to parochial schools. This ruling overturned two preceding decisions that limited public aid to religious schools and set the standard that aid provided to religious institutions does not necessarily amount to advancing religious purposes if the service is secular in nature. The use of public-school space for after-school religious clubs was deemed legal in 2001 when the court decided 6-3 in *Good News Club, Inc.* v. *Milford Central School* that an after-school club cannot be kept from using public facilities even if it is for religious instruction: "speech discussing otherwise permissible subjects cannot be excluded from a limited public forum on the ground that the subject is discussed from a religious viewpoint." On 27 June 2002 the Supreme Court ruled 5-4 in *Zelman* v. *Simmons-Harris* that a Cleveland school district was not in violation of the establishment clause by allowing state-subsidized voucher money to go to private schools run by religious organizations. The court drew a distinction between "government programs that provide aid directly to religious schools, and programs of true private choice, in which government aid reaches religious schools only as a result of the genuine and independent choice of private individuals."

Monuments. The presence of religious displays (notably the Ten Commandments) on public property was another arena for church/state debate. In October 2001 state Alabama chief justice Roy Moore was sued by the American Civil Liberties Union (ACLU), Americans for the Separation of Church and State, and Southern Poverty Law Center over a granite display of the Ten Commandments he had installed in the Alabama Supreme Court building. On 18 November 2002 the monument was declared a violation of the establishment clause, and Moore was ordered to take it down. After refusing to do so, the case was appealed to the Eleventh Circuit Court of Appeals, which upheld the decision. Still refusing to move

Former Alabama chief justice Roy Moore with the Ten Commandments monument he fought to keep at the Alabama State Supreme Court building (AP Photo/*The Albuquerque Journal*, Jaelyn deMaria Leary)

the monument, Moore was overruled unanimously by the rest of the Alabama Supreme Court, and he was eventually removed from the bench on 13 November 2003 by an ethics panel. Two similar cases were decided by the U.S. Supreme Court on 27 June 2005. In *McCreary County* v. *ACLU of Kentucky,* the court ruled 5-4 that displaying the Ten Commandments in Kentucky courthouses is unconstitutional. Two counties had argued that the commandments are a philosophical foundation for American law and government. The counties accompanied each display with other documents. The Court decided that since the commandments are part of the Judeo-Christian religious tradition they focused on a religious message, not a secular or legal one. Justice Stephen Breyer joined the majority, but later that day helped the majority rule 5-4 in *Van Orden* v. *Perry* that a monument donated to the Texas State Capitol in 1961 from the Fraternal Order of Eagles of Texas, featuring the Ten Commandments, was part of the tradition of acknowledging the role of religion. Since the central function is historical, not religious, and its placement is not in an area that raises special concerns, it does not violate the establishment clause. In *Pleasant Grove City* v. *Summum* (2009) the Court ruled that the city did not violate the First

Amendment by refusing to add a monument donated by Summum, incorporated as a tax-exempt religious organization in 1975, to the eleven religious monuments (one of which was the Ten Commandments) in a public park. This case centered on the First Amendment; since the free speech clause "restricts government regulation of private speech but not government speech," local governments have the right to choose what to convey as government speech.

Gay Marriage. The other major issue to consistently arise was same-sex marriage. On 26 June 2003 the Supreme Court struck down Texas's anti-sodomy laws, but did not address homosexuality for the rest of the decade. President Bush called for a constitutional amendment banning gay marriage, but on 14 July 2004 it was defeated by the Republican-controlled Senate 48-50. The battle concerning the definition of marriage shifted to the states, as ballot referenda to state legislatures and courts approached the issue from different legal directions resulting in an array of outcomes. More-conservative states declared outright bans on gay marriage, while moderate ones sanctioned civil unions and domestic partnerships. Only a few states created equal marriage rights for same-sex partners. The federal Defense of Marriage Act, which defined marriage as

This chart, provided by the National Conference on State Legislatures, details legislative efforts in the states to define marriage—in most cases as only a union between a man and a woman—or to codify the right of the legislatures to determine the definition of marriage (Hawaii). In Maine the measure was an attempt to overturn the legalization of same-sex marriages, while the Washington measure was a referendum to uphold rights given to same-sex couples.

State	Year	Measure #	Pass/Fail
Alabama	2006	Amendment 1	Pass
Alaska	1998	Measure 2	Pass
Arizona	2006	Proposition 107	Fail
Arizona	2008	Proposition 102	Pass
Arkansas	2004	Amendment 3	Pass
California	2000	Proposition 22	Pass
California	2008	Proposition 8	Pass
Colorado	2006	Amendment 43	Pass
Florida	2008	Amendment 2	Pass
Georgia	2004	Amendment 1	Pass
Hawaii	1998	Question 2	Pass
Idaho	2006	HJR 2	Pass
Kansas	2005	Amendment	Pass
Kentucky	2004	Amendment	Pass
Louisiana	2004	Amendment 1	Pass
Maine	2009	Question 1	Pass
Michigan	2004	Proposal 2	Pass
Mississippi	2004	Amendment 1	Pass
Missouri	2004	Amendment 2	Pass
Montana	2004	CI-96	Pass
Nebraska	2000	Initiative 416	Pass
Nevada	2002	Question 2	Pass
North Dakota	2004	ICM 1	Pass
Ohio	2004	Issue 1	Pass
Oklahoma	2004	Question 711	Pass
Oregon	2004	Measure 36	Pass
South Carolina	2006	Amendment 1	Pass
South Dakota	2006	Amendment C	Pass
Tennessee	2006	Amendment 1	Pass
Texas	2005	Proposition 2	Pass
Utah	2004	Amendment 3	Pass
Virginia	2006	Amendment 1	Pass
Washington	2009	Referendum Measure 71	Pass
Wisconsin	2006	Question 1	Pass

Source: National Conference on State Legislatures, "Same Sex Marriage on the Ballot," *ncsl.com* (25 January 2011).

the union of a man and a woman, was passed by Congress in 1996, inspiring states to pass similar amendments. Since 1998 thirty-two states addressed the issue via referendum, either as a statute or a constitutional amendment (only Wyoming, Maryland, and New Hampshire had done so in prior decades). Washington came closest to legalizing same-sex marriage, but the language of Referendum Measure 71 simply allowed all the rights and responsibilities of marriage to same-sex partners in a civil union. All other initiatives either defined marriage as being between a man and woman, gave the state legislature the right to define it as such (Hawaii), or rejected a prior legalization (Maine). Arizona became the only state to overturn a ban on gay marriage in one election (2006) and then reverse course in the next (2008). Perhaps the most famous ballot initiative was California's Proposition 8 (2008), which sought a constitutional amendment defining marriage. In 2000 California passed a statute that defined marriage in the traditional sense, but on 15 May 2008 the California Supreme Court ruled it unconstitutional under equal-protection laws. After a lengthy campaign (with $75 million spent on both sides), voters passed the referendum the following November. In August 2010, however, a federal judge ruled the marriage amendment enacted by Proposition 8 unconstitutional; that decision was appealed and a stay was placed on conducting same-sex marriages. Marriage licenses issued between 15 May and the passage of "Prop 8" were honored. California was the third state whose referendum was overturned by the courts. The Connecticut Supreme Court (October 2008) and Iowa Supreme Court (April 2009) invalidated similar same-sex-marriage bans. Iowa began issuing marriage licenses to homosexual partners in June 2009. In November 2003 the Massachusetts Supreme Court ruled that denying marriage to homosexuals was unconstitutional. The Massachusetts Senate then sought to create parallel civil unions as a replacement to civil marriage. The court responded in February 2004 that "segregating same-sex unions from opposite-sex unions cannot possibly be held rationally to advance or preserve . . . the good of the individual and of the community, especially its children." Thereafter, Massachusetts began licensing same-sex marriage in May 2004. In 2000 Vermont passed legislation that retained the traditional definition of marriage, but allowed for civil unions between same-sex partners. Then in May 2009 Vermont's legislature voluntarily allowed marriage for same-sex partners without needing a judicial mandate. In April 2005 Connecticut enacted a law for civil unions with no prompting from the court system. It later overturned the ban on marriage inherent in that civil-union bill and became the second state to allow full marriage rights for homosexuals. In 2006 New Jersey, also prompted by its Supreme Court, passed a statute allowing civil unions that went into effect on 19 February 2007. The New Hampshire legislature authorized civil unions effective 1 January 2008 and in 2009 replaced it with full same-sex marriage. Maine passed a law authorizing same-sex marriage in 2009 that was overturned via referendum in 2010.

Sources:

Mark Chaves, "Brief #6: Congregations' Social Service Activities," *Urban Institute* (December 1999);

Helen Dewar, "Ban on Gay Marriage Fails; Senate Vote on Amendment Is a Defeat for Bush," *Washington Post*, 15 July 2004;

"Faith-Based Funding Backed, But Church-State Doubts Abound," *Pew Research Center* (10 April 2001);

Nancy Gibbs and others, "The Faith Factor," *Time* (21 June 2004);

Sarah Glazer, "Faith-Based Initiatives," *CQ Researcher*, 11 (4 May 2001): 377–400;

Laurie Goodstein, "Gay Bishop Is Asked to Say Prayer at Inaugural Event," *New York Times*, 12 January 2009;

"Growing Number of Americans Say Obama is a Muslim," *Pew Forum on Religion & Public Life* (18 August 2010);

Kermit L. Hall and James W. Ely Jr., eds., *The Oxford Guide to United States Supreme Court Decisions,* second edition (Oxford & New York: Oxford University Press, 2009);

Scott Keeter and Gregory Smith, "How the Public Perceives Romney, Mormons," *pewforum.org* (4 December 2007);

David Masci, "Religion and Politics," *CQ Researcher*, 14 (30 July 2004): 637–660;

National Conference of State Legislatures, "Same-Sex Marriage, Civil Unions, and Domestic Partnerships," *ncsl.org* (February 2011);

"Too Long to Wait," *New York Times*, 7 March 2011;

U.S. Government Accountability Office, "Faith-Based and Community Initiative: Improvements in Monitoring Grantees and Measuring Performance Could Enhance Accountability" (Washington, D.C.: June 2006).

POPULAR RELIGION AND CULTURE

Believers. America remained a society of believers, but the nature of that belief proved to be unfixed and flexible. After the terrorist attacks on 11 September 2001, attendance at religious services increased. After the brief spike in attendance, the trend continued in the direction it had taken during the 1990s, in which people identified themselves less as "religious" and more as "spiritual." The 2001 American Religious Identification Survey (ARIS) indicated that 81 percent of Americans identified with a particular religious group, a decrease from 90 percent in 1990. Seventy-six percent identified themselves as Christian, but within that group 8 percent responded either "Christian-No denomination specified" (6.8 percent) or "Nondenominational" (1.2 percent). Those who considered themselves believers but did not identify with any particular religious institution totaled 14.1 percent. In February 2008 the Pew Forum on Religion & Public Life released the U.S. Religious Landscape Survey of 35,556 people conducted in 2007. The number of total believers dropped only slightly to 79.8 percent. Seventy-six percent still considered themselves Christian, but those who claimed no religious affiliation increased to 15 percent. Nearly 11 percent considered themselves "Christian-No denomination specified" (7.4 percent) or "Nondenominational" (3.5 percent). About 92 percent said that they believe in God to a certain degree. Among respondents 78.4 percent claimed to be either Catholic or Protestant. The next highest group, however, claimed to be "Unaffiliated" (16 percent), including both believers who did not adopt a particular religion (12 percent) and nonbelievers, such as

MAJOR RELIGIOUS TRADITIONS IN THE UNITED STATES

	Among all adults . . . %	
Christian..		**78.4**
Protestant		51.3
Evangelical churches	26.3	
Mainstream churches	18.1	
Hist. black churches	6.9	
Catholic..................................		23.9
Mormon..................................		1.7
Jehovah's Witnesses...............		0.7
Orthodox................................		0.6
Greek Orthodox	<0.3	
Russian Orthodox	<0.3	
Other	<0.3	
Other Christian......................		0.3
Other Religions.......................		**4.7**
Jewish....................................		1.7
Reform	0.7	
Conservative	0.5	
Orthodox	<0.3	
Other	0.3	
Buddhist.................................		0.7
Zen Buddhist	<0.3	
Theravada Buddhist	<0.3	
Tibetan Buddhist	<0.3	
Other	0.3	
Muslim*..................................		0.6
Sunni	0.3	
Shia	<0.3	
Other	<0.3	
Hindu......................................		0.4
Other world religion................		<0.3
Other faiths............................		1.2
Unitarians and other		
liberal faiths	0.7	
New Age	0.4	
Native American religion	<0.3	
Unaffiliated		**16.1**
Atheist....................................		1.6
Agnostic..................................		2.4
Nothing in particular..............		12.1
Secular unaffiliated	6.3	
Religious unaffiliated	5.8	
Don't Know/Refused		**0.8**
		100

Due to rounding, nested figures may not add to the subtotal indicated.
* From "Muslim Americans: Middle Class and Mostly Mainstream," Pew Research Center, 2007.

Source: "Muslim Americans: Middle Class and Mostly Mainstream," Pew Research Center (2007), as cited in "U.S. Religious Landscape Survey: Report 1: Religious Affiliation: Summary of Key Findings," Pew Forum on Religion and Public Life, *religions.pewforum.org* (February 2008).

atheists and agnostics (4 percent). The study showed a pattern of transience among believers as well. Forty-four percent left the denomination or religion of their upbringing for another denomination, religion, or none at all. The U.S. Census Bureau yielded comparable numbers in its *2011 Statistical Abstract,* using similar methods as the Pew Forum survey (both asked respondents in what group they identified themselves, not whether that particular group would claim them as a member). According to the *Abstract,* 76 percent identified themselves as Christian. However, 15 percent responded as having no religion at all. Of those who self-reported as Christian, 14.3 percent claimed they were "Nondenominational" (4.6 percent) or "no denomination supplied" (9.7 percent). This trend of people who were spiritual but not necessarily tied to a particular religious doctrine bears out in the political and cultural life of the nation. For every one person who joined a religion after having previously considered him or herself as unaffiliated, three people left the faith of their upbringing, making "unaffiliated" the fastest growing group of believers. Openness to a variety of religious beliefs and traditions manifested itself through choices in books, films, and television programs.

Da Vinci Code. By far the most popular, and controversial, piece of religious fiction to gain public attention was Dan Brown's *The Da Vinci Code* (2004). A mystery thriller that revolved around the puzzle-solving skills of Robert Langdon, a professor of symbology, the novel used several real-world theories about the Holy Grail, Knights Templar, and apocryphal histories of Jesus and the early church to weave a fictional mystery. Fast-paced and iconoclastic, the novel fascinated readers, and more than 80 million copies were sold worldwide by the end of the decade. The novel was adapted to a feature film in May 2006. Directed by Ron Howard and starring Tom Hanks, it earned more than $217.5 million. More than forty books analyzed or refuted statements in the novel, including Darrell L. Bock's *Breaking the Da Vinci Code: Answers to the Questions Everyone's Asking* (2004) and Daniel Burstein's *Secrets of the Code: The Unauthorized Guide to the Mysteries Behind the Da Vinci Code* (2004). Many Christians saw *The Da Vinci Code* as an attack on the church, and Catholics in particular felt it was an affront to Catholic hierarchy. The U.S. Conference of Catholic Bishops posted the website *Jesusdecoded.com* in order to distinguish historical fact from creative fiction in the novel. Brown said his intention was never to create controversy, but rather "[t]o mix facts into a fictional setting and get readers to ask questions about what they believe. But to make it fun to read." Having been labeled "controversial" without expecting it, Brown responded, "Controversy is a good thing when it gets people thinking and talking."

Passion of the Christ. Controversy marked the February 2004 premiere of Mel Gibson's movie adaptation of the crucifixion story, *The Passion of the Christ.* As a por-

Poster for a 2001 film based on the popular series of
Christian novels by Tim LaHaye and Jerry Jenkins
(<www.moviepostershop.com>)

Behind series by Tim LaHaye and Jerry Jenkins to the
screen in 2001, and he starred in *Fireproof* (2008), the
story of a firefighter who saves his marriage through
adherence to biblical principles. The romantic comedy
Keeping the Faith (2000), involving a love triangle among
three childhood friends, reflected the pluralist attitudes
of the country. A priest (Ed Norton), rabbi (Ben Stiller),
and businesswoman (Jenna Elfman) reconcile their
commitments to each other as well as to their respective
jobs/faiths. Capitalizing on the enthusiasm created by
the *Lord of the Rings* films, C. S. Lewis's three-part
Christian allegory, *The Chronicles of Narnia*, was adapted
for the screen. *The Lion, The Witch, and the Wardrobe*
premiered in 2005 (grossing $291 million), *Prince Caspian* in 2008 ($141 million), and *The Voyage of the Dawn
Treader* in 2010 ($103 million). Though filmed overseas,
the biopic *Luther* (2003)—about the German monk and
Protestant Reformation leader Martin Luther—grossed
nearly $5.8 million in the United States. The producer/
director team of brothers Joel and Ethan Coen released
A Serious Man (2009), in which a Jewish man questions
his faith as his personal and professional lives fall apart.

Television. The series *Touched by an Angel* came to an
end in 2003 after nine seasons. The series was considered "spiritual" without promoting one particular faith,
and reflected the changing attitudes of Americans
toward religious expression. The series *Joan of Arcadia*
(2003–2005) centered around a teenage girl, Joan
Girardi, who hears the voice of God through others and
embarks on "assignments" to help those around her. The
series did not preach one particular religious belief but
rather portrayed a "universal" God, appealing to a public
that was more spiritual than religious. Several series
addressed themes of the supernatural, spirituality, and
faith in general: *Lost* (2004–2010), *Saving Grace*
(2007–2010), *Medium* (2005–2011), *Ghost Whisperer*
(2005–2010), and even the science-fiction series *Battlestar Galactica* (2004–2009). The HBO hit *Big Love*
(2006–2011) did not contain elements of the supernatural but addressed specific religious issues. Set in Salt
Lake City, Utah, its protagonist Bill Henrickson (Bill
Paxton) is a polygamist who faces the challenges of living with his family while keeping their secret from the
community. The Church of Jesus Christ of Latter-Day
Saints (LDS) officially rejected polygamy more than a
century ago, and the LDS insisted that the characters
were not true Mormons.

Nonbelievers. The voice of skepticism was present
through the 2000s as well. In his inaugural address,
Barack Obama became the first president to acknowledge atheism and agnosticism as part of American life by
referring to the United States as "a nation of Christians and
Muslims, Jews and Hindus, and non-believers." Toward
the end of the decade, the rise in the number of nonbelievers coincided with discussions from people who
came to be termed the "New Atheists." Authors
regarded as leaders of New Atheism were Sam Harris

trayal of the Gospels' accounts of the last twelve hours of
Jesus' life, the movie struck a chord with Christians,
drawing $370 million at the box office. Gibson aimed
for realism on a grand scale, incorporating Aramaic
Hebrew into the script (the first film to do so) along
with Latin, and providing vividly graphic images of the
act of crucifixion. In fact, they were so graphic that
Peggy Scott of Wichita, Kansas, suffered a fatal heart
attack while watching the movie's premiere. Debate
emerged over its accuracy, but this paled in comparison
to the outcry that arose from the Jewish community.
Because of its one-sided and offensive representation of
Jewish leaders and the comparatively benign portrayal of
Pontius Pilate, many Jewish viewers felt the movie was a
restatement of the anti-Semitic position that the "Jews
killed Jesus." Gibson consistently denied these accusations, insisting that the movie's focus was on the pain
Christ endured, not on any one group who may have
caused it.

Hollywood. Religious expression through cinema
took on several additional forms. Kirk Cameron, an outspoken Christian in Hollywood, helped bring the *Left*

From **Larry Charles**
the Director of **"Borat"**

Bill Maher
Religulous
Do you smell something burning?

coming soon   LIONSGATE

Poster for the 2008 documentary film written by and
starring comedian Bill Maher
(<www.impawards.com>)

(*The End of Faith*, 2004) and *Letter to a Christian Nation*,
2006), Daniel C. Dennett (*Breaking the Spell: Religion as
a Natural Phenomenon*, 2006), Richard Dawkins (*The
God Delusion*, 2006), Victor J. Stenger (*God: The Failed
Hypothesis*, 2007), and Christopher Hitchens (*God is Not
Great: How Religion Poisons Everything*, 2007). Comedian Bill Maher provided a critique of religion with his
documentary *Religulous* (2008), which looked at faith
from an atheist's perspective. With the tagline "Heaven
help us," Maher examined the decisions made by people
on the basis of religion. The movie grossed just under
$13 million in the United States.

Sources:
"Church Responds to Questions on HBO's 'Big Love,'" *lds.org* (6
March 2006);

Dinah Eng, "Producer Explores Life and God in 'Joan of Arcadia,'"
USA Today, 14 October 2003;

Barry A. Kosmin and Ariela Keysar, "American Religious Identification Survey 2008," *americanreligionsurvey-aris.org* (March 2009);

Kosmin, Egon Mayer, and Keysar, "American Religious Identification
Survey 2001," *americanreligionsurvey-aris.org* (19 December 2001);

Bob Minzesheimer, "Nothing's Lost on Dan Brown—Author Out
Today with Long-Awaited 'Symbol,'" *USA Today*, 15 September
2009;

William Neuman, "Mel's Flock—Fans Mob N.Y. Theaters; Woman
Dies Watching 'Crucifixion,'" *New York Post*, 26 February 2004;

Barack Obama, "Inaugural Address," *White House Blog* (21 January
2009);

U.S. Census, "Table 75: Self Described Religious Identification of
Adult Population," *2011 Statistical Abstract: Religion* (20 January
2011);

"U.S. Religious Landscape Survey," *Pew Forum on Religion & Public
Life* (February 2008).

TRANSITIONS IN PROTESTANT RELIGIONS

Change. The face of Protestant evangelism changed from
2000 to 2009. Most major religious figures from the second
half of the twentieth century retired or passed away, leaving
their ministries to new leadership. Also, a wave of charismatic individuals gained national attention as part of a trend
of attendance in "megachurches," whose primary characteristic was having more than two thousand in attendance per
week. Though overall more Americans worshipped in traditional mainstream denominations, megachurches steadily
increased in power and membership.

Departures. Billy Graham was known worldwide for
his crusades and one-on-one meetings with every president
since Harry S Truman. However, he began to delegate his
work as an evangelist early in the 2000s. His son, William
Franklin Graham III, was named CEO of the Billy Graham Evangelical Association in 2000 and then named
president in 2001. Graham announced at an event in New
York in June 2005 that it would be his last crusade, though
he would make appearances at smaller events. Jerry Falwell,
a lightning rod for religion and politics, died on 15 May
2007. His sons succeeded him: Jerry Jr. as chancellor of
Liberty University and Jonathan as senior minister at
Thomas Road Baptist Church. Oral Roberts, founder of
Oral Roberts University (ORU) and a leader in taking
evangelism to the electronic media, died on 15 December
2009. He had handed the presidency of ORU to his son
Richard in 1993 and had limited activity after breaking his
hip in March 2006. After falling for a second time on 12
December 2009 (breaking his pelvis and neck), he died
three days later. D. James Kennedy, founder of Coral Ridge
Presbyterian Church and Coral Ridge Ministries, suffered
a heart attack on 28 December 2006; because of short-term
memory loss and speech impairment, he announced his
retirement on 26 August 2007 and died in his sleep on 5
September. He was replaced at Coral Ridge by Tullian
Tchividjian, grandson of Billy Graham; several hundred
members left the church in 2009 over changes in political
emphasis and service practices. Bill Bright, founder of the
Campus Crusade for Christ International, died in Orlando
on 19 July 2003 of pulmonary fibrosis.

Rise of the Megachurch. The foundation laid by crusad-
ers and televangelists was taken up by a "new guard" of charismatic Christians who either founded or expanded mega
churches that claimed thousands of members. Between 2000
and 2005 the number of megachurches reached 1,210.
The average increase in attendance was 57 percent for con-

The Crystal Cathedral, a megachurch in Garden Grove, California. The sanctuary has a seating capacity of 2,736 (photograph by Anke Meskens).

gregations that achieved megachurch status by 2000. Often a megachurch held several services at multiple locations. Craig Groeschel, for example, founded Life Covenant Church in 1996 and branched out to form LifeChurch.tv, the nation's second largest congregation. His multiple weekly services were transmitted to more than 26,000 people at thirteen campuses across the country. Though some megachurches retained a denominational identity, many were "functionally nondenominational." They constructed their congregational identity from within, instead of adhering to the requirements of outside governing bodies. Since they were self-sustaining, they rarely needed denominational support. The Hartford Institute for Religious Research published several studies on megachurches. According to Scott Thumma, author of *Beyond Megachurch Myths,* most megachurches are "Evangelical, Charismatic, or Fundamentalist." Popular author and evangelist Rick Warren founded Saddleback Church in Orange County, California, with a weekly attendance of more than twenty thousand and no denominational affiliation. His book *The Purpose Driven Church* inspired church leaders, and *The Purpose Driven Life* became the best-selling hardback in U.S. history. In 2005 he launched his "P.E.A.C.E. Plan" to fight global poverty, disease, ignorance, and spiritual starvation.

Contemporary Worship. As part of their nondenominational identity, megachurches tended to be nontraditional and contemporary. The campuses and buildings had modern architecture and few religious markers. Larger congregations often rented space at large local venues to create room for attendees. Ninety-seven percent held multiple services over multiple days, and more than half used multiple venues and satellite locations. Thirty-seven percent of Protestant churches had two or more locations under the same pastoral care in 2008. Worship services incorporated "rock and roll" style music—with full sets of drums, electrical instruments, and other attributes of modern music—and sermons focused on issues rather than texts. Bill Hybels was a pioneer of the megachurch phenomenon. In October 1975 he rented space in a theater and subsequently named it Willow Creek Community Church. He incorporated live contemporary music and brief sermons that addressed commonsense everyday issues, an approach that ballooned his congregation to 20,000 members. Leaders often have no formal religious training and are charismatic, possessing more down-to-earth qualities. Most megachurches achieve their status under the tenure of one charismatic leader; Joel Osteen fits this profile well. Having briefly attended Oral Roberts University, without completing a degree, he took over his father's ministry at Lakewood Church in 1999. Osteen gained notoriety as a charismatic preacher and "self-help" author. His services at Lakewood were televised in more than 100 countries and were seen by more than 7 million people each week. The ministry, which had the largest regularly attending congregation in the nation, grew so big that in 2004 it relocated to the Compaq Center, former basketball arena for the Houston Rockets, which seats 16,000 people. His *Your Best Life Now* and *Become a Better You* were *New York Times* best sellers.

Mainstream Concerns. Because most megachurches have vast budgets and no attachment to official denominational governing bodies, many mainstream Protestants feel the worship experience is more of a commodity than authentic religious practice. According to the 2008 Hartford Institute report, megachurches earn approximately $7.2 billion per year, with each church averaging $6.5 million. They employ a support/volunteer crew at the rate of one staff member for every ten attendees, more than 200 per church. Worship services offered to a broad demographic group can be a strength; however, traditionalists view it as a weakness. They worry that the primary purpose of ministry, to teach foundational lessons rooted in the study of scripture, has been replaced with a "feel good" atmosphere that fills pews but does not fulfill covenants with God. A common characteristic of these new churches is choice; people can choose when, how, and where to worship. This trait creates concern, since official doctrine is less of a priority when the congregation makes decisions. The biggest criticism is that megachurches are the result of a consumer culture and celebrity culture: people gather around a moving central figure and "buy into" the product being sold, creating competition for members among the churches. Huge congregations then grow like businesses, promoting the idea that bigger is better. Megachurch members and leaders deny this claim, saying that the traditional approach left a gap in the worship experience, and that their approach meets the needs of modern worshippers.

Sources:

Peter Applebome, "Jerry Falwell, Moral Majority Founder, Dies at 73," *New York Times,* 16 May 2007;

Manya A. Brachear, "Rev. Bill Hybels: The Father of Willow Creek," *Chicago Tribune,* 6 August 2006;

James D. Davis, "Forceful Evangelist Founded an Empire," *South Florida Sun-Sentinel,* 6 September 2007;

Cathy Lynn Grossman, "Billy Graham's Son Takes the Pulpit, His Own Way," *USA Today,* 7 March 2006;

Grossman, "New Face of Evangelism: 1 Church, Multiple Sites," *USA Today,* 17 December 2009;

"Joel Osteen Answers His Critics," *CBS News,* 14 October 2007;

"Oral Roberts Timeline," *Tulsa World,* 16 December 2009;

Mark I. Pinsky, "Campus Crusade's Founder Dies at 81," *Orlando Sentinel,* 21 July 2003;

Matt Sedensky, "Hundreds Leave Pioneering Megachurch Over Leadership," *Seattle Times,* 1 October 2009;

Jeffery L. Sheler, "Preacher with a Purpose," *U.S. News and World Report,* 31 October 2005;

Bill Sherman, "Oral Roberts Dies," *Tulsa World,* 15 December 2009;

Scott Thumma and Dave Travis, *Beyond Megachurch Myths: What We Can Learn from America's Largest Churches* (San Francisco: Jossey-Bass, 2007);

Thumma, Travis, and Warren Bird, "Megachurches Today: 2005 Summary of Research Findings," *Hartford Institute for Religion Research* (2005);

Thumma and Bird, "Changes in American Megachurches," *Hartford Institute for Religion Research* (2008).

HEADLINE MAKERS

ABRAHAM H. FOXMAN

1940–

ANTI-SEMITISM ACTIVIST

Fighting Bigotry. As national director of the Anti-Defamation League (ADL), Abraham H. Foxman was one of the leading activists against anti-Semitism in the United States during the 2000s. Born in Poland, he survived the Holocaust when his Catholic nanny raised him in her faith in Lithuania during World War II. After a legal battle, he was returned to his family after the war and immigrated with his parents to New York. He was part of a group known as the "Hidden Children" and in 1991 attended a celebration of this group at the First International Gathering of Children Hidden During World War II. He struggled with the conflict between his Catholic upbringing and newly found Jewish faith. He attended Yeshiva, joined pro-Zionist organizations, and earned a B.A. in political science at City College of the City University of New York (1962). Foxman earned a law degree from New York University School of Law (1965) and later studied Jewish history at the Jewish Theological Seminary and international economics at the New School for Social Research. On 18 April he was awarded the Raoul Wallenberg Humanitarian Leadership Award from the Center for Holocaust and Genocide Studies.

Controversial Leader. Foxman joined the ADL after getting his law degree. The organization was an active supporter of civil rights in the United States, although the rise of black power helped shift its attention more toward anti-Jewish extremism. One of their main targets during this period was the growth of neo-Nazi organizations. In 1987 he was named national director. The ADL sponsored antibias activities in schools and promoted respect for diversity. In the 1990s he was involved in highly publicized battles against Black Muslim leaders such as Louis Farrakhan, as well as skirmishes with mainstream black leaders such as Jesse Jackson (for once calling New York City "hymietown"). Although at times criticized for overestimating the level of anti-Jewish activity (he is called "hanging judge of anti-Semitism") and fearing that American support for Israel was waning (polls show anti-Semitism was at its lowest point in the United States by the end of the decade), he fought accusations that a "Jewish lobby" controlled U.S. foreign policy. Some critics claimed, however, that Foxman and the ADL opposed even moderate criticisms of Israeli policies, even by Jews themselves, and that he was too bombastic and divisive. In 2001 he was roundly criticized for his attempt to have a friend and fugitive financier pardoned by outgoing President Bill Clinton, although Foxman later admitted that he had erred in his support of the financial contributor to ADL. After 9/11 it condemned acts of violence carried out against Muslims, as well as criticized discriminatory measures and stereotyping. He has also steadfastly supported gay rights. In 2004 he vocally criticized Mel Gibson's *The Passion of the Christ*. In 2007 he opposed the appearance in New York of avowed anti-Semite Iranian president Mahmoud Ahmadinejad, who has denied the authenticity of the Holocaust, as well as his attempts to gain more recognition through the United Nations. At the end of the decade Foxman made headlines for criticizing former President Jimmy Carter over his allegedly anti-Israeli remarks and support for Palestinian rights.

Sources:

"Abraham H. Foxman's Story: A Life Saved, A Life of Service," Anti-Defamation League, *adl.org* (2003);

David Plotz, "Abe Foxman: The ADL Boss is the Best Kind of Pest," *slate.com* (6 April 2001);

Ben Sales, "The Two ADLs," *Jewish Week* (7 December 2010);

Joel Sprayregen, "A Tale of Two Cities: Is Abe Foxman Ruining the ADL?" *jewishdefense.org* (16 March 2007);

James Traub, "Does Abe Foxman Have an Anti-Anti-Semite Problem?" *New York Times*, 14 January 2007.

MOHAMED MAGID

1955–

IMAM

Beginnings. The daunting task of promoting interfaith understanding of Muslims in America in the wake of the September 11 attacks was taken up by Mohamed Magid, who was born in northern Sudan, the son of a Sunni cleric, and immigrated to the United States in 1987. He was deeply affected by the relationships he forged with Jewish doctors who treated his father (who died in 1990) for kidney disease. Educated by his father and at the Al-Medina Institute in New Jersey, he undertook to broaden the role of imam in the community. He met Amaarah Decuir at Howard and later married her. In 1997 he became leader of the All Dulles Area Muslim Society (a mosque serving more than five thousand Sunni and Shiite members from diverse backgrounds) in Sterling, Virginia, and instituted a more-progressive program that addressed many concerns often shunned by traditional imams, from AIDS to dating. He struggled to prevent young Muslims from adopting radical interpretations of the Koran and encouraged his congregants to support their country wholeheartedly, as well as to resist anti-Muslim sentiments in the United States. Magid taught or served as chaplain at several schools, including George Mason University, Georgetown University, Howard University, and American University.

Fostering Understanding. In the mid 2000s Magid partnered with Rabbi Robert Nosanchuk of the Northern Virginia Hebrew Congregation to foster understanding and cooperation between the two communities, especially on such topics as women and the role of terrorism. In one interview he declared, "my experience in America working with the pluralist diverse culture makes me appreciate people of different cultural backgrounds and I have become more aware of the beauty of the diversity by design that God has created." He called for an end to anti-Semitism and criticized Holocaust deniers, even visiting Auschwitz himself. Magid was instrumental in fighting radical impulses within his faith and allowed members of government agencies in 2002 to have access to his congregation to forge antiterrorist contacts, although critics have argued that there are radical elements who continue to maintain contacts and receive funding from members of the mosque. After serving two terms as vice president of the Islamic Society of North America (the largest organization of Muslims in North America), he was elected president in 2010. He stated, "The principles and values of Islam are aligned with those of America. We believe in freedom of religion, justice, celebration of diversity, equality, peace, and freedom. Many Muslims come to America seeking a better life, the freedom to pray, the freedom to discuss politics and the freedom to seek a better life for their children. In this way, America is great because it provides democracy, freedom of religion, freedom of expression and freedom of assembly. America is generous in helping people in need, raising billions of dollars in charity every year. America corrects itself in the injustices that have taken place in terms of civil rights and rights of women. When the injustice occurs again, we seek to correct our actions and learn from past mistakes rather than relive them. It truly is a land of opportunity."

Sources:

Aleisha Fishman, "Imam Mohamed Magid," *Voices on Antisemitism*, United States Holocaust Memorial Museum, *ushmm.com* (4 November 2010);

Ben Johnson, "A Troubling Presence at a Funeral," *frontpagemagazine.com* (11 June 2004);

"Meet ISNA President Imam Mohamed Magid," Islamic Society of North America, *isna.net* (2011);

Leslie Milk, "2009's Washingtonians of the Year: Imam Mohamed Magid and Rabbi Robert Nosanchuk," *washingtonian.com* (1 January 2010);

Douglas Waller Sterling, "An American Imam," *Time* (14 November 2005).

V. GENE ROBINSON

1947–

BISHOP

Early Life. V. Gene Robinson grew up in rural Nicholasville, Kentucky, and attended a fundamentalist Disciples of Christ church. He showed an early interest toward matters of faith, so much so that he was often told not to ask too many questions. During college at the University of the South in Sewanee, Tennessee, he struggled with conflicting aspects of his faith and sexuality. During his senior year (1969) he was confirmed in the Episcopal Church and earned a B.A. in American Studies/History. He enrolled at General Theological Seminary in New York only a few months after the Stonewall rebellion, a three-day-long uprising sparked by a routine raid on a gay bar in New York City, which marked the beginning of the gay rights movement. For years he tried to reconcile his sexual identity with his desire for ministry; inspired by a desire to be married and have children, he went into therapy to "cure" himself. Robinson married Isabella McDaniel in 1972, hoping to work through his homosexuality within the confines of a marriage. Ten years later they divorced amicably and maintained a close friendship. They had two daughters, Ella and Jamee.

Episcopal Church. Robinson earned his master of divinity from General Theological Seminary (1973), was ordained a deacon, and then became curate of Christ Church, Ridgewood, New Jersey. Robinson finally "came out" publicly in 1986. He served as canon to the ordinary (assistant to the bishop) for eighteen years before being elected bishop on 7 June 2003. One day before the vote, two baseless claims were leveled against him: a Vermont parishioner claimed Robinson improperly touched him, and an Episcopal bishop said that Robinson was involved with a gay counseling group with links to a porn site on its webpage. These claims did not diminish the good favor Robinson held within the New Hampshire Diocese, as the House of Bishops voted in his favor 62-43, and the House of Deputies approved him by a 2-1 margin. His former wife McDaniel served as one of his presenters at consecration, and he was invested on 7 March 2004.

Reaction. His election, however, sent a shock wave through the Episcopal Church and global Anglican Communion. Many Anglican affiliates in the southern hemisphere, such as South America and Africa, protested the decision and insisted that it would create strains between them and the Episcopal Church in the United States. Through it all, Robinson was diplomatic and courteous to those who cast blame on him for splitting the church. He insisted that the issue was not about him but rather about homosexuality in the church. He asserted that protests were a good thing: "These are fantastic discussions. Frankly, because of my election and the controversy around it, there is not an Episcopal congregation in the country that isn't asking that. This is an enormous educational and spiritual opportunity." Robinson insisted that he was theologically conservative on several doctrinal issues, defying the idea that gay clergymen automatically questioned traditional doctrine.

Civil Unions. In June 2008, six months after New Hampshire began granting civil unions for same-sex partners, he and partner Mark Andrew were joined in a civil ceremony. Andrew worked for the New Hampshire Department of Health and Human Services. They met in 1987 while on vacation in St. Croix, two months after Robinson's former wife remarried. In summer 2008 Robinson traveled to London for the Lambeth Conference that is held every ten years, though he was not granted participant status. He observed from the periphery and preached a sermon at a local church, where he was briefly heckled. Because of his stature and importance as a role model, Robinson was invited by President Barack Obama to give the invocation at the opening inaugural ceremonies at the Lincoln Memorial on 18 January 2009. Robinson delivered a nonsectarian prayer, appealing universally to "the God of our many understandings."

Service. Robinson has lobbied for state, federal, and international equal protection and civil-marriage rights for homosexuals. The Human Rights Campaign, National Gay & Lesbian Task Force, and Equality Forum have honored him for his work. *Advocate* named him their "Person of the Year" in 2003. From 1978 to 1985 he was youth ministries coordinator for seven dioceses of New England. He served two years on the National Youth Ministries Development Team and helped establish the national Episcopal Youth Event. He was founding director of Sign of the Dove Retreat Center in Temple, New Hampshire, that provides retreat programs. He developed the "Being Well in Christ" conference model for the Cornerstone Project, established a mentoring program for new clergy called "Fresh Start" (which focuses on conflict resolution), and wrote its curriculum. Robinson co-authored AIDS education curricula and worked in AIDS relief in the United States and Africa, specifically Uganda and South Africa. He advocated for antiracism training, debt relief for third-world countries, and socially responsible investment. He served on the board of New Hampshire Endowment for Health, which provides health care for the uninsured, as well as on the Church Pension Fund and New Hampshire Children's Alliance. He was featured in the award-winning documentary *For the Bible Tells Me So* (2007) and published a memoir, *In the Eye of the Storm: Swept to the Center by God* (2008).

Sources:

John Dart, "Gene Robinson Takes on More Risky Ventures," *Christian Century*, 125 (20 May 2008): 16–17;

"The Right Reverend V. Gene Robinson, IX Bishop of New Hampshire," Episcopal Diocese of New Hampshire, *nhepiscopal.org* (2010);

Bruce C. Steele and John Caldwell, "Person of the Year," *Advocate* (2003): 34–42.

KATHARINE JEFFERTS SCHORI

1954–

BISHOP

Science and Faith. Katharine Jefferts was born 26 March 1954 in Pensacola, Florida, and later attended schools in Washington and New Jersey. Schori earned a B.S. in biology from Stanford University (1974) and her M.S. (1977) and Ph.D. (1983) in oceanography from Oregon State University. She later turned to theological studies and earned a masters in divinity (1994) and doctorate of divinity (2001) at the Church Divinity School of the Pacific. In 1979 she married mathematician Richard Miles Schori. She worked as an oceanographer with the National Marine Fisheries Service in Seattle and at Oregon State University. She was ordained a priest in 1994, and while in Oregon served as a chaplain and rector in Corvallis (working largely with the Hispanic population there), and was then consecrated as a bishop in the diocese of Nevada in 2001. In 2003 she supported the election of the Episcopal Church's first openly gay bishop, V. Gene Robinson of New Hampshire.

Presiding Bishop. On 4 November 2006 in the Washington National Cathedral, Schori was invested as the twenty-sixth presiding bishop of the Episcopal Church in the United States, replacing Frank Griswold. The first woman elected as a primate of the Anglican Communion, she called for a "rich and multihued vision of a world where no one goes hungry because everyone is invited to a seat at the groaning board, it's a vision of a world where no one is sick or in prison because all sorts of disease have been healed, it's a vision of a world where every human being has the capacity to use every good gift that God has given, it's a vision of a world where no one enjoys abundance at the expense of another, where all enjoy Sabbath rest in the conscious presence of God." An outspoken feminist, she took progressive views on gays in the pulpit and on the teaching of evolution. She faced the challenge of holding together a fracturing church as it confronted the issues of gay priests and same-sex marriage. She wrote *A Wing and a Prayer: A Message of Faith and Hope* (2007) and *The Heartbeat of God: Finding the Sacred in the Middle of Everything* (2010).

Sources:

"Episcopal Church Elects Female Leader," *USA Today*, 18 June 2006;

"In Their Own Words: Katharine Jefferts Schori," *Witness Magazine* (28 February 2006);

"Our Presiding Bishop," *ecusa.anglican.org* (2011);

Mary Frances Schjonberg, "Amid Prayer and 'Shalom,' Katharine Jefferts Schori Invested as Episcopal Church's 26th Presiding Bishop," Episcopal News Service, *ecusa.anglican.org* (4 November 2006);

"Ten Questions for Katharine Jefferts Schori," *Time* (10 July 2006).

RICHARD DUANE "RICK" WARREN

1954–

PASTOR

America's Pastor. Rick Warren, who took the place of Billy Graham as "America's Pastor," was born 28 January 1954 and grew up in the small town (five hundred citizens) of Ukiah, Redwood Valley, California, and later built a congregation fifty times that size. Warren's desire to minister and write began in high school, where he started a Christian club and edited the club newsletter. He grew up as a Southern Baptist, and received a B.A. from California Baptist University in Riverside, California. While there he met his future wife, Kay; they married in 1975, the same year that he was ordained. After graduating in 1977, they moved to Fort Worth, Texas, where he attended Southwestern Baptist Theological Seminary and earned a master's in divinity. During seminary he wrote *Personal Bible Study Methods* (1981, republished as *Bible Study Methods*, 2006) that sold 100,000 copies, benefiting from distribution at some of Graham's ministerial events. While studying at seminary, he began to research the issue that became the focus of his writing career: ministry building. Warren conducted an independent study of the one hundred largest churches nationwide to discover the factors that contribute to developing successful ministries.

Saddleback. In 1979 he founded a church in Saddleback Valley, Orange County, California. Saddleback Church received financial sponsorship from five Baptist churches and was granted fifteen interns from Southwestern Baptist Seminary. He relied on the counsel of three mentors: his father Jimmy Warren Sr., Graham, and Peter Drucker, a management specialist who advised him on business strategies that laid the foundation for later success. Warren employed a "seeker-sensitive" approach, tailoring his approach to the "unchurched" using nontraditional methods. He decided not to compete with fellow Baptist ministries for membership and chose instead to research the local community to find potential congregants. In 1980 he and his volunteers canvassed on foot to learn why people did not attend church services. He found that the sermon rhetoric, atmosphere, emphasis on money, and lack of child care made many people feel unwelcome. This "market research" enabled him to form a ministry that appealed to a growing demographic: the discontented. Warren adapted his sermons to appeal to people who were unfamiliar with church doctrine or culture. Warren often interrupted his sermons with jokes, images, movie clips, music, and guest speakers so that the entire experience had an intentional rhythm, with highs and lows to keep the attention of his audience. Brief guest testimonies served as real-world examples and added a level of authenticity lacking in the traditional monologue approach.

Growth. Saddleback held its first service on Easter 1980 at Laguna Hills High School after sending out 15,000 letters of invitation targeting non-Christians. Warren emphasized membership and community action, increasing the congregation's size each year. The congregation used seventy-nine different buildings in its first thirteen years; they also used a gigantic tent that seated 2,300. By 2006 Saddleback had found its home in a 120-acre hilltop network of buildings designed by theme-park experts. The ministry grew in twenty-six years to an average attendance of 25,000 weekly. The basic business principle of designing an organization's goals around the needs of prospective clients helped create one of the top ten largest congregations in the nation. Members of Saddleback had the customary Southern California easygoing attitude: they often attended services in shorts, jeans, short-sleeved shirts, or blouses. Warren matched that attitude from the pulpit, wearing Hawaiian shirts and khakis. Like most megachurches, Saddleback offered seven services a week to cater to members who either could not or did not want to attend each Sunday morning. The services contained a variety of music and worship styles, so that members did not have the same worship experience.

Publications. Warren earned a Ph.D. from Fuller Theological Seminary and published his principles on how to build worship communities in his first major book, *The Purpose Driven Church: Growth Without Compromising Your Message & Mission* (1995). He followed with *The Purpose Driven Life: What on Earth Am I Here For?* (2002), which sold more than 30 million copies worldwide and was translated into more than forty languages. Neither Warren's books nor Saddleback Church presented new theological perspectives; rather, traditional doctrines and theologies were adapted into a more contemporary context. *The Purpose Driven Life* became part of the Brian Nichols/Ashley Smith abduction story in March 2005. Escaped convict Nichols killed a court reporter, judge, police officer, and

U.S. Customs agent, and then invaded Smith's apartment. She convinced him to let her read from the Bible and *Purpose Driven Life*, which inspired Nichols to believe that God was speaking to him through Smith. He eventually freed her and gave himself up to the police. The incident caused an increase in sales of Warren's book, which had peaked the previous year. He published *God's Answers to Life's Difficult Questions* (2006), *God's Power to Change Your Life* (2006), and *The Purpose of Christmas* (2008). Several leading magazines have named him on their most-influential-people lists.

Charities. Rick and Kay Warren consider themselves "reverse tithers," as they donate 90 percent of their earnings to charities and ministries. Warren returned twenty-five years' worth of salary to Saddleback and discontinued taking a salary. In April 2005 at Angel Stadium in Anaheim, where 30,000 people attended Saddleback's twenty-fifth anniversary service, he announced the P.E.A.C.E. Plan. The acronym stands for the plan's central purposes: "Promote reconciliation—Equip servant leaders—Assist the poor—Care for the sick—Educate the next generation." The mission seeks to motivate 10 million churches, 100 million small groups, and 1 billion Christians worldwide to achieve these goals. The underlying premise is that the Christian church's broad global network makes it better equipped to combat social ills than governments or businesses. Warren encourages activism from church members as well as people who attend his talks to help with the AIDS crisis and combat other diseases, such as Alzheimer's, cancer, and depression. Some of Saddleback's projects are a prayer garden, prison ministries, financial counseling services, food banks, support groups, a music school, a Hawaiian band, and a hula hoop team. Lay leaders help with volunteer ministries and must attend a fifty-two-week systematic-theology course. Saddleback has given money and time to assist the victims of the southeast Asia tsunami (2004), Hurricane Katrina (2005), and Haiti earthquake (2009). On 30 December 2009 Warren announced the church had received half as many donations as normal and needed an additional $900,000 to avoid an end-of-year budget shortfall. Members responded by raising $2.4 million. Despite membership declines, Saddleback was the eighth-largest congregation in the United States and remained focused on Warren's mission.

Politics. On 16 August 2008 Warren hosted presidential candidates Senators Barack Obama and John McCain at Saddleback at the "Civil Forum on the Presidency." The forum gave both candidates an opportunity to speak on matters of faith and practice in the public arena and to discuss social issues. After Obama won the presidency, he selected Warren to deliver the invocation prayer at his inauguration. The decision angered many gay-rights supporters, since Warren was an outspoken supporter of Proposition 8, California's ban on gay marriage, that passed in 2008. Warren's prayer at the inauguration was a call for unity among Americans: "May all people of good will today join together to work for a more just, a more healthy and a more prosperous nation and peaceful planet."

Sources:

Shayne Lee and Phillip Luke Sinitiere, "Surfing Spiritual Waves: Rick Warren and the Purpose-Driven Church," in *Holy Mavericks: Evangelical Innovators and the Spiritual Marketplace* (New York: New York University Press, 2009), pp. 129–148;

Erika I. Ritchie, "Church Raises $2.4 Million to Cover Financial Shortfall," *Orange County Register*, 3 January 2010;

rickwarren.com;

saddlebackchurch.com;

Martin Wisckol and Erika Ritchie, "Warren Prayer Quells Some Critics," *Orange County Register*, 21 January 2009.

JEREMIAH A. WRIGHT JR.

1941–

MINISTER AND ACTIVIST

Beginnings. Jeremiah Wright Jr. was born on 22 September 1941 and grew up in a family with a tradition of clergymen, following in the footsteps of his maternal grandfather and father. He earned four degrees: a bachelor of arts and master of arts in English from Howard University, a master of arts in history of religions from the University of Chicago Divinity School, and a doctor of ministry from the United Theological Seminary. His academic focus was on black sacred music, ethnomusicology, and African diaspora studies. Wright was hired at Trinity United Church of Christ in Chicago in April 1972, when the congregation had only eighty-seven people. An outspoken and energetic figure, he inspired the congregation to act against social ills, especially racism. Coming from a family that encouraged the discussion of diverse viewpoints, Wright took a more liberal approach to theology than conservative black Baptist churches, an approach that fit well with Trinity's slogan: "Unashamedly Black and Unapologetically Christian." Wright opposed prosperity theology and mandated school prayer; he supported black liberation theology and gay rights (sponsoring a singles group for gays). He was a unique figure among clergy, and his efforts met with great success. He oversaw groundbreakings on two sanctuaries: the first, built in 1978, held 900 people; the second, Trinity's current building, completed in 1994, holds 2,500. The congregation grew to 8,500, and so did his responsibilities, which took a toll on his home life. Wright and his wife Janet divorced; he considers this to be his biggest failure.

Obama. In 1985 community activist Barack Obama visited Trinity. Wright warned him that he might upset conservative local groups by associating himself with Trinity, which was often considered a radical church. However, Obama was drawn by Wright's ability to engage congregants from all walks of life, races, and classes of believers. At age twenty-seven, just before he left to attend law school at Harvard in 1988, Obama responded to an altar call during one of Wright's services and became a member of Trinity. Wright inspired Obama for years; this is most evident in Obama's appropriation of the Wright sermon "The Audacity to Hope" into the title of his memoir *The Audacity of Hope: Thoughts on Reclaiming the American Dream* (2006). Wright officiated at Barack and Michelle Obama's wedding ceremony and baptized their two daughters, Sasha and Malia. In February 2008 Wright delivered his final sermon as pastor of Trinity and retired after thirty-six years. Speaking about Obama, Wright observed that "children born to parents who are of two different races do not have a snowball's chance in hell of making it in America, especially if the momma was white and the daddy was black. A child born to that union is an unfortunate statistic in a racially polarized society. But, if you use your mind, instead of a lost statistic in a hate-filled universe, you just may end up a law student at Harvard University."

Controversy. As the Democratic presidential primary race between Obama and Hillary Clinton heated up in March 2008, the press received footage of some of Wright's more controversial sermons. One from 2003 featured Wright speaking out against the country's record of injustice. "'God bless America.' No, no, no, God damn America . . . God damn America for treating our citizens as less than human. God damn America, for as long as she acts like she is God, and she is supreme." In another sermon, given after the September 11 attacks, Wright criticized the government for its policies in the Middle East saying, "The stuff we have done overseas is brought right back into our homes." Obama denounced these statements, emphasizing that he would not have agreed with Wright had he attended those particular sermons. Wright was removed from the advisory position he held on Obama's campaign staff on 14 March 2008. Obama continued to provide vocal support for his pastor, however, likening him to "an uncle you love and respect but has lately said some things that you disagree with." Many tried to associate politics with the incendiary tone of the sound bites, but Obama emphasized that he had never sought political advice from Wright. In a 2007 interview, he characterized Wright as "much more of a sounding board for me to make sure that I am speaking as truthfully about what I believe as possible and that I'm not losing myself in some of the hype and hoopla and stress that's involved in national politics." Though he rarely spoke to the press, he bore no ill will toward President Obama, but rather the press for the fiasco that erupted. "I have not stopped loving him because of what the press did, and to see him beat up on because of things he is not responsible for is painful."

Retirement. Wright was succeeded at Trinity by Otis Moss III, who continues to support and defend the beleaguered reverend. Wright traveled around the country and preached at various church services and revivals, and he lectured at Union Theological Seminary in Richmond, Virginia, and the Theological School at Drew University in Madison, New Jersey. Wright published *A Sankofa Moment: The History of Trinity United Church of Christ* (2010) and lives with his second wife, Ramah Wright.

Sources:

"Bio," *jeremiahwright.com* (16 February 2010);

Manya A. Brachear, "Maverick Pastor Inspires Obama—Chicago Preacher Has Built Large Following," *Lexington Herald-Leader*, 3 February 2007;

R. Harris Hamil, "Jeremiah Wright Discusses Obama Flap, Church's History," *Houston Chronicle*, 13 March 2010;

Abdon M. Pallasch, "Obama Denounces Rhetoric But Stands Behind His Pastor," *Chicago Sun-Times*, 15 March 2008;

Karen Springen and others, "Trying Times for Trinity," *Newsweek*, 151 (2008): 50–51.

PEOPLE IN THE NEWS

Jay Scott Ballinger, an avowed Satanist, pleaded guilty on 11 July 2000 to setting fire to twenty-six churches between 1995 and 1999 in the states of Indiana, Ohio, California, Alabama, South Carolina, Missouri, Kentucky, and Tennessee.

On 13 September 2001, fundamentalist preacher **Jerry Falwell** stated on **Pat Robertson**'s *The 700 Club* that the September 11 terrorist attacks were in part divine retribution for the advancement of secular institutions in the United States. "I really believe that the pagans and the abortionists, the feminists, and the gays and the lesbians who are actively trying to make that an alternative lifestyle, the ACLU, the People for the American Way, all who try to secularize America, I point the finger in their face and say 'You helped this happen.'"

Habitat for Humanity International announced on 31 January 2005 that it had fired its cofounders—president **Millard Fuller** and his wife **Linda**—because of their behavior during an investigation into an inappropriate relationship between Fuller and a former female employee.

In November 2006 **Ted Haggard** was accused by male prostitute **Mike Jones** of having sexual relations with him and taking methamphetamines. After denying the allegations, Haggard confessed to the acts in a letter to his congregation, New Life Church in Colorado Springs; he resigned as head of the National Association of Evangelicals and was fired by his church.

Joe Hale retired in 2001 as general secretary of the World Methodist Council (WMC) after twenty-five years; he received the World Methodist Peace Award for "valiant leadership as a proponent of peace and ecumenical unity throughout the world."

Major **Nidal Malik Hasan,** a U.S. Army psychiatrist and a Muslim in charge of counseling distressed soldiers, opened fire on fellow soldiers at Fort Hood, Texas, on 5 November 2009, killing thirteen and wounding thirty-one. An open critic of the wars in Iraq and Afghanistan, Major Hasan was distraught over harassment about his faith and having recently received orders to go to the Middle East.

Bob Jones III, president of Bob Jones University in Greenville, South Carolina, announced on the 3 March 2000 episode of *Larry King Live* that the school would end its ban on interracial dating that had been in place for fifty years.

On 3 January 2006 Southern Baptist Convention executive-committee member **Lonnie Latham** was arrested for offering to engage in an act of lewdness (soliciting oral sex from a male undercover police officer). He resigned from the committee, the board of directors of the Baptist General Convention of Oklahoma, and as pastor of the South Tulsa Baptist Church. He was cleared of the charge in 2007.

Chief justice **Roy Moore** was removed from the Alabama Supreme Court on 13 November 2003 for disobeying a court order to have a 5,300-pound Ten Commandments monument removed from the statehouse rotunda. He appealed the decision on the grounds that the order forced him to violate his oath of office, but lost.

Michael Arthur Newdow, an attorney and atheist, brought several suits against the U.S. government in an attempt to augment the separation of church and state. The focus of his cases involved the words "under God" in the Pledge of Allegiance, "In God We Trust" on currency, the invocation given at President Bush's 2004 inauguration, and use of the phrase "so help me God" at President Obama's inauguration.

John Paulk, chairman of the board for Exodus International (a Christian organization that encourages homosexuals to change their behavior), was photographed visiting a gay bar in Washington, D.C., in September 2000. He was put on probation by the organization and reinstated in 2001, but he resigned in 2003.

In response to the regular picketing of military funerals by **Fred Phelps** and the Westboro Baptist Church, Congress approved the "Respect for America's Fallen Heroes Act," which was signed by President George W. Bush on 29 May 2006. The law prevents protests within three-hundred feet of a cemetery entrance from one hour before to one hour after a funeral of a deceased serviceperson.

During the interview portion of the Miss USA 2009 pageant, **Carrie Prejean** (Miss California) was asked whether homosexuals should have the right to marry. She responded, ". . . I believe that marriage should be between a man and a woman," which caused a stir among gay-rights activists. Prejean placed second in the contest.

Sally Jane Priesand, the first female rabbi ordained in the United States, retired as leader of the Monmouth Reform Temple in Tinton Falls, New Jersey, on 30 June 2006.

Due to differences regarding greater acceptance of homosexuality, the dioceses of San Joaquin, Cailfornia; Quincy, Illinois; Pittsburgh, Pennsylvania; and Fort Worth, Texas, left the Episcopal Church between 2007 and 2008. They moved under the direction of the Anglican archbishop of the Southern Cone, based in Buenos Aires, Argentina. Episcopal bishop **Katharine Jefferts Schori** stated that all churches leaving must relinquish church properties.

On 6 June 2009 **Alysa Stanton** became the first African American female rabbi, having received a master's degree at Hebrew Union College-Jewish Institute of Religion.

Mike Trout, senior vice president of the broadcast division of Focus on the Family and cohost of president **James Dobson**'s radio program, resigned from his positions in 2000 after admitting to an extramarital affair. In November 2005 the Citizens for Responsibility and Ethics in Washington (a political watchdog group) accused Focus on the Family of violating its tax-exempt status through political endorsements made by Dobson. The Internal Revenue Service eventually cleared the organization of all charges.

AWARDS

GRAWEMEYER AWARD IN RELIGION

Awarded annually since 1990, honors "ideas rather than lifelong or personal achievement"; thus winners are listed with the book for which they were recognized.

2000: Jürgen Moltmann, *The Coming of God: Christian Eschatology*

2001: James L. Kugel, *The Bible as It Was*

2002: Miroslav Volf, *Exclusion & Embrace: A Theological Exploration of Identity, Otherness, and Reconciliation*

2003: Mark Juergensmeyer, *Terror in the Mind of God: The Global Rise of Religious Violence*

2004: Jonathan Sacks, *The Dignity of Difference: How to Avoid the Clash of Civilizations*

2005: George M. Marsden, *Jonathan Edwards: A Life*

2006: Marilynne Robinson, *Gilead*

2007: Timothy B. Tyson, *Blood Done Sign My Name*

2008: Margaret A. Farley, *Just Love: A Framework for Christian Sexual Ethics*

2009: Donald W. Shriver Jr., *Honest Patriots: Loving a Country Enough to Remember Its Misdeeds*

TEMPLETON PRIZE FOR PROGRESS IN RELIGION

Awarded since 1972 to a living person who has shown "extraordinary originality in advancing humankind's understanding of God and/or spirituality."

2000: Freeman Dyson, Physicist and Mathematician

2001: No American Winner

2002: No American Winner

2003: Holmes Rolston, III, Colorado State University Professor/Presbyterian Minister

2004: No American Winner

2005: Charles H. Townes, Professor of Physics at University of California, Berkeley

2007: No American Winner

2008: No American Winner

2009: No American Winner

DEATHS

Owen Allred, 91, president of the polygamous Apostolic United Brethren (Mormon) from 1977 until his death, 14 February 2005.

William R. Bright, 81, televangelist, founder of the Campus Crusade for Christ, 19 July 2003.

Edwin Bernard Broderick, 89, Roman Catholic bishop of Albany, New York, Director of Catholic Relief Services, 2 July 2006.

Frank Forrester Church IV, 61, minister, author, and theologian, senior minister of the Unitarian Church of All Souls in New York City, 24 September 2009.

John H. Cross Jr., 82, pastor of 16th Street Baptist Church in Birmingham, Alabama (bombed during the civil-rights movement), 15 November 2007.

Billy Joe Daugherty, 57, founder of Victory Christian Center in Tulsa, Oklahoma; founder of Victory Christian School, Victory Bible Institute, and Victory World Missions Training Center, interim president of Oral Roberts University, 22 November 2009.

George MacPherson Docherty, 97, Presbyterian minister, initiated in 1952 idea to have words "under God" added to the U.S. Pledge of Allegiance, 27 November 2008.

Avery Robert Dulles, 90, theologian, taught at Fordham University, only American theologian to be elevated from priest (because of his advanced age at 82) to the College of Cardinals, 12 December 2008.

John Truscott Elson, 78, religion editor and writer, assistant managing editor of *Time*, 7 September 2009.

Aharon Zelig Epstein, 95, Orthodox rabbi, Yeshiva Shaar HaTorah-Grodno, considered last of the gedolim rabbis (most revered), 3 August 2009.

William Roscoe Estep, 80, Baptist historian, authority on the Anabaptist movement, 14 July 2000.

Jerry Falwell, 73, fundamentalist preacher, founder of Thomas Road Baptist Church, Liberty University, and the Moral Majority, 15 May 2007.

Allen Finley, 76, former president/CEO of Partners International, 30 October 2006.

Robert J. Fox, 81, Roman Catholic priest, author, director of Fatima Family Apostolate and Youth for Fatima Pilgrimages, editor of *Immaculate Heart Messenger*, 26 November 2009.

Eugene Maxwell Frank, 101, Methodist bishop, promoted racial equality, helped establish Saint Paul School of Theology in Kansas City, 13 October 2009.

John J. Geoghan, 68, defrocked Catholic priest, central figure in the Boston Catholic Diocese Church sex scandal, 23 August 2003.

Thich Man Giac, 77, leader of the Vietnamese United Buddhist Churches of America, 13 October 2006.

Langdon Brown Gilkey, 85, Protestant Ecumenical theologian, professor at Columbia University, Vanderbilt Divinity School, and University of Chicago, 19 November 2004.

Ruth Bell Graham, 87, poet, wife of evangelist Billy Graham, 14 June 2007.

Dmitry Grigorieff, 89, priest, dean emeritus of the St. Nicholas Russian Orthodox Cathedral, Washington, D.C., 8 December 2007.

Naftali Halberstam, 74, grand rabbi, head of the Bobov Hasidic sect (2000–2005), 23 March 2005.

Billy James Hargis, 79, fundamentalist evangelist, founded Christian Crusade ministries, 27 November 2004.

Carl Ferdinand Howard Henry, 90, evangelist, theologian, first editor in chief of *Christianity Today*, 7 December 2003.

Arthur Hertzberg, 84, conservative rabbi, scholar of Judaism, civil-rights activist, 17 April 2006.

Gordon B. Hinckley, 97, president of the Church of Jesus Christ of Latter-Day Saints, 27 January 2008.

Dean R. Hoge, 71, sociologist, studied American Catholicism, president of the Religious Research Association, president of the Society for the Scientific Study of Religion, 13 September 2008.

Rex Humbard, 88, televangelist, built Cathedral of Tomorrow, 21 September 2007.

Stanley L. Jaki, 84, Benedictine priest, physics professor at Seton Hall University, author of titles in philosophy of science and theology, 7 April 2009.

Dennis James Kennedy, 76, evangelist, founder of Coral Ridge Presbyterian Church, Coral Ridge Ministries, Evangelism Explosion International, Westminster Academy, Knox Theological Seminary, and Center for Reclaiming America for Christ, 5 September 2007.

Leon Klenicki, 78, rabbi, director of interfaith affairs for the Anti-Defamation League, 25 January 2009.

Kyle Lake, 33, pastor of University Baptist Church in Waco, Texas, author of *Understanding God's Will* (2004) and *(Re)understanding Prayer* (2005), electrocuted during baptismal service, died 30 October 2005.

David J. Lawson, 77, pastor, University Campus minister, bishop of the Methodist Church, 31 May 2007.

Zola Levitt, 67, Christian broadcaster, founder of Zola Levitt Ministries, 19 April 2006.

David Lieber, 83, rabbi and biblical scholar, president of the University of Judaism, 15 December 2008.

John Daido Loori, 78, abbot of Zen Mountain Monastery, Mount Tremper, New York, founder of Mountains and Rivers Order, CEO of Dharma Communications, 9 October 2009.

Robert James Marshall, 90, president of the Lutheran Church in America, helped form the Evangelical Lutheran Church in America (ELCA), 22 December 2008.

Will Maslow, 99, lawyer, civil-rights activist, executive of the American Jewish Congress, 23 February 2007.

Jarrell F. McCracken, 79, evangelist, pioneer in Christian records, founder of Word Records Inc., 7 November 2007.

William C. McInnes, 86, Jesuit academic, president of Fairfield University (1964–1973), president of University of San Francisco (1972–1977), head of Association of Jesuit Colleges and Universities (1977–1989), 8 December 2009.

Tamara "Tammy" Faye Bakker Messner, 65, singer, author, televangelist, television personality, former wife of Jim Bakker, cohost of the *PTL Club,* 20 July 2007.

Warith Deen Mohammed, 74, African American Muslim leader, disbanded the Nation of Islam, founded American Society of Muslims, 9 September 2008.

James O. Mote, 84, bishop of the Anglican Catholic Church, 29 April 2006.

Judah Nadich, 95, rabbi, president of the Rabbinical Assembly, advised General Dwight D. Eisenhower on Jewish affairs during World War II, 26 August 2007.

John Cardinal O'Connor, 80, Roman Catholic archbishop of New York, 3 May 2000.

Gilbert Earl Patterson, 67, International Presiding Bishop and Chief Apostle of the Church of God in Christ, 20 March 2007.

Jaroslav Jan Pelikan, 82, historian of Christianity and Christian theology, 13 May 2006.

Hermann Platt, 95, founded University of Judaism in Los Angeles, California, 2 January 2005.

Chaim Potok, 73, rabbi, author of *The Chosen* (1967) and *My Name is Asher Lev* (1972), 23 July 2002.

Elizabeth Clare Prophet, 70, New Age spiritual leader, helped found The Summit Lighthouse and Church Universal and Triumphant, 15 October 2009.

Granville Oral Roberts, 91, charismatic Pentecostal televangelist, founded Oral Roberts Evangelistic Association and Oral Roberts University, 15 December 2009.

Adrian Pierce Rogers, 74, two-term president of the Southern Baptist Convention, pastor of Bellevue Baptist Church in Memphis, Tennessee, 15 November 2005.

Irving D. Rubin, 57, chairman of the Jewish Defense League, accused of attempted bombing of mosque and office of Arab American congressman, allegedly of suicide while in detention, 13 November 2002.

Theresa Marie "Terri" Schiavo, 41, center of controversy over feeding tube removal while in a persistent vegetative state, 31 March 2005.

Robert L. Short, 76, Presbyterian minister and author, wrote best-selling *The Gospel According to Peanuts* (1965), *Something to Believe In: Is Kurt Vonnegut the Exorcist of Jesus Christ Superstar?* (1978), *The Gospel According to Dogs: What Our Four-Legged Saints Can Teach Us* (2007), and *The Parables of Dr. Seuss* (2008), 6 July 2009.

Frederick Earl Sontag, 84, United Church of Christ minister, professor of philosophy, author, 14 June 2009.

John Strugnell, 77, biblical scholar, member of team that edited the Dead Sea Scrolls, 30 November 2007.

Prince A. Taylor Jr., 94, bishop, United Methodist Church, longest tenure at the time and first African American bishop, 15 August 2001.

John C. Trever, 90, archaeologist and biblical scholar, first American scholar to see fragments of the Dead Sea Scrolls, 29 April 2006.

Robert Eugene Webber, 73, theologian and rabbi, leader of the Convergence Movement, 27 April 2007.

Sherwin Theodore Wine, 79, founder of Humanistic Judaism and the Birmingham Temple in Birmingham, Michigan, 21 July 2007.

Ralph Dana Winter, 84, Presbyterian missionary, founder of U.S. Center for World Mission (USCWM), William Carey International University, and International Society for Frontier Missiology, 20 May 2009.

Yosef Hayim Yerushalmi, 77, scholar of Jewish history, taught at Columbia University (1980–2008), 8 December 2009.

Maharishi Mahesh Yogi, around 91, guru, introduced the West to transcendental meditation, taught The Beatles, 5 February 2008.

PUBLICATIONS

Khaled Abou El Fadl, *The Great Theft: Wrestling Islam from the Extremists* (New York: HarperSanFrancisco, 2005);

William Y. Adams, *Religion and Adaptation* (Stanford, Cal.: CSLI Publications, 2005);

Jensine Andresen, *Religion in Mind: Cognitive Perspectives on Religious Belief, Ritual, and Experience* (Cambridge & New York: Cambridge University Press, 2001);

Reza Aslan, *No God but God: The Origins, Evolution, and Future of Islam* (New York: Random House, 2005);

Matthew C. Bagger, *The Uses of Paradox: Religion, Self-Transformation, and the Absurd* (New York: Columbia University Press, 2007);

Thomas Berry, *The Sacred Universe: Earth, Spirituality, and Religion in the Twenty-First Century,* foreword by Mary Evelyn Tucker (New York: Columbia University Press, 2009);

Ray Billington, *Religion Without God* (London & New York: Routledge, 2002);

Jenny Blain, Douglas Ezzy, and Graham Harvey, eds., *Researching Paganisms* (Walnut Creek, Cal.: AltaMira Press, 2004);

Pascal Boyer, *Religion Explained: The Evolutionary Origins of Religious Thought* (New York: Basic Books, 2001);

Lynn Bridgers, *Contemporary Varieties of Religious Experience: James's Classic Study in Light of Resiliency, Temperament, and Trauma* (Lanham, Md.: Rowman & Littlefield, 2005);

Richard Dawkins, *The God Delusion* (Boston: Houghton Mifflin, 2006);

Daniel C. Dennett, *Breaking the Spell: Religion as a Natural Phenomenon* (New York: Viking, 2006);

Jorge N. Ferrer and Jacob H. Sherman, eds., *The Participatory Turn: Spirituality, Mysticism, Religious Studies* (Albany: State University of New York Press, 2008);

David France, *Our Fathers: The Secret Life of the Catholic Church in an Age of Scandal* (New York: Broadway, 2004);

Andrew Gelman, *Red State, Blue State, Rich State, Poor State* (Princeton, N.J.: Princeton University Press, 2009);

Sam Harris, *The End of Faith: Religion, Terror, and the Future of Reason* (New York: Norton, 2004);

Harris, *Letter to a Christian Nation* (New York: Knopf, 2006):

Chris Hedges, *I Don't Believe in Atheists* (New York: Free Press, 2008);

John Hick, *The New Frontier of Religion and Science: Religious Experience, Neuroscience and the Transcendent* (Basingstoke, U.K. & New York: Palgrave Macmillan, 2006);

Christopher Hitchens, *God is Not Great: How Religion Poisons Everything* (New York: Twelve, 2007);

Laura Lyn Inglis and Peter K. Steinfeld, *Old Dead White Men's Philosophy* (Amherst, N.Y.: Humanity Books, 2000);

Hans Küng, *Islam: Past, Present and Future,* translated by John Bowden (Oxford: Oneworld, 2007);

John Lamb Lash, *Not in His Image: Gnostic Vision, Sacred Ecology, and the Future of Belief* (White River Junction, Vt.: Chelsea Green, 2006);

Timothy D. Lytton, *Holding Bishops Accountable: How Lawsuits Helped the Catholic Church Confront Clergy Abuse* (Cambridge, Mass.: Harvard University Press, 2008);

James McClenon, *Wondrous Healing: Shamanism, Human Evolution, and the Origin of Religion* (DeKalb: Northern Illinois University Press, 2002);

Alister E. McGrath and Joanna Collicutt McGrath, *The Dawkins Delusion: Atheist Fundamentalism and the Denial of the Divine* (Downers Grove, Ill.: InterVarsity Press, 2007);

Jacob Neusner, Bruce Chilton, and William A. Graham, *Three Faiths, One God: The Formative Faith and Practice of Judaism, Christianity, and Islam* (Boston: Brill, 2002);

Robert C. Neville, *Realism in Religion: A Pragmatist's Perspective* (Albany: State University of New York Press, 2009);

Pippa Norris and Ronald Inglehart, *Sacred and Secular: Religion and Politics Worldwide* (Cambridge & New York: Cambridge University Press, 2004);

Kimberley Christine Patton, *Religion of the Gods: Ritual, Paradox, and Reflexivity* (Oxford & New York: Oxford University Press, 2009);

Richard Rorty and Gianni Vattimo, *The Future of Religion*, edited by Santiago Zabala (New York: Columbia University Press, 2005);

Omid Safi, *Progressive Muslims: On Justice, Gender and Pluralism* (Oxford: Oneworld, 2003);

Alexander Saxton, *Religion and the Human Prospect* (New York: Monthly Review, 2006);

David Smith, *Hinduism and Modernity* (Malden, Mass.: Blackwell, 2003);

Raymond M. Smullyan, *Who Knows?: A Study of Religious Consciousness* (Bloomington: Indiana University Press, 2003);

C. John Sommerville, *Religion in the National Agenda: What We Mean by Religious, Spiritual, Secular* (Waco, Texas: Baylor University Press, 2009);

Lloyd H. Steffen, *Holy War, Just War: Exploring the Moral Meaning of Religious Violence* (Lanham, Md.: Rowman & Littlefield, 2007);

Victor J. Stenger, *God: The Failed Hypothesis: How Science Shows That God Does Not Exist* (Amherst, N.Y.: Prometheus, 2007);

Krista Tippett, *Speaking of Faith* (New York: Viking, 2007);

Frederick Turner, *Natural Religion* (New Brunswick, N.J.: Transaction, 2006);

Aaron Tyler, *Islam, the West, and Tolerance: Conceiving Coexistence* (New York: Palgrave Macmillan, 2008);

Graham Ward, *True Religion* (Oxford & Malden, Mass.: Blackwell, 2003);

Rick Warren, *The Purpose Driven Life: What on Earth Am I Here For?* (Grand Rapids, Mich.: Zondervan, 2002);

Harvey Whitehouse, *Modes of Religiosity: A Cognitive Theory of Religious Transmission* (Walnut Creek, Cal.: AltaMira Press, 2004);

Whitehouse and James Laidlaw, eds., *Religion, Anthropology, and Cognitive Science* (Durham, N.C.: Carolina Academic Press, 2007);

Christian Science Monitor, periodical;

Christianity Today, periodical;

Church Times, periodical;

National Catholic Reporter, periodical;

Reform Judaism Magazine, periodical;

Sojourners Magazine, periodical;

Theology Today, periodical.

Pope Benedict XVI meets with President George W. Bush at the White House during his 2008 visit to the United States.

SCIENCE AND TECHNOLOGY

by PAUL TOLLIVER BROWN

CONTENTS

Sidebars and tables are listed in italics.

2000

- Toyota begins marketing the hybrid car Prius in the United States; the manufacturer claims it has more power, better acceleration, and lower emissions than the previous model sold in Japan.

- Google begins selling advertisements associated with search keywords with bids starting at $.05 per click.

- The Society for Information Display gives Larry F. Weber its highest award for his contributions to plasma displays.

- Trek technology and IBM begin selling the first Universal Serial Bus (USB) flash drives commercially.

- Researchers at the Duke University Medical Center implant electrodes in monkeys' brains and train them to reach for food using a robotic arm operated by those electrodes.

- Paleontologist John R. Horner and his team discover the Tyrannosaurus rex skeleton, designated MOR 1125, in the Hell Creek Formation in a remote corner of the Charles M. Russell National Wildlife Refuge in Montana.

1 May   Under the executive order of President Bill Clinton, the "selective availability" restriction for the civilian use of the Global Positioning System (GPS) is lifted.

7 June   U.S. District Court judge Thomas Penfield Jackson finds that Microsoft is a monopoly and orders the company to release some of its intellectual property.

26 June   Scientists produce the first draft of the Human Genome Sequence.

July   The search engine Google indexes one billion pages.

Oct.   A public-private consortium announces plans to speed research on the sequencing of the complete genome of a laboratory mouse.

Oct.   Sony and Pioneer unveil prototypes of what will become Blu-ray Disc players at the Combined Exhibition of Advanced Technologies (CEATEC) in Japan.

2001

- The United Nations Intergovernmental Panel on Climate Change (UNIPCC) issues a report stating that human activity is the "likely" cause of global warming.

- Scientists successfully clone the endangered gaur, a species of wild ox, but the clone dies two days after birth.

- Scientists in Italy report the successful cloning of a healthy baby mouflon, an endangered wild sheep.

- Jesse Sullivan, a double amputee, controls both of his robotic arms using a method of nerve-cell operation developed at the Rehabilitation Institute of Chicago.

20 Jan.   President Clinton leaves the presidency with the best conservation record since Theodore Roosevelt.

Mar.   President George W. Bush announces that the United States will not ratify the Kyoto Protocol because it would be detrimental to its economic interests.

Aug.	President Bush restricts federally supported research to a limited number of stem-cell lines that had been previously obtained from surplus embryos at fertility clinics.
23 Oct.	Apple launches the iPod music player.
Nov.	Scientists with the biotechnology company Advanced Cell Technology (ACT) report that they have cloned the first human embryos. The only embryo to survive the process stopped developing after dividing into six cells.
Dec.	In a report titled "Abrupt Climate Change: Inevitable Surprises" the U.S. National Research Council announces that climate change may arrive quickly and have catastrophic effects.

2002

- Honda introduces the Accord Hybrid. Hybrids, particularly Toyota's Prius, start to take hold in the American marketplace.

- A British biotechnology company, PPL Therapeutics, announces that it has produced genetically modified pigs that can potentially be used to grow organs for human transplants.

- The *Odyssey* spacecraft spots what appear to be vast quantities of underground ice in the polar regions of Mars.

- The U.S. wind-energy industry wins passage of an extended production tax credit for electricity generated by wind power.

19 Feb.	The Blu-ray Disc project is officially announced.
Feb.–Mar.	The Larson B ice shelf breaks off from the Antarctic Peninsula and floats away.
26 Mar.	Elias A. Zerhouni is appointed to the National Institutes of Health by President Bush.
Oct.	The television industry awards Donald Bitzer, Gene Slottow, and Robert Wilson an Emmy for technological achievement in plasma displays.

2003

- The third-generation Prius earns several awards and becomes one of the hottest-selling cars in Toyota's line of vehicles.

- The first 3G wireless network is launched.

Jan.	The Food and Drug Administration (FDA) orders a pause in gene-therapy research involving retroviral vectors in blood stem cells.
Feb.	The FDA's Biological Response Modifiers Advisory Committee meets to discuss measures that would allow some retroviral gene-therapy trials for the treatment of life-threatening diseases.
1 Feb.	The space shuttle *Columbia* disintegrates upon reentry over Texas at approximately 9:00 A.M., killing Americans Commander Rick D. Husband, Pilot William McCool, Payload Commander Michael Anderson, Mission Specialist Kalpana Chawla, Mission Specialist David Brown, Mission Specialist Laurel Clark, and Payload Specialist Ilan Ramon, Israel's first astronaut.
2 Feb.	National Aeronautics and Space Administration (NASA) administrator Sean O'Keefe appoints retired U.S. Navy admiral Harold Gelman Jr. to head the Columbia Accident Investigation Board.

Apr.   The FDA eases the ban on gene-therapy trials that use retroviral vectors in blood stem cells.

Apr.   The Human Genome Project is completed.

9 May   NASA announces that Bill Parsons will replace Ron Dittemore as shuttle program manager.

28 July   U.S. senator James Inhofe of Oklahoma claims global warming is a hoax.

Aug.   The social-networking site MySpace is launched and soon experiences exponential growth.

21 Oct.   The first images of the new planetary body Eris are taken.

2004

- Ford introduces the first hybrid sport utility vehicle (SUV), the Ford Escape.

- Google handles upward of 84.7 percent of all search requests on the World Wide Web.

21 June   The first privately funded rocket ship to carry a human into space, *SpaceShipOne*, makes its maiden voyage to the edges of space.

19 Aug.   Google goes public, offering a total of 19,605,052 shares at $85.00 a share. At the end of the trading day, it closes at $100.34 a share.

Nov.   Google indexes eight billion web pages.

26 Dec.   An earthquake with a magnitude of between 9.1 and 9.3 on the Richter scale occurs in the Indian Ocean, causing a massive tsunami that takes the lives of more than 230,000 people in fourteen different countries.

2005

- Nicholas Negroponte, cofounder and director of the Media Lab at Massachusetts Institute of Technology (MIT) announces his plan to develop a laptop computer that costs only $100. The final product costs $199.

5 Jan.   Mike Brown, Chad Trujillo, and David Rabinowitz are recognized for discovering a new planet orbiting the Sun that is larger than Pluto.

Feb.   A research team at the University of Michigan is able to cure deafness in guinea pigs by delivering genes that promote growth of hair cells in the cochlea, the part of the inner ear that registers sound.

15 Feb.   Steve Chen, Chad Hurley, and Jawed Karim register the domain name YouTube.com for their video-sharing website.

16 Feb.   The Kyoto Protocol goes into effect. Notably, the United States and Australia do not ratify the treaty.

Mar.   Researchers announce the discovery of soft tissue inside the 68-million-year-old thighbone of a Tyrannosaurus rex.

23 Apr.   The first video gets posted on YouTube titled "Me at the Zoo."

May   YouTube's viewership surpasses that of CNN.com.

7 June   Google is valued at nearly $52 million, making it one of the world's biggest media companies by stock-market value.

29 Aug.   Hurricane Katrina ravages the U.S. Gulf Coast, causing more than 1,800 deaths and $100 million in damage to Louisiana alone.

Dec.   More than 100,000 people in more than thirty nations hold marches as part of the first worldwide demonstration calling for action against global warming.

20 Dec.   U.S. District judge John E. Jones III rules that teaching intelligent design in the classroom equates to teaching religion. Proponents of evolution see the ruling as an important victory.

20 Dec.   Members of the International Astronomical Union (IAU) meet in Prague to discuss the cultural and scientific fate of Eris and Pluto. They decide to assign Pluto, Eris, and the former asteroid Ceres the newly created status of dwarf planets.

20 Dec.   "Google" officially becomes a verb meaning to use the Google search engine to obtain information on the World Wide Web.

2006

- YouTube is the fourth-most-viewed website in the world and is named *Time* magazine's invention of the year.

- The first Blu-ray Disc players hit the market. A format war with High-Definition/Density (HD-DVD) begins.

- Evan Williams, Biz Stone, and Jack Dorsey launch the microblogging service Twitter.

Jan.   YouTube users watch approximately 25 million videos a day.

8 Feb.   Eighty-six Christian leaders form the Evangelical Climate Initiative, demanding that Congress regulate greenhouse-gas emissions.

Mar.   Gene therapy is effectively used to treat two adult patients for a myeloid disorder, a disease that affects white blood cells.

May   Researchers involved with the Human Genome Project announce the completion of the DNA sequence for the last twenty-four human chromosomes.

28 May   *An Inconvenient Truth,* a documentary on climate change starring Al Gore, opens in theaters.

8 June   The FDA announces the approval of Gardasil, a vaccine for the human papillomavirus (HPV).

Aug.   A team of researchers at the National Cancer Institute demonstrate a regression of advanced melanoma in seventeen patients whose white blood cells had been genetically engineered to recognize and attack cancer cells.

21 Aug.   Marusa Bradac of the Kavli Institute for Particle Astrophysics and Cosmology at the Stanford Linear Accelerator Center makes the first landmark observation of dark matter in the Bullet Cluster.

13 Sept.   Object 2003 UB313 and its satellite which had been informally referred to as Xena and Gabrielle, respectively, are officially named Eris and Dysnomia.

9 Oct.   Google acquires YouTube for $1.65 billion in Google stock. The deal is finalized in November.

Nov.   Microsoft launches Vista along with Office 2007 and Exchange 2007. Customers soon complain that the system is slow and has multiple programming issues.

2007

- Experts estimate that YouTube consumes as much bandwidth space as the entire World Wide Web did in 2000.

Jan.   Chevrolet introduces its Volt series hybrid sedan at the North American International Auto Show.

11 Jan.   Researchers at the University of Texas M. D. Anderson Cancer Center and the University of Texas Southwestern Medical Center deliver a combination of two tumor-suppressing genes with lipid-based nanoparticles, causing a drastic reduction in the number and size of human lung-cancer tumors in mice.

Feb.   The UNIPCC issues a report stating that global warming is "unequivocal" and human activity is "very likely" the cause.

2 Apr.   The U.S. Supreme Court rules that the Environmental Protection Agency has the authority to regulate heat-trapping gases in automobile emissions.

June   The 3G network claims its 200-millionth customer.

Sept.   Ice melt from the Arctic Ice Cap is so severe that the Northwest Passage, a shipping shortcut from Europe to Asia around the top of North America, opens for the first time since satellite records began in 1978.

Oct.   Facebook sells $240 million in shares to Microsoft, solidifying the importance of social-networking sites in the marketplace.

12 Oct.   Al Gore and the UNIPCC win the Nobel Peace Prize for disseminating greater knowledge about the man-made catastrophe of global warming and for proposing measures needed to counteract the crisis.

2008

- After years of debate, the FDA rules that meat and milk from cloned livestock are safe for consumption.

- MySpace cedes the social-networking crown to Facebook.

- YouTube is awarded the George Foster Peabody Award. *Entertainment Weekly* puts YouTube on its "best-of" list.

- Toshiba officially stops producing HD-DVD players, ending a three-year format war with Blu-ray Disc.

- Astronomers announce that they have obtained a visual picture of exoplanets—alien planets—orbiting distant stars.

24 Jan.   A team of seventeen scientists from the J. Craig Venter Institute announce that they were able to completely synthesize and assemble 582,970 base pairs of the genome of the bacterium *mycoplasma genitalium*.

12 May   The Great Sichuan Earthquake occurs in the Sichuan province of China, measuring 8.5 on the Richter magnitude scale. It claims an estimated 68,000 lives.

15 May   Due to pressure from environmental groups such as Greenpeace, the polar bear is finally listed as a threatened species under the Endangered Species Act.

21 May   President Bush signs the Genetic Nondiscrimination Act prohibiting U.S. insurance companies and employers from discrimination based on information derived from genetic testing.

25 May	NASA's *Phoenix* Mars lander lands on the Martian north pole on a quest to learn more about the planet's surface, including whether or not it contains frozen water and possibly organic-based compounds.
July	Google indexes one trillion pages.
31 July	The *Phoenix* Mars lander detects water in a Martian soil sample using its onboard Thermal and Evolved Gas Analyzer (TEGA).
Dec.	Surgeons at the Cleveland Clinic in Ohio perform the world's first near-total facial transplant surgery.
Dec.	The Federal Communications Commission (FCC) defines basic broadband as data transmission that exceeds speeds of 768 kilobits per second.
Dec.	Twenty-six percent of the world's population uses the Internet and surfs the World Wide Web.
Dec.	Google's assets total approximately $40.5 billion.
Dec.	Twitter claims more than 100 million users worldwide.
Dec.	The online encyclopedia, Wikipedia, claims more than 13 million articles.

2009

	• Toshiba releases its own Blu-ray Disc player.
	• Amputee Pierpaolo Petruzziello learns to control a biomechanical hand and becomes the first person to make complex movements with a robotic limb by using his thoughts only.
21 Jan.	Steven Chu is sworn in as the twelfth U.S. secretary of energy.
Feb.	Scientists clone a bucardo, an extinct subspecies of the Spanish ibex, from preserved skin tissue. It dies only minutes after being born.
Mar.	President Barack Obama overturns President Bush's policy on stem-cell research, allowing the National Institutes of Health to fund research on embryonic stem cells beyond the previously allotted sixty cell lines.
Apr.	The World Health Organization announces the emergence of a novel influenza virus called H1N1.
June	The Centers for Disease Control (CDC) report that more than 25 million doses of Gardasil, the HPV vaccine, have been distributed in the United States.
12 June	The last official day that full-power television stations in the United States can broadcast in analog.
18 June	NASA launches its Lunar Crater Observation and Sensing Satellite (LCROSS) as part of a double mission including the Lunar Reconnaissance Orbiter (LRO) to see if water exists on the Moon.
Aug.	Jamie Elsila at NASA's Goddard Space Flight Center in Greenbelt, Maryland, announces that her team has found glycine, an amino acid, in the tail of a comet in outer space.
Oct.	San Diego Zoo spokesperson Yadira Galindo announces that California condors have made a comeback.
1 Oct.	Scientists announce the discovery of Ardi, a 4.4-million-year-old fossilized skeleton that may be an ancestor of modern humans.

9 Oct.	NASA's LCROSS is intentionally crashed into the permanently shadowed region of Cabeus crater near the Moon's south pole, followed by a *Centaur* rocket to determine if water is present on the Moon's surface.
24 Oct.	President Obama declares the swine-flu pandemic (H1N1) a national emergency.
13 Nov.	NASA announces the discovery of water on the Moon.
Dec.	Federal health officials estimate that ten thousand Americans have died of the swine flu since April.
7–18 Dec.	Representatives from more than 193 countries convene in Copenhagen, Denmark, for the UN Climate Change Conference.

Astronauts from Space Shuttle Atlantis servicing the Hubble Space Telescope on 16 May 2009 (<www.nasa.gov>).

OVERVIEW

The International, Interdisciplinary Scientist. The major scientific and technological endeavors of the 2000s adhered to a network model, characterized by an unprecedented level of international- and cross-disciplinary collaboration. The Human Genome Project completed in 2003 involved thousands of researchers from different universities, institutes, and private companies from across the world, all working toward a common goal of identifying all of the genes in human DNA. Work on the Large Hadron Collider in the realm of particle physics crossed international borders and brought together scientists and engineers from hundreds of different countries. The scale of these projects was matched only by their ambition, as researchers successfully mapped the entire human genome and physicists explored the tiniest bits of matter, creating temperatures in the process that exceeded one hundred thousand times those found at the center of the Sun. In addition to exploring the very small, American researchers explored the very large, discovering water on Mars and on the Moon and unveiling an entirely new "dwarf planet" orbiting at the edge of the solar system. Our relationship to the larger universe altered as well as American astronomers captured the first images of potentially habitable planets outside our solar system. The concept of human evolution itself underwent change, as American and Ethiopian anthropologists finally pieced together the remains of a 4.5-million-year-old humanoid skeleton, another link in the evolutionary chain. Even though the lines blurred between nations as a growing number of seminal research projects were international in scope, American scientists continued to feature prominently in many of the major breakthroughs. Not only were these undertakings made possible by the combined efforts of sometimes tens of thousands of individuals from hundreds of different countries, but the categories that defined and separated scientists from one another were simultaneously becoming less rigid. The line dividing paleontology and biology, for example, broke down with the discovery of soft tissue in nearly 70-million-year-old fossilized dinosaur bones, bringing together experts in each field to try to figure out the complex history of prehistoric life. Medical doctors and chemists worked closely with geneticists and specialists in nanotechnology to devise better methods for the treatment of genetic disorders, cancer, and other debilitating diseases. Neuroscientists worked with engineers to create artificial limbs that users could operate with their thoughts, and computer scientists played a role in designing programs and software to assist researchers in previously unimaginable ways.

Environmental Concerns. With a greater degree of interconnectedness came an elevated sense of shared responsibility for the planet's future. Global warming was a seemingly undeniable reality that the world had to face. Gradually, nations and their leaders began to realize the impact of an ever-increasing degree of industrialization and the ever-expanding demand for energy that came with it. The United States alone contributed to nearly a quarter of the world's greenhouse gases, and its citizens and leaders started to understand the need for cleaner, "greener," sources of power. Phrases such as "green jobs," "eco-friendly driving," and "carbon footprint," became mainstream toward the end of the decade as many individuals, companies, and governments assessed their contribution to the crisis and started making efforts to reduce the amount of carbon and methane being released into the atmosphere. Many Americans focused on creating and harnessing "clean energy" in the form of wind and solar power and on improving the efficiency of their homes, vehicles, and businesses. International concern was evidenced through initiatives and conferences such as the Kyoto Protocol and the Copenhagen Summit, at which representatives from around the world attempted to make binding agreements to reduce the output of greenhouse gases and curb the longevity and severity of impending climate change. Unfortunately, legal measures and technical solutions needed to fix the growing problem were not achieved, but a rising awareness offered hope for the future.

Networking. In no other aspect of American life did the network serve as a more appropriate model than in the realm of technology. More than two-thirds of the population regularly accessed the World Wide Web (WWW), and with the advent of broadband, the Internet became an indispensable part of many personal, social, and professional lives. As educational and professional opportunities and obligations pushed families, friends, and colleagues apart geographically, social-networking sites and personal-communication technologies helped to bring them back together. Computer and communication networks kept Americans informed and in touch. With personal, pocket-sized electronic devices, people got the latest news and "tweets," updated their personal webpages and "blogs," and regularly checked their email or sent a text message. Not only did technology allow them to maintain personal and professional relationships, it enabled an apparently endless array of choices. People could shop from their computers, work from home, and form online communities with others who shared their unique concerns and interests. With Global Positioning Systems (GPS), they could find out exactly where they were and how to get to where they were going. Broadband, the 3G network, and advances in viewing and video technologies also allowed individuals to entertain themselves in novel ways. They could download their favorite songs to cell phones, play a videogame with streaming graphics online while seated in front of home computers, or watch a Blu-ray movie in vivid color on their liquid crystal display (LCD) or plasma television screens. Twenty-first-century technology allowed people to connect to a heretofore unimaginable number of other people across the planet and drastically affected the way they worked and played.

Anxieties. The United States remained at the forefront of scientific discovery that created information and technology at an astounding rate. A greater, more expansive degree of interconnectivity enabled scientists and engineers to achieve amazing results. At the same time, many Americans who benefited from these advancements also experienced a sense of being overwhelmed. As their capacity for staying connected and informed rapidly increased and the bounds of possibility pushed ever outward, there remained an undercurrent of anxiety about keeping up with the quickening pace of change. The networks that enabled large collaborative and interdisciplinary efforts and spurred scientific and technological breakthroughs also irrevocably altered Americans' role in the world. If technology caused the planet to shrink, and people enjoyed a greater degree of personal independence, an expanding industrial, digital, multicultural, and multitechnical environment simultaneously revealed the need for greater social responsibility and new concepts of privacy.

TOPICS IN THE NEWS

CLIMATE CHANGE

Growing Consensus. The first decade of the twenty-first century was the hottest on record, and only the most stubborn critics asserted that the phenomenon of global warming was merely a natural occurrence or an outright myth. One sign of the growing consensus was the worldwide demonstration in 2005 of citizens from more than thirty nations calling for direct action to stem the production of greenhouse gases. Even erstwhile skeptics began making concessions. President George W. Bush, who had retracted the U.S. commitment to the Kyoto Protocol in 2001, admitted in his 2006 State of the Union Address that America had to break its "addiction" to foreign oil. Environmentalists argued that the real solution lay in breaking America's addiction to oil itself, because the use of fossil fuels was profoundly damaging the climate. The most persuasive study confirming this assertion was conducted by six hundred scientists from the United Nations Intergovernmental Panel on Climate Change (UNIPCC) from 2002 to 2007. At the end of their exhaustive research, the panel concluded that the warming of the climate was "unequivocal" and that human activity was "very likely" the cause. A year before the panel's proclamation, former vice president Al Gore's film *An Inconvenient Truth* made headlines across the globe and spread the news about the dire facts of climate change and the need for nations to work collectively on the problem of greenhouse-gas emissions. The movie received two Oscars. On 12 October 2007 Gore and the UNIPCC won the Nobel Peace Prize for their efforts to promote knowledge of the man-made catastrophe and for proposing measures needed to counteract negative changes to the environment.

The Scale of the Problem. In 2009 representatives from 193 countries, including U.S. president Barack Obama, met at the Copenhagen Climate Conference for the purpose of drafting an effective plan of action to combat global warming. During the conference, fifty-six newspapers from around the world issued identical editorials arguing that it was no longer a question of whether or not humans were to blame for the disaster of global warming; rather, the central concern now was doing something about it. Although experts admitted that there were some natural causes for

Poster for Al Gore's 2000 documentary on climate change (<www.impawards.com>)

climate change such as subtle shifts in the Earth's orbit and increased volcanic activity, by analyzing tree rings, ice cores, ocean sediments, and other indicators of past climactic conditions, they were able to determine that humans had been responsible for most of the warming observed since 1950. Paleoclimatological readings taken from ice cores and fossils indicated that in the roughly 250 years since the beginning of the Industrial Revolution, carbon dioxide levels in the atmosphere had increased by at least 35 percent and methane levels had increased by at least 148 percent. Data collected from ships, buoys, and satellites showed that although the oceans had risen since 1978, the Sun's output had not, and the frequency of volcanic eruptions had remained approximately the same. Aside from the raw data collected by scientists, several large-scale events all pointed toward the harsh realities of a warming planet. In 2002 the Larson B ice shelf, a massive floating span of ice and snow that had been attached to the Antarctic Peninsula for thousands of years, collapsed, broke into pieces, and floated away. In 2003 a heat wave in Europe killed more than thirty thousand people. Scientists agreed that heat waves would not only be more common in the future but would also be more severe. In August 2005 Hurricane Katrina

ravaged the U.S. Gulf Coast, causing the deaths of more than 1,800 people and upward of $100 million in damages. Studies conducted in that same year revealed that in recent history the number of Category 4 and 5 hurricanes had doubled worldwide while the speed and duration of all hurricanes had risen by 50 percent. In September 2007 melt from the Arctic Ice Cap was so great that the Northwest Passage, a shipping shortcut from Europe to Asia around the top of North America, opened for the first time since satellite records began in 1978; the surface area of summer sea ice in the Arctic Ocean was nearly 23 percent below the previous record low in 2005, a loss of ice equivalent to an area the size of Alaska and Texas combined. Scientists also confirmed that the rapid melting of snow and ice in the Northern Hemisphere was causing an alarming mortality rate among polar bears. The bears were drowning because there were fewer ice platforms in the water for them to rest on between long swims in search of food. The U.S. Geological Survey projected that, due to the destruction of their habitat, two-thirds of the polar-bear population would disappear by 2050. The remaining bears would likely be relegated to the Arctic archipelago of Canada or areas off the northern Greenland coast. They would disappear from Alaska entirely. Due to pressure from environmentalist groups such as Greenpeace, the polar bear was finally listed as a threatened species in 2008 under the Endangered Species Act. In addition to the popularized plight of the polar bear, the U.S. Forest Service provided more compelling evidence of the global-warming crisis and the effect it would have on the world. It found that in just one hundred years the Sierra Nevada tree lines had shifted as much as one hundred feet up slope to escape heat and drought. It also concluded that as a result of warmer winters, pine beetles in the United States and Canada decimated tens of millions more acres of forest than they would have been able to consume in the past.

Kyoto Protocol. The Kyoto Protocol was adopted in 1997 in Kyoto, Japan, and opened in 1998 for signature by parties to the United Nations Framework Convention on Climate Change (UNFCCC). Throughout the 2000s it remained the most visible and well-known symbol of the growing international consensus on climate change. It was an agreement that aimed at reducing global industrial greenhouse-gas emissions—specifically carbon dioxide (CO_2), methane (CH_4), nitrous oxide (N_2O), hydrofluorocarbons (HFCs), perfluoro-carbons (PCFs), and sulfur hexafluoride (SF_6)—by up to 10 percent against 1990 levels over a five-year period from 2008 to 2012. President Bill Clinton signed the protocol and committed the United States to a rigorous program of pollution containment with financial penalties if it failed to meet the agreed-upon goal of a 7 percent total reduction for the United States. In 2001, however, President George W. Bush withdrew from the protocol because he deemed it detrimental to the nation's economic interests. Other critics of the protocol argued that it did not represent an extensive enough program for reducing greenhouse gases because it absolved

President Barack Obama and Secretary of State Hillary Clinton confer with world leaders during the United Nations Climate Change Conference in Copenhagen, Denmark, on 18 December 2009 (Official White House photograph by Pete Souza).

developing nations such as India, China, and Brazil from carbon restrictions and financial obligations. Furthermore, the protocol made no initial provisions for existing wilderness areas that scientists deemed carbon sinks—environmental reservoirs that absorb more carbon than they release. Compared to most developed nations, the United States had a larger portion of its overall land area covered by forests that actively pulled carbon dioxide out of the atmosphere. Therefore, despite the institution of flexible mechanisms that offered alternatives to curbing greenhouse-gas production, such as emission trading that allowed parties to purchase emission permits from other countries, the Bush administration considered the protocol unfair and impractical. Although the protocol was finally ratified by 185 nations, the United States was not among those listed. After 2000 the United States was responsible for approximately 25 percent of global greenhouse-gas emissions, a number that remained steady between 2000 and 2009. Without U.S. involvement, it became increasingly clear that even though the protocol was the first international effort to effect a positive change in harmful industrial practices, it was not extensive enough to successfully combat global warming. Many experts began warning that climate change was arriving at a faster pace than had been anticipated. The level of carbon dioxide in the atmosphere had reached 385 parts per million by 2009, and the mean global temperature over a five-year period was 14.5 degrees Celsius, the warmest in hundreds of years. Scientists

stressed the need to set strict emissions standards, reduce the world's reliance on fossil fuels, and develop pollution-free energy sources.

Copenhagen Summit. In 2009 representatives from 193 countries convened in Copenhagen, Denmark, between December 7 and 18 for the United Nations Climate Change Conference. The conference hosted the Fifteenth Conference of the Parties to the United Nations Framework Convention on Climate Change (COP 15) and the Fifth Meeting of the Parties to the Kyoto Protocol (COP 5). The goal of the conference was to commit to firm targets for midterm and long-term greenhouse-gas emissions. Requirements for the percentage of carbon-dioxide reduction varied among different nations, according to capability assessments, but the overall goal was to negotiate a binding treaty that would significantly lower the risk of dangerous climate change in the future. Characterized by disagreement and mismanagement, the talks were reported by international media outlets to be in disarray. Nevertheless, President Barack Obama managed to negotiate an accord with China, India, South Africa, and Brazil. The accord provided for a system of monitoring and reporting progress toward pollution-reduction goals and called for billions of dollars in aid to countries most vulnerable to a changing climate. It set a goal for limiting the global temperature rise to 2 degrees Celsius above preindustrial levels by 2050. However, many delegates from other nations complained that the negotiations were held

444

behind closed doors and did not reflect the open and democratic intentions of the conference. Furthermore, the accord did not commit its members to a binding treaty. Obama claimed that no agreement would have been reached otherwise. He told the American public that many nations had made progress toward recognizing the real threat of global warming, but there was still a long way to go before measures could be taken to adequately address the growing problem.

Sources:

John M. Broder, "Many Goals Remain Unmet in 5 Nations' Climate Deal," *nytimes.com* (18 December 2009);

Broder and Andrew C. Revkin, "Warming Is Seen as Wiping Out Most Polar Bears," *nytimes.com* (8 September 2007);

Eileen Claussen, "Connie Hedegaard," *time.com* (30 April 2009);

Christine Dell'Amore, "Copenhagen Climate Conference: What You Need to Know," *nationalgeographic.com* (7 December 2009);

"Emission of Greenhouse Gases Report," *eia.doe.gov* (8 December 2009);

"Global Warming and Polar Bears," *nwf.org* (n.d.);

Jeffrey Kluger, "Earth at the Tipping Point: Global Warming Heats Up," *time.com* (3 April 2006);

Heather E. Lindsay, "Global Warming and the Kyoto Protocol," *csa.com* (July 2001);

Larry Parker and John Blodgett, "Global Climate Change: Reducing Greenhouse Gases—How Much from What Baseline?" *crshead.htm* (11 March 1998);

Andrew C. Revkin, "Yelling 'Fire' on a Hot Planet," *nytimes.com* (23 April 2006);

Holli Riebeek, "Global Warming," *nasa.gov* (11 May 2007);

Spencer Weart, "The Discovery of Global Warming," *aip.org* (July 2009);

Tom Zeller Jr., "Climate Talks Open with Calls for Urgent Action," *nytimes.com* (7 December 2009).

A T-shaped Chevrolet Volt battery replica and the 2007 Chevrolet Volt lithium-ion battery-powered "electric" car from General Motors (the U.S. Department of Energy <www.doedigitalarchive.doe.gov>)

ENVIRONMENTALLY FRIENDLY AUTOMOBILES

Hybrid Technology. Although mass-marketed hybrid vehicles debuted in the 1990s, increasing concerns over greenhouse gases and rising gasoline prices caused a greater percentage of Americans to purchase hybrid vehicles during the first decade of the twenty-first century. Hybrids were more fuel efficient than their strictly internal combustion engine (ICE) predecessors, and eco-friendly, green-driving exemplified an environmentally conscious reaction to the threat of global warming. A hybrid car coupled a small internal combustion engine with a rechargeable energy-storage system, offering the acceleration benefits of a gasoline engine with the reduced pollution of an electric motor. In previous years, hybrid vehicles had failed to deliver the same level of performance as their ICE counterparts, but by 2001 Toyota sold an updated version of their Prius model that promised not only more power and better acceleration but also lower emissions. Although Toyota was the most prominent manufacturer of hybrid cars, by the end of the decade every major car company was producing versions of the popular vehicles. In addition to cars, companies created hybrid SUVs, motorcycles, trucks, and vans. Although hybrids became popular across the globe, the United States and Japan remained the leading markets for this new technology. Despite ongoing improvements in hybrid engineering, all of the mass-produced vehicles on the market functioned according to the same basic technological principles. In a parallel hybrid car, a gasoline engine and an electric motor worked in tandem, while in a series hybrid, a gasoline engine charged the batteries that powered the electric motor. Nevertheless, both types relied on regenerative braking to recharge the batteries. Hybrids converted kinetic energy created during normal brake use into potential energy by harnessing the power wasted in coasting and braking so that the natural motion of a car's wheels generated electricity. When the vehicle was stopped, the gasoline motor shut off completely. At low speeds, the electric motor operated on its own. At high speeds or during rapid acceleration, the two motors operated in conjunction to produce power. In addition to their more efficient use of energy, hybrid cars were generally constructed out of lightweight materials such as carbon fiber or aluminum and were built to be more aerodynamic. Although hybrids were far more fuel efficient and environmentally friendly than traditional ICE vehicles, getting an average of thirty miles or more per gallon, some hybrid owners expressed doubts about their safety. Based on studies conducted on subjects living near high-voltage utility lines, the National Institutes of Health and the National Cancer Institute acknowledged the potential hazards of long-term exposure to electromagnetic fields. Despite customer concerns about the effects of prolonged exposure to the weaker fields produced by hybrid cars, studies remained inconclusive.

Toyota Prius. In 1994 Akihiro Wada, executive vice president of Toyota, challenged a team of company engineers to build a car with double the fuel efficiency of contemporary vehicles. In 1997 Toyota introduced the Prius, a fifty-seven-horsepower gasoline engine linked to a forty-horsepower electric motor. By 2001 Americans were able to purchase a second-generation, more-powerful and efficient Prius, and by 2002 hybrids started to take hold in the American marketplace. In 2003 the third-generation Prius earned several awards, and Toyota Motor Sales president Jim Press hailed it as the hottest car the company had ever sold. In 2005 the Ford Motor Company marketed the first hybrid SUV to the public. In 2007, at the North American International Auto Show, Chevrolet introduced higher-grade lithium-ion batteries in the new Chevy Volt, which replaced the traditional and less-efficient nickel-metal hydride batteries used by their competitors.

Sources:

Bradley Berman, "When Old Things Turn into New Again," *nytimes.com* (24 October 2007);

"The History of the Hybrid Car," *carjunky.com* (9 November 2007);

"How Hybrid Cars Work," *hybrid-car.org* (n.d.);

"How Hybrids Work," *fueleconomy.gov* (n.d.);

Christopher Lampton, "What Is the History of Hybrid Cars?" *howstuffworks.com* (n.d.);

Jim Motavalli, "Fear, but Few Facts, on Hybrid Risk," *nytimes.com* (27 April 2008);

Don Sherman, "A History of Hybrid Vehicles," *automobilemag.com* (February 2009).

EVOLUTIONARY BIOLOGY

Ardi. On 1 October 2009 at joint press conferences in Washington, D.C., and Addis Ababa, Ethiopia, researchers announced the discovery of the 4.4-million-year-old fossilized skeletal remains of Ardi, a female member of an early humanlike species *Ardipithecus ramidus*. Tim D. White of the University of California, Berkeley, directed the research team that uncovered Ardi along with Berhane Asfaw, a paleoanthropologist and former director of the National Museum of Ethiopia, and Giday WoldeGabriel, a geologist at Los Alamos National Laboratory in New Mexico. The first fragmentary specimens of *Ardipithecus* were uncovered at Aramis in 1992, but because the fossils that made up Ardi's skeleton needed to be carefully reconstructed, it took seventeen years before the research team published a thorough account of their findings. Aramis is located in Ethiopia's Afar desert in the Middle Awash region, just forty-six miles from where Lucy, a female member of the species *Australopithecus afarensis*, was found in 1974. The team uncovered 125 pieces of the skeletal remains including the skull and teeth, pelvis, limbs, much of the feet, and virtually all of the hands. Researchers concluded that Ardi had a small brain, stood just over 4 feet tall, and weighed 110 pounds. She

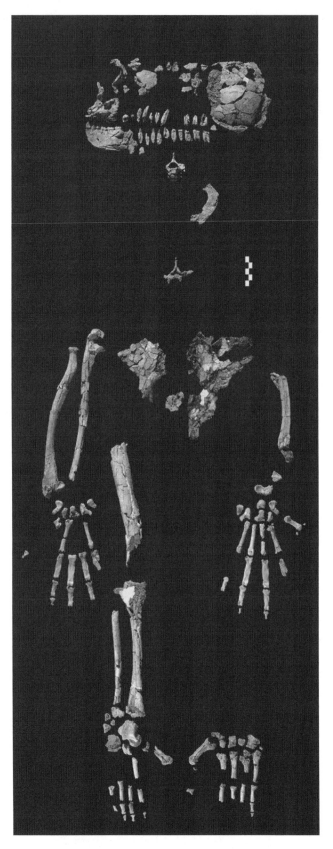

The 4.4-million-year-old fossilized skeletal remains of human ancestor *Ardipithecus ramidus* (American Association for the Advancement of Science)

Until scientists announced the discovery of soft tissue inside a thighbone of a 68-million-year-old Tyrannosaurus rex fossil in March of 2005, the study of dinosaurs had been limited to hard bones. Dinosaurs died out 65 million years ago, and scientists had long surmised that after a maximum of around a hundred thousand years, soft tissues such as collagen, blood vessels, and other organic molecules degraded to dust. In 2000 John R. Horner, a paleontologist with the Museum of the Rockies at Montana State University, and his team found a Tyrannosaurus rex skeleton they designated MOR 1125 in the Hell Creek Formation in a remote corner of the Charles M. Russell National Wildlife Refuge in Montana. For three years, Horner and his team excavated the Tyrannosaurus rex from the sandstone that encased it. Because the specimen was found in such an isolated area, they had to lift the fossilized bones out by helicopter. After a plaster-jacketed part of the fossil proved too heavy for the helicopter to lift, Horner decided to break one of the dinosaur's femurs in two. Mary Higby Schweitzer, assistant professor of paleontology at North Carolina State University, and her colleagues studied the interior of the thighbone. By soaking it in weak acid, they removed mineral fragments and exposed flexible, stretchy, transparent material that proved to be blood vessels and collagen, the main protein component of bone. Schweitzer hypothesized that the size and density of the thighbone may have helped to shield its internal structures from decay. The fact that the specimen was found in dry sandstone instead of a moist layer of soil may also have helped to preserve the soft tissues. Upon further investigation, Schweitzer found flexible bone collagen in other well-preserved prehistoric remains.

These findings changed the way scientists understood the fossilization process and enabled them to study Tyrannosaurus rex MOR 1125 at the molecular level. Examining the dinosaur's blood vessels under an electron microscope, Schweitzer found that they were virtually indistinguishable from those recovered from ostrich bones, helping to confirm the theory that birds descended from dinosaurs. Previously, the theory was based entirely upon similarities in hard body structures. In related studies, Schweitzer and John Asara of the Harvard Medical School found distinct similarities between the dinosaur sample and the bone collagen of chickens. Schweitzer exposed the dinosaur protein to a group of antibodies that normally react in the presence of chicken collagen and found that a strong reaction occurred with the dinosaur bones as well. Using mass spectrometry, Asara's team studied the amino acids present in the proteins of the Tyrannosaurus rex soft-tissue sample and was able to isolate seven fragmentary chains. The results represented the oldest such data ever recovered and affirmed the possibility that the evolutionary relationships between modern organisms and their extinct ancestors could in fact be studied at the molecular level.

Sources: Hillary Mayell, "T. Rex Soft Tissue Found Preserved," *nationalgeographic.com* (24 March 2005);

Scott Norris, "Dinosaur Soft Tissue Sequenced; Similar to Chicken Proteins," *nationalgeographic.com* (12 April 2007);

"Scientists Recover T. rex Soft Tissue," *msn.com* (24 March 2005);

"T. rex Fossils Yield Soft Tissue," *newsdiscovery.com* (24 March 2005);

John Noble Wilford, "Tissue Find Offers New Look into Dinosaurs' Lives," *nytimes.com* (24 March 2005).

showed a mix of advanced characteristics and primitive traits indicative of older apes that were unlike chimpanzees. Radiometric dating indicated that she roamed the Earth approximately 1.2 million years before Lucy. In addition to finding Ardi, scientists found bones representing at least thirty-six other individuals at the site. Researchers also uncovered and collected thousands of plant and animal fossils from the surrounding sediments that offered insights into Ardi's life. They discovered seeds from palm trees and fig trees along with fossils indicating the presence of antelope, forest-dwelling monkeys, and twenty-nine species of birds. Isotopes and wear patterns in Ardi's teeth indicated a diet that included fruits, nuts, and other forest foods. As a result of these findings, researchers concluded that Ardi inhabited a grassy woodland with patches of dense forest. Her feet, pelvis, legs, and hands suggested that she walked upright on the ground but used all four limbs when moving about in the trees. Her big toe splayed out from her foot like an ape's, but she also had a bone in her foot passed down from more-primitive ancestors that would have helped her walk bipedally on the ground. (This bone was lost in the lineages of chimps and gorillas.) Although some scientists argued that evidence for bipedality was limited, White and his team asserted that Ardi's anatomy indicated that she both climbed trees *and* walked upright. This conclusion undermined the long-held "savanna hypothesis" that held that human ancestors first stood up in response to their move into open grasslands. The theory stipulated that as upright walkers, they would have had an advantage over knuckle walkers because they could see over tall grasses to find food and avoid predators. White and his team hypothesized that perhaps human ancestors

Jack Horner with the Tyrannosaurus rex femur he discovered in Montana (Montana State University's Museum of the Rockies)

began standing upright for different reasons. The relatively small canines of *Ardipithecus* suggested that fighting between males over potential mates may not have been as common a practice as scientists once assumed. Instead, males may have started standing upright so that they could carry more food to females and their young, thereby winning favor instead of risking injury.

Sources:

Eben Harrell, "Ardi: The Human Ancestor Who Wasn't," *time.com* (27 May 2010);

Michael D. Lemonick and Andrea Dorfman, "Ardi Is a New Piece of the Evolution Puzzle," *time.com* (1 October 2009);

Jamie Shreeve, "Oldest Skeleton of Human Ancestor Found," *nationalgeographic.com* (1 October 2009);

"What Was "Lucy"? Fast Facts on an Early Human Ancestor," *nationalgeographic.com* (20 September 2006).

GENETICS

Animal Cloning. In 1997 when the Roslin Institute in Scotland created the sheep "Dolly" with reproductive cloning technology, it raised a number of ethical problems that persisted into the 2000s, including the question of cloning domestic animals for consumption, endangered animals for preservation, and human tissues for medicine. A clone is an animal that has the same nuclear DNA as another currently or previously existing animal. Scientists create clones by transferring genetic material from the nucleus of an adult donor cell to a host egg whose primary genetic material has been removed. The host egg is then treated with chemicals or an electric current to stimulate growth. After the embryo has grown sufficiently, it is transferred to the uterus of a female host where it continues to develop until birth. After Dolly, researchers successfully cloned goats, cats, mice, rabbits, and monkeys, among many other animals. In 2008, after much controversy, the FDA approved cloned livestock for consumption. In addition, however, scientists cloned several endangered species. In 2001 researchers cloned a gaur, an endangered wild ox, although it died from infection forty-eight hours after its birth. Later that same year, scientists in Italy cloned an endangered wild sheep known as a mouflon that survived and lives at a wildlife center in Sardinia. Cloning extinct animals was a greater challenge because the surrogate egg and mother needed to create and host the cloned embryo were necessarily of a different species. In February of 2009, however, scientists cloned a bucardo, an extinct subspecies of the Spanish ibex, from preserved skin tissue. In this case as well, the cloned animal died only minutes after being born.

Human Cloning. In 2001 scientists at the biotechnology company Advanced Cell Technology (ACT) cloned the first human embryos. Although the embryos stopped developing after dividing into six cells, the possibility of human cloning was no longer relegated to the realm of science fiction. The potential for genetically replicating complete human beings raised many moral and ethical issues, but most scientists agreed that reproductive cloning was an imperfect process with many practical risks involved. In addition to low success rates, cloned animals tended to die young, and many suffered from "large-offspring syndrome." They also tended to have compromised immune systems and higher rates of infection and tumor growth. Only about one or two viable candidates survived out of every one hundred attempts. The same problems could be expected with human clones. In addition, scientists could not predict how cloning would affect mental development. Consequently, physicians from the American Medical Association (AMA) and scientists with the American Association for the Advancement of Science (AAAS) issued formal public statements against human reproductive cloning, and the U.S. Congress considered passing legislation that would ban it.

Stem-Cell Research. A far more viable application of cloning technology in terms of human beings, though still controversial, derived from a process called "therapeutic cloning," also called "embryo cloning," in which scientists attempted replicating tissue cells that would genetically match a donor's cells. These "stem cells" could be used to generate virtually any type of specialized cell in the human body. When these cells were extracted from an egg, the embryo was initially destroyed in the process. This method caused ethical concerns. In August 2001 President George W. Bush restricted federally supported research to a limited number of stem-cell lines that had been previously derived

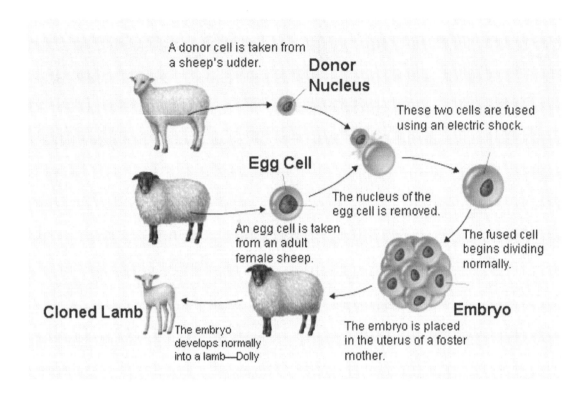

A donor cell is taken from a sheep's udder.

Donor Nucleus

These two cells are fused using an electric shock.

Egg Cell

The nucleus of the egg cell is removed.

An egg cell is taken from an adult female sheep.

The fused cell begins dividing normally.

Cloned Lamb

The embryo develops normally into a lamb—Dolly

Embryo

The embryo is placed in the uterus of a foster mother.

Chart explaining the process of genetic animal cloning (<www.theintellectualdevotional.com>)

from surplus embryos at fertility clinics. In March 2009 President Barack Obama overturned the order with support from political figures such as Nancy Reagan, who along with many others hoped that stem-cell research would lead to treatments for spinal cord injuries, Parkinson's disease, and Alzheimer's disease. Under new guidelines, the National Institutes of Health provided a review process through which scientists could use many of the hundreds of cell lines that have since been created with private funds. Scientists were also able to use new stem-cell lines provided that they came from surplus fertility embryos and were donated under strict ethical rules that stipulated donors had to be informed that the embryo would be destroyed. Donors had to give written consent and were allowed to change their minds. They could not receive payment upon donation or be promised any future medical or financial benefits. With these guidelines in place, scientists hoped that the pace of research would accelerate rapidly. In addition to some of the potential medical applications listed above, scientists believed that therapeutic cloning could be used to generate tissues and organs for transplants. DNA would be extracted from a patient and inserted into a host egg. After the egg's cells began to divide, its embryonic stem cells would be transformed into the type of tissue to be harvested. Theoretically, these stem cells could be used to generate an organ that genetically matched the donor and could be transplanted without the risk of tissue rejection. Another possible method involved the creation of genetically modified

pigs for xenotransplantation (the transplant of tissues and organs from animals to humans). Of species cloned successfully, pig's organs proved the most compatible with humans. As early as 2002 a British biotechnology company, PPL Therapeutics, based near Edinburgh, Scotland, announced that they had produced genetically modified pigs that lacked both copies of a gene involved in transplant rejection. In theory, pigs like these might be able to grow organs for human transplants.

Human Genome Project. The international effort known as the Human Genome Project (HGP) involved the collaboration of scientists from the United States and many other countries in seeking to unlock the secrets of human genetics. A genome is the entire DNA code of an organism, and the proteins that make up the human genome have strong bearing on all of the basic functions of that organism's life. Since the genome contains over 3.2 billion unique base pairs, the scale of the HGP was daunting. (The DNA sequence would fill three gigabytes of computer data storage.) The Department of Energy's (DOE) Human Genome Program, directed by Ari Patrinos, and the National Institutes of Health's (NIH) National Human Research Institute, directed by Francis Collins, sponsored the U.S. portion of the project that was initially estimated to take fifteen years and to cost $3 billion. Some goals of the project were to identify all 20,000 to 25,000 genes in human DNA; determine the sequences of the chemical base pairs; store this information in databases; improve tools for effective data analysis; transfer related technolo-

On 19 August 2008, U.S. Secretary of the Interior Dirk Kempthorne signed authorization that declared the Hanford B Reactor, the world's first, in Washington State as a U.S. National Historical Landmark on a nearly six-hundred square mile area nestled inside land now managed by the U.S. Fish and Wildlife Service. An important part of the Manhattan Project during World War II, scientists at this reactor developed the large-scale water-cooled nuclear reactor and produced the plutonium used in the test bomb (Trinity) exploded at Alamogordo, New Mexico, on 16 July 1945, and in the weapon that destroyed Nagasaki, Japan, on 9 August 1945, helping to end World War II and initiate the Cold War. In 1943, on the heels of successful experiments by Enrico Fermi at the University of Chicago, President Franklin Delano Roosevelt authorized the construction of several reactors along the Columbia River, because of its isolation and accessibility to cool water, and nearly 100,000 workers flooded to the site, with construction beginning 7 July. The first reactor was ready for production by 26 September 1944. In addition to honoring the men and women who worked at the site, the designation increases the opportunity for tourists to visit this historic landmark. The reactor stopped production in 1968 and was scheduled for dismantling and storage by 2009. Plans for the site include the construction of a museum and visitor center, and the first tourists gained access in February 2009. Special tours were also granted to government officials and local tribal leaders. Not everyone, however, was thrilled with the prospect preserving this site, nor did they applaud the efforts and results of the reactor, citing not only the damage wrought by the weapon and environmental damage, but also residual toxicity of nuclear contamination.

Sources: B Reactor Museum Association, *www.b-reactor.org*;

Department of Energy, "B Reactor," *www.hanford.gov*;

"Former Nuclear Sites to Welcome Tourists and Nature," World Nuclear News, *world-nuclear-news.org* (29 August 2008);

Michele Stenehjem Gerber, *On the Home Front: The Cold War Legacy of the Hanford Nuclear Site*, third edition (Lincoln: University of Nebraska Press, 2007);

Terry Richard, "Hanford's B Reactor to Open for Visitors," *Oregonian* (5 February 2009).

---

gies to the private sector; and address the ethical, legal, and social issues that could arise. Laboratories, colleges, and universities throughout the United States received funding for the project from the DOE and NIH. Approximately two hundred separate principal investigators were funded. The private sector was heavily involved as well, and major pharmaceutical companies along with IBM, Compaq, DuPont, and others helped to conduct genome research. GenBank, the world's largest DNA sequence repository, was developed at Los Alamos National Laboratory (LANL) in New Mexico and was later transferred to the National Library of Medicine. Chromosome-sorting capabilities used at LANL and the Lawrence Livermore National Laboratory in California enabled the development of DNA clone libraries representing the individual chromosomes. These libraries were a crucial resource for genome sequencing. Enhancements to sequencing technologies such as the development of better fluorescent dyes, chemical reagents, and enzymes along with the creation of new sequencing-machine hardware and software sped the entire process. By June 2000, scientists produced a draft of the sequence. By April 2003 they were able to reduce ambiguities and information gaps so that the margin of error allowed for only one mistake per ten thousand bases. In May 2006 researchers announced the completion of the DNA sequence for the last of the twenty-four human chromosomes. Some scientists asserted that the complete draft of the human genome represented a scientific achievement comparable to the development of the periodic table of elements. It generated an unprecedented volume of complex data. In addition to the United States, Australia, Brazil, Canada, China, Denmark, France, Germany, Israel, Italy, Japan, Korea, Mexico, the Netherlands, Russia, Sweden, and the United Kingdom all established programs. The Human Genome Organization (HUGO) helped to coordinate international collaboration on the project.

Concerns. Despite the potential benefits of mapping the human genome, several legal and ethical issues remained. Many were concerned by the potential use of genetic information by insurers, employers, courts, schools, adoption agencies, and the military; privacy and confidentiality rights; problems involving stigmatization and discrimination; educating doctors and the general public; health and environmental issues, including genetically modified foods and microbes; reproductive manipulation; and the commercialization of products in tandem with property rights and patents. Questions arose such as who owned genes and DNA, should their accessibility be limited, and to what degree? Many of these questions and concerns remained unanswered. In May 2008, however, President Bush signed into law the Genetic Nondiscrimination Act (GINA), prohibiting U.S. insurance companies and employers from discrimination based on information derived from genetic testing. The Senate passed it unanimously, and the House passed it by 414 votes to 1.

Gene Therapy. Gene therapy involved correcting defective genes responsible for the development of diseases and genetic disorders. In most cases, researchers inserted a normal gene into the genome to replace a defective gene. Scientists used a vector to deliver the therapeutic gene to the target cells. Because viruses are tiny pathogens that have evolved an efficient way of inserting their genetic material into human cells, causing everything from the common cold to cancer, scientists tried to take advantage of their natural efficiency and harness them as delivery mechanisms, or vectors, for other genetic material. By removing the disease-carrying genes from a virus and replacing them with therapeutic genes, scientists were able to target liver or lung cells that may be damaged. The viral vector inserted therapeutic genetic material into the target cell, generating a functional protein that restored damaged tissue to a normal state. Unfortunately, scientists faced several problems associated with gene therapy. Due to the rapid rate at which many cells in the body divide, it was difficult to achieve long-term effects without patients having to undergo multiple procedures. Even though targeting diseases caused by a single defective gene met with some success, conditions that arise from mutations in multiple genes such as heart disease, high blood pressure, Alzheimer's disease, arthritis, and diabetes proved especially difficult to treat using gene therapy. In addition, the human immune system is naturally designed to react defensively to foreign and potentially dangerous substances entering the body, so the highest risks involved triggering an unwanted and potentially toxic immune-system response in a patient. In 1999 eighteen-year-old Jesse Gelsinger, who was participating in a therapy trial at the University of Pennsylvania for ornithine transcarboxylase deficiency (OTDC), died from multiple organ failures four days after starting treatment. Researchers believed his death was caused by a severe immune response to the adenovirus carrier. In 2002 two children treated in a gene-therapy trial in France for X-linked severe combined immunodeficiency disease (X-SCID), also known as "bubble baby syndrome," developed leukemia-like symptoms. Consequently, in January 2003 the FDA placed a halt on all gene-therapy trials using retroviral vectors in blood stem cells. In February of that same year members of the FDA's Biological Response Modifiers Advisory Committee (BRMAC) met to discuss possible safety measures that would allow retroviral gene-therapy trials for the treatment of life-threatening diseases to proceed. In April they decided to ease the ban. Despite some tragic setbacks, scientists believed that real progress lay ahead. In February 2005 a research team at the University of Michigan was able to cure deafness in guinea pigs by delivering genes that promoted the regrowth of crucial hair cells in the cochlea, the part of the inner ear that registers sound. In March 2006 gene therapy was effectively used to treat myeloid disorders, which include bone marrow failure syndromes, in two adult patients. One significant benefit of gene therapy lay in its capacity for targeting specific damaged cells while leaving healthy cells unaffected. While chemotherapy, a traditional treatment for cancer, killed cells indiscriminately, for example, gene therapies offered a far more precise alternative. In August 2006 a team of researchers at the National Cancer Institute demonstrated a sustained regression of advanced melanoma in a study of seventeen patients whose white blood cells had been genetically engineered to recognize and attack cancer cells. British researchers announced positive results for a gene-therapy treatment used to counteract Leber's congenital amaurosis, a type of inherited childhood blindness. Even though viral carriers could successfully deliver therapeutic genetic material, in response to the tragic results of some experiments involving some of these carriers, scientists looked for other potential candidates. Nanoparticles made of biodegradable polymers less than 100 nanometers or one-billionth of a meter wide offered a promising alternative. In January 2007 researchers at the University of Texas M. D. Anderson Cancer Center and the University of Texas Southwestern Medical Center delivered a combination of two tumor-suppressing genes with lipid-based nanoparticles into lab mice, drastically reducing the number and size of human lung-cancer tumors. With these and other successes, gene therapy delivered on at least some of its promises and seemed to promise greater breakthroughs in the future.

Sources:

Anita J. Alton and others, "Biological and Environmental Research Information System: A Multifaceted Approach to DOE Systems Biology Research Communication," *ornl.gov* (n.d.);

Richard Black, "Cloned Pigs Raise Transplant Hopes," *news.bbc.co.uk* (22 August 2002;

Charles Q. Choi, "First Extinct-Animal Clone Created," *nationalgeographic.com* (10 February 2009);

"Cloning Fact Sheet," *ornl.gov* (11 May 2009);

Andy Coghlan, "Gene Therapy Is First Deafness 'Cure,'" *newscientist.com* (14 February 2005);

"Ethical, Legal, and Social Issues," *ornl.gov* (16 September 2008);

"Facts About Genome Sequencing," *ornl.gov* (19 September 2008);

"Gene Therapy," *ornl.gov* (11 June 2009);

"The Human Genome Project & the Private Sector: A Working Partnership," *ornl.gov* (10 November 2005);

"Insights Learned from the Human DNA Sequence," *ornl.gov* (9 October 2009);

Andrew Martin and Andrew Pollack, "F.D.A. Says Food from Cloned Animals Is Safe," *nytimes.com* (16 January 2008);

"Nano-treatment to Torpedo Cancer," *news.bbc.co.uk* (10 March 2009);

"New Method of Gene Therapy Alters Immune Cells for Treatment of Advanced Melanoma; Technique May Also Apply to Other Common Cancers," *cancer.gov* (31 August 2006);

"Obama Overturns Bush Policy on Stem Cells," *cnn.com* (9 March 2009);

"Public, Private Sectors Join in Mouse Consortium," *ornl.gov* (29 October 2003);

Anne Trafton, "Nanoparticles for Gene Therapy Improve," *web.mit.edu* (6 November 2009).

INTERNET TECHNOLOGY

Web-Based World. In the 2000s the Internet grew to an astounding level not only in the number of people who regularly logged on to the World Wide Web (WWW) but in the speed and capability of its technology. By December 2009, 26 percent of the world's population used the Internet and "surfed the web." Often dubbed the "information superhighway" or "global village," the Internet radically changed the way businesses operated and people communicated, interlinking markets and cultures across the world. With online media, social networking, and gaming, it also enabled the creation of virtual cultures on the web. Traditional communications media such as telephone and television services were redefined by technologies such as instant messaging, Voice over Internet Protocol (VoIP), mobile smartphones, and streaming video. The Internet changed the production, sale, and distribution of print publications, software, news, music, film, video, photography, and everyday products from soap to automobiles. Many of these changes were attributable to the advent of high-speed Internet or broadband technologies that began to expand rapidly in 2000. With broadband, Internet users could download and watch videos in a matter of seconds, media companies could offer live streaming-video newsfeeds, and peer-to-peer file sharing became efficient and commonplace. News was delivered on websites, blogs, and webfeeds, and e-commerce changed the way people shopped. Television shows, home movies, and feature films were viewed on desktop or laptop computers and even on cell phones. Students researched online, and many parents began working from home for their employers or started their own online businesses. Anyone with a little technical knowledge could broadcast audio and visual material worldwide. With the low cost of creating a personal webpage and little censorship restriction, the web was one of the most democratic forms of media and an effective way to reach a large audience. It was also becoming increasingly easy for users to access it from Internet cafés, Internet kiosks, access

terminals, and web pay phones. With the advent of wireless, customers could connect to the Internet from virtually any place that offered remote service in the form of a wireless local area network (WLAN) or Wi-Fi router.

Broadband. At the turn of the century, most users accessed the Internet by a dial-up connection in which computers used modems to connect to other computers using existing telephone lines. Typical dial-up connections ran at 56 kilobytes per second. However, the implementation of broadband technology greatly increased the speed that users could send and receive information. Between 2000 and 2003, broadband usage in the United States grew by 24 percent. Broadband referred to DSL (Digital Subscriber Line) and cable modem access; it used more-efficient coaxial cables or fiber-optic cables to transmit data. In 2009 the Federal Communications Commission (FCC) defined basic broadband as data transmission that exceeded speeds of 768 kilobits per second (Kbps), or 768,000 bits per second. For the first time since the web was invented, audio tracks and visual images could be downloaded in real time or close to real time. High-speed Internet access became standard in many homes and offices and at most public venues. The advent of broadband technology vastly changed people's relationship to the WWW and led to widespread improvements in Internet technology.

Sharing Information. Email was the general form of internet communication and allowed users to send electronic text messages. Users could also attach additional files containing text, pictures, or videos. Chat rooms and instant-messaging systems were also popular methods of online communication and were even quicker than traditional email. Broadband made other popular forms of Internet communication possible, including video chat rooms and video conferencing. Internet telephony or VoIP became increasingly popular for gaming applications. Operators of Ventrilo, Wii, Playstation 3, and Xbox 360 systems could play games and talk to one another live online. The Skype service allowed individuals to make video and phone calls, send instant messages, share files, and make calls to landlines and mobile phones from computers or other electronic devices.

Music. Between 1999 and 2001, Shawn Fanning and Sean Parker ran an online service called Napster that specialized in peer-to-peer file sharing, revolutionizing the music industry and the way many Internet users and services conducted business. Named after his hair-based moniker, nineteen-year-old Fanning created Napster while enrolled at Northeastern University in Boston. Fanning took a novel ground-up approach to running his website. Napster essentially indexed lists of all the connected systems and computer MPEG-1 Audio Layer III (MP3) music files that users uploaded and downloaded from their home computers. Although Napster had its own central servers, the system's format enabled peer-to-peer file sharing on an incredibly large scale. It was built on user-generated music files, and it operated differently from traditional hierarchical models of information sharing. Instead of storing

From left to right: Icons for social networking websites Facebook, MySpace, and Twitter (<www.facebook.com>, <www.myspace.com>, and <www.twitter.com>)

songs on a single giant database, Napster acted as a node connecting hundreds of thousands of different personal computers; therefore, its customers simultaneously used *and* provided its services. Not only did Napster enable its users to access some obscure songs, it also allowed them to bypass the established market for popular songs and led to massive copyright violations. Several high-profile music acts such as the heavy-metal band Metallica filed lawsuits against Napster for copyright infringements. Major record labels also filed lawsuits, and after a long legal battle, the site was temporarily shut down. It reemerged later as a pay service, and companies capitalized on the music downloading market. In January 2001 Apple launched the iPod digital music player, and then in April 2003 it opened the iTunes Store, allowing customers to legally purchase songs for 99 cents. Although federal courts ordered that music-sharing services such as Napster could be held liable if they were used to steal copyrighted works, Fanning's brainchild realized the power of peer-to-peer file sharing and the potential success of user-generated Internet services.

User-Generated Content. The trend of user-generated services found its complement in user-generated content when Evan Williams (who later cofounded Twitter) and Meg Hourihan launched Blogger.com in August 1999. Unlike Napster and other music services that traded or sold content generated by third-party artists, blogs were generated completely by the writers and readers that disseminated them. Blog is short for weblog, and bloggers maintained their pages by regularly publishing their thoughts and stories. Some blogs functioned as online personal diaries while others provided descriptions of news events and offered links to other webpages or additional graphics or videos. By 2005 blogging was perceived by many as a legitimate news source. Blogging, and the Internet in general, led to record declines in the circulation of major newspapers, and print publications were forced to post stories online, often allocating space for readers to give commentary. By the end of 2009, an estimated 77 percent of Internet users read or generated approximately 133,000,000 different blogs. In addition, Really Simple Syndication (RSS) allowed people to subscribe to specific blogs and other online publications. Using RSS aggregators, people could choose to get news from specialized and general publications, and mainstream media providers had to quickly adapt by providing RSS feeds.

Twitter. Williams, Biz Stone, and Jack Dorsey launched a microblogging service in 2006 called Twitter. Its creators envisioned Twitter as a means through which users could give quick status updates and organize impromptu social gatherings. People could choose to receive regular updates from their friends or "friended" celebrities about current happenings and events; they could also send "tweets," or text-based posts, of up to 140 characters. Twitter was more up to the minute than traditional blogs and approximately 80 percent of tweets were made from mobile devices. Twitter was credited with breaking news such as the Hudson River plane crash (15 January 2009). The service claimed more than 100 million users worldwide by 2009.

Webpages. Traditionally, most webpages were created as complete HyperText Markup Language (HTML) pages or structured documents that were modified only by the owner. In contrast, collaborative software known as WikiPages gained in popularity during the decade. At first, WikiPages contained little content. Visitors added their own material using a simplified markup language or text editor, so that the site grew over time. Contributors could be paid staff, members of a particular club or organization, or the general public. The largest Wiki service on the WWW was the digital encyclopedia Wikipedia; in 2009 the site contained more than 13 million articles. Its unique user-generated design allowed for breadth and scope that print publications could never match, but the fact that anyone could write or edit an article on the website raised concerns about the reliability of its information.

Social Networking. Although the WWW was a collaborative media by its very nature, it soon became a virtual community with the advent of the first social-networking site, MySpace, in August 2003. Social-networking sites followed a basic format. They typically had a representation of each user or "profile," social links, and additional services such as email and instant messaging. Members posted everything from resumes to candid photographs, and shared weblinks, blog posts, and news stories. Social-networking sites became incredibly popular as people used them to keep in touch with or reconnect with old friends, organize social events, share information about special interests or hobbies, and make and maintain professional connections. In 2008 Facebook overtook MySpace as the dominant social-networking site. By the end of the decade, social media superseded pornography as the primary activity on the web. Ninety-six percent of generation Y had joined a social network, and an estimated one out of every eight married couples in the United States met through social media. The number of users of Facebook in 2009 exceeded the population of Indonesia, the fourth largest country in the world. Along with drastically changing social and professional behaviors, sites such as MySpace, Facebook, and Friendster also enabled personalized marketing. As members of social-networking sites revealed general socioeconomic information along with personal interests and hobbies, companies sought to advertise products to potentially receptive buyers.

Advances in Play. Online gaming ranged from popular board games such as Monopoly and Scrabble that required only simple graphics to games that incorporated complex graphics and sophisticated story lines to create virtual worlds, which often hosted thousands of players simultaneously. Adobe's Flash technology allowed for streaming video and an unparalleled degree of user interactivity. Programmers could create complex graphics that were quick and easy to download. With traditional raster graphics, a program had to store information for the color and location of each individual pixel that appeared on a computer screen, which required a relatively large data file. Raster images also distorted when their size was modified. Instead of storing information for every individual pixel, Flash designs used vector images comprised of points, lines, curves, and geometric shapes such as polygons and stored them as mathematical formulae, which effectively adapted to any pixel grid and provided the best image regardless of resolution. The size of the data file remained the same even as the scale of the image changed. Flash technology was not only far more space efficient, but images scaled up and down without distorting. First-person shooter games such as Microsoft's *Halo* and massively multiplayer online role-playing games (MMORPGs) such as Blizzard Entertainment's *World of Warcraft* would not have been possible without Flash technology.

Sources:

"Flash," *techterms.com* (n.d.);

Saul Hansell, "Putting the Napster Genie Back in the Bottle," *nytimes.com* (20 November 2005);

"Internet Growth Statistics," *internetworldstats.com* (23 June 2010);

Richard MacManus, "Top Internet Trends of 2000–2009: Democratization of News Media," *readwriteweb.com* (18 November 2009);

Om Malik, "A Brief History of Twitter," *gigaom.com* (1 February 2009);

Adam Singer, "70 Usable Stats from the 2009 State of the Blogosphere," *thefuturebuzz.com* (10 December 2009);

Singer, "Social Media, Web 2.0 and Internet Stats," *thefuturebuzz.com* (12 January 2009);

"Social Media Revolution," *wn.com* (n.d.);

Jonathan Strickland, "How Twitter Works," *howstuffworks.com* (17 December 2007).

RE-IMAGINING OLD TECHNOLOGIES

The Digital Switch. On 12 June 2009, as mandated by Congress, all full-power television stations had to broadcast in digital only. Previously, most broadcast stations were transmitting in both digital and analog. Individuals who did not own a television capable of receiving digital signals had to purchase a digital-to-analog converter box. Because an analog signal conveyed all available information, transmitting an image required that every pixel be included in the signal. A standard National Television Systems Committee (NTSC) analog television

Logo of the Digital TV Converter Box Program, which offered coupons worth $40 toward the purchase of the digital converter boxes needed to update analog televisions after the 12 June 2009 digital switch (Department of Commerce)

screen included 525 lines of 720 pixels each for a total of 378,000 pixels. This information could just fit into the 6MHz (megahertz) bandwidth of a traditional analog channel. The Advanced Television Systems Committee in the United States set a screen standard for HDTVs that allotted up to 1,080 lines of 1920 pixels each, or 2,073,600 pixels total. Completely switching to an all-digital feed allowed for signal compression so that more visual information could be broadcast to HDTV users. The signal was compressed using Moving Picture Experts Group (MPEG-2) technology, which took advantage of the fact that the human brain filled in visual gaps on its own as the eye perceived variations in color and motion. An MPEG-2 encoder recorded just enough detail to make it seem like nothing was missing in a picture. It compared adjacent frames and only recorded the sections of an image that moved or changed. Implementing this technology allowed the broadcast signal to be compressed to 2 percent of its original size. Audio was sent using the Dolby Digital/AC-3 encoding system, which offered the same digital quality that compact discs (CDs) offered. It provided a total of 5.1 channels of sound—three in front (left, center, and right), two in back (left and right), and a subwoofer bass (the .1 channel). The switch to digital also enabled a station to broadcast four standard-definition signals within the same bandwidth required for one high-definition picture. In many markets, public broadcasting system (PBS) channels, for example, took advantage of this to "multicast" during the daytime. The remaining signal bandwidth saved by the switch to digital was either allocated to emergency services or auctioned off to various communications companies that then offered their customers more-advanced wireless options.

LCD Television. The switch to an all-digital broadcast signal was the inevitable response to significant changes in television technology. Cathode Ray Tube (CRT) televisions had dominated the market since they were first commercialized in 1922. CRT technology was based upon a vacuum picture tube and a screen coated in phosphors. A device at the back of the tube fired a beam of electrons at the front (or wide) end of the tube, exciting phosphor atoms. When bombarded with negatively charged particles, phosphors, from which the term phosphorescence is derived, light up. The level of voltage applied affects the relative lightness and darkness of the picture. In the 1950s manufacturers coated the front of the picture tube with three different phosphors (that lit up red, green, and blue) to produce color televisions. Triads of these three colors formed one pixel. These pixels were distributed across a grid and blended in various proportions to produce the spectrum of visible light. Although CRTs could produce excellent pictures, in order to increase the size or width of a set, the length of the tube had to be proportionally increased so that the scanning electron gun would have room to reach all parts of the screen. Consequently, large CRT sets were heavy and took up a lot of room. Liquid Crystal Display (LCD) televisions were CRT's first serious competitor, and by 2007, LCD televisions surpassed the sale of CRTs worldwide. LCD technology can be traced back to Austrian scientist Friedrich Reinitzer who first discovered the properties of liquid crystallization in 1888. Working at Charles University in the Czech Republic, Reinitzer investigated the physico-chemical properties of various derivatives of cholesteryl. He observed that when melted, cholesteryl benzoate became a cloudy liquid, but before it completely cooled, it underwent a phase transition in which it turned into a blue liquid containing tiny crystals. Eighty years later Radio Corporation of America (RCA) began experimenting with LCDs. While at RCA, George Heilmeier and his colleagues made the first efforts at putting the technology to work in digital gadgets. James Fergason, director of the Liquid Crystal Institute at Kent State University, improved upon LCD technology with his discovery of the "nematic field effect." Within a short period of time, monochrome LCD screens became commonplace as their low electrical power consumption made them ideal for battery-powered devices, including digital clocks, watches, and calculators. As the technology advanced, full-color displays became available and were prevalent in the late 1990s in devices such as cell phones. The technology also proved viable for large-screen displays and quickly became a component of many laptop computers and television sets. Although there were three liquid-crystal groups, those in the so-called nematic phase had an elongated shape like tiny cigars and could be aligned in specific directions. To harness this characteristic for use in LCD screens, the liquid crystals were spread out over two finely grooved surfaces. These alignment plates arranged the liquid crystals in different directions, causing a "twist" in the crystals. Using transistors to apply an electric current to the liquid, the crystals twisted and untwisted in a process called the "twisting nematic field effect" that alternately blocked light to a given area of the LCD screen or allowed light through. Polarizing filters were positioned on either side of the alignment plates. The level of light that passed through the polarized filters and liquid crystal produced a grayscale. Additional colorized filters—red, green, and blue—made up the pixels. A backlight made of fluorescent lights (LEDs) shone through the LCD array and provided a crisp picture. Unlike CRTs, LCDs were thin enough to hang on the wall.

Plasma Television. Plasma screens also enjoyed a distinct advantage over traditional CRTs because they could be wide and relatively thin at the same time. Plasma TVs were heavier, a little thicker, and less energy efficient than LCDs, but the image was typically brighter and better from wide angles. (LCDs looked best when the viewer was directly in front of them, whereas the picture quality degraded in proportion to less-direct viewing angles.) Panasonic, the consumer electronics company owned by Matsushita Electric Industrial Company in Japan, promoted plasma televisions as having a sharper image quality on larger screens than LCDs. The prototype for plasma-display technology was invented in 1964 at the University of Illinois at Urbana-Champaign by professors Donald Bitzer and Gene Slottow, and graduate student Robert Wilson. At the time, most computer screens only accommodated alphanumeric displays and could not render complex graphics. CRT screens did not hold a graphics-based image, and the computer memory that made this possible was not readily available. For Bitzer and Slottow, the plasma display facilitated computer-based education by making complex graphics possible. Piggybacking on their research, Larry F. Weber, Blitzer's former student, cofounded Plasmaco, Inc., in 1987. Matsushita acquired the company in 1996 and funded Weber and his colleagues as they continued to refine the technology. Weber's prototype sixty-inch plasma display bore the Panasonic label and combined the size and resolution necessary for HDTV with thinness. The Society for Information Display awarded Weber their highest award in 2000, and the television industry gave a 2002 Emmy Award to Weber's predecessors (Bitzer, Slottow, and Wilson), whose names appear on the original plasma-display patent. Fujitsu, a leading manufacturer of plasma displays, also shared the award. Plasma televisions converted xenon and neon gases into plasmas by exposing them to electric fields. When ionized, these gases contained a sufficient number of charged particles to affect their electrical properties and behavior. Under normal conditions, gas atoms carried no electrical charge. A gas became a plasma when the addition of heat or sufficient electromagnetic energy excited the atoms and caused them to release some or all of their electrons. These electrons collided with the remaining positively charged protons, releasing photons of light. The same basic process occurred in stars and in fluorescent light bulbs. In a plasma television, the gases were held in hundreds of thousands of tiny cells positioned between two plates of glass. Vertical and horizontal electrodes formed a grid connecting these cells. The cells were then charged thousands of times in a fraction of a second. These charges excited the gas atoms and caused them to release ultraviolet photons. Like CRTs before them, plasma televisions made use of the light-producing properties of phosphor. Photons released by the plasma interacted with phosphor coated on the inside of each cell wall.

Like CRT, every pixel in a plasma TV was made of three subpixels of red, green, and blue phosphor. By varying the electrical current flowing through the plasma cells, the TV's control system could increase or decrease the intensity of each subpixel hue to produce colors across the entire spectrum.

Cell Phones. Typical cell phones in the 2000s consisted of a circuit board, antenna, LCD screen, keyboard, microphone, speaker, battery, and Flash memory chip; on a complexity-per-cubic-inch scale, some were the most advanced and intricate technological devices used by Americans on a daily basis. Modern digital cell phones processed millions of calculations per second just to compress and decompress the voice stream. As the technology grew, many cell phones offered built-in MP3 players, digital cameras, Global Positioning Systems (GPS), and Bluetooth headsets for hands-free talking. Users could send and receive email from their cell phones, surf the World Wide Web, play video games, send text messages, watch television, and participate in video conferencing along with an almost endless list of other applications, or "apps." Few technologies advanced as rapidly as the cell phone. A cell phone built on the half-duplex technology of CB radios and walkie-talkies, which allowed two people to communicate on the same radio frequency. But using the same frequency meant only one user could talk at a time. The cell phone was a full-duplex device: one frequency was used for talking while a separate frequency was used for listening. This enabled two people to talk at the same time. Cell phones could have an almost limitless range as long as the user was close enough to a transmitting tower. Due to a finite number of radio frequencies available for cell-phone use (around 832 analogs), only a limited number of people could talk on their cell phones at the same time. Nevertheless, cell-phone users seldom found that all the available channels were taken. This was because service carriers divided large cities into cells of approximately ten square miles. Cell phones and base station towers used low-power transmitters—allowing them to use a relatively small battery—and radio frequencies could be reused in nonadjacent cells. With the advancements of second generation (2G) digital-transmission methods, even more frequency space became available. Digital phones converted audio signals into binary 1s and 0s and compressed them. This voice-compression technology allowed for anywhere between three and ten digital cell-phone calls to occur within the same bandwidth required for a single analog call. The first third-generation network (3G) network was launched in 2003. With even more bandwidth space available, 3G phones (often called smartphones) could process information almost as fast as home computers with a direct connection. 3G networks advertised transfer speeds of up to 3 megabits per second (Mbps), so that the average four-minute song would take about twenty seconds to download off the Internet. The fastest 2G phones took around eleven minutes. In June 2007, 3G networks claimed their 200-millionth customer.

Global Positioning System (GPS). GPS is composed of a constellation of at least twenty-four Earth-orbiting satellites that a receiving device uses to calculate its location from anywhere on the globe. These 3,000- to 4,000-pound

Advertisement for the Apple iPhone, a popular mobile device (<albumcreative.com>)

solar-powered satellites circle the planet at a rate of 12,000 miles an hour and make two complete rotations around the Earth each day. The orbits are arranged so that at any time, and from anywhere, there are at least four satellites "visible" in the sky. In a process similar to triangulation, a GPS receiver locates four or more of these satellites, determines the distance to each, and uses this information to deduce its own location. It can do so within an accuracy margin of about twenty meters (sixty-five feet) or less. When the technology was first made available to the general public, the government mandated that civilian users could only have access to "selective availability" or to limited and less-precise satellite-generated information. President Bill Clinton signed an executive order in 1996 (implemented on 2 May 2000) lifting the availability restriction. GPS was then used by a growing number of Americans in their cars and on their cell phones to help guide them. GPS receivers typically stored or had access to road maps for the entire United States and many foreign countries. A GPS receiver could upload the relevant map and display an icon on the LCD screen indicating the user's position. A user entered her or his desired destination and the GPS system provided directions. Most GPS receivers also provide verbal directions so that drivers do not have to take their eyes off the road. GPS services can also provide telephone numbers and addresses of local hotels and restaurants.

Sources:

"The Basics About Liquid Crystals," *elis.ugent.be* (2006);

Marshall Brain and Tom Harris, "How GPS Receivers Work," *howstuffworks.com* (25 September 2006);

Brain, Jeff Tyson, and Julia Layton, "How Cell Phones Work," *howstuffworks.com* (14 November 2000);

Gregg Cianfrini, "Liquid Crystal Display Technology," *buffalo.edu* (n.d.);

"Color Principles—Hue, Saturation, and Value," *ncsu.edu* (8 May 2000);

Sam Grobart, "Beyond Flat Panels: A New Generation of TV Sets," *nytimes.com* (10 June 2010);

Jerry Gurski and Lee Ming Quach, "Display Technology Overview," *lytica.com* (1 July 2005);

"History of Television," *lcd-tv-reviews.com* (n.d.);

Reynold A. Howard, "Revisiting History—How LCD TV—The World's Current Number One TV Technology—Came About," *ezinearticles.com* (24 January 2009);

Jamie Hutchinson, "The History of Plasma Display Panels," *plasmatvscience.org* (n.d.);

"LCD—Liquid Crystal Display—Technology Overview," *presentationtek.com* (n.d.);

Nor Nan, "Technological Advancements In Cell Phone," *ezinearticles.com* (n.d.);

Rick Prescott, "How LCDs Work," *chipcenter.com* (2003);

Michael Schuman, "Flat Chance," *time.com* (22 November 2004);

"The Science behind Plasma TV & Display Technology," *plasmatvscience.org* (n.d.);

Eric A. Taub, "Forget L.C.D.; Go for Plasma Says Maker of Both," *nytimes.com* (25 December 2006);

"What You Need to Know about the Digital TV Transition" *dtv.gov* (n.d.);

"What is GPS," *garmin.com* (n.d.).

SPACE

Columbia Tragedy. On 1 February 2003 the space shuttle *Columbia* disintegrated upon reentry over Texas at approximately 9:00 A.M. just before its seven-member crew was scheduled to land in Florida. Addressing the nation that Saturday afternoon, President George W. Bush said, "The *Columbia* is lost. There are no survivors." The crew included six Americans: Commander Rick D. Husband, Pilot William McCool, Payload Commander Michael Anderson, Mission Specialist Kalpana Chawla, Mission Specialist David Brown, and Mission Specialist Laurel Clark. Payload Specialist Ilan Ramon, Israel's first astronaut, also died in the accident. The crew had completed more than eighty scientific experiments while in orbit. The tragedy was the first in forty-two years of manned spaceflight to happen during a shuttle craft's descent to Earth. The last major space-shuttle disaster had occurred in 1986 when the *Challenger* exploded seventy-two seconds after takeoff, killing all seven crew members onboard. *Columbia* was the National Aeronautics and Space Administration's (NASA) oldest shuttle. This flight was the 28th for *Columbia*, the 113th flight in the shuttle program's history.

Causes. On 2 February NASA administrator Sean O'Keefe appointed retired U.S. Navy admiral Harold Gelman Jr., who led the investigation into the bombing of the USS *Cole* in Yemen in 2000, to lead the Columbia Accident Investigation Board (CAIB). The following day, Ron Dittemore, the space-shuttle program manager, told reporters that foam shed by *Columbia*'s external tank was the most likely cause of the accident. The shuttle consisted of three main components: the orbiter vehicle, two rocket boosters, and an external fuel tank. The orbiter carried the astronauts and had three engines mounted on its fuselage. The two rocket boosters provided most of the thrust needed for liftoff, while the large external tank, carrying more than 500,000 gallons of liquid hydrogen and oxygen, propelled the orbiter into space. As the shuttle thrust higher into the atmosphere, it shed its rocket boosters and finally its large external fuel tank. According to the CAIB, a piece of insulating foam that peeled from the external fuel tank when it separated had punctured a hole in the leading edge of the left orbiter wing. Sixteen days later, during the intense heat of reentry, hot gases penetrated the interior of the wing through the hole and melted the support structure of the craft, causing it to break apart and incinerate in mid-air. The impact of the 1.67-pound piece of foam had been visible in videos taken during the launch and throughout *Columbia*'s mission. It was clear from dozens of emails expressing concern over the amount of potential damage caused by the foam that NASA engineers had pleaded with mission managers to closely examine the wing. The managers held firm to a common belief that foam strikes were relatively harmless.

Recommendations. After conducting its investigation, the CAIB issued a scathing report in August that criticized NASA for being complacent about safety concerns and narrowly focused on scheduling and budgeting pressures. In addition to censuring NASA's management, the board released a list of policies to be implemented for future missions. The board found that Reinforced Carbon-Carbon Panels that line parts of the shuttle to protect against the high temperatures of reentry needed to be inspected more thoroughly for structural flaws. The board also felt that routine imaging of each shuttle while it was in orbit should be standard procedure as NASA failed to obtain clear enough images that would have enabled them to determine the amount of damage caused to the wing by the foam. The imaging system on the ground needed to be updated as well so that a minimum of three different angles of the shuttle from liftoff to at least rocket-booster separation would be available for examination. Inside the shuttle's cabin, onboard cameras captured images of the external tank after separation, but these were typically reviewed postflight. The board suggested that these images should be available during ascent so that the potential damage of debris strikes or other anomalies could be assessed. After reviewing the recommendations, NASA determined to retire the outdated shuttle-orbiter fleet in 2010. The *Columbia*, for example, had been built with materials and technology from the 1970s. NASA decided to focus on building the next generation of space vehicle, known as *Constellation*. The capsule design of *Constellation* will be more durable than the traditional airplanelike shuttle and will ride on top of the rocket where launching debris will not strike it. NASA also called for upgrades to seat hardware to provide

Columbia space shuttle crew, clockwise from top: Mission Specialist Kalpana Chawla, Commander Rick Husband, Mission Specialists Laurel Clark and David Brown, Pilot Willie McCool, Payload Specialist Ilan Ramon, and Payload Commander Michael Anderson (<www.spaceflight.nasa.gov>)

safer bodily restraint and for individual radio beacons for members of the crew. Pressure suits would be fitted with sturdier helmets, and new procedures would ensure a more reliable oxygen supply during emergencies. On 9 May 2003 NASA announced that Bill Parsons would replace Dittemore as shuttle-program manager. As a lasting tribute to the fallen astronauts, the United States Geological Survey Board of Geographic Names approved the appellation Columbia Point for a 13,980-foot mountain in Colorado's Sangre de Cristo Mountains, less than half a mile from Challenger Point.

Eris Discovered. On 5 January 2005 Mike Brown (Caltech), Chad Trujillo (Gemini Observatory), and David Rabinowitz (Yale University) discovered a new planet orbiting the Sun that was larger than Pluto. On 13 September 2006 Object 2003 UB313 and its satellite, which had been referred to as Xena and Gabrielle respectively, were officially named Eris and Dysnomia. The planet first appeared during an ongoing survey, begun in 2001, of the outer edges of the solar system at the Samuel Oschin Telescope at Palomar Observatory in San Diego County, California. In 2003 researchers installed a new QUEST camera to photograph the night sky. Distant stars and galaxies emit their own light, whereas smaller bodies in the solar system reflect light from the Sun, making it difficult to discern the nature of the body in a still photograph. However, scien-

tists trained the telescope at various areas in space for three-hour increments and used time-lapse photography at the rate of one photograph per hour to detect movement. Because of their vast distances the billions of stars and galaxies visible in the sky appear to be stationary relative to the rotation of the Earth, while much-closer satellites, planets, asteroids, and comets appear to move. Initially, researchers relied on computer models to sort through the stills to determine if any unexpected movement occurred. The first images capturing the new planet were taken on 21 October 2003. The computer, however, failed to register a moving object. Upon reanalysis, the planet was officially noticed on 5 January 2005 by Brown, despite a report later made to the press that 8 January was the discovery date, a recollection error corrected upon review. Eris was the largest object found in orbit around the Sun since Johann Gottfried Galle and Heinrich Louis d'Arrest discovered Neptune in 1846. It was 27 percent more massive than Pluto, and was part of the Kuiper belt, a cluster of icy bodies beyond Neptune. At more than 10 billion miles from the Sun, over three times more distant than Pluto, Eris took twice as long as Pluto to complete its orbit. Whereas Pluto moved from 30 to 50 times the Sun-Earth distance over its 250-year orbit, Eris moved from 38 to 97 times the Sun-Earth distance over its 560-year orbit. Sunlight takes nearly a day to reach the planet and reflect back to Earth. Its surface tem-

On 4 February 2003 at the Johnson Space Center in Houston, Texas, President George W. Bush delivered the following speech.

Their mission was almost complete and we lost them so close to home. The men and women of the Columbia had journeyed more than 6 million miles and were minutes away from arrival and reunion. The loss was sudden and terrible, and for their families the grief is heavy.

Our nation shares in your sorrow and in your pride.

We remember not only one moment of tragedy, but seven lives of great purpose and achievement.

To leave behind Earth and air and gravity is an ancient dream of humanity. For these seven, it was a dream fulfilled. Each of these astronauts had the daring and discipline required of their calling. Each of them knew that great endeavors are inseparable from great risks. And each of them accepted those risks willingly, even joyfully, in the cause of discovery.

Rick Husband was a boy of four when he first thought of being an astronaut. As a man, and having become an astronaut, he found it was even more important to love his family and serve his Lord. One of Rick's favorite hymns was, "How Great Thou Art," which offers these words of praise: "I see the stars. I hear the mighty thunder. Thy power throughout the universe displayed."

David Brown was first drawn to the stars as a little boy with a telescope in his back yard. He admired astronauts, but, as he said, "I thought they were movie stars. I thought I was kind of a normal kid." David grew up to be a physician, an aviator who could land on the deck of a carrier in the middle of the night, and a shuttle astronaut. His brother asked him several weeks ago what would happen if something went wrong on their mission. David replied, "This program will go on."

Michael Anderson always wanted to fly planes, and rose to the rank of Lt. Colonel in the Air Force. Along the way, he became a role model—especially for his two daughters and for the many children he spoke to in schools. He said to them, "Whatever you want to be in life, you're training for it now." He also told his minister, "If this thing doesn't come out right, don't worry about me, I'm just going on higher."

Laurel Salton Clark was a physician and a flight surgeon who loved adventure, loved her work, loved her husband and her son. A friend who heard Laurel speaking to Mission Control said, "There was a smile in her voice." Laurel conducted some of the experiments as Columbia orbited the Earth, and described seeing new life emerge from a tiny cocoon. "Life," she said, "continues in a lot of places, and life is a magical thing."

None of our astronauts traveled a longer path to space than Kalpana Chawla. She left India as a student, but she would see the nation of her birth, all of it, from hundreds of miles above. When the sad news reached her home town, an administrator at her high school recalled, "She always said she wanted to reach the stars. She went there, and beyond." Kalpana's native country mourns her today, and so does her adopted land.

Ilan Ramon also flew above his home, the land of Israel. He said, "The quiet that envelopes space makes the beauty even more powerful. And I only hope that the quiet can one day spread to my country." Ilan was a patriot; the devoted son of a holocaust survivor, served his country in two wars. "Ilan," said his wife, Rona, "left us at his peak moment, in his favorite place, with people he loved."

The Columbia's pilot was Commander Willie McCool, whom friends knew as the most steady and dependable of men. In Lubbock today they're thinking back to the Eagle Scout who became a distinguished Naval officer and a fearless test pilot. One friend remembers Willie this way: "He was blessed, and we were blessed to know him."

Our whole nation was blessed to have such men and women serving in our space program. Their loss is deeply felt, especially in this place, where so many of you called them friends. The people of NASA are being tested once again. In your grief, you are responding as your friends would have wished—with focus, professionalism, and unbroken faith in the mission of this agency. Captain Brown was correct: America's space program will go on.

This cause of exploration and discovery is not an option we choose; it is a desire written in the human heart. We are that part of creation which seeks to understand all creation. We find the best among us, send them forth into unmapped darkness, and pray they will return. They go in peace for all mankind, and all mankind is in their debt. Yet, some explorers do not return. And the loss settles unfairly on a few. The families here today shared in the courage of those they loved. But now they must face life and grief without them. The sorrow is lonely; but you are not alone. In time, you will find comfort and the grace to see you through. And in God's own time, we can pray that the day of your reunion will come.

The final days of their own lives were spent looking down upon this Earth. And now, on every continent, in every land they could see, the names of these astronauts are known and remembered. They will always have an honored place in the memory of this country. And today I offer the respect and gratitude of the people of the United States.

May God bless you all.

Source: "President Bush Attends Memorial for Columbia Astronauts" (4 February 2003) georgewbush-whitehouse.archives.gov.

Members of an investigation team examine debris from space shuttle *Columbia* at Barksdale Air Force Base in 2003 (United States Air Force photograph by Michael A. Kaplan).

perature varies from approximately 405 degrees Fahrenheit (243 degrees Celsius) below zero to 360 degrees Fahrenheit (218 degrees Celsius) below zero, depending on its location. Using the Hubble Space Telescope, scientists determined the size of the planet to be approximately 2,400 km in diameter. Researchers speculated that the planet was composed of about half ice and half rock. At the farthest points in its orbit, it reflects approximately 86 percent of the sunlight that strikes its surface. Scientists believe its atmosphere, composed primarily of methane and nitrogen, freezes to an icy three-inch-thick crust.

"Dwarf Planets." Brown claimed that he and his colleagues officially recommended the name Eris because she was the goddess of warfare and strife in Greek mythology, and the astronomers knew that a controversial debate over the definition of "planet" would ensue. According to legend, Eris was sister to Mars, the god of war. Her son was Strife. Her daughter Dysnomia, the appellation scientists chose for Eris's moon, represented the spirit of lawlessness. Just as Brown and his colleagues predicted, controversy ensued in the scientific community over how to categorize their discovery. To resolve the conflict, members of the International Astronomical Union (IAU) met in Prague in 2006 to discuss the cultural and scientific fate of Eris and Pluto. After all, Pluto had enjoyed planet status since its discovery by Illinois-born Clyde Tombaugh in 1930. Another lesser-known body of the Asteroid Belt—dubbed Ceres (Roman goddess of the harvest, growing plants, and motherly love) by Giuseppe Piazzi in 1801—also figured in the debate. IAU members voted

to categorize Pluto, Eris, and Ceres as "Dwarf Planets." Scientists decided to define a planet as a celestial body in orbit around the Sun with enough mass to overcome rigid body forces and form a nearly spherical shape. Furthermore, irrespective of moons, a full-sized planet must have cleared the neighborhood around its orbit. Pluto, Eris, and Ceres are all massive enough to overcome rigid forces and assume a round shape, but they have not cleared their orbits of debris.

Water Discovered on Mars. On 31 July 2008, scientists using the Thermal and Evolved Gas Analyzer (TEGA) aboard NASA's *Phoenix* Mars lander, detected water in a soil sample taken from the Red Planet. As part of a $420 million mission initially slated to last ninety days, the *Phoenix* touched down near Mars's north pole on 25 May 2008 on a quest to learn more about the planet's surface, including whether it contained frozen water and organic-based compounds essential for life. In 2002 the Mars *Odyssey* spacecraft detected what appeared to be vast quantities of underground ice at the polar regions of the planet. The arctic terrain where *Phoenix* landed had polygon shapes similar to those found in Earth's permafrost regions that are caused by seasonal expansion and shrinking of ice beneath the surface. Scientists believed that the *Phoenix* lander exposed chunks of ice while digging in the topsoil of the Martian arctic. Bits of reflective material initially photographed in a small trench that researchers had dubbed "Dodo-Goldilocks" later vanished, leading them to believe that the reflective bits were ice that had evaporated after being exposed to the Sun. There were some initial reservations that the bright matter was perhaps salt, but its disappearance clearly indicated otherwise. To be absolutely certain, the robotic arm of the *Phoenix* lander shoveled samples of the soil, surprisingly clumpy and difficult to shake from its scoop, into TEGA for analysis. TEGA heated the samples and was able to confirm that at 32 degrees Fahrenheit—the melting point of ice—water molecules were released from the soil. In general, the soil was found to be somewhat alkaline and to contain mineral nutrients such as sodium, magnesium, and potassium. No organic molecules were detected. For an additional cost of $2 million, NASA decided to extend the mission to 30 September 2008, five weeks beyond the original three-month allotment, to conduct further research. As part of the extended mission, scientists dug more trenches and took a more detailed panoramic picture of the surrounding Martian plains. The extension also allowed a weather station to gather additional meteorological information.

Water Discovered on the Moon. On 13 November 2009 Anthony Colaprete of NASA announced that his project team had discovered water on the Moon. Researchers had long speculated that frozen water, delivered perhaps by impacting comets billions of years ago, might be found in some permanently shadowed places at the bottom of craters on the lunar surface. NASA launched the Lunar Crater Observation and Sensing Satellite (LCROSS) with a *Centaur* rocket onboard along with the Lunar Reconnaissance Orbiter (LRO) on 18 June 2009 from the Kennedy Space Center in Florida as part of a $79 million mission primarily designed to determine if water existed on the Moon. After traveling approximately 113 days and nearly 5.6 million miles, LCROSS separated from LRO, which stayed in orbit to collect data. The *Centaur* rocket then separated from LCROSS and impacted the lunar surface shortly after 4:31 A.M. on 9 October 2009. LCROSS followed the rocket to collect data with its onboard instruments and then crashed into the surface approximately four minutes later. The impact of the rocket in the bottom of the crater created a two-part plume. The first part consisted of vapor and fine dust while the second contained heavier solid matter. Spectrometers aboard LCROSS were able to identify the compositional makeup of the ejected material. (A spectrometer examines the spectrum of light emitted or absorbed by materials to ascertain their composition. Excited atoms and molecules release energy at specific wavelengths, revealing their identity.) The spectrometer found that the plume contained a significant amount of water molecules. Confirmation came from an emission in the ultraviolet spectrum attributed to hydroxyl (OH), molecules that occur when water is exposed to sunlight. Based on these findings, researchers surmised that other craters would likely contain frozen water as well. It is hoped that this discovery will enable scientists to learn more about the history and evolution of the solar system (ice cores could be taken from the Moon and examined much like on Earth). The presence of water also makes the prospect of a lunar space station more viable. Not only can ice be melted and filtered for drinking water, but it can be broken down into oxygen and hydrogen for both breathable air and rocket fuel.

Sources:

Jonathan Amos, "'Significant' Water Found on Moon," *bbc.co.uk* (13 November 2009);

Jim Banke, "*Columbia* Timeline: Seven Months from Tragedy to Final Report," *space.com* (26 August 2003);

An artist's rendering of the *Phoenix* Mars lander which discovered water in the soil of the planet's northern pole in 2008 (<www.nasa.gov>)

M. E. Brown, "The Discovery of Eris, the Largest Known Dwarf Planet," *gps.caltech.edu* (n.d.);

Brown, C. A. Trujillo, and D. L. Rabinowitz, "Discovery of a Planetary-Sized Object in the Scattered Kuiper Belt," *Astronomical Journal,* 635 (10 December 2005): L97–L100;

Alicia Chang, "*Phoenix* Lander Tastes Martian Water," *discoverytechnews.blogspot.com* (2 August 2008);

Kenneth Chang, "Test of Mars Soil Sample Confirms Presence of Ice," *nytimes.com* (1 August 2008);

Jonas Dino, "LCROSS Impact Data Indicates Water on Moon," *nasa.gov* (15 November 2009);

Calvin J. Hamilton, "Dwarf Planet Ceres," *solarviews.com* (n.d.);

Edith Hamilton, *Mythology* (Boston: Little, Brown, 1942);

Brian Handwerk, "Mars Water Discovered, 'Tasted' by Lander—A First," *nationalgeographic.com* (1 August 2008);

"The Loss of the Shuttle *Columbia:* An Online NewsHour Special," *pbs.org* (28 August 2003);

"NASA Finds 'Significant' Water on Moon," *cnn.com* (13 November 2009);

Dennis Overbye, "Vote Makes It Official: Pluto Isn't What It Used to Be," *nytimes.com* (25 August 2006);

John Schwartz, "Report on Columbia Details How Astronauts Died," *nytimes.com* (30 December 2008);

"Space Shuttle Columbia Disintegrates Upon Re-entry," *pbs.org* (1 February 2003).

HEADLINE MAKERS

MIKE E. BROWN

1965–

ASTRONOMER

Dwarf Planet Discoverer. Mike Brown is best known for his discovery of Eris in 2005. Not only had Brown and his colleagues, Chad Trujillo and David Rabinowitz, found a planetary-sized object more massive than Pluto, their find began an international debate on planetary status, eventually leading Eris and Pluto (a relegation) to the newly designated classification "dwarf planet." Brown was born in Huntsville, Alabama, on 5 June 1965. He earned his A.B. (1987) in physics from Princeton University and his M.S. (1990) and Ph.D. (1994) from the University of California, Berkeley. He joined the faculty at California Institute of Technology in 1996, and later became the Richard and Barbara Rosenberg Professor of Planetary Astronomy. His specialty is the study of bodies at the edges of the solar system. Brown won several awards and honors for his scholarly pursuits, including the Urey Prize for the best young planetary scientist from the American Astronomical Society's Division of Planetary Sciences; a Presidential Early Career Award; a Sloan Fellowship; and the Richard P. Feynman Award for Outstanding Teaching at Caltech.

In 2006 he was named one of *Time* magazine's 100 Most Influential People.

Source:
"Dr. Mike E. Brown," *caltech.edu* (n.d.).

STEVEN CHU

1948–

PHYSICIST, SECRETARY OF ENERGY

Multiple Roles. In addition to his work in the field of quantum physics, Steven Chu devoted much of his career to the search for new solutions to the energy crisis and to preventing further global climate change. Chu was a distinguished scientist and co-winner of the Nobel Prize in Physics in 1997; in January 2009 he was appointed as the U.S. secretary of energy by President Barack Obama, who charged Chu with the responsibilities of investing in clean energy, creating millions of "green jobs," addressing global warming, and reducing the nation's dependence on oil.

Scholarly Life. Chu's father, Ju Chin Chu, came to the United States in 1943 to attend the Massachusetts Institute of Technology in chemical engineering. Two years later Ching Chen Li arrived to study economics. They married in 1945, and Steven was born on 28 February 1948 in St.

Louis, Missouri. Chu received an A.B. degree in mathematics before completing his B.S. degree in physics in 1970 at the University of Rochester. He entered the University of California, Berkeley, in that same year and earned his Ph.D. in theoretical physics in 1976. In the fall of 1978 he joined AT&T's Bell Laboratories. In 1983 he became head of the Quantum Electronics Research Department and moved to a branch of Bell Labs in Holmdel, New Jersey. He joined the faculty at Stanford University as a professor of physics and applied physics in 1987. His research there included work in atomic physics, quantum electronics, polymer physics, and biophysics. He developed methods for laser cooling and trapping atoms, atom interferometry, the first atomic fountain, and the manipulation of polymers and biological systems at the molecular level. He was awarded the Nobel Prize in Physics in 1997 (along with Claude Cohen-Tannoudji and William D. Phillips, who worked independently to trap atoms using laser light). In 2004 Chu returned to Berkeley as director of the Department of Energy's Lawrence Berkeley National Lab, where he pursued alternative and renewable energy technologies. His environmental work received international recognition when he was sworn into office as the twelfth secretary of energy on 21 January 2009.

Honors. Chu is a member of the National Academy of Sciences, American Philosophical Society, Chinese Academy of Sciences, Academia Sinica, Korean Academy of Sciences and Technology, and many civic and professional organizations. He holds ten patents and has published nearly 250 scientific and technical articles. He holds honorary degrees from fifteen universities.

Sources:

"Dr. Steven Chu, Secretary of Energy," *energy.gov* (n.d.);

"Steven Chu," *stanford.edu* (n.d.);

"Steven Chu—Autobiography," *nobelprize.org* (n.d.);

"Steven Chu Biography," *biography.com* (n.d.).

AL GORE

1948–

POLITICIAN AND ENVIRONMENTAL ACTIVIST

Leadership. Albert Arnold "Al" Gore Jr. is perhaps best known for being the forty-fifth vice president of the United States (1993–2001) under President Bill Clinton; however, he gained world renown for his 2006 Academy Award–winning documentary, *An Inconvenient Truth,* which brought widespread recognition of the severity of global warming. For sounding the alarm on climate change and spreading awareness on how to counteract it, Gore, along

with the Intergovernmental Panel on Climate Change (IPCC), received the Nobel Peace Prize on 12 October 2007.

Gore was born on 31 March 1948 in Washington, D.C., where his father Albert Gore Sr. was serving as a Democratic congressman from Tennessee in the U.S. House of Representatives. Gore's mother, Pauline LaFon Gore, was one of the first women to graduate with a law degree from Vanderbilt's law school. Young Gore spent his time between a hotel room in D.C. during the school year and his family's farm in Carthage, Tennessee, in the summer. After graduating from St. Albans High School, Gore attended Harvard University, where he roomed with future actor Tommy Lee Jones. In 1969 he earned a degree in government with honors after writing his senior thesis "The Impact of Television on the Conduct of the Presidency, 1947–1969." Although Gore opposed the Vietnam War, he claimed that his sense of duty compelled him to enlist in the army in August 1969. After basic training, Gore worked as a military journalist for *The Army Flier,* the newspaper at Fort Rucker. On 19 May 1970 he married Mary Elizabeth "Tipper" Aitcheson, whom he had known since high school. In January 1971 Gore was shipped to Vietnam where he served in the 20th Engineer Brigade in Bien Hoa at the Army Engineer Command in Long Binh. Upon returning to the United States, he worked as a reporter at the *Tennessean* in Nashville. On the city-politics beat he uncovered political bribery cases that led to several convictions. While working at the newspaper, he enrolled in Vanderbilt University's divinity school and then the law school. He quit law school in March 1976 to run as a representative of Tennessee in the U.S. House. He won and was reelected in 1978, 1980, and 1982. He was elected to the U.S. Senate in 1984 and 1990, and pushed for the High Performance Computer and Communication Act of 1991, which greatly expanded the Internet.

Service. Gore remained in the Senate until Clinton chose him as his running mate in 1992 and 1996. During his terms as vice president, Gore served as a central member of Clinton's economic team, president of the Senate, Cabinet member and member of the National Security Council, and led a wide range of administrative initiatives. In 2000 and 2004 he was the Democratic nominee for president. Although Gore and his running mate, Joseph Lieberman, won the popular vote by more than 500,000 votes in 2000, they lost the electoral college and the election to Republican candidate George W. Bush. In a controversial decision, the U.S. Supreme Court validated a Florida vote recount by ruling five to four in favor of Bush.

Positions. In addition to a long political career, Gore held several prominent business and academic positions and received many prestigious awards. He was a member of the board of directors at Apple Computer, Inc., and a senior advisor to Google. He was a partner in the venture capital firm Kleiner Perkins Caufield & Byers, leading the firm's climate change solutions group. He also chaired the Alliance for Climate Protection, a nonprofit organization developed to help solve the climate crisis. Gore was a chairman of Current TV, an independently owned television station based on viewer-created content and citizen journalism. He also served as chairman of Generation Investment Management, a firm focused on sustainable investing. He was a visiting professor at Middle Tennessee State University, Columbia University Graduate School of Journalism, Fisk University, and the University of California, Los Angeles. Gore's film *An Inconvenient Truth* was awarded two Academy Awards for Best Documentary Feature and Best Original Song. He also received a Primetime Emmy Award for Current TV. He was named runner-up for *Time* magazine's 2007 Person of the Year, and was given a Grammy Award for the Best Spoken Word Album in 2009. Gore wrote the best sellers *Earth in the Balance: Ecology and the Human Spirit* (1992) and *An Inconvenient Truth* (2006).

Sources:
"Al Gore Biography," *biography.com* (n.d.);

"Al's Bio," *algore.com* (n.d.);

"Biography—Al Gore," *nobelprize.org* (n.d.).

LEROY E. HOOD

1938–

BIOLOGIST

Genome Scientist. Dr. Leroy E. Hood is one of the world's leading scientists in molecular biology and genomics, and he helped to invent the technology that made the Human Genome Project possible. In addition to his contributions to mapping the sequence of human DNA, he advocated a cross-disciplinary approach to science and medicine, and pioneered systems medicine and the systems approach to disease. Born on 10 October 1938 in Missoula, Montana, Hood received an undergraduate degree in biology from the California Institute of Technology (1960), an M.D. from Johns Hopkins School of Medicine (1964), and a Ph.D. in biochemistry from Caltech (1968). At Caltech, Hood and his colleagues developed four instruments that constituted the technological foundation for contemporary molecular biology: the DNA gene sequencer and synthesizer, and the protein sequencer and synthesizer. In particular, the sequencer revolutionized genomics by enabling the rapid automated sequencing of DNA.

Systems Approach. Hood enjoyed a long and illustrious academic and professional career. From 1970 to 1992 he worked as a professor of biology at Caltech. In 1992 he founded and chaired the cross-disciplinary Department of Molecular Biotechnology (MBT) at the University of Washington. The department brought together chemists, engineers,

computer scientists, applied physicists, and biologists, and initiated systems studies on cancer biology and prion disease. In 2000 Hood cofounded the Institute for Systems Biology in Seattle, Washington, in an effort to continue the systems approach to biology and medicine. The institute pioneered research in microfluids, nanotechnology, and molecular imaging. Hood also played a role in founding more than fourteen biotechnology companies, including Amgen, Applied Biosystems, Systemix, Darwin and Rosetta, Microgenics, LYNX Therapeutics, Homestead Clinical Corporation, and the Institute for Systems Biology. He was a senior investigator at the National Cancer Institute, served as a member of the scientific advisory board for several biotechnology companies. Hood is a member of the Life Sciences Advisory Committee, National Academy of Sciences, American Academy of Arts and Sciences, American Philosophical Society, Institute of Medicine, and National Academy of Engineering, among others.

Honors. Hood has received many honors and awards, including the Albert Lasker Medical Research Award in 1987 for fundamental contributions to the understanding of immune diversity; Kyoto Prize (2002) for the development of advanced biological instrumentation; Lemelson-MIT Prize for Invention and Innovation (2003) for his automated DNA sequencer; and the Association for Molecular Pathology Award (2003) for excellence in molecular diagnostics. He earned the prestigious Biotechnology Heritage Award (2004) and the Heinz Award for Technology, the Economy, and Employment (2005–2006). In 2007 he was elected to the Inventors Hall of Fame. Hood has received fourteen honorary degrees, holds fourteen patents, and has published more than six hundred papers. He has written textbooks and co-authored a popular book on the Human Genome Project with Daniel J. Keveles titled *The Code of Codes: Scientific and Social Issues in the Human Genome Project* (1992).

Sources:
"Dr. Leroy Hood," *systemsbiology.org* (n.d.);

"Leroy E. Hood," *businessweek.com* (n.d.);

"Speaker's Biography: Leroy Hood," *milkeninstitute.org* (n.d.).

MARY HIGBY SCHWEITZER

? –

PALEONTOLOGIST

DNA Samples. One of the world's best-known paleontologists, Mary Higby Schweitzer discovered the remains of blood cells in dinosaur fossils, including the Tyrannosaurus rex specimen MOR 1125. With these discoveries, Schweitzer undermined a long-held belief that soft organic tissues could not survive for more than a few hundred thousand years inside a fossilized skeleton. Additionally, her research provided further evidence that birds are the evolutionary descendants of dinosaurs by showing the molecular similarities between the Tyrannosaurus's tissue remains and the bone collagen of ostriches and chickens. Her unconventional fusion of paleontology and molecular biology paved the way for an entirely new scientific discipline.

Education. Prior to discovering her interest in dinosaurs, Schweitzer pursued a career devoted to working with deaf children. She received a B.S. in communicative disorders from Utah State University (1977) and earned a Certificate of Secondary Education in Broadfield Science from Montana State University (1988). In 1989 she approached Professor Jack Horner, the paleontologist who led the team that discovered specimen MOR 1125, and asked if she could audit his class in vertebrate paleontology at Montana State University. From there, she set out to prove the presence of soft tissue in early prehistoric fossilized skeletal remains, earning her Ph.D. in biology in 1995. To make her case for the presence of soft tissue in the fossilized Tyrannosaurus rex skeleton, Schweitzer conducted experiments ruling out contaminants and mineral structures, and her data supported the conclusion that it contained hemoglobin and bone collagen. She published an article on her soft-tissue research in the *Proceedings of the National Academy of Sciences* in 1997 that fueled extensive debate. Horner regarded Schweitzer's work as thorough and credible, but many scientists remained skeptical. For fifteen years, molecular biologists and paleontologists disputed Schweitzer's claim to have found soft tissue inside an approximately 68-million-year-old thighbone of a Tyrannosaurus rex, but after further research, her claims were generally accepted. Scientists still had a difficult time explaining how the process of preservation worked. Nevertheless, Schweitzer continued to analyze fossilized remains and discovered collagen in 70-million-year-old sauropod dinosaur eggs found by a group of fossil hunters in Neuquén, Argentina.

Associations. Schweitzer is professor of marine, earth, and atmospheric sciences at North Carolina State University; she has received several grants from the National Science Foundation, Packard Foundation, and other foundations. She is a member of the Geological Society of America, Society of Vertebrate Paleontology, and American Chemical Society. She has reviewed in academic journals such as the *Journal of Vertebrate Paleontology* and *Journal of Experimental Zoology* and has collaborated with NASA scientists in an effort to discover trace evidence of life on other planets.

Sources:

"Mary Higby Schweitzer, Ph.D.," *ncsu.edu* (n.d.).

Barry Yeoman, "Schweitzer's Dangerous Discovery," *barryyeoman.com* (April 2006).

ELIAS A. ZERHOUNI

1951–

RADIOLOGIST, FEDERAL ADMINISTRATOR

Doctor's Work. Elias A. Zerhouni was one of the highest-profile Muslim Arab Americans to work in the administration of President George W. Bush, when he was appointed director of the National Institutes of Health (NIH) in 2002. Zerhouni pioneered important developments in Computer Axial Tomography (CAT) scans and Magnetic Resonance Imaging (MRI). He was born in 1951 in Nedroma, Algeria, earned his medical degree at the University of Algiers School of Medicine (1975), and arrived in the United States later in that same year with his wife, Nadia. He completed his residency in diagnostic radiology at Johns Hopkins in 1978 as chief resident, and served as instructor in radiology from 1978 to 1979. He became naturalized as an American citizen in the early 1980s. Between 1981 and 1985 he worked in the Department of Radiology at Eastern Virginia Medical School. He then served as Martin Donner Professor of Radiology; professor of biomedical engineering at Johns Hopkins University; executive vice dean of the Johns Hopkins School of Medicine; and chair of the Russell H. Morgan Department of Radiology and Radiological Science.

Medical Innovator. Zerhouni pioneered important advancements in diagnostic radiology, developing imaging methods for detecting cancer and cardiovascular disease. He developed the method of magnetic tagging, a noninvasive way of using magnetic resonance imaging (MRI) to track the motions and accurately measure the function of the human heart in three dimensions. He also refined the imaging technique called quantitative computed tomographic (CT) densitometry that helped doctors discriminate between noncancerous and cancerous nodules in the lung. From May 2002 until October 2008, Zerhouni oversaw the NIH's twenty-seven institutes and centers with more than 18,000 employees. He convened a series of meetings to chart a "road map" for medical research in the twenty-first century to help identify major opportunities and gaps in biomedical studies. He promoted the NIH Reform Act of 2006 that codified the NIH Common Fund to support interdisciplinary research.

Other Roles. In addition to directing the NIH, Zerhouni was a consultant to the World Health Organization (WHO) and a member of the National Cancer

Institute's Board of Scientific Advisors. He was a member of the Institute of Medicine and the National Academy of Sciences and was appointed to the boards of the Lasker Foundation and the Mayo Clinic. As the holder of eight patents, he cofounded several start-up companies, including Computerized Imaging Reference Systems, Advanced Medical Imaging, Biopsys Corporation, American Radiology Services, and Surgivision, Inc. He received the French National Order of the Legion of Honor in 2008 and has written more than two hundred academic publications.

Sources:
"Elias A. Zerhouni M.D.," *businessweek.com* (n.d.);
"Elias Zerhouni," *biovision.org* (n.d.).

PEOPLE IN THE NEWS

Commercial spaceflight became a real possibility in 2004 with the launch of *SpaceShipOne*, the first privately funded rocket ship to carry a human into space. The final stage of the flight soared approximately sixty-two miles high, past the official demarcation for the edge of space. The effort was bankrolled by billionaire **Paul Allen,** cofounder of Microsoft Corp. That same year, Virgin Galactic unveiled *SpaceShipTwo*, and the Mojave Air and Space Port became the first licensed facility dedicated to horizontal launches of reusable spacecraft in the United States.

Daniel Anderson, research associate in the David H. Koch Institute for Integrative Cancer Research at MIT along with other researchers, including **Robert Langer** and **Janet Sawicki** from the Lankenau Institute for Medical Research, found that gene therapy could be used effectively in the fight against ovarian cancer, which causes more than 15,000 deaths each year in the United States and was traditionally treated with a combination of surgery and chemotherapy. The MIT–Lankenau team successfully developed nanoparticles that delivered therapeutic DNA into infected tissues, which may lead to a drastic reduction in the number of deaths from ovarian cancer.

Trial lawyer **Peter Angelos** brought an $800 million lawsuit on behalf of Maryland resident **Christopher Newman** in 2002 against Motorola because Newman claimed that the use of his cell phone caused a brain tumor. The suit was supported by the research and testimony of **Dr. Lennart Hardell.** Judge **Catherine Blake** dismissed the case, however, ruling that the plaintiff's evidence was not sufficiently relevant or reliable.

Marusa Bradac of the Kavli Institute for Particle Astrophysics and Cosmology (KIPAC) at the Department of Energy's Stanford Linear Accelerator Center (SLAC) made the first landmark observations of dark matter in 2006. Using X-ray imaging, Bradac and her colleagues carefully estimated the weight of gas and stars flung about in the ten-million-miles-per-hour head-on collision of two galaxy clusters in what is called the Bullet Cluster. By measuring distortions with the Hubble Space Telescope and several other earth-bound telescopes, Bradac observed two large clumps of dark matter and two smaller clumps of luminous matter. Although these observations did not explain what dark matter was, they provided researchers important clues as to how it behaved.

In 2009 **Rob DeSalle,** a curator at the American Museum of Natural History, and his colleagues announced that a sperm-looking creature called monosiga was the most likely ancestor of all animals. DeSalle announced the discovery after his team compiled gene sequences from many sources and compared thousands of shared traits used to distinguish among species.

In August 2009 a research team led by **Dr. Jamie Elsila** at NASA's Goddard Space Flight Center in Greenbelt, Maryland, announced that they had found glycine, an amino acid, in outer space. Researchers followed the comet Wild 2 with a spacecraft called *Stardust*. Collection plates attached to the craft gathered materials from the comet's tail. The discovery supported the theory that some of life's ingredients may have formed in space before being delivered to Earth by meteorite and comet impacts.

In 1982 condors had been on the verge of extinction, with only 23 of them left in the wild. Conservationists captured and brought the remaining birds to the San Diego Zoo for protection and breeding. San Diego Zoo spokesperson **Yadira Galindo** announced in October 2009 that California condors had made a comeback (351 of the critically endangered birds were alive and well, with 180 living in the wild). Galindo described the comeback as "astonishing."

A team of seventeen scientists from the J. Craig Venter Institute (JCVI) in Maryland and California led by **Dan Gibson** announced on 24 January 2008 that they had completely synthesized and assembled 582,970 base pairs of the genome of the bacterium *mycoplasma genitalium*. Scientists conjectured that they would soon be able to create synthetic life.

In 2000 U.S. District Court judge **Thomas Penfield Jackson** found that Microsoft was a monopoly that used anticompetitive means to corner the Web browser market. The final judgment in the federal case established restrictions on licensing agreements and ordered Microsoft to release some of its intellectual property.

In Harrisburg, Pennsylvania, U.S. District judge **John E. Jones** ruled that members of the Dover school board promoting intelligent design—which holds that living organisms are so complex that they must have been created by a higher power—were concealing their true motive. The judge ruled that the district was not teaching science to their students but was simply trying to promote religion in schools. The 20 December 2005 decision was a clear victory for proponents of the theory of evolution.

In 2005 **Nicholas Negroponte,** cofounder and director of the Media Lab at the Massachusetts Institute of Technology, announced his plan to develop a laptop that would cost only $100. The average price for a notebook computer at the time was around $1,100. Negroponte developed the XO laptop for basic computing and accessing the Internet using a Linux operating system and a Flash memory. It came with a full-color screen and wireless capability. It ultimately cost $199; nevertheless, the charity organization One Laptop Per Child eventually distributed more than 1.2 million computers to children in thirty-one countries.

In 2006, after studying a group of bottle-nosed dolphins in Sarasota Bay, Florida, Project Leader **Laela Sayigh** of the University of North Carolina, Wilmington, and her team announced that dolphins created signature whistles that functioned like human names. Sayigh speculated that information such as the age, sex, and feelings of a dolphin may be encoded in each unique whistle.

In 2000 researchers at the Duke University Medical Center implanted electrodes in monkeys' brains and trained them to reach for food using a robotic arm. In 2001 **Jesse Sullivan,** a double amputee, controlled both of his robotic arms using a method of nerve-cell operation developed at the Rehabilitation Institute of Chicago. In 2009 amputee **Pierpaolo Petruzziello** learned to control a biomechanical hand and became the first person to make complex movements with a robotic limb by using his thoughts only.

AWARDS

NOBEL PRIZES PHYSICS

2000

Jointly for basic work on information and communication technology with one half to Russian Zhores I. Algerov and German Herbert Kroemer for developing semiconductor heterostructures used in high speed- and opto-electronics and the other half to American Jack S. Kilby for his part in the invention of the integrated electrical circuit.

2001

Americans Eric A. Cornell and Carl E. Wieman, along with German Wolfgang Ketterle, for the achievement of Bose-Einstein condensation in dilute gases of alkali atoms, and for early fundamental studies of the properties of condensates.

2002

One half shared by American Raymond Davis Jr. and Masatoshi Koshiba from Japan for pioneering contributions to astrophysics, in particular for the detection of cosmic neutrinos. The other half was awarded to American Riccardo Giacconi for pioneering contributions to astrophysics that led to the discovery of cosmic X-ray sources.

2003

Russian-born Alexei A. Abrikosov, residing in the United States at the time of the award, and Anthony J. Leggett of the United Kingdom, also residing in the United States, along with Russian Vitaly L. Ginzburg for pioneering contributions to the theory of superconductors and superfluids.

2004

Americans David J. Gross, H. David Politzer, and Frank Wilczek for the discovery of asymptotic freedom in the theory of the strong interaction.

2005

One half to Roy J. Glauber of the United States for his contributions to the quantum theory of optical coherence. The other half split between American John L. Hall and German Theodor W. Hänsch for their contributions to the development of laser-based precision spectroscopy, including the optical-frequency comb technique.

2006

John C. Mather and George F. Smoot of the United States for their discovery of the blackbody form and anisotropy of the cosmic microwave background radiation.

2007

No American winner.

2008

One half to American Yoichiro Nambu for the discovery of the mechanism of spontaneous broken symmetry in subatomic physics and one half split between Japanese Makoto Kobayashi and Toshihide Maskawa for the discovery of the origin of broken symmetry that predicts the existence of at least three families of quarks in nature.

2009

One half divided by Americans Willard S. Boyle and George E. Smith for the invention of an imaging semiconductor circuit, the CCD sensor, and one half to Charles K. Kao, born in China but residing in the United Kingdom at the time of the award, for groundbreaking achievements concerning the transmission of light in fibers for optical communication.

CHEMISTRY

2000

American Alan J. Heeger, New Zealander Alan G. MacDiarmid, residing in the United States at the time of the award, and Japanese Hideki Shirakawa for the discovery and development of conductive polymers.

2001

One half divided by William S. Knowles of the United States and Ryoji Noyori of Japan for their work on chi-

rally catalyzed hydrogenation reactions, and one half to K. Barry Sharpless of the United States for his work on chirally catalyzed oxidation reactions.

2002

Awarded for the development of methods for identification and structure analyses of biological macromolecules with one half jointly to American John B. Fenn and Japanese Koichi Tanaka for their development of soft desorption ionization methods for mass spectrometric analyses of biological macromolecules, and the other half to Swiss Kurt Wüthrich for his development of nuclear magnetic resonance spectroscopy for determining the three-dimensional structure of biological macromolecules in solution.

2003

Awarded jointly for discoveries concerning channels in cell membranes with one half to American Peter Agre for the discovery of water channels and one half to Roderick MacKinnon for structural and mechanistic studies of ion channels.

2004

To Irwin Rose of the United States, residing in Israel at the time of the award, and Aaron Ciechanover and Avram Hershko of Israel for the discovery of ubiquitin-mediated protein degradation.

2005

Robert H. Grubbs and Richard R. Schrock of the United States and Yves Chauvin of France for the development of the metathesis method in organic synthesis.

2006

American Roger D. Kornberg for his studies of the molecular basis of eukaryotic transcription.

2007

No American winner

2008

Americans Martin Chalfie and Roger Y. Tsien and Japanese Osama Shimomura for the discovery and development of the green fluorescent protein, GFP.

2009

Jointly to Thomas A. Steitz of the United States, Venkatraman Ramakrishnan of the United Kingdom, and Ada E. Yonath of Israel for studies of the structure and function of the ribosome.

DEATHS

Phillip H. Abelson, 91, co-discoverer of the element neptunium, served as editor of journal *Science,* 1 August 2004.

Ralph A. Alpher, 86, physicist, specialist on cosmic particles and the Big Bang theory, 12 August 2007.

Ralph Alphorn, 86, astrophysicist, one of the theorists of the "Big Bang," 12 August 2007.

Joseph C. Arcos, 83, science adviser at U.S. Environmental Protection Agency, expert on cancer, wrote *Chemical Induction of Cancer* (1968–1988), 31 December 2004.

Robert Bacher, 99, physicist, worked on Manhattan Project, member of U.S. Atomic Energy Commission, helped create Owens Valley Radio Observatory, 18 November 2004.

David W. Barry, 58, University of North Carolina, Chapel Hill, codiscovered AZT, the antiviral drug used to treat AIDS and a combination therapy used to treat the hepatitis B virus, 28 January 2002.

Hans A. Bethe, 98, physicist, helped develop the atomic bomb and found the field of nuclear astrophysics, winner of the Nobel Prize in Physics (1967), 6 March 2005.

Owen Chamberlain, 85, physicist, discoverer of the antiproton and winner of Nobel Prize in Physics (1959), 28 February 2006.

Martha Chase, 75, biologist and geneticist, helped discover link between DNA and heredity, 8 August 2003.

Jack Cover, 88, aerospace scientist who invented the nonlethal Taser stun gun, used to subdue individuals, 7 February 2009.

Donald J. Cram, 82, chemist, developed molecules that mimicked the operation of enzymes, winner of the Nobel Prize in Chemistry (1987), 17 June 2001.

Isidore S. Edelman, 84, helped to found Columbia Genome Center at Columbia University, codirector of Human Genome Project, 21 November 2004.

Thomas Gold, 84, founder and for twenty years director of the Cornell Center for Radiophysics and Space Research, a close colleague of Planetary Society cofounder Carl Sagan, 22 June 2004.

Stephen Jay Gould, 60, paleontologist and evolutionary biologist, one of the most frequently cited scientists in the field of evolutionary theory; he proposed that evolution was marked by long periods of stability, 20 May 2002.

Don Herbert, 89, television scientist, helped popularize the study of science to children as "Mr. Wizard," 12 June 2007.

Arthur Kantrowitz, 95, scientist and engineer, researched extremely hot gases and fluid dynamics and helped in the development of nose cones for rockets and missiles along with high-energy lasers and implanted heart-assist pumps, 29 November 2008.

Martin J. Klein, 84, physicist and historian, published Albert Einstein's papers, 28 March 2009.

Arthur Kornberg, 89, biochemist, discovered how DNA is assembled, won Nobel Prize in Medicine (1959), 26 October 2007.

Willis Lamb Jr., 94, atomic physicist, winner of the Nobel Prize in Physics (1955), advanced understanding of quantum mechanics, 15 May 2008.

Theodore H. Maiman, 79, physicist and engineer, leading developer of the laser, 5 May 2007.

Victor A. McKusick, 86, "the father of genetic medicine" who initiated the *Mendelian Inheritance in Man,* a catalogue of human genes and genetic disorders in 1966; professor emeritus of medical genetics at the Johns Hopkins University School of Medicine, 22 July 2008.

R. Bruce Merrifield, 84, chemist, winner of the Nobel Prize in Chemistry (1984), 14 May 2006.

Steven Mostow, 63, expert in the treatment of influenza and in bioterrorism at the Colorado Health Sciences Center, 25 March 2002.

Elmer R. Noble, 82, zoologist, specialist in parasitology, 8 March 2001.

Eugene Pleasants Odum, 88, and **Howard T. Odum,** 78, brothers and ecologists, advanced the study of ecosystems, 10 August 2002 and 11 September 2002, respectively.

Wolfgang K. H. Panofsky, 88, physicist, founding director of the Stanford Linear Accelerator Center, 24 September 2007.

Randy Pausch, 47, professor of computer science at Carnegie Mellon University, best known for his "The Last Lecture," 25 June 2008.

Theodore T. Puck, 89, geneticist, developed technique for growing human cells for research, 6 November 2005.

Albert Ernest Radford, 88, botanist, specialist in Southeastern flora, 12 April 2006.

Jef Raskin, 61, mathematician, helped create Apple Macintosh computer, invented "click and drag," 26 February 2005.

Melvin Schwartz, 73, winner of the Nobel Prize in Physics (1988) for constructing a beam of neutrinos, 28 August 2006.

Clifford G. Shull, 85, physicist, winner of the Nobel Prize in Physics (1994) for developing neutron diffraction, 31 March 2001.

Richard E. Smalley, 62, chemist, researcher in nanotechnology, winner of the Nobel Prize in Chemistry (1994) for discovering a round form of carbon, 28 October 2005.

George Ledyard Stebbins Jr., 94, botanist, specialized in the genetic evolution of plants, 19 January 2000.

John Wheeler, 96, theoretical physicist, coined the terms "black hole" and "wormhole," 13 April 2008.

Richard T. Whitcomb, 89, aeronautical engineer, helped solve problems in achieving supersonic flight, 13 October 2009.

Don C. Wiley, 57, microbiologist, professor at the Howard Hughes Medical Institute at Harvard University, an expert on immune-system responses to viral attacks such as HIV, ebola, and influenza, 16 November 2001.

Victor Wouk, 86, an electrical engineer and entrepreneur who built one of the first hybrid cars operating on both gasoline and electricity, 19 May 2005.

Jerry Yang, 49, reproductive biologist at the University of Connecticut, cloned the first farm animal in the United States and worked to promote cooperation between U.S. and Chinese researchers, 5 February 2009.

PUBLICATIONS

Amir D. Aczel, *Entanglement: The Greatest Mystery in Physics* (New York: Four Walls Eight Windows, 2002);

John Battelle, *The Search: How Google and Its Rivals Rewrote the Rules of Business and Transformed Our Culture* (New York: Portfolio, 2005);

Kai Bird and Martin J. Sherwin, *American Prometheus: The Triumph and Tragedy of J. Robert Oppenheimer* (New York: Knopf, 2005);

David Bodanis, *Electric Universe: The Shocking True Story of Electricity* (New York: Crown, 2005);

Bill Bryson, *A Short History of Nearly Everything* (New York: Broadway Books, 2003);

Mark Buchanan, *Nexus: Small Worlds and the Groundbreaking Science of Networks* (New York: Norton, 2002);

Nicholas Carr, *The Big Switch: Rewiring the World, from Edison to Google* (New York: Norton, 2008);

Richard Dawkins, *The Ancestor's Tale: A Pilgrimage to the Dawn of Evolution* (New York: Houghton Mifflin, 2004);

Kenneth S. Deffeyes, *Beyond Oil: The View from Hubbert's Peak* (New York: Hill & Wang, 2005);

Jared Diamond, *Collapse—How Societies Choose to Fail or Succeed* (New York: Viking, 2005);

Norman Doidge, *The Brain That Changes Itself: Stories of Personal Triumph from the Frontiers of Brain Science* (New York: Viking, 2007);

Avery Gilbert, *What the Nose Knows: The Science of Scent in Everyday Life* (New York: Crown, 2008);

Daniel Gilbert, *Stumbling on Happiness* (New York: Knopf, 2006);

Louisa Gilder, *The Age of Entanglement: When Quantum Physics Was Reborn* (New York: Knopf, 2008);

Al Gore, *An Inconvenient Truth: The Planetary Emergency of Global Warming and What We Can Do about It* (New York: Rodale 2006);

Stephen Jay Gould, *Punctuated Equilibrium* (Cambridge, Mass.: Harvard University Press, 2007);

Steve Grand, *Creation: Life and How to Make It* (Cambridge, Mass.: Harvard University Press, 2000);

Brian Green, *The Fabric of the Cosmos: Space, Time, and the Texture of Reality* (New York: Knopf, 2004);

Stephen Hawking, *The Universe in a Nutshell* (New York: Bantam, 2001);

Robert Henson, *The Rough Guide to Climate Change* (London: Rough Guides, 2006);

Hannah Holmes, *The Secret Life of Dust: From the Cosmos to the Kitchen Counter, the Big Consequences of Little Things* (New York: Wiley, 2001);

David Horrobin, *The Madness of Adam and Eve: How Schizophrenia Shaped Humanity* (London & New York: Bantam, 2001);

Donald C. Johanson and Kate Wong, *Lucy's Legacy: The Quest for Human Origins* (New York: Harmony, 2009);

Michio Kaku, *Parallel Worlds: A Journey through Creation, Higher Dimensions, and the Future of the Cosmos* (New York: Doubleday, 2005);

Robert P. Kirshner, *The Extravagant Universe: Exploding Stars, Dark Energy, and the Accelerating Cosmos* (Princeton: Princeton University Press, 2002);

Elizabeth Kolbert, *Field Notes from a Catastrophe: Man, Nature, and Climate Change* (New York: Bloomsbury, 2006);

Robert Kunzig, *Mapping the Deep: The Extraordinary Story of Ocean Science* (New York: Sort Of, 2000);

Eugene Linden, *The Winds of Change: Climate, Weather, and the Destruction of Civilization* (New York: Simon & Schuster, 2006);

Jo Marchant, *Decoding the Heavens: A 2,000-Year-Old Computer and the Century Long Search to Discover Its Secrets* (London: Heinemann, 2008);

Wil McCarthy, *Hacking Matter: Levitating Chairs, Quantum Mirages, and the Infinite Weirdness of Programmable Atoms* (New York: Basic Books, 2003);

Arthur I. Miller, *Empire of the Stars: Obsession, Friendship, and Betrayal in the Quest for Black Holes* (New York: Houghton Mifflin, 2005);

Leonard Mlodinow, *The Drunkard's Walk: How Randomness Rules Our Lives* (New York: Pantheon, 2008);

Donal O'Shea, *The Poincaré Conjecture: The Search of the Shape of the Universe* (New York: Walker, 2007);

Roger Penrose, *The Road to Reality: A Complete Guide to the Laws of the Universe* (London: Cape, 2004);

Steven Pinker, *The Blank Slate: The Modern Denial of Human Nature* (New York: Viking, 2002);

Robert M. Sapolsky, *A Primate's Memoir* (New York: Scribner, 2001);

Neil Shubin, *Your Inner Fish: A Journey into the 3.5-Billion-Year History of the Human Body* (New York: Pantheon, 2009);

Randall Stross, *Planet Google: One Company's Audacious Plan to Organize Everything We Know* (New York: Free Press, 2008);

Colin Tudge and Josh Young, *The Link: Uncovering Our Earliest Ancestor* (New York: Little, Brown, 2009);

Neil DeGrasse Tyson, *Death by Black Hole: And Other Cosmic Quandries* (New York: Norton, 2007);

Tyson and Donald Goldsmith, *Origins: Fourteen Billion Years of Cosmic Evolution* (New York: Norton, 2004);

J. Craig Venter, *A Life Decoded: My Genome, My Life* (New York: Viking, 2007);

Stephen Webb, *If the Universe Is Teeming with Aliens . . . Where Is Everybody?: Fifty Solutions to the Fermi Paradox and the Problem of Extraterrestrial Life* (New York: Copernicus Books, 2002);

Frank Wilczek, *The Lightness of Being: Mass, Ether, and the Unification of Forces* (New York: Basic Books, 2008);

American Scientist, periodical;

Discover, periodical;

National Geographic, periodical;

Natural History, periodical;

Science, periodical;

Scientific American, periodical.

After making a remarkable comeback, the Bald Eagle, America's national
symbol, was removed from the Endangered Species Act's
"threatened" list after three decades of protection
(photograph by Paul Friel).

SPORTS

by STEPHANIE TODD, GEORGE PARKER ANDERSON, JAMES F. TIDD JR.

CONTENTS

Sidebars and tables are listed in italics.

2000

4 Jan. The #1-ranked Florida State Seminoles win the college football Bowl Championship Series (BCS) national title at the Nokia Sugar Bowl in New Orleans, beating #2-ranked Virginia Tech Hokies 46–29.

30 Jan. The National Football League (NFL) St. Louis Rams defeat the Tennessee Titans 23–16 in Super Bowl XXXIV in the Georgia Dome in Atlanta. The game comes down to the last play with Titans wide receiver Kevin Dyson being stopped on the Rams's one-yard line.

3 Apr. The Michigan State Spartans defeat the University of Florida Gators 89–76 to win the National Collegiate Athletic Association (NCAA) Division I Basketball Championship.

10 June The New Jersey Devils take the Stanley Cup, four games to two, over the Dallas Stars, winning the decisive game 2–1 in double overtime.

17 June The Louisiana State University Tigers win the College World Series by defeating the Stanford University Cardinal 6–5.

19 June The Los Angeles Lakers defeat the Indiana Pacers 116–111 in the National Basketball Association (NBA) finals, winning the series four games to two, for their first title in twelve years.

8 July Venus Williams defeats Lindsay Davenport in women's singles tennis (6–3, 7–6), earning her first Grand Slam title. She and her sister Serena win the women's doubles title. Pete Sampras wins on the men's side, his thirteenth Grand Slam title.

23 July Lance Armstrong captures his second of seven consecutive Tour de France wins.

12 Aug. Evander Holyfield beats John Ruiz in twelve rounds by unanimous decision to become the first boxer in history to hold four world heavyweight championship titles.

27 Aug. The Houston Comets of the Women's National Basketball Association (WNBA) complete a two-game sweep of the New York Liberty with a 79–73 overtime victory to win the championship series; it is their fourth consecutive title.

15 Sept. The 2000 Summer Olympics open in Sydney, Australia. Marion Jones wins three gold and two bronze medals, becoming the only female track-and-field athlete to ever win five medals in a single Olympics. (She later forfeits her medals because of steriod use.) U.S. athletes take home a total of 107 medals, including 40 golds.

1 Oct. A central drug-doping monitoring body, the U.S. Anti-Doping Agency, begins operation for American athletes.

15 Oct. The Major League Soccer (MLS) Kansas City Wizards defeat the Chicago Fire 1–0 to win the MLS Cup.

26 Oct. In the first postseason "Subway Series" in nearly half of a century, the New York Yankees claim the Major League Baseball (MLB) title by defeating the New York Mets 4–2, taking the World Series four games to one.

2001

3 Jan. The #1-ranked Oklahoma Sooners defeat the #2-ranked Florida State Seminoles 13–2 in the FedEx Orange Bowl to claim the college football national title.

28 Jan. Super Bowl XXXV takes place in Tampa, Florida; the Baltimore Ravens defeat the New York Giants 34–7.

3 Feb. The XFL, an eight-team professional football league founded by Vince McMahon of the World Wrestling Federation, plays its first game. Due to its inability to attract a large audience, the league lasts only one season.

18 Feb. National Association for Stock Car Auto Racing (NASCAR) driver Dale Earnhardt dies in an accident in the final lap of the Daytona 500. Michael Waltrip wins the race.

14 Mar. Doug Swingley wins his second Iditarod dogsled race, covering the distance from Anchorage to Nome, Alaska, in just under nine days and twenty hours.

2 Apr. The Duke University Blue Devils win their third Division I Basketball championship by defeating the University of Arizona Wildcats 82–72.

8 Apr. Tiger Woods wins his second Masters Golf Tournament in Augusta, Georgia, becoming the first golfer in history to hold all four of golf's major titles at the same time.

29 May Disabled golfer Casey Martin, suffering from Klippel-Trenaunay-Weber syndrome, a progressive and untreatable circulatory disorder in his right leg, wins a ruling by the U.S. Supreme Court that he can participate on the professional tour using a motorized cart.

June Major League Lacrosse opens play with six professional teams.

9 June The Colorado Avalanche defeat the New Jersey Devils 3–1 in game seven of the Stanley Cup finals.

15 June The Los Angeles Lakers defeat the Philadelphia 76ers 108–96, winning the NBA finals in five games.

16 June The University of Miami Hurricanes win the College World Series, defeating the Stanford University Cardinal 12–1.

1 Aug. Minnesota Vikings offensive lineman Korey Stringer dies from heatstroke during practice; his death leads to discussions and changes in athletic practices held during periods of extreme heat.

1 Sept. The WNBA Los Angeles Sparks defeat the Charlotte Sting 82–54 to capture the league championship, two games to none.

8 Sept. Venus Williams wins her second consecutive U.S. Open, beating her sister Serena (6–2, 6–4), marking the first Grand Slam final competition between siblings in more than a century. The match is also the first time a women's final has been televised in prime time.

20 Sept. The University of South Carolina Gamecocks defeat the Mississippi State Bulldogs 16–14 in the first Division I football game following the September 11 terrorist attacks.

25 Sept. Former Chicago Bulls star Michael Jordan signs a contract to join the Washington Wizards; he returns to the NBA after more than three years in retirement.

7 Oct. San Francisco Giants outfielder Barry Bonds hits his seventy-third home run, setting a new record for most home runs in a single season.

21 Oct. The San Jose Earthquakes defeat the Los Angeles Galaxy, 2–1 in overtime, to win the MLS Cup.

4 Nov. In a dramatic game seven of the World Series, the Arizona Diamondbacks become the youngest franchise to win the title with a bottom-of-the-ninth walk-off hit, defeating the New York Yankees 3–2. Dubbed the "November Series," as the series did not begin until 28 October because of regular-season postponements after the September 11 terrorist attacks, it is the latest start to the series in MLB history.

14 Dec. George O'Leary, former football coach at Georgia Tech, resigns five days after being hired by the University of Notre Dame because of a falsified resume.

2002

3 Jan.   The #1-ranked University of Miami Hurricanes defeat the #2 University of Nebraska Cornhuskers in the Rose Bowl BCS National Championship game 37–14.

3 Feb.   The New England Patriots defeat the St. Louis Rams 20–17 in Super Bowl XXXVI in New Orleans, Louisiana.

8–24 Feb.   Amid allegations of cheating by French figure skating judge Marie-Reine Le Gougne in the XIX Winter Olympic Games in Salt Lake City, a second gold medal in the freestyle pair competition is awarded to Canadian duo Jamie Sale and David Pelletier. American athletes win ten gold medals, along with thirteen silver and eleven bronze. Sarah Hughes wins the gold in women's figure skating over favored countrywoman Michelle Kwan. One emerging star for the Americans is short-track speedskater Apolo Ohno, who wins a silver medal and a gold.

17 Feb.   Ward Burton wins the Daytona 500.

17 Feb.   Baltimore Orioles pitcher Steve Bechler dies in Florida of heatstroke. He had been taking weight-loss pills Xenadrine RFA-1 (containing ephedra).

1 Apr.   The NCAA Men's Division I Basketball Tournament is won 64–52 by the University of Maryland Terrapins over the Indiana University Hoosiers.

14 Apr.   Tiger Woods wins his third Masters.

30 May   Nine mountaineers fall into a crevasse on Mount Hood, Oregon; three climbers are killed. A military helicopter sent to rescue them crashes on the mountainside, resulting in injuries to six members of the crew.

8 June   Lennox Lewis knocks out Mike Tyson in the eighth round, firmly establishing Lewis as the dominant heavyweight boxing champion.

8 June   War Emblem stumbles at the start of the Belmont Stakes race, denying him a shot at the horse-racing Triple Crown. The third jewel is won by Sarava at 70–1 odds.

12 June   The Los Angeles Lakers capture their third consecutive NBA championship title, taking the last game 113–107 and sweeping the New Jersey Nets in four games.

13 June   The Detroit Red Wings win their tenth Stanley Cup with a 3–1 victory over the Carolina Hurricanes, taking the series four games to one.

22 June   The University of Texas Longhorns defeat the South Carolina Gamecocks 12–6 in the College World Series, the last time a winner-take-all final game format is used.

6 July   Serena Williams takes back the family title, beating sister Venus in straight sets (7–6, 6–3) for her first Wimbledon championship.

9 July   The MLB All-Star game goes into the eleventh inning tied 7–7; the game ends that way because of limited rosters.

25 Aug.   A team from Louisville, Kentucky, wins the Little League World Series.

30 Aug.   A last-minute labor-contract agreement is reached by MLB negotiators to avoid a players' strike. This new contract marks the first time players agree to mandatory, random testing for performance-enhancing drugs.

31 Aug.   The Los Angeles Sparks win their second WNBA championship, defeating the New York Liberty 69–66.

20 Oct.   In a double-overtime win, the Los Angeles Galaxy defeat the New England Revolution to win the series 1–0 to capture the MLS Cup.

27 Oct.   In an interstate matchup between two wild-card teams, the Anaheim Angels defeat the San Francisco Giants 4–1 in the seventh game of the World Series. It is the first championship for the Angels.

2003

3 Jan.   The #2 Ohio State Buckeyes upset the #1-ranked University of Miami Hurricanes at the Tostitos Fiesta Bowl BCS National Championship game, winning 31–24 in the second overtime.

26 Jan.   The Tampa Bay Buccaneers, led by head coach Jay Gruden, defeat the favored Oakland Raiders 48–21 in Super Bowl XXXVII, for their first-ever title. Gruden left his coaching position at Oakland the year before to coach the Tampa team.

16 Feb.   Michael Waltrip wins his second Daytona 500.

28 Mar.   American figure skater and two-time Olympic medalist Michelle Kwan wins her fifth World Figure Skating Championship title in women's singles.

30 Mar.   At the 2003 Kraft Nabisco Championship thirteen-year-old Michelle Wie, daughter of Korean immigrants, ties for ninth place, making her the youngest player to earn a Ladies Professional Golf Association (LPGA) cut. Later the same year, Wie becomes the youngest person to win a United States Golf Association (USGA) adult event.

Apr.   Aron Ralston of Aspen, Colorado, is trapped by a falling boulder while hiking Utah's Bluejohn Canyon; unable to free himself, after five days he amputates his arm and walks to safety.

4 Apr.   Chicago Cubs outfielder Sammy Sosa becomes the eighteenth player in MLB history to hit five-hundred career home runs, in a game against the Cincinnati Reds.

7 Apr.   The Syracuse University Orangemen defeat the University of Kansas Jayhawks 81–78 to capture the NCAA Men's Division I Basketball Tournament.

11 May   Texas Ranger Rafael Palmeiro becomes the nineteenth member of the five-hundred home run club in a game against the Cleveland Indians.

3 June   While playing against the Tampa Bay Rays at Wrigley Field, Chicago Cubs slugger Sammy Sosa's bat explodes, revealing that it had cork inserted into the barrel.

7 June   Funny Cide is denied the Triple Crown at the Belmont Stakes when he is beaten by Empire Maker.

9 June   In game seven of the Stanley Cup finals the New Jersey Devils shut out the Mighty Ducks of Anaheim 3–0, winning their third cup.

15 June   The San Antonio Spurs win their second NBA Championship, defeating the New Jersey Nets 88–77 to win the title in six games.

23 June   In the first three-game championship round, the Rice University Owls defeat the Stanford University Cardinal in the College World Series, taking the final game 14–2.

6 July   Los Angeles Lakers star Kobe Bryant is arrested amid allegations of sexual assault; he is formally charged at the end of the month. The charges are later dropped when the victim expresses her unwillingness to testify.

21 July   Baylor University basketball player Carlton Dotson is charged with murdering teammate Patrick Dennehy, whose body was discovered near Waco, Texas. Dotson pleads guilty the following year and is sentenced to thirty-five years in prison. Revelations of drug abuse, recruiting problems, and other problems result in the firing of the team coach and NCAA sanctions being placed on the school.

25 Aug.   Pete Sampras retires at the age of thirty-two, having won fourteen Grand Slam tennis titles.

3 Sept.   Federal agents raid Bay Area Laboratory Co-operative (BALCO) office in search of evidence of steroid misuse in sports. Many important stars, including Barry Bonds (baseball), Bill Romanowski (football), and Marion Jones (sprinter) are tied to the company.

14 Sept.   Jamal Lewis of the NFL Baltimore Ravens rushes for 295 yards against the Cleveland Browns, setting a new single-game rushing record.

16 Sept.   The Detroit Shock win their first WNBA title, defeating the Los Angeles Spark 83–78 to take the series two games to one.

14 Oct.   During the sixth game of the NLCS a fan in the left-field bleachers at Wrigley Field prevents Moises Alou of the Chicago Cubs from catching a fly ball in the eighth inning, and the Florida Marlins go on to score eight runs in the inning for an 8–3 win. The fan becomes a hated figure in Chicago, as in the following game the Marlins eliminate the Cubs from World Series contention.

25 Oct.   The Florida Marlins surprise the New York Yankees at Yankee Stadium with a 2–0 defeat in game six of the World Series, winning their second title in seven years.

16 Nov.   Denver Broncos tight end Shannon Sharpe catches his sixty-first touchdown reception, a new record for his position. He caught three touchdowns in the game that day against the San Diego Chargers.

23 Nov.   The San Jose Earthquakes defeat the Chicago Fire 4–2 to win the MLS Cup.

4 Dec.   Barry Bonds is one of several professional athletes to testify before a federal grand jury in the BALCO hearings; Bonds admits to having used a clear substance and cream but denies knowing that it was steroids.

15 Dec.   In a game against the Cleveland Browns, Indianapolis Colts wide receiver Marvin Harrison breaks Herman Moore's single-season record for receptions; he finishes the year with a record 143 catches.

28 Dec.   San Diego Chargers running back LaDainian Tomlinson becomes the first NFL player to rush for one thousand yards and catch one hundred passes in the same season.

2004

4 Jan.   The Louisiana State University Tigers, ranked #2, defeat the #1-ranked University of Oklahoma Sooners 21–14 in the Nokia Sugar Bowl National Championship Game.

10 Jan.   Hawaiian surfer and windboarder Pete Cabrinha rides a specially designed surfboard on a seventy-foot wave off the coast of Maui, the largest wave ever ridden according to the *Guinness Book of World Records*.

1 Feb.   In an exciting game in which 37 of 61 total points are scored in the fourth quarter, the New England Patriots defeat the Carolina Panthers 32–29 in Super Bowl XXXVIII. Patriots quarterback Tom Brady, Most Valuable Player (MVP), sets a Super Bowl record with thirty-two pass completions in the game.

12 Feb.   Attorney General John Ashcroft hands down a forty-two-count indictment against four men involved in the BALCO steroids scandal. All four will plead not guilty to the charges.

15 Feb.   Dale Earnhardt Jr. wins his first Daytona 500, three years after the death of his father on the same track.

16 Feb.	MLB player Alex Rodriguez (traded from the Texas Rangers) joins the New York Yankees, moving from shortstop to third baseman.
16 Mar.	Alaskan Mitch Seavey wins the Iditarod.
5 Apr.	The Connecticut University Huskies defeat the Georgia Tech Yellow Jackets 82–73 to win the NCAA Division I Basketball championship.
11 April	Phil Mickelson wins his first Masters at Augusta, Georgia.
4 May	Shot-putter Kevin Toth is banned from competition for steroid use and loses his 2003 U.S. championship. Two weeks later sprinter Kelli White accepts a similar sentence.
18 May	Arizona Diamondbacks pitcher Randy Johnson pitches a perfect game against the Atlanta Braves.
30 May	Buddy Rice wins the Indianapolis 500.
5 June	Smarty Jones falls short of earning the Triple Crown; the winner of the Belmont Stakes is Birdstone.
7 June	The Tampa Bay Lightning secure their first Stanley Cup in game seven of the NHL finals, beating the Calgary Flames 2–1.
15 June	The Detroit Pistons defeat the Los Angeles Lakers 100–87, capturing the NBA championship four games to one.
26 June	The Washington Capitals pick Alexander Ovechkin in the first selection of the 2004 NHL draft, but the 2004–2005 lockout means he does not play until the 2005–2006 season.
28 June	The California State University Fullerton Titans defeat the University of Texas Longhorns 3–2 to win the College World Series.
14 July	Center Shaquille O'Neal is traded by the Los Angeles Lakers to the Miami Heat in exchange for forwards Lamar Odom, Caron Butler, Brian Grant, and a future first-round draft pick.
17 July	Runner Regina Jacobs receives a four-year ban from competition for steroid use.
13–29 Aug.	U.S. athletes (along with those from two hundred and one other countries) participate in the Summer Olympics held in Greece. Americans take home 103 medals (35 gold, 39 silver, and 29 bronze).
21 Aug.	Swimmer Michael Phelps wins his eighth medal at the Athens Summer Olympic Games, tying the record for medals won in a single Olympics.
14 Sept.	The NFL fines three Oakland Raiders players for using the steroid tetrahydrogestrinone (THG).
16 Sept.	The Seattle Storm defeat the Connecticut Sun 74–60, winning the WNBA title two games to one.
17 Sept.	Barry Bonds hits his seven-hundredth career home run, making him only the third player in MLB history to do so.
19 Oct.	Sprinter Alvin Harrison is banned from competition for four years for steroid use.
27 Oct.	The Boston Red Sox defeat the St. Louis Cardinals 3–0 to complete a four-game sweep of the World Series, ending their eighty-six-year streak without winning the title.
14 Nov.	D.C. United defeats the Kansas City Wizards 3–2 to win the MLS Cup.

19 Nov. With less than a minute to play in an NBA game between the Detroit Pistons and Indiana Pacers, a fight breaks out on the court that escalates to a brawl including players and fans and forces officials to end the game with time remaining.

2 Dec. New York Yankees outfielder Jason Giambi admits to steroid and hormone use and implicates Barry Bonds.

10 Dec. Sprinter Michelle Collins receives an eight-year ban from track competition; it is later reduced to four after she agrees not to appeal.

26 Dec. Indianapolis Colts quarterback Peyton Manning breaks Dan Marino's single-season touchdown pass record when he throws his forty-ninth in a game against the San Diego Chargers.

2005

4 Jan. The University of Southern California (USC) Trojans easily clinch the BCS title in a 55–19 rout over the Oklahoma Sooners in the FedEx Orange Bowl, leaving lingering questions about the matchup. (In 2010 the win by the Trojans was vacated because they had used an ineligible player, Reggie Bush.)

17 Jan. *The Ultimate Fighter*, an Ultimate Fighting Championship (UFC) sponsored reality competition show featuring aspiring mixed-martial-arts fighters, debuts on SpikeTV.

6 Feb. In Jacksonville, Florida, the New England Patriots beat the Philadelphia Eagles 24–21 in Super Bowl XXXIX, their third title in four years.

16 Feb. In an unprecedented move, NHL commissioner Gary Bettman cancels the 2004–2005 season, which had never begun because of an ongoing labor dispute over salary caps; it marks the first time a professional sports team in North America lost an entire season because of failed labor negotiations.

20 Feb. Jeff Gordon wins his third Daytona 500.

7 Mar. Steve Fossett becomes the first person to fly around the world on a nonstop solo trip; he also sets records circumnavigating the globe by sailboat and balloon.

12 Mar. Bode Miller wins his first Alpine Skiing World Cup.

17 Mar. Mark McGwire, Jose Canseco, Curt Schilling, Sammy Sosa, Rafael Palmeiro, and Frank Thomas appear before the House Oversight and Government Reform Committee to testify on steroids in baseball.

4 Apr. Coach Roy Williams and the University of North Carolina Tar Heels grab a 75–70 victory over the University of Illinois in the NCAA men's basketball championship; the victory marks the team's fourth overall title and first since 1993.

4 Apr. The MLB Washington (D.C.) Nationals (formerly the Montreal Expos) begin play. Two days later they earn their first victory.

10 Apr. Tiger Woods wins his fourth Masters title, defeating Chris DiMarco in a playoff.

11 June Boxing legend Mike Tyson announces his retirement from the sport.

23 June The San Antonio Spurs beat the defending champion Detroit Pistons 81–74 in the decisive seventh game of the NBA finals.

27 June The University of Texas Longhorns win the College World Series over the University of Florida Gators with a final game 6–2 victory.

2 July Venus Williams reclaims her Wimbledon title, beating Lindsay Davenport (4–6, 7–6, 9–7) in the longest women's final to date.

15 July	BALCO owner Victor Conte and weight trainer Greg Anderson plead guilty to distributing steroids and are given short prison sentences.
22 July	The NHL and its players reach a collective-bargaining agreement that ends the lockout and allows the sport to resume for the 2005–2006 season.
24 July	Lance Armstrong wins his seventh consecutive Tour de France and announces his retirement from professional cycling.
28 Aug.	A team from Ewa Beach, Hawaii, wins the Little League World Series.
20 Sept.	In a playoff series expanded to the best of five games, the Sacramento Monarchs defeat the Connecticut Sun 62–59 to earn the WNBA title three games to one.
6 Oct.	Seventeen members of the NFL Minnesota Vikings team participate in a wild party involving prostitutes aboard a boat on Lake Minnetonka. Several players are charged with indecent conduct; a new code of conduct is implemented by the team; and fines, suspensions, and service duties are imposed.
26 Oct.	The Chicago White Sox defeat the Houston Astros 1–0 to complete a sweep and win their first World Series since 1917.
13 Nov.	The Los Angeles Galaxy defeat the New England Revolution 1–0 in overtime to win their second MLS title of the decade.
10 Dec.	University of Southern California tailback Reggie Bush wins the Heisman Trophy by an overwhelming majority, securing the second-most votes in history.
11 Dec.	St. Louis Rams running back Marshall Faulk sets the all-time receiving record for a player at his position in a game against the Minnesota Vikings. He will end his career with 6,875 receiving yards.

2006

4 Jan.	The Texas Longhorns beat the USC Trojans in the BCS Championship Rose Bowl 41–38.
5 Feb.	The Pittsburgh Steelers win Super Bowl XL, defeating the Seattle Seahawks 21–10 at Ford Field in Detroit. Steelers running back Willie Parker sets a new Super Bowl record with a seventy-five-yard run for a touchdown.
10–26 Feb.	The XX Winter Olympics are held in Turin, Italy. U.S. athletes win nine gold, nine silver, and seven bronze medals.
14 Feb.	Bode Miller is disqualified for missing gates in the Alpine combined event at the Winter Olympics. Teammate Ted Ligety wins the event.
19 Feb.	Jimmie Johnson wins the Daytona 500.
24 Feb.	The United States wins its first medal in curling, a bronze, in the Winter Olympics.
16 Mar.	Jeff King wins the Iditarod.
3 Apr.	The NCAA Men's Basketball title goes to the University of Florida Gators with their 73–57 win over the University of California, Los Angeles (UCLA) Bruins.
9 Apr.	Phil Mickelson wins his second Masters.
28 May	Barry Bonds passes Babe Ruth with home run #715; he is now second only to Hank Aaron.
28 May	Sam Hornish Jr. wins the Indianapolis 500.
19 June	The Carolina Hurricanes defeat the Edmonton Oilers 3–1 to win the Stanley Cup in seven games.

20 June   The Miami Heat defeat the Dallas Mavericks 95–92 in the NBA finals, winning their first championship four games to two.

26 June   The Oregon State University Beavers win the College World Series by defeating the University of North Carolina Tar Heels 3–2.

23 July   Floyd Landis wins the Tour de France. Four days later Landis fails his drug test, making second-place finisher, Oscar Pereiro, the new winner (only the second time in history that the winner is disqualified).

10 Aug.   Jamie M. Gold wins $12 million in the World Series of Poker, playing in the No Limit Hold'em Championship.

28 Aug.   A team from Columbus, Georgia, wins the Little League World Series.

9 Sept.   The Detroit Shock earn their second WNBA crown with a 80–75 victory over the Sacramento Monarchs, taking the series three games to two.

11 Oct.   Yankees pitcher Cory Lidle is killed in a plane crash.

27 Oct.   The St. Louis Cardinals defeat the Detroit Tigers 4–2 to win their tenth World Series title, four games to one.

12 Nov.   After playing to a 1–1 tie, the Houston Dynamo defeat the New England Revolution in penalty kicks to win the MLS Cup.

2007

8 Jan.   The University of Florida Gators defeat the Ohio State Buckeyes 41–14 in the BCS title game held in Glendale, Arizona.

11 Jan.   British star David Beckham signs a five-year contract said to be for $280 million to play soccer for the Los Angeles Galaxy.

4 Feb.   Quarterback Peyton Manning leads the Indianapolis Colts to a 29–17 Super Bowl XLI victory over the Chicago Bears. Tony Dungy becomes the first African American coach to win a Super Bowl.

18 Feb.   Kevin Harvick wins the Daytona 500.

13 Mar.   Lance Mackey wins his first Iditarod.

27 Mar.   The owners of UFC agree to buy out their rival Pride Fighting Championships.

2 Apr.   The University of Florida Gators repeat as NCAA Men's Division I champions by defeating the Ohio State Buckeyes 84–75.

8 Apr.   Zack Johnson wins the Masters.

11 Apr.   All charges are dropped against three Duke University lacrosse players who had falsely been accused of the rape and assault of a stripper at a party in March 2006; the prosecuting attorney is disciplined and disbarred. The team coach had been fired and the remainder of the season canceled; players are given an additional year of eligibility by the NCAA.

25 May   NHL Phoenix Coyotes assistant coach Rick Tocchet pleads guilty to running a gambling racket, allegedly with mafia connections.

6 June   The Anaheim Ducks defeat the Ottawa Senators 6–2 in game five to win the Stanley Cup.

14 June   The San Antonio Spurs sweep the Cleveland Cavaliers in four games to win the NBA Championship, taking the final game 83–82.

24 June	The Oregon State University Beavers repeat as champions of the College World Series by again defeating the University of North Carolina Tar Heels, winning the final game 9–3.
9 July	NBA referee Tim Donaghy, a thirteen-season veteran, resigns after allegations he bet on games in which he was officiating. He earns jail time on federal charges.
21 July	David Beckham plays in his first game with the Los Angeles Galaxy.
7 Aug.	Barry Bonds hits home run #756, passing Aaron's record.
26 Aug.	A team from Warner Robins, Georgia, wins the Little League World Series.
3 Sept.	Steve Fossett fails to return from a flight over Nevada; the search for the sixty-three-year-old sailor and aviator is unsuccessful until late 2008 when his remains are located.
16 Sept.	The Phoenix Mercury deny the Detroit Shock their third WNBA crown, taking the title three games to two with a 108–92 victory.
5 Oct.	Track star Marion Jones pleads guilty to lying to federal agents about her steroid use and forfeits all titles and results dating back to September of 2000, which includes her five medals at the 2000 Summer Olympics in Sydney.
28 Oct.	The Boston Red Sox sweep the Colorado Rockies in four games, taking the final game 4–3, to win the World Series, their second title in four years and seventh overall.
15 Nov.	Bonds is charged with perjury and obstruction of justice in relation to the federal inquiry into steroid use in professional sports.
18 Nov.	In a rematch from the previous championship, the Houston Dynamo defeat the New England Revolution 2–1 to win the MLS Cup.
21 Nov.	One hundred sky divers achieve a world record for a canopy formation (a stacking formation with a diver's feet touching the next person's parachute) over Lake Wales, Florida.
2 Dec.	The United States wins its thirty-second Davis Cup in tennis with a victory over the Russian team.

2008

7 Jan.	The #2 Louisiana State University (LSU) Tigers defeat the #1 Ohio State Buckeyes 38–24 in the BCS championship game held at the Louisiana Superdome in New Orleans.
3 Feb.	Eli Manning and the New York Giants shock the previously undefeated New England Patriots 17–14 in Super Bowl XLII. Manning is named MVP, an honor given to his brother the year before, making them the first brothers to win Super Bowl MVPs.
17 Feb.	Ryan Newman wins the Daytona 500.
15 Mar.	Bode Miller wins his second Alpine Skiing World Cup; Lindsey Vonn wins the women's World Cup (she repeats in 2009).
7 Apr.	The University of Kansas Jayhawks defeat the University of Memphis Tigers 75–68 to garner the NCAA Division I Men's Basketball crown.
20 Apr.	Danica Patrick wins the Indy Japan 300, making her the first woman to win an Indy Car race.
4 June	The Detroit Red Wings defeat the Pittsburgh Penguins 3–2 to win the Stanley Cup in six games.

7 June   Da'Tara denies the formerly unbeaten Big Brown the Triple Crown at the Belmont Stakes.

17 June   The Boston Celtics defeat the Los Angeles Lakers 131–92 to win the NBA championship in six games.

25 June   Fresno State becomes the lowest-ranked team ever to win the College Baseball World Series, beating the heavily favored University of Georgia Bulldogs 6–1.

5 July   Venus Williams wins her fifth Wimbledon, defeating sister Serena (7–5, 6–4).

8–24 Aug.   The Summer Olympics are held in Beijing, China. American athletes win 110 medals (36 gold, 38 silver, and 36 bronze).

16 Aug.   Michael Phelps wins his eighth gold medal of the 2008 Summer Olympics, marking a new record for gold won in a single Olympics.

24 Aug.   A team from Waipio, Hawaii, wins the Little League World Series.

7 Sept.   Serena Williams wins the U.S. Open, defeating Jelena Kovic (6–4, 7–5).

5 Oct.   The Detroit Shock win their third WNBA title in a three-game sweep over the San Antonio Silver Stars, taking the final game 76–60.

27 Oct.   The Philadelphia Phillies defeat the Tampa Bay Rays 4–3 in game five to win the World Series.

23 Nov.   The Columbus Crew defeat the New York Red Bulls 3–1 to win the MLS Cup.

6 Dec.   Oscar De La Hoya loses to Manny Pacquiao in the eighth round of a boxing match touted "The Dream Match."

2009

8 Jan.   Quarterback Tim Tebow and the University of Florida Gators defeat the Oklahoma Sooners 24–14 in the BCS championship game in Dolphin Stadium in Miami, Florida, winning their second championship in three years.

1 Feb.   The Pittsburgh Steelers defeat the Arizona Cardinals 27–23 in Super Bowl XLIII held in Raymond James Stadium in Tampa, Florida.

5 Feb.   Michael Phelps is suspended for three months from professional swimming for smoking marijuana.

15 Feb.   Matt Kenseth wins the Daytona 500.

6 Apr.   The University of North Carolina Tar Heels win their second basketball championship of the decade by defeating the first winner in the decade, the Michigan State Spartans.

14 Apr.   Oscar De La Hoya announces his retirement from boxing.

22 Apr.   Extreme kayaker Tyler Bradt performs a 186-foot drop off Palouse Falls, Washington.

2 May   A thunderstorm knocks down the roof of the Dallas Cowboys practice facility, injuring twelve (one with a broken back).

24 May   Danica Patrick finishes third in the Indianapolis 500, the highest-ever finish for a female driver.

12 June   In a rematch of the previous year's Stanley Cup, the Pittsburgh Penguins defeat the defending champion Detroit Red Wings four games to three, winning the climactic game 2–1.

14 June   The Los Angeles Lakers defeat the Orlando Magic 99–86 to win the NBA title in five games; this appearance is the Lakers' thirtieth in the finals, more than any other team, and their fourth championship of the decade.

24 June   The U.S. men's soccer team shocks the world when it upsets Spain (the top-rated team) at the Fédération Internationale de Football Association (FIFA) Confederations Cup. Four days later they lose 3–2 to the Brazilians for a second-place finish.

24 June   The Louisiana State University Tigers defeat the University of Texas Longhorns 11–4 to win the College World Series.

4 July   Serena Williams is back on top, defeating her sister and defending champion Venus (7–6, 6–2) to earn her third Wimbledon title.

17 July   Pittsburgh Steelers star quarterback Ben Roethlisberger is charged with sexual assault stemming from a June 2008 incident in Nevada.

23 July   Chicago White Sox pitcher Mark Buehrle throws a perfect game at the Tampa Bay Rays.

9 Aug.   The Phoenix Mercury take the five-game series with a 94–86 victory over the Indiana Fever to win the WNBA title. The first game of the title series was the highest scoring (120–116) in WNBA history.

10 Aug.   North Carolinian Rikki Cunningham plays a record 4,026 minutes of marathon billiards in a charity event.

25 Aug.   A team from Chula Vista, California, wins the Little League World Series.

20 Sept.   The Dallas Cowboys play their first regular season game in the new Cowboys Stadium, drawing an NFL regular-season record 105,121 fans.

29 Sept.   *Forbes* magazine announces that Tiger Woods is the first athlete to earn $1 billion in career earnings.

8 Oct.   The United Football League (UFL) debuts with a game between the Las Vegas Locomotives and California Redwoods.

4 Nov.   The New York Yankees defeat the Philadelphia Phillies 7–3, winning the World Series four games to two, giving the Yankees a total of twenty-seven titles, more than any other North American professional sports franchise.

22 Nov.   The MLS Cup is captured by Real Salt Lake in penalty kicks over the Los Angeles Galaxy, after playing to a 1–1 tie.

27 Nov.   Tiger Woods is injured in a car crash outside his home.

11 Dec.   Amid public accusations of infidelity and marital problems, Woods announces that he will take a temporary leave of absence from professional golf.

21 Dec.   NASCAR driver Jimmie Johnson, winner of four consecutive championships, is named the Associated Press (AP) Male Athlete of the Year, the first race-car driver to ever win this award.

OVERVIEW

Money and Sports. While professional athletes in America have long experienced high monetary compensation for their performances, the stupendous salaries of the 2000s had some fans asking if athletes were paid too much. Salaries skyrocketed in all professional sports, and in 2009 golfer Tiger Woods became the first professional athlete to earn $1 billion for his career. According to *USA Today*, the average annual salary for a National Football League (NFL) player rose from $79,000 in 1980 to $1.75 million in 2007. The National Basketball Association (NBA), the highest-paying professional sports organization in the country, featured stars such as Los Angeles Laker Kobe Bryant and Cleveland Cavalier LeBron James, both of whom *Forbes* magazine, counting endorsements as well as salary, estimated earned in excess of $40 million in 2009. In the 1980s the average professional basketball player in the United States had made around $500,000; in the 2000s he earned more than $5 million. The New York Yankees were the highest paid team in Major League Baseball (MLB), with the owner shelling out a total of $201.4 million to his players in 2009, $33 million of which went to top-earner third baseman Alex Rodriguez. The average salary for a player in MLB was nearly $3.25 million at the close of the decade, compared to an average $146,000 salary in 1980. Disconcertingly, the cost for fans to attend games also escalated wildly. In 1980, for example, the average ticket price for an MLB game was about $4.45; by 2006 that price had risen to more than $22 (with commensurate increases in the cost for parking, food, and souvenirs). In 2009 NFL ticket prices rose to an average of $75 per game, and the Fan Cost Index estimated that to take a family of four to a Dallas Cowboys game, the most expensive in the league, would cost about $759. Many fans complained that the average working-class family could no longer afford to attend professional sporting events.

Action Sports. With the introduction of snowboarding into the Winter Games in the 1990s as well as the advent of the alternative-sport X Games and its heavy promotion by the Entertainment and Sports Programming Network (ESPN), extreme sports established a loyal following in the 2000s and became a fixture on the cable network, while perhaps not attracting the large mainstream audiences for which organizers had hoped. Sports such as skateboarding, BMX biking, Moto X motorcycling, wakeboarding, and speed climbing—dubbed "action sports" by ESPN—especially attract young Generation X and Y viewers. While the "Gravity Games" faltered mid decade, the "Dew Tour," sponsored by Mountain Dew, emerged as a multisport event spanning the entire country in 2005 and offering a $2.5 million prize to the winner. With a growing viewership and the addition of major sponsors, action-sports events were able to offer successful extreme athletes the possibility of lucrative careers and widespread acclaim.

Fringe Sports. The rise of Mixed Martial Arts (MMA) and the Ultimate Fighting Championship (UFC) eclipsed the popularity of traditional boxing in the decade. MMA generally refers to any one of or combination of boxing, kickboxing, wrestling, jujitsu, and more; competitors showcased their skills at events hosted by the UFC and other promotional companies. In its infancy the UFC faced criticism for a lack of regulations in the sport, which resulted in what some felt were overly violent competitions. Consequently, the managers and promoters began reforming the sport and in 2000 held the first event sanctioned by the New Jersey State Athletic Control Board, followed by the creation of the unified rules of MMA. By 2006 the UFC was earning more than $200 million in yearly revenue from pay-per-view airings of events and attracting more than 800,000 viewers, mainly from the eighteen- to thirty-four-year-old range, a desirable demographic for advertisers. Unlike the male-dominated MMA events, roller derby—a sport that originated in America in the 1930s and that was popular in the 1970s—reemerged in the 2000s as a rough-and-tumble athletic competition among women. The 2007 documentary *Hell on Wheels* chronicles the creation of all-women leagues in Austin, Texas, and spurred the establishment of hundreds of leagues across the nation. Roller derby's return was formalized in 2004 with the founding of the Women's Flat Track Derby Association.

Mainstream Sports. America's traditional pastime, baseball, continued to be successful, despite controversy surrounding steroid use. Fans followed—and debated—the achievements of such players as Alex Rodriguez, Roger Clemens, and Barry Bonds, whose reputations were tainted by allegations of "juicing." In professional basketball stars such as Kobe Bryant, LeBron James, and Shaquille O'Neal thrilled viewers with their athleticism. Michael Jordan, perhaps the greatest player in the history of the game, had a brief comeback with the Washington Wizards from 2001 to 2003, donating his salary to help victims of the September 11 terrorist attacks. In professional football, Peyton Manning of the Indianapolis Colts and Tom Brady of the New England Patriots emerged as top quarterbacks in the league, fueling one of the most intense rivalries in the NFL. Tiger Woods was the top golfer through the decade, winning twelve major championships and becoming the highest-paid professional athlete. Professional soccer in the U.S. raised its profile when British superstar David Beckham signed to play for the Los Angeles Galaxy in 2007. In motor racing, Dale Earnhardt Jr. emerged as a popular face for NASCAR (National Association for Stock Car Auto Racing) after the death of his father, legendary driver Dale Earnhardt Sr., in 2001. Drivers such as Jeff Gordon, Jimmie Johnson, and Tony Stewart were major forces in the sport. Danica Patrick broke barriers by competing at the Indianapolis 500 and becoming the first woman to win a major international open-wheel race in 2008 at Motegi, Japan. Lance Armstrong was the star in the sport of cycling with his record-breaking six consecutive Tour de France wins from 2000 to 2005. In tennis, the Williams sisters, Venus and Serena, were the dominant force, each having been ranked #1 in singles and doubles during the decade. The sisters met in eight Grand Slam singles finals between 2001 and 2009. Notable Olympians included swimmers Michael Phelps and Jenny Thompson, volleyball stars Misty May-Treanor and Kerri Walsh, skaters Michelle Kwan and Apolo Ohno, and gymnast Shawn Johnson.

Movies and Television. With the rise of interest in reality television, sports programming entered a new era. Shows such as *Tough Enough* (2001), *The Contender* (2005), *The Ultimate Fighter* (2005), and *Dallas Cowboys Cheerleaders: Making the Team* (2006) focused on prospective athletes competing to earn contracts in their respective sports. Other shows focused on individual athletes, teams, or sports, such as *The T. O. Show* (2009), featuring NFL wide receiver Terrell Owens; HBO's series *Hard Knocks* (2001) that followed a different NFL team through training camp each year; and *Roller Girls* (2006) that portrayed various athletes and teams in female roller derby. In film, the integration of a high-school football team was the basis for the movie *Remember the Titans* (2000). *Radio* (2003) was inspired by the story of a high-school football coach and his relationship with a developmentally challenged man. Yet another movie based on a true story, *Friday Night Lights* (2005), documented a town in Texas and its obsession with high-school football. *We Are Marshall* (2006) portrayed the rebuilding of the Marshall University football program after a 1970 plane crash killed most of its team members and staff. The most successful sports film of the decade, *The Blind Side* (2009), was about the struggles of future Baltimore Ravens lineman Michael Oher, a home-less African American who was "adopted" into a white family.

Scandals. Former football star O. J. Simpson again created furor with the announcement of his book *If I Did It* in 2006, which proposed a hypothetical theory of the murders of Nicole Brown Simpson and Ronald Goldman. Public outrage cancelled its release, and a Florida court awarded rights to the book to the Goldman family, who published the book with the "If" greatly reduced in size on the cover and added the subtitle, "Confessions of the Killer." Compounding his legal trouble in 2007, Simpson was charged with robbery, kidnapping, and assault in Las Vegas, Nevada. He was found guilty in 2008 and sentenced to up to thirty-three years in prison. In other crimes involving athletes, Los Angeles Lakers star Kobe Bryant was accused of sexual assault in 2003, though the charges were later dropped. The Duke University men's lacrosse team also sparked controversy in 2006 when a woman hired by several team members to dance at a party claimed she was sexually assaulted by three of the players. Charges against the accused were eventually dropped, and the overzealous district attorney who prosecuted the case was later disbarred. In February 2004, during a live Super Bowl halftime performance with Justin Timberlake, Janet Jackson's breast was accidentally exposed to a television audience of approximately 140 million people. In an apology issued the next day, Jackson claimed that the exposure was an accident and Timberlake attributed it to a wardrobe malfunction. The incident prompted an investigation by the Federal Communications Commission (FCC). In late 2009 Tiger Woods became the object of scandal as several women came forward alleging to have had affairs with the married golfer.

Steroid Era. The use of a new type of steroid called tetrahydrogestrinone (THG) was linked to several Olympic athletes, sparking a federal investigation into the substance, its developers, and its users in 2002. THG was developed for the Bay Area Laboratory Co-operative (BALCO) and distributed by BALCO and others to several high-profile athletes and trainers. The substance was nicknamed "the clear" because it did not show up on standard drug tests. Investigators received information about the substance from an inside source and began an investigation into BALCO that linked many athletes to use of the substance, including track star Marion Jones and baseball slugger Barry Bonds. In 2004 sprinter Kelli White admitted to using steroids and was stripped of her World Championship medals and banned from the sport for two years. Faced with repeated allegations that she had used THG, Jones—who had won three gold and two bronze medals in the 2000 Summer Olympics—insisted upon her innocence. In 2007, however, Jones finally admitted to using the drugs and forfeited her medals. In addition to track and field, cycling became one of the most heavily scrutinized sports in the wake of the doping controversy, with seven-time Tour de France winner Armstrong and American cyclist Floyd Landis at the center of allegations. Landis was stripped of his title after winning the 2006 Tour de France amid accusations of using illegal performance-enhancing substances. Landis challenged the charges in a drawn-out appeal that he ultimately lost in 2007. Unlike Landis, Armstrong never failed a drug test. Throughout the latter half of his career he was often accused of doping, but Armstrong repeatedly and vehemently denied any use of illegal substances. He submitted to twenty-four unannounced drug tests in 2008 and 2009, calling himself "the most tested athlete on the planet" and reminding critics that he has "never tested positive." In concurrence with the BALCO investigation, MLB began randomly testing players for steroid use, with only minor penalties attached to a positive test. Federal investigators were much less lenient, charging BALCO in 2004 with forty-two counts related to steroid production and distribution. During federal proceedings the *San Francisco Chronicle* began publishing testimonies from various athletes who admitted to using steroids during their careers. The paper reported that Bonds admitted to using a "clear substance" and "a cream," but not to knowing that they were steroids. The public was suspicious about Bonds, who had risen late in his career to become baseball's greatest slugger, and fans were further disheartened the following year with the release of Jose Canseco's book *Juiced: Wild Times, Rampant 'Roids, Smash Hits, and How Baseball Got Big* (2005), in which he named several MLB stars who used steroids. In addition to admitting his own use, former star Canseco accused many other players, including pitching ace Roger Clemens, of steroid use and claimed to have injected slugger Mark McGwire with the drug. Canseco's revelations and congressional hearings damaged the reputations of many players. Fans felt betrayed and demanded action against those using illegal drugs.

Women in Sports. Throughout the 2000s, coverage of women's sports grew and more female competitors began participating in traditionally male-dominated sports than ever before. Most notable was the success of the Women's National Basketball Association (WNBA). The Houston Comets became in 2000 the first women's professional sports team to be invited to the White House. In 2002 Lisa Leslie became the first woman to dunk a ball in a WNBA game, and in 2009 she became the first WNBA player to score more than 6,000 career points. Pioneer players such as Leslie attracted a larger viewing audience, gaining the WNBA an eight-year television contract with ESPN in 2007. Driver Danica Patrick became only the fourth woman to compete in the Indianapolis 500 race (2005) and the first woman to win an IndyCar race (2008). Another inspiring female athlete was golfer Michelle Wie. In 2000, at age ten, Wie became the youngest player to qualify for a United States Golf Association (USGA) amateur championship. Her career skyrocketed, and at age fifteen she announced her intention to turn professional. In 2006 she became the first female to win a local qualifier for the Men's U.S. Open, but she did not make the cut for the tournament at the sectional qualifying stage. The following year she was named one of *Forbes*'s top twenty earners

under 25 with an income of $19 million. Another standout performance by female athletes occurred during the 2004 Summer Olympic Games in Athens, Greece, when American volleyball players Misty May-Treanor and Kerri Walsh won the gold medal without losing a single game. Then, at the 2008 Summer Olympic Games in Beijing, China, the pair made history by winning the gold again, becoming the first beach-volleyball team, men's or women's, to win back-to-back Olympic titles.

Post 9/11. The terrorist attacks on 11 September 2001 deeply affected all aspects of American life. Immediately following the attacks, MLB, NFL, and NCAA events were cancelled or postponed. When games did start again, there was a noticeable change in the atmosphere. Stadiums began holding tributes to honor both the victims and heroes of those dark days. On 30 October 2001 George W. Bush became the first sitting president to visit Yankee Stadium during a World Series when he threw the ceremonial first pitch in game three of the matchup between the Arizona Diamondbacks and the New York Yankees. Cheers of "USA" and signs with patriotic slogans such as "God Bless America" and "United We Stand" filled the stadium. Displays of patriotism became commonplace. The traditional seventh-inning-stretch song, "Take Me Out to the Ball Game," was typically accompanied by the singing of "God Bless America." Half-time shows became tributes to 9/11 victims or responders, with field-sized American flags, color-guard salutes, and fighter-jet flyovers becoming standard practice at football and baseball games. Rudy Giuliani, the mayor of New York City on 9/11, believed that in the wake of the attacks, when Americans felt vulnerable and dejected, sports gave them an outlet to escape the pain and confusion. There were still home runs and touchdowns, he explained, and this gave Americans a much needed sense of normalcy in a time of uncertainty.

Sports Abroad. With increased media coverage around the world and economic globalization, American sports organizations were more active internationally. Increased global access to the Internet encouraged the NBA, MLB, and the NFL to boost international broadcasting of their games in order to draw a larger audience. *NBA.com,* for example, drew more than half of its hits from international fans, many coming from China, and during the 2005–2006 season the NBA partnered with Google to begin allowing fans to purchase and watch live NBA games online. In 2001 the NBA and FIBA (International Basketball Federation) began the Basketball Without Borders program, in which camps are held around the world to promote cultural harmony through the sport. In addition to international marketing and community service, the NBA since 1988 has staged many exhibition as well as regular season games outside of the United States and Canada. NBA teams and players have participated in international competition in countries in Europe, Asia, the Middle East, Latin America, and the Caribbean. MLB created the Ambassador Program to advance baseball internationally, and several players traveled the globe helping children develop their skills and promoting the sport in areas that have historically been dominated by other sports, such as soccer or rugby. In 2006 the first World Baseball Classic, an international tournament featuring teams from all over the world, was played in seven different venues and featured sixteen teams. Japan won the inaugural series and defended their title in 2009. Baseball has particularly made efforts in Asia. Three times during the decade the MLB regular season has begun with opening series in Japan (2000, 2004, and 2008). In March 2008 the first MLB exhibition game was staged in China, a year after MLB reached an agreement with the Chinese government that allowed the All-Star Game and the World Series to be broadcast in the country for the first time. NFL Europe operated until 2007 but had difficulty competing with soccer. The NFL, however, remained dedicated to playing games and promoting "American football" internationally, and since 2005 the league has played games around the globe. The first regular-season game held outside the United States took place in Mexico City on 2 October 2005 between the Arizona Cardinals and San Francisco 49ers. International games since have usually taken place in Europe, and NFL commissioner Roger Goodell has even discussed the possibility of eventually hosting a Super Bowl in London.

TOPICS IN THE NEWS

BASEBALL

Team to Beat. After winning three of ten World Series in the 1990s, the New York Yankees of Major League Baseball (MLB) won their third consecutive World Series in 2000 in the first "Subway Series" since 1956. The Yankees beat the New York Mets in five games. In 2001 the Yankees returned to the series by defeating the Seattle Mariners in the American League Championship Series (ALCS), but, because the season had been briefly postponed due to the September 11 terrorist attacks, the World Series did not begin until 27 October. This start was the latest to date until 2009. In the World Series the Yankees were defeated in seven games by the upstart Arizona Diamondbacks, who won the final game in spectacular fashion with a bottom-of-the-ninth hit. With superstar players—such as third baseman Alex Rodriguez, shortstop Derek Jeter, second baseman Alfonso Soriano, pitcher Roger Clemens, and closer Mariano Rivera—the leadership of manager Joe Torre, and deep pockets of owner George Steinbrenner, the Yankees dominated their division with titles from 2000 to 2006 and in 2009, and American League pennants in 2001–2003 and 2009. In 2003 the Yankees returned to the World Series, falling to the Florida Marlins in six games. Although in the following years the Yankees remained competitive, making the playoffs every year until 2008, the team faced turmoil and change. In 2004 they lost the ALCS to the rival Boston Red Sox, and did so after leading the series three games to none. On 11 October 2006 promising pitcher Cory Lidle died in a plane crash in Manhattan. Following their defeat by the Cleveland Indians in the ALCS, Torre decided to depart, and his post was filled with former Yankee catcher Joe Girardi.

Even their home changed, as on 21 September 2008 the Yankees played their final game in Yankee Stadium ("The House that Ruth Built"). Nevertheless, in 2009, their first season in the new Yankee Stadium, the team returned to championship form. The Yankees won the AL East, eliminated the Minnesota Twins and Anaheim Angels in the league playoffs, and earned their twenty-seventh World Series title by defeating the defending champion Philadelphia Phillies in six games.

Best Player. The best player of the decade, according to the sports reporters at ESPN, was St. Louis Cardinals first baseman Albert Pujols, a perennial All Star, after earning Rookie of the Year honors in 2001. An immigrant to the United States from the Dominican Republic, he played high-school and college baseball in Missouri before being selected in the 1999 draft by the Cardinals; after a short stint in the minors he was called up to the majors in 2001. In 2003 he hit forty-three home runs and earned the National League (NL) batting title. Major baseball publications named him best player in the league in three separate seasons, and he won the MLB MVP three times as well (2003, 2008, and 2009). In 2004 he signed a $100 million, seven-year contract with the Cardinals. In August 2005 he became the first MLB player in history to hit thirty or more home runs in each of his first five years, and the second-fastest player to reach the two hundred mark. On the way to earning a World Series ring in 2006, he hit four consecutive home runs in a single game on 17 April. On 30 June 2009 he became the first player in history to hit more than thirty home runs and hit over .300 each year in his first nine seasons. On 3 July he hit his tenth grand slam, breaking the franchise record (formerly held by Stan Musial). Other players worthy of consideration for the honor of best of the decade were New York Yankee third baseman Rodriguez, Seattle Mariner outfielder Ichiro Suzuki, Boston Red Sox outfielder Manny Ramirez, Colorado Rockies first baseman Todd Helton, Atlanta Braves third baseman Chipper Jones, New York Yankee shortstop Jeter, Philadelphia Phillies first baseman Ryan Howard, and San Francisco Giants outfielder Barry Bonds.

New Home-Run King. Barry Bonds became synonymous not only with baseball greatness but also with scandal. In 1998 baseball fans watched Chicago Cubs outfielder Sammy Sosa and St. Louis Cardinals first baseman Mark McGwire battle to break New York Yankees outfielder Roger Maris's 1961 single-season home-run record of sixty-one. Though the Maris benchmark had held for nearly four decades, the new record survived only briefly. In 2001 Bonds, while playing outfield for the San Francisco Giants, hit an astonishing seventy-three home runs. He earned the NL's MVP title every year from 2001 to 2004, garnering a record seven MVPs over his career. In 2007 Bonds became the home-run king when he broke Hank Aaron's record by hitting home run number 756. He ended his career with a total of 762 home runs. Throughout much of the decade, however, Bonds was plagued with rumors of steroid use, most notably chronicled in the exposé *Game of Shadows* (2006). In a federal investigation, Bonds testified that he never knowingly used steroids, but he was later brought up on charges of perjury and obstruction of justice. These charges divided fans, with many calling for an asterisk to be inserted beside his name in the record books, denoting the steroid allegations. Bonds was granted free agency in 2007 but was not signed by any team. Although some squads still showed interest in signing the slugger, by the end of the decade Bonds was not on an MLB roster, though he declined to officially retire.

Steroids. Bonds was not the only baseball player tarnished by allegations of steroid use. Slugger Mark McGwire had long been suspected of using performance-enhancing drugs and in 2010 officially admitted to having used steroids. McGwire was pushed toward admitting the abuse by revelations from former teammate Jose Canseco in *Juiced: Wild Times, Rampant 'Roids, Smash Hits, and How Baseball Got Big* (2005). As a result of the book, official hearings were held by the U.S. House Committee on Oversight and Government Reform into the use of steroids. Committee member Henry A. Waxman (D-Cal.) complained that for three decades "Major League Baseball has told us to trust them, but the league hasn't honored that trust and it hasn't acted to protect the integrity of baseball or sent the right message to millions of teenagers who idolize ballplayers." In addition to McGwire, Sosa, and Canseco, Boston Red Sox pitcher Curt Schilling, Baltimore Orioles first baseman Rafael Palmeiro, and Chicago White Sox designated hitter Frank Thomas spoke before the committee. Nearly one hundred players were accused of using steroids during their MLB careers, including top players such as Roger Clemens, Eric Gagne, Jason Giambi, Jose Guillen, Todd Hundley, David Justice, Chuck Knob-

lauch, David Ortiz, Andy Pettitte, Manny Ramirez, Brian Roberts, Alex Rodriguez, Benito Santiago, Gary Sheffield, Miguel Tejada, Ismael Valdez, Mo Vaughn, and Matt Williams. In 2005 the MLB revised its existing steroids policy, increasing game suspensions for positive tests and instating regular testing. Initially league suspensions ranged around ten games, but as the decade progressed, some players served between fifty and eighty games suspensions. In a 2007 report to the commission, former U.S. senator George J. Mitchell (D-Me.) concluded that:

1. The use of steroids in Major League Baseball was widespread. The response by baseball was slow to develop and was initially ineffective. For many years, citing concerns for the privacy rights of the players, the Players Association opposed mandatory random drug testing of its members for steroids and other substances. But in 2002, the effort gained momentum after the clubs and the Players Association agreed to and adopted a mandatory random drug testing program. The current program has been effective in that detectable steroid use appears to have declined. However, that does not mean that players have stopped using performance enhancing substances. Many players have shifted to human growth hormone, which is not detectable in any currently available urine test.

2. The minority of players who used such substances were wrong. They violated federal law and baseball policy, and they distorted the fairness of competition by trying to gain an unfair advantage over the majority of players who followed the law and the rules. They—the players who follow the law and the rules—are faced with the painful choice of either being placed at a competitive disadvantage or becoming illegal users themselves. No one should have to make that choice.

3. Obviously, the players who illegally used performance enhancing substances are responsible for their actions. But they did not act in a vacuum. Everyone involved in baseball over the past two decades—Commissioners, club officials, the Players Association, and players—shares to some extent in the responsibility for the steroids era. There was a collective failure to recognize the problem as it emerged and to deal with it early on. As a result, an environment developed in which illegal use became widespread.

4. Knowledge and understanding of the past are essential if the problem is to be dealt with effectively in the future. But being chained to the past is not helpful. Baseball does not need and cannot afford to engage in a never-ending search for the name of every player who ever used performance enhancing substances. The Commissioner was right to ask for this investigation and report. It would have been impossible to get closure on this issue without it, or something like it.

5. But it is now time to look to the future, to get on with the important and difficult task that lies ahead. Everyone involved in Major League Baseball should join in a well-planned, well-executed, and sustained effort to bring the era of steroids and human growth hormone to an end and to prevent its recurrence in some other form in the future. That is the only way this cloud will be removed from the game. The adoption of the recommendations set forth in this report will be a first step in that direction.

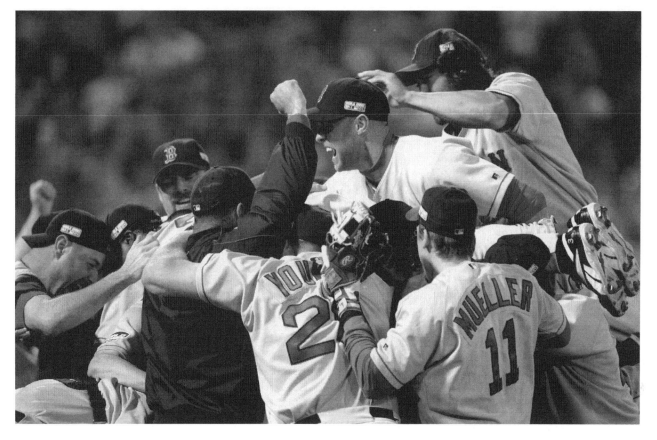

Boston Red Sox celebrate defeating the St. Louis Cardinals on 27 October 2004 in their first World Series championship since 1918 (AP Photo/Al Behrman).

Pitching Gems. Two perfect games (in which no opposing players reach base) were thrown in the major leagues during the 2000s. Arizona Diamondbacks left-handed pitcher Randy Johnson, still a towering presence on the mound at age forty, threw a perfect game on 18 May 2004 against the Atlanta Braves in a night contest at Turner Field in Atlanta. He struck out thirteen batters on the way to becoming the oldest player in MLB history to notch a perfect game. A little more than five years later on 23 July 2009, Chicago White Sox lefty Mark Buehrle threw a perfect game (only the second in team history) against the Tampa Bay Rays at U.S. Cellular Field (formerly known as the "new" Comiskey Park) in Chicago. His achievement was preserved by a spectacular just-over-the-wall catch by outfielder Dewayne Wise to rob Rays outfielder Gabe Kaplan of a home run. Buehrle nearly pitched a perfect game two years earlier against the Texas Rangers on 18 April 2007, allowing only a walk to slugger Sammy Sosa in recording the no-hitter. On 1 September 2007 rookie Boston Red Sox pitcher Clay Buchholz, in only his second start, threw a no-hitter against the Baltimore Orioles at storied Fenway Park. During the decade there were only fifteen no-hit (including the two perfect) games.

Standout Games. On 23 May 2002 Shawn Green of the Los Angeles Dodgers had a record-breaking day, as he hit four home runs (earning seven RBIs) while going six-for-six at the plate against the Milwaukee Brewers, setting the mark for most bases (nineteen) earned in a single game. He hit a first-inning double and a three-run homer against starter Glendon Rusch, following those with two home runs against reliever Brian Mallette. After hitting a weak single in the eighth inning, he topped off his performance by crushing a homer off Jose Cabrera. Green, an outfielder, played sixteen years in the majors for the Dodgers, New York Mets, Toronto Blue Jays, and Arizona Diamondbacks, and he retired from the game on 28 February 2008. On 13 June 2003 New York Yankees right-handed pitcher Clemens won career-game #300 and struck out batter number 4,000 in a 5–2 victory over the St. Louis Cardinals in Yankee Stadium. He became only the twenty-first pitcher to reach that mark and ended his career (having also played for the Boston Red Sox, Toronto Blue Jays, and Houston Astros) in 2007 with 354 wins. He played on two world championship teams (1999 and 2000) and earned eleven All Star selections. On 20 July 2004 St. Louis Cardinals first baseman Pujols went five-for-five and earned fifteen bases in a victory over the Chicago Cubs.

Curse Lifted. The famous "Curse of the Bambino" was finally lifted in the 2004 World Series when the Boston Red Sox swept the St. Louis Cardinals in four games. The curse originated in 1919 when the Red Sox sold Babe Ruth to the New York Yankees. While the Red Sox had been one of the most successful franchises up to 1918, that year winning their fifth World Series, they did not win another world championship for eighty-six years. Adding insult to injury, while the Red Sox struggled, the Yankees became the most successful franchise in professional sports. The return of the Red Sox to the championship series was that much sweeter for having come in spectacular fashion at the expense of their rivals, who had defeated the Red Sox just one season earlier to earn a trip to the World Series. In the seven-game ALCS, down by three games, the Red Sox came back to capture the final four games (the biggest comeback in MLB postseason history) against a highly touted New York pitching staff that included dreaded closer Mariano Rivera. On 20 October in Yankee Stadium the Red Sox, led on the mound by Derek Lowe, hit three home runs (including a grand slam by outfielder Johnny Damon) and won the final game ten to three. Designated hitter David "Big Papi" Ortiz, who hit two walk-off home runs during the series, captured the MVP. The World Series against the Cardinals and their star Pujols was anticlimactic. The Cardinals had defeated the Houston Astros in a hard-fought seven-game series as well. The first game of the World Series was a high-scoring affair (11–9) that went to the Red Sox, as did the second game (6–2). In the third game Cy Young Award winner Pedro Martinez dominated the Cardinals, earning a 4–1 victory. Although the Cardinals fought hard in the fourth game, the Red Sox completed the sweep with a 3–0 win and ended the curse. The Red Sox victory marked the first championship experienced by most long-suffering Boston fans.

"Feel Good" Series. In 2005 the World Series pitted the AL champion Chicago White Sox, returning to the series for the first time since 1959, against the NL Houston Astros, appearing for the first time since starting play forty-two years earlier, who squared off in what was called by one reporter the "Feel Good" series. The White Sox had last won a World Series in 1917 and were best known for the "Black Sox" scandal of 1919 when they allegedly threw the series for the benefit of gamblers. The Sox earned their slot in the series by besting the defending champion Boston Red Sox three games to none and the Anaheim Angels four games to one to claim the ALCS. The Astros defeated the Atlanta Braves three games to one (the series included an almost six-hour eighteen-inning game) and St. Louis Cardinals four games to two to earn the right to face the White Sox. The series began in Chicago with the Sox overpowering venerable starter Clemens and earning a 5–3 victory. Despite a sterling start in game two by Astro pitcher Andy Pettitte, the bullpen faltered and gave the White Sox an opening, which they took advantage of to win the game (7–6) on a ninth-inning home run by Scott Podsednik. The series moved to Houston for game three, where Chicago won a hard-fought 7–5 victory. The Astros were unable to generate any offense in game four, losing 1–0 in a pitching duel between Sox right-hander Freddie Garcia and Astro hurler Brandon Backe. Outfielder Jermaine Dye won the game with an RBI single and earned series MVP by hitting .438 during the four games. Manager Ozzie Guillen (a native of Venezuela), who had played

more than 1,700 games for the Sox during his career, was jubilant with his victory.

The Nation's Team. In 2001 Major League Baseball proposed a contraction of the league, in which the Minnesota Twins and Montreal Expos would be collectively bought by the other twenty-eight franchises and dissolved. This plan, however, was abandoned, and MLB decided to keep both teams and to move the Expos. Thus, the 2005 baseball season introduced a new team relocated in Washington, D.C., as the Nationals—or "Nats," as fans affectionately dubbed them—the first MLB team to call D.C. home since the Senators left to become the Texas Rangers in 1972. However, some controversy surrounded the move from Canada. The Expos owner lost an appeal to keep the team in Montreal and the owner of the Baltimore Orioles voted against the move, fearing that the new team would cut into his fan base. Additionally, it was unclear who would be responsible for the cost of the stadium. Finally an agreement was reached that included a shared financial burden with the MLB. The Nationals' first game was a loss to the Philadelphia Phillies on 4 April 2005, though two days later they won their first game; on 14 April they won their home opener at RFK Stadium. They played .500 ball and attracted respectable crowds for a new franchise. In 2006 the biggest name on the roster was outfielder Alfonso Soriano, who played in 158 games in a fifth-place season. While the Nationals struggled in the first years as a franchise, winning only 59 games in 2009, they were able to choose pitcher Stephen Strasberg of San Diego State University as the first pick of the draft. A right-hander with a 100-mph fastball, Strasberg excites Nats fans and is called "the most-hyped pick in draft history."

Stadiums. Many teams inaugurated new stadiums during the decade. The AL Detroit Tigers began play in the new 40,000-seat Comerica Park, which featured panoramic views of the city skyline and an amusement park. Ground was broken for the new facility in 1997, and the first game was played on 11 April 2000, with the home team defeating the Seattle Mariners. The New York Yankees began play in their new facility on 16 April 2009, the fans having said goodbye to "The House that Ruth Built," which had stood just across the street. The new Yankees Stadium, designed with the same dimensions as the previous field, held room for just over 52,000 spectators, included greater amenities, and cost more than $2.3 billion. While only two AL teams enjoyed new digs, many NL teams welcomed new facilities. The San Francisco Giants moved from the old Candlestick Park to another stadium located along the bay, AT&T Park (originally known as Pacific Bell Park, and then SBC Park until 2006), which held just under 42,000 spectators. The opening series was not auspicious as the Giants were swept by rival Los Angeles Dodgers. Also opening in 2000 was the home of the Houston Astros, which underwent several name changes as sponsorship naming rights changed. Originally known as The Ballpark at Union Station, by the end of the decade it was called Minute Maid Park (or, in fun, "The Juice

Box"). The first regular-season game was played on 7 April 2000 before a capacity crowd of nearly 42,000 fans, who saw the Astros lose to the Philadelphia Phillies. In 2001 two more teams moved to new homes. The Milwaukee Brewers left Milwaukee County Stadium to start play in Miller Park, which was named by the Miller Brewing Company. Around 42,000 fans could fill the $400 million structure, which featured a fan-shaped retractable roof. The Brewers defeated the Cincinnati Reds on opening day, 6 April 2001. Three days later the Pittsburgh Pirates opened the regular season at their new ballpark, PNC (PNC Financial Services) Park, by losing to the Reds. Nearly 39,000 fans could be seated in this traditionally styled building that featured a riverside concourse and replaced Three Rivers Stadium. In 2003 the Reds got their own new home, the Great American Ball Park, which replaced Riverfront Stadium. The Pittsburgh Pirates returned the opening day favors, by playing in the first official game on 31 March 2003. Two new parks opened in 2004. The San Diego Padres opened play against the San Francisco Giants on 8 April 2004 in the steel and sandstone PETCO Park (replacing Qualcomm Stadium), with room for approximately 42,000 people. Four days later the Philadelphia Phillies opened play at Citizens Bank Park against the Reds. Capable of handling nearly 44,000 fans, the new facility replaced Veterans Stadium, which was demolished. On 10 April 2006 the St. Louis Cardinals hosted the Brewers in their new home, the third Busch Stadium, which could hold approximately 44,000 fans. In 2008 the Washington Nationals (formerly Montreal Expos) moved from RFK Stadium to Nationals Park along the Anacostia River, hosting the Atlanta Braves on 30 March in their first official game (won by the Nats). The stadium, MLB's first "green" facility, could handle around 41,000 fans and featured views of the Capitol. In 2009, as their crosstown rivals, the Yankees, were moving into their new park, the New York Mets began play in Citi Field, a $900 million, nearly 42,000-seat facility located in Flushing Meadows. The first official MLB game played in the park featured the Mets against the Padres on 13 April 2009.

Asian Players. As baseball garnered more fans worldwide, Asian players, especially from Japan, began to join MLB teams. Foreign-born players had been commonplace in the major leagues for decades—especially from the Dominican Republic, Cuba, Canada, and several Latin American countries—but now teams also looked for stars across the Pacific. Although there had been some Japanese players as early as the 1960s, a new wave of players began entering the league in the 1990s. Probably the best-known early player was pitcher Hideo Nomo, who played eight years with the Los Angeles Dodgers, ending his MLB career in 2008 with the Kansas City Royals. Other Japanese players who began their careers in the late 1990s and played into the 2000s were pitchers Mac Suzuki, Shigetoshi Hasegawa, Hideki Irabu, Masato Yoshii, Masao Kida, and Tomokazu Ohka. The most successful Japanese player of the decade was outfielder Ichiro Suzuki, who began his

MLB career on 2 April 2001, and that year was named both the AL Rookie of the Year and the MVP. A fan favorite, Suzuki hit .333 for the decade and was a Gold Glover and an All Star each year for the Seattle Mariners. The second-most notable Japanese player in the league during the decade was outfielder and designated hitter Hideki Matsui, who played for the New York Yankees. He was a two-time All Star and was voted MVP of the 2009 World Series. Pitcher Kazuhiro Sasaki, who also played for the Mariners, won the AL Rookie of the Year in 2000. By the end of the decade there were approximately ten Japanese players on MLB squads, with more playing the minor leagues waiting their chance to be called up. The first Korean player was pitcher Chan Ho Park, who joined the Dodgers in 1994 and played with seven teams during the 2000s. Eight other South Koreans played with MLB squads during the decade. The first Taiwanese player on an MLB team was left fielder Chin-Feng Chen, who joined the Dodgers on 14 September 2002. In 2002 the Mariners signed Chinese pitcher Wang Chao, and the New York Yankees added two Chinese players to the minor-league roster in 2007. The first native Filipino to play in MLB was relief pitcher Bobby Chouinard, who broke into the major leagues in 1996 and played for the Colorado Rockies in 2000 and 2001.

Transitions. As teams left old stadiums for new ball parks, many enduring stars retired from the game. Some of the biggest names who ended their careers during the decade included Hall of Fame (HOF) second baseman Roberto Alomar; six-time All Star catcher Sandy Alomar Jr.; six-time All Star outfielder Moises Alou; four-time All Star and league MVP first baseman Jeff Bagwell; six-time All Star outfielder/designated hitter Harold Baines; four-time All Star outfielder Dante Bichette; seven-time All Star and four-time Gold Glove catcher/second baseman Craig Biggio; fourteen-time All Star, seven-time NL MVP, and all-time home-run king Barry Bonds; six-time All Star third baseman Bobby Bonilla; six-time All Star pitcher Kevin Brown; six-time All Star slugger Jose Canseco; six-time All Star and NLCS MVP first baseman Will Clark; eleven-time All Star, seven-time Cy Young awardee, and AL MVP pitcher Roger Clemens; Cy Young pitcher Bartolo Colon; five-time All Star, five-time World Series champion, and Cy Young pitcher David Cone; outfielder Eric Davis; five-time All Star pitcher Chuck Finley; four-time All Star pitcher John Franco; five-time All Star third baseman Travis Fryman; three-time All Star pitcher Eric Gagne; five-time All Star first baseman Andres Galarraga; six-time All Star and AL Rookie of the Year shortstop Nomar Garciaparra; ten-time All Star and two-time Cy Young pitcher Tom Glavine; fifteen-time All Star outfielder Tony Gwynn; ten-time All Star, HOF left fielder, and record-setting base stealer Rickey Henderson; three-time All Star, Cy Young winner, and World Series MVP pitcher Orel Hershiser; three-time All Star and ACLS MVP right fielder David Justice; five-time All Star and NL MVP second baseman Jeff Kent; twelve-time All Star and

NL MVP shortstop Barry Larkin; six-time All Star out-fielder Kenny Lofton; eight-time All Star and four-time Cy Young pitcher Greg Maddux; five-time All Star Fred McGriff; five-time All Star pitcher Mike Mussina; five-time All Star Paul O'Neill; four-time All Star Rafael Palmeiro; seven-time All Star Tim Raines; nineteen-time All Star, two-time AL MVP, HOF shortstop Cal "Iron Man" Ripken Jr. (holds the record for most consecutively played games at 2,632); five-time All Star catcher Benito Santiago; four-time All Star Ruben Sierra; seven-time All Star and NL MVP slugger Sammy Sosa; five-time All Star and two-time AL MVP designated hitter Frank Thomas; and three-time All Star and AL MVP first baseman Mo Vaughn.

Sources:

baseball-almanac.com;

baseball-reference.com;

Jose Canseco, *Juiced: Wild Times, Rampant 'Roids, Smash Hits, and How Baseball Got Big* (New York: Regan Books, 2005);

Mark Fainaru-Wada and Lance Williams, *Game of Shadows: Barry Bonds, BALCO, and the Steroids Scandal That Rocked Professional Sports* (New York: Gotham, 2006);

Mark Gonzales, "Mark Buehrle Throws a Perfect Game," *Chicago Tribune,* 23 July 2009;

Lisa Lamber, "Washington DC home to first 'green' stadium in U.S.," *reuters.com* (28 March 2008);

George J. Mitchell, "Report to the Commissioner of Baseball of an Independent Investigation into the Illegal Use of Steroids and Other Performance Enhancing Substances by Players in Major League Baseball," Office of the Commissioner of Baseball (13 December 2007);

Roger G. Noll, "The Economics of Baseball Contraction," *Journal of Sports Economics,* 4 (November 2003): 367–388;

"Randy Johnson, 40, Hurls Perfect Game," *New York Times,* 19 May 2004;

Dan Shaughnessy, "YES!! Red Sox complete sweep, win first series since 1918," *Boston Globe,* 28 October 2004.

BASKETBALL: COLLEGE

March Madness. Every March college basketball fans became students of "bracketology," poring over statistics in order to select the winners among teams in the National Collegiate Athletic Association (NCAA) Division I National Championship basketball tournament. In 2001 the tournament field was raised to sixty-five teams, to include a play-in game (allowing an additional team to earn a slot), from the former sixty-four. Nearly every game was televised nationwide, viewing figures were strong, and fans often hoped for the emergence of a "Cinderella" team to defeat one of the national powerhouses. The amount of money people spent gambling on the event (approximately $50 billion) was second only to that exchanged on wagers for the Super Bowl. CBS Sports (which had paid $6 billion for the broadcast rights) controlled the tournament television package until the end of the decade, but the NCAA was looking to change the contract to allow bids from major cable companies, with the expectation that a new arrangement would top $10 billion. Some critics complained that the vast amount earned by the tournament was not benefiting student athletes, just the NCAA and mem-

ber schools. Other voices called for greater expansion of the tournament field to ninety-six teams (those presently left out of the "Big Dance" often received a chance to play in the National Invitational Tournament [NIT]). The single-elimination format ratcheted up fan interest, as squads from basketball's dominant schools often (but not always) eliminated their lesser opponents, resulting in a "Sweet Sixteen" and "Elite Eight" that was capped with the "Final Four" playoff. Still, despite conflicts over distribution of the financial rewards or how many teams were included, the tournament boiled down to school pride and basketball enthusiasm. Television viewership during the decade for the final game ranged from a Nielsen rating of between 17.09 and 23.90 (often double its closest competitor), although overall viewership dropped from the previous decade. Nevertheless, millions also opted to catch the games using new technologies, such as viewing on televised delay, computer (video streaming), and handheld devices to follow their favorite teams.

Gator Chomp. Probably the best team during the decade was the two-time national champion University of Florida Gators, who won back-to-back NCAA tournaments (2006–2007). Representing the Southeastern Conference (SEC), the team was led by dynamic coach Billy Donovan (who had been hired in 1996) and featured an experienced group of players (including Corey Brewer, Al Horford, Lee Humphrey, Joakim Noah, and Taureen Green), many of whom decided to put off going professional early to play together an additional year. On 3 April 2006 the team won the school's first national championship in basketball by defeating the UCLA Bruins (Pacific Ten) in Indianapolis. The following year, in the Georgia Dome in Atlanta, the Gators defeated the Ohio State Buckeyes (Big Ten). The school experienced additional successes during the decade as well. The Gators won (or shared) regular season SEC titles three times and won the SEC tournament three times (2005–2007). Gator squads reached the NCAA tournament eight times (2000–2007). In 2000 they reached the final game in the NCAA tournament, losing to the Michigan State Spartans.

Tar Heel Blue. The other two-time national championship school was the University of North Carolina. The Tar Heels squads took the top prize in 2005 and 2009 (as well as earning final-four finishes in 2000 and 2008). A traditional basketball powerhouse in the Atlantic Coast Conference (ACC), the Tar Heels won five regular-season conference titles (though only two conference tournament titles). Led by coach Roy Williams (who left Kansas and took over the team in 2003) and filled with outstanding players such as Raymond Felton, Sean May, and Rashad McCants, the Tar Heels defeated the University of Illinois Fighting Illini 75–70 in St. Louis for the 2005 title, shutting out their opponent for the final two minutes of the game. The following year Williams recruited standout forward Tyler Hansbrough, who helped the team win league championships in 2007 and 2008, becoming the ACC's all-time leading scorer (2,872) and four-time unanimous selection to the ACC All-Conference team. On 6 April 2009 Hansbrough led his team (with such stars as Wayne Ellington and Ty Lawson) to the national title at Ford Field (Detroit) against the Michigan State Spartans 89–72. Nearly 73,000 fans attended the game. The ACC was well represented among the national champions during the decade. Other NCAA tournament winners included the Duke Blue Devils (2001) and Maryland Terrapins (2002), with final four appearances by four other teams.

Cinderella Teams. One of the most exciting aspects of the NCAA championship tournament is the opportunity of teams from lesser conferences to play, and possibly defeat, teams from the better-known, dominant conferences. On 27 March 2006 the eleventh-seeded George Mason Patriots of the Colonial Athletic Association defeated the number-one seeded Connecticut Huskies of the Big East Conference 86–84 (having already beaten the ACC's North Carolina and the Big Ten's Michigan State), to earn their first-ever spot in the final game, which they lost to the Florida Gators. Other notable tournament surprises included the Southern Conference's Davidson College Wildcats, lead by star Stephen Curry, defeating the Big Ten's Wisconsin Badgers and the Big East's Georgetown Hoyas in 2008; the Patriot League's Bucknell University Bison knocking off the Big Twelve's Kansas Jayhawks in 2005; and the American East Conference's Vermont Catamounts taking down the Big East's Syracuse Orangemen in 2005.

Great Players. Although it is difficult to declare one player out of the thousands of college athletes as the single best, some individuals stood out during the decade. In addition to Hansbrough, a trio of Duke Blue Devils (ACC) were usually mentioned among the best college basketball players during the decade. In 2001 small forward Shane Battier displayed tough defensive talent and helped lead the Blue Devils to two national championship games, winning the title in 2001. Point guard Jason "Jay" Williams played at Duke from 1999 to 2002, earning ACC Rookie of the Year honors and teaming with Battier to win the national title, and he was honored in 2002 with both the leading national basketball awards (Naismith and Wooden). The third recognized talent during this period was guard Jonathan "J. J." Redick, who played from 2002 until 2006. As usual, Duke was loaded with other great players as well, including center Carlos Boozer, guard Chris Duhon, guard/forward Mike Dunleavy Jr., guard Dahntay Jones, forward Josh McRoberts, and forward Sheldon Williams. Rivaling the Duke players for national attention was Oklahoma Sooners (Big Twelve) forward Blake Griffin (2007–2009), who led the league in scoring and rebounding. He played only two seasons, leaving early for an NBA career. Another dominating presence in the Big Twelve was Texas Longhorn forward Kevin Durant, who played for one season (2006–2007) and won national most-valuable honors. Other notable players during the decade included Syracuse forward Carmelo Anthony, Davidson guard Stephen Curry, Maryland guard Juan Dixon, Texas guard T. J.

A George Mason Patriots Final Four 2006 Championship ring commemorating the men's team's 27 March 2006 win over the Connecticut Huskies (<www.georgemasonbasketball.blogspot.com>)

Ford, Gonzaga forward Adam Morrison, St. Joseph's guard Jameer Nelson, Ohio State center Greg Oden, and Marquette guard Dwyane Wade.

Off-Court Scandals. Several notable scandals stained the reputation of college basketball in the decade. In 2003 the Baylor Bears basketball team was wracked by the murder of forward Patrick Dennehy by his roommate and former teammate Carlton Dotson, who was eventually sentenced to thirty-five years in prison for the crime. The tragedy apparently unfolded when the two friends had gone target shooting together. Six weeks after Dennehy's disappearance in June, his body, shot twice in the head, was found in a field near Waco, Texas. The resulting investigation uncovered a host of NCAA violations and institutional lack of control, including allegations of drug abuse and dealing, improper recruiting, illegal payments, and other misdeeds. Athletics director Tom Stanton and head coach Dave Bliss were forced to resign; sanctions and probations were levied against the program by the school administration and the NCAA. In April 2009 Louisville head coach Rick Pitino (best known for his long-time position as head coach of the Kentucky Wildcats and a short stint with the NBA Boston Celtics) was embroiled in a scandal in which he was accused of having raped a woman at a restaurant in 2003. Pitino, married and the father of five children, claimed that the sex was consensual, that he had paid for an abortion, and that he was being blackmailed. The woman was indicted and later convicted for extortion. Recruiting violations cost coach Tim Floyd at the University of Southern California his job; the University of Memphis Tigers had to vacate a NCAA tournament final appearance; and many other schools were investigated for alleged illegal payments and recruiting violations.

Women. Interest in and support of women's basketball increased during the decade. The dominant team was the Connecticut Huskies (Big East), who won five NCAA

TOP TEN NCAA MEN'S AND WOMEN'S BASKETBALL AVERAGE HOME GAME ATTENDANCE FIGURES

Men's		Women's	
Kentucky	22,554	Tennessee	13,999
North Carolina	20,497	Connecticut	10,514
Syracuse	20,345	Iowa State	9,754
Tennessee	20,267	Oklahoma	9,007
Louisville	19,481	Purdue	8,971
Maryland	17,950	Texas Tech	8,576
Wisconsin	17,190	Maryland	8,218
Arkansas	17,148	New Mexico	7,420
Indiana	16,876	Notre Dame	7,168
Memphis	16,748	Louisville	6,879

Source: "2008–09 NCAA Men's Basketball Records: Division 1 Attendance Records," *ncaa.org* (October 2009).

Source: "2009 NCAA Women's Basketball Weekly Attendance," *ncaa.org* (21 April 2009).

titles, twice enjoying undefeated seasons. Led by coach Geno Auriemma, the team featured three Naismith Award winners—Sue Bird, Diana Taurasi (twice), and Maya Moore—and often dominated their rivals in title games: 71–52 vs. Tennessee (2000); 82–70 vs. Oklahoma (2002); 73–68 vs. Tennessee (2003); 70–61 vs. Tennessee (2004); and 76–54 vs. Louisville (2009). Rivaling the Huskies were the Tennessee Volunteers (SEC), who had dominated the 1990s and won back-to-back championships (2007 and 2008). Led by Pat Summitt, the top winning coach in college basketball, the Volunteers, who had never missed earning a berth in the NCAA tournament, benefited from the special talents of Candace Parker (who could play every position). Other strong squads represented Baylor, Duke, Louisiana State, Louisiana Tech, Maryland, Stanford, and Texas. Beginning in 2007 many teams actively supported breast-cancer awareness through annual participation in the Pink Zone initiative promoted by the Women's Basketball Coaches Association (WBCA), playing in pink uniforms and wearing pink shoelaces and ribbons, helping to raise millions of dollars for research. The catalyst for the Pink Zone was Kate Yow, long-time Hall of Fame coach of the North Carolina State Wolfpack, who fought the disease for many years before finally succumbing to cancer in 2009. The women's game suffered additional shocks. On 4 April 2007, after Tennessee had downed the Rutgers Scarlet Knights in the NCAA women's tournament, radio jock Don Imus called the Rutgers players "nappy-headed hos" on air, embarrassing the women and sparking a storm of protest. CBS cancelled Imus's show eight days later, although he later gained a new spot on the FOX Business channel. Rumors of inappropriate behavior between a coach and player also raised eyebrows as LSU coach Dana "Pokey" Chatman, who led her team to three final fours in the NCAA tournament, resigned from the team in March

2007. She sued for wrongful termination (and won a settlement) and later coached in Russia and for the WNBA.

Sources:

Seth Davis, "Growing List of Scandals Have Ruined College Hoops Off-season," *si.com* (21 August 2009);

"Dotson Sentenced to 35 Years in Dennehy Murder Case," *usatoday.com* (15 June 2005);

Bill Gorman, "Will Butler Prove a Cinderella for NCAA Finals Ratings Too?" *TV by the Numbers* (5 April 2010);

Sean Gregory, "NCAA Mulls Expanding March Madness. Are They Mad?" *Time* (18 March 2010);

Elizabeth Merrill, "Chatman Mystery Continues as LSU Rolls into Cleveland," *espn.com* (31 March 2007);

naismithawards.com;

"NCAA Tournament History," *cbssports.com;*

"Pitino Says He Paid for Abortion," *espn.com* (12 August 2009);

Matt Richards, "More Bliss Violations Uncovered," The Lariat Online, *baylor.edu* (27 February 2004);

Matt Shetler, "March Madness: The 25 Biggest Upsets in the Past 10 Years," *bleacherreport.com* (13 March 2011);

"Will NCAA Opt out of March Madness Contract with CBS?" *thesportsbizblog* (17 March 2009).

BASKETBALL: PROFESSIONAL

Battle of the Titans. The Los Angeles Lakers dominated the 2000s, in large part due to two of the greatest players in basketball history: guard Kobe Bryant and center Shaquille "Shaq" O'Neal. Although the pair led their team to three consecutive NBA Championships (2000–2002), there was rumored animosity between the two men. O'Neal publicly criticized Bryant for being too selfish on the court and indicated that he needed to scale down his play. They seemed to reconcile in the early 2000s, but by the end of the 2002–2003 season, their animosity was heated and, once again, public. O'Neal omitted Bryant several times when talking to reporters about team members he was excited to play with, while Bryant openly questioned O'Neal's leadership. Many analysts believed this tension was one impetus behind O'Neal's trade in 2004 to the Miami Heat. In his first few years with the Heat, O'Neal rarely acknowledged Bryant and the feud continued; however, by mid decade the two seemed to have reconciled, and Shaq famously argued that Kobe should win MVP in 2007. Between them, these giants won six championships and five MVPs, and both appeared on the NBA All Star team throughout the decade.

Dominating Force. The Los Angeles Lakers were the most successful team of the decade as well as the most glamorous, as their star players drew Hollywood fans and regular sell-out crowds. In 1999 the team hired as their head coach Phil Jackson, who had previously won six championships with the Chicago Bulls. Jackson coached the squad during the entire decade, except for taking the 2004–2005 season off, the only year the Lakers did not make the playoffs. In the first half of the decade the team appeared in four NBA championship series (2000–2002 and 2004), winning the title back-to-back-to-back in 2000, 2001, and 2002. During this championship run, Bryant and O'Neal were aided by players such as forward A. C. Green and guards Ron Harper and Dereck Harper. In 2003–2004 season two perennial all-star players, center Karl Malone and guard Gary Payton, joined the team, but injuries marred the season and the Lakers lost in the finals to the Detroit Pistons. The Lakers became Kobe Bryant's team after O'Neal was traded to the Miami Heat in July 2004. After he returned as coach for the 2005–2006 season, Jackson began to build the team around his star player. With support from forward Lamar Odom, guard Derek Fisher, and Spanish forward Pau Gasol, the Lakers soon began to contend for the title again, returning to the finals in 2008 and winning their fourth championship of the decade in 2009 by defeating the Orlando Magic. Bryant was an All Star every year of the decade and MVP in 2008. A stellar defensive player, he was also twice the league scoring leader (2006 and 2007) and MVP of the 2009 finals.

Spurs. The other dominant team during the decade was the San Antonio Spurs, which won NBA titles in 2003, 2005, and 2007 under the guidance of head coach Gregg Popovich. The Spurs won the 2003 championship in six games over the New Jersey Nets. But with the retirement of its star center David Robinson (named a Hall of Famer in 2009), as well as teammates guard Steve Kerr and forward Danny Ferry leaving, the team looked to its emerging young center (drafted in 1997 from Wake Forest) Tim Duncan to carry much of the load. He responded by being named an All Star every year of the decade and MVP of the league in 2002 and 2003, and he often dominated opponents in the paint. To support their star, the management brought in guards William "Tony" Parker (drafted in 2001) and Manu Ginobli (an Argentine star), as well as forward Robert Horry. In 2005 they returned to championship form in a thrilling seven-game series against the defending champion Detroit Pistons, with Duncan earning MVP honors. Two years later they benefited from the playoff collapse of their rivals, the Dallas Mavericks, and then swept the Cleveland Cavaliers and their star LeBron James in the finals.

King James. In the 2003 NBA draft the Cleveland Cavaliers, one of the least successful franchises in NBA history, having begun play in 1970 and subsequently never winning a championship, selected a seventeen-year-old high-school phenom, forward/guard LeBron James, as the number one pick. He quickly rewarded their faith in him by earning Rookie of the Year honors and becoming one of the most recognizable and marketable stars in the league. Some touted him as the next Michael Jordan. Despite sterling performances from James, the team failed to make the playoffs and hired a new coach in Mike Brown. The Cavaliers made the playoffs in 2006, earned an Eastern Conference crown in 2007, and faced the San Antonio Spurs in Cleveland's first basketball championship series (although they lost in a disappointing four-game sweep). James continued to play at a high level, becoming the league scoring champ (2008), NBA First Team All Star (2006, 2008, and 2009), and two-time MVP of the annual NBA All Star game. Like Jordan, he endorsed shoes by Nike, as well as the products of many companies, becoming one of the most successful salesmen in the league.

Chinese Star. Although many important players in the NBA hailed from foreign countries, probably the best known was the giant center (7'6") Yao Ming of China. Drafted by the Houston Rockets with the first overall pick in 2002, Yao adapted quickly to the American game and placed second in Rookie of the Year balloting. He earned All Star honors from 2003 to 2009. Even as his point production and rebounding numbers improved, Yao began to suffer from nagging injuries that curtailed his playing time, as well as broken bones that sidelined him for long stretches. Not only was Yao a fan favorite in the United States, but his participation as well as that of other Chinese players made the NBA game marketable to the largest population in the world.

Gambling Referees. In August 2007 veteran NBA referee Tim Donaghy admitted that he had been gambling on league games—reportedly including games in which he officiated—as well as selling information to professional gamblers. Federal Bureau of Investigation agents tracked hundreds of cell-phone calls from Donaghy to known gamblers and their associates. He was given a fifteen-month federal jail sentence. Allegations that other referees may also have been participating in gambling schemes and fixing games also surfaced, but the NBA discovered only minor infractions.

Dream Team. Since 1989 professional basketball players have participated in the Summer Olympics on a squad commonly called the "Dream Team," reflecting the predominance of American players in the sport. Initially, superstar players jockeyed for positions on the team, but in the 2000s fewer big names chose to participate. Coached

Houston Rockets center Yao Ming dwarfing the team's trainer before a game against the Minnesota Timberwolves (AP Photo/Dave Einsel)

tured such talents as James, Anthony, Boozer, Kobe Bryant, Chris Paul, and Dwayne Wade. Again dominant, the United States won the gold-medal game over Spain 118–107.

Women. The Women's National Basketball League, which began in 1997 with eight teams, grew in popularity in the decade and expanded to twelve teams. While it often struggled financially, the league in 2008 garnered its highest television ratings ever, took in 35 percent more website visits than the previous year, and increased attendance, including more than doubling the number of sell-out games. In 2008 Candace Parker, a former University of Tennessee Lady Volunteer, joined the league and became only the second woman ever, after Lisa Leslie, to dunk a ball during a WNBA game; sales of merchandise increased as well, and Parker's jerseys became a number-one seller. In addition to Parker and Leslie, many players in the league gained recognition and fan support, including Seimone Augustus, Sue Bird, Tamika Catchings, Chamique Holdsclaw, Lauren Jackson, Sheryl Swoopes, and Diana Taurasi. Early in the decade the league was dominated by the Los Angeles Sparks, but the Detroit Shock and Phoenix Mercury were multiple-championship squads in the latter years.

Minor Leagues. In 1999 the American Basketball Association (ABA—not to be confused with the league of the same name that existed from 1967 to 1976) was founded by Joe Newman and Dick Tinkham and began minor basketball league with predominantly American teams in smaller cities. With low franchise fees and operation costs, the ABA garnered enough interest to usually have several new teams added each year. However, low attendance and advertising revenue resulted in several franchises folding each year as well. Although the ABA touted itself as the fastest-growing basketball league, the NBA Developmental League (D-League) was the official minor league. In 2001 the D-League launched its first season with eight teams and grew to a total of sixteen teams. Closer to professional style and rules than the ABA, D-League games were televised on the NBA TV and Versus networks. Players in the D-League were mostly returning and newly drafted players, who gained experience before being "called up." D-League teams typically carried a few players who remained listed on NBA teams' rosters.

Sources:
abalive.com;

Conner Ennis, "Athlete Bio: LeBron James," *New York Times,* 23 July 2008;

"Ex-NBA Ref Pleads Guilty in Betting Scandal," *cnn.com* (16 August 2007);

Lester Munson, "Donaghy's Guilty Pleas Don't Answer All the Questions," *espn.com* (15 August 2007);

nba.com;

usabasketball.com;

wnba.com;

"Women's Basketball Sees Higher Attendance, TV Ratings," *reuters.com* (16 September 2008).

by Rudy Tomjanovich, the squad included some established stars, nonetheless, including centers Kevin Garnett and Alonzo Mourning; guards Vince Carter, Jason Kidd, Gary Payton, and Tim Hardaway; and forwards Antonio McDyess and Vin Baker. The 2000 team that played in Australia did not dominate other squads as had its predecessors, barely defeating a strong Lithuanian team and gaining the gold medal in a close game with France, 85–75. In the 2004 Olympics in Athens, the Dream Team failed to live up to its name. Despite some big-name talent on the squad—including Tim Duncan, LeBron James, Carmelo Anthony, Lamar Odom, Allen Iverson, and Carlos Boozer—they made a poor showing, losing an early round match and being eliminated by Argentina. They did manage to secure the bronze medal against Lithuania, but this result was small consolation for American fans. Determined to return to prominence at the 2008 games held in China, the United States assembled a strong team that fea-

BUSINESS OF SPORTS

New Ways to View. The turn of the century ushered in a new digital component to sports media. With the rise of digital cable as well as the increase in high-definition programming and introduction of the digital video recorder (DVR), people began to consume sports in a more advanced manner. The ability to watch sports on a crystal-clear screen, as well as to record and fast forward through commercials, contributed to a greater demand for sports programming. More channels were dedicated solely to sports. Longtime industry leader ESPN and its family of networks offered new channels and high definition through ESPNHD, ESPN2HD, ESPNNewsHD, ESPNU, and an internet network called ESPN360.com. Competition was fierce and new sports networks and packages, some dedicated to a single sport or region, were available at increasingly higher prices. The NHL Network, NFL Network, and MLB Network are just a few examples, while the Big Ten Network and SportSouth were dedicated to a specific conference or region. Additionally, cable carriers registered increased demand for out-of-market sports packages such as MLB Extra Innings, NBA League Pass, and NHL Center Ice, which allowed viewers to watch games not broadcast in their area. Many networks were owned in part by the leagues and cable providers such as Comcast, Time Warner, and DIRECTTV.

Blackouts. The availability and quality of sports programming at home, especially in the case of highly produced professional football broadcasts, affected the attendance at games, especially in the latter years of the decade when the country was in an economic recession. While television ratings for games continued to reach all time highs, attendance for the league declined from 17.3 million in 2007 to 16.7 million in 2009. More and more Americans were apparently choosing to watch NFL games at home rather than pay high prices for tickets, concessions, parking, and travel. NFL commissioner Roger Goodell said that "the issue for us is we are our own competitor." The NFL's blackout rule—the practice of withholding local television coverage in markets where home games do not sell out—was invoked for only 4 percent of NFL games in 2008, down from 14 percent in 2000 and 39 percent in 1990, but league planners at the end of the decade were beginning to fear that blackouts may begin to rise again. With no plans to change their blackout rule, the NFL faced the challenge of making the experience of actually going to the stadiums to watch the games worthwhile for its fans.

Variable Pricing. Fans who bought tickets found that not all games cost them the same amount of money. In the 2000s there was a rise in "variable pricing" to sporting events, and the value of games was based on several factors. If a team was playing an important rival, ticket prices were likely to be higher. The same was true if the home team was playing a highly ranked or respected team or the opponent featured superstar athletes. Variable pricing was increasingly popularized during the Barry Bonds era, when

TOP EARNERS

In 2009 *Forbes* released its annual list of top-earning athletes of the year, and it is no surprise that Tiger Woods topped the list. Listed below are the highest-paid American athletes at the end of the decade, along with their earnings for 2009.

1. Tiger Woods, golfer. Earnings: $110 million in prize money and endorsements.

2. Kobe Bryant (tie), basketball player. Earnings: $45 million in salary from the Lakers and endorsements.

3. Michael Jordan (tie), retired basketball player. Earnings: $45 million in endorsements and brand sales.

4. LeBron James (tie), basketball player. Earnings: $40 million in salary from the Cavaliers and endorsements.

5. Phil Mickelson (tie), golfer. Earnings: $40 million in prize money and endorsements.

6. Dale Earnhardt Jr., race car driver. Earnings: $34 million in prize money, endorsements, and merchandise sales.

7. Shaquille O'Neal, basketball player. Earnings: $33 million in salary from the Phoenix Suns and endorsements.

8. Oscar De La Hoya (tie), boxer. Earnings: $32 million in prize money and endorsements.

9. Alex Rodriguez (tie), baseball player. Earnings: $32 million in salary from the New York Yankees and endorsements.

10. Kevin Garnett (tie), basketball player. Earnings: $30 million in salary from the Boston Celtics and endorsements.

11. Jeff Gordon (tie), race car driver. Earnings: $30 million in prize money and endorsements.

12. Derek Jeter (tie), baseball player. Earnings: $30 million in salary from the New York Yankees and endorsements.

Source: Kurt Bodenhausen, "The World's Highest-Paid Athletes," *Forbes* (17 June 2009).

baseball teams realized they could charge more for tickets when playing the San Francisco Giants.

Fantasy. While some fans were disinclined to attend actual games because of high costs, they were increasingly willing to spend money in other areas. Fantasy sports—games in which participants use statistics to build their own teams and compete against other "owners"—grew into nearly a $1 billion-a-year industry with an estimated 26 million Americans playing in various contrived leagues. The rise in Internet availability had probably the largest impact on fantasy sports, with several major Internet sites offering free fantasy-league management. These sites often managed individual teams for the "owners," allowing inexperienced players to join and learn as they participated. Fantasy sports were also partially responsible for the rise in sports-programming ratings, since participants watched games to evaluate the performance of their players.

Big Business. Sports in America was big business, with billion-dollar franchises, stadiums worth hundreds of millions, small towns that became sizeable cities with the influx of fans for games, impressive salaries, and labor-ownership squabbles to rival those of giant corporations and industries. The teams of the National Football League were worth a combined $33.3 billion in 2009, with the Washington Redskins being assessed as the most valuable franchise. The MLB New York Yankees were worth more than $1 billion; the NBA New York Knicks were allegedly worth more than $600 million; and NASCAR's Hendricks Motor Sports was worth more than $350 million. According to *Forbes*, some of the wealthiest Americans were athletes, including Tiger Woods (golf), Phil Mickelson (golf), LeBron James (basketball), Floyd Mayweather Jr. (boxing), Kobe Bryant (basketball), Shaquille O'Neal (basketball), Kevin Garnett (basketball), Peyton Manning (football), Alex Rodriguez (baseball), and Derek Jeter (baseball), although they were well behind owners of teams, such as George Steinbrenner, Mark Cuban, Ted Turner, and Jerry Jones. Although there was much disagreement about the social and economic impact of sports on communities—especially the question of how much communities should do to support a sports franchise—there was no denying that millions of dollars were spent by fans on travel, food, and lodging.

Sources:

Kurt Bodenhausen, "The World's Highest-Paid Athletes," *Forbes* (17 June 2009);

Eric Fisher and John Ourand, "Fitting the Pieces of the MLB Network," *Sports Business Journal/ Daily* (31 March 2008);

Jonah Freedman, "Ranking the 50 Highest-earning Athletes in the U.S.," *SI.com* (2009);

Tim Keown, "Time to Black Out the NFL's Blackout?" *espn.go.com* (25 August 2009);

Mark A. Maske, "With television ratings on the rise and attendance flagging, NFL faces a business dilemma," *Washington Post*, 19 September 2010;

Joseph Pluta, "Some Recent Experiments in Creative Pricing Strategies," *Perspectives in Business* (September 2006): 33–38;

Tom Van Riper, "The Most Valuable Teams in Sports," *forbes.com* (13 January 2009).

FIGHTING

Declining Popularity. Boxing suffered declining attendance and television viewers in the United States throughout the decade. At the end of the twentieth century, figures such as Muhammad Ali, Sugar Ray Leonard, and Mike Tyson were celebrities and significant public figures as well as boxing legends, but in the 2000s no American boxer has been able to capture the public imagination to such an extent. Other possible causes for the decline in interest in boxing were the lower number of events staged and promoted and the inability of fans to watch the top fights without having to pay pay-per-view fees. Whatever the causes, boxing experienced a downturn that aficionados feared vitally undercut the general appeal of the sport.

Leaders. While the most celebrated boxer of the new century was Filipino native Manny Pacquiao, several Americans did excel and excited fans of the sport. One star was welterweight Floyd Mayweather Jr., a skilled fighter who won nine different titles in five weight classes and who remained undefeated through the decade with a record of 40–0, including 25 knockouts. Although he defeated leading competitors, such as Oscar De La Hoya and "Sugar" Shane Mosley, he had yet to meet Pacquiao by decade's end. Another leader in the sport was Undisputed World Middleweight Champion Bernard Hopkins, who went 14–3 in the decade. The U.S. ranks had other top-rated and promising fighters, including such talents as light welterweight Devon Alexander, Haitian American welterweight Andre Berto, light welterweight Timothy Bradley, and middleweight Andre Ward. Whereas Americans once dominated the heavyweight ranks, the lack of a champion in this class has hurt domestic interest in the sport; however, a few new fighters have started to emerge, including Chris Arreola, Eddie Chambers, Seth Mitchell, Tony Thompson, and Deontay Wilder.

Scandal in the Ring. One of the biggest scandals stemmed from a 25 January 2009 bout between Shane Mosley and Antonio Margarito, who was coming off of a victory over Miguel Cotto in 2008. Before the match Margarito was forced to rewrap because someone from Mosley's camp had noticed a white powder on his hands. After Mosley went on to defeat Margarito, the substance was tested and found to be a combination of sulfur and calcium, which can turn to a hardened plaster when mixed with oxygen. Margarito and his trainer were suspended, but many critics then called into question the legitimacy of his victory over Cotto by knockout, believing he was unfairly defeated.

MMA. Mixed Martial Arts (MMA) or "full combat" fighting—in which combatants employ techniques from boxing, wrestling, martial arts, and street fighting to outpoint or knock out their opponents using strikes, kicks, and submission holds—took important steps toward becoming a mainstream sport as well as a popular spectacle in the decade. Promoters corralled the undisciplined chaos that represented early "cage" fighting or "bad man" contests by introducing new rules and eliminating dangerous strikes in order to protect fighters who were no longer capable

Floyd Mayweather Jr., left, and Oscar De La Hoya during their super welterweight world championship boxing match on 5 May 2007 (AP Photo/Kevork Djansezian)

of defending themselves. Still, the intensity of the contests was encouraged by financial incentives or bonuses based on the best fight, knockout, and submission of the night. The excitement led to growing audiences, both in person and through pay-per-view or commercial television (as well as DVDs), as fans followed their favorite fighters. MMA-related merchandise, marketed by companies such as Tapout, became popular with young men. Leading fighters began to be sought out for commercial endorsements and outside venues. Ferocious fan-favorite Chuck "The Iceman" Liddell parlayed his fighting career into an appearance on the popular reality show *Dancing With the Stars,* while others including Quinton "Rampage" Jackson were given parts in movies. MMA was dominated by the UFC, founded in the 1990s, although there were rival organizations, such as World Extreme Cage fighting (WEC), Strikeforce, and Bellator FC, each with a stable of recognized names. While leading competitors hailed from many countries—par-

ticularly Brazil, Japan, Canada, and the former Soviet bloc nations—many Americans thrived in the sport. In addition to Liddell and Jackson, some of the bigger names and draws were Mike Brown, Paul Buentello, Randy "The Natural" Couture, Rashad Evans, Urijah Faber, Kenny Florian, Rich Franklin, Forrest Griffin, Clay "The Carpenter" Guida, Matt Hughes, Brock Lesnar, Frank Mir, Tito Ortiz, B. J. Penn, Matt Serra, Ken Shamrock, Joe Stevenson, Tim Sylvia, and Frank Trigg. There was also growing interest in female fighters.

Sources:

"Boxing: Highlights and Lowlights," *si.com* (18 December 2009);

extremeprosports.com;

Scott Levinson, "Searching for the Next Great American Heavyweight: Ten Fighters to Keep an Eye On," *ringnews24.com* (14 February 2011);

Chris Mannix, "Another Sport, Another Cheat," *si.com* (11 February 2009);

Richard O'Brien, "2000s: Top 10 Boxers," *si.com* (18 December 2009);

ufc.com.

FOOTBALL: COLLEGE

Dominance and Controversy. The most successful team in college football for much of the first decade was the University of Southern California (USC) Trojans. Coach Pete Carroll's team dominated NCAA football with seven consecutive Pac-10 conference championship titles (2002–2008), seven straight Bowl Championship Series (BCS) bowl appearances (2002–2008), and two national titles (2003 and 2004). From 2003 through 2005, the team, led by running back Reggie Bush, won thirty-seven consecutive games and twice was recognized as the national champions—by the Associated Press after the 2003 season and by the BCS after the 2004 season. In 2005 Bush was awarded the Heisman Trophy, Walter Camp Award, and Doak Walker Award, and was named Associated Press (AP) Player of the Year. However, scandal marred the accomplishments when in 2006 USC faced allegations of NCAA violations, specifically a lack of institutional control that allowed Bush and his family to accept unsanctioned gifts during his time in college. The scandal sparked one of the most wide-reaching investigations in college football history with possible ramifications that included limited scholarships for the university and suspension from BCS postseason games. As part of the sentence for USC's NCAA violations, they forfeited their 2005 Orange Bowl victory and BCS National Championship title. Bush was found guilty of accepting bribes from the university and gave back or was stripped of all his major collegiate awards. While the Trojans were one of the marquee major programs, the best team record during the decade was held by the Boise State Broncos of the Western Athletic Conference, who won 112 games with only 17 losses.

SEC Remains on Top. Regarded by most as the toughest conference in college football, the Southeastern Conference (SEC) proved itself on the field, especially during the second half of the decade. Three SEC teams won five of ten national championship games: Louisiana State University Tigers (2003 and 2007), University of Florida Gators (2006 and 2008), and University of Alabama Crimson Tide (2009). Florida emerged as a premier program under the leadership of coach Urban Meyer and quarterback Tim Tebow, dominating the 2006 and 2008 seasons with 13–1 records, which included victories in SEC championship and national championship games. Tebow made his name as a hard-working signal caller who was both a passing and a rushing threat. After the team's only loss in 2008, Tebow held a press conference in which he promised that no one would work harder than he and his teammates from that point forward. He was true to his word as he led Florida to their second national title in three years. Tebow became the first underclassman to win the Heisman Trophy when as a sophomore he received the award in 2007. He was also nominated for the Heisman in 2008. By the time Tebow left college football for the NFL, he had a 34–6 record as a

Florida quarterback Tim Tebow screams to the crowd during the NCAA college football Southeastern Conference Championship against top-ranked Alabama, which Florida won 31–20 (AP Photo/Dave Martin).

starter and had set records in the SEC for total yards (11,699) and total touchdowns (141).

Championship Criticism. The BCS, which began in 1998, was disparaged by players, coaches, and fans for relying on a complicated system of computer formulas and polls to rank the top teams and select the participants for college football's national championship. Nearly every year some teams felt unjustly denied a spot in the championship game. In 2005, for example, the regular season ended with five undefeated teams—Auburn, Boise State, Utah, Oklahoma, and USC—with the latter two being selected by the BCS for the national championship game. After all the bowl games were played, there were still three undefeated teams: USC, which had beaten Oklahoma to claim the championship, but also Auburn and Utah, each of which felt unfairly denied a chance to compete for the prize. Such situations led most fans to call for the BCS to be replaced with a playoff system, as was employed by all other college sports.

Biggest Upsets. Nearly all the bigger college teams each year invite squads from smaller schools or lower divisions to play in one of their home games, often as an early season tune-up or as a breather during a difficult stretch of their schedule, in the expectation of earning an easy victory and giving their third- and fourth-string players the opportunity to see action. For the beating they often take, the visiting team experiences big-time college football, gains exposure for their program, and earns a hefty paycheck for their school. On 1 September 2007 business-as-usual backfired as the highly ranked University of Michigan Wolverines of the Big Ten experienced what many consider the biggest upset of the decade, if not in college football history, when they were defeated 34–32 by the Appalachian State University Mountaineers of the Southern Conference. More than 100,000 blue-and-maize-clad fans were stunned when the Mountaineers marched downfield late in the fourth quarter to take the lead with a long field goal and then blocked a potentially winning field goal by the home team. Two other big upsets also occurred during 2007. On New Year's Day in the Fiesta Bowl, the Boise State Broncos surprised the Oklahoma Sooners with grit and trick plays to claim a thrilling 43–42 overtime win, silencing critics who believed they did not belong in the BCS. On 6 October at the midpoint of the season, the Stanford Cardinal, a 41-point underdog, snapped the #2-ranked USC Trojans' home winning streak at thirty-five games with a last-minute touchdown for a 24–23 victory.

Coaches. Pete Carroll's nine seasons (2001–2009) with USC resulted in a 97–19 record (although later decreased to 83 official wins), seven consecutive Pac-10 titles, three Heisman Trophy players, and two national titles (although one was later tarnished). Urban Meyer, with a record of 56–10 in five seasons at Florida starting in 2005, became the second coach to win two BCS national championship titles. He announced that he was taking a leave of absence from coaching at the end of the 2009 season. Joe "JoePa" Paterno coached his fifty-ninth season at Penn State in 2009, marking his forty-fourth season as the team's head coach. Paterno held the record for most years as a head coach at a single Division I team and led his team to Big Ten conference championships in 2005 and 2008. Nick Saban became the first college football coach to win two national championships at different schools (2003 at LSU and 2009 at Alabama). Lou Holtz, head coach for six different universities over a period of more than thirty years, retired from the University of South Carolina in 2004. Holtz won one national title (1988 with Notre Dame) and is the only college football coach to have led six different programs to bowl appearances. Probably the most eye-raising change in the college coaching ranks was the forced retirement at the end of the 2009 season of Hall of Fame coach Bobby Bowden of the Florida State Seminoles, where he had coached for thirty-four years and won two national titles (1993 and 1999). In a career that also included stints at Samford and West Virginia, Bowden claimed 389 victories, second only to Paterno among major college coaches.

Conference Changes. The ability of larger conferences (particularly the SEC and the Big Twelve) to stage a championship game because they had two divisions proved to be an advantage, as it allowed their best team to play an additional game and receive greater national exposure than the champions of conferences that relied only on the regular season to determine a champion. Furthermore, conferences were interested in expanding their geographic reach to attract new television audiences. In 2004–2005 the University of Miami Hurricanes, Virginia Tech Hokies, and Boston College Eagles left the Big East Conference to join the Atlantic Coast Conference (ACC), expanding it to twelve teams and a two-division organization that allowed for a championship game. The movement of teams from one conference to another created a cascading effect as conferences vied to attract various teams. In 2005 the ACC and Conference USA (CUSA) were able to begin playing a championship game in football, joining the three conferences that had started playing a title game in the 1990s: the SEC, Big Twelve, and the Mid-American Conference (MAC).

Outstanding Players. With so many outstanding athletes in college football, it was often difficult to decide who the "top players" really were. One way to judge the true greatness of a player is to watch his performance once he reaches the NFL. Some top-performing draft picks were quarterback Tom Brady, a sixth-round pick from Michigan (2000), who seems to be on his way to a Hall of Fame career; receiver Steve Smith from the University of Utah (2001); quarterback Eli Manning from the University of Mississippi (2004); quarterback Ben Roethlisberger from Miami University (2004); receiver Larry Fitzgerald from the University of Pittsburgh (2004); safety Bob Sanders

For many universities, the size of their stadiums is almost as much of a bragging right as the performance of their teams. Each year some of the top programs add hundreds or even thousands of seats in an attempt to move up in the "biggest stadium" competition. Following is a list of the ten largest college football stadiums in the nation at the end of the decade.

Beaver Stadium, Penn State University. Capacity: 107,282. After Michigan remodeled in 2008 and lost some seats, Beaver Stadium officially took the top spot. On game day, it is the third most-populated area in the state, following only Philadelphia and Pittsburgh.

Michigan Stadium ("The Big House"), University of Michigan. Capacity: 106,201. The university plans to add more seats.

Ohio Stadium, Ohio State University. Capacity: 102,329. While boasting one of the largest capacities, the stadium lacks somewhat in function; it does not have field lights and, therefore, rarely schedules night games (when they have to bring in special lights).

Darrell K Royal–Texas Memorial Stadium, University of Texas. Capacity: 100,113. With the addition of several thousand seats before the 2009 season, the stadium took its place as the largest in the Big 12 conference.

Neyland Stadium, University of Tennessee. Capacity: 100,011. At its peak, the stadium seated more than 104,000 people, but they decreased the number of seats after criticism for reducing seat size to fit more attendees. It still remains the largest stadium in the SEC and, sitting directly on the Tennessee River, has become known as one of the most scenic stadiums.

Los Angeles Memorial Coliseum, University of Southern California. Capacity: 93,607. Nicknamed the Grand Old Lady, this stadium was built in the 1920s. Among the events hosted here are two Olympics (1932 and 1984), a Super Bowl, and a World Series.

Sanford Stadium, University of Georgia. Capacity: 92,746. Another SEC school boasts this stadium which, like USC's stadium, is nearly a century old. It too hosted Olympic events in 1996.

The Rose Bowl, University of California, Los Angeles (UCLA). Capacity: 92,542. Like numbers 6 and 7, this stadium was built in the 1920s and hosts the annual Rose Bowl. It has also been home to Olympic events and a World Cup and is listed as a national historic landmark.

Tiger Stadium, Louisiana State University. Capacity: 92,400. The third SEC stadium to make the list, it is the loudest stadium, measured at more than 130 decibels. The venue was originally nicknamed "Deaf Valley," which was mistakenly transformed into "Death Valley."

Bryant-Denny Stadium, University of Alabama. Capacity: 92,138. Also part of the SEC tradition, the structure gives the conference more large stadiums than any other. Originally named Denny Stadium, it was renamed in the 1970s to honor legendary coach Bear Bryant.

Source: "20 Largest College Football Stadiums," *rivalryfootball.com* (16 May 2010).

from the University of Iowa (2004); running back Chris Johnson from East Carolina University (2008), and quarterback Matt Ryan from Boston College (2008). Notable Heisman winners included quarterbacks Carson Palmer (2002, USC), Matt Leinart (2004, USC), Tim Tebow (2007, Florida), and Sam Bradford (2008, Oklahoma) and running backs Reggie Bush (2005, USC) and Mark Ingram (2009, Alabama). Other notable college players included quarterbacks Vince Young (Texas) and Colt McCoy (Texas), running backs Adrian Peterson (Oklahoma) and Darren McFadden (Arkansas), offensive tackle Michael Oher (Mississippi), safety Eric Berry (Tennessee), linebackers Eric Norwood (South Carolina) and Terrell Suggs (Arizona State), and receiver Michael Crabtree (Texas Tech).

Record Performances. Quarterback Timmy Chang of the University of Hawaii set the all-time record for career yardage (17,072) in 2004, while Brian James "B.J." Symons of Texas Tech set the single-season yardage record (5,833) in 2003. Brett Elliott of Linfield College set the season touchdown mark for Division III with 61 in 2004, and Colt Brennan of Hawaii set the same record for Division I with 58 in 2006. Quarterback J. J. Harp of Division II Eastern New Mexico University had a record-setting day for attempts and completions in a single game against Southeastern Oklahoma on 12 September 2009, completing 66 of 94 passes, though his 695 yards was not a record. Running back Nate Kmic of Mount Union set the all-time Division III career (8,074) and season (2,790) rushing yardage records in 2008. Freddie Barnes of Bowling Green caught a record 155 balls in thirteen games during the 2009 season. In 2002 David Kircus of Division II Grand Valley State set the mark for touchdown receptions in a season with 35, breaking his own record of 28 set a year earlier. Dwight Freeney of Syracuse set the career sacks per game record (1.61) in 2001, while Terrell Suggs of Arizona State set the mark for sacks in a season with 24 in 2002. On 10 November 2001 the San Jose State Spartans defeated the University of Nevada Wolf Pack 64–45 in a game in which the teams combined for a record 1,640 yards in a single game.

Sources:

Bob Boyles and Paul Guido, *Fifty Years of College Football: A Modern History of America's Most Colorful Sport* (New York: Skyhorse, 2007);

"Individual and Team Collegiate Records," *ncaa.org;*

Ivan Maisel, "Meyer is the Best Coach of the Decade," *espn.com* (21 January 2010);

Stewart Mandel, "College Football: Highlights and Lowlights of the Decade," *si.com* (17 December 2009);

Paul Pringle, "USC Stays Silent about NCAA Investigation," *Los Angeles Times,* 31 May 2009;

Don Yaeger and Jim Henry, *Tarnished Heisman: Did Reggie Bush Turn His Final College Season into a Six-Figure Job?* (New York: Pocket Books, 2008).

FOOTBALL: PROFESSIONAL

Super Bowl Stars. The New England Patriots, led by head coach Bill Belichick and quarterback Tom Brady, were a dominant force in professional football. The Patriots won three Super Bowls (2001, 2003, and 2004) and earned a 16-0 mark in 2007 before losing to the New York Giants in Super Bowl XLII, their fourth appearance of the decade. Brady was a six-time Pro Bowl selection, two-time Super Bowl MVP (2001 and 2003), AP Male Athlete of the Year (2007), AP NFL MVP (2007), and AP Offensive Player of the Year (2007). Brady also held records for most passing touchdowns in a regular season (50 in 2007) and combined regular season and postseason (56 in 2007), and most Super Bowl career completions (100 in four games).

Changing Sides. Brett Favre, one of the greatest quarterbacks of all time, spent most of his professional career with the Green Bay Packers (1992–2007). A daring player who seemed to symbolize the spirit of his team, Favre led the Packers to seven division championships (1995–1997, 2002–2004, and 2007), four National Football Conference (NFC) championships (1995–1997 and 2007), and two Super Bowl appearances (1996–1997), winning the championship in 1996. For the rabid supporters of the Packers, Favre was a demigod. When he announced his retirement in 2008 fans were disappointed but proud of his career. However, later that year Favre announced that he would return to professional football and play for the New York Jets, a team in the American Football Conference (AFC). While some of his fans were upset at what they regarded a betrayal, they were yet unprepared for Favre's decisions the following year. After an injury-plagued season with the Jets, Favre once again announced his retirement, but in August 2009 he signed with the Minnesota Vikings, a

Minnesota Vikings quarterback Brett Favre during a game against the Chicago Bears on 29 November 2009, which the Vikings won 36–10 (AP Photo/Andy King)

long-standing rival of the Packers and a team in their own NFC North division. While Favre's on-again-off-again retirement status became material for late-night comics, Packers fans were outraged. When Favre returned to Lambeau Field to play against the Packers on 5 October 2009, he was greeted with boos. He responded with a splendid effort, completing 24 of 31 passes for 271 yards, with no interceptions and three touchdowns. The 30–23 victory over the Packers made Favre the first quarterback in history to defeat all thirty-two NFL teams. At the end of the 2009 season—which ended with the Vikings losing in overtime to the New Orleans Saints in the NFC championship game—Favre held most of the important NFL records for a career, including regular season victories (181), passing attempts (more than 9,800), completions (more than 6,000), yards (nearly 70,000), and touchdowns (just shy of 500). He also held the record for consecutive starts as a quarterback (309, including playoff games) and was considering playing another year.

Great Quarterback Debate. While Favre's records set the bar, younger quarterbacks such as Peyton Manning of the Indianapolis Colts and Tom Brady of the New England

Patriots may be able to eclipse some of his records by the end of their careers. The debate over the superiority of Brady or Manning dominated the discussion of quarterbacks during the decade. While Brady clearly outshone Manning in postseason performance and Super Bowl appearances, Manning was on a pace to break every major quarterback record in the books. Brady has three Super Bowl rings to Manning's one, but Manning holds the highest single-season passer rating, most seasons with 4,000+ passing yards, most consecutive seasons with 4,000+ passing yards, most pass completions in a season, and most games with a perfect passer rating. Over the decade he had the most wins as a starting quarterback, most touchdown passes, most passing yards, and most completions. Other quarterbacks whose careers merited inclusion in the discussion of best quarterback were Ben Roethlisberger (Steelers), with two Super Bowl victories (2005 and 2008), and Drew Brees (Saints), the 2008 Offensive Player of the Year, who led his team to the 2009 season Super Bowl in early 2010.

Handling Troubles. On 8 August 2006 Roger Goodell succeeded Paul Tagliabue as the NFL's eighth commissioner, one of the highest profile jobs in American sports. Facing Goodell were a variety of issues including looming labor-contract negotiations, the advisability of eliminating preseason games in favor of an expanded regular season, and the question of how to market American football to world audiences. Like his predecessors, he had to run a multibillion-dollar enterprise while simultaneously balancing the concerns of owners, players, and fans. One of the first issues Goodell faced was the misbehavior of players. Tennessee Titans cornerback Adam "Pacman" Jones, Cincinnati Bengals wide receiver Chris Henry, and Chicago Bears defensive tackle Tank Johnson were all involved in various drug, violence, or gun-related incidents. Goodell handed out stiff penalties: a one-year playing suspension for Jones and eight-game suspensions for Henry and Johnson. In August 2007 Goodell dealt with the high-profile misdeeds of Atlanta Falcons star quarterback Michael Vick, who admitted that he had run a dog-fighting and gambling operation—activities that raised a storm of protest and stained the image of the league. Suspended and fined by the NFL, Vick was prosecuted and served a prison sentence for his crimes, though Goodell allowed his return to the league in 2009. As a result of DUI and manslaughter charges against Donte Stallworth, Goddell suspended the Cleveland Browns wide receiver for the 2009 season. Another type of problem concerned allegations that New England Patriots head coach Bill Belichick had allowed his staff to regularly tape opposing teams' coaches to discern their hand signals. In September 2007 Goodell handed out fines worth $750,000 to the coach and the team. The issue that seemed to have the potential to affect the way the game was played was the increased concern over the long-term consequences of concussions often suffered by players, particularly in helmet-to-helmet collisions. In testimony before Congress in October 2009

Goodell defended the league's policies on head injuries while not admitting a link between concussions and later brain diseases.

Memorable Moments. The most memorable moment of the decade, and perhaps in all of Super Bowl history, was David Tyree's unusual catch on 4 February 2008 in Super Bowl XLII, the game in which his New York Giants denied the New England Patriots a perfect season. With a little more than a minute left in the fourth quarter the Giants were down 14–10. On third and five from their own 44-yard line, Giants quarterback Eli Manning dodged a tackle attempt by linebacker Adalius Thomas and broke out of the grip of linemen Jarvis Green and Richard Seymour to avoid a sack. He then managed to lob a pass downfield that Tyree caught by pinning the ball to his helmet with one hand as he hit the ground, miraculously maintaining possession for a thirty-two-yard advance. The Giants went on to score and beat the formerly undefeated Patriots 17–14. Probably the second most memorable Super Bowl moment occurred on 30 January 2000 when St. Louis Rams linebacker Mike Jones stopped Tennessee Titans wide receiver Kevin Dyson before he stretched out to place the ball across the goal line on the final play, preserving the Rams' 23–16 vicory in Super Bowl XXXIV.

Top Coaches. In addition to the success of Bill Belichick, there were several other coaches whose accomplishments deserve noting. Four coaches retired during the decade after long, successful careers in the league: Marty Shottenheimer, who coached the Cleveland Browns, Kansas City Chiefs, Washington Redskins, and San Diego Chargers for twenty-one years (1988–2006); Bill Cowher, who guided the Pittsburgh Steelers for fifteen years (1992–2006), winning the Super Bowl in 2006; Tony Dungy, who coached the Tampa Bay Buccaneers and the Indianapolis Colts (1996–2008); and Mike Holmgren, who led the Green Bay Packers and Seattle Seahawks for seventeen years (1992–2008), winning a Super Bowl with the Packers in 1996 and taking the Seahawks to the big game in 2005. As coach of the Colts (2002–2008) Dungy led his team to the playoffs each year. When his Colts won 29–17 over the Chicago Bears in Super Bowl XLI (4 February 2007), he became the first African American head coach to win the championship game. Two years later, Mike Tomlin, an African American who followed Cower as the coach of the Steelers, led his team to a Super Bowl victory in his second season in 2008, becoming at age thirty-six the youngest coach ever to win the game.

Top Players. Aside from the quarterbacks already discussed, there were many other notable players of the decade: Randy Moss, wide receiver for the Patriots, set the record for most touchdown receptions in a season with 23 in 2007. Marvin Harrison, wide receiver for the Indianapolis Colts, averaged more than 84 receptions per season during his thirteen-year career that ended in 2008, had 1400+ receiving yards in the years 1999–2002, and is the only NFL player to catch a pass in every game he played. LaDainian Tomlinson, running back for the San Diego

Chargers, had 1,500+ rushing/receiving yards and 10+ touchdowns every year from 2001 to 2008 and holds the record for single-season touchdowns with 31. Ray Lewis, linebacker for the Baltimore Ravens, was recognized by experts as the defensive player of the decade. Named NFL AP Defensive Player of the Year twice (2000 and 2003), Lewis was also acclaimed the MVP of Super Bowl XXXV in 2001 when his Ravens dominated the Giants 34-7. Other outstanding defensive players were Ed Reed, a safety for the Ravens, who was named the 2004 NFL Defensive Player of the Year and Charles Woodson, a cornerback with the Oakland Raiders and Green Bay Packers, who received the same award in 2009. Adam Vinatieri, who was place kicker for the New England Patriots during the first six years of the decade and for their rivals the Indianapolis Colts in the last four, was a four-time Super Bowl champion and is known as one of the best clutch kickers in NFL history. He kicked the winning field goal for the Patriots in the Super Bowls played in 2002 and 2004.

Sources:

Don Banks, "NFL: 10 Signature Moments," *si.com* (8 December 2009);

Colleen Canty, "Study: Roger Goodell's Strict Discipline Helping to Keep NFL's Crime Rate Down," *nesn.com* (20 April 2010);

"Favre Throws for 271 Yards, Three Touchdowns in Vikings' Win," *espn.com* (5 October 2009);

"Goodell: Destroying Spygate Tapes Was 'right thing to do'," *espn.com* (14 February 2008);

Clark Judge, "Four NFL Coaches Stand Alone as the Decade's Best," *cbs-sports.com* (21 February 2011);

Peter King, "NFL: Highlights and Lowlights," *si.com* (8 December 2009);

pro-football-reference.com.

GOLF

Billion-Dollar Athlete. At the center of the golfing world was one athlete: Tiger Woods. He seemed to dominate every tournament in which he competed. Winner of seventy-five events, including twelve major titles, during the decade, Woods had no rival on the links. He became the youngest golfer to achieve a career Grand Slam—winning the four major annual tournaments, the Masters, the U.S. Open, the British Open, and the PGA (Professional Golfing Association) Championship—and only the second player, after Jack Nicklaus, to win each of these major titles at least three times. In 2006 Woods suffered the death to cancer of his father, Earl, who had served as his mentor and whom he described as his best friend, but he continued to

2006 Masters Golf Tournament champion Phil Mickelson receives his green jacket from 2005 champion Tiger Woods
(AP Photo/Rob Carr).

win. Americans admired Tiger's fierce competitiveness and were charmed by his smile: he was a marketing dream and became the highest-paid athlete of all time through his endorsements as well as his tour winnings. In 2009 *Forbes* named Tiger the first professional athlete ever to reach the $1 billion mark in earnings. That same year, however, after a 27 November accident in which he was injured by driving into a tree outside of his home, allegations of Woods's marital infidelity emerged as several women came forward with tawdry tales and recorded messages that titillated fans and garnered typical media coverage. The charges hurt Woods both privately and publicly, destroying the persona of a loving husband and doting father he had cultivated. In December, Woods announced that he was taking "an indefinite leave from professional golf," and his sponsors were left wondering if the superstar could recover.

Others on the Links. Jack Nicklaus, regarded as the greatest golfer of all time, made his final Masters and British Open appearances in 2005. With eighteen titles in Grand Slam tournaments over his long career, Nicklaus held more major titles than any other golfer in history. Phil "Lefty" Mickelson emerged as a leader in the sport, second only to Woods among American golfers. Mickelson followed his first major win at the 2004 Masters with two victories in quick succession at the 2005 PGA Championship and 2006 Masters. Mickelson, however, was the victim of a painful collapse at the 2006 U.S. Open, when it appeared, with a two-shot lead going into the final three holes, that he would win the tournament. He bogeyed the sixteenth hole and on the eighteenth hit a hospitality tent on a drive and then a tree on his way to a double bogey, losing the tournament to a surprised Geoff Ogilvy. Other notable American golfers who won major championships in the decade were David Duval (2001 British Open), David Toms (2001 PGA Championship), Jim Furyk (2003 U.S. Open), Shaun Micheel (2003 PGA Championship), Zach Johnson (2007 Masters), and Stewart Cink (2009 Open Championship).

Dwindling Dominance? Every two years teams of American and European golfers clash in a series of matches known as the Ryder Cup, in which each side sends twelve golfers to compete at a site alternating between the United States and Europe. The first three cups of the decade went to the European squad, with lopsided victories in 2004 and 2006. Faced with being skunked during the entire decade, in 2008, at the Valhalla Golf Club in Louisville, Kentucky, the relatively young American squad, led by Paul Azinger, defeated their heavily favored rivals 16½ to 11½. When twenty-three-year-old rookie Anthony Kim was told he had won the match, he was surprised and later said, "I'm loving every minute of it. I wouldn't trade this for $10 million. This has been an experience of a lifetime." Unlike other tournaments featuring professional golfers, there is no purse in the Ryder Cup.

Women at Masters. Controversy roiled the traditions of the Masters tournament, as women protested their exclu-

sion from membership in the private Augusta National Golf Club, host of the tournament. Martha Burk, chair of the National Council of Women's Organizations, spotlighted the issue in 2002, as she complained to tournament corporate sponsors, CBS Sports, and the PGA about the injustice. Members of the Ladies Professional Golfers Association (LPGA) called for change and some members quit the club in protest. Nevertheless, despite the loss of commercial revenue and pressure from activists, the club remained single gender at the end of the decade (although it claimed women were on its waiting list for admission).

No Need to Walk. In the 1990s PGA golfer Casey Martin, who suffered from Klippel-Trenaunay-Weber syndrome, an untreatable circulatory disorder that affected his ability to walk on the course, asked that he be allowed to utilize a cart while playing in tournaments. Tour officials denied the request on the grounds that cart-aided play changed the nature of the game. In January 2000 Martin, as a result of a lower-court ruling, was the first player to use a cart in a tour event, the Bob Hope Classic. In May 2001 the U.S. Supreme Court ruled that he could participate on the professional tour using a motorized cart because national laws insisted on providing equality for those with physical disabilities, and noted that his use of the cart did not "fundamentally change" the game.

LPGA. In women's golf, Korean American Michelle Wie became one of the most-talked-about American players when, in 2003, she became the youngest winner of the U.S. Women's Amateur Public Links Championship. Although Wie's career faltered after she turned professional at age sixteen, she proved herself in 2009 when she joined the LPGA and won her first professional event at the Solheim Cup. Sweden's Annika Sörenstam was the most successful female golfer. With fifty-four wins and eight majors, she took a commanding place as one of the greatest female golfers of all time. She won the LPGA Championship three years running (2003–2005), Women's British Open (2003), and her third U.S. Women's Open (2006). Sörenstam retired at the end of the 2008 season. Although foreign women dominated many tournaments, some Americans continued to perform well, including Paula Creamer, Juli Inkster, Cristie Kerr, and Morgan Pressel.

Sources:

Dave Andrews, "Where Are All the Great Young American Women Golfers?" *cybergolf.com*;

Larry Dorman, "United States Takes Back the Ryder Cup," *New York Times,* 21 September 2008;

Dorman, "Woods Says He'll Take 'Indefinite Break' From Golf," *New York Times,* 11 December 2009;

"Let Him Ride: Supreme Court Says Martin Can Use Cart on Tour," *cnnsi.com* (29 May 2001);

lpga.com;

Jessica Reaves, "The Casey Martin Case: The Supreme Court Takes up Golf," *Time* (29 May 2001);

rydercup.com;

Gary Van Sickle, "A Look Back at the Decade's Best, Worst and Otherwise Notable Golf Happenings," *golf.com* (18 December 2009).

HOCKEY

Lockout. The biggest story during the decade in hockey was the lockout of 2004–2005. When the 1995 collective bargaining agreement between the National Hockey League (NHL) and the NHL Players Association expired, the NHL attempted to establish a salary cap, which the players rejected. The players and league were unable to reach an agreement for nearly a year, costing the league the entire season. As a result of the impasse, fans lost respect for both the league and the players; for the first time in nearly a century the Stanley Cup was not awarded; and ice hockey became the first major professional sport in North America to cancel an entire season because of a labor dispute. In mid July the players association and the league reached an agreement, which was ratified by the players on 21 July 2005, ending the lockout 310 days after it started.

Southern Teams. NHL teams that called the South home drew good crowds and captured championships. Georgia had a professional hockey team as early as 1980. The Tampa Bay Lightning (or "Bolts"), playing out of St. Petersburg, captured the Stanley Cup in 2003–2004. The Carolina Hurricanes, formerly the Hartford Whalers, won the Stanley Cup in 2006. Other squads in the South included the Atlanta Thrashers, founded in 1999; the Florida Panthers, who were based in the Miami area; and the Nashville Predators.

Rivalry. Two of the biggest names in hockey were the dynamic young stars Sidney Crosby, a Canadian with the Pittsburgh Penguins, and Alexander Ovechkin, a Russian with the Washington Capitals. The two first competed in the 2005 World Junior Championship and entered the league for the 2005–2006 season after the lockout. That year Ovechkin won the Calder Trophy as the NHL Rookie of the Year. Crosby led the league in scoring his second season, was awarded the MVP (2007), and led his team to the Stanley Cup finals in 2008, where they were beaten by the Detroit Red Wings. Ovechkin led the league in scoring his third season and twice won the MVP (2008 and 2009). In the 2009 Eastern Conference finals Ovechkin's Capitals were defeated in seven games by Crosby's Penguins, who that year were able to beat the Red Wings for the 2009 Stanley Cup.

Players. The most impressive single player was Nicklas Lidstrom, the longtime defenseman for the Detroit Red Wings who has a career total of four Stanley Cups, the last two coming in 2002 and 2008. He won the NHL's Defensive Player of the Year six times (2001–2003, 2006–2008) as well as a gold medal as part of the Swedish team at the 2006 Winter Olympics. Other notable players include Ilya Kovalchuk, forward for the Atlanta Thrashers, who led the league in goal scoring in 2003–2004; Martin Brodeur, goaltender for the New Jersey Devils, who led his team to the playoffs every year and captured two Stanley Cups (2000 and 2003); Joe Sakic, center for the Colorado Avalanche, who scored 250 goals in the decade and was named the league's MVP in 2001, the same year his team won the

Nicklas Lidstrom, defenseman for the Detroit Red Wings, in 2006 (photograph by James Teterenko)

Stanley Cup; Martin St. Louis, forward for the Tampa Bay Lightning, the league's leading scorer and MVP in 2004, the same year his team won the Stanley Cup; Scott Niedermayer, defenseman for the New Jersey Devils and Anaheim Ducks, who won Stanley Cups with both teams (2000 and 2003 with the Devils and 2007 with the Ducks) and took home a gold medal for Canada at the 2002 Winter Olympics.

Sources:
Michael Farber, "All-Decade Team: NHL," *si.com* (14 December 2009);
Farber, "NHL: Highlights and Lowlights," *si.com* (14 December 2009);
hockey-reference.com;
Allan Muir, "NHL: 10 Signature Moments," *si.com* (14 December 2009);
nhl.com.

OLYMPICS

2000 Summer Olympics (Sydney, Australia). The initial Olympiad of the new millennium was held in the southern hemisphere for the first time in nearly half of a century. The games boasted more than 10,000 athletes from 199 countries competing in 300 different events. With the beautiful coastal city of Sydney as a backdrop, the

Michelle Kwan performs her signature spiral in practice before the 2002 U.S. Figure Skating Championships in Los Angeles (photograph by Kevin Rushforth).

games began on 15 September with an opening ceremony that celebrated the history of Australia and its coastal and inland aboriginal cultures. Two new events were added to the games—tae kwon do and the triathlon—and women participated in both weightlifting and pentathlon for the first time. At the end of the games, the United States held the highest medal count with ninety-two (thirty-seven gold). American track star Marion Jones earned three gold and two bronze medals. (She was stripped of these awards in 2007 when she was found guilty of having used performance-enhancing drugs.) In other notable performances the U.S. women's softball team had the most amazing comeback story: after losing three consecutive games, the team rebounded and beat each team they had previously lost to, and took home the gold medal. Elsewhere, the women's 4x100-meter medley relay made up of B. J. Bedford, Megan Quann, Jenny Thompson, and Dara Torres won a gold medal and set a new world record of 3:58—the first women's team to ever complete the relay in under four minutes. In men's events the U.S. basketball team won the gold, though not so comfortably as in the past. Accustomed to winning by double digits, the team had to fight to close victories over Lithuania and France. The highlight of the basketball competition was Vince Carter's amazing "dunk of death," which he performed by jumping over the head of a 7'2" French center.

2002 Winter Olympics (Salt Lake City). The nineteenth Winter Games marked the sixth time the United States hosted the Olympics. With nearly 2,400 athletes from seventy-seven nations competing in seventy-eight events, these Olympics set new records in broadcasting with more than 2 billion viewers. The games introduced women's bobsled for the first time; China and Australia won their first ever gold medals in the Winter Games. The United States came in second to Germany in total medal count with thirty-four medals, ten of which were gold, and Germany's thirty-six total medals were a new winter Olympic record for most medals in a single Games. These Olympics were especially significant for the United States since they were held at home when the country was still recovering from the September 11, 2001 terrorist attacks. Thus, a sense of national pride and camaraderie was felt during these games, and celebrations often included tributes to the victims and heroes of the tragedy. As the world-renowned Mormon Tabernacle Choir sang the National Anthem, the U.S. flag from the fallen World Trade Center was brought to the center of the stadium for the opening ceremony. Honor guards from the New York Police Department and Fire Departments attended the games, and NYPD officer Daniel Rodriguez sang "God Bless America" during the ceremonies. One of the biggest stories was the efforts of American figure skaters Sarah Hughes and Michelle Kwan. The latter was heavily favored to win the women's competition, but she fell during her long performance and received the bronze medal. Hughes, however, had a performance that included several triple jumps and combinations, and she went home with the gold. In downhill skiing Bode Miller took home two silver medals, and his performance indicated that he would be a serious contender throughout the decade. Another top story was the performance of both the men's and women's hockey teams, who took home silver medals, losing in the finals to powerhouse Canada. The men's team beat heavily favored Russia in the semifinals to move on to the final match. Canada's gold was their first in the sport in fifty years.

2004 Summer Olympics (Athens, Greece). "Welcome Home" was the motto for these games, which returned to the country where the Olympiad originated, marking the first time since 1896 that the games took place in Greece. More than 10,000 athletes competed in 301 events, and broadcast ratings soared with a record 3.9 billion television viewers. Broadcasters were allowed to provide online coverage for the first time, though athletes and coaches were not allowed to post blogs or videos pertaining to their performances while at the games. The United States again earned the most total medals (103) and most gold medals (35). Several notable performances came from swimmers. The U.S. women's 4x200-meter swimming team of Natalie

Coughlin, Carly Piper, Dana Vollmer, and Kaitlin Sandeno won the gold medal and set a new world record. While Coughlin won five medals at the games, Michael Phelps won eight medals (six gold and two bronze), setting a record for total medals at a single Olympics. The women's softball team again won the gold and outscored their opponents a combined 51–1, while the women's soccer team, led by Mia Hamm (who retired after the games), also won a gold. In a shocking defeat, the U.S. men's basketball team lost in the Olympics for the first time since professional players were allowed to compete, and took home the bronze medal. In a more pleasant surprise for the Americans, gymnast Carly Patterson became only the second U.S. gymnast in history to win the all-around gold. Controversy roiled men's gymnastics, when it was discovered that a scoring error had placed the gold medal incorrectly around the neck of Paul Hamm. Despite attempts by the South Koreans to redress the oversight and have their athlete given the gold instead of the bronze awarded, Hamm was allowed to retain the title. Beach-volleyball duo Misty May-Treanor and Kerri Walsh took home the gold medal without losing a single game.

2006 Winter Olympics (Turin, Italy). The largest city ever to host the Winter Games, Turin welcomed more than 2,500 athletes who competed in eighty-four different events. New events included team-pursuit speed skating,

Gold medalist Seth Wescott, U.S.A., in the finals of the Snowboard Cross competition at the Turin 2006 Winter Olympics in Bardonecchia, Italy (AP Photo/Peter Dejong)

team-sprint cross-country skating, and snowboard cross. While curling was not a new event, these Olympics sparked a new interest in the sport, taking in 5 million viewers, more than either ice hockey or figure skating. The highest number of viewers came from Italy and the United States, whose men's team took home the bronze medal. More people followed the games online than ever before, with the Olympic website attracting more than 700 million hits, and live coverage was provided on mobile phones for the first time. The United States was second in total medal count (25), trailing Germany (29). Bode Miller was the most controversial athlete, with a disappointing disqualification in alpine skiing. Picked as the favorite, Miller was unable to win a single medal, which was largely blamed on his partying lifestyle and lackadaisical attitude. The U.S. star of the games was short-track speedskater Apolo Ohno. Winner of a gold and silver medal at the 2002 Olympics, Ohno added another gold medal and two bronze medals to his career total. Ohno, known for his outgoing personality and television appearances, almost single-handedly garnered new interest in speed skating and became a fan favorite.

2008 Summer Olympics (Beijing, China). Although activists openly criticized the Olympic Committee for choosing a host nation with a troublesome human-rights record, the Summer Games in China were the biggest and most-watched Olympiad in history. Nearly 11,000 athletes from 204 countries competed in 302 events. China produced breathtaking opening and closing ceremonies and invested heavily in transportation and facilities, constructing twelve new venues for the varied competitions. The state-of-the-art facilities provided the stages for 40 world record and 130 Olympic record performances. In swimming, Michael Phelps and Natalie Coughlin were even more successful than they had been in the Athens Olympics in 2004. Phelps won eight gold medals and broke seven world records, while Coughlin won six medals, the only U.S. female athlete to win so many medals in a single Olympics. The American beach-volleyball team of Misty May-Treanor and Kerri Walsh became the first team in the sport to successfully defend their gold medal, continuing a 108-game winning streak that spanned more than a year. Venus and Serena Williams took the gold in doubles tennis, repeating their accomplishment of the Sydney Games in 2000.

Sources:
Brian Cazenueve, "2000s: Top Olympians," *si.com* (18 December 2009);

Craig Neff, Olympics: "10 Significant Moments," *si.com* (18 December 2009);

olympic.org.

RACING

NASCAR's Image Change. From the last decades of the twentieth century through the first decade of the twenty-first, the National Association for Stock Car Auto Racing (NASCAR) has undergone a major image change. What was once considered a pastime relegated largely to the southern

---

DARLINGTON STRIPE

Auto racers often can be heard apologizing for running into a wall or bad-mouthing the racer who sent them crashing into a wall, but racers rarely will boast about damaging their car. However, at Darlington Raceway in South Carolina, hitting the wall is a badge of honor. Unlike other tracks, where riding the white line is the quickest route, Darlington racers want to take the outside lane. Riding the wall at Darlington means that you are winning, and a driver considers the stripe worn off the outside of his car as a mark of pride. At the 2009 Southern 500 both Dale Earnhardt Jr. and Kyle Busch had so much paint scraped off their right-side doors that the numbers were barely visible at the end of the race. Darlington's egg-shaped oval is part of its charm and has made it one of the most distinctive and sacred tracks in the sport. Each year, different drivers add their paint to the wall and come away with their own, coveted "Darlington Stripe."

Sources: Gerald Hodges, "Mark Martin Wins Again," *Fulton County News*, 14 May 2009;

"Staying Alive: The Track 'Too Tough to Tame,'" *State* (Columbia, S.C.), 31 August 2008.

United States has become a national sport. Early racers such as Richard Petty, the "king" of NASCAR with seven championship titles, wore cowboy hats and boots and spoke with a Southern accent. The major speedways were mostly in the Southeast: Darlington, South Carolina; Daytona, Florida; Talladega, Alabama; Bristol, Tennessee; and Atlanta, Georgia. Televised events, too, were largely restricted to the South. However, with more drivers coming from across the country and world, NASCAR officially became one of the nation's leading sports. With tracks opening in California and New Hampshire in the 1990s, the sport began to expand. Tracks outside of the South soon regularly attracted more races and attendees. Another notable change that boosted the sport's image, making it more family friendly, was the change of NASCAR's sponsorship. From the early 1970s until 2003 the championship series was known as the Winston Cup, named after one cigarette brand of its primary sponsor, R. J. Reynolds Tobacco Company. In 2004, after the lease with Reynolds ended, NASCAR made a deal with the Sprint Nextel Corporation and changed the championship to the Nextel Cup Series. With a larger fan base due to expansion, NASCAR became more popular, experiencing increased television coverage and viewership. Ratings for all races experienced a spike between 2006 and 2008, and in 2009 there was an increase among New York audiences. With its new image and accessibility NASCAR was poised to become even more successful.

The Chase. To increase fan interest and excitement, NASCAR instituted a new championship format in 2004 called the Chase for the Cup (the Nextel Cup became the Sprint Cup in 2007). The top ten (later twelve) drivers are determined in the first twenty-six races by a points system primarily based on finishing placement. These drivers are then seeded for the last ten races, which make up the Chase for the Championship. With the top drivers vying for the overall points championship, this format creates a "race-within-a-race" competition. Jimmie Johnson was the most frequent beneficiary of the new system, winning four consecutive titles (2006–2009).

Track Tragedies. On the final lap of the 18 February 2001 Daytona 500 the racing world was stunned when NASCAR star Dale "The Intimidator" Earnhardt was killed after his car was clipped by a rival and careened into a concrete wall. Often portrayed as the villain by many fans, Earnhardt was not only an aggressive and popular figure on the track but also was respected for his skill behind the wheel. In his easily identifiable black #3 car, Earhardt won seventy-seven races and seven Winston Cup championships. As a result of an investigation into the cause of death, NASCAR instituted stricter rules for the use of seat belts and mandatory head restraint devices, while also redesigning barriers and even the cars themselves. Earnhardt was not the only NASCAR royalty to die during the decade: on 12 May 2000 nineteen-year-old Adam Petty, the fourth-generation driver of the famous Petty clan, died in a crash while preparing to race in the Busch 200 in New Hampshire.

Indy Success? Although NASCAR grabs most racing attention during the year, the premier racing event in the United States continued to be the Indianapolis 500, which features open-wheel race cars and is held over the Memorial Day weekend each year. Although American drivers dominated the race up until 1990, during the 2000s foreign drivers nearly shut out homegrown teams. In 2004 Buddy Rice of Arizona took the checkered flag in a race shortened by rain. Two years later Sam Hornish Jr. of Ohio, who also drove in NASCAR, edged out Marco Andretti in the last stretch of the race.

Sources:
Dave Caldwell, "Auto Racing: Dale Earnhardt, 49, Racing Star," *New York Times*, 18 February 2001;

"Chase for the Cup History," *espn.com* (17 September 2010);

daleearnhardt.net;

indianapolismotorspeedway.com;

nascar.com.

SOCCER

Expansion. Professional soccer grew in popularity in America through the decade. Major League Soccer (MLS) grew in size from ten to fifteen teams, with another three teams projected to join. David Beckham, one of Britain's leading players, joined the Los Angeles Galaxy in 2007, bringing more energy and a larger fan base to the league. The Galaxy, probably the best-known club in the country, also became one of the league's most successful franchises, winning the Confederation of North Central American and Caribbean Association Football (CONCACAF) Champions League championship (2000), the U.S. Open Cup (2001 and 2005), the MLS Supporters' Shield (for best regular season performance), and the MLS Championship (2002 and 2005). While the Galaxy was probably the most popular team, the most decorated squad was D.C. United, which won the MLS Cup in 2004 (their fourth), the MLS Supporter's Shield (2006 and 2007, the team's third and fourth), and the 2008 U.S. Open Cup (their second).

Biggest Moments. Many of the great moments in the sport involved the United States teams in international competition. One of the best performances was the national team's run to the quarterfinals in the 2002 World Cup, after winning the Gold Cup that same year. The United States upset heavily favored Portugal and attained their highest finish in the tournament since 1930. The team won two more Gold Cups (2005 and 2007). Another impressive win—and one of the upsets of the decade—came when the United States in the semifinals of the 2009 Confederation Cup won a 2–0 victory over Spain, which at that time was on record runs of fifteen straight victories and thirty-five games without a defeat. For the women, two of the biggest achievements came at the Summer Olympics, where the team took home gold medals (2004 and 2008). The 2008 performance was particularly impressive since Abby Wambach, a leading scorer who claimed the team's winning goal at the 2004 Olympics, broke her leg before the games began. Without Wambach, the team was not picked to do well, but they proved critics wrong by winning the gold.

Top Players. Historically, discussions of top soccer players have not included many American names, but it is impossible not to mention a few key players. Landon Donovan was easily the best American male soccer player of the decade. Playing for the San Jose Earthquakes (2001–2004) and Los Angeles Galaxy (2005–2009), Donovan became the all-time leader in both goals and assists for the national team, for whom he played in two World Cups (2002 and 2006). He was named U.S. Soccer Male Athlete of the Year three times (2003, 2004, and 2009), the only player to collect the award for two consecutive years. Donovan played a key role for his teams in attaining three MLS Cups and three CONCACAF Gold Cups, and was named the 2003 MLS Cup MVP and 2009 MLS MVP. Other exceptional male soccer players include Tim Howard, goalkeeper and member of the national team since 2002; Claudio Reyna, captain of the national team at both the 2002 and 2006 World Cups; Brian McBride, member of the 2002 and 2006 World Cup national team and MVP of the 2002 Gold Cup; and Kasey Keller, goalkeeper for the 2002 and 2006 national teams and 2005 U.S. Soccer Athlete of the Year. In women's soccer Mia Hamm was easily the most widely recognized name. During her tenure with the women's national team, Hamm contributed to winning two Olympic gold medals and two World Cup medals. She has scored more international goals (157) than any other player and was twice named the Fédération Internationale de Football Association (FIFA) World Player of the Year

(2001–2002). After Hamm's retirement in 2004 a new star emerged. Abby Wambach joined the women's national team in 2003 and played professionally for the Washington Freedom. She scored the game-winning goal for the gold medal in the 2004 Olympics and was named U.S. Soccer Female Athlete of the Year (2003, 2004, and 2007).

Sources:

Beau Dure, *Long-Range Goals: The Success Story of Major League Soccer* (Washington, D.C.: Potomac Books, 2010);

"Mia Hamm to Receive Freedom Honor," *espn.soccernet.com* (1 May 2009);

Brian Straus, "A Cup Half Full: The Decade's Best in US Soccer," *aolnews.com* (31 December 2009);

Grant Wahl, "Soccer: Highlights and Lowlights," *si.com* (18 December 2009).

TENNIS

Williams Era. American tennis belonged to the Williams sisters, Venus and Serena. During the decade Serena won ten titles, including all four majors. Her singles achievements included wins at the Australian Open (2003, 2005, 2007, and 2009); French Open (2002); Wimbledon (2002–2003 and 2009); and U.S. Open (2002 and 2008). She also twice won the World Tennis Association (WTA) Championship (2001 and 2009). Sister Venus's wins included Wimbledon (2000, 2001, 2005, 2007, and 2008) and the U.S. Open (2000 and 2001). She also won the gold medal at the 2000 Summer Olympics and WTA Championship (2008). When playing doubles, they were nearly unstoppable: they won the Australian Open (2001, 2003, and 2009); Wimbledon (2000, 2002, 2008, and 2009); and U.S. Open (2009). The pair also won gold medals in doubles at the 2000 and 2008 Olympics.

Men. In men's tennis the legendary Pete Sampras retired early in the decade, but not before winning Wimbledon (2000) and the U.S. Open (2002). Andre Agassi, who, like Sampras, is considered one of the greatest players of all time, won three major titles at the Australian Open (2000, 2001, and 2003) before his 2006 retirement. His 2003 victory was the last time an American won the tournament in the decade. Newcomer Andy Roddick made a splash by winning the 2003 U.S. Open and spent most of the decade ranked in the top ten. The Bryan brothers, Bob and Mike, dominated the doubles

WILLIAMS VS. WILLIAMS

In what is, perhaps, one of the greatest sibling rivalries of all time, Venus and Serena Williams faced off against each other in a total of eleven Grand Slam events (eight finals) this decade. Individually and together the two players have each held the number-one spot in singles and doubles tennis. Following is a record of times they matched up against one another:

Wimbledon, 2000. Victor: Venus. Although Serena was favored to win the match, Venus took the victory 6–2, 7–6 (3) and won the tournament, marking her first singles Grand Slam trophy.

U.S. Open, 2001. Victor: Venus. This first Grand Slam final between the sisters was one of the most anticipated events in recent history. Earlier that year, Venus withdrew from a match against Serena, and they were publicly accused of match fixing. Despite the hype, Venus easily won 6–2, 6–4.

French Open, 2002. Victor: Serena. Their second direct competition in a Grand Slam finals, Serena evened the score from the previous year, winning the match 7–5, 6–3.

Wimbledon, 2002. Victor: Serena. In their third Grand Slam final, Serena defended her previous victory 7–6 (4), 6–3 and edged her sister out of the top spot in women's singles rankings.

U.S. Open, 2002. Victor: Serena. In their third Grand Slam finals matchup of the year, Serena held on to her top spot 6–4, 6–3 in a heated competition.

Australian Open, 2003. Victor: Serena. After a season plagued with injuries, this meeting was the closest between the sisters in years, with Serena pulling out a narrow victory 7–6 (4), 3–6, 6–4. With this win, Serena became the first woman to hold all four Grand Slam titles at one time.

Wimbledon, 2003. Victor: Serena. With Venus still recovering from an injury, Serena narrowly won the second finals match up of the year 4–6, 6–4, 6–2. This victory marked the second consecutive Wimbledon title for Serena.

U.S. Open, 2005. Victor: Venus. In this early meeting during the fourth round, Venus beat her sister 7–6 (5), 6–2 in a Grand Slam event for the first time since 2001, although she was unable to advance to the finals.

Wimbledon, 2008. Victor: Venus. Winning 7–5, 6–4, Venus captured her first win over Serena in a Wimbledon final and her fifth singles trophy at the tournament.

U.S. Open, 2008. Victor: Serena. In what was called the best women's tennis match of the year, Serena won 7–6 (6), 7–6 (7) in the quarterfinals and later won the tournament.

Wimbledon, 2009. Victor: Serena. For the first time since 2003, Serena captured the trophy when she beat Venus 7–6 (3), 6–2.

Source: "The Williams Sisters Head-to-Head," *cbssports.com*.

Venus Williams, left, and Serena Williams holding their trophies for winning the women's double final at Wimbledon on 5 July 2008 (AP photograph/Anja Niedringhaus)

tournaments, winning more than fifty titles. Their doubles wins included three Australian Opens (2006, 2007, and 2009); the French Open (2003); Wimbledon (2006); two U.S. Opens (2005 and 2008); and one bronze medal at the 2008 Olympics.

Women. Although the Williams sisters largely dominated women's tennis, two other players stood out. Jennifer Capriati twice won the Australian Open (2001–2002) and the French Open (2001). Lindsay Davenport added a Grand Slam to her record at the Australian Open (2000).

Sources:

Jacqueline Edmondson, *Venus and Serena Williams: A Biography* (Westport, Conn.: Greenwood Press, 2005);

Jon Wertheim, "Tennis: Highlights and Lowlights," *si.com* (18 December 2009);

Wertheim, "2000s: Top Tennis Players," *si.com* (18 December 2009).

HEADLINE MAKERS

LANCE ARMSTRONG

1971–

CYCLIST

Early Years. Born in Plano, Texas, Lance Armstrong demonstrated early on that he was destined to be a great athlete. Encouraged by his mother, he trained for and won the Iron Kids Triathlon at thirteen years of age. In 1989 Armstrong qualified for the cycling junior world championships in Moscow, and in 1991 he won the U.S. National Amateur Championship. Armstrong gained a place on the U.S. Men's Olympic Cycling Team and competed in the 1992 Summer Olympics in Spain, where he finished fourteenth. Once he turned professional, Armstrong quickly became a leader in the sport, winning both the U.S. National Cycling Championships and the World Cycling Championships (1993). In 1996 in Atlanta, Armstrong again competed with the Men's Olympic Cycling Team. Later that year, the twenty-five-year-old racer received the shocking news that he had stage-three testicular cancer, which had spread to his lungs and brain. He was given less than a 50 percent chance of survival. Determined to overcome the disease, Armstrong began aggressive chemotherapy, using a combination of drugs that fought the cancer without damaging his lungs. His brain tumors were surgically removed, and by 1997 Armstrong's cancer was in remission. Inspired by this experience, Armstrong founded the Lance Armstrong Foundation to advance cancer research and provide support to sufferers and their families. His yellow rubber bracelets, sold to provide funds for cancer research, became a fashion statement.

Seven-Time Stunner. Armstrong was without a team in 1998 when he returned to professional racing.

Signed by the U.S. Postal Service team, Armstrong struggled in the early days following his recovery and had to drop out of a race in France. A determined Armstrong continued training. His hard work paid off in 1999 when he won his first Tour de France, cycling's most prestigious event, finishing seven minutes and thirty-seven seconds ahead of the next cyclist. Armstrong became only the second American to win the tour. He went on to win every Tour de France from 1999 to 2005, a record seven consecutive victories. Armstrong received national and international acclaim and was named Associated Press (AP) Male Athlete of the Year (2002–2005). He was also awarded *Sports Illustrated* Male Athlete of the Year (2002) and won the ESPY Awards Best Male Athlete title (2003–2006). Even after announcing his retirement from professional cycling in 2005, Armstrong was named one of *Time*'s 100 Most Influential People in 2008.

Second Comeback. Armstrong announced his return to professional cycling in September 2008 with the stated purpose of raising cancer awareness through his LIVESTRONG campaign. Throughout his career Armstrong has faced accusations of doping, which is believed to be widespread among professional cyclists. In 2008 and 2009 Armstrong submitted to tests, interviews, and investigations and maintained that he never engaged in any doping activities. He was allowed to officially return to cycling in January 2009 when he competed in the Australian Tour Down Under. Although he finished twenty-ninth, Armstrong considered his participation a victory, as record crowds attended the event and the Australian government pledged more than $4 million toward a cancer-research facility. Later that year, Armstrong competed in the Tour de France, finishing third. He ended the decade by announcing his intention to compete in the 2010 Tour.

Sources:

Alan Abrahamson, "Allegations Trail Armstrong Into Another Stage," *Los Angeles Times,* 9 July 2006;

lancearmstrong.com.

BARRY BONDS

1964–

BASEBALL PLAYER

In His Blood. Born in Riverside, California on 24 July 1964—the son of power hitter Bobby Bonds, the godson of Willie Mays, and the cousin of Reggie Jackson—Barry Lamar Bonds was destined to be a great baseball player. In high school Bonds stood out as an athlete in baseball, basketball, and football. He was a varsity baseball player in his sophomore year and was named an All-American in his senior year. Although drafted after high school by the San Francisco Giants, the team and Bonds were unable to agree on a salary, so he decided to go to college. At Arizona State University, Bonds excelled and was selected to the All-American team in his sophomore year (1985). The next year he tied the National Collegiate Athletic Association (NCAA) record for consecutive hits in a College World Series with seven. Bonds was chosen by the Pittsburgh Pirates in the first round of the 1985 Major League Baseball Draft and began his career in 1986. Bonds quickly established himself as a power hitter and fan favorite, leading National League rookies with sixteen home runs. Bonds rewarded the Pirates by hitting more homers each year and helping the team to capture three consecutive National League East titles (1990–1992) while setting records in attendance at home games. In 1990 Bonds hit 33 home runs and 114 RBIs. That year he won his first National League Most Valuable Player (MVP) award, which he won five more times (1992–1993 and 2001–2004). He also won Silver Slugger Awards (1990–1994, 1996–1997, and 2000–2004), and eight Gold Gloves (1990–1994 and 1996–1998). Bonds was repeatedly named an All Star selection (1990, 1992–1999, 2000–2004, and 2007).

Giant Among Giants. In 1993 Bonds returned to California to play for the Giants, signing a record six-year, $43.75 million contract. In 1996 he became only the second MLB player to hit 40 home runs and steal 40 bases in the same season, and in 1998 he was the first player in the 400–400 club in career home runs and stolen bases. In 2001 Bonds hit career home run #500, and that same year he broke the single-season home run record with 73. In 2003 Bonds became the first player in the 500–500 club; he hit home run #700 in 2004, a season in which he had more home runs (43) than strikeouts (41). In 2007 Bonds hit #756, passing Hank Aaron's career record. Bonds finished his career with 762 home runs. Allegations that Bonds had used steroids cast a shadow over his records and awards. In 2004 Bonds admitted unknowingly using an ointment that he later learned was the steroid tetrahydrogestrinone

(THG). In November 2007 Bonds was indicted on perjury and obstruction of justice charges, and the Giants decided not to renew his contract for 2008. No team picked Bonds up in 2008 or 2009.

Sources:
"Barry Bonds," *baseball-reference.com* (2011);
"Barry Bonds #25 LF," *espn.com* (2011).

KOBE BRYANT

1978–

BASKETBALL PLAYER

Early Start. Kobe Bryant was born in Philadelphia, the son of former National Basketball Association (NBA) player and coach Joe Bryant. His family moved to Italy when he was young, and he grew up as an avid athlete and fan of both soccer and basketball. After returning to the United States in 1991, Bryant continued to excel at sports and led his high-school basketball team to a state championship his senior year. Earning national recognition, Bryant received such awards as the Gatorade Men's National Basketball Player of the Year and was named an All-USA First Team Player by *USA Today*. Bryant announced his intention to enter the NBA draft his senior year and forgo college, becoming one of a handful of players to do so. In 1996 the Charlotte Hornets selected Bryant in the first round of the draft and immediately traded him to the Los Angeles Lakers. Because Bryant was only seventeen his parents had to cosign his contract. During his rookie season he became the youngest player ever to participate in an NBA game and the youngest to start. At the end of his second season Bryant was receiving more playing time and had doubled his points-per-game average, earning a spot on the All Star team—the youngest player to achieve this distinction. His early achievements included winning the Slam Dunk competition at the 1997 All Star weekend.

Lakers. With center Shaquille "Shaq" O'Neal, Bryant helped make the Lakers a dominating force in the early 2000s. Although the two stars sometimes had a strained relationship, they led the team to three consecutive NBA championships (2000–2002) and another finals appearance in 2004, a year that proved particularly difficult off the court for Bryant as he was dealing with the fallout of a 2003 sexual assault charge (the case was dropped in September 2004). With O'Neal's departure for the Miami Heat in 2004, the Lakers began to rebuild around Bryant, who soon was able to lead the team back to championship form. Bryant led the league in scoring during two seasons (2005–2006 and 2006–2007). In a 22 January 2006 game against the Toronto Raptors, he scored eighty-one points, second only to Wilt Chamberlain's 100-point effort on the list of most points scored in an NBA game. Bryant led the Lakers to another NBA final in 2008, losing to the Boston Celtics, and was named MVP that year. In 2009 Bryant and the Lakers won another championship, and Bryant was named Finals MVP. Bryant also played on the U.S. Olympic Basketball team at the 2008 Olympics, winning a gold medal.

Sources:

"Kobe Bryant," *basketball-reference.com* (2010-2011);

"Kobe Bryant," *espn.com;*

Justin Verrier, "Before they were stars: Kobe Bryant," *espn.com* (1 June 2010).

PEYTON MANNING

1976–

FOOTBALL PLAYER

Quarterback. Peyton Manning was born into a football family in New Orleans, Louisiana. His father, Archie Manning, had been a great quarterback with the New Orleans Saints. His older brother, Cooper, was a standout receiver at the high school where Peyton later starred, and his younger brother, Eli, also became a Super Bowl–winning quarterback for the New York Giants. Peyton Manning had an outstanding career as quarterback of Isidore Newman High School and was named the Gatorade National Player of the Year after his senior year (1993). He attended the University of Tennessee, where he became the all-time leading passer with more than 11,000 career yards and 89 touchdowns—two of the more than thirty school records he holds. He led his team to victory in 39 of 45 games as a starter, won a Johnny Unitas Award (1997) and an ESPY award for Best College Player (1998), and was chosen a First Team All-American quarterback. The school retired his number (16) and renamed the street leading to their football stadium Peyton Manning Pass. Manning stayed at Tennessee for his senior year, despite speculation that he would enter the draft, and won the 1997 SEC championship game against Auburn.

Colt. In the 1998 NFL draft Manning was chosen by the Indianapolis Colts as the first pick. During his first season, Manning set several rookie records, including most touchdown passes (26), and threw for more than 3,700 yards. He was named to the All-Rookie First Team. In 1999 Manning had his first 4,000+ yard season, and the Colts became AFC East champions, losing in the playoffs to the Tennessee Titans, who went to the Super Bowl that year. Manning was chosen for his first Pro Bowl that year and became a fixture at the event throughout the subsequent decade. In 2002 Tony Dungy became Colts head coach, and the team began the 2003 season with five straight victories, finishing 12–4, though they lost in the AFC Championship Game to the New England Patriots. He finished with more than 4,200 passing yards and 29 touchdowns and was awarded Associated Press (AP) co-MVP with Steve McNair, as well as an ESPY Award for Best NFL Player. In 2004 Manning finished with more than 4,500 yards, a record 121.1 passer rating, and 49 touchdowns. He was chosen NFL MVP and Offensive Player of the Year. He also won ESPY awards for Best NFL Player and Best Record-Breaking Performance. The ultimate award still eluded Manning, however, as his team again ended their season with a playoff loss to the Patriots. In 2005 Manning led the Colts to a 14–2 record, but the team lost to the Pittsburgh Steelers in the playoffs.

Super Bowl. The Colts' 2006 season opened with "Manning Bowl I," a matchup between brothers Peyton and Eli that the Colts won 26–21. The team went 12–4 in the regular season and made it to the AFC Championship Game, where they faced quarterback Tom Brady and the New England Patriots, the team that had knocked the Colts out of the playoffs in 2003 and 2004. The Colts trailed by 18 points at one point and at half-time 21–6, but Mannning mounted the greatest comeback in conference championship history by leading his team to a 38–34 victory. The Colts went on to defeat the Chicago Bears 29–17 in Super Bowl XLI. Manning was named Super Bowl MVP and won another ESPY for Best Championship performance.

Post–Super Bowl Success. The Colts opened the 2007 season with seven straight victories but were handed their first loss by Tom Brady and the New England Patriots. Manning passed the 40,000 career passing yards and won his one hundredth game. The Colts finished with five straight victories and made the playoffs, where they were eliminated by the San Diego Chargers. The season was not a disappointment for the Manning family, however, as they got to see Eli and the Giants defeat the Patriots in Super Bowl XLII. When Eli won the MVP, the Mannings were the first brothers to win back-to-back Super Bowls and MVPs. Struggling after an off-season knee surgery, Manning led the 2008 Colts to a 3–4 record. A tireless leader, however, Manning recovered, and the Colts won their next nine games to finish 12–4. Despite losing in the postseason, Manning won another NFL MVP. In 2009 the Colts won the AFC Championship and earned their second appearance in the Super Bowl this decade, but lost to the New Orleans Saints. Manning was named Player of the Decade by *Fox Sports,* and *Sporting News* listed him as the #1 player in the NFL. Manning holds many NFL records including highest single-season passer rating, most seasons and consecutive season with 4,000+ passing yards, most pass completions in a season, most games with a perfect passer rating, most consecutive regular-seasons wins as a starter, most seasons with 12+ wins as a starter, and most AP NFL MVP awards.

Sources:
"Peyton Manning," *colts.com;*

peytonmanning.com.

DANICA PATRICK

1982–

RACE CAR DRIVER

Early Racing. Danica Patrick was born in Beloit, Wisconsin, but grew up in nearby Roscoe, Illinois, where she first began go-kart racing. By the age of twelve Patrick had won several World Kart Association (WKA) races, including the WKA Grand National Championship in the Yamaha class. At fourteen, Patrick won 39 of her 49 feature races, the WKA Manufacturers Cup National Points title in the Yamaha Junior class, and five WKA series titles. In 1997, her last year of kart racing, Patrick won the WKA Grand National Championship. The next year sixteen-year-old Patrick made her formula debut in Europe, and her second-place finish at the 2000 Formula Ford Festival in England marked the highest finish for an American and for a woman. In 2002 Patrick returned to U.S. racing, driving for Letterman Rahal Racing; in 2003 she earned five top-five finishes and became the first female driver in the Toyota Atlantic Series to have a podium finish. In 2004 she again competed in the Toyota Series, this time becoming the first woman to lead in points, after her second-place finish at Portland, and the first women to have a series podium finish when she came in third in the championship.

Man's World? In 2005 Patrick entered the Indy Racing League (IRL) IndyCar Series. She became only the fourth woman to compete in the Indy 500, and her fourth place finish was the highest for a female driver. She also led for nineteen laps during the race, making her the first woman to ever lead the race. She won three pole positions that season, finished twelfth in the Indy-Car Series Championship, was named IndyCar Rookie of the Year, and was voted the IndyCar Most Popular Driver—a title she also won in 2006, 2007, and 2009. Patrick became a media sensation as well as a successful racer. She appeared in the documentary series *Girl Racers* (2005). She appeared on the cover of *FHM* magazine in 2003 and in 2005 appeared on the cover of *Sports Illustrated.* In 2006 Patrick finished fourth at

Nashville and Milwaukee, recorded six top-ten finishes, and finished ninth in the overall standings. In 2007 Patrick signed with the Andretti Green Racing team and had eleven top-ten finishes, ending seventh in the overall points standings. In 2008 she won the Twin Ring Motegi in the Indy Japan 300, marking the first time a woman won a closed-course auto race. She had three top-five finishes, recorded ten top-ten finishes, and ended the season sixth in overall points. As her popularity swelled, she became more marketable, starring in ads. In 2008 and 2009 Patrick appeared in the *Sports Illustrated Swimsuit Edition.* During 2009 Patrick had several career bests, including a third-place finish at the Indy 500, and ended the season fifth in points, the highest for an American driver. At the end of the 2009 season she announced her intention to race NASCAR.

Sources:
"Danica Patrick," *espn.com;*

danicaracing.com.

MICHAEL PHELPS

1985–

SWIMMER

First Lap. Michael Phelps was born in Baltimore, Maryland, and began swimming at seven years old. At the age of fifteen, he qualified for the 2000 Olympics and, although he did not win a medal, became the youngest male to swim on the U.S. Men's Olympic team in nearly seventy years. In 2001 Phelps set a world record for the 200-meter butterfly, becoming the youngest swimmer to hold a world record. In 2002 Phelps became a dominant force at the Pan Pacific Championships, winning three gold and two silver medals and setting a world record in the 400-meter individual medley. He also set U.S. records for the 100-meter butterfly and 200-meter individual medley. At the 2003 World Championships, Phelps won four gold and two silver medals and set another five world records.

Outstanding Olympian. Phelps became the first American to qualify for six individual events at the 2004 U.S. Olympic Trials. At the 2004 Olympic Games in Greece, Phelps won a total of eight medals, six gold and two bronze, which tied the record set by Soviet gymnast Aleksandr Dityatin. He won gold in the 100-meter and 200-meter butterfly, 200-meter and 400-meter individual medley, 4x200-meter freestyle, and the 4x100-meter medley. He also broke his world record in the 400-meter individual medley and set new Olympic records in the 100-meter and 200-meter butterfly and the 200-meter individual medley. He took home the bronze medals in the 200-meter freestyle and the 4x100-meter freestyle. At the 2005 World Championships, Phelps won five gold medals and one silver, setting a new American record in the 200-meter freestyle. At the 2006 Pan Pacific Championships, Phelps took home six medals (five gold and one silver) and set three world records in the 200-meter butterfly, 200-meter individual medley, and 4x100-meter freestyle relay. At the 2007 World Championships, Phelps tied the record for most gold medals with seven and broke five world records (200-meter butterfly, 200-meter freestyle, 200-meter and 400-meter individual medley, and 4x200-meter freestyle relay). Much of the hype surrounding the 2008 Olympics was focused on Phelps. Americans were enthralled and hopes were high. Phelps did not disappoint. He won a record-breaking eight gold medals in a single Games, bringing his total to sixteen, second only to Soviet gymnast Larissa Latynina's eighteen. Perhaps even more impressive is that Phelps set world records in seven of the eight events (200-meter butterfly, 200-meter freestyle, 200-meter and 400-meter individual medley, 4x100-meter and 4x200-meter freestyle relay, and 4x100-meter medley relay). In the eighth event, the 100-meter medley, Phelps set an Olympic record. He came home as one of the most celebrated Olympians in American history.

Legal Trouble. Being in the spotlight for much of his teen years, Phelps's reputation is not without tarnish. In 2004, shortly after returning home from the Olympics, Phelps was arrested for driving under the influence of alcohol. He pled guilty and was sentenced to eighteen months' probation. Phelps apologized publicly and promised it was an isolated incident. In 2009 a photograph emerged of Phelps smoking marijuana at a 2008 party at the University of South Carolina. Phelps admitted to and apologized for what he called inappropriate behavior. In the aftermath, Phelps faced a loss of sponsors and a three-month suspension from competition.

Sources:
beijing2008.com;

David Hancock, "Olympic Champ Sentenced for DUI," *cbsnews.com* (29 December 2004);

Juliet Macur, "Phelps Disciplined Over Marijuana Pipe Incident," *New York Times,* 5 February 2009;

"Michael Phelps Biography," *biography.com.*

TIGER WOODS

1975–

GOLFER

Early Career. Eldrick "Tiger" Woods was born in Cypress, California, and was introduced to golf by his father before his second birthday. Considered a prodigy, Woods was featured in the *Golf Digest* at five and began winning tournaments at age seven. At eight he won the 1984 Junior World Golf Championship in the nine-to-ten-year-old age group. He won the Junior World Championships every year from 1988 to 1991. In 1991 he won the U.S. Junior Amateur Golf Championship, becoming, at fifteen, the youngest player to win the event. In 1992 and 1993 he defended his U.S. Junior Amateur Golf Championship title, becoming the first multiple winner. In 1994 Woods attended Stanford University on a golf scholarship. While there, he participated for the first time in the 1995 Masters Tournament as the only amateur to qualify. In 1996 Woods became a professional golfer and quickly established himself as one of the preeminent golfers in the world. He was named PGA Rookie of the Year and Sportsman of the Year by *Sports Illustrated.* In 1997 Woods won the Masters, becoming the event's youngest winner.

Rise of the Tiger. In the 2000s Woods won three more Masters (2001, 2002, and 2005), four PGA Championships (1999, 2000, 2006, and 2007), three U.S. Open Championships (2000, 2002, and 2008), as well as the British Open Championship (2000, 2005, and 2006). Woods was named PGA Player of the Year ten times (1997, 1999–2003, 2005–2007, and 2009), AP Male Athlete of the Year (1997, 1999–2000, and 2006), and ESPY Best Male Athlete (1998, 2000–2002, and 2008). Woods's meteoric rise made him a favorite of the American public, leading to top earnings from advertisers and sponsors. The decade ended on a bad note, however, as multiple women came forward to claim they had affairs with the married golfer.

Sources:
Kurt Badenhausen, "Sport's First Billion-Dollar Man," *forbes.com* (29 September 2009);

Tracy Connor and Samuel Goldsmith, "Jamie Jungers, Las Vegas Cocktail Waitress, is Fourth Alleged Tiger Woods Mistress," *New York Daily News,* 5 December 2009;

pgatour.com;

tigerwoods.com.

PEOPLE IN THE NEWS

Andre Agassi won two consecutive Australian Opens in tennis (2000 and 2001) and a third in 2003, which marked the eighth and final Grand Slam title of his career. Agassi retired from professional tennis in 2006.

During the 2009 NCAA Men's Division I Hockey Championship tournament, the **Bemidji State University Beavers** knocked out the heavily favored Notre Dame Fighting Irish 5–1.

Tom Brady won three Super Bowl rings with the New England Patriots (2002, 2004, and 2005), claiming the Super Bowl MVP twice (2002 and 2004). He was named the AP Male Athlete of the Year and NFL Most Valuable Player in 2007, when he led the Patriots to an undefeated regular season.

Derrick Brooks won a Super Bowl ring in 2003 as a linebacker for the Tampa Bay Buccaneers. He was chosen AP NFL Defensive Player of the Year in 2002; selected for the Pro Bowl team every year from 2000 to 2006 and again in 2008; and selected for the All-Pro team in 2000 and 2002–2005.

Jennifer Capriati won her first Grand Slam title at the 2001 Australian Open, becoming the lowest seed ever to win the tournament. In 2002 she won the French Open and successfully defended her title at the Australian Open.

Roger Clemens achieved a record seven Cy Young Awards, his last two awarded in 2001 and 2004. Clemens and the New York Yankees won their second consecutive World Series in 2000.

Natalie Coughlin won five medals in swimming at the 2004 Summer Olympic Games (two golds, two silvers, and one bronze). At the 2008 Summer Olympics, she won a record-setting six medals (1 gold, 2 silvers, and 3 bronzes), the first American female to have done so in a single Olympics.

Sidney Crosby led the Pittsburgh Penguins to a Stanley Cup victory in hockey in 2009, becoming the youngest NHL captain to win the Cup.

At the 2006 Winter Olympics in Turin, Italy, speedskater **Shani Davis** became the first African American athlete to win an individual Winter Games gold medal in the 1,000-meter race.

Dale Earnhardt Jr. is the son of the late driver **Dale Earnhardt Sr.,** who died in the fourth turn of the final lap in the 2001 Daytona 500. Between 2000 and 2008 Earnhardt Jr. won eighteen Sprint Cup races, and in 2004 won the Daytona 500; he has been NASCAR's most popular driver every year from 2003 to 2009.

In 2008 record-setting quarterback **Brett Favre** announced his retirement from football after sixteen seasons with the Green Bay Packers; he stunned fans by coming out of retirement to play for the New York Jets in 2008 and then signing with the Minnesota Vikings in 2009.

Bobsledder **Vonetta Flowers** (partnered with **Jill Bakken**) became the first African American to win a Winter Olympics gold medal, at the Salt Lake City Games in 2002.

Jeff Gordon, a four-time NASCAR Sprint Cup Series winner, became the first driver to reach $100 million in lifetime winnings in 2009; he became a co-owner of the #48 Lowe's/Kobalt Tools car driven by **Jimmie Johnson.**

Mia Hamm was on the U.S. women's soccer team from 1987 to 2004 and played professionally for the Washington Freedom. She earned a silver medal at the 2000 Olympics and a gold medal at the 2004 Olympics. Hamm is credited with making soccer, particularly for women, popular with the public, and she scored more international goals than any other player by her retirement in 2004.

Indianapolis Colts wide receiver **Marvin Harrison** caught more than 1,000 yards and scored more than ten touchdowns for seven of the ten years during the decade.

Evander Holyfield made history in 2000 when he earned the world heavyweight championship in boxing for a fourth time, the only boxer to do so. After a brief hiatus to rehabilitate his shoulders, Holyfield returned to boxing in 2006 to seek a fifth heavyweight belt.

Allen Iverson was named to the All Star NBA team every year this decade and was named All Star MVP in 2001 and 2005. He was the NBA's leading scorer for the 2000–2001, 2001–2002, and 2004–2005 seasons. Iverson also played on the 2004 U.S. Men's Olympic Basketball team.

In 2003 seventeen-year-old **LeBron James** was chosen as the number-one pick by the Cleveland Cavaliers in the NBA draft. James was named 2004 NBA Rookie of the Year and has been on the NBA All Star team every year since 2005. He was named the league's MVP in 2009. James also played on the 2004 and 2008 U.S. Men's Olympic Basketball teams.

In 2000 New York Yankee **Derek Jeter** became the first baseball player to win both the All Star Game MVP and World Series MVP. He was selected as an MLB All-Star for eight out of ten years and in 2003 was named Yankees team captain.

Jimmie Johnson won the NASCAR Sprint Cup Championship every year from 2006 to 2009. He was the 2006 Daytona 500 winner and three-time NASCAR Driver of the Year (2006, 2007, and 2009) and was named 2009 AP Male Athlete of the Year.

Randy Johnson was named four times to the MLB All Star team (2000–2002, and 2004) and won five Cy Young Awards (the final three in 2000–2002). Johnson was the co-MVP of the 2001 World Series that he won with the Arizona Diamondbacks.

Swimmer **Cullen Jones** won a gold medal at the 2008 Summer Olympics in the men's 4x100-meter freestyle race (along with **Jason Lezak, Michael Phelps,** and **Garrett Weber-Gale**), in world-record time; he is the first African American swimmer to win a gold and only the third to make the U.S. team.

In 2000 **Michael Jordan,** arguably the greatest basketball player of all time, returned to the NBA as a part owner of the Washington Wizards and in 2001 returned as a player. While his comeback was plagued with injuries, Jordan was named an NBA All Star in 2002 and 2003. During the 2003 All Star game, his fourteenth and last, Jordan surpassed Kareem Abdul-Jabbar as the leading scorer in NBA All Star history. He officially retired at the end of the 2002–2003 season and now owns the Charlotte Bobcats.

Michelle Kwan is the most decorated figure skater in U.S. history with forty-two championships. She won U.S. titles (2000–2005) and World Championships (2000, 2001, and 2003) and won her second Olympic medal, a bronze, at the 2002 games.

Lisa Leslie, a pioneer in the Women's National Basketball Association, won two WNBA championships (2001–2002) with the Los Angeles Sparks. Three times the WNBA MVP (2001, 2004, and 2006), she appeared in seven WNBA All Star games (2000–2003, 2005–2006, and 2009). In 2002 Leslie became the first woman to dunk a ball in a WNBA game. She also

played on the U.S. Women's Olympic Basketball teams (2000, 2004, and 2008).

Ray Lewis, linebacker for the Baltimore Ravens, was selected for eight NFL Pro Bowls (2000–2001, 2003–2004, and 2006–2009). Lewis was awarded NFL Defensive Player of the Year in 2000 and 2003. In January 2001, Lewis won a Super Bowl XXXV ring and was named MVP of the game, becoming only the second linebacker to win the award.

Misty May-Treanor, along with teammate **Kerri Walsh,** was gold medalist in Women's Beach Volleyball at both the 2004 and 2008 Summer Olympic Games, bringing great popularity to the sport. During 2007–2008 they had a winning streak of more than 100 matches and 18 tournaments.

Phil Mickelson earned three major golf championships: the 2004 Masters, 2005 PGA Championship, and 2006 Masters. He won the World Championship and PGA Tour Championship in 2009.

Bode Miller, alpine ski racer, won the World Cup in 2005 and 2008. At the World Championships in 2003, Miller won two golds and one bronze medal in various events, and nabbed two more golds at the 2005 World Championships. At the 2002 Olympics in Salt Lake City, Miller took home two silver medals.

With 120 touchdowns this decade, **Randy Moss** stood out as one of the best receivers in the NFL. He totaled more than 11,000 yards from 2000 to 2009, playing with the Minnesota Vikings (2000–2004), Oakland Raiders (2005–2006), and New England Patriots (2007–2009). Moss was selected to five Pro Bowls (2000, 2002, 2003, 2007, and 2009) and was named the game's MVP in 2000.

Apolo Ohno won two medals (gold and silver) in speedskating at the 2002 Winter Olympic Games and another three medals (one gold and two bronze) at the 2006 Olympics. He won twenty-one World Championship medals, which included eight gold, seven silver, and six bronze medals.

Shaquille "Shaq" O'Neal won four NBA championships, three with the Los Angeles Lakers (2000–2002) and one with the Miami Heat (2006). O'Neal was NBA MVP in 2000 and NBA finals MVP (2000–2002), appeared in every NBA All Star game from 2000 to 2007 and again in 2009, and was named All-Star MVP three times (2000, 2004, and 2009).

Alexander Ovechkin was chosen number one in the 2004 NHL draft by the Washington Capitals, for whom he later played as captain. He was named NHL Rookie of the Year in 2006 and was awarded the Hart Memorial Trophy as MVP in 2008 and 2009. Ovechkin was voted to the All Star team from 2007 to 2009.

Albert Pujols won the MLB's Rookie of the Year title in 2001 and league MVP in 2005, 2008, and 2009. One of the top hitters in baseball, Pujols and the St. Louis Cardinals won the World Series in 2006. He was named an All Star in 2001 and each year from 2003 to 2009.

Andy Roddick won the U.S. Open tennis title in 2003. Roddick reached the Wimbledon singles finals three times (2004, 2005, and 2009), each time being defeated by Roger Federer. He held the record for fastest men's tennis serve at 155 miles per hour.

In 2007 **Alex "A-Rod" Rodriguez** became the youngest baseball player to hit 500 home runs. He signed a $275 million, ten-year contract with the New York Yankees, the richest contract in baseball history. Rodriguez earned nine All Star selections (2000–2008), four Silver Slugger Awards (2003, 2005, 2007, and 2008), and three American League MVPs (2003, 2005, and 2007). He won a World Series ring in 2009.

Quarterback **Ben Roethlisberger** was a first-round NFL draft pick for the Pittsburgh Steelers in 2004 and was named Offensive Rookie of the Year. In 2005, at twenty-three years old, he became the youngest quarterback to lead his team to Super Bowl victory. In 2009 he guided the team to its second Super Bowl win of the decade.

Johan Santana pitched for the Minnesota Twins (2000–2007) and the New York Mets (2008–2009). He twice won the Cy Young Award (2004 and 2006) and was named an All Star four times (2005–2007 and 2009). He was also chosen for *Sports Illustrated*'s MLB All-Decade team.

Tony Stewart won the 2002 Winston Cup and 2005 Nextel Cup.

Jenny Thompson collected twelve Olympic medals in swimming—earning three golds and one bronze in 2000 and two silver in 2004. In 2006 Thompson received her medical degree from Columbia University.

At the 2008 Summer Olympics, **Dara Torres**, 41, became the first U.S. swimmer to compete in five Olympic Games (1984, 1988, 1992, 2000, and 2008) and the oldest swimmer to be on any U.S. Olympic team. She won

three silver medals at the 2008 Olympics, bringing her career total to four apiece of gold, silver, and bronze.

Quarterback **Michael Vick** was the number-one NFL draft pick in 2001, chosen by the Atlanta Falcons. Selected for the Pro Bowl in 2002, 2004, and 2005, and awarded the ESPY Best NFL Player in 2003, Vick led the Falcons to the playoffs in two of his first six years. In 2007 he pled guilty to felony charges for running an illegal dog-fighting operation and was suspended from the NFL and sentenced to twenty-one months in prison. In 2009 Vick returned to the NFL and was signed by the Philadelphia Eagles.

Downhill ski racer **Lindsey Vonn** won the World Cup in 2008 and 2009; she also earned two gold medals at the World Championships in 2009.

In 2000 ten-year-old **Michelle Wie** became the youngest player to qualify for a United States Golf Association (USGA) amateur championship. At fifteen, Wie announced that she was turning professional. In 2009 she joined the LPGA, and the same year she earned her first professional win.

Serena Williams became the number-one player in women's tennis for the first time in 2002, a ranking she held until the following year. In singles, Williams won the Australian Open (2003, 2005, 2007, and 2009), French Open (2002), Wimbledon (2002–2003 and 2009), and U.S. Open (2002 and 2008). She also twice won the WTA Championship (2001 and 2009). In doubles, Serena and her sister **Venus** won the Australian Open (2001, 2003, and 2009), Wimbledon (2000, 2002, and 2008–2009), and U.S. Open (2009). The pair also won gold medals at the 2000 and 2008 Olympics. Serena has won more career prize money than any other female athlete.

Venus Williams was also ranked number one in women's tennis. In singles, Venus won Wimbledon (2000–2001, 2005, and 2007–2008) and the U.S. Open (2000–2001). She won the WTA Championship in 2008.

AWARDS

2000

Athletes of the Year (Associated Press) — Tiger Woods (golf) and Marion Jones (track)

Sports Illustrated **Sportsman of the Year** — Tiger Woods (golf)

Baseball Writers Association of America Most Valuable Player (American League) — Jason Giambi (Oakland Athletics)

Baseball Writers Association of America Most Valuable Player (National League) — Jeff Kent (San Francisco Giants)

Cy Young (American League) — Pedro Martinez (Boston Red Sox)

Cy Young (National League) — Randy Johnson (Arizona Diamondbacks)

Naismith College Players of the Year, Basketball — Kenyon Martin (Cincinnati) and Tamika Catchings (Tennessee)

John R. Wooden Award, Basketball — Kenyon Martin (Cincinnati)

NBA Most Valuable Player, Professional Basketball — Shaquille O'Neal (Los Angeles Lakers)

WNBA Most Valuable Player — Sheryl Swoopes (Houston Comets)

Heisman Trophy, College Football — Chris Weinke (Florida State)

Outland Trophy — John Henderson (Tennessee)

NFL Most Valuable Player, Professional Football (Associated Press) — Marshall Faulk (St. Louis Rams)

Pro Football Writers MVP — Marshall Faulk (St. Louis Rams)

NHL Hart Memorial Trophy, Hockey — Chris Pronger (St. Louis Blues)

Driver of the Year, Racing — Bobby Labonte

Chevrolet U.S. Soccer Federation Players of the Year — Chris Armas and Tiffeny Milbrett

Honda Player of the Year, Soccer — Claudio Reyna

Major League Baseball World Series — New York Yankees (American League), 4 vs. New York Mets (National League), 1

Super Bowl XXXIV — St. Louis Rams, 23 vs. Tennessee Titans, 16

National Collegiate Athletic Association Football Championship — Oklahoma Sooners

Indianapolis 500, Automobile Racing — Juan Pablo Montoya (Colombia)

Daytona 500, Automobile Racing — Dale Jarrett

National Basketball Association Championship — Los Angeles Lakers, 4 vs. Indiana Pacers, 2

Women's National Basketball Association Championship — Houston Comets, 2 vs. New York Liberty, 0

National Collegiate Athletic Association Men's Basketball Championship — Michigan State Spartans, 89 vs. University of Florida Gators, 76

National Collegiate Athletic Association Women's Basketball Championship — Connecticut Huskies, 71 vs. Tennessee Volunteers, 52

National Hockey League Stanley Cup — New Jersey Devils, 4 vs. Dallas Stars, 2

Major League Soccer Cup — Kansas City Wizards, 1 vs. Chicago Fire, 0

Kentucky Derby, Horse Racing — Fusaichi Pegasus

Ladies' Professional Golf Association Championship — Juli Inkster

U.S. Open Golf Championship — Tiger Woods

Masters Golf Tournament — Vijay Singh (Fiji)

U.S. Open Tennis Tournament — Marat Safin (Russia), Venus Williams

2001

Athletes of the Year (Associated Press) — Barry Bonds (baseball) and Jennifer Capriati (tennis)

Sports Illustrated **Sportsman of the Year** — Curt Schilling and Randy Johnson (baseball)

Baseball Writers Association of America Most Valuable Player (American League) — Ichiro Suzuki (Seattle Mariners)

Baseball Writers Association of America Most Valuable Player (National League) — Barry Bonds (San Francisco Giants)

Cy Young (American League) — Roger Clemens (New York Yankees)

Cy Young (National League) — Randy Johnson (Arizona Diamondbacks)

Naismith College Players of the Year, Basketball — Shane Battier (Duke) and Ruth Riley (Notre Dame)

John R. Wooden Award, Basketball — Shane Battier (Duke)

NBA Most Valuable Player, Professional Basketball — Allen Iverson (Philadelphia 76ers)

WNBA Most Valuable Player — Lisa Leslie (Los Angeles Sparks)

Heisman Trophy, College Football — Eric Crouch (Nebraska)

Outland Trophy — Bryant McKinnie (Miami)

NFL Most Valuable Player, Professional Football (Associated Press) — Kurt Warner (St. Louis Rams)

Pro Football Writers MVP — Marshall Faulk (St. Louis Rams)

NHL Hart Memorial Trophy, Hockey — Joe Sakic (Colorado Avalanche)

Driver of the Year, Racing — Jeff Gordon

Chevrolet U.S. Soccer Federation Players of the Year — Earnie Stewart and Tiffeny Milbrett

Honda Player of the Year, Soccer — Earnie Stewart

Major League Baseball World Series — Arizona Diamondbacks (National League), 4 vs. New York Yankees (American League), 3

Super Bowl XXXV — Baltimore Ravens, 34 vs. New York Giants, 7

National Collegiate Athletic Association Football Championship — University of Miami Hurricanes

Indianapolis 500, Automobile Racing — Helio Castroneves (Brazil)

Daytona 500, Automobile Racing — Michael Waltrip

National Basketball Association Championship — Los Angeles Lakers, 4 vs. Philadelphia 76ers, 1

Women's National Basketball Association Championship — Los Angeles Sparks, 2 vs. Charlotte Sting, 0

National Collegiate Athletic Association Men's Basketball Championship — Duke Blue Devils, 82 vs. Arizona Wildcats, 72

National Collegiate Athletic Association Women's Basketball — Notre Dame Fighting Irish, 68 vs. Purdue Boilermakers, 66

National Hockey League Stanley Cup — Colorado Avalanche, 4 vs. New Jersey Devils, 3

Major League Soccer Cup — San Jose Earthquakes, 2 vs. Los Angeles Galaxy, 1

Kentucky Derby, Horse Racing — Monarchos

Ladies' Professional Golf Association Championship — Karrie Webb (Australia)

U.S. Open Golf Championship — Retief Goosen (South Africa)

Masters Golf Tournament — Tiger Woods

U.S. Open Tennis Tournament — Lleyton Hewitt (Australia), Venus Williams

2002

Athletes of the Year (Associated Press) — Lance Armstrong (cycling) and Serena Williams (tennis)

Sports Illustrated **Sportsman of the Year** — Lance Armstrong (cycling)

Baseball Writers Association of America Most Valuable Player (American League) — Miguel Tejada (Oakland Athletics)

Baseball Writers Association of America Most Valuable Player (National League) — Barry Bonds (San Francisco Giants)

Cy Young (American League) — Barry Zito (Oakland Athletics)

Cy Young (National League) — Randy Johnson (Arizona Diamondbacks)

Naismith College Players of the Year, Basketball — Jason Williams (Duke) and Sue Bird (Connecticut)

John R. Wooden Award, Basketball — Jason Williams (Duke)

NBA Most Valuable Player, Professional Basketball — Tim Duncan (San Antonio Spurs)

WNBA Most Valuable Player — Sheryl Swoopes (Houston Comets)

Heisman Trophy, College Football — Carson Palmer (Southern California)

Outland Trophy — Rien Long (Washington State)

NFL Most Valuable Player, Professional Football (Associated Press) — Rich Gannon (Oakland Raiders)

Pro Football Writers MVP — Rich Gannon (Oakland Raiders)

NHL Hart Memorial Trophy, Hockey — Jose Theodore (Montreal Canadiens)

Driver of the Year, Racing — Cristiano da Matta

Chevrolet U.S. Soccer Federation Players of the Year — Brad Friedel and Shannon MacMillan

Honda Player of the Year, Soccer — Landon Donovan

Major League Baseball World Series — Anaheim Angels (American League), 4 vs. San Francisco Giants (National League), 3

Super Bowl XXXVI — New England Patriots, 20 vs. St. Louis Rams, 17

National Collegiate Athletic Association Football Championship — Ohio State Buckeyes

Indianapolis 500, Automobile Racing — Helio Castroneves (Brazil)

Daytona 500, Automobile Racing — Ward Burton

National Basketball Association Championship — Los Angeles Lakers, 4 vs. New Jersey Nets, 0

Women's National Basketball Association Championship — Los Angeles Sparks, 2 vs. New York Liberty, 0

National Collegiate Athletic Association Men's Basketball Championship — Maryland Terrapins, 64 vs. Indiana Hoosiers, 52

National Collegiate Athletic Association Women's Basketball Championship — Connecticut Huskies, 82 vs. Oklahoma Sooners, 70

National Hockey League Stanley Cup — Detroit Red Wings, 4 vs. Carolina Hurricanes, 1

Major League Soccer Cup — Los Angeles Galaxy, 1 vs. New England Revolution, 0

Kentucky Derby, Horse Racing — War Emblem

Ladies' Professional Golf Association Championship — Se Ri Pak (South Korea)

U.S. Open Golf Championship — Tiger Woods

Masters Golf Tournament — Tiger Woods

U.S. Open Tennis Tournament — Pete Sampras, Serena Williams

2003

Athletes of the Year (Associated Press) — Lance Armstrong (cycling) and Annika Sörenstam (golf, Sweden)

Sports Illustrated **Sportsman of the Year** — David Robinson and Tim Duncan (basketball)

Baseball Writers Association of America Most Valuable Player (American League) — Alex Rodriguez (Texas Rangers)

Baseball Writers Association of America Most Valuable Player (National League) — Barry Bonds (San Francisco Giants)

Cy Young (American League) — Roy Halladay (Toronto Blue Jays)

Cy Young (National League) — Eric Gagne (Los Angeles Dodgers)

Naismith College Players of the Year, Basketball — T. J. Ford (Texas) and Diana Taurasi (Connecticut)

John R. Wooden Award, Basketball — T. J. Ford (Texas)

NBA Most Valuable Player, Professional Basketball — Tim Duncan (San Antonio Spurs)

WNBA Most Valuable Player — Lauren Jackson (Seattle Storm)

Heisman Trophy, College Football — Jason White (Oklahoma)

Outland Trophy — Robert Gallery (Iowa)

NFL Most Valuable Player, Professional Football (Associated Press) — Peyton Manning (Indianapolis Colts) and Steve McNair (Tennessee Titans)

Pro Football Writers MVP — Jamal Lewis (Baltimore Ravens)

NHL Hart Memorial Trophy, Hockey — Peter Forsberg (Colorado Avalanche)

Driver of the Year, Racing — Ryan Newman

Chevrolet U.S. Soccer Federation Players of the Year — Landon Donovan and Abby Wambach

Honda Player of the Year, Soccer — Landon Donovan

Major League Baseball World Series — Florida Marlins (National League), 4 vs. New York Yankees (American League), 2

Super Bowl XXXVII — Tampa Bay Buccaneers, 48 vs. Oakland Raiders, 21

National Collegiate Athletic Association Football Championship — Louisiana State University Tigers

Indianapolis 500, Automobile Racing — Gil de Ferran (Brazil)

Daytona 500, Automobile Racing — Michael Waltrip

National Basketball Association Championship — San Antonio Spurs, 4 vs. New Jersey Nets, 2

Women's National Basketball Association Championship — Detroit Shock, 2 vs. Los Angeles Sparks, 1

National Collegiate Athletic Association Men's Basketball Championship — Syracuse Orangemen, 81 vs. Kansas Jayhawks, 78

National Collegiate Athletic Association Women's Basketball Championship — Connecticut Huskies, 73 vs. Tennessee Volunteers, 68

National Hockey League Stanley Cup — New Jersey Devils, 4 vs. Mighty Ducks of Anaheim, 3

Major League Soccer Cup — San Jose Earthquakes, 4 vs. Chicago Fire, 2

Kentucky Derby, Horse Racing — Funny Cide

Ladies' Professional Golf Association Championship — Annika Sörenstam (Sweden)

U.S. Open Golf Championship — Jim Furyk

Masters Golf Tournament — Mike Weir (Canada)

U.S. Open Tennis Tournament — Andy Roddick, Justine Henin (Belgium)

2004

Athletes of the Year (Associated Press) — Lance Armstrong (cycling) and Annika Sörenstam (golf, Sweden)

Sports Illustrated **Sportsman of the Year** — Boston Red Sox (baseball)

Baseball Writers Association of America Most Valuable Player (American League) — Vladimir Guerrero (Anaheim Angels)

Baseball Writers Association of America Most Valuable Player (National League) — Barry Bonds (San Francisco Giants)

Cy Young (American League) — Johan Santana (Minnesota Twins)

Cy Young (National League) — Roger Clemens (New York Yankees)

Naismith College Players of the Year, Basketball — Jameer Nelson (St. Joseph's) and Diana Taurasi (Connecticut)

John R. Wooden Award, Basketball — Jameer Nelson (St. Joseph's) and Alana Beard (Duke)

NBA Most Valuable Player, Professional Basketball — Kevin Garnett (Minnesota Timberwolves)

WNBA Most Valuable Player — Lisa Leslie (Los Angeles Sparks)

Heisman Trophy, College Football — Matt Leinart (Southern California)

Outland Trophy — Jammal Brown (Oklahoma)

NFL Most Valuable Player, Professional Football (Associated Press) — Peyton Manning (Indianapolis Colts)

Pro Football Writers MVP — Peyton Manning (Indianapolis Colts)

NHL Hart Memorial Trophy, Hockey — Martin St. Louis (Tampa Bay Lightning)

Driver of the Year, Racing — Greg Anderson

Chevrolet U.S. Soccer Federation Players of the Year — Landon Donovan and Abby Wambach

Honda Player of the Year, Soccer — Landon Donovan

Major League Baseball World Series — Boston Red Sox (American League), 4 vs. St. Louis Cardinals (National League), 0

Super Bowl XXXVIII — New England Patriots, 32 vs. Carolina Panthers, 29

National Collegiate Athletic Association Football Championship — University of Southern California Trojans

Indianapolis 500, Automobile Racing — Buddy Rice

Daytona 500, Automobile Racing — Dale Earnhardt Jr.

National Basketball Association Championship — Detroit Pistons, 4 vs. Los Angeles Lakers, 1

Women's National Basketball Association Championship — Seattle Storm, 2 vs. Connecticut Sun, 1

National Collegiate Athletic Association Men's Basketball Championship — Connecticut Huskies, 82 vs. Georgia Tech Yellow Jackets, 73

National Collegiate Athletic Association Women's Basketball Championship — Connecticut Huskies, 70 vs. Tennessee Volunteers, 61

National Hockey League Stanley Cup — Tampa Bay Lightning, 4 vs. Calgary Flames, 3

Major League Soccer Cup — D.C. United, 3 vs. Kansas City Wizards, 2

Kentucky Derby, Horse Racing — Smarty Jones

Ladies' Professional Golf Association Championship — Annika Sörenstam (Sweden)

U.S. Open Golf Championship — Retief Goosen (South Africa)

Masters Golf Tournament — Phil Mickelson

U.S. Open Tennis Tournament — Roger Federer (Switzerland), Svetlana Kuznetsova (Russia)

2005

Athletes of the Year (Associated Press) — Lance Armstrong (cycling) and Annika Sörenstam (golf, Sweden)

Sports Illustrated **Sportsman of the Year** — Tom Brady (football)

Baseball Writers Association of America Most Valuable Player (American League) — Alex Rodriguez (New York Yankees)

Baseball Writers Association of America Most Valuable Player (National League) — Albert Pujols (St. Louis Cardinals)

Cy Young (American League) — Bartolo Colon (Los Angeles Angels)

Cy Young (National League) — Chris Carpenter (St. Louis Cardinals)

Naismith College Players of the Year, Basketball — Andrew Bogut (Utah) and Seimone Augustus (LSU)

John R. Wooden Award, Basketball — Andrew Bogut (Utah) and Seimone Augustus (Louisiana)

NBA Most Valuable Player, Professional Basketball — Steve Nash (Phoenix Suns)

WNBA Most Valuable Player — Sheryl Swoopes (Houston Comets)

Heisman Trophy, College Football — Reggie Bush (Southern California) [trophy was returned]

Outland Trophy — Greg Eslinger (Minnesota)

NFL Most Valuable Player, Professional Football (Associated Press) — Shaun Alexander (Seattle Seahawks)

Pro Football Writers MVP — Shaun Alexander (Seattle Seahawks)

NHL Hart Memorial Trophy, Hockey — No Winner

Driver of the Year, Racing — Tony Stewart

Chevrolet U.S. Soccer Federation Players of the Year — Kasey Keller and Kristine Lilly

Honda Player of the Year, Soccer — Kasey Keller

Major League Baseball World Series — Chicago White Sox (American League), 4 vs. Houston Astros (National League), 0

Super Bowl XXXIX — New England Patriots, 24 vs. Philadelphia Eagles, 21

National Collegiate Athletic Association Football Championship — University of Texas Longhorns

Indianapolis 500, Automobile Racing — Dan Wheldon (Great Britain)

Daytona 500, Automobile Racing — Jeff Gordon

National Basketball Association Championship — San Antonio Spurs, 4 vs. Detroit Pistons, 3

Women's National Basketball Association Championship — Sacramento Monarchs, 3 vs. Connecticut Sun, 1

National Collegiate Athletic Association Men's Basketball Championship — North Carolina Tar Heels, 75 vs. Illinois Fighting Illini, 70

National Collegiate Athletic Association Women's Basketball Championship — Baylor Bears, 84 vs. Michigan State Spartans, 62

National Hockey League Stanley Cup — No Winner

Major League Soccer Cup — Los Angeles Galaxy, 1 vs. New England Revolution, 0

Kentucky Derby, Horse Racing — Giacomo

Ladies' Professional Golf Association Championship — Annika Sörenstam (Sweden)

U.S. Open Golf Championship — Michael Campbell (New Zealand)

Masters Golf Tournament — Tiger Woods

U.S. Open Tennis Tournament — Roger Federer (Switzerland), Kim Clijsters (Belgium)

2006

Athletes of the Year (Associated Press) — Tiger Woods (golf) and Lorena Ochoa (golf, Mexico)

Sports Illustrated **Sportsman of the Year** — Dwyane Wade (basketball)

Baseball Writers Association of America Most Valuable Player (American League) — Justin Morneau (Minnesota Twins)

Baseball Writers Association of America Most Valuable Player (National League) — Ryan Howard (Philadelphia Phillies)

Cy Young (American League) — Johan Santana (Minnesota Twins)

Cy Young (National League) — Brandon Webb (Arizona Diamondbacks)

Naismith College Players of the Year, Basketball — J. J. Redick (Duke) and Seimone Augustus (LSU)

John R. Wooden Award, Basketball — J. J. Redick (Duke) and Seimone Augustus (LSU)

NBA Most Valuable Player, Professional Basketball — Steve Nash (Phoenix Suns)

WNBA Most Valuable Player — Lisa Leslie (Los Angeles Sparks)

Heisman Trophy, College Football — Troy Smith (Ohio State)

Outland Trophy — Joe Thomas (Wisconsin)

NFL Most Valuable Player, Professional Football (Associated Press) — LaDainian Tomlinson (San Diego Chargers)

Pro Football Writers MVP — LaDainian Tomlinson (San Diego Chargers)

NHL Hart Memorial Trophy, Hockey — Joe Thornton (Boston Bruins/San Jose Sharks)

Driver of the Year, Racing — Jimmie Johnson

Chevrolet U.S. Soccer Federation Players of the Year — Oguchi Onyewu and Kristine Lilly

Honda Player of the Year, Soccer — Clint Dempsey

Major League Baseball World Series — St. Louis Cardinals (National League), 4 vs. Detroit Tigers (American League), 1

Super Bowl XL — Pittsburgh Steelers, 21 vs. Seattle Seahawks, 10

National Collegiate Athletic Association Football Championship — University of Florida Gators

Indianapolis 500, Automobile Racing — Sam Hornish Jr.

Daytona 500, Automobile Racing — Jimmie Johnson

National Basketball Association Championship — Miami Heat, 4 vs. Dallas Mavericks, 2

Women's National Basketball Association Championship — Detroit Shock, 3 vs. Sacramento Monarchs, 2

National Collegiate Athletic Association Men's Basketball Championship — Florida Gators, 73 vs. UCLA Bruins, 57

National Collegiate Athletic Association Women's Basketball Championship — Maryland Terrapins, 78 vs. Duke Blue Devils, 75

National Hockey League Stanley Cup — Carolina Hurricanes, 4 vs. Edmonton Oilers, 3

Major League Soccer Cup — Houston Dynamo, 4 vs. New England Revolution, 3

Kentucky Derby, Horse Racing — Barbaro

Ladies' Professional Golf Association Championship — Se Ri Pak (South Korea)

U.S. Open Golf Championship — Geoff Ogilvy (Australia)

Masters Golf Tournament — Phil Mickelson

U.S. Open Tennis Tournament — Roger Federer (Switzerland), Maria Sharapova (Russia)

2007

Athletes of the Year (Associated Press) — Tom Brady (football) and Lorena Ochoa (golf, Mexico)

Sports Illustrated **Sportsman of the Year** — Brett Favre (football)

Baseball Writers Association of America Most Valuable Player (American League) — Alex Rodriguez (New York Yankees)

Baseball Writers Association of America Most Valuable Player (National League) — Jimmy Rollins (Philadelphia Phillies)

Cy Young (American League) — C. C. Sabathia (Cleveland Indians)

Cy Young (National League) — Jake Peavy (San Diego Padres)

Naismith College Players of the Year, Basketball — Kevin Durant (Texas) and Lindsey Harding (Duke)

John R. Wooden Award, Basketball — Kevin Durant (Texas) and Candace Parker (Tennessee)

NBA Most Valuable Player, Professional Basketball — Dirk Nowitzki (Dallas Mavericks)

WNBA Most Valuable Player — Lauren Jackson (Seattle Storm)

Heisman Trophy, College Football — Tim Tebow (Florida)

Outland Trophy — Glenn Dorsey (Louisiana State)

NFL Most Valuable Player, Professional Football (Associated Press) — Tom Brady (New England Patriots)

Pro Football Writers MVP — Tom Brady (New England Patriots)

NHL Hart Memorial Trophy, Hockey — Sidney Crosby (Pittsburgh Penguins)

Driver of the Year, Racing — Jimmie Johnson

Chevrolet U.S. Soccer Federation Players of the Year — Clint Dempsey and Abby Wambach

Honda Player of the Year, Soccer — Landon Donovan

Major League Baseball World Series — Boston Red Sox (American League), 4 vs. Colorado Rockies (National League), 0

Super Bowl XLI — Indianapolis Colts, 29 vs. Chicago Bears, 17

National Collegiate Athletic Association Football Championship — Louisiana State University Tigers

Indianapolis 500, Automobile Racing — Dario Franchitti (Scotland)

Daytona 500, Automobile Racing — Kevin Harvick

National Basketball Association Championship — San Antonio Spurs, 4 vs. Cleveland Cavaliers, 0

Women's National Basketball Association Championship — Phoenix Mercury, 3 vs. Detroit Shock, 2

National Collegiate Athletic Association Men's Basketball Championship — Florida Gators, 84 vs. Ohio State Buckeyes, 75

National Collegiate Athletic Association Women's Basketball Championship — Tennessee Volunteers, 59 vs. Rutgers Scarlet Knights, 46

National Hockey League Stanley Cup — Mighty Ducks of Anaheim, 4 vs. Ottawa Senators, 1

Major League Soccer Cup — Houston Dynamo, 2 vs. New England Revolution, 1

Kentucky Derby, Horse Racing — Street Sense

Ladies' Professional Golf Association Championship — Suzann Pettersen (Norway)

U.S. Open Golf Championship — Angel Cabrera (Argentina)

Masters Golf Tournament — Zach Johnson

U.S. Open Tennis Tournament — Roger Federer (Switzerland), Justine Henin (Belgium)

2008

Athletes of the Year (Associated Press) — Michael Phelps (swimming) and Candace Parker (basketball)

Sports Illustrated **Sportsman of the Year** — Michael Phelps (swimming)

Baseball Writers Association of America Most Valuable Player (American League) — Dustin Pedroia (Boston Red Sox)

Baseball Writers Association of America Most Valuable Player (National League) — Albert Pujols (St. Louis Cardinals)

Cy Young (American League) — Cliff Lee (Cleveland Indians)

Cy Young (National League) — Tim Lincecum (San Francisco Giants)

Naismith College Players of the Year, Basketball — Tyler Hansbrough (North Carolina) and Candace Parker (Tennessee)

John R. Wooden Award, Basketball — Tyler Hansbrough (North Carolina) and Candace Parker (Tennessee)

NBA Most Valuable Player, Professional Basketball — Kobe Bryant (Los Angeles Lakers)

WNBA Most Valuable Player — Candace Parker (Los Angeles Sparks)

Heisman Trophy, College Football — Sam Bradford (Oklahoma)

Outland Trophy — Andre Smith (Alabama)

NFL Most Valuable Player, Professional Football (Associated Press) — Peyton Manning (Indianapolis Colts)

Pro Football Writers MVP — Peyton Manning (Indianapolis Colts)

NHL Hart Memorial Trophy, Hockey — Alexander Ovechkin (Washington Capitals)

Driver of the Year, Racing — Tony Schumacher

Chevrolet U.S. Soccer Federation Players of the Year — Tim Howard and Carli Lloyd

Honda Player of the Year, Soccer — Landon Donovan

Major League Baseball World Series — Philadelphia Phillies (National League), 4 vs. Tampa Bay Rays (American League), 1

Super Bowl XLII — New York Giants, 17 vs. New England Patriots, 14

National Collegiate Athletic Association Football Championship — University of Florida Gators

Indianapolis 500, Automobile Racing — Scott Dixon (New Zealand)

Daytona 500, Automobile Racing — Ryan Newman

National Basketball Association Championship — Boston Celtics, 4 vs. Los Angeles Lakers, 2

Women's National Basketball Association Championship — Detroit Shock, 3 vs. San Antonio Silver Stars, 0

National Collegiate Athletic Association Men's Basketball Championship — Kansas Jayhawks, 75 vs. Memphis Tigers, 68

National Collegiate Athletic Association Women's Basketball Championship — Tennessee Volunteers, 64 vs. Stanford Cardinal, 48

National Hockey League Stanley Cup — Detroit Red Wings, 4 vs. Pittsburgh Penguins, 2

Major League Soccer Cup — Columbus Crew, 3 vs. New York Red Bulls, 1

Kentucky Derby, Horse Racing — Big Brown

Ladies' Professional Golf Association Championship — Yani Tseng (Taiwan)

U.S. Open Golf Championship — Tiger Woods

Masters Golf Tournament — Trevor Immelman (South Africa)

U.S. Open Tennis Tournament — Roger Federer (Switzerland), Serena Williams

2009

Athletes of the Year (Associated Press) — Jimmie Johnson (racing) and Serena Williams (tennis)

Sports Illustrated **Sportsman of the Year** — Derek Jeter (baseball)

Baseball Writers Association of America Most Valuable Player (American League) — Joe Mauer (Minnesota Twins)

Baseball Writers Association of America Most Valuable Player (National League) — Albert Pujols (St. Louis Cardinals)

Cy Young (American League) — Zack Greinke (Kansas City Royals)

Cy Young (National League) — Tim Lincecum (San Francisco Giants)

Naismith College Players of the Year, Basketball — Blake Griffin (Oklahoma) and Maya Moore (Connecticut)

John R. Wooden Award, Basketball — Blake Griffin (Oklahoma) and Maya Moore (Connecticut)

NBA Most Valuable Player, Professional Basketball — LeBron James (Cleveland Cavaliers)

WNBA Most Valuable Player — Diana Taurasi (Phoenix Mercury)

Heisman Trophy, College Football — Mark Ingram (Alabama)

Outland Trophy — Ndamukong Suh (Nebraska)

NFL Most Valuable Player, Professional Football (Associated Press) — Peyton Manning (Indianapolis Colts)

Pro Football Writers MVP — Peyton Manning (Indianapolis Colts)

NHL Hart Memorial Trophy, Hockey — Alexander Ovechkin (Washington Capitals)

Driver of the Year, Racing — Jimmie Johnson

Chevrolet U.S. Soccer Federation Players of the Year — Landon Donovan and Hope Solo

Honda Player of the Year, Soccer — Landon Donovan

Major League Baseball World Series — New York Yankees (American League), 4 vs. Philadelphia Phillies (National League), 2

Super Bowl XLIII — Pittsburgh Steelers, 27 vs. Arizona Cardinals, 23

National Collegiate Athletic Association Football Championship — University of Alabama Crimson Tide

Indianapolis 500, Automobile Racing — Helio Castroneves (Brazil)

Daytona 500, Automobile Racing — Matt Kenseth

National Basketball Association Championship — Los Angeles Lakers, 4 vs. Orlando Magic, 1

Women's National Basketball Association Championship — Phoenix Mercury, 3 vs. Indiana Fever, 2

National Collegiate Athletic Association Men's Basketball Championship — North Carolina Tar Heels, 89 vs. Michigan State Spartans, 72

National Collegiate Athletic Association Women's Basketball Championship — Connecticut Huskies, 76 vs. Louisville Cardinals, 54

National Hockey League Stanley Cup — Pittsburgh Penguins, 4 vs. Detroit Red Wings, 3

Major League Soccer Cup — Real Salt Lake, 5 vs. Los Angeles Galaxy, 4

Kentucky Derby, Horse Racing — Mine That Bird

Ladies' Professional Golf Association Championship — Anna Nordqvist (Sweden)

U.S. Open Golf Championship — Lucas Glover

Masters Golf Tournament — Angel Cabrera (Argentina)

U.S. Open Tennis Tournament — Juan Martin del Potro (Argentina), Kim Clijsters (Belgium)

DEATHS

Sid Abel, 81, hockey player for the Detroit Red Wings and Chicago Black Hawks; won three Stanley Cups (1943, 1950, and 1952); inducted into the hockey Hall of Fame (1969), 8 February 2000.

Nicholas "Nick" Adenhart, 22, pitcher for the Los Angeles Angels of Anaheim; hours after his season debut, Adenhart was killed in a car accident by a drunk driver, 9 April 2009.

Tommie Agee, 58, center fielder for the New York Mets (1968–1972); made two famous catches during the 1969 World Series to help the Mets win the championship, 22 January 2001.

Arnold "Red" Auerbach, 89, basketball coach; won nine NBA championships with the Boston Celtics, as well as seven more titles as general manager, 28 October 2006.

Terry Albert Barr, 73, wide receiver and defensive back with the Detroit Lions (1957–1965); two-time All Pro, 28 May 2009.

Henry "Hank" Bauer, 84, right fielder for the New York Yankees (1948–1959) and the Kansas City Athletics (1960–1961); manager for the Athletics in Kansas City (1961–1962) and Oakland (1969) as well as for the Baltimore Orioles (1964–1968); during his time with the Yankees, Bauer won nine American League pennants and seven World Series; set Series record with seventeen-game hitting streak; led Orioles to their first World Series title (1966), 9 February 2007.

Sammy "Slingin' Sammy" Baugh, 94, quarterback for the Washington Redskins (1937–1952), won NFL MVP (1947–1948); his role in the development of the forward pass into play earned him a spot in the Hall of Fame (1963), 17 December 2008.

Patricia "Patty" Berg, 88, founding member of and leading competitor in the Ladies Professional Golf Association (LPGA); collected more than sixty career wins, including a record fifteen major titles; was the Associated Press's (AP) female athlete of the year (1938, 1943, and 1955); inducted into the World Golf Hall of Fame (1951), 10 September 2006.

John "Jay" Berwanger, 88, first player to receive the Heisman Trophy (1935); first player picked in the NFL's inaugural college draft (1938) but chose not to play in the league, 26 June 2002.

Felix A. "Doc" Blanchard, 84, West Point (USMA) halfback, known as "Mr. Inside"; won Heisman Award (1945), 19 April 2009.

Bobby Bonds, 57, right fielder for the San Francisco Giants (1968–1974) and seven other teams; three-time All Star (1971, 1973, and 1975), three-time Golden Glove winner (1971, 1973, and 1974); father of slugger Barry Bonds, 23 August 2003.

Lou Boudreau, 84, shortstop (1938–1950) and manager (1942–1950) for the Cleveland Indians, he led team to World Series win (1948); Baseball Hall of Famer (1970), 10 August 2001.

Myles Brand, 67, reformer, head of the NCAA (2003–2009); introduced stricter academic standards for college athletes; while president of Indiana University he fired Indiana University basketball head coach Bob Knight for abusive behavior, 16 September 2009.

Herbert Paul Brooks Jr., 66, hockey coach; led the U.S. Olympic hockey team to the gold medal in the 1980 Winter Olympics (including a victory in a semifinals match known as the "Miracle on Ice" against the heavily favored Soviet team); inducted into the Hockey Hall of Fame (2006), 11 August 2003.

Don Budge, 84, first tennis player to win the four most prestigious tournaments in a single year, the so-called Grand Slam (1938), 26 January 2000.

Chester "Chet" Bulger, 91, lineman, played nine years in the NFL; starred on the Chicago Cardinals championship team (1947), 18 February 2009.

Susan Butcher, 51, dogsled racer; second woman to win Iditarod (1986), second four-time winner of the race (1986–1988 and 1990); Alaska Sports Hall of Fame inductee (2007), 5 August 2006.

Ken Caminiti, 41, third baseman who played primarily for the Houston Astros (1987–1994 and 1999–2000); won NL MVP (1996), 10 October 2004.

Bud Carson, 75, coach; as defensive coordinator for the Pittsburgh Steelers built the "Steel Curtain" line, 7 December 2005.

Stephen P. "Steve" Courson, 50, guard; played for Pittsburgh Steelers (1978–1983) and Tampa Bay Buccaneers (1984–1985); admitted using steroids since he was a freshman playing with the University of South Carolina Gamecocks, 10 November 2005.

Henry Charles "Shag" Crawford, 90, umpire; called major-league games for twenty years and worked three World Series, 11 July 2007.

Marvin Crawford, 74, Olympic skier, fourteen-time national champion in Nordic skiing, 10 January 2005.

Edward "Eddie" Crook Jr., 76, boxer; won gold medal (165 pounds) at 1960 Olympics, 25 July 2005.

Charles "Chuck" Daly, 78, men's basketball coach; led Detroit Pistons to back-to-back NBA titles (1989–1990); coached the "Dream Team" to gold medal in 1992 Summer Olympics, 9 May 2009.

Glenn Davis, 74, sprinter and hurler, three-time gold medal winner in Olympics (1956 and 1960), 28 January 2009.

Jim Davis, 103, pioneer motorcycle racer, won 17 National Championships and 180 medals, 5 February 2000.

David "Dave" DeBusschere, 62, forward for the Detroit Pistons (1962–1969) and New York Knicks (1969–1974); won two NBA championships (1970 and 1973); Basketball Hall of Fame inductee (1983), 14 May 2003.

Mildred "Millie" Deegan, 82, pitchee and played second base with the All-American Girls Professional Baseball League (1943–1952) Rockford Peaches; nicknamed the "Babe Ruth of Women's Softball" for a home run she hit inside Madison Square Garden; her team was the focus of the movie *A League of Their Own* (1992), 21 July 2002.

Lawrence "Larry" Doby, 79, second African American player in the MLB and the first to play in the American League; centerfielder for the Cleveland Indians (1947–1955); won a World Series (1948), was a seven-time All Star player and a Baseball Hall of Fame inductee (1998), 18 June 2003.

Dale Earnhardt, 49, NASCAR driver who won 76 career races including the Daytona 500 (1998); tied Richard Petty for most all-time Winston Cup championship wins (7); was killed in a crash on turn four of the last lap of Daytona 500, 18 February 2001.

Gertrude Ederle, 98, Olympic swimmer; won gold medal (4x100-meter freestyle relay) and bronze medals (100-meter and 400-meter freestyle) at 1924 Paris Olympics; first woman to swim across the English Channel (1926), 30 November 2003.

Tom Fears, 77, wide receiver for the Los Angeles Rams (1948–1956), set a record for most catches (18) in a single game (1950); NFL Hall of Famer, 4 January 2000.

Robert "Bobby" Frankel, 68, race horse trainer; voted top trainer five times (1993 and 2000–2003); inducted into the Racing Hall of Fame (1995), 16 November 2009.

Clarence "Big House" Gaines, 81, college men's basketball coach at Winston-Salem State University (1946–1993); led team to 828 victories, won the 1967 Division II NCAA championship (first for a historically black university); Basketball Hall of Fame inductee (1982), 18 April 2005.

Kim Gallagher, 38, 800-meter runner, won two Olympic medals (silver, 1984; bronze, 1988), 18 November 2002.

Mary Garber, 92, North Carolina sportswriter; first woman to win Red Smith Award (2005); covered white and black sports in the segregated South, 21 September 2008.

Frank Gatski, 83, center; played for the Cleveland Browns, inducted into the Pro Football Hall of Fame (1985), 23 November 2005.

Althea Gibson, 76, credited with breaking the color barrier in tennis by becoming the first African American to compete on world tour and to win a Grand Slam title (1956); won Wimbledon titles (1957–1958); International Tennis Hall of Fame inductee (1971), 28 September 2003.

Herm Gilliam, 58, guard for the Portland Trail Blazers, 16 April 2005.

Curt Gowdy, 86, sports broadcaster (on ABC, NBC, and CBS), 20 February 2006.

Carole Caldwell Graebner, 65, tennis player, top-ranked American doubles player in 1963, 19 November 2008.

Otto Graham, 82, quarterback for the Cleveland Browns (1946–1955); won three league championships (1950,

1954, and 1955); awarded five Pro-Bowl selections and three league MVPs (1951, 1953, and 1955), Football Hall of Famer (1965), 17 December 2003.

Sue Gunter, 66, women's basketball coach for Louisiana State University (1982–2004); had fourteen seasons with twenty or more wins; appeared in fourteen NCAA tournaments, won two SEC championships (1991 and 2003); Basketball Hall of Famer (2005), 4 August 2005.

Frederick T. Haas Jr., 88, professional golfer; won five PGA tournaments, 26 January 2004.

Tom Haller, 67, catcher; played for the San Francisco Giants (1961–1967), Los Angeles Dodgers (1968–1971), and Detroit Tigers (1972), 26 November 2004.

Bobby Hamilton, 49, race-car driver; four time winner in the NASCAR Cup Series and 2004 Craftsman Truck Series champion, 7 January 2007.

Robert "Bob" Hayes, 59, Olympic sprinter; won two gold medals at the 1964 Tokyo Olympics (100-meter and 4x100-meter relay); played wide receiver for the Dallas Cowboys (1965–1974); won the 1971 Super Bowl, 18 September 2002.

Francis D. "Chick" Hearn, 85, announcer for the Los Angeles Lakers for forty-two years, 5 August 2002.

Curtis "Curt" Hennig, 44, professional wrestler, American Wrestling Association (AWA) and World Wrestling Foundation Intercontinental champion, 10 February 2003.

Elroy "Crazylegs" Hirsch, 80, running back, star for the Los Angeles Rams (1949–1957); three-time Pro Bowler; inducted into the Pro Football Hall of Fame (1968), 28 January 2004.

Steve Howe, 48, relief pitcher, played with the Los Angeles Dodgers; National League Rookie of the Year (1980); won World Series (1981), 28 April 2006.

Lamar Hunt, 74, leading promoter of several sports; founder of the American Football League (AFL) and of the Kansas City Chiefs; soccer's U.S. Open Cup is named after him; credited with coining the term "Super Bowl"; inducted into the Football Hall of Fame (1972), Soccer Hall of Fame (1982), International Tennis Hall of Fame (1993), 13 December 2006.

George "Larry" James, 61, sprinter; gold and silver medalist in the 1968 Olympic Games in Mexico City; famous for giving gloved "black power" salute on winners' stand, 6 November 2008.

Louis W. "Lou" Jones, 74, runner; won gold medal at 1956 Melbourne Olympics in 4x400-meter relay, 3 February 2006.

Robert Trent Jones Sr., 93, famed golf-course designer of hundreds of courses across America and the world, 14 June 2000.

Harry Kalas, 73, Philadelphia Phillies announcer and narrator for NFL films; collapsed in the press box at the new Nationals Stadium, 13 April 2009.

John A. "Johnny" Kelley, 97, long-distance runner and Olympic athlete; competed in 1936 and 1948 Olympics; won the Boston Marathon twice (1935 and 1945) and competed in it sixty-one times (last time in 1992 at age eighty-four); named "runner of the century" by *Runner's World* magazine (2000), 6 October 2004.

Jack Kemp, 73, quarterback and politician; played professionally in United States and Canada (1957–1969), including as quarterback of the Buffalo Bills (1962–1969); seven-time AFL All Star; represented New York in the U.S. House of Representatives (1971–1989); served as U.S. Secretary of Housing and Urban Development (1989–1993); Republican nominee for Vice President (1996), 2 May 2009.

Evel Knievel, 69, daredevil motorcyclist; inducted into Motorcycle Hall of Fame (1999), 30 November 2007.

Howard Komives, 67, guard; played for New York Knicks (1964–1968) and Detroit Pistons (1968–1972), 22 March 2009.

John "Jack" Kramer, 88, professional tennis player and leader in the development of the sport; won three Wimbledon titles in both singles and doubles (1946–1947) and seven U.S. Open titles in singles, doubles, and mixed doubles (1940–1941, 1943, and 1946–1947); helped establish Open Tennis (1968), erasing the distinction between amateur and professional players; founded and served as executive director of the Association of Tennis Professionals (1972); International Tennis Hall of Fame inductee (1968), 12 September 2009.

Malcolm Kutner, 77, boxer; as an amateur defeated Rocky Marciano (reportedly the only fighter to do so); acted in *The Joe Louis Story* (1953) and *Raging Bull* (1980), 30 January 2005.

Thomas W. "Tom" Landry, 75; coached the Dallas Cowboys from the team's inception in 1960 to 1988; led team to five Super Bowls (winning two); widely considered to have revolutionized football coaching with the implementation of the 4-3 defense, 12 February 2000.

Richard "Night Train" Lane, 73, defensive back who had a fourteen-year NFL career with the Los Angeles Rams, Chicago Cardinals, and Detroit Lions; seven-time Pro Bowler; intercepted fourteen passes in his rookie season with the Rams, 29 January 2002.

Bob Lemon, 79, pitcher for the Cleveland Indians (1946–1958) and manager for the New York Yankees (1978–1979 and 1981–1982); won the World Series as both a player (1948) and manager (1978); inducted into the Baseball Hall of Fame (1976), 11 January 2000.

David Little, 46, linebacker; played for the Pittsburgh Steelers and and was chosen for a Pro Bowl (1990), 17 March 2005.

Al Lopez, 97, Hall of Fame catcher and manager; played for Cleveland Indians and Chicago White Sox; managed Sox to pennant (1954), 30 October 2005.

Wellington Mara, 89, owner of the New York Giants (1959–2005); won two Super Bowls (1986 and 1990); inducted into Football Hall of Fame (1997), 25 October 2005.

Robert B. "Bob" Mathias, 75, track star, two-time Olympic decathlon champion (1948 and 1952); played football for Stanford University; four-term Californian Republican member of the U.S. House of Representatives (1967–1975), 2 September 2006.

Eddie Matthews, 69, third baseman for the Boston, Milwaukee, and Atlanta Braves (1952–1966); two-time World Series winner (1957 and 1968) and Baseball Hall of Fame inductee (1978), 18 February 2001.

Joey Maxim, 79, boxer, light heavyweight champion (1950–1952); defeated Sugar Ray Robinson to defend the title (1952), 2 June 2001.

Sherman L. "Jocko" Maxwell, 100, sports reporter; covered the Negro Baseball League; possibly the first African American sports broadcaster, 16 July 2008.

Frank "Tug" McGraw, 59, MLB relief pitcher for the New York Mets (1965–1974) and Philadelphia Phillies (1975–1984); won World Series (1969 and 1980); father of country-music musician Tim McGraw, 5 January 2004.

Jim McKay, 86, sportscaster; hosted ABC's *Wide World of Sports* for three decades; reported on the 1972 massacre of Israeli athletes at the Olympics in Berlin, 7 June 2008.

Stephen L. "Steve" McNair, 36, quarterback and all-time leading passer for the Houston Oilers/Tennessee Oilers/Tennessee Titans (1995–2005); earned three Pro Bowl selections (2000, 2003, and 2005); awarded NFL's MVP award (2003); led Titans to Super Bowl (1999), 4 July 2009.

Raymond Joseph Meyer, 92, basketball coach; led the DePaul University Blue Demons (1942–1984) to 724 victories and thirteen NCAA tournaments, 17 March 2006.

George Michael, 70, sportscaster, pathbreaker in the use of athletic highlight film for his nationally syndicated sports show, 24 December 2009.

George Mikan, 80, basketball center with the Minneapolis Lakers (1948–1956); won seven NBL, BAA, and NBA titles; named one of the greatest players of all time; inducted into the Basketball Hall of Fame (1959), 1 June 2005.

Sam Mills, 45, Pro Bowl linebacker who played with New Orleans Saints and Charlotte Panthers, 18 April 2005.

Wayne Miyata, 63, appeared in movie *The Endless Summer* (1966); made surfboards by hand, 21 March 2005.

Bobby Murcer, 62, outfielder and broadcaster; seventeen years in MLB with the New York Yankees, San Francisco Giants, and Chicago Cubs; five-time All Star; served as broadcaster for Yankees games for nearly twenty years, 12 July 2008.

Byron Nelson, 94, had the greatest year of any professional golfer when he won eleven consecutive and eighteen total tournaments in 1945; inducted into the World Golf Hall of Fame (1974); given the PGA Tour Lifetime Achievement Award (1997), 26 September 2006.

Peter "Pete" Newell, 93, coach who led the University of California's men's basketball team to the NCAA National Championship title in 1959; led the American Men's Olympic Basketball team to gold medal in 1960; ran a basketball camp and was a scout for several NBA teams; Basketball Hall of Famer (2010), 17 November 2008.

Kay Noble-Bell, 65, wrestler; active in the 1960s and 1970s (as Kay Noble), 27 April 2006.

Alfred A. "Al" Oerter, 71, track athlete, four-time Olympic champion in the discus throw (1956, 1960, 1964, and 1968), 1 October 2007.

John "Buck" O'Neil, 94, first baseman, manager, and goodwill ambassador for Negro League Baseball; became the first black coach in major league baseball, for the Chicago Cubs (1962), 6 October 2006.

Maureen Orcutt, 99, golfer and sportswriter; won or tied for first in three U.S. Women's Amateur tournaments, 9 January 2007.

Guglielmo Papaleo, better known as **Willie Pep,** 84, featherweight boxer who had 229 wins and only 11 losses; won world featherweight title (1942); inducted into the International Boxing Hall of Fame (1990), 23 November 2006.

Floyd Patterson, 71, boxer; two-time world heavyweight champion, youngest to ever win (21 years old) and regain the title; fifty-five career wins and only eight defeats; Olympic gold medalist as a middleweight in 1952, 11 May 2006.

Hyman "Hy" Peskin, 89, sports photographer; first staff photographer for *Sports Illustrated,* 2 June 2005.

Adam Kyler Petty, 19, racing driver; great-grandson of NASCAR star Lee Petty; mortally injured in practice run, 12 May 2000.

Lee Petty, 86, pioneer of NASCAR racing and one of its earliest stars with fifty-four career wins; won first Daytona 500 (1959); three-time Grand National champion; father of racer Winston Petty, grandfather of racer Kyle Petty, and great-grandfather of racer Adam Petty, 5 April 2000.

George Plimpton, 76, literary journalist; often worked out with professional athletes and wrote of the experiences—*Out of My League* (1961, baseball), *Paper Lion*

(1966, football), *The Bogey Man* (1966, golf), *Shadow Box* (1977), 26 September 2003.

Abe Pollin, 85, owner of the Washington Capitals (NHL), Washington Mystics (WNBA), and Washington Wizards (NBA); forty-six-year ownership of Wizards (known first as the Baltimore Bullets) was the longest in the NBA, 24 November 2009.

Polly Riley, 75, golfer; won more than one hundred tournaments; won the Tampa Open (1950), the first LPGA tour event, 13 March 2002.

Phil Rizzuto, 89, shortstop and broadcaster; played for the New York Yankees (1940s and 1950s), Hall of Famer, 13 August 2007.

Gerald Roberts, 85, rodeo star; won two national championships (1942 and 1948); inducted into several rodeo halls of fame, 31 December 2004.

Ronnie Robertson, 62, skater; won silver medal at 1956 Winter Olympics, 4 February 2000.

Reggie Roby, 43, punter; played sixteen seasons with the Miami Dolphins, Washington Redskins, Tampa Bay Buccaneers, Houston Oilers, and San Francisco 49ers; three-time Pro Bowler, 22 February 2005.

Lloyd Ruby, 81, race car driver; competed in eighteen straight Indy 500s; inducted into Indianapolis 500 Hall of Fame (1991), 23 March 2009.

Darrell Russell, 29, defensive tackle; played for the Oakland Raiders, earned Pro Bowl selections (1998–1999); suspended from NFL for drug violations (2004), 15 December 2005.

Glenn E. "Bo" Schembechler, 77, coach, head coach for Miami University (1963–1968) and the University of Michigan (1969–1989); inducted into College Football Hall of Fame (1993), 17 November 2006.

Otto Schnellbacher, 84, defensive back; played for the New York Giants (1950–1951); two-time All-Pro, 10 March 2008.

Margaret "Marge" Schott, 75, CEO and owner of the Cincinnati Reds (1984–1999); second woman to buy and own a North American sports team; controversial racial statements caused her to be banned from managing the team (1996–1998), 2 March 2004.

Texas "Tex" Schramm, 83, first president and general manger of the Dallas Cowboys (1960–1989); engineered merger of NFL and AFL; Football Hall of Fame inductee (1991), 15 July 2003.

William "Bill" Shoemaker, 73, jockey with more than 8,800 career wins, including eleven Triple Crown wins; National Museum of Racing Hall of Fame inductee (1958), 12 October 2003.

Seattle Slew, 28, race horse, winner of the Triple Crown (1977), 7 May 2002.

Sam Snead, 89, famed golfer who won more than eighty PGA events, including seven majors—three Masters (1949, 1952, and 1954), three PGA Championships (1942, 1949, and 1951), and one British Open (1946), 23 May 2002.

Jack Snow, 62, wide receiver; played for the Los Angeles Rams, Pro Bowl selection (1967), 9 January 2006.

Aileen Riggin Soule, 96, diver and swimmer; then-youngest American at fourteen to win Olympic gold (1920); won two additional medals in 1924 Olympics, 19 October 2002.

Warren Spahn, 82, left-handed pitcher for the Boston and Milwaukee Braves (1942 and 1946–1964); seventeen-time All Star selection; Cy Young Award winner (1957), World Series winner (1957), and Baseball Hall of Famer (1973), 24 November 2003.

Willie Stargell, 61, left fielder and first baseman for the Pittsburgh Pirates (1962–1982); helped the team win two World Series (1971 and 1979); Baseball Hall of Fame inductee (1988), 9 April 2001.

Ernie Stautner, 80, defensive lineman; played for the Pittsburgh Steelers; nine-time Pro Bowl player; defensive coach for the Dallas Cowboys; elected to the Football Hall of Fame (1969), 16 February 2006.

Henry "Hank" Stram, 82, coach of the Kansas City Chiefs (1960–1974); won three AFL championships and the Super Bowl (1969); inducted into Football Hall of Fame (2003), 4 July 2005.

Evan Tanner, 37, mixed-martial-arts fighter with a 32–8 career record; UFC middleweight champion (2005), circa 5 September 2008.

Sean Taylor, 24, free safety for the Washington Redskins (2004–2007); won 2001 National Championship with the University of Miami, selected to Pro Bowl team (2006); murdered during a home invasion, 27 November 2007.

Derrick Thomas, 33, defensive end for the Kansas City Chiefs; nine-time Pro Bowler who was one of the top pass rushers in football, 8 February 2000.

Sam Thompson Jr., 36, jockey; died after his horse threw him during a race at Los Alamitos, California, 30 December 2008.

Patrick "Pat" Tillman, 27, safety; drafted in 1998 by the Arizona Cardinals; played until 2001 when he left to serve in the U.S. Army (2002–2004); killed by "friendly fire" in Afghanistan; posthumously awarded Silver Star and Purple Heart, 22 April 2004.

Wayman Tisdale, 44, basketball forward and jazz musician; played twelve years with three NBA teams, 15 May 2009.

Burl A. Toler Sr., 81, football official, first African American official in the National Football League, 16 August 2009.

John "Johnny" Unitas, 69, famed quarterback for the Baltimore Colts (1956–1972); winner of three NFL MVP's

(1959, 1964, and 1967); two-time NFL champion (1958, "the greatest game ever played," and 1959) and Super Bowl champion (1970); ten-time Pro Bowler; inducted into the Football Hall of Fame (1979); held record for touchdown passes in forty-seven consecutive games, 11 September 2002.

William E. "Bill" Walsh, 75, football coach, head coach of the San Francisco 49ers (1979–1988); led team to three Super Bowl victories (1981, 1984, and 1988); innovator of the "West Coast offense," 30 July 2007.

Dick Weber, 75, founding member of Professional Bowlers Association (PBA), three-time bowler of the year (1961, 1963, 1965), 13 February 2005.

Mike Webster, 50, center for the Pittsburgh Steelers (1974–1988) during four-year consecutive Super Bowl victories (1974–1979); inducted into the Football Hall of Fame (1997), 24 September 2002.

Eleanor Holm Whalen, 90, swimmer; won the 100-meter backstroke in the 1932 Los Angeles Olympics; suspended from the 1936 team (for drinking at a party during a trip to Berlin); later an actress and singer, 31 January 2004.

Byron R. "Whizzer" White, 84, halfback (and highest paid player) for the Pittsburgh Pirates (1938) and Detroit Lions (1940–1941); held league rushing yards records (1938 and 1940); left football to pursue legal career and served as associate justice of the U.S. Supreme Court (1962–1993), 15 April 2002.

Reggie White, 43, defensive end for the Philadelphia Eagles (1985–1992) and Green Bay Packers (1993–1998); selected to Pro Bowl thirteen times; named NFL Defensive Player of the Year (1987 and 1998); Super Bowl winner (1996); Football Hall of Fame inductee (2006), 26 December 2004.

Ted Williams, 83, left-fielder for the Boston Red Sox (1939–1942 and 1946–1960); nineteen-time All Star player; last player to bat over .400 in a season (1941); Baseball Hall of Fame inductee (1966), 5 July 2002.

George H. Yardley III, 75, forward; played eight years in the NBA (Detroit Pistons, Syracuse Nationals); six-time All Star; enshrined in the Basketball Hall of Fame (1996), 12 August 2004.

PUBLICATIONS

Andre Agassi, *Open: An Autobiography* (New York: Knopf, 2009);

John Amaechi and Chris Bull, *Man in the Middle* (New York: ESPN Books, 2007);

Lance Armstrong and Sally Jenkins, *It's Not About the Bike: My Journey Back to Life* (New York: Putnam, 2000);

Shaun Assael, *Steroid Nation: Juiced Home Run Totals, Anti-Aging Miracles, and a Hercules in Every High School: The Secret History of America's True Drug Addiction* (New York: ESPN Books, 2007);

Bob Boyles and Paul Guido, *Fifty Years of College Football: A Modern History of America's Most Colorful Sport* (New York: Skyhorse, 2007);

J. C. Bradbury, *The Baseball Economist: The Real Game Exposed* (New York: Dutton, 2007);

Michael Bradley, *Big Games: College Football's Greatest Rivalries* (Washington, D.C.: Potomac Books, 2006);

David Browne, *Amped: How Big Air, Big Dollars, and a New Generation Took Sports to the Extreme* (New York: Bloomsbury, 2004);

Howard Bryant, *Juicing the Game: Drugs, Power, and the Fight for the Soul of Major League Baseball* (New York: Viking, 2005);

Michael L. Butterworth, *Baseball and Rhetoric of Purity: The National Pastime and American Identity during the War on Terror* (Tuscaloosa: University of Alabama Press, 2010);

Jose Canseco, *Juiced: Wild Times, Rampant 'Roids, Smash Hits, and How Baseball Got Big* (New York: Regan Books, 2005);

Leonard Cassuto and Stephen Partridge, eds., *The Cambridge Companion to Baseball* (Cambridge & New York: Cambridge University Press, 2011);

George Castle, *Baseball and the Media: How Fans Lose in Today's Coverage of the Game* (Lincoln: University of Nebraska Press, 2006);

Ronald W. Cox and Daniel Skidmore-Hess, *Free Agency and Competitive Balance in Baseball* (Jefferson, N.C.: McFarland, 2006);

Neil deMause and Joanna Cagan, *Field of Schemes: How the Great Stadium Swindle Turns Public Money into Private Profit* (Lincoln: University of Nebraska Press, 2008);

John Mark Dempsey, ed., *Sports-Talk Radio in America: Its Context and Culture* (New York: Haworth Press, 2006);

Tim Donaghy, *Personal Foul: A First-Person Account of the Scandal that Rocked the NBA* (Largo, Florida: VTI Group, 2009);

Tony Dungy and Nathan Whitaker, *Quiet Strength: The Principles, Practices, and Priorities of a Winning Life* (Carol Stream, Ill.: Tyndale, 2007);

Beau Dure, *Long-Range Goals: The Success Story of Major League Soccer* (Washington, D.C.: Potomac Books, 2010);

Mark Dyreson and J. A. Mangan, eds., *Sport and American Society: Exceptionalism, Insularity, and "Imperialism"* (New York: Routledge, 2007);

Jacqueline Edmondson, *Venus and Serena Williams: A Biography* (Westport, Conn.: Greenwood Press, 2005);

Jeremy Evans, *In Search of Powder: A Story of America's Disappearing Ski Bum* (Lincoln: University of Nebraska Press, 2010);

Mark Fainaru-Wada and Lance Williams, *Game of Shadows: Barry Bonds, BALCO, and the Steroids Scandal that Rocked Professional Sports* (New York: Gotham, 2006);

Tom Farrey, *Game On: How the Pressure to Win at All Costs Endangers Youth Sports, and What Parents Can Do About It* (New York: ESPN Books, 2009);

Franklin Foer, *How Soccer Explains the World: An Unlikely Theory of Globalization* (New York: HarperCollins, 2004);

Craig A. Forney, *The Holy Trinity of American Sports: Civil Religion in Football, Baseball, and Basketball* (Macon, Ga.: Mercer University Press, 2007);

Sharon T. Freeman, *African Americans: Reviving Baseball in Inner Cities* (Washington, D.C.: AASBEA, 2008);

Gerald R. Gems, *The Athletic Crusade: Sport and American Cultural Imperialism* (Lincoln: University of Nebraska Press, 2006);

John R. Gerdy, *Air Ball: American Education's Failed Experiment with Elite Athletics* (Jackson: University Press of Mississippi, 2006);

Billy Hawkins, *The New Plantation: Black Athletes, College Sports, and Predominantly White NCAA Institutions* (New York: Palgrave Macmillan, 2010);

Nancy Hogshead-Makar and Andrew Zimbalist, eds., *Equal Play: Title IX and Social Change* (Philadelphia: Temple University Press, 2007);

Bill James, *The New Bill James Historical Baseball Abstract* (New York: Free Press, 2001);

Richard A. Johnson and Robert Hamilton Johnson, *The Boston Marathon* (Boston: Arcadia, 2009);

Tom Jones, *Working at the Ballpark: The Fascinating Lives of Baseball People—From Peanut Vendors and Broadcasters to Players and Managers* (New York: Skyhorse, 2008);

Frank P. Jozsa Jr., *Baseball, Inc.: The National Pastime as Big Business* (Jefferson, N.C.: McFarland, 2006);

Jozsa, *Baseball in Crisis: Spiraling Costs, Bad Behavior, Uncertain Future* (Jefferson, N.C.: McFarland, 2008);

Jozsa, *Major League Baseball Expansions and Relocations: A History, 1876–2008* (Jefferson, N.C.: McFarland, 2010);

Ted A. Kluck, *Game Time: Inside College Football* (Guilford, Conn.: Lyons Press, 2007);

Dawn Knight, *Taliaferro: Breaking Barriers from the NFL Draft to the Ivory Tower* (Bloomington: Indiana University Press, 2007);

Christopher S. Kudlac, *Fair or Foul: Sports and Criminal Behavior in the United States* (Santa Barbara, Cal.: Praeger/ABC-CLIO, 2010);

Simon Kuper and Stefan Szymanski, *Soccernomics: Why England Loses, Why Germany and Brazil Win, and Why the U.S., Japan, Australia, Turkey—and Even Iraq—Are Destined to Become the Kings of the World's Most Popular Sport* (New York: Nation Books, 2009);

Kyle Kusz, *Revolt of the White Athlete: Race, Media and the Emergence of Extreme Athletes in America* (New York: Lang, 2007);

Bill Lee and Richard Lally, *The Wrong Stuff* (New York: Three Rivers Press, 2006);

Michael Lewis, *Moneyball: The Art of Winning an Unfair Game* (New York: Norton, 2003);

Lewis, *The Blind Side: Evolution of a Game* (New York: Norton, 2006);

Michael Litos, *Cinderella: Inside the Rise of Mid-Major College Basketball* (Naperville, Ill.: Sourcebooks, 2007);

Kathleen Lockwood, *Major League Bride: An Inside Look at Life Outside the Ballpark* (Jefferson, N.C.: McFarland, 2010);

Stewart Mandel, *Bowls, Polls & Tattered Souls: Tackling the Chaos and Controversy that Reign Over College Football* (Hoboken, N.J.: Wiley, 2008);

Michael Mandelbaum, *The Meaning of Sports: Why Americans Watch Baseball, Football, and Basketball, and What They See When They Do* (New York: Public Affairs, 2004);

Peyton Manning and Archie Manning, *Manning: A Father, His Sons and a Football Legacy* (New York: Harper, 2000);

Andrei S. Markovits and Lars Rensmann, *Gaming the World: How Sports are Reshaping Global Politics and Culture* (Princeton, N.J.: Princeton University Press, 2010);

Dorothy Seymour Mills, *Chasing Baseball: Our Obsession with Its History, Numbers, People and Places* (Jefferson, N.C.: McFarland, 2010);

Warren Moon and Don Yaeger, *Never Give Up on Your Dream: My Journey* (Cambridge, Mass.: Da Capo Press, 2009);

Dat Nguyen and Rusty Burson, *Dat: Tackling Life and the NFL* (College Station: Texas A&M University Press, 2005);

S. L. Price, *Heart of the Game: Life, Death, and Mercy in Minor League America* (New York: Ecco/HarperCollins, 2009);

Kirk Radomski, *Bases Loaded: The Inside Story of the Steroid Era in Baseball by the Central Figure in the Mitchell Report* (New York: Hudson Street Press, 2009);

Rick Reilly, *Who's Your Caddy?: Looping for the Great, Near Great, and Reprobates of Golf* (New York: Doubleday, 2003);

Jennifer Ring, *Stolen Bases: Why American Girls Don't Play Baseball* (Urbana: University of Illinois Press, 2009);

Betsy M. Ross, *Playing Ball with the Boys: The Rise of Women in the World of Men's Sports* (Cincinnati: Clerisy Press, 2010);

Rob Ruck, *Raceball: How the Major Leagues Colonized the Black and Latin Game* (Boston: Beacon Press, 2010);

Mike Schmidt and Glen Waggoner, *Clearing the Bases: Juiced Players, Monster Salaries, Sham Records, and a Hall of Famer's Search for the Soul of Baseball* (New York: HarperCollins, 2006);

Roy Simmons and others, *Out of Bounds: Coming Out of Sexual Abuse, Addiction, and My Life of Lies in the NFL Closet* (New York: Carroll & Graf, 2006);

Glenn Stout, ed., *The Best American Sports Writing* (New York: Houghton Mifflin, 2000–2009);

Dean A. Sullivan, ed., *Final Innings: A Documentary History of Baseball, 1972–2008* (Lincoln: University of Nebraska Press, 2010);

Stefan Szymanski and Andrew Zimbalist, *National Pastime: How Americans Play Baseball and the Rest of the World Plays Soccer* (Washington, D.C.: Brookings Institution Press, 2005);

Teri Thompson and others, *American Icon: The Fall of Roger Clemens and the Rise of Steroids in America's Pastime* (New York: Knopf, 2009);

Michael V. Uschan, *Serena Williams* (Detroit: Lucent Books, 2011);

Michael Waltrip, *In the Blink of an Eye: Dale, Daytona, and the Day That Changed Everything* (New York: Hyperion, 2011);

Venus Williams, Serena Williams, and Hilary Beard, *Venus & Serena: Serving From the Hip, Ten Rules for Living, Loving, and Winning* (Boston: Houghton Mifflin, 2005);

Tiger Woods, *How I Play Golf* (New York: Crown, 2000);

Don Yaeger and Jim Henry, *Tarnished Heisman: Did Reggie Bush Turn His Final College Season into a Six-Figure Job?* (New York: Pocket Books, 2008);

Mark Yost, *Varsity Green: A Behind the Scenes Look at Culture and Corruption in College Athletics* (Stanford, Cal.: Stanford University Press, 2010);

Dave Zirin, *Bad Sports: How Owners are Ruining the Games We Love* (New York: Scribner, 2010).

GENERAL REFERENCES

GENERAL

Bob Batchelor, *The 2000s (American Popular Culture through History)* (Westport, Conn.: Greenwood Press, 2009);

Berch Berberoglu, ed., *Globalization in the 21st Century: Labor, Capital, and the State on a World Scale* (New York: Palgrave Macmillan, 2010);

Neil Campbell and Alasdair Kean, *American Cultural Studies: An Introduction to American Culture*, third edition (New York: Routledge, 2011);

David F. Ericson, ed., *The Politics of Inclusion and Exclusion: Identity Politics in Twenty-first Century America* (New York : Routledge, 2011);

Jay Feldman, *Manufacturing Hysteria: Scapegoating, Surveillance, and Secrecy in Modern America* (New York : Pantheon Books, 2011);

Louise I. Gerdes, ed., *Perspectives on Modern History: 9/11* (Farmington Hills, Mich: Greenhaven Press, 2010);

Nicholas Kerton-Johnson, *Justifying America's Wars: The Conduct and Practice of US Military intervention* (London & New York : Routledge, 2011);

Dorothy Roberts, *Fatal Invention: How Science, Politics, and Big Business Re-create Race in the Twenty-first Century* (New York : New Press, 2011);

Deborah Schildkraut, *Americanism in the Twenty-first Century: Public Opinion in the Age of Immigration* (New York: Cambridge University Press, 2011);

Valerie Wee, *Teen Media: Hollywood and the Youth Market in the Digital Age* (Jefferson, N.C.: McFarland, 2010);

Fareed Zakaria, *The Post-American World: Release 2.0* (New York: Norton, 2011).

ARTS

Bruce Altshuler, ed., *Collecting the New: Museums and Contemporary Art* (Princeton: Princeton University Press, 2005);

Saul Austerlitz, *Another Fine Mess: A History of American Film Comedy* (Chicago: Chicago Review Press, 2010);

Julius Bailey, ed., *Jay-Z: Essays on Hip Hop's Philosopher King* (Jefferson, N.C.: McFarland, 2011);

Matthew Biberman and Julia Reinhard Lupton, eds., *Shakespeare after 9/11: How a Social Trauma Reshapes Interpretation* (Lewiston, N.Y.: Edwin Mellen Press, 2010);

Casey Nelson Blake, ed., *The Arts of Democracy: Art, Public Culture, and the State* (Washington, D.C.: Woodrow Wilson Center Press; Philadelphia: University of Pennsylvania Press, 2007);

M. Keith Booker, *Disney, Pixar, and the Hidden Messages of Children's Films* (Santa Barbara, Cal.: Praeger, 2010);

Gerald Bordman and Richard Norton, *American Musical Theatre: A Chronicle*, fourth edition (Oxford & New York: Oxford University Press, 2011);

Oscar G. Brockett and Robert J. Ball, *The Essential Theatre*, ninth edition (Boston: Wadsworth, 2008);

Paul R. Cappucci, *William Carlos Williams, Frank O'Hara, and the New York Art Scene* (Madison, N.J.: Fairleigh Dickinson University Press, 2010);

Joni Maya Cherbo, Ruth Ann Stewart, and Margaret Jane Wyszomirski, eds., *Understanding the Arts and Creative Sector in the United States* (New Brunswick, N.J.: Rutgers University Press, 2008);

Tyler Cowen, *Good & Plenty: The Creative Successes of American Arts Funding* (Princeton, N.J.: Princeton University Press, 2006);

Jessica Hoffmann Davis, *Why Our Schools Need the Arts* (New York: Teachers College Press, 2008);

Nancy Day, *Censorship, or Freedom of Expression?* (Minneapolis: Lerner Publications, 2001);

Jill Dolan, *Theatre & Sexuality* (New York: Palgrave Macmillan, 2010);

Denis Donoghue, *Speaking of Beauty* (New Haven: Yale University Press, 2003);

Charles Dorn and Penelope Orr, *Art Education in a Climate of Reform: The Need for Measurable Goals in Art Instruction* (Lanham, Md.: Rowman & Littlefield Education, 2008);

Astrid Franke, *Pursue the Illusion: Problems of Public Poetry in America* (Heidelberg: Winter, 2010);

Krin Gabbard, *Hotter than That: The Trumpet, Jazz, and American Culture* (New York: Faber & Faber, 2008);

Stanley Green, *Broadway Musicals, Show by Show*, sixth edition, revised by Kay Green (New York: Applause Theatre and Cinema Books, 2008);

Adam Gussow, *Journeyman's Road: Modern Blues Lives from Faulkner's Mississippi to Post-9/11 New York* (Knoxville: University of Tennessee Press, 2007);

Bill Ivey, *Arts, Inc.: How Greed and Neglect Have Destroyed Our Cultural Rights* (Berkeley: University of California Press, 2008);

Patricia Johnston, ed., *Seeing High & Low: Representing Social Conflict in American Visual Culture* (Berkeley: University of California Press, 2006);

Gayle Kassing, *History of Dance: An Interactive Arts Approach* (Champaign, Ill.: Human Kinetics, 2007);

Herbert H. Keyser, *Geniuses of the American Musical Theatre: The Composers and Lyricists* (New York: Applause Theatre and Cinema Books, 2009);

Dustin Kidd, *Legislating Creativity: The Intersections of Art and Politics* (New York: Routledge, 2010);

Raymond Knapp, *The American Musical and the Performance of Personal Identity* (Princeton: Princeton University Press, 2006);

Pam Korza, Barbara Schaffer Bacon, and Andrea Assaf, *Civic Dialogue, Arts & Culture: Findings from Animating Democracy* (Washington, D.C.: Americans for the Arts, 2005);

Cameron Lazerine and Devin Lazerine, *Rap-up: The Ultimate Guide to Hip-Hop and R&B* (New York: Grand Central, 2008);

Ellen Levy, *Criminal Ingenuity: Moore, Cornell, Ashbery, and the Struggle between the Arts* (Oxford & New York: Oxford University Press, 2011);

Jeffrey D. Mason, *Stone Tower: The Political Theater of Arthur Miller* (Ann Arbor: University of Michigan Press, 2008);

Kevin F. McCarthy and others, *A Portrait of the Visual Arts: Meeting the Challenges of a New Era* (Santa Monica, Cal.: RAND, 2005);

Angela L. Miller and others, *American Encounters: Art, History, and Cultural Identity* (Upper Saddle River, N.J.: Pearson/Prentice Hall, 2008);

William Murray, *Fortissimo: Backstage at the Opera with Sacred Monsters and Young Singers* (New York: Crown, 2005);

Philip Nel, *The Avant-Garde and American Postmodernity: Small Incisive Shocks* (Jackson: University Press of Mississippi, 2002);

Karen Paik, *To Infinity and Beyond!: The Story of Pixar Animation Studios* (San Francisco: Chronicle Books, 2007);

David B. Pruett, *MuzikMafia: From the Local Nashville Scene to the National Mainstream* (Jackson: University Press of Mississippi, 2010);

Annette J. Saddik, *Contemporary American Drama* (Edinburgh: Edinburgh University Press, 2007);

Anthony Shay, *Dancing across Borders: The American Fascination with Exotic Dance Forms* (Jefferson, N.C.: McFarland, 2008);

Barry Singer, *Ever After: The Last Years of Musical Theater and Beyond* (New York: Applause Theatre and Cinema Books, 2004);

Thomas M. Smith, *Raising the Barre: The Geographic, Financial, and Economic Trends of Nonprofit Dance Companies: A Study*, edited by Bonnie Nichols (Washington, D.C.: National Endowment for the Arts, 2003);

Willard Spiegelman, *How Poets See the World: The Art of Description in Contemporary Poetry* (New York: Oxford University Press, 2005);

Janis P. Stout, *Picturing a Different West: Vision, Illustration, and the Tradition of Austin and Cather* (Lubbock: Texas Tech University Press, 2007);

Steven J. Tepper and Bill Ivey, eds., *Engaging Art: The Next Great Transformation of America's Cultural Life* (New York: Routledge, 2008);

U.S. Congress, House Committee on Education and Labor, *The Economic and Employment Impact of the Arts and Music Industry: Hearing before the Committee on Education and Labor, U.S. House of Representatives, One Hundred Eleventh Congress, First Session, Hearing Held in Washington, D.C., March 26, 2009* (Washington, D.C.: Government Printing Office, 2009);

Art in America, periodical;

Art News, periodical;

Billboard, periodical;

Dance, periodical;

Entertainment Weekly, periodical;

Harper's, periodical;

Januarymagazine.com;

Jazz Review, periodical;

New Yorker, periodical;

Paris Review, periodical;

Poetry, periodical;

Rolling Stone, periodical;

Salon.com;

Spin, periodical;

Variety, periodical;

XXL, periodical.

BUSINESS

Chris Anderson, *The Long Tail: Why the Future of Business Is Selling Less of More* (New York: Hyperion, 2006);

Ken Auletta, *World War 3.0: Microsoft and Its Enemies* (New York: Random House, 2001);

John Battelle, *The Search: How Google and Its Rivals Rewrote the Rules of Business* (New York: Portfolio, 2005);

William D. Cohan, *The Last Tycoons: The Secret History of Lazard Frères & Co.* (New York: Doubleday, 2008);

Stephen Dubner and Steven D. Levitt, *Freakonomics: A Rogue Economist Explores the Hidden Side of Everything* (New York: Morrow, 2006);

Barbara Ehrenreich, *Nickel and Dimed: On (Not) Getting By in America* (New York: Metropolitan, 2001);

Mohamed El-Erian, *When Markets Collide: Investment Strategies for the Age of Global Economic Change* (New York: McGraw-Hill, 2008);

Charles Fishman, *The Wal-Mart Effect: How the World's Most Powerful Company Really Works, and How It's Transforming the American Economy* (New York: Penguin, 2006);

Malcolm Gladwell, *The Tipping Point: How Little Things Can Make a Big Difference* (Boston: Little, Brown, 2000);

Alan Greenspan, *The Age of Turbulence: Adventures in a New World* (New York: Penguin, 2007);

Michael Lewis, *Moneyball: The Art of Winning an Unfair Game* (New York: Norton, 2003);

Bethany McLean and Peter Elkind, *The Smartest Guys in the Room: The Amazing Rise and Scandalous Fall of Enron* (New York: Portfolio, 2003);

Ben Mezrich, *The Accidental Billionaires: The Founding of Facebook: A Tale of Sex, Money, Genius, and Betrayal* (New York: Doubleday, 2009);

Carmen Reinhart and Kenneth Rogoff, *This Time Is Different: Eight Centuries of Financial Folly* (Princeton, N.J.: Princeton University Press, 2009);

Pietra Rivoli, *The Travels of a T-Shirt in the Global Economy: An Economist Examines the Markets, Power, and Politics of World Trade* (New York: Wiley, 2005);

Alice Schroeder, *The Snowball: Warren Buffett and the Business of Life* (New York: Bantam, 2008);

Andrew Ross Sorkin, *Too Big to Fail: The Inside Story of How Wall Street and Washington Fought to Save the Financial System from Crisis—and Themselves* (New York: Viking, 2009);

James Stewart, *Disney War* (New York: Simon & Schuster, 2005);

James Surowiecki, *The Wisdom of Crowds: Why the Many are Smarter than the Few and How Collective Wisdom Shapes Business* (New York: Doubleday, 2004);

Nassim Nicholas Taleb, *The Black Swan: The Impact of the Highly Improbable* (New York: Random House, 2007);

Don Tapscott and Anthony D. Williams, *Wikinomics: How Mass Collaboration Changes Everything* (New York: Portfolio, 2006);

David Wessel, *In Fed We Trust: Ben Bernanke's War on the Great Panic* (New York: Random House, 2009.

EDUCATION

Karin Chenoweth, *It's Being Done: Academic Success in Unexpected Schools* (Cambridge, Mass.: Harvard Education Press, 2007);

Clayton M. Christensen, Michael B. Horn, and Curtis W. Johnson, *Disrupting Class: How Disruptive Innovation Will Change the Way the World Learns* (New York: McGraw-Hill, 2008);

David K. Cohen and Susan L. Moffitt, *The Ordeal of Equality: Did Federal Regulation Fix the Schools?* (Cambridge, Mass.: Harvard University Press, 2009);

Dave Cullen, *Columbine* (New York: Twelve, 2009);

Gareth Davies, *See Government Grow: Education Politics from Johnson to Reagan* (Lawrence: University Press of Kansas, 2007);

Richard F. Elmore, *School Reform from the Inside Out* (Cambridge, Mass.: Harvard Education Press, 2004);

Claudia D. Goldin and Lawrence F. Katz, *The Race between Education and Technology* (Cambridge, Mass.: Belknap Press of Harvard University Press, 2008);

Gerald Grant, *Hope and Despair in the American City: Why There Are No Bad Schools in Raleigh* (Cambridge, Mass.: Harvard University Press, 2009);

Jay P. Green, Greg Forster, and Marcus A. Winters, *Education Myths: What Special Interest Groups Want You to Believe about Our Schools—and Why It Isn't So* (Lanham, Md.: Rowman & Littlefield, 2005);

Eric A. Hanushek and Alfred A. Lindseth, *Schoolhouses, Courthouses, and Statehouses: Solving the Funding-Achievement Puzzle in America's Public Schools* (Princeton, N.J.: Princeton University Press, 2009);

Jeffrey R. Henig, *Spin Cycle: How Research Is Used in Policy Debates: The Case of Charter Schools* (New York: Russell Sage Foundation, 2008);

Frederick M. Hess, *Common Sense School Reform* (New York: Palgrave Macmillan, 2004);

E. D. Hirsch Jr., *The Knowledge Deficit: Closing the Shocking Education Gap for American Children* (Boston: Houghton Mifflin, 2006);

William G. Howell and Paul E. Peterson, *The Education Gap: Vouchers and Urban Schools* (Washington, D.C.: Brookings Institution Press, 2002);

Joanne Jacobs, *Our School: The Inspiring Idea of Two Teachers, One Big Idea, and the School that Beat the Odds* (New York: Palgrave Macmillan, 2005);

Richard D. Kahlenburg, *All Together Now: Creating Middle-Class Schools through Public School Choice* (Washington, D.C.: Brookings Institution Press, 2001);

Alfie Kohn, *The Homework Myth: Why Our Kids Get Too Much of a Bad Thing* (Cambridge, Mass.: Da Capo, 2006);

Daniel M. Koretz, *Measuring Up: What Educational Testing Really Tells Us* (Cambridge, Mass.: Harvard University Press, 2008);

Jay Matthews, *Work Hard. Be Nice: How Two Inspired Teachers Created the Most Promising Schools in America* (Chapel Hill, N.C.: Algonquin Books of Chapel Hill, 2009);

Deborah Meier, *In Schools We Trust: Creating Communities of Learning in an Era of Testing and Standardization* (Boston: Beacon, 2002);

Terry M. Moe, *Schools, Vouchers, and the American Public* (Washington, D.C.: Brookings Institution Press, 2001);

Moe and John E. Chubb, *Liberating Learning: Technology, Politics, and the Future of American Education* (San Francisco: Jossey-Bass, 2009);

Charles Murray, *Real Education: Four Simple Truths for Bringing America's Schools Back to Reality* (New York: Crown Forum, 2008);

William G. Ouchi and Lydia G. Segal, *Making Schools Work: A Revolutionary Plan to Get Your Children the Education They Need* (New York: Simon & Schuster, 2003);

Charles M. Payne, *So Much Reform, So Little Change: The Persistence of Failure in Urban Schools* (Cambridge, Mass.: Harvard Education Press, 2008);

Linda Perlstein, *Tested: One American School Struggles to Make the Grade* (New York: Holt, 2007);

Diane Ravitch, *Left Back: A Century of Failed School Reforms* (New York: Simon & Schuster, 2000);

Richard Rothstein, Rebecca Jacobsen, and Tamara Wilder, *Grading Education, Getting Accountability Right* (Washington, D.C.: Economic Policy Institute; New York: Teachers College Press, 2008);

Abigail Thernstrom and Stephan Thernstrom, *No Excuses: Closing the Racial Gap in Learning* (New York: Simon & Schuster, 2003);

Paul Tough, *Whatever It Takes: Geoffrey Canada's Quest to Change Harlem and America* (Boston: Houghton Mifflin, 2008);

Joe Williams, *Cheating Our Kids: How Politics and Greed Ruin Education* (New York: Palgrave Macmillan, 2005);

Daniel T. Willingham, *Why Don't Students Like School?: A Cognitive Scientist Answers Questions About How the Mind Works and What It Means for the Classroom* (San Francisco: Jossey-Bass, 2009);

Yong Zhao, *Catching Up or Leading the Way: American Education in the Age of Globalization* (Alexandria, Va.:

Association for Supervision and Curriculum Development, 2009).

FASHION

Karin Chenoweth, *It's Being Done: Academic Success in Unexpected Schools* (Cambridge, Mass.: Harvard Education Press, 2007);

Clayton M. Christensen, Michael B. Horn, and Curtis W. Johnson, *Disrupting Class: How Disruptive Innovation Will Change the Way the World Learns* (New York: McGraw-Hill, 2008);

David K. Cohen and Susan L. Moffitt, *The Ordeal of Equality: Did Federal Regulation Fix the Schools?* (Cambridge, Mass.: Harvard University Press, 2009);

Dave Cullen, *Columbine* (New York: Twelve, 2009);

Gareth Davies, *See Government Grow: Education Politics from Johnson to Reagan* (Lawrence: University Press of Kansas, 2007);

Richard F. Elmore, *School Reform from the Inside Out* (Cambridge, Mass.: Harvard Education Press, 2004);

Claudia D. Goldin and Lawrence F. Katz, *The Race between Education and Technology* (Cambridge, Mass.: Belknap Press of Harvard University Press, 2008);

Gerald Grant, *Hope and Despair in the American City: Why There Are No Bad Schools in Raleigh* (Cambridge, Mass.: Harvard University Press, 2009);

Jay P. Green, Greg Forster, and Marcus A. Winters, *Education Myths: What Special Interest Groups Want You to Believe about Our Schools—and Why It Isn't So* (Lanham, Md.: Rowman & Littlefield, 2005);

Eric A. Hanushek and Alfred A. Lindseth, *Schoolhouses, Courthouses, and Statehouses: Solving the Funding-Achievement Puzzle in America's Public Schools* (Princeton, N.J.: Princeton University Press, 2009);

Jeffrey R. Henig, *Spin Cycle: How Research Is Used in Policy Debates: The Case of Charter Schools* (New York: Russell Sage Foundation, 2008);

Frederick M. Hess, *Common Sense School Reform* (New York: Palgrave Macmillan, 2004);

E. D. Hirsch Jr., *The Knowledge Deficit: Closing the Shocking Education Gap for American Children* (Boston: Houghton Mifflin, 2006);

William G. Howell and Paul E. Peterson, *The Education Gap: Vouchers and Urban Schools* (Washington, D.C.: Brookings Institution Press, 2002);

Joanne Jacobs, *Our School: The Inspiring Idea of Two Teachers, One Big Idea, and the School that Beat the Odds* (New York: Palgrave Macmillan, 2005);

Richard D. Kahlenburg, *All Together Now: Creating Middle-Class Schools through Public School Choice*

(Washington, D.C.: Brookings Institution Press, 2001);

Alfie Kohn, *The Homework Myth: Why Our Kids Get Too Much of a Bad Thing* (Cambridge, Mass.: Da Capo, 2006);

Daniel M. Koretz, *Measuring Up: What Educational Testing Really Tells Us* (Cambridge, Mass.: Harvard University Press, 2008);

Jay Matthews, *Work Hard. Be Nice: How Two Inspired Teachers Created the Most Promising Schools in America* (Chapel Hill, N.C.: Algonquin Books of Chapel Hill, 2009);

Deborah Meier, *In Schools We Trust: Creating Communities of Learning in an Era of Testing and Standardization* (Boston: Beacon, 2002);

Terry M. Moe, *Schools, Vouchers, and the American Public* (Washington, D.C.: Brookings Institution Press, 2001);

Moe and John E. Chubb, *Liberating Learning: Technology, Politics, and the Future of American Education* (San Francisco: Jossey-Bass, 2009);

Charles Murray, *Real Education: Four Simple Truths for Bringing America's Schools Back to Reality* (New York: Crown Forum, 2008);

William G. Ouchi and Lydia G. Segal, *Making Schools Work: A Revolutionary Plan to Get Your Children the Education They Need* (New York: Simon & Schuster, 2003);

Charles M. Payne, *So Much Reform, So Little Change: The Persistence of Failure in Urban Schools* (Cambridge, Mass.: Harvard Education Press, 2008);

Linda Perlstein, *Tested: One American School Struggles to Make the Grade* (New York: Holt, 2007);

Diane Ravitch, *Left Back: A Century of Failed School Reforms* (New York: Simon & Schuster, 2000);

Richard Rothstein, Rebecca Jacobsen, and Tamara Wilder, *Grading Education, Getting Accountability Right* (Washington, D.C.: Economic Policy Institute; New York: Teachers College Press, 2008);

Abigail Thernstrom and Stephan Thernstrom, *No Excuses: Closing the Racial Gap in Learning* (New York: Simon & Schuster, 2003);

Paul Tough, *Whatever It Takes: Geoffrey Canada's Quest to Change Harlem and America* (Boston: Houghton Mifflin, 2008);

Joe Williams, *Cheating Our Kids: How Politics and Greed Ruin Education* (New York: Palgrave Macmillan, 2005);

Daniel T. Willingham, *Why Don't Students Like School?: A Cognitive Scientist Answers Questions About How the Mind Works and What It Means for the Classroom* (San Francisco: Jossey-Bass, 2009);

Yong Zhao, *Catching Up or Leading the Way: American Education in the Age of Globalization* (Alexandria, Va.: Association for Supervision and Curriculum Development, 2009).

GOVERNMENT AND POLITICS

Ari Berman, *Herding Donkeys: The Fight to Rebuild the Democratic Party and Reshape American Politics* (New York: Farrar, Straus & Giroux, 2010);

Carl Bernstein, *A Woman in Charge: The Life of Hillary Rodham Clinton* (New York: Knopf, 2007);

Douglas Brinkley, *The Great Deluge: Hurricane Katrina, New Orleans, and the Mississippi Gulf Coast* (New York: Morrow, 2006);

George W. Bush, *Decision Points* (New York: Crown, 2010);

Richard Clarke, *Against All Enemies: Inside America's War on Terror* (New York: Free Press, 2004);

Steve Coll, *Ghost Wars: The Secret History of the CIA, Afghanistan, and bin Laden, from the Soviet Invasion to September 10, 2001* (New York: Penguin, 2004);

Howard Dean and Judith Warner, *You Have the Power: How to Take Back Our Country and Restore Democracy in America* (New York: Simon & Schuster, 2004);

Robert Draper, *Dead Certain: The Presidency of George W. Bush* (New York: Free Press, 2007);

Dexter Filkins, *The Forever War.* (New York: Knopf, 2008);

Thomas Frank, *What's the Matter with Kansas?: How Conservatives Won the Heart of America* (New York: Metropolitan, 2004);

John Heilemann and Mark Halperin, *Game Change: Obama and the Clintons, McCain and Palin, and the Race of a Lifetime* (New York: Harper Perennial, 2010);

Jed Horne, *Breach of Faith: Hurricane Katrina and the Near Death of a Great American City* (New York: Random House, 2006);

Seth G. Jones, *In the Graveyard of Empires: America's War in Afghanistan* (New York: Norton, 2009);

Jill Lepore, *The Whites of Their Eyes: The Tea Party's Revolution and the Battle over American History* (Princeton, N.J.: Princeton University Press, 2010);

Michael Lewis, *The Big Short: Inside the Doomsday Machine* (New York: Norton, 2010);

Jane Mayer, *The Dark Side: The Inside Story of How the War on Terror Turned into a War on American Ideals* (New York: Doubleday, 2008);

Bethany McLean and Peter Elkind, *The Smartest Guys in the Room: The Amazing Rise and Scandalous Fall of Enron* (New York: Portfolio, 2003);

National Commission on Terrorist Attacks upon the United States, *The 9/11 Commission Report: Final Report* of the National Commission on Terrorist Attacks upon the United States (New York: Norton, 2004);

Barack Obama, *The Audacity of Hope: Thoughts on Reclaiming the American Dream* (New York: Crown, 2006);

George Packer, *The Assassins' Gate: America in Iraq* (New York: Farrar, Straus & Giroux, 2006);

Sarah Palin, *Going Rogue: An American Life* (New York: HarperCollins, 2009);

David Remnick, *The Bridge: The Life and Rise of Barack Obama* (New York: Knopf, 2010);

Thomas E. Ricks, *Fiasco: The American Military Adventure in Iraq* (New York: Penguin, 2006);

Karl Rove, *Courage and Consequence: My Life as a Conservative in the Fight* (New York: Simon & Schuster, 2010);

Larry J. Sabato, ed., *Divided States of America: The Slash and Burn Politics of the 2004 Presidential Election* (New York: Pearson-Longman, 2006);

Jeremy Scahill, *Blackwater: The Rise of the World's Most Powerful Mercenary Army* (New York: Nation, 2007);

Andrew Ross Sorkin, *Too Big to Fail: The Inside Story of How Wall Street and Washington Fought to Save the Financial System—and Themselves* (New York: Viking, 2009);

Andrew Sullivan, *The Conservative Soul: How We Lost It, How to Get it Back* (New York: HarperCollins, 2006);

Jeffrey Toobin, *Too Close to Call: The Thirty-Six-Day Battle to Decide the 2000 Election* (New York: Random House, 2002);

Rebecca Traister, *Big Girls Don't Cry: The Election that Changed Everything for American Women* (New York: Free Press, 2010);

Bob Woodward, *Bush at War* (New York: Simon & Schuster, 2002).

LAW

Michelle Alexander, *The New Jim Crow: Mass Incarceration in the Age of Colorblindness* (New York: New Press, 2010);

Akhil Reed Amar, *America's Constitution: A Biography* (New York: Random House, 2005);

Bill Barnhart and Gene Schlickman, *John Paul Stevens: An Independent Life* (Dekalb: Northern Illinois University Press, 2010);

Seyla Benhabib, *The Rights of Others: Aliens, Residents, and Citizens* (Cambridge & New York: Cambridge University Press, 2004);

Sarah A. Binder and Forrest Maltzman, *Advice & Dissent: The Struggle to Shape the Federal Judiciary* (Washington, D.C.: Brookings Institution Press, 2009);

George Chauncey, *Why Marriage?: The History Shaping Today's Debate over Gay Equality* (New York: Basic Books, 2004);

Erwin Chemerinsky, *The Conservative Assault on the Constitution* (New York: Simon & Schuster, 2010);

John Dean, *The Rehnquist Choice: The Untold Story of the Nixon Appointment that Redefined the Supreme Court* (New York: Touchstone, 2001);

Lee Epstein and Jeffrey A. Segal, *Advice and Consent: The Politics of Judicial Appointments* (Oxford & New York: Oxford University Press, 2005);

Christopher M. Finan, *From the Palmer Raids to the Patriot Act: A History of the Fight for Free Speech in America* (Boston: Beacon, 2007);

Lawrence M. Friedman, *A History of American Law*, third edition (New York: Simon & Schuster, 2005);

David Garland, *Peculiar Institution: America's Death Penalty in an Age of Abolition* (Cambridge, Mass.: Belknap Press of Harvard University Press, 2010);

Garret M. Graff, *The Threat Matrix: The FBI in the Age of Global Terror* (New York: Little, Brown, 2011);

Kermit L. Hall, ed., *The Oxford Companion to the Supreme Court of the United States*, second edition (Oxford & New York: Oxford University Press, 2005);

Michael Lewis and others, *The War on Terror and the Laws of War: A Military Perspective* (Oxford & New York: Oxford University Press, 2009);

Thomas R. Marshall, *Public Opinion and the Rehnquist Court* (Albany: SUNY Press, 2008);

Sandra Day O'Connor, *The Majesty of the Law: Reflections of a Supreme Court Justice*, edited by Craig Joyce (New York: Random House, 2003);

O'Connor and H. Alan Davis, *Lazy B: Growing Up on a Cattle Ranch in the American Southwest* (New York: Random House, 2002);

Robert Perkinson, *Texas Tough: The Rise of America's Prison Empire* (New York: Metropolitan Books, 2010);

Richard M. Pious, *The War on Terrorism and the Rule of Law* (Los Angeles: Roxbury, 2006);

Lucas A. Powe Jr., *The Supreme Court and the American Elite, 1798–2008* (Cambridge, Mass.: Harvard University Press, 2009);

David A. J. Richards, *The Sodomy Cases: Bowers v. Hardwick and Lawrence v. Texas* (Lawrence: University Press of Kansas, 2009);

Jeffrey Rosen, *The Supreme Court: The Personalities and Rivalries that Defined America* (New York: Times Books, 2006);

Gary D. Solis, *The Law of Armed Conflict: International Humanitarian Law in War* (Cambridge & New York: Cambridge University Press, 2010);

Geoffrey R. Stone, *Perilous Times: Free Speech in Wartime: from the Sedition Act of 1798 to the War on Terrorism* (New York: Norton, 2004);

Fred Strebeigh, *Equal: Women Reshape American Law* (New York: Norton, 2009);

Clarence Thomas, *My Grandfather's Son: A Memoir* (New York: Harper, 2007);

Scott Turow, *Ultimate Punishment: A Lawyer's Reflections on Dealing with the Death Penalty* (New York: Farrar, Straus, and Giroux, 2003);

Elizabeth Vrato, *The Counselors: Conversations with 18 Courageous Women Who Have Changed the World* (Philadelphia: Running Press, 2002);

Benjamin Wittes, *Law and the Long War: The Future of Justice in the Age of Terror* (New York: Penguin, 2008);

ABA Journal, periodical;

American Lawyer, periodical;

The Federal Lawyer, periodical;

National Law Journal, periodical.

LIFESTYLES

Stuart Allan, *Online News: Journalism and the Internet* (New York: Open University Press, 2006);

Ted Allen, Kyan Douglas, Thom Filicia, Carson Kressley, and Jai Rodriguez, *Queer Eye for the Straight Guy: The Fab 5's Guide to Looking Better, Cooking Better, Dressing Better, Behaving Better, and Living Better* (New York: Clarkson Potter, 2004);

James Bradley and Ron Powers, *Flags of Our Fathers* (New York: Bantam, 2000);

Hillary Rodham Clinton, *Living History* (New York: Simon & Schuster, 2003);

David Crystal, *Txtng: The Gr8 Db8* (New York: Oxford University Press, 2008);

Doug Fine, *Farewell, My Subaru: An Epic Adventure in Local Living* (New York: Villard, 2008);

Thomas L. Friedman, *Hot, Flat, and Crowded: Why We Need a Green Revolution—and How It Can Renew America* (New York: Farrar, Straus & Giroux, 2008);

David Gilmour, *The Film Club: A Memoir* (New York: Twelve, 2008);

Al Gore, *An Inconvenient Truth: The Planetary Emergency of Global Warming and What We Can Do About It* (Emmaus, Pa.: Rodale Books, 2006);

Conn Iggulden and Hal Iggulden, *The Dangerous Book for Boys* (London: HarperCollins, 2006);

Jon Krakauer, *Where Men Win Glory: The Odyssey of Pat Tillman* (New York: Doubleday, 2009);

Steven D. Levitt and Stephen J. Dubner, *Freakonomics: A Rogue Economist Explains the Hidden Side of Everything* (New York: Morrow, 2005);

Rich Ling, *The Mobile Connection: The Cell Phone's Impact on Society* (San Francisco: Morgan Kaufman, 2004);

Joseph Menn, *All The Rave: The Rise and Fall of Shawn Fanning's Napster* (New York: Crown Business, 2003);

Ben Mezrich, *The Accidental Billionaires: The Founding of Facebook: A Tale of Sex, Money, Genius, and Betrayal* (New York: Doubleday, 2009);

Barack Obama, *The Audacity of Hope: Thoughts on Reclaiming the American Dream* (New York: Crown, 2006);

Bill O'Reilly, *Culture Warrior* (New York: Broadway Books, 2006);

Michael Pollan, *The Omnivore's Dilemma: A Natural History of Four Meals* (New York: Penguin, 2006);

William Powers, *Hamlet's BlackBerry: A Practical Philosophy for Building a Good Life in the Digital Age* (New York: Harper, 2010);

Eric Schlosser, *Fast Food Nation: The Dark Side of the All-American Meal* (New York: Houghton Mifflin, 2001);

Bryant Simon, *Everything but the Coffee: Learning about America from Starbucks* (Berkeley: University of California Press, 2009);

Leslie Morgan Steiner, ed., *The Mommy Wars: Stay-at-Home and Career Moms Face Off on Their Choices, Their Lives, Their Families* (New York: Random House, 2006);

Michael Strangelove, *The Empire of the Mind: Digital Piracy and the Anti-Capitalist Movement* (Toronto: University of Toronto Press, 2005);

Morley Winograd and Michael D. Hais, *Millennial Makeover: MySpace, YouTube, and the Future of American Politics* (New Brunswick, N.J.: Rutgers University Press, 2008);

Body + Soul, periodical;

Everyday with Rachael Ray, periodical;

The New Yorker, periodical;

Newsweek, periodical;

O: The Oprah Magazine, periodical;

Rolling Stone, periodical;

Time, periodical;

Vanity Fair, periodical.

MEDIA

Sumbul Ali-Karamali, *The Muslim Next Door: The Qur'an, the Media, and That Veil Thing* (Ashland, Ore.: White Cloud, 2008);

Eric Alterman, *What Liberal Media?: The Truth about Bias and the News* (New York: Basic Books, 2003);

Robin Andersen, *A Century of Media, a Century of War* (New York: Peter Lang, 2006);

Ben H. Bagdikian, *The New Media Monopoly* (Boston: Beacon, 2004);

Steve Michael Barkin, *American Television News: The Media Marketplace and the Public Interest* (Armonk, N.Y.: M. E. Sharpe, 2002);

Joel Best, *Damned Lies and Statistics: Untangling Numbers from the Media, Politicians, and Activists* (Berkeley: University of California Press, 2001);

Eric Boehlert, *Lapdogs: How the Press Rolled Over for Bush* (New York: Free Press, 2006);

David Brock and Paul Waldman, *Free Ride: John McCain and the Media* (New York: Anchor, 2008);

Jeff Chester, *Digital Destiny: New Media and the Future of Democracy* (New York: New Press, 2007);

Lynn Schofield Clark, ed., *Religion, Media, and the Marketplace* (Rutgers, N.J.: Rutgers University Press, 2007);

Elliot D. Cohen and Bruce W. Fraser, *The Last Days of Democracy: How Big Media and Power-Hungry Government are Turning America into a Dictatorship* (Amherst, N.Y.: Prometheus, 2007);

Stuart Croft, *Culture, Crisis and America's War on Terror* (Cambridge & New York: Cambridge University Press, 2006);

David Croteau and William Hoynes, *The Business of Media: Corporate Media and the Public Interest* (Newbury Park, Cal.: Pine Forge, 2001);

Thomas De Zengotita, *Mediated: How the Media Shapes Our World and the Way We Live* (New York: Bloomsbury, 2005);

Karen E. Dill, *How Fantasy Becomes Reality: Seeing through Media Influence* (Oxford & New York: Oxford University Press, 2009);

Meenakshi Gigi Durham and Douglas Kellner, *Media and Cultural Studies: Keyworks* (Malden, Mass.: Blackwell, 2001);

Susan Faludi, *The Terror Dream: Fear and Fantasy in Post-9/11 America* (New York: Metropolitan, 2007);

Anthony R. Fellow and John Tebbel, *American Media History* (Belmont, Cal.: Thomson/Wadsworth, 2005);

Al Franken, *Lies (and the Lying Liars Who Tell Them): A Fair and Balanced Look at the Right* (New York: Dutton, 2003);

Ben Fritz, Bryan Keefer, and Brendan Nyhan, *All the President's Spin: George W. Bush, the Media, and the Truth* (New York: Simon & Schuster, 2004);

David Gauntlett, *Media, Gender and Identity: An Introduction* (London & New York: Routledge, 2002);

John Gibson, *How the Left Swiftboated America: The Liberal Media Conspiracy to Make You Think George Bush Was the Worst President in History* (New York: Harper, 2009);

Rosalind Gill, *Gender and the Media* (Cambridge & Malden, Mass.: Polity, 2007);

Dan Gillmor, *We the Media: Grassroots Journalism by the People, for the People* (Sebastopol, Cal.: O'Reilly, 2004);

Todd Gitlin, *Media Unlimited: How the Torrent of Images and Sounds Overwhelms Our Lives* (New York: Metropolitan, 2001);

Bernard Goldberg, *Bias: A CBS Insider Exposes How the Media Distort the News* (Washington, D.C.: Regnery, 2001);

Amy Goodman and David Goodman, *The Exception to the Rulers: Exposing Oily Politicians, War Profiteers, and the Media that Love Them* (New York: Hyperion, 2004);

Goodman and Goodman, *Static: Government Liars, Media Cheerleaders, and the People Who Fight Back* (New York: Hyperion, 2006);

Richard Gunther and Anthony Mughan, *Democracy and the Media: A Comparative Perspective* (Cambridge & New York: Cambridge University Press, 2000);

Theodore Hamm, *The New Blue Media: How Michael Moore, MoveOn.org, Jon Stewart and Company are Transforming Progressive Politics* (New York: New Press, 2008);

Mark B. N. Hansen, *New Philosophy for New Media* (Cambridge, Mass.: MIT Press, 2004);

Rahaf Harfoush, *Yes We Did: An Inside Look at How Social Media Built the Obama Brand* (Berkeley, Cal.: New Riders, 2009);

John Harrison and Martin Hirst, *Communication and New Media: From Broadcast to Narrowcast* (New York: Oxford University Press, 2007);

David Henderson, *Making News: A Straight-Shooting Guide to Media Relations* (Lincoln, Neb.: iUniverse Star, 2006);

Stephen Hess and Marvin L. Kalb, eds., *The Media and the War on Terrorism* (Washington, D.C.: Brookings Institution Press, 2003);

Thomas A. Hollihan, *Uncivil Wars: Political Campaigns in a Media Age* (Boston, Mass.: St. Martin's Press, 2001);

Gary Indiana, *Schwarzenegger Syndrome: Politics and Celebrity in the Age of Contempt* (New York: New Press, 2005);

Mizuko Ito and others, *Living and Learning with New Media: Summary of Findings from the Digital Youth Project* (Cambridge, Mass.: MIT Press, 2009);

Shanto Iyengar and Jennifer McGrady, *Media Politics: A Citizen's Guide* (New York: Norton, 2007);

Carrie James, *Young People, Ethics, and the New Digital Media: A Synthesis from the Good Play Project* (Cambridge, Mass.: MIT Press, 2009);

Henry Jenkins, *Convergence Culture: Where Old and New Media Collide* (New York: NYU Press, 2006);

Bill Katovsky and Timothy Carlson, eds., *Embedded: The Media at War in Iraq—An Oral History* (Guilford, Conn.: Lyons, 2003);

Eric Klinenburg, *Fighting for Air: The Battle to Control America's Media* (New York: Metropolitan, 2007);

Jonathan A. Knee, Bruce C. Greenwald, and Ava Seave, *The Curse of the Mogul: What's Wrong with the World's Leading Media Companies* (New York: Portfolio, 2009);

Paul Levinson, *New New Media* (Boston: Allyn & Bacon, 2009);

Rebecca Ann Lind, ed., *Race/Gender/Media; Considering Diversity Across Audience, Content, and Producers* (Boston: Allyn & Bacon, 2004);

Neil MacFarquhar, *The Media Relations Department of Hizbollah Wishes You a Happy Birthday: Unexpected Encounters in the Changing Middle East* (New York: PublicAffairs, 2009);

Lev Manovich, *The Language of New Media* (Cambridge, Mass.: MIT Press, 2001);

Jeremy D. Mayer, *American Media Politics in Transition* (Boston, Mass.: McGraw-Hill, 2007);

Robert W. McChesney, *The Problem of the Media: U.S. Communication Politics in the Twenty-First Century* (New York: Monthly Review, 2004);

Norman J. Medoff and Barbara Kaye, *Electronic Media: Then, Now, and Later* (Boston: Allyn & Bacon, 2004);

Bill Moyers, *Moyers on America: A Journalist and His Times*, edited by Julie Leininger Pycior (New York: New Press, 2004);

James E. Mueller, *Towel Snapping the Press: Bush's Journey from Locker-room Antics to Message Control* (Lanham, Md.: Rowman & Littlefield, 2006);

John Nichols and McChesney, *Tragedy and Farce: How the American Media Sell Wars, Spin Elections, and Destroy Democracy* (New York: New Press, 2005);

Tim O'Reilly and Sarah Milstein, *The Twitter Book* (Sebastopol, Cal.: O'Reilly, 2009);

W. James Potter, *11 Myths of Media Violence* (Thousand Oaks, Cal.: Sage, 2003);

Erik Qualman, *Socialnomics: How Social Media Transforms the Way We Live and Do Business* (Hoboken, N.J.: Wiley, 2009);

Benjamin Radford, *Media Mythmakers: How Journalists, Activists, and Advertisers Mislead Us* (Amherst, N.Y.: Prometheus, 2003);

Karen Ross, *Gendered Media: Women, Men, and Identity Politics* (Lanham, Md.: Rowman & Littlefield, 2010);

Mark J. Rozell, ed., *Media Power, Media Politics* (Lanham, Md.: Rowman & Littlefield, 2003);

Catherine R. Squires, *African Americans and the Media* (Cambridge & Malden, Mass.: Polity, 2009);

Federico Subervi-Velez, ed., *The Mass Media and Latino Politics: Studies of U.S. Media Content, Campaign Strategies and Survey Research: 1984–2004* (New York: Routledge, 2008);

Darrell M. West, *The Rise and Fall of the Media Establishment* (Boston: St. Martin's Press, 2001);

Marcy Wheeler, *Anatomy of Deceit: How the Bush Administration Used the Media to Sell the Iraq War and Out a Spy* (Berkeley, Cal.: Vaster, 2007);

James Wolcott, *Attack Poodles and Other Media Mutants: The Looting of the News in a Time of Terror* (New York: Miramax, 2004).

MEDICINE

Thomas Abraham, *Twenty-First Century Plague: The Story of SARS* (Baltimore: Johns Hopkins University Press, 2005).

Anne Davis Basting, *Forget Memory: Creating Better Lives for People with Dementia* (Baltimore: Johns Hopkins University Press, 2009).

Nancy G. Brinker and Joni Rodgers, *Promise Me: How a Sister's Love Launched the Global Movement to End Breast Cancer* (New York: Crown, 2010).

David Clark, *Germs, Genes & Civilization: How Epidemics Shaped Who We Are Today* (Upper Saddle River, N.J.: FT Press, 2010).

Michael J. Collins, *Hot Lights, Cold Steel: Life, Death and Sleepless Nights in a Surgeon's First Years* (New York: St. Martin's Press, 2005).

Thea Cooper and Arthur Ainsberg, *Breakthrough: Elizabeth Hughes, the Discovery of Insulin, and the Making of a Medical Miracle* (New York: St. Martin's Press, 2010).

Norman Doidge, *The Brain That Changes Itself: Stories of Personal Triumph from the Frontiers of Brain Science* (New York: Viking, 2007).

Madeline Drexler, *Emerging Epidemics: The Menace of New Infections* (New York: Penguin, 2009).

Jonathan Engel, *The Epidemic (A Global History of AIDS)* (Washington, D.C.: Smithsonian, 2006).

Thomas Graboys and Peter Zheutlin, *Life in the Balance: A Physician's Memoir of Life, Love, and Loss with Parkinson's Disease and Dementia* (New York: Union Square, 2008).

Sanjay Gupta, *Cheating Death: The Doctors and Medical Miracles That Are Saving Lives against All Odds* (New York: Wellness Central, 2009).

Susan Whitman Helfgot and William Novak, *The Match: Complete Strangers, a Miracle Face Transplant,*

Two Lives Transformed (New York: Simon & Schuster, 2010).

Lawrence R. Jacobs and Theda Skocpol, *Health Care Reform and American Politics* (New York: Oxford University Press, 2010).

Linda T. Kohn, Janet M. Corrigan, and Molla S. Donaldson, eds., *To Err Is Human: Building a Safer Health System* (Washington, D.C.: National Academy Press, 2000).

Joseph LeDoux, *Synaptic Self: How Our Brains Become Who We Are* (New York: Viking, 2002).

Charles R. Morris, *The Surgeons: Life and Death in a Top Heart Center* (New York: Norton, 2007).

Siddhartha Mukherjee, *The Emperor of All Maladies: A Biography of Cancer* (New York: Simon & Schuster, 2010).

Adriana Petryna, *When Experiments Travel: Clinical Trials and the Global Search for Human Subjects* (Princeton: Princeton University Press, 2009).

Michael Pollan, *In Defense of Food: An Eater's Manifesto* (New York: Penguin, 2008).

Pollan, *The Omnivore's Dilemma: A Natural History of Four Meals* (New York: Penguin, 2006).

Matt Ridley, *Genome: The Autobiography of a Species in 23 Chapters,* revised edition (New York: MJF Books, 2011).

John Elder Robison, *Look Me in the Eye: My Life with Asperger's* (New York: Crown, 2007).

Jeffrey M. Schwartz and Sharon Begley, *The Mind and the Brain: Neuroplasticity and the Power of Mental Force* (New York: ReganBooks/HarperCollins, 2002).

David Servan-Schreiber, *Anticancer: A New Way of Life* (New York: Viking, 2008).

Randy Shilts, *And the Band Played On: Politics, People and the AIDS Epidemic, 20th Anniversary Edition* (New York: St. Martin's Press, 2007).

David Snowdon, *Aging with Grace: What the Nun Study Teaches Us about Leading Longer, Healthier, and More Meaningful Lives* (New York: Bantam, 2001).

Jill Bolte Taylor, *My Stroke of Insight: A Brain Scientist's Personal Journey* (New York: Viking, 2008).

J. Craig Venter, *A Life Decoded: My Genome, My Life* (New York: Viking, 2007).

Aesthetic Surgery Journal, periodical;

Anesthesia & Analgesia, periodical;

Journal of Allergy and Clinical Immunology, periodical;

Journal of the American Medical Association, periodical;

Lancet, periodical;

New England Journal of Medicine, periodical;

Obstetrics & Gynecology, periodical;

Research in Nursing & Health, periodical.

RELIGION

Khaled Abou El Fadl, *The Great Theft: Wrestling Islam from the Extremists* (New York: HarperSanFrancisco, 2005);

William Y. Adams, *Religion and Adaptation* (Stanford, Cal.: CSLI Publications, 2005);

Jensine Andresen, *Religion in Mind: Cognitive Perspectives on Religious Belief, Ritual, and Experience* (Cambridge & New York: Cambridge University Press, 2001);

Reza Aslan, *No God but God: The Origins, Evolution, and Future of Islam* (New York: Random House, 2005);

Matthew C. Bagger, *The Uses of Paradox: Religion, Self-Transformation, and the Absurd* (New York: Columbia University Press, 2007);

Thomas Berry, *The Sacred Universe: Earth, Spirituality, and Religion in the Twenty-First Century,* foreword by Mary Evelyn Tucker (New York: Columbia University Press, 2009);

Ray Billington, *Religion Without God* (London & New York: Routledge, 2002);

Jenny Blain, Douglas Ezzy, and Graham Harvey, eds., *Researching Paganisms* (Walnut Creek, Cal.: AltaMira Press, 2004);

Pascal Boyer, *Religion Explained: The Evolutionary Origins of Religious Thought* (New York: Basic Books, 2001);

Lynn Bridgers, *Contemporary Varieties of Religious Experience: James's Classic Study in Light of Resiliency, Temperament, and Trauma* (Lanham, Md.: Rowman & Littlefield, 2005);

Richard Dawkins, *The God Delusion* (Boston: Houghton Mifflin, 2006);

Daniel C. Dennett, *Breaking the Spell: Religion as a Natural Phenomenon* (New York: Viking, 2006);

Jorge N. Ferrer and Jacob H. Sherman, eds., *The Participatory Turn: Spirituality, Mysticism, Religious Studies* (Albany: State University of New York Press, 2008);

David France, *Our Fathers: The Secret Life of the Catholic Church in an Age of Scandal* (New York: Broadway, 2004);

Andrew Gelman, *Red State, Blue State, Rich State, Poor State* (Princeton, N.J.: Princeton University Press, 2009);

Sam Harris, *The End of Faith: Religion, Terror, and the Future of Reason* (New York: Norton, 2004);

Harris, *Letter to a Christian Nation* (New York: Knopf, 2006):

Chris Hedges, *I Don't Believe in Atheists* (New York: Free Press, 2008);

John Hick, *The New Frontier of Religion and Science: Religious Experience, Neuroscience and the Transcendent* (Basingstoke, U.K. & New York: Palgrave Macmillan, 2006);

Christopher Hitchens, *God is Not Great: How Religion Poisons Everything* (New York: Twelve, 2007);

Laura Lyn Inglis and Peter K. Steinfeld, *Old Dead White Men's Philosophy* (Amherst, N.Y.: Humanity Books, 2000);

Hans Küng, *Islam: Past, Present and Future*, translated by John Bowden (Oxford: Oneworld, 2007);

John Lamb Lash, *Not in His Image: Gnostic Vision, Sacred Ecology, and the Future of Belief* (White River Junction, Vt.: Chelsea Green, 2006);

Timothy D. Lytton, *Holding Bishops Accountable: How Lawsuits Helped the Catholic Church Confront Clergy Abuse* (Cambridge, Mass.: Harvard University Press, 2008);

James McClenon, *Wondrous Healing: Shamanism, Human Evolution, and the Origin of Religion* (DeKalb: Northern Illinois University Press, 2002);

Alister E. McGrath and Joanna Collicutt McGrath, *The Dawkins Delusion: Atheist Fundamentalism and the Denial of the Divine* (Downers Grove, Ill.: InterVarsity Press, 2007);

Jacob Neusner, Bruce Chilton, and William A. Graham, *Three Faiths, One God: The Formative Faith and Practice of Judaism, Christianity, and Islam* (Boston: Brill, 2002);

Robert C. Neville, *Realism in Religion: A Pragmatist's Perspective* (Albany: State University of New York Press, 2009);

Pippa Norris and Ronald Inglehart, *Sacred and Secular: Religion and Politics Worldwide* (Cambridge & New York: Cambridge University Press, 2004);

Kimberley Christine Patton, *Religion of the Gods: Ritual, Paradox, and Reflexivity* (Oxford & New York: Oxford University Press, 2009);

Richard Rorty and Gianni Vattimo, *The Future of Religion*, edited by Santiago Zabala (New York: Columbia University Press, 2005);

Omid Safi, *Progressive Muslims: On Justice, Gender and Pluralism* (Oxford: Oneworld, 2003);

Alexander Saxton, *Religion and the Human Prospect* (New York: Monthly Review, 2006);

David Smith, *Hinduism and Modernity* (Malden, Mass.: Blackwell, 2003);

Raymond M. Smullyan, *Who Knows?: A Study of Religious Consciousness* (Bloomington: Indiana University Press, 2003);

C. John Sommerville, *Religion in the National Agenda: What We Mean by Religious, Spiritual, Secular* (Waco, Texas: Baylor University Press, 2009);

Lloyd H. Steffen, *Holy War, Just War: Exploring the Moral Meaning of Religious Violence* (Lanham, Md.: Rowman & Littlefield, 2007);

Victor J. Stenger, *God: The Failed Hypothesis: How Science Shows That God Does Not Exist* (Amherst, N.Y.: Prometheus, 2007);

Krista Tippett, *Speaking of Faith* (New York: Viking, 2007);

Frederick Turner, *Natural Religion* (New Brunswick, N.J.: Transaction, 2006);

Aaron Tyler, *Islam, the West, and Tolerance: Conceiving Coexistence* (New York: Palgrave Macmillan, 2008);

Graham Ward, *True Religion* (Oxford & Malden, Mass.: Blackwell, 2003);

Rick Warren, *The Purpose Driven Life: What on Earth Am I Here For?* (Grand Rapids, Mich.: Zondervan, 2002);

Harvey Whitehouse, *Modes of Religiosity: A Cognitive Theory of Religious Transmission* (Walnut Creek, Cal.: AltaMira Press, 2004);

Whitehouse and James Laidlaw, eds., *Religion, Anthropology, and Cognitive Science* (Durham, N.C.: Carolina Academic Press, 2007);

Christian Science Monitor, periodical;

Christianity Today, periodical;

Church Times, periodical;

National Catholic Reporter, periodical;

Reform Judaism Magazine, periodical;

Sojourners Magazine, periodical;

Theology Today, periodical.

SCIENCE

Amir D. Aczel, *Entanglement: The Greatest Mystery in Physics* (New York: Four Walls Eight Windows, 2002);

John Battelle, *The Search: How Google and Its Rivals Rewrote the Rules of Business and Transformed Our Culture* (New York: Portfolio, 2005);

Kai Bird and Martin J. Sherwin, *American Prometheus: The Triumph and Tragedy of J. Robert Oppenheimer* (New York: Knopf, 2005);

David Bodanis, *Electric Universe: The Shocking True Story of Electricity* (New York: Crown, 2005);

Bill Bryson, *A Short History of Nearly Everything* (New York: Broadway Books, 2003);

Mark Buchanan, *Nexus: Small Worlds and the Groundbreaking Science of Networks* (New York: Norton, 2002);

Nicholas Carr, *The Big Switch: Rewiring the World, from Edison to Google* (New York: Norton, 2008);

Richard Dawkins, *The Ancestor's Tale: A Pilgrimage to the Dawn of Evolution* (New York: Houghton Mifflin, 2004);

Kenneth S. Deffeyes, *Beyond Oil: The View from Hubbert's Peak* (New York: Hill & Wang, 2005);

Jared Diamond, *Collapse—How Societies Choose to Fail or Succeed* (New York: Viking, 2005);

Norman Doidge, *The Brain That Changes Itself: Stories of Personal Triumph from the Frontiers of Brain Science* (New York: Viking, 2007);

Avery Gilbert, *What the Nose Knows: The Science of Scent in Everyday Life* (New York: Crown, 2008);

Daniel Gilbert, *Stumbling on Happiness* (New York: Knopf, 2006);

Louisa Gilder, *The Age of Entanglement: When Quantum Physics Was Reborn* (New York: Knopf, 2008);

Al Gore, *An Inconvenient Truth: The Planetary Emergency of Global Warming and What We Can Do about It* (New York: Rodale 2006);

Stephen Jay Gould, *Punctuated Equilibrium* (Cambridge, Mass.: Harvard University Press, 2007);

Steve Grand, *Creation: Life and How to Make It* (Cambridge, Mass.: Harvard University Press, 2000);

Brian Green, *The Fabric of the Cosmos: Space, Time, and the Texture of Reality* (New York: Knopf, 2004);

Stephen Hawking, *The Universe in a Nutshell* (New York: Bantam, 2001);

Robert Henson, *The Rough Guide to Climate Change* (London: Rough Guides, 2006);

Hannah Holmes, *The Secret Life of Dust: From the Cosmos to the Kitchen Counter, the Big Consequences of Little Things* (New York: Wiley, 2001);

David Horrobin, *The Madness of Adam and Eve: How Schizophrenia Shaped Humanity* (London & New York: Bantam, 2001);

Donald C. Johanson and Kate Wong, *Lucy's Legacy: The Quest for Human Origins* (New York: Harmony, 2009);

Michio Kaku, *Parallel Worlds: A Journey through Creation, Higher Dimensions, and the Future of the Cosmos* (New York: Doubleday, 2005);

Robert P. Kirshner, *The Extravagant Universe: Exploding Stars, Dark Energy, and the Accelerating Cosmos* (Princeton: Princeton University Press, 2002);

Elizabeth Kolbert, *Field Notes from a Catastrophe: Man, Nature, and Climate Change* (New York: Bloomsbury, 2006);

Robert Kunzig, *Mapping the Deep: The Extraordinary Story of Ocean Science* (New York: Sort Of, 2000);

Eugene Linden, *The Winds of Change: Climate, Weather, and the Destruction of Civilization* (New York: Simon & Schuster, 2006);

Jo Marchant, *Decoding the Heavens: A 2,000-Year-Old Computer and the Century Long Search to Discover Its Secrets* (London: Heinemann, 2008);

Wil McCarthy, *Hacking Matter: Levitating Chairs, Quantum Mirages, and the Infinite Weirdness of Programmable Atoms* (New York: Basic Books, 2003);

Arthur I. Miller, *Empire of the Stars: Obsession, Friendship, and Betrayal in the Quest for Black Holes* (New York: Houghton Mifflin, 2005);

Leonard Mlodinow, *The Drunkard's Walk: How Randomness Rules Our Lives* (New York: Pantheon, 2008);

Donal O'Shea, *The Poincaré Conjecture: The Search of the Shape of the Universe* (New York: Walker, 2007);

Roger Penrose, *The Road to Reality: A Complete Guide to the Laws of the Universe* (London: Cape, 2004);

Steven Pinker, *The Blank Slate: The Modern Denial of Human Nature* (New York: Viking, 2002);

Robert M. Sapolsky, *A Primate's Memoir* (New York: Scribner, 2001);

Neil Shubin, *Your Inner Fish: A Journey into the 3.5-Billion-Year History of the Human Body* (New York: Pantheon, 2009);

Randall Stross, *Planet Google: One Company's Audacious Plan to Organize Everything We Know* (New York: Free Press, 2008);

Colin Tudge and Josh Young, *The Link: Uncovering Our Earliest Ancestor* (New York: Little, Brown, 2009);

Neil DeGrasse Tyson, *Death by Black Hole: And Other Cosmic Quandries* (New York: Norton, 2007);

Tyson and Donald Goldsmith, *Origins: Fourteen Billion Years of Cosmic Evolution* (New York: Norton, 2004);

J. Craig Venter, *A Life Decoded: My Genome, My Life* (New York: Viking, 2007);

Stephen Webb, *If the Universe Is Teeming with Aliens . . . Where Is Everybody?: Fifty Solutions to the Fermi Paradox and the Problem of Extraterrestrial Life* (New York: Copernicus Books, 2002);

Frank Wilczek, *The Lightness of Being: Mass, Ether, and the Unification of Forces* (New York: Basic Books, 2008);

American Scientist, periodical;

Discover, periodical;

National Geographic, periodical;

Natural History, periodical;

Science, periodical;

Scientific American, periodical.

SPORTS

Andre Agassi, *Open: An Autobiography* (New York: Knopf, 2009);

John Amaechi and Chris Bull, *Man in the Middle* (New York: ESPN Books, 2007);

Lance Armstrong and Sally Jenkins, *It's Not About the Bike: My Journey Back to Life* (New York: Putnam, 2000);

Shaun Assael, *Steroid Nation: Juiced Home Run Totals, Anti-Aging Miracles, and a Hercules in Every High School: The Secret History of America's True Drug Addiction* (New York: ESPN Books, 2007);

Bob Boyles and Paul Guido, *Fifty Years of College Football: A Modern History of America's Most Colorful Sport* (New York: Skyhorse, 2007);

J. C. Bradbury, *The Baseball Economist: The Real Game Exposed* (New York: Dutton, 2007);

Michael Bradley, *Big Games: College Football's Greatest Rivalries* (Washington, D.C.: Potomac Books, 2006);

David Browne, *Amped: How Big Air, Big Dollars, and a New Generation Took Sports to the Extreme* (New York: Bloomsbury, 2004);

Howard Bryant, *Juicing the Game: Drugs, Power, and the Fight for the Soul of Major League Baseball* (New York: Viking, 2005);

Michael L. Butterworth, *Baseball and Rhetoric of Purity: The National Pastime and American Identity during the War on Terror* (Tuscaloosa: University of Alabama Press, 2010);

Jose Canseco, *Juiced: Wild Times, Rampant 'Roids, Smash Hits, and How Baseball Got Big* (New York: Regan Books, 2005);

Leonard Cassuto and Stephen Partridge, eds., *The Cambridge Companion to Baseball* (Cambridge & New York: Cambridge University Press, 2011);

George Castle, *Baseball and the Media: How Fans Lose in Today's Coverage of the Game* (Lincoln: University of Nebraska Press, 2006);

Ronald W. Cox and Daniel Skidmore-Hess, *Free Agency and Competitive Balance in Baseball* (Jefferson, N.C.: McFarland, 2006);

Neil deMause and Joanna Cagan, *Field of Schemes: How the Great Stadium Swindle Turns Public Money into Private Profit* (Lincoln: University of Nebraska Press, 2008);

John Mark Dempsey, ed., *Sports-Talk Radio in America: Its Context and Culture* (New York: Haworth Press, 2006);

Tim Donaghy, *Personal Foul: A First-Person Account of the Scandal that Rocked the NBA* (Largo, Florida: VTI Group, 2009);

Tony Dungy and Nathan Whitaker, *Quiet Strength: The Principles, Practices, and Priorities of a Winning Life* (Carol Stream, Ill.: Tyndale, 2007);

Beau Dure, *Long-Range Goals: The Success Story of Major League Soccer* (Washington, D.C.: Potomac Books, 2010);

Mark Dyreson and J. A. Mangan, eds., *Sport and American Society: Exceptionalism, Insularity, and "Imperialism"* (New York: Routledge, 2007);

Jacqueline Edmondson, *Venus and Serena Williams: A Biography* (Westport, Conn.: Greenwood Press, 2005);

Jeremy Evans, *In Search of Powder: A Story of America's Disappearing Ski Bum* (Lincoln: University of Nebraska Press, 2010);

Mark Fainaru-Wada and Lance Williams, *Game of Shadows: Barry Bonds, BALCO, and the Steroids Scandal that Rocked Professional Sports* (New York: Gotham, 2006);

Tom Farrey, *Game On: How the Pressure to Win at All Costs Endangers Youth Sports, and What Parents Can Do About It* (New York: ESPN Books, 2009);

Franklin Foer, *How Soccer Explains the World: An Unlikely Theory of Globalization* (New York: HarperCollins, 2004);

Craig A. Forney, *The Holy Trinity of American Sports: Civil Religion in Football, Baseball, and Basketball* (Macon, Ga.: Mercer University Press, 2007);

Sharon T. Freeman, *African Americans: Reviving Baseball in Inner Cities* (Washington, D.C.: AASBEA, 2008);

Gerald R. Gems, *The Athletic Crusade: Sport and American Cultural Imperialism* (Lincoln: University of Nebraska Press, 2006);

John R. Gerdy, *Air Ball: American Education's Failed Experiment with Elite Athletics* (Jackson: University Press of Mississippi, 2006);

Billy Hawkins, *The New Plantation: Black Athletes, College Sports, and Predominantly White NCAA Institutions* (New York: Palgrave Macmillan, 2010);

Nancy Hogshead-Makar and Andrew Zimbalist, eds., *Equal Play: Title IX and Social Change* (Philadelphia: Temple University Press, 2007);

Bill James, *The New Bill James Historical Baseball Abstract* (New York: Free Press, 2001);

Richard A. Johnson and Robert Hamilton Johnson, *The Boston Marathon* (Boston: Arcadia, 2009);

Tom Jones, *Working at the Ballpark: The Fascinating Lives of Baseball People—From Peanut Vendors and Broadcasters to Players and Managers* (New York: Skyhorse, 2008);

Frank P. Jozsa Jr., *Baseball, Inc.: The National Pastime as Big Business* (Jefferson, N.C.: McFarland, 2006);

Jozsa, *Baseball in Crisis: Spiraling Costs, Bad Behavior, Uncertain Future* (Jefferson, N.C.: McFarland, 2008);

Jozsa, *Major League Baseball Expansions and Relocations: A History, 1876–2008* (Jefferson, N.C.: McFarland, 2010);

Ted A. Kluck, *Game Time: Inside College Football* (Guilford, Conn.: Lyons Press, 2007);

Dawn Knight, *Taliaferro: Breaking Barriers from the NFL Draft to the Ivory Tower* (Bloomington: Indiana University Press, 2007);

Christopher S. Kudlac, *Fair or Foul: Sports and Criminal Behavior in the United States* (Santa Barbara, Cal.: Praeger/ABC-CLIO, 2010);

Simon Kuper and Stefan Szymanski, *Soccernomics: Why England Loses, Why Germany and Brazil Win, and Why the U.S., Japan, Australia, Turkey—and Even Iraq—Are Destined to Become the Kings of the World's Most Popular Sport* (New York: Nation Books, 2009);

Kyle Kusz, *Revolt of the White Athlete: Race, Media and the Emergence of Extreme Athletes in America* (New York: Lang, 2007);

Bill Lee and Richard Lally, *The Wrong Stuff* (New York: Three Rivers Press, 2006);

Michael Lewis, *Moneyball: The Art of Winning an Unfair Game* (New York: Norton, 2003);

Lewis, *The Blind Side: Evolution of a Game* (New York: Norton, 2006);

Michael Litos, *Cinderella: Inside the Rise of Mid-Major College Basketball* (Naperville, Ill.: Sourcebooks, 2007);

Kathleen Lockwood, *Major League Bride: An Inside Look at Life Outside the Ballpark* (Jefferson, N.C.: McFarland, 2010);

Stewart Mandel, *Bowls, Polls & Tattered Souls: Tackling the Chaos and Controversy that Reign Over College Football* (Hoboken, N.J.: Wiley, 2008);

Michael Mandelbaum, *The Meaning of Sports: Why Americans Watch Baseball, Football, and Basketball, and What They See When They Do* (New York: Public Affairs, 2004);

Peyton Manning and Archie Manning, *Manning: A Father, His Sons and a Football Legacy* (New York: Harper, 2000);

Andrei S. Markovits and Lars Rensmann, *Gaming the World: How Sports are Reshaping Global Politics and Culture* (Princeton, N.J.: Princeton University Press, 2010);

Dorothy Seymour Mills, *Chasing Baseball: Our Obsession with Its History, Numbers, People and Places* (Jefferson, N.C.: McFarland, 2010);

Warren Moon and Don Yaeger, *Never Give Up on Your Dream: My Journey* (Cambridge, Mass.: Da Capo Press, 2009);

Dat Nguyen and Rusty Burson, *Dat: Tackling Life and the NFL* (College Station: Texas A&M University Press, 2005);

S. L. Price, *Heart of the Game: Life, Death, and Mercy in Minor League America* (New York: Ecco/HarperCollins, 2009);

Kirk Radomski, *Bases Loaded: The Inside Story of the Steroid Era in Baseball by the Central Figure in the Mitchell Report* (New York: Hudson Street Press, 2009);

Rick Reilly, *Who's Your Caddy?: Looping for the Great, Near Great, and Reprobates of Golf* (New York: Doubleday, 2003);

Jennifer Ring, *Stolen Bases: Why American Girls Don't Play Baseball* (Urbana: University of Illinois Press, 2009);

Betsy M. Ross, *Playing Ball with the Boys: The Rise of Women in the World of Men's Sports* (Cincinnati: Clerisy Press, 2010);

Rob Ruck, *Raceball: How the Major Leagues Colonized the Black and Latin Game* (Boston: Beacon Press, 2010);

Mike Schmidt and Glen Waggoner, *Clearing the Bases: Juiced Players, Monster Salaries, Sham Records, and a Hall of Famer's Search for the Soul of Baseball* (New York: HarperCollins, 2006);

Roy Simmons and others, *Out of Bounds: Coming Out of Sexual Abuse, Addiction, and My Life of Lies in the NFL Closet* (New York: Carroll & Graf, 2006);

Glenn Stout, ed., *The Best American Sports Writing* (New York: Houghton Mifflin, 2000–2009);

Dean A. Sullivan, ed., *Final Innings: A Documentary History of Baseball, 1972–2008* (Lincoln: University of Nebraska Press, 2010);

Stefan Szymanski and Andrew Zimbalist, *National Pastime: How Americans Play Baseball and the Rest of the World Plays Soccer* (Washington, D.C.: Brookings Institution Press, 2005);

Teri Thompson and others, *American Icon: The Fall of Roger Clemens and the Rise of Steroids in America's Pastime* (New York: Knopf, 2009);

Michael V. Uschan, *Serena Williams* (Detroit: Lucent Books, 2011);

Michael Waltrip, *In the Blink of an Eye: Dale, Daytona, and the Day That Changed Everything* (New York: Hyperion, 2011);

Venus Williams, Serena Williams, and Hilary Beard, *Venus & Serena: Serving From the Hip, Ten Rules for Living, Loving, and Winning* (Boston: Houghton Mifflin, 2005);

Tiger Woods, *How I Play Golf* (New York: Crown, 2000);

Don Yaeger and Jim Henry, *Tarnished Heisman: Did Reggie Bush Turn His Final College Season into a Six-Figure Job?* (New York: Pocket Books, 2008);

Mark Yost, *Varsity Green: A Behind the Scenes Look at Culture and Corruption in College Athletics* (Stanford, Cal.: Stanford University Press, 2010);

Dave Zirin, *Bad Sports: How Owners are Ruining the Games We Love* (New York: Scribner, 2010).

CONTRIBUTORS

WORLD EVENTS

JAMES F. TIDD JR.
Manly, Inc.
Columbia, South Carolina

THE ARTS

GEORGE PARKER ANDERSON
Manly, Inc.
Columbia, South Carolina

PHILIP B. DEMATTEIS
Manly, Inc.
Columbia, South Carolina

HEATHER PENFIELD
Upton, Massachusetts

BUSINESS AND THE ECONOMY

JOE MORRIS
Charleston, West Virginia

EDUCATION

ASHLEY COOK
Fort Scott, Kansas

PAUL COOK
Cottey College
Nevada, Missouri

FASHION

EMILY MURRAY
University of South Carolina
Columbia, South Carolina

GOVERNMENT AND POLITICS

MEEGHAN KANE
University of South Carolina
Columbia, South Carolina

LAW AND JUSTICE

ERIC BARGERON
University of South Carolina
Columbia, South Carolina

LIFESTYLES AND SOCIAL TRENDS

TRACY BEALER
The Citadel
Charleston, South Carolina

MEDIA   RACHEL LURIA
                                             Florida Atlantic University
                                             Jupiter, Florida

MEDICINE AND HEALTH   ROBERT J. WILENSKY
                                             Washington, D.C.

RELIGION   KEVIN KYZER
                                             University of South Carolina
                                             Columbia, South Carolina

SCIENCE AND TECHNOLOGY   PAUL TOLLIVER BROWN
                                             University of South Carolina
                                             Columbia, South Carolina

SPORTS   GEORGE PARKER ANDERSON
                                             Manly, Inc.
                                             Columbia, South Carolina
                                             JAMES F. TIDD JR.
                                             Manly, Inc.
                                             Columbia, South Carolina
                                             STEPHANIE TODD
                                             University of Tennessee at Chattanooga
                                             Chattanooga, Tennessee

INDEX OF PHOTOGRAPHS

on 29 November 2009, which the Vikings won 36–10 (AP Photo/ Andy King) 505

Federal abstinence education: Map showing state participation in federal abstinence education program (AP Photo/Damiko Morris) 144

Federer, Roger: *Vogue* editor in chief Anna Wintour (second from right) watches from the front row along with tennis star Roger Federer and other *Vogue* editors during Oscar de la Renta's 2008 spring/summer collection. 192

Ford, Tom: A model wearing a dress designed by Tom Ford for Yves Saint Laurent Rive Gauche's fall-winter 2004–2005 collection (AP Photo/Michel Euler) 173

Franklin, Aretha: Aretha Franklin sports a gray felt hat designed by Luke Song for her performance at the inauguration of President Barack Obama in 2009 (AP Photo/ Ron Edmonds). 167

Freakonomics: A Rogue Economist Explores the Hidden Side of Everything: University of Chicago economics professor Steven Levitt poses with his book, coauthored with Stephen Dubner, *Freakonomics: A Rogue Economist Explores the Hidden Side of Everything*, in Chicago, 2005 (AP Photo/ Charles Rex Arbogast). 104

Futuresex/Lovesounds: Cover for Justin Timberlake's last solo album of the decade, released in 2006 (Jive Records) 56

Gates, Bill: Microsoft chairman Bill Gates speaks to business and government leaders at the Microsoft Government Leaders' Conference in Seattle, 4 April 2000 (AP Photo/Stevan Morgian). 93

Gehry, Frank: The Walt Disney Concert Hall (2003) in Los Angeles, designed by Frank Gehry (photograph by Arturo Ramos) 164

Geoghan, John: Former priest John Geoghan is taken into custody by a court officer after being convicted of child sexual abuse in Cambridge, Massachusetts, on 18 January 2002. Geoghan was murdered in prison on 22 February 2003 (AP Photo/Pool, Kevin Wisniewski). 403

George Mason Patriots basketball: A George Mason Patriots Final Four 2006 Championship ring commemorating the men's team's 27 March 2006 win over the Connecticut Huskies (<www.george-masonbasketball.blogspot.com>) 495

Gettelfinger, Ron: Auto executives, from left, General Motors chief executive officer Richard Wagoner, United Auto Workers president Ron Gettelfinger, Ford chief executive officer Alan Mulally, and Chrysler chief executive officer Robert Nardelli, testify on Capitol Hill in Washington on 4 December 2008, before a Senate Banking Committee hearing on the auto industry bailout (AP Photo/Gerald Herbert, File). 95

Ginsburg, Ruth Bader: The United States Supreme Court in 2009; top row (left to right): Samuel A. Alito, Ruth Bader Ginsburg, Stephen G. Breyer, and Sonia Sotomayor; bottom row: Anthony M. Kennedy, John Paul Stevens, John G. Roberts, Antonin G. Scalia, and Clarence Thomas (photograph by Steve Petteway, staff photographer of the Supreme Court) 274

Goldberg, Whoopi: The women of ABC's daytime talk show *The View*—from left, Whoopi Goldberg, Barbara Walters, Joy Behar, Sherri Shepherd, and Elisabeth Hasselbeck—interview President Barack Obama (official White House photograph by Pete Souza). 342

Goodridge, Hillary, and Julie: Julie Goodridge, left, and her spouse, Hillary Goodridge, cross the street from the Unitarian Universalist Church to the State House in Boston after their marriage on 17 May 2004 (AP Photo/Winslow Townson). 405

Google: Google cofounders Larry Page, left, and Sergey Brin at their company's headquarters on 15 January 2004 in Mountain View, California (AP Photo/Ben Margot) 103

Gore, Al: Democratic presidential candidate Vice President Al Gore at a campaign rally in Nashville, Tennessee, on 7 March 2000 after his Super Tuesday victories (AP Photo/Amy Sancetta) 205

Guantánamo Bay Detention Camp: Detainees are held for in-processing at U.S. naval base Guantánamo Bay, Cuba, on 11 January 2002 (Department of Defense photograph by Petty Officer 1st Class Shane T. Mc-Coy, U.S. Navy). 277

Gunn, Tim: Tim Gunn, a former faculty member at the Parsons School of Design and on-air mentor for the fashion-design reality program *Project Runway*, interviewed during New York fashion week 2009 (The Heart Truth) 176

H&M Garden Collection: Advertisement for fashion retailer H&M promoting its environmentally friendly Garden Collection (from <www.pourfemme.it>) 166

H1N1 vaccine: A health-care practitioner administers a nasal-spray flu vaccine for the H1N1 virus to a patient in 2009 (<www.cdc.gov>). 381

Harry Potter series: Teachers capitalized on students' interest in J. K. Rowling's Harry Potter and Stephenie Meyer's *Twilight* series to promote good reading habits, incorporating these popular novels into the curriculum. Dust jackets above are from the last two Harry

Potter novels (2005, 2007, respectively), and the first two *Twilight* novels (2005, 2006, respectively). 156

Hasselbeck, Elisabeth: The women of ABC's daytime talk show *The View*—from left, Whoopi Goldberg, Barbara Walters, Joy Behar, Sherri Shepherd, and Elisabeth Hasselbeck—interview President Barack Obama (official White House photograph by Pete Souza). 342

Healthy Kids Fair: First Lady Michelle Obama participates in the Healthy Kids Fair on the South Lawn of the White House on 21 October 2009 (<www.whitehouse.gov>). 369

Hood, Leroy E. 464

Horner, Jack: Jack Horner with the *Tyrannosaurus rex* femur he discovered in Montana (Montana State University's Museum of the Rockies) 448

Houston Astros ballpark: Workers remove an Enron logo from the Houston Astros ballpark on 28 February 2002. The ballpark, named for Enron, briefly became Astros Field until Minute Maid bought the naming rights (AP Photo/Pat Sullivan). 99

HPV vaccine: A nurse administers the HPV vaccine to a young woman in 2006 (<www.cdc.gov>). 375

Hubble Space Telescope: Astronauts from Space Shuttle *Atlantis* servicing the Hubble Space Telescope on 16 May 2009 (from <www.nasa.gov>). 440

Huffington, Arianna: Arianna Huffington, cofounder of the liberal news website *The Huffington* Post (photograph by David Shankbone) 335

Husband, Rick: Columbia space shuttle crew, clockwise from top: Mission Specialist Kalpana Chawla, Mission Specialists Laurel Clark and David Brown, Pilot Willie McCool, Payload Specialist Ilan Ramon and Payload Commander Michael Anderson

(<www.spaceflight.nasa.gov>) 458

Hussein, Saddam: U.S. soldiers and Iraqi civilians watch as the statue of Saddam Hussein is toppled in Firdous Square, in downtown Bagdhad, on 9 April 2003 (AP Photo/Jerome Delay). 233

Imus, Don: Radio and television personality Don Imus speaks with civil-rights activist Al Sharpton about Imus's racially charged comments about the Rutgers women's basketball team on 9 April 2007 (AP Photo/Richard Drew). 334

Individuals with Disabilities Education Improvement Act of 2004: President George W. Bush with Carolyn Bailey and her daughter, Isabelle, at the signing of the Individuals with Disabilities Education Improvement Act of 2004 (AP Photo/Lawrence Jackson) 143

Iraq War, invasion: Map showing the strategic locations of various forces involved in the invasion of Iraq (<www.army.mil>) 232

Jacobs, Marc 181

Jay-Z 66

Jena, Louisiana: Demonstration in Jena, Louisiana, 20 September 2007, in support of six black teenagers initially charged with attempted murder in the beating of Justin Barker, a white classmate (AP Photo/*The Chronicle*, Sharon Steinmann) 134

JetBlue: A February 2009 JetBlue airline advertisement capitalizes on popular dissatisfaction with Wall Street to promote its low-fare services (<http://when-growthstalls.com>). 97

Jobs, Steve 112

Katrina, Air National Guard: Air National Guard members deliver water and food to stranded citizens of New Orleans after the city was devastated by Hurricane Katrina (U.S. Navy photograph by Photographer's Mate First Class Brien Aho). 219

Katrina: Technical Sergeant Lem Torres surveys houses in New Orleans on 2 September 2005 looking for victims of Hurricane Katrina (U.S. Air Force photograph by Staff Sergeant Manuel J. Martinez). 218

Kennedy, Anthony M.: The United States Supreme Court in 2009; top row (left to right): Samuel A. Alito, Ruth Bader Ginsburg, Stephen G. Breyer, and Sonia Sotomayor; bottom row: Anthony M. Kennedy, John Paul Stevens, John G. Roberts, Antonin G. Scalia, and Clarence Thomas (photograph by Steve Petteway, staff photographer of the Supreme Court) 274

Kerry, John: President George W. Bush, left, and Democratic candidate Senator John Kerry during their second presidential debate at Washington University in St. Louis, Missouri, on 8 October 2004 (AP Photo/Charlie Riedel) 207

Kwan, Michelle: Michelle Kwan performs her signature spiral in practice before the 2002 U.S. Figure Skating Championships in Los Angeles (photograph by Kevin Rushforth). 510

Lansbury, Angela 66

Lead-based paint in China-made toys: Following a 2007 recall a darkly humorous "de-motivational" Internet poster highlights the hidden dangers of lead-based paint used in toys produced in China (<www.motifake.com>). 107

Left Behind: Poster for a 2001 film based on the popular series of Christian novels by Tim LaHaye and Jerry Jenkins (<www.moviepostershop.com>) 417

Lehman Brothers: Robin Radaetz holds a sign in front of the Lehman Brothers headquarters in New York on 15 September 2008, the day the 158-year-old investment bank filed for Chapter 11 protection in the biggest bank-

GENERAL INDEX

A

Aaliyah (Aaliyah Dana Haughton) 28, 73
Aaron, Hank 481, 483, 490
Abandon (Iyer) 31
ABBA (musical group) 62
Abbott, Darrell 73
Abboud, Francois 389
ABC 46, 102, 105, 120, 158–159, 178, 250, 253, 256, 282, 324–327, 334–335, 340, 344, 347, 353–354
ABC World News Tonight (television show) 326
Abdul, Paula 338
Abdul-Jabbar, Kareem 346, 522
Abel, Elie 352
Abelson, Phillip H. 469
Abercrombie and Fitch (store) 168
abortion 211, 239, 250, 253, 256, 269, 376, 391
    antiabortion activists 200
    partial-birth 199, 206, 268, 360
About Schmidt (movie) 29
Abramoff, Jack 198, 217, 239
Abramovitz, Max 189
Abrams, Frederick R. 388
Abrikosov, Alexei A. 467
"Abrupt Climate Change: Inevitable Surprises" 435
The Absolutely True Diary of a Part-time Indian (Alexie) 37
The Abstinence Teacher (Perrotta) 37
Absurdistan (Shetyngart) 35
Abu Ghraib prison 197, 208–209, 230, 236, 326
Academia Sinica 463
Academy Awards 65, 158, 166–167, 182, 463–464
Academy of Country Music (ACM) 56
Accreditation Council for Graduate Medical Education (ACGME), 125, 369

Acemoglu, Daron 119
Acheron (Kenyon) 38
Ackerman, Gary 94
Acquanetta, Burna 73
Acquired Immune Deficiency Syndrome (AIDS) 364
Act for the Relief of the Parents of Theresa Marie Schiavo 270
The Actors Studio 77
Actors Theatre (Louisville) 61
ACTPass 62
Acura MDX 188
Adair, Virginia 73
Adam-12 (television show) 74
Adams, Eddie 352
Adams, Victoria Gray 250
Adams, William James, Jr. 346
Adaptation (movie) 29
Addington, Whitney W. 389
Adelphia Communications 85, 87, 100
Adequate Yearly Progress 142
Adler, Mortimer J. 152
Adobe Flash 454
Adrover, Miguel 185
Advanced Cell Technology (ACT) 378, 435, 448
Advanced Medical Imaging 466
Advanced Television Systems Committee 454
The Adventures of Augie March (Bellow) 73
Advertising 327
Advertising Age (magazine) 348
Advertising Standards Authority (Great Britain) 182
Advocate (magazine) 422
Advocates for Youth 144
AdWords 102
Aéropostale 160
Aesthetic Surgery Journal 365
affirmative action 132–133, 154, 254, 267

education 271
workplace 272
The Affluent Society (Galbraith) 252
Afghanistan 162, 194, 197, 201, 207–208, 210, 214, 224, 226–232, 235–236, 243, 245, 247, 249, 276–277, 334, 352, 360, 372, 395, 401, 410, 426
    Kabul 228–229, 231
    Northern Alliance 228
    poppy cultivation in 230
    Qandahar 228
    teacher training 148
    troop escalation in 200
Africa 255, 350
    AIDS in 422
African American Lives (Gates) 149
African Americans 77–78, 124–125, 131, 133, 149, 181, 189, 203, 212–213, 220, 242, 246–247, 253, 254, 256, 272, 284, 334, 340, 411, 429, 482, 487, 506, 521–522
    education 143
    first rabbi 427
    movies 42
    obesity 369
Africana
    The Encyclopedia of the African and African American Experience 149
The African Queen (movie) 76
After This (McDermott) 35
Against the Day (Pynchon) 35, 47
Agassi, Andre 521
Agins, Teri 186
Agnes of God (movie) 73
Agnew, Spiro 252
Agre, Peter C. 389, 468
Agriprocessors Inc. 88
Aguilera, Christina 42, 58, 171
Ahmadinejad, Mahmoud 421
A.I. Artificial Intelligence (movie) 27
Aida (musical) 70

AIDS 144, 158, 252, 256, 359, 363, 390–391, 421–422, 424, 469
  drugs 358
Aiken, Clay 338
"Ain't It Funny" (song) 30
"Ain't No Stoppin' Us Now" (song) 78
The Air Castle That Blew Up (Larsson) 49
Air Force One 223
Air National Guard 209
Akerlof, George A. 119
Al Qaeda 194, 195, 197–198, 201, 224, 226–227, 229, 232–234, 236, 276, 278, 325, 394–395, 406
Alabama 118, 190, 197, 209, 396
  children's campaign 250
  Ten Commandments controversy 412
Alamogordo, N.Mex. 450
Al-Arian, Sami 125, 151
Alaska 129
  oil dividends 244
  polar bears 443
Albee, Edward 70
Albert, Carl Bert 250
Albert, Eddie 73
Albert, Stew 250
Albert Lasker Medical Research Award 464
Alcaide, Chris 73
Alderson, Samuel W. 389
Alentejo Blue (Ali) 35
Alex Cross's Trial (Patterson and DiLallo) 40
Alexander, Devon 500
Alexis, Kim 176
Algerov, Zhores I. 467
Ali (movie) 27
Ali, Muhammad 27, 500
Alice (television show) 75
Alison, Jane 31
Alito, Samuel A. 245, 267–268, 280–281
All Dulles Area Muslim Society 421
"All for You" (song) 28
"All I Have" (song) 31
All in the Family (television show) 77, 354
All My Children (television show) 80
All My Sons (play) 39
The All New Mickey Mouse Club (television show) 58, 171
All over Creation (Ozeki) 31
All Songs Considered (web show) 337
All That Jazz (movie) 79
All the Pretty Horses (movie) 26

All Things Considered (radio show) 51, 337
"All You Wanted" (song) 30
Allen, Dayton 73
Allen, Donald M. 73
Allen, Paul 466
Allen, Richard 388
Allen, Ted 176
Allen, Tina 73
Allen Room 57
Allergies 370
Alley, Vernon 73
Alliance Capital 116
Alliance for Climate Protection 463
Alliance of Motion Picture and Television Producers 88
Alligator Records 79
Allred, Owen 428
Al-Medina Institute (New Jersey) 421
Almost (Benedict) 28
Almost Famous (movie) 26
Aloft (Lee) 31
Alomar, Roberto 493
Alomar, Sandy, Jr. 493
Alou, Moises 478, 493
Alpher, Ralph A. 469
Alphorn, Ralph 469
Alpine Skiing World Cup 480, 483
Alter, Harvey J. 386, 389
Altman, Robert 73
Alvin Ailey American Dance Theater 80
Alzheimer's disease 64, 207, 358, 360, 378, 384, 424, 449, 451
"Amazed" (song) 27
The Amazing Adventures of Kavalier & Clay (Chabon) 26, 47
The Amazing Race (television show) 348, 349
Amazon.com 41, 55, 327, 340
Ambros, Victor 386
Ambrose, Stephen A. 152, 250
AMC 59, 160, 327, 330
  Matador 189
Amendment B 405
America Online (AOL) 84, 103, 347
"America the Beautiful" (song) 45
America (The Book) (Stewart and others) 333
America's Got Talent (television show) 327, 338
America's Next Top Model (television show) 159, 175, 181, 184, 325, 338
"America's Song" (song) 346
American Academy of Arts and Sciences 464

American Airlines 96
American Apparel 160, 169, 173
American Association of Christian Schools 410
American Association of Medical Colleges (AAMC) 369
American Association of Pediatricians 144
American Association of Plastic Surgeons 390
American Association of Retired Persons (AARP) 274
American Association of School Administrators 142
American Astronomical Society Division of Planetary Sciences 462
American Ballet Theatre 45, 74
American Bankers Association 101
American Baptist Churches (ABC), USA 397
American Basketball Association 498
American Beauty (movie) 340
American Chemical Society 465
American Civil Liberties Union (ACLU) 276, 284, 407, 426, 412
American College of Obstetricians and Gynecologists (ACOG) 375
American Dialect Society 333
American Eagle 166
American East Conference 495
American Economic Association 119
American Federation of Labor 87
American Football Conference (AFC) 505
American Football League 252
American Gangster (movie) 36
American High (television show) 348
American Idol (television show) 42, 57, 366, 325, 327–328, 338
American Institute of Architects 164, 183
American International Group (AIG) 89, 110, 112
  A.I.G. Financial Products 222
American Jewish Congress 153, 400, 429
American League Championship Series (ALCS) 489
American Lung Association 380
American Masters (television show) 348–349
  "Finding Lucy" 348
  "Hitchcock, Selznick and the End of Hollywood" 348
American Medical Association (AMA) 144
  cloning 448

American Morning (television show) 347

American Movie Classics (AMC) 170, 331

American Museum of Natural History 466

American Music Awards 167

American Muslim Alliance 407

American Muslim Council 407

American Muslims for Jerusalem 407

American Pastoral (Roth) 47

American Philosophical Society 463–464

American Podiatric Medical Association 170

American Psycho (movie) 26

American Public Health Association 144

American Radiology Services 466

American Recovery and Reinvestment Act (ARRA) 222, 242, 372

American Religious Identification Survey 395, 399, 415

American Revolution 65

American Rust (Meyer) 40

American Society of Interior Designers 178

American Society of Muslims 429

American Son (Roley) 28

American Stock Exchange (ASE) 84

American University 421

American Wife (Sittenfeld) 38

American Woman (Choi) 31

Americans for the Separation of Church and State 412

Americans with Disabilities Act 253

Ames, Joe 73

Ames Brothers (musical group) 73

Amgen 464

Amish 128, 132, 146

"Amman Message" 407

Amway Corporation 120

Amyotrophic lateral sclerosis (ALS) 390

Anabolic Steroid Control Act 360

Anacostia River 493

Anaheim Angels 477, 489

Anaheim Ducks 482

Anarchy, State, and Utopia (Nozick) 153

Anathem (Stephenson) 38

Anbar Awakening 236

Anchorage, Alaska 475

Anchorman: The Legend of Ron Burgundy (movie) 32

And Now You Can Go (Vida) 31

Anderson, Daniel 466

Anderson, Elmer L. 250

Anderson, Greg 481

Anderson, Michael 435, 457

Anderson, Nick 351

Anderson, Pamela 169, 184

Anderson, Paul Thomas 52

Anderson, Phyllis B. 396

Anderson, Wes 52

Anderson Cooper 360 (television show) 347

ANDi (genetically altered primate) 358

Ando, Tadao 187

Andre the Giant 63

André 3000 173

Andrew, Mark 422

Andrew Mellon Foundation 29

Andrews, Mason 389

The Andromeda Strain (movie) 75

The Andy Griffith Show (television show) 74, 78, 353

"Angel" (song) 28

Angela's Ashes (McCourt) 77

Angelos, Peter 466

Angels and Demons (Brown) 54–55

Angels & Demons (movie) 39, 55

Angels Fall (Roberts) 35

Angelus (Findlay), Muriel 73

Anger, Hal O. 389

Anglican Catholic Church 429

Anglican Church of North America 399, 404

Anglican Communion 423

Aniston, Jennifer 343

Anja the Liar (Moran) 31

Anna Karenina (Tolstoy) 49

The Anna Nicole Show (television show) 354

Annenberg, Walter 120

Another World (television show) 78

Answered Prayers (Steel) 30

Antarctica 390
     Larson B ice shelf 435, 443

The Anthologist (Baker) 39

Anthony, Carmelo 495, 498

anthrax 194, 226, 333, 363, 374, 384

Anti-Ballistic Missile Treaty 195

Anti-Defamation League (ADL) 420, 429

Antiochian Orthodox Christian Archdiocese of North America 397

Anti-Semitism 65, 398, 421, 417

Antrim, Donald 64

Ants on the Melon (Adair) 73

AOL Time Warner 85, 92–93, 102–103, 324–325, 347

Apex Hides the Hurt (Whitehead) 36

Apocalypse Now (movie) 74

Apocalypto (movie) 35

"Apologize" (song) 38

Apostolic United Brethren (Mormon) 428

Appalachian Mountains 200

Appalachian State University Mountaineers 503

Appalachian Trail 217

Appaloosa (movie) 37

The Appeal (Grisham) 38

Appelbaum, Paul Stuart 388

Apple, Inc. 41, 58, 112–113, 324, 327, 340, 435, 453, 463, 470

Applegate, William T. 388

Applied Biosystems 464

The Apprentice (television show) 217, 325, 347

Aprahamian, Charles 388

Aqua Dots 107

Arab Americans 226

Archerd, Army 352

Architectural Forum 189

architecture
     green design 163
     sustainable design 163–164

Architecture for Humanity 188

Archives of Internal Medicine 360

Arcos, Joseph C. 469

Arctic Ice Cap 438, 443

Arctic Ocean 443

Ardi (human ancestor) 439, 446–447

Ardipithecus ramidus 446, 448

Are You Smarter Than a 5th Grader? (television show) 347

Arens, James F. 388

Argentina
     basketball 498
     Buenos Aires 217
     financial crisis 115
     Neuquén 465

Arizona
     Glendale 482

Arizona Cardinals 484, 489

Arizona Diamondbacks 475, 479, 488–489, 491, 522

Arizona State University 505

Arkansas 284
     same-sex marriage 272

Arky, Ronald A. 387

Arledge, Roone 120

Arlington High School (LaGrange, New York) 130

Armageddon (LeHaye and Jenkins) 31

Armed Services and Veterans Affairs 256

Armendariz, Albert 284

Armey, Dick 251

Armies of the Night (Mailer) 77

Bakker, Jim 429
Bal, Dileep 387
Balanchine, George 45, 74
Balilty, Oded 351
Ball, Alan 340
"The Ballad of Jed Clampett" (song) 79
Ballas, Mark 46
Ballet 45, 73, 76
Ballinger, Jay Scott 426
Ballpark at Union Station 492
Baltimore, David 388
Baltimore, Maryland 332
Baltimore Orioles 360, 476, 490–492
Baltimore Ravens 474, 478, 487, 507, 522
Baltimore Science Fiction Society 74
Baltimore Sun 84, 324
Bampton, Rose 73
Banana Republic 167
Bancroft, Anne 73
Bangkok 8 (Burdett) 31
Bangladesh 203
Bang the Drum Slowly (Harris) 76
Bank, Aaron 250
Bank of America 89, 100, 108–110, 112, 116
Bank of America Tower (New York City) 165
Bank One 100, 104
Banking 92, 108
  investment 94
Banks, Tyra 159, 170, 175, 181, 184, 325
Banksy 63
Baptist General Convention of Oklahoma 426
Baptist General Convention of Texas 394
Baquet, Dean 347
Barbera, Joseph 73
Barbie doll 189
Barclays Bank 108–109
Baretta (television show) 80
Bariatric surgery 365
Barksdale Air Force Base 223
Barnes, Edward Larrabee 187
Barnes, Freddie 504
Barnes & Noble 41, 55
Barnes-Jewish Hospital Cardiac Catheterization Laboratory 384
Barnett, Martha 283
Barney's (store) 167
Barnyard (movie) 35
Barrie Black, Ira 390
Barry, Barbara 188
Barry, David W. 469
Barry, Keith 180

Barry Lyndon (movie) 79
Barstow, David 351
Bartlett-Stewart, Breanna Lynn 389
Barton Fink (movie) 52
Baseball 489–494
  world popularity 488
Basic Educational Opportunity Grants (Pell Grants) 153, 254
Basie, Count 73
Basketball
  college 494–496
  professional 496–498
  scandals 495
  women (college) 495
  women (professional) 498
The Basketball Diaries (Carroll) 74
Basketball Without Borders 488
Bass, Lance 46, 58, 306
Batali, Mario 170
Bates, Alan 70
Bates, Doug 351
Batman Begins (movie) 33, 55
Baton Rouge 130
Batten, Frank, Sr. 352
Battier, Shane 495
Battleground (movie) 81
Battlestar Galactica (television show) 417
Bauer, Gary 398
Baulcombe, David 386
Baum, L. Frank 62
Baxter, Charles R. 389
Baxter, J. Clifford 221
Bay Area Laboratory Co-operative (BALCO) 478, 481, 487–488
Bay of Souls (Stone) 31
Baylor University 477
Baylor University Bears 495–496
BCS National Championship 477
"Be without You" (song) 36
The Beach House (Patterson and de Jonge) 30
Beach Road (de Jonge) 35
The Bear and the Dragon (Clancy) 26
Bear Stearns 88, 100, 108–109, 112, 115
Bearak, Barry 350
Beard, Amanda 160
BearShare 58
Beat Generation 77, 353
"Beat It" (song) 76
The Beatles 29, 79, 429
"Beautiful" (song) 31
Beautiful Children (Bock) 38
A Beautiful Mind (movie) 27
Beauty and the Geek (television show) 338

Beaver Stadium, Penn State University 504
Bebop 79
"Because of You" (song) 34
Bechler, Steve 360, 476
Beck, Aaron T. 386, 389
Beck, Glenn 335, 347
Beck, John C. 388
Becker, Edward R. 284
Becker, Jo 352
Beckham, David 482–483, 487
Beckham, Victoria 168
Become a Better You (Osteen) 397, 420
Bedbug Advisory Board (New York City) 362
Bee Season (Goldberg) 26
Beene, Geoffrey 159, 189
"Before He Cheats" (song) 37
Before I Say Goodbye (Clark) 26
"Begin the Beguine" (song) 79
Beginner's Greek (Collins) 38
Begley, Ed, Jr. 330
Behar, Joy 342
"Behind These Hazel Eyes" (song) 34
Behte, Hans A. 469
Beijing Evening News 333
Being Well in Christ conference 422
Bel Air, California 197
Bel Canto (Patchett) 28, 47
Belichick, Bill 505–506
Beliefs and Blasphemies (Adair) 73
Bell, Joshua 37, 59
Bell, Kristin Melissa 388
Bellator FC 501
Bellevue Baptist Church (Memphis, Tennessee) 429
Bellow, Saul 73
Belmont Stakes 476–477, 479, 484
Bemidji State University Beavers 521
Benadryl 391
Benchley, Peter 73
Benedict XVI (Pope) 396, 401
  visits the United States 398
Ben-Hur (movie) 76
Benjamin, Regina M. 362, 384
Bennett, Clay 350
Bensimon, Gilles 186
Benson, George 77
Benson, John A., Jr. 388
Benson, Lenore 189
"Bent" (song) 27
Bentsen, Lloyd Millard, Jr. 120, 250
Beowulf (movie) 36
Berberian, Ara 73
Berenstain, Jan 73
Berenstain, Stan 73
Berenstain Bears (characters) 73
Berg, Leonard 389

professor slurs McCain 203
Bobov Hasidic sect 428
bobsledding 521
Bocconi University (Italy) 114
Bock, Darrell L. 416
Bodanya, Natalie 74
The Body Artist (DeLillo) 47
Body Mass Index (BMI) 365
Boehner, John 141, 245
Bogdanich, Walt 351
Boho chic 168
Boho style 159, 177
Boies, David 281
Boilen, Bob 337
Boise State University Broncos 502–503
Bolender, Todd 74
Bolin, Jane 284
Bolinder, Scott 399
Bollinger, Lee 133
Bolt (movie) 37
Bonda, Penny 188
Bonds, Barry 475, 478–481, 483, 486–488, 490, 493, 499
Bonilla, Bobby 493
Bonnie and Clyde (movie) 75
Bono 186
Bonow, Robert O. 388
Boo, Katherine 349
Boogie Nights (movie) 52
The Book of Fate (Melzer) 35
"Book of Order" (Presbyterian Church USA) 405
Book of the Dead (Cornwell) 37
"Boom Boom Pow" (song) 40
Boorstin, Daniel J. 152
Boozer, Carlos 495, 498
Borat (movie) 35
Border Patrol 275
Borland, James L., Jr. 389
Boston Celtics 484, 495
Boston College 504
Boston College Eagles 503
Boston Globe 350–351, 402
Boston Red Sox 479, 483, 489–492, 524
Both Ways Is the Only Way I Want It (Meloy) 40
Bottle Rocket (movie) 52
Botts, Mike 74
Botulinum toxin 377
Bouder, Ashley 45
Boulder Community Hospital, Foothills Campus (Colorado) 165
Boumediene v. *Bush* 277
Bound for Glory (movie) 79
The Bounty (movie) 65
The Bourne Identity (movie) 29, 54

The Bourne Supremacy (movie) 32, 54
The Bourne Ultimatum (movie) 36, 54
Bow Wow 42
Bowden, Bobby 503
Bowie, Iman 45
Bowl Championship Series (BCS) 474, 502
Bowling Green University 504
A Box of Matches (Baker) 31
Boxer, Barbara 253
Boxing 474, 486, 500, 521
scandal 500
The Boy from Oz (musical) 70
Boy Scouts of America
homosexuality, policy on 272, 394
Boy Scouts of America v. *Dale* 394
Boyd, David R. 388
Boyett, William 74
Boyett Ostar Productions 70
Boyle, Lara Flynn 167
Boyle, Peter 74
Boyle, Willard S. 468
Boys Choir of Harlem 80
Boys Don't Cry (movie) 42
The Boys from Brazil (movie) 77
The Boys from Syracuse (play) 73
Boyse, Edward A. 390
Bradac, Marusa 437, 466
Braden, Loyer D. 130
Bradford, Sam 504
Bradley, Bill 203, 204
Bradley, Timothy 500
Bradt, Tyler 484
Brady, Tom 478, 487, 503, 505, 521
Branded (street artist) 44
Brando, Jocelyn 74
Brando, Marlon 74
Brandt, Edward N., Jr. 390
Brant, Henry 74
The Brass Verdict (Connelly) 38
Braveheart (movie) 65
Bravo, Rose Marie 186
Bravo Network 159, 161–162, 171, 329, 348
Braxton, Toni 46
Brazil 215, 444, 450
financial crisis 115
MMA fighters 501
Brazill, Nathaniel 124
Bread (band) 74, 76
"Breakaway" (song) 33
The Breakfast Club (movie) 76, 332
Breakfast of Champions (Vonnegut) 80
Breaking Bad (television show) 332
Breaking Dawn (Meyer) 51, 340
Breaking the Spell: Religion as a Natural Phenomenon (Dennett) 418
Breast implants 358

silicone 376
A Breath of Snow and Ashes (Gabaldon) 34
"Breathe" (song) 27
Brecker, Michael 74
Breen, Steve 352
Brees, Drew 506
Brennan, Colt 504
Brennan, Murray F. 388
Brenner, Sydney 385, 386
The Brethren (Grisham) 26
Brewer, Corey 494
Breyer, Stephen 413
Bridge of Sighs (Russo) 37
Bridgestone-Firestone Inc. 84
Bridget Jones's Diary (movie) 27
The Brief Wondrous Life of Oscar Wao (Diaz) 37, 47, 69
Brigham and Women's Hospital (Boston) 367
Bright, William R. "Bill" 410, 418, 428
Bring It On (movie) 26
"Bring Me to Life" (song) 31
Brinker, Nancy 387
Brinkley, David 250, 352
Brinkley, Douglas 208
Bristol-Myers Squibb 358
British Open 507
Britney (album) 58
Broadband 439, 441–442, 452
Broadcast networks 92
Broadcasting
digital 328
Broadway 27, 32, 34, 39, 42, 61–62, 73–74, 77–79, 185
The American Musical (television show) 349
Broderick, Edwin Bernard 428
Broderick, Matthew 28
Brokaw, Tom 326, 333
Brokeback Mountain (movie) 33, 42
The Broker (Grisham) 34
Brominated flame retardants (PBDEs) 363
Bronson, Charles 74
Brooklyn (Toibin) 40
Brooklyn Children's Museum 165
Brooklyn Law School 113
Brooks, Derrick 521
Brooks, Donald 189
Brooks, Mel 62, 70
Brooks & Dunn (musical group) 56
Brosnan, Pierce 62
Brother Rat (movie) 78
Brown, Dan 395, 397, 416
Brown, Danny Joe 74
Brown, David 435, 457

Church of God in Christ 429

Church of Jesus Christ of Latter-Day Saints (Mormons) 398, 417, 428

Church Pension Fund 423

Church Universal and Triumphant 429

Churchill, Ward 129, 151

Ciechanover, Aaron 385, 468

Cigarettes 362, 390

Cille, Michel du 352

Cincinnati Bengals 506

Cincinnati Pops Orchestra 77

Cincinnati Reds 477, 493

Cinderella Man (movie) 33

Cinemark 59

Cinnamon Kiss (Mosley) 34

Ciprofloxacin 374

Circuit City 89

Cirque du Soleil
Fire Within (television show) 348

Citi Field 493

Citigroup 88–89, 94, 97, 99, 108, 111, 222

Citizen Kane (movie) 80

Citizens Bank Park 493

Citizens for a Sound Economy 138

Citizens for Responsibility and Ethics in Washington 427

City of Bones (Connelly) 30

City Slickers (movie) 78

City University of New York
City College 420
Graduate Center 395

"Civil Forum on the Presidency" 399, 424

Civil rights 252, 255

Civil Rights Act of 1964 213, 252, 411

Civil-rights movement 256

Civil unions
Connecticut 415
New Hampshire 415, 422
New Jersey 415

Civil War 226

Cizik, Richard 398

Claiborne, Liz 160, 185, 189

Clancy, Tom 47

Clarabel the Clown 325

Clark, Jim 284

Clark, Kenneth B. 153

Clark, Laurel 435, 457

Clark, Mary Higgins 26, 28, 30, 34–35, 37–39

Clark, Ramsey 281

Clark, Wesley 207

Clark, Will 493

Clarke, Richard Alan 227

Clarkson, Kelly 338

Clean Air Act 116

Clear Channel Entertainment 70

Clemens, Roger 486, 488–490, 492–493, 521

Clemson University 152

Cleveland, Ohio 130, 147, 158

Cleveland Browns 478, 506

Cleveland Cavaliers 482, 486, 497, 522

Cleveland Clinic 362, 366, 384, 439
human-face transplant 376

Cleveland Indians 477, 489

Climate Change
"An Evangelical Call for Action" 397

Cline, Patsy 76

Clinton, Al 204

Clinton, Hillary 181, 198–199, 212–214, 242, 246–247, 358, 382, 336, 341, 345, 425

Clinton, William J. (Bill) 51, 84, 150, 202, 212–213, 238, 242, 246, 252–253, 280, 284, 333, 396, 411, 421, 434, 443, 463
conservation record 434
lifts GPS restrictions 456

Clinton administration 115, 227
achievements 202
health-care initiative 372
regulation of online pharmaceutical sales 358

Cloning 391, 434–435, 439, 448–451
human 378, 448

Clooney, George 159

Close, Glenn 390

Close, William T. 390

"Closer" (song) 38

The Closers (Connelly) 34

Clothing
vintage 168

Clyburn, James 246

CNBC 335

CNN 251, 327, 334–335, 344, 346–347, 436

Coach Carter (movie) 33

Coach Leatherwear (fashion line) 189

Coast Guard 226, 275

Coca-Cola Company 84

Cochran, Johnnie L., Jr. 284

Coddington, Boyd 189

Coddington, Grace 185

The Code of Codes: Scientific and Social Issues in the Human Genome Project (Hood and Keveles) 464

Coen, Ethan 52, 417

Coen, Joel 52, 417

The Coffee Trader (Liss) 31

Coffin, William Sloan 251

Cohen, Claudia 353

Cohen-Tannoudji, Claude 463

Colbert, Stephen 333

The Colbert Report (television show) 333

Cold Case (television show) 268

Cold Mountain (movie) 30

Cold War 253, 255–257, 450

Coleman, Cy 74

Coleman, Jacquelyn T. 388

Coleman, Ornette 69

Colgate-Palmolive Company 107

Collateral Damage (movie) 29

Collateral (movie) 32

College Dropout (album) 173

College of Cardinals 428

College World Series 474–477, 479, 480, 482–485

Collicott, Paul E. 388

Collins, Billy 48

Collins, Francis S. 388–389, 449

Collins, Michelle 480

Collins, Suzanne 42

Colon, Bartolo 493

Colonial Athletic Association 495

Colonoscopy 358, 360

The Color of Money (movie) 78

The Color Purple (musical) 34

Colorado 358, 359, 458
Aspen 477

Colorado Avalanche 475

Colorado Health Sciences Center 469

Colorado Rockies 483, 490, 493

Colson, Chuck 410

Coltrane, John 75

Columbia (spacecraft) 435, 457

Columbia Accident Investigation Board (CAIB) 435, 457

Columbia Point 458

Columbia Records 57

Columbia River 450

Columbia University 242, 428–429, 523
Genome Center 469
Graduate School of Journalism 464

Columbine High School (Colorado) 125, 130, 132, 145

Columbus, Georgia 482

Columbus Crew 484

Colvin, Steven 384

Combined Exhibition of Advanced Technologies (CEATEC) 434

Combs, Sean "Diddy" 162, 173, 186

Comcast 91, 100, 328, 348, 499

Comedy Central 102, 324, 333, 341

Comerica Park 492

Comiskey Park 491

The Commissariat of Enlightenment (Kalfus) 31

Commission on Campus Unrest 284

Committee on Jewish Law and Standards (Conservative Judaism) 397

A Common Life (Karon) 28

"A Common Word between Us and You" 398, 407

Common Word conferences 399, 400, 407

Communications 442

Communism 354

Como, Perry 75

The Company: A Novel of the CIA (Littell) 30

The Company You Keep (Gordon) 31

Compaq 118, 450

Compaq Center 396, 420

Complexions Contemporary Ballet (New York City) 45

"Complicated" (song) 30

Compulsion (Kellerman) 38

CompuServe 99

Computer Axial Tomography (CAT) 465

Computer generated imagery (CGI) 41

Computerized Imaging Reference Systems 466

computers 442, 470
    laptop 436, 455

Conal, Robbie 63

Concerts 59

Condé Nast 160

Condoms 358

Cone, David 493

Cone beam computed tomography (CBCT) 368

Confederate flag 240

Conference USA 503

Confessions of a Dangerous Mind (movie) 29

The Confessions of Edward Day (Martin) 40

The Confessions of Nat Turner (Styron) 80

Congo 350

Congress, U.S. 84–86, 88–89, 94–96, 101, 115, 133, 141, 252, 256
    bailout legislation 110
    cloning 448
    Enron testimony 117

Congress of Industrial Organizations 87

Congressional Black Caucus 252

Congressional Record 48

Conn, David 284

Connecticut 46, 394
    New Haven 272, 280
    New London 273
    same-sex marriage 272

Connecticut Sun 479, 481

Connelly, Michael 28, 30–31, 33–35, 38, 40, 47

conservatism 201, 239
    social 239

Conservative Committee on Jewish Law and Standards 406

Consolidated Omnibus Budget Reconciliation Act (COBRA) 372

Constellation (spacecraft) 457

Constitution 276, 277

Contact (musical) 70

Conte, Victor 481

Contemporary Theatre 61

The Contender (television show) 487

Continental Airlines 96–97

Contraception 376

Contract with America 251

Controlled Substances Act (1970) 359, 361

Convergence Movement 429

Converse (shoe) 172

Conway, Arkansas 130

Cony, Edward R. 353

Cook, David A. 388

Cooke, Alistair 75

Cool Hand Luke (movie) 78

Coombs, Alice A. Tolbert 387

Cooper, Anderson 333, 346–347

Cooper, Brice 178

Cooper, Leroy 75

Cooper, Matthew 216

Cooper, Roy 129

Cooper Union for the Advancement of Science and Art 79, 161, 183

Coors, Joseph, Sr., 120

Copeland, Robert B. 389

Copenhagen (play) 70

Copenhagen Climate Conference 441–442

Copley News Service 351

Coppola, Francis Ford 53

Coppola, Sofia 53

Coptics 397

Copyright 49, 324, 341

Coraline (movie) 39

Coral Ridge Presbyterian Church 410, 418, 429

Cornejo, Maria 187

Cornell, Eric A. 467

Cornell Center for Radiophysics and Space Research 469

Cornerstone Project 422

Cornwell, Patricia 26, 31, 33–35, 38, 40

Corporate fraud 92, 97, 98

The Corrections (Franzen) 28, 47, 49, 64

Corridor of Shame: The Neglect of South Carolina's Rural Schools (movie) 127

Cosmopolis (DeLillo) 31, 47

Costa, Francisco 186–187

Costa, Max 373

Cost Plus 179

Cotto, Miguel 500

The Cotton Club (movie) 76

Coty American Fashion Critics' Hall of Fame 189

Coughlin, Natalie 521

Coulter, Ann 273

Coulter, Catherine 34, 40

Council of Economic Advisers 115

Council of Fashion Designers of America (CFDA) 167, 173–174

Council on American-Islamic Relations (CAIR) 407

Counterinsurgency 236

The Country and the City (Powell) 28

Country Music Association 56

Country Music Hall of Fame 74, 78, 80

Country Music Television 57

Couric, Katie 244, 327, 334, 342, 344, 358, 360

"Courtesy of the Red, White and Blue (The Angry American)" (song) 41, 56

Couture, Randy "The Natural" 501

Covad Communications 93

Cover, Jack 469

Cowboys Stadium 485

Cowell, Simon 338

Cowher, Bill 506

Cox, Christopher 87

Crabtree, Michael 504

Crackpots (Pritchard) 31

Craig, Larry 215

Cram, Donald J. 469

Crangi, Philip 186

Crankshaw, Patrick 75

"Crank That" (song) 37

Cranston, Alan 251

Crash (movie) 32

"Crazy" (song) 36

"Crazy in Love" (song) 31

Creation (Govier) 31

Creationism 401

Creative Artists Agency 284

"Creed" (song) 27

Dolphin Stadium 484
Dominican Republic 489
    baseball players from 493
Domino's Pizza 126, 151
Domitro, Taras 45
Donaghy, Tim 483, 497
Donald, Jim 118
Donaldson, William 87
Donnie Darko (movie) 27
Donovan, Billy 494
Don't Ask, Don't Tell 267
"Don't Cha" (song) 34
"Don't Forget about Us" (song) 34
"Don't Let Me Get Me" (song) 30
"Don't Matter" (song) 37
"Don't Phunk with My Heart" (song) 34
"Don't Stop the Music" (song) 38
"Don't Tell Me" (song) 28
Doobie Brothers (musical group) 77
Dora the Explorer (character) 107
Dorsey, Jack 347, 437, 453
Doss, Desmond T. 251
dot-com crash 93, 113
Dotson, Carlton 477, 495
DoubleClick 102
Double Cross (Patterson) 37
Double Sextet (album) 69
Doubt (play) 70
Douglas, C. Dillon 120
Douglas, Kyan 176
Douglas, Michael 27
Dow Jones Corporation 118
Dow Jones Industrial Average 84, 88–89, 94, 200
Dowling, Robert D. 359
"Down" (song) 40
Downie, Leonard 336
Down Syndrome 244, 375
Downtown Owl (Klosterman) 38
Doyle, Jim 379
Dr. Dre 56, 58
Drachenberg, Katherine von 184
"Dragostea din tei" (song) 341
Dreamcatcher (King) 28
Dreamgirls (movie) 35, 338
Dreams of My Father (Obama) 241
Dream Team 497, 498
DreamWorks 41, 102
Drew, Lori 281
Drew University 426
Dreyfus, Lee Sherman 251
The Drifters (musical group) 78
Drinan, Robert F. 251, 283
Droney, Damien 44
"Drops of Jupiter" (song) 28
Drowning Ruth (Schwarz) 26
Druce, Joseph L. 395

Drucker, Peter F. 120, 423
Drudge, Matt 336
The Drudge Report 336
drug testing
    involuntary 359
Druker, Brian 386
Drusin, Lewis M. 388
Dryden, Spencer 75
Dubner, Stephen 105
DuBrow, Kevin 75
Dude, Where's My Car? (movie) 26
Duff, Hilary 42
Duhon, Chris 495
Dukakis, Michael 250, 253
The Dukes of Hazzard (television show) 75
Duke University 129–130, 152, 391
Duke University Blue Devils 475, 495–496
    lacrosse scandal 482, 487
Duke University Medical Center 434, 467
Dulles, Avery Robert 428
Duma Key (King) 38
Dumbarton Oaks 190
Dunaway, Faye 189
Duncan, Arne 130, 137–138, 147, 151
Duncan, David 98
Duncan, Lindsay 70
Duncan, Robert 399
Duncan, Tim 497–498
Dungeons & Dragons (game) 120
Dungy, Tony 482, 506
Dunkin' Donuts 121
Dunleavy, Mike, Jr. 495
Dunn, Jennifer 251
DuPont 450
Duquesne University 128
Durant, Kevin 495
Dust Bowl 220
DVD 104
Dwarf Planets 460
Dye, Jermaine 492
Dykstra, Lenny 101
Dynasty (television show) 354
Dynegy 85, 98
Dysnomia (planetary body) 437, 458, 460
Dyson, Freeman 427
Dyson, Kevin 474, 506

E

E&J Gallo Winery 120
E! Channel 354
Eagle Eye (movie) 37
Eagle Scout 272

Eagleton, Thomas F. 251
Earle, Ronnie 281
Earnhardt, Dale, Jr. 478, 487, 499, 521
Earnhardt, Dale, Sr. 475, 487, 521
Earth Day 254
Earth in the Balance: Ecology and the Human Spirit (Gore) 464
"East Bound and Down" (song) 79
East Carolina University 504
East of Eden (movie) 77, 79
East of Eden (Steinbeck) 49
Eastern New Mexico University 504
Eastern Virginia Medical School 465
Easton, Richard 70
Easy Prey (Sandford) 26
Eaton, William J. 353
eBay 119, 162
Ebbers, Bernard 86, 99–101
Ebersole, Christine 70
Ebert, Roger 53
Ebola virus 390
Ebony 120
Ebooks 41
The Echo Maker (Powers) 35
Echo Park (Connelly) 35
Eckerd, Jack 120
Eckerd's Drugs 120
Eckstine, Billy 77
Eclipse (Meyer) 37, 51, 340
Ecofashion 166
E-commerce 452
Economy 92–121
Eddie Bauer (clothing retailer) 161
Edelman, Isidore S. 469
Edelman, Norman 380
Edmonton Oilers 481
Edmund Pettus Bridge 284
Education 132–155
    affirmative action in 271
Education Consolidation and Improvement Act 124
Education Department Office of Civil Rights 124
Education for All Handicapped Children Act (1975) 153
Edward R. Murrow Award 344
Edwards, Bob 337
Edwards, Don 283
Edwards, Elizabeth 217
Edwards, John 196, 199, 207–209, 212, 216–217, 246
Edwards, Ralph 353
Edwards, Robert 386
Efron, Zac 42
Egan, Philip S. 189
Eggers, Dave 54

Egypt
   Cairo 200
Ehle, Jennifer 70
"Eight Elvises" 40
8 Mile (movie) 29
8 Simple Rules (television show) 354
The 8th Confession and Swimsuit (Patterson and Paetro) 40
Einstein, Albert 390, 469
Eisenhower, Dwight D. 148, 253, 256, 429
Eisenman, Peter 187
Eisner, Will 75
Elbaz, Alber 186
ELCA 400
The Elderberry Tree (Petite) 78
Elections Research Center 255
Electoral College 205, 273
Electromagnetic fields 445
Eleven on Top (Evanovich) 34
Elfman, Jenna 417
Elizabeth and James (fashion line) 184
Elk Grove Unified School District v. *Newdow* 126
Elle (magazine) 159, 162, 190
Ellen (television show) 317
The Ellen DeGeneres Show (television show) 317
The Ellen Show (television show) 317
Ellen Tracy (fashion line) 189
Ellenberger, Arthur R. 388
Ellington, Wayne 495
Elliott, Brett 504
Ellis, Perry 182, 189
Ellison, Keith Maurice 397
Ellsberg, Daniel 284
Elmo (character) 107
Elo, Jorma 45
Elsila, Jamie 439, 466
Elson, John Truscott 428
Elswit, Robert 53
Emergency Economic Stabilization Act 110, 200
Emerson, William A., Jr. 353
Emerson College 345
Emily's List 257
Eminem 42, 56, 173
Eminent domain 87
Emmy Awards 189, 317, 464
Emory University Hospital 382
The Emperor's Children (Messud) 35, 48
The Emperor's New Groove (movie) 26
Emphysema 373
Empire (magazine) 65
Empire Falls (Russo) 28
Empire Maker (horse) 477

Empire Rising (Kelly) 34
Enchanted (movie) 36
Encyclopaedia Britannica 152
The End of Faith (Harris) 418
Endangered Species Act 251, 438, 443
Endeavour (space shuttle) 130
Endo, Akira 386
Enemy at the Gates (movie) 27
Engle, Howard A. 390
Engle, Robert 119
Enron 85, 87, 92, 98–99, 116–117, 120, 194, 198, 221, 239, 324, 329
   The Smartest Guys in the Room: The Amazing Rise and Scandalous Fall of Enron (movie) 329
Ensign, John 217
Entertainment and Sports Programming Network (ESPN) 486, 489, 499
   ESPNHD 499
   ESPN2HD 499
   ESPN360.com 499
   ESPNNewsHD 499
   ESPNU 499
Entertainment Weekly 345, 438
Entourage (television show) 332
Environment
   design 162
Environmental Protection Agency (EPA) 360, 374, 438, 469
Environmental Science: How the World Works and Your Place in It 138
Environmentalism 254, 329
Envy (Harrison) 34
Ephedra 360
Ephron, Nora 54
Episcopal Church 399, 412, 422, 423, 427
   Episcopal Youth Event 422
   female bishop 397
   General Convention 400
   homosexuality, policy on 395, 400, 404, 422
   New Hampshire 395
"E Pluribus Venom" (art exhibition) 63
Epstein, Adam 70
Epstein, Aharon Zelig 428
Equal Rights Amendment 250
Equality Forum 422
Equilibrium (movie) 29
ER (television show) 75
Erdrich, Louise 28, 31, 34
Erin Brokovitch (movie) 26
Eris (planetary body) 436–437, 458, 460, 462
Eskew, Tucker 241

Esquire 173
Essential Norms for Diocesan/Eparchial Policies Dealing with Allegations of Sexual Abuse of Minors by Priests or Deacons 395, 403
Essex University (England) 183
Estep, William Roscoe 428
Eternal Sunshine of the Spotless Mind (movie) 32
Ethics
   medical 363, 378
Ethiopia
   Addis Ababa 446
   Afar Desert 446
Etsy 162, 178
Eugenides, Jeffrey 30, 47, 53
Eukanuba 106
Europe
   heat wave (2003) 443
   steel tariffs 85
Europe Central (Vollman) 34
Evangelical Christians 239
Evangelical Climate Initiative 437
Evangelical Lutheran Church in America (ELCA) 394, 404, 429
Evangelism 418
Evangelism Explosion International 429
Evanovich, Janet 26, 28, 30–31, 33, 35, 37–38, 40
Evans, Bob 120
Evans, Dale 75
Evans, Dwight L. 389
Evans, Heidi 351
Evans, Martin J. 385
Evans, Rashad 501
Evans, Ray 75
Evans, Ronald 386
Evans, Rowland 251, 254, 354
Evans & Novak (television show) 251
Everhart Museum 34
Everybody Loves Raymond (television show) 74, 348
Everyman (Roth) 35
Everything Is Illuminated (Foer) 30, 47
Everything's Eventual (King) 30
"Everything You Want" (song) 27
Evidence of Things Unseen (Wiggins) 31
Evolution
   human 446–448
   teaching of 124, 127–128, 139, 140, 151
   theory of 153, 401, 467, 469
EV1 (automobile) 179
Exchange 2007 437
The Executioner's Song (Mailer) 77

Fox, Robert J. 428
Fox, Sylvan 353
Fox Television 102, 324–325, 327, 328
   Fox Business Channel 334
   Fox News Channel 205, 210, 247, 249, 267, 334–335, 347
Fox Theater (Atlanta) 59
Fox Theatricals 70
Foxman, Abraham H. 420
France 49, 112, 215, 226, 450, 451
   basketball 498
   Cannes 158
   human-face transplant 376
   Paris 195
France, Bill R. 120
Franciosa, Anthony "Tony" 75
Franco, John 493
Frank, Barney 152
Frank, Eugene Maxwell 428
Frank A. McCourt High School of Writing 153
Frankel-Baruch-Viertel-Routh Group, The 70
Frankfurt, Suzie 189
Frankfurt Book Fair 48
Franklin, Aretha 167
Franklin, John Hope 252
Franklin, Rich 501
Franklin D. Roosevelt Memorial (Washington, D.C.) 189
Franklin Templeton 100
Franks, Thomas 234
Franzen, Jonathan 47, 49, 64
Fraternal Order of Eagles of Texas 413
Frayn, Michael 70
Freakonomics: A Rogue Economist Explores the Hidden Side of Everything (Levitt and Dubner) 105
Frederic C. Hamilton building (Denver) 183
Frederick, Joseph 151
Free Speech Movement 154, 255
Freedom Rider 251, 252, 256
Freedom Tower 159, 163, 183
Freeland, Richard M. 138
Freeman, Harold 387
Freeman, Orville L. 252
Freenet 58
Freeney, Dwight 505
Freie Universität (Berlin) 64
Freis, Edward D. 390
The French Connection (Moore) 78
The French Connection (movie) 79
French National Order of the Legion of Honor 466
French Open 521, 523

Fresh Start (curriculum) 422
Fresno State University 484
Frey, James 50
Friday Night Lights (movie) 32, 487
Friedan, Betty 153, 252
Friedman, Jon 347
Friedman, Milton 120, 153
Friedman, Stephen 85
Friedman, Tom 334
Friendly, Henry 279
Friends (television show) 348
Friendster 325, 454
Frist, Bill 270
From a Buick 8 (King) 30
From the Corner of His Eye (Koontz) 26
Frost, David 332
Frühlings Erwachen (play) 62
Fryman, Travis 493
Fuels
   alternative 87
FUH2.com 180
Fujitsu 455
Fulbright Fellowship 64
The Full Monty (musical) 27
Fuller, Linda 426
Fuller, Millard 426
Fuller Theological Seminary 424
Fundamentalism 240
Fundamentalist Church of Jesus Christ of Latter-Day Saints 398, 401
Funny Cide (horse) 477
Furnas, David W. 387
Furstenberg, Diane von 186
Fusion (automobile) 179
The Future of Industrial Man (Drucker) 120
FutureSex/LoveSounds (album) 58

G

G suit 391
Gabellini, Michael 187
Gabrielle (planetary body) 437, 458
Gagne, Eric 490, 493
Galarraga, Andres 493
Galbraith, John Kenneth 120, 252
Galindo, Yadira 439, 466
Gall, Joseph 387
Gallaudet University 129
Galle, Johann Gottfried 458
Gallen, Herbert 189
Galliano, John 177
Gallo, Ernest 120
Gambino crime family 115
Gambling 482–483, 497
"The Game of Love" (song) 30

Game of Shadows (Fainaru-Wada and Williams) 490
The Game Plan (movie) 36
Gamma-hydroxybutyrate 107
Gammon, Reginald 75
Gan, Stephen 185
Gandolfini, James 330
Gang of Four 256
Gangs of New York (movie) 29, 41
Ganong, William F. 390
Gap 158, 166, 168
Garabedian, Mitchell 402
Garbus, Marvin 282
Garcia, Freddie 492
Garcia, Nina 162, 176
Garciaparra, Nomar 493
Gardasil 361, 375, 437, 439
Garland, Hank 76
Garner, Tyron 272
Garnett, Kevin 498–500
Garrett, George 76
Garrison, Samuel Alexander 284
Gasol, Pau 497
The Gate House (DeMille) 38
Gates, Bill 84
Gates, Henry Louis, Jr. 131–132, 149
"The Gates" (art installation) 34
The Gates of the Alamo (Harrigan) 26
The Gathering Storm (Sanderson) 40
Gatorade 153, 390
Gaucher's disease 389
Gaultier, Jean-Paul 185
Gauthe, Gilbert 402
Gawker Media 347
Gay, Lesbian, Bi-Sexual, Transgender, and Queer (GLBTQ) 404
Gay Liberation Front 252
Gay rights 252, 256
Gaylord, Edward Lewis 353
Gaylord, Norman G. 390
Geertz, Clifford 153
Geffen, David 36
Gehringer, George 179
Gehry, Frank 44, 164, 187
Geithner, Timothy 109–110, 115
Gellman, Barton 352
Gelman, Harold, Jr. 435, 457
Gelsinger, Jesse 358, 451
Gemini Observatory 458
GenBank 450
Gene therapy 361, 437, 450–451
   research 435
   stem cell trials 436
   stopped at University of Pennsylvania 358
General Accounting Office 145
General Electric 91, 116, 120, 328, 348

General Medical Council (Great Britain) 380

General Motors 87–92, 94–95, 179, 200

General Theological Seminary 422

Generation Investment Management 464

Generation X 486

Genetic Nondiscrimination Act (GINA), 438, 450

Genetics 384, 441, 448–451

Geneva Conventions 195, 198, 226, 249, 276–277

Genie 172

"Genie in a Bottle" (song) 172

Genital warts 376

Genocchio, Benjamin 63

Genome research 434, 438

Gentleman's Agreement (movie) 77

Geoffrey Beene, Inc. 189

Geoghan, John J. 395, 402, 428

Geological Society of America 465

Geology 446

George, Sara 168

George (magazine) 324

George Foster Peabody Award 438

George Fox University 130

George Mason University 421

George Mason University Patriots 495

George Washington Bridge 92

Georgetown Steel 92

Georgetown University 400, 407, 421

Georgetown University Hoyas 495

Georgia 107
    same-sex marriage 272

Georgia Dome 474, 494

"Georgia on My Mind" (song) 74

Georgia Tech 475

Georgia Tech Yellow Jackets 479

German Berlin Orchestra 183

Germany 49, 226, 450
    automakers 95
    Green Party 203

Gersten, Bernard 70

Gertner, Nancy 283

"Get the Party Started" (song) 30

Getting Mother's Body (Parks) 31

Getty, J. Paul, Jr. 120

Ghesquière, Nicolas 185

Ghirradelli Square (San Francisco) 189

Ghost (movie) 80

Ghost Rider (movie) 36

Ghost Whisperer (television show) 417

Giac, Thich Man 428

Giacconi, Riccardo 467

Giambi, Jason 480, 490, 524

Gibson, Dan 467

Gibson, Mel 33, 64–65, 396, 416–417, 421

Gibson, Truman K. 284

Gibson, William 31

Gidget (movie) 75

Gilead (Robinson) 33, 47

Gilkey, Langdon Brown 428

Gillespie, Dizzy 75

Gilligan's Wake (Carson) 31

Gingrich, Newt 245

Ginobli, Manu 497

Ginsberg, Allen 353

Ginzburg, Vitaly L. 467

Gioia, Dana 43

Girardi, Joe 489

The Girl Who Kicked the Hornets' Nest (Larsson) 49

The Girl Who Played with Fire (Larsson) 49

The Girl with the Dragon Tattoo (Larsson) 49

"Girlfriend" (song) 30, 37

Giuliani, Rudolph W. 211, 246, 358, 488

Giunta, Justin 187

The Given Day (Lehane) 38

"Gives You Hell" (song) 40

Givhan, Robin 186

Gladiator (movie) 26

"Glamorous" (song) 37

Glamour (magazine) 161

Glaser, Milton 187

Glass House 190

Glasspool, Mary 404

Glauber, Roy J. 468

Glavine, Tom 493

Gleason, Paul 76

Glee (television show) 328

Glenn Beck (television show) 347

Glens Falls (N.Y.) *Post-Star* 352

Glick, M. 70

Global Anglican Communion 400, 404

Global Crossing 93

Global Positioning System (GPS), 442, 456

Global Security Institute 251

Global Settlement 94

Global warming 132, 397, 434, 436–438, 441–443, 445, 463
    greenhouse gases, 437, 441

Glorious Appearing (LaHaye and Jenkins) 33

Gluck, Suzanne 105

Gluckman, Richard 187

Glushien, Morris P. 284

Glycine 439

GMC 95
    Envoy 188

Gnosticism 397

Gnutella 58

Go Green campaign 330

The Goat or Who Is Sylvia? (play) 70

God: The Failed Hypothesis (Stenger) 418

The God Delusion (Dawkins) 418

God Is Not Great: How Religion Poisons Everything (Hitchens) 418

"God Loveth His Children" 398, 406

God's Answers to Life's Difficult Questions (Warren) 424

God's Power to Change Your Life (Warren) 424

Goddard Space Flight Center 439, 466

The Godfather (movie) 53, 74

Going Rogue: An American Life (Palin) 244, 342

"Gold Digger" (song) 34

Gold, Glen David 47

Gold, Jamie M. 482

Gold, Thomas 469

Goldberg, Michael 76

Goldberg, Whoopi 70, 149, 343

Goldberger, Paul 164

The Golden Compass (movie) 36

Golden Fleece Awards 255

The Golden Girls (television show) 352

Golden Globe Awards 167

Golden parachutes 222

Goldman, Lee 388

Goldman, Ronald 487

Goldman Sachs 85, 88, 94, 108, 110, 118, 222

Goldwater, Barry 214, 240, 250, 256

Golf 487, 507–508

Golub, Leon 76

Gone (Kellerman) 35

"Gone" (song) 28

Gone Tomorrow (Child) 39

Gone with the Wind (movie) 77

"Gonna Fly Now" (song) 75

Gonorrhea 358

Gonzaga University Zags 495

Gonzales, Alberto R. 199, 246, 252, 279, 281, 374

González, Elián 194, 349

Gonzáles, Jeffrey 282

Gonzales v. Carhart 398, 412

Gonzales v. Oregon 361

Good Faith (Smiley) 31

The Good Life (McInerney) 48

Good Morning America (television show) 49, 335

Gulfport, Mississippi 87
Gullah 78
Gun rights 254
Gunga Din (movie) 75
Gunn, Tim 176
Gunsmoke (television show) 79
Gupta, Damyanti 382
Gupta, Sanjay 382
Gupta, Subhash 382
Gurdon, John 386
Guterson, David 31
Gutierrez, Daphne 185
Guys and Dolls (musical) 62
Gwathmey, Charles 189
Gwathmey Siegel & Associates 189
Gwynn, Tony 493
Gygax, Gary 120
Gyllenhall, Jake 42
Gynecology 374
    cosmetic 375

H

H&M 167
H&R Block 120
H1N1 influenza 363, 381
Habeas corpus, suspension of 226
Habitat for Humanity International 188, 426
Hackett, Buddy 76
Hadid, Zaha 188
Hagee, John 399, 412
Haggard, Ted 397, 401, 426
Hainstock, Eric 128
Hairspray (movie) 36
Hairspray (musical) 30, 62, 70
Haiti 352
    earthquake 424
Halberstam, David 353
Halberstam, Naftali 428
Hale, Joe 426
Hall, John L. 468
Hall, Michael C. 331
Hall of Fame (HOF) 493
Halliburton 239, 245
Halloween (movie) 76
Halmos, Jeff 186
Halo (game) 454
Halpern, Abraham L. 389
Halprin, Lawrence 189
Hamacher, Patrick 271
Hamdan, Salim Ahmed 277, 282
Hamdan v. *Rumsfeld* 277, 280, 282
Hamdi, Yaser 277
Hamdi v. *Rumsfeld* 277
Hamilton, Tim 187
Hamlet (movie) 65

Hamm, Mia 521
Hammersley, Frederick 76
Hammerstein, Oscar 62
Hammond, Michael 29
Hampton, Lionel 73
Hamrick, Edna Hipps 189
Hamrick's (store) 189
Handelsman, Walt 351
Handle with Care (Picoult) 40
Handler, Ruth 120, 189
Hanford B Reactor 450
"Hanging by a Moment" (song) 28
Hanging chads 206
The Hangover (movie) 39
Hanks, Tom 416
Hanna, Bill 73
Hannibal (movie) 27, 55
Hannity, Sean 335
Hänsch, Theodore W. 468
Hansen, Joseph 76
Hanson, Mark S. 394, 404
Happy Days (television show) 78
"Happy Trails" (song) 75
Harcourt Brace Jovanovich 120
Hard Eight (Evanovich) 30
Hard Eight (movie) 52
Hard Knocks (television show) 487
Hard Times (Terkel) 80
Hardaway, Tim 498
Hardball (television show) 336
Hardell, Lennart 466
"Harder to Breathe" (song) 31
Hardwick, Chris 341
Hargis, Billy James 428
Harkin, Tom 268
Harlem Renaissance 75
Harold Melvin & the Blue Notes (musical group) 74
Harper, Dereck 497
Harper, Ron 497
HarperCollins 244
Harper's Bazaar (magazine) 189–190
Harriman, W. Averill 251
Harrington, Noreen 118
Harris, Charlaine 340
Harris, Dean 185
Harris, Katherine 273
Harris, Mark 76
Harris, Neil Patrick 306
Harris, Radie 353
Harris, Sam 417
Harris, Thomas 55
Harrison, Alvin 479
Harrison, Charles 187
Harrison, George 29
Harrison, Marvin 478, 506, 521
Harry Potter (novel and movie series) 41–42, 49

Harry Potter and the Chamber of Secrets (movie) 29
Harry Potter and the Deathly Hollows (movie) 42
Harry Potter and the Deathly Hallows (Rowling) 50
Harry Potter and the Goblet of Fire (movie) 33
Harry Potter and the Half-Blood Prince (movie) 39
Harry Potter and the Half-Blood Prince (Rowling) 50
Harry Potter and the Order of the Phoenix (movie) 36
Harry Potter and the Order of the Phoenix (Rowling) 50
Harry Potter and the Prisoner of Azkaban (movie) 32
Harry Potter and the Sorcerer's Stone (movie) 27, 29
Harry Potter and the Sorcerer's Stone (Rowling) 50
Hart, Johnny 76
Hartford Institute for Religious Research 419
Hartford Seminary 394
Hartke, Vance 252
Harvard University 49, 64, 111, 114, 119, 125, 128–129, 131–132, 148–150, 152–154, 183, 214, 241–242, 279, 325, 425, 463
    Harvard Business School 209, 237
    Harvard Corporation 149–150
    Harvard Law Review 242, 279
    Harvard Law School 115, 242, 279
    Harvard Medical School 447
    Howard Hughes Medical Institute 470
Harvey, Paul 353
Harvey, Thomas Stoltz 390
Harvey Milk High School (New York City) 126
Harvick, Kevin 482
Hasan, Nidal Malik 200, 400, 407, 426
Hasbro 63
Hasegawa, Shigetoshi 493
Hass, Robert 69
Hasselbeck, Elisabeth 342, 348
Hatch, Orrin 372, 379
Hatch, Richard 338
Hatfill, Steven 374
Hathaway, Anne 159, 175, 177, 185
Hathaway, Stanley K. 252
Hattoy, Bob 252
Hawaii 129, 214, 415

Ewa Beach 481
Waipio 484
Hawkins, Augustus F. 252
Hay, Harry 252
Hayden, Melissa 76
Hayden, Tom 214
Hayek, Salma 345
Hayes, Isaac 76
Haynesworth, Clement 353
Headley, Heather 70
Headline News Channel 334
Head Start 153
Health-care reform 236
Health Reimbursement Accounts (HRAs) 371
Health Savings Accounts (HSAs) 371
HealthSouth 86, 118
Hearst Castle (California) 40
Hearst Tower (New York City) 165
Heart disease 378, 451
The Heartbeat of God: Finding the Sacred in the Middle of Everything (Schori) 423
The Heartbreak Kid (movie) 73
A Heartbreaking Work of Staggering Genius (Eggers) 26
"Heartless" (song) 40
Heart's Needle (Snodgrass) 80
The Heartsong of Charging Elk (Welch) 26
Heatwave (musical group) 81
Hebrew Union College-Jewish Institute of Religion 427
Heche, Anne 317
Heckman, James J. 119
Hedgepeth v. *Washington Metropolitan Area Transit Authority* 280
Hedison, Alexandra 317
Heeger, Alan J. 468
Hee Haw (television show) 78
Heene, Falcon 335
Heene, Mayumi 335
Heene, Richard 335
The Heidi Chronicles (play) 80
Heilbroner, Robert 120
Heilmeier, George 455
Heinz Award for Technology, the Economy, and Employment 464
Heisman Trophy 481, 502–503
Held, Al 76
Helder, Lucas John 125
Hellboy (movie) 32
Heller, Dick Anthony 274
Heller, Joseph 26
Hell on Wheels (movie) 486
Helms, Jesse 153, 252
Helmsley, Leona 120

"He Loves U Not" (song) 28
The Help (Stockett) 40
"Help Me Make It through the Night" (song) 79
Helton, Todd 490
Helú, Carlos Slim 92
Henderson, Billy 76
Henderson, Fritz 91, 95
Henderson, Ricky 493
Henderson, Skitch 76
Hendricks Motor Sports 500
Hendrix, Jimi 79
Henry, Carl Ferdinand Howard 428
Henry, Chris 506
Henry, Richard 76
Hentel, Nat H. 284
Hepatitis 359
    Hepatitis B 469
Hepburn, Audrey 75
Hepburn, Katharine 76
Herald, Mary T. 389
Herbalife 390
Herbert, Don 469
Herbster, Carl D. 410
"Here without You" (song) 31
Her Fearful Symmetry (Niffenegger) 40
Herman, George 353
Herman, Richard 131, 151
Herman, Stan 186
Hernandez, Lazaro 186
"Hero" (song) 28
Herrera, Carolina 186–187
Herring, John A. (Tony) 387
Hersh, Seymour M. 197, 326
Hershiser, Orel 493
Hershko, Avram 385, 468
Hertzberg, Arthur 428
Herzog, Jacques 188
Hess, Orvan W. 390
Heston, Charlton 76
Hetch Hetchy Valley 351
"He Wasn't Man Enough" (song) 27
Hewitt, Don 252, 353
Hewlett, William Redington 120, 153
Hewlett-Packard 112, 118, 120, 153, 222
Hewson, Ali 186
"Hey Baby" (song) 30
"Hey Mama" (song) 33
"Hey There Delilah" (song) 37
Heywood, Stephen 390
"Hey Ya" (song) 31
Higginbotham, Brooks Evelyn 149
High blood pressure 451
High-Definition/Density Digital Video Disc (HD-DVD) 437

High Definition Television (HDTV) 339
Higher Education Act (1965) 141
Higher Education Opportunity Act (2008) 141
"Higher" (song) 27
High Fidelity (movie) 26
High Line 184
High Performance Computer and Communication Act (1991) 463
High School Musical (television show) 42
High School Reunion (television show) 338
Highly Active Antiretroviral Therapy (HAART) 364
Hightower, Rosella 76
Hilco Consumer Capital 104
Hill, Debra 76
Hill, Faith 56
Hill, Oliver W. 283
Hill, Paul Jennings 390
Hilleman, Maurice Ralph 390
Hillerman, Tony 76
Hillman, Douglas W. 284
Hilton, Nicky 159
Hilton, Paris 168
Hilton, Perez 347, 405
Hinckley, Gordon B. 398, 428
Hines, Gregory 76
Hinrichs, Joel Henry, III 128
Hip-hop 42, 162, 173
"Hip-Hop Won't Stop: The Beat, the Rhymes, the Life" (exhibition) 56
"Hips Don't Lie" (song) 36
Hipster 172
Hirsch, Samuel 360
Hirschfeld, Al 76
Hispanic Americans 249, 267, 280
The Historian (Kostova) 34
Hitchens, Christopher 418
"Hit 'Em Up Style (Oops!)" (song) 28
Hitler, Adolf 213, 400
HIV/AIDS 62
Ho, Don 76
The Hobbit (Tolkien) 50
Hockey 521
Hockney, David 28
Hodgins, William 187
Hodgson, Jane Elizabeth 390
Hofstra College 113
Hoge, Dean R. 428
HOK Community Service Project 188
Hold Tight (Coben) 38
Holdsclaw, Chamique 498
Holl, Steven 187
"Hollaback Girl" (song) 34

Holloway, Natalee 268, 281–282, 335
Hollywood 105, 166, 190, 327, 417, 497
Hollywood and Highland Center (California) 166
Hollywood Reporter 353
Hollywood Squares (television show) 354
Hollywood 10, 80
Hollywood Walk of Fame 56
Holman, Halsted R. 388
Holmes, Katie 39
Holmgren, Mike 506
Holocaust 50, 399, 412
    denial of 421
Holtz, Lou 503
Holy Blood, Holy Grail (Baigent and Leigh) 55
Holy Grail 55, 416
Holyfield, Evander 101, 474, 521
Home (Robinson) 38
Home and Garden Television (HGTV) 178
Home Box Office (HBO) 173, 177, 324–327, 330, 332, 340, 397, 417, 487
Home Land (Lipsyte) 34
Homebody/Kabul (play) 29
Homer 52
Homestead Clinical Corporation 464
Homosexuality 42, 126, 128, 130, 145, 160, 171, 182, 215–216, 242, 252, 256, 267, 272, 306, 317, 324, 332, 340, 397–398, 400, 422, 427
    marriage 206, 214, 239, 248, 251, 317, 394, 399, 413
    marriage, ban on, defeated 396
    religion 401, 404–406
    sodomy laws 395
Homosexuality, Human Dignity, and Halakha 397, 406
Honda
    Accord Hybrid 435
    Civic 188
    Ridgeline 188
Honeymoon (Roughan) 34
Hong Kong
    SARS 384
Hood, Leroy E. 464
Hooker, John Lee 76
Hoover Dam 92
Hope, Bob 76
Hopkins, Bernard 500
Horford, Al 494
Hormone replacement therapy (HRT) 376
Horner, John R. "Jack" 434, 447, 465
Hornish, Sam, Jr. 481

Horowitz, Lawrence 70
Horry, Robert 497
Horsey, David 350
Horton, Odell 284
Horton Hears a Who! (movie) 37
Horvitz, H. Robert 385
Horyn, Cathy 182, 185
The Host (Meyer) 38
The Hostage (Griffin) 34
"Hot in Here" (song) 30
The Hot Kid (Leonard) 34
Hot Six (Evanovich) 26
Hotel Dorset 44
Hotel Rwanda (movie) 32
Hough, Derek 46
Houghton, Michael 386
Hour Game (Baldacci) 33
Hourihan, Meg 453
The Hours (movie) 29
The House (Steel) 36
The House at Sugar Beach (Cooper) 38
House Call with Dr. Sanjay Gupta (television show) 383
House Lights (Cohen) 37
House of Deréon (fashion line) 184
House of Leaves (Danielewski) 26
House of Meetings (Amis) 37
House of Representatives, U.S. 89, 101, 129, 198
    Armed Services investigations subcommitte 254
    Education Committee 141
    Committee on Oversight and Government Reform 480, 490
    Internal Security Committee251
    majority whip 246
    minority whip 247
    Un-American Activities Committee 77, 80, 251, 285
    Ways and Means Committee 217
The House on Hope Street (Steel) 26
Housekeeping (Robinson) 47
Housing bubble 115
Houston, Charles Snead 390
Houston (Texas) Independent School District 149
Houston Astros 481, 491–493
Houston Comets 474, 488
Houston Dynamo 482–483
Houston Rockets 396, 420, 497
How the Grinch Stole Christmas (movie) 26
How to Be Alone: Essays (Franzen) 64
How to Be Very, Very Popular (movie) 78
Howard, Brenda 252
Howard, George, Jr. 284
Howard, Ron 416

Howard, Ryan 490
Howard University 421, 425
The Howdy Doody Show (television show) 325
Hoyt, David B. 388
Hubble Space Telescope 460, 466
Huckabee, Mike 211, 246
Hudgens, Vanessa 42
Hudson, Jennifer 338
Hudson, Kate 175
Hudson River 327
    plane crash (2009) 453
    pollution 116
The Hudsucker Proxy (movie) 52, 75
Huffington, Arianna 336
The Huffington Post 326, 336, 346
Huffman, Felicity 42
Hughes, Karen 204
Hughes, Mark R. 390
Hughes, Matt 501
Hughes, Sarah 476
Hugo Award 74
Hulk (movie) 30, 55
Hull, Anne 352
Hull, Brian 242
Hulu.com 102, 340
Human Genome Organization (HUGO) 450
Human Genome Project 436–437, 441, 449, 464, 469
Human Genome Sequence 434
Human Immunodeficiency Virus (HIV) 62, 364
Human papillomavirus (HPV) 375, 437
Human Rights Campaign 422
The Human Stain (Roth) 26, 47
Humana Festival 61
Humanistic Judaism 429
Humbard, Rex 428
Hummer (automobile) 180
    H2 158, 180
Humphrey, Hubert 254
Humphrey, Lee 494
Humvee (automobile) 180
Hundley, Todd 490
Hundley, William G. 284
Hung, William 338
The Hunger Games (Collins) 42
Hunt, E. Howard 253
Hunt, Scott 388
Hunter, Rielle 199, 216–217, 246
Huntley, Chet 352
Huntsville, Alabama 129
Hurley, Chad 347, 436
Hurley, Elizabeth 162
Hurley, Wilson 76
Hurricane Ike 352

Jeter, Derek 489, 490, 499–500, 522
The Jetsons (cartoon characters) 73
Jewish Americans
    first vice-presidential candidate 394
Jewish Defense League 429
Jewish Hospital (Louisville, Kentucky) 359, 366
Jewish Museum Berlin 163, 183
Jewish Theological Seminary 420
Jim Crow laws 215, 253
Jim the Boy (Earley) 26
Jimenez, Luis 77
Jimmy Eat World (musical group) 172
Jindal, Bobby 247
JLO (fashion line) 173
Joan of Arcadia (television show) 395, 417
Joan Shorenstein Center on the Press, Politics, and Policy 341
Jobs, Steve 112–113
Jobs and Growth Tax Relief Reconciliation Act 86
Joel, Billy 74
Joffrey Ballet 73
Johansson, Scarlett 53, 346
John Birch Society 250
John F. Kennedy Center for the Performing Arts (Washington, D.C.) 45
John Henry Days (Whitehead) 28
John Jay College of Criminal Justice 404
John Paul II (Pope) 396, 401
John Q (movie) 29
Johnny Angel (Steel) 31
Johns Hopkins University 465
    School of Medicine 464, 469
Johnson, Betsey 162, 170
Johnson, Chris 504
Johnson, Denis 26, 37
Johnson, Diane 31
Johnson, Ian 350
Johnson, Jimmie 481, 485, 487, 521–522
Johnson, John 120
Johnson, Lady Bird 153
Johnson, Lyndon B. 251–257, 354
Johnson, Philip 190
Johnson, Randy 479, 491, 522
Johnson, Robert 118
Johnson, Samuel Curtis 120
Johnson, Shawn 487
Johnson, Tank 506
Johnson, Zack 482
Johnston, Levi 244
Joint Chiefs of Staff 248

Joint replacement 366
Jolie Blon's Bounce (Burke) 30
Jolie, Angelina 343
Jon & Kate Plus 8 (television show) 343
Jonas Brothers (musical group) 42
Jonathan LeVine Gallery 63
Jones, Adam "Pacman" 506
Jones, Arthur 390
Jones, Bob, III 426
Jones, Carol 138
Jones, Cherry 70
Jones, Chipper 490
Jones, Cullen 522
Jones, Dahntay 495
Jones, Jerry 500
Jones, John E. 467
Jones, John E., III 128, 437
Jones, Marion 474, 478, 483, 487
Jones, Mike 397, 426, 506
Jones, Palmer P. 388
Jones, Quincy 149
Jones, Reginald 120
Jones, Star 342, 366
Jones, Stephanie Tubbs 253
Jones, Tommy Lee 463
Jonze, Spike 54
Jordan
    Amman 407
Jordan, Mary 350
Jordan, Michael 203, 475, 487, 497, 499, 522
Journal News 350
Journal of Experimental Zoology 465
Journal of the American Medical Association 359, 363
Journal of Vertebrate Paleontology 465
Journalism
    gonzo 80
    political allegiances 201
Journey through Heartsongs (Stepanek) 28
Journey Together Faithfully: The Church and Homosexuality 404
Jovanovich, William A. 120
Joy, Rick 187
Judaism 428
    homosexuality and 406
Judas Iscariot 397
The Judas Field (Bahr) 35
Judge Advocate General Corps 282
Judge & Jury (Gross) 35
Juergensmeyer, Mark 427
Juiced: Wild Times, Rampant 'Roids, Smash Hits, and How Baseball Got Big (Canseco) 101, 488, 490
Juicy Couture 184
Julavits, Heidi 26

Julie & Julia (movie) 39, 54
"Jumpin', Jumpin'" (song) 27
Jungle Fever (movie) 75
Juno (movie) 36
Jurassic Park (movie) 75
"Just Dance" (song) 40
Just Take My Heart (Clark) 39
Justice, David 490, 493
Justice, William Wayne 283
Justice Department, U.S. 84–85, 93, 153, 217, 223, 245–246, 249, 253

K

Kael, Pauline 77
Kagan, Elena 249
Kahn, Joseph 351
Kahneman, Daniel 119
Kaine, Tim 146
Kamali, Norma 186
Kamehameha Preparatory School (Hawaii) 129
Kammer, Jerry 351
Kandahar 194
Kandel, Eric R. 385
Kaner, Joan 186
Kanovitz, Howard 77
Kansas
    evolution, teaching of 124, 132
    Fort Hood 200
    sodomy laws 272
    State Board of Education 124, 139
Kansas City Chiefs 506
Kansas City Royals 493
Kansas City Wizards 474, 479
Kantrowitz, Arthur 469
Kao, Charles K. 468
Kaplan, Gabe 491
Karan, Donna 45, 160, 167, 186, 190
Karapetyan, Davit 45
The Karate Kid (movie) 78
Karim, Jawed 436
"Karma" (song) 34
Karmazin, Mel 347
Karzai, Hamid 229–230, 247
Kassel, Tichi Wilkerson 353
Kathy Griffin: My Life on the D-List (television show) 349
Katrina Cottages 188
Katz, Martin 159
Kaufman, Millard 77
Kavli Institute for Particle Astrophysics and Cosmology (KIPAC) 466
Kayaking 484
Kazaa 58
Kazan, Elia 77
Kazmierczak, Stephen P. 130
Keating, Charles 240, 251

Kuiper belt 458
Kulikova, Irina 175
Kundig, Tom 187
Kunitz, Stanley 77
Kunzel, Erich 77
Kurtzman, Ray 284
Kushner, Tony 29
Kuwait 232
Kwan, Michelle 476–477, 487, 522
Kydland, Finn E. 119
Kyoto Prize 464
Kyoto Protocol 238, 434, 436, 441–443
Kyrgyzstan 226

L

L.A. Ink (television show) 184
L'Affaire (Johnson) 31
L'Enfant Plaza Metro Station (Washington, D.C.) 37, 59
L'Engle, Madeleine 50, 77
La Bohème (opera) 62
Labor Department 254
Lacrosse 482
The Lacuna (Kingsolver) 40
Lacy, Paul E. 390
Ladder 49 (movie) 32
Ladies' Home Journal 190
Ladies Professional Golf Association (LPGA) 477, 523
Ladykillers (movie) 52
"Lady Love" (song) 79
Lagarde, Christine 112
Lagerfeld, Karl 185
Laguna Hills High School (California) 424
LaHara, Brianna 32
LaHaye, Tim 394, 417
Lahiri, Jhumpa 26, 31, 38
Laine, Frankie 77
The Lake House (Patterson) 31
Lake, Kyle 429
Lake Minnetonka 481
Lake Pontchartrain 219
Lake Worth Middle School (Florida) 124
Lakewood Church 396, 419
Lam, Derek 186
Lamantia, Philip 77
Lamb, Willis, Jr. 469
Lambeau Field 505
Lamberto-Egan, Josia 186
Lambertson, Richard 185
Lambeth Conference 422
The Lancet 380
Land Rover (automobile) 96
    LR3 188

Land, Richard 410
Landers, Alan 390
Landesman, Rocco 40, 70
Landis, Floyd 482, 487–488
Landon, Christophe 30
Lane, Bernard 396
Lane, Nathan 28
Lane, Stewart F. 70
Lang, David 69
Lang, Helmut 185
Langer, Robert 466
Lankenau Institute for Medical Research 466
Lantz, Francess 77
Lapham, Anthony A. 284
Large Hadron Collider 441
Lark and Termite (Phillips) 40
Larkin, Barry 494
Larrick, Nancy 153
Larry King Live (television show) 335, 426
Larson, Jonathan 39
Larson B ice shelf 443
Larsson, Stieg 49
Las Vegas, Nevada 129, 487
Las Vegas Locomotives 485
Las Vegas Sun 352
Lasala, John M. 384
Lasker Foundation 466
Last Exit to Brooklyn (Selby) 79
The Last Juror (Grisham) 33
"The Last Lecture" 470
The Last Patriot (Thor) 38
The Last Precinct (Cornwell) 26
The Last Report on the Miracles at Little No Horse (Erdrich) 28
The Last Samurai (movie) 30
The Last Song (Sparks) 40
The Last Stand (movie) 35
Late Night with Conan O'Brien (television show) 335, 345, 348
Late Night with Jimmy Fallon (television show) 335
The Late Show with David Letterman (television show) 347–348
Latham, Lonnie 426
Latif, Adrees 352
Latin America
    baseball players from 493
Latta, Hugh 187
Lattimer, John K. 390
Lauder, Estée 120, 182, 190
Lauder, Evelyn 185
Laura Bush Foundation 148
Lauren, Ralph 158, 186
Lauterbur, Paul C. 385
Law, Bernard Francis 395, 402
Law Abiding Citizen (movie) 39

Law and Justice 267–286
Law & Order (television show) 78, 267
Lawrence, Jacob 77
Lawrence, John 272
Lawrence (Massachusetts) *Eagle-Tribune* 350
Lawrence Livermore National Laboratory (California) 450
Lawrence v. *Texas* 272, 395
Lawson, David J. 429
Lawson, Ty 495
Lawton, Harry W. 353
The Lay of the Land (Ford) 35
Lay, Donald P. 284
Lay, Kenneth L. 87, 98, 117, 120, 198, 221
Le Gougne, Marie-Reine 476
"Le Maurien" 30
Leadership in Energy and Environmental Design (LEED) 163
    structures 165
LEAF (automobile) 179
Lean Mean Thirteen (Evanovich) 37
The Learning Channel (TLC) 158, 178
"Leave (Get Out)" (song) 33
Leavitt, Michael 70, 360
Lebanon 240, 253
Leber's congenital amaurosis 451
Ledger, Heath 42, 55
Lee, Ang 42, 55
Lee, Harper 75
Lee, Kahi 178
Lee, Spike 203
Leeson, David 350
Left Behind: The Movie 394, 417
Legend, John 346
Leggett, Anthony J. 467
Leggings 169
Legorreta, Ricardo 187
Lehman Brothers 89, 108–109, 112, 199, 222
Leibrock, Cynthia 188
Leigh, Dorian 190
Leigh, Richard 55
Leinart, Matt 504
Leiserowitz, Nila 188
Lemelson-MIT Prize for Invention and Innovation 464
Lemmon, Jack 77
Lemony Snicket's A Series of Unfortunate Events (movie) 32
Leno, Jay 328, 336, 345, 348
Leo Baeck Medal 183
Leonard, Sugar Ray 500
Leonardo da Vinci, 32
Lerer, Kenneth 336

Measles, mumps, and rubella (MMR) vaccine 380

Medal of Freedom 252

Medal of Honor 251, 252

Media 329–356

Medicaid 372

Medical Device User Fee and Modernization Act (MDUFMA) 372

Medicare 204, 238, 239, 371

Medicare Advantage 371

Medicare Modernization Act 196

Medicare Prescription Drug Improvement and Modernization Act 360, 371, 384

Medicare+Choice 371

Medicine and Health 363–392
  military 372

Medium (television show) 417

Meeds, Lloyd 153

Meet the Parents (movie) 26, 75

Meet the Press (television show) 255, 354

Meet the Robinsons (movie) 36

Mehta, Sonny 50

Melamine 107

Mello, Craig C. 385

Mello, Dawn 185

Melrose Place (television show) 354

Meltzer, Bernard D. 285

Memento (movie) 26

Memoirs of a Geisha (movie) 33, 184

Memorial Medical Center (New Orleans) 361

Memory Foundations 183

A Memory of War (Busch) 31

Men's Vogue 159, 160, 185

Menand, Louis 48

Mendes da Rocha, Paulo 188

Menendez, Eric and Lyle 284

Menotti, Giancarlo 45, 78

Menu Foods Inc. 106–107

Menzel, Idina 32, 70

Mercedes Benz 179, 188, 450

Mercer, Heather 395

Merck 285, 358

A Mercy (novel) 47

Meredith v. *Jefferson County [Kentucky] Board of Education* 271

The Mermaid Chair (Kidd) 34

Merrifield, R. Bruce 469

Merrill Lynch 88, 89, 94, 108–110, 112, 116, 222

The Merv Griffin Show (television show) 353

Merwin, W. S. 69

Meselson, Matthew 387

Mesereau, Thomas 282

Messner, Tamara "Tammy" Faye Bakker 429

Messud, Claire 48

Metallica (band) 58, 453

Methodist Church
  homosexuality, policy on 405

Metro Girl (novel) 33

Metropolitan Museum of Art (The Met) 32, 36, 37, 40, 44, 173

Metropolitan Opera 59, 73–74, 79, 185

Metrosexuality 162, 171

Meuron, Pierre de 188

Mexican-American Legal Defense & Educational Fund 284

Mexican Americans 77, 79

Mexico 104, 450, 489
  financial crisis 115

Meyer, Cheryl Diaz 350

Meyer, Douglas L. 70

Meyer, Stephenie 35, 37, 39–40, 42, 50–51, 340

Meyer, Urban 502

MFS Communications 99

MGM 49

MGM Studios v. *Grokster Ltd.* 87

Mi Reflejo (album) 58

Miami (Fla.) 168
  Police Department 331
  City Ballet 45

Miami Heat 479, 482, 497, 522

Miami Herald (newspaper) 349, 352

Miami Ink (television show) 184

Miami Twice (store) 168

Miami University 503

Michael Clayton (movie) 36

Michael J. Fox Foundation for Parkinson's Research 358

Michigan 127, 132, 142, 163, 201, 205, 272, 379
  Mount Morris Township school shooting 124

Michigan Opera Theatre 73

Michigan Stadium 504

Michigan State University Spartans 474, 484, 494–495

Mickelson, Phil 479, 481, 499–500, 508, 522

Microgenics 464

Microsoft 84, 93, 113, 119, 325, 434, 437, 438, 454, 466–467

Mid-American Conference (MAC) 503

Middle East 202, 208, 224, 231–232, 235, 401, 425
  oil prices 86
  women in 148

Middle Tennessee State University 464

"The Middle" (song) 30

Middlesex (Eugenides) 30, 47

Midnight at the Well of Souls (novel) 74

Midnight Bayou (novel) 28

Miers, Harriet 198, 273

Mifepristone 376

Mighty Ducks of Anaheim 477

Mikulski, Barbara 141

Mikva, Abner J. 283

Milan (automobile) 179

Milk (movie) 38

The Milkmaid (painting) 40

Miller Brewing Company 493

Miller Park 493

Miller, Alan 350

Miller, Arthur 78

Miller, Bode 480, 481, 483, 522

Miller, George 141, 238

Miller, John Parr 78

Miller, Judith 216

Miller, Richard McDermott 78

Miller, Sienna 168

Million Dollar Baby (movie) 32

A Million Little Pieces (Frey) 50

Mills, Heather 46

Milwaukee Brewers 491, 493

Milwaukee County Stadium 493

Minami, Dale 283

The Mineral Palace (novel) 26

Ming, Yao 497

Minneapolis, Minn. 130

Minnesota 127

Minnesota Democratic-Farmer-Labor Party 252

Minnesota Twins 489, 492, 523

Minnesota Vikings 359, 475, 481, 505, 521–522

Minnesota-St. Paul International Airport 215

Minority Report (movie) 29

Minority whip 248

Minute Maid Park 492

Minyard, Frank 383

Minzner, Pamela 285

Mir, Frank 501

The Miracle Life of Edgar Mint (Udall) 28

Miracle on the Hudson 327

The Miracle Worker (movie) 73

Miró, Joan 28

Mirren, Helen 184

"Miss Independent" (song) 31

Mission Impossible II (movie) 26

Mission Impossible III (movie) 35

"Mission Accomplished" 209, 234, 329

Music
   country 42, 56
   digital 113
   electronic sharing of 452
   emo 172
   fashion 162
   grunge (Seattle) 168
   hip-hop 42, 56
   jazz 57
   rap 56
"Music" (song) 27
Musicals 62
Muslim Alliance in North America 407
Muslim American Society 407
Muslim Americans 226, 401, 406–407, 421
   fatwa against terrorism 397
   first congressman 397
Muslim Public Affairs Council 407
Muslim-Christian dialogue 399
Muslims 200
Mussina, Mike 494
Mustang (automobile) 159, 162, 180
My Big Fat Greek Wedding (movie) 29
"My Boo" (song) 33
"My Happy Ending" (song) 33
"My Immortal" (song) 33
My Name is Asher Lev (Potok) 429
"My Sacrifice" (song) 30
My Sister's Keeper (movie) 55
MySpace 281, 325, 341, 436, 438, 453–454
Mycoskie, Blake 159
Myerson, Roger B. 119
Mystic River (novel, Lehane) 28 (movie) 31

N

NAACP (National Association for the Advancement of Colored People) 206, 234, 254, 274
Nabel, Elizabeth G. 389
Nader, Ralph 203
Nadich, Judah 429
Nagin, C. Ray 220, 247
Nahrwold, David L. 388
The Naked and the Dead (Mailer) 77
The Naked City (movie) 80
Naked Economics 105
Naked Prey (Sandford) 31
Nambu, Yoichiro 468
The Name of the World (Johnson) 26
Name That Tune 353
"The Names" (poem) 48
The Namesake (Lahiri) 31

The Nanny Diaries (McLaughlin and Kraus) 30
Nanotechnology 441
Napster 58, 452, 453
Nardoza, Edward 187
The Narrows (Connelly) 33
Nas 56
NASA (National Aeronautics and Space Administration) 435, 436, 439–440, 457–461, 465
   Goddard Space Flight Center 466
NASCAR (National Association for Stock Car Auto Racing) 120, 475, 485, 487, 500, 521–522
NASDAQ (National Association of Securities Dealers Automated Quotations) 84, 93–94, 113
Nash-Taylor, Gela 184
Nashville (movie) 73
Nation of Islam 429
The Nation 116
National 466
National Academy of Engineering 464
National Academy of Sciences 463–464, 466
National Arts Education Foundation 137
National Assessment of Educational Progress 126
National Association of Criminal Defense Lawyers 285
National Association of Evangelicals 397–398, 401, 426
National Association of Securities Dealers 86, 114
National Basketball Association (NBA) 474, 482, 486
   Developmental League (D-League) 498
   League Pass 499
   NBA.com 488
National Book Award 64, 74, 80
National Book Festival 148
National Cancer Institute 359, 361, 379, 437, 445, 451, 464, 465
National Center for Education Statistics 128
National Commission on Marijuana and Drug Use 255
National Council of Churches 234
National Council of Churches (NCC) 397
National D-Day Museum 250
National debt 202
National Economic Council 85, 150
National Education Association 126, 142, 150

National Endowment for the Arts (NEA) 29, 40, 43, 77, 252, 254
National Football Conference (NFC) 505
National Football League (NFL) 474, 486, 500
   NFL Europe 489
   NFL Network 499
National Foundation for the Arts and the Humanities Act 254
National Gay & Lesbian Task Force 422
National Geographic Society 397
National Guard 220, 255
National Heart, Lung, and Blood Institute (NHLBI)
   Framingham Heart Study 365
National Historical Landmark 450
National Hockey League (NHL) 481
   NHL Center Ice 499
   NHL Network 499
National Instant Criminal Background Check System 146
National Institute of Child Health and Human Development 256, 359
National Institute of Mental Health 142
National Institutes of Health (NIH) 359, 362, 378, 435, 439, 445, 449, 465
National League (NL) 489
National Library of Medicine 450
National Marine Fisheries Service 423
National Medal of Art 77
National Museum of Ethiopia 446
National Organization of Women 252
National Prayer Breakfast 399, 412
National Public Radio (NPR) 329, 336
National Research Council 435
National Review 250
National Rifle Association (NRA) 243, 252, 274
National Rod & Custom Hall of Fame Museum 189
National Science Foundation 150, 465
National Security Administration 279
National Security Agency 246, 267, 278
National Security and Homeland Security Presidential Directive 199
National Security Council 463
National Sleep Conference 360
National Steel 92

Nichols, Brian 424
Nickel Mines shooting 128–129, 132, 146
Nicklaus, Jack 507–508
Nielsen SoundScan 56
Nielubowicz, Mary Joan 391
Nifong, Michael 129–130, 152
Niger 216, 233–234
Nigeria 149
Night (Wiesel) 50
Night at the Museum: Battle of the Smithsonian (movie) 39
A Night at the Opera (movie) 74
Night Fall (DeMille) 33
Nights in Rodanthe (Sparks) 30
Nike 63, 184, 497
Nine Dragons (Connelly) 40
9/11 attacks 93–94, 163, 194, 198, 201, 207, 210, 221, 223, 226, 228, 238, 267, 275–276, 329, 333, 350, 395, 401, 407, 415
    conspiracy theories 227
    impact on airlines 96–97
    impact on arts 41
    impact on fashion 162
    impact on health 373–374
    impact on sports 475, 487–489
    novels 47
    response by Muslim Americans 406
9/11 Commission 227, 234
9/11 Commission Report 197, 227
Nineteen Minutes (Picoult) 37
Nirvana 182
Nissan 179, 188
(NIT) National Invitational Tournament 494
Nixon, Pat 354
Nixon, Richard M. 205, 247, 250–253, 255–257, 284, 326, 354
"No Air" (song) 38
No Child Left Behind (NCLB) 125–127, 132, 135, 137, 141–143, 150–153, 195, 238–239, 245, 253
No Country for Old Men (McCarthy) 34, 47, 52
No Country for Old Men (movie) 36, 52
No Limit Hold'em Championship 482
"No One" (song) 38
No Place Like Home (Clark) 34
Noah, Joakim 494
Nobel Prizes
    Chemistry 469–470
    Economics 256
    Literature 73
    Peace 200, 242, 246, 438, 442, 463

Physiology and Medicine 389, 469
Physics 462–463, 469–470
Noble, Elmer R. 469
Noble, John York 70
Nokia Sugar Bowl 474, 478
Nolan, Christopher 55
Nomo, Hideo 493
Nomura Holdings 108
Nooyi, Indra 118
Norell, Norman 158
Norplant 391
North, Sheree 78
North American Free Trade Agreement (NAFTA) 256
North American International Auto Show 438, 446
North American Lutheran Church 400, 404
North Atlantic Treaty Organization (NATO) 231
North Carolina 107, 129
North Carolina Agricultural & Technical State University 255
North Carolina State University 447, 465
North Carolina State University Wolfpack 496
North Dakota 272
North Hopewell-Winterstown Elementary School 124
North Korea 195, 201, 226, 229, 233, 246
North Texas State Hospital 343
Northeastern Ohio College of Medicine 366
Northeastern University 58, 452
Northern Alliance 395
Northern Illinois University 130
Northern Lights (novel) 33
Northern Virginia Hebrew Congregation 421
Northland Pines High School (Eagle River, Wis.) 165
NorthPoint Communications 93
Northwest Airlines Inc. 87, 96–97
Northwest Passage 438, 443
Norton, Ed 417
Norville, Deborah 333
Norwegian National Theatre 183
Norwood, Charles W., Jr. 254
Nosanchuk, Robert 421
Noselli, Nicole 185
The Notebook (movie) 32
"Nothing from Nothing" (song) 79
Nothing to Lose (Child) 38
Notre Dame University Fighting Irish 503, 521
Nottage, Lynn 69

"Notturno" (song) 77
Nouvel, Jean 188
Novak, Robert 196, 216, 251, 254, 354
Nowell, Peter C. 389
Noyori, Ryoji 468
Nozick, Robert 153
NPD Group 104
*NSYNC (band) 58
Nuclear power 87
Numa Numa kid 341
Numann, Patricia J. 388
Number 5, 1948 (Pollock) 36
Nun Study 384
Nuremberg trials 285
Nurse Jackie (television show) 332
NYPD Blue (television show) 317

O

O: The Oprah Magazine 119, 324
O Brother, Where Art Thou? (movie) 26, 42, 52
Oakland Athletics 101, 524
Oakland Raiders 477, 479, 507, 522
Obama administration
    bank bailout 110
    charter schools 137
    financial stimulus 222
    gay rights 267
    industry bailouts 95
    reform of No Child Left Behind 143
Obama, Barack 63, 90, 94, 112, 132, 135, 145, 147, 149–151, 162, 167, 181, 183, 198–201, 212–215, 217, 222, 231, 236, 239, 241, 244–247, 267, 277, 280, 282, 329, 335, 336, 341, 345–347, 372, 383, 398–399, 401, 412, 417, 422, 424–425, 445, 462
    Cairo speech 200
    climate issues 442
    declared flu emergency 440
    effigy of 130
    Nobel Peace Prize 200
    overturns restrictions on stem-cell research 449
    stem-cell research 362, 379, 399, 439
Obama, Malia 183, 425
Obama, Michelle 140, 183, 187, 242, 247, 384, 425
    election night dress 167
    fights childhood obesity 369
    inaugural dress 161, 167
Obama, Sasha 183, 425
O'Bannon, Frank L. 153, 254

"Over and Over" (song) 33
"Over My Head (Cable Car)" (song) 36
Owens Valley Radio Observatory 469
Owens, Bill 359
Owens, Buck 78
Owens, Rick 185, 187
Owens, Terrell 487
Oxfam America 234
Oxford University 49
Oxley, Michael 101
OxyClean 353

P
"P" Is for Peril (Grafton) 28
P.E.A.C.E. Plan 397, 419, 424
Pac-10 Conference 502–503
Pacific Bell Park 492
Pacific Coast Highway 51
Pacific Gas & Electric 84
Pacific Lutheran Theological Seminary 396
Packard Foundation 465
Pacquiao, Manny 484, 500
Page, James O. 391
Paige, Rod 126, 127, 149, 152
The Painted Drum (Erdrich) 34
A Painted House (Grisham) 28
Paisley, Brad 56
Pajama Game (movie) 79
Pakistan 195, 228–229, 231, 236, 243, 247–248, 325, 352, 354
Palance, Jack 78
Paleoanthropology 446
Paleoclimatology 443
Palestine 421
Palestinian Islamic Jihad 151
Palin, Bristol 244
Palin, Sarah 160, 199, 213–214, 241–244, 341, 342, 344–345
Palm Sunday Compromise 270
Palmeiro, Rafael 477, 480, 490, 494
Palmer, Carson 504
Palomar Observatory 458
Paltrow, Gwyneth 167
Panasonic 455
Pancreatic cancer 344
Panichgul, Thakoon 183
Panofsky, Wolfgang K. H. 470
Pantera (band) 73
Paquin, Anna 340
The Parables of Dr. Seuss 429
Paradise Hotel (television show) 338
Paramount Pictures 102
Parents 353
Parents Involved in Community Schools v. Seattle School District No. 1 271

Paretsky, Sara 47
Paris Match 190
The Paris Review 78
Park City 55
Park, Chan Ho 493
Parker, Candace 496, 498
Parker, Mary-Louise 70, 330
Parker, Sarah Jessica 162, 173, 186
Parker, Sean 58, 452
Parker, Suzy 190
Parker, William "Tony" 497
Parker, Willie 481
Parkinson's disease 358, 378–379, 449
Parkland Memorial Hospital (Texas) 389
Parks, Gordon 78
Parks, Rosa 153, 254
Parsons School of Design 175–176, 181–182
Parsons, Bill 436, 458
Partial-Birth Abortion Ban Act 196, 268, 398, 412
Partners International 428
Parton, Dolly 80
"Party Like a Rock Star" (song) 37
Pasadena EcoHouse (Pasadena, California) 165
Paschke, Ed 78
The Passion of the Christ (movie) 33, 65, 396, 416, 421
Pataki, George 163
A Patch of Blue (movie) 81
Patchett, Ann 47
Patchett, Jean 190
Patel, Marilyn Hall 58
Paterno, Joe "JoePa" 503
Paterson, David 216
Patterson, James 34
Patient Protection and Affordable Care Act 243
Patina (restaurant) 164
Patrick, Danica 483–484, 487–488
Patrinos, Ari 449
Patriot Act 194, 199, 226, 238, 249, 275, 279
Patriot League 495
The Patriot (movie) 26, 65
Pattern of Recognition (Gibson) 31
Patterson, Gilbert Earl 429
Paul, Chris 498
Paul, Les 78
Paul, Rand 213, 247
Paul, Ron 247
Paulk, John 426
Paulson, Henry 88, 89, 109–110, 221
Pausch, Randy 470
The Pawnbroker (movie) 80

Paxton, Bill 417
Pay It Forward (movie) 26
Paycheck, Johnny 78
Payton, Gary 497–498
PCPA Theaterfest (Santa Maria, California) 61
Peabody Award 333
Peace Accords (1973) 240
"Peace, Unity, and Purity" commission 405
Peake, James 373
Peanuts (comic strip) 79, 354
Pearl Jam 182
Pearl, Daniel 195, 247, 325, 354
Pearson-Prentice Hall 138
Peche Platinum 170
Peck, Gregory 78
Pediatrics 369
Pei, I. M. 187
Pejoski, Marjan 167
Pelikan, Jaroslav Jan 429
Pell Grants 129, 153, 243
Pell, Claiborne 153, 254
Pelletier, David 476
Pelosi, Nancy 198, 213, 248
PEN/Newman's Own First Amendment Award 153
Penn, B. J. 501
Penn, Irving 186, 190
Penn, John Garrett 285
Pennington, Ty 178
Pennsylvania 84, 107, 124, 128–129, 132, 140, 146, 194, 204, 223, 324, 395
Pennsylvania Ballet 45
Pennsylvania State University 503, 504
Pentagon 85, 194, 196, 223, 249, 395, 406
People for the American Way 426
People for the Ethical Treatment of Animals (PETA) 160, 170, 335
The People's Court (television show) 353
People 65
Pepper, Claude 256
PepsiCo 63, 112, 118
Percy Jackson (series) 42
Perdido Street Station (Mieville) 30
Pereiro, Oscar 482
Peretti, Jonah 336
The Perfect Storm (movie) 26
Perkins, Tony 398
Perkoff, Kathy 317
Permeable contact lens 390
Perry, Katy 170
Perry, Malcolm O. 391
Perry, Matthew J., Jr. 283

Perry, Rick 375
Personal Bible Study Methods 423
PETA 175
PETCO Park 493
Peterson, Adrian 504
Petite, Irving 78
Petraeus, David H. 236
Petruzziello, Pierpaolo 439, 467
Pets.com 93
Pett, Joel 349
Petters Group Worldwide 104
Pettitte, Andy 490, 492
Pew Forum 407, 411
Pew Forum on Religion & Public Life 398, 412, 415
Pew Research Center 324, 333
    Project for Excellence in Journalism 333
Pfizer, Inc. 84
PGA (Professional Golfing Association) Championship 507, 522
Phair, John P. 388
Phantom (Goodkind) 35
Phat Farm (fashion line) 162
Phelps, Edmund S. 119
Phelps, Fred 427
Phelps, Michael 479, 484, 487, 522
Philadelphia 76ers 475
Philadelphia Eagles 480, 523
Philadelphia Inquirer 120
Philadelphia Phillies 484–485, 489–490, 492–493
Phillips, William D. 463
Philp, Tom 351
Phish (band) 59
Phoenix 498
Phoenix Coyotes 482
Phoenix Mercury 483, 485, 498
Phoenix University 133
Phoenix Mars lander (spacecraft) 439, 460, 461
"Phone Call to God" (comedy routine)
"Photograph" (song) 34
Phthalates 363
The Pianist (movie) 29
Piano Concerto: Chiavi in Mano (album) 69
Piano, Renzo 44, 187
Piazza, Guiseppe 460
Picarello, John 59
Pickens, T. Boone 118
Pickering, John H. 283
Pickett, Wilson 78
Picoult, Jodi 37–38, 40, 55
"Picture" (song) 31
"Pieces of Me" (song) 33
Pier One (store) 179

Pigasus 250
Pilot Project Scholarship 147
Pinckney, Joe 78
Pineapple Express (movie) 38
Pink Zone 496
Pinkney, Bill 78
Pinsky, David Drew 384
Pioneer 434
Pioneer Telephone 100
Pioneer Theatre Company (Salt Lake City) 62
Pirates of the Caribbean: At World's End (movie) 36
Pirates of the Caribbean: The Curse of the Black Pearl (movie) 31
Pirates of the Caribbean: Dead Man's Chest (movie) 35, 36
Pitchmen (television show) 353
Pitino, Rick 495
Pitt, Brad 343
Pitt, Harvey 85
The Pittsburgh Cycle (play) 81
Pittsburgh Penguins 483, 484, 521
Pittsburgh Pirates 493
Pittsburgh Steelers 481, 484–485, 506, 523
Pittsburgh Symphony Orchestra 32
Pixar 41, 113
Plagiarism 152, 325
Plame, Valerie 196, 199, 216, 246–247, 254
Plan B (morning-after pill) 361, 376
Planet Earth (television show) 349
Planetary Society 469
Planned Parenthood 268
Planned Parenthood v. *Casey* 251
Plasmaco, Inc. 455
Plato's Closet (store) 168
Platt, Hermann 429
Platte Canyon High School (Colorado) 128
Playboy 354
Playing for Pizza (Grisham) 37
Playstation 3 452
Pleasant Grove City v. *Summum* 399, 413
PleatsPlease.com 185
Pledge of Allegiance 125–126, 151, 426, 428
Plimpton, George 78
Plokhov, Alexandre 186
The Plot Against America (Roth) 33
Plum Lovin' (Evanovich) 37
Plum Lucky (Evanovich) 38
Plum Spooky (Evanovich) 40
Pluto 436, 437, 458, 460, 462
Plutonium 450
PNC Financial Services Park 493

Pneumococcal vaccine 389
"Pocketful of Sunshine" (song) 38
Podsednik, Scott 492
Poehler, Amy 345
Point Blank (Coulter) 34
The Pointer Sisters (musical group) 79
Pointer, June 79
"Poker Face" (song) 40
Polanski, Roman 267
Polar bears 438, 443
Polar Shift (Cussler and Kemprecos) 34
Polaroid 85, 103–104
Polidori, Robert 36
Politically Incorrect 324
PolitiFact 352
Politzer, H. David 468
Pollack, Sydney 79
Pollock, Jackson 34, 36
Pollock (movie) 26
Polshek Partnership 187
Polygamy 417
"Pon de Replay" (song) 34
Ponce De Leon High School (Fla.) 160
Ponder, Julie 359
Pontiac 95
Pontiac Fiero 189
Pontiac Firebird 189
Pontiac GTO 120, 189
Ponzi scheme 90, 114, 394
Pop Art 78
Pop Idol (television show) 338
Pope Benedict XVI 396
Pope John Paul II 251
Popovich, Gregg 497
Populous (archtecture firm) 184
Porter, John Edward, Jr. 387
Porter, James 402
Portland Oregonian 350–351
Portman, Natalie 167
Portrait of an Artist, as an Old Man (Heller) 26
Posen, Zac 167, 186
Posner, Victor 121
Possokhov, Yuri 45
Postman, Neil 154
Posttraumatic stress disorder 373
Potok, Chaim 429
Pottermania 50
Pou, Anna 361–362, 384
Powell, Billy 79
Powell, Colin 195, 216, 226, 232–233, 248
Powell, Jody 255
PPL Therapeutics 435, 449
Practice of Management 120
Prada 170

Prada, Miuccia 186
Prasad, Ananda S. 389
Precious (movie) 39, 54
Predator (Cornwell) 34
Predock, Antoine 187
Prejean, Carrie 405, 427
Presbyterian Church USA (PCUSA) 405
Prescott, Edward C. 119
Presidential Early Career Award 462
Presidential Medal of Freedom 250, 255, 282
Presidential Medal of Honor 250
Presley, Lisa Marie 58
Press, Jim 446
The Prestige (movie) 35
Preston, Billy 79
Prey (Crichton) 30
Price, Candy Pratts 186
Price, William A. 255, 354
Pride Fighting Championships 482
Priesand, Sally Jane 427
Priest, Dana 352
Primal Fear (Diehl) 75
Prime Time Live (television show) 354
Prince 59
Prince, Charles O., III 88
Prince, Erik 248
Prince-Ramus, Joshua 159
The Princess and the Frog (movie) 39
Princeton University 111, 115, 125, 150, 152, 183, 280, 462
Prison Fellowship Ministries 410
Prius (Toyota) 179
Privacy Act 374
Private Choice 147
Private Lives (play) 70
Proceedings of the National Academy of Sciences 465
The Producers (musical) 28, 42, 62, 70
Project C 250
Project for Excellence in Journalism 341
Project Head Start 154, 391
Project Runway (television show) 159, 161–162, 175
"Promiscuous" (song) 36
Promises in Death (Robb) 40
Proof (play) 70
Prophet, Elizabeth Clare 429
The Proposal (movie) 39
Proposition 8 (California) 317, 399, 406, 415, 424
Proposition 22 (California) 398
Proposition 215 (California) 359
Prosthetics 372
Prostitution 216, 397

Protect America Act 278
Protect and Defend (Flynn) 37
Proxmire, William 255
Prudential Financial 100
Pryor, Richard 79
Pryor, Terrelle 503
PTL Club (television show) 429
Public Broadcasting Service (PBS) 75, 149, 152, 354, 454
Public Charter Schools Grant Program 136
Public Company Accounting Oversight Board 101
Public Enemies (movie) 39
Public Eye 326
Public Health Service 391
Public-Private Investment Program 90
Publishers Clearinghouse 353
Puccini, Giacomo 59, 62
Puck, Theodore T. 470
Puerto Rican Legal Defense and Education Fund 280
Pujols, Albert 489, 491, 492, 522
Pulitzer Prize 47, 152, 153, 255, 353, 354, 402
Punch Drunk Love (movie) 52
Purdue University 137
The Purpose Driven Church 395, 419, 424
The Purpose of Christmas 424
The Pursuit of Happyness (movie) 35
Push (Sapphire) 54
The Pussycat Dolls 346
Putnam 100
Pynchon, Thomas 47

Q

"Q" *Is for Quarry* (Grafton) 30
Quaker Oats 118
Qualcomm Stadium 493
The Quality of Life Report (Daum) 31
Quantum of Solace (movie) 38
Queen Latifah 56
Queen of the Damned (movie) 73
The Queen (movie) 35
Queer as Folk (television show) 324, 332
Queer Eye for the Straight Guy (television show) 162, 171, 176, 349
QUEST camera 458
Quick, William 325
The Quickie (Patterson and Ledwidge) 37
A Quiet Genius (Munro) 28
Quiet Riot (band) 75
Quill, Timothy E. 389

Quinn, Anthony 79
Quinn, Dan 138

R

"R" *Is for Ricochet* (Grafton) 33
Rabbinical Assembly 429
Rabbit Hole (play) 69
Rabin, Matthew 119
Rabinowitz, David 436, 458, 462
Race to the Top grants 132
Radcliffe Institute for Advanced Study 148
Radford, Albert Ernest 470
Radio 336–337
Radio Corporation of America (RCA) 455
Radio (movie) 487
Radiohead (band) 42
Raines, Tim 494
A Raisin in the Sun (play) 70, 79
Raitt, Bonnie 79
Raitt, John 79
Raksin, Alex 350
Ralston, Aron 477
Ramakrishnan, Venkatraman 468
Ramirez, Manny 490
Ramirez, Michael 352
Ramon, Ilan 435, 457
Ramone, Dee Dee 79
Ramone, Johnny 79
The Ramones (band) 79
Rampart Investment Management Company 113
Randall, Jessie 186
Randall, Tony 317
Random House 50, 55
Rangel, Charles 217
Rankin, Nell 79
Ransohoff, Joseph 391
Raoul Wallenberg Humanitarian Leadership Award 421
Rascal Flatts (band) 56
Rashad, Phylicia 70
Raskin, Jef 470
Rassmann, Jim 208
Rat Pack 74
Ratatouille (movie) 36
Rather, Dan 209, 252, 333
Ratmansky, Alexei 45
The Raw Shark Texts (Hall) 37
Rawls, John 154
Rawls, Lou 79
Ray (movie) 32
Ray-Ban 160
Ray, Rachael 304, 318
Raymond James Stadium 484
RC2 107

Reagan administration 146, 232
Reagan, Nancy 168, 189, 378, 449
Reagan, Ronald 81, 121, 154, 197, 204, 240, 250, 252, 254–255, 280, 282, 358, 360, 379
Real Housewives (television show) 329
Real Salt Lake 485
The Real Thing (play) 70
The Real World (television show) 338
Really Simple Syndication (RSS) 453
"The Reason" (song) 33
Rebirthing 358–359
Recession 93, 200, 221
Reconstructionist Rabbinical Assembly 398
Recording Industry Association of America (RIAA) 32, 58
Recycling 163
Red (Republican) states 201
Red Dragon (movie) 29, 55
Red Lake High School (Minnesota) shooting 127
Red Lion School District (Pennsylvania) violence 124, 126
Red Rabbit (Clancy) 30
Redbox 104, 105
Redgrave, Vanessa 70
Redick, Jonathan "J. J." 495
Redwall (Jacque) 50
Reed, Ed 507
Reed, Jerry 79
Reeve, Christopher 387, 391
Reeve, Dana 391
Referendum Measure 71 (Washington) 415
Reform Party 203
Reformation Lutheran Church (Wichita, Kansas) 200
Regal 59
Regan, Donald 121
Regent University 279
Regents of the University of California v. Bakke 271
"Regreen: The Nation's First Green Residential Remodeling Guidelines" 178
Rehabilitation Institute of Chicago 358, 434, 467
Rehn, Trista 339
Rehnquist, William H. 147, 197, 248, 267, 273, 280
Reich, Steve 69
Reichlin, Seymour 389
Reid, Harry 213, 248
Reid, Richard 195, 247, 333
Reid, Whitelaw 354
Reid, William 185

Reiling, Richard B. 388
Reilly, Charles Nelson 354
Reilly, Thomas 402
Reinitzer, Friedrich 455
Relentless (Koontz) 40
Relenza 381
Religion 401–432
Religious Landscape Survey 398, 415
Religious Research Association 428
Religulous (movie) 399, 418
The Reluctant Debutante (movie) 75
Rembrandt 37
Remember the Titans (movie) 26, 487
Remington Products 120
The Remnant (LaHaye and Jenkins) 30
Reno, Janet 283
Reno, Nev. 374
Rent (movie) 34 (musical) 39, 62
Renta, Oscar de la 177, 185–186
Report to the People of God: Clergy Sexual Abuse in the Archdiocese of Los Angeles, 1930–2003 396, 403
Republican National Committee 160, 245, 250
Republican National Convention 214, 244, 250
Republican Party 201–202, 204, 210–212, 214–217, 221, 239–241, 245, 247, 249, 253, 255–256
Requiem for a Dream (movie) 26
Requiem for a Heavyweight (movie) 78
The Rescue (Sparks) 26
Research in Nursing & Health 379
Resolution 1441 (UN) 233
The Return of the King (movie) 54
(Re)understanding Prayer 429
Reuters 352
Reuther, Victor 121
Revenge of the Sith (movie) 42
Revlon 73, 190
Reynolds, Gerald A. 124
Reynolds, Nick 79
Reynolds, William A. 389
Reynoso, Cruz 283
RFK Stadium 492, 493
Rhoades, Jason 79
Rhode Island School of Design 63
Rhodes, James A. 255
Rhodes-Armstead, Izora 73
Ricci v. *DeStefano* 271, 280
Rice University 477
Rice, Buddy 479
Rice, Condoleezza 227, 233
Rich, Marc 84
Rich, Norman M. 388
Richard and Barbara Rosenberg Professor of Planetary Astronomy 462

Richard P. Feynman Award for Outstanding Teaching 462
Richards, Ann 255
Richards, Lloyd 79
Richardson, Desmond 45
Richardson-Merrill 284
Richenburg, Robert 79
Richmond, Julius B. 154, 391
Riddick, Frank A., Jr. 387
Ridge, Tom 195, 226, 248, 275
Ridin (song) 36
Riding the Bullet (King) 27
Rieveschl, George 391
Rigas, John 85, 87, 100
Rigas, Michael 100
Rigas, Timothy 100
"Right Round" (song) 40
Rigotti, Nancy A. 388
"Rikrok" (song) 28
Riley, Joe 45
Riley, Robert 190
"Ring of Fire" (song) 74
The Ring Two (movie) 34
The Ring (movie) 29
Ripken, Cal "Iron Man" 494
Rise and Shine (Quindlen) 35
Risen, James 351
The Rising (LaHaye and Jenkins) 34
Rit Sun Guard 368
Ritter, John 354
Ritter, Jordan 58
Rivera, Mariano 489
Riverfront Stadium 493
Roach, Max 79
Road to Perdition (movie) 29, 78
The Road (McCarthy) 35, 47, 69
The Road (movie) 55
Rob, J. D. 37, 40
Robert Mondavi Winery 121
Robert T. Stafford Student Loan Program 154
Robert Wood Johnson School of Medicine 390
Roberts IV, Charles Carl 128
Roberts, John G. 245, 248–249, 267, 273, 279
   becomes Chief Justice 198
Roberts, Brian 490
Roberts, Charles C. 146
Roberts, Julia 158
Roberts, Nora 28, 30–31, 33, 34–35, 38, 40
Roberts, Oral 401, 418, 429
Roberts, Richard 398, 401, 418
Robertson, Nan C. 354
Robertson, Pat 126, 152, 203, 407, 426
Robin Hood Foundation 188

Robinson, Anne 168
Robinson, David 497
Robinson, Gene 395, 399
Robinson, Luther D. 389
Robinson, Marilynne 47, 427
Robinson, V. Gene 404, 412
Robotics 434, 439, 467
    in surgery 376, 384
Rocawear (fashion line) 118, 162, 173, 184
Rock and Roll Hall of Fame 74, 76, 78
"Rock Your Body" (song) 31
Rockefeller, Laurance 121
Rockwell Group 187
Rockwell, Norman 63
Rocky Mountain News 349, 350
Roddick, Andy 523
Rodgers, Richard 62
Rodin, Auguste 28
Rodino, Peter W. 255
Rodriguez, Alex 118, 479, 486, 489–490, 499–500, 523
Rodriguez, Jai 176
Rodriguez, Narciso 167, 183, 185
Roe v. *Wade* 211, 268, 360, 412
Roeder, Robert 385
Roeder, Scott 200, 391
Roethlisberger, Ben 485, 503, 506, 523
Rogers, Adrian Pierce 429
Rogers, Fred 354
Rogers, Richard 188
Rogers, Roy 75
Rogers, William P. 255
Rogers, Wilson, Jr. 402
Roker, Al 366
Roller derby 486, 487
Roller Girls (television show) 487
Rolling Stone 58, 76, 80, 175
Rolling Stones (band) 79
Rolston, Holmes 427
Roman Catholic Church 350
    sex abuse scandal 127, 402–404
Romanowski, Bill 478
Rome (television show) 332
Romeo Must Die (movie) 73
Romer, Christina 90
Romney, Mitt 211, 248, 272, 412
Roosevelt, Franklin D. 252, 450
Roosevelt, Theodore 434
Roraback, Catherine 285
Rose Bowl 476, 481, 504
Rose Hall 57
Rose, Irwin 468
Rose, Judd 354
Rosenberg, Barnett 391
Rosenberg, William 121

Rosengarden, Bobby 79
Rosenman, Leonard 79
Rosie Radio 348
Rosie 324
Roslin Institute (Scotland) 448
Ross, Robert 391
Rossellini, Isabella 45
Rossman, Michael 154, 255
Rostow, Walt Whitman 255
Roth Individual Retirement Account 121
Roth, Philip 47
Roth, William V., Jr. 121, 255
Rothenberg, Stanley 285
Rothman, James 385
Roubini, Nouriel 114–115
Rounds, Mike 268
Roussimoff, Andre 63
Rove, Karl 199, 202, 205, 207–208, 216, 241, 248
The Row (fashion line) 160, 184
Rowley, Janet D. 389
Rowling, J. K. 41–42, 50–51
Roxio, Inc 58
Roy, Elsijane Trimble 285
Roy, Rachel 162
Royal Aal al-Bayt Institute for Islamic Thought (Amman, Jordan) 407
Royal Free Hospital (London, England) 380
Royal Institute of British Architects Award 183
The Royal Tenenbaums (movie) 28, 52
RU-486 (mifepristone) 376
Rubin, Irving D. 429
Rubin, Rick 74
Rubinow, David R. 389
Rucci, Ralph 187
Ruined (play) 69
The Ruins (Smith) 35
Ruiz, John 474
Rukeyser, Louis 121
Rumsfeld v. *Forum for Academic and Institutional Rights* 128
Rumsfeld, Donald H. 195, 220, 226, 236, 249
"Run It" (song) 34, 36
Run-DMC (rap group) 76
Rusch, Glendon 491
Rush, Bobby 242
Rushdie, Salman 45
Rushmore (movie) 52
Russell, Mary Jane 190
Russert, Tim 216, 255, 273, 354
Russia 195, 450
    financial crisis 115
Rutgers University 272, 282, 327, 334, 496

women's basketball team controversy 129
Ruth, Babe 481, 491
Rutland (Vt.) Herald 350
Rutstein, David C. 388
Ruttenstein, Kal 185, 190
Ruvkun, Gary 386
Rwanda 175, 351
Ryan, Jack 242
Ryan, Matt 504

S

S-10 EV (automobile) 179
Sabiston, David C., Jr. 391
Sachs, Jonathan 427
Sachs, Mel A. 285
Sack, Kevin 350
Sacramento Bee 351
Sacramento Monarchs 481–482
Saddleback Church (California) 399, 412, 419, 423
Saez, Emmanuel 119
Safeguard the Children (program) 396, 403
"Safety of Silicone Breast Implants" 377
Safire, William 255, 354
Sag Harbor (Whitehead) 40
Sagan, Carl 469
Sago Mine 87
Sail (Patterson and Roughan) 38
Saint Laurent, Yves 158, 182
Saint Paul School of Theology (Kansas City) 428
Saks Fifth Avenue 160, 185, 342
Sale, Jamie 476
Salomon Smith Barney 94
Salon 182
Salopek, Paul 350
Salter, Mark 241
Salvation Army 168
Samaritan (Price) 31
Sam's Letters to Jennifer (Patterson) 33
Same-sex marriage 267, 272, 317, 404, 415
Samford University 503
Sampras, Pete 474, 478
San Antonio Silver Stars 484
San Antonio Spurs 477, 480, 482, 497
San Diego Chargers 478, 480, 506
San Diego Padres 493
San Diego State University 492
San Diego Union-Tribune 351–352
San Diego Zoo 439, 466
San Francisco 49ers 489
San Francisco Ballet 45

Selby, Hubert 79
Seller, Jeffrey 70
Selzer, Richard Sylvan (Mr. Blackwell) 168, 190
Senate 101, 198, 251
    anthrax scare 374
    Health, Education, Labor, and Pensions Committee 270
    Ethics Committee 240
    Foreign Relations Committee 209, 245
    majority leader 253
The Senator's Wife (Miller) 38
Sendak, Maurice 54
September 11 attacks (see 9/11 attacks)
"Serenade" (ballet) 45
Serenity (movie) 34
A Serious Man (movie) 417
Serra, Matt 501
Seton Hall University 429
"The 7 Words You Can't Say on Television" (comedy routine) 353
The 700 Club (television show) 407, 426
Seven Up (Evanovich) 28
7th Heaven (television show) 354
Sex and the City (movie) 38, 162, 177
Sex and the City (television show) 162, 170, 173, 177, 325, 348
sex education 133
    abstinence emphasis 130, 132, 143–145
Sex Pistols (band) 63
Sexually transmitted diseases 144–145, 358
"Sexy Back" (song) 36
Sexy Beast (movie) 26
"Sexy Can I" (song) 38
Seymour, Richard 506
SFX Theatrical Group 70
Shadel, Billy 354
Shadid, Anthony 350
Shadow of a Doubt (movie) 81
The Shadow of Sirius (Merwin) 69
Shadow of the Law (movie) 79
Shady Ltd (fashion line) 173
Shafer Commission 255
Shafer, Raymond P. 255
Shaft (movie) 78
Shaheen, Alfred 190
"Shake It Off" (song) 34
"Shake Ya Tailfeather" (song) 31
Shalala, Donna 358
Shamrock, Ken 501
Shane (movie) 78
Shanghai Knights (movie) 31
Shanley, John Patrick 70

Shannon, Claude Elwood 154
Shapiro, Carl 114
Shark Tale (movie) 32
Shark Tank (television show) 347
Sharky's Machine (Diehl) 75
Sharpe, Shannon 478
Sharpless, K. Barry 468
Sharpton, Al 130, 334
Shaw, Artie 79
The Shawshank Redemption (movie) 81
"She Bangs" (song) 338
"She Will Be Loved" (song) 33
She's Got the Look (television show) 176
Shearer, Harry 336
Sheets, James 126
Sheffield, Gary 490
Shelby, Richard 112
Sheldon, Sidney 79
The Shelters of Stone (Auel) 30
Sheridan, Nicollette 168
Sherlock Holmes (movie) 39
Sherman Antitrust Act 93
Shestack, Jerome J. 283
The Shield (television show) 268
Shilling, Marion 79
Shimomura, Osama 468
Shipley, Sam 186
Shirakawa, Hideki 468
SHoP Architects 187
Shopaholic & Baby (Kinsella) 37
Shore, Grace 138
Short, Robert L. 429
Shottenheimer, Marty 506
"Show and Tell" (song) 81
Showtime 324, 330–332
Shrek 2 (movie) 32
Shrek the Third (movie) 36
Shrek! (Steig) 80
Shrek (movie) 28
Shriver, Donald W., Jr. 427
Shriver, Eunice Kennedy 256
Shubert Organization 70
Shull, Clifford G. 470
Shumway, Norman E. 391
Sichuan Tengzhong Heavy Industrial Machinery 180
Sideways (movie) 32
Sidley Austin (law firm) 183
Siegel, Robert 51, 189
Siegelman, Don 118
Siemienow, Maria 384
Sierra Club 234
Sierra Nevada 443
Sierra, Ruben 494
Sign of the Dove Retreat Center (Temple, N. H.) 422

Signs (movie) 29
Silber, Sherman 378
Siler, Jamar B. 130
Sillerman, Robert F. X. 70
Sills, Beverly 79
Silver Star 197
Silver Streak (movie) 79
Silverman v. Major League Baseball Player Relations Committee, Inc. 280
Silverstein, Larry 163
Simmons, Kimora Lee 184
Simmons, Russell 162
Simmons, Ruth J. 124
Simon, Herbert A. 154
Simon, Paul 256
Simple Genius (Baldacci) 37
Simply Vera (fashion line) 175
Simpson, Jessica 162, 168, 173
Simpson, Nicole Brown 487
Simpson, O. J. 284, 487
The Simpsons Movie (movie) 37
Sims, Naomi 190
Simulcasts 59
Sin City (movie) 34
"Since U Been Gone" (song) 34
Sinclair, Cameron 188
Sinclair, Upton 53
"Single Ladies (Put a Ring on It)" (song) 40
Sinkford, William G. 404
Sioux Valley Hospitals and Health System 384
Sipchen, Bob 350
Sirius 60, 325–326, 337, 347–348
Sirius XM Radio 60, 337, 347–348
Sisqó 172
Sitowitz, Hal 79
Six Easy Pieces: Easy Rawlins Stories (Mosley) 31
Six Feet Under (television show) 330, 340
16th Street Baptist Church (Birmingham, Ala.) 428
The 6th Target (Patterson and Paetro) 37
60 Minutes (television show) 252, 353, 407
60 Minutes II (television show) 208–209, 236
Skaist-Levy, Pamela 184
Skilling, Jeffrey 98–99, 101, 117, 198, 221
Skin Trade (Hamilton) 40
Skipping Christmas (Grisham) 28, 47
Sky diving 483
Skype 452
Slatkin, Leonard 59

Waxman, Henry A. 490
Waxman, Herbert S. 389
"The Way I Are" (song) 37
"The Way You Move" (song) 33
Wayfarer (sunglasses) 160
Wayne, John 77
We Are Marshall (movie) 487
"We Belong Together" (song) 34
We Were Soldiers (movie) 30, 65
Weapons of mass destruction (WMD) 195, 201, 210, 216, 232, 233, 284
Weather Channel 352
The Weather Girls (musical group) 73
Weather Underground 214, 255
Web Soup (television show) 341
Webber, Robert Eugene 429
Weber, Bruce 186
Weber, Larry F. 434, 455
Weber-Gale, Garrett 522
Webfeeds 452
Websites 336, 452
Wedding Crashers (movie) 34
The Wedding (Steel) 26
Wedekind, Frank 62, 64
Weeds (television show) 330
Weil, Jack Arnold 190
Weinberger, Caspar W. 256
Weinstein, Bob 70
Weinstein, Harvey 70
Weintraub, Beverly 351
Weirton Steel 92
Weis, Charlie 366
Weisberger, Lauren 177, 185
Weise, Jeff 127
Weisfeldt, Myron L. 388
Weisman, Joel D. 391
Weiss, Stephan 190
Welch, Laura 148, 237
Welfare Reform Act 411
Weller, Thomas Huckle 391
Wells Fargo 89, 111
Welnick, Vince 80
Wenger, Nanette K. 388
Wesley, Paul 341
West Nile virus 358, 359–360, 363, 381
West Point (See United States Military Academy)
The West Point Story (movie) 78
West Virginia 87, 98
West Virginia University Mountaineers 503
The West Wing (television show) 348
West, Cornel 125, 149–150, 152
West, Kanye 56, 57, 173, 345
Westboro Baptist Church 427

Western Athletic Conference 502
Westminster Academy 429
Westmoreland, William C. 257
Weston High School (Cazenovia, Wisconsin) 128
Weyco 379
Wham-O 120
"What a Girl Wants" (song) 27
What Not To Wear (television show) 176
What Perez Sez (television show) 347
What Women Want (movie) 65
"Whatever You Like" (song) 38
Wheel of Fortune (television show) 353
Wheeldon, Christopher 45
Wheeler, John 470
"When I'm Gone" (song) 31
When Will There Be Good News? (Atkinson) 38
Where Are You Now? (Clark) 38
"Where Is the Love?" (song) 31
Where the Wild Things Are (book) 54, (movie) 39
"Wherever You Will Go" (song) 30
Whistle-blower 117
The Whistling Season (Doig) 35
Whitacre, Edward 91
Whitcomb, Richard T. 470
White House 149, 150, 223, 241, 246 blog 327
White House Correspondents' Association Dinner 333
White House Council of Economic Advisers 90
White House Office of Faith-Based Initiatives 394, 399, 411–412
White House Office of Women's Programs 250
White Noise (DeLillo) 47
White Noise (movie) 34
White Oleander (movie) 55
The White Stripes (band) 42
White, Barry 80
White, Byron Raymond "Whizzer" 154
White, Kelli 479, 487
White, Onna 80
White, Thelma 80
White, Tim D. 446
Whitewater 284
Whitfield, Vantile 80
Whitledge, John 186
Whitman, Christine Todd 374
Whitman, Meg 119
Whitmore, James 81
Who Wants to Be a Millionaire? (television show) 338

Whole Foods Market 57
The Whole Truth (Baldacci) 38
Why Did I Ever (Robison) 28
"Why Don't You & I" (song) 31
Whyte, Jenny Bechtel 190
Wicked: The Life and Times of the Wicked Witch of the West (Maguire) 62
Wicked Prey (Sanford) 40
Wicked (musical) 32, 62, 70
Wide World of Sports 120
The Widows of Eastwick (Updike) 38
Wie, Michelle 477, 488, 523
Wiegenstein, John G. 387
Wieman, Carl E. 467
Wiesel, Elie 50
Wiest, Dianne 39
Wife Swap (television show) 335
Wi-Fi 452
Wii 452
WikiLeaks 327
WikiPages 453
Wikipedia 324, 333, 439, 453
Wilco (band) 42
Wilczek, Frank 468
Wild 2 (comet) 466
Wild, John J. 391
Wilde, John 81
Wilder, Johnnie, Jr. 81
Wilder, Billy 81
Wilder, Deontay 500
Wiley, Don C, 470
Will & Grace (television show) 348
Will.i.am 346
William and Flora Hewlett Foundation 124, 153
William Carey International University 429
William J. Clinton Presidential Library (Little Rock, Ark.) 165
William Tyndale College 396
Williams, Armstrong 127, 150, 152
Williams, Brian 333
Williams, Evan 347, 437, 453
Williams, Jason "Jay" 495
Williams, Matt 490
Williams, Roy 480, 494
Williams, Serena 474–476, 484, 485, 487, 523
Williams, Sheldon 495
Williams, Tod 187
Williams, Vanessa 159
Williams, Venus 474–476, 480, 484, 485, 487, 523
Williamson, Oliver E. 119
Williams-Sonoma 57
Willie Boy: A Desert Manhunt 353

Willow Creek Community Church 419

Willy Wonka and the Chocolate Factory (movie) 332

Wilson, Al 81

Wilson, August 81

Wilson, Harriet E. 149

Wilson, Joe 216

Wilson, Owen 52

Wilson, Patrick 39

Wilson, Robert 187, 435, 455

Wilson, Roger 279

Wilson, William Julius 149

Wilson, Woodrow 210

Wimbledon 480, 484–485, 523

Win Without War 234

Wind energy 435

Wind Talkers (movie) 30

Windows 93

Windsor, Duchess of 189

Wine, Sherwin Theodore 429

Winfrey, Oprah 41, 50, 64, 119, 149, 369, 324, 328–329, 345
book club 49

A Wing and a Prayer: A Message of Faith and Hope 423

Winokur, Marissa Jaret 70

Winslet, Kate 167

Winston Cup 523

Winter Solstice (Pilcher) 26

Winter, Ralph Dana 429

Winter's Bone (Woodrell) 36

Winter's Heart (Jordan) 26

Winters, Shelley 81

Wintour, Anna 159, 177, 185–186

The Wire (television show) 332

Wired 180

Wireless local area network (WLAN) 452

Wiretapping 255, 278–279

Wiretaps 276

Wisconsin 128, 147, 379

Wisconsin Institute for Discovery 379

Wise, Dewayne 491

Wiseman, Paul Vincent 187

"With You" (song) 33, 38

WoldeGabriel, Giday 446

Wolf Lake (television show) 341

Wolf, Naomi 204

Wolfe, David 172

Wolfe, Tom 353

Wolferth, Charles C., Jr. 388

Wolff, Tobias 31, 38

Womack, LeAnn 56

Woman III (de Kooning, Willem) 36

Women's Basketball Coaches Association (WBCA) 496

Women's Flat Track Derby Association 486

Women's Health and Human Life Protection Act (South Dakota) 268

Women's National Basketball Association (WNBA) 474, 488, 498, 522

Women's Wear Daily 182, 189–190

Wonder Boy (movie) 26

The Wonderful Wizard of Oz (Baum) 62

Wong, Jade Snow 81

Wood, Earl H. 391

Woods, Earl 507

Woods, Harriet 257

Woods, Rose Mary 257

Woods, Tiger 475, 476, 480, 485–487, 499, 500, 507–508, 524

Woods, Timmy 177

Woodson, Charles 507

Woodstock 75

Woodward, Bob 198, 251, 281

Wootan, Margo G. 140

Wooten, Mike 244

Word Records, Inc. 429

World Bank 223

World Baseball Classic 489

World Cup (skiing) 523

World Cup (women's) 483

World Economic Forum 115

World Extreme Cage fighting (WEC) 501

World Figure Skating Championship 477

World Health Organization (WHO) 358, 439, 465
Global AIDS program 364

World Market (store) 179

World Methodist Council 426

World Methodist Peace Award 426

World Music Awards 58

World News Tonight (television show) 120, 253, 353

The World Newser 326

World of Warcraft (game) 454

World Series 474–475, 477–479, 481–485, 488, 489, 492, 521, 522

World Series of Poker 482

World Trade Center 28, 41, 48, 94, 141, 159, 162–163, 183, 194, 195, 223, 227, 246, 373, 324, 395, 406
casualties 224

World Trade Center Syndrome 373

World Trade Center (movie) 35

World War I 27, 47
amputations 372

World War II 229, 240, 248, 251–252, 254, 256, 284, 391, 354, 429, 450
amputations 372
internment of Japanese Americans 226

World Wide Web 58, 327, 336, 341, 352, 436, 438–439, 441, 451, 456

World Without End (Follett) 37

World Wrestling Federation 474

WorldCom 85, 86, 93, 99–101, 117

The Worldly Philosophers: The Lives, Times & Ideas of the Great Economic Thinkers 120

Worthington, Christa 190

Wouk, Victor 470

Wozniak, Stephen 112

Wray, Fay 81

Wright, Doug 70

Wright, Frank Lloyd 189

Wright, Jeremiah 398, 412, 425

Wright, Teresa 81

Wrigley Field 477, 478

A Wrinkle in Time (L'Engle) 50, 77

Writers Guild of America (WGA) 88, 327, 345

Wu, Jason 161, 167, 183

Wu-Tang Clan (rap group) 56, 78

Wüthrich, Kurt 468

Wyeth, Andrew 77, 81

Wyeth, N. C. 77

Wyman, Jane 81

Wyner, Yehudi 69

Wyoming 415

X

X Games 486

X2 (movie) 31, 55

Xbox 360 452

Xe Services 248

Xena (planetary body) 437, 458

Xenadrine RFA-1 360, 476

Xenotransplantation 449

Xerox 339

XFL 474

X-linked severe combined immuno-deficiency disease (X-SCID) 451

XM Satellite Radio 60, 324, 337, 347

X-Men: The Last Stand (movie) 55

X-Men Origins: Wolverine (movie) 39

X-Men (movie) 26, 35, 42, 55

XO Communications 93

Y

Y2K bug 84

Yahoo! 93

Yale Law Journal 280